CISCO

Course Booklet

CCNA Security

Version 1.1

ciscopress.com

Cisco | Networking Academy
Mind Wide Open

CCNA Security Course Booklet Version 1.1

Cisco Networking Academy

Copyright© 2012 Cisco Systems, Inc.

Published by:
Cisco Press
800 East 96th Street
Indianapolis, IN 46240 USA

Printed in the United States of America

Second Printing December 2012

Library of Congress Cataloging-in-Publication Data is available upon request.

ISBN-13: 978-1-58713-307-7

ISBN-10: 1-58713-307-5

Warning and Disclaimer

This book is designed to provide information about networking. Every effort has been made to make this book as complete and as accurate as possible, but no warranty or fitness is implied.

The information is provided on an "as is" basis. The authors, Cisco Press, and Cisco Systems, Inc. shall have neither liability nor responsibility to any person or entity with respect to any loss or damages arising from the information contained in this book or from the use of the discs or programs that may accompany it.

The opinions expressed in this book belong to the author and are not necessarily those of Cisco Systems, Inc.

Publisher
Paul Boger

Associate Publisher
Dave Dusthimer

Cisco Representative
Erik Ullanderson

**Cisco Press
Program Manager**
Anand Sundaram

Executive Editor
Mary Beth Ray

Managing Editor
Sandra Schroeder

Editorial Assistant
Vanessa Evans

Designer
Sandra Schroeder

Composition
Mark Shirar

This book is part of the Cisco Networking Academy® series from Cisco Press. The products in this series support and complement the Cisco Networking Academy curriculum. If you are using this book outside the Networking Academy, then you are not preparing with a Cisco trained and authorized Networking Academy provider.

For more information on the Cisco Networking Academy or to locate a Networking Academy, Please visit www.cisco.com/edu.

CISCO

Trademark Acknowledgments

All terms mentioned in this book that are known to be trademarks or service marks have been appropriately capitalized. Cisco Press or Cisco Systems, Inc., cannot attest to the accuracy of this information. Use of a term in this book should not be regarded as affecting the validity of any trademark or service mark.

Feedback Information

At Cisco Press, our goal is to create in-depth technical books of the highest quality and value. Each book is crafted with care and precision, undergoing rigorous development that involves the unique expertise of members from the professional technical community.

Readers' feedback is a natural continuation of this process. If you have any comments regarding how we could improve the quality of this book, or otherwise alter it to better suit your needs, you can contact us through email at feedback@ciscopress.com. Please make sure to include the book title and ISBN in your message.

We greatly appreciate your assistance.

Americas Headquarters
Cisco Systems, Inc.
San Jose, CA

Asia Pacific Headquarters
Cisco Systems (USA) Pte. Ltd.
Singapore

Europe Headquarters
Cisco Systems International BV
Amsterdam, The Netherlands

Cisco has more than 200 offices worldwide. Addresses, phone numbers, and fax numbers are listed on the Cisco Website at **www.cisco.com/go/offices.**

CCDE, CCENT, Cisco Eos, Cisco HealthPresence, the Cisco logo, Cisco Lumin, Cisco Nexus, Cisco StadiumVision, Cisco TelePresence, Cisco WebEx, DCE, and Welcome to the Human Network are trademarks; Changing the Way We Work, Live, Play, and Learn and Cisco Store are service marks; and Access Registrar, Aironet, AsyncOS, Bringing the Meeting To You, Catalyst, CCDA, CCDP, CCIE, CCIP, CCNA, CCNP, CCSP, CCVP, Cisco, the Cisco Certified Internetwork Expert logo, Cisco IOS, Cisco Press, Cisco Systems, Cisco Systems Capital, the Cisco Systems logo, Cisco Unity, Collaboration Without Limitation, EtherFast, EtherSwitch, Event Center, Fast Step, Follow Me Browsing, FormShare, GigaDrive, HomeLink, Internet Quotient, IOS, iPhone, iQuick Study, IronPort, the IronPort logo, LightStream, Linksys, MediaTone, MeetingPlace, MeetingPlace Chime Sound, MGX, Networkers, Networking Academy, Network Registrar, PCNow, PIX, PowerPanels, ProConnect, ScriptShare, SenderBase, SMARTnet, Spectrum Expert, StackWise, The Fastest Way to Increase Your Internet Quotient, TransPath, WebEx, and the WebEx logo are registered trademarks of Cisco Systems, Inc. and/or its affiliates in the United States and certain other countries.

All other trademarks mentioned in this document or website are the property of their respective owners. The use of the word partner does not imply a partnership relationship between Cisco and any other company. (0812R)

Contents at a Glance

Contents

Command Syntax Conventions

The conventions used to present command syntax in this book are the same conventions used in the IOS Command Reference. The Command Reference describes these conventions as follows:

- **Boldface** indicates commands and keywords that are entered literally as shown. In actual configuration examples and output (not general command syntax), boldface indicates commands that are manually input by the user (such as a **show** command).

- *Italic* indicates arguments for which you supply actual values.

- Vertical bars (|) separate alternative, mutually exclusive elements.

- Square brackets ([ ]) indicate an optional element.

- Braces ({ }) indicate a required choice.

- Braces within brackets ([{ }]) indicate a required choice within an optional element.

About this Course Booklet

Your Cisco Networking Academy Course Booklet is designed as a study resource you can easily read, highlight, and review on the go, wherever the Internet is not available or practical:

- The text is extracted directly, word-for-word, from the online course so you can highlight important points and take notes in the "Your Chapter Notes" section.

- Headings with the exact page correlations provide a quick reference to the online course for your classroom discussions and exam preparation.

- An icon system directs you to the online curriculum to take full advantage of the images imbedded within the Networking Academy online course interface and reminds you to perform the labs and Packet Tracer activities for each chapter.

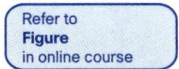
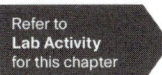

The *Course Booklet* is a basic, economical paper-based resource to help you succeed with the Cisco Networking Academy online course.

0.0 Course Introduction

0.0.1.1 Welcome

Welcome to the CCNA Security course. The goal of this course is to develop a detailed understanding of network security principles as well as the tools and configurations available. These online course materials will assist you in developing the skills necessary to design and support network security.

More than Just Information

This computer-based learning environment is an important part of the overall course experience for students and instructors in the Networking Academies. These online course materials are designed to be used along with several other instructional tools and activities. These include:

- Class presentation, discussion and practice with your teacher

- Hands-on labs that use networking equipment within the Networking Academy classroom

- Online scored assessments and grade book

- Packet Tracer simulation tool

A Global Community

When you participate in the Networking Academies, you are joining a global community linked by common goals and technologies. Schools in over 160 countries participate in the program. You can see an interactive network map of the global Cisco Networking Academy community at http://www.academynetspace.com

The material in this course addresses a range of technologies that facilitate how people work, live, play and learn by communicating with voice, video, and other data. We have worked with instructors around the world to create these materials. It is important that you work with your instructor and fellow students to adapt the material in this course to your local situation.

Keep in Touch

These on-line instructional materials, and the rest of the course tools, are part of the larger Cisco Networking Academy. The portal for the program is located at http://www.cisco.com/web/learning/netacad/index.htm. This portal is where you access tools, informational updates and other relevant links, including the assessment server and student grade book.

Mind Wide Open™

An important goal in education is to enrich you, the student, by expanding what you know and can do. It is important to realize, however, that the instructional materials and the instructor can only *facilitate* the change. *You* must make the commitment yourself to learn new skills. Below are a few suggestions to help you learn:

1.Take notes. Professionals in the networking field often keep Engineering Journals in which they write down the things they observe and learn. Taking notes is an important way to help your understanding improve over time.

2. Think about it. The course provides information both to change what you know, and what you can do. As you go through the course, ask yourself what makes sense and what doesn't. Stop and ask questions when you are confused. Try to find out more about topics which interest you. If you are not sure why something is being taught, consider asking your instructor or a friend. Think about how the different parts of the course fit together.

3. Practice. Learning new skills requires practice. We believe this is so important to e-learning that we have a special name for it. We call it e-Doing. It is very important that you complete the activities in the online instructional materials and that you complete the hands-on labs and Packet Tracer activities.

4. Practice again. Have you ever thought you knew how to do something and then, when it was time to show it on a test or at work, you discovered you really hadn't mastered it? Just like learning any new skill, such as a sport, game, or language, learning a professional skill requires patience and repeated practice before you can say you have truly learned it. The on-line instructional materials in this course provide repeated practice for many skills. Take full advantage of them. Work with your instructor to create additional practice opportunities using Packet Tracer and other tools.

5. Teach it. Teaching a friend or colleague is often a good way to improve your own learning. To teach well, you need to work through details you may have overlooked on your first reading. Conversations about the course material with fellow students, colleagues, and the instructor can help solidify your understanding of networking concepts.

6. Make changes as you go. The course is designed to provide feedback through interactive activities and quizzes, the online assessment system, and through interactions with your instructor. You can use this feedback to better understand where your strengths and weaknesses are. If there is an area you are having trouble with, focus on studying or practicing more in that area. Seek feedback from your instructor and other students.

Explore the World of Networking

This version of the course includes a special tool called Packet Tracer. Packet Tracer is a networking learning tool that supports a wide range of physical and logical simulations. It also provides visualization tools to help you to understand the internal workings of a network. The Packet Tracer activities included with the course consist of network simulations, games, activities, and challenges that provide a broad range of learning experiences.

Create your own worlds

You can also use Packet Tracer to create your own experiments and networking scenarios. We hope that, over time, you consider using Packet Tracer – not only for experiencing the activities included with the course, but also to become an author, explorer, and experimenter.

0.0.1.2

More and more, we interact and share ideas using a network built on IP services. With more being done in this environment security is a constantly growing requirement. Behind the scenes, the architects of secure communications are network security specialists.

We expect the network applications and services we use to be available and secure. And, as the underlying networks become more complex with more services offered, securing these networks becomes a top priority. We rely on network security specialists to ensure our networks can meet our expectations. A well secured network protects our investment in networking technology and provides our organizations with a competitive edge. Career opportunities in network security are growing quickly, as organizations large and small understand the importance of maintaining a secure network.

0.0.1.3

Upon successful completion of this course, you will be able to:

- Describe the security threats facing modern network infrastructures.
- Secure Cisco routers.
- Implement AAA on Cisco routers using local router databases and external servers.
- Mitigate threats to Cisco routers and networks using ACLs.
- Implement secure network management and reporting.
- Mitigate common Layer 2 attacks.
- Implement the Cisco IOS firewall feature set.
- Implement the Cisco IOS IPS feature set.
- Implement site-to-site IPsec VPNs.

Chapter Summary

Refer to
Figure
in online course

Refer to **Packet
Tracer Activity**
for this chapter

Refer to
Lab Activity
for this chapter

Your Chapter Notes

CHAPTER 1

Modern Network Security Threats

Chapter Introduction

Refer to **Figure** in online course

Network security is now an integral part of computer networking. Network security involves protocols, technologies, devices, tools, and techniques to secure data and mitigate threats. Network security solutions emerged in the 1960s but did not mature into a comprehensive set of solutions for modern networks until the 2000s.

Network security is largely driven by the effort to stay one step ahead of ill-intentioned hackers. Just as medical doctors attempt to prevent new illness while treating existing problems, network security professionals attempt to prevent potential attacks while minimizing the effects of real-time attacks. Business continuity is another major driver of network security.

Network security organizations have been created to establish formal communities of network security professionals. These organizations set standards, encourage collaboration, and provide workforce development opportunities for network security professionals. It is important for network security professionals to be aware of the resources provided by these organizations.

The complexity of network security makes it difficult to master all it encompasses. Different organizations have created domains that subdivide the world of network security into more manageable pieces. This division allows professionals to focus on more precise areas of expertise in their training, research, and employment.

Network security policies are created by companies and government organizations to provide a framework for employees to follow during their day-to-day work. Network security professionals at the management level are responsible for creating and maintaining the network security policy. All network security practices relate to and are guided by the network security policy.

Just as network security is composed of domains of network security, network attacks are classified so that it is easier to learn about them and address them appropriately. Viruses, worms, and Trojan Horses are specific types of network attacks. More generally, network attacks are classified as reconnaissance, access, or Denial of Service attacks.

Mitigating network attacks is the job of a network security professional. In this chapter, the learner masters the underlying theory of network security, which is essential before beginning an in-depth practice of network security. The methods of network attack mitigation are introduced here, and the implementation of these methods comprises the remainder of this course.

A hands-on lab for the chapter, *Researching Network Attacks and Security Audit Tools*, guides learners through researching network attacks and security audit tools.

1.1 Fundamental Principles of a Secure Network

1.1.1 Evolution of Network Security

Refer to
Figure
in online course

In July 2001, the Code Red worm attacked web servers globally, infecting over 350,000 hosts. The worm not only disrupted access to the infected servers, but also affected the local networks hosting the servers, making them very slow or unusable. The Code Red worm caused a Denial of Service (DoS) to millions of users.

If the network security professionals responsible for these Code Red-infected servers had developed and implemented a security policy, security patches would have been applied in a timely manner. The Code Red worm would have been stopped and would only merit a footnote in network security history.

Network security relates directly to an organization's business continuity. Network security breaches can disrupt e-commerce, cause the loss of business data, threaten people's privacy (with the potential legal consequences), and compromise the integrity of information. These breaches can result in lost revenue for corporations, theft of intellectual property, and lawsuits, and can even threaten public safety.

Maintaining a secure network ensures the safety of network users and protects commercial interests. To keep a network secure requires vigilance on the part of an organization's network security professionals. Network security professionals must constantly be aware of new and evolving threats and attacks to networks, and vulnerabilities of devices and applications. This information is used to adapt, develop, and implement mitigation techniques. However, security of the network is ultimately the responsibility of everyone who uses it. For this reason, it is the job of the network security professional to ensure that all users receive security awareness training. Maintaining a secure, protected network provides a more stable, functional work environment for everyone.

Refer to
Figure
in online course

"Necessity is the mother of invention." This saying applies perfectly to network security. In the early days of the Internet, commercial interests were negligible. The vast majority of users were research and development experts. Early users rarely engaged in activities that would harm other users. The Internet was not a secure environment because it did not need to be.

Early on, networking involved connecting people and machines through communications media. The job of a networker was to get devices connected to improve people's ability to communicate information and ideas. The early users of the Internet did not spend much time thinking about whether or not their online activities presented a threat to the network or to their own data.

When the first viruses were unleashed and the first DoS attack occurred, the world began to change for networking professionals. To meet the needs of users, network professionals learned techniques to secure networks. The primary focus of many network professionals evolved from designing, building, and growing networks to securing existing networks.

Today, the Internet is a very different network compared to its beginnings in the 1960s. The job of a network security professional includes ensuring that appropriate personnel are well-versed in network security tools, processes, techniques, protocols, and technologies. It is critical that network security professionals manage the constantly evolving threats to networks.

Refer to
Figure
in online course

As network security became an integral part of everyday operations, devices dedicated to particular network security functions emerged.

One of the first network security tools was the intrusion detection system (IDS), first developed by SRI International in 1984. An IDS provides real-time detection of certain types of attacks while they are in progress. This detection allows network security professionals to more quickly mitigate the negative impact of these attacks on network devices and users. In the late 1990s, the intrusion prevention system or sensor (IPS) began to replace the IDS solution. IPS devices enable the detection of malicious activity and have the ability to automatically block the attack in real-time.

In addition to IDS and IPS solutions, firewalls were developed to prevent undesirable traffic from entering prescribed areas within a network, thereby providing perimeter security. In 1988, Digital Equipment Corporation (DEC) created the first network firewall in the form of a packet filter. These early firewalls inspected packets to see if they matched sets of predefined rules, with the option of forwarding or dropping the packets accordingly. Packet filtering firewalls inspect each packet in isolation without examining whether a packet is part of an existing connection. In 1989, AT&T Bell Laboratories developed the first stateful firewall. Like packet filtering firewalls, stateful firewalls use predefined rules for permitting or denying traffic. Unlike packet filtering firewalls, stateful firewalls keep track of established connections and determine if a packet belongs to an existing flow of data, providing greater security and more rapid processing.

The original firewalls were software features added to existing networking devices, such as routers. Over time, several companies developed standalone, or dedicated firewalls that enable routers and switches to offload the memory and processor-intensive activity of filtering packets. Cisco's Adaptive Security Appliance (ASA) is available as a standalone context-aware firewall. For organizations that do not require a dedicated firewall, modern routers, like the Cisco Integrated Services Router (ISR), can be used as sophisticated stateful firewalls.

Traditional security relied on the layering of products and using multiple filters. However, as threats became more sophisticated, these filters were required to look deeper into Network and Application Layer traffic. Security requirements included more dynamic updates of information and quicker response times to threats. For this reason, Cisco designed the Security Intelligence Operations (SIO). SIO is a cloud-based service that connects global threat information, reputation-based services, and sophisticated analysis to Cisco network security devices to provide stronger protection with faster response times.

Refer to **Figure** in online course

In addition to dealing with threats from outside of the network, network security professionals must also be prepared for threats from inside the network. Internal threats, whether intentional or accidental, can cause even greater damage than external threats because of direct access to, and knowledge of the corporate network and data. Despite this fact, it has taken more than 20 years after the introduction of tools and techniques for mitigating external threats to develop tools and techniques for mitigating internal threats.

A common scenario for a threat originating from inside the network is a disgruntled employee with some technical skills and a willingness to do harm. Most threats from within the network leverage the protocols and technologies used on the local area network (LAN) or the switched infrastructure. These internal threats fall into two categories: spoofing and Denial of Service (DoS).

Spoofing attacks are attacks in which one device attempts to pose as another by falsifying data. There are multiple types of spoofing attacks. For example, MAC address spoofing occurs when one computer accepts data packets based on the MAC address of another computer.

DoS attacks make computer resources unavailable to intended users. Attackers use various methods to launch DoS attacks.

As a network security professional, it is important to understand the methods designed specifically for targeting these types of threats and ensuring the security of the LAN.

Refer to **Figure** in online course

In addition to preventing and denying malicious traffic, network security also requires that data stay protected. Cryptography, the study and practice of hiding information, is used pervasively in modern network security. Today, each type of network communication has a corresponding protocol or technology designed to hide that communication from anyone other than the intended user.

Wireless data can be encrypted (hidden) using various cryptography applications. The conversation between two IP phone users can be encrypted. The files on a computer can also be hidden with encryption. These are just a few examples. Cryptography can be used almost anywhere that there is data communication. In fact, the trend is toward all communication being encrypted.

Cryptography ensures data confidentiality, which is one of the three components of information security: confidentiality, integrity, and availability. Information security deals with protecting information and information systems from unauthorized access, use, disclosure, disruption, modification, or destruction. Encryption provides confidentiality by hiding plaintext data. Data integrity, meaning that the data is preserved unaltered during any operation, is achieved by the use of hashing mechanisms. Availability, which is data accessibility, is guaranteed by network hardening mechanisms and backup systems.

1.1.2 Drivers for Network Security

Refer to
Figure
in online course

The word 'hackers' has a variety of meanings. For many, it means Internet programmers who try to gain unauthorized access to devices on the Internet. It is also used to refer to individuals who run programs to prevent or slow network access to a large number of users, or corrupt or wipe out data on servers. But for some, the term hacker has a positive interpretation as a network professional that uses sophisticated Internet programming skills to ensure that networks are not vulnerable to attack. Good or bad, hacking is a driving force in network security.

From a business perspective, it is important to minimize the effects of hackers with bad intentions. Businesses lose productivity when the network is slow or unresponsive. Business profits are impacted by data loss and data corruption.

The job of a network security professional is to stay one step ahead of the hackers by attending training and workshops, participating in security organizations, subscribing to real-time feeds regarding threats, and perusing security websites on a daily basis. The network security professional must also have access to state-of-the art security tools, protocols, techniques, and technologies. Network security professionals should have many of the same traits as law enforcement professionals. They should always remain aware of malicious activities and have the skills and tools to minimize or eliminate the threats associated with those activities.

Hacking has the unintended effect of creating a high demand for network security professionals. However, relative to other technology professions, network security has the steepest learning curve and requires a commitment to continuous professional development.

Refer to
Figure
in online course

Hacking started in the 1960s with phone freaking, or phreaking, which refers to using various audio frequencies to manipulate phone systems. Phreaking began when AT&T introduced automatic switches to their phone systems. The AT&T phone switches used various tones, or tone dialing, to indicate different functions, such as call termination and call dialing. A few AT&T customers realized that by mimicking a tone using a whistle, they could exploit the phone switches to make free long-distance calls.

As communication systems evolved, so did hacking methods. Wardialing became popular in the 1980s with the use of computer modems. Wardialing programs automatically scanned telephone numbers within a local area, dialing each one in search of computers, bulletin board systems, and fax machines. When a phone number was found, password-cracking programs were used to gain access.

Wardriving began in the 1990s and is still popular today. With wardriving, users gain unauthorized access to networks via wireless access points. This is accomplished using a wireless-enabled portable computer or PDA. Password-cracking programs are used to authenticate, if necessary, and there is even software to crack the encryption scheme required to associate to the access point.

Other threats have evolved since the 1960s. These include network scanning tools such as Nmap and SATAN, as well as remote system administration hacking tools such as Back Orifice. Network security professionals must be familiar with all of these tools.

Refer to
Figure
in online course

Transactions worth trillions of dollars are conducted over the Internet on a daily basis, and the livelihoods of millions of people depend on Internet commerce. For this reason, criminal laws are in place to protect individual and corporate assets. There are numerous cases of individuals who have had to face the court system due to these laws.

The first email virus, the Melissa virus, was written by David Smith of Aberdeen, New Jersey. This virus resulted in memory overflows in Internet mail servers. David Smith was sentenced to 20 months in federal prison and a US $5,000 fine.

Robert Morris created the first Internet worm with 99 lines of code. When the Morris Worm was released, 10% of Internet systems were brought to a halt. Robert Morris was charged and received three years probation, 400 hours of community service, and a fine of US $10,000.

One of the most notorious Internet hackers, Kevin Mitnick, was incarcerated for hacking credit card accounts in the early 1990s.

Whether the attack is via spam, a virus, DoS, or simply breaking into accounts, when the creativity of hackers is used for malicious purposes, they often end up going to jail, paying large fines, and losing access to the very environment in which they thrive.

Refer to
Figure
in online course

As a result of hacker exploits, the sophistication of hacker tools, and government legislation, network security solutions developed rapidly in the 1990s. By the late 1990s, many sophisticated network security solutions had been developed for organizations to strategically deploy within their networks. With these solutions came new job opportunities and increased compensation in the field of network security.

The annual income for a network security professional is on the high end of the scale for careers in technology because of the depth and breadth of knowledge required. Network security professionals must constantly upgrade their skill set to keep abreast of the latest threats. The challenge of gaining and maintaining the necessary knowledge often translates into a shortage of network security professionals.

Network security professionals are responsible for maintaining data assurance for an organization and ensuring the integrity and confidentiality of information. A network security professional might be responsible for setting up firewalls and intrusion prevention systems as well as ensuring encryption of company data. Implementing enterprise authentication schemes is another important task. The job entails maintaining detailed logs of suspicious activity on the network to use for reprimanding or prosecuting violators. As a network security professional, it is also important to maintain familiarity with network security organizations. These organizations often have the latest information on threats and vulnerabilities.

1.1.3 Network Security Organizations

Refer to
Figure
in online course

Network security professionals must collaborate with professional colleagues more frequently than most other professions. This includes attending workshops and conferences that are often affiliated with, sponsored or organized by local, national, or international technology organizations.

Three of the more well-established network security organizations are:

- SysAdmin, Audit, Network, Security (SANS) Institute

- Computer Emergency Response Team (CERT)

- International Information Systems Security Certification Consortium (pronounced (ISC)2 as "I-S-C-squared")

A number of other network security organizations are also important to network security professionals. InfoSysSec is a network security organization that hosts a security news portal, providing the latest breaking news pertaining to alerts, exploits, and vulnerabilities. The Mitre Corporation maintains a list of common vulnerabilities and exposures (CVE) used by prominent security organizations. Forum of Incident Response and Security Teams (FIRST) is a security organization that brings together a variety of computer security incident response teams from government, commercial, and educational organizations to foster cooperation and coordination in information sharing, incident prevention and rapid reaction. Finally, the Center for Internet Security (CIS) is a non-profit enterprise that develops security configuration benchmarks through a global consensus to reduce the risk of business and e-commerce disruptions.

Refer to
Figure
in online course

SANS was established in 1989 as a cooperative research and education organization. The focus of SANS is information security training and certification. SANS develops research documents about various aspects of information security.

A range of individuals, from auditors and network administrators to chief information security officers, share lessons and solutions to various challenges. At the heart of SANS are security practitioners in varied global organizations, from corporations to universities, working together to help the entire information security community.

SANS resources are largely free upon request. This includes the popular Internet Storm Center, the Internet's early warning system; NewsBites, the weekly news digest; @RISK, the weekly vulnerability digest; flash security alerts; and more than 1,200 award-winning, original research papers.

SANS develops security courses that can be taken to prepare for Global Information Assurance Certification (GIAC) in auditing, management, operations, legal issues, security administration, and software security. GIAC validates the skills of network security professionals, ranging from entry-level information security to advanced subject areas like auditing, intrusion detection, incident handling, firewalls and perimeter protection, data forensics, hacker techniques, Windows and UNIX operating system security, and secure software and application coding.

Refer to
Figure
in online course

CERT is part of the U.S. federally funded Software Engineering Institute (SEI) at Carnegie Mellon University. CERT is chartered to work with the Internet community in detecting and resolving computer security incidents. The Morris Worm motivated the formation of CERT at the directive of the Defense Advanced Research Projects Agency (DARPA). The CERT Coordination Center (CERT/CC) focuses on coordinating communication among experts during security emergencies to help prevent future incidents.

CERT responds to major security incidents and analyzes product vulnerabilities. CERT works to manage changes relating to progressive intruder techniques and to the difficulty of detecting attacks and catching attackers. CERT develops and promotes the use of appropriate technology and systems management practices to resist attacks on networked systems, to limit damage, and to ensure continuity of services.

CERT focuses on five areas: software assurance, secure systems, organizational security, coordinated response, and education and training.

CERT disseminates information by publishing articles, research and technical reports, and papers on a variety of security topics. CERT works with the news media to raise awareness of the risks on the Internet and the steps that users can take to protect themselves. CERT works with other major technology organizations, such as FIRST and Internet Engineering Task Force (IETF), to increase the commitment to security and survivability. CERT also advises U.S. government organizations, such as the National Threat Assessment Center, the National Security Council, and the Homeland Security Council.

Refer to
Figure
in online course

(ISC)2 provides vendor-neutral education products and career services in more than 135 countries. Its membership includes over 75,000 certified industry professionals worldwide.

The mission of (ISC)2 is to make the cyber world a safer place by elevating information security to the public domain, and supporting and developing network security professionals around the world.

(ISC)2 develops and maintains the (ISC)2 Common Body of Knowledge (CBK). The CBK defines global industry standards, serving as a common framework of terms and principles that (ISC)2 credentials are based upon. The CBK allows professionals worldwide to discuss, debate, and resolve matters pertaining to the field.

Most notably, (ISC)2 is universally recognized for its four information security certifications, including one of the most popular certifications in the network security profession, the Certified Information Systems Security Professional (CISSP). These credentials help to ensure that employers with certified employees maintain the safety of information assets and infrastructures.

(ISC)2 promotes expertise in handling security threats through its education and certification programs. As members, individuals have access to current industry information and networking opportunities unique to its network of certified information security professionals.

Refer to
Figure
in online course

In addition to the websites of the various security organizations, one of the most useful tools for the network security professional is Really Simple Syndication (RSS) feeds.

RSS is a family of XML-based formats used to publish frequently updated information, such as blog entries, news headlines, audio, and video. RSS uses a standardized format. An RSS feed includes complete or summarized text, plus metadata, such as publishing dates and authorships.

RSS benefits professionals who want to subscribe to timely updates from favored websites or to aggregate feeds from many sites into one place. RSS feeds can be read using a web-based RSS reader, typically built into a web browser. The RSS reader software checks the user's subscribed feeds regularly for new updates and provides an interface to monitor and read the feeds. By using RSS, a network security professional can acquire up-to-date information on a daily basis and aggregate real-time threat information for review at any time.

For example, the US-CERT Current Activity web page is a regularly updated summary of the most frequent, high-impact types of security incidents being reported to the US-CERT. A text-only RSS feed is available at http://www.us-cert.gov/current/index.rdf. This feed reports at all hours of the day and night, with information regarding security advisories, email scams, backup vulnerabilities, malware spreading via social network sites, and other potential threats.

1.1.4 Domains of Network Security

Refer to
Figure
in online course

It is vital for a network security professional to understand the drivers for network security and be familiar with the organizations dedicated to network security. It is also important to have an understanding of the various network security domains. Domains provide an organized framework to facilitate learning about network security.

There are 12 network security domains specified by the International Organization for Standardization (ISO)/International Electrotechnical Commission (IEC). Described by ISO/IEC 27002, these 12 domains serve to organize (at a high level) the vast realm of information under the umbrella of network security. These domains have some significant parallels with domains defined by the CISSP certification.

The 12 domains are intended to serve as a common basis for developing organizational security standards and effective security management practices, and to help facilitate communication between organizations.

Refer to
Figure
in online course

The 12 domains of network security provide a convenient separation for the elements of network security. While it is not important to memorize these 12 domains, it is important to be aware of their existence and formal declaration by the ISO. They will serve as a useful reference in your work as a network security professional.

One of the most important domains is security policy. A security policy is a formal statement of the rules by which people must abide who are given access to the technology and information assets of an organization. The concept, development, and application of a security policy are critical to keeping an organization secure. It is the responsibility of a network security professional to weave the security policy into all aspects of business operations within an organization.

1.1.5 Network Security Policies

Refer to
Figure
in online course

The network security policy is a broad, end-to-end document designed to be clearly applicable to an organization's operations. The policy is used to aid in network design, convey security principles, and facilitate network deployments.

The network security policy outlines rules for network access, determines how policies are enforced, and describes the basic architecture of the organization's network security environment. Because of its breadth of coverage and impact, it is usually compiled by a committee. It is a complex document meant to govern items such as data access, web browsing, password usage, encryption, and email attachments.

A security policy should keep ill-intentioned users out and have control over potentially risky users. When a policy is created, it must be first understood what services are available to which users. The network security policy establishes a hierarchy of access permissions, giving employees only the minimal access necessary to perform their work.

The network security policy outlines what assets need to be protected and gives guidance on how they should be protected. This will then be used to determine the security devices and mitigation strategies and procedures that should be implemented on the network. One possible guideline that administrators can use when developing the security policy and determining various mitigation strategies is the Cisco SecureX architecture.

Refer to
Figure
in online course

The Cisco SecureX architecture is designed to provide effective security for any user, using any device, from any location, and at any time. This new security architecture uses a higher-level policy language that takes into account the full context of a situation - who, what, where, when and how. With highly distributed security policy enforcement, security is pushed closer to where the end user is working.

This architecture includes the following five major components:

- Scanning Engines
- Delivery Mechanisms
- Security Intelligence Operations (SIO)
- Policy Management Consoles
- Next-generation Endpoint

Refer to
Figure
in online course

Increased user mobility, the influx of consumer devices, and movement of information to non-traditional locations has created complexities for securing the IT infrastructure. Deploying piecemeal security solutions can lead to duplicated efforts and inconsistent access policies, and requires increased integration and staffing to support.

Cisco SecureX products work together to provide effective security for any user, using any device, from any location, at any time. This is one of the primary reasons for relying on the Cisco SecureX architecture to help shape the security policy.

Refer to
Figure
in online course

A network security policy drives all the steps to be taken to secure network resources, not just equipment requirements and procedures.

A security policy is a set of objectives for the company, rules of behavior for users and administrators, and requirements for system and management that collectively ensure the security of network and computer systems in an organization. A security policy is a "living document," meaning that the document is never finished and is continuously updated as technology, business, and employee requirements change.

For example, an organization's employee laptops will be subject to various types of attacks, such as email viruses. A network security policy explicitly defines how frequently virus software updates and virus definition updates must be installed. Additionally, the network security policy includes guidelines for what users can and cannot do. This is normally stipulated as a formal acceptable use policy (AUP). The AUP must be as explicit as possible to avoid ambiguity or misunderstanding. An AUP might, for example, list the Usenet newsgroups that are prohibited.

While the security policy should be comprehensive, it should also be succinct enough to be usable by the technology practitioners in the organization.

1.2 Viruses, Worms, and Trojan Horses

1.2.1 Viruses

Refer to
Figure
in online course

The primary vulnerabilities for end user computers are virus, worm, and Trojan Horse attacks:

- A virus is malicious software which attaches to another program to execute a specific unwanted function on a computer.

- A worm executes arbitrary code and installs copies of itself in the memory of the infected computer, which then infects other hosts.

- A Trojan Horse is an application written to look like something else. When a Trojan Horse is downloaded and opened, it attacks the end user computer from within.

Refer to
Figure
in online course

Traditionally, the term virus refers to an infectious organism that requires a host cell to grow and replicate. A University of Southern California student named Frederick Cohen suggested the term "computer virus" in 1983. A computer virus, referred to as a virus in the rest of this course, is a program that can copy itself and infect a computer without the knowledge of the user.

A virus is a malicious code that is attached to legitimate programs or executable files. Most viruses require end user activation and can lay dormant for an extended period and then activate at a specific time or date. A simple virus may install itself at the first line of code on an executable file. When activated, the virus might check the disk for other executables, so that it can infect all the files it has not yet infected. Viruses can be harmless, such as those that display a picture on the screen, or they can be destructive, such as those that modify or delete files on the hard drive. Viruses can also be programmed to mutate to avoid detection.

In the past, viruses were usually spread via floppy disks and computer modems. Today, most viruses are spread by USB memory sticks, CDs, DVDs, network shares, or email. Email viruses are now the most common type of virus.

1.2.2 Worms

Refer to
Figure
in online course

Worms

Worms are a particularly dangerous type of hostile code. They replicate themselves by independently exploiting vulnerabilities in networks. Worms usually slow down networks.

Whereas a virus requires a host program to run, worms can run by themselves. They do not require user participation and can spread very quickly over the network.

Worms are responsible for some of the most devastating attacks on the Internet. For example, the SQL Slammer Worm of January 2003 slowed global Internet traffic as a result of Denial of Service. Over 250,000 hosts were affected within 30 minutes of its release. The worm exploited a buffer overflow bug in Microsoft's SQL Server. A patch for this vulnerability was released in mid-2002, so the servers that were affected were those that did not have the update patch applied. This is a great example of why it is so important for the security policy of an organization to require timely updates and patches for operating systems and applications.

Refer to
Figure
in online course

Despite the mitigation techniques that have emerged over the years, worms have continued to evolve with the Internet and still pose a threat. While worms have become more sophisticated over time, they still tend to be based on exploiting weaknesses in software applications. Most worm attacks have three major components:

- *Enabling vulnerability* A worm installs itself using an exploit mechanism (email attachment, executable file, Trojan Horse) on a vulnerable system.

- *Propagation mechanism* After gaining access to a device, the worm replicates itself and locates new targets.

- *Payload* Any malicious code that results in some action. Most often this is used to create a backdoor to the infected host.

Worms are self-contained programs that attack a system to exploit a known vulnerability. Upon successful exploitation, the worm copies itself from the attacking host to the newly exploited system and the cycle begins again.

Refer to
Figure
in online course

When studying the major worm and virus attacks over the past 20 years, it becomes clear that the various phases of attack methods employed by hackers have similarities.

- *Probe phase* Vulnerable targets are identified. The goal is to find computers that can be subverted. Internet Control Message Protocol (ICMP) ping scans are used to map networks. Then the application scans and identifies operating systems and vulnerable software. Hackers can obtain passwords using social engineering, dictionary attack, brute-force attack, or network sniffing.

- *Penetrate phase* Exploit code is transferred to the vulnerable target. The goal is to get the target to execute the exploit code through an attack vector, such as a buffer overflow, ActiveX or Common Gateway Interface (CGI) vulnerabilities, or an email virus.

- *Persist phase* After the attack is successfully launched in the memory, the code tries to persist on the target system. The goal is to ensure that the attacker code is running and available to the attacker even if the system reboots. This is achieved by modifying system files, making registry changes, and installing new code.

- *Propagate phase* The attacker attempts to extend the attack to other targets by looking for vulnerable neighboring machines. Propagation vectors include emailing copies of the attack to other systems, uploading files to other systems using file shares or FTP services, active web connections, and file transfers through Internet Relay Chat (IRC).

- *Paralyze phase*   Actual damage is done to the system. Files can be erased, systems can crash, information can be stolen, and distributed DoS (DDoS) attacks can be launched.

The five basic phases of attack allow security experts to conveniently describe worms and viruses according to their particular implementation mechanism for each phase. This makes it easier to categorize worms and viruses.

Viruses and worms are two methods of attack. Another method is the Trojan Horse, which leverages viruses or worms with the added element of masquerading as a benign program.

1.2.3 Trojan Horses

Refer to **Figure** in online course

Trojan Horse

The term Trojan Horse originated from Greek mythology. Greek warriors offered the people of Troy (Trojans) a giant hollow horse as a gift. The Trojans brought the giant horse into their walled city, unaware that it contained many Greek warriors. At night, after most Trojans were asleep, the warriors burst out of the horse and overtook the city.

A Trojan Horse in the world of computing is malware that carries out malicious operations under the guise of a desired function. A Trojan Horse contains hidden, malicious code that exploits the privileges of the user that runs it. Games can often have a Trojan Horse attached to them. When running the game, the game works, but in the background, the Trojan Horse has been installed on the user's system and continues running after the game has been closed.

The Trojan Horse concept is flexible. It can cause immediate damage, provide remote access to the system (a back door), or perform actions as instructed remotely, such as "send me the password file once per week."

Custom-written Trojan Horses, such as Trojan Horses with a specific target, are difficult to detect.

Refer to **Figure** in online course

Trojan Horses are usually classified according to the damage that they cause or the manner in which they breach a system:

- **Remote-access Trojan Horse** - enables unauthorized remote access
- **Data sending Trojan Horse** - provides the attacker with sensitive data such as passwords
- **Destructive Trojan Horse** - corrupts or deletes files
- **Proxy Trojan Horse** - user's computer functions as a proxy server
- **FTP Trojan Horse** - opens port 21
- **Security software disabler Trojan Horse** - stops antivirus programs or firewalls from functioning
- **Denial of Service Trojan Horse** - slows or halts network activity

1.2.4 Mitigating Viruses, Worms, and Trojan Horses

Refer to **Figure** in online course

A majority of the software vulnerabilities that are discovered relate to buffer overflows. A buffer is an allocated area of memory used by processes to store data temporarily. A buffer overflow occurs when a fixed-length buffer reaches its capacity and a process attempts to store data above and beyond that maximum limit. This can result in extra data overwriting adjacent memory locations as well as causing other unexpected behaviors. Buffer overflows are usually the primary conduit through which viruses, worms, and Trojan Horses do their damage. In fact, there are reports that suggest that one-third of the software vulnerabilities identified by CERT relate to buffer overflows.

Viruses and Trojan Horses tend to take advantage of local root buffer overflows. A root buffer overflow is a buffer overflow intended to attain root privileges to a system. Local root buffer overflows require the end user or system to take some type of action. A local root buffer overflow is typically initiated by a user opening an email attachment, visiting a website, or exchanging a file via instant messaging.

Worms such as SQL Slammer and Code Red exploit remote root buffer overflows. Remote root buffer overflows are similar to local root buffer overflows, except that local end user or system intervention is not required.

Refer to
Figure
in online course

Viruses, worms, and Trojan Horses can cause serious problems on networks and end systems. Network administrators have several means of mitigating these attacks. Note that mitigation techniques are often referred to in the security community as 'countermeasures'.

The primary means of mitigating virus and Trojan Horse attacks is antivirus software. Antivirus software helps prevent hosts from getting infected and spreading malicious code. It requires much more time to clean up infected computers than it does to maintain up-to-date antivirus software and antivirus definitions on the same machines.

Antivirus software is the most widely deployed security product on the market today. Several companies that create antivirus software, such as Symantec, Computer Associates, McAfee, and Trend Micro, have been in the business of detecting and eliminating viruses for more than a decade. Many corporations and educational institutions purchase volume licensing for their users. The users are able to log in to a website with their account and download the antivirus software on their desktops, laptops, or servers.

Antivirus products have update automation options so that new virus definitions and new software updates can be downloaded automatically or on demand. This practice is the most critical requirement for keeping a network free of viruses and should be formalized in a network security policy.

Antivirus products are host-based. These products are installed on computers and servers to detect and eliminate viruses. However, they do not prevent viruses from entering the network, so a network security professional needs to be aware of the major viruses and keep track of security updates regarding emerging viruses.

Refer to
Figure
in online course

Worms are more network-based than viruses. Worm mitigation requires diligence and coordination on the part of network security professionals. The response to a worm infection can be broken down into four phases: containment, inoculation, quarantine, and treatment.

The containment phase involves limiting the spread of a worm infection to areas of the network that are already affected. This requires compartmentalization and segmentation of the network to slow down or stop the worm and prevent currently infected hosts from targeting and infecting other systems. Containment requires using both outgoing and incoming ACLs on routers and firewalls at control points within the network.

The inoculation phase runs parallel to or subsequent to the containment phase. During the inoculation phase, all uninfected systems are patched with the appropriate vendor patch for the vulnerability. The inoculation process further deprives the worm of any available targets. A network scanner can help identify potentially vulnerable hosts. The mobile environment prevalent on modern networks poses significant challenges. Laptops are routinely taken out of the secure network environment and connected to potentially unsecure environments, such as home networks. Without proper patching of the system, a laptop can be infected with a worm or virus and then bring it back into the secure environment of the organization's network where it can infect other systems.

The quarantine phase involves tracking down and identifying infected machines within the contained areas and disconnecting, blocking, or removing them. This isolates these systems appropriately for the treatment phase.

During the treatment phase, actively infected systems are disinfected of the worm. This can involve terminating the worm process, removing modified files or system settings that the worm introduced, and patching the vulnerability the worm used to exploit the system. Alternatively, in more severe cases, the system may need to be reinstalled to ensure that the worm and its byproducts are removed.

<table>
<tr><td>Refer to Figure in online course</td></tr>
</table>

In the case of the SQL Slammer worm, malicious traffic was detected on UDP port 1434. This port should normally be blocked by a firewall on the perimeter. However, most infections enter by way of back doors and do not pass through the firewall; therefore, to prevent the spreading of this worm it would be necessary to block this port on all devices throughout the internal network.

In some cases, the port on which the worm is spreading might be critical to business operation. For example, when SQL Slammer was propagating, some organizations could not block UDP port 1434 because it was required to access the SQL Server for legitimate business transactions. In such a situation, alternatives must be considered.

If the network devices using the service on the affected port are known, permitting selective access is an option. For example, if only a small number of clients are using SQL Server, one option is to open UDP port 1434 to critical devices only. Selective access is not guaranteed to solve the problem, but it certainly lowers the probability of infection.

Viruses, worms, and Trojan Horses can slow or stop networks and corrupt or destroy data. Good security policies and antivirus software options are available for mitigating these types of threats. Network security professionals must maintain constant vigilance. It is not enough to react efficiently to an attack. A good network security professional examines the whole network to find vulnerabilities and fixes them before an attack occurs.

1.3 Attack Methodologies

1.3.1 Reconnaissance Attacks

<table>
<tr><td>Refer to Figure in online course</td></tr>
</table>

There are many different types of network attacks other than viruses, worms, and Trojan Horses. To mitigate attacks, it is useful to first categorize the various types of attacks. By categorizing network attacks, it is possible to address types of attacks rather than individual attacks. There is no standardized way of categorizing network attacks. The method used in this course classifies attacks in three major categories.

Reconnaissance Attacks

Reconnaissance attacks involve the unauthorized discovery and mapping of systems, services, or vulnerabilities. Reconnaissance attacks often employ the use of packet sniffers and port scanners, which are widely available as free downloads on the Internet. Reconnaissance is analogous to a thief surveying a neighborhood for vulnerable homes to break into, such as an unoccupied residence or a house with an easy-to-open door or window.

Access Attacks

Access attacks exploit known vulnerabilities in authentication services, FTP services, and web services to gain entry to web accounts, confidential databases, and other sensitive information. An access attack can be performed in many different ways. An access attack often employs a dictionary attack to guess system passwords. There are also specialized dictionaries for different languages that can be used.

Denial of Service Attacks

Denial of service attacks send extremely large numbers of requests over a network or the Internet. These excessive requests cause the target device to run sub-optimally. Consequently, the attacked device becomes unavailable for legitimate access and use. By executing exploits or combinations of exploits, DoS attacks slow or crash applications and processes.

Refer to **Figure** in online course

Reconnaissance is also known as information gathering and, in most cases, precedes an access or DoS attack. In a reconnaissance attack, the malicious intruder typically begins by conducting a ping sweep of the target network to determine which IP addresses are active. The intruder then determines which services or ports are available on the live IP addresses. Nmap is the most popular application for performing port scans. From the port information obtained, the intruder queries the ports to determine the type and version of the application and operating system that is running on the target host. In many cases, the intruders look for vulnerable services that can be exploited later when there is less likelihood of being caught.

Reconnaissance attacks use various tools to gain access to a network:

- Packet sniffers

- Ping sweeps

- Port scans

- Internet information queries

Refer to **Figure** in online course

A packet sniffer is a software application that uses a network adapter card in promiscuous mode to capture all network packets that are sent across a LAN. Promiscuous mode is a mode in which the network adapter card sends all packets that are received to an application for processing. Some network applications distribute network packets in unencrypted plaintext. Because the network packets are not encrypted, they can be understood by any application that can pick them off the network and process them.

Packet sniffers can only work in the same collision domain as the network being attacked, unless the attacker has access to the intermediary switches.

Numerous freeware and shareware packet sniffers, such as Wireshark, are available and do not require the user to understand anything about the underlying protocols.

Refer to **Figure** in online course

When used as legitimate tools, ping sweep and port scan applications run a series of tests against hosts and devices to identify vulnerable services. The information is gathered by examining IP addressing and port, or banner, data from both TCP and UDP ports. An attacker uses this information to compromise the system.

Internet information queries can reveal information such as who owns a particular domain and what addresses have been assigned to that domain. They can also reveal who owns a particular IP address and which domain is associated with the address.

A ping sweep is a basic network scanning technique that determines which range of IP addresses map to live hosts. A single ping indicates whether one specified host computer exists on the network. A ping sweep consists of ICMP echo requests sent to multiple hosts. If a given address is live, the address returns an ICMP echo reply. Ping sweeps are among the older and slower methods used to scan a network.

Each service on a host is associated with a well-known port number. Port scanning is a scan of a range of TCP or UDP port numbers on a host to detect listening services. It consists of sending a message to each port on a host. The response that the sender receives indicates whether the port is used.

Ping sweeps of addresses revealed by Internet information queries can present a picture of the live hosts in a particular environment. After such a list is generated, port scanning tools can cycle through all well-known ports to provide a complete list of all services that are running on the hosts that the ping sweep discovered. Hackers can then examine the characteristics of active applications, which can lead to specific information that is useful to a hacker whose intent is to compromise that service.

Refer to **Figure** in online course

Keep in mind that reconnaissance attacks are typically the precursor to further attacks with the intention of gaining unauthorized access to a network or disrupting network functionality. A network security professional can detect when a reconnaissance attack is underway by configured alarms that are triggered when certain parameters are exceeded, such as the number of ICMP requests per second. A variety of technologies and devices can be used to monitor this type of activity and generate an alarm. Cisco's Adaptive Security Appliance (ASA) provides intrusion prevention in a standalone device. Additionally, the Cisco ISR supports network-based intrusion prevention through the Cisco IOS security image.

1.3.2 Access Attacks

Refer to **Figure** in online course

Hackers use access attacks on networks or systems for three reasons: retrieve data, gain access, and escalate access privileges.

Access attacks often employ password attacks to guess system passwords. Password attacks can be implemented using several methods, including brute-force attacks, Trojan Horse programs, IP spoofing, and packet sniffers. However, most password attacks refer to brute-force attacks, which involve repeated attempts based on a built-in dictionary to identify a user account or password.

A brute-force attack is often performed using a program that runs across the network and attempts to log in to a shared resource, such as a server. After an attacker gains access to a resource, the attacker has the same access rights as the user whose account was compromised. If this account has sufficient privileges, the attacker can create a back door for future access without concern for any status and password changes to the compromised user account.

As an example, a user can run the L0phtCrack, or LC5, application to perform a brute-force attack to obtain a Windows server password. When the password is obtained, the attacker can install a keylogger, which sends a copy of all keystrokes to a desired destination. Or, a Trojan Horse can be installed to send a copy of all packets sent and received by the target to a particular destination, thus enabling the monitoring of all the traffic to and from that server.

Refer to **Figure** in online course

There are five types of access attacks:

- *Password attack* An attacker attempts to guess system passwords. A common example is a dictionary attack.

- *Trust exploitation* An attacker uses privileges granted to a system in an unauthorized way, possibly leading to compromising the target.

- *Port redirection* A compromised system is used as a jump-off point for attacks against other targets. An intrusion tool is installed on the compromised system for session redirection.

- *Man-in-the-middle attack* An attacker is positioned in the middle of communications between two legitimate entities in order to read or modify the data that passes between the two parties. A popular man-in-the-middle attack involves a laptop acting as a rogue access point to capture and copy all network traffic from a targeted user. Often the user is in a public location on a wireless hotspot.

- *Buffer overflow* A program writes data beyond the allocated buffer memory. Buffer overflows usually arise as a consequence of a bug in a C or C++ program. A result of the overflow is that valid data is overwritten or exploited to enable the execution of malicious code.

Refer to
Figure
in online course

Access attacks in general can be detected by reviewing logs, bandwidth utilization, and process loads.

The network security policy should specify that logs are formally maintained for all network devices and servers. By reviewing logs, network security personnel can determine if an unusual number of failed login attempts have occurred. Software packages such as ManageEngine EventLog Analyzer or Cisco Secure Access Control Server (CSACS) maintain information regarding failed login attempts to network devices. UNIX and Windows servers also keep a log of failed login attempts. Cisco routers and firewall devices can be configured to prevent login attempts for a given time from a particular source after a prescribed number of failures in a specified amount of time.

Man-in-the-middle attacks often involve replicating data. An indication of such an attack is an unusual amount of network activity and bandwidth utilization, as indicated by network monitoring software.

Similarly, an access attack resulting in a compromised system would likely be revealed by sluggish activity due to ongoing buffer overflow attacks, as indicated by active process loads viewable on a Windows or a UNIX system.

1.3.3 Denial of Service Attacks

Refer to
Figure
in online course

A DoS attack is a network attack that results in some sort of interruption of service to users, devices, or applications. Several mechanisms can generate a DoS attack. The simplest method is to generate large amounts of what appears to be valid network traffic. This type of network DoS attack saturates the network so that valid user traffic cannot get through.

A DoS attack takes advantage of the fact that target systems such as servers must maintain state information. Applications may rely on expected buffer sizes and specific content of network packets. A DoS attack can exploit this by sending packet sizes or data values that are not expected by the receiving application.

There are two major reasons a DoS attack occurs:

- A host or application fails to handle an unexpected condition, such as maliciously formatted input data, an unexpected interaction of system components, or simple resource exhaustion.

- A network, host, or application is unable to handle an enormous quantity of data, causing the system to crash or become extremely slow.

DoS attacks attempt to compromise the availability of a network, host, or application. They are considered a major risk because they can easily interrupt a business process and cause significant loss. These attacks are relatively simple to conduct, even by an unskilled attacker.

Refer to
Figure
in online course

One example of a DoS attack is sending a poisonous packet. A poisonous packet is an improperly formatted packet designed to cause the receiving device to process the packet in an improper fashion. The poisonous packet causes the receiving device to crash or run very slowly. This attack can cause all communications to and from the device to be disrupted.

In another example, an attacker sends a continuous stream of packets, which overwhelms the available bandwidth of network links. In most cases, it is impossible to differentiate between the attacker and legitimate traffic and to trace an attack quickly back to its source. If many systems in the Internet core are compromised, the attacker may be able to take advantage of virtually unlimited bandwidth to unleash packet storms toward desired targets.

A Distributed Denial of Service Attack (DDoS) is similar in intent to a DoS attack, except that a DDoS attack originates from multiple coordinated sources. A DDoS attack requires the network security professional to identify and stop attacks from distributed sources while managing an increase in traffic.

As an example, a DDoS attack could proceed as follows:

- A hacker scans for systems that are accessible.

- After the hacker accesses several "handler" systems, the hacker installs zombie software on them.

- Zombies then scan and infect agent systems.

- When the hacker accesses the agent systems, the hacker loads remote-control attack software to carry out the DDoS attack.

Refer to
Figure
in online course

It is useful to detail three common DoS attacks to get a better understanding of how DoS attacks work.

Ping of Death

In a ping of death attack, a hacker sends an echo request in an IP packet larger than the maximum packet size of 65,535 bytes. Sending a ping of this size can crash the target computer. A variant of this attack is to crash a system by sending ICMP fragments, which fill the reassembly buffers of the target.

Smurf Attack

In a smurf attack, a perpetrator sends a large number of ICMP requests to directed broadcast addresses, all with spoofed source addresses on the same network as the respective directed broadcast. If the routing device delivering traffic to those broadcast addresses forwards the directed broadcasts, all hosts on the destination networks send ICMP replies, multiplying the traffic by the number of hosts on the networks. On a multi-access broadcast network, hundreds of machines might reply to each packet.

TCP SYN Flood

In a TCP SYN flood attack, a flood of TCP SYN packets is sent, often with a forged sender address. Each packet is handled like a connection request, causing the server to spawn a half-open connection by sending back a TCP SYN-ACK packet and waiting for a packet in response from the sender address. However, because the sender address is forged, the response never comes. These half-open connections saturate the number of available connections the server is able to make, keeping it from responding to legitimate requests until after the attack ends.

Refer to
Figure
in online course

The TCP SYN flood, ping of death, and smurf attacks demonstrate how devastating a DoS attack can be. There are five basic ways that DoS attacks can do harm:

- Consumption of resources, such as bandwidth, disk space, or processor time

- Disruption of configuration information, such as routing information

- Disruption of state information, such as unsolicited resetting of TCP sessions

- Disruption of physical network components

- Obstruction of communication between the victim and others.

It is usually not difficult to determine if a DoS attack is occurring. A large number of complaints about not being able to access resources is a first sign of a DoS attack. To minimize the number of attacks, a network utilization software package should be running at all times. This should also be required by the network security policy. A network utilization graph showing unusual activity could indicate a DoS attack.

Keep in mind that DoS attacks could be a component of a larger offensive. DoS attacks can lead to problems in the network segments of the computers being attacked. For example, the packet-per-second capacity of a router between the Internet and a LAN might be exceeded by an attack, compromising not only the target system but also the entire network. If the attack is conducted on a sufficiently large scale, entire geographical regions of Internet connectivity could be compromised.

Not all service outages, even those that result from malicious activity, are necessarily DoS attacks. In any case, DoS attacks are among the most dangerous types of attacks, and it is critical that a network security professional act quickly to mitigate the effects of such attacks.

1.3.4 Mitigating Network Attacks

Refer to
Figure
in online course

There are a variety of network attacks, network attack methodologies, and categories of network attacks. The important question is, 'How do I mitigate these network attacks?'

The type of attack, as specified by the categorization of reconnaissance, access, or DoS attack, determines the means of mitigating a network threat.

Refer to
Figure
in online course

Reconnaissance attacks can be mitigated in several ways.

Using strong authentication is a first option for defense against packet sniffers. Strong authentication is a method of authenticating users that cannot easily be circumvented. A One-Time Password (OTP) is a form of strong authentication. OTPs utilize two-factor authentication. Two-factor authentication combines something one has, such as a token card, with something one knows, such as a PIN. Automated teller machines (ATMs) use two-factor authentication.

Encryption is also effective for mitigating packet sniffer attacks. If traffic is encrypted, using a packet sniffer of little use because captured data is not readable.

Anti-sniffer software and hardware tools detect changes in the response time of hosts to determine whether the hosts are processing more traffic than their own traffic loads would indicate. While this does not completely eliminate the threat, as part of an overall mitigation system, it can reduce the number of instances of threat.

A switched infrastructure is the norm today, which makes it difficult to capture any data except for that data that is in your immediate collision domain, which probably contains only one host. A switched infrastructure does not eliminate the threat of packet sniffers, but can greatly reduce the sniffer's effectiveness.

It is impossible to mitigate port scanning. But using an IPS and firewall can limit the information that can be discovered with a port scanner. Ping sweeps can be stopped if ICMP echo and echo-reply are turned off on edge routers. However, when these services are turned off, network diagnostic data is lost. Additionally, port scans can be run without full ping sweeps. The scans simply take longer because inactive IP addresses are also scanned.

Network-based IPS and host-based IPS can usually notify an administrator when a reconnaissance attack is under way. This warning enables the administrator to better prepare for the coming attack or to notify the ISP from where the reconnaissance probe is being launched.

Refer to
Figure
in online course

Several techniques are also available for mitigating access attacks.

A surprising number of access attacks are carried out through simple password guessing or brute-force dictionary attacks against passwords. The use of encrypted or hashed authentication protocols, along with a strong password policy, greatly reduces the probability of successful access attacks. There are specific practices that help to ensure a strong password policy:

- Disable accounts after a specific number of unsuccessful logins. This practice helps to prevent continuous password attempts.

- Do not use plaintext passwords. Use either a one-time password (OTP) or encrypted password.

- Use strong passwords. Strong passwords are at least eight characters and contain uppercase letters, lowercase letters, numbers, and special characters.

The network should be designed using the principle of minimum trust. This means that systems should not use one another unnecessarily. For example, if an organization has a server that is used by untrusted devices, such as web servers, the trusted device (server) should not trust the untrusted devices (web servers) unconditionally.

Cryptography is a critical component of any modern secure network. Using encryption for remote access to a network is recommended. Routing protocol traffic should be encrypted as well. The more that traffic is encrypted, the less opportunity hackers have for intercepting data with man-in-the-middle attacks.

Refer to **Figure** in online course

Companies with a high-profile Internet presence should plan in advance how to respond to potential DoS attacks. Historically, many DoS attacks were sourced from spoofed source addresses. These types of attacks can be thwarted using antispoofing technologies on perimeter routers and firewalls. Many DoS attacks today are distributed DoS attacks carried out by compromised hosts on several networks. Mitigating DDoS attacks requires careful diagnostics, planning, and cooperation from ISPs.

The most important elements for mitigating DoS attacks are firewalls and IPSs. Both host-based and network-based IPSs are strongly recommended.

Cisco routers and switches support a number of antispoofing technologies, such as port security, DHCP snooping, IP Source Guard, Dynamic ARP Inspection, and ACLs.

Lastly, although Quality of Service (QoS) is not designed as a security technology, one of its applications, traffic policing, can be used to limit ingress traffic from any given customer on an edge router. This limits the impact a single source can have on ingress bandwidth utilization.

Refer to **Figure** in online course

Defending your network against attack requires constant vigilance and education. There are 10 best practices that represent the best insurance for your network:

Step 1. Keep patches up-to-date by installing them weekly or daily, if possible, to prevent buffer overflow and privilege escalation attacks.

Step 2. Shut down unnecessary services and ports.

Step 3. Use strong passwords and change them often.

Step 4. Control physical access to systems.

Step 5. Avoid unnecessary web page inputs. Some websites allow users to enter usernames and passwords. A hacker can enter more than just a username. For example, entering "jdoe; rm -rf /" might allow an attacker to remove the root file system from a UNIX server. Programmers should limit input characters and not accept invalid characters such as | ; < > as input.

Step 6. Perform backups and test the backed up files on a regular basis.

Step 7.   Educate employees about the risks of social engineering, and develop strategies to validate identities over the phone, via email, or in person.

Step 8.   Encrypt and password protect sensitive data.

Step 9.   Implement security hardware and software such as firewalls, IPSs, virtual private network (VPN) devices, antivirus software, and content filtering.

Step 10.   Develop a written security policy for the company.

These methods are only a starting point for sound security management. Organizations must remain vigilant at all times to defend against continually evolving threats.

Using these proven methods of securing a network and applying the knowledge gained in this chapter, you are now prepared to begin deploying network security solutions. One of the first deployment considerations involves securing access to network devices.

1.4 Cisco Network Foundation Protection Framework

1.4.1 NFP

Refer to
Figure
in online course

The Cisco Network Foundation Protection (NFP) framework provides comprehensive guidelines for protecting the network infrastructure. These guidelines form the foundation for continuous delivery of service.

NFP logically divides routers and switches into three functional areas:

- *Control Plane* Responsible for routing data correctly. Control plane traffic consists of device-generated packets required for the operation of the network itself such as ARP message exchanges or OSPF routing advertisements.

- *Management Plane* Responsible for managing network elements. Management plane traffic is generated either by network devices or network management stations using processes and protocols such as Telnet, SSH, TFTP, FTP, NTP, AAA, SNMP, syslog, TACACS+, RADIUS, and NetFlow.

- *Data Plane (Forwarding Plane)* Responsible for forwarding data. Data plane traffic normally consists of user-generated packets being forwarded between endstations. Most traffic travels through the router, or switch, via the data plane. Data plane packets are typically processed in fast-switching cache.

Refer to
Figure
in online course

Control plane traffic consists of device-generated packets required for the operation of the network itself. Control plane security can be implemented using the following features:

- *Cisco AutoSecure* Cisco AutoSecure provides a one-step device lockdown feature to protect the control plane as well as the management and data planes. It is a script that is initiated from the CLI to configure the security posture of routers. The script disables nonessential system processes and services. It first makes recommendations to address security vulnerabilities and then modifies the router configuration.

- *Routing protocol authentication* Routing protocol authentication, or Neighbor authentication, prevents a router from accepting fraudulent routing updates. Most routing protocols support neighbor authentication.

- *Control Plane Policing (CoPP)* CoPP is a Cisco IOS feature designed to allow users to control the flow of traffic that is handled by the route processor of a network device.

CoPP is designed to prevent unnecessary traffic from overwhelming the route processor. The CoPP feature treats the control plane as a separate entity with its own ingress (input) and egress (output) ports. A set of rules can be established and associated with the ingress and egress ports of the control plane.

CoPP consists of the following features:

- **Control Plane Policing (CoPP)** - lets users configure a QoS filter that manages the traffic flow of control plane packets. This protects the control plane against reconnaissance and DoS attacks.

- **Control Plane Protection (CPPr)** - an extension of CoPP but allows for policing granularity. For example, CPPr can filter and rate-limit the packets that are going to the control plane of the router and discard malicious and error packets (or both).

- **Control Plane Logging** - enables logging of the packets that CoPP or CPPr drop or permit. It provides the logging mechanism needed to deploy, monitor, and troubleshoot CoPP features efficiently.

Note: Further detail on securing the control plane is beyond the scope of this course.

<table>
<tr><td>Refer to Figure in online course</td></tr>
</table>

Management plane traffic is generated either by network devices or network management stations using processes and protocols such as Telnet, SSH, TFTP, and FTP, etc. The management plane is a very attractive target to hackers. For this reason, the management module was built with several technologies designed to mitigate such risks.

The information flow between management hosts and the managed devices can be out-of-band (OOB) (information flows within a network on which no production traffic resides) or in-band (information flows across the enterprise production network, the Internet, or both).

Management plane security can be implemented using the following features:

- *Login and password policy* Restricts device accessibility. Limits the accessible ports and restricts the "who" and "how" methods of access.

- *Present legal notification* Displays legal notices. These are often developed by legal counsel of a corporation.

- *Ensure the confidentiality of data* Protects locally stored sensitive data from being viewed or copied. Uses management protocols with strong authentication to mitigate confidentiality attacks aimed at exposing passwords and device configurations.

- *Role-based access control (RBAC)* Ensures access is only granted to authenticated users, groups, and services. RBAC and authentication, authorization, and accounting (AAA) services provide mechanisms to effectively manage access control.

- *Authorize actions* Restricts the actions and views that are permitted by any particular user, group, or service.

- *Enable management access reporting* Logs and accounts for all access. Records who accessed the device, what occurred, and when it occurred.

RBAC restricts user access based on the role of the user. Roles are created according to job or task functions, and assigned access permissions to specific assets. Users are then assigned to roles, and are granted the permissions that are defined for that role.

In Cisco IOS, the role-based CLI access feature implements RBAC for router management access. The feature creates different "views" that define which commands are accepted and what configuration information is visible. For scalability, users, permissions, and roles are usually created and maintained in a central repository server. This makes the access control policy available to multiple devices. The central repository server can be a AAA server, such as the Cisco Secure Access Control System (ACS), which provides AAA services to a network for management purposes.

Refer to
Figure
in online course

Data plane traffic consists mostly of user-generated packets being forwarded through the router via the data plane. Data plane security can be implemented using ACLs, antispoofing mechanisms, and Layer 2 security features.

ACLs perform packet filtering to control which packets move through the network and where those packets are allowed to go. ACLs are used to secure the data plane in a variety of ways, including:

- *Blocking unwanted traffic or users* ACLs can filter incoming or outgoing packets on an interface. They can be used to control access based on source addresses, destination addresses, or user authentication.

- *Reducing the chance of DoS attacks* ACLs can be used to specify whether traffic from hosts, networks, or users access the network. The TCP intercept feature can also be configured to prevent servers from being flooded with requests for a connection.

- *Mitigating spoofing attacks* ACLs allow security practitioners to implement recommended practices to mitigate spoofing attacks.

- *Providing bandwidth control* ACLs on a slow link can prevent excess traffic.

- *Classifying traffic to protect the Management and Control planes* ACLs can be applied on VTY line.

ACLs can also be used as an antispoofing mechanism by discarding traffic that has an invalid source address. This forces attacks to be initiated from valid, reachable IP addresses, allowing the packets to be traced to the originator of an attack.

Features such as Unicast Reverse Path Forwarding (uRPF) can be used to complement the antispoofing strategy.

Cisco Catalyst switches can use integrated features to help secure the Layer 2 infrastructure. The following are Layer 2 security tools integrated into the Cisco Catalyst switches:

- *Port security* Prevents MAC address spoofing and MAC address flooding attacks.

- *DHCP snooping* Prevents client attacks on the DHCP server and switch.

- *Dynamic ARP Inspection (DAI)* Adds security to ARP by using the DHCP snooping table to minimize the impact of ARP poisoning and spoofing attacks.

- *IP Source Guard* Prevents spoofing of IP addresses by using the DHCP snooping table.

This course focuses on the various technologies and protocols used to secure the Management and Data planes.

Chapter Summary

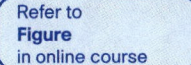

Your Chapter Notes

CHAPTER 2

Securing Network Devices

Chapter Introduction

Refer to
Figure
in online course

Securing outgoing network traffic and scrutinizing incoming traffic are critical aspects of network security. Securing the edge router, which connects to the outside network, is an important first step in securing the network.

Device hardening is a critical task when securing the network. It involves implementing proven methods for physically securing the router and protecting the router's administrative access using the Cisco IOS command-line interface (CLI) as well as the Cisco Configuration Professional (CCP). Some of these methods involve securing administrative access, including maintaining passwords, configuring enhanced virtual login features, and implementing Secure Shell (SSH). Because not all information technology personnel should have the same level of access to the infrastructure devices, defining administrative roles in terms of access is another important aspect of securing infrastructure devices.

Securing the management and reporting features of Cisco IOS devices is also important. Recommended practices for securing syslog, using Simple Network Management Protocol (SNMP), and configuring Network Time Protocol (NTP) are examined.

Many router services are enabled by default. A number of these features are enabled for historical reasons but are no longer required today. This chapter discusses some of these services and examines router configurations with the Security Audit feature of CCP. This chapter also examines the One-Step Lockdown mode of the CCP Security Audit and the `auto secure` command, which can be used to automate device-hardening tasks.

A hands-on lab for the chapter, *Securing the Router for Administrative Access*, is a comprehensive lab that provides an opportunity to practice the wide-ranging security features introduced in this chapter. The lab introduces the various means of securing administrative access to a router, including password best practices, appropriate banner configuration, enhanced login features, and SSH. The role-based CLI access feature relies on creating *views* as a means of providing different levels of access to routers. The Cisco IOS Resilient Configuration feature permits securing router images and configuration files. Syslog and SNMP are used for management reporting. Cisco AutoSecure is an automated tool for securing Cisco routers using the CLI. The CCP Security Audit feature is based on the Cisco IOS AutoSecure feature.

A Packet Tracer activity, *Configure Cisco Routers for Syslog, NTP, and SSH Operations*, provides learners additional practice implementing the technologies introduced in this chapter. In particular, learners configure routers with NTP, syslog, timestamp logging of messages, local user accounts, exclusive SSH connectivity, and RSA key pairs for SSH servers. Using SSH client access from a Windows PC and from a Cisco router is also explored.

2.1 Securing Device Access

2.1.1 Securing the Edge Router

Refer to
Figure
in online course

Securing the network infrastructure is critical to overall network security. The network infrastructure includes routers, switches, servers, endpoints, and other devices.

Consider a disgruntled employee casually looking over the shoulder of a network administrator while the administrator is logging in to an edge router. This is known as shoulder surfing, and it is a surprisingly easy way for an attacker to gain unauthorized access.

If an attacker gains access to a router, the security and management of the entire network can be compromised, leaving servers and endpoints at risk. It is critical that the appropriate security policies and controls be implemented to prevent unauthorized access to all infrastructure devices. Although all infrastructure devices are at risk, routers are a primary target for network attackers. This is because routers act as traffic police, directing traffic into, out of, and between networks.

The edge router is the last router between the internal network and an untrusted network such as the Internet. All of an organization's Internet traffic goes through this edge router; therefore, it often functions as the first and last line of defense for a network. Through initial and final filtering, the edge router helps to secure the perimeter of a protected network. It is also responsible for implementing security actions that are based on the security policies of the organization. For these reasons, securing network routers is imperative.

Refer to
Figure
in online course

The edge router implementation varies depending on the size of the organization and the complexity of the required network design. Router implementations can include a single router protecting an entire inside network or a router as the first line of defense in a defense-in-depth approach.

Single Router Approach

In the single router approach, a single router connects the protected network, or internal LAN, to the Internet. All security policies are configured on this device. This is more commonly deployed in smaller site implementations such as branch and SOHO sites. In smaller networks, the required security features can be supported by ISRs without impeding the router's performance capabilities.

Defense-in-Depth Approach

A defense-in-depth approach is more secure than the single router approach. In this approach, the edge router acts as the first line of defense and is known as a screening router. It passes all connections that are intended for the internal LAN to the firewall.

The second line of defense is the firewall. The firewall typically picks up where the edge router leaves off and performs additional filtering. It provides additional access control by tracking the state of the connections and acts as a checkpoint device.

The edge router has a set of rules specifying which traffic it allows and denies. By default, the firewall denies the initiation of connections from the outside (untrusted) networks to the inside (trusted) network. However, it allows the internal users to establish connections to the untrusted networks and permits the responses to come back through the firewall. It can also perform user authentication (authentication proxy) where users must be authenticated to gain access to network resources.

DMZ Approach

A variation of the defense-in-depth approach is to offer an intermediate area, often called the demilitarized zone (DMZ). The DMZ can be used for servers that must be accessible from the Internet or some other external network. The DMZ can be set up between two routers, with an internal router connecting to the protected network and an external router connecting to the unprotected network. Alternatively, the DMZ can simply be an additional port off of a single router. The firewall, located between the protected and unprotected networks, is set up to permit the required connections (for example, HTTP) from the outside (untrusted) networks to the public servers in the DMZ. The firewall serves as the primary protection for all devices on the DMZ. In the DMZ approach, the router provides some protection by filtering some traffic, but leaves the bulk of the protection to the firewall.

Securing the edge router is a critical first step in securing the network. If there are other internal routers, they must be securely configured as well. Three areas of router security must be maintained.

Refer to **Figure** in online course

Physical Security

Provide physical security for the routers:

- Place the router and physical devices that connect to it in a secure locked room that is accessible only to authorized personnel, is free of electrostatic or magnetic interference, has fire suppression, and has controls for temperature and humidity.

- Install an uninterruptible power supply (UPS) and keep spare components available. This reduces the possibility of a DoS attack from power loss to the building.

Router Hardening

Eliminate potential abuse of unused ports and services:

- Secure administrative control. Ensure that only authorized personnel have access and that their level of access is controlled.

- Disable unused ports and interfaces. Reduce the number of ways a device can be accessed.

- Disable unnecessary services. Similar to many computers, a router has services that are enabled by default. Some of these services are unnecessary and can be used by an attacker to gather information or for exploitation.

Operating System Security

Secure the features and performance of the router operating systems:

- Configure the router with the maximum amount of memory possible. The availability of memory can help protect the network from some DoS attacks, while supporting the widest range of security services.

- Use the latest stable version of the operating system that meets the feature requirements of the network. Security features in an operating system evolve over time. Keep in mind that the latest version of an operating system might not be the most stable version available.

- Keep a secure copy of the router operating system image and router configuration file as a backup.

Refer to **Figure** in online course

Administrative access is required for router management purposes; therefore, securing administrative access is an extremely important security task. If an unauthorized person were to gain administrative access to a router, that person could alter routing parameters, disable routing functions, or discover and gain access to other systems in the network.

Several important tasks are involved in securing administrative access to an infrastructure device:

- *Restrict device accessibility* Limit the accessible ports, restrict the permitted communicators, and restrict the permitted methods of access.

- *Log and account for all access* For auditing purposes, record anyone who accesses a device, including what occurs and when.

- *Authenticate access* Ensure that access is granted only to authenticated users, groups, and services. Limit the number of failed login attempts and the time between logins.

- *Authorize actions* Restrict the actions and views permitted by any particular user, group, or service.

- *Present legal notification* Display a legal notice, developed in conjunction with company legal counsel, for interactive sessions.

- *Ensure the confidentiality of data* Protect locally stored sensitive data from viewing and copying. Consider the vulnerability of data in transit over a communication channel to sniffing, session hijacking, and man-in-the-middle (MITM) attacks.

Refer to
Figure
in online course

There are two ways to access a device for administrative purposes: locally and remotely.

Local Access

All network infrastructure devices can be accessed locally. Local access to a router usually requires a direct connection to a console port on the Cisco router using a computer that is running terminal emulation software.

Remote Access

Some network devices can be accessed remotely. Remote access typically involves allowing Telnet, Secure Shell (SSH), HTTP, HTTPS, or Simple Network Management Protocol (SNMP) connections to the router from a computer. The computer can be on the same subnet or a different subnet. Some remote access protocols send the data, including usernames and passwords, to the router in plaintext. If an attacker can collect network traffic while an administrator is remotely logged in to a router, the attacker can capture passwords or router configuration information.

For this reason, it is preferable to allow only local access to the router. However, remote access might still be necessary. When accessing the network remotely, a few precautions should be taken:

- Encrypt all traffic between the administrator computer and the router. For example, instead of using Telnet, use SSH. Or instead of using HTTP, use HTTPS.

- Establish a dedicated management network. The management network should include only identified administration hosts and connections to a dedicated interface on the router.

- Configure a packet filter to allow only the identified administration hosts and preferred protocols to access the router. For example, permit only SSH requests from the IP address of the administration host to initiate a connection to the routers in the network.

These precautions are valuable, but they do not protect the network completely. Other methods of defense must also be implemented. One of the most basic and important methods is the use of a secure password.

2.1.2 Configuring Secure Administrative Access

Refer to
Figure
in online course

Attackers deploy various methods of discovering administrative passwords. They can shoulder surf, attempt to guess passwords based on the user's personal information, or sniff TFTP packets containing plaintext configuration files. Attackers can also use tools such as L0phtCrack and Cain & Abel to attempt brute force attacks and guess passwords.

To protect assets such as routers and switches, follow these common guidelines for choosing strong passwords. These guidelines are designed to make passwords less easily discovered by intelligent guessing and cracking tools:

- Use a password length of 10 or more characters. A longer password is a better password.

- Make passwords complex. Include a mix of uppercase and lowercase letters, numbers, symbols, and spaces.

- Avoid passwords based on repetition, dictionary words, letter or number sequences, usernames, relative or pet names, biographical information, such as birthdates, ID numbers, ancestor names, or other easily identifiable pieces of information.

- Deliberately misspell a password. For example, Smith = Smyth = 5mYth or Security = 5ecur1ty.

- Change passwords often. If a password is unknowingly compromised, the window of opportunity for the attacker to use the password is limited.

- Do not write passwords down and leave them in obvious places such as on the desk or monitor.

On Cisco routers and many other systems, password-leading spaces are ignored, but spaces after the first character are not ignored. Therefore, one method to create a strong password is to use the space bar in the password and create a phrase made of many words. This is called a pass phrase. A pass phrase is often easier to remember than a simple password. It is also longer and harder to guess.

Administrators should ensure that strong passwords are used across the network. One way to accomplish this is to use the same cracking and brute force attack tools that attackers use as a way to verify password strength.

> Refer to
> **Figure**
> in online course

Many access ports require passwords on a Cisco router, including the console port, auxiliary port, and virtual terminal connections. Password management in a large network should be maintained using a central TACACS+ or RADIUS authentication server such as the Cisco Secure Access Control Server (ACS). All routers must be configured with the user and privileged EXEC passwords. A local username database is also recommended as backup if access to an authentication, authorization, and accounting (AAA) server is compromised. Using a password and assigning privilege levels is a simple way to provide terminal access control in a network. Passwords must be established for privileged EXEC mode access and individual lines such as the console and auxiliary lines.

Enable Secret Password

The `enable secret` *password* global configuration command restricts access to privileged EXEC mode. The enable secret password is always hashed inside the router configuration using a Message Digest 5 (MD5) hashing algorithm. If the enable secret password is lost or forgotten, it must be replaced using the Cisco router password recovery procedure.

Console Line

By default, the console port does not require a password for console administrative access; however, it should always be configured as a console port line-level password. Use the `line console 0` command followed by the `login` and `password` subcommands to require login and establish a login password on the console line.

Virtual Terminal Lines

By default, Cisco routers support up to five simultaneous virtual terminal vty (Telnet or SSH) sessions. On the router, the vty ports are numbered from 0 through 4. Use the `line vty 0 4` command followed by the **login** and **password** subcommands to require login and establish a login password on incoming Telnet sessions.

Auxiliary Line

By default, Cisco router auxiliary ports do not require a password for remote administrative access. Administrators sometimes use this port to remotely configure and monitor the router using a dialup modem connection.

To access the auxiliary line use the **line aux 0** command. Use the **login** and **password** subcommands to require login and establish a login password on incoming connections.

By default, with the exception of the enable secret password, all Cisco router passwords are stored in plaintext within the router configuration. These passwords can be viewed with the **show running-config** command. Sniffers can also see these passwords if the TFTP server configuration files traverse an unsecured intranet or Internet connection. If an intruder gains access to the TFTP server where the router configuration files are stored, the intruder is able to obtain these passwords.

Refer to
Figure
in online course

There are multiple actions that can be taken to increase password security:

- Enforce minimum password lengths.

- Disable unattended connections.

- Encrypt all passwords in the configuration file.

Minimum Character Length

Beginning with the Cisco IOS Release 12.3(1) and later, administrators can set the minimum character length for all router passwords from 0 to 16 characters using the global configuration command **security passwords min-length** *length*. It is strongly recommended that the minimum password length be set to at least 10 characters to eliminate common passwords that are short and prevalent on most networks, such as "lab" and "cisco."

This command affects user passwords, enable secret passwords, and line passwords that are created after the command is executed. Existing router passwords remain unaffected. Any attempt to create a new password that is less than the specified length fails and results in an error message similar to the following.

```
Password too short - must be at least 10 characters. Password configuration failed.
```

Disable Unattended Connections

By default, an administrative interface stays active and logged in for 10 minutes after the last session activity. After that, the interface times out and logs out of the session.

If an administrator is away from the terminal while the console connection is active, an attacker has up to 10 minutes to gain privilege level access. It is recommended that these timers be fine-tuned to limit the amount of time to within a two or three minute maximum. These timers can be adjusted using the **exec-timeout** command in line configuration mode for each of the line types that are used.

It is also possible to turn off the exec process for a specific line, such as on the auxiliary port, using the **no exec** command within the line configuration mode. This command allows only an outgoing connection on the line. The **no exec** command allows you to disable the EXEC process for connections that may attempt to send unsolicited data to the router.

Encrypt All Passwords

By default, some passwords are shown in plaintext, which means that they are not encrypted, in the Cisco IOS software configuration. With the exception of the enable secret password, all other plaintext passwords in the configuration file can be encrypted in the configuration file using the **service password-encryption** command. This command hashes current and future plaintext passwords in the configuration file into an encrypted ciphertext. To stop encrypting passwords, use the **no** form of the command. Only passwords created after the **no** command is issued will be unencrypted. Existing passwords that have been previously encrypted will remain so.

The **service password-encryption** command is primarily useful for keeping unauthorized individuals from viewing passwords in the configuration file. The algorithm used by the **service password-encryption** command is simple and can be easily reversed by someone with access to the encrypted ciphertext and a password-cracking application. For that reason, this command should not be used with the intention to protect configuration files against serious attacks.

The **enable secret** command is far more secure because it encrypts the password using MD5, which is a stronger algorithm.

Refer to
Figure
in online course

Another available security feature is authentication. Cisco routers can maintain a list of usernames and passwords in a local database on the router for performing local login authentication. There are two methods of configuring local username accounts.

```
username name password password
username name secret password
```

The **username secret** command is more secure because it uses the stronger algorithm, MD5 hashing, for concealing passwords. MD5 is a much better algorithm than the standard type 7 used by the **service password-encryption** command. The added layer of MD5 protection is useful in environments in which the password crosses the network or is stored on a TFTP server. Keep in mind that when configuring a username and password combination, password length restrictions must be followed. Use the **login local** command on the line configuration to enable the local database for authentication.

All of the remaining examples in this chapter are using the **username secret** configuration instead of **username password**.

2.1.3 Configuring Enhanced Security for Virtual Logins

Refer to
Figure
in online course

Assigning passwords and local authentication does not prevent a device from being targeted for attack. DoS attacks flood a device with so many connection requests that the device might not provide normal login service to legitimate system administrators. A dictionary attack, which is used to gain administrative access to a device, floods a device with thousands of username and password combinations. The end result is much the same as a DoS attack, in that the device cannot process legitimate user requests. The network needs to have systems in place to detect and help prevent these attacks.

By enabling a detection profile, a network device can be configured to react to repeated failed login attempts by refusing further connection requests (login blocking). This block can be configured for a period of time, which is called a quiet period. Legitimate connection attempts can still be permitted during a quiet period by configuring an access control list (ACL) with the addresses that are known to be associated with system administrators.

The Cisco IOS login enhancements feature provides more security for Cisco IOS devices when creating a virtual connection, such as Telnet, SSH, or HTTP, by slowing down dictionary attacks and stopping DoS attacks. To better configure security for virtual login connections, the login process should be configured with specific parameters:

- Delays between successive login attempts

- Login shutdown if DoS attacks are suspected

- Generation of system logging messages for login detection

These enhancements do not apply to console connections. It is assumed that only authorized personnel have physical access to the devices.

Refer to
Figure
in online course

The following commands are available to configure a Cisco IOS device to support the enhanced login features.

```
Router# configure terminal
Router(config)# login block-for seconds attempts tries within seconds
Router(config)# login quiet-mode access-class {acl-name ¦ acl-number}
Router(config)# login delay seconds
Router(config)# login on-failure log [every login]
Router(config)# login on-success log [every login]
```

Authentication on vty lines must be configured to use a username and password combination. If the vty lines are configured to use only a password, the enhanced login features are not enabled.

What does each command accomplish?

Refer to
Figure
in online course

All login enhancement features are disabled by default. Use the **login block-for** command to enable login enhancements. The **login block-for** feature monitors login device activity and operates in two modes:

- *Normal mode (watch mode)* The router keeps count of the number of failed login attempts within an identified amount of time.

- *Quiet mode (quiet period)* If the number of failed logins exceeds the configured threshold, all login attempts using Telnet, SSH, and HTTP are denied.

When quiet mode is enabled, all login attempts, including valid administrative access, are not permitted. However, to provide critical hosts access at all times, this behavior can be overridden using an ACL. The ACL must be created and identified using the **login quiet-mode access-class** command.

By default, Cisco IOS devices can accept connections, such as Telnet, SSH, and HTTP, as quickly as they can be processed. This makes devices susceptible to dictionary attack tools, such as Cain or L0phtcrack, which are capable of thousands of password attempts per second. The **login block-for** command invokes an automatic delay of 1 second between login attempts. Attackers have to wait 1 second before they can try a different password.

This delay time can be changed using the **login delay** command. The **login delay** command introduces a uniform delay between successive login attempts. The delay occurs for all login attempts, including failed or successful attempts.

The **login block-for**, **login quiet-mode access-class**, and **login delay** commands help block failed login attempts for a limited period of time but cannot prevent an attacker from trying again. How can an administrator know when someone tries to gain access to the network by guessing the password?

Refer to
Figure
in online course

The command **auto secure** enables message logging for failed login attempts. Logging successful login attempts is not enabled by default.

These commands can be used to keep track of the number of successful and failed login attempts.

login on-failure log [**every** *login*] generates logs for failed login requests.

login on-success log [**every** *login*] generates log messages for successful login requests.

The number of login attempts before a logging message is generated can be specified using the [**every** *login*] parameter. The default value is 1 attempt. The valid range is from 1 to 65,535.

As an alternative, the `security authentication failure rate` *threshold-rate* `log` command generates a log message when the login failure rate is exceeded.

To verify that the `login block-for` command is configured and which mode the router is currently in, use the `show login` command. The router is in either normal or quite mode, depending on whether login thresholds were exceeded.

The `show login failures` command displays more information regarding the failed attempts, such as the IP address from which the failed login attempts originated.

Refer to
Figure
in online course

Use banner messages to present legal notification to potential intruders to inform them that they are not welcome on a network. Banners are very important to the network from a legal perspective. Intruders have won court cases because they did not encounter appropriate warning messages when accessing router networks. In addition to warning would-be intruders, banners are also used to inform remote administrators of use restrictions.

Choosing what to place in banner messages is important and should be reviewed by legal counsel before putting them on network routers. Never use the word welcome or any other familiar greeting that may be misconstrued as an invitation to use the network.

Banners are disabled by default and must be explicitly enabled. Use the `banner` command from global configuration mode to specify appropriate messages.

```
banner {exec ¦ incoming ¦ login ¦ motd ¦ slip-ppp} d message d
```

Tokens are optional and can be used within the message section of the `banner` command:

`$(hostname)`-Displays the host name for the router.

`$(domain)`-Displays the domain name for the router.

`$(line)`-Displays the vty or tty (asynchronous) line number.

`$(line-desc)`-Displays the description that is attached to the line.

Be careful in placing this information in the banner because it provides more information to a possible intruder.

CCP can also be used to configure banner messages.

2.1.4 Configuring SSH

Refer to
Figure
in online course

When enabling remote administrative access, it is also important to consider the security implications of sending information across the network. Traditionally, remote access on routers was configured using Telnet on TCP port 23. However, Telnet was developed in the days when security was not an issue, therefore, all Telnet traffic is forwarded in plaintext. Using this protocol, critical data, such as router configurations, is easily accessible to attackers. Hackers can capture packets forwarded by an administrator's computer using a protocol analyzer such as Wireshark. If the initial Telnet stream is discovered and followed, attackers can learn the administrator's username and password.

However, having remote access capability can save an organization time and money when making necessary configuration changes. How can a secure remote access connection be established to manage Cisco IOS devices?

SSH has replaced Telnet as the recommended practice for providing remote router administration with connections that support confidentiality and session integrity. It provides functionality that is similar to an outbound Telnet connection, except that the connection is encrypted and operates on port 22. With authentication and encryption, SSH allows for secure communication over a non-secure network.

Four steps must be completed prior to configuring routers for the SSH protocol:

Step 1. Ensure that the target routers are running a Cisco IOS Release 12.1(1)T image or later to support SSH. Only the Cisco IOS cryptographic images containing the IPsec feature set support SSH. Specifically, Cisco IOS 12.1 or later IPsec DES or Triple Data Encryption Standard (3DES) cryptographic images support SSH. Typically, these images have image IDs of k8 or k9 in their image names. For example, c1841-advipservicesk9-mz.124-10b.bin is an image that can support SSH.

Step 2. Ensure that each of the target routers has a unique host name.

Step 3. Ensure that each of the target routers is using the correct domain name of the network.

Step 4. Ensure that the target routers are configured for local authentication or AAA services for username and password authentication. This is mandatory for a router-to-router SSH connection.

Using the CLI, there are four steps to configure a Cisco router to support SSH:

Step 1. If the router has a unique host name, configure the IP domain name of the network using the `ip domain-name` *domain-name* command in global configuration mode.

Step 2. One-way secret keys must be generated for a router to encrypt the SSH traffic. These keys are referred to as asymmetric keys. Cisco IOS software uses the Rivest, Shamir, and Adleman (RSA) algorithm to generate keys. To create the RSA key, use the `crypto key generate rsa general-keys modulus` *modulus-size* command in global configuration mode. The modulus determines the size of the RSA key and can be configured from 360 bits to 2048 bits. The larger the modulus, the more secure the RSA key. However, keys with large modulus values take slightly longer to generate and longer to encrypt and decrypt as well. The minimum recommended modulus key length is 1024 bits.

To verify SSH and display the generated keys, use the `show crypto key mypubkey rsa` command in privileged EXEC mode. If there are existing key pairs, it is recommended that they are overwritten using the `crypto key zeroize rsa` command.

Step 3. Ensure that there is a valid local database username entry. If not, create one using the `username` *name* `secret` *secret* command.

Step 4. Enable vty inbound SSH sessions using the line vty commands `login local` and `transport input ssh`.

SSH is automatically enabled after the RSA keys are generated. The router SSH service can be accessed using SSH client software.

Additional SSH Commands

Optionally, SSH commands can be used to configure the following:

- SSH version
- SSH timeout period
- Number of authentication retries

Cisco routers support two versions of SSH: SSH version 1 (SSHv1) and the newer, more secure SSH version 2 (SSHv2). SSHv2 provides better security using the Diffie-Hellman key exchange and the strong integrity-checking message authentication code (MAC).

Cisco IOS Release 12.1(1)T and later supports SSHv1. Cisco IOS Release 12.3(4)T and later operates in compatibility mode and supports both SSHv1 and SSHv2. To change from compatibility mode to a specific version, use the `ip ssh version {1 | 2}` global configuration command.

The time interval that the router waits for the SSH client to respond during the SSH negotiation phase can be configured using the `ip ssh time-out` *seconds* command in global configuration mode. The default is 120 seconds. When the EXEC session starts, the standard exec timeout configured for the vty applies.

By default, a user logging in has three attempts before being disconnected. To configure a different number of consecutive SSH retries, use the `ip ssh authentication-retries` *integer* command in global configuration mode.

To verify the optional SSH command settings, use the `show ip ssh` command.

After SSH is configured, an SSH client is required to connect to an SSH-enabled router.

> Refer to
> **Figure**
> in online course

There are two different ways to connect to an SSH-enabled router:

- Connect using an SSH-enabled Cisco router using the privileged EXEC mode `ssh` command.

- Connect using a publicly and commercially available SSH client running on a host. Examples of these clients are PuTTY, OpenSSH, and TeraTerm.

Cisco routers are capable of acting as the SSH server and as an SSH client connecting to another SSH-enabled device. By default, both of these functions are enabled on the router when SSH is enabled. As a server, a router can accept SSH client connections. As a client, a router can SSH to another SSH-enabled router.

The procedure for connecting to a Cisco router varies depending on the SSH client application that is being used. Generally, the SSH client initiates an SSH connection to the router. The router SSH service prompts for the correct username and password combination. After the login is verified, the router can be managed as if the administrator was using a standard Telnet session.

Use the `show ssh` command to verify the status of the client connections.

> Refer to
> **Figure**
> in online course

CCP can be used to configure an SSH daemon on a router. To see the current SSH key settings, choose **Configure > Router > Router Access > SSH**. The SSH key settings have two status options.

- *RSA key is not set on this router* This notice appears if there is no cryptographic key configured for the device. If there is no key configured, enter a modulus size and generate a key.

- *RSA key is set on this router* This notice appears if a cryptographic key has been generated, in which case SSH is enabled on this router.

Some Cisco routers are shipped with Cisco Configuration Professional Express and a default configuration. These files are loaded into the router's flash memory. The default configuration includes the basic settings needed for a local PC to access CCP Express. These basic settings include an HTTP or HTTPS server with local authentication, a local user account, and SSH access to the vty lines. This default configuration generates an RSA key.

The **Generate RSA** Key button configures a cryptographic key if one is currently set. The Key Modulus Size dialog box appears. If the modulus value needs to be between 512 and 1024, enter an integer value that is a multiple of 64. If the modulus value needs to be higher than 1024, enter 1536 or 2048. If a value greater than 512 is entered, key generation can take a minute or longer.

After SSH is enabled on the router, the vty lines to support SSH need to be configured. Choose **Configure > Router > Router Access > VTY**. The VTY Lines window displays the vty settings on the router. Click the **Edit** button to configure vty parameters.

2.2 Assigning Administrative Roles

2.2.1 Configuring Privilege Levels

Refer to
Figure
in online course

While it is important that a system administrator can securely connect to and manage a device, still more configurations are needed to keep the network secure. For example, should complete access be provided for all employees in a company? The answer to that question is usually no. Most company employees require only specific areas of access to the network. What about complete access for all employees in the IT department? Keep in mind that large organizations have many various job functions within an IT department. For example, job titles include Chief Information Officer (CIO), Security Operator, Network Administrator, WAN Engineer, LAN Administrator, Software Administrator, PC Tech support, Help Desk support, and others. Not all job functions should have the same level of access to the infrastructure devices.

As an example, a senior network administrator leaves for vacation and, as a precaution, provides a junior administrator with the privileged EXEC mode passwords to all infrastructure devices. A few days later, the curious junior administrator accidentally disables the company network. This is not an uncommon scenario, because all too often a router is secured with only one privileged EXEC password. Anyone with knowledge of this password has open access to the entire router.

Configuring privilege levels is the next step for the system administrator who wants to secure the network. Privilege levels determine who should be allowed to connect to the device and what that person should be able to do with it. The Cisco IOS software CLI has two levels of access to commands.

- User EXEC mode (privilege level 1) - Provides the lowest EXEC mode user privileges and allows only user-level commands available at the `router>` prompt.

- Privileged EXEC mode (privilege level 15) - Includes all enable-level commands at the `router#` prompt.

Although these two levels do provide control, sometimes a more precise level of control is required.

Cisco IOS software has two methods of providing infrastructure access: privilege level and role-based CLI.

Refer to
Figure
in online course

Assigning Privilege Levels

Since Cisco IOS Release 10.3, Cisco routers enable an administrator to configure multiple privilege levels. Configuring privilege levels is especially useful in a help desk environment where certain administrators must be able to configure and monitor every part of the router (level 15), and other administrators need only to monitor, not configure, the router (customized levels 2 to 14). There are 16 privilege levels in total. Levels 0, 1, and 15 have predefined settings.

An administrator can define multiple customized privilege levels and assign different commands to each level. The higher the privilege level, the more router access a user has. Commands that are available at lower privilege levels are also executable at higher levels, because a privilege level includes the privileges of all lower levels. For example, a user authorized for privilege level 10 is granted access to commands allowed at privilege levels 0 through 10 (if also defined). A privilege-level-10 user cannot access commands granted to privilege level 11 (or higher). A user authorized for privilege level 15 can execute all Cisco IOS commands.

To assign commands to a custom privilege level, use the `privilege` command from global configuration mode.

```
Router(config)# privilege mode {level level command ¦ reset} command
```

It is important to note that assigning a command with multiple keywords, such as `show ip route`, to a specific privilege level automatically assigns all commands associated with the first few keywords to the specified privilege level. For example, both the `show` command and the `show ip` command are automatically set to the privilege level where `show ip route` is set. This is necessary because the `show ip route` command cannot be executed without access to the `show` and `show ip` commands. Subcommands coming under `show ip route` are also automatically assigned to the same privilege level. Assigning the `show ip route` command allows the user to issue all `show` commands, such as `show version`.

<table>
<tr><td>Refer to
Figure
in online course</td></tr>
</table>

Privilege levels should also be configured for authentication. There are two methods for assigning passwords to the different levels:

- To the privilege level using the global configuration command `enable secret level` *level* *password*.

- To a user that is granted a specific privilege level, using the global configuration command `username` *name* `privilege` *level* `secret` *password*.

For example, an administrator could assign four levels of device access within an organization:

- A USER account (requiring level 1, not including `ping`)

- A SUPPORT account (requiring all level 1 access, plus the `ping` command)

- A JR-ADMIN account (requiring all level 1 and 5 access, plus the `reload` command)

- An ADMIN account (requiring complete access)

Implementing privilege levels varies depending on the organization's structure and the different job functions that require access to the infrastructure devices.

In the case of the USER, which requires default level 1 (Router>) access, no custom privilege level is defined. This is because the default user mode is equivalent to level 1.

The SUPPORT account could be assigned a higher level access such as level 5. Level 5 automatically inherits the commands from levels 1 through 4, plus additional commands can be assigned. Keep in mind that when a command is assigned at a specific level, access to that command is taken away from any lower level. For example, to assign level 5 the `ping` command, use the following command sequence.

```
privilege exec level 5 ping
```

The USER account (level 1) no longer has access to the ping command, because a user must have access to level 5 or higher to perform the ping function.

To assign a password to level 5, enter the following command.

```
enable secret level 5 cisco5
```

To access level 5, the password cisco5 must be used.

To assign a specific username to privilege level 5, enter the following command.

```
username support privilege 5 secret cisco5
```

A user that logs in under the username support is only able to access privilege level 5, which also inherits privilege level 1.

Refer to
Figure
in online course

The JR-ADMIN account needs access to all level 1 and level 5 commands as well as the **reload** command. This account must be assigned a higher level access, such as level 10. Level 10 automatically inherits all the commands from the lower levels.

To assign level 10 to the privileged EXEC mode **reload** command, use the following command sequence.

```
privilege exec level 10 reload
username jr-admin privilege 10 secret cisco10
enable secret level 10 cisco10
```

By performing these commands, the **reload** command is only available to users with level 10 access or higher. The username jr-admin is given access to privilege level 10 and all associated commands, including those commands assigned to any lower privilege levels. To access level 10 mode, the password cisco10 is required.

An ADMIN account could be assigned the default level 15 access for privileged EXEC mode. In this instance, no custom commands need to be defined. A custom password could be assigned using the **enable secret level 15 cisco123** command, however, that does not override the enable secret password, which could also be used to access level 15. Use the **username admin privilege 15 secret cisco15** command to assign level 15 access to the user ADMIN with a password of cisco15.

Keep in mind that when assigning usernames to privilege levels, the **privilege** and **secret** keywords are not interchangeable. For example, the **username USER secret cisco privilege 1** command does not assign the USER account level 1 access. Instead, it creates an account requiring the password "**cisco privilege 1**".

To access established privilege levels, enter the **enable** *level* command from user mode, and enter the password that was assigned to the custom privilege level. Use the same command to switch from a lower level to a higher level.

- To switch from level 1 to level 5, use the **enable 5** command at the EXEC prompt.

- To switch to level 10, use **enable 10** with the correct password.

- To switch from level 10 to level 15, use the **enable** command. If no privilege level is specified, level 15 is assumed.

It is sometimes easy to forget which level of access a user currently has. Use the **show privilege** command to display and confirm the current privilege level. Remember that the higher privilege levels automatically inherit the command access of the lower levels.

Refer to
Figure
in online course

Although assigning privilege levels does provide some flexibility, some organizations might not find them suitable because of the following limitations:

- No access control to specific interfaces, ports, logical interfaces, and slots on a router.

- Commands available at lower privilege levels are always executable at higher levels.

- Commands specifically set on a higher privilege level are not available for lower privileged users.

- Assigning a command with multiple keywords to a specific privilege level also assigns all commands associated with the first keywords to the same privilege level. An example is the **show ip route** command.

The biggest limitation however is that if an administrator needs to create a user account that has access to most but not all commands, `privilege exec` statements must be configured for every command that must be executed at a privilege level lower than 15. This can be a tedious process.

How can the limitations of assigning privilege levels be overcome?

2.2.2 Configuring Role-Based CLI Access

Refer to
Figure
in online course

Role-Based CLI

To provide more flexibility than privilege levels, Cisco introduced the Role-Based CLI Access feature in Cisco IOS Release 12.3(11)T. This feature provides finer, more granular access by controlling specifically which commands are available to specific roles. Role-based CLI access enables the network administrator to create different views of router configurations for different users. Each view defines the CLI commands that each user can access.

Security

Role-based CLI access enhances the security of the device by defining the set of CLI commands that is accessible by a particular user. Additionally, administrators can control user access to specific ports, logical interfaces, and slots on a router. This prevents a user from accidentally or purposely changing a configuration or collecting information to which they should not have access.

Availability

Role-based CLI access prevents unintentional execution of CLI commands by unauthorized personnel, which could result in undesirable results. This minimizes downtime.

Operational Efficiency

Users only see the CLI commands applicable to the ports and CLI to which they have access; therefore, the router appears to be less complex, and commands are easier to identify when using the help feature on the device.

Refer to
Figure
in online course

Role-based CLI provides three types of views:

- Root view
- CLI view
- Superview

Each view dictates which commands are available.

Root View

To configure any view for the system, the administrator must be in root view. Root view has the same access privileges as a user who has level 15 privileges. However, a root view is not the same as a level 15 user. Only a root view user can configure a new view and add or remove commands from the existing views.

CLI View

A specific set of commands can be bundled into a CLI view. Unlike privilege levels, a CLI view has no command hierarchy and, therefore, no higher or lower views. Each view must be assigned all commands associated with that view, and a view does not inherit commands from any other views. Additionally, the same commands can be used in multiple views.

Superview

A superview consists of one or more CLI views. Administrators can define which commands are accepted and which configuration information is visible. Superviews allow a network administrator to assign users and groups of users multiple CLI views at once, instead of having to assign a single CLI view per user with all commands associated to that one CLI view.

Superviews have the following characteristics:

- A single CLI view can be shared within multiple superviews.

- Commands cannot be configured for a superview. An administrator must add commands to the CLI view and add that CLI view to the superview.

- Users who are logged into a superview can access all the commands that are configured for any of the CLI views that are part of the superview.

- Each superview has a password that is used to switch between superviews or from a CLI view to a superview.

Deleting a superview does not delete the associated CLI views. The CLI views remain available to be assigned to another superview.

Refer to
Figure
in online course

Before an administrator can create a view, AAA must be enabled using the **aaa new-model** CLI command or CCP. To configure and alter views, an administrator must log in as the root view, using the **enable view** privileged EXEC command. The **enable view root** command can also be used. When prompted, enter the enable secret password.

There are five steps to create and manage a specific view:

Step 1.   Enable AAA with the **aaa new-model** global configuration command. Exit and enter the root view with the **enable view** command.

Step 2.   Create a view using the **parser view** *view-name* command. This enables the view configuration mode. Excluding the root view, there is a maximum limit of 15 views in total.

Step 3.   Assign a secret password to the view using the **secret** *encrypted-password* command.

Step 4.   Assign commands to the selected view using the **commands** *parser-mode* {**include** ¦ **include-exclusive** ¦ **exclude**} [**all**] [**interface** *interface-name* ¦ *command*] command in view configuration mode.

Step 5.   Exit view configuration mode by typing the **exit** command.

Refer to
Figure
in online course

The steps to configure a superview are essentially the same as configuring a CLI view, except that instead of using the **commands** command to assign commands, use the **view** *view-name* command to assign views. The administrator must be in root view to configure a superview. To confirm that root view is being used, use either the **enable view** or **enable view root** command. When prompted, enter the enable secret password.

There are four steps to create and manage a superview:

Step 1.   Create a view using the **parser view** *view-name* **superview** command and enter superview configuration mode.

Step 2.   Assign a secret password to the view using the **secret** *encrypted-password* command.

Step 3.   Assign an existing view using the **view** *view-name* command in view configuration mode.

Step 4.   Exit superview configuration mode by typing the **exit** command.

More than one view can be assigned to a superview, and views can be shared between superviews.

To access existing views, enter the **enable view** *view-name* command in user mode and enter the password that was assigned to the custom view. Use the same command to switch from one view to another.

Refer to
Figure
in online course

To verify a view, use the **enable view** command. Enter the name of the view to verify, and provide the password to log in to the view. Use the question mark (**?**) command to verify that the commands available in the view are correct.

From the root view, use the **show parser view all** command to see a summary of all views.

2.3 Monitoring and Managing Devices

2.3.1 Securing the Cisco IOS Image and Configuration Files

Refer to
Figure
in online course

If attackers gain access to a router there are many things that they could do. For example, they could alter traffic flows, alter configurations, and even erase the startup configuration file and Cisco IOS image. If the configuration or IOS image is erased, the operator might need to retrieve an archived copy to restore the router. The recovery process must then be performed on each affected router, adding to the total network downtime.

The Cisco IOS Resilient Configuration feature allows for faster recovery if someone reformats flash memory or erases the startup configuration file in NVRAM. This feature allows a router to withstand malicious attempts at erasing the files by securing the router image and maintaining a secure working copy of the running configuration.

When a Cisco IOS image is secured, the resilient configuration feature denies all requests to copy, modify, or delete it. The secure copy of the startup configuration is stored in flash along with the secure IOS image. This set of Cisco IOS image and router running configuration files is referred to as the bootset.

The Cisco IOS resilient configuration feature is only available for systems that support a PCMCIA Advanced Technology Attachment (ATA) flash interface. The Cisco IOS image and backup running configuration on the Flash drive are hidden from view, so the files are not included in any directory listing on the drive.

Two global configurations commands are available to configure the Cisco IOS resilient configuration features: **secure boot-image** and **secure boot-config**.

Refer to
Figure
in online course

The **secure boot-image** command enables Cisco IOS image resilience. When enabled for the first time, the running Cisco IOS image is secured, and a log entry is generated. This feature can be disabled only through a console session using the **no** form of the command.

This command functions properly only when the system is configured to run an image from a flash drive with an ATA interface. Additionally, the running image must be loaded from persistent storage to be secured as primary. Images that are booted from the network, such as a TFTP server, cannot be secured.

The Cisco IOS resilient configuration feature detects image version mismatches. If the router is configured to boot with Cisco IOS resilience and an image with a different version of the Cisco IOS software is detected, a message, similar to the one shown below, is displayed at bootup:

```
ios resilience: Archived image and configuration version 12.2 differs from running
version 12.3
```

To upgrade the image archive to the new running image, reenter the **secure boot-image** command from the console. A message about the upgraded image is displayed. The old image is released and is visible in the **dir** command output.

To take a snapshot of the router running configuration and securely archive it in persistent storage, use the **secure boot-config** command in global configuration mode. A log message is displayed on the console notifying the user that configuration resilience is activated. The configuration archive is hidden and cannot be viewed or removed directly from the CLI prompt.

The configuration upgrade scenario is similar to an image upgrade. This feature detects a different version of Cisco IOS configurations and notifies the user of a version mismatch. The **secure boot-config** command can be run to upgrade the configuration archive to a newer version after new configuration commands have been issued.

Refer to
Figure
in online course

Secured files do not appear in the output of a **dir** command that is issued from the CLI. This is because the Cisco IOS file system prevents secure files from being listed. Because the running image and running configuration archives are not visible in the **dir** command output, use the **show secure bootset** command to verify the existence of the archive. This step is important to verify that the Cisco IOS image and configuration files have been properly backed up and secured.

While the Cisco IOS file system prevents these files from being viewed, ROM monitor (ROMmon) mode does not have any such restrictions and can list and boot from secured files.

There are five steps to restore a primary bootset from a secure archive after the router has been tampered with (by an NVRAM erase or a disk format):

Step 1. Reload the router using the **reload** command.

Step 2. From ROMmon mode, enter the **dir** command to list the contents of the device that contains the secure bootset file. From the CLI, the device name can be found in the output of the **show secure bootset** command.

Step 3. Boot the router with the secure bootset image using the **boot** command with the filename found in Step 2. When the compromised router boots, change to privileged EXEC mode and restore the configuration.

Step 4. Enter global configuration mode using **conf t**.

Step 5. Restore the secure configuration to the supplied filename using the **secure boot-config restore** *filename* command.

Refer to
Figure
in online course

In the event that a router is compromised or needs to be recovered from a misconfigured password, an administrator must understand password recovery procedures. For security reasons, password recovery requires the administrator to have physical access to the router through a console cable.

Recovering a router password involves several steps:

Step 1. Connect to the console port.

Step 2. Use the **show version** command to view and record the configuration register.

The configuration register is similar to the BIOS setting of a computer, which controls the boot process. A configuration register, represented by a single hexadecimal value, tells a router what specific steps to take when powered on. Configuration registers have many uses, and password recovery is probably the most used. To view and record the configuration register, use the **show version** command.

```
R1> show version
<Output omitted>
Configuration register is 0x2102
```

The configuration register is usually set to 0x2102 or 0x102. If there is no longer access to the router (because of a lost login or TACACS password), an administrator can safely assume that the configuration register is set to 0x2102.

Step 3. Use the power switch to power cycle the router.

Step 4. Issue the break sequence within 60 seconds of power up to put the router into ROMmon.

Step 5. Type **confreg 0x2142** at the rommon 1> prompt.

This changes the default configuration register and causes the router to bypass the startup configuration where the forgotten enable password is stored.

Step 6. Type **reset** at the rommon 2> prompt. The router reboots, but ignores the saved configuration.

Step 7. Type **no** after each setup question, or press Ctrl-C to skip the initial setup procedure.

Step 8. Type **enable** at the Router> prompt. This puts the router into enable mode and allows you to see the Router# prompt.

Step 9. Type **copy startup-config running-config** to copy the NVRAM into memory. Be careful not to type **copy running-config startup-config** or the startup configuration will be erased.

Step 10. Type **show running-config**. In this configuration, the **shutdown** command appears under all interfaces because all interfaces are currently shut down. An administrator can now see the passwords (enable password, enable secret, vty, and console passwords) either in encrypted or unencrypted format. Unencrypted passwords can be reused, but encrypted passwords need a new password to be created.

Step 11. Enter global configuration and type the **enable secret** command to change the enable secret password. For example:

```
R1(config)# enable secret cisco
```

Step 12. Issue the **no shutdown** command on every interface to be used. Then issue the **show ip interface brief** command in privileged EXEC mode to confirm that the interface configuration is correct. Every interface to be used should display "up up."

Step 13. From global configuration mode type **config-register** *configuration_register_setting*. The configuration register setting is either the value recorded in step 2 or 0x2102. For example:

```
R1(config)# config-register 0x2102
```

Step 14. Save the configuration changes using the **copy running-config startup-config** command.

Password recovery is now complete. Enter the **show version** command to confirm that the router is using the configured configuration register setting on the next reboot.

Refer to
Figure
in online course
If someone gained physical access to a router, they could potentially gain control of that device through the password recovery procedure. This procedure, if performed correctly, leaves the router configuration intact. If the attacker makes no major changes, this type of attack is difficult to detect. An attacker can use this attack method to discover the router configuration and other pertinent information about the network, such as traffic flows and access control restrictions.

An administrator can mitigate this potential security breach by using the **no service password-recovery** global configuration command. This command is a hidden Cisco IOS command and has no arguments or keywords. If a router is configured with the **no service password-recovery** command, all access to ROMmon mode is disabled.

When the **no service password-recovery** command is entered, a warning message is displayed and must be acknowledged before the feature is enabled.

The **show running configuration** command displays a **no service password-recovery** statement. Additionally, when the router is booted, the initial boot sequence displays a message stating "PASSWORD RECOVERY FUNCTIONALITY IS DISABLED."

To recover a device after the **no service password-recovery** command is entered, initiate the break sequence within five seconds after the image decompresses during the boot. You are prompted to confirm the break key action. After the action is confirmed, the startup configuration is completely erased, the password recovery procedure is enabled, and the router boots with the factory default configuration. If you do not confirm the break action, the router boots normally with the **no service password-recovery** command enabled.

CAUTION: If the router flash memory does not contain a valid Cisco IOS image because of corruption or deletion, the ROMmon **xmodem** command cannot be used to load a new flash image. To repair the router, an administrator must obtain a new Cisco IOS image on a flash SIMM or on a PCMCIA card. Refer to Cisco.com for more information regarding backup flash images.

2.3.2 Secure Management and Reporting

Refer to
Figure
in online course

Network administrators need to securely manage all devices and hosts in the network. In a small network, managing and monitoring network devices, is a straightforward operation. However, in a large enterprise with hundreds of devices, monitoring, managing, and processing log messages can be challenging.

Several factors should be considered when implementing secure management. This includes configuration change management. When a network is under attack, it is important to know the state of critical network devices and when the last known modifications occurred. Configuration change management also includes ensuring that the right people have access when new management methodologies are adopted, and having a plan for handling tools and devices that are no longer used. Creating a plan for change management should be part of a comprehensive security policy; however, at a minimum, record changes using authentication systems on devices and archive configurations using FTP or TFTP.

Automated logging and reporting of information from identified devices to management hosts are also important considerations. These logs and reports can include content flow, configuration changes, and new software installs, to name a few. To identify the priorities of reporting and monitoring, it is important to get input from management and from the network and security teams. The security policy should also play a large role in answering the questions of what information to log and report.

From a reporting standpoint, most networking devices can send syslog data that can be invaluable when troubleshooting network problems or security threats. Data from any device can be sent to a syslog analysis host for viewing. This data can be viewed in real time, on demand, and in scheduled reports. There are various logging levels to ensure that the correct amount of data is sent, based on the device sending the data. It is also possible to flag device log data within the analysis software to permit granular viewing and reporting. For example, during an attack, the log data that is provided by Layer 2 switches might not be as interesting as the data that is provided by the intrusion prevention system (IPS).

Many applications and protocols are also available, such as SNMP, which is used in network management systems to monitor and make configuration changes to devices remotely.

When logging and managing information, the information flow between management hosts and the managed devices can take two paths:

Refer to
Figure
in online course

- *Out-of-band (OOB)* Information flows on a dedicated management network on which no production traffic resides.

- *In-band* Information flows across an enterprise production network, the Internet, or both using regular data channels.

For example, a network has two network segments that are separated by a Cisco IOS router that acts as a firewall and a virtual private network (VPN) termination device. One side of the firewall connects to all management hosts and to Cisco IOS routers that act as terminal servers. The terminal servers offer OOB direct connections to any device requiring management on the production network. Most devices should be connected to this management segment and be configured using OOB management.

The other side of the firewall connects to the production network itself. The connection to the production network is only provided for selective Internet access by the management hosts, limited in-band management traffic, and encrypted management traffic from predetermined hosts. In-band management occurs only when a management application does not use OOB, or when the Cisco device being managed does not physically have enough interfaces to support the normal connection to the management network. If a device must contact a management host by sending data across the production network, that traffic should be sent securely using a private encrypted tunnel or VPN tunnel. The tunnel should be preconfigured to permit only the traffic that is required for management and reporting of these devices. The tunnel should also be locked down so that only appropriate hosts can initiate and terminate tunnels. The Cisco IOS firewall is configured to allow syslog information into the management segment. In addition, Telnet, SSH, and SNMP are allowed on the condition that these services are first initiated by the management network.

Because the management network has administrative access to nearly every area of the network, it can be a very attractive target to hackers. The management module on the firewall has been built with several technologies designed to mitigate such risks. The primary threat is a hacker attempting to gain access to the management network itself. This can possibly be accomplished through a compromised managed host that a management device must access. To mitigate the threat of a compromised device, strong access control should be implemented at the firewall and at every other device. Additionally, management devices should be set up in a fashion that prevents direct communication with other hosts on the same management subnet, using separate LAN segments or VLANs.

Refer to
Figure
in online course

As a general rule, for security purposes, OOB management is appropriate for large enterprise networks. However, it is not always desirable. The decision to use OOB management depends on the type of management applications running and the protocols being monitored. For example, consider a situation in which two core switches are being managed and monitored using an OOB network. If a critical link between these two core switches fails on the *production* network, the application monitoring those devices may never determine that the link has failed and alert the administrator. This is because the OOB network makes all devices appear to be attached to a single OOB management network. The OOB management network remains unaffected by the downed link. With management applications such as these, it is preferable to run the management application in-band in a secure fashion.

In-band management is also recommended in smaller networks as a means of achieving a more cost-effective security deployment. In such architectures, management traffic flows in-band in all cases. It is made as secure as possible using secure variants to insecure management protocols, such as using SSH instead of Telnet. Another option is to create secure tunnels, using protocols such as IPsec, for management traffic. If management access is not necessary at all times, perhaps temporary holes can be placed in a firewall while management functions are performed. This technique should be used cautiously, and all holes should be closed immediately when management functions are completed.

Finally, if using remote management tools with in-band management, be wary of the underlying security vulnerabilities of the management tool itself. For example, SNMP managers are often used to ease troubleshooting and configuration tasks on a network. However, SNMP should be treated with the utmost care because the underlying protocol has its own set of security vulnerabilities.

2.3.3 Using Syslog for Network Security

Refer to
Figure
in online course

Implementing a router logging facility is an important part of any network security policy. Cisco routers can log information regarding configuration changes, ACL violations, interface status, and many other types of events. Cisco routers can send log messages to several different facilities. You should configure the router to send log messages to one or more of the following items:

- *Console* Console logging is on by default. Messages log to the console and can be viewed when modifying or testing the router using terminal emulation software while connected to the console port of the router.

- *Terminal lines* Enabled EXEC sessions can be configured to receive log messages on any terminal lines. Similar to console logging, this type of logging is not stored by the router and, therefore, is only valuable to the user on that line.

- *Buffered logging* Buffered logging is a little more useful as a security tool because log messages are stored in router memory for a time. However, events are cleared whenever the router is rebooted.

- *SNMP traps* Certain thresholds can be preconfigured on routers and other devices. Router events, such as exceeding a threshold, can be processed by the router and forwarded as SNMP traps to an external SNMP server. SNMP traps are a viable security logging facility but require the configuration and maintenance of an SNMP system.

- *Syslog* Cisco routers can be configured to forward log messages to an external syslog service. This service can reside on any number of servers or workstations, including Microsoft Windows and UNIX-based systems. Syslog is the most popular message logging facility, because it provides long-term log storage capabilities and a central location for all router messages.

Cisco router log messages fall into one of eight levels. The lower the level number, the higher the severity level.

Cisco router log messages contain three main parts:

- Timestamp

- Log message name and severity level

- Message text

Refer to
Figure
in online course

Syslog is the standard for logging system events. Syslog implementations contain two types of systems.

- *Syslog servers* Also known as log hosts, these systems accept and process log messages from syslog clients.

■ *Syslog clients* Routers or other types of equipment that generate and forward log messages to syslog servers.

The syslog protocol allows login messages to be sent from a syslog client to the syslog server. While the ability to send logs to a central syslog server is part of a good security solution, it can also potentially be part of a security problem. The biggest issue is the enormity of the task of evaluating the information. This includes sifting through the various logs and events, correlating the events from several different network devices and application servers, and determining the type of action to take based on a vulnerability assessment of the incident.

Use the following steps to configure system logging:

Refer to **Figure** in online course

Step 1. Set the destination logging host using the `logging host` command.

Step 2. (Optional) Set the log severity (trap) level using the `logging trap` *level* command.

Step 3. Set the source interface using the `logging source-interface` command. This specifies that syslog packets contain the IPv4 or IPv6 address of a specific interface, regardless of which interface the packet uses to exit the router.

Step 4. Enable logging with the `logging on` command. You can turn logging on and off for these destinations individually using the `logging buffered`, `logging monitor`, and `logging` global configuration commands. However, if the `logging on` command is disabled, no messages are sent to these destinations. Only the console receives messages.

Refer to **Figure** in online course

To enable syslog logging on a router using CCP, follow these steps:

Step 1. Choose **Configure > Router > Logging**.

Step 2. From the Logging pane, click **Edit**.

Step 3. In the Logging window, select **Enable Logging Level** and choose the logging level from the **Logging Level** list box. Messages will be logged for the level selected and below.

Step 4. Click **Add**, and enter an IP address of a logging host in the **IP Address/Hostname** field.

Step 5. Click **OK** to return to the Logging dialog box.

Step 6. Click **OK** to accept the changes and return to the Logging pane.

Refer to **Figure** in online course

CCP can be used to monitor logging by choosing **Monitor > Logging**.

From the Syslog tab, you can perform the following functions:

■ See the logging hosts to which the router logs messages.

■ Choose the minimum severity level to view.

■ Monitor the router syslog messages, update the screen to show the most current log entries, and erase all syslog messages from the router log buffer.

2.3.4 Using SNMP for Network Security

Refer to **Figure** in online course

Another common monitoring tool is SNMP. SNMP was developed to manage nodes, such as servers, workstations, routers, switches, hubs, and security appliances, on an IP network. SNMP is an Application Layer protocol that facilitates the exchange of management information between network devices. SNMP is part of the TCP/IP protocol suite. SNMP enables network administrators to manage network performance, find and solve network problems, and plan for network growth. There are different versions of SNMP: SNMP version 1 (SNMPv1), SNMP version 2 (SNMPv2), and SNMP version 3 (SNMPv3). All three versions use managers (network management systems [NMSs]), agents (managed nodes), and Management Information Bases (MIBs).

In any configuration, at least one manager node runs SNMP management software. Network devices that need to be managed, such as switches, routers, servers, and workstations, are equipped with an SMNP agent software module. The agent is responsible for providing access to a local MIB of objects that reflects the resources and activity at its node. MIBs store data about the device operation and are meant to be available to authenticated remote users.

The SNMP manager can get information from the agent, and change, or set, information in the agent. Sets can change configuration variables in the agent device. Sets can also initiate actions in devices. A reply to a set indicates the new setting in the device. For example, a set can cause a router to reboot, send a configuration file, or receive a configuration file. SNMP traps enable an agent to notify the management station of significant events by sending an unsolicited SNMP message. The actions 'get' and 'set' are the vulnerabilities that open SNMP to attack.

Refer to
Figure
in online course

SNMP agents accept commands and requests from SNMP management systems only if those systems have a correct community string. An SNMP community string is a text string that can authenticate messages between a management station and an SNMP agent and allow access to the information in MIBs. Community strings are essentially used for password-only authentication of messages between the NMS and the agent.

There are two types of community strings:

- *Read-only community strings* Provides read-only access to all objects in the MIB, except the community strings.

- *Read-write community strings* Provides read-write access to all objects in the MIB, except the community strings.

If the manager sends one of the correct read-only community strings, it can get information but not set information in an agent. If the manager uses one of the correct read-write community strings, it can get or set information in the agent. In effect, having set access to a router is equivalent to having the enable password of the router.

By default, most SNMP systems use "public" as a community string. If you configure your router SNMP agent to use this commonly known community string, anyone with an SNMP system is able to read the router MIB. Because router MIB variables can point to things such as routing tables and other security-critical parts of the router configuration, it is extremely important that you create your own custom SNMP community strings. However, even if the community string is changed, the strings are sent in plaintext. This is a huge vulnerability of the SNMPv1 and SNMPv2 architecture.

If using in-band management, to reduce security risks, SNMP management should be configured to only pull information from devices rather than being allowed to push 'set' changes to the devices. To ensure management information is pulled, each device should be configured with a read-only SNMP community string.

Keeping SNMP traffic on a management segment allows the traffic to traverse an isolated segment when management information is pulled from devices and when configuration changes are pushed to a device. Therefore, if using an OOB network, it is acceptable to configure an SNMP read-write community string. However, be aware of the increased security risk of a plaintext string that allows modification of device configurations.

Refer to
Figure
in online course

SNMPv3 is a standards-based protocol for network management. To address vulnerabilities of earlier versions of SNMP, SNMPv3 authenticates and encrypts packets over the network to provide secure access to devices. SNMPv3 provides the following security features:

- *Message integrity* Ensures that a packet has not been tampered with in transit.

- *Authentication* Determines that the message is from a valid source.

- *Encryption* Scrambles the contents of a packet to prevent it from being seen by an unauthorized source.

- *Access Control* Restricts each principal to certain actions on specific portions of data.

While it is recommended that SNMPv3 be used where possible because of the added security features, configuring SNMPv3 is beyond the scope of this course.

Refer to
Figure
in online course

When enabling SNMP, it is important to consider the security model and the security level. The security model is an authentication strategy that is set up for a user and the group in which the user resides. Currently, Cisco IOS software supports three security models: SNMPv1, SNMPv2c, and SNMPv3. A security level is the permitted level of security within a security model. The security level is a type of security algorithm that is performed on each SNMP packet.

There are three security levels:

- *noAuth* Authenticates a packet by a string match of the username or community string.

- *auth* Authenticates a packet by using either the Hashed Message Authentication Code (HMAC) with MD5 method or Secure Hash Algorithms (SHA) method. The HMAC method is described in RFC 2104, HMAC: Keyed-Hashing for Message Authentication.

- *priv* Authenticates a packet by using either the HMAC MD5 or HMAC SHA algorithms and encrypts the packet using the Data Encryption Standard (DES), Triple DES (3DES), or Advanced Encryption Standard (AES) algorithms.

The combination of the model and level determines which security mechanism is employed when handling an SNMP packet. Only SNMPv3 supports the auth and priv security levels. However, CCP does not support configuration of SNMPv3.

To enable SNMPv1 and SNMPv2 using CCP follow these steps:

Step 1. Choose **Configure > Router > SNMP**. Click the **Edit** button.

Step 2. From the SNMP Properties window, select **Enable SNMP** to enable SNMP support.

Set community strings and enter trap manager information from the same SNMP Properties window used to enable support.

Step 3. In the SNMP Properties window, click **Add** to create new community strings, click **Edit** to edit an existing community string, or click **Delete** to delete a community string.

An example CLI command that CCP would generate based on a read only community string of cisco123 is `snmp-server community cisco123 ro`:

- `ro` Assigns a read-only community string.

- `rw` Assigns a read-write community string.

Refer to
Figure
in online course

The administrator can also configure devices to which a router sends traps. These devices are referred to as trap receivers. CCP can be used to add, edit, or delete a trap receiver:

Step 1. From the SNMP pane in CCP, click **Edit**. The SNMP Properties window displays.

Step 2.   To add a new trap receiver, click **Add** in the Trap Receiver section of the SNMP Properties window. The Add a Trap Receiver window displays.

Step 3.   Enter the IP address or host name of the trap receiver and the password that is used to connect to the trap receiver. Typically, this is the IP address of the SNMP management station that monitors the domain. Check with the site administrator to determine the address if unsure.

Step 4.   Click **OK** to finish adding the trap receiver.

Step 5.   To edit an existing trap receiver, choose a trap receiver from the trap receiver list and click **Edit**. To delete an existing trap receiver, choose a trap receiver from the trap receiver list and click **Delete**.

Step 6.   When the trap receiver list is complete, click **OK** to return to the SNMP pane.

The SNMP Properties window also contains the SNMP Server Device Location field and the SNMP Server Administrator Contact field. Both of these fields are text fields that can be used to enter descriptive information about the SNMP server location and the contact information for a person managing the SNMP server. These fields are not required and do not affect the operation of the router.

2.3.5 Using NTP

Refer to
Figure
in online course

Many things involved in the security of a network, such as security logs, depend on an accurate date and timestamp. When dealing with an attack, seconds matter, because it is important to identify the order in which a specified attack occurred. To ensure that log messages are accurately timestamped, clocks on hosts and network devices must be synchronized and maintained.

Typically, the date and time settings of the router can be set using one of two methods:

- Manually editing the date and time

- Configuring the Network Time Protocol (NTP)

Although the manual method works in a small network environment, as a network grows, it becomes difficult to ensure that all infrastructure devices are operating with synchronized time. Even in a smaller network environment, the manual method is not ideal. If a router reboots, where would it get an accurate date and timestamp?

A better solution is to configure NTP on the network. NTP allows routers on the network to synchronize their time settings with an NTP server. A group of NTP clients that obtain time and date information from a single source have more consistent time settings. When NTP is implemented in the network, it can be set up to synchronize to a private master clock, or it can synchronize to a publicly available NTP server on the Internet.

NTP uses UDP port 123 and is documented in RFC 1305.

Refer to
Figure
in online course

When determining whether to use a private clock synchronization versus a public clock, it is necessary to weigh the risks and benefits of both.

If a private master clock is implemented, it could be synchronized to Coordinated Universal Time (UTC) via satellite or radio. The administrator does need to ensure that the time source is valid and from a secure site; otherwise, it can introduce vulnerabilities. For example, an attacker can launch a DoS attack by sending bogus NTP data across the Internet to the network in an attempt to change the clocks on network devices, possibly causing digital certificates to become invalid. An attacker could attempt to confuse a network administrator during an attack by disrupting the clocks on network devices. This scenario would make it difficult for the network administrator to determine the order of syslog events on multiple devices.

Pulling the clock time from the Internet means that unsecured packets are allowed through the firewall. Many NTP servers on the Internet do not require any authentication of peers; therefore, the network administrator must trust that the clock itself is reliable, valid, and secure.

The communications (known as associations) between machines that run NTP are usually statically configured. Each device is given the IP address of NTP masters. Accurate timekeeping is possible by exchanging NTP messages between each pair of machines with an association. In an NTP configured network, one or more routers are designated as the master clock keeper (known as an NTP master) using the `ntp master` global configuration command.

NTP clients either contact the master or listen for messages from the master to synchronize their clocks. To contact the master, use the `ntp server` *ntp-server-address* command.

In a LAN environment, NTP can be configured to use IP broadcast messages instead by using the `ntp broadcast client` command. This alternative reduces configuration complexity because each machine can be configured to send or receive broadcast messages. The accuracy of timekeeping is marginally reduced because the information flow is one-way only.

<table>
<tr><td>Refer to
Figure
in online course</td><td>The time that a device keeps is critical; therefore, the security features of NTP should be used to avoid the accidental or malicious setting of incorrect times. There are two security mechanisms available:</td></tr>
</table>

- ACL-based restriction scheme

- Encrypted authentication mechanism offered by NTP version 3 or later

NTP version 3 (NTPv3) and later support a cryptographic authentication mechanism between NTP peers. This authentication mechanism, in addition to ACLs that specify which network devices are allowed to synchronize with other network devices, can be used to help mitigate such an attack.

To secure NTP traffic, it is strongly recommended that NTP version 3 or later is implemented. Use the following commands on both the NTP master and the NTP client:

```
ntp authenticate
ntp authentication-key key-number md5 key-value
ntp trusted-key key-number
```

The authentication is for the benefit of a client to ensure that it is getting the time from an authenticated server. Clients configured without authentication still get the time from the server. The difference is that these clients do not authenticate the server as a secure source.

Use the `show ntp associations detail` command to confirm that the server is an authenticated source.

Note: The key value can also be set as an argument in the `ntp server` *ntp-server-address* command.

<table>
<tr><td>Refer to
Figure
in online course</td><td>CCP allows a network administrator to view the configured NTP server information, add new information, and edit or delete existing information.</td></tr>
</table>

There are seven steps to add an NTP server using CCP:

Step 1.   Choose **Configure > Router > Time > NTP and SNTP**. The NTP pane appears, displaying the information for all configured NTP servers.

Step 2.   To add a new NTP server, click **Add**. The Add NTP Server Details window appears.

Step 3. Add an NTP server by name (if the router is configured to use a Domain Name System server) or by IP address. To add an NTP server by IP address, enter the IP address in the field next to the NTP Server IP Address option. If the organization does not have an NTP server, the administrator might want to use a publicly available server. There is a list of these servers at: http://support.ntp.org/bin/view/Servers/WebHome.

Step 4. (Optional) From the **NTP Source Interface** drop-down list, choose the interface that the router uses to communicate with the NTP server. The NTP Source Interface is an optional field. If this field is left blank, NTP messages are sent out the closest interface per the routing table.

Step 5. Select **Prefer** if this NTP server has been designated as a preferred NTP server. Preferred NTP servers are contacted before nonpreferred NTP servers. There can be more than one preferred NTP server.

Step 6. If the NTP server uses authentication, select **Authentication Key** and enter the key number and key value.

Step 7. Click **OK** to finish adding the server.

2.4 Using Automated Security Features

2.4.1 Performing a Security Audit

Refer to
Figure
in online course

Cisco routers are initially deployed with many services that are enabled by default. This is done for convenience and to simplify the configuration process required to get the device operational. However, some of these services can make the device vulnerable to attack if security is not enabled. Administrators can also enable services on Cisco routers that can expose the device to significant risk. Both of these scenarios must be taken into account when securing the network.

For example, Cisco Discovery Protocol (CDP) is an example of a service that is enabled by default on Cisco routers. It is used primarily to obtain protocol addresses of neighboring Cisco devices and to discover the platforms of those devices. Unfortunately, an attacker on the network can use CDP to discover devices on the local network. In addition, attackers do not need to have CDP-enabled devices. Readily available software, such as Cisco CDP Monitor, can be downloaded to gain the information. The intent of CDP is to make it easier for administrators to discover and troubleshoot other Cisco devices on the network. However, because of the security implications, CDP should be used with caution. While it is an extremely helpful tool, it should not be everywhere in the network. Edge devices are an example of a device that should have this feature disabled.

Refer to
Figure
in online course

Attackers choose services and protocols that make the network more vulnerable to malicious exploitation.

Depending on the security needs of an organization, many of these services should be disabled or, at a minimum, restricted in their capabilities. These features range from Cisco proprietary protocols, such as Cisco Discovery Protocol (CDP), to globally available protocols such as ICMP and other scanning tools.

Some of the default settings in Cisco IOS software are there for historical reasons. They were logical default settings at the time the software was originally written. Other defaults make sense for most systems but can create security exposures if they are used in devices that form part of a network perimeter defense. Still other defaults are actually required by standards but are not always desirable from a security point of view.

Many practices help ensure a device is secure:

- Disable unnecessary services and interfaces.

- Disable and restrict commonly configured management services, such as SNMP.

- Disable probes and scans, such as ICMP.

- Ensure terminal access security.

- Disable gratuitous and proxy Address Resolution Protocol (ARP).

- Disable IP-directed broadcasts.

Refer to
Figure
in online course

To secure network devices, administrators must first determine the vulnerabilities that exist with the current configuration. The best way to accomplish this is through the use of a security audit tool. A security audit tool performs checks on the security level of a configuration by comparing that configuration to recommended settings and tracking discrepancies. After vulnerabilities are identified, network administrators must modify the configuration to reduce or eliminate those vulnerabilities to secure the device and the network.

The three security audit tools that are available include:

- **Security Audit wizard** - a security audit feature provided through CCP. The Security Audit wizard provides a list of vulnerabilities and then allows the administrator to choose which potential security-related configuration changes to implement on a router.

- **Cisco AutoSecure** - a security audit feature available through the Cisco IOS CLI. The `autosecure` command initiates a security audit and then allows for configuration changes. Based on the mode selected, configuration changes can be automatic or require network administrator input.

- **One-Step Lockdown** - a security audit feature provided through CCP. The One-Step Lockdown feature provides a list of vulnerabilities and then automatically makes all recommended security-related configuration changes.

Both Security Audit wizard and One-Step Lockdown are based on the Cisco IOS AutoSecure feature.

Refer to
Figure
in online course

Security Audit Wizard

The Security Audit wizard tests the router configuration to determine if any potential security problems exist in the configuration, and then presents a screen that lets the administrator determine which of those security problems to fix. At this point, Security Audit wizard makes the necessary changes to the router configuration to fix those problems.

The Security Audit wizard compares a router configuration against recommended settings and performs the following:

- Shuts down unneeded servers.

- Disables unneeded services.

- Applies the firewall to the outside interfaces.

- Disables or hardens SNMP.

- Shuts down unused interfaces.

- Checks password strength.

- Enforces the use of ACLs.

When a security audit is initiated, the Security Audit wizard must know which router interfaces connect to the inside network and which connect to the outside of the network. The Security Audit wizard then tests the router configuration to determine possible security problems that may exist. A window shows all configuration options tested and whether the current router configuration passes those tests.

When the audit is complete, the Security Audit wizard identifies possible vulnerabilities in the configuration and provides a way to correct those problems. It also gives the administrator the option to fix problems automatically, in which case it determines the necessary configuration commands. A description of specific problems and a list of the Cisco IOS commands used to correct those problems are provided.

Before any configuration changes are made, a summary page displays a list of all the configuration changes that the Security Audit wizard will make. The administrator must click **Finish** to send those configurations to the router.

2.4.2 Locking Down a Router Using AutoSecure

Cisco AutoSecure

Refer to
Figure
in online course

Released in IOS version 12.3, Cisco AutoSecure is a feature that is initiated from the CLI and executes a script. AutoSecure first makes recommendations for fixing security vulnerabilities and then modifies the security configuration of the router.

AutoSecure can lock down the management plane functions and the forwarding plane services and functions of a router.

The management plane is the logical path of all traffic related to the management of a routing platform. It is used to control all other functions of routing and to manage a device through its connection to the network. There are several management plane services and functions:

- Secure BOOTP, CDP, FTP, TFTP, PAD, UDP, and TCP small servers, MOP, ICMP (redirects, mask-replies), IP source routing, Finger, password encryption, TCP keepalives, gratuitous ARP, proxy ARP, and directed broadcast

- Legal notification using a banner

- Secure password and login functions

- Secure NTP

- Secure SSH access

- TCP intercept services

The forwarding plane is responsible for packet forwarding (or packet switching), which is the act of receiving packets on the router interfaces and sending them out on other interfaces.

There are three forwarding plane services and functions that AutoSecure enables:

- Cisco Express Forwarding (CEF)

- Traffic filtering with ACLs

- Cisco IOS firewall inspection for common protocols

AutoSecure is often used in the field to provide a baseline security policy on a new router. Features can then be altered to support the security policy of the organization.

Refer to
Figure
in online course

Use the `auto secure` command to enable the Cisco AutoSecure feature setup. This setup can be interactive or non-interactive.

```
auto secure [no-interact]
```

In interactive mode, the router prompts with options to enable and disable services and other security features. This is the default mode, but it can also be configured using the `auto secure full` command.

The non-interactive mode is similar to the CCP Security Audit One-Step Lockdown feature because it automatically executes the Cisco AutoSecure command with the recommended Cisco default settings. This mode is enabled using the `auto secure no-interact` privileged EXEC command.

The `auto secure` command can also be entered with keywords to configure specific components, such as the management plane and forwarding plane.

Note: If you are using CCP, you must manually enable the HTTP server through the `ip http server` command, or HTTPS using the `ip http secure-server` command after AutoSecure completes.

Refer to
Figure
in online course

When the `auto secure` command is initiated, a wizard is displayed to step the administrator through the configuration of the device. User input is required. When the wizard is complete, a running configuration displays all configuration settings and changes.

2.4.3 Locking Down a Router Using CCP

Refer to
Figure
in online course

Cisco One-Step Lockdown

One-Step Lockdown tests a router configuration for any potential security problems and automatically makes the necessary configuration changes to correct any problems.

Cisco One-Step Lockdown disables:

- Finger service
- PAD service
- TCP small servers service
- UDP small servers service
- IP BOOTP server service
- IP identification service
- Cisco Discovery Protocol
- IP source route
- IP GARPs
- SNMP
- IP redirects
- IP proxy ARP
- IP directed broadcast
- MOP service
- IP unreachables

- IP mask reply

- IP unreachables on null interface

Cisco One-Step Lockdown enables:

- Password encryption service

- TCP keepalives for inbound and outbound Telnet sessions

- Sequence numbers and timestamps on debugs

- Cisco Express Forwarding with integrated NetFlow switching

- Unicast Reverse Path Forwarding (RPF) on outside interfaces

- Firewall on all outside interfaces

- SSH for access to the router

- AAA

Cisco One-Step Lockdown configures:

- Minimum password length to six characters

- Authentication failure rate to less than three retries

- TCP synwait time

- Notification banner

- Logging parameters

- Enable secret password

- Scheduler interval

- Scheduler allocate

- Users

- Telnet settings

- Access class on HTTP server service

- Access class on vty lines

<table>
<tr><td>Refer to
Figure
in online course</td><td>Deciding which automated lockdown feature to use, AutoSecure or CCP Security Audit One-Step Lockdown, is basically a matter of preference. There are differences in how they implement good security practices.</td></tr>
</table>

CCP does not implement all the features of Cisco AutoSecure. Since CCP version 2.4, the following Cisco AutoSecure features are not part of the CCP One-Step Lockdown:

- *Disabling NTP* Based on input, Cisco AutoSecure disables NTP if it is not necessary. Otherwise, NTP is configured with MD5 authentication. CCP does not support disabling NTP.

- *Configuring AAA* If the AAA service is not configured, Cisco AutoSecure configures local AAA and prompts for the configuration of a local username and password database on the router. CCP does not support AAA configuration.

- *Setting Selective Packet Discard (SPD) values* CCP does not set SPD values.

- ***Enabling TCP intercepts*** CCP does not enable TCP intercepts.

- ***Configuring antispoofing ACLs on outside interfaces*** Cisco AutoSecure creates three named access lists to prevent antispoofing source addresses. CCP does not configure these ACLs.

The following features are implemented differently in Cisco AutoSecure than they are in the CCP One-Step Lockdown:

- ***Enabling SSH for access to the router*** CCP enables and configures SSH on Cisco IOS images that have the IPsec feature set; however, unlike Cisco AutoSecure, CCP does not enable Secure Copy Protocol (SCP) or disable other access and file transfer services, such as FTP.

- ***Disabling SNMP*** CCP disables SNMP; however, unlike Cisco AutoSecure, CCP does not provide an option for configuring SNMPv3. The SNMPv3 option is not available on all routers.

Regardless of which automated feature is preferred, it should be used as a baseline and then altered to meet the needs of the organization.

Chapter Summary

Refer to **Figure** in online course

Refer to **Packet Tracer Activity** for this chapter

Refer to **Lab Activity** for this chapter

Your Chapter Notes

CHAPTER 3

Authentication, Authorization and Accounting

Chapter Introduction

Refer to **Figure** in online course

A network must be designed to control who is allowed to connect to it and what they are allowed to do when they are connected. These design specifications are identified in the network security policy. The policy specifies how network administrators, corporate users, remote users, business partners, and clients access network resources. The network security policy can also mandate the implementation of an accounting system that tracks who logged in and when and what they did while logged in.

Managing network access using only the user mode or privilege mode password commands is limited and does not scale well. Instead, using the Authentication, Authorization, and Accounting (AAA) protocol provides the necessary framework to enable scalable access security.

Cisco IOS routers can be configured to use AAA to access a local username and password database. Using a local username and password database provides greater security than a simple password and is a cost effective and easily implemented security solution. Cisco IOS routers can also be configured to use AAA to access a Cisco Secure Access Control Server (ACS). Using Cisco ACS is very scalable because all infrastructure devices access a central server. The Cisco Secure ACS solution is also fault tolerant because multiple servers can be configured. The Cisco Secure ACS solution is often implemented by large organizations.

A hands-on lab for the chapter, *Securing Administrative Access Using AAA and RADIUS*, allows learners to use CLI and CCP to configure and test local authentication with and without AAA. Centralized authentication using AAA and RADIUS is also explored.

A Packet Tracer activity, *Configure AAA Authentication on Cisco Routers*, provides learners additional practice implementing the technologies introduced in this chapter. Learners configure local authentication with and without AAA. Server-based AAA authentication is configured with TACACS+ and RADIUS.

3.1 Purpose of AAA

3.1.1 AAA Overview

Refer to **Figure** in online course

Network intruders can potentially gain access to sensitive network equipment and services. Access control limits who or what can use specific resources as well as the services or options available once access is granted. Many types of authentication methods can be performed on a Cisco device, and each method offers varying levels of security.

The simplest form of authentication is passwords. This method is configured using a login and password combination on console, and vty lines and aux ports. This method is the easiest to implement, but it is also the weakest and least secure. Password-only logins are very vulnerable to brute-force attacks. Additionally, this method provides no accountability. Anyone with the password can gain entry to the device and alter the configuration.

To help provide accountability, local database authentication may be implemented using one of the following commands:

```
username username password password
username username secret password
```

This method creates individual user accounts on each device with a specific password assigned to each user. The local database method provides additional security, because an attacker is required to know a username and a password. It also provides more accountability, because the username is recorded when a user logs in. Keep in mind that the **username password** command combination displays the password in plaintext in the configuration file if the **service password-encryption** command is not configured. The **username secret** combination is highly recommended because it provides MD5-style encryption.

The local database method has some limitations. The user accounts must be configured locally on each device. In a large enterprise environment that has multiple routers and switches to manage, it can take time to implement and change local databases on each device. Additionally, the local database configuration provides no fallback authentication method. For example, what if the administrator forgets the username and password for that device? With no backup method available for authentication, password recovery becomes the only option.

A better solution is to have all devices refer to the same database of usernames and passwords from a central server. This chapter explores the various methods of securing network access using Authentication, Authorization, and Accounting (AAA) to secure Cisco routers.

Refer to
Figure
in online course

AAA network security services provide the primary framework to set up access control on a network device. AAA is a way to control who is permitted to access a network (authenticate), what they can do while they are there (authorize), and to audit what actions they performed while accessing the network (accounting). It provides a higher degree of scalability than the con, aux, vty and privileged EXEC authentication commands alone.

Network and administrative AAA security in the Cisco environment has several functional components:

- *Authentication* Users and administrators must prove that they are who they say they are. Authentication can be established using username and password combinations, challenge and response questions, token cards, and other methods. For example: "I am user 'student'. I know the password to prove that I am user 'student'."

- *Authorization* After the user is authenticated, authorization services determine which resources the user can access and which operations the user is allowed to perform. An example is "User 'student' can access host serverXYZ using Telnet only."

- *Accounting and auditing* Accounting records what the user does, including what is accessed, the amount of time the resource is accessed, and any changes that were made. Accounting keeps track of how network resources are used. An example is "User 'student' accessed host serverXYZ using Telnet for 15 minutes."

This concept is similar to the use of a credit card. The credit card identifies who can use it, how much that user can spend, and keeps account of what items the user spent money on.

3.1.2 AAA Characteristics

Refer to
Figure
in online course

AAA Authentication

AAA can be used to authenticate users for administrative access or it can be used to authenticate users for remote network access. These two access methods use different modes to request AAA services:

- *Character mode* A user sends a request to establish an EXEC mode process with the router for administrative purposes.

- *Packet mode* A user sends a request to establish a connection through the router with a device on the network.

With the exception of accounting commands, all AAA commands apply to both character mode and packet mode. This topic focuses on securing character mode access. For a truly secure network, it is important to also configure the router for secure administrative access and remote LAN network access using AAA services as well. Cisco provides two common methods of implementing AAA services.

Local AAA Authentication

Local AAA uses a local database for authentication. This method stores usernames and passwords locally in the Cisco router, and users authenticate against the local database. This database is the same one required for establishing role-based CLI. Local AAA is ideal for small networks.

Server-Based AAA Authentication

The server-based method uses an external database server resource that leverages RADIUS or TACACS+ protocols. Examples include Cisco Secure Access Control Server (ACS) for Windows Server, Cisco Secure ACS Solution Engine, or Cisco Secure ACS Express. If there are multiple routers, server-based AAA is more appropriate.

Refer to
Figure
in online course

AAA Authorization

After users are successfully authenticated against the selected AAA data source (local or server-based), they are then authorized for specific network resources. Authorization is basically what a user can and cannot do on the network after that user is authenticated, similar to how privilege levels and role-based CLI give users specific rights and privileges to certain commands on the router.

Authorization is typically implemented using a AAA server-based solution. Authorization uses a created set of attributes that describes the user's access to the network. These attributes are compared to the information contained within the AAA database, and a determination of restrictions for that user is made and delivered to the local router where the user is connected.

Authorization is automatic and does not require users to perform additional steps after authentication. Authorization is implemented immediately after the user is authenticated.

Refer to
Figure
in online course

AAA Accounting

Accounting collects and reports usage data so that it can be employed for purposes such as auditing or billing. The collected data might include the start and stop connection times, executed commands, number of packets, and number of bytes.

Accounting is implemented using a AAA server-based solution. This service reports usage statistics back to the ACS server. These statistics can be extracted to create detailed reports about the configuration of the network.

One widely deployed use of accounting is combining it with AAA authentication for managing access to internetworking devices by network administrative staff. Accounting provides more security than just authentication. The AAA servers keep a detailed log of exactly what the authenticated user does on the device. This includes all EXEC and configuration commands issued by the user. The log contains numerous data fields, including the username, the date and time, and the actual command that was entered by the user. This information is useful when troubleshooting devices. It also provides leverage against individuals who perform malicious actions.

3.2 Local AAA Authentication

3.2.1 Configuring Local AAA Authentication with CLI

Refer to
Figure
in online course

Local AAA Authentication, also referred to as self-contained authentication, should be configured for smaller networks. Smaller networks are those networks that have one or two routers that provide access to a limited number of users. This method uses the local usernames and passwords stored on a router. The system administrator must populate the local security database by specifying username and password profiles for each user that might log in.

The Local AAA Authentication method is similar to using the `login local` command with one exception. AAA also provides a way to configure backup methods of authentication.

Configuring local AAA services to authenticate administrator access (character mode access) requires a few basic steps:

Step 1.   Add usernames and passwords to the local router database for users that need administrative access to the router.

Step 2.   Enable AAA globally on the router.

Step 3.   Configure AAA parameters on the router.

Step 4.   Confirm and troubleshoot the AAA configuration.

Refer to
Figure
in online course

To enable AAA, use the `aaa new-model` global configuration command. To disable AAA, use the `no` form of this command.

After AAA is enabled, to configure authentication on vty ports, asynchronous lines (tty), the auxiliary port, or the console port, define a named list of authentication methods and then apply that list to the various interfaces.

To define a named list of authentication methods, use the `aaa authentication login` command. This command requires a list name and the authentication methods. The *list name* identifies the list of authentication methods activated when a user logs in. The method list is a sequential list describing the authentication methods to be queried for authenticating a user. Method lists enable an administrator to designate one or more security protocols for authentication. Using more than one protocol provides a backup system for authentication in case the initial method fails.

Several keywords can be used to indicate the method. To enable local authentication using a preconfigured local database, use the keyword `local` or `local-case`. The difference between the two options is that `local` accepts a username regardless of case, and `local-case` is case-sensitive. To specify that a user can authenticate using the enable password, use the `enable` keyword. To ensure that the authentication succeeds even if all methods return an error, specify `none` as the final method. For security purposes, use the `none` keyword only when testing the AAA configuration. It should never be applied on a live network. For example, the `enable` method could be configured as a fallback mechanism in case the username and password is forgotten.

```
aaa authentication login TELNET-ACCESS local enable
```

In this example, a AAA authentication list named TELNET-ACCESS is created that requires users to attempt to authenticate to the router local user database first. If that attempt returns an error, such as a local user database which is not configured, the user can attempt to authenticate by knowing the enable password.

A minimum of one method and a maximum of four methods can be specified for a single method list. When a user attempts to log in, the first method listed is used. Cisco IOS software attempts authentication with the next listed authentication method only when there is no response or an error from the previous method occurs. If the authentication method denies the user access, the authentication process stops and no other authentication methods are allowed.

Refer to
Figure
in online course

The defined list of authentication methods must be applied to specific interfaces or lines. For flexibility, different method lists can be applied to different interfaces and lines. For example, an administrator could apply a special login for Telnet and then have a different login method for the line console. To enable a specific list name, use the **aaa login authentication** *list-name* command in line configuration mode.

The option also exists to configure a default list name. When AAA is first enabled, the default method list named "default" is automatically applied to all interfaces and lines, but it has no authentication methods defined. To assign multiple authentication methods to the default list, use the command **aaa authentication login default** *method1...*[*method2*].

The authentication methods in the default method list are used on all lines, unless a custom authentication method list is created. If an interface or line has a custom authentication method list applied to it, that method list overrides the default method list for that interface. If the default method list is not set and there is no other list, only the local user database is checked. This has the same effect as the command **aaa authentication login default local**. On the console, login succeeds without any authentication checks if default is not set.

Once a custom authentication method list is applied to an interface, it is possible to return to the default method list by using the **no aaa authentication login** *list-name* command. If the default list has not been defined, then AAA authentication does not occur.

Refer to
Figure
in online course

Additional security can be implemented on the line using the **aaa local authentication attempts max-fail** *number-of-unsuccessful-attempts* command in global configuration mode. This command secures AAA user accounts by locking out accounts that have excessive failed attempts. To remove the number of unsuccessful attempts that was set, use the **no** form of this command.

To display a list of all locked-out users, use the **show aaa local user lockout** command in privileged EXEC mode. Use the **clear aaa local user lockout {username** *username* ¦ **all}** command in privileged EXEC mode to unlock a specific user or to unlock all locked users.

The **aaa local authentication attempts max-fail** command differs from the **login delay** command in how it handles failed attempts. The **aaa local authentication attempts max-fail** command locks the user account if the authentication fails. This account stays locked until it is cleared by an administrator. The **login delay** command introduces a delay between failed login attempts without locking the account.

When a user logs into a Cisco router and uses AAA, a unique ID is assigned to the session. Throughout the life of the session, various attributes that are related to the session are collected and stored internally within the AAA database. These attributes can include the IP address of the user, the protocol that is used to access the router, such as PPP or Serial Line Internet Protocol (SLIP), the speed of the connection, and the number of packets or bytes that are received or transmitted.

To display the attributes that are collected for a AAA session, use the **show aaa user {all** ¦ *unique id*} command in privileged EXEC mode. This command does not provide information for all users who are logged into a device, but only for those who have been authenticated or authorized using AAA or whose sessions are being accounted for by the AAA module.

The `show aaa sessions` command can be used to show the unique ID of a session.

3.2.2 Configuring Local AAA Authentication with CCP

Refer to
Figure
in online course

AAA can be enabled using CCP. To verify the AAA configuration and to enable or disable AAA, choose **Configure > Router > AAA > AAA Summary**. The current status of AAA will display in the window along with a button to either enable or disable AAA depending on the current setting. If AAA is currently disabled, click the **Enable AAA** button. CCP will display an informational message stating that configuration changes will be made to prevent loss of access to the device. Click **Yes** to continue.

If the **Disable AAA** button is clicked, CCP displays an informational message stating that it will make configuration changes to ensure that the router can be accessed after AAA is disabled.

Refer to
Figure
in online course

The first task when using CCP to configure AAA services for local authentication is to create users:

Step 1.   Choose **Configure > Router > Router Access > User Accounts/View**.

Step 2.   Click **Add** to add a new user.

Step 3.   In the Add an Account window, enter the username and password in the appropriate fields to define the user account.

Step 4.   From the Privilege Level drop-down list, choose **15**, unless there are lesser privilege levels defined.

Step 5.   If views have been defined, check the **Associate a View with the user** check box and choose a view from the View Name list that is associated with a user.

Step 6.   Click **OK**.

The CLI command that CCP generates is `username AAAadmin privilege 15 secret 5 $1$f16u$uKOO6J/UnojZ0bCEzgnQi1 view root`.

Refer to
Figure
in online course

To configure AAA authentication, an administrator must first either define a list of authentication methods for the default method or configure a named method list and apply it. Different method lists can be created and applied to different interfaces or lines. Configure the default method list for login authentication using the local database:

Step 1.   Choose **Configure > Router > AAA > Authentication Policies > Login**. Any defined method lists will be displayed.

Step 2.   To view the options for a method list, select the list name and click **Edit**.

Step 3.   From the Edit a Method List for Authentication Login window, click **Add**.

Step 4.   From the Select Method List(s) for Authentication Login window, choose **local** from the method list if it is not already selected.

Step 5.   Click **OK**.

The CLI command that CCP generates is `aaa authentication login default local`.

3.2.3 Troubleshooting Local AAA Authentication

Refer to
Figure
in online course

The Cisco router has debug commands that are useful for troubleshooting authentication issues. The `debug aaa` command contains several keywords that can be used for this purpose. Of special interest is the `debug aaa authentication` command.

It is important to analyze debug output when everything is working properly. Knowing how debug output displays when all is well helps identify problems when things are not working properly. Exercise caution when using the `debug` command in a production environment because these commands place a significant load on router resources and can affect network performance.

Refer to
Figure
in online course

The `debug aaa authentication` command is instrumental when troubleshooting AAA problems. To disable this command, use the `no` form of the command or the all-encompassing `undebug all` statement.

Look specifically for GETUSER and GETPASS status messages. The message is also helpful when identifying which method list is being referenced.

3.3 Server-Based AAA

3.3.1 Server-Based AAA Characteristics

Refer to
Figure
in online course

Local implementations of AAA do not scale well. Most corporate environments have multiple Cisco routers with multiple router administrators and hundreds or thousands of users needing access to the corporate LAN. Maintaining a local database for each Cisco router for this size of network is not feasible.

To solve this challenge, one or more AAA servers, such as Cisco Secure ACS, can be used to manage the user and administrative access needs for an entire corporate network. Cisco Secure ACS can create a central user and administrative access database that all devices in the network can access. It can also work with many external databases, including Active Directory and Lightweight Directory Access Protocol (LDAP). These databases store user account information and passwords, allowing for central administration of user accounts.

Refer to
Figure
in online course

The Cisco Secure ACS family of products supports both Terminal Access Control Access Control Server Plus (TACACS+) and Remote Authentication Dial-In User Services (RADIUS) protocols, which are the two predominant protocols used by Cisco security appliances, routers, and switches for implementing AAA.

While both protocols can be used to communicate between client and AAA servers, TACACS+ is considered the more secure protocol. This is because all TACACS + protocol exchanges are encrypted; RADIUS only encrypts the user password. It does not encrypt user names, accounting information, or any other information carried in the RADIUS message.

3.3.2 Server-Based AAA Communication Protocols

Refer to
Figure
in online course

TACACS+ and RADIUS are both authentication protocols. Each supports different capabilities and functionality. Whether TACACS+ or RADIUS is selected depends on the needs of the organization. For example, a large ISP might select RADIUS because it supports detailed accounting required for billing users. An organization with various user groups might select TACACS+ because it requires select authorization policies to be applied on a per-user or per-group basis.

It is important to understand the many differences between the TACACS+ and RADIUS protocols.

Critical factors for TACACS+ include:

- Is incompatible with its predecessors TACACS and XTACACS

- Separates authentication and authorization

- Encrypts all communication

- Utilizes TCP port 49

Critical factors for RADIUS include:

- Uses RADIUS proxy servers for scalability

- Combines RADIUS authentication and authorization as one process

- Encrypts only the password

- Utilizes UDP

- Supports remote-access technologies, 802.1X, and Session Initiation Protocol (SIP)

Refer to
Figure
in online course

TACACS+ is a Cisco enhancement to the original TACACS protocol. Despite its name, TACACS+ is an entirely new protocol that is incompatible with any previous version of TACACS. TACACS+ is supported by the Cisco family of routers and access servers.

TACACS+ provides separate AAA services. Separating the AAA services provides flexibility in implementation, because it is possible to use TACACS+ for authorization and accounting while using another method of authentication.

The extensions to the TACACS+ protocol provide more types of authentication requests and response codes than were in the original TACACS specification. TACACS+ offers multiprotocol support, such as IP and AppleTalk. Normal TACACS+ operation encrypts the entire body of the packet for more secure communications and utilizes TCP port 49.

Refer to
Figure
in online course

RADIUS, developed by Livingston Enterprises, is an open IETF standard AAA protocol for applications such as network access or IP mobility. RADIUS works in both local and roaming situations and is commonly used for accounting purposes. RADIUS is currently defined by RFCs 2865, 2866, 2867, and 2868.

The RADIUS protocol hides passwords during transmission, even with the Password Authentication Protocol (PAP), using a rather complex operation that involves Message Digest 5 (MD5) hashing and a shared secret. However, the rest of the packet is sent in plaintext.

RADIUS combines authentication and authorization as one process. When a user is authenticated, that user is also authorized. RADIUS uses UDP port 1645 or 1812 for authentication and UDP port 1646 or 1813 for accounting.

RADIUS is widely used by VoIP service providers. It passes login credentials of a SIP endpoint, such as a broadband phone, to a SIP registrar using digest authentication, and then to a RADIUS server using RADIUS. RADIUS is also a common authentication protocol that is utilized by the 802.1X security standard.

The Diameter protocol is the planned replacement for RADIUS. Diameter uses a new transport protocol called Stream Control Transmission Protocol (SCTP) and TCP instead of UDP.

3.3.3 Cisco Secure ACS

Refer to
Figure
in online course

Many enterprise-level authentication servers are on the market today, but they lack the ability to combine both the TACACS+ and RADIUS protocols into a single solution. Fortunately, Cisco Secure ACS for Windows Server is a single solution that offers AAA for both TACACS+ and RADIUS.

The Cisco ACS family of products are highly scalable, high-performance access control servers that can be leveraged to control administrator access and configuration for all network devices in a network supporting RADIUS or TACACS+ or both. Cisco Secure ACS offers several benefits:

- Extends access security by combining authentication, user access, and administrator access with policy control within a centralized identity networking solution.

- Allows greater flexibility and mobility, increased security, and user-productivity gains.

- Enforces a uniform security policy for all users, regardless of how they access the network.

- Reduces the administrative and management burden when scaling user and network administrator access to the network.

Refer to **Figure** in online course

Cisco Secure ACS can authenticate users against an internal Cisco Secure user database, or it can be configured to leverage external databases that can be centrally managed. This centralizes the control of all user privileges and distributes them to access points throughout the network. Cisco Secure ACS provides detailed reporting and monitoring capabilities of user behavior, access connections, and device configuration changes. This feature is extremely important for organizations trying to comply with various government regulations. Cisco Secure ACS supports a broad variety of access connections, including wired and wireless LAN, dialup, broadband, content, storage, VoIP, firewalls, and virtual private networks (VPNs).

Cisco Secure ACS provides a variety of advanced features:

- Automatic service monitoring

- Database synchronization and importing of tools for large-scale deployments

- LDAP user authentication support

- User and administrative access reporting

- Restrictions to network access based on criteria such as the time of day and the day of week

- User and device group profiles

Refer to **Figure** in online course

Cisco Secure ACS is a core component of the Cisco TrustSec solution. Cisco TrustSec is deployed in either an 802.1X infrastructure-based approach or a NAC appliance-based approach.

In the 802.1X infrastructure-based TrustSec approach, the Cisco ACS is the policy server which authenticates users connecting to the network. ACS offers central management of access policies for device administration and for wireless and wired 802.1X network access scenarios. Cisco ACS supports both RADIUS and TACACS+ protocols for authentication, authorization and accounting. It is a next-generation network identity and access solution that serves as an administration point and decision point for policy-based access control.

In the NAC appliance-based TrustSec approach the Cisco NAC Manager is the policy server that works with the Cisco NAC Server to authenticate users and their devices over wired, wireless, and VPN connections. Both approaches can include the Cisco NAC Profiler and the Cisco NAC Guest Server to enhance policy-based access control for employees and guests. Cisco TrustSec integrates with the Cisco SecureX architecture to allow the Cisco security portfolio to use network-based identity context for full context-aware firewalling and policy enforcement.

Refer to **Figure** in online course

Cisco Secure ACS has many high-performance and scalability features:

- *Ease of use* A web-based user interface simplifies and distributes the configuration for user profiles, group profiles, and Cisco Secure ACS configuration.

- *Scalability* Cisco Secure ACS is built to provide large networked environments with support for redundant servers, remote databases, and database replication and backup services.

- *Extensibility* LDAP authentication forwarding supports the authentication of user profiles that are stored in directories from leading directory vendors, including Sun, Novell, and Microsoft.

- *Management* Microsoft Windows Active Directory support consolidates Windows username and password management and uses the Windows Performance Monitor for real-time statistics viewing.

- *Administration* Different access levels for each Cisco Secure ACS administrator and the ability to group network devices together make it easier and more flexible to control the enforcement and changes of security policy administration for all devices in a network.

- *Product flexibility* Because Cisco IOS software has embedded support for AAA, Cisco Secure ACS can be used across virtually any network access server that Cisco sells (the Cisco IOS software release must support RADIUS or TACACS+). Cisco Secure ACS is available in three options: Cisco Secure ACS Solution Engine, Cisco Secure ACS Express, and Cisco Secure ACS for Windows.

- *Integration* Tight coupling with Cisco IOS routers and VPN solutions provides features such as multi-chassis multilink PPP and Cisco IOS software command authorization.

- *Third-party support* Cisco Secure ACS offers token server support for any one-time password (OTP) vendor that provides an RFC-compliant RADIUS interface, such as RSA, PassGo, Secure Computing, ActiveCard, Vasco, or CryptoCard.

- *Control* Cisco Secure ACS provides dynamic quotas to restrict access based on the time of day, network use, number of logged sessions, and the day of the week.

Refer to **Figure** in online course

Cisco Secure ACS is available as software installed on a Windows Server or on a 1U, rack-mountable, security-hardened server, such as ACS Solution Engine or ACS Express. All are server-based examples of providing AAA services using a remote security database. The Cisco Secure ACS for Windows option enables the AAA services on a router to contact an external Cisco Secure ACS installed on a Windows server system for user and administrator authentication.

Cisco Secure ACS Solution Engine is a 1U rack-mountable unit, security-hardened appliance with a pre-installed Cisco Secure ACS license. It should be used in large organizations where more than 350 users need to be supported. Compared to the Cisco Secure ACS for Windows product, Cisco Secure ACS Solution Engine reduces the total cost of ownership by eliminating the need to install and maintain a Microsoft Windows server machine.

Cisco Secure ACS Express is also a 1U rack-mountable unit, security-hardened appliance with a pre-installed Cisco Secure ACS Express license. The difference is that the ACS Express option is intended for commercial (less than 350 users), retail, and enterprise branch office deployments. ACS Express offers a comprehensive yet simplified feature set, a user-friendly GUI, and a lower price point that allows administrators to deploy this product in situations where Cisco Secure ACS for Windows Server or Cisco Secure ACS Solution Engine might not be suitable.

While this chapter focuses on deploying Cisco Secure ACS for Windows Server, the concepts and features discussed are also available on the ACS Solution Engine and ACS Express.

3.3.4 Configuring Cisco Secure ACS

Refer to **Figure** in online course

Before installing the Cisco Secure ACS, it is important to prepare the server. Third-party software requirements and the network and port requirements of the server and AAA devices must be considered.

Third-Party Software Requirements

Software products that are mentioned in the release notes are supported for interoperability by Cisco. Support for interoperability issues with software products that are not mentioned in the release notes might be difficult to attain. The most recent version of the Cisco Secure ACS release notes are posted on Cisco.com.

Keep in mind that in the Cisco Secure ACS application, a client is a router, switch, firewall, or VPN concentrator that uses the services of the server.

Network and Port Prerequisites

The network should meet specified requirements before administrators begin deploying Cisco Secure ACS:

- For full TACACS+ and RADIUS support on Cisco IOS devices, AAA clients must run Cisco IOS Release 11.2 or later.

- Cisco devices that are not Cisco IOS AAA clients must be configured with TACACS+, RADIUS, or both.

- Dial-in, VPN, or wireless clients must be able to connect to the applicable AAA clients.

- The computer running Cisco Secure ACS must be able to reach all AAA clients using `ping`.

- Gateway devices between the Cisco Secure ACS and other network devices must permit communication over the ports that are needed to support the applicable feature or protocol.

- A supported web browser must be installed on the computer running Cisco Secure ACS. For the most recent information about tested browsers, see the release notes for the Cisco Secure ACS product on Cisco.com.

- All NICs in the computer running Cisco Secure ACS must be enabled. If there is a disabled network card on the computer running Cisco Secure ACS, installing Cisco Secure ACS might proceed slowly because of delays caused by the Microsoft CryptoAPI.

After successfully installing Cisco Secure ACS, some initial configuration must be performed. The only way to configure a Cisco Secure ACS server is through an HTML interface.

To access the Cisco Secure ACS HTML interface from the computer that is running Cisco Secure ACS, use the Cisco Secure icon labeled ACS Admin that appears on the desktop. Alternatively, enter the following URL into a supported web browser: http://127.0.0.1:2002.

The Cisco Secure ACS can also be accessed remotely after an administrator user account is configured. To remotely access the Cisco Secure ACS, enter http://ip_address[hostname]:2002. After the initial connection, a different port is dynamically negotiated.

Refer to **Figure** in online course

The home page of the Cisco Secure ACS contains a navigation bar with buttons that represent functions that can be configured:

- User Setup

- Group Setup

- Shared Profile Components

- Network Configuration

- System Configuration

- Interface Configuration

- Administration Control

- External User Databases

- Posture Validation

- Network Access Profiles

- Reports and Activity

- Online Documentation

Button titles may vary between versions. If the RADIUS options are not displayed, the AAA client that uses the RADIUS protocol must be added. Additionally, the interface configuration is directly affected by the settings in the network configuration.

Refer to
Figure
in online course

Before configuring a router, switch, or firewall as a TACACS+ or RADIUS client, those devices should be added as clients within the ACS server.

In the Cisco Secure ACS application, a client is a router, switch, firewall, or VPN concentrator that uses the services of the ACS server.

By default, ACS allows the user to add AAA clients individually, but it is also possible to use a network device group (NDG) to simplify configuration of common devices by grouping them as AAA clients. To use an NDG, it is necessary to enable the NDG option within ACS.

The specific steps to add and configure a client within ACS varies between different ACS versions, but is done through the Network Configuration page (4.x) or the Network Resources page (5.x) by clicking an **Add Entry** button. When configuring a client, it is necessary to provide information such as the client host name, IP address, the secret key that the client will use for encryption, and the appropriate AAA protocol (TACACS+ or RADIUS) to be used.

The Interface Configuration page allows the administrator to control the display of properties on the User Setup page. The specific options displayed depend on whether TACACS+ or RADIUS clients have been added to the server:

- User Data Configuration

- TACACS+ (Cisco IOS)

- RADIUS (Microsoft)

- RADIUS (Ascend)

- RADIUS (IETF)

- RADIUS (IOS/PIX)

- Advanced Options

The User Data Configuration link on the Interface Configuration page enables administrators to customize the fields that appear in the user setup and configuration windows. Administrators can add fields such as phone number, work location, supervisor name, or any other pertinent information. The TACACS+ (Cisco IOS) link enables the administrator to configure TACACS+ settings as well as add new TACACS+ services. Administrators can also configure advanced options that affect what is displayed in the user interface.

Refer to
Figure
in online course

Cisco Secure ACS can be configured to forward authentication of users to one or more external user databases. Support for external user databases means that Cisco Secure ACS does not require duplicate user entries to be created in the Cisco Secure user database. In organizations in which a substantial user database already exists, such as an Active Directory environment, Cisco Secure ACS can leverage the work already invested in building the database without any additional input.

For most database configurations, except for Windows databases, Cisco Secure ACS supports only one instance of a username and password. If Cisco Secure ACS is configured to use multiple user databases with common usernames stored in each, be careful with the database configurations. The first database to match the authentication credentials of the user is the only one that Cisco Secure ACS uses for that user. It is for this reason that it is recommended that there be only one instance of a username in all the external databases.

To establish an external user database connection, you must access the External User Databases page.

When configuring the ACS external databases, there are three major configuration options:

- *Unknown User Policy* Configures the authentication procedure for users that are not located in the Cisco Secure ACS database.

- *Database Group Mappings* Configures what group privileges external database users inherit when Cisco Secure ACS authenticates them. In most cases, when a user is authenticated by an external user database, the actual privileges are drawn from Cisco Secure ACS and not the external database.

- *Database Configuration* Defines the external servers that Cisco Secure ACS works with.

The Database Configuration screen is used to define the parameters of the external server. Options include:

- RSA SecurID Token Server

- RADIUS Token Server

- External ODBC Database

- Windows Database

- LEAP Proxy RADIUS Server

- Generic LDAP

The Windows database configuration has more parameters than the other external database configurations. Because Cisco Secure ACS is native to the Windows operating system, administrators can configure additional functionality on the Windows External User Database Configuration pane. Administrators can gain more control over who is able to authenticate to the network, as well as configuring Dialin Permissions.

In the Dialin Permission section, check the **Verify That "Grant dialin permissions to user" setting has been enabled from within the Windows Users Manager for users configured for Windows User Database authentication** check box. Also make sure that the Grant Dial-in Permissions check box is checked in the Windows profile within Windows Users Manager. The Dialin Permissions option of Cisco Secure ACS applies to more than just the dialup connections. If a user has this option enabled, it applies to any access that user tries to make.

Another option that can be configured using the Windows external database is mapping databases to domains. Mapping allows an administrator to have the same username across different domains, all with different passwords.

3.3.5 Configuring Cisco Secure ACS Users and Groups

Refer to
Figure
in online course

When Cisco Secure ACS is configured to communicate with an external user database, it can be configured to authenticate users with the external user database in one of two ways:.

- *By specific user assignment* Authenticate specific users with an external user database.

- *By unknown user policy* Use an external database to authenticate users not found in the Cisco Secure user database. This method does not require administrators to define users in the Cisco Secure user database.

The External User Database configuration page can be used to configure the unknown user policy, by selecting the **Unknown User Policy** link.

When configuring the unknown user policy, the database must be selected from the External Databases list and placed into the Selected Databases list. This must be done for each database that Cisco Secure ACS is to use when attempting to authenticate unknown users. The order in which the external databases are listed is the same order in which Cisco Secure ACS checks the selected external databases when attempting to authenticate an unknown user.

Refer to
Figure
in online course

After a user is authenticated to an external database, the authorization that takes place is determined by Cisco Secure ACS. This can complicate things because users that are authenticated by a Windows server might require different authorization than users that are authenticated by the LDAP server.

Because of this potential need for different authorizations, place users that are authenticated by the Windows server in one group and users that are authenticated by the LDAP server in another group. To do this, use database group mappings.

Database group mappings enable an administrator to map an authentication server (i.e., LDAP, Windows, ODBC, etc.) to a group that has been configured in Cisco Secure ACS. For some databases, a user can belong to only one group. For other databases, such as LDAP and Windows, support for group mapping by external database group membership is possible.

One of the things that can be configured in a group setup is per group command authorization, which uses Cisco Secure ACS to authorize which router commands the users that belong to a group can execute. For example, a group can be permitted to execute any router commands except `show running-config`.

Refer to
Figure
in online course

Adding a user account and configuring user access is a critical task for Cisco Secure ACS. The steps to configure user access vary between different ACS versions, but all occur from the User Setup page. In the Edit pane, enter data in the fields to define the user account. Some fields typically configured are the user password fields, TACACS+ enable control, TACACS+ enable password, and TACACS+ shell authorized commands.

Remember that the Interface Configuration page allows the administrator to control the display of properties on the User Setup page. If there are necessary user properties that are not present on the User Setup page, the interface configuration must be modified.

3.4 Server-Based AAA Authentication

3.4.1 Configuring Server-Based AAA Authentication with CLI

Refer to
Figure
in online course

Unlike Local AAA Authentication, server-based AAA must identify various TACACS+ and RADIUS servers that the AAA service should consult when authenticating and authorizing users.

There are a few basic steps to configure server-based authentication:

Step 1.   Globally enable AAA to allow the use of all AAA elements. This step is a prerequisite for all other AAA commands.

Step 2. Specify the Cisco Secure ACS that will provide AAA services for the router. This can be a TACACS+ or RADIUS server.

Step 3. Configure the encryption key needed to encrypt the data transfer between the network access server and Cisco Secure ACS.

Step 4. Configure the AAA authentication method list to refer to the TACACS+ or RADIUS server. For redundancy, it is possible to configure more than one server.

Refer to
Figure
in online course

Configure a TACACS+ Server and Encryption Key

To configure a TACACS+ server, use the `tacacs-server host` *ip-address* `single-connection` command.

The `single-connection` keyword enhances TCP performance by maintaining a single TCP connection for the life of the session. Otherwise, by default, a TCP connection is opened and closed for each session. If required, multiple TACACS+ servers can be identified by entering their respective IP address using the `tacacs-server host` command.

Next, use the `tacacs-server key` *key* command to configure the shared secret key to encrypt the data transfer between the TACACS+ server and AAA-enabled router. This key must be configured exactly the same on the router and the TACACS+ server.

Configure a RADIUS Server and Encryption Key

To configure a RADIUS server, use the `radius-server host` *ip-address* command. Because RADIUS uses UDP, there is no equivalent `single-connection` keyword. If required, multiple RADIUS servers can be identified by entering a `radius-server host` command for each server.

To configure the shared secret key for encrypting the password, use the `radius-server key` *key* command. This key must be configured exactly the same on the router and the RADIUS server.

Configure Authentication to Use the AAA Server

When the AAA security servers have been identified, the servers must be included in the method list of the `aaa authentication login` command. AAA servers are identified using the `group tacacs+` or `group radius` keywords. For example, to configure a method list for the default login to authenticate using a RADIUS server, a TACACS+ server, or a local username database, use the command `aaa authentication login default group radius group tacacs+ local-case`.

3.4.2 Configuring Server-Based AAA Authentication with CCP

Refer to
Figure
in online course

If using CCP for TACACS+ support, it is necessary to specify a list of available Cisco Secure ACS servers that provide TACACS+ services for the router:

Step 1. From the CCP home page, choose **Configure > Router > AAA > AAA Servers and Groups > Servers**.

Step 2. From the AAA Servers pane, click **Add**. The Add AAA Server window appears. Choose **TACACS+** from the Server Type list box.

Step 3. Enter the IP address or host name of the AAA server in the Server IP or Host field. If the router has not been configured to use a DNS server, enter a DNS server IP address.

Step 4.   The router can be configured to maintain a single open connection to the TACACS+ server rather than opening and closing a TCP connection each time it communicates with the server. To do so, check the **Single connection to server(for CiscoSecure)** check box.

Step 5.   To override AAA server global settings and specify a server-specific timeout value in the Server-Specific Setup section, enter a value in the **Timeout (seconds)** field. This field determines how long the router waits for a response from this server before going on to the next server in the group list. If a value is not entered, the router uses the value that is configured in the AAA Servers Global Settings window. The default setting is five seconds.

Step 6.   To configure a server-specific key, check the **Configure Key** check box and enter the key that is used to encrypt traffic between the router and this server in the New Key field. Re-enter the key in the Confirm Key field for confirmation. If this option is not checked and a value is not entered, the router uses the value that was configured in the AAA Servers Global Settings window.

Step 7.   Click **OK**.

An example CLI command that CCP would generate based on a TACACS+ server at IP address 10.0.1.1 and key TACACS+Pa55w0rd is `tacacs-server host 10.0.1.1 key TACACS+Pa55w0rd`.

Refer to
Figure
in online course

After AAA is enabled and the TACACS+ servers are configured, the router can be configured to use the Cisco Secure ACS server to authenticate user access to the router. To configure the router to use the Cisco Secure ACS server for login authentication, a user-defined (or custom) authentication method list must be created, or the default method list must be edited. Keep in mind, the default method list is automatically applied to all interfaces and lines, except those that have a user-defined method list explicitly applied. The administrator can use CCP to configure a user-defined authentication login method list:

1. From the CCP home page, choose **Configure > Router > AAA > Authentication Policies > Login**.

2. From the Authentication Login pane, click **Add**.

3. To create a new authentication login method, choose **User Defined** from the Name drop-down list.

4. Enter the authentication login method list name in the **Specify** field, for example TACACS_SERVER.

5. Click **Add** to define the methods that this policy uses. The Select Method List(s) for Authentication Login window appears.

6. Choose **group tacacs+** from the method list.

7. Click **OK** to add group tacacs+ to the method list and return to the Add a Method List for Authentication Login window.

8. Click **Add** to add a backup method to this policy. The Select Method List(s) for Authentication Login window appears.

9. Choose **enable** from the method list to use the enable password as the backup login authentication method.

10. Click **OK** to add enable to the method list and return to the Add a Method List for Authentication Login window.

11. In the Deliver Configuration to Device window, click the **Deliver** button to deliver the configuration to the router.

The resulting CLI command that CCP generates is `aaa authentication login TACACS_SERVER group tacacs+ enable`.

Refer to
Figure
in online course

After the authentication login method lists are created, apply the lists to lines and interfaces on the router.

CCP can be used to apply an authentication policy to a router line:

Step 1. Choose **Configure > Router > Router Access > VTY**.

Step 2. From the VTY Lines window, click the **Edit** button to make changes to the vty lines. The Edit VTY Lines window appears.

Step 3. From the Authentication Policy list box, choose the authentication policy to apply to the vty lines. For example, applying the authentication policy named TACACS_SERVER to vty lines 0 through 4 results in the `login authentication TACACS_SERVER` CLI command.

The CLI can also be used to apply an authentication policy to lines or interfaces with the `login authentication {default | list-name}` command in line configuration mode or interface configuration mode.

3.4.3 Troubleshooting Server-Based AAA Authentication

Refer to
Figure
in online course

When AAA is enabled, it is often necessary to monitor authentication traffic and troubleshoot configurations.

The `debug aaa authentication` command is a useful AAA troubleshooting command because it provides a high-level view of login activity.

The command indicates a status message of PASS when a TACACS+ login attempt is successful. If the status message returned is FAIL, verify the secret key and troubleshoot as necessary.

Refer to
Figure
in online course

Two other very useful server-based AAA troubleshooting commands include the `debug tacacs` and `debug radius` commands. These commands can be used to provide more detailed AAA debugging information. To disable debugging output, use the `no` form of these commands.

Similar to the `debug aaa authentication` command, the `debug tacacs` also indicates status messages of PASS or FAIL.

To see all TACACS+ messages use the `debug tacacs` command. To narrow the results and display information from the TACACS+ helper process, use the `debug tacacs events` command in privileged EXEC mode. The `debug tacacs events` command displays the opening and closing of a TCP connection to a TACACS+ server, the bytes read and written over the connection, and the TCP status of the connection. Use the `debug tacacs events` command with caution, because it can generate a substantial amount of output. To disable debugging output, use the `no` form of this command.

3.5 Server-Based AAA Authorization and Accounting

3.5.1 Configuring Server-Based AAA Authorization

Refer to
Figure
in online course

While authentication is concerned with ensuring that the device or end user is legitimate, authorization is concerned with allowing and disallowing authenticated users access to certain areas and programs on the network.

The TACACS+ protocol allows the separation of authentication from authorization. A router can be configured to restrict the user to performing only certain functions after successful authentication. Authorization can be configured for both character mode (exec authorization) and packet mode (network authorization). Keep in mind that RADIUS does not separate the authentication from the authorization process.

Another important aspect of authorization is the ability to control user access to specific services. Controlling access to configuration commands greatly simplifies the infrastructure security in large enterprise networks. Per-user permissions on the Cisco Secure ACS simplify network device configuration.

For example, an authorized user can be permitted to access the `show version` command but not the `configure terminal` command. The router queries the ACS for permission to execute the commands on behalf of the user. When the user issues the `show version` command, the ACS sends an ACCEPT response. If the user issues a `configure terminal` command, the ACS sends a REJECT response.

By default, TACACS+ establishes a new TCP session for every authorization request, which can lead to delays when users enter commands. Cisco Secure ACS supports persistent TCP sessions to improve performance.

Refer to
Figure
in online course

To configure command authorization, use the `aaa authorization {network ¦ exec ¦ commands level} {default ¦ list-name} method1...[method4]` command. The service type can specify the types of commands or services:

- `commands` *level* - for exec (shell) commands
- `exec` - for starting an exec (shell)
- `network` - for network services (PPP, SLIP, ARAP)

When AAA authorization is not enabled, all users are allowed full access. After authentication is started, the default changes to allow no access. This means that the administrator must create a user with full access rights before authorization is enabled. Failure to do so immediately locks the administrator out of the system the moment the `aaa authorization` command is entered. The only way to recover from this is to reboot the router. If this is a production router, rebooting might be unacceptable. Be sure that at least one user always has full rights.

Refer to
Figure
in online course

To configure the router to use the Cisco Secure ACS server for authorization, create a user-defined (or custom) authorization method list or edit the default authorization method list. The default authorization method list is automatically applied to all interfaces except those that have a user-defined authorization method list explicitly applied. A user-defined authorization method list overrides the default authorization method list. CCP can be used to configure the default authorization method list for character mode (exec) access:

Step 1. From the CCP home page, choose **Configure > Router > AAA > Authorization Policies > EXEC Command Mode**.

Step 2. From the Exec Authorization pane, select the default list and click **Edit**.

Step 3. From the Edit a Method List for Exec Authorization window, click **Add** to define the methods that this policy uses.

Step 4. From the Select Method List(s) for Exec Authorization window, choose **group tacacs+** from the method list.

Step 5. Click **OK** to return to the Edit a Method List for Exec Authorization window.

Step 6. Click **OK** to return to the Exec Authorization pane.

The resulting CLI command that CCP generates is `aaa authorization exec default group tacacs+`.

Refer to
Figure
in online course

CCP can also be used to configure the default authorization method list for packet mode (network):

Step 1. From the CCP home page, choose **Configure > Router > AAA > Authorization Policies > Network**.

Step 2. From the Network Authorization pane, click **Add**.

Step 3. From the Add a Method List for Network Authorization window, choose **Default** from the Name drop-down list.

Step 4. Click **Add** to define the methods that this policy uses.

Step 5. From the Select Method List(s) for Network Authorization window, choose **group tacacs+** from the method list.

Step 6. Click **OK** to return to the Add a Method List for Network Authorization window.

Step 7. Click **OK** to return to the Network Authorization pane.

The resulting CLI command that CCP generates is `aaa authorization network default group tacacs+`.

3.5.2 Configuring Server-Based AAA Accounting

Refer to
Figure
in online course

Companies often need to keep track of which resources individuals or groups use. Examples of this include one department charging another department for access, or one company providing internal support to another company. AAA accounting enables usage tracking, such as dial-in access, to log the data gathered to a database, and to produce reports on the data gathered.

Although accounting is generally considered a network management or financial management issue, it is discussed briefly here because it is so closely linked with security. One security issue that is addressed by accounting is the creation of a list of users and the time of day they dialed into the system. If, for example, the administrator knows that a worker logs in to the system in the middle of the night, this information can be used to further investigate the purpose of the login.

Another reason to implement accounting is to create a list of changes occurring on the network, the user that made the changes, and the exact nature of the changes. Knowing this information helps the troubleshooting process if the changes cause unexpected results.

Cisco Secure ACS serves as a central repository for accounting information, essentially tracking events that occur on the network. Each session that is established through Cisco Secure ACS can be fully accounted for and stored on the server. This stored information can be very helpful for management, security audits, capacity planning, and network usage billing.

Like authentication and authorization method lists, method lists for accounting define the way accounting is performed and the sequence in which these methods are performed. After it is enabled, the default accounting method list is automatically applied to all interfaces, except those that have a user-defined (or custom) accounting method list explicitly defined.

Refer to
Figure
in online course

To configure AAA accounting, use the **aaa accounting** {**network** ¦ **exec** ¦ **connection**} {**default** ¦ *list-name*} {**start-stop** ¦ **stop-only** ¦ **none**} [**broadcast**] *method1...*[*method4*] global configuration mode command. The **network**, **exec**, and **connection** parameters are commonly used keywords.

- *Network* Runs accounting for all network-related service requests, including Serial Line Internet Protocol (SLIP), PPP, PPP Network Control Protocols (NCPs).

- *Exec* Runs accounting for the EXEC shell session.

- *Connection* Runs accounting on all outbound connections made from the network access server, such as Telnet or local-area transport (LAT).

- *Default* Uses the listed accounting methods that follow this keyword as the default list of methods.

- *List-name* Character string used to name a custom accounting method list.

- *Start-stop* Sends a "start" accounting notice at the beginning of a process and a "stop" accounting notice at the end of a process.

- *Stop-only* Sends a "stop" accounting record for all cases including authentication failures.

- *None* Disables accounting services on a line or interface.

- *Broadcast* (Optional) Enables sending accounting records to multiple AAA servers.

As with AAA authentication, either the keyword **default** or a *list-name* is used. Next, the record type, or trigger, is configured. The trigger specifies what actions cause accounting records to be updated. Possible triggers are **none**, **start-stop**, and **stop-only**.

For example, to log the use of EXEC commands and network connections, use the global configuration commands.

```
R1(config)# aaa accounting exec start-stop group tacacs+
R1(config)# aaa accounting network start-stop group tacacs+
```

Chapter Summary

Refer to **Figure** in online course

Refer to **Packet Tracer Activity** for this chapter

Refer to **Lab Activity** for this chapter

Your Chapter Notes

Implementing Firewall Technologies

Chapter Introduction

As networks continued to grow over time, they were increasingly used to transfer and store sensitive data. This intensified the need for stronger security technologies, which led to the invention of the firewall. The term firewall originally referred to a fireproof wall, usually made of stone or metal that prevented flames from spreading between connected structures. Similarly, in networking, firewalls separate protected areas from non-protected areas. This prevents unauthorized users from accessing protected network resources.

Initially, basic Access Control Lists (ACLs), including standard, extended, numbered and named, were the only means of providing firewall protection. Other firewall technologies began to mature in the late 1990s. Stateful firewalls use tables to track the real-time state of end-to-end sessions. Stateful firewalls take into account the session-oriented nature of network traffic. The first stateful firewalls used the "TCP established" option for ACLs. Later, reflexive ACLs were used to dynamically reflect certain types of inside-to-outside traffic upon the return of that traffic. Dynamic ACLs were developed to open a hole in the firewall for approved traffic for a finite period of time. Time-based ACLs were created to apply ACLs during certain times of the day on specified days of the week. With the proliferation of ACL types, it became more and more important to be able to verify the proper behavior of these ACLs with **show** and **debug** commands.

Today there are many types of firewalls in existence, including packet filtering, stateful, application gateway (proxy), address-translation, host-based, transparent, and hybrid firewalls. Modern network design must carefully include proper placement of one or more firewalls to protect those resources that must be protected while allowing secure access to those resources that must remain available.

In a hands-on lab for the chapter, *Configuring CBAC and Zone-Based Firewalls*, learners use CLI and CCP to configure and test Context-Based Access Control and Zone-Based Policy Firewall. The lab is found in the lab manual on Academy Connection at cisco.netacad.net.

A Packet Tracer activity, *Configure IP ACLs to Mitigate Attacks*, provides learners additional practice implementing the technologies introduced in this chapter. In particular, learners configure ACLs to ensure that remote access to routers is available only from management stations. Edge routers are configured with ACLs to mitigate common network attacks and these ACLs are tested for proper operation.

In a second Packet Tracer activity, *Configuring Context-Based Access Control (CBAC)*, learners configure and IOS firewall with CBAC on a perimeter router. CBAC functionality is verified with ping, Telnet, and HTTP.

Refer to
Figure
in online course

The last Packet Tracer activity for the chapter, *Configuring a Zone-Based Policy Firewall (ZPF)*, has learners configure a ZPF policy on a perimeter router. ZPF functionality is verified with ping, Telnet and HTTP.

4.1 Access Control Lists

4.1.1 Configuring Standard and Extended IP ACLs with CLI

Refer to
Figure
in online course

Access control lists (ACLs) are widely used in computer networking and in network security for mitigating network attacks and controlling network traffic. Administrators use ACLs to define and control classes of traffic on networking devices based on various parameters. These parameters are specific to Layer 2, 3, 4, and 7 of the OSI model.

Virtually any type of traffic can be defined explicitly by using an appropriately numbered ACL. For example, in the past, the Ethernet type field of an Ethernet frame header was used to define certain types of traffic. An Ethernet type of 0x8035 indicated a reverse address resolution protocol (RARP) frame. Numbered ACLs with a range of 200-299 were used to control traffic according to Ethernet type.

It was also common to create ACLs based on MAC addresses. An ACL numbered 700-799 indicates traffic is classified and controlled based on MAC addresses.

After the type of classification is specified, control parameters required for that ACL can be set. For example, an ACL numbered 700-799 could be used to block a client with a specific MAC address from associating with a predetermined access point.

Today, when classifying traffic, the most common types of parameters used in security-related ACLs involve IPv4 and IPv6 addresses as well as TCP and UDP port numbers. For example, an ACL can permit all users with a specific IP network address to download files from the Internet using secure FTP. That same ACL can be used to deny all IP addresses from traditional FTP access.

Standard ACLs

Refer to
Figure
in online course

ACLs numbered 1-99 or 1300-1999 are standard IPv4 ACLs. Standard ACLs match packets by examining the source IP address field in the IP header of that packet. These ACLs are used to filter packets based solely on Layer 3 source information.

The command syntax for configuring a standard numbered IP ACL is as follows:

```
Router(config)# access-list {1-99} {permit | deny} source-addr [source-wildcard]
```

The first value specifies the ACL number. The second value specifies whether to permit or deny the configured source IP address traffic. The third value is the source IP address that must be matched. The fourth value is the wildcard mask to be applied to the previously configured IP address to indicate the range.

Extended ACLs

Extended ACLs match packets based on Layer 3 and Layer 4 source and destination information. Layer 4 information can include TCP and UDP port information. Extended ACLs give greater flexibility and control over network access than standard ACLs. The command syntax for configuring an extended numbered IP ACL is as follows:

```
Router(config)# access-list {100-199} {permit | deny} protocol source-addr
[source-wildcard] [operator operand] destination-addr [destination-wildcard]
[operator operand] [established]
```

Similar to standard ACLs, the first value specifies the ACL number. ACLs numbered 100-199 or 2000-2699 are extended ACLs. The next value specifies whether to permit or deny according to the criteria that follows. The third value indicates protocol type. The administrator must specify IP, TCP, UDP, or other specific IP sub-protocols. The source IP address and wildcard mask determine where traffic originates. The destination IP address and its wildcard mask are used to indicate the final destination of the network traffic. Although the port parameter is defined as optional, if the administrator does not specify the port either by number or by a well-known port name, all traffic to that destination will either be dropped or permitted.

All ACLs assume an implicit deny, meaning that if a packet does not match any of the criteria specified in the ACL, the packet is denied. After creating an ACL, include at least one permit statement, otherwise all traffic will be dropped when that ACL is applied to an interface.

Both standard and extended ACLs can be used to describe packets entering or exiting an interface. The list is searched sequentially. The first statement matched stops the search through the list and defines the action to be taken.

After creating the standard or extended ACL, the administrator must apply it to the appropriate interface. The command to apply the ACL to an interface is as follows:

Refer to
Figure
in online course

```
Router(config-if)# ip access-group access-list-number {in ¦ out}
```

The command to apply the ACL to a vty line is as follows:

```
Router(config-line)# access-class access-list-number {in ¦ out}
```

It is possible to create a named ACL instead of a numbered ACL. Named ACLs must be specified as either standard or extended.

```
Router(config)# ip access-list [standard ¦ extended] name_of_ACL
```

Executing this command places a user into subconfiguration mode where **permit** and **deny** commands are entered. The **permit** and **deny** commands have the same basic syntax as those in the numbered IP ACL commands.

A standard named ACL can use **deny** and **permit** statements.

```
Router(config-std-nacl)# deny {source [source-wildcard] ¦ any}
Router(config-std-nacl)# permit {source [source-wildcard] ¦ any}
```

An extended named ACL offers additional parameters.

```
Router(config-ext-nacl)# {permit ¦ deny} protocol source-addr [source-wildcard]
[operator operand] destination-addr [destination-mask] [operator operand]
[established]
```

Once the ACL statements are created, the administrator activates the ACL on an interface with the **ip access-group** command, specifying the name of the ACL.

```
Router(config-if)# ip access-group access-list-name {in ¦ out}
```

An ACL can also be used to permit or deny specific IP addresses from gaining virtual access. Standard ACLs allow restrictions to be enforced on the originator source IP address or IP address range. An extended ACL does the same but can also enforce the access protocol such as port 23 (Telnet) or port 22 (SSH). The access-class extended ACL only supports the **any** keyword as the destination. The access list must be applied to the vty port.

Refer to
Figure
in online course

```
Router(config-line)# access-class access-list-name {in ¦ out}
```

At the end of an ACL statement, the administrator has the option to configure the **log** parameter.

```
R1(config)# access-list 101 permit tcp 192.168.1.0 0.0.0.255 192.168.2.0 0.0.0.255
eq 22 log
```

If this parameter is configured, when the Cisco IOS software compares packets to the ACL and finds a match, the router logs this information to any enabled logging facility. An enabled logging facility could be the console, the internal buffer of the router, or a syslog server. Several pieces of information are logged:

- **Action** - permit or deny

- **Protocol** - TCP, UDP, or ICMP

- **Source and destination** - IPv4 or IPv6 addresses

- **TCP and UDP** - source and destination port numbers

- **For ICMP** - message types

Log messages are generated on the first packet match and then at five minute intervals after that first packet match.

Enabling the **log** parameter on a Cisco router or switch seriously affects the performance of that device. When logging is enabled, packets are either process- or fast-switched. The log parameter should only be used when the network is under attack and an administrator is trying to determine who the attacker is. In this instance, an administrator should enable logging for the period required to gather the appropriate information and then disable logging.

Refer to
Figure
in online course

An ACL is made up of one or more access control entries (ACEs). Several caveats should be considered when working with ACLs:

- *Implicit deny all* All Cisco ACLs end with an implicit "deny all" statement. Even if this statement is not apparent in an ACL, it is there.

- *Standard ACL packet filtering* Standard ACLs are limited to packet filtering based on source addresses only. Extended ACLs might need to be created to fully implement a security policy.

- *Order of statements* ACLs have a policy of first match. When a statement is matched, the list is no longer examined. Certain ACEs are more specific than others and, therefore, must be placed higher in the ACL. For example, blocking all UDP traffic at the top of the list negates the statement for allowing SNMP packets, which use UDP, that is lower in the list. An administrator must ensure that statements at the top of the ACL do not negate any statements found lower.

- *Directional filtering* Cisco ACLs have a directional filter that determines whether inbound packets (toward the interface) or outbound packets (away from the interface) are examined. An administrator should double-check the direction of data that an ACL is filtering.

- *Modifying ACLs* When a router compares a packet to an ACL, the ACEs are examined from the top down. When a router locates an entry with matching criteria, the ACL processing stops and the packet is either permitted or denied based on the ACE. When new entries are added to an ACL, they are, by default, added to the bottom of the list. This can render new entries unusable if a previous entry is more general. For example, if an ACL has an entry that denies network 172.16.1.0/24 access to a server in one line, but the next line down permits a single host, host 172.16.1.5, access to that same server, that host will still be denied. This is because the router matches packets from 172.16.1.5 to the 172.16.1.0/24 network and denies the traffic without reading the next line. When a new ACE renders the ACL unusable, a new ACL must be created with the correct statement ordering. The old ACL should be deleted, and the new ACL assigned to the router interface. If using Cisco IOS Release 12.3 and later, sequence numbers can be used to ensure that ACEs are added in the correct location. The ACL is processed top-down based on the sequence numbers of the ACEs (lowest to highest).

- *Special packets* Router-generated packets, such as routing table updates, are not subject to outbound ACL statements on the source router. If the security policy requires filtering these types of packets, inbound ACLs on adjacent routers or other router filter mechanisms using ACLs must do the filtering task.

Now that the syntax and guidelines for standard and extended IP ACLs are defined, what are some specific scenarios for which ACLs provide a security solution?

4.1.2 Using Standard and Extended IP ACLs

Refer to **Figure** in online course

Determining whether to use standard or extended ACLs is based on the overall objective of the entire ACL. For example, imagine a scenario in which all traffic from a single subnet, 172.16.4.0, must be denied access to another subnet, but all other traffic should be permitted.

In this case, a standard ACL can be applied outbound on interface Fa0/0:

```
R1(config)# access-list 1 deny 172.16.4.0 0.0.0.255
R1(config)# access-list 1 permit any
R1(config)# interface FastEthernet 0/0
R1(config-if)# ip access-group 1 out
```

All hosts on subnet 172.16.4.0 are blocked from going out on interface Fa0/0 to subnet 172.16.3.0.

These are the **access-list** command parameters:

- The **1** parameter indicates that this ACL is a standard list.

- The **deny** parameter indicates that traffic matching the selected parameters is not forwarded.

- The **172.16.4.0** parameter is the IP address of the source subnet.

- The **0.0.0.255** parameter is the wildcard mask. Zeros (0) indicate positions that must match in the anding process; ones (1) indicate positions that will be ignored. The mask with zeros (0) in the first three octets indicates those positions must match. The 255 indicates the last octet will be ignored.

- The **permit** parameter indicates that traffic matching the selected parameters is forwarded.

- The **any** parameter is an abbreviation for the IP address of the source. Indicates a source address of 0.0.0.0 and a wildcard mask of 255.255.255.255; all source addresses will match.

Because of the implicit deny at the end of all ACLs, the command **access-list 1 permit any** must be included to ensure that only traffic from the 172.16.4.0 subnet is blocked and that all other traffic is allowed.

Refer to **Figure** in online course

As compared to standard ACLs, extended ACLs allow for specific types of traffic to be denied or permitted. Imagine a scenario in which FTP traffic from one subnet must be denied on another subnet. In this case, an extended ACL is required because a specific traffic type is filtered.

```
R1(config)# access-list 101 deny tcp 172.16.4.0 0.0.0.255 172.16.3.0 0.0.0.255 eq 21
R1(config)# access-list 101 deny tcp 172.16.4.0 0.0.0.255 172.16.3.0 0.0.0.255 eq 20
R1(config)# access-list 101 permit ip any any
```

In this ACL, FTP access is denied from subnet 172.16.4.0/24 to subnet 172.16.3.0/24. All other traffic is allowed. TCP port 21 is used for FTP program commands. TCP port 20 is used for FTP data transfer. Both ports are denied.

A **permit ip any any** statement is required at the end of the ACL; otherwise, all traffic is denied because of the implicit deny.

The best placement of this ACL is inbound on the Fa0/1 interface. This ensures that the unwanted FTP traffic is dropped before wasting router processing resources.

```
Router(config)# interface fastethernet 0/1
Router(config-if)# ip access-group 101 in
```

Keep in mind, with this ACL, a **permit any any** entry overrides the implicit **deny all** entry at the end of every ACL. This means that all other traffic, including FTP traffic originating from the 172.16.4.0/24 network destined for any network other than the 172.16.3.0/24 network, would be permitted.

Refer to
Figure
in online course

After an ACL is created and applied, editing that ACL requires special attention. For example, if you intend to delete a specific entry (ACE) from a numbered ACL, specifying the **no** parameter followed by the ACE will result in deleting the entire ACL.

```
Router# configure terminal
Enter configuration commands, one per line. End with CNTL/Z.
Router(config)# no access-list 101 deny icmp any any
Router(config)# ^Z
Router# show access-lists
Router#
*Mar 9 00:43:29.832: %SYS-5-CONFIG_I: Configured from console by console
```

In Cisco IOS Release 12.3 and later, with the use of sequence numbers, it is possible to delete specific ACEs in standard and extended ACLs without deleting the ACL. It is also possible to add new ACEs to a specific location.

In an extended ACL, sequence numbers are used to indicate the order in which the ACL is processed. To use sequence numbers to add or delete ACEs, you must first enter the ACL subconfiguration mode of the named or numbered ACL. Next, if deleting an entry, use the **no** parameter, followed by the sequence number of the entry. If adding an entry, specify a new sequence number that falls between the two ACEs where the new entry should appear.

```
Router# show access-lists
Extended IP access list 101
10 permit tcp any any
20 permit udp any any
30 permit icmp any any
Router(config)# ip access-list extended 101
Router(config-ext-nacl)# no 20
Router(config-ext-nacl)# 5 deny tcp any any eq telnet
Router(config-ext-nacl)# 20 deny udp any any
```

For backward compatibility with previous releases, if entries with no sequence numbers are applied, the first entry is assigned a sequence number of 10, and successive entries are incremented by 10. If a sequence number is not specified for a new entry, the router will automatically place the entry at the bottom of the list and assign an appropriate sequence number.

Refer to
Figure
in online course

On standard access lists, the Cisco IOS will add new entries by descending order of the IP address, regardless of the sequence number. Therefore, the sequence number in a standard ACL is used as an identifier of a specific ACE for deletion purposes.

This example shows the different entries of an existing standard ACL 19. All entries, regardless of the order in which they were entered, were placed in order of descending IP address, from specific to general.

```
Router# show access-lists
Standard IP access list 19
10 permit 192.168.100.1
20 permit 10.10.10.0, wildcard bits 0.0.0.255
```

```
30 permit 201.101.110.0, wildcard bits 0.0.0.255
40 deny any
```

An administrator attempts to add an entry in access list 19 in order to permit the IP Address 172.22.1.1 using sequence number 25.

```
Router(config)# ip access-list standard 19
Router(config-std-nacl)# 25 permit 172.22.1.1
```

Even though the sequence number specified is larger than the sequence number of the network 10.10.10.0, the entry is added prior to the 10.10.10.0 ACE in order to give priority to the specific IP address rather than to the network.

```
Router# show access-lists
Standard IP access list 19
10 permit 192.168.100.1
25 permit 172.22.1.1
20 permit 10.10.10.0, wildcard bits 0.0.0.255
30 permit 201.101.110.0, wildcard bits 0.0.0.255
40 deny any
```

While the sequence number does not dictate processing order in a standard ACL, it can be used as an identifier for deleting a specific entry.

4.1.3 Topology and Flow for ACLs

Refer to
Figure
in online course

The direction of traffic through a networking device is defined by the ingress (inbound) and egress (outbound) interfaces for the traffic. Inbound traffic refers to traffic as it enters into the router, prior to the routing table being accessed. Outbound traffic refers to traffic that entered the router and has been processed by the router to determine where to forward that data. Prior to the data being forwarded out of that interface, an outbound ACL is examined.

Depending on the type of device and the type of ACL configured, the return traffic can be dynamically tracked.

Refer to
Figure
in online course

In addition to flow, it is important to keep the placement of ACLs in mind. Placement depends on the type of ACL being used.

Standard ACL placement - Standard ACLs are placed as close to the destination as possible. Standard ACLs filter packets based on the source address only. Placing these ACLs too close to the source can adversely affect packets by denying all traffic, including valid traffic.

Extended ACL placement - Extended ACLs are placed on routers as close as possible to the source that is being filtered. Placing Extended ACLs too far from the source is inefficient use of network resources. For example, packets can be sent a long way only to be dropped or denied.

Refer to
Figure
in online course

Most often, ACLs are used to prevent a majority of traffic from entering a network. At the same time they selectively permit some more secure types of traffic, such as HTTPS (TCP port 443), to be used for business purposes. This generally requires using Extended ACLs and a clear understanding of which ports must be blocked versus permitted.

The Nmap program can be used to determine which ports are open on a given device. For example, an ACL blocks POP3 traffic from downloading email through the Internet from a mail server on the company network, but allows email to be downloaded from a workstation inside the company network. The output of an Nmap scan on the POP3 server depends on where the scan originates. If the scan is done from a PC inside the network, the POP3 port appears open (TCP port 110).

Refer to
Figure
in online course

After an ACL is applied to an interface, it is important to verify that it is functioning as intended. That is, traffic that should be denied is denied and valid traffic is permitted.

While the `log` option shows matches of logged packets as they happen, it can be an excessive resource burden on the networking device. The `log` option is best used to verify or troubleshoot configuration of an ACL.

The `show ip access-lists` command can be used as a basic means of checking the intended effect of an ACL. With this command, only the number of packets matching a given ACE is recorded.

The `show running-config` command can be used to view which interfaces have ACLs applied.

4.1.4 Configuring Standard and Extended ACLs with CCP

Refer to
Figure
in online course

Standard and Extended ACLs can be configured from the CLI or by using CCP.

To configure ACLs on a routing device using CCP, the router must be selected from the drop down box under Select Community Member. If the router IP address does not appear, the router has not yet been discovered by CCP.

After the device is selected, click the **Configure** button at the top of the CCP application window to open the task list. Select the **Router** drop down box, followed by the **ACL** drop down box to access the ACL configuration options.

Configure > Router > ACL

Refer to
Figure
in online course

Rules define how a router responds to a particular kind of traffic. Using CCP, an administrator can create access rules that cause the router to deny certain types of traffic while permitting other types. CCP provides default rules that an administrator can use when creating access rules.

An administrator can also view rules that were not created using CCP, called external rules, and rules with syntax that CCP does not support, which are called unsupported rules.

The CCP Rules (ACLs) Summary window provides a summary of the rules in the router configuration and access to other windows to create, edit, and delete rules. To access this window, choose **Configure > Router > ACL > ACL Summary**. These are the types of rules that CCP manages:

- *Access rules* Govern the traffic that can enter and leave the network. An administrator can apply access rules to router interfaces and to vty lines.

- *NAT rules* Determine which private IP addresses are translated into valid Internet IP addresses.

- *IPsec rules* Determine which traffic is encrypted on secure connections.

- *NAC rules* Specify which IP addresses are admitted to the network or blocked from the network.

- *Firewall rules* Specify the source and destination addresses and whether the traffic is permitted or denied.

- *QoS rules* Specify traffic that belongs to the quality of service (QoS) class to which the rule is associated.

- *Unsupported rules* Not created using CCP and not supported by CCP. These rules are read only and cannot be modified using CCP.

- *Externally defined rules* Not created using CCP, but supported by CCP. These rules cannot be associated with any interface.

- *Cisco CP default rules* Predefined rules that are used by CCP wizards.

Refer to
Figure
in online course

CCP refers to ACLs as access rules. Using CCP, an administrator can create and apply standard rules (Standard ACLs) and extended rules (Extended ACLs). These are the steps for configuring a standard rule using CCP:

Step 1.   Choose **Configure > Router > ACL > ACL Editor**.

Step 2.   Click **Add**. The Add a Rule window appears.

Step 3.   In the Add a Rule window, enter a name or number in the **Name/Number** field.

Step 4.   From the Type drop-down list, choose **Standard Rule**. Optionally, enter a description in the **Description** field.

Step 5.   Click **Add**. The Add a Standard Rule Entry window appears.

Step 6.   From the Select an Action drop-down list, choose **Permit** or **Deny**.

Step 7.   From the Type drop-down list, choose an address type:

- *A Network* Applies to all IP addresses in a network or subnet.

- *A Host Name or IP Address* Applies to a specific host or IP address.

- *Any IP address* Applies to any IP address.

Step 8.   Depending on what was selected from the Type drop-down list, these additional fields must be completed:

- *IP Address* If in the Type field, 'A Network' was selected, enter the IP address.

- *Wildcard Mask* If in the Type field, 'A Network' was selected; specify a wildcard mask from the Wildcard mask drop-down list or enter a custom wildcard mask.

- *Hostname/IP* If in the Type field, 'A Host Name or IP Address' was selected; enter the name or the IP address of the host. If a host name is entered, the router must be configured to use a DNS server.

Step 9.   (Optional) Enter a description in the **Description** field. The description must be less than 100 characters.

Step 10.   (Optional) Check the **Log matches against this entry**. Depending on how the syslog settings are configured on the router, the matches are recorded in the local logging buffer, sent to a syslog server, or both.

Step 11.   Click **OK**.

Step 12.   Continue adding or editing rule entries until the standard rule is complete. If at any time the order of the rule entries in the Rule Entry list needs to be rearranged, use the **Move Up** and **Move Down** buttons.

Refer to
Figure
in online course

After the Rule Entry list is complete, the next step is to apply the rule to an interface. These are the steps for applying a rule to an interface:

Step 1.   From the Add a Rule window, click **Associate**. The Associate with an Interface window appears. Only interfaces with a status of up/up will appear in the drop-down list.

Step 2. From the Select an Interface drop-down list, choose the interface to which this rule will be applied.

Step 3. From the Specify a Direction section, click either the **Inbound** or the **Outbound** radio button. If the router is to check packets inbound to the interface, click **Inbound**. If the router is to forward the packet to the outbound interface before comparing it to the entries in the access rule, click **Outbound**.

Step 4. If a rule is already associated with the designated interface in the desired direction, a query box appears asking if you would like to continue with the association. If **No** is clicked, the Associate with an Interface window reappears to allow you to change the association. If **Yes** is clicked, another box appears with the following options:

- *Merge* combine the new access rule with the existing rule and associate the new combined rule to the interface. Any duplicate ACEs will be removed.

- *Replace* replace the existing access rule with the new access rule and associate the new rule with the interface.

- *Preview* preview the existing access rule prior to making a decision.

Refer to
Figure
in online course

After the access rule is created, click the **OK** button in the Add a Rule window. The Deliver Configuration to Device window appears. It displays the configuration commands generated by the new access rule that will be sent to the router. Click the check box next to **Save running config. to device's startup config**. Then click the **Deliver** button.

4.1.5 Configuring TCP Established and Reflexive ACLs

Refer to
Figure
in online course

Over time, engineers have created more sophisticated types of access control filters based on increasingly precise parameters. Engineers have also expanded the range of platforms and the range of ACLs which can be processed at wire speed. These improvements to platforms and ACLs allow network security professionals to implement cutting-edge firewall solutions without sacrificing network performance.

In a modern network, a network firewall must be placed between the inside of the network and the outside of the network. The basic idea is that all traffic from the outside should be blocked from entering the inside unless it is explicitly permitted by an ACL, or if it is returning traffic initiated from the inside of the network. This is the fundamental role of a network firewall, whether it is a dedicated hardware device or a Cisco router with IOS Firewall.

Many common applications rely on TCP, which builds a virtual circuit between two endpoints. The first generation IOS traffic filtering solution to support the two-way nature of TCP virtual circuits was the TCP `established` keyword for extended IP ACLs. Introduced in 1995, the TCP `established` keyword for extended IP ACLs enabled a primitive network firewall to be created on a Cisco router. It blocked all traffic coming from the Internet except for the TCP reply traffic associated with established TCP traffic initiated from the inside of the network.

The second generation IOS solution for session filtering was reflexive ACLs. Reflexive ACLs were introduced to the IOS in 1996. These ACLs filter traffic based on source and destination addresses, and port numbers, and keep track of sessions. Reflexive ACL session filtering uses temporary filters which are removed when a session is over.

The TCP `established` option and reflexive ACLs are examples of complex ACLs.

Refer to
Figure
in online course

The syntax for the TCP **established** option in a numbered extended IP ACL is as follows:

```
Router(config)# access-list {100-199} {permit ¦ deny} protocol source-addr
[source-wildcard] [operator operand] destination-addr [destination-wildcard]
[operator operand] [established]
```

The **established** keyword forces the router to check whether the TCP ACK or RST control flag is set. If the ACK flag is set, the TCP traffic is allowed in. If not, it is assumed that the traffic is associated with a new connection initiated from the outside.

Using the **established** keyword does not implement a stateful firewall on a router. No stateful information is maintained to keep track of traffic initiated from the inside of the network. The established parameter permits any TCP segments with the appropriate control flag set. The router does not keep track of conversations. Therefore, it cannot guarantee that traffic is return traffic associated with a connection initiated from the inside.

Using the **established** keyword to allow return traffic into a network opens a hole in the router. Hackers can take advantage of this hole by using a packet generator or scanner, such as Nmap, to sneak TCP packets into a network by masquerading them as returning traffic. Hackers accomplish this by using a packet generator to set the appropriate bit or bits in the TCP control field.

The **established** option does not apply to UDP or ICMP traffic, because UDP and ICMP traffic does not rely on any control flags as used with TCP traffic.

Refer to
Figure
in online course

Despite the security hole, using the **established** keyword provides a more secure solution since a match occurs only if the TCP packet has the ACK or RST control bits set.

```
R1(config)#access-list 100 permit tcp any eq 443 192.168.1.0 0.0.0.255 established
R1(config)#access-list 100 permit tcp any 192.168.1.3 0.0.0.0 eq 22
R1(config)#access-list 100 deny ip any any
R1(config)#interface s0/0/0
R1(config-if)#ip access-group 100 in
```

If the keyword **established** is not included, then any TCP traffic with source port 443 would be permitted. With the keyword, only traffic from source port 443 with the ACK, FIN, PSH, RST, SYN, or URG TCP control flag set is permitted.

As is typical with a firewall configuration, all incoming traffic is denied unless explicitly permitted (SSH, port 22, traffic in this case) or unless it is associated with traffic initiated from the inside of the network (HTTPS traffic in this case). Any TCP source port 443 traffic initiated from outside the network with the appropriate control flag set is allowed in.

Refer to
Figure
in online course

Reflexive ACLs were introduced to Cisco IOS in 1996, about a year after the TCP **established** option became available. Reflexive ACLs provide a truer form of session filtering than is possible with TCP **established**. Reflexive ACLs are much harder to spoof because more filter criteria must be matched before a packet is permitted through. For example, source and destination addresses and port numbers are checked, not just ACK and RST bits. Also, session filtering uses temporary filters that are removed when a session is over. This adds a time limit on a hacker's attack opportunity.

The **established** keyword is available only for the TCP upper layer protocol. The other upper layer protocols, such as UDP and ICMP, must either permit all incoming traffic or define all possible permissible source and destination, host, and port address pairs for each protocol.

The biggest limitation of standard and extended ACLs is that they are designed to filter unidirectional rather than bidirectional connections. Standard and extended ACLs do not keep track of the state of a connection. If someone inside sends traffic to the Internet, it is difficult to safely allow the returning traffic back into the network without opening a large hole on the perimeter router.

Reflexive ACLs were developed for this reason. Reflexive ACLs allow an administrator to perform actual session filtering for any type of IP traffic.

Reflexive ACLs work by using temporary ACEs inserted into an extended ACL, which is applied on the external interface of the perimeter router. When the session ends or the temporary entry times out, it is removed from the ACL configuration of the external interface. This reduces network exposure to DoS attacks.

To make this work, a named extended ACL examines the traffic as it exits the network. The ACL can be applied inbound on an internal interface or outbound on the external interface. ACEs examine traffic associated with new sessions using the **reflect** parameter. Based on these statements (using **reflect**), the connection ACEs are built dynamically to permit return traffic. Without the **reflect** statements, return traffic is dropped by default. For example, an administrator could set up the ACL statements to examine only HTTP connections, thus allowing only temporary reflexive ACEs to be created for HTTP traffic.

As traffic is leaving the network, if it matches a permit statement with a **reflect** parameter, a temporary entry is added to the reflexive ACL. For each permit-reflect statement, the router builds a separate reflexive ACL.

A reflexive ACE is an inverted entry: the source and destination information is flipped. For example, a reflexive ACE is created if a user on a workstation with IP address 192.168.1.3 Telnets to 209.165.200.5, where the source port number is 11000.

```
R1(config-ext-nacl)#permit host 209.165.200.5 eq 23 host 192.168.1.3 eq 11000
```

Any temporary reflexive ACEs that are created contain the permit action to allow the returning traffic for this session.

Refer to
Figure
in online course

To configure a router to use reflexive ACLs involves just a few steps:

Step 1. Create an internal ACL that looks for new outbound sessions and creates temporary reflexive ACEs.

Step 2. Create an external ACL that uses the reflexive ACLs to examine return traffic.

Step 3. Activate the Named ACLs on the appropriate interfaces.

The syntax for the internal ACL is as follows:

```
Router(config)# ip access-list extended internal_ACL_name
Router(config-ext-nacl)# permit protocol source-addr [source-mask] [operator
operand] destination-addr [destination-mask] [operator operand] [established]
reflect reflexive_ACL_name [timeout seconds]
```

For example, these are the commands for matching internal users surfing the Internet with a web browser and relying on DNS:

```
R1(config)# ip access-list extended internal_ACL
R1(config-ext-nacl)# permit tcp any any eq 80 reflect web-only-reflexive-ACL
R1(config-ext-nacl)# permit udp any any eq 53 reflect dns-only-reflexive-ACL
timeout 10
```

Cisco IOS creates two reflexive ACEs that maintain session information for outbound web connections (web-only-reflexive-ACL) and DNS queries (dns-only-reflexive-ACL). Notice that a 10-second timeout for DNS queries is set.

After building the internal extended Named ACL, which creates the reflexive ACEs, the temporary entries need to be referenced as traffic flows back into the network. This is done by building a second extended Named ACL. In this Named ACL, use the **evaluate** statement to reference the reflexive ACEs that were created from the internal ACL.

```
Router(config)# ip access-list extended external_ACL_name
Router(config-ext-nacl)#evaluate reflexive_ACL_name
```

Continuing the example with HTTP and DNS traffic, this syntax creates an external ACL that denies all traffic originating from the outside, but permits return HTTP and DNS traffic.

```
R1(config)# ip access-list extended external_ACL
R1(config-ext-nacl)#evaluateweb-only-reflexive-ACL
R1(config-ext-nacl)#evaluatedns-only-reflexive-ACL
R1(config-ext-nacl)#deny ip any any
```

The last step is to apply the ACLs.

```
R1(config)# interface s0/0/0
R1(config-if)# description connection to the ISP.
R1(config-if)# ip access-group internal_ACL out
R1(config-if)# ip access-group external_ACL in
```

Reflexive ACLs provided the first solution for session filtering on Cisco routers. Reflexive ACLs are one of the many types of complex ACLs supported on Cisco networking devices. Some complex ACLs are designed to permit dynamic connections through routers to be built on a per-user basis. Other complex ACLs are automatically enabled during particular dates and times.

4.1.6 Configuring Dynamic ACLs

Refer to
Figure
in online course

Dynamic ACLs, also known as lock-and-key ACLs, were added as an option to Cisco IOS in 1996, before ACL logging and reflexive ACLs were available as options. Dynamic ACLs are available for IP traffic only. Dynamic ACLs are dependent on Telnet connectivity, authentication (local or remote), and Extended ACLs.

Dynamic ACL configuration starts with the application of an Extended ACL to block traffic through the router. Users who want to traverse the router are blocked until they use Telnet to connect to the router and are authenticated. The Telnet connection is then dropped, and a single-entry dynamic ACL is added to the existing extended ACL. This permits traffic for a particular period. Both idle and absolute timeouts are possible.

One reason to use dynamic ACLs is to provide a specific remote user or group of remote users access to a host within the network. Another reason to use dynamic ACLs is when a subset of hosts on a local network needs to access a host on a remote network that is protected by a firewall.

Dynamic ACLs offer these security benefits over standard and static Extended ACLs:

- Challenge mechanism to authenticate individual users

- Simplified management in large internetworks

- Reduced router processing for ACLs

- Less opportunity for network break-ins by network hackers

- Creation of dynamic user access through a firewall, without compromising other configured security restrictions

Refer to
Figure
in online course

A combination of user-prompted and automated device activities occur when a dynamic ACL is implemented and invoked.

First, a remote user must open a Telnet or SSH connection to the router. The external ACL of the router must permit this connection. The router prompts the user for a username and password, which the user must enter.

Next, the router authenticates the connection using either the local username database defined with **username** commands, an AAA server using RADIUS or TACACS+, or the **password** command on the vty lines. If the authentication is successful, the Telnet or SSH connection is terminated, because the function of the connection is for authentication only.

After the user successfully authenticates, Cisco IOS adds a dynamic ACL entry that grants the user access to the configured internal resources. It is not possible to set up per-user access policies. Instead, the administrator defines one policy for all dynamic ACL users, and this single policy is applied to all the authenticated users.

Finally, the user can access the internal resources that would otherwise be denied without the dynamic ACL entry.

There are a few basic steps for setting up a dynamic ACL:

Refer to
Figure
in online course

Step 1.   Create an Extended ACL.

A dynamic ACL supports both numbered and named extended ACLs. One of the first entries in the ACL permits Telnet or SSH access to an IP address on the router that the external users can use. Also, at a minimum, a placeholder entry is created in the ACL. The user's successful authentication creates this dynamic entry.

Step 2.   Define the authentication.

A dynamic ACL supports these methods of authentication: local (the username database), an external AAA server, and the line password. Typically, the line password is not used because all users must use the same password.

Step 3.   Enable the dynamic authentication method.

This occurs on the vty lines of the router. When enabled, the router can create dynamic ACL entries on the interface ACL that has the dynamic ACL reference.

This is the command to create the dynamic ACL entry:

```
Router(config)# access-list {100-199} dynamic dynamic_ACL_name [timeout minutes]
{permit ¦ deny} protocol source-addr [source-wildcard] [operator operand]
destination-addr [destination-wildcard] [operator operand] [established]
```

The **dynamic** keyword lets an administrator specify the name of the dynamic ACL that is to be used. This name must be unique among all named ACLs on the router. The **timeout** parameter is optional. It specifies an absolute timeout for the dynamic entry that an authenticated user creates. The timeout can range from 1 to 9999 minutes.

Refer to
Figure
in online course

Two timeouts are associated with dynamic ACL entries: absolute and idle. The absolute timer is specified in the dynamic ACL entry. The idle timeout value is specified in the **autocommand** command, which enables lock-and-key authentication on the vty lines. If timeouts are not specified, the default is to never time out the entry. Therefore, it is recommended that an idle or an absolute timeout be configured.

Following the timeout parameter in the ACL statement, specify which user traffic is permitted. Normally, the IP address of the external user is unknown, so use the keyword **any**.

After creating the Extended ACL to enable Telnet and/or SSH permission and the dynamic entries, activate it on the router interface with the **ip access-group** command.

With a local username database configured, the last thing to do is enable lock-and-key authentication on the vty lines.

```
Router(config)# line vty 0 4
Router(config-line)# autocommand access-enable host [timeout minutes]
```

The **autocommand access-enable** command specifies lock-and-key authentication. After a user successfully authenticates, a temporary ACL entry is inserted into the Extended ACL. This entry is placed at the **dynamic** parameter placeholder in the Extended ACL. The temporary entry is added only on the one interface to which the user connects. Without the **autocommand access-enable** command, the router will not create the temporary ACL entries.

The **host** parameter is optional. By specifying this parameter, the Cisco IOS replaces the dynamic ACL entry's keyword **any** with the user's IP address. If the Extended ACL is applied inbound, the source keyword **any** is replaced with the user's IP address; if it is applied outbound, the destination keyword **any** is replaced.

The optional timeout parameter is used to set the idle timeout for the user's temporary ACL entry.

4.1.7 Configuring Time-Based ACLs

Refer to
Figure
in online course

Another useful complex ACL is the time-based ACL. Time-based ACLs, introduced to Cisco IOS in 1998, are similar to Extended ACLs in function, but they allow for access control based on time. Timed-based ACLs enable traffic to be restricted based on the time of day, the day of the week, or the day of the month.

Time-based ACLs offer the security professional more control over permitting or denying access to resources. Sometimes it is necessary to open a hole in the filter of a router to allow a specific type of traffic. This hole should not be allowed to remain indefinitely. For example, users could be allowed to access the Internet during lunch, but not during regular business hours. Timed ACLs enable the enforcement of this kind of policy.

Time-based ACLs also allow security professionals to control logging messages. ACL entries can log traffic at certain times of the day, but not constantly. The administrator can simply deny access without analyzing the many logs that are generated during peak hours.

Time-based ACLs are an extension of numbered and named Extended ACLs. The administrator creates time-based entries and uses the **time-range** parameter to specify the period of time that the ACL statement is valid. The period of time specified can be recurring or a specific instance that happens only once.

Refer to
Figure
in online course

When creating a time range with the **time-range** command, it must have a unique name. The name must begin with a letter and cannot contain a space. Use this name later to associate a specific ACL statement with this range. Executing the **time-range** command places the router in ACL sub-configuration mode. In this mode, two types of ranges can be specified: one-time only (absolute) and recurring (periodic).

These are the commands for creating a time range:

```
Router(config)# time-range time_range_name
Router(config-time-range)# absolute [start_time start_date] [end_time end_date]
Router(config-time-range)# periodic day_of_the_week hh:mm to [day_of_the_week] hh:mm
```

The **absolute** command specifies a single time period for which the time range is valid. ACL statements that reference this time range are not used after this period. The administrator can specify a beginning time, an ending time, or both. The time is specified in 24-hour time: *hh:mm*, where the hours range from 0 to 23 and the minutes range from 0 to 59. For example, 3 p.m. is represented as 15:00. The date is specified as day month year. The day is specified as a number from 1 to 31; the month is the name of the month, such as May, and the year is a four-digit value, such as 2003. Examples of date specification are 19 November 2009 and 07 July 2010. If the starting time is omitted, it defaults to the current time on the router. If the ending time is omitted, it defaults to 23:59 31 December 2035.

The **periodic** command specifies a recurring time period for which the time range is valid. Multiple **periodic** commands are permitted within the same time range. Specify a beginning and ending time. The ending time can be on a different day. The first parameter specified is the day of the week:

- monday
- tuesday
- wednesday
- thursday
- friday
- saturday
- sunday
- daily (every day)
- weekdays (Monday through Friday)
- weekend (Saturday and Sunday)

The next parameter is the beginning time, specified as *hh:mm*. This is followed by the **to** parameter and the ending time. If the day of week parameter is omitted, it defaults to the day of week configured for the beginning time. Following this is the ending time, specified as *hh:mm*. It is important to note that the router clock must be set in order for this command to operate as expected.

After creating time ranges, the administrator must activate them. This is done by adding the **time-range** parameter to the ACL statement. This is supported in both named and numbered extended ACLs. This is the configuration syntax for a numbered ACL.

```
Router(config)# access-list {100-199} {permit | deny} protocol source-addr
[source-mask] [operator operand] destination-addr [destination-mask] [operator
operand] [established] [log | log-input] [established] [time-range
name_of_time_range]
```

The time range needs to be added to the ACL statement. When this is done, the ACL statement is processed by the Cisco IOS only when the time of the router falls within the period specified by the **periodic** or **absolute** commands defined in the **time-range** configuration.

Refer to
Figure
in online course

A network administrator has a situation that requires time-based ACLs. Users are not allowed to access the Internet during business hours, except during lunch and after hours until 7 p.m. when the office closes. This is a time-based ACL that supports the requirement:

```
R1(config)# time-range employee-time
R1(config-time-range)# periodic weekdays 12:00 to 13:00
R1(config-time-range)# periodic weekdays 17:00 to 19:00
R1(config-time-range)# exit
R1(config)# access-list 100 permit ip 192.168.1.0 0.0.0.255 any time-range em-
ployee-time
R1(config)# access-list 100 deny ip any any
R1(config)# interface FastEthernet 0/1
R1(config-if)# ip access-group 100 in
R1(config-if)# exit
```

In this example, the commands allow IP access to the Internet during lunch time and after work hours. ACL 100 permits employee traffic to the Internet during lunch and after work hours between 5 PM and 7 PM.

4.1.8 Troubleshooting Complex ACL Implementations

Refer to
Figure
in online course

To verify ACL configuration, use the `show access-lists` command.

```
Router# show access-lists [access-list-number ¦ access-list-name]
```

The command output shows how many packets have been matched against each entry in the ACLs, enabling the user to monitor the particular packets that have been permitted or denied.

To troubleshoot an ACL configuration, use the `debug ip packet` command.

```
Router# debug ip packet [access-list-number] [detail]
```

The `debug ip packet` command is useful for analyzing the messages traveling between the local and remote hosts. IP packet debugging captures the packets that are process-switched, including received, generated, and forwarded packets.

The `detail` option displays detailed IP packet debugging information. This information includes the packet types and codes as well as source and destination port numbers.

Because the `debug ip packet` command generates a substantial amount of output and uses a substantial amount of system resources, use this command with caution in production networks.

Refer to
Figure
in online course

An ACL counter counts how many packets are matched (permitted or denied) by each line of the ACL. This number is displayed as the number of matches.

By checking the number of matches with the `show access-lists` command, an administrator can determine if the configured standard and extended IP ACLs are filtering properly. For example, if an entry has significantly more matches than expected, the entry may be too broad. This could indicate that the ACL is not having the intended effect on network traffic.

Refer to
Figure
in online course

In the `debug ip packet` output, the denial of a packet is explicitly displayed. This enables granular real-time determination of successful ACL implementation.

The "g" in the `debug ip packet` output indicates the next hop gateway.

The `debug` output can be stopped with the `undebug all` command. Sometimes it takes a few moments before the output stops scrolling, depending on which `debug` commands were configured and the amount of traffic traversing the router.

The verification and troubleshooting commands for ACLs are relatively easy to use, and there are not many commands to remember. It is critical that ACLs are tested after they have been implemented to ensure their proper operation.

4.1.9 Mitigating Attacks with ACLs

Refer to
Figure
in online course

ACLs can be used to mitigate many network threats:

- IP address spoofing, inbound and outbound

- DoS TCP SYN attacks

- DoS smurf attacks

ACLs can also filter the following traffic:

- ICMP messages, inbound and outbound

- traceroute

DoS attacks tend to be the most devastating network attacks. Cisco IOS supports several technologies designed to minimize damage caused by DoS attacks. Most DoS attacks use some type of spoofing. There are many well-known classes of IP addresses that should never be seen as source IP addresses for traffic entering an organization's network. By specifying IP source address within an ACL, it is possible to control whether traffic from hosts, networks, or users access the network. Additionally, it is possible to filter on specific Time to Live (TTL) values in packets to control how many hops a packet can take before reaching a router in the network.

ICMP has been used extensively in network attacks over the years. Cisco IOS now supports specific technologies to prevent ICMP-based attacks from affecting a network.

Refer to Figure in online course

ACLs can be used as an antispoofing mechanism. Spoofing protection involves discarding traffic that has an invalid source address. As a rule, administrators should not allow any IP packets containing the source address of any internal hosts or networks inbound to a private network. An administrator can create an ACL that denies all packets containing the following IP addresses in their source field:

- Any local host addresses (127.0.0.0/8)

- Any reserved private addresses (RFC 1918, *Address Allocation for Private Internets*)

- Any addresses in the IP multicast address range (224.0.0.0/4)

Administrators should not allow any outbound IP packets with a source address other than a valid IP address of the internal network. An administrator can create an ACL that permits only those packets that contain source addresses from inside the network and denies all others.

Refer to Figure in online course

DNS, SMTP, and FTP are common services that often must be allowed through a firewall.

It is also quite common that a firewall needs to be configured to permit protocols that are necessary to administer a router. For example, it may be necessary to allow traffic through an internal router that permits router maintenance traffic from an outside device. Telnet, SSH, syslog, and SNMP are examples of services that a router may need to include. SSH is always preferred over Telnet. Keep in mind, while many of these services are useful, it is important that they are controlled and monitored, as exploitation of these services does lead to security vulnerabilities.

Refer to Figure in online course

Hackers use several ICMP message types to attack networks. However, various management applications use ICMP messages to gather information. Network management uses ICMP messages that are automatically generated by the router.

Hackers can use ICMP echo packets to discover subnets and hosts on a protected network and to generate DoS flood attacks. Hackers can use ICMP redirect messages to alter host routing tables. Both ICMP echo and redirect messages should be blocked inbound by the router.

Several ICMP messages are recommended for proper network operation and should be allowed inbound:

- *Echo reply* Allows users to ping external hosts.

- *Source quench* Requests the sender to decrease the traffic rate of messages.

- *Unreachable* Unreachable messages are generated for packets that are administratively denied by an ACL.

Several ICMP messages are required for proper network operation and should be allowed outbound:

- *Echo* Allows users to ping external hosts.

- *Parameter problem* Informs the host of packet header problems.

- *Packet too big* Required for packet maximum transmission unit (MTU) discovery.

- *Source quench* Throttles down traffic when necessary.

As a rule, block all other ICMP message types outbound.

ACLs are used to block IP address spoofing, selectively permit specific services through a firewall, and to allow only required ICMP messages.

Management protocols such as SNMP, while useful for remote monitoring and management of networked devices, can be exploited. If SNMP is necessary, exploitation of SNMP vulnerabilities can be mitigated by applying interface ACLs to filter SNMP packets from non-authorized systems. The ACL can then permit known source addresses that are destined for the IOS device itself, such as those devices within a management network. It should be noted that an exploit may still be possible if the SNMP packet is sourced from an address that has been spoofed and is permitted by the ACL.

While these security measures are helpful, the most effective means of exploitation prevention is to disable the SNMP server on IOS devices that do not require it. To disable SNMP processing on the Cisco IOS devices, issue the command:

```
Router(config)# no snmp-server
```

4.1.10 IPv6 ACLs

In recent years, many networks have begun the transition to an IPv6 environment. Part of the need for the transition to IPv6 is because of the weaknesses inherent in IPv4. IPv4 was designed without a number of modern-day network requirements such as:

- *Security* IPsec

- *Device roaming* Mobile IP

- *Quality of service* RSVP

- *Address scarcity* DHCP, NAT, CIDR, VLSM

Unfortunately, as the migration to IPv6 continues, IPv6 attacks are becoming more pervasive. This is, in part, due to the transitional nature of switching between the two. IPv4 will not disappear overnight. Rather, it will coexist with, and then gradually be replaced by, IPv6. This potentially creates security holes. An example of a security concern is attackers leveraging IPv6 to exploit IPv4 in dual stack. Dual stack is an integration method in which a node has implementation and connectivity to both an IPv4 and IPv6 networks. As a result, the node and its corresponding routers have two protocol stacks.

Combining multiple techniques, attackers can accomplish stealth attacks that result in trust exploitation using dual stacked hosts, rogue neighbor discovery protocol (NDP) messages, and tunneling techniques. The attacker gains a foothold in the IPv4 network. The compromised host sends rogue router advertisements, triggering dual stacked hosts to obtain an IPv6 address. The attacker can also use the routing header to pivot around multiple hosts in the internal network before sending traffic out.

It is necessary to develop and implement a strategy to mitigate attacks against IPv6 infrastructures and protocols. This mitigation strategy should include filtering at the edge using various techniques such as IPv6 ACLs.

Refer to
Figure
in online course

Refer to
Figure
in online course

Refer to
Figure
in online course

The standard ACL functionality in IPv6 is similar to standard ACLs in IPv4. These ACLs determine what traffic is blocked and what traffic is forwarded at router interfaces. They allow filtering based on source and destination addresses, inbound and outbound to a specific interface. IPv6 ACLs are defined using the ipv6 access-list command with the **deny** and **permit** keywords in global configuration mode.

In Cisco IOS Release 12.0(23)S and 12.2(13)T or later releases, the standard IPv6 ACL functionality is extended. It can support traffic filtering based on IPv6 option headers and optional, upper-layer protocol type information for finer granularity of control, similar to extended ACLs in IPv4. To configure an IPv6 ACL, first enter into the IPv6 access-list configuration mode:

```
Router(config)# ipv6 access-list access-list-name
```

Next, configure each access list entry to specifically permit or deny traffic.

```
Router(config-ipv6-acl)# {permit | deny} protocol {source-ipv6-prefix/prefix-
length | any | host source-ipv6-address | auth} [operator [port-number]]
{destination-ipv6-prefix/prefix-length | any | host destination-ipv6-address |
auth} [operator [port-number]]
```

After the ACL statements are created, the administrator activates the ACL on an interface with the **ipv6 traffic-filter** command, specifying the name of the ACL and the direction of traffic to which the ACL applies.

Refer to
Figure
in online course

```
Router(config-if)# ipv6 traffic-filter access-list-name {in | out}
```

Each IPv6 ACL contains implicit permit rules to enable IPv6 neighbor discovery. The IPv6 neighbor discovery process makes use of the IPv6 Network Layer service. Therefore, by default, IPv6 ACLs implicitly allow IPv6 neighbor discovery packets to be sent and received on an interface. Other than the IPv6 neighbor discovery protocol, IPv6 access lists implicitly deny all other services not specifically permitted.

These rules can be overridden by the user by placing a **deny ipv6 any any** statement at the end of the ACL. If, however, this statement is used, then the administrator must also specifically permit the neighbor discovery process as follows:

```
permit icmp any any nd-na
permit icmp any any nd-ns
deny ipv6 any any
```

4.1.11 Using Object Groups in ACEs

Refer to
Figure
in online course

In large networks, ACLs can be large (hundreds of lines) and difficult to configure and manage, especially if the ACLs frequently change.

Object group-based ACLs are smaller, more readable, and easier to configure and manage than conventional ACLs. They simplify static and dynamic ACL deployments for large user access environments on Cisco IOS routers. Both IPv4 and IPv6 ACLs support object groups.

The object groups for ACLs feature lets an administrator classify users, devices, or protocols into groups. These groups can then be applied to ACLs to create access control policies for a group of objects. This feature lets the administrator use object groups instead of individual IP addresses, protocols, and ports, which are used in conventional ACLs. This results in fewer, more manageable ACEs.

Refer to
Figure
in online course

By grouping like objects together, you can use the object group in an ACE instead of having to enter an ACE for each object separately. It is possible to create the following types of object groups:

- Network

- Service

The following guidelines and limitations apply to object groups:

- Object groups must have unique names. While you might want to create a network object group named "Engineering" and a service object group named "Engineering," you need to add an identifier (or "tag") to the end of at least one of the object group names to make it unique. For example, use "Engineering_admins" and "Engineering_svcs".

- After an object group is created, it is possible to append additional objects to the group by simply following the same procedure that is used for creating a new object group; in this instance, specifying the existing group name and then specifying the additional objects.

- Objects such as hosts or services can be grouped. After objects are grouped, if that group name is used in a single command, the command will apply to every item in the group.

- You cannot delete an object group or make an object group empty if it is being used in an ACE.

When you define a group with the **object-group** command and then use any security appliance command, the command applies to every item in that group. This feature can significantly reduce your configuration size.

Network Object Groups

Refer to **Figure** in online course

A network object group is a group of any of the following objects:

- Hostnames, IP addresses, or subnets
- Ranges of IP addresses
- Existing network object groups

To create a network group, enter the following commands:

```
Router(config)# object-group network nw_grp_id
Router(config-network-group)# description description-text ¦ host {host-address ¦
host-name} ¦ network-address {/prefix-length ¦ network-mask} ¦ range host-address1
host-address2 ¦ any ¦ group-object nested-object-group-name
```

Service Object Groups

A service object group is a group of any of the following objects:

- Top-level protocols (such as TCP, UDP, or ESP)
- Source and destination protocol ports (such as Telnet or SNMP)
- ICMP types (such as echo, echo-reply, or host-unreachable)
- Existing service object groups

To create a service group, enter the following commands:

Refer to **Figure** in online course

```
Router(config)# object-group service svc_grp_id
Router(config-service-group)# protocol ¦ [tcp ¦ udp ¦ tcp-udp [source {{[eq]¦ lt ¦
gt} port1 ¦ range port1 port2}] {destination-prefix/wildcard mask ¦ any ¦ host
destination-address ¦ object-group network_obj_grp_id} [operator {port [port] ¦
object-group service_obj_grp_id}] {[log [level]]}
```

Object groups can also be used in an IPv6 ACL configuration in the following manner:

```
Router(config)# ipv6 access-list access-list-name
```

```
Router(config-ipv6-acl)# {permit | deny} {protocol | object-group
protocol_obj_grp_id} {source-ipv6-prefix/prefix-length | any | host source-ipv6-
address | object-group network_obj_grp_id}[operator {port [port] | object-group
service_obj_grp_id}] {destination-ipv6-prefix/prefix-length | any | host destina-
tion-ipv6-address | object-group network_obj_grp_id}
```

Note that an ACE can contain a mixture of object groups and individual objects, such as specific protocols, networks or services.

After an object group is applied to an ACE, the object group cannot be deleted nor emptied. If additional objects are appended to the object group after it has been applied to the ACE, there is no need to reapply the object group to the ACE. The ACE will automatically adjust to include any newly appended objects.

4.2 Firewall Technologies

4.2.1 Securing Networks with Firewalls

Refer to
Figure
in online course

The term firewall originally referred to a fireproof wall (usually made of stone or metal) that prevented flames from spreading to connected structures. Later the term firewall was applied to the metal sheet that separated the engine compartment of a vehicle or aircraft from the passenger compartment. Eventually the term was adapted for use with computer networks: a firewall prevents undesirable traffic from entering prescribed areas within a network.

A firewall is a system or group of systems that enforces an access control policy between networks. It can include options such as a packet filtering router, a switch with two VLANs, and multiple hosts with firewall software.

Firewalls are different things to different people and organizations, but all firewalls share some common properties:

- They are resistant to attacks.

- They are the only transit point between networks (all traffic flows through the firewall).

- They enforce the access control policy.

In 1988, DEC created the first network firewall in the form of a packet filter firewall. These early firewalls inspected packets to see if they matched sets of rules, with the option of forwarding or dropping the packets accordingly. This type of packet filtering, known as stateless filtering, occurs regardless of whether a packet is part of an existing flow of data. Each packet is filtered based solely on the values of certain parameters in the packet header, similar to how ACLs filter packets.

In 1989, AT&T Bell Laboratories developed the first stateful firewall. Stateful firewalls filter packets on information stored in the firewall based on data flowing through the firewall. The stateful firewall is able to determine if a packet belongs to an existing flow of data. Static rules, as in packet filter firewalls, are supplemented with dynamic rules created in real time to define these active flows. Stateful firewalls help to mitigate DoS attacks that exploit active connections through a networking device.

The original firewalls were not standalone devices, but routers or servers with software features added to provide firewall functionality. Over time, several companies developed standalone firewalls. Dedicated firewall devices enabled routers and switches to offload the memory- and processor-intensive activity of filtering packets. Modern routers, such as the Cisco Integrated Services Routers (ISRs), can also be used as sophisticated stateful firewalls for organizations that may not require a dedicated firewall.

Refer to
Figure
in online course

There are several benefits of using a firewall in a network:

- Exposure of sensitive hosts and applications to untrusted users can be prevented.
- The protocol flow can be sanitized, preventing the exploitation of protocol flaws.
- Malicious data can be blocked from servers and clients.
- Security policy enforcement can be made simple, scalable, and robust with a properly configured firewall.
- Offloading most of the network access control to a few points in the network can reduce the complexity of security management.

Firewalls also present some limitations:

- If misconfigured, a firewall can have serious consequences (single point of failure).
- The data from many applications cannot be passed over firewalls securely.
- Users might proactively search for ways around the firewall to receive blocked material, exposing the network to potential attack.
- Network performance can slow down.
- Unauthorized traffic can be tunneled or hidden as legitimate traffic through the firewall.

It is important to understand the different types of firewalls and their specific capabilities, so that the right firewall is used for each situation.

4.2.2 Types of Firewalls

Refer to
Figure
in online course

A firewall system can be composed of many different devices and components. One component is traffic filtering, which is what most people commonly call a firewall. The following four firewalls are covered in this chapter:

- *Packet filtering firewall* Typically is a router with the capability to filter some packet content, such as Layer 3 and sometimes Layer 4 information.
- *Stateful firewall* Monitors the state of connections, whether the connection is in an initiation, data transfer, or termination state.
- *Application gateway firewall (proxy firewall)* A firewall that filters information at Layers 3, 4, 5, and 7 of the OSI reference model. Most of the firewall control and filtering is done in software.
- *Network address translation (NAT) firewall* A firewall that expands the number of IP addresses available and hides network addressing design.

Other methods of implementing firewalls include:

- *Host-based (server and personal) firewall* A PC or server with firewall software running on it.
- *Transparent firewall* A firewall that filters IP traffic between a pair of bridged interfaces.
- *Hybrid firewall* A firewall that is a combination of the various firewall types. For example, an application inspection firewall combines a stateful firewall with an application gateway firewall.

Refer to
Figure
in online course

Packet filtering firewalls work primarily at the Network Layer of the OSI model. Firewalls are generally considered Layer 3 constructs. However, they permit or deny traffic based on Layer 4 information, such as protocol as well as source and destination port numbers. Packet filtering uses ACLs to determine whether to permit or deny traffic, based on source and destination IP addresses, protocol, source and destination port numbers, and packet type. Packet filtering firewalls are usually part of a router firewall.

Services rely on specific ports to function. For example, SMTP servers listen to port 25 by default. Because packet filtering firewalls filter traffic according to static packet header information, they are sometimes referred to as static filters. By restricting certain ports, an administrator can restrict the services that rely on certain ports. For example, blocking port 25 on a specific workstation prevents an infected workstation from broadcasting email viruses across the Internet.

Packet filtering firewalls use a simple policy table lookup that permits or denies traffic based on specific criteria:

- Source IP address
- Destination IP address
- Protocol
- Source port number
- Destination port number
- Synchronize/start (SYN) packet receipt

Packet filters do not represent a complete firewall solution, but they are an important element.

Refer to
Figure
in online course

Stateful firewalls are the most versatile and the most common firewall technologies in use. Stateful firewalls provide stateful packet filtering using connection information maintained in a state table. Stateful filtering is a firewall architecture that is classified at the Network Layer, although for some applications it can also analyze traffic at Layer 4 and Layer 5.

Unlike static packet filtering, which examines a packet based on the information in a packet header, stateful filtering tracks each connection traversing all interfaces of the firewall and confirms that they are valid. Stateful firewalls use a state table to keep track of the actual communication process. The firewall examines information in the headers of Layer 3 packets and Layer 4 segments. For example, the firewall looks at the TCP header for synchronize (SYN), reset (RST), acknowledgment (ACK), finish (FIN), and other control codes to determine the state of the connection.

When an outside service is accessed, the stateful packet filter firewall retains certain details of the request by saving the state of the request in the state table. Each time a TCP or UDP connection is established for inbound or outbound connections, the firewall logs the information in a stateful session flow table. When the outside system responds to a request, the firewall server compares the received packets with the saved state to allow or deny network access.

The stateful session flow table contains the source and destination addresses, port numbers, TCP sequencing information, and additional flags for each TCP or UDP connection that is associated with that particular session. This information creates a connection object that is used by the firewall to compare all inbound and outbound packets against session flows in the stateful session flow table. The firewall permits data only if an appropriate connection exists to validate the passage of that data.

More advanced stateful firewalls include the ability to parse FTP port commands and update the state table to allow FTP to work transparently through the firewall. Advanced stateful firewalls can also provide TCP sequence number interpretation and DNS query and response matching to ensure that the firewall allows packets to return only in response to queries that originate from inside the network. These features reduce the threat of TCP RST flood attacks and DNS cache poisoning.

There is a potential disadvantage of using stateful filtering. While stateful inspection provides speed and transparency, packets inside the network must make their way to the outside network. This can expose internal IP addresses to potential hackers. Most firewalls incorporate stateful inspection, NAT, and proxy servers for added security.

Refer to
Figure
in online course

Cisco Systems provides several options for network security professionals to implement a firewall solution. These include the Cisco IOS Firewall, the PIX Security Appliances (this product is now end of life), and the Adaptive Security Appliances.

Cisco IOS Firewall is a specialized Cisco IOS feature that runs on Cisco routers. It is an enterprise-class firewall for support of small and medium-sized business (SMB) and enterprise branch offices.

The Cisco PIX Security Appliance is a standalone device that delivers robust user and application policy enforcement, multivector attack protection, and secure connectivity services. The Cisco PIX Security Appliances can scale to meet a range of requirements and network sizes.

Cisco Adaptive Security Appliances (ASA) are easy-to-deploy solutions that integrate firewall capabilities, Cisco Unified Communications (voice and video) security, Secure Sockets Layer (SSL) and IPsec VPN, IPS, and content security services. Designed as a key component of the Cisco SecureX architecture, ASA provides intelligent threat defense and secure communications services that stop attacks before they affect business continuity. ASA was designed to protect networks of all sizes and lower organizations' overall deployment and operation costs by providing comprehensive multilayer security.

When choosing between the various options for a firewall solution, it is important to perform a cost versus risk analysis. Whatever decision is made for the purchase of a firewall solution, the proper network security design is critical for the successful deployment of a firewall.

4.2.3   Firewalls in Network Design

Refer to
Figure
in online course

In network security, there is often reference to a demilitarized zone (DMZ). A DMZ is a portion of a network bounded by a firewall or set of firewalls. The term was originally used as a military description for an area between military powers where conflict is not permitted.

DMZs define the portions of a network that are trusted and the portions that are untrusted. Firewall design is primarily about device interfaces permitting or denying traffic based on the source, the destination, and the type of traffic.

Some designs are as simple as designating an outside network and inside network, determined by two interfaces on a firewall. The public network (or outside network) is untrusted and the private network (or inside network) is trusted. Typically a firewall with two interfaces is configured as follows:

- Traffic originating from the private network is inspected as it traverses toward the public network, and is permitted with little or no restriction; inspected traffic returning from the public network, that is associated with traffic that originated from the private network, is permitted.

- Traffic originating from the public network, and traveling to the private network, is generally blocked entirely.

More complicated designs involve three or more interfaces on a firewall. In this case, there is typically one inside interface connected to the private network, one outside interface connected to the public network, and one DMZ interface. In this configuration, a typical firewall implementation is as follows:

- Traffic originating from the private network is inspected as it traverses toward the public or DMZ network, and is permitted with little or no restriction; inspected traffic returning from the DMZ or public network to the private network is permitted.

- Traffic originating from the DMZ network and traveling to the private network is generally blocked.

- Traffic originating from the DMZ network and traveling to the public network is selectively permitted based on service requirements

- Traffic originating from the public network and traveling toward the DMZ is selectively permitted and inspected. This type of traffic is typically email, DNS, HTTP, or HTTPS traffic. Return traffic from the DMZ to the public network is dynamically permitted.

- Traffic originating from the public network and traveling to the private network is blocked.

Refer to **Figure** in online course

In a layered defense scenario, firewalls provide perimeter security of the entire network and of internal network segments in the core. For example, network security professionals can use a firewall to separate the human resources or financial networks of an organization from other networks or network segments within the organization.

A layered defense uses different types of firewalls that are combined in layers to add depth to the security of an organization. For example, traffic that comes in from the untrusted network first encounters a packet filter on the outer router. The traffic goes to the screened firewall or bastion host system that applies more rules to the traffic and discards suspect packets. A bastion host is a hardened computer that is typically located in the DMZ. The traffic now goes to an interior screening router. The traffic moves to the internal destination host only after successfully passing through all filtering between the outside router and the inside network. This type of DMZ setup is called a screened subnet configuration.

A common misconception is that a layered firewall topology is all that is needed to ensure a safe internal network. This myth is probably encouraged by the rapidly growing firewall business. A network administrator must consider many factors when building a complete in-depth defense:

- A significant number of intrusions come from hosts within the network. For example, firewalls often do little to protect against viruses that are downloaded through email.

- Firewalls do not protect against rogue modem installations.

- Firewalls do not replace backup and disaster recovery mechanisms resulting from attack or hardware failure. An in-depth defense also includes offsite storage and redundant hardware topologies.

- Most importantly, firewalls are no substitute for informed administrators and users.

Refer to **Figure** in online course

A network security professional is responsible for creating and maintaining a security policy, including a firewall security policy. This is a partial generic list that can serve as a starting point for firewall security policy:

- Position firewalls at critical security boundaries.

- Firewalls are a critical part of network security, but it is unwise to rely exclusively on a firewall for security.

- Deny all traffic by default, and permit only services that are needed.

- Ensure that physical access to the firewall is controlled.

- Regularly monitor firewall logs.

- Practice change management for firewall configuration changes.

- Firewalls primarily protect from technical attacks originating from the outside. Inside attacks tend to be nontechnical in nature.

4.3 Context-Based Access Control

4.3.1 CBAC Characteristics

Refer to
Figure
in online course

Context-based access control (CBAC) is a solution available within the Cisco IOS Firewall. CBAC intelligently filters TCP and UDP packets based on Application Layer protocol session information. It provides stateful Application Layer filtering, including protocols that are specific to unique applications, as well as multimedia applications and protocols that require multiple channels for communication, such as FTP and H.323.

CBAC can also examine supported connections for embedded NAT and PAT information and perform the necessary address translations. CBAC can block peer-to-peer (P2P) connections, such as those used by the Gnutella and KaZaA applications. Instant messaging traffic, such as Yahoo!, AOL, and MSN, can be blocked.

CBAC provides four main functions: traffic filtering, traffic inspection, intrusion detection, and generation of audits and alerts.

Traffic Filtering

CBAC can be configured to permit specified TCP and UDP return traffic through a firewall when the connection is initiated from within the network. It accomplishes this by creating temporary openings in an ACL that would otherwise deny the traffic. CBAC can inspect traffic for sessions that originate from either side of the firewall. It can also be used for intranet, extranet, and Internet perimeters of the network. CBAC examines not only Network Layer and Transport Layer information but also examines the Application Layer protocol information (such as FTP connection information) to learn about the state of the session. This allows support of protocols that involve multiple channels created as a result of negotiations in the control channel. Most of the multimedia protocols as well as some other protocols (such as FTP, RPC, and SQL*Net) involve multiple channels.

Traffic Inspection

Because CBAC inspects packets at the Application Layer and maintains TCP and UDP session information, it can detect and prevent certain types of network attacks such as SYN-flooding. A SYN-flood attack occurs when a network attacker floods a server with a barrage of connection requests and does not complete the connection. The resulting volume of half-open connections overwhelms the server, causing it to deny service to valid requests. CBAC also helps to protect against DoS attacks in other ways. It inspects packet sequence numbers in TCP connections to see if they are within expected ranges and drops any suspicious packets. CBAC can also be configured to drop half-open connections, which require firewall processing and memory resources to maintain.

Intrusion Detection

CBAC provides a limited amount of intrusion detection to protect against specific SMTP attacks. With intrusion detection, syslog messages are reviewed and monitored for specific attack signatures. Certain types of network attacks have specific characteristics or signatures. When CBAC detects an attack based on those specific characteristics, it resets the offending connections and sends syslog information to the syslog server.

Alert and Audit Generation

CBAC also generates real-time alerts and audit trails. Enhanced audit trail features use syslog to track all network transactions and record timestamps, source and destination hosts, ports used, and the total number of transmitted bytes for advanced session-based reporting. Real-time alerts send syslog error messages to central management consoles upon detecting suspicious activity.

Refer to
Figure
in online course

The first CBAC commands were introduced to Cisco IOS software in 1997. CBAC is a dramatic improvement over the TCP established and reflexive ACL firewall options in several fundamental ways:

- Monitors TCP connection setup

- Tracks TCP sequence numbers

- Monitors UDP session information

- Inspects DNS queries and replies

- Inspects common ICMP message types

- Supports applications that rely on multiple connections

- Inspects embedded addresses

- Inspects Application Layer information

It is important to note that CBAC only provides filtering for those protocols that are specified by an administrator. If a protocol is not specified, the existing ACLs determine how that protocol is filtered, and no temporary opening is created. Additionally, CBAC only detects and protects against attacks that travel through the firewall. It does not typically protect against attacks originating from within the protected network unless that traffic travels through an internal router with the Cisco IOS Firewall enabled.

While there is no such thing as a perfect defense, CBAC detects and prevents most of the popular attacks on a network. However, there is no impenetrable defense. Determined, skilled attackers can still find ways to launch effective attacks.

4.3.2 CBAC Operation

Refer to
Figure
in online course

Without CBAC, traffic filtering is limited to ACL implementations that examine packets at the Network Layer or, at most, the Transport Layer. CBAC relies on a stateful packet filter that is application-aware. This means that the filter is able to recognize all sessions of a dynamic application. CBAC examines not only Network Layer and Transport Layer information but also examines Application Layer protocol information (such as FTP connection information) to learn about the state of the session. For example, CBAC can monitor TCP, UDP, and ICMP connections and maintain information in a state table (or connection table) to keep track of these active sessions. This allows support of protocols that involve multiple channels created as a result of negotiations in the control channel. Most of the multimedia protocols as well as some other protocols (such as FTP, RPC, and SQL*Net) involve multiple channels.

The state table tracks the sessions and inspects all packets that pass through the stateful packet filter firewall. CBAC then uses the state table to build dynamic ACL entries that permit returning traffic through the perimeter router or firewall.

How does CBAC work? CBAC creates openings in ACLs at firewall interfaces by adding a temporary ACL entry for a specific session. These openings are created when specified traffic exits the internal protected network through the firewall. The temporary openings allow returning traffic that would normally be blocked and additional data channels to enter the internal network back through the firewall. The traffic is allowed back through the firewall only if it is part of the same session and has the expected properties as the original traffic that triggered CBAC when exiting through the firewall. Without this temporary ACL entry, this traffic would be denied by the preexisting ACL. The state table dynamically changes and adapts with the traffic flow.

Refer to **Figure** in online course

Assume that a user initiates an outbound connection, such as Telnet, from a protected network to an external network, and CBAC is enabled to inspect Telnet traffic. Also assume that an ACL is applied on the external interface preventing Telnet traffic from entering the protected network. This connection goes through a multistep operation:

Step 1. When the traffic is first generated, as it passes through the router, the ACL is processed first if an inbound ACL is applied. If the ACL denies this type of outbound connection, the packet is dropped. If the ACL permits this outbound connection, the CBAC inspection rules are examined.

Step 2. Based on the inspection rules for CBAC, the Cisco IOS software might inspect the connection. If Telnet traffic is not inspected, the packet is allowed through, and no other information is gathered. Otherwise, the connection goes to the next step.

Step 3. The connection information is compared to entries in the state table. If the connection does not currently exist, the entry is added. If it does exist, the idle timer for the connection is reset.

Step 4. If a new entry is added, a dynamic ACL entry is added on the external interface in the inbound direction (from the external network to the internal protected network). This allows the returning Telnet traffic, that is, packets that are part of the same Telnet connection previously established with the outbound packet, back into the network. This temporary opening is only active for as long as the session is open. These dynamic ACL entries are not saved to NVRAM.

Step 5. When the session terminates, the dynamic information from the state table and the dynamic ACL entry are removed.

This is very similar to how reflexive ACLs are processed. CBAC creates temporary openings in the ACLs to allow returning traffic. These entries are created as inspected traffic leaves the network and are removed whenever the connection terminates or the idle timeout period for the connection is reached. Also, as with reflexive ACLs, the administrator can specify which protocols to inspect, as well as on which interface and in which direction the inspection occurs.

CBAC is flexible in its configuration, especially in choosing which direction to inspect traffic. In a typical setup, CBAC is used on the perimeter router or firewall to allow returning traffic into the network. CBAC can also be configured to inspect traffic in two directions - in and out. This is useful when protecting two parts of a network, where both sides initiate certain connections and allow the returning traffic to reach its source.

Refer to **Figure** in online course

CBAC TCP Handling

Recall that TCP uses a three-way handshake. The first packet contains a random sequence number and sets the TCP SYN flag. When the first packet from a TCP flow with the TCP SYN flag is received by the router, the inbound ACL on the inside secured interface is checked. If the packet is permitted, a dynamic session entry is created. The session is described by endpoint addresses, port numbers, sequence numbers, and flags.

All subsequent packets belonging to this session are checked against the current state and discarded if the packets are invalid. How does CBAC determine if a packet is a subsequent packet belonging to an already established session?

When the TCP SYN packet is transmitted, the second packet contains a random sequence number that the responding host generates, as well as an acknowledgment sequence number (the received sequence number incremented by one), and the TCP SYN and ACK flags are set. The third packet acknowledges the received packet by incrementing the packet sequence number in the acknowledgment sequence, raising the sequence number by the appropriate number of transmitted octets, and setting the ACK flag.

All subsequent segments increment their sequence numbers by the number of transmitted octets and acknowledge the last received segment by an increment of one, according to the TCP state machine. After the three-way handshake, all packets have the ACK flag set until the session is terminated. The router tracks the sequence numbers and flags to determine the session to which the packet belongs.

CBAC UDP Handling

With UDP, the router cannot track the sequence numbers and flags. There is no three-way handshake and no teardown process. If the first packet from a UDP flow is permitted through the router, a UDP entry is created in the connection table. The endpoint addresses and port numbers describe the UDP connection entry. When no data is exchanged within the connection for a configurable UDP timeout, the connection description is deleted from the connection table.

CBAC Handling of Other IP Protocols

Stateful firewalls do not usually track other protocols, such as GRE and IPsec, but handle protocols in a stateless manner, similar to how a classic packet filter handles these protocols. If stateful support is provided for other protocols, the support is usually similar to the support for UDP. When a protocol flow is initially permitted, all packets matching the flow are permitted until an idle timer expires.

Dynamic applications, such as FTP, SQLnet, and many protocols that are used for voice and video signaling and media transfer, open a channel on a well-known port and then negotiate additional channels through the initial session. Stateful firewalls support these dynamic applications through application inspection features. The stateful packet filter snoops the initial session and parses the application data to learn about the additional negotiated channels. Then the stateful packet filter enforces the policy that if the initial session was permitted, any additional channels of that application should be permitted as well.

Refer to
Figure
in online course

With CBAC, the protocols to inspect are specified in an inspection rule. An inspection rule is applied to an interface in a direction (in or out) where the inspection applies. The firewall engine inspects only the specified protocol packets if they first pass the inbound ACL that is applied to the inside interface. If a packet is denied by the ACL, the packet is dropped and not inspected by the firewall.

Packets that match the inspection rule generate a dynamic ACL entry that allows return traffic back through the firewall. The firewall creates and removes ACLs as required by the applications. When the application terminates, CBAC removes all dynamic ACLs for that session.

The Cisco IOS Firewall engine can recognize application-specific commands such as illegal SMTP commands in the control channel and detect and prevent certain Application Layer attacks. When an attack is detected, the firewall can take several actions:

- Generate alert messages

- Protect system resources that could impede performance

- Block packets from suspected attackers

The timeout and threshold values are used to manage connection state information. These values help determine when to drop connections that do not become fully established or that time out.

Cisco IOS Firewall provides three thresholds against TCP-based DoS attacks:

- Total number of half-opened TCP sessions
- Number of half-opened sessions in a time interval
- Number of half-opened TCP sessions per host

If a threshold for the number of half-opened TCP sessions is exceeded, the firewall has two options:

- It sends a reset message to the endpoints of the oldest half-opened session, making resources available to service newly arriving SYN packets.
- It blocks all SYN packets temporarily for the duration that the threshold value is configured. When the router blocks a SYN packet, the TCP three-way handshake is never initiated, which prevents the router from using memory and processing resources that valid connections need.

4.3.3 Configuring CBAC

Refer to
Figure
in online course

There are four steps to configure CBAC:

Step 1.   Pick an interface - internal or external.

Step 2.   Configure IP ACLs at the interface.

Step 3.   Define inspection rules.

Step 4.   Apply an inspection rule to an interface.

Refer to
Figure
in online course

Pick an Interface

First determine the internal and external interfaces for applying inspection. With CBAC, internal and external refers to the direction of conversation. The interface in which sessions can be initiated must be selected as the internal interface. Sessions that originate from the external interface will be blocked.

In a typical two-interface scenario in which one interface connects to the external network and the other connects to the protected network, CBAC prevents the specified protocol traffic from entering the firewall and the internal network, unless the traffic is part of a session initiated from within the internal network.

In a three-interface scenario in which the first interface connects to the external network, the second interface connects to a network in a DMZ, and the third interface connects to the internal protected network, the firewall can permit external traffic to resources within the DMZ, such as DNS and web services. The same firewall can then prevent specified protocol traffic from entering the internal network unless the traffic is part of a session initiated from within the internal network.

CBAC can also be configured in two directions at one or more interfaces. Configure the firewall in two directions when the networks on both sides of the firewall require protection, such as with extranet or intranet configurations, and for protection against DoS attacks. If configuring CBAC in two directions, configure one direction first, using the appropriate internal and external interface designations. When configuring CBAC in the other direction, the interface designations must be swapped.

Refer to
Figure
in online course

Configure IP ACLs at the Interface

For Cisco IOS Firewall to work properly, an administrator must configure IP ACLs at the inside, outside, and DMZ interfaces.

To provide the security benefits of ACLs, an administrator should, at a minimum, configure ACLs on border routers situated at the edge of the network between the internal and external networks. This provides a basic buffer from the outside network or from a less controlled area of an organization's network into a more sensitive area of the network.

ACLs can also be used on a router positioned between two internal parts of a network to control traffic flow. For example, if the research and development (R&D) network of an organization is separated from the human resources network by a router, an ACL can be implemented to prevent the R&D employees from accessing the human resources network.

ACLs can be configured on an interface to filter inbound traffic, outbound traffic, or both. The administrator must define ACLs for each protocol enabled on an interface to control traffic flow for that protocol. Use ACLs to determine what types of traffic to forward or block at the router interfaces. For example, an administrator might permit email traffic and at the same time block all Telnet traffic.

These are the guidelines for configuring IP ACLs on a Cisco IOS Firewall:

- Start with a basic configuration. A basic initial configuration allows all network traffic to flow from protected networks to unprotected networks while blocking network traffic from unprotected networks.

- Permit traffic that the Cisco IOS Firewall is to inspect. For example, if the firewall is set to inspect Telnet, Telnet traffic should be permitted on all ACLs that apply to the initial Telnet flow.

- Use extended ACLs to filter traffic that enters the router from unprotected networks. For a Cisco IOS Firewall to dynamically create temporary openings, the ACL for the return traffic must be an extended ACL. If the firewall only has two connections, one to the internal network and one to the external network, applying ACLs inbound on both interfaces works well because packets are stopped before they have a chance to affect the router.

- Set up antispoofing protection by denying any inbound traffic (incoming on an external interface) from a source address that matches an address on the protected network. Antispoofing protection prevents traffic from an unprotected network from assuming the identity of a device on the protected network.

- Deny broadcast messages with a source address of 255.255.255.255. This entry helps prevent broadcast attacks.

- By default, the last entry in an ACL is an implicit denial of all IP traffic that is not specifically allowed by other entries in the ACL. Optionally, an administrator can add an entry to the ACL that denies IP traffic with any source or destination address, thus making the denial rule explicit. Adding this entry is especially useful if it is necessary to log information about the denied packets.

Define inspection Rules

Refer to
Figure
in online course

The administrator must define inspection rules to specify which Application Layer protocols to inspect at an interface. Normally, it is only necessary to define one inspection rule. The only exception occurs if it is necessary to enable the firewall engine in two directions at a single firewall interface. In this instance, the administrator can configure two rules, one for each direction.

An inspection rule should specify each desired Application Layer protocol to inspect, as well as generic TCP, UDP, or ICMP, if desired. Generic TCP and UDP inspection dynamically permits return traffic of active sessions. ICMP inspection allows ICMP echo reply packets forwarded as a response to previously seen ICMP echo messages.

The inspection rule consists of a series of statements, each listing a protocol and specifying the same inspection rule name. Inspection rules include options for controlling alert and audit trail messages.

Inspection rules are configured in global configuration.

```
Router(config)# ip inspect name inspection_name protocol [alert {on ¦ off}]
[audit-trail {on ¦ off}] [timeout seconds]
```

Example 1

In this example, the IP inspection rule is named FWRULE. FWRULE inspects extended SMTP and FTP with alert and audit trails enabled. FWRULE has an idle timeout of 300 seconds.

```
ip inspect name FWRULE smtp alert on audit-trail on timeout 300
ip inspect name FWRULE ftp alert on audit-trail on timeout 300
```

Example 2

In this example, the PERMIT_JAVA rule allows all users permitted by standard ACL 10 to download Java applets.

```
ip inspect name PERMIT_JAVA http java-list 10
access-list 10 permit 10.224.10.0 0.0.0.255
```

Example 3

In this example, a list of protocols, including generic TCP with an idle timeout of 12 hours (normally 1 hour) is defined for the Cisco IOS Firewall to inspect.

Refer to
Figure
in online course

```
ip inspect name in2out rcmd
ip inspect name in2out ftp
ip inspect name in2out tftp
ip inspect name in2out tcp timeout 43200
ip inspect name in2out http
ip inspect name in2out udp
```

Apply an Inspection Rule to an Interface

The last step for configuring CBAC is to apply an inspection rule to an interface.

This is the command syntax used to activate an inspection rule on an interface:

```
Router(config-if)# ip inspect inspection_name {in ¦ out}
```

For the Cisco IOS Firewall to be effective, both inspection rules and ACLs must be strategically applied to all router interfaces. There are two guiding principles for applying inspection rules and ACLs on the router:

- On the interface where traffic initiates, apply the ACL in the inward direction that permits only wanted traffic and apply the rule in the inward direction that inspects wanted traffic.

- On all other interfaces, apply the ACL in the inward direction that denies all traffic, except traffic that has not been inspected by the firewall, such as GRE and ICMP traffic that is not related to echo and echo reply messages.

For example, an administrator needs to permit inside users to initiate TCP, UDP, and ICMP traffic with all external sources. Outside clients are allowed to communicate with the SMTP server (209.165.201.1) and HTTP server (209.165.201.2) that are located in the enterprise DMZ. It is also necessary to permit certain ICMP messages to all interfaces. All other traffic from the external network is denied.

For this example, first create an ACL that allows TCP, UDP, and ICMP sessions and denies all other traffic.

```
R1(config)# access-list 101 permit tcp 10.10.10.0 0.0.0.255 any
R1(config)# access-list 101 permit udp 10.10.10.0 0.0.0.255 any
R1(config)# access-list 101 permit icmp 10.10.10.0 0.0.0.255 any
R1(config)# access-list 101 deny ip any any
```

This ACL is applied to the internal interface in the inbound direction. The ACL processes traffic initiating from the internal network prior to leaving the network.

```
R1(config)# interface Fa0/0
R1(config-if)# ip access-group 101 in
```

Next, create an extended ACL in which SMTP and HTTP traffic is permitted from the external network to the DMZ network only, and all other traffic is denied.

```
R1(config)# access-list 102 permit tcp any 209.165.201.1 0.0.0.0 eq 80
R1(config)# access-list 102 permit tcp any 209.165.201.2 0.0.0.0 eq smtp
R1(config)# access-list 102 permit icmp any any echo-reply
R1(config)# access-list 102 permit icmp any any unreachable
R1(config)# access-list 102 permit icmp any any administratively-prohibited
R1(config)# access-list 102 permit icmp any any packet-too-big
R1(config)# access-list 102 permit icmp any any echo
R1(config)# access-list 102 permit icmp any any time-exceeded
R1(config)# access-list 102 deny ip any any
```

This ACL is applied to the interface connecting to the external network in the inbound direction.

```
R1(config)# interface S0/0/0
R1(config-if)#ip access-group 102 in
```

If the configuration stopped here, all returning traffic, with the exception of ICMP messages, would be denied because of the external ACL. Next, create inspection rules for TCP inspection and UDP inspection.

```
R1(config)#ip inspect name MYSITE tcp
R1(config)#ip inspect name MYSITE udp
```

These inspection rules are applied to the internal interface in the inbound direction.

```
R1(config)# interface Fa0/0
R1(config-if)#ip inspect MYSITE in
```

The inspection list automatically creates temporary ACL statements in the inbound ACL applied to the external interface for TCP and UDP connections. This permits TCP and UDP traffic that is in response to requests generated from the internal network.

To remove CBAC from the router, use the global **no ip inspect** command.

```
Router(config)#no ip inspect
```

This command removes all CBAC commands, the state table, and all temporary ACL entries created by CBAC. It also resets all timeout and threshold values to their factory defaults. After CBAC is removed, all inspection processes are no longer available, and the router uses only the current ACL implementations for filtering.

4.3.4 Troubleshooting CBAC

Refer to **Figure** in online course

CBAC inspection supports two types of logging functions: alerts and audits.

Alerts

Alerts display messages concerning CBAC operation, such as insufficient router resources, DoS attacks, and other threats. Alerts are enabled by default and automatically display on the console line of the router. The administrator can globally disable alerts, although it is highly recommended that alerts are left enabled.

```
Router(config)#ip inspect alert-off
```

The administrator can also disable and enable alerts per inspection rule; however, it is strongly recommended that alerts are left enabled.

This is an example of an alert informing that someone is trying to send an unapproved SMTP command to an email server:

```
%FW-4-SMTP_INVALID_COMMAND: Invalid SMTP command from initiator(209.165.201.5:49387)
```

CBAC can also detect other types of SMTP attacks:

- Sending a pipe (|) in the To or From fields of an email message

- Sending :decode@ in the email header

- Using old SMTP wiz or debug commands on the SMTP port

- Executing arbitrary commands to exploit a bug in the Majordomo email program.

This is an example of an alert that is generated when a hacker tries to exploit the SMTP Majordomo bug:

Refer to
Figure
in online course

```
02:04:55: %FW-4-TCP_MAJORDOMO_EXEC_BUG: Sig:3107:Majordomo Execute Attack - from
209.165.201.5 to 192.168.1.1:
```

Audits

Auditing keeps track of the connections that CBAC inspects, including valid and invalid access attempts. For example, it displays messages when CBAC adds or removes an entry from the state table. The audit record gives some basic statistical information about the connection. Auditing is disabled by default, but can be enabled with the following command:

```
Router(config)#ip inspect audit-trail
```

For example, this audit message is being created from a telnet connection initiated from 192.1.1.2:

```
%FW-6-SESS_AUDIT_TRAIL: tcp session initiator (192.168.1.2:32782) sent 22 bytes
responder (209.165.201.1:23) sent 200 bytes
```

By default, alerts and audits are displayed on the console line. This information can be logged to other locations, including the internal buffer of the router or an external syslog server.

Refer to
Figure
in online course

CBAC supports many show commands that can be used to view the temporary ACL entries created, the state table, and CBAC operation. To view information about CBAC inspections, use the **show ip inspect** command.

```
Router# show ip inspect [parameter]
```

The following output shows the inspection rules configured for the inspect_outbound inspection rule. This rule inspects TCP and UDP traffic, both with their default idle timeouts.

```
Router# show ip inspect name inspect_outbound
Inspection name inspect_outbound
 cuseeme alert is on audit-trail is on timeout 3600
 ftp alert is on audit-trail is on timeout 3600
 http alert is on audit-trail is on timeout 3600
 rcmd alert is on audit-trail is on timeout 3600
 realaudio alert is on audit-trail is on timeout 3600
 smtp max-data 20000000 alert is on audit-trail is on timeout 3600
 tftp alert is on audit-trail is on timeout 30
 udp alert is on audit-trail is on timeout 15
 tcp alert is on audit-trail is on timeout 3600
```

In the next example, the state table has two entries: 192.168.1.2 is inside the network, and 209.165.201.1 is outside. The second entry shows the internal device opening a connection to an external FTP server. The first connection displays the data connection that the FTP server opened back to the internal client. This shows the CBAC dynamic ACL entries created in the inbound extended ACL. The **show ip access-list** command displays the dynamic ACL entries created by the inbound extended ACL.

```
Router# show ip inspect sessions
Established Sessions
 Session 25A3378 (209.165.201.1:20)=>(192.168.1.2:32704) ftp-data SIS_OPEN
 Session 25A5AC2 (192.168.1.2:32703)=>(209.165.201.1:21) ftp SIS_OPEN
Router# show ip access-list
Extended IP access list 100
 permit tcp host 209.165.201.1 eq 21 host 192.168.1.2 eq 32703 (24 matches)
 permit tcp host 209.165.201.1 eq 20 host 192.168.1.2 eq 32704 (88 matches)
<output omitted>
```

There are two dynamic ACL entries to allow return traffic from the FTP server, 209.165.201.1, to the FTP client, 192.168.1.1.

Refer to
Figure
in online course

For detailed troubleshooting of CBAC, the administrator can use **debug** commands. With **debug** commands, the administrator sees in real time the operation of CBAC on the router. The **debug ip inspect** command can inspect various applications and other operation details.

```
Router# debug ip inspect protocol parameter
```

The application names to use for inspection are **cuseeme**, **dns**, **ftp-cmd**, **ftp-token**, **h323**, **http**, **netshow**, **rcmd**, **realaudio**, **rpc**, **rtsp**, **sip**, **skinny**, **smtp**, **sqlnet**, **streamworks**, **tftp**, and **vdolive**.

This output from the **debug ip inspect timers** command enables an administrator to determine, among other things, when idle timeouts are reached.

```
Router# debug ip inspect timers
*Mar 2 01:20:43: CBAC* sis 25A3604 pak 2541C58 TCP P ack 4223720032 seq
4200176225(22)
(10.0.0.1:46409) => (10.1.0.1:21)
*Mar 2 01:20:43: CBAC* sis 25A3604 ftp L7 inspect result: PROCESS-SWITCH packet
*Mar 2 01:20:43: CBAC sis 25A3604 pak 2541C58 TCP P ack 4223720032 seq
4200176225(22)
(10.0.0.1:46409) => (10.1.0.1:21)
*Mar 2 01:20:43: CBAC sis 25A3604 ftp L7 inspect result: PASS packet
*Mar 2 01:20:43: CBAC* sis 25A3604 pak 2544374 TCP P ack 4200176247 seq
4223720032(30)
(10.0.0. 1:46409) <= (10.1.0.1:21)
*Mar 2 01:20:43: CBAC* sis 25A3604 ftp L7 inspect result: PASS packet
*Mar 2 01:20:43: CBAC* sis 25A3604 pak 25412F8 TCP P ack 4223720062 seq
4200176247(15)
(10.0.0. 1:46409) => (10.1.0.1:21)
*Mar 2 01:20:43: CBAC* sis 25A3604 ftp L7 inspect result: PASS packet
*Mar 2 01:20:43: CBAC sis 25C1CC4 pak 2544734 TCP S seq 4226992037(0)
(10.1.0.1:20) =>
(10.0.0.1:46411)
*Mar 2 01:20:43: CBAC* sis 25C1CC4 pak 2541E38 TCP S ack 4226992038 seq
4203405054(0)
(10.1.0.1:20) <= (10.0.0.1:46411)
```

Beginning with Cisco IOS Release 12.4(20)T, the **debug policy-firewall** command replaces the **debug ip inspect** command.

CBAC has dramatically transformed the capability of Cisco routers to serve as firewalls. CBAC has incredible versatility, enabling a Cisco router to act as a true stateful firewall. Despite the extreme usefulness of CBAC in securing modern networks, it does have some shortcomings. Newer technologies enable a more intuitive and structured implementation of Cisco routers as Cisco IOS Firewalls while building on the functionality of CBAC.

4.4 Zone-Based Policy Firewall

4.4.1 Zone-Based Policy Firewall Characteristics

Refer to
Figure
in online course

In 2006, Cisco Systems introduced the zone-based policy firewall configuration model with Cisco IOS Release 12.4(6)T. With this new model, interfaces are assigned to zones and then an inspection policy is applied to traffic moving between the zones. A zone-based firewall allows different inspection policies to be applied to multiple host groups connected to the same router interface. It also has the ability to prohibit traffic via a default deny-all policy between firewall zones.

The zone-based policy firewall (ZPF or ZBF or ZFW) inspection interface supports previous firewall features, including stateful packet inspection, application inspection, URL filtering, and DoS mitigation.

Firewall policies are configured using the Cisco Common Classification Policy Language (C3PL), which uses a hierarchical structure to define network protocol inspection and allows hosts to be grouped under one inspection policy.

Refer to
Figure
in online course

The primary motivations for network security professionals to migrate to the ZPF model are structure and ease of use. The structured approach is useful for documentation and communication. The ease of use makes network security implementations more accessible to a larger community of security professionals.

Implementing CBAC is complex and can be overwhelming. Unlike ZPF, CBAC does not utilize any dedicated hierarchical data structures to modularize the implementation. CBAC has these limitations:

- Multiple inspection policies and ACLs on several interfaces on a router make it difficult to correlate the policies for traffic between multiple interfaces.

- Policies cannot be tied to a host group or subnet with an ACL. All traffic through a given interface is subject to the same inspection.

- The process relies too heavily on ACLs.

Zones establish the security borders of a network. The zone itself defines a boundary where traffic is subjected to policy restrictions as it crosses over into another region of a network. The default policy between zones is deny all. If no policy is explicitly configured, all traffic moving between zones is blocked. This is a significant departure from the CBAC model in which traffic was implicitly allowed until it was explicitly blocked with an ACL.

While many ZPF commands appear similar to CBAC commands, they are not the same. A second significant change is the introduction of Cisco Common Classification Policy Language (C3PL). This new configuration policy language allows a modular approach to firewall implementation.

Some of the benefits of ZPF include the following:

- It is not dependent on ACLs.

- The router security posture is to block unless explicitly allowed.

- Policies are easy to read and troubleshoot with C3PL.

- One policy affects any given traffic, instead of needing multiple ACLs and inspection actions.

When deciding whether to implement CBAC or zones, one important note is that both configuration models can be enabled concurrently on a router. However, the models cannot be combined on a single interface. For example, an interface cannot be configured as a security zone member and configured for IP inspection simultaneously.

Refer to
Figure
in online course

Common ZPF designs are LAN-to-Internet firewall, a firewall with public servers, redundant firewalls, and complex firewalls.

Designing zone-based firewalls involves a few steps:

Step 1.   **Determine the Zones** - The internetworking infrastructure under consideration must be split into separate zones with various security levels. In this step, the administrator does not consider physical implementation of the firewall (number of devices, defense depth, redundancy, etc.), but focuses instead on the separation of the infrastructure into zones. For example, the public network to which the internal network is connected is one zone.

Step 2.   **Establish policies between zones** - For each pair of "source-destination" zones (for example, from inside network to Internet), define the sessions that clients in the source zones can request from servers in destination zones. These sessions are most commonly TCP and UDP sessions, but also ICMP sessions such as ICMP echo. For traffic that is not based on the concept of sessions, such as IPsec Encapsulating Security Payload [ESP], the administrator must define unidirectional traffic flows from source to destination and vice versa. As in Step 1, this step is about the traffic requirements between zones, not the physical setup.

Step 3.   **Design the physical infrastructure** - After the zones have been identified and the traffic requirements between them documented, the administrator must design the physical infrastructure, taking into account security and availability requirements. This includes dictating the number of devices between most-secure and least-secure zones and determining redundant devices.

Step 4.   **Identify subset within zones and merge traffic requirements** - For each firewall device in the design, the administrator must identify zone subsets connected to its interfaces and merge the traffic requirements for those zones. For example, multiple zones might be indirectly attached to a single interface of a firewall, resulting in a device-specific interzone policy.

4.4.2 Zone-Based Policy Firewall Operation

Refer to
Figure
in online course

The Cisco IOS zone-based policy firewall can take three possible actions when configured using CCP:

- *Inspect* Configures Cisco IOS stateful packet inspection. This action is equivalent to the CBAC **ip inspect** command. It automatically allows for return traffic and potential ICMP messages. For protocols requiring multiple parallel signaling and data sessions (for example, FTP or H.323), the inspect action also handles the proper establishment of data sessions.

- *Drop* Analogous to a deny statement in an ACL. A **log** option is available to log the rejected packets.

- *Pass* Analogous to a permit statement in an ACL. The pass action does not track the state of connections or sessions within the traffic. Pass allows the traffic only in one direction. A corresponding policy must be applied to allow return traffic to pass in the opposite direction.

To apply rate limits to the traffic of a specified class, the **police** option can be used in conjunction with the **inspect** or **pass** command.

Refer to
Figure
in online course

The membership of the router network interfaces in zones is subject to several rules governing interface behavior, as is the traffic moving between zone member interfaces:

- A zone must be configured before an administrator can assign interfaces to the zone.

- If traffic is to flow between all interfaces in a router, each interface must be a member of a zone.

- An administrator can assign an interface to only one security zone.

- Traffic is implicitly allowed to flow by default among interfaces that are members of the same zone.

- To permit traffic to and from a zone member interface, a policy allowing or inspecting traffic must be configured between that zone and any other zone.

- Traffic cannot flow between a zone member interface and any interface that is not a zone member. An administrator can apply pass, inspect, and drop actions only between two zones.

- Interfaces that have not been assigned to a zone function can still use a CBAC stateful packet inspection configuration.

- If an administrator does not want an interface on the router to be part of the zone-based firewall policy, it might still be necessary to put that interface in a zone and configure a pass-all policy (also known as a dummy policy) between that zone and any other zone to which traffic flow is desired.

Refer to
Figure
in online course

The rules for a zone-based policy firewall are different when the router is involved in the traffic flow. The rules depend on whether the router is the source or the destination of the traffic.

When an interface is configured to be a zone member, the hosts that are connected to the interface are included in the zone, but traffic flowing to and from the interfaces of the router is not controlled by the zone policies. Instead, all the IP interfaces on the router are automatically made part of the self zone. To limit IP traffic moving to the IP addresses of the router from the various zones on a router, policies must be applied. The policies can be set to block, allow, or inspect traffic between the zone and the self zone of the router, and vice versa. If there are no policies between a zone and the self zone, all traffic is permitted to the interfaces of the router without being inspected.

A policy can be defined using the self zone as either the source or the destination zone. The self zone is a system-defined zone. It does not require any interfaces to be configured as members. A zone pair that includes the self zone, along with the associated policy, applies to traffic that is directed to the router or traffic that the router generates. It does not apply to traffic traversing the router.

When the router is involved in the traffic flow, additional rules for zone-based policy firewalls govern interface behavior:

- All traffic to and from a given interface is implicitly blocked when the interface is assigned to a zone, except traffic to or from other interfaces in the same zone and traffic to any interface on the router.

- All the IP interfaces on the router are automatically made part of the self zone when ZPF is configured. The self zone is the only exception to the default deny all policy. All traffic to any router interface is allowed by default until traffic is explicitly denied.

4.4.3 Configuring a Zone-Based Policy Firewall with CLI

Refer to
Figure
in online course

There are several steps for configuring ZPF with the CLI:

Step 1.   Create the zones for the firewall with the `zone security` command.

Step 2.   Define traffic classes with the `class-map type inspect` command.

Step 3.   Specify firewall policies with the `policy-map type inspect` command.

Step 4.   Apply firewall policies to pairs of source and destination zones using the `zone-pair security` command.

Step 5.   Assign router interfaces to zones using the `zone-member security` interface command.

When configuring ZPF with the CLI, there are several factors to consider:

- Only policy maps defined with `type inspect` can be used in the `zone-pair security` command.

- Only class maps defined with `type inspect` can be used in policy maps with `type inspect`.
- There can be no name overlap with other types of class maps or policy maps. For example, there cannot be a quality-of-service class map and an inspect class map with the same name.
- A zone must be configured with the `zone security` global command before it can be used in the `zone-member security` interface configuration command.
- An interface cannot belong to multiple zones. To create a union of security zones, specify a new zone and appropriate policy map and zone pairs.
- The zone-based policy firewall feature is a replacement for CBAC. Remove the `ip inspect` interface configuration command before applying the `zone-member security` command.
- The zone-based policy firewall can coexist with CBAC. The `ip inspect` command can still be used on interfaces that are not members of security zones.
- Traffic can never flow between an interface assigned to a zone and an interface without a zone assignment. Applying the `zone-member` configuration command always results in temporary interruption of service.
- The default interzone policy is to drop all traffic unless specified otherwise in the `zone-pair` configuration command.
- The router never filters the traffic between interfaces in the same zone.
- The `zone-member` command does not protect the router itself (traffic to and from the router is not affected) unless the zone- pairs are configured using the predefined self zone.

CBAC dynamically creates entries in ACLs attached to interfaces on which the `ip inspect` command is configured. ZPF does not change ACLs. Review ACL usage before entering the `zone-member` command.

Create the Zones

Refer to **Figure** in online course

The administrator creates the zones for the firewall with the **zone security** command. An optional description is recommended.

```
Router(config)# zone security zone-name
Router(config-sec-zone)# description line-of-description
```

Think about what should constitute the zones. The general guideline is to group together interfaces that are similar when viewed from a security perspective. In other words, interfaces that have similar security needs should be placed into a zone.

Define Traffic Classes

Refer to **Figure** in online course

ZPF traffic classes enable the network security professional to define traffic flows in as granular a fashion as desired.

This is the syntax for creating ZPF traffic classes:

```
Router(config)# class-map type inspect [match-any | match-all] class-map-name
```

For Layer 3 and Layer 4, top-level class maps, the **match-any** option is the default behavior:

```
Router(config)# class-map type inspect protocol-name [match-any | match-all] class-map-name
```

For Layer 7 application-specific class maps, check documentation found on www.cisco.com for more construction details.

The syntax for referencing access lists from within the class map is:

```
Router(config-cmap)# match access-group {access-group | name access-group-name}
```

Protocols are matched from within the class map with the syntax:

```
Router(config-cmap)# match protocol protocol-name
```

Nested class maps can be configured as well using the syntax:

```
Router(config-cmap)# match class-map class-map-name
```

The ability to create a hierarchy of classes and policies by nesting is one of the reasons that ZPF is such a powerful approach to creating Cisco IOS firewalls.

Refer to **Figure** in online course

Specify Firewall Policies

Similar to other modular CLI constructs with Cisco IOS software, the administrator has to specify what to do with the traffic matching the desired traffic class. The options are **pass**, **inspect**, **drop**, and **police**.

This is the syntax for creating ZPF policy maps.

```
Router(config)# policy-map type inspect policy-map-name
```

Traffic classes on which an action must be performed are specified within the policy map.

```
Router(config-pmap)# class type inspect class-name
```

The default class (matching all remaining traffic) is specified using this command.

```
Router(config-pmap)# class class-default
```

Finally, the action to take on the traffic is specified.

```
Router(config-pmap-c)# pass ¦ inspect ¦ drop [log] ¦ police
```

Refer to **Figure** in online course

Apply Firewall Policies

After the firewall policy has been configured, the administrator applies it to traffic between a pair of zones using the **zone-pair security** command. To apply a policy, a zone pair must first be created. Specify the source zone, the destination zone, and the policy for handling the traffic between them.

```
Router(config)# zone-pair security zone-pair-name [source source-zone-name ¦ self]
destination [self ¦ destination-zone-name]
```

Use the **service-policy type inspect** *policy-map-name* command to attach a policy-map and its associated actions to a zone pair. Enter the command after entering the **zone-pair security** command.

Deep-packet inspection (attaching a Layer 7 policy map to a top-level policy map) can also be configured. This is the syntax used with Cisco IOS Release 12.4(20)T.

```
Router(config-pmap-c)# service-policy {h323 ¦ http ¦ im ¦ imap ¦ p2p ¦ pop3 ¦ sip
¦ smtp ¦ sunrpc ¦ urlfilter} policy-map
```

The policy map is the name of the Layer 7 policy map being applied to the top-level Layer 3 or Layer 4 policy map.

Assign Router Interfaces

Finally, the administrator must assign interfaces to the appropriate security zones using the **zone-member** interface command.

```
Router(config-if)# zone-member security zone-name
```

The **zone-member security** command puts an interface into a security zone. When an interface is in a security zone, all traffic to and from that interface (except traffic going to the router or initiated by the router) is dropped by default. To permit traffic through an interface that is a zone member, the zone must be part of a zone pair to which a policy is applied. If the policy permits traffic (via inspect or pass actions), traffic can flow through the interface.

ZPF configuration with the CLI might appear a little intimidating at first. The good news is that there are two ways to configure ZPF. Use the Cisco IOS CLI or CCP.

4.4.4 Configuring Zone-Based Policy Firewall with CCP Wizard

Refer to
Figure
in online course

When using CCP, a zone-based policy firewall is created using the Basic or Advanced Firewall wizards.

The Basic Firewall wizard of CCP helps implement a firewall with two zones: an in-zone and an out-zone. The wizard goes through the creation of the firewall by asking for information about the interfaces on the router, as well as what rules to use in the firewall. The difference between the Basic and Advanced Firewall Wizard is that the Advanced Firewall Wizard can be used to define a security DMZ used for Internet accessible services. Additionally, the Advanced Firewall Wizard allows the user to select the level of default security that is initially implemented.

These are the steps for accessing the Advanced Firewall Configuration wizard using CCP:

Step 1.   From CCP, choose **Configuration > Firewall > Firewall**.

Step 2.   In the Create Firewall tab, click the **Advanced Firewall** option and click **Launch the selected task** button.

Step 3.   The Advanced Firewall Configuration Wizard window appears. Click **Next** to begin the configuration.

Refer to
Figure
in online course

The first task to enable an advanced firewall configuration is to define inside and outside interfaces. An outside interface is typically the router interface that is connected to the Internet or to a WAN. An inside interface is typically a physical or logical interface that connects to the LAN. It is possible to select multiple inside and outside interfaces:

Step 1.   From the Advanced Firewall Interface Configuration window, use the **outside (untrusted)** check boxes to select the outside interface. Use the **inside (trusted)** check boxes to identify each interface that is an inside interface. Outside interfaces connect to an organization's WAN or to the Internet. Inside interfaces connect to the LAN. These interfaces will be associated with one of two default zones created by CCP, the out-zone and the in-zone. There can be more than one interface selected for each zone.

Step 2.   If a DMZ is necessary, use the DMZ Interface drop down box to select the interface connected to the DMZ.

Step 3.   (Optional) Check the **Allow secure Cisco CP access from outside interfaces** check box if the intent is to allow users outside the firewall access to the router using CCP. Choosing this option permits secure HTTP access to the outside interface. Because it is a secure CCP connection to the firewall, it is not possible to browse the outside interface via HTTP after the firewall wizard completes the configuration. Click **Next**.

Step 4.   If the **Allow secure Cisco CP access from the outside interfaces** check box is checked, the Configuring Firewall for Remote Access window appears. Specify the source host or network from which CCP is allowed to remotely manage the router. Choose **Network address**, **Host IP address**, or **any** from the Type drop-down list, and then fill in the IP address and Subnet Mask fields as appropriate. The firewall is modified to allow access to the address specified.

If the **Allow secure Cisco CP access from outside interfaces** box is not checked, a warning will appear to inform you that access to CCP from the outside interface will no longer be allowed after configuration is complete. Click **OK**.

Refer to
Figure
in online course

After interface configuration, the Advanced Firewall Security Configuration window appears. Use the slider bar to view a description of the security each level provides and select the security level desired. Security levels include low, medium and high. Note that when using the Basic Firewall wizard, this option is not available. Once the appropriate security level is selected, click **Next**.

In the Advanced Firewall Security Configuration window, click the **Preview Commands** button to view the Cisco IOS commands that make up the selected policy. The router must be configured with the IP address of at least one DNS server for application security to work.

Refer to
Figure
in online course

The Firewall Configuration Summary window displays the policy name chosen, CCP_HIGH, CCP_MEDIUM, or CCP_LOW, and the configuration statements in the policy.

Click **Finish** to complete the configuration. If a routing protocol is enabled on the router, a routing traffic configuration window will appear. This box enables you to specify that routing updates are allowed through the firewall.

In the Deliver Configuration to Device window, click the **Deliver** button to enable the zone-based policy firewall commands.

The commands executed by the Basic and Advanced Firewall wizards are often quite lengthy. The configurations created by wizards are generally more extensive than those created by a manual configuration.

4.4.5 Configuring a Zone-Based Policy Firewall Manually with CCP

Refer to
Figure
in online course

Zone-Based Policy Firewall configuration can also performed manually with CCP.

There are four steps to manual configuration of ZPF with CCP:

Step 1.   Define zones.

Step 2.   Configure class maps to describe traffic between zones.

Step 3.   Create policy maps to apply actions to the traffic of the class maps.

Step 4.   Define zone pairs and assign policy maps to the zone pairs.

Unlike the CCP Basic Firewall Wizard, with manual CCP ZPF configuration, zones, zone pairs, traffic classification, policy maps, and application of the various elements are performed independently.

Refer to
Figure
in online course

Task 1. Define Zones

The first step in configuring a Cisco IOS ZPF with CCP is to define zones. A zone, or security zone, is a named group of interfaces to which a security policy can be applied. A zone can contain a single interface or multiple interfaces; however, an interface cannot be a member of more than one zone. The interfaces in a zone share common functions, features, or security requirements. For example, an administrator might place two interfaces that connect to the local LAN in one security zone, and the interfaces that connect to the Internet into another security zone.

For traffic to flow between all interfaces in a router, all interfaces must be a member of a security zone. However, it is not required that all router interfaces be members of security zones.

These are the steps for creating a zone using CCP:

Step 1.   Choose **Configure > Security > Firewall > Firewall Components > Zones**.

Step 2.   From the Zone panel, click **Add** to create a new zone.

Step 3.   The Add a Zone window appears. Enter a zone name in the **Zone Name** field.

Step 4.   Choose the interfaces for this zone by checking the check box in front of the interface name. Because physical interfaces can be placed in only one zone, they do not appear in the list if they have already been assigned to a zone.

As you assign interfaces to zones, keep in mind the ZPF rules that govern interface behavior.

Step 5.   Click **OK** to create the zone, and click **OK** in the Commands Delivery Status window.

When a zone is created, the interfaces associated with that zone can be changed, but the name of the zone cannot. Click **Edit** in the Zone panel to choose different interfaces for an existing zone. Click **Delete** in the Zone panel to remove a zone. A zone that is a member of a zone pair cannot be deleted.

Refer to
Figure
in online course

Task 2. Configure Class Maps

After a zone is created and the interfaces are applied, the next step in configuring ZPF is to configure class maps. Class maps identify traffic and traffic parameters for policy application.

Layer 3 and 4 class maps sort the traffic based on specific criteria:

- *Access group*   A numbered or named ACL (either standard or extended) can filter traffic based on source and destination IP addresses and source and destination ports.

- *Protocol*   The class map can identify Layer 4 protocols, such as TCP, UDP, and ICMP, and application services such as HTTP, SMTP, and DNS. Any well-known or user-defined service known to Port-to-Application Mapping (PAM) can be specified.

- *Class map*   A subordinate class map that provides additional match criteria can be nested inside another class map.

Class maps can apply match-any or match-all operators to determine how to apply the match criteria. If match-any is specified, traffic must meet just one of the match criteria in the class map. If match-all is specified, traffic must match all of the class map criteria to belong to that particular class.

These are the steps to create a class map using CCP:

Step 1.   Choose **Configure > Security > C3PL > Class Map > Inspection**.

Step 2.   From the Inspect Class Maps window, click **Add**.

Step 3.   Enter a class map name in the Class Map field and optionally add a description in the **Description** field. Select the desired protocols from the list and click **Add >>** to add them to the inspection list for this class map.

Class maps can be reviewed, created, and edited in the Inspect Class Map window. The Class Map Name area of the window lists the configured class maps, and the lower portion of the window displays the details of the selected class map. If it is necessary to edit a class map or see more details, choose the class map from the list and click **Edit**.

Refer to
Figure
in online course

Task 3. Create Policy Maps

Now that the class maps are created, it is time to create policy maps. Class maps are applied within policy maps. Policy maps specify the actions to be taken when traffic matches the criteria. A policy map associates traffic classes with actions.

Inspection policy maps specify the action the router is to take for traffic that matches the criteria in the associated class maps. These are the actions that a policy map supports:

- *Pass*   Traffic is allowed to pass from one zone to another only in one direction. The router does not monitor the state of connections or session.

- *Drop*   The router drops unwanted traffic and can optionally log the event.

■ *Inspect* The router maintains state-based session and connection information so that the router permits traffic returning from a destination zone to a source zone.

These are the steps to create a policy map using CCP:

Step 1. Choose **Configure > Security > C3PL > Policy Map > Protocol Inspection**.

Step 2. From the Protocol Inspection Policy Maps window, click **Add**.

Step 3. Enter a policy name in the **Policy Name** field and optionally add a description in the **Description** field. The name and description that you enter will be visible in the Protocol Inspection Policy Maps window.

Step 4. The Class Map and Action columns display the class maps that are associated with this policy map, and the action that the router takes for the traffic that the class map describes. Click **Add** to add a new class map to the list and configure the action.

Step 5. The Associate Class map window appears. In the **Class Name** field, enter the name of the class map to apply. If the class map name is unknown, or a new class map is to be created, click the down arrow to the right of the **Class Name** field. A pop-up menu appears for adding a class map, choosing a class map, or choosing the class default.

Step 6. After selecting the class map, define the action that the policy map takes for traffic that matches this class map. From the Action section, choose **Pass**, **Drop**, or **Inspect**, based on the particular needs for this class map. Click **OK**.

Step 7. To add another class map to the policy, click **Add**. To modify the actions of an existing class map, choose the class map from the Class Map list and click **Edit**. To delete a class map, choose the class map from the Class Map list and click **Delete**. Use the **Move Up** and **Move Down** buttons to change the order in which the class maps are evaluated.

Step 8. Click **OK**. In the Command Delivery Status window, click **OK**.

Refer to
Figure
in online course

Task 4. Define Zone Pairs

A zone-pair allows a unidirectional firewall policy between two security zones to be specified. The direction of the traffic is determined by specifying a source and destination security zone. The same zone cannot be defined as both the source and the destination.

If the intent is for traffic to flow in both directions between two zones, a zone pair must be created for each direction. If the intent is for traffic to flow freely among all interfaces, each interface must be configured in a zone.

These are the steps for configuring a new zone pair using CCP:

Step 1. Choose **Configure > Security > Firewall > Firewall Components > Zone Pairs**.

Step 2. In the Zone Pairs panel, click **Add**. The Add a Zone Pair window appears.

Step 3. In the **Zone Pair** field, enter a name for the zone pair. Choose a source zone from which traffic originates, a destination zone to which traffic is sent, and the policy that determines which traffic can be sent across the zones.

The **Source zone** and **Destination zone** lists contain the zones that are configured on the router and the self zone. The self zone can be used when configuring zone pairs for traffic originating from the router itself, or destined for the router itself, such as a zone pair that is configured for SNMP traffic. The **Policy** list contains the name of each policy map that is configured on the router.

Step 4.   Click **OK** in the Add a Zone Pair window, and click **OK** in the Command Delivery Status window.

Step 5.   To edit a zone pair, in the Zone Pairs panel choose the zone pair to edit and click **Edit**. If editing a zone pair, the policy map can be changed, but the name or the source or destination zones cannot be changed.

4.4.6 Troubleshooting Zone-Based Policy Firewall

Refer to
Figure
in online course

After creating the zone-based policy firewall, examine it in CCP within the **Configure > Security > Firewall > Firewall** menu, under the **Edit Firewall Policy** tab. A graphical view of the firewall displays. It is possible to modify the firewall configuration from this window.

The CLI ZPF commands generated by a two-interface firewall with default inspection parameters are not that lengthy. Typically, protocols such as HTTP, SMTP, and FTP are inspected in this type of scenario. A policy map applies stateful inspection to these protocols listed in a class map. Two zones, such as private and Internet, are created. The inside interface is made a member of the private zone, and the WAN interface is a member of the Internet zone. Lastly, a zone pair, such as priv-to-internet, is created. This pair has a source zone of private, a destination zone of Internet, and the policy map is applied to it.

Refer to
Figure
in online course

CCP can be used to display the status of the firewall activity for each zone pair that is configured on the router. To view active sessions monitored by ZPF, or to view statistics for dropped packets and allowed packets related to the implemented ZPF policy, use the Monitor option in CCP:

Monitor > Security > Firewall Status.

Refer to
Figure
in online course

Use the `show policy-map type inspect zone-pair session` command to examine the active connections in the ZPF state table.

Cisco IOS Zone-Based Policy Firewall provides state-of-the-art firewall design and configuration. What began with TCP `established` in 1995 has evolved into a rich set of technologies for securing networks.

But firewalls alone can never provide a complete security solution. Other technologies are required to build a secure infrastructure. Network intrusion prevention is another security technology that is required to support the network firewall. Intrusion prevention goes a long way toward closing any security gaps in a modern network.

Summary

Refer to **Figure** in online course

Refer to **Packet Tracer Activity** for this chapter

Refer to **Lab Activity** for this chapter

Your Chapter Notes

CHAPTER 5

Implementing Intrusion Prevention

Chapter Introduction

Refer to
Figure
in online course

The security challenges that face today's network administrators cannot be successfully managed by any single application. Although implementing device hardening, AAA access control, and firewall features are all part of a properly secured network, these features still cannot defend the network against fast-moving Internet worms and viruses. A network must be able to instantly recognize and mitigate worm and virus threats.

It is also no longer possible to contain intrusions at a few points in the network. Intrusion prevention is required throughout the entire network to detect and stop an attack at every inbound and outbound point.

A networking architecture paradigm shift is required to defend against fast-moving and evolving attacks. This must include cost-effective detection and prevention systems, such as intrusion detection systems (IDS) or, the more scalable, intrusion prevention systems (IPS). The network architecture integrates these solutions into the entry and exit points of the network.

When implementing IDS and/or IPS, it is important to be familiar with the types of systems available, host-based and network-based approaches, the placement these systems, the role of signature categories, and possible actions that a Cisco IOS router can take when an attack is detected.

In a comprehensive hands-on lab for the chapter, *Configuring an Intrusion Prevention System (IPS) Using the CLI and CCP*, learners configure IPS using the CLI, modify IPS signatures, verify IPS functionality, and log IPS messages to a syslog server. Next, learners configure IPS using CCP, modify signatures, use a scanning tool to simulate an attack, and use CCP Monitor to verify IPS functionality.

A Packet Tracer activity, *Configure IOS Intrusion Prevention System (IPS) using CLI*, provides learners additional practice implementing the technologies introduced in this chapter. Learners configure IPS using CLI, modify IPS signatures, and verify IPS functionality.

5.1 IPS Technologies

5.1.1 IDS and IPS Characteristics

Refer to
Figure
in online course

Internet worms and viruses can spread across the world in a matter of minutes. A network must instantly recognize and mitigate worm and virus threats. Firewalls can only do so much and cannot protect against malware and zero-day attacks.

A zero-day attack, sometimes referred to as a zero-day threat, is a computer attack that tries to exploit software vulnerabilities that are unknown or undisclosed by the software vendor. The term zero-hour describes the moment when the exploit is discovered. During the time it takes the software vendor to develop and release a patch, the network is vulnerable to these exploits. To defend against these fast-moving attacks requires network security professionals to expand the way they view network architecture. It is no longer possible to contain intrusions at a few points in the network.

Refer to **Figure** in online course

One approach to prevent worms and viruses from entering a network is for an administrator to continuously monitor the network and analyze the log files generated by the network devices. This solution is not very scalable. Manually analyzing log file information is a time-consuming task and provides a limited view of the attacks being launched against a network. By the time that the logs are analyzed, the attack has already begun.

Intrusion Detection Systems (IDSs) were implemented to passively monitor the traffic on a network. An IDS-enabled device copies the traffic stream, and analyzes the monitored traffic rather than the actual forwarded packets. Working offline, it compares the captured traffic stream with known malicious signatures, similar to software that checks for viruses. This offline IDS implementation is referred to as promiscuous mode.

The advantage of operating with a copy of the traffic is that the IDS does not negatively affect the actual packet flow of the forwarded traffic. The disadvantage of operating on a copy of the traffic is that the IDS cannot stop malicious single-packet attacks from reaching the target before responding to the attack. An IDS often requires assistance from other networking devices, such as routers and firewalls, to respond to an attack.

It is better to implement a solution that detects and immediately addresses a network problem as required.

Refer to **Figure** in online course

An Intrusion Prevention System (IPS) builds upon IDS technology. Unlike IDS, an IPS device is implemented in inline mode. This means that all ingress and egress traffic must flow through it for processing. An IPS does not allow packets to enter the trusted side of the network without first being analyzed. It can detect and immediately address a network problem as required.

An IPS monitors Layer 3 and Layer 4 traffic and analyzes the contents and the payload of the packets for more sophisticated embedded attacks that might include malicious data at Layers 2 through 7. Cisco IPS platforms use a blend of detection technologies, including signature-based, profile-based, and protocol analysis intrusion detection. This deeper analysis lets the IPS identify, stop, and block attacks that would normally pass through a traditional firewall device. When a packet comes in through an interface on an IPS, that packet is not sent to the outbound or trusted interface until the packet has been analyzed.

The advantage of operating in inline mode is that the IPS can stop single-packet attacks from reaching the target system. The disadvantage is that a poorly configured IPS or an inappropriate IPS solution can negatively affect the packet flow of the forwarded traffic.

The biggest difference between IDS and IPS is that an IPS responds immediately and does not allow any malicious traffic to pass, whereas an IDS might allow malicious traffic to pass before responding.

Refer to **Figure** in online course

IDS and IPS technologies do share several characteristics. IDS and IPS technologies are both deployed as sensors. An IDS or IPS sensor can be any of the following devices:

- Router configured with Cisco IOS IPS software
- Appliance specifically designed to provide dedicated IDS or IPS services
- Network module installed in an adaptive security appliance, switch, or router

IDS and IPS technologies use signatures to detect patterns of misuse in network traffic. A signature is a set of rules that an IDS or IPS uses to detect typical intrusive activity. Signatures can be used to detect severe breaches of security, common network attacks, and information gathering. IDS and IPS technologies can detect atomic signature patterns (single-packet) or composite signature patterns (multi-packet).

Does an IPS sensor completely replace an IDS sensor?

IDS Advantages and Disadvantages

One main advantage of an IDS platform is that it is deployed in promiscuous mode. Because the IDS sensor is not inline, it has no impact on network performance. It does not introduce latency, jitter, or other traffic flow issues. In addition, if a sensor fails, it does not affect network functionality. It only affects the ability of the IDS to analyze the data.

But there are many disadvantages of deploying an IDS platform in promiscuous mode. IDS sensor response actions cannot stop the trigger packet and are not guaranteed to stop a connection. They are also less helpful in stopping email viruses and automated attacks such as worms.

Users deploying IDS sensor response actions must have a well thought-out security policy, combined with a good operational understanding of their IDS deployments. Users must spend time tuning IDS sensors to achieve expected levels of intrusion detection.

Finally, because IDS sensors are not inline, an IDS implementation is more vulnerable to network security evasion techniques used by various network attach methods.

IPS Advantages and Disadvantages

Deploying an IPS platform in inline mode also has advantages and disadvantages.

One advantage over IDS is that an IPS sensor can be configured to perform a packet drop that can stop the trigger packet, the packets in a connection, or packets from a source IP address. Additionally, being inline, an IPS sensor can use stream normalization techniques to reduce or eliminate many of the network security evasion capabilities that exist.

A disadvantage of IPS is that errors, failure, and overrunning the IPS sensor with too much traffic can have a negative effect on network performance. This is because IPS must be deployed inline, and traffic must be able to pass through it. An IPS sensor can affect network performance by introducing latency and jitter. An IPS sensor must be appropriately sized and implemented so that time-sensitive applications, such as VoIP, are not negatively affected.

Deployment Considerations

Using one of these technologies does not negate the use of the other. In fact, IDS and IPS technologies can complement each other. For example, an IDS can be implemented to validate IPS operation, because IDS can be configured for deeper packet inspection offline. This allows the IPS to focus on fewer but more critical traffic patterns inline.

Deciding which implementation to use is based on the security goals of the organization as stated in the network security policy.

5.1.2 Network-Based IPS Implementations

A network IPS can be implemented using a dedicated IPS appliance, such as the IPS 4200 series. Alternatively, it can be added to an ISR router, an ASA firewall appliance, or Catalyst 6500 switch.

Sensors detect malicious and unauthorized activity in real time and can take action when required. Sensors are deployed at designated network points that enable security managers to monitor network activity while it is occurring, regardless of the location of the attack target.

Sensors can be implemented in several ways:

- Added to an ISR router using an IPS Advanced Integration Module (AIM) or a Network Module Enhanced (IPS NME).

- Added to an ASA firewall appliance using an Advanced Inspection and Prevention Security Services Module (ASA AIP-SSM).

- Added to a Catalyst 6500 switch using an Intrusion Detection System Services Module (IDSM-2).

Network IPS sensors are usually tuned for intrusion prevention analysis. The underlying operating system of the platform on which the IPS module is mounted is stripped of unnecessary network services, and essential services are secured. This is known as hardening. The hardware includes three components.

- *Network interface card (NIC)* The network IPS must be able to connect to any network (Ethernet, Fast Ethernet, Gigabit Ethernet).

- *Processor* Intrusion prevention requires CPU power to perform intrusion detection analysis and pattern matching.

- *Memory* Intrusion detection analysis is memory-intensive. Memory directly affects the ability of a network IPS to efficiently and accurately detect an attack.

Network IPS gives security managers real-time security insight into their networks regardless of growth. Additional hosts can be added to protected networks without requiring more sensors. Additional sensors are only required when their rated traffic capacity is exceeded, when their performance does not meet current needs, or when a revision in security policy or network design requires additional sensors to help enforce security boundaries. When new networks are added, additional sensors are easy to deploy.

Refer to
Figure
in online course

Cisco 1900, 2900, and 3900 ISR G2s can be configured (using CLI or CCP) to support IPS features using Cisco IOS IPS, which is part of the Cisco IOS Firewall feature set. This does not require the installation of an IPS module but does require downloading signature files and adequate memory to load the signatures. However, this deployment should be limited to a small organization with limited traffic patterns.

For larger volumes of traffic, Cisco IPS sensors can be implemented using standalone appliances or as modules added to network devices.

In addition to Cisco IOS IPS, Cisco offers a variety of modular and appliance-based IPS solutions:

- *Cisco IPS Advanced Integration Module (AIM) and Network Module Enhanced (IPS NME)* Integrates IPS onto a Cisco ISR used for small and medium-sized business (SMB) and branch office environments. It provides advanced, enterprise-class IPS functions and meets the ever-increasing security needs of branch offices. It can also scale in performance to match branch office WAN bandwidth requirements, while keeping the solution cost low for businesses of all sizes. Not all Cisco IOS images support IPS features. Administrators must check the Cisco IOS software and hardware to ensure compatibility. Cisco IOS IPS and Cisco IPS AIM / IPS NME cannot be used together. Cisco IOS IPS must be disabled when the Cisco IPS AIM is installed.

- *Cisco IPS 4200 Series Sensors* Combines inline intrusion prevention services with innovative technologies that improve accuracy in detecting, classifying, and stopping threats including worms, spyware and adware, and network viruses. As a result, more threats can be stopped without the risk of dropping legitimate network traffic. Cisco IPS Sensor Software Version 5.1 includes enhanced detection capabilities and improved scalability, resiliency, and performance features.

■ ***Cisco Catalyst 6500 Series Intrusion Detection System Services Module (IDSM-2)*** As part of the Cisco IPS solution, it works in combination with the other components to efficiently protect the data infrastructure.

■ ***IPS functionality for the ASAs*** IPS functionality within the ASA can be provided in the form of integrated services or through a separate module. The Cisco Adaptive Security Appliance Advanced Inspection and Prevention Security Services Module (ASA AIP-SSM) and the Cisco ASA Advanced Inspection and Prevention Security Services Card (AIP-SSC) use advanced inspection and prevention technology to provide high-performance security services such as intrusion prevention services and advanced anti-X services.

With the increased complexity of security threats, achieving efficient network intrusion security solutions is critical to maintaining a high level of protection. Vigilant protection ensures business continuity and minimizes the effect of costly intrusions.

Refer to
Figure
in online course

The choice of a sensor varies depending on the requirements of the organization. There are several factors that affect the IPS sensor selection and deployment:

■ Amount of network traffic

■ Network topology

■ Security budget

■ Available security staff to manage IPS

Small implementations such as branch offices might only require a Cisco IOS IPS-enabled ISR router. As traffic patterns increase, the ISR can be configured to offload IPS functions using an IPS Network Module Enhanced (NME) or IPS Advanced Integration Module (AIM).

Larger installations can be deployed using an existing ASA 5500 appliance with an ASA Advanced Inspection and Prevention (AIP).

Enterprises and service providers might require a dedicated IPS appliance or a Catalyst 6500 using an IDSM-2 network module.

Refer to
Figure
in online course

Network IPS has several advantages and disadvantages. One advantage is that a network-based monitoring system can easily see attacks that are occurring across the entire network. This provides a clear indication of the extent to which the network is being attacked. In addition, because the monitoring system is examining traffic only from the network, it does not have to support every type of operating system that is used on the network.

There are also disadvantages of network IPS. If network data is encrypted this can essentially blind network IPS, allowing attacks to go undetected. Another problem is that IPS has a difficult time reconstructing fragmented traffic for monitoring purposes. Finally, as networks become larger in terms of bandwidth, it becomes more difficult to place network IPS at a single location and successfully capture all traffic. Eliminating this problem requires using more sensors throughout the network, which increases costs.

5.2 IPS Signatures

5.2.1 IPS Signature Characteristics

Refer to
Figure
in online course

To stop incoming malicious traffic, the network must first be able to identify it. Fortunately, malicious traffic displays distinct characteristics or "signatures." A signature is a set of rules that an IDS and an IPS use to detect typical intrusive activity, such as DoS attacks. These signatures uniquely identify specific worms, viruses, protocol anomalies, or malicious traffic. IPS sensors are tuned to look for matching signatures or abnormal traffic patterns. IPS signatures are conceptually similar to the virus.dat file used by virus scanners.

As sensors scan network packets, they use signatures to detect known attacks and respond with predefined actions. A malicious packet flow has a specific type of activity and signature. An IDS or IPS sensor examines the data flow using many different signatures. When a sensor matches a signature with a data flow, it takes action, such as logging the event or sending an alarm to IDS or IPS management software.

Signatures have three distinctive attributes:

- Type
- Trigger (alarm)
- Action

Signature Types

Refer to
Figure
in online course

Signature types are generally categorized as atomic or composite.

Atomic

An atomic signature is the simplest type of signature. It consists of a single packet, activity, or event that is examined to determine if it matches a configured signature. If it does, an alarm is triggered, and a signature action is performed. Because these signatures can be matched on a single event, they do not require an intrusion system to maintain state information. State refers to situations in which multiple packets of information are required that are not necessarily received at the same time. For example, if there was a requirement to maintain state, it would be necessary for the IDS or IPS to track the three-way handshake of established TCP connections. With atomic signatures, the entire inspection can be accomplished in an atomic operation that does not require any knowledge of past or future activities.

Detecting atomic signatures consumes minimal resources (such as memory) on the IPS or IDS device. These signatures are easy to identify and understand because they are compared against a specific event or packet. Traffic analysis for these atomic signatures can usually be performed very quickly and efficiently. For example, a LAND attack is an atomic signature because it sends a spoofed TCP SYN packet (connection initiation) with the IP address of the target host and an open port as both source and destination. The reason a LAND attack works is because it causes the machine to reply to itself continuously. One packet is required to identify this type of attack. An IDS is particularly vulnerable to an atomic attack because, until it finds the attack, malicious single packets are allowed into the network. However, an IPS prevents these packets from entering the network altogether.

Composite

A composite signature is also called a stateful signature. This type of signature identifies a sequence of operations distributed across multiple hosts over an arbitrary period of time. Unlike atomic signatures, the stateful properties of composite signatures usually require several pieces of data to match an attack signature, and an IPS device must maintain state. The length of time that the signatures must maintain state is known as the event horizon.

The length of an event horizon varies from one signature to another. An IPS cannot maintain state information indefinitely without eventually running out of resources. Therefore, an IPS uses a configured event horizon to determine how long it looks for a specific attack signature when an initial signature component is detected. Configuring the length of the event horizon is a tradeoff between consuming system resources and being able to detect an attack that occurs over an extended period of time.

Refer to **Figure** in online course

Network security threats are occurring more frequently and spreading more quickly. As new threats are identified, new signatures must be created and uploaded to an IPS. To make this process easier, all signatures are contained in a signature file and uploaded to an IPS on a regular basis.

The signature file contains a package of network signatures intended as an update to the signature database resident in a Cisco product with IPS or IDS functions. This signature database is used by the IPS or IDS solution to compare network traffic against data patterns within the signature-file library. The IPS or IDS uses this comparison to detect suspected malicious network traffic behavior.

For example, the LAND attack is identified in the "Impossible IP Packet" signature (signature 1102.0). A signature file contains that signature and many more. Networks deploying the latest signature files are better protected against network intrusions.

Refer to **Figure** in online course

To make the scanning of signatures more efficient, Cisco IOS software relies on signature micro-engines (SME), which categorize common signatures in groups. Cisco IOS software can then scan for multiple signatures based on group characteristics, instead of one at a time.

When IDS or IPS is enabled, an SME is loaded or built on the router. When an SME is built, the router might need to compile the regular expression found in a signature. A regular expression is a systematic way to specify a search for a pattern in a series of bytes.

The SME then looks for malicious activity in a specific protocol. Each engine defines a set of legal parameters with allowable ranges or sets of values for the protocols and the fields the engine inspects. Atomic and composite packets are scanned by the micro-engines that recognize the protocols contained in the packets. Signatures can be defined using the parameters offered by the SME.

Each SME extracts values from the packet and passes portions of the packet to the regular expression engine. The regular expression engine can search for multiple patterns at the same time.

The available SMEs vary depending on the platform, Cisco IOS version, and version of the signature file. Cisco IOS Release 12.4(6)T defines five micro-engines:

- *Atomic* Signatures that examine simple packets, such as ICMP and UDP.

- *Service* Signatures that examine the many services that are attacked.

- *String* Signatures that use regular expression-based patterns to detect intrusions.

- *Multi-string* Supports flexible pattern matching and Trend Labs signatures.

- *Other* Internal engine that handles miscellaneous signatures.

SMEs are constantly being updated. For example, before Release 12.4(11)T, the Cisco IPS signature format used version 4.x. Since IOS 12.4(11)T, Cisco introduced version 5.x, an improved IPS signature format. The new version supports encrypted signature parameters and other features such as signature risk rating, which rates the signature on security risk.

There are a few factors to consider when determining router requirements for maintaining signatures. First, compiling a regular expression requires more memory than the final storage of the regular expression. Determine the final memory requirements of the finished signature before loading and merging signatures. Assess how many signatures the various router platforms can actually support. The number of signatures and engines that can adequately be supported depends only on the memory available. For this reason, configure Cisco IOS IPS-enabled routers with the maximum amount of memory possible.

Refer to
Figure
in online course

Cisco investigates and creates signatures for new threats and malicious behavior as they are discovered and publishes them regularly. Typically, lower priority IPS signature files are published bi-weekly. If the threat is severe, Cisco publishes signature files within hours of identification.

To protect a network, the signature file must be updated regularly. Each update includes new signatures and all the signatures in the previous version. For example, signature file IOS-S595-CLI.pkg includes all signatures in file IOS-S594-CLI.pkg plus signatures created for threats discovered subsequently.

Just as virus checkers must constantly update their virus database, network administrators must be vigilant and regularly update the IPS signature file. New signatures are available from cisco.com. A CCO login is required to retrieve signatures.

5.2.2 IPS Signature Alarms

Signature Alarm

Refer to
Figure
in online course

The heart of any IPS signature is the signature alarm, often referred to as the signature trigger. Consider a home security system. The triggering mechanism for a burglar alarm could be a motion detector that detects the movement of an individual entering a room protected by an alarm.

The signature trigger for an IPS sensor could be anything that can reliably signal an intrusion or security policy violation. A network IPS might trigger a signature action if it detects a packet with a payload containing a specific string going to a specific port. A host-based IPS might trigger a signature action when a specific function call is invoked. Anything that can reliably signal an intrusion or security policy violation can be used as a triggering mechanism.

The Cisco IDS and IPS sensors (Cisco IPS 4200 Series Sensors and Cisco Catalyst 6500 - IDSM) can use four types of signature triggers:

- Pattern-based detection

- Anomaly-based detection

- Policy-based detection

- Honey pot-based detection

These triggering mechanisms can be applied to both atomic and composite signatures. The triggering mechanisms can be simple or complex. Every IPS incorporates signatures that use one or more of these basic triggering mechanisms to trigger signature actions.

Another common triggering mechanism is called protocol decodes. Instead of simply looking for a pattern anywhere in a packet, protocol decodes break down a packet into the fields of a protocol and then search for specific patterns in a specific protocol field or some other malformed aspect of the protocol fields. The advantage of protocol decodes is that it enables a more granular inspection of traffic and reduces the number of false positives (traffic that generates an alert but is not a threat to the network).

Pattern-Based Detection

Refer to
Figure
in online course

Pattern-based detection, also known as signature-based detection, is the simplest triggering mechanism because it searches for a specific, pre-defined pattern. A signature-based IDS or IPS sensor compares the network traffic to a database of known attacks and triggers an alarm or prevents communication if a match is found.

The signature trigger might be textual, binary, or even a series of function calls. It can be detected in a single packet (atomic) or in a sequence of packets (composite). In most cases, the pattern is matched to the signature only if the suspect packet is associated with a particular service or destined to and from a particular port. This matching technique helps to lessen the amount of inspection done on every packet. However, it makes it more difficult for systems to deal with protocols and attacks that do not utilize well-defined ports, such as Trojan Horses and their associated traffic, which can move at will.

At the initial stage of incorporating pattern-based IDS or IPS, before the signatures are tuned, there can be many false positives. After the system is tuned and adjusted to the specific network parameters, there are fewer false positives than with a policy-based approach.

Anomaly-Based Detection

Refer to **Figure** in online course

Anomaly-based detection, also known as profile-based detection, involves first defining a profile of what is considered normal for the network or host. This normal profile can be learned by monitoring activity on the network or specific applications on the host over a period of time. It can also be based on a defined specification, such as an RFC. After defining normal activity, the signature triggers an action if excessive activity occurs beyond a specified threshold that is not included in the normal profile.

The advantage of anomaly-based detection is that new and previously unpublished attacks can be detected. Instead of having to define a large number of signatures for various attack scenarios, the administrator simply defines a profile for normal activity. Any activity that deviates from this profile is then abnormal and triggers a signature action.

Despite this obvious advantage, several disadvantages can make anomaly-based signatures hard to use. For example, an alert from an anomaly signature does not necessarily indicate an attack. It indicates only a deviation from the defined normal activity, which can sometimes occur from valid user traffic. As the network evolves, the definition of normal usually changes, so the definition of normal must be redefined.

Another consideration is that the administrator must guarantee that the network is free of attack traffic during the learning phase. Otherwise, the attack activity will be considered normal traffic. Precautions should be taken to ensure that the network is free of attacks while establishing normal activity. However, it can be difficult to define normal traffic because most networks consist of a heterogeneous mixture of systems, devices, and applications that continually change.

When a signature does generate an alert, it might be difficult to correlate that alert back to a specific attack, because the alert indicates only that non-normal traffic has been detected. More analysis is required to determine whether the traffic represents an actual attack and what the attack actually accomplished. In addition, if the attack traffic happens to be similar to normal traffic, the attack might go undetected altogether.

Policy-Based Detection

Refer to **Figure** in online course

Policy-based detection, also known as behavior-based detection, is similar to pattern-based detection, but instead of trying to define specific patterns, the administrator defines behaviors that are suspicious based on historical analysis.

The use of behaviors enables a single signature to cover an entire class of activities without having to specify each individual situation. For example, having a signature that triggers an action when an email client invokes cmd.exe enables the administrator to apply the signature to any application whose behavior mimics the basic characteristics of an email client without having to apply the signature to each email client application individually. Therefore, if a user installs a new email application, the signature still applies.

Honey Pot-Based Detection

Honey pot-based detection uses a dummy server to attract attacks. The purpose of the honey pot approach is to distract attacks away from real network devices. By staging different types of vulnerabilities in the honey pot server, administrators can analyze incoming types of attacks and malicious traffic patterns. They can then use this analysis to tune their sensor signatures to detect new types of malicious network traffic. Honey pot systems are rarely used in production environments. Antivirus and other security vendors tend to use them for research.

Refer to
Figure
in online course

Cisco has implemented IPS functions into its Cisco IOS software. Cisco IOS IPS uses technology from Cisco IDS and IPS sensor product lines, including Cisco IPS 4200 Series Sensors and Cisco Catalyst 6500 Series Intrusion Detection System Services Module (IDSM).

There are many benefits to using the Cisco IOS IPS solution:

- It uses the underlying routing infrastructure to provide an additional layer of security.

- Because Cisco IOS IPS is inline and is supported on a broad range of routing platforms, attacks can be effectively mitigated by denying malicious traffic from both inside and outside the network.

- When used in combination with Cisco IDS, Cisco IOS Firewall, VPN, and Network Admission Control (NAC) solutions, Cisco IOS IPS provides threat protection at all entry points to the network.

- It is supported by easy and effective management tools, such as CCP.

- The size of the signature database supported by the device depends on the amount of available memory in the router.

5.2.3 Tuning IPS Signature Alarms

Refer to
Figure
in online course

Triggering False Alarms

Triggering mechanisms can generate alarms that are false positives or false negatives. These alarms must be addressed when implementing an IPS sensor.

A false positive alarm is an expected but undesired result. A false positive occurs when an intrusion system generates an alarm after processing normal user traffic that should not have triggered an alarm. Analyzing false positives limits the time that a security analyst has to examine actual intrusive activity on a network. If this occurs, the administrator must be sure to tune the IPS to change these alarm types to true negatives. A true negative describes a situation in which normal network traffic does not generate an alarm.

A false negative is when an intrusion system fails to generate an alarm after processing attack traffic that the intrusion system is configured to detect. It is imperative that the intrusion system does not generate false negatives, because it means that known attacks are not being detected. The goal is to render these alarm types as true positive. A true positive describes a situation in which an intrusion system generates an alarm in response to known attack traffic.

Refer to
Figure
in online course

Alarms trigger when specific parameters are met. An administrator must balance the number of incorrect alarms that can be tolerated with the ability of the signature to detect actual intrusions. If there are too few alarms, suspect packets might be allowed into the network, but network traffic flows more quickly. But if IPS systems use untuned signatures, they produce many false positive alarms.

A signature is tuned to one of four levels (listed alphabetically), based on the perceived severity of the signature:

- *High* Attacks used to gain access or cause a DoS attack are detected, and an immediate threat is extremely likely.

- *Informational* Activity that triggers the signature is not considered an immediate threat, but the information provided is useful information.

- *Low* Abnormal network activity is detected that could be perceived as malicious, but an immediate threat is not likely.

- *Medium* Abnormal network activity is detected that could be perceived as malicious, and an immediate threat is likely.

There are several factors to consider when implementing the alarms that a signature uses:

- The level assigned to the signature determines the alarm severity level.

- When tuning a signature alarm, the severity level of the signature should be the same as the severity level of the alarm.

- To minimize false positives, the administrator must study the existing network traffic patterns and then tune the signatures to recognize intrusion patterns that are atypical.

Signature tuning should be based on the actual network traffic patterns.

5.2.4 IPS Signature Actions

Refer to
Figure
in online course

Whenever a signature detects the activity for which it is configured, the signature triggers one or more actions. Several actions can be performed:

- Generate an alert.

- Log the activity.

- Drop or prevent the activity.

- Reset a TCP connection.

- Block future activity.

- Allow the activity.

The available actions depend on the signature type and the platform.

Refer to
Figure
in online course

Generating an Alert

Monitoring the alerts generated by network-based and host-based IPS systems is vital to understanding the attacks being launched against the network. If an attacker causes a flood of bogus alerts, examining these alerts can overload the security analysts. Both network- and host-based IPS solutions incorporate two types of alerts to enable an administrator to efficiently monitor the operation of the network: atomic alerts and summary alerts. Understanding these types of alerts is critical to providing the most effective protection for a network.

Atomic Alerts

Atomic alerts are generated every time a signature triggers. In some situations, this behavior is useful and indicates all occurrences of a specific attack. However, an attacker might be able to flood the monitor console with alerts by generating thousands of bogus alerts against the IPS device or applications.

Summary Alerts

Instead of generating alerts for each instance of a signature, some IPS solutions enable the administrator to generate summary alerts. A summary alert is a single alert that indicates multiple occurrences of the same signature from the same source address or port. Alarm summary modes limit the number of alerts generated and make it difficult for an attacker to consume resources on the sensor.

With the summarization modes, the administrator also receives information on the number of times that the activity that matches a signature's characteristics was observed during a specific period of time. When using alarm summarization, the first instance of intrusive activity usually triggers a normal alert. Then, other instances of the same activity (duplicate alarms) are counted until the end of the signature's summary interval. When the length of time specified by the summary interval has elapsed, a summary alarm is sent, indicating the number of alarms that occurred during the time interval.

Some IPS solutions also enable automatic summarization even though the default behavior is to generate atomic alerts. In this situation, if the number of atomic alerts exceeds a configured threshold in a specified amount of time, the signature automatically switches to generating summary alerts instead of atomic alerts. After a defined period of time, the signature reverts to its original configuration. Automatic summarization enables the administrator to automatically regulate the number of alerts being generated.

As a hybrid between atomic alerts and summary alerts, some IPS solutions also enable the generation of a single atomic alert and then disable alerts for that signature and source address for a specific period of time. This prevents an administrator from getting overwhelmed with alerts while still indicating that a specific system shows suspicious activity.

Logging the Activity

Refer to
Figure
in online course

In some situations, an administrator does not necessarily have enough information to stop an activity. Therefore, logging the actions or packets that are seen so that they can be analyzed later in more detail is very important. By performing a detailed analysis, an administrator can identify exactly what is taking place and make a decision as to whether it should be allowed or denied in the future.

For example, if an administrator configures a signature to look for the string **/etc/password** and to log the action with the attacker's IP address whenever the signature triggers, the IPS device begins logging the traffic from the attacker's IP address for a specified period of time or number of bytes. This log information is usually stored on the IPS device in a specific file. Because the signature also generates an alert, the administrator can observe the alert on the management console. Then the log data can be retrieved from the IPS device, and the activity that the attacker performed on the network after triggering the initial alarm can be analyzed.

Dropping or Preventing the Activity

Refer to
Figure
in online course

One of the most powerful actions that an IPS device can perform is to drop packets or prevent an activity from occurring. This action enables the device to stop an attack before it has the chance to perform malicious activity. Unlike a traditional IDS device, the IPS device actively forwards packets across two of its interfaces. The analysis engine determines which packets should be forwarded and which packets should be dropped.

Besides dropping individual packets, the drop action can be expanded to drop all packets for a specific session or even all packets from a specific host for a certain amount of time. By dropping traffic for a connection or host, the IPS conserves resources without having to analyze each packet separately.

Refer to
Figure
in online course

Resetting a TCP Connection

The TCP Reset Signature Action is a basic action that can be used to terminate TCP connections by generating a packet for the connection with the TCP RST flag set. Many IPS devices use the TCP reset action to abruptly end a TCP connection that is performing unwanted operations. The reset TCP connection action can be used in conjunction with deny packet and deny connection actions. Deny packet and deny flow actions do not automatically cause TCP reset actions to occur.

Blocking Future Activity

Most IPS devices have the capability to block future traffic by having the IPS device update the access control lists (ACLs) on one of the infrastructure devices. The ACL stops traffic from an attacking system without requiring the IPS to consume resources analyzing the traffic. After a configured period of time, the IPS device removes the ACL. Network IPS devices usually provide this blocking functionality along with other actions such as dropping unwanted packets. One advantage of the blocking action is that a single IPS device can stop traffic at multiple locations throughout the network, regardless of the location of the IPS device. For example, an IPS device located deep within the network can apply ACLs at the perimeter router or firewall.

Allowing the Activity

The final action is the Allow Signature action. It might seem a little confusing, because most IPS devices are designed to stop or prevent unwanted traffic on a network. The allow action is necessary so that an administrator can define exceptions to configured signatures. When an IPS device is configured to disallow certain activities, sometimes there is a need to allow a few systems or users to be exceptions to the configured rule. Configuring exceptions enables administrators to take a more restrictive approach to security because they can first deny everything and then allow only the activities that are needed.

For example, suppose that the IT department routinely scans its network using a common vulnerability scanner. This scanning causes the IPS to trigger various alerts. These are the same alerts that the IPS generates if an attacker scans the network. By allowing the alerts from the approved IT scanning host, an administrator can protect the network from intrusive scans while eliminating the false positives generated by the routine IT-approved scanning.

Some IPS devices provide the allow action indirectly through other mechanisms, such as signature filters. If an IPS does not provide the allow action directly through an action such as permit or allow, the administrator needs to search the product documentation to find the mechanism used to enable exceptions to signatures.

5.2.5 Managing and Monitoring IPS

Refer to
Figure
in online course

Monitoring the security-related events on a network is also a crucial aspect of protecting a network from attack. Although an IPS can prevent numerous attacks against a network, understanding which attacks are being launched against the network enables an administrator to assess how strong the current protections are and what enhancements may be required as the network grows. Only by monitoring the security events on a network can an administrator accurately identify the attacks and security policy violations that are occurring.

Refer to
Figure
in online course

Management Method

IPS sensors can be managed individually or centrally. Configuring each IPS device individually is the easiest process if there are only a couple of sensors. For example, a network deploying Cisco IOS IPS on a few routers could be managed using CCP. Managing many IPS routers and IPS sensors individually becomes difficult and time-consuming.

In a larger network, a centralized management system that allows the administrator to configure and manage all IPS devices from a single central system should be deployed. Using a centralized management approach for large sensor deployments reduces time and staffing requirements and enables greater visibility to all events occurring on a network.

Event Correlation

Event correlation refers to the process of correlating attacks and other events that are happening simultaneously at different points across a network. Using Network Time Protocol (NTP) and having the devices derive their time from an NTP server enables all alerts generated by the IPS to be accurately time-stamped. A correlation tool can then correlate the alerts based on their time-stamps. The administrator should enable NTP on all network devices to time-stamp events with a common system time. These time-stamps can then be used to accurately assess when specific network events happened in relation to other events, regardless of which device detected the event.

Another factor that facilitates event correlation is deploying a centralized monitoring facility on a network. By monitoring all IPS events at a single location, an administrator greatly improves the accuracy of event correlation.

Security Staff

IPS devices tend to generate numerous alerts and other events during network traffic processing. Large enterprises require the appropriate security staff to analyze this activity and determine how well the IPS is protecting the network. Examining these alerts also enables security operators to tune the IPS and optimize the IPS operation to the unique requirements of the network.

Incident Response Plan

If a system is compromised on a network, a response plan must be implemented. The compromised system should be restored to the state it was in before the attack. It must be determined if the compromised system led to a loss of intellectual property or the compromise of other systems on the network.

Refer to
Figure
in online course

Although the CLI can be used to configure an IPS deployment, it is simpler to use a GUI-based device manager. Several Cisco device management software solutions are available to help administrators manage an IPS solution. Some provide locally managed IPS solutions while others provide more centrally managed solutions.

CCP is used on an ISR router to manage an IPS implementation. Multiple IPS sensors can be managed using either Cisco IPS Manager Express (IME) or Cisco Security Manager (CSM).

Refer to
Figure
in online course

IPS sensors and Cisco IOS IPS, generate alarms when an enabled signature is triggered. These alarms are stored on the sensor and can be viewed locally, or through a management application, such as IPS Manager Express.

Upon detecting an attack signature, the Cisco IOS IPS feature can send a syslog message or an alarm in Secure Device Event Exchange (SDEE) format. This format was developed to improve communication of events generated by security devices. It primarily communicates IDS events, but the protocol is intended to be extensible and allows additional event types to be included as they are defined.

CCP can monitor syslog and SDEE-generated events and keep track of alarms that are common in SDEE system messages, including IPS signature alarms.

An SDEE system alarm message has this type of format:

Refer to
Figure
in online course

```
%IPS-4-SIGNATURE:Sig:1107 Subsig:0 Sev:2 RFC1918 address [192.168.121.1:137 -
>192.168.121.255:137]
```

Managing signatures on many IPS devices can be difficult. To improve IPS efficiency in a network, consider using these recommended configuration best practices:

- The need to upgrade sensors with the latest signature packs must be balanced with the momentary downtime during which the network becomes vulnerable to attack.

- When setting up a large deployment of sensors, update signature packs automatically rather than manually upgrading each sensor. This gives security operations personnel more time to analyze events.

- When new signature packs are available, download them to a secure server within the management network. Use another IPS to protect this server from attack by an outside party.

- Place signature packs on a dedicated FTP server within the management network. If a signature update is not available, a custom signature can be created to detect and mitigate a specific attack.

- Configure the FTP server to allow read-only access to the files within the directory on which the signature packs are placed.

- Configure the sensors to regularly check the FTP server for new signature packs. Stagger the time of day for each sensor to check the FTP server for new signature packs, perhaps through a predetermined change window. This prevents multiple sensors from overwhelming the FTP server by asking for the same file at the same time.

- Keep the signature levels that are supported on the management console synchronized with the signature packs on the sensors.

5.2.6 IPS Global Correlation

Refer to
Figure
in online course

In addition to maintaining signature packs, Cisco IPS includes a security feature called Cisco Global Correlation. With global correlation, Cisco IPS devices receive regular threat updates from a centralized Cisco threat database called the Cisco SensorBase Network. The Cisco SensorBase Network contains real-time, detailed information about known threats on the Internet.

Participating IPS devices are part of the SensorBase Network, and receive global correlation updates that include information on network devices with a reputation for malicious activity. Similar to human social interaction, reputation is an opinion about a device on the Internet. A network device with reputation is most likely either malicious or infected. The reputation analysis data contained in the global correlation updates is factored into the analysis of network traffic. This increases IPS effectiveness, because traffic is denied or allowed based on the reputation of the source IP address.

Cisco Global Correlation is available only on the AIP-SSM.

Refer to
Figure
in online course

The IPS sensor can be configured to participate in the global correlation updates and/or in sending telemetry data. Conversely both services can be turned off.

When participating in global correlation, the Cisco SensorBase Network provides information to the IPS sensor about IP addresses with a reputation. The sensor uses this information to determine which actions, if any, to perform when potentially harmful traffic is received from a host with a known reputation. Because the global correlation database changes rapidly, the sensor must periodically download global correlation updates from the global correlation servers. It is possible to view reputation scores in events and see the reputation score of attackers. It is also possible to view statistics from the reputation filter.

Sensors installed at customer sites can also enable network participation, in which they send data to the SensorBase Network. This allows the SensorBase Network to collect nearly real-time data from sensors around the world. Communication between sensors and the SensorBase Network involves an HTTPS request and response over TCP/IP. Network participation requires a network connection to the Internet. There are three modes for network participation: off, partial participation and full participation.

Refer to
Figure
in online course

For global correlation to occur, the raw information is first collected by the SensorBase Network. The SensorBase Network is part of a larger, back-end security ecosystem, known as the Cisco Security Intelligence Operation (SIO). The purpose of Cisco SIO is to detect threat activity, research and analyze threats, and provide real-time updates and best practices to keep organizations informed and protected. Cisco SIO consists of three elements:

- Threat intelligence from the Cisco SensorBase Network

- The automatic and human development process, called the Threat Operations Center

- The automated and best practices content that is pushed to network elements in the form of dynamic updates

Cisco SIO is a security intelligence center that baselines the current state of threats on a worldwide basis, and provides the network administrative systems with valuable information to detect, prevent, and react to threats. SIO acts as an early warning system by correlating threat information from the SensorBase which has been analyzed by the Threat Operations Center. SIO then feeds this information to enforcement elements, such as an IPS device configured with global correlation. These enforcement elements provide live threat prevention based on malware outbreaks, current vulnerabilities, and zero-day attacks.

5.3 Implementing IPS

5.3.1 Configuring Cisco IOS IPS with CLI

Refer to
Figure
in online course

Cisco IOS IPS enables administrators to manage intrusion prevention on routers. Cisco IOS IPS monitors and prevents intrusions by comparing traffic against signatures of known threats and blocking the traffic when a threat is detected.

Several steps are necessary to use the Cisco IOS CLI to work with IOS IPS 5.x format signatures. Cisco IOS version 12.4(10) or earlier used IPS 4.x format signatures and some IPS commands have changed.

To implement IOS IPS:

Step 1. Download the IOS IPS files.

Step 2. Create an IOS IPS configuration directory in flash.

Step 3. Configure an IOS IPS crypto key.

Step 4. Enable IOS IPS.

Step 5. Load the IOS IPS signature package to the router.

Refer to
Figure
in online course

Cisco IOS release 12.4(10)T and earlier, provided built-in signatures in the Cisco IOS software image, as well as support for imported signatures. IPS signature selection involved loading an XML file onto the router. This file, called the signature definition file (SDF), contained a detailed description of each selected signature in Cisco IPS Sensor software 4.x signature format.

With newer IOS versions, there are no built-in (hard-coded) signatures within the Cisco IOS software. Instead, all signatures are stored in a separate signature file and must be imported. The recommended IOS release, 12.4(15)T4 or later, uses the newer 5.x format signature files. These files can be can be downloaded from Cisco.com (requires log in).

Step 1. Download the IOS IPS files.

Prior to configuring IPS, it is necessary to download the IOS IPS signature package files and public crypto key from Cisco.com. The specific IPS files to download vary depending on the current release. Only registered customers can download the package files and key.

- *IOS-Sxxx-CLI.pkg*   This is the latest signature package.

- *realm-cisco.pub.key.txt*   This is the public crypto key used by IOS IPS.

Step 2. Create an IOS IPS configuration directory in flash.

The second step is to create a directory in flash to store the signature files and configurations. Use the `mkdir` *directory-name* privileged EXEC command to create the directory. IOS IPS supports any Cisco IOS file system as the configuration location with proper write access. A Cisco USB flash drive connected to the USB port of the router can be used as an alternative location to store the signature files and configurations. The USB flash drive must remain connected to the USB port of the router if it is used as the IOS IPS configuration directory location.

Other commands that are useful include `rename` *current-name new-name*. This allows the administrator to change the name of the directory. To verify the contents of flash, enter the `dir flash:` privileged EXEC command.

Refer to
Figure
in online course

Step 3. Configure an IOS IPS crypto key.

Next, configure the crypto key used by IOS IPS. This key is located in the realm-cisco.pub.key.txt file that was downloaded in Step 1.

The crypto key verifies the digital signature for the master signature file (sigdef-default.xml). The content of the file is signed by a Cisco private key to guarantee its authenticity and integrity.

To configure the IOS IPS crypto key, open the text file, copy the contents of the file, and paste the contents to the router at the global configuration prompt. The text file issues the various commands to generate the RSA key.

At the time of signature compilation, an error message is generated if the public crypto key is invalid. This is an example of an error message:

`%IPS-3-INVALID_DIGITAL_SIGNATURE: Invalid Digital Signature found (key not found)`

If the key is configured incorrectly, the key must be removed and then reconfigured. Use the `no crypto key pubkey-chain rsa` and the `no named-key realm-cisco.pub signature` commands to reconfigure the key.

Enter the `show run` command at the router prompt to confirm that the crypto key is configured.

Refer to
Figure
in online course

Step 4. Enable IOS IPS.

The fourth step is to configure IOS IPS, which is a process that consists of four substeps.

Step 1.   Identify the IPS rule name and specify the location.

Use the **ip ips name** [*rule name*] [*optional ACL*] command to create a rule name. An optional extended or standard access control list (ACL) can be configured to filter the scanned traffic. All traffic that is permitted by the ACL is subject to inspection by the IPS. Traffic that is denied by the ACL is not inspected by the IPS.

Use the **ip ips config location flash:***directory-name* command to configure the IPS signature storage location. Prior to IOS 12.4(11)T, the **ip ips sdf location** command was used.

Step 2. **Enable SDEE and logging event notification.**

To use SDEE, the HTTP server must first be enabled with the **ip http server** command. If the HTTP server is not enabled, the router cannot respond to the SDEE clients because it cannot see the requests. SDEE notification is disabled by default and must be explicitly enabled. Use the **ip ips notify sdee** command to enable IPS SDEE event notification. IOS IPS also supports logging to send event notification. SDEE and logging can be used independently or enabled at the same time. Logging notification is enabled by default. If the logging console is enabled, IPS log messages are displayed on the console. Use the **ip ips notify log** command to enable logging.

Step 3. **Configure the signature category.**

All signatures are grouped into categories, and the categories are hierarchical. This helps classify signatures for easy grouping and tuning. The three most common categories are **all**, **basic**, and **advanced**.

The signatures that IOS IPS uses to scan traffic can be retired or unretired. Retiring a signature means that IOS IPS does not compile that signature into memory for scanning. Unretiring a signature instructs IOS IPS to compile the signature into memory and use it to scan traffic. When IOS IPS is first configured, all signatures in the **all** category should be retired. Then selected signatures should be unretired in a less memory-intensive category. To retire and unretired signatures, first enter IPS category mode using the **ip ips signature-category** command. Next use the **category** *category-name* command to change a category. For example, use the **category all** command to enter IPS category **all** action mode. To retire a category, use the **retired true** command. To unretire a category, use the **retired false** command.

CAUTION: Do not unretire the **all** category. The **all** signature category contains all signatures in a signature release. The IOS IPS cannot compile and use all the signatures at one time, because it will run out of memory.

The order in which the signature categories are configured on the router is also important. IOS IPS processes the category commands in the order listed in the configuration. Some signatures belong to multiple categories. If multiple categories are configured and a signature belongs to more than one of them, IOS IPS uses the signature's properties in the last configured category, for example, retired, unretired, or actions.

Step 4. **Apply the IPS rule to a desired interface, and specify the direction.**

Use the **ip ips** *rule-name* [**in** | **out**] interface configuration command to apply the IPS rule. The **in** argument means that only traffic going into the interface is inspected by IPS. The **out** argument specifies that only traffic going out of the interface is inspected.

Step 5. Load the IOS IPS Signature Package to the Router.

Refer to **Figure** in online course

The last step is for the administrator to upload the signature package to the router. The most common methods are either FTP or TFTP. To copy the downloaded signature package from the FTP server to the router, make sure to use the `idconf` parameter at the end of the command.

```
copy ftp://ftp_user:password@Server_IP_address/signature_package idconf
```

To verify that the signature package is properly compiled, the administrator uses the `show ip ips signature count` command.

5.3.2 Configuring Cisco IOS IPS with CCP

Refer to
Figure
in online course

CCP provides controls for applying Cisco IOS IPS on interfaces, importing and editing signature files from Cisco.com, and configuring the action that Cisco IOS IPS takes if a threat is detected. The tasks for managing routers and security devices are displayed in a task pane on the left side of the CCP home page. Choose **Configure > Security > Intrusion Prevention** to display the intrusion prevention options in CCP.

For the CCP host computer, a minimum Java memory heap size of 256MB is required to configure IOS IPS. If an error is generated when attempting to access the Intrusion Prevention window, the Java memory heap size must be changed on the host computer. To do so, exit CCP and open the Windows Control Panel. Click on the **Java** option which opens the Java Control Panel. Select the Java tab and click on the **View** button under the Java Applet Runtime Settings. In the Java Runtime Parameter field enter exactly **-Xmx256m** and click **OK**.

After the Java memory heap size is correctly configured, CCP displays five tabs in the Intrusion Prevention Systems (IPS) window. Use the tabs at the top of the IPS window to configure or monitor IPS.

- *Create IPS* Launch the IPS Rule wizard used to create a new IPS rules on an interface and specify the location of the signature definition file.
- *Edit IPS* Edit Cisco IOS IPS rules and apply or remove them from interfaces.
- *Security Dashboard* View the Top Threats table and deploy signatures associated with those threats.
- *IPS Sensor* Manage the IPS sensor, make failover settings, and configure ACLs for the monitored interfaces.
- *IPS Migration* Migrate Cisco IOS IPS configurations that were created using earlier releases of the Cisco IOS Software. IPS Migration is not available in releases prior to Cisco IOS Release 12.4(11)T.

The administrator can use CCP to create a new rule on a Cisco router either manually through the Edit IPS tab, or automatically using the IPS Rule wizard.

The Cisco IOS IPS Deployment Guide recommends using the IPS Rule wizard. The wizard does more than just configure a rule. It performs all the Cisco IOS IPS configuration steps.

Refer to
Figure
in online course

Prior to configuring IPS with CCP, download the latest IPS signature file and public key, if required, from Cisco.com. Configuring Cisco IOS IPS on a router or security device using CCP involves several steps:

Step 1.   Launch CCP. Choose **Configure > Security > Intrusion Prevention > Create IPS**.

Step 2.   Click the **Launch IPS Rule Wizard** button. If SDEE notification is not enabled on the router, a notice will appear stating that CCP will open a subscription with the router to get SDEE events. Click **OK**.

Step 3.   Read the Welcome to the IPS Policies Wizard screen and click **Next**.

Step 4.   In the Select Interfaces window, choose the interfaces to which to apply the IPS rule and the direction of traffic by checking one or both of the boxes. Checking the inbound and the outbound boxes applies the rule to traffic flowing in both directions. Click **Next**.

Refer to
Figure
in online course

Cisco IOS IPS examines traffic by comparing it against signatures contained in a signature definition file (SDF). The SDF can be located in router flash memory or on a remote system that the router can reach. You can specify multiple SDF locations so that if the router is not able to contact the first location, it can attempt to contact other locations until it obtains an SDF

Step 5. In the Signature File pane in the Signature File and Public Key window, select either the **Specify the signature file you want to use with IOS IPS** or **Get the latest signature file from Cisco.com and save to PC** option and fill in the appropriate text box. The signature file is an IOS IPS update package with the naming convention of IOS-S*nnn*-CLI.pkg, where *nnn* is the number of the signature set.

Step 6. If you already have a copy of the signature file and do not need to download it from Cisco.com, then click the [. . .] button beside the **Specify the signature file you want to use with IOS IPS** option. The Specify Signature File window appears. In the Specify Signature File window, select how you would like the router to access the file. For example, the router can access the signature file using a flash file, through TFTP, or via a saved location on the PC. If you do not have a copy of the signature file and want to download the latest signature file from Cisco.com, select **Get the latest signature file from Cisco.com and save to PC** option button. Click the **Browse** button to specify the location on the PC where the file should be downloaded to and then click **Download**.

The Cisco IOS IPS signature file contains default signature information. Any changes made to this configuration are not saved to the signature file but rather in a special file called the delta file. The delta file is saved to router flash memory. For security, the delta file must be digitally signed by a key which is also obtained from Cisco.com.

Refer to **Figure** in online course

Step 7. If the public crypto-key was not previously downloaded and saved to the PC, download the public crypto-key from Cisco.com. Open the public key file in a text editor and copy the text after the phrase "named-key" into the **Name** field. For example, if the line of text is "named-key realm-cisco.pub signature" copy "realm-cisco.pub signature" to the **Name** field.

Step 8. Copy the text between the phrase "key-string" and the word "quit" into the **Key** field. The text might look as follows:

```
30820122 300D0609 2A864886 F70D0101 01050003 82010F00 3082010A 02820101
00C19E93 A8AF124A D6CC7A24 5097A975 206BE3A2 06FBA13F 6F12CB5B 4E441F16
17E630D5 C02AC252 912BE27F 37FDD9C8 11FC7AF7 DCDD81D9 43CDABC3 6007D128
B199ABCB D34ED0F9 085FADC1 359C189E F30AF10A C0EFB624 7E0764BF 3E53053E
5B2146A9 D7A5EDE3 0298AF03 DED7A5B8 9479039D 20F30663 9AC64B93 C0112A35
FE3F0C87 89BCB7BB 994AE74C FA9E481D F65875D6 85EAF974 6D9CC8E3 F0B08B85
50437722 FFBE85B9 5E4189FF CC189CB9 69C46F9C A84DFBA5 7A0AF99E AD768C36
006CF498 079F88F8 A3B3FB1F 9FB7B3CB 5539E1D1 9693CCBB 551F78D2 892356AE
2F56D826 8918EF3C 80CA4F4D 87BFCA3B BFF668E9 689782A5 CF31CB6E B4B094D3
F3020301 0001
```

Click **Next**.

Refer to **Figure** in online course

If using Cisco IOS Release 12.4(11) or later, the location for storing signature information and the type of signature category can be specified.

Step 9. In the Config Location and Category window, in the Config Location section, click the ellipsis [. . .] button next to the **Config Location** field to specify where to store the XML signature files, including the delta file that is created when changes are made to the signature file.

Step 10. Because router memory and resource constraints can limit using all the available signatures, choose a category in the **Choose Category** field that allows the Cisco IOS IPS to function efficiently on the router. The **basic** signature category is appropriate for routers with less than 128 MB of flash memory, and the **advanced** signature category is appropriate for routers with more than 128 MB of flash memory. Click **Next**.

Step 11.   Click **Finish**. The IPS Policies Wizard confirms the configured information in a summary screen.

Use the `show running-config` command to verify the IPS configuration generated by the CCP IPS Wizard.

5.3.3 Modifying Cisco IOS IPS Signatures

Refer to
Figure
in online course

The Cisco IOS CLI can be used to retire or unretire individual signatures or a group of signatures that belong to a signature category. When a group of signatures are retired or unretired, all signatures in that category are retired or unretired.

Some unretired signatures (either unretired as an individual signature or within an unretired category) might not compile because of insufficient memory, invalid parameters, or if the signature is obsolete.

Refer to
Figure
in online course

The IOS CLI can also be used to change signature actions for one signature or a group of signatures based on signature categories. To change an action, the `event-action` command must be used in IPS Category Action mode or Signature Definition Engine mode.

The `event-action` command has several parameters, including `produce-alert`, `deny-packet-in-line`, and `reset-tcp-connection`.

Refer to
Figure
in online course

IPS signatures are loaded as part of the procedure to create a Cisco IOS IPS rule using the IPS rule wizard. To view the configured signatures on the router, choose **Configure > Security > Intrusion Prevention > Edit IPS > Signatures**. Confirm that all the correct signatures are loaded on the router or security device. From this window, administrators can add customized signatures or import signatures that are downloaded from Cisco.com. They can also edit, delete, enable, and disable signatures.

The signature tree enables an administrator to filter the signature list according to the type of signature to be viewed. To modify a signature, right-click it and select an option from the context menu. To change the severity of the signature, select **Set Severity To**, and select the appropriate severity level from the list.

Refer to
Figure
in online course

CCP can be used to tune a signature configuration. To tune a signature, choose **Configure > Security > Intrusion Prevention > Edit IPS > Signatures**. The list of available signatures appears.

To modify a signature action, right-click the signature and select **Actions** from the context menu. The Assign Actions window appears. The available actions depend on the signature, but the following are the most common actions:

- **Deny Attacker Inline** Create an ACL that denies all traffic from the IP address that is considered the source of the attack by the Cisco IOS IPS system.

- **Deny Connection Inline** Drop the packet and all future packets from this TCP flow.

- **Deny Packet Inline** Do not transmit this packet (inline only).

- **Produce Alert** Generate an alarm message.

- **Reset TCP Connection** Send TCP resets to terminate the TCP flow.

Refer to
Figure
in online course

To access and configure signature parameters, choose the signature and then click the **Edit** button in the Intrusion Prevention System (IPS) window.
Signatures have different parameters:

- **Signature ID** Displays the unique numerical value that is assigned to this signature. This value allows Cisco IOS IPS to identify a particular signature.

- **SubSignature ID** Displays the unique numerical value that is assigned to this subsignature. A subsignature ID identifies a more granular version of a broad signature.

- *Alert Severity* Displays the severity of the alert for this signature.

- *Sig Fidelity Rating* Displays the confidence level of detecting a true positive.

- *Promiscuous Delta* Displays the value used to determine the seriousness of the alert. It is not recommended to change the promiscuous delta setting.

- *Sig Description* Includes the signature name, alert notes, user comments, alert traits, and release number.

- *Engine* Contains information about which engine the signature uses and characteristics about how the engine operates.

- *Event Counter* Displays the event count, the event count key, and whether an alert interval is to be specified. An alert interval allows the administrator to define special handling for timed events.

- *Alert Frequency* Includes settings to define the frequency of the alert.

- *Status* Shows whether the signature is enabled or retired.

5.4 Verify and Monitor IPS

5.4.1 Verifying Cisco IOS IPS

Refer to
Figure
in online course

After IPS is implemented, it is necessary to verify the configuration to ensure correct operation. There are several **show** commands which can be used to verify the IOS IPS configuration.

- The **show ip ips** privileged EXEC command can be used with other parameters to provide specific IPS information.

- The **show ip ips all** command displays all IPS configuration data. The output can be lengthy depending on the IPS configuration.

- The **show ip ips configuration** command displays additional configuration data that is not displayed with the **show running-config** command.

- The **show ip ips interfaces** command displays interface configuration data. The output shows inbound and outbound rules applied to specific interfaces.

- The **show ip ips signatures** command verifies the signature configuration. The command can also be used with the key word **detail** to provide more explicit output.

- The **show ip ips statistics** command displays the number of packets audited and the number of alarms sent. The optional **reset** keyword resets output to reflect the latest statistics.

Use the **clear ip ips configuration** command to disable IPS, remove all IPS configuration entries, and release dynamic resources. The **clear ip ips statistics** command resets statistics on packets analyzed and alarms sent.

Refer to
Figure
in online course

To verify the IPS configuration on the router using CCP, choose **Configure > Security > Intrusion Prevention > Edit IPS**. The default window for the Edit IPS tab is IPS Policies, which shows all the interfaces on the router and whether they are configured for Cisco IOS IPS. If "Enabled" appears in either the Inbound or Outbound column, Cisco IOS IPS is enabled for that direction of traffic on that interface. If "Disabled" appears in either column, Cisco IOS IPS is disabled for that direction on the interface.

The Virtual Fragment Reassembly (VFR) Status field shows the status of VFR on an interface. If VFR is enabled on the interface, the column displays "On." If VFR is disabled, the column displays "Off."

The Edit IPS tab also contains buttons that allow the administrator to configure and manage Cisco IOS IPS policies, security messages, and signatures.

5.4.2 Monitoring Cisco IOS IPS

Refer to
Figure
in online course

Cisco IOS IPS provides two methods to report IPS intrusion alerts:

- CCP Security Device Event Exchange (SDEE)

- Cisco IOS logging via syslog

To specify the method of event notification, use the `ip ips notify [log ¦ sdee]` global configuration command:

- The `log` keyword sends messages in syslog format.

- The `sdee` keyword sends messages in SDEE format.

Refer to
Figure
in online course

SDEE is the preferred method of reporting IPS activity. SDEE uses HTTP and XML to provide a standardized interface. It can be enabled on an IOS IPS router using the `ip ips notify sdee` command. The Cisco IOS IPS router can still send IPS alerts via syslog.

Administrators must also enable HTTP or HTTPS on the router when enabling SDEE. The use of HTTPS ensures that data is secured as it traverses the network.

When Cisco SDEE notification is disabled, all stored events are lost. A new buffer is allocated when the notifications are re-enabled. SDEE uses a pull mechanism. With a pull mechanism, requests come from the network management application, and the IDS or IPS router responds. SDEE becomes the standard format for all vendors to communicate events to a network management application.

The buffer stores up to 200 events by default. If a smaller buffer is requested, all stored events are lost. If a larger buffer is requested, all stored events are saved. The default buffer size can be altered with the `ip sdee events` *events* command. The maximum number of events is 1,000. The `clear ip ips sdee {events ¦ subscription}` command clears SDEE events or subscriptions.

The `ip ips notify` command replaces the older `ip audit notify` command. If the `ip audit notify` command is part of an existing configuration, the IPS interprets it as the `ip ips notify` command.

Refer to
Figure
in online course

Management software such as Cisco IPS Manager Express or CCP must be used to view SDEE messages. For example, to view SDEE alarm messages in CCP, choose **Monitor > Router > Logging**. Select the SDEE Message Log tab. Syslog messages can also be viewed from this page.

To monitor IPS signature statistics and alert statistics, select **Monitor > Security > IPS Status**.

Chapter Summary

Refer to **Figure** in online course

Refer to **Packet Tracer Activity** for this chapter

Refer to **Lab Activity** for this chapter

Your Chapter Notes

CHAPTER 6

Securing the Local Area Network

Chapter Introduction

Refer to
Figure
in online course

A secure network is only as strong as its weakest link. For this reason, in addition to securing the network edge, it is also important to secure the end devices that reside within the network. Endpoint security includes securing the network infrastructure devices in the LAN as well as the end systems, such as workstations, servers, IP phones, access points, and storage area networking (SAN) devices. There are several endpoint security applications and devices available to accomplish this, including Cisco IronPort security appliances and Network Admission Control (NAC).

Endpoint security also encompasses securing Layer 2 of the network infrastructure to prevent against Layer 2 attacks such as MAC address spoofing and STP manipulation attacks. Layer 2 security configurations include enabling port security, BPDU guard, root guard, storm control, and PVLAN Edge.

Finally, the type of security solutions implemented depends upon the type of LAN technologies used. For example, networks that employ wireless, VoIP, and SANs technologies have additional security considerations and solutions.

In a comprehensive hands-on lab for the chapter, *Securing Layer 2 Switches*, learners configure the following on a Layer 2 switch: SSH access, storm control for broadcasts, PortFast, BPDU guard, root guard, port security, Switched Port Analyzer, and PVLAN Edge. Learners also verify the configurations, monitor port activity using Wireshark, and analyze a sourced attack.

A Packet Tracer activity, *Layer 2 Security*, provides learners additional practice implementing the technologies introduced in this chapter. Learners secure STP parameters to mitigate STP attacks, enable storm control to prevent broadcast storms, and enable port security to prevent MAC address table overflow attacks.

In a second Packet Tracer activity, *Layer 2 VLAN Security*, learners create a management VLAN, attach a management PC to the management VLAN, and implement an ACL to prevent outside users from accessing the management VLAN.

6.1 Endpoint Security

6.1.1 Introducing Endpoint Security

Refer to
Figure
in online course

The high-profile threats most often discussed in the media are external threats, such as Internet worms and DoS attacks. But securing an internal local area network (LAN) is just as important as securing the perimeter of a network. Without a secure LAN, users in an organization may not be able to access the network, which can significantly reduce productivity.

Many network administrators develop their security strategy from the perimeter of a network and work toward the LAN. Other administrators develop their network security strategy at the LAN and work toward the perimeter. Regardless of the approach, two specific areas that are vital to secure are the endpoints and the network infrastructure.

The LAN is made up of network endpoints. An endpoint, or host, is an individual computer system or device that acts as a network client. Common endpoints are laptops, desktops, IP phones, and personal digital assistants (PDAs). Servers can also be considered endpoints. The LAN-to-perimeter security strategy is based on the idea that if users are not practicing security in their desktop operations, no amount of security precautions will guarantee a secure network.

The network infrastructure is the other area of focus for securing the LAN. Part of securing a LAN is mitigating attacks. These attacks include MAC address spoofing attacks, STP manipulation attacks, MAC address table overflow attacks, LAN storm attacks, and VLAN attacks. Another element to securing the network infrastructure is securing the non-endpoint LAN devices. These include switches, wireless devices, IP telephony devices, and storage area networking (SAN) devices.

Refer to
Figure
in online course

In the past, company employees worked and data resources resided within a clearly defined perimeter. This perimeter was protected by firewalls at the border. Employees typically used company-issued computers connected to a corporate LAN. Today, consumerized devices, such as iPhones, BlackBerrys, and netbooks are blurring the network border. It is increasingly common that primary business resources, including data centers, applications, endpoints, as well as users, all exist outside the traditional business perimeter. Cisco calls this the borderless network. In this new borderless network, access to resources can be initiated by users from many locations, on many types of endpoint devices, using various connectivity methods.

In addition to the concept of borderless networks, cloud computing has blurred the network border. Cloud computing allows organizations to use services such as data storage or cloud-based applications to extend their capacity or capabilities without adding infrastructure. By its very nature, the cloud is outside of the traditional network perimeter. So, an organization may be faced with a data center that may or may not reside behind the traditional perimeter.

Traditional network security consists of two major components: a heavy endpoint protection suite (antivirus, personal firewall, etc.) and perimeter-based, network-scanning devices (firewalls, web proxies, and email gateways). This architecture worked well in a world of high-powered PCs that were mainly on the LAN and behind the firewall. But, in a network of mobile workers using personal devices from a variety of locations, this model does not work.

The new network devices are not good candidates for the traditional antivirus endpoint suite. They were designed to be lightweight and portable. Additionally, with blurred network borders, there are many entrances into the network. There is no longer a network perimeter. The challenge is how to allow these heterogeneous devices to connect to enterprise resources securely. To address these very issues, Cisco created the SecureX architecture.

The SecureX security architecture for the borderless network relies on a lightweight, pervasive endpoint. Its role is not to scan content or run signatures. Instead, its sole focus is making sure every connection coming on or off the endpoint is pointed at a network scanning element somewhere in a Cisco security cloud. These scanning elements are now capable of running many more layers of scanning than a single endpoint possibly could: five layers of malware signatures, data loss prevention and acceptable use policies, content scanning, and more.

Refer to
Figure
in online course

Operating systems provide basic security services to applications:

- *Trusted code and trusted path* Ensures that the integrity of the operating system is not violated. Trusted code refers to the assurance that the operating system code is not compromised. An operating system might provide integrity checking of all running code by using hash message authentication codes (HMACs) or digital signatures. Integrity verification of add-on software might be necessary at installation. Digital signatures can also be used. Trusted path refers to a facility that ensures that the user is using a genuine system and not a Trojan Horse. An example of a trusted path is the Ctrl-Alt-Delete key sequence for locking the screen or logging off Windows Server and Windows 7 operating systems.

- *Privileged context of execution* Provides identity authentication and certain privileges based on the identity.

- *Process memory protection and isolation* Provides separation from other users and their data.

- *Access control to resources* Ensures confidentiality and integrity of data.

An attacker can undermine all of these services. If either the trusted code or a trusted path is not present or is compromised, the operating system and all applications can easily be subverted by hostile code. An operating system might be made more vulnerable if there is a need to provide support for legacy protocols.

Refer to
Figure
in online course

Modern operating systems provide each process with an identity and privileges. Privilege switching is possible during program operation or during a single login session. For example, UNIX uses the **suid** (**set user ID**) facility and Windows uses the **runas** utility.

These are a few techniques that help protect an endpoint from operating system vulnerabilities:

- *Least privilege concept* To better protect en endpoint, a process should never be given more privilege than is necessary to perform a job.

- *Isolation between processes* Isolation between processes can be virtual or physical. For example, memory protection can be done in hardware. Some trusted operating systems provide isolation using logical execution compartments.

- *Reference monitor* A reference monitor is an access control concept that refers to a mechanism or process that mediates all access to objects. It provides a central point for all policy decisions, typically implementing auditing functions to keep track of access.

- *Small, verifiable pieces of code* For all security functionality, it is desirable to have small, easily verifiable pieces of code that are managed and monitored by a reference monitor.

The ultimate target of an attacker is often an application running on a host that processes sensitive data that the attacker wants to obtain. Attacks to applications can be direct or indirect. In a direct attack, the attacker fools the application into performing a task with the application's privileges. In an indirect attack, the attacker first compromises another subsystem and attacks the application through the compromised subsystem (privilege escalation).

When an attacker has the option of communicating directly with the target application, the application must be suitably protected. For example, an attacker might attempt a DoS attack to a specific application. Another example of a direct attack to a target application is if an attacker uses flaws in the application to bypass its access controls to obtain read or write access to sensitive data.

In another scenario, an attacker indirectly gains access to sensitive data through a chain of compromises of other system components. For example, an attacker first obtains basic user-level access to the system on which the sensitive data resides. Then, by exploiting a flaw in any local application, the attacker attains system administration privileges (privilege escalation). Using those privileges, the attacker might be able to read or write to most objects on the system, including sensitive data of the target application.

Refer to
Figure
in online course

Cisco Systems provides several components to ensure a robust endpoint security solution. Two primary components of this solution are: IronPort and Cisco NAC.

Cisco IronPort perimeter security appliances protect enterprises against Internet threats, with a focus on email and web security, two of the main endpoint security considerations. Endpoints in this case are secured by devices working on the network perimeter.

NAC uses the network infrastructure to enforce security policy compliance on all devices seeking to access network computing resources. With NAC, network security professionals can authenticate, authorize, evaluate, and remediate wired, wireless, and remote users and their machines prior to network access. NAC identifies whether networked devices are compliant with the network security policies and repairs any vulnerability before permitting access to the network.

IronPort and NAC have some overlap in their functional support of endpoint security. These technologies, when used in parallel, add layers of protection and are interoperable. They combine to provide protection of operating system vulnerabilities against both direct and indirect attacks.

While there are a number of alternatives to the endpoint security solutions provided by Cisco Systems, the limitation of these other systems is that they do not provide a comprehensive end-to-end approach to securing the network. Some of the major players in providing endpoint security solutions are McAfee, Symantec, Juniper, SonicWALL, and Fortinet.

6.1.2 Endpoint Security with IronPort

Refer to
Figure
in online course

Cisco Systems acquired IronPort Systems in 2007. IronPort is a leading provider of anti-spam, antivirus, and anti-spyware appliances. IronPort uses SenderBase, the world's largest threat detection database, to help provide preventive and reactive security measures.

IronPort offers different security appliances:

- *C-Series* An email security appliance for virus and spam control.

- *S-Series* A web security appliance for spyware filtering, URL filtering, and anti-malware.

- *M-Series* A security management appliance that compliments the email and web security appliances by managing and monitoring an organization's policy settings and audit information.

The M-Series appliance is a flexible management tool for centralizing and consolidating policy and runtime data, providing security professionals a single interface to manage all of their application layer security systems.

IronPort helps prevent Internet threats of all types from reaching the desktops of employees.

Refer to
Figure
in online course

IronPort SenderBase is the world's largest email traffic monitoring service. SenderBase collects data from more than 100,000 ISPs, universities, and corporations. It measures more than 120 different parameters for any email server on the Internet. This massive database receives more than five billion queries per day, with real-time data streaming in from every continent and both small and large network providers. SenderBase has the most accurate view of the sending patterns of any given mail sender because of the size of the database. It has remained the largest in the world because of the accuracy of the data. IronPort licenses SenderBase data to the open-source community and other institutions that are participating in the fight against spam.

The eight largest ISPs and more than 20 percent of the largest enterprises in the world use the IronPort C-Series email security appliances. By protecting the email systems of enterprises of all sizes, the downtime that is associated with spam, viruses, and a wide variety of other threats has been reduced. The system also reduces the burden on technical staff.

Refer to
Figure
in online course

Spyware has become one of the most significant corporate security issues. More than 80 percent of corporate PCs are infected with spyware, yet less than 10 percent of corporations have deployed perimeter spyware defenses. The speed, variety, and maliciousness of spyware and web-based malware attacks have highlighted the importance of a robust, secure platform to protect the enterprise network perimeter from such threats. The IronPort S-Series is a fast web security appliance that offers multiple anti-malware scanning engines on a single, integrated appliance. The S-Series includes IronPort's exclusive Web Reputation technology and Dynamic Vectoring and Streaming engine, a new scanning technology that enables signature-based spyware filtering.

A security professional can run the scanning engines simultaneously to offer greater protection against malware threats, with minimal performance degradation. It provides protection against a wide variety of web-based threats, ranging from adware, phishing, and pharming attacks to more malicious threats such as Trojan Horses, worms, and other system monitoring attacks.

6.1.3 Endpoint Security with Network Admission Control

Refer to
Figure
in online course

The purpose of Cisco NAC is twofold: allow only authorized and compliant systems (whether managed or unmanaged) to access the network, and to enforce network security policy.

NAC helps maintain network stability by providing four important features: authentication and authorization, posture assessment (evaluating an incoming device against the policies of the network), quarantining of noncompliant systems, and remediation of noncompliant systems.

Cisco NAC products come in two general categories:

- *NAC framework* The NAC framework uses the existing Cisco network infrastructure and third-party software to enforce security policy compliance on all endpoints. The NAC framework is suited for high-performance network environments with diverse endpoints. These environments require a consistent LAN, WAN, wireless, extranet, and remote access solution that integrates into the existing security and patch software, tools, and processes. Different devices in the network, not necessarily one device, can provide the four features of NAC.

- *Cisco NAC Appliance* The Cisco NAC Appliance solution condenses the four NAC functions into an appliance form and provides a turnkey solution to control network access. This solution is a natural fit for medium-sized networks requiring a self-contained, turnkey solution. The Cisco NAC Appliance is ideal for organizations that need simplified and integrated tracking of operating system and antivirus patches and vulnerability updates. It does not require a Cisco network.

With Cisco NAC Appliance (formerly Cisco Clean Access), the network infrastructure is used to enforce security policy compliance on all devices that attempt to gain access. The Cisco NAC Appliance can be used to authenticate, authorize, evaluate, and remediate wired, wireless, and remote users before they can access the network. The Cisco NAC Appliance can be used to:

- Recognize users, their devices, and their roles in the network

- Evaluate whether machines are compliant with security policies

- Enforce security policies by blocking, isolating, and repairing noncompliant machines

- Provide easy and secure guest access

- Simplify non-authenticating device access

- Audit and report whom is on the network

Cisco NAC Appliance extends NAC to all network access methods, including access through LANs, remote-access gateways, and wireless access points. It also supports posture assessment for guest users.

Refer to
Figure
in online course

The components of a NAC framework provide compliance-based access control. NAC works in conjunction functions, including authentication, authorization, and accounting (AAA), scanning, and remediation, are performed by other Cisco products, such as a Cisco Secure Access Control Server (ACS), or partner products such as TrendMicro.

The goal of both the NAC framework and the Cisco NAC Appliance is to ensure that only hosts that are authenticated and have had their security posture examined and approved are permitted onto the network. For example, company laptops used offsite for a period of time might not have received current security updates or could have become infected from other systems. Those systems cannot connect to the network until they are examined, updated and approved.

Network access devices function as the enforcement layer. They force the clients to query a RADIUS server for authentication and authorization. The RADIUS server can query other devices, such as a TrendMicro antivirus server, and reply to the network enforcers.

Refer to
Figure
in online course

Cisco Secure Access Control products are part of the NAC Appliance-based Cisco TrustSec solution. TrustSec is a core component of the Secure Borderless Networks architecture. In the NAC Appliance-based TrustSec approach, Cisco NAC Manager (NAM) is a policy server that works with Cisco NAC Server (NAS) to authenticate users and assess their devices over LAN, wireless, or VPN connections. Access to the network and resources is based on user credentials and their roles in the organization, as well as the policy compliance of endpoint devices.

- *Cisco NAC Manager (NAM)* the policy and management center for an appliance-based NAC deployment environment, Cisco NAC Manager defines role-based user access and endpoint security policies.

- *Cisco NAC Server (NAS)* assesses and enforces security policy compliance in an appliance-based NAC deployment environment.

- *Cisco NAC Agent (NAA)* an optional lightweight agent running on an endpoint device. It performs deep inspection of the device's security profile by analyzing registry settings, services, and files.

Additional TrustSec Policy enforcement tools:

- *Cisco NAC Guest Server* manages guest network access, including provisioning, notification, management, and reporting of all guest user accounts and network activities

- *Cisco NAC Profiler* helps to deploy policy-based access control by providing discovery, profiling, policy-based placement, and post-connection monitoring of all endpoint devices.

Refer to
Figure
in online course

Cisco NAC Guest Server provides guest policy enforcement to either the Cisco NAC Appliance or the Cisco Wireless LAN Controller, where guest policies are enforced. Cisco NAC Guest Server, a component of the Cisco TrustSec solution, provides full guest access lifecycle support, including provisioning, notification, management, and reporting.

The Cisco NAC Guest Server solution helps IT and security administrators to:

- Cut operational costs and reduce the workload for IT and support staff

- Improve guest access security by applying consistent policies, reducing human errors, and terminating guest access after each visit

- Boost customer and partner productivity and satisfaction, by helping guests easily access online resources

- Address compliance and audit requirements by generating guest-user activity and history reports

Cisco NAC Guest Server provides the ability for sponsors (employees of the company) to create guest accounts. Sponsors are authenticated on the guest server and are granted permissions based upon their roles. Sponsors can be given role-based permissions to create accounts, edit accounts, suspend accounts and run reporting. These permissions can be granted in one of three ways: to accounts they created, to all accounts, or to none. After a guest account is created, guests can log into the network with the details provided to them by the sponsor.

Refer to
Figure
in online course

Cisco NAC Profiler enables the dynamic discovery, identification, and monitoring of all network-attached endpoints within an enterprise network. It manages these devices intelligently, based on user-defined security policies.

When deployed as part of a broader Network Admission Control (NAC) implementation, Cisco NAC Profiler facilitates deployment and management of Cisco NAC systems. It discovers and tracks the location and type of all LAN-attached endpoints, including those that cannot authenticate.

Cisco NAC Profiler enables security administrators to:

- Simplify deployment of Cisco NAC by automating device identification and authentication and easing administrative tasks.

- Facilitate deployment and management of the Cisco ACS 802.1x-based infrastructure or Cisco NAC overlay solutions.

- Gather endpoint device profiling information and maintain a real-time, contextual inventory of networked devices.

- Monitor and manage device behavior anomalies, such as port swapping, MAC address spoofing, and profile changes.

- Secure all company-owned endpoints, including non-authenticating devices such as printers and IP phones.

Cisco NAC Profiler has two components: the NAC Profiler Server and the NAC Profiler Collector application.

The Profiler Server houses the database, provides access to the administrator's user interface, and communicates with the Cisco NAC Appliance Manager (NAM). The Cisco NAM provides a web-based interface for creating security policies and managing online users. It can also act as an authentication proxy to authenticate servers on the back end. Administrators can use it to establish user roles, compliance checks, and remediation requirements. The Cisco NAM communicates with and manages the enforcement component of the Cisco NAC Appliance.

The NAC Profiler Collector application resides on each NAC Appliance Server. The NAC Profiler Collector application comprises the following modules:

- *NetWatch* the "sniffer" component of the Cisco NAC Profiler system. It is designed to collect as much profile information as possible to populate the modeling engine.

- *NetMap* consults with every network device through SNMP to determine network topology information. As part of the Profiler Collector, NetMap uses the Cisco NAC Appliance Server's host address to communicate with the network devices.

- *NetInquiry* the active profiling component, used to communicate directly with network endpoints to learn information about the end system.

- *NetTrap* collects link-state and MAC information from network access devices to provide real-time data of endpoints joining and leaving the network.

Cisco NAC Profiler generates an automated inventory of all endpoints, including those known to be non-responsive hosts, and automatically populates them into the Filters List of the Cisco NAM. Information contained within the Filters List includes the MAC address of each endpoint, the device type (i.e., network printer, IP phone, wireless access point, etc.), and the appropriate level of access for that endpoint.

Changes in the endpoint environment are detected and made to the Filters List automatically. For example, if a network printer is moved and connected to a new port, the Filters List will be dynamically updated. This feature also enhances security. For example, if a device is doing something on the network that is inconsistent with its profiled device type, Cisco NAC Profiler will notify the Cisco NAC Appliance to remove the suspect endpoint from the Filters List.

6.2 Layer 2 Security Considerations

6.2.1 Introducing Layer 2 Security

Refer to **Figure** in online course

Network security professionals must mitigate attacks within the Layer 2 infrastructure. These attacks include MAC address spoofing, STP manipulation, MAC address table overflows, LAN storms, and VLAN attacks.

The first step in mitigating attacks such as these is to understand the underlying threats posed by the Layer 2 infrastructure. Layer 2 can be a very weak link to the higher OSI Layers because if Layer 2 is compromised, hackers can work their way up. It is important for the network security professional to remember that Layer 2 attacks typically require internal access, either from an employee or visitor.

Another fundamental consideration is buffer overflows. Buffer overflows are often the source of a DoS attack. Buffer overflows can be used to enable the execution of arbitrary code into a program and unauthorized privilege escalation.

Refer to **Figure** in online course

Layer 2 is the Data Link Layer in the OSI model. It is one of the seven layers designed to work together but with autonomy. Layer 2 operates above the Physical Layer and below the Network and Transport Layers. Layer 2 independence enables interoperability and interconnectivity. From a security perspective, Layer 2 independence creates a challenge because when the layer is compromised, other layers are not aware of that fact, leaving them open to being compromised. Network security is only as strong as the weakest link, and that link is often the Data Link Layer.

To help prevent Layer 2 exploitations, an application must carefully validate user input. The input might contain improperly formatted data, control sequences, or too much data, such as with buffer overflows. Remember, buffer overflow exploits try to overwrite memory on an application.

Buffer overflows are perhaps the most common method of application subversion on the Internet today. They are mostly used to gain access to root privileges or cause a DoS attack.

Various tools are available to prevent buffer overflows.

6.2.2 MAC Address Spoofing Attacks

Refer to **Figure** in online course

Unlike hubs, switches regulate the flow of data between ports by creating instant networks that contain only the two endpoint devices communicating with each other at that moment in time. Switches accomplish this by forwarding data out specific ports based on the MAC address. Switches maintain MAC address tables, also known as content-addressable memory (CAM) lookup tables, to track the source MAC addresses associated with each switch port. These lookup tables are populated by an address-learning process on the switch.

It is important to note that data frames are sent by end systems, and their source and destination addresses are not changed throughout the switched domain. If a switch receives an incoming data frame and the destination MAC address is not in the table, the switch forwards the frame out all ports, except for the port on which it was received. When the destination node responds, the switch records the MAC address of the node in the address table from the frame source address field. Switches populate the MAC address table by recording the source MAC address of a frame, and associating that address with the port on which the frame is received.

In networks with multiple interconnected switches, the MAC address tables record multiple MAC addresses for the ports interconnecting switches. These MAC addresses reflect remote nodes or nodes that are connected to another switch within the switched domain.

The method used by switches to populate the MAC address table leads to a vulnerability known as MAC spoofing. Spoofing attacks occur when one host masquerades or poses as another to receive otherwise inaccessible data or to circumvent security configurations.

Refer to
Figure
in online course

MAC spoofing attacks occur when an attacker alters the MAC address of their host to match another known MAC address of a target host. The attacking host then sends a frame throughout the network with the newly configured MAC address. When the switch receives the frame, it examines the source MAC address. The switch overwrites the current MAC address table entry and assigns the MAC address to the new port. It then inadvertently forwards frames destined for the target host to the attacking host.

When the switch changes the MAC address table, the target host does not receive any traffic until it sends traffic. When the target host sends traffic, the switch receives and examines the frame, resulting in the MAC address table being rewritten once more, realigning the MAC address to the original port.

6.2.3 MAC Address Table Overflow Attacks

Refer to
Figure
in online course

In addition to MAC spoofing attacks, Layer 2 devices are vulnerable to MAC address table overflow attacks. Remember that switches use MAC addresses to direct network communications through their switch fabric to the appropriate port toward the destination node. The term fabric refers to the integrated circuits and the accompanying machine programming that enables device operation. For example, the switch fabric is responsible for controlling the data paths through the switch. The MAC address table in a switch contains the MAC addresses that can be reached from a given physical port of a switch and the associated VLAN parameters for each. When a Layer 2 switch receives a frame, the switch looks in the MAC address table for the destination MAC address and forwards the frames appropriately.

The key to understanding how MAC address overflow attacks work is to know that MAC address tables are limited in size. MAC flooding takes advantage of this limitation by bombarding the switch with fake source MAC addresses until the switch MAC address table is full. If enough entries are entered into the MAC address table before older entries expire, the table fills up to the point that no new entries can be accepted. When this occurs, the switch begins to flood all incoming traffic to all ports because there is no room in the table to learn any legitimate MAC addresses. The switch, in essence, acts like a hub. As a result, the attacker can see all of the frames sent from one host to another. Traffic is flooded only within the local VLAN, so the intruder sees only traffic within the local VLAN to which the intruder is connected.

If the intruder does not maintain the flood of invalid source MAC addresses, the switch eventually ages out the older MAC address entries from the table and begins to act like a switch again.

Refer to
Figure
in online course

The most common way of implementing a MAC address table overflow attack is using the **macof** tool. This tool floods a switch with frames containing randomly generated source and destination MAC and IP addresses. Over a short period of time, the MAC address table fills up. When the MAC address table is full of invalid source MAC addresses, the switch begins to flood all frames that it receives. As long as **macof** is left running, the table on the switch remains full, and the switch continues to flood all received frames out of every port.

Both MAC spoofing and MAC address table overflow attacks can be mitigated by configuring port security on the switch. With port security, the administrator can either statically specify the MAC addresses on a particular switch port or allow the switch to dynamically learn a fixed number of MAC addresses for a switch port. To statically specify the MAC addresses is not a manageable solution for a production environment. Allowing the switch to dynamically learn a fixed number of MAC addresses is an administratively scalable solution.

6.2.4 STP Manipulation Attacks

Refer to
Figure
in online course

Another vulnerability of Layer 2 devices is the Spanning Tree Protocol (STP). STP is a Layer 2 protocol that ensures a loop-free topology. STP operates by electing a root bridge and building a tree topology from that root. STP allows for redundancy, but at the same time, ensures that only one link is operational at a time and no loops are present.

Network attackers can manipulate STP to conduct an attack by changing the topology of a network. An attacker can make it appear that the attacking host is a root bridge, thereby spoofing the root bridge. All traffic for the immediate switched domain then passes through the rogue root bridge (the attacking system).

Refer to
Figure
in online course

To conduct an STP manipulation attack, the attacking host broadcasts STP configuration and topology change BPDUs to force spanning-tree recalculations. The BPDUs sent by the attacking host announce a lower bridge priority in an attempt to be elected as the root bridge. If successful, the attacking host becomes the root bridge and sees a variety of frames that otherwise are not accessible.

This attack can be used to defeat all three of the security objectives: confidentiality, integrity, and availability.

Mitigation techniques for STP manipulation include enabling PortFast as well as root guard and BPDU guard.

6.2.5 LAN Storm Attack

Refer to
Figure
in online course

Layer 2 devices are also vulnerable to LAN storm attacks. A LAN storm occurs when packets flood the LAN, creating excessive traffic and degrading network performance. Errors in the protocol stack implementation, mistakes in network configurations, or users issuing a DoS attack can cause a storm. Broadcast storms can also occur on networks. Remember that switches always forward broadcasts out all ports. Some necessary protocols, such as ARP and DHCP, use broadcasts; therefore, switches must be able to forward broadcast traffic.

Refer to
Figure
in online course

While it is not possible to prevent all types of packet storms and excessive broadcasts, it is possible to suppress them using storm control. Storm control prevents traffic on a LAN from being disrupted by a broadcast, multicast, or unicast storm on one of the physical interfaces. Storm control (or traffic suppression) monitors packets passing from an interface to the switching bus and determines if the packet is unicast, multicast, or broadcast. The switch counts the number of packets of a specified type received within a certain time interval and compares the measurement with a predefined suppression-level threshold. Storm control then blocks traffic when the rising threshold is reached.

6.2.6 VLAN Attacks

Refer to
Figure
in online course

A VLAN is a logical broadcast domain that can span multiple physical LAN segments. Within the switched internetwork, VLANs provide segmentation and organizational flexibility. A VLAN structure can be designed to enable grouping of stations logically by function, project team, or application, without regard to the physical location of the users. Each switch port can be assigned to only one VLAN, thereby adding a layer of security. Ports in a VLAN share broadcasts; ports in different VLANs do not share broadcasts. Containing broadcasts within a VLAN improves the overall performance of the network.

Using VLAN technology, switch ports and their connected users can be grouped into logically defined communities, such as coworkers in the same department, a cross-functional product team, or diverse user groups sharing the same network application. A VLAN can exist on a single switch or span multiple switches. VLANs can include hosts in a single building or multiple-building infrastructures. VLANs can also connect across metropolitan area networks.

There are a number of different types of VLAN attacks prevalent in modern switched networks. Rather than list all the types of attacks, it is important to understand the general methodology behind these attacks and the primary approaches to mitigate them.

Refer to
Figure
in online course

The VLAN architecture simplifies network maintenance and improves performance, but it also opens the door to abuse. VLAN hopping enables traffic from one VLAN to be seen by another VLAN with the aid of a router. Under certain circumstances, attackers can sniff data and extract passwords and other sensitive information. The attack works by taking advantage of an incorrectly configured trunk port. By default, trunk ports have access to all VLANs and pass traffic for multiple VLANs across the same physical link, generally between switches. The data moving across these links might be encapsulated with IEEE 802.1Q or inter-switch link (ISL).

In a basic VLAN hopping attack, the attacker takes advantage of the default automatic trunking configuration on most switches. The network attacker configures a system to spoof itself as a switch. This spoofing requires that the network attacker be capable of emulating either ISL or 802.1Q signaling along with Cisco-proprietary Dynamic Trunking Protocol (DTP) signaling. By tricking a switch into thinking it is another switch that needs to trunk, an attacker can gain access to all the VLANs allowed on the trunk port. This attack requires a configuration on the port that supports trunking with *auto or dynamic* mode to succeed. As a result, the attacker is a member of all the VLANS that are trunked on the switch and can hop, that is, send and receive traffic on all the VLANs.

A VLAN hopping attack can be launched in one of two ways:

- Spoofing DTP messages from the attacking host to cause the switch to enter trunking mode. From here, the attacker can send traffic tagged with the target VLAN, and the switch then delivers the packets to the destination.

- Introducing a rogue switch and enabling trunking. The attacker can then access all the VLANs on the victim switch from the rogue switch.

The best way to prevent a basic VLAN hopping attack is to turn off trunking on all ports, except the ones that specifically require trunking. On the required trunking ports, disable DTP (auto trunking) negotiations and manually enable trunking.

Refer to
Figure
in online course

Another type of VLAN attack is a double-tagging (or double-encapsulated) VLAN hopping attack. This type of attack takes advantage of the way that hardware on most switches operates. Most switches perform only one level of 802.1Q decapsulation; this can allow an attacker in specific situations to embed a hidden 802.1Q tag inside the frame. This tag allows the frame to go to a VLAN that the original 802.1Q tag did not specify. An important characteristic of the double-encapsulated

VLAN hopping attack is that it works even if trunk ports are disabled (a host typically sends a frame on a segment that is not a trunk link).

A double-tagging VLAN hopping attack follows four steps:

Step 1.   The attacker sends a double-tagged 802.1Q frame to the switch. The outer header has the VLAN tag of the attacker, which is the same as the native VLAN of the trunk port. For the purposes of this example, assume that this is VLAN 10. The inner tag is the victim VLAN, in this example, VLAN 20.

Step 2.   The frame arrives on the switch, which looks at the first 4-byte 802.1Q tag. The switch sees that the frame is destined for VLAN 10, which is the native VLAN. The switch forwards the packet out on all VLAN 10 ports after stripping the VLAN 10 tag. On the trunk port the VLAN 10 tag is stripped, and the packet is not retagged since it is part of the Native VLAN. At this point, the VLAN 20 tag is still intact and has not been inspected by the first switch.

Step 3.   The frame arrives at the second switch but has no knowledge that it was supposed to be for VLAN 10. Native VLAN traffic is not tagged by the sending switch as specified in the 802.1Q specification.

Step 4.   The second switch looks only at the inner 802.1Q tag that the attacker sent and sees that the frame is destined for VLAN 20, the target VLAN. The second switch sends the frame on to the victim port or floods it, depending on whether there is an existing MAC address table entry for the victim host.

This type of attack is unidirectional and works only when the attacker is connected to a port residing in the same VLAN as the native VLAN of the trunk port. Thwarting this type of attack is not as easy as stopping basic VLAN hopping attacks. The best approach is to ensure that the native VLAN of the trunk ports is different from the VLAN of the user ports. In fact, it is considered a security best practice to use a dummy VLAN that is unused throughout the switched LAN as the native VLAN for all 802.1Q trunks in a switched LAN.

6.3 Configuring Layer 2 Security

6.3.1 Configuring Port Security

Refer to
Figure
in online course

After the vulnerabilities of a Layer 2 device are understood, the next step is to implement mitigation techniques to prevent the attacks that take advantage of those vulnerabilities. For example to prevent MAC spoofing and MAC table overflows, enable port security.

Port security allows an administrator to statically specify MAC addresses for a port or to permit the switch to dynamically learn a limited number of MAC addresses. By limiting the number of permitted MAC addresses on a port to one, port security can be used to control unauthorized expansion of the network.

When MAC addresses are assigned to a secure port, the port does not forward frames with source MAC addresses outside the group of defined addresses. When a port configured with port security receives a frame, the source MAC address of the frame is compared to the list of secure source addresses that were manually configured or autoconfigured (learned) on the port. If a MAC address of a device attached to the port differs from the list of secure addresses, the port either shuts down until it is administratively enabled (default mode) or drops incoming frames from the insecure host (restrict option). The behavior of the port depends on how it is configured to respond to a security violator.

It is recommended that an administrator configure the port security feature to issue a shutdown rather than dropping frames from insecure hosts with the restrict option. The restrict option might fail under the load of an attack.

Refer to
Figure
in online course

These are the steps for configuring port security on an access port:

Step 1.   Configure an interface as an access interface.

```
Switch(config-if)# switchport mode access
```

If an interface is in the default mode (dynamic auto), it cannot be configured as a secure port.

Step 2.   Enable port security on the interface using the `switchport port-security` command.

The complete syntax includes a number of optional parameters.

```
Switch(config-if)# switchport port-security [mac-address mac-address
[vlan {vlan-id ¦ {access ¦ voice}}]] ¦ [mac-address sticky [mac-address ¦
vlan {vlan-id ¦ {access ¦ voice}}]] [maximum value [vlan {vlan-list¦
{access ¦ voice}}]]
```

Note: Available configuration parameters are dependent on the switch model and IOS version.

Step 3.   (Optional) Set the maximum number of secure MAC addresses for the interface.

```
Switch(config-if)# switchport port-security maximum value
```

The range is 1 to 132. The default is 1.

Refer to
Figure
in online course

After port security is enabled, it is necessary to establish the violation rules for the access port. Violation rules refer to the actions that the switch takes if a security violation occurs.

These are the steps for configuring port security violation on an access port:

Step 1.   Set the violation mode. This is the action that the switch takes when a security violation is detected. If the violation mode is not specified, the default is to shut down the port.

```
Switch(config-if)# switchport port-security violation {protect ¦ restrict
¦ shutdown ¦ shutdown vlan}
```

When a secure port is in the error-disabled state, this means that a violation has occurred and the port is disabled. To bring it out of this state, enter the **errdisable recovery cause psecure-violation** global configuration command, or manually re-enable it by entering the **shutdown** and **no shutdown** interface configuration commands.

Step 2.   Enter a static secure MAC address for the interface.

```
Switch(config-if)# switchport port-security mac-address mac-address
```

Repeat this command as many times as necessary for each secure MAC address.

Step 3.   Enable sticky learning on the interface.

```
Switch(config-if)# switchport port-security mac-address sticky
```

When sticky learning is enabled, the interface adds all secure MAC addresses that are dynamically learned, up to the maximum number configured, to the running configuration and converts these addresses to sticky secure MAC addresses.

Use the **no switchport port-security** interface configuration command to return the interface to the default condition as an unsecure port. The sticky secure addresses remain part of the running configuration.

Use the **no switchport port-security maximum** value interface configuration command to return the interface to the default number of secure MAC addresses.

Use the **no switchport port-security violation {protect ¦ restrict}** interface configuration command to return the violation mode to the default condition (shutdown mode).

Refer to
Figure
in online course

Port security aging can be used to set the aging time for static and dynamic secure addresses on a port. Two types of aging are supported per port:

- *Absolute* The secure addresses on the port are deleted after the specified aging time.

- *Inactivity* The secure addresses on the port are deleted only if they are inactive for the specified aging time.

Use aging to remove secure MAC addresses on a secure port without manually deleting the existing secure MAC addresses. Aging time limits can also be increased to ensure past secure MAC addresses remain, even while new MAC addresses are added. Keep in mind the maximum number of secure addresses per port can be configured. Aging of statically configured secure addresses can be enabled or disabled on a per-port basis.

Use the **switchport port-security aging {static ¦ time** *time*¦ **type {absolute ¦ inactivity}}** command to enable or disable static aging for the secure port or to set the aging time or type.

Refer to
Figure
in online course

A typical port security configuration for a voice port requires three secure MAC addresses in order to support an IP phone and a PC. This is because when the port is connected to a Cisco IP phone, the IP phone requires up to two MAC addresses. The IP phone address is learned on the voice VLAN and might also be learned on the access VLAN. Connecting a PC to the IP phone requires an additional MAC address.

The addresses are usually learned dynamically. However, when configuring port security with an IP phone, the voice addresses cannot be made sticky.

Violations of this policy result in the port being shut down. The aging timeout for the learned MAC addresses is set to two hours.

Note: In higher-end switches, such as the Catalyst 4500 Series, using IOS versions 12.2(31)SG or later, port security is VLAN aware. Therefore only two MAC addresses are required, one for the IP phone and one for the connected PC.

6.3.2 Verifying Port Security

Refer to
Figure
in online course

When port security is enabled, the administrator should use **show** commands to verify that the port learned the MAC address. Additionally, **show** commands are useful when monitoring and troubleshooting port-security configurations. They can be used to view information such as the maximum number of MAC addresses that can be associated with a port, the violation count, and the current violation mode.

Use the **show port-security** command to view port security settings for the switch, including violation count, configured interfaces, and security violation actions.

Use the **show port-security [interface** *interface-id*] command to view port security settings for the specified interface, including the maximum allowed number of secure MAC addresses for the interface, the number of secure MAC addresses on the interface, the number of security violations that have occurred, and the violation mode.

Refer to
Figure
in online course

Use the **show port-security [interface** *interface-id*] **address** command to view all secure MAC addresses configured on all switch interfaces or on a specified interface with aging information for each address.

Refer to
Figure
in online course

Network managers need a way of monitoring who is using the network and where they are. For example, if port Fa0/1 is secure on a switch, an SNMP trap is generated when a MAC address entry for that port disappears from the MAC address table.

The MAC address notification feature sends SNMP traps to the network management station (NMS) whenever a new MAC address is added to or an old address is deleted from the forwarding tables. MAC address notifications are generated only for dynamic and secure MAC addresses.

MAC address notification allows the network administrator to monitor MAC addresses that are learned as well as MAC addresses that age out and are removed from the switch.

Use the `mac address-table notification` global configuration command to enable the MAC address notification feature on a switch.

6.3.3 Configuring BPDU Guard, BPDU Filter, and Root Guard

Refer to
Figure
in online course

To mitigate STP manipulation, the PortFast, root guard, and BPDU guard STP enhancement commands can be enabled. These features enforce the placement of the root bridge in the network and enforce the STP domain borders.

PortFast

The spanning-tree PortFast feature causes an interface configured as a Layer 2 access port to transition from the blocking to the forwarding state immediately, bypassing the listening and learning states. PortFast can be used on Layer 2 access ports that connect to a single workstation or server to allow those devices to connect to the network immediately, instead of waiting for STP to converge.

Because the purpose of PortFast is to minimize the time that access ports must wait for STP to converge, it should be used only on access ports. If PortFast is enabled on a port connecting to another switch, there is a risk of creating a spanning-tree loop.

This command configures PortFast for all non-trunking ports at once:

```
Switch(config)# spanning-tree portfast default
```

This command configures Portfast on an interface:

```
Switch(config-if)# spanning-tree portfast
```

This command verifies that PortFast has been configured on an interface:

Refer to
Figure
in online course

```
Switch# show running-config interface FastEthernet 0/8
```

BPDU Guard

The STP BPDU guard feature allows network designers to keep the active network topology predictable. BPDU guard is used to protect the switched network from the problems caused by receiving BPDUs on ports that should not be receiving them. The receipt of unexpected BPDUs might be accidental or part of an unauthorized attempt to add a switch to the network.

If a port that is configured with PortFast receives a BPDU, STP can put the port into the disabled state by using BPDU guard.

BPDU guard is best deployed toward user-facing ports to prevent rogue switch network extensions by an attacking host.

Use this command to enable BPDU guard on all ports with PortFast enabled:

```
Switch(config)# spanning-tree portfast bpduguard default
```

Refer to
Figure
in online course

To display information about the state of spanning tree, use the `show spanning-tree summary` command. In this output, BPDU guard is enabled:

```
Switch# show spanning-tree summary
Root bridge for: VLAN0001, VLAN0004-VLAN1005
```

```
VLAN1013-VLAN1499, VLAN2001-VLAN4094
EtherChannel misconfiguration guard is enabled
Extended system ID is enabled
Portfast is enabled by default
PortFast BPDU Guard is enabled
Portfast BPDU Filter is disabled by default
Loopguard is disabled by default
UplinkFast is disabled
BackboneFast is disabled
Pathcost method used is long
<output omitted>
```

Another useful command to verify BPDU guard configuration is the **show spanning-tree summary totals** command.

Refer to
Figure
in online course

BPDU Filtering

The BPDU filtering feature can be globally enabled on the switch or can be enabled per interface. There are some differences in how the feature operates based on how it is enabled. At the global level, you can enable BPDU filtering on PortFast-enabled interfaces by using the **spanning-tree portfast bpdufilter default** global configuration command. This command prevents interfaces that are in a PortFast-operational state from sending or receiving BPDUs. The interfaces still send a few BPDUs at link-up before the switch begins to filter outbound BPDUs. Globally enable BPDU filtering on a switch so that hosts connected to these interfaces do not receive BPDUs. If a BPDU is received on a PortFast-enabled interface because it is connected to a switch, the interface loses its PortFast-operational status, and BPDU filtering is disabled.

At the interface level, you can enable BPDU filtering on any interface by using the **spanning-tree bpdufilter enable** interface configuration command without also enabling the PortFast feature. This command prevents the interface from sending or receiving BPDUs. Note that enabling BPDU filtering on an interface is the same as disabling spanning tree on it and can result in spanning-tree loops.

BPDU filtering is supported with PVST+, rapid PVST+, and MSTP.

To display information about the state of spanning tree, use the **show spanning-tree summary** command.

Refer to
Figure
in online course

Root Guard

The Cisco switch root guard feature provides a way to enforce the placement of root bridges in the network. Root guard limits the switch ports out of which the root bridge can be negotiated. If a root-guard-enabled port receives BPDUs that are superior to those that the current root bridge is sending, that port is moved to a root-inconsistent state. This is effectively equal to an STP listening state, and no data traffic is forwarded across that port.

Because an administrator can manually set the bridge priority of a switch to zero, root guard may seem unnecessary. Setting the priority of a switch to zero does not guarantee that switch will be elected as the root bridge. This is because there might be another switch with a priority of zero and a lower MAC address, and therefore a lower bridge ID.

Root guard is best deployed toward ports that connect to switches that should not be the root bridge.

With root guard, if an attacking host sends out spoofed BPDUs in an effort to become the root bridge, the switch, upon receipt of a BPDU, ignores the BPDU and puts the port in a root-inconsistent state. The port recovers as soon as the offending BPDUs cease.

BPDU guard and root guard are similar, but their impact is different. BPDU guard disables the port upon BPDU reception if PortFast is enabled on the port. The disablement effectively denies devices behind such ports from participating in STP. The administrator must manually re-enable the port that is put into an errdisable state or configure an errdisable timeout.

Root guard allows the device to participate in STP as long as the device does not try to become the root. If root guard blocks the port, subsequent recovery is automatic. Recovery occurs as soon as the offending device ceases to send superior BPDUs.

This is the command for configuring root guard on an interface:

```
Switch(config-if)#spanning-tree guard root
```

To verify root guard, use the **show spanning-tree inconsistentports** command. Keep in mind that a switch places a port in a root-inconsistent state if it receives BPDUs on a port that should not be receiving BPDUs. The port recovers as soon as the offending BPDUs cease.

6.3.4 Configuring Storm Control

Refer to
Figure
in online course

LAN storm attacks can be mitigated by using storm control to monitor predefined suppression-level thresholds. When enabling storm control, both a rising threshold and a falling threshold can be set.

Storm control uses one of these methods to measure traffic activity:

- Bandwidth as a percentage of the total available bandwidth of the port that can be used by the broadcast, multicast, or unicast traffic.

- Traffic rate in packets per second at which broadcast, multicast, or unicast packets are received.

- Traffic rate in bits per second at which broadcast, multicast, or unicast packets are received.

- Traffic rate in packets per second and for small frames. This feature is enabled globally. The threshold for small frames is configured for each interface.

With each method, the port blocks traffic when the predefined rising threshold is reached. The port remains blocked until the traffic rate drops below the falling threshold if one is specified, and then resumes normal forwarding. If the falling threshold is not specified, the switch blocks all traffic until the traffic rate drops below the rising threshold. The threshold, or suppression level, refers to the number of packets allowed before action is taken. In general, the higher the suppression level the less effective the protection against broadcast storms.

Use the **storm-control** interface configuration command to enable storm control on an interface and set the threshold value for each type of traffic. The storm-control suppression level can be configured as a percentage of total bandwidth of the port, as a rate in packets per second at which traffic is received, or as a rate in bits per second at which traffic is received.

Refer to
Figure
in online course

When the traffic suppression level is specified as a percentage (up to two decimal places) of the total bandwidth, the level can be from 0.00 to 100.00. A threshold value of 100 percent means that no limit is placed on the specified type of traffic (broadcast, multicast or unicast). A value of 0.0 means that all traffic of that type on that port is blocked.

Threshold percentages are approximations because of hardware limitations and the way in which packets of different sizes are counted. Depending on the packet sizes that make up the incoming traffic, the actual enforced threshold might differ from the configured level by several percentage points.

Storm control is supported on physical interfaces. With Cisco IOS Release 12.2(25), storm control can also be configured on EtherChannels. When configuring storm control on an EtherChannel, the storm control settings propagate to the EtherChannel physical interfaces.

This is the complete syntax for the **storm-control** command.

```
storm-control {{broadcast | multicast | unicast} level {level [level-low] | bps
bps [bps-low] | pps pps [pps-low]}} | {action {shutdown | trap}}
```

The **trap** and **shutdown** options are independent of each other.

If the **trap** action is configured, the switch will send an SNMP log message when a storm occurs.

If the **shutdown** action is configured, the port is error-disabled during a storm, and the **no shut-down** interface configuration command must be used to bring the interface out of this state.

When a storm occurs and the action is to filter traffic, if the falling suppression level is not specified, the switch blocks all traffic until the traffic rate drops below the rising suppression level. If the falling suppression level is specified, the switch blocks traffic until the traffic rate drops below this level.

Refer to
Figure
in online course

Use the **show storm-control [interface]** command to verify storm control settings. This command displays storm control suppression levels set on all interfaces, or the specified interface, for the specified traffic type. If no traffic type is specified, the default is broadcast traffic.

6.3.5 Configuring VLAN Trunk Security

Refer to
Figure
in online course

The best way to mitigate VLAN hopping attacks is to ensure that trunking is only enabled on ports that require trunking. Additionally, be sure to disable DTP (auto trunking) negotiations and manually enable trunking.

To prevent a VLAN hopping attack that uses double 802.1Q encapsulation, the switch must look further into the frame to determine whether more than one VLAN tag is attached to it. Unfortunately, most switches have hardware that is optimized to look for one tag and then to switch the frame. The issue of performance versus security requires administrators to balance their requirements carefully.

Mitigating VLAN hopping attacks that use double 802.1Q encapsulation requires several modifications to the VLAN configuration. One of the more important elements is to use a dedicated native VLAN for all trunk ports. This attack is easy to stop when following the recommended practice of not using native VLANs for trunk ports anywhere else on the switch. In addition, disable all unused switch ports and place them in an unused VLAN.

Refer to
Figure
in online course

To control trunking for ports, several options are available.

For links that are not intended as trunks, use the **switchport mode access** interface configuration command to disable trunking.

There are three steps to create trunk links:

Step 1. Use the **switchport mode trunk** interface configuration command to cause the interface to become a trunk link.

Step 2. Use the **switchport nonegotiate** interface configuration command to prevent the generation of DTP frames.

Step 3. Use the **switchport trunk native vlan** *vlan_number* interface configuration command to set the native VLAN on the trunk to an unused VLAN. The default native VLAN is VLAN 1.

6.3.6 Configuring Cisco Switched Port Analyzer

Refer to
Figure
in online course

In addition to the mitigation techniques, it is also possible to configure a Layer 2 device to support traffic analysis. Network traffic passing through ports or VLANs can be analyzed by using switched port analyzer (SPAN). SPAN can send a copy of traffic from one port to another port on the same switch where a network analyzer or monitoring device is connected. SPAN copies (or mirrors) traffic received, sent, or both on source ports or source VLANs to a destination port for analysis. SPAN does not affect the switching of network traffic on the source ports or VLANs. The destination port is dedicated for SPAN use. Except for traffic that is required for the SPAN, destination ports do not receive or forward traffic. Interfaces should usually be monitored in both directions, while VLANs should be monitored in only one direction.

SPAN is not required for syslog or SNMP. SPAN is used to mirror traffic, while syslog and SNMP are configured to send data directly to the appropriate server. SPAN does not mitigate attacks, but it does enable monitoring of malicious activity.

Refer to
Figure
in online course

A SPAN session can be configured to monitor source port traffic to a destination port. For example, configure SPAN session 1 by first deleting session 1. Then configure bidirectional traffic mirroring from source Gigabit Ethernet port 0/1 to destination Gigabit Ethernet port 0/2, retaining the encapsulation method.

```
Switch(config)# monitor session 1 source interface gigabitethernet0/1
Switch(config)# monitor session 1 destination interface gigabitethernet0/2 encap-
sulation replicate
Switch(config)# end
```

Another example illustrates the capture of received and transmitted traffic for VLANs 10 and 20, respectively.

```
Switch(config)# monitor session 1 source vlan 10 rx
Switch(config)# monitor session 1 source vlan 20 tx
Switch(config)# monitor session 1 destination interface FastEthernet 3/4
```

To verify SPAN configuration, use the **show monitor session** *session-number* command.

Refer to
Figure
in online course

An intrusion detection system (IDS) has the ability to detect misuse, abuse, and unauthorized access to networked resources. SPAN can be used to mirror traffic to another port where a probe or an IDS sensor is connected. When an IDS sensor detects an intruder, the sensor can send out a TCP reset that tears down the intruder connection within the network, immediately removing the intruder from the network.

SPAN is commonly deployed when an IDS is added to a network. IDS devices need to read all packets in one or more VLANs, and SPAN can be used to get the packets to the IDS devices.

6.3.7 Configuring PVLAN Edge

Refer to
Figure
in online course

Some applications require that no traffic be forwarded at Layer 2 between ports on the same switch so that one neighbor does not see the traffic generated by another neighbor. In such an environment, the use of the Private VLAN (PVLAN) Edge feature, also known as protected ports, ensures that there is no exchange of unicast, broadcast, or multicast traffic between these ports on the switch.

The PVLAN Edge feature has the following characteristics:

- A protected port does not forward any traffic (unicast, multicast, or broadcast) to any other port that is also a protected port. Data traffic cannot be forwarded between protected ports at Layer 2; only control traffic is forwarded because these packets are processed by the CPU and forwarded in software. All data traffic passing between protected ports must be forwarded through a Layer 3 device.

- Forwarding behavior between a protected port and a nonprotected port proceeds as usual.

- The default is to have no protected ports defined.

Refer to
Figure
in online course

To configure the PVLAN Edge feature, enter the command **switchport protected** in interface configuration mode.

The PVLAN Edge feature can be configured on a physical interface or an EtherChannel group. When the PVLAN Edge feature is enabled for a port channel, it is enabled for all ports in the port-channel group. To disable protected port, use the `no switchport protected` interface configuration command.

To verify the configuration of the PVLAN Edge feature, use the `show interfaces interface-id switchport` global configuration mode command.

6.3.8 Recommended Practices for Layer 2

Refer to
Figure
in online course

Layer 2 guidelines are dependent on the particular security policy of an organization.

It is important to manage switches, like routers, using secure protocols or out-of-band methods if policy permits it. Turn off services that are not necessary and ports that are not being used. Implement various security services, such as port security and STP enhancements, as necessary and as supported by the hardware. Disable CDP on ports that do not connect to network devices, with the exception of ports that connect to Cisco IP phones.

Refer to
Figure
in online course

To mitigate risks to the network, deterministic VLANs should be used instead of default VLANs.

By default, VLAN 1 is the management VLAN. Also, by default, all ports are members of VLAN 1 (VLAN1 is the default user VLAN). In addition, VLAN1 is the default native VLAN used by trunk ports. For this reason, it is strongly recommended to avoid using VLAN 1 in a production network. All unused ports should be assigned to an alternate, unused VLAN. Additionally, the management VLAN should be reassigned to an unused VLAN that is neither a user VLAN or the native VLAN.

6.4 Wireless, VoIP, and SAN Security

6.4.1 Enterprise Advanced Technology Security Considerations

Refer to
Figure
in online course

Wireless LAN technology has been a powerful driver for advances in network security. With greater ease of access via wireless devices comes a greater need for comprehensive wireless security solutions.

Similarly, the advent of Voice over IP (VoIP) and all the accompanying devices and technologies (IP telephony), has motivated several advances in security. Who would want their telephone call intercepted by a hacker? It is worthwhile to describe the drivers for VoIP implementations, the components that are required in VoIP networks, and VoIP service issues. The natural progression is to explore the implications of implementing security measures in IP networks that transport voice.

Storage area networks (SANs) offer a solution to the increasing cost of network and server downtime. Given that the purpose of network security is to secure data (including voice and video), and the fact that data now typically resides on a SAN, it is essential that the SAN be secured.

Refer to
Figure
in online course

Modern enterprise networks typically employ wireless controllers, access points, and a wireless management system to deliver comprehensive protection against wireless attacks. The wireless environment is secured with infrastructure-integrated threat protection, advanced visibility into the RF environment, and wired network security collaboration.

An infrastructure-integrated approach to comprehensive wireless security reduces costs while streamlining security operations. Such a solution has a number of benefits:

- Proactive threat and intrusion detection capabilities detect wireless attacks and prevent them.

- Comprehensive protection safeguards confidential data and communications.

- A single user identity and policy simplifies user management and protects against unauthorized access.

- Collaboration with wired security systems enables a superset of wireless security functionality and protection.

Refer to
Figure
in online course

IP phones, IP Private Branch Exchanges (PBXs), voice gateways, voice mail systems, and the requisite protocols are also common in an enterprise network. These technologies and protocols enhance productivity and ultimately save the organization on telephony costs. By using an IP PBX, organizations can eliminate the legacy PBX and enjoy IP telephony benefits over a converged network. An IP PBX provides call-control functionality and, when used in conjunction with IP phone sets or a soft phone application, it can provide PBX functionality in a distributed and scalable fashion. Cisco IP telephony solution deployment models fall into one of these categories:

- Single-site deployment

- Centralized call processing with remote branches

- Distributed call processing deployment

- Clustering over the IP WAN

Selection of the deployment model depends on the organization's requirements, such as the size of the network, features, and availability of the WAN bandwidth.

Refer to
Figure
in online course

Enterprise networks also utilize storage area networking. Storage area networking is central to the contemporary data center architecture, providing a networking platform that helps IT departments achieve lower total cost of ownership, enhanced resiliency, and greater agility. Storage network solutions provide:

- *Investment protection* First, second, and third generations can all coexist in existing customer chassis and new switch configurations.

- *Virtualization* IT managers can provision their storage infrastructure.

- *Security* Data is protected when it is at rest and while it is being transported and replicated.

- *Consolidation* Storage professionals can consolidate resources by taking advantage of highly scalable, intelligent SAN platforms.

- *Availability* Instantaneous access to data is available from multiple tiers for disaster recovery.

Wireless LANs rely on radio frequency (RF) technology. RF technology has existed since the late nineteenth century. VoIP technology became commercially available in the 1990s. SAN technology did not formally enter the market until the early 2000s. The approach here follows the historical order.

6.4.2 Wireless Security Considerations

Refer to
Figure
in online course

In the early 2000s, the autonomous access point (AP) deployment model was quickly replaced by the lightweight access point deployment model. Lightweight APs depend on wireless LAN controllers (WLCs) for their configurations. This differs from autonomous APs, which require individual configuration of each device. The lightweight AP-wireless controller solution has several benefits that were not previously available, such as rogue AP detection and location.

Cisco WLCs are responsible for system-wide wireless LAN functions, such as security policies, intrusion prevention, RF management, QoS, and mobility. These functions work in conjunction with APs and the Cisco Wireless Control System (WCS) to support wireless applications. From voice and data services to location tracking, Cisco WLCs provide the control, scalability, security, and reliability to build secure, enterprise-scale wireless networks from branch offices to main campuses.

Cisco WLCs smoothly integrate into existing enterprise networks. They communicate with lightweight APs over any Layer 2 or Layer 3 infrastructure using the Lightweight Access Point Protocol (LWAPP). These devices support automation of numerous WLAN configuration and management functions across all enterprise locations.

Because the Cisco WLCs support IEEE 802.11a/b/g and the 802.11n standards, organizations can deploy the solution that best meets their individual requirements. Organizations can offer robust coverage with 802.11a/b/g or deliver greater performance with five times the throughput and the increased reliability of 802.11n.

Refer to
Figure
in online course

With pervasive wireless Internet access available, hackers now have expanded opportunities to covertly connect to remote networks. Whether a skilled hacker or a novice to wireless technology, opportunities abound for exploiting weaknesses in wireless networks.

The most popular form of wireless hacking is called war driving, where a hacker attempts to gain access to wireless networks on their laptop while driving around a metropolitan or suburban area. A neighbor might hack into another neighbor's wireless network to get free Internet access or to access confidential information. Airports, fast food restaurants, and coffee shops frequently offer Internet access, which again gives hackers the opportunity to compromise the data of other users. A hacker might even try to connect to another computer using ad hoc mode in a public area.

It is never safe to connect to an open wireless network, especially in a public area, unless the connection is followed by an encrypted VPN connection to another network. With respect to the enterprise network, remember that most security attacks come from the inside. These attacks can be intentionally launched by a disgruntled employee, or they might be unintentionally activated by a computer that is infected by a virus. Many organizations, as part of their security policies, do not allow employees to install their own APs in the worksite.

Refer to
Figure
in online course

Wireless hackers have an array of tools at their disposal, depending on their level of sophistication and determination:

- Network Stumbler software finds wireless networks.

- Kismet software displays wireless networks that do not broadcast their SSIDs.

- AirSnort software sniffs and cracks WEP keys.

- CoWPAtty cracks WPA-PSK (WPA1).

- ASLEAP gathers authentication data.

- Wireshark can scan wireless Ethernet data and 802.11 SSIDs.

For the more determined hacker, a spectrum analyzer can be used to identify, classify, and find sources of Wi-Fi RF signals. Modern spectrum analyzers can identify the specific types of devices that are causing RF interference and track them to their physical location.

6.4.3 Wireless Security Solutions

Refer to
Figure
in online course

The first wireless LANs (WLANs) emerged in 1990. These WLANs were totally open, with no authentication or encryption required. The first security option for WLANs was a service set identifier (SSID). Later implementations enabled the use of SSIDs without the APs broadcasting the SSIDs.

The IEEE 802.11b standard defined the Wired Equivalent Privacy (WEP) security protocol for encrypting data between radio endpoints. For several years, WEP implementations were the only means for securing WLANs. Weaknesses in WEP led to the development of newer technologies, based on protocols such as Temporal Key Integrity Protocol (TKIP) and ciphers such as Advanced Encryption Standard (AES). Wi-Fi Protected Access (WPA) implements TKIP and is more secure than WEP. WPA2 implements AES and is more secure than WPA. WPA2, an interoperable implementation of 802.11i, is currently the state of the art in wireless security.

Along the way, authentication was added as an option to securing WLANs and is now a fundamental component of enterprise wireless policy. The 802.11i architecture specifies 802.1X for authentication, entailing the use of EAP and an authentication server.

> **Refer to Figure** in online course

When designing and using wireless networks, it is a good idea for the network security professional to maintain an appropriate level of paranoia. Wireless networks are extremely inviting to hackers.

Fortunately, if a few precautions are taken, network administrators can decrease the risk for wireless users. The network administrator should keep several security considerations in mind:

- Wireless networks using WEP or WPA/TKIP are not very secure and are vulnerable to hacking attacks.

- Wireless networks using WPA2/AES should have a pass phrase of at least 21 characters.

- If an IPsec VPN is available, use it on any public wireless LAN.

- If wireless access is not needed, disable the wireless radio or wireless NIC.

As a network security professional, deploying a wireless solution should absolutely require WPA2/AES together with authentication. Authentication should be handled by a centralized authentication server.

6.4.4 VoIP Security Considerations

> **Refer to Figure** in online course

VoIP is the transmission of voice traffic over IP-based networks. IP was originally designed for data networking, but its success in data networking has led to its adaptation to voice traffic.

VoIP has become popular largely because of the cost savings over traditional telephone networks. On traditional telephone networks, most people pay a flat monthly fee for local telephone calls and a per-minute charge for long-distance calls. VoIP calls are placed using the Internet, with most Internet connections being charged a flat monthly fee. Using the Internet connection for both data traffic and voice calls allows consumers to reduce their monthly phone bill. For international calls, the monetary savings can be enormous.

The business advantages that drive implementations of VoIP networks have changed over time. Starting with simple media convergence, these advantages have evolved to include the convergence of call-switching intelligence and the total user experience. Originally, return on investment (ROI) calculations centered on toll-bypass and converged-network savings. Although these savings are still relevant today, advances in voice technologies allow organizations and service providers to differentiate their product offerings by providing advanced features.

VoIP has a number of business advantages:

- Lower telecom call costs are significant. VoIP service providers charge up to 50 percent less for phone connectivity service than traditional phone companies.

- Productivity increases with VoIP phone service can be substantial. Some businesses have reported productivity increases of up to three hours per week, per employee. Features such as find me/follow me, remote office, click-to-call, Outlook integration, unified voice mail, conference calling, and collaboration tools enable productivity increases.

- Move, add, and change costs are much lower. VoIP flexibility enables easily moving a phone between workstations.

- Ongoing service and maintenance costs can be lower.

- Many VoIP systems require little or no training for users.

- Mobile phone charges decrease as employees make calls via their laptop instead of their mobile phone. These network calls are part of the network charges and cost only the amount of the Internet connection itself.

- Telecommuting phone costs are decreased and there are no major setup fees. Voice communication takes place over a broadband connection.

- VoIP enables unified messaging. Information systems are integrated.

- Encryption of voice calls is supported.

- Fewer administrative personnel are needed for answering telephones.

Refer to
Figure
in online course

A packet voice network, or network that supports voice traffic, has a number of possible components:

- *IP phones* Provide IP voice to the desktop.

- *Gatekeeper* Provides Call Admission Control (CAC), bandwidth control and management, and address translation.

- *Gateway* Provides translation between VoIP and non-VoIP networks, such as the PSTN. Gateways also provide physical access for local analog and digital voice devices, such as telephones, fax machines, key sets, and PBXs.

- *Multipoint control unit (MCU)* Provides real-time connectivity for participants in multiple locations to attend the same videoconference or meeting.

- *Call agent* Provides call control for IP phones, CAC, bandwidth control and management, and address translation. Cisco Unified Communications Managers and Cisco Unified Communications Manager Business Edition both function as the call agents.

- *Application servers* Provide services such as voice mail and unified messaging, such as Cisco Unity.

- *Videoconference station* Provides access for end user participation in videoconferencing. The videoconference station contains a video capture device for video input and a microphone for audio input. The user can view video streams and hear the audio that originates at a remote user station.

Other components, such as software voice applications, interactive voice response (IVR) systems, and softphones, provide additional services to meet the needs of enterprise sites.

VoIP depends on a number of specialized protocols, including H.323, Media Gateway Control Protocol (MGCP), Session Initiation Protocol (SIP), skinny call control protocol (SCCP), and real-time protocol RTP.

Refer to
Figure
in online course

VoIP communication occurs over the traditional data network. That means that securing voice communication is directly related to securing the data network. There are several threats specific to VoIP networks:

Unauthorized Access to Voice Resources

Hackers can tamper with voice systems, user identities, and telephone configurations, and intercept voice-mail messages. If hackers gain access to the voice-mail system, they can change the voice-mail greeting, which can have a negative impact on the image and reputation of the company. A hacker who gains access to the PBX or voice gateway can shut down voice ports or change voice-routing parameters, affecting voice access into and through the network.

Compromising Network Resources

The goal of a secure network is to ensure that applications, processes, and users can reliably and securely interoperate using the shared network resources. Because the shared network infrastructure carries voice and data, security and access to the network infrastructure are critical in securing voice functions. Because IP voice systems are installed on a data network, they are potential targets for hackers who previously targeted only PCs, servers, and data applications. Hackers are aided in their search for vulnerabilities in IP voice systems by the open and well-known standards and protocols that are used by IP networks.

Eavesdropping

Eavesdropping involves the unauthorized interception of voice packets or RTP media streams. Eavesdropping exposes confidential or proprietary information that is obtained by intercepting and reassembling packets in a voice stream. Hackers use a variety of tools to eavesdrop.

DoS Attacks

DoS attacks are defined as the malicious attacking or overloading of call-processing equipment to deny access to services by legitimate users. Most DoS attacks fall into one of three categories:

- **Network resource overload** involves overloading a network resource that is required for proper functioning of a service. The network resource is most often bandwidth. The DoS attack uses up all available bandwidth, causing authorized users to be unable to access the required services.

- **Host resource starvation** involves using up critical host resources. When use of these resources is maximized by the DoS attack, the server can no longer respond to legitimate service requests.

- **Out-of-bounds attack** involves using illegal packet structure and unexpected data, which can cause the operating system of the remote system to crash. One example of this type of attack is using illegal combinations of TCP flags. Most TCP/IP stacks are developed to respond to appropriate use; they are not developed for anomalies. When the stack receives illegal data, it might not know how to handle the packet, causing a system crash.

Refer to **Figure** in online course Spam over Internet Telephony (SPIT), or VoIP spam, is unsolicited and unwanted bulk messages broadcast over VoIP to the endusers of an enterprise network. In addition to being annoying, high-volume bulk calls can significantly affect the availability and productivity of the endpoints. Because bulk calls are also difficult to trace, they can be used for fraud, unauthorized use, and privacy violations.

SPIT has the potential to become a major problem. SPIT could be generated in a similar way to email spam with botnets targeting millions of VoIP users from compromised machines. Unsolicited commercial and malicious email spam now makes up the majority of email worldwide. There is concern that VoIP will suffer the same fate as email.

Another concern about SPIT is that email anti-spam methods will not work. The real-time nature of voice calls makes dealing with SPIT much more challenging than email spam. New methods have to be invented to address SPIT problems.

Authenticated Transport Layer Security (TLS) stops most SPIT attacks, because endpoints only accept packets from trusted devices.

Refer to
Figure
in online course

Two common types of fraud in VoIP networks are vishing and toll fraud.

Vishing

Vishing (voice phishing) uses telephony to glean information, such as account details directly from users. One of the first reported cases of vishing affected PayPal. Victims first received an email pretending to come from PayPal asking them to verify their credit card details over the phone. Those who called the number were then asked to enter their credit card number using the keypad. After the credit card number had been entered, the perpetrators of this fraud were able to steal money from the account of their victims.

Because of the lower cost of making VoIP calls as compared to standard phone systems, attackers can call thousands of people for very little cost. Users still trust the telephone more than the web, but these spamming techniques can undermine user confidence in VoIP.

Toll Fraud

Toll fraud is the theft of long-distance telephone service by unauthorized access to a PSTN trunk (an outside line) on a PBX or voice-mail system. Toll fraud is a multibillion-dollar illegal industry, and all organizations are vulnerable. Theft can also be defined as the use of the telephony system by both authorized and unauthorized users to access unauthorized numbers, such as charge-per-call numbers.

This fraud is not new and PBXs have always been vulnerable. The difference is that few people could hack into PBXs, compared to the numbers of people actively breaking into IP systems. To protect against such fraud, network administrators use features that exist in Cisco Unified Communications Manager to control phone calls, such as dial plan filters, partitions, or Forced Authorization Codes (FACs).

SIP Vulnerabilities

Another growing VoIP security issue concerns the Session Initiation Protocol (SIP). SIP is a signaling protocol widely used for controlling communication sessions such as VoIP sessions. The increasing adoption of SIP for VoIP is expected to open up a completely new front in the security war. SIP is a relatively new protocol that offers little inherent security. Some of its characteristics also leave it vulnerable to hackers, such as using text for encoding and SIP extensions that can create security holes.

Examples of hacks for SIP include: registration hijacking, message tampering, and session tear-down. Registration hijacking allows a hacker to intercept incoming calls and reroute them. Message tampering allows a hacker to modify data packets traveling between SIP addresses. Session tear-down allows a hacker to terminate calls or carry out a VoIP-targeted DoS attack by flooding the system with shutdown requests.

6.4.5 VoIP Security Solutions

Refer to
Figure
in online course

Many IP security solutions can be implemented only on Layer 3 devices. Because of protocol architecture, Layer 2 offers very little or no inherent security. Understanding and establishing broadcast domains is one of the fundamental concepts in designing secure IP networks. Many simple yet dangerous attacks can be launched if the attacking device resides within the same broadcast domain as the target system. For this reason, IP phones, VoIP gateways, and network management workstations should always be on their own subnet, separate from the rest of the data network and from each other.

To ensure communications privacy and integrity, voice media streams must be protected from eavesdropping and tampering. Data-networking technologies such as VLANs can segment voice traffic from data traffic, preventing access to the voice VLAN from the data VLAN. Using separate

VLANs for voice and data prevents any attacker or attacking application from snooping or capturing other VLAN traffic as it traverses the physical wire. By making sure that each device connects to the network using a switched infrastructure, packet-sniffing tools can also be rendered less effective for capturing user traffic.

Assigning voice traffic to specific VLANs to logically segment voice and data traffic is an industry-wide recommended practice. As much as possible, devices that are identified as voice devices should be restricted to dedicated voice VLANs. This approach ensures that they can communicate only with other voice resources. More importantly, voice traffic is kept away from the general data network, where it could be more easily intercepted or tampered with. Having a voice-specific VLAN makes it easier to apply VLAN access control lists (VACLs) to protect voice traffic.

By understanding the protocols that are used between devices in the VoIP network, effective ACLs can be implemented on the voice VLANs. IP phones send only RTP traffic to each other, and they never have a reason to send TCP or ICMP traffic to each other. IP phones do send a few TCP and UDP protocols to communicate with servers. Many of the IP phone attacks can be stopped by using ACLs on the voice VLANs to prevent deviations from these principles.

<table>
<tr><td>Refer to
Figure
in online course</td></tr>
</table>

Firewalls inspect packets and match them against configured rules based on the ports specified. It is difficult to specify in advance which ports will be used in a voice call because the ports are dynamically negotiated during call setup.

Cisco ASA inspects voice protocols to ensure that SIP, SCCP, H.323, and MGCP requests conform to voice standards. Cisco ASA can also provide these capabilities to help protect voice traffic:

- Ensure SIP, SCCP, H.323, and MGCP requests conform to standards.

- Prevent inappropriate SIP methods from being sent to Cisco Unified Communications Manager.

- Rate limit SIP requests.

- Enforce the policy of calls (whitelist, blacklist, caller/called party, SIP Uniform Resource Identifier).

- Dynamically open ports for Cisco applications.

- Enable only "registered phones" to make calls.

- Enable inspection of encrypted phone calls.

Cisco IOS firewalls also provide many of these secure features.

<table>
<tr><td>Refer to
Figure
in online course</td></tr>
</table>

VPNs are widely used to provide secure connections to the corporate network. The connections can originate from a branch office, a small office/home office (SOHO), a telecommuter, or a roaming user. IPsec can be used for authentication and confidentiality services. To facilitate performance, it is recommended that VPN tunnels terminate inside of a firewall. The firewall is used to inspect and protect the plaintext protocols.

When deploying VPNs across the Internet or a public network, it is important to consider the absence of QoS. Where possible, QoS should be addressed with the provider through a service level agreement (SLA). An SLA is a document that details the expected QoS parameters for packets that go through the provider network.

Voice communications do not work well (or sometimes at all) with latency. Because secure VPNs encrypt data, they can create a throughput bottleneck when they process packets through their encryption algorithm. The problem usually gets worse as security increases.

VoIP and either DES or 3DES encryptions are fully compatible with each other as long as the VPN delivers the necessary throughput. Internationally, corporations might face other issues that affect voice communications. The U.S. Department of Commerce places restrictions on the export of certain encryption technology. Usually, DES is exportable while 3DES is not. However, regulations take numerous forms, from total export exclusions that are applied to certain countries, to allowing 3DES export to specific industries and users. Most corporations with VPNs that extend outside the United States must find out if their VPN provider has exportable products and how export regulations affect networks built with those products.

Refer to
Figure
in online course

When securing voice traffic, do not forget to secure the voice application servers. The newer versions of Cisco Unified Communications Manager disable unnecessary services, disable default usernames, allow only signed images to be installed, and support secure management protocols.

By combining the transport security that is provided by secure LANs, firewalls, and VPNs with the application and host security features available with the Cisco Unified Communications Manager and Cisco IP phones, it is possible to have a highly secure IP telephony environment.

6.4.6 SAN Security Considerations

Refer to
Figure
in online course

A SAN is a specialized network that enables fast, reliable access among servers and external storage resources. In a SAN, a storage device is not the exclusive property of any one server. Rather, storage devices are shared among all networked servers as peer resources. Just as a LAN can be used to connect clients to servers, a SAN can be used to connect servers to storage, servers to each other, and storage to storage.

A SAN does not need to be a physically separate network. It can be a dedicated subnet that carries only business-critical I/O traffic between servers and storage devices. A SAN, for example, would not carry general-purpose traffic such as email or other end user applications. It would be limited to I/O traffic, such as reading a file from a disk or writing a file to a disk. This network approach helps avoid the unacceptable compromise and reduced performance that is inherent when a single network is used for all applications.

Network and server downtime costs companies large sums of money in business and productivity losses. At the same time, the amount of information to be managed and stored is increasing dramatically every year.

SANs offer an answer to the increasing volume of data that must be stored in an enterprise network environment. By implementing a SAN, users can offload storage traffic from the daily network operations and establish a direct connection between storage media and servers.

SANs in enterprise infrastructures are evolving rapidly to meet three primary business requirements:

- Reduce capital and operating expenses.

- Increase agility to support changing business priorities, application requirements, and revenue growth.

- Improve long-distance replication, backup, and recovery to meet regulatory requirements and industry best practices.

Cisco provides an enterprise-wide approach to deploying scalable, highly available, and more easily administered SANs. Cisco solutions for intelligent SANs are an integral part of an enterprise data center architecture. Cisco SAN solutions provide a preferred means of accessing, managing, and protecting information resources across a variety of SAN transport technologies. These include consolidated Fibre Channel, Fibre Channel over IP (FCIP), Internet Small Computer Systems Interface (iSCSI), Gigabit Ethernet, or optical network.

Refer to
Figure
in online course

All the major SAN transport technologies are based on the SCSI communications model. In many ways, a SAN can be described as the merging of SCSI and networking. SCSI command protocol is the de facto standard that is used extensively in high-performance storage applications. The command part of SCSI can be transported over a Fibre Channel SAN or encapsulated in IP and carried across IP networks.

There are three major SAN transport technologies:

- *Fibre Channel* This technology is the primary SAN transport for host-to-SAN connectivity. Traditionally, SANs have required a separate dedicated infrastructure to interconnect hosts and storage systems. The primary transport protocol for this interconnection has been Fibre Channel. Fibre Channel networks provide a serial transport for the SCSI protocol.

- *iSCSI* Maps SCSI over TCP/IP. This is another host-to-SAN connectivity model that is typically used in the LAN. An iSCSI leverages an investment in existing IP networks to build and extend the SANs. This is accomplished by using TCP/IP to transport SCSI commands, data, and status between hosts or initiators and storage devices or targets, such as storage subsystems and tape devices.

- *FCIP* Popular SAN-to-SAN connectivity model that is often used over the WAN or MAN (metropolitan area network). SAN designers can use the open-standard FCIP protocol to break the distance barrier of current Fibre Channel solutions and enable interconnection of SAN islands over extended distances.

In computer storage, a logical unit number (LUN) is a 64-bit address for an individual disk drive and, by extension, the disk device itself. The term is used in the SCSI protocol as a way to differentiate individual disk drives within a common SCSI target device such as a disk array.

LUN masking is an authorization process that makes a LUN available to some hosts and unavailable to other hosts. LUN masking is implemented primarily at the host bus adapter (HBA) level. LUN masking that is implemented at this level is vulnerable to any attack that compromises the HBA.

The security benefits of LUN masking are limited because, with many HBAs, it is possible to forge source addresses. LUN masking is mainly a way to protect against misbehaving servers corrupting disks belonging to other servers.

For example, Windows servers that are attached to a SAN sometimes corrupt non-Windows volumes by attempting to write Windows volume labels to them. By hiding the LUNs of the non-Windows volumes from the Windows server, this can be prevented because the Windows server does not even realize the non-Windows volumes exist.

Today, LUNs are normally not individual disk drives but virtual partitions (or volumes) of a Redundant Array of Independent Disks (RAID) set.

Refer to **Figure** in online course

A world wide name (WWN) is a 64-bit address that Fibre Channel networks use to uniquely identify each element in a Fibre Channel network.

Zoning can utilize WWNs to assign security permissions. Zoning can also use name servers in the switches to either allow or block access to particular WWNs in the fabric.

The use of WWNs for security purposes is inherently insecure, because the WWN of a device is a user-configurable parameter. Zoning that uses WWNs is susceptible to unauthorized access because the zone can be bypassed if an attacker is able to spoof the WWN of an authorized host bus adapter (HBA). An HBA is an I/O adapter that sits between the bus of the host computer and the Fibre Channel loop and manages the transfer of information between the two channels.

Refer to **Figure** in online course

In storage area networking, Fibre Channel zoning is the partitioning of a Fibre Channel fabric into smaller subsets. If a SAN contains several storage devices, one device should not necessarily be allowed to interact with all the other devices in the SAN.

Zoning is sometimes confused with LUN masking, because both processes have the same objectives. The difference is that zoning is implemented on fabric switches while LUN masking is performed on endpoint devices. Zoning is also potentially more secure. Zone members see only other members of the zone. Devices can be members of more than one zone.

There are some simple rules to keep in mind for zoning operation:

- Zone members see only other members of the zone.

- Zones can be configured dynamically based on WWN.

- Devices can be members of more than one zone.

- Switched fabric zoning can take place at the port or device level, based on the physical switch port, device WWN, or LUN ID.

Fibre Channel fabric zoning has the benefit of securing device access and allowing operating system coexistence. Zoning applies only to the switched fabric topology; it does not exist in simpler Fibre Channel topologies.

Refer to
Figure
in online course

A virtual storage area network (VSAN) is a collection of ports from a set of connected Fibre Channel switches that form a virtual fabric. Ports can be partitioned within a single switch into multiple VSANs. Additionally, multiple switches can join any number of ports to form a single VSAN. In this manner, VSANs strongly resemble VLANs. Like VLANs, traffic is tagged as it crosses inter-switch links with the VSAN ID.

Fabric events are isolated per VSAN. VSANs utilize hardware-based isolation, meaning that traffic is explicitly tagged across inter-switch links with VSAN membership information. Statistics can also be gathered on a per-VSAN basis.

VSANs were originally invented by Cisco, but they have now been adopted as an ANSI standard.

6.4.7 SAN Security Solutions

Refer to
Figure
in online course

In order to secure SANs, it is necessary to secure the SAN fabric, any attaching hosts, and the actual disks.

There are six critical areas to consider when securing a SAN:

- *SAN management*   Secure the management services that are used to administer the SAN.

- *Fabric access*   Secure access to the fabric. The SAN fabric refers to the hardware that connects servers to storage devices.

- *Target access*   Secure access to storage devices (targets) and LUNs.

- *SAN protocols*   Secure the protocols that are used in switch-to-switch communication.

- *IP storage*   Secure FCIP and iSCSI.

- *Data integrity and secrecy*   Encrypt data as it crosses networks as well as when stored on disks.

Refer to
Figure
in online course

There are several types of SAN-management tools available that can manage device-level performance and application-level performance, as well as offer reporting and monitoring of services. Whatever SAN-management tool is used, ensure that access to the management tool is secure. When managing a SAN, there are other security concerns to consider:

- *Disruption of switch processing*   A DoS attack can cause excessive load on the CPU, rendering the CPU unable to react to fabric events.

- *Compromise of fabric* Changed configurations or lost configurations can result in changes to the configured services or ports.

- *Compromise of data integrity and confidentiality* Breaching the actual data compromises the integrity and confidentiality of stored information.

Refer to
Figure
in online course

To ensure application data integrity, LUN integrity, and application performance, it is necessary to secure both fabric and target access.

If fabric and target access are not secure, this can result in unauthorized access to data. Unauthorized access means that integrity and confidentiality have both been breached. Data may also be corrupted or deleted. If the LUN is compromised either accidentally or intentionally, data can be lost and availability can be threatened. Finally, application performance and availability can be affected by unnecessary I/O or fabric events because the processor is kept busier than required.

To prevent these types of issues, use VSANs and zoning.

Refer to
Figure
in online course

VSANs and zones are complementary technologies that work well together as a security control in a SAN. The first step in configuring these complimentary protocols is to associate the physical ports with a VSAN, much like associating switch ports with VLANs, and then logically dividing the VSANs into zones.

Zoning is the prime mechanism for securing access to SAN targets (disk and tape). There are two main methods of zoning, hard and soft. Soft zoning restricts the fabric name services, showing a device only an allowed subset of devices. When a server looks at the content of the fabric, it sees only the devices that it is allowed to see. However, any server can still attempt to contact other devices on the network based on their addresses.

In contrast, hard zoning restricts communication across a fabric. This zoning is more commonly used because it is more secure.

Refer to
Figure
in online course

To secure data during transmission, a number of techniques are employed. iSCSI leverages many strategies that are common to IP networking. For example, IP ACLs are analogous to Fibre Channel zones, VLANs are similar to VSANs, and IEEE 802.1X port security resembles Fibre Channel port security.

For data transmission security, a number of encryption and authentication protocols are supported:

- Diffie-Hellman Challenge Handshake Authentication Protocol (DH-CHAP)

- Fibre Channel Authentication Protocol (FCAP)

- Fibre Channel Password Authentication Protocol (FCPAP)

- Encapsulating Security Payload (ESP)

- Fibre Channel Security Protocol (FC-SP)

FCIP security leverages many IP security features in Cisco IOS-based routers:

- IPsec for security over public carriers

- High-speed encryption services in specialized hardware

- Firewall filtering

Securing SANs completes the process of securing the LAN: secure the endpoints, the switches, the wireless environment, the VoIP infrastructure, and the SANs.

In securing the LAN, a number of references to IPsec have been made. IPsec is a means of encrypting data between endpoints, such as within a VPN tunnel. To understand how IPsec works, a basic understanding of cryptography is necessary.

Chapter Summary

Refer to **Figure** in online course

Refer to **Packet Tracer Activity** for this chapter

Refer to **Lab Activity** for this chapter

Your Chapter Notes

CHAPTER 7

Cryptographic Systems

Chapter Introduction

Refer to
Figure
in online course

A network can be secured through device hardening, AAA access control, firewall features, and IPS implementations. These combined features protect the infrastructure devices as well as the end devices within the local network. But how is network traffic protected when traversing the public Internet? The answer is through cryptographic methods.

Cryptology is the science of making and breaking secret codes. The development and use of codes is called cryptography, and breaking codes is called cryptanalysis. Cryptography has been used for centuries to protect secret documents. For example, Julius Caesar used a simple alphabetic cipher to encrypt messages to his generals in the field. His generals would have knowledge of the cipher key required to decrypt the messages. Today, modern day cryptographic methods are used in multiple ways to ensure secure communications.

Secure communication requires a guarantee that the message is not a forgery and does actually come from whom it states (authentication). It also requires a guarantee that no one intercepted the message and altered it (integrity). Finally, secure communication ensures that if the message is captured, it cannot be deciphered (confidentiality).

The principles of cryptology can be used to explain how modern day protocols and algorithms are used to secure communications. Many modern networks ensure authentication with protocols such as HMAC. Integrity is ensured by implementing either MD5 or SHA-1. Data confidentiality is ensured through symmetric encryption algorithms, including DES, 3DES, and AES, or asymmetric algorithms, including RSA and the public key infrastructure (PKI). Symmetric encryption algorithms are based on the premise that each communicating party knows the pre-shared key. Asymmetric encryption algorithms are based on the assumption that the two communicating parties have not previously shared a secret and must establish a secure method to do so.

In a hands-on lab for the chapter, *Exploring Encryption Methods*, learners decipher a pre-encrypted message using the Vigenere cipher, create and decipher a Vigenere cipher message, and use steganography to embed a secret message in a graphic. The lab is found in the lab manual on Academy connection at cisco.netacad.net.

7.1 Cryptographic Services

7.1.1 Securing Communications

Refer to **Figure** in online course

The first goal for network administrators is to secure the network infrastructure, including routers, switches, servers, and hosts. This is accomplished using hardening, AAA access control, ACLs, firewalls, and monitoring threats using IPS.

The next goal is to secure the data as it travels across various links. This may include internal traffic, but of greater concern is protecting the data that travels outside of the organization to branch sites, telecommuter sites, and partner sites.

Secure communications involves a few primary tasks:

- *Authentication* Guarantees that the message is not a forgery and does actually come from who it states it comes from.

- *Integrity* Similar to a checksum function in a frame, guarantees that no one intercepted the message and altered it.

- *Confidentiality* Guarantees that if the message is captured, it cannot be deciphered.

Refer to **Figure** in online course

Authentication

Authentication guarantees that a message comes from the source that it claims to come from. Authentication is similar to entering a secure personal information number (PIN) for banking at an ATM. The PIN should only be known to the user and the financial institution. The PIN is a shared secret that helps protect against forgeries.

Authentication can be accomplished with cryptographic methods. This is especially important for applications or protocols, such as email or IP, that do not have built-in mechanisms to prevent spoofing of the source.

Data nonrepudiation is a similar service that allows the sender of a message to be uniquely identified. With nonrepudiation services in place, a sender cannot deny having been the source of that message. It might appear that the authenticity service and the nonrepudiation service are fulfilling the same function. Although both address the question of the proven identity of the sender, there is a difference between the two.

The most important part of nonrepudiation is that a device cannot repudiate, or refute, the validity of a message sent. Nonrepudiation relies on the fact that only the sender has the unique characteristics or signature for how that message is treated. Not even the receiving device can know how the sender treated this message to prove authenticity, because the receiver could then pretend to be the source.

If the major concern is for the receiving device to validate the source and there is no concern about the receiving device imitating the source, it does not matter whether the sender and receiver both know how to treat a message to provide authenticity. An example of authenticity versus nonrepudiation is a data exchange between two computers of the same company versus a data exchange between a customer and an e-commerce website. The two computers exchanging data within an organization do not have to prove to the other which of them sent a message. The only thing that must be proven is that whatever was received by one was sent by the other. In this instance, the two computers can share the same way of transforming their messages.

This practice is not acceptable in business applications, such as when purchasing items online through a web shop. If the web shop knows how a customer transforms messages to prove authenticity of the source, the web shop could easily fake "authentic" orders. In such a scenario, the sender must be the only party having the knowledge of how to transform messages. The web shop can prove to others that the order was, in fact, sent by the customer, and the customer cannot argue that the order is invalid.

Refer to
Figure
in online course

Integrity

Data integrity ensures that messages are not altered in transit. With data integrity, the receiver can verify that the received message is identical to the sent message and that no manipulation occurred.

European nobility ensured the data integrity of documents by creating a wax seal to close an envelope. The seal was often created using a signet ring. These bore the family crest, initials, a portrait, or a personal symbol or motto of the owner of the signet ring. An unbroken seal on an envelope guaranteed the integrity of its contents. It also guaranteed authenticity based on the unique signet ring impression.

Refer to
Figure
in online course

Confidentiality

Data confidentiality ensures privacy so that only the receiver can read the message. Encryption is the process of scrambling data so that it cannot be read by unauthorized parties.

When enabling encryption, readable data is called plaintext, or cleartext, while the encrypted version is called ciphertext. The plaintext readable message is converted to ciphertext, which is the unreadable, disguised message. Decryption reverses the process. A key is required to encrypt and decrypt a message. The key is the link between the plaintext and ciphertext.

Historically, various encryption algorithms and methods have been used. Julius Caesar is said to have secured messages by putting two sets of the alphabet side by side and then shifting one of them by a specific number of places. The number of places in the shift serves as the key. He converted plaintext into ciphertext using this key, and only his generals, who also had the key, knew how to decipher the messages. This method is now known as the Caesar cipher.

Using a hash function is another way to ensure data confidentiality. A hash function transforms a string of characters into a usually shorter, fixed-length value or key that represents the original string. The difference between hashing and encryption is in how the data is stored. With encrypted text, the data can be decrypted with a key. With the hash function, after the data is entered and converted using the hash function, the plaintext is gone. The hashed data is simply there for comparison. For example, when a user enters a password, the password is hashed and then compared to the stored hashed value. If the user forgets the password, it is impossible to decrypt the stored value, and the password must be reset.

The purpose of encryption and hashing is to guarantee confidentiality so that only authorized entities can read the message.

7.1.2 Cryptography

Refer to
Figure
in online course

Authentication, integrity, and confidentiality are components of cryptography. Cryptography is both the practice and the study of hiding information.

Cryptographic services are the foundation for many security implementations and are used to ensure the protection of data when that data might be exposed to untrusted parties. Understanding the basic functions of cryptography and how encryption provides confidentiality and integrity is important in creating a successful security policy. It is also important to understand the issues that are involved in managing the encryption key.

The history of cryptography starts in diplomatic circles thousands of years ago. Messengers from a king's court took encrypted messages to other courts. Occasionally, other courts not involved in the communication attempted to steal any message sent to a kingdom that they considered an adversary. Not long after, military commanders started using encryption to secure messages.

Various cipher methods, physical devices, and aids have been used to encrypt and decrypt text:

- One of the earliest methods may have been the scytale of ancient Greece, a rod allegedly used by the Spartans as an aid for a transposition cipher. The sender and receiver had identical rods (scytale) on which to wrap a transposed messaged.

- The Caesar cipher is a simple substitution cipher that was used by Julius Caesar on the battlefield to quickly encrypt a message that could easily be decrypted by his commanders. The method to encrypt could compare two scrolls of letters, moving one scroll over by a single key number or by turning the inner dial of a cipher wheel by a single key number.

- The Vigenere Cipher was invented by Frenchman Blaise de Vigenere in the 16th century using a polyalphabetic system of encryption. Based on the Caesar cipher, it encrypted plaintext using a multi-letter key.

- Thomas Jefferson, the third president of the United States, invented an encryption system that was believed to have been used when he served as secretary of state from 1790 to 1793.

- Arthur Scherbius invented an electro-mechanical encoding device called the Enigma in 1918 that he had sold to Germany. It served as a template for the machines that all the major participants in World War II used. It was estimated that if 1,000 cryptanalysts tested four keys per minute, all day, every day, it would take 1.8 billion years to try them all. Germany knew their ciphered messages could be intercepted by the allies, but never thought they could be deciphered.

- Also during World War II, Japan was deciphering every code the Americans came up with. A more elaborate coding system was needed, and the answer came in the form of the Navajo code talkers. Not only were there no words in the Navajo language for military terms, the language was unwritten and less than 30 people outside of the Navajo reservations could speak it, and not one of them was Japanese. By the end of the war, more than 400 Navajo Indians were working as code talkers.

Each of these encryption methods uses a specific algorithm, called a cipher, to encrypt and decrypt messages. A cipher is a series of well-defined steps that can be followed as a procedure when encrypting and decrypting messages.

There are several methods of creating cipher text:

- Transposition

- Substitution

- Vernam

Refer to
Figure
in online course

In transposition ciphers, no letters are replaced; they are simply rearranged. An example of this type of cipher is taking the message FLANK EAST ATTACK AT DAWN and transposing it to read NWAD TAKCATTA TSAE KNALF. In this example, the key is to reverse the letters.

Another example of a transposition cipher is known as the rail fence cipher. In this transposition, the words are spelled out as if they were a rail fence, meaning some in front and some in back across several parallel lines. For example, a rail fence cipher that uses a key of three specifies that three lines are required when creating the encrypted code. To read the message, read diagonally up and down, following the rail fence.

```
F...K...T...A...T...N.
.L.N.E.S.A.T.C.A.D.W..
..A...A...T...K...A...
```

Modern encryption algorithms, such as the Data Encryption Standard (DES) and the Triple Data Encryption Standard (3DES), still use transposition as part of the algorithm.

Refer to
Figure
in online course

Substitution ciphers substitute one letter for another. In their simplest form, substitution ciphers retain the letter frequency of the original message.

The Caesar cipher was a simple substitution cipher. Every day there was a different key to use for adjusting the alphabet. For example, if the key for the day was 3, the letter A was moved three spaces to the right, resulting in an encoded message that used the letter D in place of the letter A. The letter E would be the substitute for the letter B, and so on. If the key for the day was 8, A becomes I, B becomes J, and so on.

Because the entire message relied on the same single key shift, the Caesar cipher is referred to as a monoalphabetic substitution cipher. It is also fairly easy to crack. For this reason, polyalphabetic ciphers, such as the Vigenere cipher, were invented. The method was originally described by Giovan Battista Bellaso in 1553, but the scheme was later misattributed to the French diplomat and cryptographer, Blaise de Vigenere.

The Vigenere cipher is based on the Caesar cipher, except that it encrypts text by using a different polyalphabetic key shift for every plaintext letter. The different key shift is identified using a shared key between sender and receiver. The plaintext message can be encrypted and decrypted using the Vigenere Cipher Table.

To illustrate how the Vigenere Cipher Table works, suppose that a sender and receiver have a shared secret key composed of these letters: SECRETKEY. The sender uses this secret key to encode the plaintext FLANK EAST ATTACK AT DAWN:

- The F (**F**LANK) is encoded by looking at the intersection of column F and the row starting with S (**S**ECRETKEY), resulting in the cipher letter X.

- The L (F**L**ANK) is encoded by looking at the intersection of column L and the row starting with E (S**E**CRETKEY), resulting in the cipher letter P.

- The A (FL**A**NK) is encoded by looking at the intersection of column A and the row starting with C (SE**C**RETKEY), resulting in the cipher letter C.

- The N (FLA**N**K) is encoded by looking at the intersection of column N and the row starting with R (SEC**R**ETKEY), resulting in the cipher letter E.

- The K (FLAN**K**) is encoded by looking at the intersection of column K and the row starting with E (SECR**E**TKEY), resulting in the cipher letter O.

The process continues until the entire text message FLANK EAST ATTACK AT DAWN is encrypted. The process can also be reversed. For instance, the F is still the cipher letter X if encoded by looking at the intersection of *row* F (**F**LANK) and the *column* starting with S (**S**ECRETKEY).

When using the Vigenere cipher and the message is longer than the key, the key is repeated. For example, SECRETKEYSECRETKEYSEC is required to encode FLANK EAST ATTACK AT DAWN:

Secret key: SECRE TKEY SECRET KE YSEC

Plaintext: FLANK EAST ATTACK AT DAWN

Cipher text: XPCEO XKUR SXVRGD KX BSAP

Although the Vigenere cipher uses a longer key, it can still be cracked. For this reason, a better cipher method was required.

Refer to
Figure
in online course

Gilbert Vernam was an AT&T Bell Labs engineer who, in 1917, invented and patented the stream cipher and later co-invented the one-time pad cipher. Vernam proposed a teletype cipher in which a prepared key consisting of an arbitrarily long, non-repeating sequence of numbers was kept on paper tape. It was then combined character by character with the plaintext message to produce the ciphertext. To decipher the ciphertext, the same paper tape key was again combined character by character, producing the plaintext. Each tape was used only once, hence the name one-time pad. As long as the key tape does not repeat or is not reused, this type of cipher is immune to cryptanalytic attack because the available ciphertext does not display the pattern of the key.

Several difficulties are inherent in using one-time pads in the real world. One difficulty is the challenge of creating random data. Computers, because they have a mathematical foundation, are incapable of creating true random data. Additionally, if the key is used more than once, it is easy to break. RC4 is an example of this type of cipher that is widely used on the Internet. Again, because the key is generated by a computer, it is not truly random. In addition to these issues, key distribution is also challenging with this type of cipher.

7.1.3 Cryptanalysis

Refer to **Figure** in online course

As long as there has been cryptography, there has been cryptanalysis. Cryptanalysis is the practice and study of determining the meaning of encrypted information (cracking the code), without access to the shared secret key.

Refer to **Figure** in online course

A variety of methods are used in cryptanalysis.

Brute-Force Attack

In a brute-force attack, an attacker tries every possible key with the decryption algorithm knowing that eventually one of them will work. All encryption algorithms are vulnerable to this attack. On average, a brute-force attack succeeds about 50 percent of the way through the keyspace, which is the set of all possible keys. The objective of modern cryptographers is to have a keyspace large enough that it takes too much money and too much time to accomplish a brute-force attack.

Recently, a DES cracking machine was used to recover a 56-bit DES key in 22 hours using brute force. It is estimated that on the same equipment it would take 149 trillion years to crack Advanced Encryption Standard (AES) using the same method.

Ciphertext-Only Attack

In a ciphertext-only attack, the attacker has the ciphertext of several messages, all of which have been encrypted using the same encryption algorithm, but the attacker has no knowledge of the underlying plaintext. The job of the attacker is to recover the ciphertext of as many messages as possible. Even better for the attacker is to deduce the key or keys used to encrypt the messages to decrypt other messages encrypted with the same keys. The attacker could use statistical analysis to deduce the key. These kinds of attacks are no longer practical, because modern algorithms produce pseudorandom output that is resistant to statistical analysis.

Known-Plaintext Attack

In a known-plaintext attack, the attacker has access to the ciphertext of several messages, but also knows something about the plaintext underlying that ciphertext. With knowledge of the underlying protocol, file type, or some characteristic strings that appear in the plaintext, the attacker uses a brute-force attack to try keys until decryption with the correct key produces a meaningful result. This attack might be the most practical attack, because attackers can usually assume some features of the underlying plaintext if they can only capture the ciphertext. Modern algorithms with enormous keyspaces make it unlikely for this attack to succeed because, on average, an attacker must search through at least half of the keyspace to be successful.

Refer to **Figure** in online course

Chosen-Plaintext Attack

In a chosen-plaintext attack, the attacker chooses which data the encryption device encrypts and observes the ciphertext output. A chosen-plaintext attack is more powerful than a known-plaintext attack because the chosen plaintext might yield more information about the key. This attack is not very practical because, unless the trusted network has been breached and the attacker already has access to confidential information, it is often difficult or impossible to capture both the ciphertext and plaintext.

Chosen-Ciphertext Attack

In a chosen-ciphertext attack, the attacker can choose different ciphertext to be decrypted and has access to the decrypted plaintext. With the pair, the attacker can search through the keyspace and determine which key decrypts the chosen ciphertext in the captured plaintext. For example, the attacker has access to a tamperproof encryption device with an embedded key. The attacker must deduce the embedded key by sending data through the box. This attack is analogous to the chosen-plaintext attack. Like the chosen-plaintext attack, this attack is not very practical. Unless the trusted network has been breached, and the attacker already has access to confidential information, it is difficult or impossible for the attacker to capture both the ciphertext and plaintext.

Meet-in-the-Middle

The meet-in-the-middle attack is a known plaintext attack. The attacker knows a portion of the plaintext and the corresponding ciphertext. The plaintext is encrypted with every possible key, and the results are stored. The ciphertext is then decrypted using every key, until one of the results matches one of the stored values.

Refer to **Figure** in online course

As an example of how to choose the cryptanalysis method, consider the Caesar cipher encrypted code. The best way to crack the code is to use brute force. Because there are only 25 possible rotations, it is not a big effort to try all possible rotations and see which one returns something that makes sense.

A more scientific approach is to use the fact that some characters in the English alphabet are used more often than others. This method is called frequency analysis. For example, the letters E, T, and A are the most popular letters used in the English language. The letters J, Q, X, and Z are the least popular. Understanding this pattern can help discover which letters are probably included in the cipher message.

For example, in the Caesar ciphered message IODQN HDVW DWWDFN DW GDZQ, the cipher letter D appears six times, while the cipher letter W appears four times. There is a good possibility that the cipher letters D and W represent either the plaintext E, T, or A. In this case, the D represents the letter A, and the W represents the letter T.

7.1.4 Cryptology

Refer to **Figure** in online course

Cryptology is the science of making and breaking secret codes. Cryptology combines the two separate disciplines of cryptography, which is the development and use of codes, and cryptanalysis, which is the breaking of those codes. There is a symbiotic relationship between the two disciplines, because each makes the other one better. National security organizations employ members of both disciplines and put them to work against each other.

There have been times when one of the disciplines has been ahead of the other. For example, during the Hundred Years War between France and England, the cryptanalysts were ahead of the cryptographers. France believed that the Vigenere cipher was unbreakable; however, the British were able to crack it. Some historians believe that World War II largely turned on the fact that the winning side on both fronts was much more successful than the losing side at cracking the encryption of its adversary. Currently, it is believed that cryptographers have the edge.

Refer to **Figure** in online course

Cryptanalysis is often used by governments in military and diplomatic surveillance, by enterprises in testing the strength of security procedures, and by malicious hackers in exploiting weaknesses in websites.

While cryptanalysis is often linked to mischievous purposes, it is actually a necessity. It is an ironic fact of cryptography that it is impossible to prove an algorithm secure. It can only be proven that it is not vulnerable to known cryptanalytic attacks. Therefore, there is a need for mathematicians, scholars, and security forensic experts to keep trying to break the encryption methods.

Refer to
Figure
in online course

In the world of communications and networking, authentication, integrity, and data confidentiality are implemented in many ways using various protocols and algorithms. The choice of protocol and algorithm varies based on the level of security required to meet the goals in the network security policy.

For example, for message integrity, message-digest 5 (MD5) is faster but less secure than SHA2. Confidentiality can be implemented using DES, 3DES, or the very secure AES. Again, the choice varies depending on the security requirements specified in the network security policy document.

Old encryption algorithms, such as the Caesar cipher or the Enigma machine, were based on the secrecy of the algorithm to achieve confidentiality. With modern technology, where reverse engineering is often simple, public-domain algorithms are often used. With most modern algorithms, successful decryption requires knowledge of the appropriate cryptographic keys. This means that the security of encryption lies in the secrecy of the keys, not the algorithm. How can the keys be kept secret?

7.2 Basic Integrity and Authenticity

7.2.1 Cryptographic Hashes

Refer to
Figure
in online course

A hash function takes binary data, called the message, and produces a condensed representation, called the message digest. Hashing is based on a one-way mathematical function that is relatively easy to compute, but significantly harder to reverse. Grinding coffee is a good example of a one-way function. It is easy to grind coffee beans, but it is almost impossible to put all of the tiny pieces back together to rebuild the original beans.

The cryptographic hashing function is designed to verify and ensure data integrity. It can also be used to verify authentication. The procedure takes a variable block of data and returns a fixed-length bit string called the hash value or message digest.

Hashing is similar to calculating cyclic redundancy check (CRC) checksums, but it is much stronger cryptographically. For instance, given a CRC value, it is easy to generate data with the same CRC. With hash functions, it is computationally infeasible for two different sets of data to come up with the same hash output. Every time the data is changed or altered, the hash value also changes. Because of this, cryptographic hash values are often called digital fingerprints. They can be used to detect duplicate data files, file version changes, and similar applications. These values are used to guard against an accidental or intentional change to the data and accidental data corruption.

The cryptographic hash function is applied in many different situations:

- To provide proof of authenticity when it is used with a symmetric secret authentication key, such as IP Security (IPsec) or routing protocol authentication.

- To provide authentication by generating one-time and one-way responses to challenges in authentication protocols such as the PPP Challenge Handshake Authentication Protocol (CHAP).

- To provide a message integrity check proof, such as those used in digitally signed contracts, and public key infrastructure (PKI) certificates, such as those accepted when accessing a secure site using a browser.

Refer to
Figure
in online course

Mathematically, a hash function (H) is a process that takes an input (x) and returns a fixed-size string, which is called the hash value (h). The formula for the calculation is $h = H(x)$.

A cryptographic hash function should have the following properties:

- The input can be any length.

- The output has a fixed length.

- H(x) is relatively easy to compute for any given x.

- H(x) is one way and not reversible.

- H(x) is collision free, meaning that two different input values will result in different hash values.

If a hash function is hard to invert, it is considered a one-way hash. Hard to invert means that given a hash value of h, it is computationally infeasible to find some input, (x), such that H(x) = h.

Refer to **Figure** in online course

Hash functions are helpful when ensuring data is not changed accidentally, but they cannot ensure that data is not changed deliberately. For instance, the sender wants to ensure that the message is not altered on its way to the receiver. The sending device inputs the message into a hashing algorithm and computes its fixed-length digest or fingerprint. Both the message and the hash are in plaintext. This fingerprint is then attached to the message and sent to the receiver. The receiving device removes the fingerprint from the message and inputs the message into the same hashing algorithm. If the hash that is computed by the receiving device is equal to the one that is attached to the message, the message has not been altered during transit.

When the message traverses the network, a potential attacker could intercept the message, change it, recalculate the hash, and append it to the message. Hashing only prevents the message from being changed accidentally, such as by a communication error. There is nothing unique to the sender in the hashing procedure, so anyone can compute a hash for any data, as long as they have the correct hash function.

These are two well-known hash functions:

- Message Digest 5 (MD5) with 128-bit digests

- Secure Hash Algorithm 1 (SHA-1) with 160-bit digests

7.2.2 Integrity with MD5 and SHA-1

Refer to **Figure** in online course

The MD5 algorithm is a hashing algorithm that was developed by Ron Rivest and is used in a variety of Internet applications today.

MD5 is a one-way function that makes it easy to compute a hash from the given input data, but makes it unfeasible to compute input data given only a hash value. MD5 is also collision resistant, which means that two messages with the same hash are very unlikely to occur. MD5 is essentially a complex sequence of simple binary operations, such as exclusive OR (XORs) and rotations, that are performed on input data and produce a 128-bit digest.

The main algorithm is based on a compression function, which operates on blocks. The input is a data block plus a feedback of previous blocks. 512-bit blocks are divided into 16 32-bit subblocks. These blocks are then rearranged with simple operations in a main loop, which consists of four rounds. The output of the algorithm is a set of four 32-bit blocks, which concatenate to form a single 128-bit hash value. The message length is also encoded into the digest.

MD5 is based on MD4, an earlier algorithm. MD4 has been broken, and MD5 is now considered less secure than SHA-1 by many authorities on cryptography. These authorities consider MD5 less secure because some noncritical weaknesses have been found in one of the MD5 building blocks.

Refer to **Figure** in online course

The U.S. National Institute of Standards and Technology (NIST) developed the Secure Hash Algorithm (SHA), the algorithm that is specified in the Secure Hash Standard (SHS). SHA-1, published in 1994, corrected an unpublished flaw in SHA. Its design is very similar to the MD4 and MD5 hash functions that Ron Rivest developed.

The SHA-1 algorithm takes a message of less than 2^64 bits in length and produces a 160-bit message digest. The algorithm is slightly slower than MD5, but the larger message digest makes it more secure against brute-force collision and inversion attacks.

NIST published four additional hash functions in the SHA family, each with longer digests:

- SHA-224 (224 bit)

- SHA-256 (256 bit)

- SHA-384 (384 bit)

- SHA-512 (512 bit)

These four versions are collectively known as SHA-2, although the term SHA-2 is not standardized. SHA-1, SHA-224, SHA-256, SHA-384, and SHA-512 are the secure hash algorithms required by law for use in certain U.S. government applications, including use within other cryptographic algorithms and protocols, for the protection of sensitive unclassified information.

A newer more secure cryptographic hashing algorithm called SHA-3 has been developed by NIST. SHA-3 will eventually replace SHA-1 and SHA-2 and it should be used if available.

Refer to
Figure
in online course

Both MD5 and SHA-1 are based on MD4. This makes MD5 and SHA-1 similar in many ways. SHA-1 and SHA-2 are more resistant to brute-force attacks because their digest is at least 32 bits longer than the MD5 digest.

SHA-1 involves 80 steps, and MD5 involves 64 steps. The SHA-1 algorithm must also process a 160-bit buffer instead of the 128-bit buffer of MD5. Because there are fewer steps, MD5 usually executes more quickly, given the same device.

When choosing a hashing algorithm, SHA-1 or SHA-2 is preferred over MD5. MD5 has not been proven to contain any critical flaws, but its security is questionable today. If performance is an issue, the MD5 algorithm is slightly faster than the algorithm for SHA-1. Keep in mind that MD5 may prove to be substantially less secure than SHA-1.

Are hashes only used to provide data integrity?

7.2.3 Authenticity with HMAC

Refer to
Figure
in online course

In cryptography, a keyed-hash message authentication code (HMAC or KHMAC) is a type of message authentication code (MAC). An HMAC is calculated using a specific algorithm that combines a cryptographic hash function with a secret key. Hash functions are the basis of the protection mechanism of HMACs.

Only the sender and the receiver know the secret key, and the output of the hash function now depends on the input data and the secret key. Only parties who have access to that secret key can compute the digest of an HMAC function. This characteristic defeats man-in-the-middle attacks and provides authentication of the data origin.

If two parties share a secret key and use HMAC functions for authentication, a properly constructed HMAC digest of a message that a party has received indicates that the other party was the originator of the message, because it is the only other entity possessing the secret key.

The cryptographic strength of the HMAC depends on the cryptographic strength of the underlying hash function, on the size and quality of the key, and the size of the hash output length in bits.

Cisco technologies use two well-known HMAC functions:

■ Keyed MD5 (HMAC-MD5), based on the MD5 hashing algorithm

■ Keyed SHA-1 (HMAC-SHA-1), based on the SHA-1 hashing algorithm

When an HMAC digest is created, data of an arbitrary length is input into the hash function, together with a secret key. The result is a fixed-length hash that depends on the data and the secret key.

Care must be taken to distribute secret keys only to the parties who are involved because, if the secret key is compromised, the other party can forge and change packets, violating data integrity.

Refer to
Figure
in online course

Consider an example where a sender wants to ensure that the message is not altered in transit, and wants to provide a way for the receiver to authenticate the origin of the message.

The sending device inputs data and the secret key into the hashing algorithm and calculates the fixed-length HMAC digest or fingerprint. This authenticated fingerprint is then attached to the message and sent to the receiver.

The receiving device removes the fingerprint from the message and uses the plaintext message with its secret key as input to the same hashing function. If the fingerprint that is calculated by the receiving device is equal to the fingerprint that was sent, the message has not been altered. Additionally, the origin of the message is authenticated, because only the sender possesses a copy of the shared secret key. The HMAC function has ensured the authenticity of the message.

IPsec virtual private networks (VPNs) rely on HMAC functions to authenticate the origin of every packet and provide data integrity checking.

Refer to
Figure
in online course

Cisco products use hashing for entity authentication, data integrity, and data authenticity purposes:

■ Cisco IOS routers use hashing with secret keys in an HMAC-like manner to add authentication information to routing protocol updates.

■ IPsec gateways and clients use hashing algorithms, such as MD5 and SHA-1 in HMAC mode, to provide packet integrity and authenticity.

■ Cisco software images that are downloaded from Cisco.com have an MD5-based checksum available so that customers can check the integrity of downloaded images.

■ Hashing can also be used in a feedback-like mode to provide a shared secret key to encrypt data. For example, TACACS+ uses an MD5 hash as the key to encrypt the session.

Digital signatures are an alternative to HMAC.

7.2.4 Key Management

Refer to
Figure
in online course

Key management is often considered the most difficult part of designing a cryptosystem. Many cryptosystems have failed because of mistakes in their key management, and all modern cryptographic algorithms require key management procedures. In practice, most attacks on cryptographic systems are aimed at the key management level, rather than at the cryptographic algorithm itself. There are several essential characteristics of key management to consider:

■ *Generation* It was up to Caesar to choose the key of his cipher. The Vigenere cipher key is also chosen by the sender and receiver. In a modern cryptographic system, key generation is usually automated and not left to the end user. The use of good random number generators is needed to ensure that all keys are likely to be equally generated so that the attacker cannot predict which keys are more likely to be used.

- *Verification* Some keys are better than others. Almost all cryptographic algorithms have some weak keys that should not be used. With the help of key verification procedures, these keys can be regenerated if they occur. With the Caesar cipher, using a key of 0 or 25 does not encrypt the message, so it should not be used.

- *Storage* On a modern multi-user operating system that uses cryptography, a key can be stored in memory. This presents a possible problem when that memory is swapped to the disk, because a Trojan Horse program installed on the PC of a user could then have access to the private keys of that user.

- *Exchange* Key management procedures should provide a secure key exchange mechanism that allows secure agreement on the keying material with the other party, probably over an untrusted medium.

- *Revocation and Destruction* Revocation notifies all interested parties that a certain key has been compromised and should no longer be used. Destruction erases old keys in a manner that prevents malicious attackers from recovering them.

Two terms that are used to describe keys are key length and keyspace. The key length is the measure in bits, and the keyspace is the number of possibilities that can be generated by a specific key length. As key lengths increase, the keyspace increases exponentially:

- A 2-bit (2^2) key length = a keyspace of 4, because there are four possible keys ($00, 01, 10,$ and 11).

- A 3-bit (2^3) key length = a keyspace of 8, because there are eight possible keys ($000, 001, 010, 011, 100, 101, 110, 111$).

- A 4-bit (2^4) key length = a keyspace of 16 possible keys.

- A 40-bit (2^{40}) key length = a keyspace of $1,099,511,627,776$ possible keys.

Refer to
Figure
in online course

The keyspace of an algorithm is the set of all possible key values. A key that has n bits produces a keyspace that has 2^n possible key values. By adding one bit to the key, the keyspace is effectively doubled. For example, DES with its 56-bit keys has a keyspace of more than $72,000,000,000,000,000$ (2^{56}) possible keys. By adding one bit to the key length, the keyspace doubles, and an attacker needs twice the amount of time to search the keyspace.

Almost every algorithm has some weak keys in its keyspace that enable an attacker to break the encryption via a shortcut. Weak keys show regularities in encryption or poor encryption. For instance, DES has four keys for which encryption is the same as decryption. This means that if one of these weak keys is used to encrypt plaintext, an attacker can use the weak key to encrypt the ciphertext and reveal the plaintext.

The DES weak keys are those that produce 16 identical subkeys. This occurs when the key bits are:

- Alternating ones plus zeros (0101010101010101)

- Alternating F plus E (FEFEFEFEFEFEFEFE)

- E0E0E0E0F1F1F1F1

- 1F1F1F1F0E0E0E0E

It is very unlikely that such keys would be chosen, but implementations should still verify all keys and prevent weak keys from being used. With manual key generation, take special care to avoid defining weak keys.

Refer to
Figure
in online course

Several types of cryptographic keys can be generated:

- Symmetric keys, which can be exchanged between two routers supporting a VPN

- Asymmetric keys, which are used in secure HTTPS applications

- Digital signatures, which are used when connecting to a secure website

- Hash keys, which are used in symmetric and asymmetric key generation, digital signatures, and other types of applications

Regardless of the type of key, all keys share similar issues. Choosing a suitable key length is one issue. If the cryptographic system is trustworthy, the only way to break it is with a brute-force attack. A brute-force attack is a search through the entire keyspace, trying all the possible keys to find a key that decrypts the data. If the keyspace is large enough, the search requires an enormous amount of time, making such an exhaustive effort impractical.

On average, an attacker has to search through half of the keyspace before the correct key is found. The time that is needed to accomplish this search depends on the computer power that is available to the attacker. Current key lengths can easily make any attempt insignificant, because it takes millions or billions of years to complete the search when a sufficiently long key is used. With modern algorithms that are trusted, the strength of protection depends solely on the length of the key. Choose the key length so that it protects data confidentiality or integrity for an adequate period of time. Data that is more sensitive and needs to be kept secret longer must use longer keys.

Refer to **Figure** in online course

Performance is another issue that can influence the choice of a key length. An administrator must find a good balance between the speed and protective strength of an algorithm, because some algorithms, such as the Rivest, Shamir, and Adleman (RSA) algorithm, run slowly because of large key sizes. Strive for adequate protection, while enabling unhindered communication over untrusted networks.

The estimated funding of the attacker should also affect the choice of key length. When assessing the risk of someone breaking the encryption algorithm, estimate the resources of the attacker and how long the data must be protected. For example, classic DES can be broken by a $1 million machine in a couple of minutes. If the data that is being protected is worth significantly more than $1 million dollars needed to acquire a cracking device, then, classic DES is a bad choice. It would take an attacker a million years or more to crack 168-bit 3DES or 128-bit RC4, which makes either of these key length choices more than adequate.

Because of the rapid advances in technology and cryptanalytic methods, the key size that is needed for a particular application is constantly increasing. For example, part of the strength of the RSA algorithm is the difficulty of factoring large numbers. If a 1024-bit number is hard to factor, a 2048-bit number is going to be even harder. Even with the fastest computers available today, it would take many lifetimes to factor a 1024-bit number that is a factor of two 512-bit prime numbers. Of course, this advantage is lost if an easy way to factor large numbers is found, but cryptographers consider this possibility unlikely. The rule "the longer the key, the better" is valid, except for possible performance reasons.

7.3 Confidentiality

7.3.1 Encryption

Refer to **Figure** in online course

Cryptographic encryption can provide confidentiality at several layers of the OSI model by incorporating various tools and protocols:

- Proprietary link-encrypting devices provide Data Link Layer confidentiality.

- Network Layer protocols, such as the IPsec protocol suite, provide Network Layer confidentiality.

- Protocols such as Secure Sockets Layer (SSL) or Transport Layer Security (TLS) provide Session Layer confidentiality.

- Secure email, secure database session (Oracle SQL*net), and secure messaging (Lotus Notes sessions) provide Application Layer confidentiality.

There are two approaches to ensuring the security of data when using various encryption methods. The first is to protect the algorithm. If the security of an encryption system is based on the secrecy of the algorithm itself, the algorithm code must be heavily guarded. If the algorithm is revealed, every party that is involved must change the algorithm. The second approach is to protect the keys. With modern cryptography, all algorithms are public. The cryptographic keys ensure the secrecy of the data. Cryptographic keys are sequences of bits that are input into an encryption algorithm together with the data to be encrypted.

Two basic classes of encryption algorithms protect the keys: symmetric and asymmetric. Each differs in its use of keys. Symmetric encryption algorithms use the same key, sometimes called a secret key, to encrypt and decrypt data. The key must be pre-shared. A pre-shared key is known by the sender and receiver before any encrypted communications commence. Because both parties are guarding a shared secret, the encryption algorithms used can have shorter key lengths. Shorter key lengths mean faster execution. Symmetric algorithms are generally much less computationally intensive than asymmetric algorithms.

Asymmetric encryption algorithms use different keys to encrypt and decrypt data. Secure messages can be exchanged without having to have a pre-shared key. Because both parties do not have a shared secret, very long key lengths must be used to thwart attackers. These algorithms are resource intensive and slower to execute. In practice, asymmetric algorithms are typically hundreds to thousands times slower than symmetric algorithms.

Refer to **Figure** in online course

To help understand the differences between both types of algorithms, consider an example where Alice and Bob live in different locations and want to exchange secret messages to one another through the mail system. In this example, Alice wants to send a secret message to Bob.

Symmetric Algorithm

In the symmetric algorithm example, Alice and Bob have identical keys to a single padlock. These keys were exchanged prior to sending any secret messages. Alice writes a secret message and puts it in a small box that she locks using the padlock with her key. She mails the box to Bob. The message is safely locked inside the box as the box makes its way through the post office system. When Bob receives the box, he uses his key to unlock the padlock and retrieve the message. Bob can use the same box and padlock to send a secret reply back to Alice.

Asymmetric Algorithm

In the asymmetric algorithm example, Bob and Alice do not exchange keys prior to sending secret messages. Instead, Bob and Alice each have a separate padlock with separate corresponding keys. For Alice to send a secret message to Bob, she must first contact him and ask him to send his open padlock to her. Bob sends the padlock but keeps his key. When Alice receives the padlock, she writes her secret message and puts it in a small box. She also puts her open padlock in the box, but keeps her key. She then locks the box with Bob's padlock. When Alice locks the box, she is no longer able to get inside because she does not have a key to that padlock. She mails the box to Bob. As the box is sent through the mail system, no one is able to open the box. When Bob receives the box, he can use his key to unlock the box and retrieve the message from Alice. To send a secure reply, Bob puts his secret message in the box along with his open padlock and locks the box using Alice's padlock. Bob mails the secured box back to Alice.

Refer to **Figure** in online course

Symmetric, or secret key, encryption is the most commonly used form of cryptography, because the shorter key length increases the speed of execution. Additionally, symmetric key algorithms are based on simple mathematical operations that can easily be accelerated by hardware. Symmetric encryption is often used for wire-speed encryption in data networks and to provide bulk encryption when data privacy is required, such as to protect a VPN.

With symmetric encryption, key management can be a challenge. The encryption and decryption keys are the same. The sender and the receiver must exchange the symmetric, secret key using a secure channel before any encryption can occur. The security of a symmetric algorithm rests in the secrecy of the symmetric key. By obtaining the key, anyone can encrypt and decrypt messages.

DES, 3DES, AES, Software Encryption Algorithm (SEAL), and the Rivest ciphers (RC) series, which includes RC2, RC4, RC5, and RC6, are all well-known encryption algorithms that use symmetric keys. There are many other encryption algorithms, such as Blowfish, Twofish, Threefish, and Serpent. However, these protocols are either not supported on Cisco platforms or have yet to gain wide acceptance.

Refer to
Figure
in online course

The most commonly used techniques in symmetric encryption cryptography are block ciphers and stream ciphers.

Block Ciphers

Block ciphers transform a fixed-length block of plaintext into a common block of ciphertext of 64 or 128 bits. Block size refers to how much data is encrypted at any one time. Currently the block size, also known as the fixed length, for many block ciphers is either 64 bits or 128 bits. The key length refers to the size of the encryption key that is used. This ciphertext is decrypted by applying the reverse transformation to the ciphertext block, using the same secret key.

Block ciphers usually result in output data that is larger than the input data, because the ciphertext must be a multiple of the block size. For example, DES encrypts blocks in 64-bit chunks using a 56-bit key. To accomplish this, the block algorithm takes data one chunk at a time, for example, 8 bytes each chunk, until the entire block size is full. If there is less input data than one full block, the algorithm adds artificial data (blanks) until the full 64 bits are used.

Common block ciphers include DES with a 64-bit block size, AES with a 128-bit block size, and RSA with a variable block size.

Stream Ciphers

Unlike block ciphers, stream ciphers encrypt plaintext one byte or one bit at a time. Stream ciphers can be thought of as a block cipher with a block size of one bit. With a stream cipher, the transformation of these smaller plaintext units varies, depending on when they are encountered during the encryption process. Stream ciphers can be much faster than block ciphers, and generally do not increase the message size, because they can encrypt an arbitrary number of bits.

The Vigenere cipher is an example of a stream cipher. This cipher is periodic, because the key is of finite length, and the key is repeated if it is shorter than the message.

Common stream ciphers include A5, which is used to encrypt GSM cell phone communications, and the RC4 cipher. DES can also be used in stream cipher mode.

Refer to
Figure
in online course

Choosing an encryption algorithm is one of the most important decisions a security professional makes when building a cryptosystem. Two main criteria should be considered when selecting an encryption algorithm for an organization:

- *The algorithm is trusted by the cryptographic community.* Most new algorithms are broken very quickly, so algorithms that have been resisting attacks for a number of years are preferred. Inventors and promoters often oversell the benefits of new algorithms.

- *The algorithm adequately protects against brute-force attacks.* A good cryptographic algorithm is designed in such a way that it resists common cryptographic attacks. The best way to break data that is protected by the algorithm is to try to decrypt the data using all the possible keys. The amount of time that such an attack needs depends on the number of possible keys, but is generally a very long time. With appropriately long keys, such attacks are usually considered unfeasible. If the algorithm is considered trusted, there is no shortcut to break it, and the attacker must search through the keyspace to guess the correct key. The algorithm must allow key lengths that satisfy the confidentiality requirements of an organization. For example, DES does not provide enough protection for most modern needs because of its short key.

Other criteria to consider:

- *The algorithm supports variable and long key lengths and scalability.* Variable key lengths and scalability are also desirable attributes of a good encryption algorithm. The longer the encryption key, the longer it takes an attacker to break it. For example, a 16-bit key has 65,536 possible keys, but a 56-bit key has 7.2 x 10^16 possible keys. Scalability provides flexible key length and enables the administrator to select the strength and speed of the encryption required.

- *The algorithm does not have export or import restrictions.* Carefully consider export and import restrictions when using encryption internationally. Some countries do not allow the export of encryption algorithms, or allow only the export of these algorithms with shorter keys. Some countries impose import restrictions on cryptographic algorithms.

7.3.2 Data Encryption Standard

Refer to **Figure** in online course

Data Encryption Standard (DES) is a symmetric encryption algorithm that usually operates in block mode. It encrypts data in 64-bit blocks. The DES algorithm is essentially a sequence of permutations and substitutions of data bits combined with an encryption key. The same algorithm and key are used for both encryption and decryption.

DES has a fixed key length. The key is 64-bits long, but only 56 bits are used for encryption. The remaining 8 bits are used for parity. The least significant bit of each key byte is used to indicate odd parity.

A DES key is always 56 bits long. When DES is used with a weaker encryption of a 40-bit key, the encryption key is 40 secret bits and 16 known bits, which make the key length 56 bits. In this case, DES has a key strength of 40 bits.

Refer to **Figure** in online course

Although DES typically uses block cipher mode, it can also encrypt using stream cipher mode. To encrypt or decrypt more than 64 bits of data, DES uses two standardized block cipher modes, Electronic Code Book (ECB) or Cipher Block Chaining (CBC).

Both cipher modes use the logical operation XOR with the following definition:

1 XOR 1 = 0

1 XOR 0 = 1

0 XOR 1 = 1

0 XOR 0 = 0

Block Cipher Mode

ECB mode serially encrypts each 64-bit plaintext block using the same 56-bit key. If two identical plaintext blocks are encrypted using the same key, their ciphertext blocks are the same. Therefore, an attacker could identify similar or identical traffic flowing through a communications channel. The attacker could then, without even knowing the meaning behind the traffic, build a catalog of messages and replay them later to possibly gain unauthorized entry. For example, an attacker might unknowingly capture a login sequence of someone with administrative privilege whose traffic is protected by DES-ECB and then replay it. That risk is undesirable, so CBC mode was invented to mitigate this risk.

In CBC mode, each 64-bit plaintext block is exclusive ORed (XORed) bitwise with the previous ciphertext block and then is encrypted using the DES key. The encryption of each block depends on previous blocks. Encryption of the same 64-bit plaintext block can result in different ciphertext blocks.

CBC mode can help guard against certain attacks, but it cannot help against sophisticated cryptanalysis or an extended brute-force attack.

Stream Cipher Mode

To encrypt or decrypt more than 64 bits of data, DES uses two common stream cipher modes:

- Cipher feedback (CFB), which is similar to CBC and can encrypt any number of bits, including single bits or single characters.

- Output feedback (OFB) generates keystream blocks, which are then XORed with the plaintext blocks to get the ciphertext.

In stream cipher mode, the cipher uses previous ciphertext and the secret key to generate a pseudo-random stream of bits, which only the secret key can generate. To encrypt data, the data is XORed with the pseudo-random stream bit by bit, or sometimes byte by byte, to obtain the ciphertext. The decryption procedure is the same. The receiver generates the same random stream using the secret key, and XORs the ciphertext with the pseudo-random stream to obtain the plaintext.

Refer to **Figure** in online course

There are several things to consider when securing DES-encrypted data:

- Change keys frequently to help prevent brute-force attacks.

- Use a secure channel to communicate the DES key from the sender to the receiver.

- Consider using DES in CBC mode. With CBC, the encryption of each 64-bit block depends on previous blocks. CBC is the most widely used mode of DES.

- Test a key to see if it is a weak key before using it. DES has 4 weak keys and 12 semi-weak keys. Because there are 2^{56} possible DES keys, the chance of picking one of these keys is very small. However, because testing the key has no significant impact on the encryption time, testing is recommended.

Because of its short key length, DES is considered a good protocol to protect data for a very short time. 3DES is a better choice to protect data. It has an algorithm that is very trusted and has higher security strength.

7.3.3 3DES

Refer to **Figure** in online course

With advances in computer-processing power, the original 56-bit DES key became too short to withstand attack from those with a medium-sized budget for hacking technology. One way to increase the DES effective key length, without changing the well-analyzed algorithm itself, is to use the same algorithm with different keys several times in a row.

The technique of applying DES three times in a row to a plaintext block is called 3DES. Today, brute-force attacks on 3DES are considered unfeasible because the basic algorithm has been well tested in the field for more than 35 years. It is considered very trustworthy.

The Cisco IPsec implementation uses DES and 3DES in CBC mode.

Refer to
Figure
in online course

3DES uses a method called 3DES-Encrypt-Decrypt-Encrypt (3DES-EDE) to encrypt plaintext. First, the message is encrypted using the first 56-bit key, known as K1. Next, the data is decrypted using the second 56-bit key, known as K2. Finally, the data is encrypted again, using the third 56-bit key, known as K3.

The 3DES-EDE procedure is much more effective at increasing security than simply encrypting the data three times with three different keys. Encrypting data three times in a row using different 56-bit keys equals a 58-bit key strength. The 3DES-EDE procedure, on the other hand, provides encryption with an effective key length of 168 bits. If keys K1 and K3 are equal, as in some implementations, a less secure encryption of 112 bits is achieved.

To decrypt the message, the opposite of the 3DES-EDE method is used. First, the ciphertext is decrypted using key K3. Next, the data is encrypted using key K2. Finally, the data is decrypted using key K1.

Although 3DES is very secure, it is also very resource intensive. For this reason, the AES encryption algorithm was developed. It has proven to be as secure as 3DES, but with much faster results.

7.3.4 Advanced Encryption Standard

Refer to
Figure
in online course

For a number of years, it was recognized that DES would eventually reach the end of its usefulness. In 1997, the AES initiative was announced, and the public was invited to propose encryption schemes to replace DES. After a five-year standardization process in which 15 competing designs were presented and evaluated, the U.S. National Institute of Standards and Technology (NIST) selected the Rijndael block cipher as the AES algorithm.

The Rijndael cipher, developed by Joan Daemen and Vincent Rijmen, has a variable block length and key length. Rijndael is an iterated block cipher, which means that the initial input block and cipher key undergo multiple transformation cycles before producing output. The algorithm can operate over a variable-length block using variable-length keys. A 128-, 192-, or 256-bit key can be used to encrypt data blocks that are 128, 192, or 256 bits long, and all nine combinations of key and block length are possible.

The accepted AES implementation of Rijndael contains only some of the capabilities of the Rijndael algorithm. The algorithm is written so that the block length or the key length or both can easily be extended in multiples of 32 bits, and the system is specifically designed for efficient implementation in hardware or software on a range of processors.

The AES algorithm has been analyzed extensively and is now used worldwide. Although it has not been proven in day-to-day use to the degree that 3DES has, AES with the Rijndael cipher is the more efficient algorithm. It can be used in high-throughput, low-latency environments, especially when 3DES cannot handle the throughput or latency requirements. AES is expected to gain trust as time passes and more attacks have been attempted against it.

Refer to
Figure
in online course

AES was chosen to replace DES for a number of reasons. The key length of AES makes the key much stronger than DES. AES runs faster than 3DES on comparable hardware. AES is more efficient than DES and 3DES on comparable hardware, usually by a factor of five when it is compared with DES. AES is more suitable for high-throughput, low-latency environments, especially if pure software encryption is used.

Despite these advantages, AES is a relatively young algorithm. The golden rule of cryptography states that a mature algorithm is always more trusted. 3DES is therefore a more trusted choice in terms of strength, because it has been tested and analyzed for 35 years.

AES is available in the following Cisco VPN devices as an encryption transform:

- IPsec-protected traffic using Cisco IOS Release 12.2(13)T and later

- Cisco PIX Firewall software version 6.3 and later

- Cisco ASA software version 7.0 and later

- Cisco VPN 3000 software version 3.6 and later

7.3.5 Alternate Encryption Algorithms

Refer to **Figure** in online course

The Software-optimized Encryption Algorithm (SEAL) is an alternative algorithm to software-based DES, 3DES, and AES. Phillip Rogaway and Don Coppersmith designed SEAL in 1993. It is a stream cipher that uses a 160-bit encryption key. Because it is a stream cipher, data to be encrypted is continuously encrypted and, therefore, much faster than block ciphers. However, it has a longer initialization phase during which a large set of tables is created using SHA.

SEAL has a lower impact on the CPU compared to other software-based algorithms. SEAL support was added to Cisco IOS Software Release 12.3(7)T.

SEAL has several restrictions:

- The Cisco router and the peer must support IPsec.

- The Cisco router and the other peer must run an IOS image with k9 long keys (the k9 subsystem).

- The router and the peer must not have hardware IPsec encryption.

Refer to **Figure** in online course

The RC algorithms were designed all or in part by Ronald Rivest, who also invented MD5. The RC algorithms are widely deployed in many networking applications because of their favorable speed and variable key-length capabilities.

There are a number of widely used RC algorithms:

- *RC2* Variable key-size block cipher that was designed as a "drop-in" replacement for DES.

- *RC4* World's most widely used stream cipher. This algorithm is a variable key-size Vernam stream cipher that is often used in file encryption products and for secure communications, such as within SSL. It is not considered a one-time pad, because its key is not random. The cipher can be expected to run very quickly in software and is considered secure, although it can be implemented insecurely, as in Wired Equivalent Privacy (WEP).

- *RC5* A fast block cipher that has a variable block size and key size. RC5 can be used as a drop-in replacement for DES if the block size is set to 64-bit.

- *RC6* Developed in 1997, RC6 was an AES finalist (Rijndael won). A 128-bit to 256- bit block cipher that was designed by Rivest, Sidney, and Yin and is based on RC5. Its main design goal was to meet the requirement of AES.

7.3.6 Diffie-Hellman Key Exchange

Refer to **Figure** in online course

Whitfield Diffie and Martin Hellman invented the Diffie-Hellman (DH) algorithm in 1976. The DH algorithm is the basis of most modern automatic key exchange methods and is one of the most common protocols used in networking today. Diffie-Hellman is not an encryption mechanism and is not typically used to encrypt data. Instead, it is a method to securely exchange the keys that encrypt data.

In a symmetric key system, both sides of the communication must have identical keys. Securely exchanging those keys has always been a challenge. Asymmetric key systems address this challenge because they use two keys. One key is called the private key, and the other is the public key. The private key is secret and known only to the user. The public key is openly shared and easily distributed.

DH is a mathematical algorithm that allows two computers to generate an identical shared secret on both systems, without having communicated before. The new shared key is never actually exchanged between the sender and receiver. But because both parties know it, it can be used by an encryption algorithm to encrypt traffic between the two systems. Its security is based on the difficulty of calculating the discrete logarithms of very large numbers.

DH is commonly used when data is exchanged using an IPsec VPN, data is encrypted on the Internet using either SSL or TLS, or when SSH data is exchanged.

Unfortunately, asymmetric key systems are extremely slow for any sort of bulk encryption. This is why it is common to encrypt the bulk of the traffic using a symmetric algorithm such as DES, 3DES, or AES and use the DH algorithm to create keys that will be used by the encryption algorithm.

Refer to **Figure** in online course

To help understand how DH is used, consider this example of communication between Alice and Bob.

Step 1. To start a DH exchange, Alice and Bob must agree on two non-secret numbers. The first number, **g**, is a base number (also called the generator). The second number, **p**, is a prime number that is used as the modulus. These numbers are usually public and are chosen from a table of known values. Typically, **g** is a very small number, such as 2, 3, 4, or 5 and **p** is a larger prime number.

Step 2. Next, Alice generates a secret number **Xa**, and Bob generates his secret number **Xb**.

Step 3. Based on **g**, **p**, and Alice's **X** number, Alice calculates a public value (**Ya**) using the DH algorithm. She sends her public value (**Ya**) to Bob.

Step 4. Bob also calculates a public value (**Yb**) using **g**, **p** and his secret number. Bob sends his public value (**Yb**) to Alice. These values are not the same.

Step 5. Alice now performs a second DH algorithm using Bob's public value (**Yb**) as the new base number.

Step 6. Bob also performs a second DH algorithm using Alice's public value (**Ya**) as the new base number.

The result is that Alice and Bob both come up with the same result (**Z**). This new value is now a shared secret between Alice and Bob and can be used by an encryption algorithm as a shared secret key between Alice and Bob.

Anyone listening on the channel cannot compute the secret value, because only **g**, **p**, **Ya,** and **Yb** are known, and at least one secret value is needed to calculate the shared secret. Unless the attackers can compute the discrete algorithm of the above equation to recover **Xa** or **Xb**, they cannot obtain the shared secret.

Although DH is used with symmetric algorithms to create shared keys, it is important to remember that it is actually an asymmetric algorithm.

What other asymmetric algorithms are there and what are they used for?

7.4 Public Key Cryptography

7.4.1 Symmetric Versus Asymmetric Encryption

Refer to
Figure
in online course

Asymmetric algorithms, also sometimes called public-key algorithms, are designed so that the key that is used for encryption is different from the key that is used for decryption. The decryption key cannot, in any reasonable amount of time, be calculated from the encryption key and vice versa.

In the example of Alice and Bob, they did not exchange pre-shared keys prior to communication. Instead, they each had separate padlocks and corresponding keys. In this same manner, asymmetric algorithms are used to exchange secret messages without ever having had a shared secret before the exchange.

There are four protocols that use asymmetric key algorithms:

- Internet Key Exchange (IKE), a fundamental component of IPsec VPNs
- Secure Socket Layer, now implemented as IETF standard TLS
- SSH
- Pretty Good Privacy (PGP), a computer program that provides cryptographic privacy and authentication and often used to increase the security of email communications

Asymmetric algorithms use two keys: a public key and a private key. Both keys are capable of the encryption process, but the complementary matched key is required for decryption. For example, if a public key encrypts the data, the matching private key decrypts the data. The opposite is also true. If a private key encrypts the data, the corresponding public key decrypts the data.

This process enables asymmetric algorithms to achieve authentication, integrity, and confidentiality.

Refer to
Figure
in online course

The confidentiality objective of asymmetric algorithms is achieved when the encryption process is started with the public key. The process can be summarized using the formula:

Public Key (Encrypt) + Private Key (Decrypt) = Confidentiality

When the public key is used to encrypt the data, the private key must be used to decrypt the data. Only one host has the private key, therefore, confidentiality is achieved.

If the private key is compromised, another key pair must be generated to replace the compromised key.

Refer to
Figure
in online course

The authentication objective of asymmetric algorithms is achieved when the encryption process is started with the private key. The process can be summarized using the formula:

Private Key (Encrypt) + Public Key (Decrypt) = Authentication

When the private key is used to encrypt the data, the corresponding public key must be used to decrypt the data. Because only one host has the private key, only that host could have encrypted the message, providing authentication of the sender. Typically, no attempt is made to preserve the secrecy of the public key, so any number of hosts can decrypt the message. When a host successfully decrypts a message using a public key, it is trusted that the private key encrypted the message, which verifies who the sender is. This is a form of authentication.

Refer to
Figure
in online course

When sending a message that ensures message confidentiality, authentication and integrity, the combination of two encryption phases is necessary.

Phase 1 - Confidentiality

Alice wants to send a message to Bob ensuring message confidentiality (only Bob can read the document in plaintext). Alice uses the public key of Bob to cipher the message. Only Bob can decipher it, using his private key.

Phase 2 - Authentication and Integrity

Alice also wants to ensure message authentication and integrity (Bob is sure that the document was not modified, and was sent by Alice). Alice uses her private key to cipher a hash of the message. In this way, Bob can use the public key of Alice to verify that the message was not modified (the received hash is equal to the locally determined hash based on Alice's public key). Additionally, this verifies that Alice is definitely the sender of the message because nobody else has Alice's private key.

By sending a message that was ciphered using Bob's public key and a ciphered hash that was encrypted using Alice's private key, confidentiality, authenticity and integrity are ensured.

A variety of well-known asymmetric key algorithms are available:

- Diffie-Hellman

- Digital Signature Standard (DSS), which incorporates the Digital Signature Algorithm

- RSA encryption algorithms

- ElGamal

- Elliptical curve techniques

Although the mathematics differ with each algorithm, they all share one trait in that the calculations required are complicated. Their design is based on computational problems, such as factoring extremely large numbers or computing discrete logarithms of extremely large numbers. As a result, computation takes more time for asymmetric algorithms. In fact, asymmetric algorithms can be up to 1,000 times slower than symmetric algorithms. Because they lack speed, asymmetric algorithms are typically used in low-volume cryptographic mechanisms, such as key exchanges that have no inherent key exchange technology, and digital signatures.

The key management of asymmetric algorithms tends to be simpler than that of symmetric algorithms, because usually one of the two encryption or decryption keys can be made public.

Typical key lengths for asymmetric algorithms range from 512 to 4096 bits. Key lengths greater than or equal to 1024 are considered to be trustworthy, while key lengths that are shorter than 1024 bits are considered unreliable for most algorithms.

It is not relevant to compare the key length of asymmetric and symmetric algorithms because the underlying design of the two algorithm families differs greatly. To illustrate this point, it is generally thought that a 2048-bit encryption key of RSA is roughly equivalent to a 128-bit key of RC4 in terms of resistance against brute-force attacks.

7.4.2 Digital Signatures

Refer to **Figure** in online course

Handwritten signatures have long been used as a proof of authorship of the contents of a document. Digital signatures can provide the same functionality as handwritten signatures, and much more. For example, assume a customer sends transaction instructions via an email to a stockbroker, and the transaction turns out badly for the customer. It is conceivable that the customer could claim never to have sent the transaction order or that someone forged the email.

The brokerage could protect itself by requiring the use of digital signatures before accepting instructions via email. In fact, digital signatures are often used in the following situations:

- To provide a unique proof of data source, which can only be generated by a single party, such as contract signing in e-commerce environments.

- To authenticate a user by using the private key of that user and the signature it generates.

- To prove the authenticity and integrity of PKI certificates.

- To provide a secure timestamp using a trusted time source.

Specifically, digital signatures provide three basic security services:

- *Authenticity of digitally signed data* Digital signatures authenticate a source, proving that a certain party has seen and signed the data in question.

- *Integrity of digitally signed data* Digital signatures guarantee that the data has not changed from the time it was signed.

- *Nonrepudiation of the transaction* The recipient can take the data to a third party, and the third party accepts the digital signature as a proof that this data exchange did take place. The signing party cannot repudiate that it has signed the data.

To better understand nonrepudiation, consider using HMAC functions, which also provide authenticity and integrity guarantees. With HMAC functions, two or more parties share the same authentication key and can compute the HMAC fingerprint. Therefore, taking received data and its HMAC fingerprint to a third party does not prove that the other party sent this data. Other users could have generated the same HMAC fingerprint, because they have a copy of the HMAC authentication key. With digital signatures, each party has a unique, secret signature key, which is not shared with any other party, making nonrepudiation possible.

Refer to
Figure
in online course

Digital signatures have specific properties that enable entity authentication and data integrity:

- The signature is authentic and not forgeable. The signature is proof that the signer, and no one else, signed the document.

- The signature is not reusable. The signature is part of the document and cannot be moved to a different document.

- The signature is unalterable. After a document is signed, it cannot be altered.

- The signature cannot be repudiated. For legal purposes, the signature and the document are considered physical things. Signers cannot claim later that they did not sign it.

In some countries, including the United States, digital signatures are considered equivalent to handwritten signatures if they meet certain provisions. Some of these provisions include the proper protection of the certificate authority, the trusted signer of all other public keys, and the proper protection of the private keys of the users. In such a scenario, users are responsible for keeping their private keys private, because a stolen private key can be used to steal their identity.

Many Cisco products use digital signatures:

- IPsec gateways and clients use digital signatures to authenticate their Internet Key Exchange (IKE) sessions if the administrator chooses digital certificates and the IKE RSA signature authentication method.

- Cisco SSL endpoints, such as Cisco IOS HTTP servers, and the Cisco Adaptive Security Device Manager (ASDM) use digital signatures to prove the identity of the SSL server.

- Some of the service provider-oriented voice management protocols for billing and settlement use digital signatures to authenticate the involved parties.

Refer to
Figure
in online course

The current signing procedures of digital signatures are not simply implemented by public-key operations. In fact, a modern digital signature is based on a hash function and a public-key algorithm.

There are six steps to the digital signature process:

Step 1.   The sending device (signer) creates a hash of the document.

Step 2. The sending device encrypts the hash with the private key of the signer.

Step 3. The encrypted hash, known as the signature, is appended to the document.

Step 4. The receiving device (verifier) accepts the document with the digital signature and obtains the public key of the sending device.

Step 5. The receiving device decrypts the signature using the public key of the sending device. This step unveils the assumed hash value of the sending device.

Step 6. The receiving device makes a hash of the received document, without its signature, and compares this hash to the decrypted signature hash. If the hashes match, the document is authentic; it was signed by the assumed signer and has not changed since it was signed.

Both encryption and digital signatures are required to ensure that the message is private and has not changed.

Refer to **Figure** in online course

In addition to ensuring authenticity and integrity of messages, digital signatures are commonly used to provide assurance of the authenticity and integrity of mobile and classic software codes. The executable files, or possibly the entire installation package of a program, are wrapped with a digitally signed envelope, which allows the end user to verify the signature before installing the software.

Digitally signing code provides several assurances about the code:

- The code has not been modified since it left the software publisher.

- The code is authentic and is actually sourced by the publisher.

- The publisher undeniably publishes the code. This provides nonrepudiation of the act of publishing.

The digital signature could be forged only if someone obtained the private key of the publisher. The assurance level of digital signatures is extremely high if the private key is protected properly.

The user of the software must also obtain the public key, which is used to verify the signature. The user can obtain the key in a secure fashion. For example, the key could be included with the installation of the operating system or transferred securely over the network.

Protecting the private key is of the highest importance when using digital signatures. If the signature key of an entity is compromised, the attacker can sign data in the name of that entity, and repudiation is not possible. To exchange verification keys in a scalable fashion, a secure but accessible method must be deployed.

Refer to **Figure** in online course

Well-known asymmetric algorithms, such as RSA or Digital Signature Algorithm (DSA), are typically used to perform digital signing.

DSA

In 1994, the U.S. NIST selected the DSA as the Digital Signature Standard (DSS). DSA is based on the discrete logarithm problem and can only provide digital signatures.

DSA, however, has had several criticisms. Critics claim that DSA lacks the flexibility of RSA. The verification of signatures is too slow, and the process by which NIST chose DSA was too secretive and arbitrary. In response to these criticisms, the DSS now incorporates two additional algorithm choices: Digital Signature Using Reversible Public Key Cryptography (which uses RSA) and the Elliptic Curve Digital Signature Algorithm (ECDSA).

A network administrator must decide whether RSA or DSA is more appropriate for a given situation. DSA signature generation is faster than DSA signature verification. On the other hand, RSA signature verification is much faster than signature generation.

7.4.3 Rivest, Shamir, and Alderman

Refer to
Figure
in online course

RSA is one of the most common asymmetric algorithms. Ron Rivest, Adi Shamir, and Len Adleman invented the RSA algorithm in 1977. It was a patented public-key algorithm. The patent expired in September 2000, and the algorithm is now in the public domain. Of all the public-key algorithms that were proposed over the years, RSA is by far the easiest to understand and implement.

The RSA algorithm is very flexible because it has a variable key length, so the key can be shortened for faster processing. There is a tradeoff; the shorter the key, the less secure it is.

The RSA keys are usually 512 to 2048 bits long. RSA has withstood years of extensive cryptanalysis. Although the security of RSA has been neither proved nor disproved, it does suggest a confidence level in the algorithm. The security of RSA is based on the difficulty of factoring very large numbers. If an easy method of factoring these large numbers were discovered, the effectiveness of RSA would be destroyed.

The RSA algorithm is based on a public key and a private key. The public key can be published and given away, but the private key must be kept secret. It is not possible to determine the private key from the public key using any computationally feasible algorithm and vice versa.

RSA keys are long term and are usually changed or renewed after some months or even years. It is currently the most common method for signature generation and is used widely in e-commerce systems and Internet protocols.

Refer to
Figure
in online course

RSA is about a hundred times slower than DES in hardware, and about a thousand times slower than DES in software. This performance problem is the main reason that RSA is typically used only to protect small amounts of data.

RSA is mainly used to ensure confidentiality of data by performing encryption, and to perform authentication of data or nonrepudiation of data, or both, by generating digital signatures.

7.4.4 Public Key Infrastructure

Refer to
Figure
in online course

In large organizations, it is impractical for all parties to continually exchange identification documents. With trusted third-party protocols, all individuals agree to accept the word of a neutral third party. Presumably, the third party does an in-depth investigation prior to the issuance of credentials. After this in-depth investigation, the third party issues credentials that are difficult to forge. From that point forward, all individuals who trust the third party simply accept the credentials that the third party issues. Certificate servers are an example of a trusted third party.

As an example, a large organization such as Cisco goes to reasonable lengths to identify employees and contractors, and then issues an ID badge. This badge is relatively difficult to forge. Measures are in place to protect the integrity of the badge and the badge issuance. Because of these measures, all Cisco personnel accept this badge as authoritative of the identity of any individual.

If this method did not exist and 10 individuals needed to validate each other, 90 validations would need to be performed before everyone would have validated everyone else. Adding a single individual to the group would require an additional 20 validations because each one of the original 10 individuals would need to authenticate the new individual, and the new individual would need to authenticate the original 10. This method does not scale well.

For another example, assume that Alice applies for a driver's license. In this process, she submits evidence of her identity and her qualifications to drive. Her application is approved, and a license is issued. Later, Alice needs to cash a check at the bank. Upon presenting the check to the bank teller, the bank teller asks her for ID. The bank, because it trusts the government agency that issued the driver's license, verifies her identity and cashes her check.

Certificate servers function like the driver's license bureau. The driver's license is analogous to a certificate in a Public Key Infrastructure (PKI) or another technology that supports certificates.

How does PKI actually work?

Refer to
Figure
in online course

PKI is the service framework that is needed to support large-scale public key-based technologies. A PKI allows for very scalable solutions and is becoming an extremely important authentication solution for VPNs.

PKI is a set of technical, organizational, and legal components that are needed to establish a system that enables large-scale use of public key cryptography to provide authenticity, confidentiality, integrity, and nonrepudiation services. The PKI framework consists of the hardware, software, people, policies, and procedures needed to create, manage, store, distribute, and revoke digital certificates.

Two very important terms must be defined when talking about a PKI: certificates and certificate authority (CA).

Certificates are used for various purposes in a network. Certificates are public information. They contain the binding between the names and public keys of entities and are usually published in a centralized directory so that other PKI users can easily access them.

The CA is a trusted third-party entity that issues certificates. The certificate of a user is always signed by a CA. Every CA also has a certificate containing its public key, signed by itself. This is called a CA certificate or, more properly, a self-signed CA certificate.

A single CA server can facilitate many applications that require digital certificates for authentication purposes. Using CA servers is a solution that simplifies the management of authentication and provides strong security due to the strength of the cryptographic mechanisms that are used in combination with digital certificates.

Refer to
Figure
in online course

PKI is more than just a CA and its users. In addition to implementing the enabling technology, building a large PKI involves a huge amount of organizational and legal work. There are five main components of a PKI:

- PKI users, such as people, devices, and servers
- CAs for key management
- Storage and protocols
- Supporting organizational framework, known as practices and user authentication using Local Registration Authorities (LRAs)
- Supporting legal framework

Many vendors offer CA servers as a managed service or as an end user product, including VeriSign, Entrust Technologies, RSA, CyberTrust, Microsoft, and Novell. CAs, especially outsourced ones, can issue certificates of a number of classes, which determine how trusted a certificate is. A single outsourcing vendor such as VeriSign might run a single CA, issuing certificates of different classes, and its customers use the CA they need depending on the desired level of trust.

A certificate class is usually identified by a number. The higher the number, the more trusted the certificate. The trust in the certificate is usually determined by how rigorous the procedure was that verified the identity of the holder when the certificate was issued:

- Class 0 is for testing purposes in which no checks have been performed.
- Class 1 is for individuals with a focus on verification of email.

- Class 2 is for organizations for which proof of identity is required.

- Class 3 is for servers and software signing for which independent verification and checking of identity and authority is done by the issuing certificate authority.

- Class 4 is for online business transactions between companies.

- Class 5 is for private organizations or governmental security.

For example, a class 1 certificate might require an email reply from the holder to confirm the wish to enroll. This kind of confirmation is a weak authentication of the holder. For a class 3 or 4 certificate, the future holder must prove identity and authenticate the public key by showing up in person with at least two official ID documents.

Refer to **Figure** in online course

Some PKIs offer the possibility, or even require the use, of two key pairs per entity. The first public and private key pair is intended only for encryption operations. The public key encrypts, and the private key decrypts. The second public and private key pair is intended for digital signing operations. The private key signs, and the public key verifies the signature.

These keys are sometimes called usage or special keys. They may differ in key length and even in the choice of the public key algorithm. If the PKI requires two key pairs per entity, a user has two certificates. An encryption certificate contains the public key of the user, which encrypts the data, and a signature certificate contains the public key of the user, which verifies the digital signature of the user.

The following scenarios typically employ usage keys:

- When an encryption certificate is used much more frequently than a signing certificate, the public and private key pair is more exposed because of its frequent usage. In this case, it might be a good idea to shorten the lifetime of the key pair and change it more often, while having a separate signing private and public key pair with a longer lifetime.

- When different levels of encryption and digital signing are required because of legal, export, or performance issues, usage keys allow an administrator to assign different key lengths to the two pairs.

- When key recovery is desired, such as when a copy of a user's private key is kept in a central repository for various backup reasons. Usage keys allow the user to back up only the private key of the encrypting pair. The signing private key remains with the user, enabling true nonrepudiation.

7.4.5 PKI Standards

Refer to **Figure** in online course

Standardization and interoperability of different PKI vendors is still an issue when interconnecting PKIs. Interoperability between a PKI and its supporting services, such as Lightweight Directory Access Protocol (LDAP) and X.500 directories, is a concern because many vendors have proposed and implemented proprietary solutions instead of waiting for standards to develop. The state of interoperability is very basic, even after 10 years of PKI software development.

To address this interoperability concern, the IETF formed the Public-Key Infrastructure X.509 (PKIX) workgroup, which is dedicated to promoting and standardizing PKI in the Internet. This workgroup has published a draft set of standards, X.509, detailing common data formats and PKI-related protocols in a network.

Refer to **Figure** in online course

X.509 is a well-known standard that defines basic PKI formats such as the certificate and certificate revocation list (CRL) format to enable basic interoperability. The standard has been widely used for years with many Internet applications, such as SSL and IPsec.

The X.509 version 3 (X.509v3) standard defines the format of a digital certificate. Certificates were traditionally used at the Application Layer to provide strong authentication for applications. Each application can have a different implementation of the actual authentication process, but they all use a similar type of certificate in the X.509 format.

This format is already extensively used in the infrastructure of the Internet:

- Secure web servers use X.509v3 for website authentication in the SSL and TLS protocols.

- Web browsers use X.509v3 to implement HTTPS client certificates in the SSL protocol. SSL is the most widely used certificate-based authentication. Other well-known applications, such as Simple Mail Transfer Protocol (SMTP), LDAP, and Post Office Protocol version 3 (POP3) that were using poor authentication and no encryption, were modified to use SSL.

- User mail agents that support mail protection using the Secure/Multipurpose Internet Mail Extensions (S/MIME) protocol use X.509.

- IPsec VPNs where certificates can be used as a public key distribution mechanism for IKE RSA-based authentication use X.509.

- Pretty Good Privacy (PGP) is an application that was originally developed by Phil Zimmerman, a privacy advocate, so that end users could engage in confidential communications using encryption. The most frequent use of PGP has been to secure email. PGP also recognizes the x.509 certificate.

Certificates are also used at the Network Layer or Application Layer by network devices. Cisco routers, Cisco VPN concentrators, and Cisco PIX firewalls can use certificates to authenticate IPsec peers.

Cisco switches can use certificates to authenticate end devices connecting to LAN ports. Authentication uses 802.1X between the adjacent devices. The authentication can be proxied to a central ACS via the Extensible Authentication Protocol with TLS (EAP-TLS).

Cisco routers can also provide TN3270 support that does not include encryption or strong authentication. Cisco routers can now use SSL to establish secure TN3270 sessions.

> **Refer to Figure in online course**

Another important PKI standard is the Public-Key Cryptography Standards (PKCS). PKCS refers to a group of Public Key Cryptography Standards devised and published by RSA Laboratories. PKCS provides basic interoperability of applications that use public-key cryptography. PKCS defines the low-level formats for the secure exchange of arbitrary data, such as an encrypted piece of data or a signed piece of data.

As the RSA Laboratories website states, "The Public-Key Cryptography Standards are specifications produced by RSA Laboratories in cooperation with secure systems developers worldwide for the purpose of accelerating the deployment of public-key cryptography."

> **Refer to Figure in online course**

Public key technology is increasingly deployed and becoming the basis for standards-based security, such as the IPsec and IKE protocols. With the use of public key certificates in network security protocols comes the need for a certificate management protocol for PKI clients and CA servers. These clients and servers can support certificate lifecycle operations, such as certificate enrollment and revocation and certificate and CRL access.

For example, an end entity starts an enrollment transaction by creating a certificate request using PKCS #10 (certification request syntax standard) and sends it to the CA that is enveloped using the PKCS #7 (cryptographic message syntax standard). After the CA receives the request, it can perform one of three functions:

- Automatically approve the request.

- Send the certificate back.

- Compel the end entity to wait until the operator can manually authenticate the identity of the requesting end entity.

The end goal is that any network user should be able to request a digital certificate easily and electronically. Previously, these processes required intensive input from network administrators and were not suited to large scale deployments. The IETF designed the Simple Certificate Enrollment Protocol (SCEP) to make issuing and revocation of digital certificates as scalable as possible. The goal of SCEP is to support the secure issuance of certificates to network devices in a scalable manner using existing technology whenever possible.

SCEP is now being referenced by network equipment manufacturers and software companies who are developing simplified means of handling certificates for large-scale implementation to everyday users.

7.4.6 Certificate Authorities

Refer to
Figure
in online course

PKIs can form different topologies of trust, including single-root PKI topologies, hierarchical CA topologies, and cross-certified CA topologies.

Single-root PKI Topology

In the single-root PKI model, a single CA, which is also known as the root CA, issues all the certificates to the end users. The benefit is simplicity. There are also disadvantages:

- It is difficult to scale to a large environment.

- It needs a strictly centralized administration.

- Using a single signing private key has a critical vulnerability; if this key is stolen, the whole PKI falls apart because the CA can no longer be trusted as a unique signer.

Because of its simplicity, VPNs that are managed by a single organization often use this topology.

Refer to
Figure
in online course

Hierarchical CA Topology

Going beyond the single-root CA, more complex topologies involve multiple CAs within the same organization. In the hierarchical CA topology, CAs can issue certificates to end users and to subordinate CAs, which in turn issue their certificates to end users, other CAs, or both. In this way, a tree of CAs and end users is built in which every CA can issue certificates to lower level CAs and end users.

The main benefits of a hierarchical PKI topology are increased scalability and manageability. Trust decisions can now be hierarchically distributed to smaller branches. This distribution works well in most large organizations. For example, a large company might have a root CA, which issues certificates to level-2 CAs. These level-2 CAs issue the certificates to the end users. Because the root-signing key is seldom used after the subordinate CA certificates are issued, the root-signing key is less exposed and therefore much more trusted. Additionally, if a subordinate CA has its private key stolen, only a branch of the PKI is rendered untrusted.

One issue with hierarchical PKI topologies lies in finding the certification path for a certificate. It can be difficult to determine the chain of the signing process. This task increases in difficulty as more CAs are placed between the root CA and the end user.

Cross-certified CA Topology

Another approach to hierarchical PKIs is called a cross-certified CA or cross-certifying. In this approach, multiple, flat, single-root CAs establish trust relationships horizontally by cross-certifying their own CA certificates.

Refer to
Figure
in online course

As PKIs are hierarchical in nature, the issuing certificate authority may be a root CA (the top-level CA in the hierarchy) or a subordinate CA. The PKI might employ additional hosts, called registration authorities (RAs) to accept requests for enrollment in the PKI. RAs are employed to reduce the burden on CAs in an environment that supports a large number of certificate transactions or where the CA is offline.

In a more complex environment, the RA might be tasked with verifying user identity, establishing passwords for certificate management transactions, submitting enrollment requests along with appropriate organizational attributes or other information to the CA, and handling assorted tasks such as certificate revocation and re-enrollment.

Usually, these tasks are offloaded to the RA:

- Authentication of users when they enroll with the PKI

- Key generation for users that cannot generate their own keys

- Distribution of certificates after enrollment

It is important to note that the RA only has the power to accept registration requests and forward them to the CA. It is not allowed to issue certificates or publish CRLs. The CA is responsible for these functions.

How are certificates retrieved, enrolled, and used in authentication?

7.4.7 Digital Certificates and CAs

Refer to
Figure
in online course

In the CA authentication procedure, the first step when contacting the PKI is to securely obtain a copy of the public key of the CA. The public key verifies all the certificates issued by the CA and is vital for the proper operation of the PKI.

The public key, called the self-signed certificate, is also distributed in the form of a certificate issued by the CA itself. Only a root CA issues self-signed certificates.

To explain how CA certificates are retrieved, consider this example:

Step 1.   Alice and Bob request the CA certificate that contains the CA public key.

Step 2.   Upon receipt of the CA certificate, each requesting system verifies the validity of the certificate using public key cryptography.

Step 3.   Alice and Bob follow up the technical verification done by their system by telephoning the CA administrator and verifying the public key and serial number of the certificate.

CA certificates are retrieved in-band over a network, and the authentication is done out-of-band using the telephone.

Refer to
Figure
in online course

After retrieving the CA certificate, Alice and Bob submit certificate requests to the CA:

Step 1.   Both systems forward a certificate request that includes their public key along with some identifying information. All of this information is encrypted using the public key of the CA.

Step 2.   Upon the receipt of the certificate requests on the CA server, the CA administrator telephones Alice and Bob to confirm their submittal and the public key. The CA administrator issues the certificate by adding some additional data to the certificate request and digitally signing it all.

Step 3.   Either the end user manually retrieves the certificate or SCEP automatically retrieves the certificate, and the certificate is installed onto the system.

Refer to
Figure
in online course

Having installed certificates signed by the same CA, Bob and Alice are now ready to authenticate each other:

Step 1.   Bob and Alice exchange certificates. The CA is no longer involved.

Step 2.   Each party verifies the digital signature on the certificate by hashing the plaintext portion of the certificate, decrypting the digital signature using the CA public key, and comparing the results. If the results match, the certificate is verified as being signed by a trusted third party, and the verification by the CA that Bob is Bob and Alice is Alice is accepted.

Authentication no longer requires the presence of the CA server, and each user exchanges their certificates containing public keys.

Refer to
Figure
in online course

PKI as an authentication mechanism has several characteristics:

- To authenticate each other, users have to obtain the certificate of the CA and their own certificate. These steps require out-of-band verification. After this verification is complete, the presence of the CA is no longer required until one of the involved certificates expires.

- Public-key systems use asymmetric keys in which one is public and the other one is private. One of the features of these algorithms is that whatever is encrypted using one key can only be decrypted using the other key. This provides nonrepudiation.

- Key management is simplified because two users can freely exchange the certificates. The validity of the received certificates is verified using the public key of the CA, which the users have in their possession.

- Because of the strength of the algorithms that are involved, administrators can set a very long lifetime for the certificates, typically a lifetime that is measured in years.

The disadvantages of using trusted third parties relate to key management:

- A user certificate is compromised (stolen private key).

- The certificate of the CA is compromised (stolen private key).

- The CA administrator makes an error (the human factor).

Which type of PKI to implement varies depending on the needs of the organization. Administrators might need to combine public-key authentication with another authentication mechanism to increase the level of security and provide more authorization options. For example, IPsec using certificates for authentication and Extended Authentication (XAUTH) with one-time password hardware tokens is a superior authentication scheme when compared to certificates alone.

Whatever choice the administrator makes, the PKI implementation must be based on the requirements specified in the network security policy.

Chapter Summary

Refer to **Figure** in online course

Refer to **Packet Tracer Activity** for this chapter

Refer to **Lab Activity** for this chapter

Your Chapter Notes

CHAPTER 8

Implementing Virtual Private Networks

Chapter Introduction

Refer to
Figure
in online course

Organizations use virtual private networks (VPNs) to create an end-to-end private network connection (tunnel) over third-party networks such as the Internet or extranets. The tunnel eliminates the distance barrier and enables remote users to access central site network resources. However, VPNs cannot guarantee that the information remains secure while traversing the tunnel. For this reason, modern cryptographic methods are applied to VPNs to establish secure, end-to-end, private network connections.

The IP Security (IPsec) protocol provides a framework for configuring secure VPNs and is commonly deployed over the Internet to connect branch offices, remote employees, and business partners. It is a reliable way to maintain communication privacy while streamlining operations, reducing costs, and allowing flexible network administration.

Secure site-to-site VPNs, between central and remote sites, can be implemented using the IPsec protocol. IPsec can also be used in remote-access tunnels for telecommuter access. The Cisco VPN Client is one method for establishing the IPsec remote-access VPN. In addition to IPsec, the Secure Sockets Layer (SSL) protocol can be used to established remote-access VPN connections.

In the first hands-on lab for the chapter, *Configuring a Site-to-Site VPN Using Cisco IOS and CCP*, learners configure IPsec VPN settings with the CLI on perimeter routers and then verify IPsec VPN operation. Another site-to-site IPsec VPN is configured and verified using CCP.

In a second hands-on lab, *Configuring a Remote Access VPN Server and Client*, learners configure ZPF with CCP on a perimeter router, followed by Cisco Easy VPN Server. Next, Cisco VPN client is installed and configured on a PC. A remote access VPN connection is then tested.

A Packet Tracer activity, *Configure and Verify a Site-to-Site IPsec VPN Using CLI*, provides learners additional practice implementing the technologies introduced in this chapter. Learners secure and test a WAN connection between two remote networks with a site-to-site IPsec VPN.

8.1 VPNs

8.1.1 VPN Overview

Refer to
Figure
in online course

Solutions, such as the various encryption methods and PKI, enable businesses to securely extend their networks through the Internet. One way in which businesses accomplish this extension is through Virtual Private Networks (VPNs).

A VPN is a private network that is created via tunneling over a public network, usually the Internet. Instead of using a dedicated physical connection, a VPN uses virtual connections routed through the Internet from the organization to the remote site. The first VPNs were strictly IP tunnels that did not include authentication or encryption of the data. For example, Generic Routing Encapsulation (GRE) is a tunneling protocol developed by Cisco that can encapsulate a wide variety of Network Layer protocol packet types inside IP tunnels. This creates a virtual point-to-point link to Cisco routers at remote points over an IP internetwork. Other examples of VPNs that do not automatically include security measures are Frame Relay, ATM PVCs, and Multiprotocol Label Switching (MPLS) networks.

A VPN is a communications environment in which access is strictly controlled to permit peer connections within a defined community of interest. Confidentiality is achieved by encrypting the traffic within the VPN. Today, a secure implementation of VPN with encryption is what is generally equated with the concept of virtual private networking.

VPNs have many benefits:

- *Cost savings*   VPNs enable organizations to use cost-effective, third-party Internet transport to connect remote offices and remote users to the main corporate site. VPNs eliminate expensive dedicated WAN links and modem banks. Additionally, with the advent of cost-effective, high-bandwidth technologies, such as DSL, organizations can use VPNs to reduce their connectivity costs while simultaneously increasing remote connection bandwidth.

- *Security*   VPNs provide the highest level of security by using advanced encryption and authentication protocols that protect data from unauthorized access.

- *Scalability*   VPNs enable corporations to use the Internet infrastructure that is within Internet service providers (ISPs) and devices. This makes it easy to add new users, so that corporations can add significant capacity without adding significant infrastructure.

- *Compatibility with broadband technology*   VPNs allow mobile workers, telecommuters, and people who want to extend their workday to take advantage of high-speed, broadband connectivity to gain access to their corporate networks, providing workers significant flexibility and efficiency. High-speed broadband connections provide a cost-effective solution for connecting remote offices.

Refer to
Figure
in online course

In the simplest sense, a VPN connects two endpoints over a public network to form a logical connection. The logical connections can be made at either Layer 2 or Layer 3 of the OSI model. VPN technologies can be classified broadly on these logical connection models as Layer 2 VPNs or Layer 3 VPNs. Establishing connectivity between sites over a Layer 2 or Layer 3 VPN is the same. A delivery header is added in front of the payload to get it to the destination site. This chapter focuses on Layer 3 VPN technology.

Common examples of Layer 3 VPNs are GRE, MPLS, and IPsec. Layer 3 VPNs can be point-to-point site connections such as GRE and IPsec, or they can establish any-to-any connectivity to many sites using MPLS.

Generic routing encapsulation (GRE) was originally developed by Cisco and later standardized as RFC 1701. An IP delivery header for GRE is defined in RFC 1702. A GRE tunnel between two sites that have IP reachability can be described as a VPN, because the private data between the sites is encapsulated in a GRE delivery header.

Pioneered by Cisco, MPLS was originally known as tag switching and later standardized via the IETF as MPLS. Service providers are increasingly deploying MPLS to offer MPLS VPN services to customers. MPLS VPNs use labels to encapsulate the original data, or payload, to form a VPN.

How does a network administrator prevent eavesdropping of data in a VPN? Encrypting the data is one way to protect it. Data encryption is achieved by deploying encryption devices at each site. IPsec is a suite of protocols developed with the backing of the IETF to achieve secure services over IP packet-switched networks. The Internet is the most ubiquitous packet-switched public network; therefore, an IPsec VPN deployed over the public Internet can provide significant cost savings to a corporation as compared to a leased-line VPN.

IPsec services allow for authentication, integrity, access control, and confidentiality. With IPsec, the information exchanged between remote sites can be encrypted and verified. Both remote-access and site-to-site VPNs can be deployed using IPsec.

8.1.2 VPN Topologies

Refer to **Figure** in online course

There are two basic types of VPN networks: site-to-site and remote-access

A site-to-site VPN is created when connection devices on both sides of the VPN connection are aware of the VPN configuration in advance. The VPN remains static, and internal hosts have no knowledge that a VPN exists. Frame Relay, ATM, GRE, and MPLS VPNs are examples of site-to-site VPNs.

A remote-access VPN is created when VPN information is not statically set up, but instead allows for dynamically changing information and can be enabled and disabled. Consider a telecommuter who needs VPN access to corporate data over the Internet. The telecommuter does not necessarily have the VPN connection set up at all times. The telecommuter's PC is responsible for establishing the VPN. The information required to establish the VPN connection, such as the IP address of the telecommuter, changes dynamically depending on the location of the telecommuter.

Refer to **Figure** in online course

Site-to-Site VPN

A site-to-site VPN is an extension of a classic WAN network. Site-to-site VPNs connect entire networks to each other, for example, they can connect a branch office network to a company headquarters network. In the past, a leased line or Frame Relay connection was required to connect sites, but because most corporations now have Internet access, these connections can be replaced with site-to-site VPNs.

In a site-to-site VPN, hosts send and receive normal TCP/IP traffic through a VPN gateway, which can be a router, firewall, Cisco VPN concentrator, or Cisco ASA. The VPN gateway is responsible for encapsulating and encrypting outbound traffic from a particular site and sending it through a VPN tunnel over the Internet to a peer VPN gateway at the target site. Upon receipt, the peer VPN gateway strips the headers, decrypts the content, and relays the packet toward the target host inside its private network.

Refer to **Figure** in online course

Remote-Access VPN

Remote-access VPNs are an evolution of circuit-switching networks, such as plain old telephone service (POTS) or ISDN. Remote-access VPNs support a client / server architecture where a VPN client (remote host) requires secure access to the enterprise network via a VPN server device at the network edge.

In the past, corporations supported remote users by using dial-in networks and ISDN. With the advent of VPNs, a mobile user simply needs access to the Internet to communicate with the central office. In the case of telecommuters, their Internet connectivity is typically a broadband connection.

Refer to **Figure** in online course

In a remote-access VPN, each host typically has Cisco VPN client software. Whenever the host tries to send traffic intended for the VPN, the Cisco VPN Client software encapsulates and encrypts that traffic before sending it over the Internet to the VPN gateway at the edge of the target network. Upon receipt, the VPN gateway behaves as it does for site-to-site VPNs.

Refer to
Figure
in online course

The Cisco IOS SSL VPN is a technology that provides remote-access connectivity from almost any Internet-enabled location with a web browser and its native SSL encryption. SSL VPN provides the flexibility to support secure access for all users, regardless of the endpoint host from which they establish a connection. SSL VPN currently delivers three modes of SSL VPN access: clientless, thin client, and full client. SSL VPNs allow users to access web pages and services. This includes accessing files, sending and receiving email, and running TCP-based applications without IPsec VPN Client software. If application access requirements are modest, meaning access is limited to a few services or servers, SSL VPN does not require a software client to be preinstalled on the endpoint host. This ability enables companies to extend their secure enterprise networks to any authorized user by providing remote-access connectivity to corporate resources from any Internet-enabled location. For broader application access, a dynamically downloadable tunneling client is delivered, when needed, to the client machine to support full SSL VPN capabilities.

SSL VPNs are appropriate for user populations that require per-application or per-server access control, or access from non-enterprise-owned desktops. In many cases, IPsec and SSL VPNs are complementary because they solve different problems. This complementary approach allows a single device to address all remote-access user requirements. The primary benefit of SSL VPN is that it is compatible with Dynamic Multipoint VPNs (DMVPNs), Cisco IOS Firewalls, IPsec, intrusion prevention systems (IPSs), Cisco Easy VPN, and Network Address Translation (NAT).

8.1.3 VPN Solutions

Refer to
Figure
in online course

The Cisco VPN product line includes several devices to support remote and site-to-site VPN:

- *Cisco VPN-enabled routers and switches* A good option for customers of all sizes looking to take advantage of their existing network infrastructures to deploy VPNs and security while integrating all services into a single device with the widest selection of WAN and LAN interfaces.

- *Cisco PIX 500 Series Security Appliances* Provide robust, enterprise-class, integrated network security services, including stateful inspection firewall, deep protocol and application inspection and IPsec VPN. PIX 500 Series Security Appliances are an excellent option for organizations whose security policies recommend separate management of the security infrastructure to set a clear demarcation between security and network operation. The Cisco PIX 500 Series is End-of-Sale (EOS). This means it is no longer being sold; however, there is a large installed base.

- *Cisco ASA* All-in-one security appliances that deliver enterprise-class security and IPsec VPN to small- and medium-sized businesses and large enterprise networks in a modular, purpose-built appliance. The appliances incorporate a wide range of integrated security services, including firewall, IPS, and VPN. Cisco ASA 5500 Series Appliances are ideal for clients who are looking for a robust firewall combined with comprehensive VPN support.

- *Cisco VPN 3000 Series Concentrators* Offer both IPsec and SSL VPN connectivity on a single platform without the expense of individual feature licensing. Cisco VPN 3000 Series Concentrators are EOS.

- *SOHO routers* Many newer broadband home routers such as Linksys also support VPNs.

In most networks, devices are already in place. If this is the case, it is necessary to verify if interoperability among the different devices is possible. For example, a customer network might have a Cisco ASA 5500 Series Adaptive Security Appliance at one site and a Cisco router at another. This site-to-site VPN interoperability is possible by choosing, at a minimum, the following software versions: Cisco IOS Release 12.2(8)T and Cisco ASA 5500 Series Adaptive Security Appliance Version 8.0.

With Cisco routers running Cisco IOS software, organizations can deploy and scale site-to-site VPNs of any topology, from hub-and-spoke to the more complex, fully meshed VPNs. In addition, the Cisco IOS security features combine the VPN feature set with firewall, intrusion prevention, and extensive Cisco IOS capabilities, including quality of service (QoS), multiprotocol, multicast, and advanced routing support.

Refer to **Figure** in online course

Cisco provides a suite of VPN-optimized routers. Cisco IOS software for routers combines VPN services with routing services. The Cisco VPN software adds strong security using encryption and authentication. These Cisco VPN-enabled routers provide high performance for site-to-site, intranet, and extranet VPN solutions.

The Cisco IOS feature sets incorporate many VPN features:

- *Voice and Video Enabled VPN (V3PN)* Integrates IP telephony, QoS, and IPsec, providing an end-to-end VPN service that helps ensure the timely delivery of latency-sensitive applications such as voice and video.

- *IPsec stateful failover* Provides fast and scalable network resiliency for VPN sessions between remote and central sites. With both stateless and stateful failover solutions available, such as Hot Standby Router Protocol (HSRP), IPsec stateful failover ensures maximum uptime of mission-critical applications.

- *Dynamic Multipoint Virtual Private Network (DMVPN)* Enables the auto-provisioning of site-to-site IPsec VPNs, combining three Cisco IOS software features: Next Hop Resolution Protocol (NHRP), multipoint GRE, and IPsec VPN. This combination eases the provisioning challenges for customers and provides secure connectivity between all locations.

- *IPsec and MPLS integration* Enables ISPs to map IPsec sessions directly into an MPLS VPN. This solution can be deployed on co-located edge routers that are connected to a Cisco IOS software MPLS provider edge (PE) network. This approach enables the ISP to securely extend its VPN service beyond the boundaries of the MPLS network by using the public IP infrastructure that securely connects enterprise customer remote offices, telecommuters, and mobile users from anywhere to the corporate network.

- *Cisco Easy VPN* Simplifies VPN deployment for remote offices and teleworkers. The Cisco Easy VPN solution centralizes VPN management across all Cisco VPN devices, thus reducing the management complexity of VPN deployments.

Refer to **Figure** in online course

For VPN services, Cisco ASA offer flexible technologies that deliver tailored solutions to suit remote-access and site-to-site connectivity requirements. These appliances provide easy-to-manage IPsec and SSL VPN-based remote-access and network-aware, site-to-site VPN connectivity. Businesses can create secure connections across public networks to mobile users, remote sites, and business partners.

As an important component of the Cisco SecureX Architecture, Cisco ASA provides proactive threat mitigation, control network activity and application traffic, and deliver flexible VPN connectivity while remaining cost effective.

Cisco ASA offer other services, such as intrusion prevention, Cisco SSL VPN, and advanced integration module (AIM) to enhance the processing capabilities of the appliances. These are some of the features that Cisco ASA provides:

- *Flexible platform* Offers both IPsec and SSL VPN on a single platform, eliminating the need to provide parallel solutions. In addition to VPN services, Cisco ASA offer application inspection firewall and intrusion prevention services.

- *Resilient clustering* Allows remote-access deployments to scale cost-effectively by evenly distributing VPN sessions across all Cisco ASA and Cisco VPN 3000 Series Concentrators, without requiring user intervention.

- *Cisco Easy VPN* Delivers scalable, cost-effective, and easy-to-manage remote-access VPN architecture. Cisco ASA dynamically push the latest VPN security policies to remote VPN devices and clients, making sure that those endpoint policies are up to date before a connection is established.

- *Automatic Cisco VPN Client updates* Enables Cisco VPN Client software operating on remote desktops to be automatically upgraded.

- *Cisco IOS SSL VPN* Offers Cisco SSL VPN with clientless and thin client Cisco SSL VPN capabilities.

- *VPN infrastructure for contemporary applications* Enables converged voice, video, and data across a secure IPsec network by combining robust site-to-site VPN support with rich inspection capabilities, QoS, routing, and stateful failover features.

- *Integrated web-based management* Provides management of the Cisco ASA using the integrated web-based Cisco Adaptive Security Device Manager (ASDM). Cisco ASDM manages all security and VPN functions of the appliances.

Each Cisco ASA supports a number of VPN peers:

- *Cisco ASA 5505* 10 IPsec VPN peers and 25 SSL VPN peers, with a Base license, and 25 VPN peers (IPsec or SSL) with the Security Plus license

- *Cisco ASA 5510* 250 VPN peers

- *Cisco ASA 5520* 750 VPN peers

- *Cisco ASA 5540* 5000 IPsec VPN peers and 2500 SSL VPN peers

- *Cisco ASA 5550* 5000 VPN peers

- *Cisco ASA 5585-X* 10000 VPN peers

Refer to
Figure
in online course

Cisco remote-access VPNs can use four IPsec clients:

- *Certicom client* A wireless client that is loaded on to wireless personal digital assistants (PDAs) running the Palm or Microsoft Windows Mobile operating systems. Certicom wireless client software allows companies to extend critical enterprise applications, such as email and customer relationship management (CRM) tools, to mobile professionals by enabling handheld devices to connect to corporate VPN gateways for secure wireless access.

- *Cisco VPN Client software* Installed on the PC or laptop of an individual, the Cisco VPN Client allows organizations to establish end-to-end, encrypted VPN tunnels for secure connectivity for mobile employees or teleworkers. The Cisco Easy VPN feature allows the Cisco VPN Client to receive security policies from the central site VPN device, the Cisco

Easy VPN Server, when a VPN tunnel connection is made, minimizing configuration requirements at the remote location.

■ *Cisco Remote Router VPN Client* A Cisco remote router, configured as a VPN client, that connects small office, home office (SOHO) LANs to the VPN.

■ *Cisco AnyConnect VPN Client* Next-generation VPN client that provides remote users with secure VPN connections to the Cisco ASA. The Cisco AnyConnect VPN Client is available for the Windows, Mac OS X, and Linux platforms. It is also supported on some smart devices including iPhones, iPads, BlackBerry, and Android smartphones.

Refer to
Figure
in online course

To enhance performance and offload the encryption task to specialized hardware, the Cisco VPN family of devices offers hardware acceleration modules:

■ *Advanced integration modules (AIM)* A broad range of Cisco routers can be equipped with AIM. The module is installed inside the router chassis to offload encryption tasks from the router CPU.

■ *Cisco IPsec VPN Shared Port Adapter (SPA)* Delivers scalable and cost-effective VPN performance for Cisco Catalyst 6500 Series Switches and Cisco 7600 Series Routers. Using the Cisco 7600 Series/Catalyst 6500 Series Services SPA Carrier-400, each slot of the Cisco Catalyst 6500 Series Switch or the Cisco 7600 Series Router can support up to two Cisco IPsec VPN SPAs.

■ *Cisco VPN Accelerator Module 2+ (VAM2+)* Provides high performance encryption/compression and key generation services for IPsec VPN applications.

8.2 GRE VPNs

8.2.1 Configuring a Site-to-Site GRE Tunnel

Refer to
Figure
in online course

Generic routing encapsulation (GRE) is a tunneling protocol defined in RFC 1702 and RFC 2784. It was originally developed by Cisco Systems for creating a virtual point-to-point link to Cisco routers at remote points over an IP internetwork.

GRE supports multiprotocol tunneling. It can encapsulate multiple protocol packet types inside an IP tunnel. Adding an additional GRE header between the payload and the tunneling IP header provides the multiprotocol functionality. IP tunneling using GRE enables network expansion by connecting multiprotocol subnetworks across a single-protocol backbone environment. GRE also supports IP multicast tunneling. Routing protocols that are used across the tunnel enable dynamic exchange of routing information in the virtual network.

GRE tunnels are stateless. Each tunnel endpoint keeps no information about the state or availability of the remote tunnel endpoint. This feature helps service providers (SPs) provide IP tunnels to customers who are not concerned about the internal tunneling architecture at the SP end. Customers then have the flexibility to configure or reconfigure their IP architecture but still maintain connectivity. It creates a virtual point-to-point link to routers at remote points over an IP internetwork. GRE does not include any strong security mechanisms to protect its payload.

Refer to
Figure
in online course

GRE encapsulates the entire original IP packet with a standard IP header and GRE header. A GRE tunnel header contains at least two 2-byte mandatory fields:

■ GRE flag

■ Protocol type

GRE uses a protocol type field in the GRE header to support the encapsulation of any OSI Layer 3 protocol. The GRE header, together with the tunneling IP header, creates at least 24 bytes of additional overhead for tunneled packets.

There are five steps to configuring a GRE tunnel:

Refer to **Figure** in online course

Step 1.   Create a tunnel interface using the `interface tunnel 0` command.

Step 2.   Assign the tunnel an IP address.

Step 3.   Identify the source tunnel interface using the `tunnel source` command.

Step 4.   Identify the destination of the tunnel using the `tunnel destination` command.

Step 5.   Configure which protocol GRE encapsulates using the `tunnel mode gre` command.

Refer to **Figure** in online course

The advantages of GRE are that it can be used to tunnel non-IP traffic over an IP network. Unlike IPsec, which only supports unicast traffic, GRE supports multicast and broadcast traffic over the tunnel link. Therefore, routing protocols are supported in GRE.

GRE does not provide encryption. If that is needed, IPsec should be configured.

8.3 IPsec VPN Components and Operation

8.3.1 Introducing IPsec

Refer to **Figure** in online course

IPsec is an IETF standard (RFC 2401-2412) that defines how a VPN can be configured using the IP addressing protocol. IPsec is not bound to any specific encryption, authentication, security algorithms, or keying technology. IPsec is a framework of open standards that spells out the rules for secure communications. IPsec relies on existing algorithms to implement the encryption, authentication, and key exchange.

IPsec works at the Network Layer, protecting and authenticating IP packets between participating IPsec devices (peers). As a result, IPsec can protect virtually all application traffic because the protection can be implemented from Layer 4 through Layer 7. All implementations of IPsec have a plaintext Layer 3 header, so there are no issues with routing. IPsec functions over all Layer 2 protocols, such as Ethernet, ATM, Frame Relay, Synchronous Data Link Control (SDLC), and High-Level Data Link Control (HDLC).

The IPsec framework consists of five building blocks:

- The first represents the IPsec protocol. Choices include ESP or AH.

- The second represents the type of confidentiality implemented using an encryption algorithm such as DES, 3DES, AES, or SEAL. The choice depends on the level of security required.

- The third represents integrity that can be implemented using either MD5 or SHA.

- The fourth represents how the shared secret key is established. The two methods are pre-shared or digitally signed using RSA.

- The fifth represents the DH algorithm group. There are four separate DH key exchange algorithms to choose from including DH Group 1 (DH1), DH Group 2 (DH2), DH Group 5 (DH5), and DH Group 7 (DH7). The type of group selected depends on the specific needs.

IPsec provides the framework, and the administrator chooses the algorithms that are used to implement the security services within that framework. By not binding IPsec to specific algorithms, it allows newer and better algorithms to be implemented without patching the existing IPsec standards.

IPsec can secure a path between a pair of gateways, a pair of hosts, or a gateway and host. Using the IPsec framework, IPsec provides these essential security functions:

- *Confidentiality* IPsec ensures confidentiality by using encryption.

- *Integrity* IPsec ensures that data arrives unchanged at the destination using a hash algorithm such as MD5 or SHA.

- *Authentication* IPsec uses Internet Key Exchange (IKE) to authenticate users and devices that can carry out communication independently. IKE uses several types of authentication, including username and password, one-time password, biometrics, pre-shared keys (PSKs), and digital certificates.

- *Secure key exchange* IPsec uses the DH algorithm to provide a public key exchange method for two peers to establish a shared secret key.

Confidentiality

Refer to **Figure** in online course

Confidentiality is achieved through encryption of traffic as it travels down the VPN. The degree of security depends on the length of the key of the encryption algorithm. If someone tries to hack the key through a brute-force attack, the number of possibilities to try is a function of the length of the key. The time to process all the possibilities is a function of the computer power of the attacking device. The shorter the key, the easier it is to break. A 64-bit key can take approximately one year to break with a relatively sophisticated computer. A 128-bit key with the same machine can take roughly 10^19 years to decrypt.

The following are some encryption algorithms and key lengths that VPNs use:

- *DES* Uses a 56-bit key, ensuring high-performance encryption. DES is a symmetric key cryptosystem.

- *3DES* A variant of the 56-bit DES. 3DES uses three independent 56-bit encryption keys per 64-bit block, providing significantly stronger encryption strength over DES. 3DES is a symmetric key cryptosystem.

- *AES* Provides stronger security than DES and is computationally more efficient than 3DES. AES offers three different key lengths: 128 bits, 192 bits, and 256 bits. AES is a symmetric key cryptosystem.

- *Software-Optimized Encryption Algorithm (SEAL)* A stream cipher developed in 1993 by Phillip Rogaway and Don Coppersmith, which uses a 160-bit key. SEAL is a symmetric key cryptosystem.

Integrity

Refer to **Figure** in online course

The next VPN-critical function is data integrity. Assume that a check for $100 is written to Sonya from Jeremy. The check is then mailed to Sonya but intercepted by an attacker. The attacker changes the name and amount on the check and attempts to cash it. Depending on the forged quality of the altered check, the attacker could be successful.

This scenario applies to VPNs because data is transported over the public Internet. Potentially, this data could be intercepted and modified. A method of proving data integrity is required to guarantee that the content has not been altered. A data integrity algorithm can provide this guarantee.

Hashed Message Authentication Codes (HMAC) is a data integrity algorithm that guarantees the integrity of the message using a hash value. At the local device, the message and a shared-secret key are processed through a hash algorithm, which produces a hash value. This value is appended to the message, and the message is sent over the network. At the remote device, the hash value is recalculated and compared to the sent hash value. If the transmitted hash matches the received hash, the message integrity is verified. However, if they do not match, the message was altered and is invalidated.

There are two common HMAC algorithms:

- *HMAC-Message Digest 5 (HMAC-MD5)* Uses a 128-bit shared-secret key. The variable-length message and 128-bit shared secret key are combined and run through the HMAC-MD5 hash algorithm. The output is a 128-bit hash.

- *HMAC-Secure Hash Algorithm 1 (HMAC-SHA-1)* Uses a 160-bit secret key. The variable-length message and the 160-bit shared secret key are combined and run through the HMAC-SHA-1 hash algorithm. The output is a 160-bit hash.

HMAC-SHA-1 is considered cryptographically stronger than HMAC-MD5. It is recommended when slightly superior security is important.

Authentication

Refer to **Figure** in online course

When conducting business over long distance, it is necessary to know (authenticate) the individual at the other end of the phone, email, or fax. The same is true of VPN networks. The device on the other end of the VPN tunnel must be authenticated before the communication path is considered secure.

In the middle ages, a seal guaranteed the authenticity of a document. In modern times, a signed document is notarized with a seal and a signature. In the electronic era, a document is signed using the sender's private encryption key called a digital signature. A signature is authenticated by decrypting the signature with the sender's public key.

There are two primary methods of configuring peer authentication.

- *Pre-shared Keys (PSKs)* A pre-shared secret key value is entered into each peer manually and is used to authenticate the peer. At each end, the PSK is combined with other information to form the authentication key. Each peer must authenticate its opposite peer before the tunnel is considered secure. Pre-shared keys are easy to configure manually but do not scale well, because each IPsec peer must be configured with the pre-shared key of every other peer with which it communicates.

- *RSA signatures* The exchange of digital certificates authenticates the peers. The local device derives a hash and encrypts it with its private key. The encrypted hash is attached to the message and is forwarded to the remote end and acts like a signature. At the remote end, the encrypted hash is decrypted using the public key of the local end. If the decrypted hash matches the recomputed hash, the signature is genuine. Each peer must authenticate its opposite peer before the tunnel is considered secure.

A less common way of accomplishing authentication is through RSA-encrypted nonces. A nonce is a random number that is generated by the peer. RSA-encrypted nonces use RSA to encrypt the nonce value and other values. This method requires that the public key of the two peers be present on the other peer before the third and fourth messages of an IKE exchange can be accomplished. For this reason, public keys must be manually copied to each peer as part of the configuration process.

Refer to
Figure
in online course

Secure Key Exchange

Encryption algorithms such as DES, 3DES, and AES as well as the MD5 and SHA-1 hashing algorithms require a symmetric, shared secret key to perform encryption and decryption. How do the encrypting and decrypting devices get the shared secret key?

Email, courier, or overnight express can be used to send the shared secret keys to the administrators of the devices. But the easiest key exchange method is a public key exchange method between the encrypting and decrypting devices.

The Diffie-Hellman (DH) key agreement is a public key exchange method that provides a way for two peers to establish a shared secret key that only they know, even though they are communicating over an insecure channel. Variations of the DH key exchange are specified as DH groups. There are several DH groups:

- DH groups 1, 2, and 5 support exponentiation over a prime modulus with a key size of 768 bits, 1024 bits, and 1536 bits, respectively. These groups are not recommended for use after 2012.

- DH groups 14, 15, and 16 use larger key sizes with 2048 bits, 3072 bits, and 4096 bits, respectively, and are recommend for use until 2030.

- DH groups 19, 20 and 24 support Elliptical Curve Cryptography (ECC), which reduces the time needed to generate keys. With respective key sizes 256 bits, 384 bits, and 2048 bits. DH group 24 is preferred for longevity of use.

- Newer Cisco IOS versions support more advanced DH groups.

The DH group chosen must be strong enough (have enough bits) to protect the IPsec keys during negotiation. For example, DH group 1 is strong enough to support only DES and 3DES encryption, but not AES. During tunnel setup, VPN peers negotiate which DH group to use.

8.3.2 IPsec Security Protocols

Refer to
Figure
in online course

IPsec is a framework of open standards. IPsec spells out the messaging to secure the communications but relies on existing algorithms. The two main IPsec framework protocols are AH and ESP. The IPsec protocol is the first building block of the framework. The choice of AH or ESP establishes which other building blocks are available:

- *Authentication Header (AH)*   AH, which is IP protocol 51, is the appropriate protocol to use when confidentiality is not required or permitted. It provides data authentication and integrity for IP packets that are passed between two systems. It ensures that the origin of the data is either R1 or R2 and verifies that the data has not been modified during transit. AH does not provide data confidentiality (encryption) of packets. All text is transported unencrypted. If the AH protocol is used alone, it provides weak protection.

- *Encapsulating Security Payload (ESP)*   ESP, which is IP protocol 50, can provide confidentiality and authentication. It provides confidentiality by performing encryption on the IP packet. IP packet encryption conceals the data payload and the identities of the ultimate source and destination. ESP provides authentication for the inner IP packet and ESP header. Authentication provides data origin authentication and data integrity. Although both encryption and authentication are optional in ESP, at a minimum, one of them must be selected.

Refer to
Figure
in online course

Authentication Header

AH achieves authenticity by applying a keyed one-way hash function to the packet to create a hash or message digest. The hash is combined with the text and is transmitted. The receiver detects changes in any part of the packet that occur during transit by performing the same one-way hash function on the received packet and comparing the result to the value of the message digest that the sender supplied. The fact that the one-way hash also involves a shared secret key between the two systems means that authenticity is assured.

The AH function is applied to the entire packet, except for any mutable IP header fields that change in transit. For example, Time to Live (TTL) fields that are modified by the routers along the transmission path are mutable fields.

The AH process occurs in this order:

Step 1.   The IP header and data payload are hashed using the shared secret key.

Step 2.   The hash builds a new AH header, which is inserted into the original packet.

Step 3.   The new packet is transmitted to the IPsec peer router.

Step 4.   The peer router hashes the IP header and data payload using the shared secret key, extracts the transmitted hash from the AH header, and compares the two hashes.

The hashes must match exactly. If one bit is changed in the transmitted packet, the hash output on the received packet changes and the AH header will not match.

AH supports the HMAC-MD5 and HMAC-SHA-1 algorithms. AH can have problems if the environment uses NAT.

ESP

Refer to
Figure
in online course

ESP provides confidentiality by encrypting the payload. It supports a variety of symmetric encryption algorithms. If ESP is selected as the IPsec protocol, an encryption algorithm must also be selected. The default algorithm for IPsec is 56-bit DES. Cisco products also support the use of 3DES, AES, and SEAL for stronger encryption.

ESP can also provide integrity and authentication. First, the payload is encrypted. Next, the encrypted payload is sent through a hash algorithm, HMAC-MD5 or HMAC-SHA-1. The hash provides authentication and data integrity for the data payload.

Optionally, ESP can also enforce anti-replay protection. Anti-replay protection verifies that each packet is unique and is not duplicated. This protection ensures that a hacker cannot intercept packets and insert changed packets into the data stream. Anti-replay works by keeping track of packet sequence numbers and using a sliding window on the destination end. When a connection is established between a source and destination, their counters are initialized at zero. Each time a packet is sent, a sequence number is appended to the packet by the source. The destination uses the sliding window to determine which sequence numbers are expected. The destination verifies that the sequence number of the packet is not duplicated and is received in the correct order. For example, if the sliding window on the destination is set to one, the destination is expecting to receive the packet with the sequence number one. After it is received, the sliding window moves to two. When detection of a replayed packet occurs, such as the destination receiving a second packet with the sequence number of one, an error message is sent, the replayed packet is discarded, and the event is logged.

Anti-replay is typically used in ESP, but it is also supported in AH.

Refer to
Figure
in online course

The original data is well protected by ESP because the entire original IP datagram and ESP trailer are encrypted. With ESP authentication, the encrypted IP datagram and trailer, and the ESP header, are included in the hashing process. Last, a new IP header is attached to the authenticated payload. The new IP address is used to route the packet through the Internet.

When both authentication and encryption are selected, encryption is performed first. One reason for this order of processing is that it facilitates rapid detection and rejection of replayed or bogus packets by the receiving device. Prior to decrypting the packet, the receiver can authenticate inbound packets. By doing this, it can quickly detect problems and potentially reduce the impact of DoS attacks.

ESP and AH can be applied to IP packets in two different modes, transport mode and tunnel mode.

Refer to
Figure
in online course

Transport Mode

In transport mode, security is provided only for the Transport Layer of the OSI model and above. Transport mode protects the payload of the packet but leaves the original IP address in plaintext. The original IP address is used to route the packet through the Internet.

ESP transport mode is used between hosts. Transport mode works well with GRE, because GRE hides the addresses of the end devices by adding its own IP.

Tunnel Mode

Tunnel mode provides security for the complete original IP packet. The original IP packet is encrypted and then it is encapsulated in another IP packet. This is known as IP-in-IP encryption. The IP address on the outside IP packet is used to route the packet through the Internet.

ESP tunnel mode is used between a host and a security gateway or between two security gateways. For gateway-to-gateway applications, rather than load IPsec on all of the computers at the remote and corporate offices, it is easier to have the security gateways perform the IP-in-IP encryption and encapsulation.

ESP tunnel mode is used in the IPsec remote-access application. A home office might not have a router to perform the IPsec encapsulation and encryption. In this case, an IPsec client running on the PC performs the IPsec IP-in-IP encapsulation and encryption. At the corporate office, the router de-encapsulates and decrypts the packet.

The VPN process involves selecting and applying many parameters. How does IPsec actually negotiate these security parameters?

8.3.3 Internet Key Exchange

Refer to
Figure
in online course

The IPsec VPN solution negotiates key exchange parameters, establishes a shared key, authenticates the peer, and negotiates the encryption parameters. The negotiated parameters between two devices are known as a security association (SA).

Security Associations

An SA is a basic building block of IPsec. Security associations are maintained within a SA database (SADB), which is established by each device. A VPN has SA entries defining the IPsec encryption parameters as well as SA entries defining the key exchange parameters.

All cryptographic systems, including the Caesar cipher, Vigenere cipher, Enigma machine, to modern encryption algorithms, must deal with key management issues. DH is used to create the shared secret key. However, IPsec uses the Internet Key Exchange (IKE) protocol to establish the key exchange process.

Instead of transmitting keys directly across a network, IKE calculates shared keys based on the exchange of a series of data packets. This disables a third party from decrypting the keys even if the third party captured all exchanged data that is used to calculate the keys.

IKE is layered on UDP and uses UDP port 500 to exchange IKE information between the security gateways. UDP port 500 packets must be permitted on any IP interface involved in connecting a security gateway peer.

IKE is defined in RFC 2409. It is a hybrid protocol, combining the Internet Security Association and Key Management Protocol (ISAKMP) and the Oakley and Skeme key exchange methods. ISAKMP defines the message format, the mechanics of a key-exchange protocol, and the negotiation process to build an SA for IPsec. ISAKMP does not define how keys are managed or shared between the two IPsec peers. Oakley and Skeme have five defined key groups. Of these groups, Cisco routers support Group 1 (768-bit key), Group 2 (1024-bit key), and Group 5 (1536-bit key).

IKE combines these protocols to build secure IPsec connections between devices. It establishes SAs that are mutually agreeable to each peer. Each peer must have identical ISAKMP and IPsec parameters to establish an operational and secure VPN. Note that the terms ISAKMP and IKE are commonly used by industry people to refer to IKE.

An alternative to using IKE is to manually configure all parameters required to establish a secure IPsec connection. This process is impractical because it does not scale.

How does IKE work?

Refer to Figure in online course

To establish a secure communication channel between two peers, the IKE protocol executes two phases:

- *Phase 1* Two IPsec peers perform the initial negotiation of SAs. The basic purpose of Phase 1 is to negotiate IKE policy sets, authenticate the peers, and set up a secure channel between the peers. It can be implemented in main mode (longer, initial contact) or aggressive mode (after initial contact).

- *Phase 2* SAs are negotiated by the IKE process ISAKMP on behalf of IPsec. It can be negotiated in quick mode.

In Phase 1, the transform sets, hash methods, and other parameters are determined. An IKE session begins with a router (the initiator) sending a proposals to another router (the responder). The proposal sent by the initiator defines which encryption and authentication protocols are acceptable, how long keys should remain active, and whether perfect forward secrecy (PFS) should be enforced. PFS is a property that states that keys used to protect data are not used to derive any other keys. PFS ensures that if one key is compromised, previous and subsequent keys remain secure.

Refer to Figure in online course

Three exchanges transpire during IKE Phase 1. These are referred to as the first, second, and third exchanges.

First Exchange

The first exchange between the initiator and the responder establishes the basic security policy. Peers negotiate and agree on the algorithms and hashes that are used to secure the IKE communications. Rather than negotiate each protocol individually, the protocols are grouped into sets, called IKE policy sets. The IKE policy sets are exchanged first.

The initiator first transmits proposals for the encryption and authentication schemes to be used. The responder looks for a matching ISAKMP policy. The responder chooses a proposal that is best suited to the security situation and then sends that proposal to the initiator. If a policy match is found between the peers, IKE Phase 1 continues. If no match is found, the tunnel is torn down.

Policy set numbers are only locally significant to a VPN device. The policy set numbers do not have to match between two VPN peers. In a point-to-point application, each end might need only a single IKE policy set to be defined. In a hub-and-spoke environment, the central site might require multiple IKE policy sets to satisfy all the remote peers.

Second Exchange

The second exchange creates and exchanges the DH public keys between the two endpoints. DH allows two parties that have no prior knowledge of each other to establish a shared secret key over an insecure communications channel.

The two peers run the DH key exchange protocol to acquire the keying material that is needed by the various encryption and hashing algorithms upon which IKE and IPsec will ultimately agree. Using the DH algorithm, each peer generates a shared secret without actually exchanging secrets. All further negotiations are encrypted using the DH-generated secret key.

Third Exchange

Each end device must authenticate the other end device before the communication path is considered secure. The last exchange of IKE Phase 1 authenticates the remote peer.

The initiator and recipient authenticate each other using one of the three data-origin authentication methods:

- PSK
- RSA signature
- RSA encrypted nonce

The Phase 1 SA negotiations are bidirectional, which means that data can be sent and received using the same encryption key. Even if the SA negotiation data stream between the two IPsec peers is compromised, there is little chance that the encryption keys could be decrypted.

Refer to **Figure** in online course

The three exchanges of IKE Phase 1 occur during what is called main mode. The outcome of main mode is a secure communication path for subsequent exchanges between the peers.

Aggressive mode is another option for IKE Phase 1. Aggressive mode is faster than main mode because there are fewer exchanges. Aggressive mode compresses the IKE SA negotiation phases into one exchange with three packets, whereas main mode requires three exchanges with six packets.

Aggressive mode packets include:

- *First packet* The initiator packages everything needed for the SA negotiation in the first message, including its DH public key.
- *Second packet* The recipient responds with the acceptable parameters, authentication information, and its DH public key.
- *Third packet* The initiator then sends a confirmation that it received that information.

Aggressive mode negotiation is quicker, and the initiator and responder IDs pass in plaintext.

After the IKE SA is established, Phase 2 negotiation begins.

Refer to **Figure** in online course

The purpose of IKE Phase 2 is to negotiate the IPsec security parameters that will be used to secure the IPsec tunnel. IKE Phase 2 is called quick mode and can only occur after IKE has established the secure tunnel in Phase 1. SAs are negotiated by the IKE process ISAKMP on behalf of IPsec, which needs encryption keys for operation. Quick mode negotiates the IKE Phase 2 SAs. In this phase, the SAs that IPsec uses are unidirectional; therefore, a separate key exchange is required for each data flow.

IKE Phase 2 performs the following functions:

- Negotiates IPsec security parameters, known as IPsec transform sets
- Establishes IPsec SAs

- Periodically renegotiates IPsec SAs to ensure security

- Optionally performs an additional DH exchange

Quick mode also renegotiates a new IPsec SA when the IPsec SA lifetime expires. Basically, quick mode refreshes the keying material that creates the shared secret key based on the keying material that is derived from the DH exchange in Phase 1.

8.4 Implementing Site-to-Site IPsec VPNs with CLI

8.4.1 Configuring a Site-to-Site IPsec VPN

Refer to
Figure
in online course

A VPN is a communications channel that is used to form a logical connection between two end-points over a public network. VPNs do not necessarily include encryption or authentication. IPsec VPNs rely on the IKE protocol to establish secure communications.

IPsec VPN negotiation involves several steps, which include Phase 1 and Phase 2 of IKE negotiation.

Step 1. An IPsec tunnel is initiated when host A sends "interesting" traffic to host B. Traffic is considered interesting when it travels between the IPsec peers and meets the criteria that is defined in the crypto ACL.

Step 2. IKE Phase 1 begins. The IPsec peers negotiate the established IKE SA policy. When the peers are authenticated, a secure tunnel is created using ISAKMP.

Step 3. IKE Phase 2 begins. The IPsec peers use the authenticated secure tunnel to negotiate IPsec SA transforms. The negotiation of the shared policy determines how the IPsec tunnel is established.

Step 4. The IPsec tunnel is created and data is transferred between the IPsec peers based on the IPsec parameters that are configured in the IPsec transform sets.

Step 5. The IPsec tunnel terminates when the IPsec SAs are deleted, or when their lifetime expires.

Refer to
Figure
in online course

Some basic tasks must be completed to configure a site-to-site IPsec VPN.

Task 1. Ensure that ACLs configured on interfaces are compatible with the IPsec configuration. Usually there are restrictions on the interface that the VPN traffic uses. For example, block all traffic that is not IPsec or IKE.

Task 2. Create an ISAKMP policy. This policy determines the ISAKMP parameters that will be used to establish the tunnel.

Task 3. Configure the IPsec transform set. The transform set defines the parameters that the IPsec tunnel uses. The set can include the encryption and integrity algorithms.

Task 4. Create a crypto ACL. The crypto ACL defines which traffic is sent through the IPsec tunnel and protected by the IPsec process.

Task 5. Create and apply a crypto map. The crypto map groups the previously configured parameters together and defines the IPsec peer devices. The crypto map is applied to the outgoing interface of the VPN device.

8.4.2 Task 1 - Configure Compatible ACLs

Refer to
Figure
in online course

The first step in configuring Cisco IOS ISAKMP is to ensure that the existing ACLs on perimeter routers, firewalls, or other routers do not block IPsec traffic. Perimeter routers typically implement a restrictive security policy with ACLs, where only specific traffic is permitted, and all other traffic is denied. Such a restrictive policy blocks IPsec traffic. Therefore, specific permit statements must be added to the ACL.

Ensure that the ACLs are configured so that ISAKMP, Encapsulating Security Payload (ESP), and Authentication Header (AH) traffic is not blocked at the interfaces used by IPsec.

- ESP is assigned IP protocol number 50.

- AH is assigned IP protocol number 51.

- ISAKMP uses UDP port 500.

Refer to **Figure** in online course

To permit AH, ESP, and ISAKMP on an IPsec interface while denying any other unnecessary traffic, an existing ACL must be edited or a new ACL created.

- To permit AH traffic, use the **access-list** *acl* **permit ahp** *source wildcard destination wildcard* command.

- To permit ESP traffic, use the **access-list** *acl* **permit esp** *source wildcard destination wildcard* command.

- To permit ISAKMP traffic, use the **access-list** *acl* **permit udp** *source wildcard destination wildcard* **eq isakmp** command.

Use the **show access-lists** command to verify the entries.

8.4.3 Task 2 - Configure IKE

Refer to **Figure** in online course

The second major task in configuring Cisco IOS ISAKMP support is to define the parameters within the IKE policy. IKE uses these parameters during negotiation to establish ISAKMP peering between two IPsec endpoints.

Multiple ISAKMP policies can be configured on each peer participating in IPsec. When configuring policies, each policy must be given a unique priority number. Use the command **crypto isakmp policy** *priority*, where the priority is a number that uniquely identifies the IKE policy and assigns a priority to the policy. Use an integer from 1 to 10,000, with 1 being the highest priority and 10,000 the lowest. Assign the most secure policy the smallest available number.

The **crypto isakmp policy** command invokes ISAKMP policy configuration command mode. Set the ISAKMP parameters in this mode. If commands are not explicitly configured, default values are used. For example, if the **hash** command is not explicitly configured, IKE uses the default SHA value.

Refer to **Figure** in online course

Two endpoints must negotiate ISAKMP policies before they agree on the SA to use for IPsec.

When the ISAKMP negotiation begins in IKE Phase 1 main mode, the peer that initiates the negotiation sends all its policies to the remote peer. The remote peer tries to find a match with its own policies. The remote peer looks for a match by comparing its own highest priority policy against the policies it received from the other peer. The remote peer checks each of its policies in order of its priority (highest priority first) until a match is found.

A match is made when both policies from the two peers contain the same encryption, hash, authentication, DH parameter values, and when the policy of the remote peer specifies a lifetime less than or equal to the lifetime of the policy that is being compared. If the lifetimes are not identical, the shorter lifetime from the remote peer policy is used. Assign the most secure policy the smallest available priority number so that the most secure policy finds a match before any less secure policies are configured.

If an acceptable match is not found, ISAKMP refuses negotiation, and IPsec is not established. If a match is found, ISAKMP completes the main mode negotiation, and IPsec SAs are created during IKE Phase 2 quick mode.

Refer to
Figure
in online course

PSKs are required for encryption. At a given peer, the same key can be configured to be shared with multiple remote peers. A more secure approach is to specify different keys to share between different pairs of peers.

Configure a PSK with the **crypto isakmp key** global configuration command. This key must be configured if the **authentication pre-share** command was configured in the ISAKMP policy.

```
crypto isakmp key keystring address peer-address
crypto isakmp key keystring hostname hostname
```

By default, the ISAKMP identity is set to use the IP address. To use the *hostname* parameter, the ISAKMP identity must be configured to use the host name with the **crypto isakmp identity hostname** global configuration mode command. In addition, DNS must be accessible to resolve the hostname.

8.4.4 Task 3 - Configure the Transform Sets

Refer to
Figure
in online course

A transform set is a combination of individual IPsec transforms that are designed to enact a specific security policy for traffic. During the ISAKMP IPsec SA negotiation that occurs in IKE Phase 2 quick mode, the peers agree to use a particular transform set for protecting a particular data flow.

Transform sets consist of a combination of an AH transform, an ESP transform, and the IPsec mode (either tunnel or transport mode). Transform sets are limited to one AH transform and one or two ESP transforms. Multiple transform sets can be configured. Then one or more of these transform sets can be specified in a crypto map entry. The IPsec SA negotiation uses the transform set that is defined in the crypto map entry to protect the data flows that are specified by the ACL of that crypto map entry.

To define a transform set, specify one to four transforms using the **crypto ipsec transform-set** global configuration command. This command invokes crypto-transform configuration mode.

```
crypto ipsec transform-set transform-set-name transform1 [transform2] [transform3]
[transform4]
```

Each transform represents an IPsec security protocol (AH or ESP) plus the associated algorithm. These protocols and algorithms are specified within the crypto-transform configuration mode. In a transform set, specify the AH protocol, the ESP protocol, or both. If an ESP protocol is specified in a transform set, an ESP encryption transform set or an ESP encryption transform set and an ESP authentication transform set must be specified.

During the negotiation, the peers search for a transform set that has the same criteria (the combination of protocols, algorithms, and other settings) at both peers. When a transform set is found, it is selected and applied to the protected traffic as part of the IPsec SAs of both peers.

When ISAKMP is not used to establish SAs, a single transform set must be used. In this instance, the transform set is not negotiated.

Refer to
Figure
in online course

Transform sets are negotiated during IKE Phase 2 quick mode. When configuring multiple transform sets, configure the transforms from most to least secure, according to the network security policy.

IPsec peers search for a transform set that matches at both ends and agree on one unidirectional transform proposal per SA. For example, assume R1 and R2 are negotiating a transform set. R1 has transform sets ALPHA, BETA, and CHARLIE configured, while R2 has RED, BLUE, and YELLOW configured. Each R1 transform set is compared against each R2 transform set in succession. R1 transform sets ALPHA, BETA, and CHARLIE are compared to R2 transform set RED. The result is no match. All the R1 transform sets are then compared against R2 transform set BLUE. Finally, the R1 transform sets are compared to R2 transform set YELLOW. YELLOW is matched against the R1 transform set CHARLIE. When a transform set match is found, it is selected and applied to the protected traffic as part of the IPsec SAs of both peers.

8.4.5 Task 4 - Configure the Crypto ACLs

Refer to
Figure
in online course

Crypto ACLs identify the traffic flows to protect. Outbound crypto ACLs select outbound traffic that IPsec should protect. Traffic that is not selected is sent in plaintext. If desired, inbound ACLs can be created to filter and discard traffic that should have been protected by IPsec.

Extended IP ACLs select IP traffic to encrypt based on protocol, IP address, network, subnet, and port. Although the ACL syntax is unchanged from extended IP ACLs, the meanings are slightly different for crypto ACLs. For example, **permit** specifies that matching packets must be encrypted, and **deny** specifies that matching packets are not encrypted. Traffic is not necessarily dropped because of a deny statement. Crypto ACLs are processed in a similar fashion to an extended IP ACL applied to outbound traffic on an interface.

Refer to
Figure
in online course

The command syntax for the basic form of an extended IP ACL is:

```
access-list access-list-number {permit | deny} protocol source source-wildcard
destination destination-wildcard
```

Outbound crypto ACLs define the interesting traffic to be encrypted. All other traffic passes as plaintext.

Inbound crypto ACLs inform the router of which traffic should be received as encrypted traffic. When traffic matches the permit statement, the router expects that traffic to be encrypted. If inbound plaintext traffic is received that matches a permit statement in the crypto ACL, that traffic is dropped. This drop occurs because the plaintext traffic was expected to be protected by IPsec and encrypted, but was not.

An administrator might want specific traffic to receive one combination of IPsec protection (authentication only) and other traffic to receive a different combination (both authentication and encryption). To do so, create two different crypto ACLs to define the two different types of traffic. Different crypto map entries then use these ACLs to specify different IPsec policies.

Try to be as restrictive as possible when defining which packets to protect in a crypto ACL. Using the **any** keyword to specify source or destination addresses is not recommended. The **permit any any** statement is strongly discouraged because it causes all outbound traffic to be protected and all protected traffic to be sent to the peer that is specified in the corresponding crypto map entry. Then, all inbound packets that lack IPsec protection are silently dropped, including packets for routing protocols, NTP, echo, echo response, and others. If the **any** keyword must be used in a permit statement, preface the statement with a series of deny statements to filter out traffic that should not be protected.

The crypto ACL is associated with a crypto map, which in turn is assigned to a specific interface.

Refer to
Figure
in online course

Symmetric crypto ACLs must be configured for use by IPsec. When a router receives encrypted packets back from an IPsec peer, it uses the same ACL to determine which inbound packets to decrypt by viewing the source and destination addresses in the ACL in reverse order. The ACL criteria are applied in the forward direction to traffic exiting a router, and in the backward direction to traffic entering the router, so that the outbound ACL source becomes the inbound ACL destination.

For example, assume that for Site 1, IPsec protection is applied to traffic between hosts on the 10.0.1.0/24 network as the data exits the R1 S0/0/0 interface in route to Site 2 hosts on the

10.0.2.0/24 network. For traffic from Site 1 hosts on the 10.0.1.0/24 network to Site 2 hosts on the 10.0.2.0/24 network, the ACL entry on R1 is evaluated as follows:

- Source = hosts on 10.0.1.0/24 network

- Destination = hosts on 10.0.2.0/24 network

For incoming traffic from Site 2 hosts on the 10.0.2.0/24 network to Site 1 hosts on the 10.0.1.0/24 network, that same ACL entry on R1 is evaluated as follows:

- Source = hosts on 10.0.2.0/24 network

- Destination = hosts on 10.0.1.0/24 network

8.4.6 Task 5 - Apply the Crypto Map

Refer to **Figure** in online course

Crypto map entries that are created for IPsec combine the needed configuration parameters of IPsec SAs, including the following parameters:

- Which traffic to protect using a crypto ACL

- Granularity of the flow to be protected by a set of SAs

- Who the remote IPsec peer is, which determines where the IPsec-protected traffic is sent

- Local address used for the IPsec traffic (optional)

- Which type of IPsec security is applied to this traffic, choosing from a list of one or more transform sets

Crypto map entries with the same crypto map name but different map sequence numbers are grouped into a crypto map set.

Only one crypto map can be set to a single interface. The crypto map set can include a combination of Cisco Encryption Technology (CET) and IPsec using IKE. Multiple interfaces can share the same crypto map set if the same policy is applied to multiple interfaces. If more than one crypto map entry is created for a given interface, use the sequence number (*seq-num*) of each map entry to rank the map entries. The smaller the sequence number, the higher the priority. At the interface that has the crypto map set, traffic is evaluated against higher priority map entries first.

Create multiple crypto map entries for a given interface if any of these conditions exist:

- Separate IPsec peers handle different data flows.

- Different IPsec security must be applied to different types of traffic (to the same or separate IPsec peers). For example, if traffic between one set of subnets needs to be authenticated, and traffic between another set of subnets needs to be both authenticated and encrypted. In this case, define the different types of traffic in two separate ACLs, and create a separate crypto map entry for each crypto ACL.

- IKE is not used to establish a particular set of SAs, and multiple ACL entries must be specified, create separate ACLs (one per permit entry) and specify a separate crypto map entry for each ACL.

Refer to **Figure** in online course

Use the `crypto map` global configuration command to create or modify a crypto map entry and enter crypto map configuration mode. Set the crypto map entries that reference dynamic maps to the lowest priority in a crypto map set (they should have the largest sequence numbers). The command syntax and parameter definitions are as follows:

```
crypto map map-name seq-num cisco
```

```
crypto map map-name seq-num ipsec-manual
crypto map map-name seq-num ipsec-isakmp [dynamic dynamic-map-name]
no crypto map map-name [seq-num]
```

Using the **crypto map** command in global configuration mode enters crypto-map configuration mode. From here, various IPsec components are configured, including which crypto ACL, peer address, and transform set to use.

ACLs for crypto map entries that are tagged as IPsec-manual are restricted to a single permit entry, and subsequent entries are ignored. The SAs that are established by that particular crypto map entry are for a single data flow only. To support multiple manually established SAs for different kinds of traffic, define multiple crypto ACLs and then apply each one to a separate IPsec-manual crypto map entry. Each ACL includes one permit statement that defines the traffic that it must protect.

Two peers can be specified in a crypto map for redundancy. If the first peer cannot be contacted, the second peer is used. There is no limit to the number of redundant peers that can be configured.

After the crypto map parameters are configured, assign the crypto map to interfaces using the **crypto map** interface configuration command.

Refer to
Figure
in online course

The crypto map is applied to the outgoing interface of the VPN tunnel using the **crypto map** command in interface configuration mode.

```
crypto map map-name
map-name is the name of the crypto map set to apply to the interface.
```

Make sure that the routing information that is needed to send packets into the tunnel is also configured.

All IP traffic passing through the interface where the crypto map is applied is evaluated against the applied crypto map set. If a crypto map entry sees outbound IP traffic that should be protected and the crypto map specifies the use of IKE, an SA is negotiated with the remote peer according to the parameters that are included in the crypto map entry.

8.4.7 Verify and Troubleshoot the IPsec Configuration

Refer to
Figure
in online course

VPNs can be complex and sometimes do not operate as expected. For this reason, there are a variety of useful commands to verify the operation of VPNs and to troubleshoot when necessary.

The best time to become familiar with these commands and their output is when the network is operating correctly. This way, anomalies can be detected when using them for troubleshooting.

Refer to
Figure
in online course

To view all configured crypto maps, use the **show crypto map** command. This command verifies configurations and shows the SA lifetime. The **show running-config** command also reveals many of these same settings.

Use the **show crypto isakmp policy** command to display configured IKE policies and the default IKE policy settings. This command is useful because it reveals all ISAKMP (IKE) configuration information.

Use the **show crypto ipsec transform-set** command to show all configured transform sets. Because transform sets determine the level of protection that the data will have as it is tunneled, it is important to verify the strength of the IPsec protection policy.

Refer to
Figure
in online course

One of the more useful commands is **show crypto ipsec sa**. If the output indicates that an SA is established, the rest of the configuration is assumed to be working. Within the output, the pkts encrypt and pkts decrypt values indicate that traffic is flowing through the tunnel.

A similar useful command is **show crypto isakmp sa**. This command displays all current IKE SAs. QM_IDLE status indicates an active IKE SA.

Refer to
Figure
in online course

To use debugging commands to troubleshoot VPN connectivity, connect to the Cisco IOS router with a terminal connection.

The `debug crypto isakmp` command displays detailed information about the IKE Phase 1 and IKE Phase 2 negotiation processes. The `debug crypto ipsec` command displays detailed information about IPsec events.

As with other debug commands, use the `debug crypto isakmp` command with caution, because debug processes can cause performance problems on the device. Use the `undebug all` command to turn off the debug as soon as possible.

8.5 Implementing Site-to-Site IPsec VPNs with CCP

8.5.1 Configuring IPsec Using CCP

Refer to
Figure
in online course

In addition to configuring IPsec VPNs via CLI, it is possible to configure them using a CCP wizard.

To select and start a VPN wizard, follow these steps:

Step 1.   Click **Configure** in the main toolbar.

Step 2.   Click the **Security** folder and then click the **VPN** subfolder.

Step 3.   Choose a wizard from the VPN list.

Step 4.   Click the VPN implementation subtype.

Step 5.   Click the **Launch the selected task** button to start the wizard.

Refer to
Figure
in online course

CCP VPN wizards use two sources to create a VPN connection: user input during a Step by Step wizard process, and preconfigured VPN components.

CCP provides some default VPN components for the Quick Setup wizard: two IKE policies and an IPsec transform set.

The VPN wizards create other components during the step-by-step configuration process. Some components must be configured before the wizards can be used. For instance, PKI components must be configured before using the PKI wizard.

The main VPN folder contains a VPN design guide, the wizards to create a site-to-site VPN, Easy VPN Remote, Easy VPN Server, and dynamic multipoint VPN. The VPN wizards simplify the configuration of individual VPN components. The individual IPsec components section can then be used to modify parameters that might have been misconfigured during the VPN wizard step-by-step configuration.

Under the VPN folder are three subfolders:

- *The SSL VPN* Is used to configure SSL VPNs parameters.

- *The GET VPN* Is used to configure GET VPN parameters.

- *VPN components* Are used to configure VPN components such as IPsec, IKE, Easy VPN Server group policies and browser proxy settings, and VPN Keys Encryption. The VPN keys encryption option appears if the Cisco IOS software image on the router supports type 6 encryption, also referred to as VPN key encryption. Use this window to specify a master key when encrypting VPN keys, such as PSKs, Cisco Easy VPN keys, and Extended Authentication (XAuth) keys. When the keys are encrypted, they are not readable by someone viewing the router configuration file.

Refer to
Figure
in online course

Use a web browser to start the CCP on a router. Select the VPN wizard by choosing **Configure > Security > VPN > Site-to-Site VPN**.

To create and configure a classic site-to-site VPN, click the **Create a Site-to-Site VPN** radio button on the Create Site-to-Site VPN tab.

Then click the **Launch the selected task** button.

Refer to
Figure
in online course

A window displays the Quick setup option and the Step by Step wizard option.

The **Quick setup** option uses the CCP default IKE policies and IPsec transform sets. It enables a junior administrator to quickly set up an IPsec VPN using best practice security parameters.

The **Step by step wizard** option allows the administrator to specify the details of the IPsec VPN.

Click the **Next** button to configure the parameters of the VPN connection.

8.5.2 VPN Wizard - Quick Setup

Refer to
Figure
in online course

The Quick Setup option uses a single window to configure the VPN connection and includes the following parameters:

- Interface to use for the VPN connection (usually the outside interface)

- Peer identity information, which includes the type of peer and IP address of the peer

- Authentication method, either PSKs (specify the secret) or digital certificates (choose a certificate that has been created beforehand)

- Traffic to encrypt by identifying the source interface and destination IP subnet

CCP provides a default IKE policy to govern authentication, a default transform set to control data encryption, and a default IPsec rule that encrypts all traffic between the router and the remote device.

Refer to
Figure
in online course

When all parameters are set, verify the configuration on the summary page before clicking **Finish**.

Quick Setup is best used when both the local router and the remote system are Cisco routers using CCP. Quick setup configures 3DES encryption if it is supported by the Cisco IOS image. Otherwise, it configures DES encryption. If AES or SEAL encryption is required, the Step by Step wizard must be used.

8.5.3 VPN Wizard – Step by Step Setup

Refer to
Figure
in online course

The Step by Step wizard requires multiple steps to configure the VPN connection and includes the following parameters:

- Connection settings, including outside interface, peer identity, and authentication credentials

- IKE proposals, such as priority, encryption, the Hashed Message Authentication Code (HMAC) algorithm, IKE authentication method, Diffie-Hellman (DH) group, and IKE lifetime

- IPsec transform set information, including name, integrity algorithm, encryption algorithm, mode of operation (tunnel or transport), and compression

- Traffic to protect by identifying the single source and destination subnets or defining an ACL to use for more complex VPNs

The first task in the Step by Step wizard is to configure the connection settings.

Step 1. Choose the outside interface to connect to the IPsec peer over the untrusted network.

Step 2. Specify the IP address of the peer.

Step 3. Choose the authentication method and specify the credentials. Use long, random PSKs to prevent brute-force and dictionary attacks against IKE.

Step 4. Click **Next**.

Refer to **Figure** in online course

The second task in the Step by Step wizard is to configure IKE proposals. A custom IKE proposal can be created, or the default IKE proposal can be used.

Custom IKE Proposal

To create a custom IKE proposal, a new IKE must be added.

Step 1. Click the **Add** button to define a proposal and specify the IKE proposal priority, encryption algorithm, hashing algorithm, IKE authentication method, DH group, and IKE lifetime.

Step 2. Click **OK** when configuring the IKE proposal is completed.

Step 3. When finished with adding IKE policies, choose the proposal to use. Click **Next**.

Predefined IKE Proposal

To use the predefined IKE proposal, click **Next** on the IKE Proposal page. The predefined IKE proposal is chosen by default.

Refer to **Figure** in online course

The third task in the Step by Step wizard is to configure a transform set. A custom IPsec transform set can be created, or a predefined IPsec transform set can be used.

Custom IPsec Transform Set

To create a custom IPsec transform set, a new IPsec transform set must be added.

Step 1. Click the **Add** button to define the transform set and specify the name, integrity algorithm, encryption algorithm, mode of operation, and optional compression.

Step 2. Click **OK** when configuring the transform set is completed.

Step 3. When finished adding transform sets, choose the transform set to use, and click **Next** to proceed to the next task.

Predefined IPsec Transform Set

To use the IPsec transform set, click **Next** on the Transform Set page. The predefined transform set is chosen by default.

Refer to **Figure** in online course

The fourth task in the Step by Step wizard is to configure which traffic needs protection.

To protect all traffic from one IP subnet to another:

Step 1. From the Traffic to Protect window, click the **Protect all traffic between the following subnets** radio button.

Step 2.   Define the IP address and subnet mask of the local network where IPsec traffic originates.

Step 3.   Define the IP address and subnet mask of the remote network where IPsec traffic is sent.

To specify a Custom ACL (IPsec rule) that defines the traffic types to be protected:

Step 1.   From the Traffic to Protect window, click the **Create/Select an access-list for IPsec traffic** radio button.

Step 2.   Click the ellipsis (**...**) button to choose an existing ACL or to create a new one.

Step 3.   To use an existing ACL, choose the **Select an existing rule (ACL)** option. To create a new ACL, choose the **Create a new rule (ACL) and select** option.

Refer to
Figure
in online course

When creating a new ACL to define traffic that needs protection, a window that lists the created access rule entries is displayed:

Step 1.   Give the access rule a name and description.

Step 2.   Click the **Add** button to start adding rule entries.

After a new ACL is created, entries must be specified within the ACL:

Step 1.   Choose an action from the **Select an action** list box and enter a description of the rule entry in the **Description** text box.

Step 2.   Define the source hosts or networks in the Source Host/Network pane, and the destination hosts or networks in the Destination Host/Network pane. Each rule entry defines one pair of source and destination addresses or networks. Be sure to use wildcard bits and not the subnet mask bits in the Wildcard Mask field.

Step 3.   (Optional) To provide protection for a specific protocol, choose the protocol radio button (TCP, UDP, or ICMP) and the port numbers. If IP is chosen as the protocol, the rule applies to all IP traffic.

At the end of the configuration, the wizard presents a summary of the configured parameters. To modify the configuration, click the **Back** button. Click the **Finish** button to complete the configuration.

8.5.4 Verifying, Monitoring, and Troubleshooting VPNs

After the IPsec VPN is configured, it is necessary to test the VPN to verify operation.

Refer to
Figure
in online course

To test the configuration of the VPN tunnel, choose **Configure > Security > VPN > Site-to-Site VPN > Edit Site to Site VPN** and click the **Test Tunnel** button.

The **Generate Mirror** button can also be clicked to generate a mirroring configuration that is required on the other end of the tunnel. This is useful if the other router does not have CCP and must use the CLI to configure the tunnel.

Refer to
Figure
in online course

To see all IPsec tunnels, their parameters, and status, choose **Monitor > Security > VPN Status > IPsec Tunnels**.

8.6 Implementing Remote-Access VPNs

8.6.1 A Shift to Telecommuting

Refer to
Figure
in online course

How many hours are spent by employees traveling to and from work every day? What if there are traffic jams? How could these hours be put to productive use? The answer is telecommuting.

Telecommuting is sometimes referred to as teleworking. Telecommuting employees have flexibility in location and hours. Employers offer telecommuting because they can save on real estate, utility, and other overhead costs. Organizations that have the greatest success with a telecommuting program ensure that telecommuting is voluntary, subject to management discretion, operationally feasible, and results in no additional costs.

Telecommuting organizations take full advantage of new technologies and new ways of working. With telecommuting, the focus is on the actual work performed rather than on the location where it is performed. This aspect of telecommuting moves us closer to a global society, allowing individuals across the world to work together. As one of the critical workplace transformers of the next decade, there is little doubt that telecommuting will inevitably and dramatically reshape how work is performed.

Refer to
Figure
in online course

Telecommuting offers organizational, social, and environmental benefits. Studies have shown that telecommuting improves employee lifestyles by decreasing job-related stresses. It can also accommodate those with health problems or disabilities. Telecommuting helps reduce energy consumption by decreasing transportation related pollution. It also increases organizational profits, improves recruitment and retention, and can offer possibilities for increased service and international reach. Telecommuters in different time zones can ensure that a company is virtually open for business around the clock.

Although telecommuting has many benefits, there may be some drawbacks. For example, telecommuters working from home can experience distractions that they would not have at work. Additionally, companies that offer telecommuting programs have to manage more risk, because data must travel across public networks, and organizations must rely on employees to maintain secure systems.

Refer to
Figure
in online course

Telecommuters typically need high-speed access to the Internet. This access can be provided using broadband connections, such as DSL, Cable or satellite Internet connections. Although a dialup connection can be used to access the Internet, the access speed is very slow and is not generally considered adequate for telecommuting.

Laptop or desktop computers are also required, and many implementations also require a VoIP phone to provide seamless telephone services.

Security is a huge concern for companies. Remote access to corporate locations is implemented using remote VPN access.

8.6.2 Introducing Remote-Access VPNs

Refer to
Figure
in online course

The ubiquity of the Internet, combined with today's VPN technologies, allows organizations to cost-effectively and securely extend the reach of their networks to anyone, anyplace, anytime.

VPNs have become the logical solution for remote-access connectivity for many reasons. VPNs provide secure communications with access rights tailored to individual users, such as employees, contractors, and partners. They also enhance productivity by extending the corporate network and applications securely while reducing communication costs and increasing flexibility.

Using VPN technology, employees can essentially take their office, including access to emails and network applications, with them. VPNs can also allow contractors and partners to have limited access to the specific servers, web pages, or files required. This network access allows them to contribute to business productivity without compromising network security.

There are two primary methods for deploying remote-access VPNs:

- Secure Sockets Layer (SSL)

- IP Security (IPsec)

Refer to **Figure** in online course

The type of VPN method implemented is based on the access requirements of the users and the organization's IT processes.

Both IPsec and SSL VPN technologies offer access to virtually any network application or resource. SSL VPNs offer such features as easy connectivity from non-company-managed desktops, little or no desktop software maintenance, and user-customized web portals upon login.

IPsec exceeds SSL in many significant ways:

- Number of applications that are supported

- Strength of encryption

- Strength of authentication

- Overall security

When security is an issue, IPsec is the superior choice. If support and ease of deployment are the primary issues, consider SSL.

IPsec and SSL VPN are complementary because they solve different problems. Depending on its needs, an organization can implement one or both. This complementary approach allows a single device such as an ISR router or an ASA firewall appliance to address all remote-access user requirements. While many solutions offer either IPsec or SSL, Cisco remote-access VPN solutions offer both technologies integrated on a single platform with unified management. Offering both IPsec and SSL technologies enables organizations to customize their remote-access VPN without any additional hardware or management complexity.

8.6.3 SSL VPNs

Refer to **Figure** in online course

Cisco IOS SSL VPN technology provides remote-access connectivity from almost any Internet-enabled location using a web browser and its native SSL encryption. Originally developed by Netscape, SSL has been universally accepted on the Web.

An SSL VPN does not require a software client to be preinstalled on the endpoint host. It provides remote-access connectivity for corporate resources to any authorized user from any Internet-enabled location.

The SSL protocol supports a variety of different cryptographic algorithms for operations such as authenticating the server and client to each other, transmitting certificates, and establishing session keys. Cisco SSL VPN solutions can be customized for businesses of any size. These solutions deliver many remote-access connectivity features and benefits:

- Web-based clientless access and full network access without preinstalled desktop software. This facilitates customized remote access based on user and security requirements, and minimizes desktop support costs.

- Protection against viruses, worms, spyware, and hackers on a VPN connection by integrating network and endpoint security in the Cisco SSL VPN platform. This reduces cost and management complexity by eliminating the need for additional security equipment and management infrastructure.

- Simple, flexible, and cost-effective licensing. SSL uses a single license. There is no per-feature license to purchase or manage. User count upgrades are flexible and cost effective. An implementation can start with as few as 10 users and scale as the needs change.

- Single device for both SSL VPN and IPsec VPN. This reduces cost and management complexity by facilitating robust remote access and site-to-site VPN services from a single platform with unified management.

Refer to
Figure
in online course

SSL VPNs provide different types of access:

- Clientless

- Thin client

- Full client

An SSL VPN provides three modes of remote access on Cisco IOS routers: clientless, thin client, and full client. ASA devices have two modes: clientless (which includes clientless and thin client port forwarding) and AnyConnect client (which replaces full tunnel).

Clientless Access Mode

In clientless mode, the remote user accesses the internal or corporate network using a web browser on the client machine. Clientless access requires no specialized VPN software or applet on the user desktop. All VPN traffic is transmitted and delivered through a standard web browser. No other software is required, eliminating many support issues. Using a clientless connection, all web-enabled and some client/server applications, such as intranets, applications with Web interfaces, email, calendaring, and file servers, can be accessed.

Not all client/server applications are accessible to SSL clients; however, this limited access is often a perfect fit for business partners or contractors who should have access only to a limited set of resources on the organization's network. It does not work for employees that require full network access.

Thin Client Mode

Thin client mode, sometimes called TCP port forwarding, assumes that the client application uses TCP to connect to a well-known server and port. In this mode, the remote user downloads a Java applet by clicking the link provided on the portal page. The Java applet acts as a TCP proxy on the client machine for the services configured on the SSL VPN gateway. The Java applet starts a new SSL connection for every client connection.

The Java applet initiates an HTTP request from the remote user client to the SSL VPN gateway. The name and port number of the internal email server is included in the HTTP request. The SSL VPN gateway creates a TCP connection to that internal email server and port.

Thin client mode is often referred to as a type of clientless mode and can be used anywhere that clientless VPNs are supported. It extends the capability of the cryptographic functions of the web browser to enable remote access to TCP-based applications such as POP3, SMTP, IMAP, Telnet, and SSH.

Refer to
Figure
in online course

Full Client Access Mode

Full client mode enables complete access to the corporate network over an SSL VPN tunnel, which is used to move data at the Network (IP) Layer. This mode supports most IP-based applications, such as Microsoft Outlook, Microsoft Exchange, Lotus Notes Email, and Telnet. Being part of the SSL VPN is transparent to the applications run on the client. A Java applet is downloaded to handle the tunneling between the client host and the SSL VPN gateway. The user can use any application as if the client host was on the internal network.

This is a dynamically downloaded and updated VPN client. No software distribution or interaction from the end user is needed. It requires little or no desktop support by IT organizations, thereby minimizing deployment and operations costs. Like clientless access, full network access offers full access control customization based on the access privileges of the end user. Full network access is a natural choice for employees who need remote access to the same applications and network resources that they use when in the office. Full network access is also appropriate for any client/server application that cannot be delivered across a web-based clientless connection.

Refer to **Figure** in online course

Establishing an SSL session involves five steps:

Step 1. The user makes an outbound connection to TCP port 443.

Step 2. The router responds with a digital certificate, which contains a public key that is digitally signed by a trusted certificate authority (CA).

Step 3. The user's computer generates a shared secret key that both parties use.

Step 4. The shared secret is encrypted with the public key of the router and transmitted to the router. The router software is able to easily decrypt the packet using its private key. Now both participants in the session know the shared secret key.

Step 5. The key is used to encrypt the SSL session.

SSL utilizes encryption algorithms with key lengths from 40 to 256 bits.

Refer to **Figure** in online course

Before SSL VPN services are implemented in Cisco IOS routers, the current environment must be analyzed to determine which features and modes might be useful in the implementation.

There are many SSL VPN design considerations:

- *User connectivity* Determine whether the users connect to the corporate network from public shared computers, such as a computer in a library or at an Internet kiosk. In this case, use clientless SSL VPN mode.

- *Router feature* A Cisco IOS router can run various features, such as IPsec VPN tunnels, routing engines, and firewall processes. Enabling the SSL VPN feature can add considerable load if the router is already running a number of features.

- *Router hardware* The SSL VPN process is fairly CPU and memory intensive. Before implementing an SSL VPN on the Cisco IOS router, make sure to leverage the hardware-accelerated SSL VPN engines such as AIM-VPN/SSL-1, AIM-VPN/SSL-2, and AIM-VPN/SSL-3. Check www.cisco.com for more information about the SSL VPN hardware modules.

- *Infrastructure planning* It is important to consider the placement of the VPN termination devices. Before implementing the SSL VPN feature in Cisco IOS, ask questions such as: Should the SSL VPN be placed behind a firewall? If so, what ports should be opened? Should the decrypted traffic be passed through another set of firewalls? If so, what ports should be allowed?

- *Implementation scope* Network security administrators need to determine the size of the SSL VPN deployment, especially the number of simultaneous users that will connect to gain network access. If one Cisco IOS router is not enough to support the required number of users, traditional load balancers or server-clustering schemes must be considered to accommodate all potential remote users.

SSL VPNs are a viable option for many organizations, however, the configuration of SSL VPNs is beyond the scope of this course. Visit www.cisco.com to learn about the required configuration commands to implement SSL VPNs as well as to download reference guides.

8.6.4 Cisco Easy VPN

Refer to
Figure
in online course

While SSL VPNs are useful in many instances, many applications require the security of an IPsec VPN connection for authentication and encryption of data. Establishing a VPN connection between two sites can be complicated and typically requires coordination between the network administrators at each site to configure the VPN parameters. When deploying VPNs for telecommuters and small branch offices, ease of deployment is critical if technical resources are not available for VPN configuration on the remote site router.

The Cisco Easy VPN solution feature offers flexibility, scalability, and ease of use for site-to-site and remote-access VPNs. It consists of three components:

- *Cisco Easy VPN Server* A Cisco IOS router or Cisco ASA Firewall acting as the VPN head-end device in site-to-site or remote-access VPNs.

- *Cisco Easy VPN Remote* A Cisco IOS router or Cisco ASA Firewall acting as a remote VPN client.

- *Cisco VPN Client* An application supported on a PC used to access a Cisco VPN server.

Most of the VPN parameters are defined on the Cisco IOS Easy VPN Server to simplify deployment. When a remote client initiates a VPN tunnel connection, the Cisco Easy VPN Server pushes the IPsec policies to the client and creates the corresponding IPsec VPN tunnel connection.

The remote device can be a mobile worker running the Cisco Easy client software on a PC. This PC can easily establish a VPN connection with the Cisco Easy VPN Server-enabled device through the Internet. It can also be a Cisco device running the Cisco Easy VPN Remote feature, enabling it to be a client of the Easy VPN Server. This means that individuals at small branch offices no longer need to run VPN client software on their PCs.

Refer to
Figure
in online course

The Cisco Easy VPN Server makes it possible for mobile and remote workers using VPN Client software on their PCs to create secure IPsec tunnels to access their headquarters' intranet where critical data and applications exist. It enables Cisco IOS routers and Cisco ASA Firewalls to act as VPN head-end devices in site-to-site or remote-access VPNs. Remote office devices use the Cisco Easy VPN Remote feature or the Cisco VPN Client application to connect to the server, which then pushes defined security policies to the remote VPN device. This ensures that those connections have up-to-date policies in place before the connection is established.

The Cisco Easy VPN Remote enables Cisco IOS routers or software clients to act as remote VPN clients. These devices can receive security policies from a Cisco Easy VPN Server, minimizing VPN configuration requirements at the remote location. This cost-effective solution is ideal for remote offices with little IT support or for large customer premises equipment (CPE) deployments where it is impractical to individually configure multiple remote devices.

Refer to
Figure
in online course

When a client connects to a server, the negotiation to secure the VPN occurs:

Step 1.   The VPN client initiates the IKE Phase 1 process. If a pre-shared key is used for authentication, the VPN Client initiates aggressive mode. If digital certificates are used for authentication, the VPN Client initiates main mode.

Step 2. The VPN client establishes an ISAKMP SA. To reduce the amount of manual configuration on the VPN Client, Easy VPN ISAKMP proposals include every combination of encryption and hash algorithms, authentication methods, and DH group sizes.

Step 3. The Easy VPN Server accepts the SA proposal. The ISAKMP policy can consist of several proposals, but the Easy VPN Server uses the first match, so always configure the most secure policies first. Device authentication ends and user authentication begins at this point.

Step 4. The Easy VPN Server initiates a username and password challenge. The information that is entered is checked against authentication entities using authentication, authorization, and accounting (AAA) protocols such as RADIUS and TACACS+. Token cards can also be used via AAA proxy. VPN devices that are configured to handle remote VPN clients should always enforce user authentication.

Step 5. The mode configuration process is initiated. The remaining system parameters (i.e., IP address, DNS, split tunnel attributes, etc.) are pushed to the VPN client at this time using mode configuration.

Step 6. The reverse route injection (RRI) process is initiated. RRI ensures that a static route is created on the Cisco Easy VPN Server for the internal IP address of each VPN client.

Step 7. IPsec quick mode completes the connection. The connection is complete after IPsec SAs have been created.

8.6.5 Configuring a VPN Server with CCP

Refer to
Figure
in online course

Configuring Cisco Easy VPN Server functionality using CCP consists of two major tasks:

Task 1. Configure prerequisites, such as AAA, privileged users, and the enable secret password, based on the chosen VPN design.

Task 2. Configure the Cisco Easy VPN Server.

From the CCP main page, click the **Configure** button, click the **Security** folder, click the **VPN** subfolder, and then select the **Easy VPN Server** option. If AAA has not been previously configured, the wizard asks to configure it. If AAA is disabled on the router, configure AAA before Easy VPN Server configuration begins and create at least one administrative user.

Refer to
Figure
in online course

After the Easy VPN Server wizard is launched, the Interface and Authentication window displays. Specify the router interface where the VPN connection will terminate and the authentication method (e.g., pre-shared keys, digital certificates, or both).

Click **Next** to display the IKE Proposals window. When configuring IKE proposals, use the default policy that is predefined by CCP or add a custom IKE Policy specifying these required parameters:

- Interface on which client connections terminate

- IKE policy

- Authentication (PRE_SHARE or RSA_SIG)

- D-H group (group1, group2, or group5)

- Encryption algorithm (DES, 3DES or AES)

- Hash (SHA_1 or MD5)

- IKE lifetime

Refer to Figure in online course

CCP provides a default transform set. Use the default or create a new IPsec transform set configuration using these parameters:

- Transform set name
- Encryption algorithm (DES, 3DES, AES, or SEAL)
- HMAC (SHA_1 or MD5)
- Optional compression
- Mode of operation (tunnel or transport)

Refer to Figure in online course

The Group Authorization and Group Policy Lookup window appears next. There are three options to choose from for the location where Easy VPN group policies can be stored:

- *Local* All groups are in the router configuration in NVRAM.
- *RADIUS* The router uses the RADIUS server for group authorization.
- *RADIUS and Local* The router can look up policies stored in an AAA server database that can be reached via RADIUS.

Click **Next** to configure optional user authentication (XAuth). Click **Next** again to configure the Group Authorization parameters. Click the **Add** button to add a new group policy. The General tab allows configuration of the following parameters:

- Group name
- Pre-shared keys
- IP Address pool information
- Maximum connections allowed

Other tabs address the following options:

- DNS/WINS
- Split Tunneling
- Client Settings
- XAuth Options

Refer to Figure in online course

After all the steps are completed, the Easy VPN Server wizard presents a summary of the configured parameters. Click **Back** to correct any errors in the configuration. Otherwise, click **Finish** to apply the configuration to the router.

The Easy VPN Server configuration can then be verified. Run a test to confirm the correct tunnel configuration by clicking the **Test VPN Server** button at the bottom of the Edit Easy VPN Server page. This will present the VPN Troubleshooting window which displays the VPN validation results.

8.6.6 Connecting with a VPN Client

Refer to Figure in online course

The Cisco VPN Client is simple to deploy and operate. It allows organizations to establish end-to-end, encrypted VPN tunnels for secure connectivity for mobile employees or telecommuters. This thin design IPsec-implementation is compatible with all Cisco VPN products.

When preconfigured for mass deployments, initial logins require little user intervention. Cisco VPN Client supports the innovative Cisco Easy VPN capabilities, delivering a uniquely scalable, cost-effective, and easy-to-manage remote access VPN architecture. It eliminates the operational costs associated with maintaining a consistent policy and key management method.

The Cisco Easy VPN feature allows the Cisco VPN Client to receive security policies on a VPN tunnel connection from the central site VPN device (Cisco Easy VPN Server), minimizing configuration requirements at the remote location. This simple and highly scalable solution is ideal for large remote access deployments where it is impractical to configure policies individually for multiple remote PCs.

Refer to
Figure
in online course

When the Cisco VPN client is installed, open the Cisco VPN client window to start an IPsec VPN connection on a PC.

The application lists the available preconfigured sites. Double-click a site. In the user authentication dialog box, authenticate the site. After authentication, the Cisco VPN Client displays a connected status.

Configuring the Cisco VPN client is beyond the scope of this course. Check www.cisco.com for more information.

Chapter Summary

Refer to
Figure
in online course

Refer to **Packet
Tracer Activity**
for this chapter

Refer to
Lab Activity
for this chapter

Your Chapter Notes

CHAPTER 9

Managing a Secure Network

Chapter Introduction

Refer to
Figure
in online course

Mitigating network attacks requires a comprehensive, end-to-end approach that includes creating and maintaining security policies based on the security needs of an organization. The first step in establishing the security needs of an organization is to identify likely threats and perform a risk analysis. The results of the risk analysis are used to establish the security hardware and software implementations, mitigation policies, and network design.

To help simplify network design, it is recommended that all security mechanisms come from a single vendor. The Cisco SecureX architecture is a comprehensive, end-to-end solution for network security that includes solutions to secure the network, email, web, access, mobile users and data center resources. Cisco Security Manager and CCP provide network management options for Cisco SecureX solutions.

After the network is designed, operations security entails the day-to-day practices necessary to first deploy and later maintain the secure system. Part of maintaining a secure system is network security testing. Security testing is performed by the operations team, to ensure that all security implementations are operating as expected. Testing is also used to provide insight into business continuity planning, which addresses the continuing operations of an organization in the event of a disaster, disruption, or prolonged service interruption.

After a secure network is implemented and continuity plans are established, those plans and documents must be continuously updated based on the changing needs of the organization. For this reason, it is necessary to understand the system development life cycle (SDLC) for the purposes of evaluating system changes and adjusting security implementations. The SDLC includes five phases: initiation, acquisition and development, implementation, operations and maintenance, and disposition. It is important to include security considerations in all phases of the SDLC.

A network security system cannot completely prevent assets from being vulnerable to threats. New attacks are developed and vulnerabilities identified that can be used to circumvent security solutions. Additionally, technical, administrative, and physical security systems can be defeated if the end user community does not adhere to security practices and procedures. A comprehensive security policy must be maintained which identifies an organization's assets, specifies the security hardware and software requirements for protecting those assets, clarifies the roles and responsibilities of personnel, and establishes the proper protocol for responding to security breaches. If security policies are established and followed, organizations can minimize the loss and damages resulting from attacks.

In a comprehensive hands-on lab for the chapter, *Security Policy Development and Implementation*, learners create a basic security policy, harden network routers, configure remote-access and authentication options, configure NTP and logging, configure a CBAC firewall, configure a firewall using ZPF, configure IPS using CLI and SDM, back up and secure router images and configuration files, harden network switches, configure remote-access and authentication options, mitigate STP attacks, and configure and test remote-access IPsec VPNs.

A comprehensive Packet Tracer activity, *Configure a Network for Secure Operation*, provides learners additional practice implementing the technologies introduced in this final chapter. Learners secure the routers with strong passwords and password encryption, secure the console and VTY lines, configure login banners, configure local AAA authentication, configure SSH, configure syslog, configure NTP, harden the network routers, configure CBAC, configure ZPF, and secure the network switches.

9.1 Principles of Secure Network Design

9.1.1 Ensuring a Network is Secure

Refer to
Figure
in online course

Mitigating network attacks requires a comprehensive, end-to-end approach:

- Secure network devices with AAA, SSH, role-based CLI, syslog, SNMP, and NTP.

- Secure services using AutoSecure and CCP one-step lockdown.

- Protect network endpoints (such as workstations and servers) against viruses, Trojan Horses, and worms, with Cisco NAC and Cisco IronPort.

- Use Cisco IOS Firewall and accompanying ACLs to secure resources internally while protecting those resources from outside attacks.

- Supplement Cisco IOS Firewall with Cisco IPS technology to evaluate traffic using an attack signature database.

- Protect the LAN by following Layer 2 and VLAN recommended practices and by using a variety of technologies, including BPDU guard, root guard, PortFast, and SPAN.

Despite these security techniques, hackers are continuously developing new ways to attack networks. An important part of implementing a secure network is creating and maintaining security policies to mitigate existing, as well as new kinds of attacks. These policies enforce a structured, informed, consistent approach to securing the network. When developing security policies, several questions must be answered:

- *Business needs* What does the organization want to do with the network? What are the organizational needs? Regardless of the security implications, business needs must come first.

- *Threat identification* What are the most likely types of threats given the organization's purpose? For example, a financial institution will face different threats than a university.

- *Risk analysis* What is the cost versus benefit analysis of implementing various security technologies? How do the latest security techniques affect the network environment and what is the risk if they are not implemented?

- *Security needs* What are the policies, standards, and guidelines needed to address business needs and risks?

- *Industry-recommended practices* What are the reliable, well-understood, and recommended security practices that similar organizations currently employ?

- *Security operations* What are the current procedures for incident response, monitoring, maintenance, and auditing of the system for compliance?

Refer to
Figure
in online course

Many security assumptions are made when designing and implementing a secure network. Unfortunately, assumptions about how and where the system will be used can lead to broken, misconfigured, or bypassed security mechanisms. An example of a bad assumption is that more users need to use a protocol, such as FTP, than is actually the case.

A wrong assumption has negative ramifications for all design work. It might influence one design decision, and then propagate to other decisions that depend on it. Wrong decisions are especially dangerous in early stages of secure system design when threats are modeled and risks are assessed. It is often easy to correct or enhance a single implementation aspect of a system, such as a firewall configuration. However, design errors, such as where that firewall is placed, are either extremely hard or impossible to correct without substantial investments in time and technology.

There are guidelines to help you avoid making wrong assumptions:

- Expect that any aspect of a security system might fail. When designing a system, perform what-if analysis for failures of every element, assess the probability of failure, and analyze all possible consequences of a failure, taking into account cascading failures of other elements.

- Identify any elements that fail-open. Fail-open occurs when a failure results in a complete bypass of the security function. Ideally, any security element should be fail-safe. If the element fails, it should default to a secure state, such as blocking all traffic.

- Try to identify all attack possibilities. One way to accomplish this is with a top-down analysis of possible system failures, which involves evaluating the simplicity and probability of every attack on a system. This type of analysis is commonly referred to as an attack tree analysis.

- Evaluate the probability of exploitation. Focus on the resources that are needed to create an attack, not the obscurity of a particular vulnerability. Be sure to account for technological advances.

- Assume that people make mistakes. For example, end users might use a system improperly, compromising its security unintentionally.

- Attackers might not use common and well-established techniques to compromise a system. Instead, they might hammer the system with seemingly random attacks, looking for possible information on how the system behaves under unexpected conditions.

- Check all assumptions with other people. They might have a fresh perspective on potential threats and their probability. The more people that question the assumptions, the more likely a wrong assumption will be identified.

9.1.2 Threat Identification and Risk Analysis

Refer to
Figure
in online course

Threat identification provides an organization with a list of threats that a system is subject to in a particular environment. When identifying threats, it is important to ask two questions:

- What are the possible vulnerabilities of a system?

- What are the consequences if system vulnerabilities are exploited?

For example, threat identification for connecting an e-banking system would include:

- *Internal system compromise* The attacker uses the exposed e-banking servers to break into an internal bank system.

- *Stolen customer data* An attacker steals the personal and financial data of bank customers from the customer database.

- *Phony transactions from an external server* An attacker alters the code of the e-banking application and runs arbitrary transactions impersonating a legitimate user.

- *Phony transactions using a stolen customer PIN or smart card* An attacker steals the identity of a customer and runs malicious transactions from the compromised account.

- *Insider attack on the system* A bank employee finds a flaw in the system from which to mount an attack.

- *Data input errors* A user inputs incorrect data or makes incorrect transaction requests.

- *Data center destruction* A cataclysmic event severely damages or destroys the data center.

Identifying vulnerabilities on a network entails understanding the important applications that are used as well as the different vulnerabilities of that application and hardware. This can require a significant amount of research on the part of the network administrator.

Refer to
Figure
in online course

Risk analysis is the systematic study of uncertainties and risks. It estimates the probability and severity of threats to a system and provides an organization with a prioritized list. Risk analysts identify the risks, determine how and when those risks might arise, and estimate the impact (financial or otherwise) of adverse outcomes.

The first step in developing a risk analysis is to evaluate each threat to determine its severity and probability:

- *Internal system compromise* Extremely severe and likely if untrusted software is used to pass data to the inside network.

- *Stolen customer data* Severe and likely if the external server is vulnerable to intrusions, which could compromise the operating system or application.

- *Phony transactions if external server is breached* Severe and likely if the external server is vulnerable to intrusions, which could compromise the operating system or application.

- *Phony transactions using a stolen customer PIN or smart card* Limited severity because individual accounts are compromised. Likely only if the stolen credentials are not detected quickly.

- *Insider attack on the system* Extremely severe and likely based on past insider attacks on company data.

- *Data input errors* Moderate severity and likely because of human error.

- *Data center destruction* Extremely severe but not likely because it requires an event of epic proportions, such as a natural disaster.

After the threats are evaluated for severity and likelihood, the information is used in a risk analysis. There are two types of risk analysis in information security, quantitative and qualitative.

Quantitative Risk Analysis

Quantitative risk analysis uses a mathematical model that assigns a monetary figure to the value of assets, the cost of threats being realized, and the cost of security implementations. Monetary figures are typically based on an annual cost.

Qualitative Risk Analysis

There are various ways of conducting qualitative risk analysis. One method uses a scenario-based model. This approach is best for large cities, states, and countries because it is impractical to try to list all the assets, which is the starting point for any quantitative risk analysis. For example, by the time a typical national government lists all of its assets, the list would have hundreds or thousands of changes and would no longer be accurate.

With qualitative risk analysis, research is exploratory and cannot always be graphed or proven mathematically. It focuses mostly on the understanding of why risk is present and how various solutions work to resolve the risk. Quantitative risk analysis is more mathematically precise and typically used by organizations as cost justification for proposed countermeasures. For this reason, the next topic investigates the specifics of building a quantitative risk analysis.

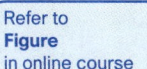
Refer to **Figure** in online course

Quantitative Risk Analysis

Quantitative risk analysis relies on specific formulas to determine the value of the risk decision variables. These include formulas that calculate the asset value (AV), exposure factor (EF), single loss expectancy (SLE), annualized rate of occurrence (ARO), and annualized loss expectancy (ALE).

Asset Value

The asset value includes the purchase price, the cost of deployment, and the cost of maintenance. In the instance of a database or a web server, the AV should also include the cost of development. AV is not an easy number to calculate.

Exposure Factor

The exposure factor is an estimate of the degree of destruction that could occur. For example, suppose water flooding is a possibility that could affect the e-banking data center. What is the likelihood that it could destroy the data center? Would the destruction be 60 percent, 80 percent, or 100 percent? The risk assessment team must evaluate all possibilities and then make a determination. Assuming that a backup copy of all media and data is stored offsite, the only losses are to the hardware and productivity. Therefore, a flood would have a 60 percent destruction factor.

As another example, consider data entry errors, which are much less damaging than a flood. A single data entry error is most likely less than a fraction of a percent in exposure, or .001 percent.

Single Loss Expectancy

The single loss expectancy calculation represents the expected loss from a single occurrence of the threat. The SLE is defined as AV multiplied by EF. Using the previous examples, the SLE calculations result in the following:

```
Flood threat
```

- Exposure Factor is 60 percent

- AV of the enterprise is US$10,000,000

- SLE is US$10,000,000 * .60 = US$6,000,000

```
Data entry error
```

- Exposure Factor is .001 percent

- AV of data and databases is US$1,000,000

- SLE is US$1,000,000 * 0.00001 = US$10

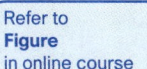
Refer to **Figure** in online course

Annualized Rate of Occurrence

The annualized rate of occurrence estimates the frequency of an event and is used to calculate the ALE.

Using the previous examples, the type of flood to affect the data center would be a flood-of-the-century event, so it has a 1/100 chance of occurring this year, making the ARO for the flood 1/100.

Expect a data entry error to occur 500 times a day. Because the organization is open for business 250 days per year, estimate the ARO for the data entry error to be 500 * 250, or 125,000 total occurrences.

Annualized Loss Expectancy

Risk analysts calculate the ALE in annualized terms to address the cost to the organization if the organization does nothing to counter existing threats. The ALE is derived from multiplying the SLE by the ARO. The ALE calculations for the examples are surprising.

Flood threat

- SLE is US$6,000,000

- ARO is .01

- ALE is US$6,000,000 * .01 = US$60,000

Data input error

- SLE is US$10

- ARO is 125,000

- ALE is US$10 * 125,000 = US$1,250,000

It is a justifiable decision to spend US$50,000 to enhance the security of database applications, in order to significantly reduce data entry errors. It is equally justifiable to reject a proposal to spend US$3,000,000, to enhance the defenses against a possible flood.

Refer to **Figure** in online course

It is necessary to perform a quantitative risk analysis for all threats identified during the threat identification process.

A list of all identified threats should state each expected issue, the relative cost of that issue, and the total cost if all expected threats are realized. This list should then be prioritized based on the most serious threat and relative cost.

If an organization had a list of 10 expected threats, it could then prioritize the threats and address the most serious ones first. This prioritization enables management to focus resources where they do the most good. For example, suppose an organization compiled this list of threats and costs:

- Insider network abuse - US$1,000,000

- Data input error - US$500,000

- Worm outbreak - US$100,000

- Viruses - US$10,000

- Laptop theft - US$10,000

Assume that a current antivirus solution is in place and decision-makers must decide whether to update it. Based on quantitative analysis, decision makers could determine that resources are best used toward addressing insider network abuse and not toward the new antivirus solution.

In incidents that involve national security, it is not advisable to base decisions on cost.

9.1.3 Risk Management and Risk Avoidance

Refer to
Figure
in online course

When the threats are identified and the risks are assessed, a protection strategy must be deployed to protect against the risks. There are two very different methods to handle risks:

- *Risk management* This method deploys protection mechanisms to reduce risks to acceptable levels. Risk management is perhaps the most basic and the most difficult aspect of building secure systems, because it requires a good knowledge of risks, risk environments, and mitigation methods.

- *Risk avoidance* This method eliminates risk by avoiding the threats altogether, which is usually not an option in the commercial world, where controlled, or managed, risk enables profits.

Refer to
Figure
in online course

Consider the bank that wants to provide e-banking services. Risk management can be illustrated by high-level strategy decisions, which describe how to mitigate each risk. Keep in mind that not all mitigation techniques are implemented based on the risk versus cost formula used in the quantitative risk analysis:

- *Internal system compromise* Provide the minimum necessary privileges to internal users to perform specific tasks, and use secure applications that minimizes inside access.

- *Stolen customer data* Keep all customer data on inside servers, and only transfer data to the outside on demand.

- *Phony transactions if external server is broken into* Allow only man-in-the-middle attacks on the external server, and design the external server application so that it does not allow arbitrary transactions to be called for any customer account.

- *Phony transactions using a stolen customer PIN or smart card* Use a quick refresh of revocation lists, and have a contract with the user that forces the user to assume responsibility for stolen token cards.

- *Insider attack on the system* Strictly limit inside access to the application, and provide strict auditing of all accesses from the inside.

- *Data input error* Enhance the security of database applications, and provide a redundant checking system to reduce data entry errors.

- *Data center destruction* Ensure that backups are kept off campus and that additional equipment is on hand. Enhance defenses against flooding by raising equipment off the ground and taking other precautions.

Refer to
Figure
in online course

Using the risk avoidance approach, a company might decide against offering e-banking services as it is deemed too risky. Such an attitude might be valid for some military organizations, but is usually not an option in the commercial world. Organizations that can manage the risks are traditionally the most profitable.

After an organization identifies threats, it performs the appropriate analysis. If they decide to manage the risk, the next step is to create a security solution.

9.2 Security Architecture

9.2.1 Introducing the Cisco SecureX Architecture

Refer to
Figure
in online course

In the past, threats from internal and external sources moved more slowly than they do today. Employees and data resources were within a predefined perimeter protected by firewall technology. Employees typically used company-issued computers connected to a corporate LAN that were continuously monitored and updated to meet security requirements.

Traditional network security consisted of two major components: a heavy endpoint protection suite (i.e., antivirus, personal firewall, etc.) and perimeter-based network-scanning devices (i.e., firewalls, web proxies, and email gateways, etc.). This architecture worked well in a world of high-powered PCs that were mainly on the LAN and behind the firewall.

Today, Internet worms and other security threats spread across the world in a matter of minutes requiring that the security system, and the network itself, react instantaneously. Additionally, consumer endpoints such as iPhones, BlackBerrys, netbooks, and thousands of other devices are becoming powerful substitutes for, or complements to, the traditional PC. More and more people are using these devices to access enterprise information. Even the workforce itself is changing. A new workforce is emerging, accustomed to the always-on, anytime, anywhere connectivity on their device of choice.

In addition, the rapid onset of cloud computing has introduced new security concerns. Cloud computing allows organizations to use services such as data storage or cloud-based applications to extend their capacity or capabilities without adding infrastructure. By its very nature, the cloud is outside of the traditional network perimeter, allowing an organization to have a data center that may or may not reside behind the traditional perimeter.

Cisco calls this the Borderless Network. In this new Borderless Network, access to resources can be initiated by users from many locations, on many types of endpoint devices, using various connectivity methods.

What does this mean for network security? In today's network of mobile workers using personal devices from a variety of locations, the traditional network security model does not work. The new network devices are not good candidates for the traditional antivirus endpoint suite. They were designed to be lightweight and portable. Additionally, with blurred network borders, multiple entrances into the network can exist. Because there is no longer a network perimeter, the challenge is how to allow these heterogeneous devices to connect to enterprise resources securely. To address these very issues, Cisco has outlined a security architecture called Cisco SecureX.

Refer to
Figure
in online course

The SecureX security architecture for the Borderless Network relies on a lightweight, pervasive endpoint. Its role is not to scan content or run signatures. Instead, its sole focus is making sure every connection coming on or off the endpoint is pointed at a network scanning element somewhere in a Cisco security cloud. These scanning elements are now capable of running many more layers of scanning than a single endpoint possibly could: five layers of malware signatures, data loss prevention and acceptable use policies, content scanning, and more.

This architecture is designed to provide effective security for any user, using any device, from any location, and at any time.

This new security architecture uses a high-level policy language that can describe the full context of a situation, including who, what, where, when and how. With highly distributed security policy enforcement, security is pushed closer to where the end user is working, anywhere on the planet. This architecture is comprised of five major components:

- *Scanning engines* These are the foundation of security enforcement and can be viewed as the workhorses of policy enforcement. They are the proxies or network-level devices that examine content, identify applications, and authenticate users. A scanning engine can be a firewall/IPS, a proxy, or a fusion of the two. Scanning engines can run multiple layers of anti-malware signatures, behavioral analyses, and content inspection engines.

- *Delivery mechanisms* These are the mechanisms by which scanning elements are introduced into the network. This includes the traditional network appliance, a module in a switch or a router, or an image in a Cisco security cloud.

- *Security intelligence operations (SIO)* These distinguish good traffic from bad. The Cisco SIO encompasses multi-terabyte traffic monitoring databases, thousands of servers in multiple data centers, and hundreds of engineers and technicians with a single purpose - identifying and stopping malicious traffic.

- *Policy management consoles* These consoles are separate from the scanners that enforce policy. By separating policy creation and management from enforcement, the Cisco SecureX architecture makes it possible to have a single point of policy definition that spans multiple enforcement points such as email, instant messaging, and the Web.

- *The next-generation endpoint* A wave of consumer devices that are flooding the enterprise, these devices must be equipped with the capability to automatically find the nearest scanning element somewhere in the virtual security fabric and make a seamless connection. The role of the next-generation endpoint is not to scan content or run signatures, but rather to guarantee every connection coming on or off the endpoint

The endpoint of tomorrow will not have just an antivirus suite, but an intelligent connection manager that sits on the edge of every device imaginable. In the Borderless Network, security must begin with the endpoint.

Refer to **Figure** in online course

The Borderless Network has significantly improved business efficiency and flexibility. Workers can accomplish their tasks from anywhere, anytime and using any device. However, that flexibility creates complexities for the IT infrastructure, and any efforts to keep the infrastructure secure.

How does IT support this new computing model in a way that scales and ensures that resources are secure? By using a context-aware network scanning element that uses central polices to enforce security.

A context-aware scanning element is a network security device that does more than just examining packets on the wire. It looks at external information to understand the full context of the situation. To be context aware, the scanner has to consider the who, what, where, when and how of security.

These scanning elements are available as stand-alone appliances, software modules running in a router, or an image in the cloud. They are managed from a central policy console that uses a high level language that mirrors an organization's business language and understands the context of the situation.

A context-aware policy uses a simplified descriptive business language to define security policies based on five parameters:

- The person's identity

- The application in use

- The type of device being used for access

- The location

- The time of access

This centralized policy is pushed across the entire networked environment for distributed enforcement. This distributed enforcement ensures consistent security implementation across network zones, branch offices, remote workers, virtualized devices, remote workers, and cloud-based services.

Refer to
Figure
in online course

The context-aware scanning architecture uses local network context from Cisco TrustSec technology. This is a packet tagging technology that allows security elements to share information gathered from the scanning elements as well as the endpoint client. It is all governed by real-time global threat intelligence from Cisco Security Intelligence Operations (SIO), which helps distinguish good traffic from bad traffic.

Cisco SIO is the world's largest cloud-based security ecosystem, using almost a million live data feeds from deployed Cisco email, web, firewall, and IPS solutions. Cisco SIO weighs and processes the data, automatically categorizing threats and creating rules using more than 200 parameters. Rules are dynamically delivered to deployed Cisco security devices every three to five minutes. The Cisco SIO team also publishes security best practice recommendations and tactical guidance for preventing attacks.

AnyConnect 3.0 adds real-time client-based threat telemetry to Cisco. With a footprint of more than 150 million AnyConnect and legacy VPN clients, this enhances the visibility and actionable threat intelligence.

9.2.2 Solutions for the Cisco SecureX Architecture

Refer to
Figure
in online course

The Cisco SecureX architecture refers to five product families: secure edge and branch, secure email and web, secure access, secure mobility, and secure data center and virtualization.

Secure Edge and Branch

The goal of the Cisco secure edge and branch is to deploy devices and systems to detect and block attacks and exploits, and prevent intruder access. With firewall and intrusion prevention in stand-alone and integrated deployment options, organizations can avoid attacks and meet compliance requirements. A number of devices and systems work together to ensure the secure network.

Cisco ASA 5500 Series:

- Combines industry-leading firewall, VPN, and intrusion prevention in a unified platform

- Provides comprehensive real-time threat protection and highly secure communications services to stop attacks before they affect business continuity

- Reduces deployment and operational costs while delivering comprehensive security for networks of all sizes

- Versatile, always-on remote-access integrated with IPS and web security for highly secure mobility and enhanced productivity

Cisco Intrusion Prevention System:

- Identifies, classifies, and stops malicious traffic, including worms, spyware, adware, viruses, and application abuse

- Delivers high-performance, intelligent threat detection and protection over a range of deployment options

- Uses global threat correlation with reputation filtering to prevent threats with confidence

- Provides peace of mind with guarantees for coverage, response time, and effectiveness for Microsoft, Cisco, and critical enterprise application vulnerabilities

- Promotes business continuity and helps businesses meet compliance needs

Cisco Integrated Services Router Generation 2:

- Delivers suite of built-in capabilities, including firewall, intrusion prevention, VPN, and cloud-based web security

- Promotes the integration of new network security features on existing routers

- Provides additional protection without adding hardware and maximizes network security

- Decreases ongoing support and manageability costs by reducing the total number of devices required

Cisco Security Manager:

- Provides a comprehensive management solution for Cisco network and security devices

- Enables consistent policy enforcement, quick troubleshooting of security events, and summarized reports across the deployment

- Supports role-based access control and an approval framework for proposing and integrating changes

- Integrates powerful capabilities, including policy, object, and event management; reporting; and troubleshooting

Secure Email and Web

Refer to **Figure** in online course

Cisco secure email and web solutions reduce costly downtime associated with email-based spam, viruses, and web threats, and are available in a variety of form factors, including on-premise appliances, cloud services, and hybrid security deployments with centralized management.

Cisco IronPort Email Security Appliances:

- Fights spam, viruses, and blended threats for organizations of all sizes

- Enforces compliance and protects reputation and brand assets

- Reduces downtime and simplifies administration of corporate mail systems

- Deployed by more than 40 percent of the world's largest enterprises

Cisco IronPort Web Security Appliances:

- Integrates web-usage controls, data security, reputation and malware filtering

- Applies Cisco Security Intelligence Operations and global threat technology

- Combats sophisticated web-based threats with layered security technology

- Supports built-in management for visibility of threat-related activity

Cisco ScanSafe Cloud Web Security:

- Analyzes web requests for malicious, inappropriate, or acceptable content

- Offers granular control over open and encrypted web content

- Extends real-time protection and policy enforcement to remote employees

- Blocks unwanted and malicious emails, while protecting confidential data

Refer to
Figure
in online course

Secure Access

Secure access technologies are put in place to enforce network security policies, secure user and host access controls, and control network access based on dynamic conditions.

Cisco Identity Services Engine:

- Apply policy-based access control
- Support greater flexibility to use devices and applications of choice
- Provide a single IT interface for policy creation and enforcement
- Deploy in active standby mode to help ensure high availability

Network Admission Control Appliance:

- Recognize users, their devices, and their roles in the network
- Evaluate whether machines are compliant with security policies
- Enforce security policies by blocking, isolating, and repairing noncompliant machines
- Provide easy and secure guest access
- Simplify non-authenticating device access
- Audit and report whom is on the network

Cisco Secure Access Control System:

- Controls network access based on dynamic conditions and attributes
- Meets evolving access requirements with rule-based policies
- Increases compliance with integrated monitoring, reporting, and troubleshooting capabilities
- Takes advantage of built-in integration capabilities and distributed deployment

Cisco Virtual Office:

- Extends highly secure, and manageable network services to remote employees
- Cost-effectively scales through standard or express versions
- Includes Cisco and approved partner services, remote site aggregation and head-end systems
- Delivers full IP phone, wireless, data, and video services

Refer to
Figure
in online course

Secure Mobility

Cisco secure mobility solutions promote highly secure mobile connectivity with VPN, wireless security, and remote workforce security solutions that extend network access safely and easily to a wide range of users and devices. Cisco Secure Mobility solutions offer the most comprehensive and versatile connectivity options, endpoints, and platforms to meet an organization's changing mobility needs.

VPN Services for Cisco ASA Series:

- Provides remote access for up to 10,000 SSL or true IPsec connections
- Supports functionality unavailable to a clientless, browser-based VPN connection
- Connects users to IPv6 resources over IPv4 network tunnels
- Facilitates creating user profiles and defining names and addresses of host

Cisco Adaptive Wireless IPS Software:

- Provides automated wireless vulnerability and performance monitoring
- Maintains a constant awareness of the RF environment
- Automatically monitors and identifies unauthorized access and RF attacks
- Collaborates with Cisco network security products to create a layered security approach

Cisco AnyConnect Secure Mobility Solutions:

- Provides an intelligent, smooth, and reliable connectivity experience
- Gives users a choice of how, when, and where they access their information
- Provides comprehensive remote-access connectivity
- Enforces context-aware policy, and protection from malware

Refer to
Figure
in online course

Secure Data Center and Virtualization

Cisco secure data center and virtualization solutions protect high-value data and data center resources with threat defense, secure virtualization, segmentation and policy control.

Cisco ASA 5585-X:

- Combines a proven firewall, comprehensive intrusion prevention, and VPN
- Delivers eight times the performance density of competitive firewalls
- Integrates intrusion prevention with global correlation
- Supports context-aware firewall capabilities

Cisco Catalyst 6500 ASA Services Module:

- Combines full-featured switching with best-in-class security
- Places security directly into the data center backbone
- Provides up to 16 Gbps multiprotocol throughput for 300,000 connections per second
- Supports up to four modules in a single chassis

Cisco Virtual Security Gateway (VSG):

- Integrates with Cisco Nexus 1000V virtual switch and hypervisors
- Delivers security policy enforcement and visibility at a virtual machine level
- Logically isolates applications in virtual data centers and multi-tenant environments
- Enforces separation of duties between security and server administrators

Cisco ASA 1000V Cloud Firewall

- Integrates with the Cisco Nexus 1000V virtual switch
- Employs mainstream, proven ASA technology
- Spans and helps to secure multiple VMware ESX hosts
- Enables consistency across physical, virtual, and cloud infrastructures

9.2.3 Future Trends for Network Security

Refer to
Figure
in online course

The security industry is always changing. The next few years are going to be a period of significant change, driven by three major trends: the consumerization of the endpoint, the increasing use of high-definition video conferencing systems like Cisco TelePresence, and the adoption of cloud computing. These trends necessitate a shift in the way businesses deploy IT resources as well as how information is securely stored and accessed.

New endpoint technologies entering the enterprise are redefining the workplace experience. Work is no longer a place where people go to sit in a cubicle for eight hours using a company-provided PC. The workforce of the future will demand access anytime, from anywhere, and on any device. Considering the significant change in endpoint capabilities in the past few years, there is every reason to think that this rate of change will continue into the future.

As collaboration tools, such as high-definition video conferencing, become more commonplace, future workers will expect face-to-face interaction from anywhere in the world to customers, partners and colleagues. These high bandwidth tools will require a secure infrastructure to meet employee expectations.

As more companies embrace cloud-computing we will see cloud-based apps that enable easy sharing and access to data. This, coupled with the virtualization of the data center, will challenge IT departments to stay ahead of security threats in an increasingly distributed environment.

9.3 Operations Security

9.3.1 Introducing Operations Security

Refer to
Figure
in online course

While the Cisco SecureX architecture does increase the level of security, it cannot guarantee a completely invulnerable network. New types of attacks and advances in hacking technologies are still threats to even the most secure systems. Additionally, all networks are vulnerable to attack if the planning, implementation, operations, and maintenance of the network do not adhere to operational security practices. Operations security is concerned with the day-to-day practices necessary to first deploy and later maintain a secure system.

Operations security starts with the planning and implementation process of a network. During these phases, the operations team proactively analyzes designs, identifies risks and vulnerabilities, and makes the necessary adaptations. After a network is set up, the actual operational tasks begin, including the continual day-to-day maintenance of the environment. These activities are regular in nature and enable the environment, systems, and applications to continue to run correctly and securely.

Refer to
Figure
in online course

The responsibilities of the operations team pertain to everything that takes place to keep the network, computer systems, applications, and the environment up and running in a secure and protected manner. These individuals are concerned with the controls or security solutions used to protect hardware, software, and media on a day-to-day basis. This includes protection from threats in the operating environment, internal and external intruders, and operators who access resources inappropriately.

The operations team usually has the objectives of preventing reoccurring problems, reducing hardware failures to an acceptable level, and reducing the impact of hardware failure or disruption. They should investigate any unusual or unexplained occurrences, unscheduled initial program loads, deviations from standards, and other abnormal conditions occurring on the network. While the people within operations are responsible for ensuring that systems are protected and continue to run in a predictable manner, it is important to note that management is responsible for the behavior and correction of personnel. For this reason, it is necessary that management work closely with the operations team to ensure the continued security of the network.

To ensure a secure working environment within the operations department, certain core principles should be integrated into the day-to-day activities:

- Separation of duties

- Rotation of duties

- Trusted recovery

- Change and configuration controls

9.3.2 Principles of Operations Security

Separation of Duties

> Refer to
> **Figure**
> in online course

Separation (or segregation) of duties (SoD) is one of the main concepts of internal control and is the most difficult and sometimes the most costly control to achieve. SoD states that no single individual has control over two or more phases of a transaction or operation. Instead, responsibilities are assigned in a way that incorporates checks and balances. This makes a deliberate fraud more difficult to perpetrate because it requires a collusion of two or more individuals or parties.

The term SoD is already well known in financial systems. These companies do not combine roles such as receiving checks, approving discounts, depositing cash, reconciling bank statements, and approving time cards. This helps to reduce the potential damage from the actions of one person. Similarly, IT departments should be organized in a way that achieves adequate separation of duties. There are two methods to accomplish this.

The first method is known as the two-person control principle. It states that a task requires two individuals, and each is responsible for reviewing and approving the work of the other. In addition to providing accountability and reducing opportunities for fraud, this principle has the added benefit of reducing errors within configurations. Because of the overhead costs involved, this practice is usually limited to sensitive duties that are considered potential security risks.

Another method of implementing SoD is the dual operator principle in which a task is broken down and each part of the task is assigned to a different individual. The task is not complete until both individuals complete their part. An example of the dual operator principle is a check that requires two signatures for the bank to accept it.

Rotation of Duties

> Refer to
> **Figure**
> in online course

Rotation of duties, or job rotation, is a security measure in which individuals are given a specific assignment for a certain amount of time before moving to a new assignment. To successfully implement this principle, it is important that individuals have the training necessary to complete more than one job.

Peer review is built into the practice of rotation of duties. For example, suppose that a job rotation scheme has five people rotating through five different roles during the course of a week. Peer review of work occurs whether or not it was intended. When five people do one job in the course of the week, each person is effectively reviewing the work of the others.

In addition to providing security, rotation of duties also prevents boredom and gives individuals a greater breadth of exposure to the entire network operation. This creates a strong and flexible operations department because everyone is capable of doing multiple jobs.

Refer to
Figure
in online course

Trusted Recovery

One of the easiest ways to compromise a system is to make the system restart and gain control of it before all of its defenses are reloaded. For this reason, trusted recovery is an important principle of operations security. This principle states that systems fail at some point, so a process for recovery must be established. The most common way to prepare for failure is to back up data on a regular basis.

Backing up data is standard practice in most IT departments. Keep in mind that many backup software programs use an account that bypasses file security. Therefore, individuals with the right to back up data can have access to files that they would not ordinarily be able to access. The same is true if those individuals who have the right to restore data.

Network security professionals propose that a secure backup program contain some of the following practices:

- A junior staff member is responsible for loading blank media.

- Backup software uses an account that is unknown to individuals to bypass file security.

- A different staff member removes the backup media and securely stores it onsite while being assisted by another member of the staff.

- A separate copy of the backup is stored off site and handled by a third staff member who is accompanied by another staff member.

One of the easiest ways for an attacker to obtain a password file (or any other data) is to get a copy of the backup tape because the backup tape is not always handled or stored very securely.

Being prepared for system failure is also an important part of operations security:

- Back up critical data on a regular basis

- Evaluate who has access to the files to back them up and what kind of access they have

- Secure the backup media

System recovery follows system failure. There are several examples of programs and applications that incorporate system recovery features:

- The ability of operating systems to recover from a system crash by implementing single-user or safe mode.

- The ability to recover files that were open at the time of a system crash. The autosave process in many desktop applications is an example of this ability. Memory dumps that many operating systems perform upon system failure are also an example of this ability.

- The ability to recover other files and retain the security settings of those file after a system crash is critical so that the security is not bypassed by forcing a crash.

- The ability to recover and retain security settings for critical system files such as the registry, configuration files, and password files.

Refer to
Figure
in online course

Configuration and Change Control

Configuration and change control is a process that should be implemented to ensure that standardized methods and procedures are used to efficiently handle all changes. A change is defined as an event that results in a new status of one or more configuration items. A change should be approved by management, be cost effective, and be an enhancement to business processes with a minimum of risk to the IT infrastructure and security.

The configuration and change controls should address three major components: the processes in place to minimize system and network disruption, backups and reversing changes that go badly, and guidance on the economical use of resources and time.

A few suggestions are recommended to accomplish configuration changes in an effective and safe manner:

- Ensure that the change is implemented in an orderly manner with formalized testing

- Ensure that the end users are aware of the coming change when necessary

- Analyze the effects of the change after it is implemented

Although the change control process differs from organization to organization, certain patterns emerge in change management. There are five steps in a typical change control process:

Step 1.   Apply to introduce the change.

Step 2.   Catalog the proposed change.

Step 3.   Schedule the change.

Step 4.   Implement the change.

Step 5.   Report the change to the relevant parties.

Operations security minimizes harm to the network by providing organized processes for security personnel. The effectiveness of an operations security solution can be tested without waiting for a real threat to take place. Network security testing makes this possible.

9.4 Network Security Testing

9.4.1 Introducing Network Security Testing

Refer to **Figure** in online course

Network security testing is performed on a network to ensure all security implementations are operating as expected. Typically, network security testing is conducted during the implementation and operational stages, after the system has been developed, installed, and integrated.

Security testing provides insight into various administrative tasks such as risk analysis and contingency planning. It is important to document the results of security testing and make them available for staff involved in other IT areas.

During the implementation stage, security testing is conducted on specific parts of the security system.

After a network is fully integrated and operational, a Security Test and Evaluation (ST&E) is performed. ST&E is an examination or analysis of the protective measures that are placed on an operational network.

Tests should be repeated periodically and whenever a change is made to the system. For security systems that protect critical information or protect hosts that are exposed to constant threat, security testing should be conducted more frequently.

Refer to
Figure
in online course

After a network is operational, it is important to ascertain its security status. Many tests can be conducted to assess the operational status of the system:

- Network scanning

- Vulnerability scanning

- Password cracking

- Log review

- Integrity checkers

- Virus detection

- Wardialing

- Wardriving (802.11 or wireless LAN testing)

- Penetration testing

Some testing techniques are predominantly manual and other tests are highly automated. Regardless of the type of testing, the staff that sets up and conducts the security testing should have significant security and networking knowledge, including expertise in the following areas: network security, firewalls, intrusion prevention systems (IPSs), operating systems, programming, and networking protocols, such as TCP/IP.

Refer to
Figure
in online course

Network security testing results can be used in several ways:

- As a reference point for corrective action

- To define mitigation activities to address identified vulnerabilities

- As a benchmark to trace the progress of an organization in meeting security requirements

- To assess the implementation status of system security requirements

- To conduct cost and benefit analysis for improvements to system security

- To enhance other activities such as risk assessments, certification and authorization (C&A), and performance improvement efforts

9.4.2 Network Security Testing Tools

Refer to
Figure
in online course

There are many tools available to test the security of systems and networks. Some of these tools are open source while others are commercial tools that require licensing.

Two of the most common security testing tools are Nmap and SuperScan.

Refer to
Figure
in online course

Nmap

Nmap is the best-known low-level scanner available to the public. It has an array of excellent features which can be used for network mapping and reconnaissance. The basic functionality of Nmap allows the user to accomplish several tasks:

- Classic TCP and UDP port scanning - looking for different services on one host.

- Classic TCP and UDP port sweeping - looking for the same service on multiple hosts.

- Stealth TCP and UDP port scans and sweeps - similar to classic scans and sweeps but harder to detect by the target host or IPS.

- Remote operating system identification, known as OS fingerprinting.

Advanced features of Nmap include protocol scanning, known as Layer 3 port scanning. This feature identifies Layer 3 protocol support on a host. Examples of protocols that can be identified include GRE and OSPF.

While Nmap can be used for security testing, it can also be used for malicious purposes. Nmap has an additional feature that allows it to use decoy hosts, on the same LAN as the target host, to mask the source of the scan.

Nmap has no Application Layer features and runs on UNIX, Linux, Windows, and OS X.

Both console and graphical versions are available. The Nmap program and Zenmap GUI can be downloaded from the internet.

SuperScan

Refer to **Figure** in online course

SuperScan is a Microsoft Windows port scanning tool. It runs on most versions of Windows and requires administrator privileges. Windows XP SP2 removed support for raw sockets, which limits the ability of SuperScan and other scanning tools.

A raw socket is a socket that allows a user to directly access and manipulate the header of a data packet.

While SP2 increased the security aspect of this tool, some functionality can be restored by entering the `net stop SharedAccess` command at the Windows command prompt.

SuperScan version 4 has a number of useful features:

- Adjustable scanning speed
- Support for unlimited IP ranges
- Improved host detection using multiple ICMP methods
- TCP SYN scanning
- UDP scanning (two methods)
- Simple HTML report generation
- Source port scanning
- Fast hostname resolving
- Extensive banner grabbing
- Massive built-in port list description database
- IP and port scan order randomization
- A selection of useful tools (ping, traceroute, and whois)
- Extensive Windows host enumeration capability

Refer to **Figure** in online course

Tools such as **Nmap** and **SuperScan** can provide effective penetration testing on a network and determine network vulnerabilities while helping to anticipate possible attack mechanisms. However network testing cannot prepare a network administrator for every security problem.

The good news is that networks can recover from most security issues by adapting the security solution. The bad news is that prior to adapting the security solution it is possible for an attack to cause disruption and even catastrophic damage. Catastrophic damage is serious disruption to network services or complete destruction of data or network systems. Catastrophic damage can also be caused by a cataclysmic event. A business must have a plan in place to recover and remain in business in the event of serious disruption or network destruction.

9.5 Business Continuity Planning and Disaster Recovery

9.5.1 Continuity Planning and Disaster Recovery

Refer to **Figure** in online course

Business continuity planning addresses the continuing operations of an organization in the event of a disaster or prolonged service interruption that affects the mission of the organization. These plans address an emergency response phase, a recovery phase, and a return to normal operation phase. These phases should include a short to medium-term framework to continue the organizational operations. Each phase also identifies the responsibilities of personnel and the available resources during an incident.

In reality, contingency and disaster recovery plans do not address every possible scenario or assumption. Rather, they focus on the events most likely to occur and identify an acceptable method of recovery. Periodically, the plans and procedures should be practiced to ensure that they are effective and well understood.

Business continuity planning may address the following concerns:

- Moving or relocating critical business components and people to a remote location while the original location is being repaired

- Using different channels of communication to deal with customers, shareholders, and partners until operations are returned to normal

Refer to **Figure** in online course

Disaster recovery is the process of regaining access to the data, hardware, and software necessary to resume critical business operations after a natural or human-induced disaster. It also includes plans for coping with the unexpected or sudden loss of key personnel. A disaster recovery plan is part of business continuity planning.

9.5.2 Disruptions and Backups

Refer to **Figure** in online course

When planning for disaster recovery and business continuity, the first step is identifying the possible types of disasters and disruptions. Not all disruptions to business operations are equal. A good disaster recovery plan takes into account the magnitude of the disruption, recognizing that there are differences between catastrophes, disasters, and minor incidents.

Refer to **Figure** in online course

The only way to deal with destruction is redundancy. When a component is destroyed, it must be replaced with a redundant component. This component can be a standby component that is owned by the organization for disaster recovery purposes or a new device that is provided by the service provider with which the organization has contracted services. If the service provider is responsible for providing redundant components, this information must be contained within the service level agreement (SLA). The SLA should also cover redundancy when service is disrupted, or provide for some type of compensation.

On a much larger scale, an organization might require a redundant facility if some catastrophic event results in facility destruction. Redundant facilities are referred to as hot, warm, and cold sites.

Each type of facility is available for a different price with different resulting downtimes. With hot sites, a completely redundant facility is required with almost identical equipment. The copying of data to this redundant facility is part of normal operations, so in the case of a catastrophe, only the latest data changes must be applied to restore full operations. Organizations that need to respond in seconds often employ global load balancing (GLB) and distributed SANs to respond quickly. With this type of redundancy in place, an organization can quickly recover from disruption or even destruction.

Warm sites are physically redundant facilities, but software and data are not stored and updated on the equipment. A disaster recovery team is required to physically go to the redundant facility and get it operational. Depending on how much software and data is involved, it can take days before operations are ready to resume.

A cold site is usually an empty data center with racks, power, WAN links, and heating, ventilation, and air conditioning (HVAC) already present, but no equipment. In this instance, an organization must first acquire routers, switches, firewalls, servers, and other equipment to rebuild everything. When the backups are uploaded onto the new equipment, operations can continue. This option is the least expensive in terms of money spent annually, but usually requires weeks to resume operations.

9.5.3 Secure Copy

Refer to
Figure
in online course

The primary goal of disaster recovery is to restore the network to a fully functional state. Two of the most critical components of a functional network are the router configuration and the router image files. Every disaster recovery plan should include backup and retrieval of these files. Because an organization's network configuration includes private or proprietary information, these files must be copied in a secure manner. The secure copy (SCP) feature provides a secure and authenticated method for copying router configuration or router image files.

The behavior of SCP is similar to that of remote copy (RCP), which comes from the Berkeley R-tools suite, except that SCP relies on SSH for security. In addition, SCP requires that authentication, authorization, and accounting (AAA) authorization be configured so that the router can determine whether the user has the correct privilege level.

SCP allows a user who has appropriate authorization to copy any file that exists in the Cisco IOS File System (IFS) to and from a router by using the **copy** command. An authorized administrator may also perform this action from a workstation.

SCP Server Configuration

Refer to
Figure
in online course

Because SCP relies on SSH for secure transport, before enabling SCP, you must correctly configure SSH, and the router must have an RSA key pair, To configure the router for server-side SCP, perform these steps:

Step 1. Enable AAA with the **aaa new-model** global configuration command.

Step 2. Define a named list of authentication methods, with the **aaa authentication login** {**default** |*list*-name} *method1* [*method2...*] command.

Step 3. Configure command authorization, use the **aaa authorization** {**network** | **exec** | **commands** *level*} {**default** | *list-name*} *method1...*[*method4*] command.

Step 4. Configure a username and password to use for local authentication with the **username** *name* [**privilege** *level*] {**password** *encryption-type password*} command. This step is optional if using network-based authentication such as TACACS+ or RADIUS.

Step 5. Enable SCP server-side functionality with the **ip scp server enable** command.

Router to Workstation SCP Transfer

A workstation running a command-line SCP client can authenticate to the SCP server on the router to securely transfer files from the router flash memory. This allows a network administrator to store backup copies of a router's configuration and IOS files to any secure network location. An example of a command-line SCP client is the PuTTY Secure Copy client included in the PuTTY suite of utilities.

Router to Router SCP Transfer

When transferring files between routers, one router acts as the SCP client. This router can authenticate to and copy files from the SCP server enabled router.

To troubleshoot SCP authentication issues, use the `debug ip scp` privileged EXEC command. A successful transfer will have several lines of output ending with <OK>. The most common authentication issue is an incorrect username/password combination. There will also be an authentication failure if the username/password combination was not configured with the `privilege 15` keyword on the SCP server.

9.6 System Development Life Cycle

9.6.1 Introducing the SDLC

Refer to
Figure
in online course

Business continuity and disaster recovery plans are ever-changing documents. They must be adjusted to changes in environment, equipment, and business needs. These changes not only affect continuity plans, but all aspects of network operations. Documentation should be maintained and updated regularly, and security needs should be continuously evaluated.

Evaluating system changes and adjusting plans are all part of a system life cycle. Keep in mind that the term "system" can refer to a single device or a group of devices that operate together within a network.

Refer to
Figure
in online course

A general system development life cycle (SDLC) includes five phases:

Step 1. Initiation

Step 2. Acquisition and development

Step 3. Implementation

Step 4. Operation and maintenance

Step 5. Disposition

When using the SDLC to design a network, each phase should include a minimum set of security requirements. This results in less expensive and more effective security as compared to adding security to an operational system after the fact. This purposeful inclusion of security in every phase of the life cycle is part of the secure network life cycle management process.

9.6.2 Phases of the SDLC

Refer to
Figure
in online course

Initiation

These are the security tasks related to the initiation phase of the SDLC:

- *Security categorization* Define three levels of potential impact on organizations or individuals if there is a breach of security: low, moderate, and high. Security categorization standards help organizations make the appropriate selection of security controls for their information systems.

- *Preliminary risk assessment* Initial description of the basic security needs of the system that defines the threat environment in which the system operates.

Refer to **Figure** in online course

Acquisition and Development

These are the security tasks related to the acquisition and development phase of the SDLC:

- *Risk assessment* Identify the protection requirements for the system through a formal risk assessment process. This analysis builds on the risk assessment that was performed during the initiation phase, but is more in-depth and specific.

- *Security functional requirements* Analyze the operating necessities addressing the system security environment, the enterprise information security policy, and enterprise security architecture.

- *Security assurance requirements* Address the developmental activities that are required and the assurance evidence that is needed to produce the desired level of confidence that the information security is working correctly and effectively. The analysis, which is based on legal and functional security requirements, serves as the basis for determining how much and what kinds of assurance are required.

- *Security cost considerations and reporting* Determine how much of the development cost to attribute toward information security over the life cycle of the system. These costs include hardware, software, personnel, and training.

- *Security planning* Complete document of the agreed-upon security controls. The security plan also fully describes the information system and includes attachments or references to key documents that support the information security program of the organization. Examples of documents that support the information security program include, such as a configuration management plan, contingency plan, incident response plan, security awareness and training plan, rules of behavior, risk assessment, security test and evaluation results, system interconnection agreements, security authorizations and accreditations, and a plan of action and milestones.

- *Security control development* Ensure that the security controls that are described by the various security plans are designed, developed, and implemented. The security plans for information systems that are currently in operation might call for the development of additional security controls to supplement the controls that are already in place or the modification of selected controls that are deemed less than effective.

- *Developmental security test and evaluation* Ensure that security controls that are developed for a new information system are working properly and are effective. Some types of security controls, primarily those of a non-technical nature, cannot be tested and evaluated until the information system is deployed. These controls are typically management and operational controls.

- *Other planning components* Consider all the necessary components of the development process when incorporating security into the network life cycle. These components include the appropriate contract, the participation of all necessary functional groups within an organization, the participation of the certifier and accreditor, and the development and execution of the contracting plans and processes.

Refer to **Figure** in online course

Implementation

These are the security tasks related to the implementation phase of the SDLC:

- *Inspection and acceptance* Validate and verify that the functionality the specification describes is included in the deliverables.

- *System integration* Ensure that the system is integrated at the operational site where the information system is deployed. The security control settings and switches must be enabled in accordance with the vendor instructions and the available security implementation guidance.

- *Security certification* Use established verification techniques and procedures. This step gives organization officials confidence that the appropriate safeguards and countermeasures are in place. Security certification also uncovers and describes the known vulnerabilities in the information system.

- *Security accreditation* Provide the necessary security authorization to process, store, and transmit the information that is required. This authorization is granted by a senior organization official and is based on the verified effectiveness of security controls to some agreed-upon level of assurance and an identified residual risk to organization assets or operations.

Refer to **Figure** in online course

Operations and Maintenance

These are the security tasks related to the operations and maintenance phase of the SDLC:

- *Configuration management and control* Consider the potential security impacts caused by specific changes to an information system or its surrounding environment. Configuration management and configuration control procedures are critical to establishing an initial baseline of hardware, software, and firmware components and subsequently controlling and maintaining an accurate inventory of any changes to the system.

- *Continuous monitoring* Ensure that controls continue to be effective through periodic testing and evaluation. Reporting the security status of the information system to the appropriate officials is an essential activity of a comprehensive information security program.

Refer to **Figure** in online course

Disposition

These are the security tasks related to the disposition phase of the SDLC:

- *Information preservation* Retain information as necessary to conform to legal requirements and to accommodate future technology changes that can render the retrieval method obsolete.

- *Media sanitization* Ensure that data is deleted, erased, and written over, as necessary.

- *Hardware and software disposal* Dispose of hardware and software as directed by the information system security officer.

9.7 Developing a Comprehensive Security Policy

9.7.1 Security Policy Overview

Refer to **Figure** in online course

The Secure Network Life Cycle is a process of assessment and re-evaluation of equipment and security needs as the network changes. One important aspect of this ongoing evaluation is understanding which assets an organization must protect, even as those assets are changing.

Determine what the assets of an organization are by asking questions:

- What does the organization have that others want?

- What processes, data, or information systems are critical to the organization?

- What would stop the organization from doing business or fulfilling its mission?

The answers might identify assets such as critical databases, vital applications, important customer and employee information, classified commercial information, shared drives, email servers, and web servers.

Network security systems help protect these assets, but a security system alone cannot prevent assets from being vulnerable to threat. Technical, administrative, and physical security systems can all be defeated if the end user community does not adhere to security policies and procedures.

Refer to
Figure
in online course

A security policy is a set of security objectives for a company, rules of behavior for users and administrators, and system requirements. These objectives, rules, and requirements collectively ensure the security of a network and the computer systems in an organization. Much like a continuity plan, a security policy is a constantly evolving document based on changes in technology, business, and employee requirements.

A comprehensive security policy has a number of benefits:

- Demonstrates an organization's commitment to security.

- Sets the rules for expected behavior.

- Ensures consistency in system operations, software and hardware acquisition and use, and maintenance.

- Defines the legal consequences of violations.

- Gives security staff the backing of management.

Security policies are used to inform users, staff, and managers of an organization's requirements for protecting technology and information assets. A security policy also specifies the mechanisms that are needed to meet security requirements and provides a baseline from which to acquire, configure, and audit computer systems and networks for compliance.

One of the most common security policy components is an acceptable (or appropriate) use policy (AUP). This component defines what users are allowed and not allowed to do on the various system components. This includes the type of traffic that is allowed on the network. The AUP should be as explicit as possible to avoid misunderstanding. For example, an AUP might list specific websites, newsgroups, or bandwidth intensive applications that are prohibited from being accessed by company computers or from the company network.

Refer to
Figure
in online course

The audience for the security policy is anyone who has access to the network. The internal audience includes various personnel, such as managers and executives, departments and business units, technical staff, and employees. The external audience is also a varied group that includes partners, customers, suppliers, consultants, and contractors. It is likely that one document cannot meet the needs of the entire audience of a large organization. The goal is to ensure that the various information security policy documents are consistent with the needs of the intended audience.

The audience determines the content of the policy. For example, it is probably unnecessary to include a description of why something is necessary in a policy that is intended for the technical staff. It can be assumed that the technical staff already knows why a particular requirement is included. Managers are not likely to be interested in the technical aspects of why a particular requirement is needed. Instead, they want a high-level overview or the principles supporting the requirement. Employees often require more information on why particular security rules are necessary. If they understand the reasons for the rules, they are more likely to comply with them.

9.7.2 Structure of a Security Policy

Refer to **Figure** in online course

Most corporations use a suite of policy documents to meet their wide and varied needs. These documents are often broken into a hierarchical structure:

- *Governing policy* High-level treatment of the security guidelines that are important to the entire company. Managers and technical staff are the intended audience. The governing policy controls all security-related interactions among business units and supporting departments in the company.

- *Technical policy* Used by security staff members as they carry out security responsibilities for the system. These policies are more detailed than the governing policy and are system-specific or issue-specific. For example, access control and physical security issues are described in a technical policy.

- *End user policy* Covers all security topics that are important to end users. End users can include employees, customers, and any other individual user of the network.

Refer to **Figure** in online course

Governing Policy

The governing policy outlines the company's overall security goals for managers and technical staff. It covers all security-related interactions among business units and supporting departments in the company.

The governing policy aligns closely with existing company policies and is placed at the same level of importance as these other policies. This includes human resource policies and other policies that mention security-related issues, such as email, computer use, or related IT subjects.

A governing policy includes several components:

- Statement of the issue that the policy addresses

- How the policy applies in the environment

- Roles and responsibilities of those affected by the policy

- Actions, activities, and processes that are allowed and those that are not

- Consequences of noncompliance

Refer to **Figure** in online course

Technical Policy

Technical policies are detailed documents that are used by technical staff in the conduct of their daily security responsibilities. These policies are system-specific or issue-specific, such as router security and physical security issues. They are essentially security handbooks that describe what the technical staff does, but not how they perform the functions.

Technical policies are broken down into specified technical areas, including:

- General

- Email

- Remote-access

- Telephony

- Application usage

- Network usage

- Wireless communication

Refer to
Figure
in online course

End User Policy

End user policies cover all rules pertaining to information security that end users should know about and follow. End user policies might overlap with technical policies. These policies are generally grouped together into a single document for ease of use.

Several different target groups require end user policies. Each group might have to agree to a different end user policy. For example, an employee end user policy would probably be different from a customer end user policy.

9.7.3 Standards, Guidelines, and Procedures

Refer to
Figure
in online course

The security policy documents are high-level overview documents. The security staff uses detailed documents to implement the security policies. These include the standards, guidelines, and procedures documents.

Standards, guidelines, and procedures contain the actual details defined in the policies. Each document serves a different function, covers different specifications, and targets a different audience. Separating these documents makes it is easier to update and maintain them.

Refer to
Figure
in online course

Standards Documents

Standards help an IT staff maintain consistency in the operations of the network. Standards documents include the technologies that are required for specific uses, hardware and software versioning requirements, program requirements, and any other organizational criteria that must be followed. This helps IT staff improve efficiency and simplicity in design, maintenance, and troubleshooting.

One of the most important security principles is consistency. For this reason it is necessary for organizations to establish standards. Each organization develops standards to support its unique operating environment. For example, if an organization supports 100 routers, it is important that all 100 routers are configured using the established standards. Device configuration standards are defined in the technical section of an organization's security policy.

Refer to
Figure
in online course

Guideline Documents

Guidelines provide a list of suggestions on how to do things better. They are similar to standards, but are more flexible and are not usually mandatory. Guidelines can be used to define how standards are developed and to guarantee adherence to general security policies.

Some of the most helpful guidelines are found in organizational repositories called best practices. In addition to an organization's defined best practices, a number of guidelines are widely available, including:

- National Institute of Standards and Technology (NIST) Computer Security Resource Center

- National Security Agency (NSA) Security Configuration Guides

- The Common Criteria standard

Refer to
Figure
in online course

Procedure Documents

Procedure documents are longer and more detailed than standards and guidelines. Procedure documents include implementation details, usually with step-by-step instructions and graphics. Procedure documents are extremely important for large organizations to have the consistency of deployment that is necessary for a secure environment.

9.7.4 Roles and Responsibilities

Refer to
Figure
in online course

All persons in an organization, from the chief executive officer (CEO) to the newest hires, are considered end users of the network and must abide by the organization's security policy. Developing and maintaining the security policy is delegated to specific roles within the IT department.

Executive-level management must always be consulted during security policy creation to ensure that the policy is comprehensive, cohesive, and legally binding. Smaller organizations might have a single executive position that oversees all aspects of operation, including network operations. Larger organizations might break up the executive task into several positions. The business and reporting structure of an organization depends on the organization's size and industry.

Refer to
Figure
in online course

Some of the more common executive titles include:

- *Chief Executive Officer (CEO)* Is ultimately responsible for the success of an organization. All executive positions report to the CEO.

- *Chief Technology Officer (CTO)* Identifies and evaluates new technologies and drives new technology development to meet organization objectives. Maintains and enhances the current enterprise systems, while providing direction in all technology-related issues in support of operations.

- *Chief Information Officer (CIO)* Responsible for the information technology and computer systems that support enterprise goals, including successful deployment of new technologies and work processes. Small- to medium-sized organizations typically combine the responsibilities of CTO and CIO into a single position that can use either title. When an organization has both a CTO and CIO, the CIO is generally responsible for processes and practices supporting the flow of information, and the CTO is responsible for technology infrastructure.

- *Chief Security Officer (CSO)* Develops, implements, and manages the organization's security strategy, programs, and processes associated with all aspects of business operation, including intellectual property. A major aspect of this position is to limit exposure to liability in all areas of financial, physical, and personal risk.

- *Chief Information Security Officer (CISO)* Similar to the CSO, except that this position has a specific focus on IT security. One of the major responsibilities of the CISO is developing and implementing the security policy. The CISO might choose to be the primary author of the security policy or to delegate some or all of the authoring. In either case, the CISO is responsible and accountable for security policy content.

9.7.5 Security Awareness and Training

Refer to
Figure
in online course

Technical, administrative, and physical security is easily breached if the end user community is not purposefully abiding security policies. To help ensure the enforcement of the security policy, a security awareness program must be put in place. Leadership must develop a program that keeps everyone aware of security issues and educates staff on how to work together to maintain the security of their data.

A security awareness program reflects the business needs of an organization tempered by known risks. It informs users of their IT security responsibilities and explains the rules of behavior for using the IT systems and data within a company. This program must explain all IT security policies and procedures. A security awareness program is crucial to the financial success of any organization. It disseminates the information that all end users need to effectively conduct business in a way that protects the organization from loss of intellectual capital, critical data, and even physical equipment. The security awareness program also details the sanctions that the organization imposes for noncompliance. This portion of the program should be part of all new hire orientation.

A security awareness program usually has two major components:

- Awareness campaigns

- Training and education

Awareness Campaigns

Refer to **Figure** in online course

Awareness campaigns are usually aimed at all levels of the organization, including executive positions. Security awareness efforts are designed to change behavior or reinforce good security practices. Awareness is defined in NIST Special Publication 800-16:

"Awareness is not training. The purpose of awareness presentations is simply to focus attention on security. Awareness presentations are intended to allow individuals to recognize IT security concerns and respond accordingly. In awareness activities, the learner is the recipient of information Awareness relies on reaching broad audiences with attractive packaging techniques."

An example of a topic for an awareness session (or awareness material to be distributed) is virus protection. The subject can be briefly addressed by describing what a virus is, what can happen if a virus infects a user system, what the user must do to protect the system, and what users do if they discover a virus.

There are several methods of increasing security awareness:

- Lectures, videos

- Posters, newsletter articles, and bulletins

- Awards for good security practices

- Reminders, such as login banners, mouse pads, coffee cups, and notepads

Training and Education

Refer to **Figure** in online course

Training strives to impart needed security skills to end users who may or may not be members of the IT staff. The most significant difference between training and awareness is that training teaches skills that allow a person to perform a specific task, while awareness campaigns simply focus an individual's attention on security issues. The skills that users acquire during training build upon the information learned in security awareness campaigns. Following a security awareness campaign with training targeted to specific audiences helps cement the information and skills imparted. A training curriculum does not necessarily lead to a formal degree from an institution of higher learning, but it might contain much of the same material found in a course that a college or university includes in a certificate or degree program.

An example of a training course for non-IT personnel is one that addresses appropriate security practices specific to those applications that the end user must use, such as database applications.

An example of training for IT personnel is an IT security course that addresses in detail the management, operational, and technical controls that must be implemented.

An effective security training course requires proper planning, implementation, maintenance, and periodic evaluation. The life cycle of a security training course includes several steps:

Step 1. **Identify course scope, goals, and objectives.** The scope of the course provides training to all types of people who interact with IT systems. Because users need training that relates directly to their use of particular systems, it is necessary to supplement a large organization-wide program by more system-specific courses.

Step 2. **Identify and educate training staff.** It is important that trainers have sufficient knowledge of computer security issues, principles, and techniques. It is also vital that they know how to communicate information and ideas effectively.

Step 3. **Identify target audiences.** Not everyone needs the same degree or type of computer security information to perform an assigned job. Security training courses that present only the information that is needed by the particular audience and omit irrelevant information have the best results.

Step 4. **Motivate management and employees.** Consider using motivational techniques to show management and employees how their participation in a training course benefits the organization.

Step 5. **Administer the courses.** Important considerations for administering the course include selecting appropriate training methods, topics, materials, and presentation techniques.

Step 6. **Maintain the courses.** Stay informed of changes in computer technology and security requirements. Training courses that meet the needs of an organization today can become ineffective when the organization starts to use a new application or changes its environment, such as the deployment of VoIP.

Step 7. **Evaluate the courses.** An evaluation seeks to ascertain how much information is retained, to what extent computer security procedures are being followed, and the general attitude toward computer security.

Refer to **Figure** in online course

Education integrates all the security skills and competencies of the various functional specialties into a common body of knowledge, adds a multidisciplinary study of concepts, issues, and principles (technological and social), and strives to produce IT security specialists and professionals capable of vision and proactive response.

An example of an educational program is a degree program at a college or university. Some people take a course or several courses to develop or enhance their skills in a particular discipline. This is training as opposed to education. Many colleges and universities offer certificate programs, in which a student can take two or more classes in a related discipline and be awarded a certificate upon completion. Often, these certificate programs are conducted as a joint effort between schools and software or hardware vendors. These programs are more characteristic of training than education. Those responsible for security training must assess both types of programs and decide which one better addresses the identified needs.

A successfully implemented security awareness program measurably reduces unauthorized actions by insiders, increases the effectiveness of existing controls, and helps fight waste, fraud, and abuse of information systems resources.

9.7.6 Laws and Ethics

Refer to
Figure
in online course

Laws

For many businesses today, one of the biggest considerations for setting security policies and implementing awareness programs is compliance with the law. Network security professionals must be familiar with the laws and codes of ethics that are binding on Information Systems Security (INFOSEC) professionals. Most countries have three types of laws: criminal, civil (also called tort), and administrative.

Criminal law is concerned with crimes, and its penalties usually involve fines or imprisonment, or both.

Civil law focuses on correcting situations in which entities have been harmed and an economic award can help. Imprisonment is not possible in civil law. An example of a civil law case is if one company sues another company for infringing on a patent. The penalty in civil law is usually monetary, although there can also be performance requirements such as ceasing to infringe on the patent.

Administrative law involves government agencies enforcing regulations. For example, a company might owe its employees vacation pay. An administrative court could force the company to pay its employees as well as levy a fine that is payable to the court.

Not all governments accept or classify their laws the same way. This can impede prosecution for computer and networking crimes that cross international boundaries.

Ethics

Ethics is a standard that is higher than the law. It is a set of moral principles that govern civil behavior. Ethical principles are often the foundation of many of the laws currently in place. These principles are frequently formalized into codes of ethics. Individuals that violate the code of ethics can face consequences such as loss of certification, loss of employment, and even prosecution by criminal or civil court. The information security profession has a number of formalized codes:

- International Information Systems Security Certification Consortium, Inc (ISC)2 Code of Ethics

- Computer Ethics Institute (CEI)

- Internet Activities Board (IAB)

- Generally Accepted System Security Principles (GASSP)

Refer to
Figure
in online course

(ISC)2 Code of Ethics

The (ISC)2 code of ethics consists of the preamble and the ethics canons. The canons are explained in more detail at the (ISC)2 website.

Code of Ethics Preamble

Safety of the commonwealth, duty to our principals, and to each other requires that we adhere, and be seen to adhere, to the highest ethical standards of behavior. Therefore, strict adherence to this Code is a condition of certification.

Code of Ethics Canons

- Protect society, the commonwealth, and the infrastructure.

- Act honorably, honestly, justly, responsibly, and legally.

- Provide diligent and competent service to principals.

- Advance and protect the profession.

Computer Ethics Institute Code of Ethics

The CEI formalized its code of ethics as the Ten Commandments of Computer Ethics:

Step 1.   Thou shalt not use a computer to harm other people.

Step 2.   Thou shalt not interfere with other people's computer work.

Step 3.   Thou shalt not snoop around in other people's computer files.

Step 4.   Thou shalt not use a computer to steal.

Step 5.   Thou shalt not use a computer to bear false witness.

Step 6.   Thou shalt not copy or use proprietary software which is not paid for.

Step 7.   Thou shalt not use other people's computer resources without authorization or proper compensation.

Step 8.   Thou shalt not appropriate other people's intellectual output.

Step 9.   Thou shalt think about the social consequences of the program being written or the system being designed.

Step 10.   Thou shalt always use a computer in ways that ensure consideration and respect for fellow humans.

IAB Code of Ethics

The IAB issued a statement that constitutes its code of ethics:

The Internet is a national facility whose utility is largely a consequence of its wide availability and accessibility. Irresponsible use of this critical resource poses an enormous threat to its continued availability to the technical community. The U.S. government, sponsors of this system, suffers when highly disruptive abuses occur. Access to and use of the Internet is a privilege and should be treated as such by all users of this system. The IAB strongly endorses the view of the Division Advisory Panel of the National Science Foundation Division of Network, Communications Research and Infrastructure which, in paraphrase, characterized as unethical and unacceptable any activity which purposely:

- Seeks to gain unauthorized access to the resources of the Internet

- Disrupts the intended use of the Internet

- Wastes resources, such as people, capacity, and computer, through such actions

- Destroys the integrity of computer-based information

- Compromises the privacy of users

GASSP Code of Ethics

The GASSP Code of Ethics states that information systems and the security of information systems should be provided and used in accordance with the Code of Ethical Conduct of information security professionals. The Code of Ethical Conduct prescribes the relationships of ethics, morality, and information.

As social norms for using IT systems evolve, the Code of Ethical Conduct will change and information security professionals will spread the new concepts throughout their organizations and products. Safeguards may require an ethical judgment for use or to determine limits or controls.

For example, entrapment is a process for luring someone into performing an illegal or abusive act. As a security safeguard, a security professional might set up an easy-to-compromise hole in the access control system, and then monitor attempts to exploit the hole. This form of entrapment is useful in providing warning that penetration has occurred. It can also provide enough information to identify the perpetrator. Due to laws, regulations, or ethical standards, it may be unethical to use data that is collected via entrapment in prosecution, but it may be ethical to use entrapment as a detection and prevention strategy. One should seek both legal and ethical advice when designing network security.

9.7.7 Responding to a Security Breach

Refer to **Figure** in online course

Laws and codes of ethics are in place to allow organizations and individuals a means of reclaiming lost assets and preventing crimes. Different countries have different legal standards. In most countries and courts, to successfully prosecute an individual, it is necessary to establish motive, opportunity, and means.

Motive answers the question of why a person committed the illegal act. As a crime is investigated, it is important to start with individuals who might have been motivated to commit the crime. For example, employees who believe they were wrongly passed over for advancement may be motivated to sell confidential company data to a competitor. Having identified likely suspects, the next thing to consider is whether the suspects had the opportunity to commit the crime.

Opportunity answers the question of when and where the person committed the crime. For example, if it can be established that three of the suspects were all participating in a wedding at the time of the security breach, they might have been motivated, but they did not have the opportunity because they were busy doing something else.

Means answers the question of how the person committed the crime. It is pointless to accuse someone who does not have the knowledge, skills, or access to accomplish the crime.

While establishing motive, opportunity, and means is a standard for finding and prosecuting individuals of all types of crimes, in computer crimes, it is fairly easy to manipulate and cover up evidence because of the complexity of computer systems, global accessibility via the Internet, and the knowledge of many attackers. For this reason, it is necessary to have strict protocols in place for security breaches. These policies should be outlined in the security policy of an organization.

Refer to **Figure** in online course

Computer data is virtual data, meaning that there are rarely physical, tangible representations. For this reason, data can be easily damaged or modified. When working with computer data as part of a forensics case, the integrity of the data must be maintained if it is to be used as evidence in a court of law. For example, changing a single bit of data can change a timestamp from August 2, 2001 to August 3, 2001. A perpetrator can easily adjust data to establish a false alibi. Therefore, strict procedures are required to guarantee the integrity of forensics data recovered as part of an investigation. Some of the procedures that must be established are proper data collection, data chain of custody, data storage, and data backups.

The process of collecting data must be done precisely and quickly. When a security breach occurs, it is necessary to isolate the infected system immediately. Systems should not be shut down or rebooted before the memory is dumped to a file because the system flushes the memory every time a device is powered off. Additionally, a drive image should be taken before working with data on the hard drive. Multiple copies of the hard drive are usually made after the device is powered down to establish master copies. These master copies are usually locked up in a safe, and investigators use working copies for both the prosecution and the defense. Investigators can determine if data tampering has occurred by comparing working copies to the master copy that has been secured and untouched since the beginning of the investigation.

After data is collected but before equipment is disconnected, it is necessary to photograph the equipment in place. All evidence must be handled while maintaining a proper chain of custody, meaning that only those individuals with authorization have access to evidence, and all access is documented.

If security protocols are established and followed, organizations can minimize the loss and damages resulting from attacks.

Chapter Summary

Refer to **Figure** in online course

Refer to **Packet Tracer Activity** for this chapter

Refer to **Lab Activity** for this chapter

Your Chapter Notes

Implementing the Cisco Adaptive Security Appliance (ASA)

Chapter Introduction

Refer to
Figure
in online course

For over two decades, firewall solutions have evolved to meet the increasing security requirements. Today there are many types of firewalls, including packet-filtering, stateful, application gateway (proxy), address-translation, host-based, transparent, and hybrid firewalls. Modern network design must include proper placement of one or more firewalls to protect resources. Cisco provides two firewall solutions: the firewall-enabled ISR and the Cisco Adaptive Security Appliance (ASA).

An ASA provides a proven, comprehensive firewall solution. The Cisco ASA 5500 series is a primary component of the Cisco Secure Borderless Network. It delivers superior scalability, a broad range of technology and solutions, and effective, always-on security designed to meet the needs of a wide array of deployments.

The Cisco ASA 5500 series helps organizations provide secure, high performance connectivity and protect critical assets by integrating the following:

- Proven firewall technology

- Comprehensive, highly effective intrusion prevention system (IPS) with Cisco Global Correlation and guaranteed coverage

- High-performance VPNs and always-on remote-access

- Failover feature for fault tolerance

This chapter will provide an introduction to the ASA platform and to the firewall and VPN features of the ASA 5505 series device.

In the first hands-on lab for the chapter, *Configuring ASA Basic Settings and Firewall Using CLI*, learners configure the ASA 5505 as a basic firewall by setting up three interfaces, the outside, inside, and DMZ.

In a second hands-on lab, *Configuring ASA Basic Settings and Firewall Using ASDM*, learners configure the ASA 5505 as a basic firewall, but this time, by using the ASA GUI interface, ASDM.

In a third hands-on lab, *Configuring Clientless and AnyConnect Remote Access SSL VPNs Using ASDM*, learners will use the ASDM VPN Wizard to configure a clientless SSL remote access VPN and verify access using a remote PC. Next, learners will configure an AnyConnect client-based SSL remote access VPN and verify connectivity.

Finally, in a fourth hands-on lab, *Configuring a Site-to-Site IPsec VPN Using CCP and ASDM*, learners will configure the ASA as a Site-to-Site IPsec VPN endpoint using both the CCP VPN Wizard and the ASDM VPN Wizard.

10.1 Introduction to the ASA

10.1.1 Overview of the ASA

Refer to
Figure
in online course

An IOS router firewall solution is appropriate for small branch deployments and for administrators who are experienced with Cisco IOS. However, an IOS firewall solution does not scale well and typically cannot meet the needs of a large enterprise.

The ASA is a standalone firewall device that is a primary component of the Cisco SecureX architecture. There are six ASA models, ranging from the basic 5505 branch office model to the 5585 data center version. All provide advanced stateful firewall features and VPN functionality. The biggest difference between the models is the maximum traffic throughput handled by each model and the number and type of interfaces. Cisco ASA devices scale to meet a range of requirements and network sizes. The choice of ASA model will depend on an organization's requirements, such as maximum throughput, maximum connections per second, and budget.

The ASA software combines firewall, VPN concentrator, and intrusion prevention functionality into one software image. Previously, these functions were available in three separate devices, each with its own software and hardware. Combining the functionality into one software image provides significant improvements in the available features.

Other advanced ASA features include these:

- *ASA virtualization* A single ASA can be partitioned into multiple virtual devices. Each virtual device is called a security context. Each context is an independent device, with its own security policy, interfaces, and administrators. Multiple contexts are similar to having multiple standalone devices. Many features are supported in multiple context mode, including routing tables, firewall features, IPS, and management. Some features are not supported, including VPN and dynamic routing protocols.

- *High availability with failover* Two identical ASAs can be paired into an active / standby failover configuration to provide device redundancy. One physical device is designated as primary, the other as secondary. One of the ASAs is elected to be in active state (forwarding traffic) and the other in hot standby state (waiting). The status of the active ASA device is monitored over the LAN failover interface by the standby ASA. Both platforms must be identical in software, licensing, memory, and interfaces, including the Security Services Module (SSM).

- *Identity firewall* The ASA provides optional granular access control based on an association of IP addresses to Windows Active Directory login information. The ASA uses Active Directory as the source to retrieve the current user identity information for specific IP addresses and allows transparent authentication for Active Directory users. Identity-based firewall services enhance the existing access control and security policy mechanisms by allowing users or groups to be specified in place of source IP addresses. Identity-based security policies can be interleaved without restriction between traditional IP address-based rules.

- *Threat control and containment services* All ASA models support basic IPS features. However, advanced IPS features can only be provided by integrating special hardware modules with the ASA architecture. IPS capability is available using the Advanced Inspection and Prevention (AIP) modules, while anti-malware capabilities can be deployed integrating the Content Security and Control (CSC) module. The Cisco Advanced Inspection and Prevention Security Services Module (AIP-SSM) and Cisco Advanced Inspection and Prevention Security Services Card (AIP-SSC) deliver protection against tens of thousands of known exploits. They also protect against millions more potential unknown exploit variants using specialized IPS detection engines and thousands of signatures. Cisco Services for IPS provides signature updates through a global intelligence team working 24 hours a day to help ensure protection against the latest threats.

All ASA models can be configured and managed using either the command line interface or the Adaptive Security Device Manager (ASDM). ASDM is a browser-based, Java applet used to configure and monitor the software on the ASA. ASDM is loaded from the ASA, onto the PC. ASDM is used to configure, monitor, and manage the device.

The focus of this chapter will be on the entry level ASA 5505 which is designed for small business, branch office, and enterprise teleworker implementations.

Note: The four advanced features listed above are out of scope for this course and will not be explored further. For technical specifications of each ASA, refer to: www.cisco.com/en/US/products/ps6120/prod_models_comparison.html

Refer to **Figure** in online course

When discussing networks connected to a firewall, there are some general terms to keep in mind:

- Outside network -Network that is outside the protection of the firewall.

- Inside network - Network that is protected and behind the firewall.

- DMZ - Demilitarized zone, while protected by the firewall, limited access is allowed to outside users.

Firewalls protect inside networks from unauthorized access by users on an outside network. They also protect inside network users from each other. For example, by creating zones, an administrator can keep the network hosting the accounting servers separate from other networks in an organization.

Cisco ISRs can provide firewall features by using either zone-based policy firewall (ZPF) or by using the older context-based access control (CBAC) feature. An ASA provides the same features but the configuration differs markedly from the IOS router configuration of ZPF.

The ASA is a dedicated firewall appliance. By default, it treats a defined inside interface as the trusted network, and any defined outside interfaces as untrusted networks.

Each interface has an associated security level. These trust levels enable the ASA to implement security policies. For example, inside users can access outside networks based on certain addresses, by requiring authentication or authorization, or by coordinating with an external URL filtering server.

Network resources that are needed by outside users, such as a web or FTP server, can be located in a DMZ. The firewall allows limited access to the DMZ, while protecting the inside network from outside users.

Refer to **Figure** in online course

A stateful firewall, such as the ASA, tracks the state of the TCP or UDP network connections traversing it. The firewall is programmed to determine legitimate packets for different types of connections. Only packets matching a known active connection will be allowed by the firewall; others will be rejected.

All traffic forwarded through an ASA is inspected using the Adaptive Security Algorithm and is either allowed to pass through or is dropped. The algorithm takes into consideration the state, if any, of a connection associated with the packet.

If the packet creates a new connection, the ASA has to check the packet against access lists and perform other tasks to determine if the packet is permitted or denied. To perform this check, the first packet of the session goes through the "session management path," which is part of the management plane. Depending on the type of traffic, it might also pass through the "control plane path."

The session management path is responsible for the following tasks:

- Performing the access list checks

- Performing route lookups

- Allocating NAT translations (xlates)

- Establishing sessions in the "fast path"

Some packets require Layer 7 inspection. Layer 7 inspection engines are required for protocols that have two or more channels: a data channel (which uses well-known port numbers), and a control channel (which uses different port numbers for each session). When a packet requires Layer 7 inspection, the packet payload must be inspected or altered and the packets are passed on to the control plane path. Protocols that require Layer 7 inspection include FTP, H.323, and SNMP. To support these protocols, the packet filter snoops the initial session and parses the application data to learn about the additional negotiated channels. Then the packet filter enforces the policy that states that if the initial session was permitted, then any additional channels of that application should also be permitted.

If the connection is already established, the ASA does not need to re-check packets. Most matching packets can go through the "fast" path in both directions. The fast path is responsible for the following tasks:

- IP checksum verification

- Session lookup

- TCP sequence number check

- NAT translations based on existing sessions

- Layer 3 and Layer 4 header adjustments

For UDP or other connectionless protocols, the ASA creates connection state information so that it can also use the fast path.

Refer to
Figure
in online course

There are two firewall modes of operation available on ASA devices: routed mode and transparent mode.

Routed Mode

Routed mode is the traditional mode for deploying a firewall where there are two or more interfaces that separate Layer 3 networks. The ASA is considered to be a router hop in the network and can perform NAT between connected networks. Routed mode supports multiple interfaces. Each interface is on a different subnet and requires an IP address on that subnet.

Transparent Mode

In transparent mode the ASA functions like a Layer 2 device. Transparent mode is often referred to as a "bump in the wire," or a "stealth firewall." In transparent mode, the ASA is not considered a router hop. Similar to a Layer 2 switch, the ASA requires only one management IP address configured in global configuration mode. This address is for remote management purposes and is required before the device will forward traffic. Once the address is assigned, all interfaces start "listening" on this address to ensure the device is responsive to its administrator. This global IP address assigned to the device must be in the same subnet that the forwarding interfaces are participating in. A transparent firewall may be used to simplify a network configuration or be deployed where the existing IP addressing cannot be altered. Transparent mode is also useful for making the firewall invisible to attackers. However, the drawbacks to using transparent mode include no support for dynamic routing protocols, VPNs, QoS, or DHCP Relay.

The focus of this chapter will be on routed mode.

Refer to
Figure
in online course

A license specifies the options that are enabled on a given ASA. Most ASA appliances come preinstalled with either a Base license or a Security Plus license. For example, the Cisco ASA 5505 model comes with a Base license and the option to upgrade to the Security Plus license. The Security Plus upgrade license enables the Cisco ASA 5505 to scale to support a higher connection capacity and up to 25 IPsec VPN users. It adds full DMZ support, and integrates into switched network environments through VLAN trunking support. Furthermore, the Security Plus license maximizes business continuity by enabling support for redundant ISP connections and stateless active/standby high-availability services.

To provide additional features to the ASA, additional time-based or optional licenses can be purchased. For example, an administrator can install a Botnet Traffic Filter time-based license that is valid for one year. Another example would be if the ASA must handle a short-term surge in the number of concurrent SSL VPN users. In this case, an optional AnyConnect Premium license can be purchased.

Combining these additional licenses to the pre-installed licenses creates a permanent license. The permanent license is then activated by installing a permanent activation key using the **activation-key** command. The permanent activation key includes all licensed features in a single key. A product activation key can be purchased from a Cisco account representative.

Note that only one permanent license key can be installed and once it is installed, it is referred to as the running license.

To verify the license information on an ASA device, use the **show version** or the **show activation-key** command.

For more information on licenses, refer to: www.cisco.com/en/US/docs/security/asa/asa84/license/license_management/license.html

10.1.2 Basic ASA Configuration

> Refer to
> **Figure**
> in online course

The Cisco ASA 5505 is a full-featured security appliance for small businesses, branch offices, and enterprise teleworker environments. It delivers a high-performance firewall, SSL VPN, IPsec VPN, and rich networking services in a modular, plug-and-play appliance.

The front panel of the ASA 5505 features:

- *USB Port* Reserved for future use.
- *Speed and link activity LEDs* A solid green speed indicator LED indicates 100 Mb/s. If the LED is off, this indicates 10 Mb/s. When the link activity indicator LED is on, it indicates that a network link is established. When it is blinking, it indicates network activity.
- *Power LED* Solid green indicates that the appliance is powered on.
- *Status LED* Flashing green indicates that the system is booting and power-up tests are running. Solid green indicates that the system tests passed and the system is operational. Amber solid indicates that the system tests failed.
- *Active LED* Green indicates that this Cisco ASA is active when configured for failover.
- *VPN LED* Solid green indicates that one or more VPN tunnels are active.
- *Security Services Card (SSC) LED* Solid green indicates that an SSC card is present in the SSC slot.

The back panel of the Cisco ASA 5505 features:

- An 8-port 10/100 Fast Ethernet switch. Each port can be dynamically grouped to create up to three separate VLANs or zones to support network segmentation and security. Ports 6 and 7 are Power over Ethernet (PoE) ports to simplify the deployment of Cisco IP phones and external wireless access points.

- Three USB ports. These ports (one on the front and two on the backplane) can be used to enable additional services and capabilities.

- One Security Service Card (SSC) slot for expansion. The slot can be used to add the Cisco Advanced Inspection and Prevention Security Services Card (AIP-SSC). The AIP-SSC card enables the Cisco ASA 5500 to provide intrusion prevention services to stop malicious traffic before it can affect a network. Cisco IPS with Global Correlation increases the efficacy of traditional IPS. With updates every five minutes, Cisco IPS with Global Correlation provides fast and accurate threat protection with real-time global intelligence from Cisco IPS, firewall, e-mail, and web appliances.

The default DRAM memory is 256 MB (upgradable to 512 MB) and the default internal flash memory is 128 MB for the Cisco ASA 5505. In a failover configuration, the two units must be identical models with the same hardware configuration, the same number and types of interfaces, and the same amount of RAM.

To view an interactive model of the Cisco ASA 5505, refer to: www.cisco.com/en/US/prod/collateral/vpndevc/ps6032/ps6094/ps6120/ps6913/prod_presentation0900aecd805ac1dd.html

Refer to **Figure** in online course

The ASA assigns security levels to distinguish between inside and outside networks. Security levels define the level of trustworthiness of an interface. The higher the level, the more trusted the interface. The security level numbers range between 0 (untrustworthy) to 100 (very trustworthy). Each operational interface must have a name and a security level from 0 (lowest) to 100 (highest) assigned.

For example, assign level 100 to the most secure network, such as the inside host network, while the outside network connected to the Internet can be assigned level 0. DMZs and other networks can be assigned a security level between 0 and 100. When traffic moves from an interface with a higher security level to an interface with a lower security level, it is considered outbound traffic. Conversely, traffic moving from an interface with a lower security level to an interface with a higher security level is considered inbound traffic.

Security levels help control:

- *Network access* By default, there is an implicit `permit` from a higher security interface to a lower security interface (outbound). Hosts on the higher security interface can access hosts on a lower security interface. Multiple interfaces can be assigned the same security level. If communication is enabled for same security interfaces, there is an implicit `permit` for interfaces to access other interfaces at the same security level or lower.

- *Inspection engines* Some application inspection engines are dependent on the security level. When interfaces have the same security level, the ASA inspects traffic in either direction.

- *Filtering* Filtering applies only for outbound connections (from a higher level to a lower level). If communication is enabled for same security interfaces, traffic can be filtered in either direction.

Outbound traffic is allowed and inspected by default. Returning traffic is allowed because of stateful packet inspection. For example, internal users on the inside interface can access resources on the DMZ freely. They can also initiate connections to the Internet with no restrictions and without the need for an additional policy or additional commands. However, traffic that is sourced on the outside network and going into either the DMZ or the inside network, is denied by default. Return traffic, originating on the inside network and returning via the outside interface, would be allowed. Any exception to this default behavior requires configuration of an ACL to explicitly permit traffic from an interface with a lower security level to an interface with a higher security level (e.g. outside to inside).

The ASA 5505 is different from the other 5500 series ASA models. With other ASAs, the physical port can be assigned a Layer 3 IP address directly, much like a Cisco router. With the ASA 5505, the eight integrated switch ports are Layer 2 ports, and therefore cannot be assigned IP addresses directly.

On an ASA 5505, Layer 3 parameters are configured on a switch virtual interface (SVI). An SVI, a logical VLAN interface, requires a name, interface security level, and IP address. The Layer 2 switch ports are then assigned to a specific VLAN. Switch ports on the same VLAN can communicate with each other using hardware switching. But when a switch port on VLAN 1 wants to communicate with a switch port on VLAN 2, then the ASA applies the security policy to the traffic and routes between the two VLANs.

Refer to Figure in online course

The ASA 5505 is commonly used as an edge security device that connects a small business to an ISP device, such as a DSL or cable modem, for access to the Internet. It can be deployed to interconnect and protect several workstations, network printers, and IP phones.

In a small branch deployment, a common deployment would include an inside network (VLAN 1) with security level 100 and an outside network (VLAN 2) with security level 0. Fast Ethernet switch ports 6 and 7 are PoE ports. They can be assigned to VLAN 1 and are used to connect IP phones.

In a small business, the ASA 5505 can be deployed with two different protected network segments: The inside network (VLAN 1) to connect workstations and IP phones, and the DMZ (VLAN 3) to connect a company web server. The outside interface (VLAN 2) is used to connect to the Internet.

In an enterprise deployment, the ASA 5505 can be used by telecommuters and home users to connect to a centralized location using a VPN.

Refer to Figure in online course

Higher-end ASA models such as the Cisco ASA 5510 are designed to deliver advanced security services for medium-sized businesses and enterprise branch offices. The ASA 5510 supports 300 Mb/s throughput and 9,000 firewall connections per second capacity. This makes the ASA 5510 very suitable for most office deployments.

The Cisco ASA 5510, 5520, 5540, and 5550 are all one-rack units (1RU). Each of these has an expansion slot for security-services modules.

The front panel of the ASA 5510 features Power, Status, Active, VPN, and Flash LEDs.

The back panel of the Cisco ASA 5510 features:

- One Security Services Module (SSM) slot for expandability

- Two USB ports that can be used to enable additional services and capabilities

- One Fast Ethernet out-of-band (OOB) management interface

- Four Fast Ethernet interfaces

- One Flash card slot to provide storage for system images and configuration files

- Power, status, active, VPN, and flash LED indicators

- One serial console port

- One auxiliary port to connect an external modem for OOB management

The four integrated 10/100 Fast Ethernet network interfaces and the OOB combine to create 5 possible interfaces. Three of these five Fast Ethernet ports are enabled by default (0 to 2). The fourth is disabled by default and the fifth is reserved for OOB management. Depending on the ASA software version, restrictions on the OOB port may be removed. Therefore, all five Fast Ethernet interfaces can be used for transit traffic and can have security levels applied.

The Security Services Module (SSM) slot can be used to add the following:

- A 4-Port Gigabit Ethernet Security Services Module (4GE SSM) to better segment network traffic into separate security zones. This high-performance module has four 10/100/1000 RJ-45 ports and four Small Form-Factor Pluggable (SFP) ports to support both copper and optical connections.
- The Advanced Inspection and Prevention Security Services Module (AIP-SSM) to provide proactive, full-featured intrusion prevention services to stop malicious traffic, including worms and network viruses, before they can affect a network.
- The Series Content Security and Control Security Services Module (CSC-SSM) to provide industry-leading threat protection and content control at the Internet edge. It provides comprehensive antivirus, anti-spyware, file blocking, anti-spam, anti-phishing, URL blocking and filtering, and content filtering.

For more information, go to: www.cisco.com/en/US/docs/security/asa/quick_start/5500/inst5500.html

Refer to
Figure
in online course

The default factory configuration for the ASA 5510 and higher includes configuration of the management interface, DHCP server support, and ASDM support. The default factory configuration includes the following:

- The management interface, Management 0/0, is preconfigured with the IP address 192.168.1.1 and mask 255.255.255.0.
- The DHCP server is enabled on the ASA, so a PC connecting to the interface receives an address between 192.168.1.2 and 192.168.1.254.
- The HTTP server is enabled for ASDM and is accessible to users on the 192.168.1.0 network.

Note: Configuring ASA 5510 and higher models is beyond the scope of this chapter.

10.2 ASA Firewall Configuration

10.2.1 Introduction to the ASA Firewall Configuration

Refer to
Figure
in online course

ASA devices can be configured and managed using either the command-line interface (CLI) or the Adaptive Security Device Manager (ASDM) GUI.

The ASA CLI is a proprietary OS which has a similar look and feel to the router IOS. There are many similar commands between the ASA CLI and the IOS CLI. There are also many different commands.

The Cisco ASA contains a command set structure similar to that of a Cisco IOS router and offers the following access modes:

- User EXEC mode - `ciscoasa>` **en**
- Privileged EXEC mode - `ciscoasa#` **config t**
- Global configuration mode - `ciscoasa(config)#`
- Various sub-configuration modes, for example - `ciscoasa(config-if)#`
- ROMMON mode - `ROMMON>`

Like a Cisco IOS router, the ASA also recognizes the following:

- Abbreviation of commands and keywords

- Tab key to complete a partial command

- The help key (**?**) after the command

Unlike an ISR, the ASA performs as follows:

- Execute any ASA CLI command regardless of the current configuration mode prompt. The IOS **do** command is not required or recognized.

- Provide a brief description and command syntax when **help** is entered followed by the command. For example, typing **help reload** will display the command syntax for reload, a description, and the supported arguments.

- Interrupt **show** command output using **Q**. The IOS requires the use of Ctrl+C (^C).

Note: The security appliance uses ROMMON mode (Read-Only-Memory Monitor mode) when it does not find a bootable image or when an administrator forces it to enter into that mode. In ROM-MON mode, an administrator can use a TFTP server to load a system image into the security appliance. ROMMON mode is also used to recover the system password.

> Refer to
> **Figure**
> in online course

The ASA 5505 ships with a default configuration that, in most cases, is sufficient for a basic SOHO deployment. The configuration includes two preconfigured VLAN networks: VLAN1 and VLAN2. VLAN 1 is for the inside network and VLAN 2 is for the outside network.

The inside interface also provides DHCP addressing and NAT features. Clients on the inside network obtain a dynamic IP address from the ASA so that they can communicate with each other and with devices on the Internet.

Specifically, the default factory configuration for the ASA 5505 configures the following:

- A default host name of ciscoasa.

- Console or enable passwords which are blank.

- An inside VLAN 1 interface that includes the Ethernet 0/1 through 0/7 switch ports. The VLAN 1 IP address and mask are 192.168.1.1 and 255.255.255.0.

- An outside VLAN 2 interface that includes the Ethernet 0/0 switch port. VLAN 2 derives its IP address from the ISP using DHCP.

- The default route that is derived from DHCP.

- All inside IP addresses to be translated when accessing the outside using interface PAT.

- The HTTP server to support ASDM access.

- An internal DHCP server to provide addresses between 192.168.1.5 and 192.168.1.36 for hosts that connect to a VLAN 1 interface.

These settings can be changed manually using the CLI or interactively using either the CLI Setup Initialization wizard or by using the ASDM Startup wizard.

The ASA can be restored to its factory default configuration by using the **configure factory-default** global configuration command.

For more information, refer to: www.cisco.com/en/US/docs/security/asa/quick_start/5505/5505-poster.html

Refer to
Figure
in online course

The ASA startup configuration can be erased using the **write erase** and **reload** commands.

Note: Unlike router IOS, the ASA does not recognize the **erase startup-config** command.

Once rebooted, the ASA displays the following prompt "**Pre-configure Firewall now through interactive prompts [yes]?**"

Entering **no**, cancels the Setup Initialization wizard and the ASA will display its default prompt. Pressing Enter accepts the default [yes] and the ASA will interactively guide an administrator to configure the following:

- Firewall mode
- Enable password
- Enable password recovery
- Time and date settings
- Inside IP address and mask
- ASA device host name
- Domain name

The security appliance displays the default values in brackets ([ ]) before prompting the user to accept or change them. To accept the default input, press Enter.

After the interactive portion of the Setup Initialization wizard is completed, the security appliance displays the summary of the new configuration and prompts the user to save or reject the settings. Answering **yes** saves the configuration to flash and displays the configured hostname prompt. Answering **no** restarts the Setup Initialization wizard from the beginning with any changes that had been made as the new default settings. This enables the administrator to correct a misconfigured setting.

The Setup Initialization wizard is an optional method for initially configuring an ASA. It also provides most of the settings needed to access the ASA using ASDM.

10.2.2 Configuring Management Settings and Services

Refer to
Figure
in online course

Like router IOS, ASA basic settings can be configured using the CLI. If the user entered **no** at the Setup Initialization wizard prompt, then the basic management settings must be configured manually using the ASA OS CLI.

Configure Basic Settings

Basic management settings are configured in global configuration mode. The first time global configuration mode is accessed, a message prompting you to enable the Smart Call Home feature appears. This feature offers proactive diagnostics and real-time alerts on select Cisco devices, which provides higher network availability and increased operational efficiency. To participate, a CCO ID is required and the ASA device must be registered under a Cisco SMARTnet Service contract.

For more information on Smart Call Home, refer to: www.cisco.com/go/smartcall

In global configuration mode, configure the ASA host name, domain name, and privileged EXEC mode password using the following commands:

- **hostname** *name* Changes the name of the ASA.
- **domain-name** *name* Changes the domain name.

- **`enable password `*`password`*** Configures the privileged EXEC mode password. Note that there is no secret option.

- **`passwd `*`password`*** Configures the Telnet / SSH password.

Optionally, a master passphrase can be created to encrypt all passwords. This feature is similar to the IOS **`service password-encryption`** command. The master passphrase securely stores plaintext passwords in encrypted format. The master passphrase provides a key that is used to universally encrypt or mask all passwords, without changing any functionality. To configure a master passphrase, use the following commands:

- **`key config-key password-encryption [`*`new-passphrase`* `[`*`old-passphrase`*`]]`** Creates or changes an existing master passphrase. The passphrase must be 8 to 128 characters in length and all characters except a backspace and double quote are accepted. If a new passphrase is not included in the command, then the ASA will prompt for it. To change the passphrase, the old passphrase will first have to be entered.

- **`password encryption aes`** Enables password encryption. As soon as password encryption is turned on and the master passphrase is available, all the user passwords will be encrypted. The running configuration will show the passwords in the encrypted format. If the key config-key password-encryption passphrase is not configured at the time that password encryption is enabled, the command will still be accepted and passwords will become encrypted when the passphrase is configured.

To determine if password encryption is enabled, use the **`show password encryption`** command.

Configure the Interfaces

Next the interfaces should be configured. Recall that the ASA 5505 has 8 Layer 2 switch ports. Therefore, two types of interfaces must be configured: the logical VLAN interface which is also referred to as a switch virtual interface (SVI), and the Layer 2 ports which are assigned to VLANs.

Use the following commands to configure the logical VLAN interface:

- **`interface vlan `*`vlan-number`*** Creates a switch virtual interface (SVI).

- **`nameif `*`name`*** Assigns a name to the SVI interface.

- **`security-level `*`value`*** Assigns a security level to the SVI interface.

Default security level values are assigned to the inside interface and outside interface. Therefore, the **`security-level`** command is required only if an administrator chooses to change those values. Any other interface should be assigned a security level value.

The IP address of an interface can be configured using three options:

- Manually
- Using DHCP
- Using PPPoE

To manually configure an IP address, use the following:

- **`ip address `*`ip-address netmask`*** Command to assign an IP address and mask to the SVI.

Refer to
Figure
in online course

If the interface is connecting to an upstream device providing DHCP services, then the interface can be a DHCP client and can discover its IP address and DHCP-related information using the following:

- `ip address dhcp` Interface configuration command that requests an IP address from the upstream device.

- `ip address dhcp setroute` Same command but it also requests and installs a default route to the upstream device.

If the interface is connecting to an upstream DSL device providing point-to-point over Ethernet services, then it can discover its IP address by using the following:

- `ip address pppoe` Interface configuration command that requests an IP address from the upstream device.

- `ip address pppoe setroute` Same command but it also requests and installs a default route to the upstream device.

CAUTION: An ASA 5505 with a Base license does not allow three fully functioning VLAN interfaces to be created. However, a third "limited" VLAN interface can be created if it is first configured with the `no forward interface vlan` command. This command limits the interface from initiating contact to another VLAN. Therefore, when the inside and outside VLAN interfaces are configured, the `no forward interface vlan` *number* command must be entered before the `nameif` command is entered on the third interface. The *number* argument specifies the VLAN ID to which this VLAN interface cannot initiate traffic. The Security Plus license is required to achieve full functionality.

The Layer 2 ports must be assigned to a VLAN. By default, all Layer 2 switch ports are assigned to VLAN 1. Therefore, to change the default VLAN assignment, the Layer 2 port must be configured with the following commands:

- `switchport access vlan` *vlan-id* Changes the VLAN assignment of the port from the default of VLAN 1.

- `no shutdown` Enables the Layer 2 port.

Note: The running configuration will only display the `switchport access vlan` command for interfaces whose VLAN membership has been changed from the default VLAN 1. Interfaces in the default VLAN 1 do not display the `switchport access vlan 1` command.

To verify VLAN settings, use the `show switch vlan` command. To verify interface settings use the `show interface` or `show int ip brief` commands.

Configure a Default Route

If an ASA is configured as a DHCP client, then it can receive and install a default route from the upstream device. Otherwise, a default static route will have to be configured using the using the `route` *interface-name* `0.0.0.0 0.0.0.0` *next-hop-ip-address* command. To verify the route entry, use the `show route` command.

Note: Additional HTTP commands are required to allow ASDM to connect to the ASA.

Refer to
Figure
in online course

Configure Telnet Access

The ASA can be configured to accept Telnet connections from a single host or a range of hosts on the inside network. To enable the Telnet service, use the following commands:

- `passwd` *password* Configures the Telnet / SSH password.

- **telnet** Identifies which inside host can telnet to the ASA.

- **telnet timeout** *minutes* Alters the default exec timeout of 5 minutes.

SSH is also supported but requires AAA authentication to be enabled. Use the following commands to enable SSH support:

- **username** *name* **password** *password* Creates a local database entry.

- **aaa authentication ssh console LOCAL** Configures SSH to refer to the local database for authentication. The LOCAL keyword is case sensitive and is a predefined server tag.

- **crypto key generate rsa modulus 1024** Generates the RSA key required for SSH encryption.

- **ssh** *ip-addresssubnet-maskinterface-name* Identifies which inside host can SSH to the ASA.

- **ssh timeout** *minutes* Alters the default exec timeout of 5 minutes.

To verify the SSH configuration, use the **show ssh** command.

Configure NTP Services

Network Time Protocol (NTP) services can be configured on an ASA. Use the following global configuration commands to enable and configure NTP:

- **ntp server** *ip-address* Identifies the NTP server address.

- **ntp authentication-key** Configures the authentication key and password.

- **ntp trusted-key** *value* Identifies which configured key is to be trusted.

- **ntp authenticate** Enables NTP authentication.

To verify the NTP configuration and status, use the **show ntp status** and **show ntp associations** commands.

Refer to
Figure
in online course

Configure DHCP Services

An ASA can be configured to be a DHCP client and a DHCP server.

As a DHCP client, an interface is configured to receive its IP address and DHCP-related information from an upstream device. To configure an ASA interface as a DHCP client, use the **ip address dhcp [setroute]** interface configuration command. The **setroute** option can be added to request and install a default route from the upstream device.

As a DHCP server, the ASA provides IP addresses and DHCP-related information to inside hosts. To enable an ASA as a DHCP server and provide DHCP services to inside hosts, configure the following:

- **dhcpd enable inside** Enables the DHCP server service (daemon) on the inside interface of the ASA.

- **dhcpd address** [*start-of-pool*]-[*end-of-pool*] **inside** Defines the pool of IP addresses and assigns the pool to inside users. Notice that the *start-of-pool* and *end-of-pool* IP addresses are separated by a hyphen.

Note: The ASA 5505 Base license is a 10-user license and therefore the maximum number of DHCP clients supported is 32. For a 50-user license, the maximum is 128 clients. For an unlimited user license, the maximum is 250 (which is the same as all other ASA models).

DHCP options such as DNS, domain name, WINS, and lease time can all be manually configured as follows:

- `dhcpd domain domain-name` Configures the DNS domain name.

- `dhcpd dns dns-ip-address` Configures the DNS server IP address.

- `dhcpd wins wins-ip-address` Command to configure the WINS server address.

- `dhcpd lease seconds` Configures the lease time in seconds. The default is 3600 seconds (1 hour).

- `dhcpd option value` Configures the DHCP option code. Option code is in the range 0 - 250.

If the ASA outside interface was configured as a DHCP client, then the `dhcpd auto_config outside` global configuration command can be used to pass DNS, WINS, and domain information obtained from the DHCP client on the outside interface to the DHCP clients on the inside interface.

To verify DHCP settings, use the following commands:

- `show dhcpd state` Displays the current DHCP state for inside and outside interfaces.

- `show dhcpd binding` Displays the current DHCP bindings of inside users.

- `show dhcpd statistics` Displays the current DHCP statistics.

To clear the DHCP bindings or statistics, use the `clear dhcpd binding` or `clear dhcpd statistics` command.

Note: NAT service is covered later in this chapter.

10.2.3 Introduction to ASDM

Refer to **Figure** in online course

Cisco ASDM is a Java-based GUI tool that facilitates the setup, configuration, monitoring, and troubleshooting of Cisco ASAs. The application hides the complexity of commands from administrators, and allows streamlined configurations without requiring extensive knowledge of the ASA CLI. It works with SSL to ensure secure communication with the ASA. Cisco ASDM can be used to monitor and configure multiple ASAs that run the same ASDM version.

ASDM is now preloaded in flash memory on any ASA running versions 7.0 and later. ASDM can be run as a Java Web Start application that is dynamically downloaded from the ASA flash. This allows an administrator to configure and monitor that ASA device. Otherwise ASDM can also be downloaded from flash and installed locally on a host as an application. This allows an administrator to use ASDM to configure and manage multiple ASA devices.

ASDM access requires some minimal configurations to communicate over the network with a management interface. The management interface depends on the model of ASA:

- *Cisco ASA 5505* The management switch port can be any port, except for Ethernet 0/0.

- *Cisco ASA 5510 and higher* The interface to connect is Management 0/0.

To allow access to ASDM, configure the ASA to allow HTTPS connections from any host on the inside network. Use these commands:

- `http server enable` Enables the ASA HTTP server.

- `http ip-address subnet-mask interface-name` Specifies a host or hosts that can access the ASA HTTP server using ASDM.

Note: To remove and disable the ASA HTTP server service, use the global configuration command `clear configure http`.

Refer to
Figure
in online course

The ASDM interface can be accessed from any workstation with an IP address included in the HTTP trusted network list. Before attempting to establish a secure connection to the ASA, verify that IP connectivity exists between the workstation and the Cisco ASA.

With a factory default configuration, a host on the 192.168.1.0/24 network can connect to the ASA default management IP address of 192.168.1.1 using ASDM. The host must establish a connection through a browser to the inside interface IP address using the HTTPS protocol. Depending on the browser settings, a security certificate window may appear. Select **Yes** to continue to the ASDM launcher window.

The ASDM launcher window provides three choices:

- *Install ASDM Launcher and Run ASDM* Install ASDM as an application on the host. The advantage of doing so is that one application can be used to manage several ASA devices. An Internet browser will no longer be required to start ASDM.

- *Run ASDM* Run ASDM as a Java Web start application. The advantage is that the ASDM application is not installed on the local host. An Internet browser is required to establish a connection.

- *Run Startup Wizard* Run the ASDM Startup Wizard. This choice is similar to the Setup Initialization wizard and provides step-by-step windows to help initially configure the ASA.

Selecting the Run ASDM option will open an ASDM authentication window. If starting ASDM for the first time after running a Startup wizard, the fields should be left empty. If SSH has been configured, then a local database username and password should be used.

When authentication is successful, the ASDM Home page will be displayed.

Refer to
Figure
in online course

The Cisco ASDM Home page displays important information about the ASA. Status information in the Home page is updated every 10 seconds. Although many of the details available in the Home page are available elsewhere in ASDM, this page provides a quick view of the operational status of ASA.

The Cisco ASDM user interface is designed to provide easy access to the many features that the ASA supports. All pages include the following elements:

- *Menu bar* Provides quick access to files, tools, wizards, and help.

- *Toolbar* Provides easy navigation of Cisco ASDM. From the toolbar an administrator can access the Home, Configuration, and Monitoring views as well as save, refresh, navigate between views, and access Help.

- *Device List button* Opens a dockable page that lists other ASA devices. Use this page to switch to another device running the same version of ASDM. When managing only one ASA device, the Device List page is hidden and must be opened using the Device List button.

- *Status bar* Displays the time, connection status, user, memory status, running configuration status, privilege level, and SSL status at the bottom of the application window.

By default, the Home page also displays two tabs:

- *Device Dashboard* Provides a view of important information about the ASA, such as the status of interfaces, the OS version, licensing information, and performance related information.

- *Firewall Dashboard* Provides security related information about traffic that passes through the ASA, such as connection statistics, dropped packets, scan and syn attack detection.

Other tabs the Home page may display include:

- *Intrusion Prevention* Appears only if an IPS module or card is installed. The additional tab displays status information about the IPS software.

- *Content Security* Appears only if a CSC-SSM is installed in the ASA. The Content Security tab displays status information about the CSC-SSM software.

The Configuration and Monitoring views also feature a dockable navigation pane that can be maximized, restored, or made to float so that it can be moved, hidden, or closed. The navigation pane of the Configuration view displays the following tabs:

- Device Setup

- Firewall

- Remote-Access VPN

- Site-to-Site VPN

- Device Management

The navigation pane of the Monitoring view displays the following tabs:

- Interfaces

- VPN

- Routing

- Properties

- Logging

The options listed in the navigation pane will vary depending on the view and tab that is selected.

Refer to
Figure
in online course

The ASDM Configuration view is required to configure basic device management settings via the Device Setup tab. Settings that can be configured include the system time, hostname, passwords, interface settings, and routing. Click the **Apply** button to save any changes made.

The Device Setup tab also features the Startup wizard, which is similar to the interactive Setup Initialization wizard. Launching the wizard will guide an administrator through creating a basic configuration for the ASA. Any values previously configured are used as the current values.

To configure the hostname, domain name, enable, and Telnet passwords, choose **Configuration > Device Setup > Device Name/Password**. The hostname appears in the command line prompt and is also used in system messages. The ASA appends the domain name as a suffix to unqualified names. The Telnet password sets the login password which by default is set to "cisco." The Telnet password applies to Telnet and SSH access.

Optionally, a master passphrase can be created to encrypt all passwords. To do so, choose **Configuration > Device Management > Advanced > Master Passphrase**.

To change the system time, choose **Configuration > Device Setup > System Time > Clock**. From this screen, the time zone, date, and time can be configured manually. The date and time can also be configured dynamically using an NTP server. The time is displayed in the status bar in the bottom right hand corner.

To configure the Layer 3 interfaces, choose **Configuration > Device Setup > Interfaces**. In this window, the ASA inside and outside interfaces can be created or edited.

To configure the Layer 2 ports, choose **Configuration > Device Setup > Interfaces > Switch Ports**. In this window, Layer 2 ports can be enabled and associated with a specific VLAN interface.

To configure a default route, choose **Configuration > Device Setup > Routing > Static Routes**. In this window, static and default static routes can be entered or edited.

Refer to
Figure
in online course

To configure NTP, choose **Configuration > Device Setup > System Time > NTP**. In this window, the administrator can add, edit, or delete an NTP server. When adding a server, the IP address and authentication parameters can be configured. Time derived from an NTP server overrides any time set manually.

To configure management access for Telnet and SSH services, choose **Configuration > Device Management > Management Access > ASDM/HTTPS/Telnet/SSH**. In this window, an administrator can identify which host or networks can have access to the ASA via ASDM/HTTPS, Telnet, or SSH.

To enable DHCP server services, choose **Configuration > Device Management > DHCP > DHCP Server**. In this window, the general DHCP settings can be modified. The inside and outside DHCP settings can be edited by clicking the **Edit** button.

Be sure to click the **Apply** button any time a change is made.

10.2.4 ASDM Wizards

Refer to
Figure
in online course

Cisco ASDM offers several wizards to help simplify the configuration of the appliance:

- Startup Wizard

- VPN Wizards

- High Availability and Scalability Wizard

- Unified Communication Wizard

- Packet Capture Wizard

Refer to
Figure
in online course

The Startup wizard guides the administrator through the initial configuration of the ASA and helps to define basic settings. The Startup wizard can be activated by choosing either **Wizards > Startup Wizard**, or **Configuration > Device Setup > Startup Wizard**. After the Startup wizard page appears, click the **Launch Startup Wizard** button.

The actual number of steps in the wizard may vary depending on the specific ASA model and modules installed. However, most ASA models can be configured in a nine-step process.

After the Startup wizard has been launched, follow these steps:

Step 1. The Starting Point window (also referred to as the Welcome window) is displayed and provides a choice to **Modify an Existing Configuration** or to **Reset the Configuration to Factory Defaults**. Select an option and click **Next** to continue.

Step 2. In the Basic Configuration window, complete the basic ASA management configuration consisting of a host name, domain name, and privileged EXEC password. Optionally, this step also allows the administrator to deploy the ASA for a remote worker. Complete the options and click **Next** to continue.

Step 3. In the Interface Selection window, create the VLAN switch interfaces. This step is specific to the ASA 5505 model. Complete the options and click **Next** to continue.

Step 4. In the Switch Port Allocation window, map the physical Layer 2 switch ports to the logically named VLANs in the previous step. By default, all switch ports are assigned to VLAN 1 (Inside). Click **Next** to continue.

Step 5. In the Interface IP Address Configuration window, identify the inside and outside IP addresses for the defined VLANs. Note that these addresses could also be created using DHCP or PPPoE. Complete the options and click **Next** to continue.

Step 6. The DHCP window allows the administrator to enable the DHCP service for inside hosts. All DHCP related options are defined in this window. Complete the options and click **Next** to continue.

Step 7. The Address Translation (NAT/PAT) window allows the administrator to enable PAT or NAT. Complete the options and click **Next** to continue.

Step 8. In the Administrative Access window, specify which host or hosts are allowed to access the ASA using either HTTPS/ASDM, SSH, or Telnet. Complete the options and click **Next** to continue.

Step 9. The final window is the Startup Wizard Summary. Review the proposed configuration. Changes can be made by clicking the **Back** button or saved by clicking the **Finish** button.

Refer to
Figure
in online course

The VPN wizard allows an administrator to configure basic site-to-site and remote-access VPN connections and assign either pre-shared keys or digital certificates for authentication.

To launch the VPN wizard from the Menu Bar, click **Wizards** and choose **VPN Wizards**.

The VPN wizards include:

- Site-to-site VPN wizard

- AnyConnect VPN wizard

- Clientless SSL VPN wizard

- IPsec (IKEv1) Remote Access VPN wizard

To compliment the wizards, ASDM also provides the ASDM Assistant. For example to view the remote-access ASDM Assistant, choose **Configurations > Remote-Access VPN > Introduction**.

After an initial configuration, ASDM can be used to edit and configure advanced features.

Refer to
Figure
in online course

Three other wizards are available in ASDM: the High Availability and Scalability wizard, the Unified Communication wizard, and the Packet Capture wizard.

The High Availability and Scalability wizard can guide an administrator to configure failover with high availability and VPN cluster load balancing. VPN cluster mode requires two ASA devices establishing VPN sessions to the same destination network and performing load balancing. Note that the ASA 5505 with Base license is unable to support this wizard.

There are two methods for accessing the wizard:

- Choose **Wizards > High Availability and Scalability Wizard**.

- Choose **Configuration > Device Management > High Availability > HA/Scalability Wizard**, and then click **Launch High Availability and Scalability Wizard**.

The Unified Communication wizard can be used to configure the ASA to support the Cisco Unified Communications Proxy feature. There are two methods for accessing the wizard:

- Choose **Wizards > Unified Communication Wizard**.

- Choose **Configuration > Firewall > Unified Communications** followed by **Unified Communication Wizard**.

Finally, the Packet Capture wizard is useful to configure and run captures for troubleshooting errors. It is also useful for validating a NAT policy. The captures can use access lists to limit the type of traffic captured, the source and destination addresses and ports, and one or more interfaces. The wizard runs one capture on each of the ingress and egress interfaces. Captures can be saved to a host and examined in a packet analyzer.

To initiate the Packet Capture wizard, choose **Wizards > Packet Capture Wizard**.

Note: The three wizards named above are out-of-scope for this chapter and will not be explored further.

10.2.5 Object Groups

Refer to **Figure** in online course

The ASA supports objects and object groups. Objects are created and used by the ASA in place of an inline IP address in any given configuration. An object can be defined with a particular IP address and netmask pair or a protocol (and, optionally, a port) and it can be re-used in several configurations. The advantage is that when an object is modified, the change is automatically applied to all rules that use the specified object. Therefore, objects make it easy to maintain configurations.

Objects can be attached or detached from one or more object groups when needed, ensuring that the objects are not duplicated but can be re-used wherever needed. These objects can be used in NAT, access lists, and object groups. Specifically, network objects are a vital part of configuring NAT.

There are two types of objects that can be configured:

- *Network object* Contains a single IP address/mask pair. Network objects can be of three types: host, subnet, or range.

- *Service object* Contains a protocol and optional source and/or destination port.

Note: A network object is required to configure NAT in ASA image versions 8.3 and higher.

Refer to **Figure** in online course

To create a network object, use the `object network` *object-name* global configuration command. The prompt will change to the network object configuration mode.

A network object name can contain only one IP address and mask pair. Therefore, there can only be one statement in the network object. Entering a second IP address/mask pair will replace the existing configuration.

Network objects can be defined using one of the following three methods:

- `host` *ip-addr* Assigns an IP address to the named object.

- `subnet` *net-address net-mask* Assigns a network subnet to the named object.

- `range` *ip-addr-1 ip-addr-n* Assigns IP addresses in a range.

Use the **no** form of any of these three commands to remove a network object. To erase all network objects, use the `clear config object network` command. Note that this command clears all network objects.

To create a service object, use the **object service** *object-name* global configuration command. The prompt will change to the service object configuration mode. The service object can contain a protocol, ICMP, ICMPv6, TCP, or UDP port or port ranges.

A service object name can only be associated with one protocol and port (or ports). If an existing service object is configured with a different protocol and port (or ports), the new configuration replaces the existing protocol and port (or ports) with the new ones.

There are five service options:

- **service** *protocol* [**source** [*operator port*]] [**destination** [*operator port*]] Specifies an IP protocol name or number.

- **service tcp** [**source** [*operator port*]] [**destination** [*operator port*]] Specifies that the service object is for the TCP protocol.

- **service udp** [**source** [*operator port*]] [**destination** [*operator port*]] Specifies that the service object is for the UDP protocol.

- **service icmp** *icmp-type* Specifies that the service object is for the ICMP protocol.

- **service icmp6** *icmp6-type* Specifies that the service object is for the ICMPv6 protocol.

Optional keywords are used to identify source port or destination port or both. Operators, such as **eq**, **neq**, **lt**, **gt**, and **range** support configuring a port for a given protocol. If no operator is specified, the default operator is eq.

Use the **no** form of the command to remove a service object. To erase all service objects, use the **clear config object service** command. This command clears all service objects.

To verify, use the **show running-config object** command.

Refer to **Figure** in online course

Objects can be grouped together to create an object group. By grouping like objects together, an object group can be used in an access control entry (ACE) instead of having to enter an ACE for each object separately.

The following guidelines and limitations apply to object groups:

- Objects and object groups share the same name space.

- Object groups must have unique names.

- An object group cannot be removed or emptied if it is used in a command.

- The ASA does not support IPv6 nested object groups.

The ASA supports the following types of object groups:

- Network

- Protocol

- ICMP-type

- Service

Refer to **Figure** in online course

To configure a network object group, use the **object-group network** *grp-name* global configuration command. After entering the command, add network objects to the network group with the following commands:

- **network-object**

- **group-object**

Note: A network object group cannot be used to implement NAT. A network object is required to implement NAT.

To configure a protocol object group, use the `object-group protocol` *grp-name* global configuration command. After entering the command, define a group of protocols such as TCP and UDP. Add network objects to the protocol group with the following commands:

- `protocol-object`

- `group-object`

To configure an ICMP object group, use the `object-group icmp-type` *grp-name* global configuration command. After entering the command, add ICMP objects with the following commands:

- `icmp-object`

- `group-object`

To configure a service object group, use the `object-group service` *grp-name* global configuration command. The service object group can define a mix of TCP services, UDP services, ICMP-type services, and any protocol. After entering the `object-group service` command, add service objects to the service group with the following commands:

- `service-object`

- `group-object`

To configure a service object group for TCP, UDP, or TCP and UDP, specify the option in the `object-group service` *grp-name* [`tcp` ¦ `udp` ¦ `tcp-udp`] global configuration command. When `tcp`, `udp`, or `tcp-udp` is optionally specified on the command line, service defines a standard service object group of TCP/UDP port specifications such as "eq smtp" and "range 2000 2010." After entering the command, add port objects to the service group with the following commands:

- `port-object`

- `group-object`

To remove all the object groups from the configuration, use the `clear configure object-group` global configuration command.

To verify group object configurations, use the `show running-config object-group` command.

Practical examples of object groups will be presented when configuring ACLs and NAT.

Refer to **Figure** in online course
To configure a network object or a network object group in ASDM, choose **Configuration > Firewall > Objects > Network Objects/Groups**. From this window, the administrator can add, edit, or delete a network object or a network object group.

To configure service objects, service object groups, ICMP object groups, or protocol object groups, choose **Configuration > Firewall > Objects > Service Objects/Groups**. From this window, the administrator can add, edit, or delete a service object or a service object groups, ICMP object groups, and/or protocol object groups.

10.2.6 ACLs

Refer to **Figure** in online course
The Cisco ASA 5500 provides basic traffic filtering capabilities with ACLs. ACLs control access in a network by preventing defined traffic from entering or exiting.

There are many similarities between ASA ACLs and IOS ACLs. For example, both are made up of ACEs, processed sequentially from top down, and there is an implicit **deny all**. Additionally, the rule of only one ACL per interface, per protocol, per direction still applies.

ASA ACLs differ from IOS ACLs in that they use a network mask (e.g., 255.255.255.0) instead of a wildcard mask (e.g. 0.0.0.255). Also most ASA ACLs are named instead of numbered.

Another difference is due to the ASA interface security levels. By default, security levels apply access control without an ACL configured. For instance, traffic from a more secure interface (such as security level 100) is allowed to access less secure interfaces (such as level 0). Traffic from a less secure interface is blocked from accessing more secure interfaces.

For example, a host from the inside interface with security level 100 can access the outside interface with security level 0. But an outside host from an outside interface with security level 0 cannot access the inside higher level interface. Therefore an ACL would be required to permit traffic from a lower security level to a higher security level.

Note: To allow connectivity between interfaces with the same security levels, the **same-security-traffic permit inter-interface** global configuration command is required. To enable traffic to enter and exit the same interface, such as when encrypted traffic enters an interface and is then routed out the same interface unencrypted, use the **same-security-traffic permit intra-interface** global configuration command. These commands are beyond the scope of this chapter.

ACLs on a security appliance can be used not only to filter out packets passing through the appliance but also to filter out packets destined to the appliance.

- *Through-traffic filtering* Traffic that is passing through the security appliance from one interface to another interface. The configuration is completed in two steps; Set up an ACL and apply that ACL to an interface.

- *To-the-box-traffic filtering* Also known as a management access rule, applies to traffic that terminates on the ASA. Introduced in version 8.0 to filter traffic destined to the control plane of the ASA. It is completed in one step but requires an additional set of rules to implement access control.

The ASA supports five types of access lists:

- *Extended access lists* The most common type of ACL. Contains one or more ACEs to specify source and destination addresses and protocol, ports (for TCP or UDP), or the ICMP type (for ICMP).

- *Standard access lists* Unlike IOS where a standard ACL identifies the source host/network, ASA standard ACLs are used to identify the destination IP addresses. They are typically only used for OSPF routes and can be used in a route map for OSPF redistribution. Standard access lists cannot be applied to interfaces to control traffic.

- *EtherType access lists* An EtherType ACL can be configured only if the security appliance is running in transparent mode.

- *Webtype access lists* Used in a configuration that supports filtering for clientless SSL VPN.

- *IPv6 access lists* Used to determine which IPv6 traffic to block and which traffic to forward at router interfaces.

Use the **help access-list** privileged EXEC command to display the syntax for all of the ACLs supported on an ASA platform.

Note: The focus of this chapter will be on extended ACLs.

Refer to
Figure
in online course

The ACL configuration syntax options for the ASA can be a little overwhelming considering the number of parameters supported. These parameters not only give an administrator full control over what to inspect, but also provide full logging capabilities in order to analyze traffic flows at a later time.

IOS and ASA ACLs have similar elements, but some options vary with the ASA. For example:

- *ACL name* Can be any alphanumeric name up to 241 characters.
- *Type* Can be extended, standard, or webtype.
- *Action* Can be **permit** or **deny**.
- *Protocol number* Can be **ip** for all traffic, or the name / IP protocol number (0-250) including **icmp (1)**, **tcp (6)**, **udp (17)**. Can also be a protocol object-group.
- *Source* Identifies the source and can be **any**, a **host**, a network, or a network object group. For to-the-box-traffic filtering, the interface keyword is used to specify the source interface of the ASA.
- *Source port operator* (Optional) Operand is used in conjunction with the source port. Valid operands include **lt** (less than), **gt** (greater than), **eq** (equal), **neq** (not equal), and **range** for an inclusive range.
- *Source port* (Optional) Can be the actual TCP or UDP port number, select port name, or service object group.
- *Destination* Identifies the destination and like the source, it can be **any**, a **host**, a network, or a network object group. For to-the-box-traffic filtering, the **interface** keyword is used to specify the destination interface of the ASA.
- *Destination port operator* (Optional) Operand is used in conjunction with the destination port. Valid operands are the same as the source port operands.
- *Destination port* (Optional) Can be the actual TCP or UDP port number, select port name, or service object group.
- *Log* Can set elements for syslog. Options include setting the severity level number or name, the log interval from the default of 300 seconds. Logging can also be reset to the default, or disabled for this ACE.
- *Time range* (Optional) Specify a time range for this ACE.

Note: Explanation of all ACL syntax is beyond the scope of this chapter and will not be explored further.

There are many options that can be used with ACLs. However, for most needs, a more useful and condensed version of the syntax is as follows:

```
access-list id extended {deny ¦ permit} protocol {source-addr source-mask} ¦ any ¦
host src-host interface src-if-name [operator port [port]] {dest-addr dest-mask} ¦
any ¦ host dst-host ¦ interface dst-if-name [operator port [port]]
```

After you configure an ACL to identify traffic allowed or denied by the ASA, the next step is to apply the ACL to an interface in either the inbound or the outbound direction. Apply the ACL as follows:

```
access-group access-list {in ¦ out} interface interface-name [per-user-override ¦
control-plane]
```

To verify ACLs, use the **show access-list** and **show running-config access-list** commands.

To erase a configured ACL, use the **clear configure access-list** id command.

Refer to
Figure
in online course

Consider a situation that requires access from two external hosts to two internal servers providing web and e-mail services. All other traffic attempting to pass through the ASA should be dropped and logged.

The ACL would require two ACEs for each PC. The implicit **deny all** will drop and log any packets that do not match email or web services. ACLs should always be well documented using the **remark** command.

To verify the ACL syntax, use the **show running-config access-list** and **show access-list** commands.

Refer to
Figure
in online course

Object grouping is a way to group similar items together to reduce the number of ACEs. By grouping like objects together, object groups can be used in an ACL instead of having to enter an ACE for each object separately. Without object grouping, the security appliance configuration may contain thousands of lines of ACEs, which can become hard to manage.

The following is a condensed version of the **access-list** command highlighting the configurable object group parameters:

```
access-list id [line line-num] [extended] {deny ¦ permit} object-group protocol-
obj-grp-id object-group network-obj-grp-id object-group service-obj-grp-id]
object-group network-obj-grp-id object-group service-obj-grp-id] [log level]
[interval secs] [[disable ¦ default] ¦ [time-range time-range-ID]] ¦ [inactive]
```

The security appliance follows the multiplication factor rule when ACEs are defined. For example, if two outside hosts need to access two internal servers running HTTP and SMTP services, the ASA will have 8 host-based ACEs. They should be calculated as follows:

Number of ACEs = (2 internal servers) x (2 outside hosts) x (2 services) = 8

Object grouping can cluster network objects such as internal servers into one group and outside hosts into another. The security appliance can also combine both TCP services into a service object group.

For example, consider the previous extended ACL example had a total of 9 ACEs (8 permit ACEs plus the implicit deny ACE). Creating the following objects can help simplify the actual ACL-IN ACL to one ACE. For example, the following object groups are created:

- *Protocol object group named TCP* Identifies all of the TCP protocols.

- *Network object group named Internet-Hosts* Identifies two external hosts.

- *Network object group named Internal-Servers* Identifies servers providing e-mail and web services.

- *Service object group HTTP-SMTP* Identifies SMTP and HTTP protocols.

After object groups have been configured, they can be used in any ACL and multiple ACLs. A single ACE could be used to allow trusted hosts to make specific service requests to a group of internal servers.

Although the configuration of object groups may seem tedious, the advantage is that these objects can be reused in other ASA commands and they can easily be altered. For instance, if a new internal mail server needs to be added, then all that is required is to edit the Internal-Servers object group.

Note: Object groups can also be nested in other object groups.

Refer to
Figure
in online course

In ASDM, access rules can be created and maintained using the Access Rules window. To open the window, choose **Configuration > Firewall > Access Rules**.

From this page, a new toolbar appears providing options to add, edit, or delete rules. These options are also available by right-clicking a particular rule.

Other tools are available to simplify the process of rule management. In-pane editing is available for specific components of each rule, for instance changing the source or destination IP addresses or ports on each line, without having to enter the rule edit options. Rules can also be moved up or down, copied and cloned, or temporarily disabled and re-enabled.

A diagram is displayed at the bottom of the rule set, providing a more visual statement to understand and troubleshoot specific rules.

10.2.7 NAT Services on an ASA

Refer to
Figure
in online course

Like IOS routers, the ASA supports NAT and PAT and these addresses can also be provided either statically or dynamically.

NAT and PAT can be deployed using one of these methods:

- *Inside NAT* The typical NAT deployment method is when a host from a higher-security interface has traffic destined for a lower-security interface and the ASA translates the internal host address to a global address. The ASA then restores the original inside IP address for return traffic.

- *Outside NAT* This method is used when traffic from a lower-security interface is destined for a host on the higher-security interface is translated. This method may be useful to make a host on the outside appear as one from a known internal IP address.

- *Bidirectional NAT* Indicates that both inside NAT and outside NAT are used together.

By default, Cisco ASA does not require an address translation policy to be created when the higher level security interfaces need to access resources on lower security-level interfaces. However, if a packet matches a NAT/PAT policy, the ASA translates the address.

Refer to
Figure
in online course

Traditionally, NAT was configured using the **nat**, **global**, and **static** commands. However, Auto-NAT is a new feature introduced in ASA version 8.3 that has replaced that method of configuring NAT. The **global** and **static** commands are no longer supported. Auto-NAT has considerably simplified the configuration and troubleshooting of NAT.

Auto-NAT takes advantage of using network objects as the building blocks to configure all variations of NAT. A network object is created and it is within this object that the NAT is configured. Recall that network objects can be used to identify a host, subnet, or range of IP addresses using one of three methods:

- **host** *ip-addr* Command assigns an IP address to the named object.

- **subnet** *net-address net-mask* Assigns a network subnet to the named object.

- **range** *ip-addr-1 ip-addr-n* Assigns an IP addresses in a range.

Additionally the **nat** command parameters must be specified in the object using the following command:

- **nat** [(*real-ifc*,*mapped-ifc*)] **dynamic** {*mapped-inline-host-ip* [**interface**] ¦ [*mapped-obj*] [**pat-pool** *mapped-obj* [**round-robin**]] [**interface**]} [**dns**]

The choice of parameters to choose from is directly related to the type of NAT required.

The ASA divides the NAT configuration into two sections. The first section defines the network to be translated using a network object. The second section defines the actual **nat** command parameters. These appear in two different places in the running-config.

Therefore, two commands are required to display the NAT configuration. Use the **show run object** command to display the network object and use the **show run nat** command to display the NAT running configuration.

Cisco ASA supports the following common types of network address translation:

- *Dynamic NAT* Many-to-many translation. Usually an inside pool of private addresses requiring public addresses from another pool.

- *Dynamic PAT* Many-to-one translation. Usually an inside pool of private addresses overloading an outside interface or outside address.

- *Static NAT* A one-to-one translation. Usually an outside address mapping to an internal server.

Another ASA version 8.3 feature is called Twice-NAT. Twice-NAT identifies both the source and destination address in a single rule (**nat** command). Twice-NAT is used when configuring remote-access IPsec and SSL VPNs.

Note: Twice-NAT is beyond the scope of the chapter and will not be explored further.

Refer to
Figure
in online course

To configure Dynamic NAT, two network objects are required. The first network object identifies the pool of public IP addresses that internal addresses will be translated to. The second network object binds the two objects together. Use the following commands:

- **object network** *mapped-obj* Names the network object that identifies the pool of public addresses.

- **range** *ip-addr-1 ip-addr-n* Assigns IP addresses in a range.

- **object network** *nat-object-name* Names the NAT object.

- **subnet** *net-address net-mask* Assigns a network subnet to the named object. Alternatively the **range** command could be used.

- **nat (**real-ifc,mapped-ifc**) dynamic** *mapped-obj* Maps a static address to a mapped-inline-host-ip address.

To configure Dynamic PAT, use the following commands:

- **object network** *nat-object-name* Names the PAT object.

- **subnet** *net-address net-mask* Assigns a network subnet to the named object. Alternatively the **range** command could also be used.

- **nat (**real-ifc,mapped-ifc**) dynamic interface** Provides inside hosts on the *real-ifc* to overload the outside address of the *mapped-ifc* interface.

A variation to this configuration is called Dynamic PAT. This is when an actual external IP address is configured and overloaded instead of the ASA interface IP address.

To configure Static NAT, where an inside address is mapped to an outside address, use the following commands:

- **object network** *nat-object-name* Names the static NAT object.

- **host** *ip-addr* Identifies the host inside IP address.

- **nat (**real-ifc,mapped-ifc**) static** *mapped-inline-host-ip* Statically maps an inside address to an outside address.

Note: The **any** keyword could be used instead of the *mapped-ifc* parameter. This allows the translation of an object between multiple interfaces with just one CLI command. For example, **nat** `(dmz, any) static 209.165.200.227` would allow any device on any internal network access to the DMZ server using the outside IP address.

An ACL is required for the translation to be successful. Unlike IOS ACLs, the ASA must permit access to the internal private DMZ address from the outside. External hosts access the server using its public static NAT address and the ASA translates it to the internal host IP address and applies the ACL.

Use the `show nat` and `show xlate` commands to verify translations. It may be necessary to use the `clear nat counters` command when testing NAT.

Refer to
Figure
in online course

Dynamic NAT Configuration

To configure Dynamic NAT in ASDM, choose **Configurations > Firewall > Objects > Network Objects/Groups** and then click **Add > Network Object**. The Add Network Object window will appear. Complete the following:

- *Name* Enter a network object name.

- *Type* Choose **Network** or **Range**.

- *IP Address* Enter the network address of the internal hosts.

- *Netmask* Enter the netmask.

- *Description* Enter an optional description.

If the NAT section is hidden, click **NAT** to expand the section and continue:

- Check the **Add Automatic Address Translation Rules** check box.

- *Type* Choose **Dynamic**.

- *Translated Addr* To the right of the field, click the browse button and choose an existing network object or create a new object from the Browse Translated Addr dialog box.

Dynamic PAT Configuration

To configure Dynamic PAT in ASDM, choose **Configurations > Firewall > Objects > Network Objects/Groups** and then click **Add > Network Object**. The Add Network Object window will appear. Complete the following:

- *Name* Enter a network object name.

- *Type* Choose **Network** or **Range**.

- *IP Address* Enter the network address of the internal hosts.

- *Netmask* Enter the netmask.

- *Description* Enter an optional description.

If the NAT section is hidden, click **NAT** to expand the section and continue:

- Check the **Add Automatic Address Translation Rules** check box.

- *Type* Choose **Dynamic**.

- *Translated Addr* Leave it empty

- Check the **PAT Translated Address** checkbox and click the browse button and choose an existing network object or create a new object.

Static NAT Configuration

To configure Static NAT in ASDM, choose **Configurations > Firewall > Objects > Network Objects/Groups** and then click **Add > Network Object**. The Add Network Object window will appear. Complete the following:

- *Name* Enter a network object name.
- *Type* Choose **Host**.
- *IP Address* Enter the IP address of the internal host.
- *Description* Enter an optional description.

If the NAT section is hidden, click **NAT** to expand the section and continue:

- Check the **Add Automatic Address Translation Rules** check box.
- *Type* Choose **Dynamic**.
- *Translated Addr* Enter the public IP address to translate to.

To verify the NAT rules, choose **Configurations > Firewall > NAT Rules** to open the NAT Rules window.

10.2.8 Access Control on an ASA

Refer to
Figure
in online course

Authentication, Authorization, and Accounting (AAA) provides an extra level of protection and user control. Using AAA only, authenticated and authorized users can be permitted to connect through the ASA. Authentication can be used alone or with authorization and accounting. Authorization always requires a user to be authenticated first. Accounting can be used alone, or with authentication and authorization.

Authentication controls access by requiring valid user credentials, which are usually a username and password. The ASA can authenticate all administrative connections to the ASA, including Telnet, SSH, console, ASDM using HTTPS, and privileged EXEC.

Authorization controls access, per user, after users are authenticated. Authorization controls the services and commands that are available to each authenticated user. Without authorization enabled, authentication alone would provide the same access to services for all authenticated users. The ASA can authorize the following items:

- Management commands
- Network access
- VPN access

The ASA caches the first 16 authorization requests per user. Therefore, if the user accesses the same services during the current authentication session, the ASA does not resend the request to the authorization server.

Accounting tracks traffic that passes through the ASA, enabling administrators to have a record of user activity. Accounting information includes session start and stop times, usernames, the number of bytes that pass through the ASA for the session, the service used, and the duration of each session.

Refer to
Figure
in online course

Cisco ASA can be configured to authenticate using a local user database or an external server for authentication or both.

Local AAA uses a local database for authentication. This method stores usernames and passwords locally on the ASA, and users authenticate against the local database. Local AAA is ideal for small networks that do not need a dedicated AAA server.

Note: Unlike the ISR, ASA devices do not support local authentication without using AAA.

Use the **username** *name* **password** *password* [**privilege** *priv-level*] command to create local user accounts.

To erase a user from the local database, use the **clear config username** [*name*] command. To view all user accounts, use the **show running-conf username** command.

Server-based AAA authentication is a far more scalable method than local AAA authentication. Server-based AAA authentication uses an external database server resource leveraging RADIUS or TACACS+ protocols. Examples include Cisco Secure Access Control Server (ACS) for Windows Server, Cisco Secure ACS Solution Engine, or Cisco Secure ACS Express. If there are multiple networking devices, server-based AAA is more appropriate.

To configure a TACACS+ or RADIUS server, use the following commands:

- **aaa-server** *server-tag* **protocol** *protocol* Creates a TACACS+ or RADIUS AAA server group.

- **aaa-server** *server-tag* [(*interface-name*)] **host** {*server-ip* ¦ *name*} [*key*] Configures a AAA server as part of a AAA server group. Also configures AAA server parameters that are host-specific.

Parameters available will vary depending on the type of server chosen.

To erase all AAA server configurations, use the **clear config aaa-server** command. To view all user accounts, use the **show running-conf aaa-server** command.

Refer to
Figure
in online course

To authenticate users who access the ASA CLI over a console, SSH, HTTPS (ASDM), or Telnet connection, or to authenticate users who access privileged EXEC mode using the **enable** command, use the **aaa authentication console** command in global configuration mode.

The command syntax is as follows:

- **aaa authentication** {**serial** ¦ **enable** ¦ **telnet** ¦ **ssh** ¦ **http**} **console** {**LOCAL** ¦ *server-group* [**LOCAL**]}

To erase all AAA parameters, use the **clear config aaa** command. To view all user accounts, use the **show running-conf username** command.

Refer to
Figure
in online course

To enable AAA on an ASA:

Step 1. Create the local database entries.

To add or edit local database entries, choose **Configuration > Device Management > Users/AAA > User Accounts**. To add a user, click **Add**. Complete the Add User Account windows.

Step 2. Create the AAA server groups.

To create or edit a local AAA server group, choose **Configuration > Device Management > Users/AAA > AAA Server Groups**. To add a server, click the **Add** button on the right side of the AAA Server Groups window. Complete the Add AAA Server Group window.

Step 3. Add the AAA servers to the server groups.

To add AAA servers to group, choose **Configuration > Device Management > Users/AAA > AAA Server Groups**. To add a server to a specific Server Group, select a server in the AAA Server Group window and then click the **Add** button on the right side of the Servers in the Selected Group window. Complete the Add AAA Server window.

Step 4.   Click **Apply** to commit the changes.

Refer to
Figure
in online course

To bind the authentication with the AAA Server Groups and local database, choose **Configuration > Device Management > Users/AAA > AAA Access**.

From this window, an administrator can choose to configure Authentication, Authorization, and Accounting.

10.2.9 Service Policies on an ASA

Refer to
Figure
in online course

Modular Policy Framework (MPF) configuration defines a set of rules for applying firewall features, such as traffic inspection and QoS, to the traffic that traverses the ASA. MPF allows granular classification of traffic flows, to apply different advanced policies to different flows. MPF is used with hardware modules to redirect traffic granularly from the ASA to the modules that use Cisco MPF. MPF can be used for advanced Application Layer inspection of traffic by classifying at Layers 5 through 7. Rate limiting and QoS features can also be implemented using MPF.

Cisco MPF uses these three configuration objects to define modular, object-oriented, hierarchical policies:

- *Class maps* Define match criterion by using the `class-map` global configuration command.

- *Policy maps* Associate actions to the class map match criteria by using the `policy-map` global configuration command.

- *Service policies* Enable the policy by attaching it to an interface, or globally to all interfaces using the `service-policy` interface configuration command.

Although the MPF syntax is similar to the Cisco Modular QoS CLI (MQC) syntax, and the Cisco Common Classification Policy Language (C3PL) syntax, used on IOS routers, the configurable parameters differ. The ASA platform provides more configurable actions as compared to an ISR for Cisco IOS ZPF. The ASA supports Layer 5 through Layer 7 inspections using a richer set of criteria for application-specific parameters. For instance, the ASA MPF feature can be used to do the following:

- Match HTTP URLs and request methods.

- Prevent users from surfing to specific sites during specific times.

- Prevent users from downloading music (MP3) and video files via HTTP/FTP or HTTPS/SFTP.

Refer to
Figure
in online course

There are four steps to configure MPF on an ASA:

Step 1.   Configure extended ACLs to identify specific granular traffic. This step may be optional.

Step 2.   Configure the class map to identify traffic.

Step 3.   Configure a policy map to apply actions to those class maps.

Step 4.   Configure a service policy to attach the policy map to an interface.

Configure ACL

Extended ACLs are typically used to define traffic flows. These ACLs can be specifically referenced in the class map. For example, ACLs can be used to match:

- All TCP traffic

- All UDP traffic

- All HTTP traffic

- All traffic to a specific server

Configure Class Map

Class maps are configured to identify Layer 3/4 traffic. To create a class map and enter class-map configuration mode, use the **class-map** *class-map-name* global configuration command. The names "class-default" and any name that begins with "_internal" or "_default" are reserved. The class map name must be unique and can be up to 40 characters in length. The name should also be descriptive.

Note: A variation of the **class-map** command is used for management traffic that is destined to the ASA. In this case, use the **class-map type management** *class-map-name* command.

In class-map configuration mode, ciscoasa(config-cmap)#, define the traffic to include in the class by matching one of the following characteristics.

- **description** Add description text.

- **match any** Class map matches all traffic.

- **match access-list** *access-list-name* Class map matches traffic specified by an extended access list.

Note: Unless otherwise specified, only include one **match** command in the class map.

Default Global Policy

The class map configuration also includes a default Layer 3/4 class map that the ASA uses in the default global policy. It is called **inspection_default** and matches the default inspection traffic. For example:

```
class-map inspection_default
match default-inspection-traffic
```

The **match default-inspection-traffic** is a special CLI shortcut to match the default ports for all inspections. When used in a policy map, this class map ensures that the correct inspection is applied to each packet, based on the destination port of the traffic. For example, when UDP traffic for port 69 reaches the ASA, the ASA applies the TFTP inspection. In this case only, multiple inspections can be configured for the same class map. Normally, the ASA does not use the port number to determine which inspection to apply. This provides flexibility to apply inspections to non-standard ports.

To display information about the class map configuration, use the **show running-config class-map** command.

To remove all class maps, use the **clear configure class-map** command in global configuration mode.

Configure Policy Map

Refer to
Figure
in online course

Policy maps are used to bind class maps with actions. To apply actions to the Layer 3 and 4 traffic, use the **policy-map** *policy-map-name* global configuration command. The policy map name must be unique and up to 40 characters in length. The name should also be descriptive.

In policy-map configuration mode (config-pmap), use the following commands:

- **Description** Add description text.

- **class** *class-map-name* Identify a specific class map on which to perform actions.

The maximum number of policy maps is 64. There can be multiple Layer 3/4 class maps in one policy map, and multiple actions can be assigned from one or more feature types to each class map.

Note: The configuration includes a default Layer 3/4 policy map that the ASA uses in the default global policy. It is called `global_policy` and performs inspection on the default inspection traffic. There can only be one global policy. Therefore, to alter the global policy, either edit it or replace it.

Although there are a number of different commands available in this sub configuration mode, the most common ones include:

- `set connection` Sets connection values.

- `Inspect` Provides protocol inspection servers.

- `Police` Sets rate limits for traffic in this class.

Actions are applied to traffic bidirectionally or unidirectionally depending on the feature.

To display information about the policy map configuration, use the `show running-config policy-map` command.

To remove all policy maps, use the `clear configure policy-map` command in global configuration mode.

Configure the Service Policy

To activate a policy map globally on all interfaces or on a targeted interface, use the `service-policy` global configuration command. Use the command to enable a set of policies on an interface. The command syntax is as follows:

- `service-policy` *policy-map-name* [`global` | `interface` *intf*]

The ASA default configuration includes a global policy that matches all default application inspection traffic and applies inspection to the traffic globally. Otherwise, the service policy can be applied to an interface or globally.

Interface service policies take precedence over the global service policy for a given feature. For example, if there is a global policy with inspections, and an interface policy with inspections, then only the interface policy inspections are applied to that interface.

To alter the global policy, an administrator needs to either edit the default policy, or disable the default policy and apply a new policy.

To display information about the service policy configuration, use the `show service-policy` or the `show running-config service-policy` command.

To remove all service policies, use the `clear configure service-policy` command in global configuration mode. The `clear service-policy` command clears the service policy statistics.

To configure a service policy using ASDM, choose **Configuration > Firewall > Service Policy Rules**, and click **Add**.

Complete the following:

- *Name* Enter a network object name.

- *Type* Choose **Network** or **Range**.

- *IP Address* Enter the network address of the internal hosts.

- *Netmask* Enter the netmask.

Refer to **Figure** in online course

Refer to **Figure** in online course

10.3 ASA VPN Configuration

10.3.1 ASA Remote-Access VPN Options

Refer to
Figure
in online course

Organizations must support the needs of mobile users while ensuring security of corporate resources. Enterprise IT is evolving from localized desktop computers to mobile users accessing information from anywhere, on any device. Enterprise users are requesting support for their mobile devices including smart phones, tablets, notebooks, and a broader range of laptop manufacturers and operating systems.

This shift has created a challenge for IT security.

A solution to securing remote-access is the use of SSL VPNs help provide the flexibility to support secure access for all users, regardless of the endpoint from which they establish a connection.

Refer to
Figure
in online course

Cisco ISRs provide IPsec and SSL VPN capabilities. Specifically, ISRs are capable of supporting as many as 200 concurrent users. The Cisco ASA 5500 series provides IPsec and SSL VPN capabilities as well. However, they are Cisco's most advanced SSL VPN solution capable of supporting concurrent user scalability from 10 to 10,000 sessions per device. For this reason, the ASA is usually the choice when supporting a large remote networking deployment.

The ASA supports three types of remote-access VPNs:

- Clientless SSL VPN Remote Access (using a web browser)

- SSL or IPsec (IKEv2) VPN Remote Access (using Cisco AnyConnect client)

- IPsec (IKEv1) VPN Remote Access (using Cisco VPN client)

The ASA supports IKEv1 for connections from the legacy Cisco VPN client. IKEv2 is required for the AnyConnect VPN client. For IKEv2, it is possible to configure multiple encryption and authentication types, and multiple integrity algorithms for a single policy. With IKEv1 for each parameter, only one value can be set per security policy.

When security is the issue, IPsec is the superior choice as it exceeds SSL in:

- IP application support

- Strength of encryption

- Strength of authentication

If support and ease of deployment are the primary issues, then consider SSL. The benefits of SSL are its ease of use and ease of deployment. SSL is appropriate for user populations that require per-application or per-server access control or access from non-enterprise owned hosts.

SSL is a cryptosystem that was created by Netscape in the mid-1990s and was designed to enable secure communications on an insecure network such as the Internet. It provides encryption and integrity of communications along with strong authentication using digital certificates.

The conventional teleworker remote-access solution is IPsec VPN which requires a VPN client to be pre-installed on the host. An advantage of SSL is that it does not require any pre-installed, special-purpose client software. SSL VPNs allow users to access web pages, access services, access files, send and receive e-mail, and run TCP-based applications using a browser.

This means SSL VPNs are capable of "anywhere" connectivity from company-managed desktops and non-company-managed desktops. This can include employee-owned PCs, contractor or business partner desktops, Internet kiosks, and even smart handheld devices.

In many cases, IPsec and SSL VPNs are complementary because they solve different problems. This complementary approach allows a single device to address all remote-access user requirements.

The focus of this section is on SSL VPNs.

The ASA provides two main deployment modes that are found in Cisco SSL VPN solutions:

Refer to
Figure
in online course

- *Clientless SSL VPN* Clientless, browser-based VPN that lets users establish a secure, remote-access VPN tunnel to the ASA using a web browser. After authentication, users access a portal page and can access specific, supported internal resources.

- *Client-Based SSL VPN* Provides full tunnel SSL VPN connection but requires a VPN client application to be installed on the remote host.

Clientless SSL VPN

The clientless SSL VPN deployment model enables corporations to have the additional flexibility of providing access to corporate resources even when the remote device is not corporately managed. In this deployment model, the Cisco ASA is used as a proxy device to network resources and provides a web portal interface for remote devices to navigate the network using port-forwarding capabilities. The remote device system requires a supported web browser with built-in SSL functionality to access the SSL VPN network. Although easier to deploy and more flexible than client-based SSL VPNs, clientless SSL VPNs provide only limited network application or resource access and include additional security risks when using non-corporate managed clients.

Client-Based SSL VPN

Client-Based SSL VPNs provide authenticated users with LAN-like, full network access to corporate resources such as Microsoft Outlook, Cisco Unified Personal Communicator, Lotus Notes, Lotus Sametime, Meeting Maker, Telnet, Secure Shell (SSH), and X-Windows. However, the remote devices require a client application such as the Cisco VPN Client or the newer AnyConnect client to be installed on the end user device.

A full tunnel SSL VPN requires more planning for network deployment due to the fact that a client must be installed on the remote systems. The VPN client can be manually pre-installed on a host or it can be downloaded as needed by initially establishing a clientless SSL VPN.

Client-based SSL VPN supports a wider variety of applications, but it does present additional operational challenges in downloading and maintaining the client software on remote hosts. This requirement will make it difficult to deploy on non-corporate managed systems because most SSL VPN clients require administrator privileges to install.

The focus of this section is on clientless SSL VPN using a Web browser and SSL VPN using the Cisco AnyConnect client.

Refer to
Figure
in online course

Client-based SSL VPN requires a client, such as the Cisco AnyConnect VPN client to be installed on the host. The AnyConnect client can be manually pre-installed on the host, or downloaded on-demand to a host via a browser.

When the AnyConnect client is pre-installed on the host, the VPN connection can be initiated by starting the application. Once the user authenticates, the ASA examines the revision of the client and upgrades it as necessary.

Without a pre-installed client, remote users can connect to the ASA using an HTTPS browser connection, and authenticate to the ASA. Once authenticated, the ASA uploads the AnyConnect client to the host. Host operating systems supported include Microsoft Windows, Mac OS, and Linux. The AnyConnect client then installs and configures itself and finally establishes an SSL VPN connection.

Depending on the ASA SSL VPN policy configured, when the connection terminates the AnyConnect client application will either remain installed on the host or it will uninstall itself.

Refer to
Figure
in online course

To support IT consumerization, the Cisco AnyConnect client is available at no cost for select platforms such as iPhones, iPad, Android, and BlackBerry devices. Each application is qualified for use only for certain smart phone models, or is (in some cases) provided as a native application that is shipped by the manufacturer.

Cisco AnyConnect is available for the following platforms:

- iOS devices (iPhone, iPad, and iPod Touch)

- Android OS (select models)

- BlackBerry

- Windows Mobile 6.1

- HP webOS

- Nokia Symbian

For more information, go to www.cisco.com/go/asm.

10.3.2 Clientless SSL VPN

Refer to
Figure
in online course

ASDM provides two tools for initially configuring a clientless SSL VPN on an ASA:

- *ASDM Assistant* This feature guides an administrator through the SSL VPN configuration.

- *VPN wizard* This is an ASDM wizard that simplifies the SSL VPN configuration.

To use the ASDM assistant to configure a clientless SSL VPN, choose **Configurations > Remote Access VPN > Introduction** and then click the **Clientless SSL VPN Remote Access (using Web Browser)**.

To use the VPN wizard, from the Menu Bar, click **Wizards** and then choose **VPN Wizards > Clientless SSL VPN Wizard**.

This topic will use the VPN wizard to configure a remote-access clientless SSL VPN.

Refer to
Figure
in online course

The topology in this example is as follows:

- An inside network with security level 100

- A DMZ with security level 50

- An outside network with a security level of 0

Access to the DMZ server is already provided using static NAT.

Assume the outside host requires access to specific applications which do not need a full tunnel SSL VPN. For this reason, the remote host will use a secure web browser connection to access select corporate resources.

10.3.3 Configuring Clientless SSL VPN

Refer to
Figure
in online course

To create a clientless SSL VPN configuration, use the VPN wizard and complete the following steps:

Step 1.   Launch the Clientless SSL VPN wizard.

From the menu bar, select the **Wizards** menu and choose **VPN Wizards > Clientless SSL VPN Wizard**. The VPN wizard Introduction window is displayed. Click **Next** to continue.

Step 2. Configure the SSL VPN interface.

Configure a connection profile name for the connection and identify the interface to which outside users will connect.

By default, the ASA will use a self-signed certificate to send to the client for authentication. Optionally, the ASA may be configured to use a third-party certificate that is purchased from a well-known certificate authority, such as VeriSign, to connect clients. In the event that a certificate is purchased, it may be selected in the Digital Certificate drop-down menu.

The SSL VPN Interface screen provides links in the Information section. These links identify the URLs that need to be used for the SSL VPN service access (login) and for Cisco ASDM access (to access the Cisco ASDM software download). Click **Next** to continue.

Step 3. Configure user authentication.

In this window, the authentication method can be defined. Authentication using a AAA server can be configured by checking the radio button. Click **New** to enter the location of the AAA Server.

Alternatively, the local database can be used. To add a new user, enter the username and password and then click **Add**. Click **Next** to continue.

Step 4. Create a group policy.

> Refer to **Figure** in online course

In this window, a custom group policy for the clientless SSL VPN connection can be created or modified.

If configuring a new policy, the policy name cannot contain any spaces.

By default, the created user group policy will inherit its settings from the DfltGrpPolicy. These settings may be modified after the wizard has been completed by navigating to the **Configuration > Remote Access VPN > Clientless SSL VPN Access > Group Policies** submenu. Click **Next** to continue.

Step 5. Configure a bookmark list for clientless connections only.

A bookmark list is a set of URLs that is configured to be used in the clientless SSL VPN web portal. If there are bookmarks already listed, use the Bookmark List drop-down menu, select the bookmark of choice and click **Next** to continue with the SSL VPN wizard.

However, there are no configured bookmark lists by default and therefore they must be configured by the network administrator. To create an HTTP server bookmark in the bookmark list, choose **Manage** and the Configure GUI Customization Objects window opens. Choose **Add** to open the Add Bookmark List window. Finally, choose **Add** once more to open the Add Bookmark window.

Specifics to enter include:

- Enter a name for the bookmark in the Bookmark Title field. The name cannot contain spaces.
- Enter the HTTP URL value.
- Enter the server destination IP address or hostname to be used with the bookmark entry.
- (Optional) Enter the name in the Subtitle field. The subtitle will appear under the bookmark entry on the web portal.
- (Optional) Enter the name of the thumbnail image to be used with this bookmark entry in the Thumbnail field. In order to use thumbnails with bookmarks, the images must first be uploaded to the ASA.

When the specifics are configured, click **OK** in the Add Bookmark window to return to the Edit Bookmark List window. Select the desired bookmark and click **OK** to return to the Configure GUI Customization Objects window. Select the bookmark list that will be displayed in the Web portal page and click **OK**. Click **Next** to continue.

Step 6. Verify and commit the configuration.

The summary page is displayed next. Verify that the information configured in the SSL VPN wizard is correct. Use the **Back** button to alter any of the configuration parameters. Click **Finish** to finish the wizard and deliver the commands to the ASA.

To verify the Clientless SSL VPN configuration, complete four steps:

> Refer to
> **Figure**
> in online course

Step 1. Open the ASDM Clientless SSL VPN Access window.

In ASDM, open the Network Client Access window. Choose **Configurations > Remote Access VPN > Clientless SSL VPN Access > Connection Profiles**. From this window the VPN configuration can be verified and edited.

Step 2. Login from the remote host.

Open a compliant web browser and enter the login URL for the SSL VPN into the address field. Be sure to use secure HTTP (HTTPS) as SSL is required to connect to the ASA.

The login window should appear. Enter a previously configured username and password and click **Logon** to continue.

Step 3. View web portal bookmarks.

Once the user authenticates, the ASA SSL Web portal webpage will be displayed listing the various bookmarks previously assigned to the profile.

Step 4. Logout.

The user should log out of the web portal window when done. However, the web portal will timeout if there is no activity. In either case a logout window will be displayed informing users that for additional security, they should clear the browser cache, delete the downloaded files, and close the browser window.

> Refer to
> **Figure**
> in online course

The clientless SSL VPN wizard generates configuration settings for the following:

- WebVPN

- Group policy

- Remote user

- Tunnel group

Note: Detailed explanation of the commands is beyond the scope of this course and will not be explored further.

10.3.4 AnyConnect SSL VPN

> Refer to
> **Figure**
> in online course

Cisco AnyConnect SSL VPN for remote-access provides remote users with secure access to corporate networks. The Cisco ASA must be configured to support the SSL VPN connection.

ASDM provides two tools for initially configuring an SSL VPN on an ASA:

- *ASDM assistant* This feature guides an administrator through the SSL VPN configuration.

- *VPN wizard* An ASDM wizard which simplifies the SSL VPN configuration.

To use the ASDM assistant, choose **Configurations > Remote-Access VPN > Introduction** and then click the **SSL or IPsec(IKEv2) VPN Remote Access (using Cisco AnyConnect Client)**.

To use the VPN wizard, from the Menu Bar, click **Wizards** and then choose **VPN Wizards > AnyConnect VPN Wizard**.

This topic will use the VPN wizard to configure a remote-access SSL VPN.

Refer to
Figure
in online course

The topology in this example is as follows:

- An inside network with security level 100

- A DMZ with security level 50

- An outside network with a security level of 0

The outside host requires an SSL VPN connection to the inside network. Outside access to the DMZ server is already provided via static NAT.

The outside host does not have the Cisco AnyConnect client pre-installed. Therefore, the remote user will have to initiate a clientless SSL VPN connection using a web browser, and then download and install the AnyConnect client on the remote host.

Refer to
Figure
in online course

Once installed, the host can exchange traffic with the ASA using a full tunnel SSL VPN connection.

10.3.5 Configuring AnyConnect SSL VPN

To create a full tunnel SSL VPN configuration, use the VPN wizard and complete the following steps:

Step 1.   Launch the AnyConnect VPN Wizard.

From the menu bar, choose the **Wizards** menu and choose **VPN Wizards >
AnyConnect VPN Wizard**. The VPN wizard Introduction window is displayed. Click
Next to continue.

Step 2.   Configure a connection profile identification.

Configure a connection profile name for the connection and identify the interface to which outside users will connect. Click **Next** to continue.

Step 3.   Select the VPN protocol(s).

Select how the traffic will be protected. The choices are SSL and or IPsec. A third-party certificate can also be configured. Uncheck **IPsec** and then click **Next** to continue.

Step 4.   Add the AnyConnect client images.

In order for client systems to download the Cisco AnyConnect SSL VPN Client automatically from the ASA, the location of the SSL VPN Client must be specified in the configuration. To configure the location of the Cisco AnyConnect SSL VPN Client, click **Add** to identify the location of the image and open the Add AnyConnect Client Image window. Now click the **Browse Flash** button if the image file is already located on the Cisco ASA. Browse to the location of the Cisco AnyConnect SSL VPN Client in the flash memory and click **OK**. Notice that there are images for Linux, MAC OS, and Windows hosts.

Note: If there is no image file on the ASA, click **Upload** to upload a copy from the local machine.

Click **OK** again to accept the location of the Cisco AnyConnect SSL VPN Client and then click **Next** to continue.

Step 5.   Configure the authentication methods.

In this window, the authentication method can be defined. The location of the AAA authentication server can be added. Click **New** to enter the location of the AAA Server. If a server is not identified, then the local database will be used. To add a new user, enter the username and password and then click **Add**. Click **Next** to continue.

Refer to
Figure
in online course

Step 6.   Create and assign the client IP address pool.

The IP address pool configuration is required for successful client-based SSL VPN connectivity. Without an available IP address pool, the connection to the security appliance will fail.

A preconfigured IP address pool can be selected from the Address Pool drop-down menu. Otherwise, click **New** to create a new one. The following items must be included in the IP address pool configuration:

- *Name* A name to be associated with the IP address pool. This name cannot contain any spaces.

- *Starting IP Address* Starting IP address of the range to be assigned to client SSL VPN connections.

- *Ending IP Address* Ending IP address of the range to be assigned to the client SSL VPN connections.

- *Subnet Mask* Choose the desired subnet mask of the IP address pool from the drop-down menu.

Click **Next** to continue.

Step 7. Specify the network name resolution servers.

Specify the DNS server and WINS server locations (if any) and provide the Domain Name. Click **Next** to continue.

Step 8. Enable NAT exemption for VPN traffic.

If NAT is configured on the ASA, then a NAT exemption rule must be for the configured IP address pool. Like IPsec, SSL client address pools must be exempt from the NAT process because NAT translation occurs before encryption functions. Click **Next** to continue.

Step 9. View the AnyConnect client deployment methods.

An informational page explaining how the AnyConnect client is deployed is displayed. There are two methods of deploying AnyConnect:

- Web launched, which means a clientless AnyConnect connection using a browser is required to initially access the ASA and install the client on the host.

- Download the application and manually install it.

Click **Next** to continue.

Step 10. Verify and commit the configuration.

The summary page is displayed next. Verify that the information configured in the SSL VPN wizard is correct. Use the **Back** button to alter any of the configuration parameters. Click **Finish** to finish the wizard and deliver the commands to the ASA.

Several steps must be performed to verify the VPN configuration. Some of these steps may be optional depending on whether the AnyConnect client is already installed on the remote host.

> Refer to
> **Figure**
> in online course

To verify the ASA AnyConnect VPN configuration, complete the following steps:

Step 1. (Optional) Open the ASDM Network (Client) Access Window.

The VPN configuration can be altered, customized, and verified in the AnyConnect Connections Profile page. To open the Network Client Access window, choose **Configurations > Remote Access VPN > Network (Client) Access > AnyConnect Connection Profiles**.

Step 2. Login from the remote host.

Establish a clientless SSL VPN connection to the ASA. Open a compliant web browser and enter the login URL for the SSL VPN into the address field. Be sure to use secure HTTP (HTTPS) as SSL is required to connect to the ASA. Enter a previously configured username and password and click **Logon** to continue.

Step 3. Accept the security certificate (if required).

The ASA may request confirmation that this is a trusted site. If requested then click **Yes** to proceed.

Step 4. Begin the platform detection.

The ASA will begin a software auto-download process consisting of a series of compliance checks for the target system. The ASA performs the platform detection by querying the client system in an attempt to identify the type of client connecting to the security appliance. Based on the platform that is identified, the proper software package may be auto-downloaded.

Step 5. Install AnyConnect (if required).

If the AnyConnect client must be downloaded, then a security warning will be displayed on the remote host. To continue, choose **Install**.

Step 6. Detect ActiveX (if required).

Refer to **Figure** in online course

If the AnyConnect client must be downloaded, the host requires ActiveX to be installed. For ActiveX to operate properly with the Cisco ASA, it is important that the security appliance is added as a trusted network site. ActiveX will be used for client download in the event that a web portal is not in use. If prompted, click **Yes**.

Step 7. Accept the security certificate (if required).

The VPN Client Installer will begin and another security alert window may appear. If so, then click **Yes** to continue.

Step 8. Review the connection established message.

After the client completes the auto-download of the Cisco AnyConnect SSL VPN Client, the web session will automatically launch the Cisco AnyConnect SSL VPN Client. It will attempt to log the user into the network using the same credentials that were supplied when logging into the web portal.

Step 9. Confirm connectivity.

When the full tunnel SSL VPN connection is established, an icon will appear in the system tray identifying that the client has successfully connected to the SSL VPN network. Additional connection statistics and information may be shown by double-clicking the icon in the system tray. This client interface may also be used to log the user out.

Finally, verify the IP address on the remote host using the `ipconfig` command. There should be two IP addresses listed: one for the remote host local IP address and the other is the IP address assigned for the SSL VPN tunnel. Ping an inside host to verify connectivity.

Future SSL VPN sessions may be launched through the web portal or through the installed Cisco AnyConnect SSL VPN Client.

Refer to **Figure** in online course

The AnyConnect SSL VPN wizard generates configuration settings for the following:

- NAT
- WebVPN
- Group policy
- Tunnel group

Note: Detailed explanation of the commands is beyond the scope of this course and will not be explored further.

Chapter Summary

Refer to **Figure** in online course

Refer to **Packet Tracer Activity** for this chapter

Refer to **Lab Activity** for this chapter

Your Chapter Notes

AAA   Authentication, Authorization, and Accounting - AAA is a protocol, specified in RFC 2903 and several other RFCs, for specifying who can access a system or network, how they can access it, and what they did while they were connected.

ABR   1) Available Bit Rate - QOS class defined by the ATM Forum for ATM networks. ABR is used for connections that do not require timing relationships between source and destination. ABR provides no guarantees in terms of cell loss or delay, providing only best-effort service. Traffic sources adjust their transmission rate in response to information they receive describing the status of the network and its capability to successfully deliver data. Compare with CBR, UBR, and VBR. 2) Area Border Router - Router located on the border of one or more OSPF areas that connects those areas to the backbone network. ABRs are considered members of both the OSPF backbone and the attached areas. They therefore maintain routing tables describing both the backbone topology and the topology of the other areas.

absorption   Absorption is the physical phenomenon that occurs when radio frequency waves are absorbed by objects such as walls.

Abstract Syntax Notation One   See ASN.1

AC   Alternating Current - Electrical current that reverses its direction regularly and continually. It is the form of electrical power found in residential and commercial buildings.

access card   I/O card in the LightStream 2020 ATM switch. Together with their associated line cards, access cards provide data transfer services for a switch using physical interfaces such as OC-3c. A LightStream 2020 switch can have up to 10 access cards. Access card is also known as a paddle card.

access control list   List kept by Cisco routers to control access to or from the router for a number of services (for example, to prevent packets with a certain IP address from leaving a particular interface on the router).

access gateway   A gateway that supports both bearer traffic and signaling traffic. For example, a gateway that terminates ISDN is an access gateway.

access method   1) Generally, the way in which network devices access the network medium. 2) Software within an SNA processor that controls the flow of information through a network.

access point   See AP.

access server   Communications processor that connects asynchronous devices to a LAN or WAN through network and terminal emulation software. Performs both synchronous and asynchronous routing of supported protocols. Sometimes called a network access server. Compare with communication server.

accounting management   One of five categories of network management defined by ISO for management of OSI networks. Accounting management subsystems are responsible for collecting network data relating to resource usage.

ACK   Acknowledgment - Notification sent from one network device to another to acknowledge that some event (for example, receipt of a message) has occurred. Compare to NAK.

acknowledgment   See ACK.

acknowledgment number   Next expected TCP octet.

ACL   Access Control List - List kept by Cisco routers to control access to or from the router for a number of services (for example, to prevent packets with a certain IP address from leaving a particular interface on the router).

ACR   Allowed Cell Rate - Parameter defined by the ATM Forum for ATM traffic management. ACR varies between the MCR and the PCR, and is dynamically controlled using congestion control mechanisms.

ACSE   Association Control Service Element - An OSI convention used to establish, maintain, or terminate a connection between two applications.

active hub   Multiported device that amplifies LAN transmission signals.

ad hoc   Ad hoc describes a WLAN topology, also called independent basic service set, where mobile clients connect directly without an intermediate access point.

adapter   See NIC (network interface card).

adaptive routing   See dynamic routing.

address   Data structure or logical convention used to identify a unique entity, such as a particular process or network device.

address mapping   Technique that allows different protocols to interoperate by translating addresses from one format to another. For example, when routing IP over X.25, the IP addresses must be mapped to the X.25 addresses so that the IP packets can be transmitted by the X.25 network.

address mask   Bit combination used to describe which portion of an address refers to the network or subnet and which part refers to the host. An address mask is also known as a mask.

address resolution   Generally, a method for resolving differences between computer addressing schemes. Address resolution usually specifies a method for mapping network layer (Layer 3) addresses to data link layer (Layer 2) addresses.

Address Resolution Protocol   See ARP.

adjacency   Relationship formed between selected neighboring routers and end nodes for the purpose of exchanging routing information. Adjacency is based upon the use of a common media segment.

administrative distance   A rating of the trustworthiness of a routing information source. In Cisco routers, administrative distance is expressed as a numerical value between 0 and 255. The higher the value, the lower the trustworthiness rating.

admission control   See traffic policing.

ADSU   ATM Data Service Unit - Terminal adapter used to access an ATM network via an HSSI-compatible device.

ADU   Aironet Desktop Utility - ADU is a utility used by Cisco Aironet 802.11a/b/g network cards for wireless configuration.

Advanced Program-to-Program Communication   See APPC.

Advanced Research Projects Agency   See ARPA.

Advanced Research Projects Agency Network   See ARPANET.

advertising   Router process in which routing or service updates are sent at specified intervals so that other routers on the network can maintain lists of usable routes.

AES   Advanced Encryption Standard - AES replaced WEP as the most secure method of encrypting data. AES is an option for WPA2.

AFI   1) Authority and Format ID - One byte of the NSAP address, actually a binary value between 0 and 99, used to specify the IDI format and DSP syntax of the address and the authority that assigned the address. See NSAP address. 2) Adress Family Identifier - A 2 byte field in a RIP message. It identifies the routed protocol and is normally set to two for IP. The only exception is a request for a router's (or host's) full routing table, in which case it will be set to zero. AFI is set to all 1s if authentication is enabled in RIPv2.

agent   1) Generally, software that processes queries and returns replies on behalf of an application. 2) In NMSs, process that resides in all managed devices and reports the values of specified variables to management stations. 3) In Cisco hardware architecture, an individual processor card that provides one or more media interfaces.

AGS+   Multiprotocol, high-end Cisco router optimized for large corporate internetworks. The AGS+ runs the Cisco IOS software and features a modular approach that provides for easy and efficient scalability.

AIS   Alarm Indication Signal - In a T1 transmission, an all-ones signal transmitted in lieu of the normal signal to maintain transmission continuity and to indicate to the receiving terminal that there is a transmission fault that is located either at, or upstream from, the transmitting terminal.

alarm   Message notifying an operator or administrator of a network problem.

alarm indication signal   See AIS.

a-law   The ITU-T companding standard used in the conversion between analog and digital signals in PCM systems. A-law is used primarily in European telephone networks and is similar to the North American mu-law standard.

algorithm   Well-defined rule or process for arriving at a solution to a problem. In networking, algorithms are commonly used to determine the best route for traffic from a particular source to a particular destination.

alias   See entity.

allowed cell rate   See ACR.

alternate mark inversion   See AMI.

AM   Amplitude Modulation - Modulation technique whereby information is conveyed through the amplitude of the carrier signal. Compare with FM and PAM.

American National Standards Institute   See ANSI.

American Standard Code for Information Interchange   See ASCII.

AMI   Alternate Mark Inversion - Line-code type used on T1 and E1 circuits. In AMI, zeros are represented by 01 during each bit cell, and ones are represented by 11 or 00, alternately, during each bit cell. AMI requires that the sending device maintain ones density. Ones density is not maintained independent of the data stream. Compare with B8ZS. AMI is also know as binary coded alternate mark inversion.

amplitude   Maximum value of an analog or a digital waveform.

amplitude modulation   See AM.

analog transmission   Signal transmission over wires or through the air in which information is conveyed through variation of some combination of signal amplitude, frequency, and phase.

ANSI   American National Standards Institute - Voluntary organization comprised of corporate, government, and other members that coordinates standards-related activities, approves U.S. national standards, and develops positions for the United States in international standards organizations. ANSI helps develop international and U.S. standards relating to, among other things, communications and networking. ANSI is a member of the IEC and the ISO.

anycast A type of IPv6 network addressing and routing scheme whereby data is routed to the "nearest" or "best" destination as viewed by the routing topology. A packet sent to an anycast address is delivered to the closest interface, as defined by the routing protocols in use, identified by the anycast address. It shares the same address format as an IPv6 global unicast address.

AON Application-Oriented Networking - Technology that changes how applications are deployed, integrated, and managed. It does so by delivering common application infrastructure functions as network-based services. Cisco AON helps to dramatically lower the cost and complexity of deploying applications and maintaining application infrastructure by relocating these repeatable functions, such as application security, messaging, logging, and event capture, into the network and onto routers and switches.

AP Access Point - Device that connects wireless communication devices together to form a wireless network, analogous to a hub connecting wired devices to form a LAN. The AP usually connects to a wired network, and can relay data between wireless devices and wired devices. Several Aps can link together to form a larger network that allows roaming.

APaRT Automated Packet Recognition/Translation - Technology that allows a server to be attached to CDDI or FDDI without requiring the reconfiguration of applications or network protocols. APaRT recognizes specific data link layer encapsulation packet types and, when these packet types are transferred from one medium to another, translates them into the native format of the destination device.

API Application Programming Interface - Specification of function-call conventions that defines an interface to a service.

Apollo Domain Proprietary network protocol suite developed by Apollo Computer for communication on proprietary Apollo networks.

APPC Advanced Program-to-Program Communication - IBM SNA system software that allows high-speed communication between programs on different computers in a distributed computing environment. APPC establishes and tears down connections between communicating programs, and consists of two interfaces, a programming interface and a data-exchange interface. The former replies to requests from programs requiring communication; the latter establishes sessions between programs. APPC runs on LU 6.2 devices.

AppleTalk Series of communications protocols designed by Apple Computer. Two phases currently exist. Phase 1, the earlier version, supports a single physical network that can have only one network number and be in one zone. Phase 2, the more recent version, supports multiple logical networks on a single physical network and allows networks to be in more than one zone.

application Program that performs a function directly for a user. FTP and Telnet clients are examples of network applications.

Application layer Layer 7 of the OSI reference model. This layer provides services to application processes (such as electronic mail, file transfer, and terminal emulation) that are outside of the OSI model. The application layer identifies and establishes the availability of intended communication partners (and the resources required to connect with them), synchronizes cooperating applications, and establishes agreement on procedures for error recovery and control of data integrity. Corresponds roughly with the transaction services layer in the SNA model.

application programming interface See API.

Application-Oriented Networking See AON.

ARCnet Attached Resource Computer Network - A 2.5-Mbps token-bus LAN developed in the late 1970s and early 1980s by Datapoint Corporation.

area Logical set of network segments (either CLNS-, DECnet-, or OSPF-based) and their attached devices. Areas are usually connected to other areas via routers, making up a single autonomous system.

area border router   See ABR.

ARM   Asynchronous Response Mode - HDLC communication mode involving one primary station and at least one secondary station, where either the primary or one of the secondary stations can initiate transmissions.

ARP   Address Resolution Protocol - Internet protocol used to map an IP address to a MAC address. Defined in RFC 826. Compare with RARP.

ARPA   Advanced Research Projects Agency - Research and development organization that is part of DoD. ARPA is responsible for numerous technological advances in communications and networking. ARPA evolved into DARPA, and then back into ARPA again in 1994.

ARPANET   Advanced Research Projects Agency Network - Landmark packet-switching network established in 1969. ARPANET was developed in the 1970s by BBN and funded by ARPA (and later DARPA). It eventually evolved into the Internet. The term ARPANET was officially retired in 1990.

ARQ   1) Automatic Repeat Request - Communication technique in which the receiving device detects errors and requests retransmissions. 2) Admission Request - In VoIP, ARQ is used with the H.323 protocol.

AS   Collection of networks under a common administration sharing a common routing strategy. Autonomous systems are subdivided by areas. An autonomous system must be assigned a unique 16-bit number by the IANA.

ASBR   Autonomous System Boundary Router - ABR located between an OSPF autonomous system and a non-OSPF network. ASBRs run both OSPF and another routing protocol, such as RIP. ASBRs must reside in a nonstub OSPF area.

ASCII   American Standard Code for Information Interchange - 8-bit code for character representation (7 bits plus parity).

ASM-CS   Cisco multiprotocol communication server designed to connect asynchronous devices to any LAN or WAN using TCP/IP, LAT, or SLIP. It can be configured to interface with Ethernet or Token Ring LANs or synchronous serial networks.

ASN.1   Abstract Syntax Notation One - OSI language for describing data types independent of particular computer structures and representation techniques. Described by ISO International Standard 8824.

associated   A station is configured properly to allow it to wirelessly communicate with an access point.

association control service element   See ACSE.

associative memory   Memory that is accessed based on its contents, not on its memory address. Associative memory is also known as content addressable memory (CAM).

AST   Automatic Spanning Tree - Function that supports the automatic resolution of spanning trees in SRB networks, providing a single path for spanning explorer frames to traverse from a given node in the network to another. AST is based on the IEEE 802.1 standard.

asynchronous response mode   See ARM.

asynchronous time-division multiplexing   See ATDM.

Asynchronous Transfer Mode   See ATM.

asynchronous transmission   Term describing digital signals that are transmitted without precise clocking. Such signals generally have different frequencies and phase relationships. Asynchronous transmissions usually encapsulate individual characters in control bits (called start and stop bits) that designate the beginning and end of each character. Compare with isochronous transmission, plesiochronous transmission, and synchronous transmission.

ATDM   Asynchronous Time-Division Multiplexing - Method of sending information that resembles normal TDM, except that time slots are allocated as needed rather than preassigned to specific transmitters. Compare with FDM, statistical multiplexing, and TDM.

ATM   Asynchronous Transfer Mode - International standard for cell relay in which multiple service types (such as voice, video, or data) are conveyed in fixed-length (53-byte) cells. Fixed-length cells allow cell processing to occur in hardware, thereby reducing transit delays. ATM is designed to take advantage of high-speed transmission media such as E3, SONET, and T3.

ATM data service unit   See ADSU.

ATM Forum   International organization jointly founded in 1991 by Cisco Systems, NET/ADAP-TIVE, Northern Telecom, and Sprint that develops and promotes standards-based implementation agreements for ATM technology. The ATM Forum expands on official standards developed by ANSI and ITU-T, and develops implementation agreements in advance of official standards.

ATM management   See ATMM.

ATM UNI   See UNI.

ATMM   ATM Management - Process that runs on an ATM switch that controls VCI translation and rate enforcement.

Attached Resource Computer Network   See ARCnet.

attachment unit interface   See AUI.

attenuation   Loss of communication signal energy.

attribute   Configuration data that defines the characteristics of database objects such as the chassis, cards, ports, or virtual circuits of a particular device. Attributes might be preset or user-configurable. On a LightStream 2020 ATM switch, attributes are set using the configuration program or CLI commands.

AUI   Attachment Unit Interface - IEEE 802.3 interface between an MAU and a network interface card (NIC). The term AUI can also refer to the rear panel port to which an AUI cable might attach, such as those found on a Cisco LightStream Ethernet access card. AUI is also known as transceiver cable.

authentication   In security, the verification of the identity of a person or process.

authority zone   Associated with DNS, an authority zone is a section of the domain-name tree for which one name server is the authority.

Automated Packet Recognition/Translation   See APaRT.

automatic call reconnect   Feature permitting automatic call rerouting away from a failed trunk line.

automatic repeat request   See ARQ.

automatic spanning tree   See AST.

autonomous access point   An autonomous access point is the type used in a distributed WLAN solution. Each autonomous access point is configured individually and does not rely on a wireless controller.

autonomous system   See AS.

autonomous system boundary router   See ASBR.

AutoQoS   Cisco AutoQoS is a feature that automates consistent deployment of QoS features across Cisco routers and switches to ensure high-quality application performance. Once enabled, it automatically configures the device with QoS features and variables which are based on Cisco best-practice recommendations. Users can subsequently tune parameters that are generated by Cisco AutoQoS to suit their particular application needs, as desired.

autoreconfiguration   Process performed by nodes within the failure domain of a Token Ring network. Nodes automatically perform diagnostics in an attempt to reconfigure the network around the failed areas.

available bit rate   See ABR.

average rate   The average rate, in kilobits per second (kbps), at which a given virtual circuit will transmit.

B channel   Bearer channel - In ISDN, a full-duplex, 64-kbps channel used to send user data. Compare to D channel, E channel, and H channel.

B8ZS   Binary 8-zero Substitution - Line-code type, used on T1 and E1 circuits, in which a special code is substituted whenever 8 consecutive zeros are sent through the link. This code is then interpreted at the remote end of the connection. This technique guarantees ones density independent of the data stream. Sometimes called bipolar 8-zero substitution. Compare with AMI.

back end   Node or software program that provides services to a front end.

backbone   The part of a network that acts as the primary path for traffic that is most often sourced from, and destined for, other networks.

backbone cabling   Cabling that provides interconnections between wiring closets, wiring closets and the POP, and between buildings that are part of the same LAN. Backbone cabling is also known as vertical cabling.

backoff   The retransmission delay enforced when a collision occurs.

backplane   Physical connection between an interface processor or card and the data buses and power distribution buses inside a Cisco chassis.

backward explicit congestion notification   See BECN.

balanced configuration   In HDLC, a point-to-point network configuration with two combined stations.

bandwidth   The difference between the highest and lowest frequencies available for network signals. Bandwidth is also used to describe the rated throughput capacity of a given network medium or protocol.

bandwidth allocation   See bandwidth reservation.

bandwidth reservation   Process of assigning bandwidth to users and applications served by a network. Involves signing priority to different flows of traffic based on how critical and delay-sensitive they are. This makes the best use of available bandwidth, and if the network becomes congested, lower-priority traffic can be dropped. Bandwidth reservation is also known as bandwidth allocation.

Banyan VINES   See VINES.

BARRNet   Bay Area Regional Research Network - Regional network serving the San Francisco Bay Area. The BARRNet backbone is composed of four University of California campuses (Berkeley, Davis, Santa Cruz, and San Francisco), Stanford University, Lawrence Livermore National Laboratory, and NASA Ames Research Center. BARRNet is now part of BBN Planet.

baseband   Characteristic of a network technology where only one carrier frequency is used. Ethernet is an example of a baseband network. Contrast with broadband. Baseband is also known as narrowband.

bash   Bourne-again shell - Interactive UNIX shell based on the traditional Bourne shell, but with increased functionality. The LynxOS bash shell is presented when you log in to a LightStream 2020 ATM switch as root (bash#) or fldsup (bash$).

basic configuration   The minimal configuration information entered when a new router, switch, or other configurable network device is installed on a network. The basic configuration for a LightStream 2020 ATM switch, for example, includes IP addresses, the date, and parameters for at least one trunk line. The basic configuration enables the device to receive a full configuration from the NMS.

basic encoding rules   See BER.

Basic Rate Interface   See BRI.

basic service area   See BSA.

basic service set   See BSS.

baud   Unit of signaling speed equal to the number of discrete signal elements transmitted per second. Baud is synonymous with bits per second (bps), if each signal element represents exactly 1 bit.

Bay Area Regional Research Network   See BARRNet.

BBN   Bolt, Beranek, and Newman, Inc. - High-technology company located in Massachusetts that developed and maintained the ARPANET (and later, the Internet) core gateway system.

BBN Planet   Subsidiary company of BBN that operates a nationwide Internet access network composed in part by the former regional networks BARRNET, NEARNET, and SURAnet.

Bc   Committed Burst - Negotiated tariff metric in Frame Relay internetworks. The maximum amount of data (in bits) that a Frame Relay internetwork is committed to accept and transmit at the CIR.

Be   Excess Burst - Negotiated tariff metric in Frame Relay internetworks. The number of bits that a Frame Relay internetwork will attempt to transmit after Bc is accommodated. Be data is, in general, delivered with a lower probability than Bc data because Be data can be marked as DE by the network.

beacon   1) Frame from a Token Ring or FDDI device indicating a serious problem with the ring, such as a broken cable. A beacon frame contains the address of the station assumed to be down. See failure domain. 2) In wireless technology, a beacon is a wireless LAN packet that signals the availability and presence of the wireless device. Beacon packets are sent by access points and base stations; however, client radio cards send beacons when operating in computer to computer (Ad Hoc) mode.

bearer channel   See B channel.

Because It's Time Network   See BITNET.

BECN   Backward Explicit Congestion Notifcation - Bit set by a Frame Relay network in frames traveling in the opposite direction of frames encountering a congested path. DTE receiving frames with the BECN bit set can request that higher-level protocols take flow control action as appropriate. Compare with FECN.

Bell Communications Research   See Bellcore.

Bell operating company   See BOC.

Bellcore   Bell Communications Research - Organization that performs research and development on behalf of the RBOCs.

Bellman-Ford routing algorithm   See distance vector routing algorithm.

BER   1) Bit Error Rate - The ratio of received bits that contain errors. 2) Basic Encoding Rules - Rules for encoding data units described in the ISO ASN.1 standard.

Berkeley Standard Distribution   See BSD.

BERT   Bit Error Rate Tester - Device that determines the BER on a given communications channel.

best-effort delivery Describes a network system that does not use a sophisticated acknowledgment system to guarantee reliable delivery of information.

BGP Border Gateway Protocol - Interdomain routing protocol that replaces EGP. BGP exchanges reachability information with other BGP systems. BGP is defined by RFC 1163.

BGP4 BGP Version 4 - Version 4 of the predominant interdomain routing protocol used on the Internet. BGP4 supports CIDR and uses route aggregation mechanisms to reduce the size of routing tables.

big-endian Method of storing or transmitting data in which the most significant bit or byte is presented first. Compare with little-endian.

binary A numbering system characterized by ones and zeros (1 = on, 0 = off).

binary 8-zero substitution See B8ZS.

binary coded alternate mark inversion See AMI.

biphase coding Bipolar coding scheme originally developed for use in Ethernet. Clocking information is embedded into and recovered from the synchronous data stream without the need for separate clocking leads. The biphase signal contains no direct current energy.

bipolar 8-zero substitution See B8ZS.

BISDN Broadband ISDN - ITU-T communication standards designed to handle high-bandwidth applications such as video. BISDN currently uses ATM technology over SONET-based transmission circuits to provide data rates from 155 to 622 Mbps and beyond. Contrast with N-ISDN.

bit Binary digit used in the binary numbering system. A bit can be 0 or 1.

bit error rate See BER.

bit error rate tester See BERT.

bit rate Speed at which bits are transmitted, usually expressed in bits per second (bps).

BITNET Because It's Time Network - Low-cost, low-speed academic network consisting primarily of IBM mainframes and 9600-bps leased lines. BITNET is now part of CREN.

BITNET III Dial-up service providing connectivity for members of CREN.

bit-oriented protocol Class of data link layer communication protocols that can transmit frames regardless of frame content. Compared with byte-oriented protocols, bit-oriented protocols provide full-duplex operation and are more efficient and reliable. Compare with byte-oriented protocol.

bits per second Abbreviated bps.

black hole Routing term for an area of the internetwork where packets enter, but do not emerge, due to adverse conditions or poor system configuration within a portion of the network.

block multiplexer channel IBM-style channel that implements the FIPS-60 channel, a U.S. channel standard. This channel is also referred to as OEMI channel and 370 block mux channel.

blocking In a switching system, a condition in which no paths are available to complete a circuit. Blocking is also used to describe a situation in which one activity cannot begin until another has been completed.

blower Internal cooling fan used in larger router and switch chassis such as the Cisco AGS+, the Cisco 7000, and the LightStream 2020.

BNC connector Standard connector used to connect IEEE 802.3 10BASE2 coaxial cable to an MAU.

BNN   boundary network node In SNA terminology, a subarea node that provides boundary function support for adjacent peripheral nodes. This support includes sequencing, pacing, and address translation. BNN is also known as a boundary node.

BOC   Abbreviation for Bell Operating Company.

Bolt, Beranek, and Newman, Inc.   See BBN.

boot programmable read-only memory   See boot PROM.

boot PROM   boot Programmable Read-Only Memory - Chip mounted on a printed circuit board used to provide executable boot instructions to a computer device.

BOOTP   Bootstrap Protocol - Protocol used by a network node to determine the IP address of its Ethernet interfaces, in order to affect network booting.

CA   Congestion Avoidance - The mechanism by which a LightStream-based ATM network controls traffic entering the network to minimize delays. In order to use resources most efficiently, lower-priority traffic is discarded at the edge of the network if conditions indicate that it cannot be delivered.

cable   Transmission medium of copper wire or optical fiber wrapped in a protective cover.

cable television   See CATV.

caching   Form of replication in which information learned during a previous transaction is used to process later transactions.

call admission control   Traffic management mechanism used in ATM networks that determines whether the network can offer a path with sufficient bandwidth for a requested VCC.

call priority   Priority assigned to each origination port in circuit-switched systems. This priority defines the order in which calls are reconnected. Call priority also defines which calls can or cannot be placed during a bandwidth reservation.

call setup time   The time required to establish a switched call between DTE devices.

CAM   Content-Addressable Memory - See associative memory.

carrier   Electromagnetic wave or alternating current of a single frequency, suitable for modulation by another, data-bearing signal.

carrier detect   See CD.

carrier sense multiple access/collision detect   See CSMA/CD.

CAS   Channel-Associated Signaling - The transmission of signaling information within the voice channel. CAS signaling often is referred to as robbed-bit signaling because user bandwidth is being robbed by the network for other purposes.

Case Management   A process of identifying individuals at high risk for problems associated with complex health care needs and coordinating care to optimize the outcome.

Catalyst 1600 Token Ring Switch   Cisco Token Ring switch that offers full-duplex dedicated LAN segments to individual servers and other workstations that require high-speed switching access. The Catalyst 1600 provides up to 12 switched Token Ring interfaces and low latency switching between servers and clients across a backbone.

Catalyst 5000   Cisco modular switching system that allows connection to Ethernet, CDDI, FDDI, and ATM LANs and backbones. The Catalyst 5000 switch performs store-and-forward packet switching and allows the user to dedicate 10- or 100-Mbps connections to existing LAN segments or high-performance end stations.

Catalyst Workgroup Switch Series of Cisco workgroup switches that enhance the network performance of Ethernet client/server workgroups. The Catalyst Workgroup Switch integrates software enhancements for network management and provides a 100-Mbps interface to servers and dedicated Ethernet-to-desktop workstations.

catchment areas Zone that falls within an area that can be served by an internetworking device such as a hub.

Category 1 cabling One of five grades of UTP cabling described in the EIA/TIA-568B standard. Category 1 cabling is used for telephone communications and is not suitable for transmitting data. Compare with Category 2 cabling, Category 3 cabling, Category 4 cabling, and Category 5 cabling.

Category 2 cabling One of five grades of UTP cabling described in the EIA/TIA-568B standard. Category 2 cabling is capable of transmitting data at speeds up to 4 Mbps. Compare with Category 1 cabling, Category 3 cabling, Category 4 cabling, and Category 5 cabling.

Category 3 cabling One of five grades of UTP cabling described in the EIA/TIA-568B standard. Category 3 cabling is used in 10BASE-T networks and can transmit data at speeds up to 10 Mbps. Compare with Category 1 cabling, Category 2 cabling, Category 4 cabling, and Category 5 cabling.

Category 4 cabling One of five grades of UTP cabling described in the EIA/TIA-568B standard. Category 4 cabling is used in Token Ring networks and can transmit data at speeds up to 16 Mbps. Compare with Category 1 cabling, Category 2 cabling, Category 3 cabling, and Category 5 cabling.

Category 5 cabling One of five grades of UTP cabling described in the EIA/TIA-568B standard. Category 5 cabling is used for running CDDI and can transmit data at speeds up to 100 Mbps. Compare with Category 1 cabling, Category 2 cabling, Category 3 cabling, and Category 4 cabling.

catenet Network in which hosts are connected to diverse networks, which themselves are connected with routers. The Internet is a prominent example of a catenet.

CATV Cable Television - Communication system where multiple channels of programming material are transmitted to homes using broadband coaxial cable. Formerly called Community Antenna Television.

CBDS Connectionless Broadband Data Service - European high-speed, packet-switched, datagram-based WAN networking technology. Similar to SMDS.

CBR Constant Bit Rate - QOS class defined by the ATM Forum for ATM networks. CBR is used for connections that depend on precise clocking to ensure undistorted delivery. Compare with ABR, UBR, and VBR.

CBWFQ Class-Based Weighted Fair Queueing - Extends the standard WFQ functionality to provide support for user-defined traffic classes. For CBWFQ, you define traffic classes based on match criteria including protocols, access control lists (ACLs), and input interfaces.

CCITT Consultative Committee for International Telegraph and Telephone - International organization responsible for the development of communications standards. CCITT is now known as the ITU-T.

CCK Complementary Code Keying - CCK is a modulation technique used in IEEE 802.11b-compliant wireless LANs for transmission at 5.5 and 11 Mbps.

CCS Common Channel Signaling - Signaling system used in telephone networks that separates signaling information from user data. A specified channel is exclusively designated to carry signaling information for all other channels in the system.

CCX Cisco Compatible Extensions - The CCX program for WLAN devices is an evolving set of specification for interoperabililty, which facilitates testing of vendor clients and provides tested compatibility with licensed Cisco infrastructure innovations.

CD Carrier Detect - Signal that indicates whether an interface is active. Also, a signal generated by a modem indicating that a call has been connected.

CDDI Copper Distributed Data Interface - Implementation of FDDI protocols over STP and UTP cabling. CDDI transmits over relatively short distances, about 325 feet (100 m), providing data rates of 100 Mbps using a dual-ring architecture to provide redundancy. Based on the ANSI Twisted-Pair Physical Medium Dependent (TPPMD) standard. Compare with FDDI.

CDDI/FDDI workgroup concentrator See Cisco Workgroup Concentrator.

CDP Cisco Discovery Protocol - Media- and protocol-independent device-discovery protocol that runs on all Cisco-manufactured equipment including routers, access servers, bridges, and switches. Using CDP, a device can advertise its existence to other devices and receive information about other devices on the same LAN or on the remote side of a WAN. Runs on all media that support SNAP, including LANs, Frame Relay, and ATM media.

CDPD Cellular Digital Packet Data - Open standard for two-way wireless data communication over high-frequency cellular telephone channels. Allows data transmissions between a remote cellular link and a NAP. Operates at 19.2 Kbps.

CDVT Cell Delay Variation Tolerance - Parameter defined by the ATM Forum for ATM traffic management. In CBR transmissions, determines the level of jitter that is tolerable for the data samples taken by the PCR.

cell 1) The basic unit for ATM switching and multiplexing. Cells contain identifiers that specify the data stream to which they belong. Each cell consists of a 5-byte header and 48 bytes of payload. See also cell relay. 2) In wireless technology, a cell is the area of radio range or coverage in which the wireless devices can communicate with the base station. The size of the cell depends upon the speed of the transmission, the type of antenna used, and the physical environment, as well as other factors.

cell delay variation tolerance See CDVT.

cell line card See CLC.

cell loss priority See CLP.

cell payload scrambling Technique used on the LightStream 2020 ATM switch to maintain framing on some medium-speed edge and trunk interfaces.

cell relay Network technology based on the use of small, fixed-size packets, or cells. Because cells are fixed-length, they can be processed and switched in hardware at high speeds. Cell relay is the basis for many high-speed network protocols including ATM, IEEE 802.6, and SMDS.

cells per second See cps.

Cellular Digital Packet Data See CDPD.

cellular radio Technology that uses radio transmissions to access telephonecompany networks. Service is provided in a particular area by a low-power transmitter.

CEMAC Circuit Emulation Access Card - T1 or E1 circuit emulation card in the LightStream 2020 ATM switch.

central office See CO.

Centrex AT and T PBX that provides direct inward dialing and automatic number identification of the calling PBX.

CFRAD See Cisco FRAD.

CGMP   Cisco Group Management Protocol - A Cisco-developed protocol that runs between Cisco routers and Catalyst switches to leverage IGMP information on Cisco routers to make Layer 2 forwarding decisions on Catalyst switch ports that are attached to interested receivers.

CGS   Compact Gateway Server - Cisco midrange multiprotocol router designed for medium to small regional and district environments. The CGS is a 2-slot router that supports up to four interfaces (all of the same type).

Challenge Handshake Authentication Protocol   See CHAP.

channel   1) A communication path. Multiple channels can be multiplexed over a single cable in certain environments. 2) In IBM, the specific path between large computers (such as mainframes) and attached peripheral devices.

Channel Interface Processor   See CIP.

channel service unit   See CSU.

channel-attached   Pertaining to attachment of devices directly by data channels (input/output channels) to a computer.

channelized E1   Access link operating at 2.048 Mbps that is subdivided into 30 B-channels and 1 D-channel. Supports DDR, Frame Relay, and X.25. Compare with channelized T1.

channelized T1   Access link operating at 1.544 Mbps that is subdivided into 24 channels (23 B-channels and 1 D-channel) of 64 Kbps each. The individual channels or groups of channels connect to different destinations. Supports DDR, Frame Relay, and X.25. Compare with channelized E1. Channelized T1 is also known as fractional T1.

CHAP   Challenge Handshake Authentication Protocol - Security feature supported on lines using PPP encapsulation that prevents unauthorized access. CHAP does not itself prevent unauthorized access, it merely identifies the remote end. The router or access server then determines whether that user is allowed access. Compare to PAP.

chat script   String of text that defines the login "conversation" that occurs between two systems. Consists of expect-send pairs that define the string that the local system expects to receive from the remote system and what the local system should send as a reply.

Cheapernet   Industry term used to refer to the IEEE 802.3 10BASE2 standard or the cable specified in that standard. Compare with Thinnet.

checksum   1) Method for checking the integrity of transmitted data. A checksum is an integer value computed from a sequence of octets taken through a series of arithmetic operations. The value is recomputed at the receiving end and compared for verification. 2) Calculated checksum of the header and data fields.

choke packet   Packet sent to a transmitter to tell it that congestion exists and that it should reduce its sending rate.

CIA   Specification for running IP over ATM in a manner that takes full advantage of the features of ATM. Defined in RFC 1577.

CICNet   Regional network that connects academic, research, nonprofit, and commercial organizations in the Midwestern United States. Founded in 1988, CICNet was a part of the NSFNET and was funded by the NSF until the NSFNET dissolved in 1995.

CIDR   Classless Interdomain Routing - Technique supported by BGP4 and based on route aggregation. CIDR allows routers to group routes together in order to cut down on the quantity of routing information carried by the core routers. With CIDR, several IP networks appear to networks outside the group as a single, larger entity.

CIO Cisco Information Online - Online service available to Cisco customers that provides electronic services and online information relating to Cisco products. CIO services include product information, software updates, release notes, technical tips, configuration notes, brochures, and download offerings.

CIP Channel Interface Processor - Channel attachment interface for Cisco 7000 series routers. The CIP is used to connect a host mainframe to a control unit, eliminating the need for an FEP for channel attachment.

CIR Committed Information Rate - The rate at which a Frame Relay network agrees to transfer information under normal conditions, averaged over a minimum increment of time. CIR, measured in bits per second, is one of the key negotiated tariff metrics.

circuit Communications path between two or more points.

circuit emulation access card See CEMAC.

circuit group Grouping of associated serial lines that link two bridges. If one of the serial links in a circuit group is in the spanning tree for a network, any of the serial links in the circuit group can be used for load balancing. This load-balancing strategy avoids data ordering problems by assigning each destination address to a particular serial link.

circuit switching Switching system in which a dedicated physical circuit path must exist between sender and receiver for the duration of the "call." Used heavily in the telephone company network. Circuit switching can be contrasted with contention and token passing as a channel-access method, and with message switching and packet switching as a switching technique.

Cisco 1000 Any of the Cisco 1000 series LAN Extenders and routers. The Cisco 1000 series are easy-to-install, inexpensive, multiprotocol access products designed for small offices and other remote sites. The Cisco 1000 series includes an ISDN router, an asynchronous router, and LAN extenders.

Cisco 2500 Any of the Cisco 2500 series routers and access servers, including single LAN routers; mission-specific, low-end routers; router/hub combinations; access servers; and dual LAN routers. The Cisco 2500 is designed for small offices and other remote sites and runs the Cisco IOS software. The Cisco 2500 series is also known as Cisco Access Server 2500 series.

Cisco 4000 Any of the Cisco 4000 series routers designed for a wide variety of network computing environments. The Cisco 4000 series routers run the Cisco IOS software and can be optimized for particular environments with custom configurations.

Cisco 5100 Cisco data communications platform that combines the functions of a Cisco access server with analog and digital modems, CSUs, and T1 channel banks. The Cisco 5100 is optimized for high-speed modem access and is well-suited for dial-up applications, including host access, electronic mail, file transfer, and dial-in access to a LAN. Cisco 5100 is also kknown as Cisco Access Server 5100.

Cisco 7000 Any of the Cisco 7000 series of routers (the Cisco 7000 or the Cisco 7010), a high-end router platform that supports a wide range of network interfaces and media types and is designed for use in enterprise networks. Cisco 7000 series routers run the Cisco IOS software and support online software reconfiguration, OIR, fast boot, environmental monitoring, self-diagnostics, redundant power supplies, and Flash memory.

Cisco 7500 Any of the Cisco 7500 series of routers, a high-end multiprotocol router platform designed for use in enterprise networks. Cisco 7500 series routers run the Cisco IOS software and implement a distributed multiprocessor architecture consisting of the CyBus, the RSP, and the VIP.

Cisco Access Server 2500 See Cisco 2500.

Cisco Access Server 5100 See Cisco 5100.

Cisco Discovery Protocol See CDP.

Cisco Extended Bus   See CxBus.

Cisco FRAD   Cisco Frame Relay Access Device - Cisco product that supports Cisco IOS Frame Relay SNA services and can be upgraded to be a full-function multiprotocol router. The Cisco FRAD connects SDLC devices to Frame Relay without requiring an existing LAN. However, the Cisco FRAD does support attached LANs and can perform conversion from SDLC to Ethernet and Token Ring.

Cisco Frame Relay access device   See Cisco FRAD.

Cisco Information Online   See CIO.

Cisco Internetwork Operating System software   See Cisco IOS software.

Cisco IOS software   Cisco Internetwork Operating System software - Cisco system software that provides common functionality, scalability, and security for all products under the CiscoFusion architecture. The Cisco IOS software allows centralized, integrated, and automated installation and management of internetworks, while ensuring support for a wide variety of protocols, media, services, and platforms.

Cisco LightStream 100   Cisco LightStream 100 ATM switch A fully nonblocking ATM switch operating at up to 2.4 Gbps and supporting multiple ATM lines of 155-Mbps data speed as well as a variety of LAN and WAN interfaces. The LightStream 100 switch can serve as part of an ATM workgroup or small campus backbone connecting a number of ATM routers, multilayer LAN switches, and high-performance servers and clients.

Cisco LightStream 2020   Cisco LightStream 2020 Enterprise ATM switch For campus and wide-area applications. The LightStream 2020 ATM switch supports trunks operating at T1/E1 data rates and provides a migration path through T3/E3 into a SONET/SDH OC-3 trunk. The LightStream 2020 intelligent edge modules support a variety of services including frame forwarding, Frame Relay, ATM UNI, and LAN internetworking.

Cisco Workgroup Adapter   Series of Cisco workgroup adapters that allow workstations to connect to CDDI or FDDI interfaces operating at 100 Mbps.

Cisco Workgroup Concentrator   Series of Cisco workgroup concentrators that combines the compact form factor of workgroup concentrators with the versatility of modular hubs. Supports from 4 to 32 combinations of CDDI or FDDI ports.

ciscoBus controller   See SP.

CiscoFusion   Cisco internetworking architecture that "fuses" together the scalability, stability, and security advantages of the latest routing technologies with the performance benefits of ATM and LAN switching, and the management benefits of VLANs.

CiscoView   GUI-based device-management software application that provides dynamic status, statistics, and comprehensive configuration information for Cisco internetworking devices. In addition to displaying a physical view of Cisco device chassis, CiscoView also provides device monitoring functions and basic troubleshooting capabilities, and can be integrated with several leading SNMP-based network management platforms.

CiscoWorks   Series of SNMP-based internetwork management software applications. CiscoWorks includes applications for monitoring router and access server status, managing configuration files, and troubleshooting network problems. CiscoWorks applications are integrated on several SNMP-based network management platforms, including SunNet Manager, HP OpenView, and IBM NetView.

CKIP   Cisco Key Integrity Protocol - CKIP is the Cisco implementation of PPK.

class of service   See COS.

Class-based weighted fair queueing   See CBWFQ.

classfull network   Network that uses traditional IP network addresses of class A, class B, and class C.

classical IP over ATM   See CIA.

classless interdomain routing   See CIDR.

classless network   Network that does not use the traditional IP network addressing (class A, class B, and class C), but defines the network boundary using a prefix value that indicates the number of bits used for the network portion.

CLAW   Common Link Access for Workstations - Data link layer protocol used by channel-attached RISC System/6000 series systems and by IBM 3172 devices running TCP/IP off-load. CLAW improves efficiency of channel use and allows the CIP to provide the functionality of a 3172 in TCP/IP environments and support direct channel attachment. The output from TCP/IP mainframe processing is a series of IP datagrams that the router can switch without modifications.

CLC   Cell Line Card - Card on the LightStream 2020 ATM switch that, in conjunction with an access card, supports up to two OC-3c edge ports or one OC-3c trunk port. A CLC can be configured as an edge card or a trunk card.

Clear To Send   See CTS.

CLEC   Competitive Local Exchange Carrier - A company that builds and operates communication networks in metropolitan areas and provides its customers with an alternative to the local telephone company.

CLI   Command-Line Interface - The command-line interface on the LightStream 2020 that runs on NPs and Sun SPARCstations and is used to monitor and control an ATM network.

client   1) Node or software program (front-end device) that requests services from a server. See also back end, front end, and server. 2) In wireless technology, a client is a radio device that uses the services of an Access Point to communicate wirelessly with other devices on a local area network.

client-server computing   Term used to describe distributed computing (processing) network systems in which transaction responsibilities are divided into two parts: client (front end) and server (back end). Both terms (client and server) can be applied to software programs or actual computing devices. Compare with peer-to-peer computing. Client-server computing is also known as distributed computing.

client-server model   Common way to describe network services and the model user processes (programs) of those services. Examples include the nameserver/nameresolver paradigm of the DNS and fileserver/file-client relationships such as NFS and diskless hosts.

clinical information   Data related to, or founded on actual observation and treatment of patients.

CLNP   Connectionless Network Protocol - Protocol stack developed originally as a replacement for TCP/IP with the anticipation that this OSI suite would take over being based upon the standard OSI 7-layer model. This has not happened, however one protocol within CLNP called IS-IS has become very popular within the Internet community due to its scalability as the Internet grows.

CLNS   Connectionless Network Service - The OSI network layer service similar to bare IP service. A CLNS entity communicates over Connectionless Network Protocol (CLNP) with its peer CLNS entity. CLNP is the OSI equivalent of IP. CLNP provides the interface between CLNS and upper layers. CLNS does not perform connection setup or termination because paths are determined independently for each packet that is transmitted through a network. In addition, CLNS provides best-effort delivery, which means that no guarantee exists that data will not be lost, corrupted, miss-ordered, or duplicated. CLNS relies on transport layer protocols to perform error detection and correction.

CLP   Cell Loss Priority - Field in the ATM cell header that determines the probability of a cell being dropped if the network becomes congested. Cells with CLP = 0 are insured traffic, which is unlikely to be dropped. Cells with CLP = 1 are best-effort traffic, which might be dropped in congested conditions in order to free up resources to handle insured traffic.

cluster controller   1) Generally, an intelligent device that provides the connections for a cluster of terminals to a data link. 2) In SNA, a programmable device that controls the input/output operations of attached devices. Typically, an IBM 3174 or 3274 device.

CMI   Coded Mark Inversion - ITU-T line coding technique specified for STS-3c transmissions. Also used in DS-1 systems.

CMIC   Cisco Message Integrity Check - The Cisco implementation of MIC.

CMIP   Common Management Information Protocol - OSI network management protocol created and standardized by ISO for the monitoring and control of heterogeneous networks.

CMIS   Common Management Information Services - OSI network management service interface created and standardized by ISO for the monitoring and control of heterogeneous networks.

CMNS   Connection-Mode Network Service - Extends local X.25 switching to a variety of media (Ethernet, FDDI, Token Ring).

CMT   Connection Management - FDDI process that handles the transition of the ring through its various states (off, active, connect, and so on), as defined by the ANSI X3T9.5 specification.

CO   Central Office - Local telephone company office to which all local loops in a given area connect and in which circuit switching of subscriber lines occurs.

coaxial cable   Cable consisting of a hollow outer cylindrical conductor that surrounds a single inner wire conductor. Two types of coaxial cable are currently used in LANs: 50-ohm cable, which is used for digital signaling, and 75-ohm cable, which is used for analog signal and high-speed digital signaling.

code bits   Control functions, such as setup and termination of a session.

CODEC   Coder-Decoder - Device that typically uses PCM to transform analog signals into a digital bit stream, and digital signals back into analog.

coded mark inversion   See CMI.

coder-decoder   See CODEC.

coding   Electrical techniques used to convey binary signals.

collapsed backbone   Nondistributed backbone in which all network segments are interconnected by way of an internetworking device. A collapsed backbone might be a virtual network segment existing in a device such as a hub, a router, or a switch.

collision   In Ethernet, the result of two nodes transmitting simultaneously. The frames from each device impact and are damaged when they meet on the physical media.

collision detection   See CSMA/CD.

collision domain   In Ethernet, the network area within which frames that have collided are propagated. Repeaters and hubs propagate collisions; LAN switches, bridges and routers do not.

command-line interface   The command-line interface on the LightStream 2020 that runs on NPs and Sun SPARCstations and is used to monitor and control an ATM network.

Committed Burst   See Bc.

committed information rate   See CIR.

common carrier   Licensed, private utility company that supplies communication services to the public at regulated prices.

common channel signaling   See CCS.

Common Link Access for Workstations   See CLAW.

Common Management Information Protocol   See CMIP.

Common Management Information Services   See CMIS.

common mode   Term used to describe problems involving either the hot or neutral wires and the safety ground wire on a power line.

Common Programming Interface for Communications   See CPI-C.

communication   Transmission of information.

communication controller   In SNA, a subarea node (such as an IBM 3745 device) that contains an NCP.

communication server   Communications processor that connects asynchronous devices to a LAN or WAN through network and terminal emulation software. Performs only asynchronous routing of IP and IPX. Compare with access server.

communications line   The physical link (such as wire or a telephone circuit) that connects one or more devices to one or more other devices.

community   In SNMP, a logical group of managed devices and NMSs in the same administrative domain.

Community Antenna Television   Now known as CATV. See CATV.

Community Health Information network   Information network linking providers, insurers, patients and suppliers throughout a community.

community string   Text string that acts as a password and is used to authenticate messages sent between a management station and a router containing an SNMP agent. The community string is sent in every packet between the manager and the agent.

Compact Gateway Server   See CGS.

companding   Contraction derived from the opposite processes of compression and expansion. Part of the PCM process whereby analog signal values are logically rounded to discrete scale-step values on a nonlinear scale. The decimal step number is then coded in its binary equivalent prior to transmission. The process is reversed at the receiving terminal using the same nonlinear scale. Compare with compression and expansion.

Compressed Serial Link Internet Protocol   See CSLIP.

compression   The running of a data set through an algorithm that reduces the space required to store or the bandwidth required to transmit the data set. Compare with companding and expansion.

Computer Science Network   See CSNET.

concentrator   See hub.

conductor   Any material with a low resistance to electrical current. Any material capable of carrying an electrical current.

configuration management   One of five categories of network management defined by ISO for management of OSI networks. Configuration management subsystems are responsible for detecting and determining the state of a network.

configuration register   In Cisco routers, a 16-bit, user-configurable value that determines how the router functions during initialization. The configuration register can be stored in hardware or software. In hardware, the bit position is set using a jumper. In software, the bit position is set by specifying a hexadecimal value using configuration commands.

congestion   Traffic in excess of network capacity.

congestion avoidance   See CA.

connection management   See CMT.

connectionless   Term used to describe data transfer without the existence of a virtual circuit. Compare with connection-oriented.

Connectionless Broadband Data Service   See CBDS.

Connectionless Network Protocol   See CLNP.

Connectionless Network Service   See CLNS.

Connection-Mode Network Service   See CMNS.

connection-oriented   Term used to describe data transfer that requires the establishment of a virtual circuit.

Connection-Oriented Network Protocol   See CONP.

CONP   Connection-Oriented Network Protocol - OSI protocol providing connection-oriented operation to upper-layer protocols.

console   DTE through which commands are entered into a host.

constant bit rate   See CBR.

Consultative Committee for International Telegraph   See CCITT.

content-addressable memory   See associative memory.

contention   Access method in which network devices compete for permission to access the physical medium. Contrast with circuit switching and token passing.

ControlStream traffic management   Traffic management scheme used by the LightStream 2020 ATM switch. Includes congestion avoidance, traffic shaping, and traffic policing, and allows links to operate at high levels of utilization by scaling back lower-priority, delay-tolerant traffic at the edge of the network when congestion begins to occur.

convergence   The speed and ability of a group of internetworking devices running a specific routing protocol to agree on the topology of an internetwork after a change in that topology.

conversation   In SNA, an LU 6.2 session between two transaction programs.

Copper Distributed Data Interface   See CDDI.

core gateway   The primary routers in the Internet.

core router   In a packet-switched star topology, a router that is part of the backbone and that serves as the single pipe through which all traffic from peripheral networks must pass on its way to other peripheral networks.

Corporation for Open Systems   See COS.

Corporation for Research and Educational Networkin   See CREN.

COS   1) Class of Service - Indication of how an upper-layer protocol requires that a lower-layer protocol treat its messages. In SNA subarea routing, COS definitions are used by subarea nodes to determine the optimal route to establish a given session. A COS definition comprises a virtual route number and a transmission priority field. Also known as type of service (TOS). 2) Corporation for Open Systems - Organization that promulgates the use of OSI protocols through conformance testing, certification, and related activities.

cost Arbitrary value, typically based on hop count, media bandwidth, or other measures, that is assigned by a network administrator and used to compare various paths through an internetwork environment. Cost values are used by routing protocols to determine the most favorable path to a particular destination: the lower the cost, the better the path. Cost is also known as path cost.

count to infinity Problem that can occur in routing algorithms that are slow to converge, in which routers continuously increment the hop count to particular networks. Typically, some arbitrary hop-count limit is imposed to prevent this problem.

CPE Customer Premises Equipment - Terminating equipment, such as terminals, telephones, and modems, supplied by the telephone company, installed at customer sites, and connected to the telephone company network.

CPI-C Common Programming Interface for Communications - Platform-independent API developed by IBM and used to provide portability in APPC applications.

cps Cells Per Second

CPU Central Processing Unit - The part of a computer that controls all the other parts. It fetches instructions from memory and decodes them. This may cause it to transfer data to or from memory or to activate peripherals to perform input or output.

CQ Custom Queuing - Queuing method that is used to guarantee bandwidth for traffic by assigning queue space to each protocol.

CRC Cyclic Redundancy Check - Error-checking technique in which the frame recipient calculates a remainder by dividing frame contents by a prime binary divisor and compares the calculated remainder to a value stored in the frame by the sending node.

CREN Corporation for Research and Educational Networking - The result of a merger of BITNET and CSNET. CREN is devoted to providing Internet connectivity to its members, which include the alumni, students, faculty, and other affiliates of participating educational and research institutions, via BITNET III.

cross talk Interfering energy transferred from one circuit to another.

CSLIP Compressed Serial Link Internet Protocol - Extension of SLIP that, when appropriate, allows just header information to be sent across a SLIP connection, reducing overhead and increasing packet throughput on SLIP lines.

CSMA/CD Carrier Sense Multiple Access/Collision Detect - Media-access mechanism wherein devices ready to transmit data first check the channel for a carrier. If no carrier is sensed for a specific period of time, a device can transmit. If two devices transmit at once, a collision occurs and is detected by all colliding devices. This collision subsequently delays retransmissions from those devices for some random length of time. CSMA/CD access is used by Ethernet and IEEE 802.3.

CSNET Computer Science Network - Large internetwork consisting primarily of universities, research institutions, and commercial concerns. CSNET merged with BITNET to form CREN.

CSU Channel Service Unit - Digital interface device that connects end-user equipment to the local digital telephone loop. Often referred to together with DSU, as CSU/DSU.

csumon Tool available on the LightStream 2020 ATM switch, accessible from the bash shell. Csumon allows connection to an external CSU/DSU on a low-speed line for monitoring and control purposes, and can display statistics on the internal CSU/DSU of a medium-speed line.

CTS Clear To Send - Circuit in the EIA/TIA-232 specification that is activated when DCE is ready to accept data from DTE.

custom queuing See CQ.

Custom report creator The software function that allows users to create reports or report templates that meet their specific requirements.

customer premises equipment   See CPE.

cut sheet   A rough diagram indicating where cable runs are located and the numbers of rooms they lead to.

cut-through packet switching   Packet switching approach that streams data through a switch so that the leading edge of a packet exits the switch at the output port before the packet finishes entering the input port. A device using cut-through packet switching reads, processes, and forwards packets as soon as the destination address is looked up, and the outgoing port determined. Contrast with store and forward packet switching. Cut-through packet switching is also known as on-the-fly packet switching.

CxBus   Cisco Extended Bus - Data bus for interface processors on Cisco 7000 series routers that operates at 533 Mbps.

CyBus   1.067-Gbps data bus for interface processors. Used in the Cisco 7500 series routers.

cycles per second   See hertz.

cyclic redundancy check   See CRC.

D channel   Data Channel - 1) Full-duplex, 16-kbps (BRI) or 64-kbps (PRI) ISDN channel. Compare to B channel, E channel, and H channel. 2) In SNA, a device that connects a processor and main storage with peripherals.

D4 framing   See SF.

DARPA   Defense Advanced Research Projects Agency - U.S. government agency that funded research for and experimentation with the Internet. Evolved from ARPA, and then, in 1994, back to ARPA.

DARPA Internet   Obsolete term referring to the Internet. See Internet.

data   Upper-layer protocol data.

data bus connector   See DB connector.

data channel   See D channel.

data circuit-terminating equipment   See DCE.

data communications equipment   See DCE.

Data Encryption Standard   See DES.

data flow control layer   Layer 5 of the SNA architectural model. This layer determines and manages interactions between session partners, particularly data flow. Corresponds to the session layer of the OSI model.

data link control layer   Layer 2 in the SNA architectural model. Responsible for the transmission of data over a particular physical link. Corresponds roughly to the data link layer of the OSI model.

data link layer   Layer 2 of the OSI reference model. This layer provides reliable transit of data across a physical link. The data link layer is concerned with physical addressing, network topology, line discipline, error notification, ordered delivery of frames, and flow control. The IEEE has divided this layer into two sublayers: the MAC sublayer and the LLC sublayer. Sometimes simply called link layer. Roughly corresponds to the data link control layer of the SNA model.

Data mining   The process of extracting patterns from data.

Data Movement Processor   See DMP.

data service unit   See DSU.

data set ready   See DSR.

data sink Network equipment that accepts data transmissions.

data stream All data transmitted through a communications line in a single read or write operation.

data terminal equipment See DTE.

data terminal ready See DTR.

Database A digital collection of information that is organized so that it can easily be accessed, managed, and updated.

datagram Logical grouping of information sent as a network layer unit over a transmission medium without prior establishment of a virtual circuit. IP datagrams are the primary information units in the Internet. The terms frame, message, packet, and segment are also used to describe logical information groupings at various layers of the OSI reference model and in various technology circles.

data-link connection identifier See DLCI.

data-link switching See DLSw.

dB decibel - The ratio between two signal levels. It is a unit-less physical measurement of signal strength.

DB connector Data Bus Connector - Type of connector used to connect serial and parallel cables to a data bus. DB connector names are of the format DB-x, where x represents the number of (wires) within the connector. Each line is connected to a pin on the connector, but in many cases, not all pins are assigned a function. DB connectors are defined by various EIA/TIA standards.

dBi A ratio of decibels to an isotropic antenna that is commonly used to measure antenna gain. The greater the dBi value, the higher the gain, and the more acute the angle of coverage.

DC Direct Current - Electrical current that travels in only one direction. Direct current is generally used in electronic circuits.

DCA Defense Communications Agency - U.S. government organization responsible for DDN networks such as MILNET. DCA is now known as DISA.

DCE Data Communications Equipment - Data communications equipment (EIA expansion) or data circuit-terminating equipment (ITU-T expansion). The devices and connections of a communications network that comprise the network end of the user-to-network interface. The DCE provides a physical connection to the network, forwards traffic, and provides a clocking signal used to synchronize data transmission between DCE and DTE devices. Modems and interface cards are examples of DCE.

dCEF Cisco Express Forwarding - Advanced Layer 3 IP forwarding technology designed to optimize network performance and scalability.

DDM Distributed Data Management - Software in an IBM SNA environment that provides peer-to-peer communication and file sharing. One of three SNA transaction services.

DDN Defense Data Network - U.S. military network composed of an unclassified network (MILNET) and various secret and top-secret networks. DDN is operated and maintained by DISA.

DDR Dial-on-Demand Routing - Technique whereby a Cisco router can automatically initiate and close a circuit-switched session as transmitting stations demand. The router spoofs keepalives so that end stations treat the session as active. DDR permits routing over ISDN or telephone lines using an external ISDN terminal adaptor or modem.

DE Discard Eligible - See tagged traffic.

de facto standard Standard that exists by nature of its widespread use. Compare with de jure standard.

de jure standard Standard that exists because of its approval by an official standards body. Compare with de facto standard.

decibels See dB.

DECnet Digital Equipment Corporation Network - Group of communications products (including a protocol suite) developed and supported by Digital Equipment Corporation. DECnet/OSI (also called DECnet Phase V) is the most recent iteration and supports both OSI protocols and proprietary Digital protocols. Phase IV Prime supports inherent MAC addresses that allow DECnet nodes to coexist with systems running other protocols that have MAC address restrictions.

DECnet routing Digital Equipment Corporation Network routing - Proprietary routing scheme introduced by Digital Equipment Corporation in DECnet Phase III. In DECnet Phase V, DECnet completed its transition to OSI routing protocols (ES-IS and IS-IS).

decorative raceway Type of wall-mounted channel with removable cover used to support horizontal cabling. Decorative raceway is big enough to hold two cables.

decryption The reverse application of an encryption algorithm to encrypted data, thereby restoring that data to its original, unencrypted state.

dedicated LAN Network segment allocated to a single device. Used in LAN switched network topologies.

dedicated line Communications line that is indefinitely reserved for transmissions, rather than switched as transmission is required.

default route Routing table entry that is used to direct frames for which a next hop is not explicitly listed in the routing table.

Defense Advanced Research Projects Agency See DARPA.

Defense Communications Agency See DCA.

Defense Data Network See DDN.

Defense Information Systems Agency See DISA.

Defense Intelligence Agency See DIA.

delay 1) The time between the initiation of a transaction by a sender and the first response received by the sender. 2) The time required to move a packet from source to destination over a given path.

demand priority Media access method used in 100VG-AnyLAN that uses a hub that can handle multiple transmission requests and can process traffic according to priority, making it useful for servicing time-sensitive traffic such as multimedia and video. Demand priority eliminates the overhead of packet collisions, collision recovery, and broadcast traffic typical in Ethernet networks.

demarc Demarcation point between carrier equipment and CPE.

demodulation Process of returning a modulated signal to its original form. Modems perform demodulation by taking an analog signal and returning it to its original (digital) form.

demultiplexing The separating of multiple input streams that have been multiplexed into a common physical signal back into multiple output streams.

dense mode PIM See PIM dense mode.

Department of Defense See DoD.

Department of Defense Intelligence Information Sys See DNSIX.

Dependent LU See DLU.

DES Data Encryption Standard - Standard cryptographic algorithm developed by the U.S. NBS.

designated bridge   The bridge that incurs the lowest path cost when forwarding a frame from a segment to the route bridge.

Designated Intermediate System   See DIS.

designated router   OSPF router that generates LSAs for a multiaccess network and has other special responsibilities in running OSPF. Each multiaccess OSPF network that has at least two attached routers has a designated router that is elected by the OSPF Hello protocol. The designated router enables a reduction in the number of adjacencies required on a multiaccess network, which in turn reduces the amount of routing protocol traffic and the size of the topological database.

destination address   Address of a network device that is receiving data.

destination MAC   See DMAC.

destination port   Number of the called port.

destination service access point   See DSAP.

deterministic load distribution   Technique for distributing traffic between two bridges across a circuit group. Guarantees packet ordering between source-destination pairs and always forwards traffic for a source-destination pair on the same segment in a circuit group for a given circuit-group configuration.

Deutsche Industrie Norm   See DIN.

Deutsche Industrie Norm connector   See DIN connector.

device   See node.

DFS   Dynamic Frequency Selection - DFS dynamically instructs a transmitter to switch to another channel whenever a particular condition (such as the presence of a radar signal) is met. Prior to transmitting, the DFS mechanism of a device monitors its available operating spectrum, listening for a radar signal. If a signal is detected, the channel associated with the radar signal is vacated or flagged as unavailable for use by the transmitter.

DIA   Document Interchange Architecture - Defines the protocols and data formats needed for the transparent interchange of documents in an SNA network. One of three SNA transaction services.

Diagnosis   The nature and cause of a disease or injury determined through evaluation of patient history, examination, and review of laboratory data.

dial backup   Feature supported by Cisco routers that provides protection against WAN downtime by allowing the network administrator to configure a backup serial line through a circuit-switched connection.

dial-on-demand routing   See DDR.

dial-up line   Communications circuit that is established by a switched-circuit connection using the telephone company network.

differential encoding   Digital encoding technique whereby a binary value is denoted by a signal change rather than a particular signal level.

differential Manchester encoding   Digital coding scheme where a mid-bit-time transition is used for clocking, and a transition at the beginning of each bit time denotes a zero. The coding scheme used by IEEE 802.5 and Token Ring networks.

Diffusing Update Algorithm   See DUAL.

Digital Network Architecture   See DNA.

digital signal   Language of computers comprising only two states, on and off which are indicated by a series of voltage pulses.

digital signal level 0   See DS-0.

digital signal level 1   See DS-1.

digital signal level 3   See DS-3.

Dijkstra's algorithm   See SPF.

DIN   Deutsche Industrie Norm - German national standards organization.

DIN connector   Deutsche Industrie Norm connector - Multipin connector used in some Macintosh and IBM PC-compatible computers, and on some network processor panels.

dipole   A type of low-gain (2.2-dBi) antenna consisting of two (often internal) elements. Compare with isotropic.

direct memory access   See DMA.

directed search   Search request sent to a specific node known to contain a resource. A directed search is used to determine the continued existence of the resource and to obtain routing information specific to the node. See also broadcast search.

directionality   The coverage around the antenna. An omnidirectional WLAN antenna transmits and receives signals in all horizontal directions equally. A directional antenna focuses the signal from the access point into a smaller coverage area resulting in a stronger signal in this direction.

directory services   Services that help network devices locate service providers.

DIS   Designated Intermediate System - Elected and will conduct the flooding over the media. The DIS is analogous to the designated router in Open Shortest Path First (OSPF) Protocol, even though the details including election process and adjacencies within a multi-access media differ significantly. The DIS is elected by priority. The highest priority becomes the DIS. This is configurable on an interface basis. In the case of a tie, the router with the highest SNPA (MAC) address will become the DIS.

DISA   Defense Information Systems Agency - U.S. military organization responsible for implementing and operating military information systems, including the DDN.

discard eligible   See DE.

disk assembly   The combination of a hard disk drive, a floppy disk drive, and a disk power supply on a LightStream 2020 ATM switch. Each NP card in a LightStream 2020 chassis has its own disk assembly.

Distance Vector Multicast Routing Protocol   See DVMRP.

distance vector routing algorithm   Class of routing algorithms that iterate on the number of hops in a route to find a shortest-path spanning tree. Distance vector routing algorithms call for each router to send its entire routing table in each update, but only to its neighbors. Distance vector routing algorithms can be prone to routing loops, but are computationally simpler than link state routing algorithms. Distance vector routing algorithm is also known as Bellman-Ford routing algorithm.

distortion delay   Problem with a communication signal resulting from nonuniform transmission speeds of the components of a signal through a transmission medium. Also called group delay.

distributed computing (processing)   See client-server computing.

Distributed Data Management   See DDM.

Distributed Queue Dual Bus   See DQDB.

Distributed Software System   A distributed system consists of a collection of autonomous computers linked by a computer network and equipped with distributed system software. This software enables computers to coordinate their activities and to share the resources of the system hardware, software, and data.

Distributed Weighted Fair Queuing   See dWFQ.

DLCI   Data-Link Connection Identifier - Value that specifies a PVC or SVC in a Frame Relay network. In the basic Frame Relay specification, DLCIs are locally significant (connected devices might use different values to specify the same connection). In the LMI extended specification, DLCIs are globally significant (DLCIs specify individual end devices).

DLSw   Data-Link Switching - Interoperability standard, described in RFC 1434, that provides a method for forwarding SNA and NetBIOS traffic over TCP/IP networks using data link layer switching and encapsulation. DLSw uses Switch-to-Switch Protocol (SSP) instead of SRB, eliminating the major limitations of SRB, including hop-count limits, broadcast and unnecessary traffic, timeouts, lack of flow control, and lack of prioritization schemes.

DLSw+   Data Link Switching Plus - Cisco implementation of the DLSw standard for SNA and NetBIOS traffic forwarding. DLSw+ goes beyond the standard to include the advanced features of the current Cisco RSRB implementation, and provides additional functionality to increase the overall scalability of data-link switching.

DLU   Dependent Logical Unit - An LU that depends on the SSCP to provide services for establishing sessions with other Lus.

DMA   Direct Memory Access - The transfer of data from a peripheral device, such as a hard disk drive, into memory without that data passing through the microprocessor. DMA transfers data into memory at high speeds with no processor overhead.

DMAC   Destination MAC - The MAC address specified in the Destination Address field of a packet. Compare with SMAC.

DMP   Data Movement Processor - Processor on the Catalyst 5000 that, along with the multiport packet buffer memory interface, performs the frame-switching function for the switch. The DMP also handles translational bridging between the Ethernet and FDDI interfaces, IP segmentation, and intelligent bridging with protocol-based filtering.

DNA   Digital Network Architecture - Network architecture developed by Digital Equipment Corporation. The products that embody DNA (including communications protocols) are collectively referred to as DECnet.

DNIS   Dialed Number Identification Service - DNIS is also known as called number.

DNS   Domain Naming System - System used in the Internet for translating names of network nodes into addresses.

DNS ALG   Domain Naming System Application Level Gateway - Protocol that can be used in NAT-PT translations to map network addresses dynamically based on DNS queries. Compare with NAT-PT and SIIT.

DNSIX   Department of Defense Intelligence Information System Network Security for Information Exchange - Collection of security requirements for networking defined by the U.S. Defense Intelligence Agency.

Document Interchange Architecture   See DIA.

DoD   Department of Defense - U.S. government organization that is responsible for national defense. The DoD has frequently funded communication protocol development.

domain   1) In the Internet, a portion of the naming hierarchy tree that refers to general groupings of networks based on organization-type or geography. 2) In SNA, an SSCP and the resources it controls. 3) In IS-IS, a logical set of networks. 4) Networking system developed by Apollo Computer (now part of Hewlett-Packard) for use in its engineering workstations.

Domain Naming System   See DNS.

domain specific part   See DSP.

dot address   Refers to the common notation for IP addresses in the form a.b.c.d where each number a represents, in decimal, 1 byte of the 4-byte IP address. Dot address is also known as dotted notation or four-part dotted notation.

dotted notation   See dot address.

downlink station   See ground station.

downstream physical unit   See DSPU.

DQDB   Distributed Queue Dual Bus - Data link layer communication protocol, specified in the IEEE 802.6 standard, designed for use in MANs. DQDB, which permits multiple systems to interconnect using two unidirectional logical buses, is an open standard that is designed for compatibility with carrier transmission standards, and is aligned with emerging standards for BISDN. SMDS Interface Protocol (SIP) is based on DQDB.

DRAM   Dynamic Random-Access Memory - RAM that stores information in capacitors that must be periodically refreshed. Delays can occur because DRAMs are inaccessible to the processor when refreshing their contents. However, DRAMs are less complex and have greater capacity than SRAMs.

drop   Point on a multipoint channel where a connection to a networked device is made.

drop cable   Generally, a cable that connects a network device (such as a computer) to a physical medium. A type of AUI.

DS-0 or DSO   Digital Signal Level 0 - Framing specification used in transmitting digital signals over a single channel at 64-kbps on a T1 facility. Compare with DS-1 and DS-3.

DS-1   Digital Signal Level 1 - Framing specification used in transmitting digital signals at 1.544-Mbps on a T1 facility (in the United States) or at 2.108-Mbps on an E1 facility (in Europe). Compare with DS-0 and DS-3.

DS-1 domestic trunk interface   See DS-1/DTI.

DS-1/DTI   Digital Signal Level 1/Domestic Trunk Interface - Interface circuit used for DS-1 applications with 24 trunks.

DS-3   Digital Signal Level 3 - Framing specification used for transmitting digital signals at 44.736-Mbps on a T3 facility. Compare with DS-0 and DS-1.

DSAP   Destination Service Access Point - The SAP of the network node designated in the Destination field of a packet. Compare to SSAP.

DSP   Domain Specific Part - The part of a CLNS address that contains an area identifier, a station identifier, and a selector byte.

DSPU   Downstream Physical Unit - 1) In SNA, a PU that is located downstream from the host. 2) Cisco IOS software feature that enables a router to function as a PU concentrator for SNA PU 2 nodes. PU concentration at the router simplifies the task of PU definition at the upstream host while providing additional flexibility and mobility for downstream PU devices. This feature is sometimes referred to as DSPU concentration. See also PU and SNA.

DSPU concentration   See DSPU and PU.

DSR   Data Set Ready - EIA/TIA-232 interface circuit that is activated when DCE is powered up and ready for use.

DSSS   Direct Sequence Spread Spectrum - DSSS is one of the modulation techniques provided for by the IEEE 802.11 and the one chosen by the 802.11 Working Group for the widely used IEEE 802.11b devices.

DSU Data Service Unit - Device used in digital transmission that adapts the physical interface on a DTE device to a transmission facility such as T1 or E1. The DSU is also responsible for such functions as signal timing. Often referred to together with CSU, as CSU/DSU.

DSX-1 Cross-connection point for DS-1 signals.

DTE Data Terminal Equipment - Device at the user end of a user-network interface that serves as a data source, destination, or both. DTE connects to a data network through a DCE device (for example, a modem) and typically uses clocking signals generated by the DCE. DTE includes such devices as computers, protocol translators, and multiplexers. Compare with DCE.

DTMF Dual Tone Multifrequency - Use of two simultaneous voice-band tones for dialing (such as touch tone).

DTR Data Terminal Ready - EIA/TIA-232 circuit that is activated to let the DCE know when the DTE is ready to send and receive data.

DUAL Diffusing Update Algorithm - Convergence algorithm used in Enhanced IGRP that provides loop-free operation at every instant throughout a route computation. Allows routers involved in a topology change to synchronize at the same time, while not involving routers that are unaffected by the change.

dual counter-rotating rings Network topology in which two signal paths, whose directions are opposite one another, exist in a token-passing network. FDDI and CDDI are based on this concept.

dual homing Network topology in which a device is connected to the network by way of two independent access points (points of attachment). One access point is the primary connection, and the other is a standby connection that is activated in the event of a failure of the primary connection.

Dual IS-IS See Integrated IS-IS.

dual stack A common transition mechanism to enable a smooth integration of IPv4 to IPv6. Compare with IPv6-over-IPv4 tunnels.

dual tone multifrequency See DTMF.

dual-homed station Device attached to multiple FDDI rings to provide redundancy.

DVMRP Distance Vector Multicast Routing Protocol - Internetwork gateway protocol, largely based on RIP, that implements a typical dense mode IP multicast scheme. DVMRP uses IGMP to exchange routing datagrams with its neighbors.

dWFQ Distributed Weighted Fair Queuing - Special high-speed version of WFQ that provides bandwidth allocations and delay bounds to specified IP traffic sources by segregating the traffic into flows or classes and then providing non-first-in, first-out (FIFO) service to the various queues according to their assigned weights. In order to use dWFQ, dCEF switching must be enabled on the interface.

dynamic address resolution Use of an address resolution protocol to determine and store address information on demand.

dynamic random-access memory See DRAM.

dynamic routing Routing that adjusts automatically to network topology or traffic changes. Dynamic routing is also known as adaptive routing.

E channel echo channel - 64-kbps ISDN circuit-switching control channel. The E channel was defined in the 1984 ITU-T ISDN specification, but was dropped in the 1988 specification. Compare with B channel, D channel, and H channel.

E.164 ITU-T recommendation for international telecommunication numbering, especially in ISDN, BISDN, and SMDS. An evolution of standard telephone numbers.

E1 Wide-area digital transmission scheme used predominantly in Europe that carries data at a rate of 2.048 Mbps. E1 lines can be leased for private use from common carriers. Compare with T1.

E3 Wide-area digital transmission scheme used predominantly in Europe that carries data at a rate of 34.368 Mbps. E3 lines can be leased for private use from common carriers. Compare with T3.

EAP Extensible Authentication Protocol - Universal authentication framework frequently used in wireless networks defined by RFC 3748. Although the EAP protocol is not limited to WLANs and can be used for wired LAN authentication, it is most often used in WLANs. The WPA and WPA2 standards have adopted five EAP types as their official authentication mechanisms.

early token release Technique used in Token Ring networks that allows a station to release a new token onto the ring immediately after transmitting, instead of waiting for the first frame to return. This feature can increase the total bandwidth on the ring.

EBCDIC Extended Binary Coded Decimal Interchange Code - Any of a number of coded character sets developed by IBM consisting of 8-bit coded characters. This character code is used by older IBM systems and telex machines. Compare with ASCII.

ECC Edge Card Control - Process on the NP of a LightStream 2020 ATM switch that performs per-card processing for an edge card. Such processing includes protocol management (ATM connection management) and media-specific (Ethernet and FDDI) management tasks, internetworking operations such as packet forwarding and filtering, and network management tasks.

echo channel See E channel.

ECMA European Computer Manufacturers Association - Group of European computer vendors who have done substantial OSI standardization work.

ECNM Enterprise Composite Network Model - Framework used by network professionals to describe and analyze any modern enterprise network. It takes a complex enterprise network design and breaks it down into three functional areas including the Enterprise Campus, Enterprise Edge, and the Service Provider Edge.

edge card Line card on the LightStream 2020 ATM switch that is configured to communicate with devices outside the ATM network. Edge cards offer Ethernet, FDDI, frame forwarding, Frame Relay, OC-3c, and UNI interfaces.

edge card control See ECC.

edge device Network entity such as a LAN segment, host, or router that connects to a LightStream 2020 ATM switch via an edge card. Edge devices send and receive the data that passes through the ATM network.

EDI Electronic Data Interchange - The electronic communication of operational data such as orders and invoices between organizations.

EDIFACT Electronic Data Interchange for Administration, Commerce, and Transport - Data exchange standard administered by the United Nations to be a multi-industry EDI standard.

EEPROM Electrically Erasable Programmable Read-Only Memory - EPROM that can be erased using electrical signals applied to specific pins.

EIA Electronic Industries Association - Group that specifies electrical transmission standards. The EIA and TIA have developed numerous well-known communications standards, including EIA/TIA-232 and EIA/TIA-449.

EIA/TIA-232 Electronic Industries Association/Telecommunications Industry Association 232 - Common physical layer interface standard, developed by EIA and TIA, that supports unbalanced circuits at signal speeds of up to 64 kbps. Closely resembles the V.24 specification. EIA/TIA-232 was formerly known as RS-232.

EIA/TIA-449 Electronic Industries Association/Telecommunications Industry Association 449 - Popular physical layer interface developed by EIA and TIA. Essentially, a faster (up to 2 Mbps) version of EIA/TIA-232 capable of longer cable runs. EIA/TIA-449 was formerly known as RS-449.

EIA/TIA-568 Electronic Industries Association/Telecommunications Industry Association 568 - Standard that describes the characteristics and applications for various grades of UTP cabling.

EIA/TIA-606 Electronic Industries Association/Telecommunications Industry Association 606 - Administration standard for the telecommunications infrastructure of commercial buildings. It includes the following administration areas: terminations, media, pathways, spaces, and bounding and grounding.

EIA-530 Electronic Industries Association 530 - Refers to two electrical implementations of EIA/TIA-449: RS-422 (for balanced transmission) and RS-423 (for unbalanced transmission).

EIGRP Enhanced Interior Gateway Routing Protocol - Advanced version of IGRP developed by Cisco. Provides superior convergence properties and operating efficiency, and combines the advantages of link state protocols with those of distance vector protocols.

EIP Ethernet Interface Processor - Interface processor card on the Cisco 7000 series routers. The EIP provides high-speed (10-Mbps) AUI ports that support Ethernet Version 1 and Ethernet Version 2 or IEEE 802.3 interfaces, and a high-speed data path to other interface processors.

EIRP Effective Isotropic Radiated Power - EIRP is the effective power in front of the antenna. The EIRP of a transmitter is the power that the transmitter appears to have if the transmitter were an isotropic radiator (if the antenna radiated equally in all directions). By virtue of the gain of a radio antenna (or dish), a beam is formed that preferentially transmits the energy in one direction. The EIRP is estimated by adding the gain (of the antenna) and the transmitter power (of the radio).

EISA Extended Industry-Standard Architecture - 32-bit bus interface used in PCs, PC-based servers, and some UNIX workstations and servers.

ELAN Emulated Local Area Network - ATM network in which an Ethernet or Token Ring LAN is emulated using a client-server model. ELANs are composed of an LEC, an LES, a BUS, and an LECS. Multiple ELANs can exist simultaneously on a single ATM network. ELANs are defined by the LANE specification.

electrically erasable programmable read-only memor See EEPROM.

electromagnetic interference See EMI.

electromagnetic pulse See EMP.

electronic data interchange See EDI.

Electronic Data Interchange for Administration, Co See EDIFACT.

Electronic Industries Association See EIA.

electronic mail See email.

Electronic Messaging Association See EMA.

electrostatic discharge See ESD.

EMA 1) Enterprise Management Architecture - Digital Equipment Corporation network management architecture, based on the OSI network management model. 2) Electronic Messaging Association - Forum devoted to standards and policy work, education, and development of electronic messaging systems such as electronic mail, voice mail, and facsimile.

email electronic mail - Widely used network application in which mail messages are transmitted electronically between end users over various types of networks using various network protocols.

EMI   Electromagnetic Interference - Interference by electromagnetic signals that can cause reduced data integrity and increased error rates on transmission channels.

EMIF   ESCON Multiple Image Facility - Mainframe I/O software function that allows one ESCON channel to be shared among multiple logical partitions on the same mainframe.

EMP   Electromagnetic Pulse - Caused by lightning and other high-energy phenomena. Capable of coupling enough energy into unshielded conductors to destroy electronic devices.

emulated LAN   See ELAN.

emulation mode   Function of an NCP that enables it to perform activities equivalent to those performed by a transmission control unit. For example, with CiscoWorks, the NetView PU 2 emulates the IBM 3274.

encapsulation   The wrapping of data in a particular protocol header. For example, Ethernet data is wrapped in a specific Ethernet header before network transit. Also, when bridging dissimilar networks, the entire frame from one network is simply placed in the header used by the data link layer protocol of the other network.

encapsulation bridging   Carries Ethernet frames from one router to another across disparate media, such as serial and FDDI lines. Contrast with translational bridging.

encoder   Device that modifies information into the required transmission format.

encoding   Process by which bits are represented by voltages.

encryption   The application of a specific algorithm to data so as to alter the appearance of the data making it incomprehensible to those who are not authorized to see the information.

end of transmission   See EOT.

end point   Device at which a virtual circuit or virtual path begins or ends.

end system   See ES.

End System Hello   See ESH.

End System-to-Intermediate System   See ES-IS.

Energy Sciences Network   See ESnet.

Enhanced IGRP   See EIGRP.

Enhanced Interior Gateway Routing Protocol   See EIGRP.

Enhanced Monitoring Services   Set of analysis tools on the Catalyst 5000 switch, consisting of an integrated RMON agent and the SPAN. These tools provide traffic monitoring, and network segment analysis and management.

Enterprise Composite Network Model   See ECNM.

Enterprise Management Architecture   See EMA.

enterprise network   Large and diverse network connecting most major points in a company or other organization. Differs from a WAN in that it is privately owned and maintained.

Enterprise Network Model   Also known as Enterprise Composite Network Model. See ECNM.

Enterprise System Connection   See ESCON.

Enterprise System Connection channel   See ESCON channel.

entity   Generally, an individual, manageable network device. An entity is also known as an alias.

EOT   End of Transmission - Generally, a character that signifies the end of a logical group of characters or bits.

EPROM   Erasable Programmable Read-Only Memory - Nonvolatile memory chips that are programmed after they are manufactured, and, if necessary, can be erased by some means and reprogrammed. Compare with EEPROM and PROM.

equalization   Technique used to compensate for communications channel distortions.

erasable programmable read-only memory   See EPROM.

error control   Technique for detecting and correcting errors in data transmissions.

error-correcting code   Code having sufficient intelligence and incorporating sufficient signaling information to enable the detection and correction of many errors at the receiver.

error-detecting code   Code that can detect transmission errors through analysis of received data based on the adherence of the data to appropriate structural guidelines.

ES   End System - Any non-routing host or node. ES lives in a particular area.

ESCON   Enterprise System Connection - IBM channel architecture that specifies a pair of fiber-optic cables, with either LEDs or lasers as transmitters and a signaling rate of 200 Mbps.

ESCON channel   IBM channel for attaching mainframes to peripherals such as storage devices, backup units, and network interfaces. This channel incorporates fiber channel technology. The ESCON channel replaces the bus and tag channel. Compare with parallel channel.

ESCON Multiple Image Facility   See EMIF.

ESD   Electrostatic Discharge - A flow or spark of electricity that originates from a static source such as a carpet and arcs across a gap to another object.

ESF   Extended Superframe Format - Framing type used on T1 circuits that consists of 24 frames of 192 bits each, with the 193rd bit providing timing and other functions. ESF is an enhanced version of SF.

ESH   End System Hello - An IS-IS hello packet type. It is part of the ES-IS spec 9542; similar to IRDP in TCP/IP; used for routers (Iss) and End Systems (Ess) to detect each other and form adjacencies.

ES-IS   End System-to-Intermediate System - ES-IS discovery protocols used for routing between end systems and intermediate systems. ES-IS is an analogous to ARP in IP. Although not technically a routing protocol, ES-IS is commonly used with routing protocols to provide end-to-end data movement through an internetwork. Routing between end systems and intermediate systems is sometimes referred to as Level 0 routing.

ESnet   Energy Sciences Network - Data communications network managed and funded by the U.S. Department of Energy Office of Energy Research (DOE/OER). Interconnects the DOE to educational institutions and other research facilities.

ESS   Extended Service Set - WLAN infrastruce mode whereby two or more basic service sets are connected by a common distribution system. An ESS generally includes a common SSID to allow roaming from access point to access point without requiring client configuration.

Ethernet   Baseband LAN specification invented by Xerox Corporation and developed jointly by Xerox, Intel, and Digital Equipment Corporation. Ethernet networks use CSMA/CD and run over a variety of cable types at 10 Mbps. Ethernet is similar to the IEEE 802.3 series of standards.

Ethernet Interface Processor   See EIP.

ETSI   European Telecommunication Standards Institute - Organization created by the European PTTs and the European Community (EC) to propose telecommunications standards for Europe.

EUI-64   Extended Universal Identifier (EUI)-64 address - This is an IPv6 address format created by taking an interface's MAC address (which is 48 bits in length) and inserting another 16-bit hexadecimal string (FFFE) between the OUI (first 24 bits) and unique serial number (last 24 bits) of the MAC address. To ensure that the chosen address is from a unique Ethernet MAC address, the seventh bit in the high-order byte is set to 1 (equivalent to the IEEE G/L bit) to indicate the uniqueness of the 48-bit address.

EUnet European Internet - European commercial Internet service provider. Eunet is designed to provide electronic mail, news, and other Internet services to European markets.

European Computer Manufacturers Association See ECMA.

European Internet See EUnet.

European Telecommunication Standards Institute See ETSI.

event Network message indicating operational irregularities in physical elements of a network or a response to the occurrence of a significant task, typically the completion of a request for information.

Excess Burst See Be.

excess rate Traffic in excess of the insured rate for a given connection. Specifically, the excess rate equals the maximum rate minus the insured rate. Excess traffic is delivered only if network resources are available and can be discarded during periods of congestion. Compare with insured rate and maximum rate.

exchange identification See XID.

EXEC The interactive command processor of the Cisco IOS software.

expansion The process of running a compressed data set through an algorithm that restores the data set to its original size. Compare with companding and compression.

expectational acknowledgment Type of acknowledgment scheme in which the acknowledgment number refers to the octet expected next.

expedited delivery Option set by a specific protocol layer telling other protocol layers (or the same protocol layer in another network device) to handle specific data more rapidly.

explicit route In SNA, a route from a source subarea to a destination subarea, as specified by a list of subarea nodes and transmission groups that connect the two.

explorer frame Frame sent out by a networked device in a SRB environment to determine the optimal route to another networked device.

Extended Binary Coded Decimal Interchange Code See EBCDIC.

Extended Industry-Standard Architecture See EISA.

extended service set See ESS.

Extended Superframe Format See ESF.

Extended Universal Identifier (EUI)-64 See EUI-64.

Extensible Authentication Protocol See EAP.

exterior gateway protocol Any internetwork protocol used to exchange routing information between autonomous systems.

failure domain Area in which a failure has occurred in a Token Ring, defined by the information contained in a beacon. When a station detects a serious problem with the network (such as a cable break), it sends a beacon frame that includes the station reporting the failure, its NAUN, and everything in between. Beaconing in turn initiates a process called autoreconfiguration.

fan-out unit Device that allows multiple devices on a network to communicate using a single network attachment.

Fast Ethernet   Any of a number of 100-Mbps Ethernet specifications. Fast Ethernet offers a speed increase ten times that of the 10BASE-T Ethernet specification, while preserving such qualities as frame format, MAC mechanisms, and MTU. Such similarities allow the use of existing 10BASE-T applications and network management tools on Fast Ethernet networks. Based on an extension to the IEEE 802.3 specification. Compare with Ethernet.

Fast Ethernet Interface Processor   See FEIP.

Fast Sequenced Transport   See FST.

Fast Serial Interface Processor   See FSIP.

fast switching   Cisco feature whereby a route cache is used to expedite packet switching through a router. Contrast with slow switching.

fault management   One of five categories of network management defined by ISO for management of OSI networks. Fault management attempts to ensure that network faults are detected and controlled.

Fault tolerance   Describes a computer system or component designed so that, in the event that a component fails, a backup component or procedure can immediately take its place with no loss of service. Fault tolerance can be provided with software, or embedded in hardware, or provided by some combination.

FCC   Federal Communications Commission - U.S. government agency that supervises, licenses, and controls electronic and electromagnetic transmission standards.

fcload   function card load - Low-level software module in the LightStream 2020 ATM switch that is invoked by higher-level modules to load software from the NP to a function card.

FCS   Frame Check Sequence - Refers to the extra characters added to a frame for error control purposes. Used in HDLC, Frame Relay, and other data link layer protocols.

FDDI   Fiber Distributed Data Interface - LAN standard, defined by ANSI X3T9.5, specifying a 100-Mbps token-passing network using fiber-optic cable, with transmission distances of up to 2 km. FDDI uses a dual-ring architecture to provide redundancy. Compare with CDDI and FDDI II.

FDDI II   Fiber Distributed Data Interface II - ANSI standard that enhances FDDI. FDDI II provides isochronous transmission for connectionless data circuits and connection-oriented voice and video circuits. Compare with FDDI.

FDDI Interface Processor   See FIP.

FDM   Frequency-Division Multiplexing - Technique whereby information from multiple channels can be allocated bandwidth on a single wire based on frequency. Compare with ATDM, statistical multiplexing, and TDM.

FECN   Forward Explicit Congestion Notification - Bit set by a Frame Relay network to inform DTE receiving the frame that congestion was experienced in the path from source to destination. DTE receiving frames with the FECN bit set can request that higher-level protocols take flow-control action as appropriate. Compare with BECN.

Federal Communications Commission   See FCC.

Federal Networking Council   See FNC.

FEIP   Fast Ethernet Interface Processor - Interface processor on the Cisco 7000 series routers. The FEIP supports up to two 100-Mbps 100BASE-T ports.

FEP   Front-End Processor - Device or board that provides network interface capabilities for a networked device. In SNA, typically an IBM 3745 device.

FF Frame Forwarding - Interface on the LightStream 2020 ATM switch that allows any traffic based on HDLC or SDLC frames to traverse the ATM network. Frame forwarding circuits are port-to-port, and only one PVC is allowed between a pair of ports. Frame forwarding is supported by the low-speed interface module, which offers V.35, EIA/TIA-449, or X.21 physical interfaces.

FF02::1 IPv6 multicast address identifying all nodes on a link.

FF02::2 IPv6 multicast address identifying all routers on a link.

FF02::5 IPv6 multicast address identifying all OSPF routers on the link-local scope. It is equivalent to the multicast address 224.0.0.5 in OSPFv2.

FF02::6 IPv6 multicast address identifying all OSPF designated routers on the link-local scope. It is equivalent to the multicast address 224.0.0.6 in OSPFv2.

FF02::9 IPv6 multicast address identifying all IPv6 RIPng routers on link.

FF05::1:FFXX:XXXX IPv6 multicast address used to create neighbor solicitation messages which are sent on a local link when a node wants to determine the link-layer address of another node on the same local link. Similar to ARP in IPv4.

FF05::101 IPv6 multicast address identifying all NTP servers in the site (site-local scope).

Fiber Distributed Data Interface See FDDI.

Fiber Distributed Data Interface II See FDDI II.

fiber-optic cable Physical medium capable of conducting modulated light transmission. Compared with other transmission media, fiber-optic cable is more expensive, but is not susceptible to electromagnetic interference, and is capable of higher data rates. Fiber-optic cable is also known as optical fiber.

fiber-optic interrepeater link See FOIRL.

Fibre Channel over IP Fibre Channel over IP (FCIP or FC/IP, also known as Fibre Channel tunneling or storage tunneling), is an Internet Protocol (IP)-based storage networking technology developed by the Internet Engineering Task Force (IETF) and defined in RFC 3821. FCIP mechanisms enable the transmission of Fibre Channel (FC) information by tunneling data between storage area network (SAN) facilities over IP networks; this capacity facilitates data sharing over a geographically distributed enterprise.

FID0 Format Indicator 0 - One of several formats that an SNA TH can use. An FID0 TH is used for communication between an SNA node and a non-SNA node.

FID1 Format Indicator 1 - One of several formats that an SNA TH can use. An FID1 TH encapsulates messages between two subarea nodes that do not support virtual and explicit routes.

FID2 Format Indicator 2 - One of several formats that an SNA TH can use. An FID2 TH is used for transferring messages between a subarea node and a PU 2, using local addresses.

FID3 Format Indicator 3 - One of several formats that an SNA TH can use. An FID3 TH is used for transferring messages between a subarea node and a PU 1, using local addresses.

FID4 Format Indicator 4 - One of several formats that an SNA TH can use. An FID4 TH encapsulates messages between two subarea nodes that are capable of supporting virtual and explicit routes.

field-replaceable unit See FRU.

FIFO queuing First In First Out queuing - Classic algorithm for packet transmission. With FIFO, transmission occurs in the same order as messages are received. Until recently, FIFO queuing is the default for all router interfaces with the bandwidth greater then 2.048 Mbps.

file transfer Popular network application that allows files to be moved from one network device to another.

File Transfer Protocol   See FTP.

File Transfer, Access, and Management   See FTAM.

filter   Generally, a process or device that screens network traffic for certain characteristics, such as source address, destination address, or protocol, and determines whether to forward or discard that traffic based on the established criteria.

FIP   FDDI Interface Processor - Interface processor on the Cisco 7000 series routers. The FIP supports SASs, DASs, dual homing, and optical bypass, and contains a 16-mips processor for high-speed (100-Mbps) interface rates. The FIP complies with ANSI and ISO FDDI standards.

firewall   Router or access server, or several routers or access servers, designated as a buffer between any connected public networks and a private network. A firewall router uses access lists and other methods to ensure the security of the private network.

firmware   Software instructions set permanently or semipermanently in ROM.

First In First Out queuing   See FIFO queuing.

fish tape   Retractable coil of steel tape used to guide cable through a wall from above or below.

flapping   Routing problem where an advertised route between two nodes alternates (flaps) back and forth between two paths due to a network problem that causes intermittent interface failures.

Flash memory   Technology developed by Intel and licensed to other semiconductor companies. Flash memory is nonvolatile storage that can be electrically erased and reprogrammed. Allows software images to be stored, booted, and rewritten as necessary.

flash update   Routing update sent asynchronously in response to a change in the network topology. Compare with routing update.

fldsup account   field service personnel account - One of the four default user accounts that are created in the factory on each LightStream 2020 ATM switch. The fldsup account is for the use of field service personnel. Its default interface is the bash shell.

flooding   Traffic passing technique used by switches and bridges in which traffic received on an interface is sent out all of the interfaces of that device except the interface on which the information was originally received.

flow   Stream of data traveling between two endpoints across a network (for example, from one LAN station to another). Multiple flows can be transmitted on a single circuit.

flow control   Technique for ensuring that a transmitting entity, such as a modem, does not overwhelm a receiving entity with data. When the buffers on the receiving device are full, a message is sent to the sending device to suspend the transmission until the data in the buffers has been processed. In IBM networks, this technique is called pacing.

FM   Frequency Modulation - Modulation technique in which signals of different frequencies represent different data values. Compare with AM and PAM.

FNC   Federal Networking Council - Group responsible for assessing and coordinating U.S. federal agency networking policies and needs.

FOIRL   Fiber-Optic Interrepeater Link - Fiber-optic signaling methodology based on the IEEE 802.3 fiber-optic specification. FOIRL is a precursor of the 10BASE-FL specification, which is designed to replace it.

format indicator 0   See FID0.

format indicator 1   See FID1.

format indicator 2   See FID2.

format indicator 3   See FID3.

format indicator 4   See FID4.

forward channel   Communications path carrying information from the call initiator to the called party.

forward delay interval   Amount of time an interface spends listening for topology change information after that interface has been activated for bridging and before forwarding actually begins.

forward explicit congestion notification   See FECN.

forwarding   Process of sending a frame toward its ultimate destination by way of an internetworking device.

forwarding priority   See transmit priority.

Fourier transform   Technique used to evaluate the importance of various frequency cycles in a time series pattern.

four-part dotted notation   See dot address.

fractional T1   See channelized T1.

FRAD   Frame Relay Access Device - Any network device that provides a connection between a LAN and a Frame Relay WAN.

fragment   Piece of a larger packet that has been broken down to smaller units.

fragmentation   Process of breaking a packet into smaller units when transmitting over a network medium that cannot support the original size of the packet.

frame   Logical grouping of information sent as a data link layer unit over a transmission medium. Often refers to the header and trailer, used for synchronization and error control, that surround the user data contained in the unit. The terms datagram, message, packet, and segment are also used to describe logical information groupings at various layers of the OSI reference model and in various technology circles.

frame check sequence   See FCS.

frame forwarding   See FF.

Frame Relay   Industry-standard, switched data link layer protocol that handles multiple virtual circuits using HDLC encapsulation between connected devices. Frame Relay is more efficient than X.25, the protocol for which it is generally considered a replacement.

Frame Relay Access Device   See FRAD.

Frame Relay Access Support   See FRAS.

Frame Relay bridging   Bridging technique, described in RFC 1490, that uses the same spanning-tree algorithm as other bridging functions, but allows packets to be encapsulated for transmission across a Frame Relay network.

frame switch   See LAN switch.

FRAS   Frame Relay Access Support - Cisco IOS software feature that allows SDLC, Token Ring, Ethernet, and Frame Relay-attached IBM devices to connect to other IBM devices across a Frame Relay network.

frequency   Number of cycles, measured in hertz, of an alternating current signal per unit time.

frequency modulation   See FM.

frequency-division multiplexing   See FDM.

from switch unit   See FSU.

front end   Node or software program that requests services of a back end.

front-end processor   See FEP.

FRU   Field-Replaceable Unit - Hardware component that can be removed and replaced by Cisco-certified service providers. Typical FRUs include cards, power supplies, and chassis components.

FSIP   Fast Serial Interface Processor - The default serial interface processor for Cisco 7000 series routers. The FSIP provides four or eight high-speed serial ports.

FST   Fast Sequenced Transport - Connectionless, sequenced transport protocol that runs on top of the IP protocol. SRB traffic is encapsulated inside of IP datagrams and is passed over an FST connection between two network devices (such as routers). Speeds up data delivery, reduces overhead, and improves the response time of SRB traffic.

FSU   From Switch Unit - Subsystem of each line card on a LightStream 2020 ATM switch that accepts calls from the switch card, verifies their checksums, and passes them to the reassembly unit. The FSU selectively drops cells if the network becomes congested.

FTAM   File Transfer, Access, and Management - In OSI, an application layer protocol developed for network file exchange and management between diverse types of computers.

FTP   File Transfer Protocol - Application protocol, part of the TCP/IP protocol stack, used for transferring files between network nodes. FTP is defined in RFC 959.

full duplex   Capability for simultaneous data transmission between a sending station and a receiving station. Compare with half duplex and simplex.

full mesh   Term describing a network in which devices are organized in a mesh topology, with each network node having either a physical circuit or a virtual circuit connecting it to every other network node. A full mesh provides a great deal of redundancy, but because it can be prohibitively expensive to implement, it is usually reserved for network backbones.

function card   Line card or an NP card in a LightStream 2020 ATM switch.

function card load   See fcload.

Fuzzball   Digital Equipment Corporation LSI-11 computer system running IP gateway software. The NSFnet used these systems as backbone packet switches.

G.703/G.704   ITU-T electrical and mechanical specifications for connections between telephone company equipment and DTE using BNC connectors and operating at E1 data rates.

G.804   ITU-T framing standard that defines the mapping of ATM cells into the physical medium.

gain   The amount of increase in energy that an antenna appears to add to an RF signal. There are different methods for measuring this, depending on the reference point chosen.

gateway   In the IP community, an older term referring to a routing device. Today, the term router is used to describe nodes that perform this function, and gateway refers to a special-purpose device that performs an application layer conversion of information from one protocol stack to another. Compare with router.

Gateway Discovery Protocol   See GDP.

gateway host   In SNA, a host node that contains a gateway SSCP.

gateway NCP   NCP that connects two or more SNA networks and performs address translation to allow cross-network session traffic.

Gateway-to-Gateway Protocol   See GGP.

generic routing encapsulation   See GRE.

Get Nearest Server   See GNS.

GGP   Gateway-to-Gateway Protocol - MILNET protocol specifying how core routers (gateways) should exchange reachability and routing information. GGP uses a distributed shortest-path algorithm.

GID Global Information Distribution - Process that runs on the NP of every LightStream 2020 ATM switch in a network. GID maintains a database and keeps nodes in the network apprised of changes in topology such as ports, cards, and nodes being added or removed, and trunks going up or down. This information is supplied by the ND process. Global information distribution is also known as global information distribution daemon (GIDD).

GIDD Global Information Distribution Daemon - See GID.

gigabit In data communications, a gigabit is 1,000,000,000 (10^9) bits. Abbreviated Gb.

gigabits per second Abbreviated Gbps.

gigabyte Abbreviated GB.

gigabytes per second Abbreviated GBps.

gigahertz Abbreviated GHz.

GLBP Gateway Load Balancing Protocol - GLBP is an improvement to HSRP and VRRP, allowing automatic selection and simultaneous use of multiple available gateways as well as automatic failover between those gateways. With GLBP, resources can be fully utilized without the administrative burden of configuring multiple groups and managing multiple default gateway configurations as is required with HSRP and VRRP.

global information distribution See GID.

global information distribution daemon See GID.

global unicast address An IPv6 unicast address that is globally unique. It can be routed globally with no modification. It shares the same address format as an IPv6 anycast address. Global unicast addresses are assigned by the Internet Assigned Numbers Authority (IANA). Compare with local unicast address.

GNS Get Nearest Server - Request packet sent by a client on an IPX network to locate the nearest active server of a particular type. An IPX network client issues a GNS request to solicit either a direct response from a connected server or a response from a router that tells it where on the internetwork the service can be located. GNS is part of the IPX SAP.

GOSIP Government OSI Profile - U.S. government procurement specification for OSI protocols. Through GOSIP, the government has mandated that all federal agencies standardize on OSI and implement OSI-based systems as they become commercially available.

Government OSI Profile See GOSIP.

grade of service Measure of telephone service quality based on the probability that a call will encounter a busy signal during the busiest hours of the day.

graphical user interface See GUI.

GRE Generic Routing Encapsulation - Tunneling protocol developed by Cisco that can encapsulate a wide variety of protocol packet types inside IP tunnels, creating a virtual point-to-point link to Cisco routers at remote points over an IP internetwork. By connecting multiprotocol subnetworks in a single-protocol backbone environment, IP tunneling using GRE allows network expansion across a single-protocol backbone environment.

ground Electrically neutral contact point.

ground loop Arrangement that exists when a multi-path connection exists between computers. Usually this occurs when computers are connected to each other through a ground wire and when computers are attached to the same network using twisted pair cable.

ground station Collection of communications equipment designed to receive signals from (and usually transmit signals to) satellites. Ground station is also known as downlink station.

group address See multicast address.

group delay   See distortion delay.

guard band   Unused frequency band between two communications channels that provides separation of the channels to prevent mutual interference.

GUI   Graphical User Interface - User environment that uses pictorial as well as textual representations of the input and output of applications and the hierarchical or other data structure in which information is stored. Conventions such as buttons, icons, and windows are typical, and many actions are performed using a pointing device (such as a mouse). Microsoft Windows and the Apple Macintosh are prominent examples of platforms utilizing a GUI.

gutter   Type of wall-mounted channel with removable cover used to support horizontal cabling. Gutter is big enough to hold several cables.

H channel   High-speed channel - Full-duplex ISDN primary rate channel operating at 384 Kbps. Compare with B channel, D channel, and E channel.

H.323   H.323 allows dissimilar communication devices to communicate with each other by using a standardized communication protocol. H.323 defines a common set of CODECs, call setup and negotiating procedures, and basic data transport methods.

half duplex   Capability for data transmission in only one direction at a time between a sending station and a receiving station. Compare with full duplex and simplex.

hammer drill   Tool resembling an oversized electric drill used for drilling into masonry. As it turns the bit, it hammers rapidly.

handshake   Sequence of messages exchanged between two or more network devices to ensure transmission synchronization.

hardware address   See MAC address.

HBD3   Line code type used on E1 circuits.

HCC   Horizontal Cross-Connect - Wiring closet where the horizontal cabling connects to a patch panel which is connected by backbone cabling to the main distribution facility.

HDLC   High-Level Data Link Control - Bit-oriented synchronous data link layer protocol developed by ISO. Derived from SDLC, HDLC specifies a data encapsulation method on synchronous serial links using frame characters and checksums.

headend   The end point of a broadband network. All stations transmit toward the headend; the headend then transmits toward the destination stations.

header   Control information placed before data when encapsulating that data for network transmission. Compare with trailer.

header checksum   Field within an IP datagram that indicates the integrity check on the header.

HELLO   Interior routing protocol used principally by NSFnet nodes. HELLO allows particular packet switches to discover minimal delay routes. Not to be confused with the Hello protocol.

hello packet   Multicast packet that is used by routers for neighbor discovery and recovery. Hello packets also indicate that a client is still operating and network-ready.

Hello protocol   Protocol used by OSPF systems for establishing and maintaining neighbor relationships. Not to be confused with HELLO.

helper address   Address configured on an interface to which broadcasts received on that interface will be sent.

HEPnet   High-Energy Physics Network - Research network that originated in the United States, but that has spread to most places involved in high-energy physics. Well-known sites include Argonne National Laboratory, Brookhaven National Laboratory, Lawrence Berkeley Laboratory, and the Stanford Linear Accelerator Center (SLAC).

hertz Measure of frequency. Synonymous with cycles per second. Abbreviated Hz.

heterogeneous network Network consisting of dissimilar devices that run dissimilar protocols and in many cases support dissimilar functions or applications.

hexadecimal Base 16. A number representation using the digits 0 through 9, with their usual meaning, plus the letters A through F to represent hexadecimal digits with values of 10 to 15. The right-most digit counts ones, the next counts multiples of 16, then $16^2=256$, etc.

hierarchical routing Routing based on a hierarchical addressing system. For example, IP routing algorithms use IP addresses, which contain network numbers, subnet numbers, and host numbers.

hierarchical star topology Extended star topology where a central hub is connected by vertical cabling to other hubs that are dependent on it.

High-Level Data Link Control See HDLC.

High-Order DSP See HODSP.

High-Performance Parallel Interface See HIPPI.

High-Speed Communications Interface See HSCI.

High-Speed Serial Interface See HSSI.

highway See bus.

HIP HSSI Interface Processor - Interface processor on the Cisco 7000 series routers. The HIP provides one HSSI port that supports connections to ATM, SMDS, Frame Relay, or private lines at speeds up to T3 or E3.

HIPPI High-Performance Parallel Interface - High-performance interface standard defined by ANSI. HIPPI is typically used to connect supercomputers to peripherals and other devices.

HLEN Number of 32-bit words in the header.

HODSP High-Order DSP - NSAP address field that is used for subdividing the domain into areas. This is roughly equivalent to a subnet in IP.

holddown State into which a route is placed so that routers will neither advertise the route nor accept advertisements about the route for a specific length of time (the holddown period). Holddown is used to flush bad information about a route from all routers in the network. A route is typically placed in holddown when a link in that route fails.

homologation Conformity of a product or specification to international standards, such as ITU-T, CSA, TUV, UL, or VCCI. Enables portability across company and international boundaries.

hop Term describing the passage of a data packet between two network nodes (for example, between two routers).

hop count Routing metric used to measure the distance between a source and a destination. RIP uses hop count as its sole metric.

10 Mbps 10 million bits per second A unit of information transfer rate. Ethernet carries 10 Mbps.

100BASE-FX 100-Mbps baseband Fast Ethernet specification using two strands of multimode fiber-optic cable per link. To guarantee proper signal timing, a 100BASE-FX link cannot exceed 1310 feet (400 m) in length. Based on the IEEE 802.3 standard.

100BASE-T 100-Mbps baseband Fast Ethernet specification using UTP wiring. Like the 10BASE-T technology on which it is based, 100BASE-T sends link pulses over the network segment when no traffic is present. However, these link pulses contain more information than those used in 10BASE-T. Based on the IEEE 802.3 standard.

100BASE-T4   100-Mbps baseband Fast Ethernet specification using four pairs of Category 3, 4, or 5 UTP wiring. To guarantee proper signal timing, a 100BASE-T4 segment cannot exceed 325 feet (100 m) in length. Based on the IEEE 802.3 standard.

100BASE-TX   100-Mbps baseband Fast Ethernet specification using two pairs of either UTP or STP wiring. The first pair of wires is used to receive data; the second is used to transmit. To guarantee proper signal timing, a 100BASE-TX segment cannot exceed 325 feet (100 m) in length. Based on the IEEE 802.3 standard.

100BASE-X   100-Mbps baseband Fast Ethernet specification that refers to the 100BASE-FX and 100BASE-TX standards for Fast Ethernet over fiber-optic cabling. Based on the IEEE 802.3 standard.

100VG-AnyLAN   100-Mbps Fast Ethernet and Token Ring media technology using four pairs of Category 3, 4, or 5 UTP cabling. This high-speed transport technology, developed by Hewlett-Packard, can be made to operate on existing 10BASE-T Ethernet networks. Based on the IEEE 802.12 standard.

10BASE2   10-Mbps baseband Ethernet specification using 50-ohm thin coaxial cable. 10BASE2, which is part of the IEEE 802.3 specification, has a distance limit of 600 feet (185 m) per segment.

10BASE5   10-Mbps baseband Ethernet specification using standard (thick) 50-ohm baseband coaxial cable. 10BASE5, which is part of the IEEE 802.3 baseband physical layer specification, has a distance limit of 1640 feet (500 m) per segment.

10BASE-F   10-Mbps baseband Ethernet specification that refers to the 10BASE-FB, 10BASE-FL, and 10BASE-FP standards for Ethernet over fiber-optic cabling.

10BASE-FB   10-Mbps baseband Ethernet specification using fiber-optic cabling. 10BASE-FB is part of the IEEE 10BASE-F specification. It is not used to connect user stations, but instead provides a synchronous signaling backbone that allows additional segments and repeaters to be connected to the network. 10BASE-FB segments can be up to 6560 feet (2000 m) long.

10BASE-FL   10-Mbps baseband Ethernet specification using fiber-optic cabling. 10BASE-FL is part of the IEEE 10BASE-F specification and, while able to interoperate with FOIRL, is designed to replace the FOIRL specification. 10BASE-FL segments can be up to 3280 feet (1000 m) long if used with FOIRL, and up to 6560 feet (2000 m) if 10BASE-FL is used exclusively.

10BASE-FP   10-Mbps fiber-passive baseband Ethernet specification using fiber-optic cabling. 10BASE-FP is part of the IEEE 10BASE-F specification. It organizes a number of computers into a star topology without the use of repeaters. 10BASE-FP segments can be up to 1640 feet (500 m) long.

10BASE-T   10-Mbps baseband Ethernet specification using two pairs of twisted-pair cabling (Category 3, 4, or 5): one pair for transmitting data and the other for receiving data. 10BASE-T, which is part of the IEEE 802.3 specification, has a distance limit of approximately 328 feet (100 m) per segment.

10Broad36   10-Mbps broadband Ethernet specification using broadband coaxial cable. 10Broad36, which is part of the IEEE 802.3 specification, has a distance limit of 11810 feet (3600 m) per segment.

370 block mux channel   See block multiplexer channel.

4B/5B local fiber   4-byte/5-byte local fiber - Fiber channel physical media used for FDDI and ATM. Supports speeds of up to 100 Mbps over multimode fiber.

4-byte/5-byte local fiber   See 4B/5B local fiber.

500-CS   500 series communication server - Cisco multiprotocol communication server that combines the capabilities of a terminal server, a telecommuting server, a protocol translator, and an asynchronous router in one unit.

6to4 Common transition mechanism to enable a smooth integration of IPv4 to IPv6. This mechanism uses the reserved prefix 2002::/16 to allow an IPv4 Internet-connected site to create and use a /48 IPv6 prefix based on a single globally routable or reachable IPv4 address. 6to4 is also known as 6to4 tunneling.

8B/10B local fiber 8-byte/10-byte local fiber - Fiber channel physical media that supports speeds up to 149.76 Mbps over multimode fiber.

8-byte/10-byte local fiber See 8B/10B local fiber.

Bootstrap Protocol See BOOTP.

border gateway Router that communicates with routers in other autonomous systems.

Border Gateway Protocol See BGP.

bot Application that runs automated tasks.

boundary network node See BNN.

boundary node See BNN.

BPDU Bridge Protocol Data Unit - Spanning-Tree Protocol hello packet that is sent out at configurable intervals to exchange information among bridges in the network.

BRI Basic Rate Interface - ISDN interface composed of two B channels and one D channel for circuit-switched communication of voice, video, and data. Compare with PRI.

bridge Device that connects and passes packets between two network segments that use the same communications protocol. Bridges operate at the data link layer (layer 2) of the OSI reference model. In general, a bridge will filter, forward, or flood an incoming frame based on the MAC address of that frame.

bridge forwarding Process that uses entries in a filtering database to determine whether frames with a given MAC destination address can be forwarded to a given port or ports. Described in the IEEE 802.1 standard.

bridge group Cisco bridging feature that assigns network interfaces to a particular spanning-tree group. Bridge groups can be compatible with the IEEE 802.1 or the DEC specification.

bridge number Number that identifies each bridge in an SRB LAN. Parallel bridges must have different bridge numbers.

bridge protocol data unit See BPDU.

bridge static filtering Process in which a bridge maintains a filtering database consisting of static entries. Each static entry equates a MAC destination address with a port that can receive frames with this MAC destination address and a set of ports on which the frames can be transmitted. Defined in the IEEE 802.1 standard.

broadband Transmission system that multiplexes multiple independent signals onto one cable. In telecommunications terminology, any channel having a bandwidth greater than a voice-grade channel (4 kHz). In LAN terminology, a coaxial cable on which analog signaling is used. Also called wideband. Contrast with baseband.

Broadband ISDN See BISDN.

broadcast Data packet that will be sent to all nodes on a network. Broadcasts are identified by a broadcast address. Compare with multicast and unicast.

broadcast address Special address reserved for sending a message to all stations. Generally, a broadcast address is a MAC destination address of all ones. Compare with multicast address and unicast address.

broadcast domain   The set of all devices that will receive broadcast frames originating from any device within the set. Broadcast domains are typically bounded by routers because routers do not forward broadcast frames.

broadcast search   Propagation of a search request to all network nodes if the location of a resource is unknown to the requester.

broadcast storm   Undesirable network event in which many broadcasts are sent simultaneously across all network segments. A broadcast storm uses substantial network bandwidth and, typically, causes network time-outs.

browser   See WWW browser.

BSA   Basic Service Area - Area of radio frequency coverage provided by an access point. To extend the BSA, or to simply add wireless devices and extend the range of an existing wired system, you can add an access point. A BSA is also known as a microcell.

BSD   Berkeley Standard Distribution - Term used to describe any of a variety of UNIX-type operating systems based on the UC Berkeley BSD operating system.

BSS   Basic Service Set - WLAN infrastructure mode whereby mobile clients use a single access point for connectivity to each other or to wired network resources.

BT   Burst Tolerance - Parameter defined by the ATM Forum for ATM traffic management. For VBR connections, BT determines the size of the maximum burst of contiguous cells that can be transmitted.

buffer   Storage area used for handling data in transit. Buffers are used in internetworking to compensate for differences in processing speed between network devices. Bursts of data can be stored in buffers until they can be handled by slower processing devices. A buffer is also known as a packet buffer.

buffering   Storing data until it can be handled by other devices or processes. Buffering is typically used when there is a difference between the rate at which data is received and the rate at which it can be processed.

burst tolerance   See BT.

bus   1) Common physical signal path composed of wires or other media across which signals can be sent from one part of a computer to another. Bus is also known as highway. 2) See bus topology.

bus and tag channel   IBM channel, developed in the 1960s, incorporating copper multiwire technology. Replaced by the ESCON channel.

bus topology   Linear LAN architecture in which transmissions from network stations propagate the length of the medium and are received by all other stations. Compare with ring topology, star topology, and tree topology.

bypass mode   Operating mode on FDDI and Token Ring networks in which an interface has been removed from the ring.

bypass relay   Allows a particular Token Ring interface to be shut down and thus effectively removed from the ring.

byte   Term used to refer to a series of consecutive binary digits that are operated upon as a unit (for example, an 8-bit byte).

byte reversal   Process of storing numeric data with the least-significant byte first. Used for integers and addresses on devices with Intel microprocessors.

byte-oriented protocol   Class of data-link communications protocols that use a specific character from the user character set to delimit frames. These protocols have largely been replaced by bit-oriented protocols. Compare with bit-oriented protocol.

horizontal cross connect   See HCC.

host   Computer system on a network. Similar to the term node except that host usually implies a computer system, whereas node generally applies to any networked system, including access servers and routers.

host address   See host number.

host node   SNA subarea node that contains an SSCP.

host number   Part of an IP address that designates which node on the subnetwork is being addressed. A host number is also known as a host address.

Hot Standby Router Protocol   See HSRP.

hot swapping   See OIR and POS.

hot wire   Ungrounded lead wire that connects the transformer and electrical devices or appliances via an electrical outlet and power plug.

HSCI   High-Speed Communications Interface - Single-port interface, developed by Cisco, providing full-duplex synchronous serial communications capability at speeds up to 52 Mbps.

HSRP   Hot Standby Router Protocol - Provides high network availability and transparent network topology changes. HSRP creates a Hot Standby router group with a lead router that services all packets sent to the Hot Standby address. The lead router is monitored by other routers in the group, and if it fails, one of these standby routers inherits the lead position and the Hot Standby group address.

HSSI   High-Speed Serial Interface - Network standard for high-speed (up to 52 Mbps) serial connections over WAN links.

HSSI Interface Processor   See HIP.

HTML   Hypertext Markup Language - Simple hypertext document formatting language that uses tags to indicate how a given part of a document should be interpreted by a viewing application, such as a WWW browser. See also hypertext and WWW browser.

hub   1) Generally, a term used to describe a device that serves as the center of a star-topology network. 2) Hardware or software device that contains multiple independent but connected modules of network and internetwork equipment. Hubs can be active (where they repeat signals sent through them) or passive (where they do not repeat, but merely split, signals sent through them). 3) In Ethernet and IEEE 802.3, an Ethernet multiport repeater, sometimes referred to as a concentrator.

hybrid network   Internetwork made up of more than one type of network technology, including LANs and WANs.

hypertext   Electronically-stored text that allows direct access to other texts by way of encoded links. Hypertext documents can be created using HTML, and often integrate images, sound, and other media that are commonly viewed using a WWW browser.

hypertext markup language   See HTML.

I/O   Abbreviation for input/output.

IAB   Internet Architecture Board - Board of internetwork researchers who discuss issues pertinent to Internet architecture. Responsible for appointing a variety of Internet-related groups such as the IANA, IESG, and IRSG. The IAB is appointed by the trustees of the ISOC.

IANA   Internet Assigned Numbers Authority - Organization operated under the auspices of the ISOC as a part of the IAB. IANA delegates authority for IP address-space allocation and domain-name assignment to the NIC and other organizations. IANA also maintains a database of assigned protocol identifiers used in the TCP/IP stack, including autonomous system numbers.

IBNS   Identity Based Network Services - Integrated solution combining several Cisco products that offer authentication, access control, and user policies to secure network connectivity and resources.

ICC   Intermediate Cross Connect - IDF that connects the horizontal cross-connect to the main cross-connect. See HCC and MCC.

ICMP   Internet Control Message Protocol - Network layer Internet protocol that reports errors and provides other information relevant to IP packet processing. Documented in RFC 792.

ICMP Router Discovery Protocol   See IRDP.

Identification, Flags, Frag Offset   Field within an IP datagram that provides fragmentation of datagrams to allow differing MTUs in the internet.

Identity Based Network Services   See IBNS.

IDF   Intermediate Distribution Facility - Secondary communications room for a building using a star networking topology. The IDF is dependent on the MDF.

IDI   Initial Domain Identifier - NSAP address field that identifies the domain.

IDN   International Data Number. See X.121.

IDP   Interdomain Part - NSAP address field that consists of the AFI and IDI together. This is roughly equivalent to a classful IP network, in decimal format.

IDPR   Interdomain Policy Routing - Interdomain routing protocol that dynamically exchanges policies between autonomous systems. IDPR encapsulates interautonomous system traffic and routes it according to the policies of each autonomous system along the path. IDPR is currently an IETF proposal.

IDRP   IS-IS Interdomain Routing Protocol - OSI protocol that specifies how routers communicate with routers in different domains.

IEC   International Electrotechnical Commission - Industry group that writes and distributes standards for electrical products and components.

IEEE   Institute of Electrical and Electronics Engineers - Professional organization whose activities include the development of communications and network standards. IEEE LAN standards are the predominant LAN standards today.

IEEE 802.1   IEEE specification that describes an algorithm that prevents bridging loops by creating a spanning tree. The algorithm was invented by Digital Equipment Corporation. The Digital algorithm and the IEEE 802.1 algorithm are not exactly the same, nor are they compatible.

IEEE 802.11   IEEE specification developed to eliminate the problems inherent with proprietary WLAN technologies. It began with a 1 Mbps standard and has evolved into several other standards, including 802.11a, 802.11b, and 802.11g.

IEEE 802.11a   IEEE WLAN standard for 54 Mbps at 5 GHz.

IEEE 802.11b   IEEE WLAN standard for 11 Mbps at 2.4 GHz.

IEEE 802.11g   IEEE WLAN standard for 54 Mbps at 2.4 GHz.

IEEE 802.11h   IEEE specification that radios must comply with in order to use the 11 channels for the 802.11a standard. IEEE 802.11h includes the TPC and DFS features.

IEEE 802.11i   IEEE 802.11 specification for WPA.

IEEE 802.12   IEEE LAN standard that specifies the physical layer and the MAC sublayer of the data link layer. IEEE 802.12 uses the demand priority media-access scheme at 100 Mbps over a variety of physical media.

IEEE 802.1x   IEEE standard specifying authentication protocols, such as EAP.

IEEE 802.2   IEEE LAN protocol that specifies an implementation of the LLC sublayer of the data link layer. IEEE 802.2 handles errors, framing, flow control, and the network layer (Layer 3) service interface. Used in IEEE 802.3 and IEEE 802.5 LANs.

IEEE 802.3   IEEE LAN protocol that specifies an implementation of the physical layer and the MAC sublayer of the data link layer. IEEE 802.3 uses CSMA/CD access at a variety of speeds over a variety of physical media. Extensions to the IEEE 802.3 standard specify implementations for Fast Ethernet. Physical variations of the original IEEE 802.3 specification include 10BASE2, 10BASE5, 10BASE-F, 10BASE-T, and 10Broad36. Physical variations for Fast Ethernet include 100BASE-T, 100BASE-T4, and 100BASE-X.

IEEE 802.3i   Physical variation of the original IEEE 802.3 specification that calls for using Ethernet type signaling over twisted pair networking media. The standard sets the signaling speed at 10 megabits per second using a baseband signaling scheme transmitted over twisted pair cable employing a star or extended star topology.

IEEE 802.4   IEEE LAN protocol that specifies an implementation of the physical layer and the MAC sublayer of the data link layer. IEEE 802.4 uses token-passing access over a bus topology and is based on the token bus LAN architecture.

IEEE 802.5   IEEE LAN protocol that specifies an implementation of the physical layer and MAC sublayer of the data link layer. IEEE 802.5 uses token passing access at 4 or 16 Mbps over STP cabling and is similar to IBM Token Ring.

IEEE 802.6   IEEE MAN specification based on DQDB technology. IEEE 802.6 supports data rates of 1.5 to 155 Mbps.

IESG   Internet Engineering Steering Group - Organization, appointed by the IAB, that manages the operation of the IETF.

IETF   Internet Engineering Task Force - Task force consisting of over 80 working groups responsible for developing Internet standards. The IETF operates under the auspices of ISOC.

IFIP   International Federation for Information Processing - Research organization that performs OSI prestandardization work. Among other accomplishments, IFIP formalized the original MHS model.

IGMP   Internet Group Management Protocol - Used by IP hosts to report their multicast group memberships to an adjacent multicast router.

IGP   Interior Gateway Protocol - Internet protocol used to exchange routing information within an autonomous system. Examples of common Internet IGPs include IGRP, OSPF, and RIP.

IGRP   Interior Gateway Routing Protocol - IGP developed by Cisco to address the problems associated with routing in large, heterogeneous networks. Compare with Enhanced IGRP.

IIH   Intermediate System-to-Intermediate System Hello - Used by routers to detect neighbors and form adjacencies. In addition to the IIH, which is an IS-IS PDU, there is an ISH and an ESH, which are ES-IS PDUs.

IIN   Intelligent Information Network - Network that seamlessly supports new IP strategies, including service-oriented architecture (SOA), Web services and virtualization. It is implemented using SONA. Compare with SONA.

ILEC   Incumbent Local Exchange Carrier - Traditional telephone company. In the U.S., the Regional Bell Operation Companies (RBOCs) that were formed after the divestiture of AT and T and the Independent Operating Companies (IOCs) that usually are located in more rural areas or single cities are ILECs. In other areas of the world, ILECs are the Post, Telephone, and Telegraphs (PTTs), government-managed monopolies.

ILMI   Interim Local Management Interface - Specification developed by the ATM Forum for incorporating network-management capabilities into the ATM UNI.

IMP   Interface Message Processor - Former name for ARPANET packet switches. An IMP is now known as a packet-switch node (PSN).

in-band signaling   Transmission within a frequency range normally used for information transmission. Compare with out-of-band signaling.

Industry-Standard Architecture   See ISA.

Information Technology   The development, installation, and implementation of computer systems and applications.

infrared   Electromagnetic waves whose frequency range is above that of microwaves, but below that of the visible spectrum. LAN systems based on this technology represent an emerging technology.

infrastructure   Infrastructure mode indicates a WLAN topology where clients connect through an access point.

initial domain identifier   See IDI.

initial domain part   See IDP.

INOC   Internet Network Operations Center - BBN group that in the early days of the Internet monitored and controlled the Internet core gateways (routers). INOC no longer exists in this form.

input/output   See I/O.

Institute of Electrical and Electronics Engineers   See IEEE.

insulator   Any material with a high resistance to electrical current. See conductor.

insured burst   The largest burst of data above the insured rate that will be temporarily allowed on a PVC and not tagged by the traffic policing function for dropping in the case of network congestion. The insured burst is specified in bytes or cells. Compare with maximum burst.

insured rate   The long-term data throughput, in bits or cells per second, that an ATM network commits to support under normal network conditions. The insured rate is 100 percent allocated; the entire amount is deducted from the total trunk bandwidth along the path of the circuit. Compare with excess rate and maximum rate.

insured traffic   Traffic within the insured rate specified for the PVC. This traffic should not be dropped by the network under normal network conditions.

Integrated Application Software   A tightly interconnected suite of software applications that share a common database and user interface.

Integrated IS-IS   Integrated Intermediate System-to-Intermediate System - Routing protocol based on the OSI routing protocol IS-IS, but with support for IP and other protocols. Integrated IS-IS implementations send only one set of routing updates, making it more efficient than two separate implementations. Compare with IS-IS. Integrated IS-IS was formerly known as Dual IS-IS.

Integrated Services Digital Network   See ISDN.

Intelligent Information Network   See IIN.

interarea routing   Term used to describe routing between two or more logical areas. Compare with intra-area routing.

interdomain ID   See IDI.

interdomain part   See IDP.

Interdomain Policy Routing   See IDPR.

interface   1) Connection between two systems or devices. 2) In routing terminology, a network connection. 3) In telephony, a shared boundary defined by common physical interconnection characteristics, signal characteristics, and meanings of interchanged signals. 4) The boundary between adjacent layers of the OSI model.

interface message processor   See IMP.

interface module   Combination of a line card and an access card that together allow you to connect a LightStream 2020 ATM switch to other devices.

interface processor   Any of a number of processor modules used in the Cisco 7000 series routers.

interference   Unwanted communication channel noise.

Interim Local Management Interface   See ILMI.

Interior Gateway Protocol   See IGP.

Interior Gateway Routing Protocol   See IGRP.

intermediate cross connect   See ICC.

intermediate distribution facility   See IDF.

intermediate routing node   See IRN.

intermediate system   See IS.

Intermediate System Hello   See ISH.

Intermediate System-to-Intermediate System   See IS-IS.

Intermediate System-to-Intermediate System Hello   See IIH.

Internal Medicine   The branch of medicine concerned with nonsurgical diseases in adults.

International Data Number   See X.121.

International Electrotechnical Commission   See IEC.

International Federation for Information Processin   See IFIP.

International Organization for Standardization   See ISO.

International Standards Organization   Erroneous expansion of the acronym ISO. See ISO.

International Telecommunication Union Telecommunic   See ITU-T.

Internet   1) Internet. Term used to refer to the largest global internetwork, connecting tens of thousands of networks worldwide and having a "culture" that focuses on research and standardization based on real-life use. Many leading-edge network technologies come from the Internet community. The Internet evolved in part from ARPANET. At one time, called the DARPA Internet. Not to be confused with the general term internet. See also ARPANET. 2) internet. Not to be confused with the Internet. See internetwork.

Internet address   See IP address.

Internet Architecture Board   See IAB.

Internet Assigned Numbers Authority   See IANA.

Internet Control Message Protocol   See ICMP.

Internet Engineering Steering Group   See IESG.

Internet Engineering Task Force   See IETF.

Internet Group Management Protocol   See IGMP.

Internet Network Operations Center   See INOC.

Internet Protocol   1) See IP. 2) Any protocol that is part of the TCP/IP protocol stack. See TCP/IP.

Internet Research Steering Group   See IRSG.

Internet Research Task Force   See IRTF.

Internet Society   See ISOC.

internetwork   Collection of networks interconnected by routers and other devices that functions (generally) as a single network. The term internetwork is also known as internet, which is not to be confused with the Internet.

Internetwork Packet Exchange   See IPX.

internetworking   General term used to refer to the industry that has arisen around the problem of connecting networks together. The term can refer to products, procedures, and technologies.

interNIC   Organization that serves the Internet community by supplying user assistance, documentation, training, registration service for Internet domain names, and other services. InterNIC was formerly known as Network Information Center (NIC).

interoperability   1) The capability to provide successful communication between end-users across a mixed environment of different domains, networks, facilities and equipment. 2) Ability of computing equipment manufactured by different vendors to communicate with one another successfully over a network.

Inter-Switching System Interface   See ISSI.

intra-area routing   Term used to describe routing within a logical area. Compare with interarea routing.

Inverse Address Resolution Protocol   See Inverse ARP.

Inverse ARP   Inverse Address Resolution Protocol - Method of building dynamic routes in a network. Allows an access server to discover the network address of a device associated with a virtual circuit.

IOS   See Cisco IOS software.

IOS commands/Cisco IOS software   The software used on the vast majority of Cisco Systems routers and current Cisco network switches. IOS is a package of routing, switching, internetworking and telecommunications functions tightly integrated with a multitasking operating system.

IP (Internet Protocol)   The network layer protocol in the TCP/IP stack that offers internetwork service. IP provides features for addressing, type-of-service specification, fragmentation and reassembly, and security.

IP address   1) 32-bit address assigned to hosts using TCP/IP. An IP address belongs to one of five classes (A, B, C, D, or E) and is written as 4 octets separated with periods (dotted decimal format). Each address consists of a network number, an optional subnetwork number, and a host number. The network and subnetwork numbers together are used for routing, while the host number is used to address an individual host within the network or subnetwork. A subnet mask is used to extract network and subnetwork information from the IP address. IP address is also known as an Internet address. 2) Command used to establish the logical network address of this interface. See also IP and subnet mask.

IP datagram   Fundamental unit of information passed across the Internet. Contains source and destination addresses along with data and a number of fields that define such things as the length of the datagram, the header checksum, and flags to indicate whether the datagram can be (or was) fragmented.

IP multicast   Routing technique that allows IP traffic to be propagated from one source to a number of destinations or from many sources to many destinations. Rather than sending one packet to each destination, one packet is sent to a multicast group identified by a single IP destination group address.

IP options   Field within an IP datagram that deals with network testing, debugging, security, and others.

IPng   Internet Protocol next generation. See IPv6.

IPSO   IP Security Option - U.S. government specification that defines an optional field in the IP packet header that defines hierarchical packet security levels on a per interface basis.

IPv4   Internet Protocol version 4 - Network layer protocol in the TCP/IP stack offering a connectionless internetwork service. IPv4 provides features for addressing, type-of-service specification, fragmentation and reassembly, and security. Documented in RFC 791.

IPv6   Internet Protocol version 6 - Network layer IP standard used by electronic devices to exchange data across a packet-switched internetwork. It follows IPv4 as the second version of the Internet Protocol to be formally adopted for general use. IPv6 includes support for flow ID in the packet header, which can be used to identify flows. IPv6 was formerly known as IP next generation (Ipng).

IPv6-over-IPv4 tunnels   See 6to4.

IPX   Internetwork Packet Exchange - NetWare network layer (Layer 3) protocol used for transferring data from servers to workstations. IPX is similar to IP and XNS.

IPXWAN   Internetwork Packet Exchange - Protocol that negotiates end-to-end options for new links. When a link comes up, the first IPX packets sent across are IPXWAN packets negotiating the options for the link. When the IPXWAN options have been successfully determined, normal IPX transmission begins. Defined by RFC 1362.

IRDP   ICMP Router Discovery Protocol - Enables a host to determine the address of a router that it can use as a default gateway. Similar to ESIS, but used with IP.

IRN   intermediate Routing Node - In SNA, a subarea node with intermediate routing capability.

IRSG   Internet Research Steering Group - Group that is part of the IAB and oversees the activities of the IRTF.

IRTF   Internet Research Task Force - Community of network experts that consider Internet-related research topics. The IRTF is governed by the IRSG and is considered a subsidiary of the IAB.

IS   Intermediate System - Router which participates in routing IS-IS information.

ISA   Industry-Standard Architecture - 16-bit bus used for Intel-based personal computers.

isarithmic flow control   Flow control technique in which permits travel through the network. Possession of these permits grants the right to transmit. Isarithmic flow control is not commonly implemented.

ISATAP   Intra-Site Automatic Tunnel Addressing Protocol - Allows an IPv4 private intranet (which may or may not be using RFC 1918 addresses) to incrementally implement IPv6 nodes without upgrading the network.

iSCSI   In computing, iSCSI is Internet SCSI (Small Computer System Interface), an Internet Protocol (IP)-based storage networking standard for linking data storage facilities. By carrying SCSI commands over IP networks, iSCSI is used to facilitate data transfers over intranets and to manage storage over long distances. iSCSI can be used to transmit data over local area networks (LANs), wide area networks (WANs), or the Internet and can enable location-independent data storage and retrieval.

ISDN   Integrated Services Digital Network - Communication protocol, offered by telephone companies, that permits telephone networks to carry data, voice, and other source traffic.

ISH   Intermediate System Hello - ISH packets are a type of a hello packet. ISH is part of the ES-IS spec 9542; similar to IRDP in TCP/IP; used for Iss and Ess to detect each other. ISH packets are sent out to all IS-IS-enabled interfaces. On LANs they are sent out periodically, destined to a special multicast address. Routers will become neighbors when they see themselves in their neighbor's hello packets and link authentication information matches.

IS-IS   Intermediate System-to-Intermediate System - OSI link-state hierarchical routing protocol based on DECnet Phase V routing whereby Iss (routers) exchange routing information based on a single metric to determine network topology. Compare with Integrated IS-IS.

IS-IS Hello   See IIH.

IS-IS Interdomain Routing Protocol   See IDRP.

ISM   Industrial, Scientific, and Medical - The 900-MHz and 2.4-GHz bands are referred to as the ISM bands.

ISO   International Organization for Standardization - International organization that is responsible for a wide range of standards, including those relevant to networking. ISO developed the OSI reference model, a popular networking reference model.

ISO 3309   HDLC procedures developed by ISO. ISO 3309:1979 specifies the HDLC frame structure for use in synchronous environments. ISO 3309:1984 specifies proposed modifications to allow the use of HDLC in asynchronous environments as well.

ISO 9000   Set of international quality-management standards defined by ISO. The standards, which are not specific to any country, industry, or product, allow companies to demonstrate that they have specific processes in place to maintain an efficient quality system.

ISO development environment   See ISODE.

ISOC   Internet Society - International nonprofit organization, founded in 1992, that coordinates the evolution and use of the Internet. In addition, ISOC delegates authority to other groups related to the Internet, such as the IAB. ISOC is headquartered in Reston, Virginia, U.S.A.

isochronous transmission   Asynchronous transmission over a synchronous data link. Isochronous signals require a constant bit rate for reliable transport. Compare with asynchronous transmission, plesiochronous transmission, and synchronous transmission.

ISODE   International Organization for Standardization Development Environmen - Large set of libraries and utilities used to develop upper-layer OSI protocols and applications.

isotropic   An antenna that radiates its signal in a spherical pattern. Compare with dipole.

ISSI   Inter-Switching System Interface - Standard interface between SMDS switches.

ITU-T   International Telecommunication Union Telecommunication Standardization Sector - International Telecommunication Union Telecommunication Standardization Sector (ITU-T) (formerly the Committee for Internatiional Telegraph and Telephone ([CCITT]). An international organization that develops communication standards.

jabber   1) Error condition in which a network device continually transmits random, meaningless data onto the network. 2) In IEEE 802.3, a data packet whose length exceeds that prescribed in the standard.

JANET   Joint Academic Network - X.25 WAN connecting university and research institutions in the United Kingdom.

Japan UNIX Network   See JUNET.

jitter Analog communication line distortion caused by the variation of a signal from its reference timing positions. Jitter can cause data loss, particularly at high speeds.

John von Neumann Computer Network See JvNCnet.

Joint Academic Network See JANET.

jumper 1) Term used for patchcords found in a wiring closet. 2) Electrical switch consisting of a number of pins and a connector that can be attached to the pins in a variety of different ways. Different circuits are created by attaching the connector to different pins.

JUNET Japan UNIX Network - Nationwide, noncommercial network in Japan, designed to promote communication between Japanese and other researchers.

JvNCnet John von Neumann Computer Network - Regional network, owned and operated by Global Enterprise Services, Inc., composed of T1 and slower serial links providing midlevel networking services to sites in the Northeastern United States.

Karn's algorithm Algorithm that improves round-trip time estimations by helping transport layer protocols distinguish between good and bad round-trip time samples.

keepalive interval Period of time between each keepalive message sent by a network device.

keepalive message Message sent by one network device to inform another network device that the virtual circuit between the two is still active.

Kermit Popular file-transfer and terminal-emulation program.

KERN Kernel trap logging facility. Process that runs on each NP of every LightStream 2020 ATM switch in a network. KERN converts LynxOS kernel messages, sent to the console, into SNMP messages.

kilobit Approximately 1,000 bits. Abbreviated kb.

kilobits per second A bit rate expressed in thousands of bits per second. Abbreviated kbps.

kilobyte Approximately 1,000 bytes. Abbreviated KB.

kilobytes per second A bit rate expressed in thousands of bytes per second. Abbreviated KBps.

LAN Local-Area Network - High-speed, low-error data network covering a relatively small geographic area (up to a few thousand meters). LANs connect workstations, peripherals, terminals, and other devices in a single building or other geographically limited area. LAN standards specify cabling and signaling at the physical and data link layers of the OSI model. Ethernet, FDDI, and Token Ring are widely used LAN technologies. Compare with MAN and WAN.

LAN emulation See LANE.

LAN Emulation Client See LEC.

LAN Emulation Configuration Server See LECS.

LAN Emulation Server See LES.

LAN Extender Any of the products in the Cisco 1000 series. Cisco LAN Extenders provide a transparent connection between a central site and a remote site, logically extending the central network to include the remote LAN. LAN Extender products support all standard network protocols and are configured and managed through a host router at the central site, requiring no technical expertise at the remote end. See also Cisco 1000.

LAN Manager Distributed NOS, developed by Microsoft, that supports a variety of protocols and platforms.

LAN Manager for UNIX See LM/X.

LAN Network Manager See LNM.

LAN or Local Area Network   High-speed, low-error data transfer system that encompasses a small geographic area. A LAN connects workstations, peripherals, terminals, and other devices in a single building or other geographically limited area. LAN standards specify cabling and signaling at the Physical Layer and the Data Link Layer of the OSI reference model. Examples of LAN technologies are Ethernet, FDDI, and Token Ring.

LAN Server   Server-based NOS developed by IBM and derived from LNM.

LAN switch   High-speed switch that forwards packets between data-link segments. Most LAN switches forward traffic based on MAC addresses. This variety of LAN switch is sometimes called a frame switch. LAN switches are often categorized according to the method they use to forward traffic: cut-through packet switching or store-and-forward packet switching. Multilayer switches are an intelligent subset of LAN switches. An example of a LAN switch is the Cisco Catalyst 5000. Compare with multilayer switch.

LANE   LAN emulation - Technology that allows an ATM network to function as a LAN backbone. The ATM network must provide multicast and broadcast support, address mapping (MAC-to-ATM), SVC management, and a usable packet format. LANE also defines Ethernet and Token Ring ELANs.

LAPB   Link Access Procedure, Balanced - Data link layer protocol in the X.25 protocol stack. LAPB is a bit-oriented protocol derived from HDLC.

LAPD   Link Access Procedure on the D channel - ISDN data link layer protocol for the D channel. LAPD was derived from the LAPB protocol and is designed primarily to satisfy the signaling requirements of ISDN basic access. Defined by ITU-T Recommendations Q.920 and Q.921.

LAPF   Link Access Procedure for Frame Relay - The international draft standard that defines the structure of frame relay frames. All frame relay frames entering a frame relay network automatically conform to this structure.

LAPM   Link Access Procedure for Modems - ARQ used by modems implementing the V.42 protocol for error correction.

laser   light amplification by stimulated emission of radiation Analog transmission device in which a suitable active material is excited by an external stimulus to produce a narrow beam of coherent light that can be modulated into pulses to carry data. Networks based on laser technology are sometimes run over SONET.

LAT   Local-Area Transport - A network virtual terminal protocol developed by Digital Equipment Corporation.

LATA   Local Access and Transport Area - Geographic telephone dialing area serviced by a single local telephone company. Calls within LATAs are called "local calls." There are well over 100 LATAs in the United States.

latency   1) Delay between the time a device requests access to a network and the time it is granted permission to transmit. 2) Delay between the time when a device receives a frame and the time that frame is forwarded out the destination port.

LCC   Line Card Control - Process that runs on the NP for each CLC, LSC, and MSC of a LightStream 2020 ATM switch. LCC establishes VCCs, maintains the link management protocol for the line card, continually monitors line quality on each trunk using TUD, and performs other functions.

LCI   Logical Channel Identifier - See VCN.

LCN   Logical Channel Number. See VCN.

LCP   Link Control Protocol - Protocol that establishes, configures, and tests data-link connections for use by PPP.

leaf internetwork   In a star topology, an internetwork whose sole access to other internetworks in the star is through a core router.

learning bridge   Bridge that performs MAC address learning to reduce traffic on the network. Learning bridges manage a database of MAC addresses and the interfaces associated with each address.

leased line   Transmission line reserved by a communications carrier for the private use of a customer. A leased line is a type of dedicated line.

LEC   1) LAN Emulation Client - Entity in an end system that performs data forwarding, address resolution, and other control functions for a single ES within a single ELAN. A LEC also provides a standard LAN service interface to any higher-layer entity that interfaces to the LEC. Each LEC is identified by a unique ATM address, and is associated with one or more MAC addresses reachable through that ATM address. See also ELAN and LES. 2) Local Exchange Carrier - Local or regional telephone company that owns and operates a telephone network and the customer lines that connect to it.

LECS   LAN Emulation Configuration Server - Entity that assigns individual LANE clients to particular ELANs by directing them to the LES that corresponds to the ELAN. There is logically one LECS per administrative domain, and this serves all ELANs within that domain.

LED   Light Emitting Diode - Semiconductor device that emits light produced by converting electrical energy. Status lights on hardware devices are typically LEDs.

LES   LAN Emulation Server - Entity that implements the control function for a particular ELAN. There is only one logical LES per ELAN, and it is identified by a unique ATM address.

Level 1 IS   Level 1 Intermediate System - Provides routing within an area. It keeps track of the routing within its own area. For a packet destined for another area, a Level 1 IS sends the packet to the nearest Level 2 IS in its own area, regardless of what the destination area is.

Level 1 router   Device that routes traffic within a single DECnet or OSI area.

Level 2 IS   Level 2 Intermediate System - Provides routing between Level 1 areas and form an intradomain routing backbone. It keeps track of the paths to destination areas. A level 1 must go through a level 2 IS to communicate with another area.

Level 2 router   Device that routes traffic between DECnet or OSI areas. All Level 2 routers must form a contiguous network.

Level 3 IS   Level 3 Intermediate System - Provides routing between separate domains.

light amplification by stimulated emission of radi   See laser.

light emitting diode   See LED.

lightweight access point   A lightweight access point is the type of access point used in a centralized WLAN solution where a wireless controller monitors and manages the access points.

limited resource link   Resource defined by a device operator to remain active only when being used.

line   1) In SNA, a connection to the network. 2) See link.

line card   Card on a LightStream 2020 ATM switch that, together with its access card, provides I/O services for the switch. There are four types of line cards: CLC, LSC, MSC, and PLC.

line card control   See LCC.

line code type   One of a number of coding schemes used on serial lines to maintain data integrity and reliability. The line code type used is determined by the carrier service provider.

line conditioning   Use of equipment on leased voice-grade channels to improve analog characteristics, thereby allowing higher transmission rates.

line driver Inexpensive amplifier and signal converter that conditions digital signals to ensure reliable transmissions over extended distances.

Line Interface See LINF.

line of sight Characteristic of certain transmission systems such as laser, microwave, and infrared systems in which no obstructions in a direct path between transmitter and receiver can exist.

line printer daemon See LPD.

line turnaround Time required to change data transmission direction on a telephone line.

LINF Line Interface - Interface card used on the LightStream 100 ATM switch. The LINF receives cells sent over a line, checks them for errors, and forwards them toward their destination.

link Network communications channel consisting of a circuit or transmission path and all related equipment between a sender and a receiver. Most often used to refer to a WAN connection. A link is also known as a line or a transmission link.

Link Access Procedure for Frame Relay See LAPF.

Link Access Procedure for Modems See LAPM.

Link Access Procedure on the D channel See LAPD.

Link Access Procedure, Balanced See LAPB.

link layer See data link layer.

link state routing algorithm Routing algorithm in which each router broadcasts or multicasts information regarding the cost of reaching each of its neighbors to all nodes in the internetwork. Link state algorithms create a consistent view of the network and are therefore not prone to routing loops, but they achieve this at the cost of relatively greater computational difficulty and more widespread traffic (compared with distance vector routing algorithms). Compare with distance vector routing algorithm.

link-layer address See MAC address.

link-local address IPv6 uses link-local addresses to identify interfaces on a link that are meant to stay within a given broadcast domain. They may also be thought of as the host portion of an IPv6 address. These addresses are used for features such as stateless Autoconfiguration. Link-local addresses start with the prefix FE80::/10, and then include an interface ID. Compare with site-local unicast address.

link-state advertisement See LSA.

link-state packet See LSA.

link-state PDU database See LSPD.

little-endian Method of storing or transmitting data in which the least significant bit or byte is presented first. Compare with big-endian.

LLC Logical Link Control - Higher of the two data link layer sublayers defined by the IEEE. The LLC sublayer handles error control, flow control, framing, and MAC-sublayer addressing. The most prevalent LLC protocol is IEEE 802.2, which includes both connectionless and connection-oriented variants.

LLC2 Connection-oriented OSI LLC-sublayer protocol.

LLQ Low Latency Queueing - Brings strict priority queueing to Class-Based Weighted Fair Queueing (CBWFQ).

LM/X LAN Manager for UNIX - Monitors LAN devices in UNIX environments.

LMI Local Management Interface - Set of enhancements to the basic Frame Relay specification.

LMI includes support for a keepalive mechanism, which verifies that data is flowing; a multicast mechanism, which provides the network server with its local DLCI and the multicast DLCI; global addressing, which gives DLCIs global rather than local significance in Frame Relay networks; and a status mechanism, which provides an on-going status report on the DLCIs known to the switch. LMI is known as LMT in ANSI terminology.

LMT See LMI.

LNM LAN Network Manager - SRB and Token Ring management package provided by IBM. Typically running on a PC, it monitors SRB and Token Ring devices, and can pass alerts up to NetView.

load balancing In routing, the ability of a router to distribute traffic over all its network ports that are the same distance from the destination address. Good load-balancing algorithms use both line speed and reliability information. Load balancing increases the utilization of network segments, thus increasing effective network bandwidth.

local access and transport area See LATA.

local acknowledgment Method whereby an intermediate network node, such as a router, responds to acknowledgments for a remote end host. Use of local acknowledgments reduces network overhead and, therefore, the risk of time-outs. Local acknowledgment is also known as local termination.

local bridge Bridge that directly interconnects networks in the same geographic area.

local exchange carrier See LEC.

local loop Line from the premises of a telephone subscriber to the telephone company CO.

Local Management Interface See LMI.

local termination See local acknowledgment.

local traffic filtering Process by which a bridge filters out (drops) frames whose source and destination MAC addresses are located on the same interface on the bridge, thus preventing unnecessary traffic from being forwarded across the bridge. Defined in the IEEE 802.1 standard.

local unicast address An IPv6 address whose scope is configured to a single link. The address is unique only on this link and it is not routable off the link. Compare with a global unicast address.

local-area network See LAN.

local-area transport See LAT.

logical address See network address.

logical channel Nondedicated, packet-switched communications path between two or more network nodes. Packet switching allows many logical channels to exist simultaneously on a single physical channel.

logical channel identifier See LCI.

logical channel number See LCN.

Logical Link Control See LLC.

Logical Link Control, type 2 See LLC2.

logical unit See LU.

logical unit 6.2 See LU 6.2.

loop Route where packets never reach their destination, but simply cycle repeatedly through a constant series of network nodes.

loopback test   Test in which signals are sent and then directed back toward their source from some point along the communications path. Loopback tests are often used to test network interface usability.

lossy   Characteristic of a network that is prone to lose packets when it becomes highly loaded.

Low Latency Queueing   See LLQ.

low-speed line card   See LSC.

LPD   Line Printer Daemon - Protocol used to send print jobs between UNIX systems.

LSA   Link-State Advertisement - Broadcast packet used by link-state protocols that contains information about neighbors and path costs. LSAs are used by the receiving routers to maintain their routing tables. Link-state advertisement is also known as link-state packet (LSP).

LSC   Low-Speed Line Card - Card on the LightStream 2020 ATM switch that can be configured as an edge or a trunk card. An LSC, in conjunction with an access card, supports eight trunk or edge ports (Frame Relay or frame forwarding) at individual port speeds up to 3.584 Mbps, or an aggregate rate of 6 Mbps per line card.

LSP   Link-State Packet

LSPD   Link-State PDU Database - Database maintained by each router running a link-state routing protocol. It provides a global view of the area itself and the exit points to neighboring areas.

LU   Logical Unit - Primary component of SNA, an LU is an NAU that enables end users to communicate with each other and gain access to SNA network resources.

LU 6.2   Logical Unit 6.2 - In SNA, an LU that provides peer-to-peer communication between programs in a distributed computing environment. APPC runs on LU 6.2 devices.

LWAPP   Lightweight Access Point Protocol - LWAPP encapsulates and encrypts (with AES) control traffic between access points and wireless controllers. The data traffic between the access points and controllers is also encapsulated by LWAPP, but not encrypted.

LynxOS   Real-time, UNIX-like operating system that runs on the NP of a LightStream 2020 ATM switch.

MAC   Media Access Control - Lower of the two sublayers of the data link layer defined by the IEEE. The MAC sublayer handles access to shared media, such as whether token passing or contention will be used.

MAC address   Media Access Control address - Standardized data link layer address that is required for every port or device that connects to a LAN. Other devices in the network use these addresses to locate specific ports in the network and to create and update routing tables and data structures. MAC addresses are 6 bytes long and are controlled by the IEEE. Compare with network address. MAC address is also known as hardware address, MAC-layer address, or physical address.

MAC address learning   Service that characterizes a learning bridge, in which the source MAC address of each received packet is stored so that future packets destined for that address can be forwarded only to the bridge interface on which that address is located. Packets destined for unrecognized addresses are forwarded out every bridge interface. This scheme helps minimize traffic on the attached LANs. MAC address learning is defined in the IEEE 802.1 standard.

MAC-layer address   See MAC address.

main cross connect   See MCC.

main distribution facility   See MDF.

Maintenance Operation Protocol   See MOP.

MAN   Metropolitan-Area Network - Network that spans a metropolitan area. Generally, a MAN spans a larger geographic area than a LAN, but a smaller geographic area than a WAN. Compare with LAN and WAN.

managed object   In network management, a network device that can be managed by a network management protocol.

Management Information Base   See MIB.

Management Information Base collection   See MIB collection.

Management Information Base reporting   See MIB reporting.

management services   SNA functions distributed among network components to manage and control an SNA network.

Manchester encoding   Digital coding scheme, used by IEEE 802.3 and Ethernet, in which a mid-bit-time transition is used for clocking, and a 1 is denoted by a high level during the first half of the bit time.

Manufacturing Automation Protocol   See MAP.

MAP   Manufacturing Automation Protocol - Network architecture created by General Motors to satisfy the specific needs of the factory floor. MAP specifies a token-passing LAN similar to IEEE 802.4.

mask   See address mask and subnet mask.

master management agent   See MMA.

MAU   Media Attachment Unit - Device used in Ethernet and IEEE 802.3 networks that provides the interface between the AUI port of a station and the common medium of the Ethernet. The MAU, which can be built into a station or can be a separate device, performs physical layer functions including the conversion of digital data from the Ethernet interface, collision detection, and injection of bits onto the network. Sometimes referred to as a media access unit, also abbreviated MAU, or as a transceiver. In Token Ring, a MAU is known as a multistation access unit and is usually abbreviated MSAU to avoid confusion.

maximum burst   Specifies the largest burst of data above the insured rate that will be allowed temporarily on an ATM PVC, but will not be dropped at the edge by the traffic policing function, even if it exceeds the maximum rate. This amount of traffic will be allowed only temporarily; on average, the traffic source needs to be within the maximum rate. Specified in bytes or cells. Compare with insured burst.

maximum rate   Maximum total data throughput allowed on a given virtual circuit, equal to the sum of the insured and uninsured traffic from the traffic source. The uninsured data might be dropped if the network becomes congested. The maximum rate, which cannot exceed the media rate, represents the highest data throughput the virtual circuit will ever deliver, measured in bits or cells per second. Compare with excess rate and insured rate.

maximum transmission unit   See MTU.

Mb/s   Megabits Per Second - A megabit per second is a unit of data transfer rate equal to 1,000,000 bits per second.

MBONE   Multicast Backbone - The multicast backbone of the Internet. MBONE is a virtual multicast network composed of multicast LANs and the point-to-point tunnels that interconnect them.

MCA   Micro Channel Architecture - Bus interface commonly used in PCs and some UNIX workstations and servers.

MCC   Main Cross-Connect - Wiring closet that serves as the most central point in a star topology and where LAN backbone cabling connects to the Internet.

MCI Multiport Communications Interface - Card on the AGS+ that provides two Ethernet interfaces and up to two synchronous serial interfaces. The MCI processes packets rapidly, without the interframe delays typical of other Ethernet interfaces.

MCR Minimum Cell Rate - Parameter defined by the ATM Forum for ATM traffic management. MCR is defined only for ABR transmissions, and specifies the minimum value for the ACR.

MD5 Message Digest 5 - Algorithm used for message authentication in SNMP v.2. MD5 verifies the integrity of the communication, authenticates the origin, and checks for timeliness.

MDF Main Distribution Facility - Primary communications room for a building. Central point of a star networking topology where patch panels, hub, and router are located.

media The various physical environments through which transmission signals pass. Common network media include twisted-pair, coaxial and fiber-optic cable, and the atmosphere (through which microwave, laser, and infrared transmission occurs). Media is also known as physical media. Media is the plural of medium.

Media Access Control See MAC.

Media Access Control Address See MAC address.

media access unit See MAU.

media attachment unit See MAU.

media interface connector See MIC.

media rate Maximum traffic throughput for a particular media type.

medium See media.

medium-speed line card See MSC.

megabit Abbreviated Mb.

megabits per second See Mb/s.

megabyte Abbreviated MB.

mesh Network topology in which devices are organized in a manageable, segmented manner with many, often redundant, interconnections strategically placed between network nodes.

message Application layer (Layer 7) logical grouping of information, often composed of a number of lower-layer logical groupings such as packets. The terms datagram, frame, packet, and segment are also used to describe logical information groupings at various layers of the OSI reference model and in various technology circles.

Message Digest 5 See MD5.

message handling system See MHS.

Message Queuing Interface See MQI.

message switching Switching technique involving transmission of messages from node to node through a network. The message is stored at each node until such time as a forwarding path is available. Contrast with circuit switching and packet switching.

message unit Unit of data processed by any network layer.

metering See traffic shaping.

metric See routing metric.

metropolitan-area network See MAN.

MHS Message Handling System - ITU-T X.400 recommendations that provide message handling services for communications between distributed applications. NetWare MHS is a different (though similar) entity that also provides message-handling services.

MIB Management Information Base - Database of network management information that is used and maintained by a network management protocol such as SNMP or CMIP. The value of a MIB object can be changed or retrieved using SNMP or CMIP commands. MIB objects are organized in a tree structure that includes public (standard) and private (proprietary) branches.

MIC 1) Media Interface Connector - FDDI is the de facto standard connector. 2) Message Integrity Check - MIC is a method use to overcome the exploitation of encryption keys by utilizing integrity checks.

micro channel architecture See MCA.

microcode Translation layer between machine instructions and the elementary operations of a computer. Microcode is stored in ROM and allows the addition of new machine instructions without requiring that they be designed into electronic circuits when new instructions are needed.

microsegmentation Division of a network into smaller segments, usually with the intention of increasing aggregate bandwidth to network devices.

microwave Electromagnetic waves in the range 1 to 30 GHz. Microwave-based networks are an evolving technology gaining favor due to high bandwidth and relatively low cost.

Military Network See MILNET.

millions of instructions per second See mips.

MILNET Military Network - Unclassified portion of the DDN. Operated and maintained by the DISA.

minimum cell rate See MCR.

MIP MultiChannel Interface Processor - Interface processor on the Cisco 7000 series routers that provides up to two channelized T1 or E1 connections via serial cables to a CSU. The two controllers on the MIP can each provide up to 24 T1 or 30 E1 channel-groups, with each channel-group presented to the system as a serial interface that can be configured individually.

mips Millions of Instructions Per Second - Number of instructions executed by a processor per second.

MMA Master Management Agent - SNMP agent that runs on the NP of a LightStream 2020 ATM switch. MMA translates between an external network manager using SNMP and the internal switch management mechanisms.

Mobile IP An IETF standard for IPv4 and IPv6 which enables mobile devices to move without breaking current connections. In IPv6, mobility is built in, which means that any IPv6 node can use it as needed.

modem Modulator-Demodulator - Device that converts digital and analog signals. At the source, a modem converts digital signals to a form suitable for transmission over analog communication facilities. At the destination, the analog signals are returned to their digital form. Modems allow data to be transmitted over voice-grade telephone lines.

modulation Any of several techniques for combining user information with a transmitter's carrier signal. It is a process by which the characteristics of electrical signals are transformed to represent information. Types of modulation include AM, FM, and PAM.

modulator-demodulator See modem.

monitor Management tool on the LightStream 2020 ATM switch that allows a user to examine individual nodes in the network and learn the status of interface modules and power supplies. The monitor is an HP OpenView-based application that runs on an NMS.

monomode fiber   See single-mode fiber.

MOP   Maintenance Operation Protocol - Digital Equipment Corporation protocol, a subset of which is supported by Cisco, that provides a way to perform primitive maintenance operations on DECnet systems. For example, MOP can be used to download a system image to a diskless station.

Mosaic   Public-domain WWW browser, developed at the National Center for Supercomputing Applications (NCSA).

MP-BGP   Multiprotocol-Border Gateway Protocol - Used to enable BGP4 to carry information of other protocols, for example, Multiprotocol Label Switching (MPLS) and IPv6.

MPLS   Multiprotocol Label Switching - Labeling technique used to increase the speed of traffic flow. Each packet is tagged with the path sequence to the destination. This saves time by not have to do a lookup of the routing table. In another word packet switching is done at layer 2 instead of layer 3. MPLS support multiple protocols such as IP, ATM, and frame relay.

MPLS/TE   Multiprotocol Label Switching/Traffic Engineering - Provides a way to integrate TE capabilities (such as those used on Layer 2 protocols like ATM) into Layer 3 protocols (IP). MPLS TE uses an extension to existing protocols (Resource Reservation Protocol (RSVP), IS-IS, Open Shortest Path First (OSPF))to calculate and establish unidirectional tunnels that are set according to the network constraint. Traffic flows are mapped on the different tunnels depending on their destination.

MQI   Message Queuing Interface - International standard API that provides functionality similar to that of the RPC interface. In contrast to RPC, MQI is implemented strictly at the application layer.

MSAU   Multistation Access Unit - Wiring concentrator to which all end stations in a Token Ring network connect. The MSAU provides an interface between these devices and the Token Ring interface of, for example, a Cisco 7000 TRIP. MSAU is also abbreviated MAU.

MSC   Medium-Speed Line Card - Card on the LightStream 2020 ATM switch that can be configured as an edge or a trunk card. The MSC, in conjunction with an access card, supports two trunk or edge (UNI) ports at data rates up to T3 or E3.

MTU   Maximum Transmission Unit - Maximum packet size, in bytes, that a particular interface can handle.

mu-law   North American companding standard used in conversion between analog and digital signals in PCM systems. Similar to the European alaw.

multiaccess network   Network that allows multiple devices to connect and communicate simultaneously.

multicast   Single packets copied by the network and sent to a specific subset of network addresses. These addresses are specified in the destination address field. Compare with broadcast and unicast.

multicast address   Single address that refers to multiple network devices. Synonymous with group address. Compare with broadcast address and unicast address.

multicast backbone   See MBONE.

multicast group   Dynamically determined group of IP hosts identified by a single IP multicast address.

multicast router   Router used to send IGMP query messages on their attached local networks. Host members of a multicast group respond to a query by sending IGMP reports noting the multicast groups to which they belong. The multicast router takes responsibility for forwarding multicast datagrams from one multicast group to all other networks that have members in the group.

multicast server Establishes a one-to-many connection to each device in a VLAN, thus establishing a broadcast domain for each VLAN segment. The multicast server forwards incoming broadcasts only to the multicast address that maps to the broadcast address.

MultiChannel Interface Processor See MIP.

multihomed host Host attached to multiple physical network segments in an OSI CLNS network.

multihoming Addressing scheme in IS-IS routing that supports assignment of multiple area addresses.

multilayer switch Switch that filters and forwards packets based on MAC addresses and network addresses. A subset of LAN switch. The Catalyst 5000 is an example of a multilayer switch. Compare with LAN switch.

multimode fiber Optical fiber supporting propagation of multiple frequencies of light.

multipath distortion The echoes created as a radio signal bounces off of physical objects. Multipath distortion occurs when an RF signal has more than one path between a receiver and a transmitter. RF waves can take more than one path when going from a transmitting to a receiving antenna. These multiple signals arrive at the receiving antenna at different times and phases which causes distortion of the signal.

multiple domain network SNA network with multiple SSCPs.

multiplexing Scheme that allows multiple logical signals to be transmitted simultaneously across a single physical channel. Compare with demultiplexing.

Multiport Communications Interface See MCI.

Multiprotocol BGP See MP-BGP.

Multiprotocol Label Switching (MPLS) See MPLS.

Multiprotocol Label Switching/Traffic Engineering See MPLS/TE.

multistation access unit See MSAU.

NAC Network Admission Control - Method of controlling access to a network in order to prevent the introduction of computer viruses. Using a variety of protocols and software products, NAC assesses the condition of hosts when they attempt to log onto the network, and handles the request based on the host's condition, called its posture. Infected hosts can be placed in quarantine; hosts without up-to-date virus protection software can be directed to obtain updates, and uninfected hosts with up-to-date virus protection can be allowed onto the network.

Nagle's algorithm Actually two separate congestion control algorithms that can be used in TCP-based networks. One algorithm reduces the sending window; the other limits small datagrams.

NAK Negative Acknowledgment - Response sent from a receiving device to a sending device indicating that the information received contained errors. Compare to ACK.

name caching Method by which remotely discovered host names are stored by a router for use in future packet-forwarding decisions to allow quick access.

name resolution Generally, the process of associating a name with a network location.

name server Server connected to a network that resolves network names into network addresses.

NAP Network Access Point - Location for interconnection of Internet service providers in the United States for the exchange of packets.

narrowband See baseband.

Narrowband ISDN See N-ISDN.

NAT   Network Address Translation - Only globally unique in terms of the public internet. A mechanism for translating private addresses into publicly usable addresses to be used within the public internet. An effective means for hiding actual device addressing within a private network. Network Address Translation is also known as Network Address Translator.

National Bureau of Standards   See NBS.

National Institute of Standards and Technology   See NIST.

National Science Foundation   See NSF.

National Science Foundation Network   See NSFnet.

native client interface architecture   See NCIA.

NAT-PT   Network Address Translation - Protocol Translation Translation mechanism that sits between an IPv6 network and an IPv4 network. The job of the translator is to translate IPv6 packets into IPv4 packets and vice versa. Compare with Stateless IP/Internet Control Message Protocol (ICMP) Translation (SIIT) algorithm and DNS ALG.

NAU   Network Addressable Unit - SNA term for an addressable entity. Examples include Lus, Pus, and SSCPs. NAUs generally provide upper-level network services. Compare with path control network.

NAUN   Nearest Active Upstream Neighbor - In Token Ring or IEEE 802.5 networks, the closest upstream network device from any given device that is still active.

NBMA   Nonbroadcast Multiaccess - Term describing a multiaccess network that either does not support broadcasting (such as X.25) or in which broadcasting is not feasible (for example, an SMDS broadcast group or an extended Ethernet that is too large).

NBS   National Bureau of Standards - Organization that was part of the U.S. Department of Commerce. National Bureau of Standards is now known as National Institute of Standards and Technology (NIST).

NCIA   Native Client Interface Architecture - SNA applications-access architecture, developed by Cisco, that combines the full functionality of native SNA interfaces at both the host and client with the flexibility of leveraging TCP/IP backbones. NCIA encapsulates SNA traffic on a client PC or workstation, thereby providing direct TCP/IP access while preserving the native SNA interface at the end-user level. In many networks, this capability obviates the need for a standalone gateway and can provide flexible TCP/IP access while preserving the native SNA interface to the host.

NCP   Network Control Protocol - In SNA, a program that routes and controls the flow of data between a communications controller (in which it resides) and other network resources.

ND   Neighborhood Discovery - Process that runs on the NP of each LightStream 2020 ATM switch in the ATM network. For call routing purposes, every node in the network needs to know about changes in network topology, such as trunks and ports going up or down. ND learns about such changes at the chassis level and forwards this information to the GID process, which sends the information throughout the network. Neighborhood discovery is also known as neighborhood discovery daemon (NDD).

NDD   Neighborhood Discovery Daemon.

NDIS   Network Driver Interface Specification - Specification for a generic, hardware- and protocol-independent device driver for NICs. Produced by Microsoft.

nearest active upstream neighbor   See NAUN.

NEARNET   Regional network in New England (United States) that links Boston University, Harvard University, and MIT. Now part of BBN Planet.

negative acknowledgment   See NAK.

neighborhood discovery   See ND.

neighborhood discovery daemon   See ND.

neighboring routers   In OSPF, two routers that have interfaces to a common network. On multi-access networks, neighbors are dynamically discovered by the OSPF Hello protocol.

NET   Network Entity Title - NSAP with an n-selector of zero. All router NETs have an n-selector of zero, implying the network layer of the IS itself (0 means no transport layer). For this reason, the NSAP of a router is always referred to as a NET.

NetBEUI   NetBIOS Extended User Interface - Enhanced version of the NetBIOS protocol used by network operating systems such as LAN Manager, LAN Server, Windows for Workgroups, and Windows NT. NetBEUI formalizes the transport frame and implements the OSI LLC2 protocol.

NetBIOS   Network Basic Input/Output System - API used by applications on an IBM LAN to request services from lower-level network processes. These services might include session establishment and termination, and information transfer.

NetView   IBM network management architecture and related applications. NetView is a VTAM application used for managing mainframes in SNA networks.

NetWare   Popular distributed NOS developed by Novell. Provides transparent remote file access and numerous other distributed network services.

NetWare Link Services Protocol   See NLSP.

NetWare Loadable Module   See NLM.

Network   A system for communication among two or more computers.

network   1) Collection of computers, printers, routers, switches, and other devices that are able to communicate with each other over some transmission medium. 2) Command that assigns a NIC-based address to which the router is directly connected. 3) Command that specifies any directly connected networks to be included.

network access point   See NAP.

network access server   See access server.

network address   Network layer address referring to a logical, rather than a physical, network device. Compare with MAC address. Network address is also known as protocol address.

network addressable unit   See NAU.

network administrator   Person responsible for the operation, maintenance, and management of a network.

Network Admission Control   See NAC.

network analyzer   Network monitoring device that maintains statistical information regarding the status of the network and each device attached to it. More sophisticated versions using artificial intelligence can detect, define, and fix problems on the network.

Network architecture   The design of a communications network. It is a framework for the specification of a network's physical components and their functional organization and configuration, its operational principles and procedures, as well as data formats used in its operation.

Network Basic Input/Output System   See NetBIOS.

Network byte order   Internet-standard ordering of the bytes corresponding to numeric values.

Network Control Program   See NCP.

network driver interface specification   See NDIS.

network entity title   See NET.

Network File System   See NFS.

Network Information Center   See NIC.

Network Information Service   See NIS.

Network infrastructure   The architecture, in terms of equipment and connections, that makes up a network.

network interface   Boundary between a carrier network and a privately-owned installation.

network interface card   See NIC.

network layer   Layer 3 of the OSI reference model. This layer provides connectivity and path selection between two end systems. The network layer is the layer at which routing occurs. Corresponds roughly with the path control layer of the SNA model.

network management   Generic term used to describe systems or actions that help maintain, characterize, or troubleshoot a network.

Network Management Processor   See NMP.

network management system   See NMS.

network management vector transport   See NMVT.

network number   Part of an IP address that specifies the network to which the host belongs.

network operating system   See NOS.

Network Operations Center   See NOC.

network operator   Person who routinely monitors and controls a network, performing such tasks as reviewing and responding to traps, monitoring throughput, configuring new circuits, and resolving problems.

network processor card   See NP card.

network service access point   See NSAP.

networking   Connecting of any collection of computers, printers, routers, switches, and other devices for the purpose of communication over some transmission medium.

Network-to-Network Interface   See NNI.

neutral wire   Circuit wire that is connected to an earth ground at the power plant and at the transformer.

Next Hop Resolution Protocol   See NHRP.

NFS   Network File System - As commonly used, a distributed file system protocol suite developed by Sun Microsystems that allows remote file access across a network. In actuality, NFS is simply one protocol in the suite. NFS protocols include NFS, RPC, External Data Representation (XDR), and others. These protocols are part of a larger architecture that Sun refers to as ONC.

NHRP   Next Hop Resolution Protocol - Protocol Used by routers to dynamically discover the MAC address of other routers and hosts connected to a NBMA network. These systems can then directly communicate without requiring traffic to use an intermediate hop, increasing performance in ATM, Frame Relay, SMDS, and X.25 environments.

NIC   1) Network Interface Card - Board that provides network communication capabilities to and from a computer system. A network interface card is also known as an adapter. 2) Network Information Center - Organization whose functions have been assumed by the InterNIC. See interNIC.

NIS Network Information Service - Protocol developed by Sun Microsystems for the administration of network-wide databases. The service essentially uses two programs: one for finding a NIS server and one for accessing the NIS databases.

N-ISDN Narrowband ISDN - Communication standards developed by the ITU-T for baseband networks. Based on 64-kbps B channels and 16- or 64-kbps D channels. Contrast with BISDN.

NIST National Institute of Standards and Technology - Formerly the NBS, this U.S. government organization supports and catalogs a variety of standards.

NLM NetWare Loadable Module - Individual program that can be loaded into memory and function as part of the NetWare NOS.

NLRI Network Layer Reachability Information - BGP sends routing update messages containing NLRI to describe a route and how to get there. In this context, an NLRI is a prefix. A BGP update message carries one or more NLRI prefixes and the attributes of a route for theNLRI prefixes; the route attributes include a BGP next hop gateway address, community values, and other information.

NLSP NetWare Link Services Protocol - Link-state routing protocol based on IS-IS. The Cisco implementation of NLSP also includes MIB variables and tools to redistribute routing and SAP information between NLSP and other IPX routing protocols.

NMP Network Management Processor - Processor module on the Catalyst 5000 switch used to control and monitor the switch.

NMS Network Management System - System responsible for managing at least part of a network. An NMS is generally a reasonably powerful and well-equipped computer such as an engineering workstation. NMSs communicate with agents to help keep track of network statistics and resources.

NMVT Network Management Vector Transport - SNA message consisting of a series of vectors conveying network management specific information.

NNI Network-to-Network Interface - ATM Forum standard that defines the interface between two ATM switches that are both located in a private network or are both located in a public network. The interface between a public switch and private one is defined by the UNI standard. Also, the standard interface between two Frame Relay switches meeting the same criteria.

NOC Network Operations Center - Organization responsible for maintaining a network.

node 1) Endpoint of a network connection or a junction common to two or more lines in a network. Nodes can be processors, controllers, or workstations. Nodes, which vary in routing and other functional capabilities, can be interconnected by links, and serve as control points in the network. Node is sometimes used generically to refer to any entity that can access a network, and is frequently used interchangeably with device. 2) In SNA, the basic component of a network, and the point at which one or more functional units connect channels or data circuits.

noise Undesirable communications channel signals.

nominal velocity of propagation See NVP.

nonbroadcast multiaccess See NBMA.

non-stub area Resource-intensive OSPF area that carries a default route, static routes, intra-area routes, interarea routes, and external routes. Nonstub areas are the only OSPF areas that can have virtual links configured across them, and are the only areas that can contain an ASBR. Compare with stub area.

nonvolatile random-access memory See NVRAM.

normal mode Term used to describe problems between the hot and neutral wires on a power line.

normal response mode   See NRM.

NOS   Network Operating System - Generic term used to refer to what are really distributed file systems. Examples of NOSs include LAN Manager, NetWare, NFS, and VINES.

Novell IPX   See IPX.

NP card   Network Processor Card - Main computational and storage resource for the LightStream 2020 ATM switch. Each LightStream 2020 switch has one or two NPs. The second card, if present, serves as a backup for the first. Each NP is associated with a floppy disk drive for loading software and a hard disk drive for storing software and configuration data. Each NP also has an access card that provides an Ethernet port.

NP module   On a LightStream 2020 ATM switch, the combination of the NP card, the NP access card, and the disk assembly.

NP TCS monitoring module   See NPTMM.

npadmin account   One of the four default user accounts that are created in the factory on each LightStream 2020 ATM switch. The npadmin account is for privileged users. Its default interface is the CLI.

NPTMM   Network Processor Test and Control System Monitoring Module - Process that runs on the NP of every LightStream 2020 ATM switch in an ATM network. NPTMM monitors the health of the system through the TCS and coordinates switch cutover when redundant switch cards are present.

NRM   Normal Response Mode - HDLC mode for use on links with one primary station and one or more secondary stations. In this mode, secondary stations can transmit only if they first receive a poll from the primary station.

NSAP   Network Service Access Point - Conceptual point on the boundary between the network and the transport layers. The NSAP is the location at which OSI network services are provided to the transport layer. Each transport layer entity is assigned a single NSAP.

NSAP Address   Network Service Access Point Address - Network-layer address for CLNS packets. An NSAP describes an attachment to a particular service at the network layer of a node, similar to the combination of IP destination address and IP protocol number in an IP packet. NSAP encoding and format are specified by ISO 8348/Ad2. NSAP address has two major parts: the initial domain part (IDP) and the domain specific part (DSP). The IDP consists of a 1-byte authority and format identifier (AFI) and a variable-length initial domain identifier (IDI), and the DSP is a string of digits identifying a particular transport implementation of a specified AFI authority. Everything to the left of the system ID can be thought of as the area address of a network node.

NSEL   Network Service Access Point Selector - Part of the NSAP address field that identifies a process on the device. It is roughly equivalent to a socket or a TCP port number in TCP/IP. The NSEL is not used in routing decisions. Domain-Specific Part (DSP): comprised of the HODSP, the system ID, and the NSEL in binary format. The last byte is the N-Selector (NSEL) and must be specified as a single-byte length preceded by a '.'. A NET definition must set the N-Selector to \rquote 00\rquote.

NSF   National Science Foundation - U.S. government agency that funds scientific research in the United States. The now-defunct NSFNET was funded by the NSF.

NSFnet   National Science Foundation Network - Large network that was controlled by the NSF and provided networking services in support of education and research in the United States, from 1986 to 1995. NSFnet is no longer in service.

NTP   Network Time Protocol - Protocol built on top of TCP that assures accurate local timekeeping with reference to radio and atomic clocks located on the Internet. This protocol is capable of synchronizing distributed clocks within milliseconds over long time periods.

null modem   Small box or cable used to join computing devices directly, rather than over a network.

NVP   Nominal Velocity of Propagation - Speed at which a signal moves through a cable, expressed as a percentage or fraction of the speed of light in a vacuum. To calculate a cable length, a cable tester uses NVP together with the time a signal takes to return to the testing device.

NVRAM   Nonvolatile RAM - RAM that retains its contents when a unit is powered off. In Cisco products, NVRAM is used to store configuration information.

NYSERNet   Network in New York (United States) with a T1 backbone connecting NSF, many universities, and several commercial concerns.

OAM cell   Operation, Administration, and Maintenance cell - ATM Forum specification for cells used to monitor virtual circuits. OAM cells provide a virtual circuit-level loopback in which a router responds to the cells, demonstrating that the circuit is up, and the router is operational.

OC   Optical Carrier - Series of physical protocols (OC-1, OC-2, OC-3, and so on), defined for SONET optical signal transmissions. OC signal levels put STS frames onto multimode fiber-optic line at a variety of speeds. The base rate is 51.84 Mbps (OC-1); each signal level thereafter operates at a speed divisible by that number (thus, OC-3 runs at 155.52 Mbps).

octet   8 bits. In networking, the term octet is often used (rather than byte) because some machine architectures employ bytes that are not 8 bits long.

ODA   Open Document Architecture - ISO standard that specifies how documents are represented and transmitted electronically. Open document Architecture was known as Office Document Architecture.

ODI   Open Data-Link Interface - Novell specification providing a standardized interface for NICs that allows multiple protocols to use a single NIC.

OEMI channel   See block multiplexer channel.

OFDM   Orthogonal Frequency Division Multiplexing - OFDM is a modulation technique used with IEEE 802.11g.

Office Document Architecture   See ODA.

OIM   OSI Internet Management - Group tasked with specifying ways in which OSI network management protocols can be used to manage TCP/IP networks.

OIR   Online Insertion and Removal - Feature that permits the addition, replacement, or removal of interface processors in a Cisco router without interrupting the system power, entering console commands, or causing other software or interfaces to shut down. Online insertion and removal is also known as hot swapping.

omni-directional   This typically refers to a primarily circular antenna radiation pattern.

ONC   Open Network Computing - Distributed applications architecture designed by Sun Microsystems, currently controlled by a consortium led by Sun. The NFS protocols are part of ONC.

ones density   Scheme that allows a CSU/DSU to recover the data clock reliably. The CSU/DSU derives the data clock from the data that passes through it. In order to recover the clock, the CSU/DSU hardware must receive at least one 1 bit value for every 8 bits of data that pass through it. Ones density is also known as pulse density.

online insertion and removal   See OIR.

on-the-fly packet switching   See cut-through packet switching.

open architecture   Architecture with which third-party developers can legally develop products and for which public domain specifications exist.

open circuit   Broken path along a transmission medium. Open circuits will usually prevent network communication.

Open Document Architecture   See ODA.

Open Network Computing   See ONC.

Open Shortest Path First   See OSPFv2 and OSPFv3.

Open System Interconnection   See OSI.

Open System Interconnection reference model   See OSI reference model.

oper account   One of the four default user accounts that are created in the factory on each LightStream 2020 ATM switch. The oper account is for general users. Its default interface is the CLI.

Operation, Administration, and Maintenance cell   See OAM cell.

Optical Carrier   See OC.

optical fiber   See fiber-optic cable.

Organizational Unique Identifier   See OUI.

Orthogonal Frequency Division Multiplex (OFDM)   A wireless modulation technique used by IEEE 802.11a-compliant wireless LANs for transmission at 6, 9, 12, 18, 24, 36, 48, and 54 Mbps.

oscillation   Secondary signal on top of the 60-Hz waveform. It has a magnitude that ranges from 15% to 100% of the normal voltage carried on the power line.

OSI   Open System Interconnection - International standardization program created by ISO and ITU-T to develop standards for data networking that facilitate multivendor equipment interoperability.

OSI Internet Management   See OIM.

OSI Presentation Address   Address used to locate an OSI Application entity. It consists of an OSI Network Address and up to three selectors, one each for use by the transport, session, and presentation entities.

OSI reference model   Open System Interconnection reference model - Network architectural model developed by ISO and ITU-T. The model consists of seven layers, each of which specifies particular network functions such as addressing, flow control, error control, encapsulation, and reliable message transfer. The highest layer (the application layer) is closest to the user; the lowest layer (the physical layer) is closest to the media technology. The next to lowest layer are implemented in hardware and software, while the upper five layers are implemented only in software. The OSI reference model is used universally as a method for teaching and understanding network functionality. Similar in some respects to SNA.

OSINET   International association designed to promote OSI in vendor architectures.

OSPFv2   Open Shortest Path First version 2 - OSPFv2 is an IPv4 link-state, hierarchical IGP routing algorithm proposed as a successor to RIP in the Internet community. OSPF features include least-cost routing, multipath routing, and load balancing. OSPF was derived from an early version of the ISIS protocol.

OSPFv3   Open Shortest Path First version 3 - Protocol implementation for IPv6. It is based on OSPF version 2 (OSPFv2), with enhancements.

OUI   Organizational Unique Identifie - The 3 octets assigned by the IEEE in a block of 48-bit LAN addresses.

outframe   Maximum number of outstanding frames allowed in an SNA PU 2 server at any time.

out-of-band signaling   1) Transmission using frequencies or channels outside the frequencies or channels normally used for information transfer. Out-of-band signaling is often used for error reporting in situations in which in-band signaling can be affected by whatever problems the network might be experiencing. Contrast with in-band signaling. 2) Out-of-band management is the use of a dedicated management channel for device management. This channel is isolated from the data channel and not vulnerable to network connectivity issues.

P/F   Poll/Final bit - Bit in bit-synchronous data link layer protocols that indicates the function of a frame. If the frame is a command, a 1 in this bit indicates a poll. If the frame is a response, a 1 in this bit indicates that the current frame is the last frame in the response.

pacing   See flow control.

packet   Logical grouping of information that includes a header containing control information and (usually) user data. Packets are most often used to refer to network layer units of data. The terms datagram, frame, message, and segment are also used to describe logical information groupings at various layers of the OSI reference model and in various technology circles.

packet assembler/disassembler   See PAD.

packet buffer   See buffer.

packet Internet groper   See ping.

Packet Level Protocol   See PLP.

packet line card   See PLC.

packet switch   WAN device that routes packets along the most efficient path and allows a communications channel to be shared by multiple connections. A packet switch is also known as a packet switch node (PSN), and was formerly known as an interface message processor (IMP).

packet switch exchange   See PSE.

packet switching   Networking method in which nodes share bandwidth with each other by sending packets. Compare with circuit switching and message switching.

packet-switched data network   See PSN.

packet-switched network   See PSN.

packet-switching node   See PSN.

PAD   Packet Assembler/Disassembler - Device used to connect simple devices (like character-mode terminals) that do not support the full functionality of a particular protocol to a network. PADs buffer data and assemble and disassemble packets sent to such end devices.

paddle card   See access card.

Palo Alto Research Center   See PARC.

PAM   Pulse Amplitude Modulation - Modulation scheme where the modulating wave is caused to modulate the amplitude of a pulse stream. Compare with AM and FM.

PAP   Password Authentication Protocol - Authentication protocol that allows PPP peers to authenticate one another. The remote router attempting to connect to the local router is required to send an authentication request. Unlike CHAP, PAP passes the password and host name or username in the clear (unencrypted). PAP does not itself prevent unauthorized access, but merely identifies the remote end. The router or access server then determines if that user is allowed access. PAP is supported only on PPP lines. Compare with CHAP.

parallel channel   Channel that uses bus and tag cables as a transmission medium. Compare with ESCON channel.

parallel transmission   Method of data transmission in which the bits of a data character are transmitted simultaneously over a number of channels. Compare with serial transmission.

parallelism   Indicates that multiple paths exist between two points in a network. These paths might be of equal or unequal cost. Parallelism is often a network design goal: if one path fails, there is redundancy in the network to ensure that an alternate path to the same point exists.

PARC   Palo Alto Research Center - Research and development center operated by XEROX. A number of widely-used technologies were originally conceived at PARC, including the first personal computers and LANs.

PARC Universal Protocol   See PUP.

parity check   Process for checking the integrity of a character. A parity check involves appending a bit that makes the total number of binary 1 digits in a character or word (excluding the parity bit) either odd (for odd parity) or even (for even parity).

partial mesh   Term describing a network in which devices are organized in a mesh topology, with some network nodes organized in a full mesh, but with others that are only connected to one or two other nodes in the network. A partial mesh does not provide the level of redundancy of a full mesh topology, but is less expensive to implement. Partial mesh topologies are generally used in the peripheral networks that connect to a fully meshed backbone.

partial sequence number PDU   See PSNP.

passive interface   A passive interface receives updates, but does not send them. It is used to control routing update. The passive-interface command can be used with all IP interior gateway protocols. That is that it can be use with RIP, IGRP, EIGRP, OSPF, and IS-IS.

Password Authentication Protocol   See PAP.

patch panel   An assembly of pin locations and ports which can be mounted on a rack or wall bracket in the wiring closet. Patch panels act like switchboards that connect workstations cables to each other and to the outside.

path control layer   Layer 3 in the SNA architectural model. This layer performs sequencing services related to proper data reassembly. The path control layer is also responsible for routing. Corresponds roughly with the network layer of the OSI model.

path control network   SNA concept that consists of lower-level components that control the routing and data flow through an SNA network and handle physical data transmission between SNA nodes. Compare with NAU.

path cost   See cost.

path name   Full name of a UNIX, DOS, or LynxOS file or directory, including all directory and subdirectory names. Consecutive names in a path name are typically separated by a forward slash (/) or a backslash (\), as in /usr/app/base/config.

payload   Portion of a frame that contains upper-layer information (data).

PBX   Private Branch Exchange - Digital or analog telephone switchboard located on the subscriber premises and used to connect private and public telephone networks.

PCI   Protocol Control Information - Control information added to user data to comprise an OSI packet. The OSI equivalent of the term header.

PCM   Pulse Code Modulation - Transmission of analog information in digital form through sampling and encoding the samples with a fixed number of bits.

PCR   Peak Cell Rate - Parameter defined by the ATM Forum for ATM traffic management. In CBR transmissions, PCR determines how often data samples are sent. In ABR transmissions, PCR determines the maximum value of the ACR.

PDAs Personal Digital Assistant - Handheld device. Depending on the model and version, they can offer a varying amount of features including some of the following: personal organizers, address book, calculators, clock and calendar functions, computer games, Internet access, e-mail, radio and MP3 playback, video recording, GPS, mobile phones (smartphone), web browsers or media players.

PDN Public Data Network - Network operated either by a government (as in Europe) or by a private concern to provide computer communications to the public, usually for a fee. PDNs enable small organizations to create a WAN without all the equipment costs of long-distance circuits.

PDU Protocol Data Unit - OSI term for packet. See also BPDU and packet.

peak cell rate See PCR.

peak rate Maximum rate, in kilobits per second, at which a virtual circuit can transmit.

peer-to-peer computing Peer-to-peer computing calls for each network device to run both client and server portions of an application. Also describes communication between implementations of the same OSI reference model layer in two different network devices.

performance management One of five categories of network management defined by ISO for management of OSI networks. Performance management subsystems are responsible for analyzing and controlling network performance including network throughput and error rates.

peripheral node In SNA, a node that uses local addresses and is therefore not affected by changes to network addresses. Peripheral nodes require boundary function assistance from an adjacent subarea node.

permanent virtual circuit See PVC.

permanent virtual connection See PVC.

permanent virtual path See PVP.

permit processing See traffic policing.

Personal digital assistants See PDAs.

PGP Pretty Good Privacy - Public-key encryption application that allows secure file and message exchanges. There is some controversy over the development and use of this application, in part due to U.S. national security concerns.

phase Location of a position on an alternating wave form.

phase shift Situation in which the relative position in time between the clock and data signals of a transmission becomes unsynchronized. In systems using long cables at higher transmission speeds, slight variances in cable construction, temperature, and other factors can cause a phase shift, resulting in high error rates.

PHY Physical Sublayer - One of two sublayers of the FDDI physical layer. See also PMD.

physical address See MAC address.

physical control layer Layer 1 in the SNA architectural model. This layer is responsible for the physical specifications for the physical links between end systems. Corresponds to the physical layer of the OSI model.

Physical layer Layer 1 of the OSI reference model. The physical layer defines the electrical, mechanical, procedural and functional specifications for activating, maintaining, and deactivating the physical link between end systems. Corresponds with the physical control layer in the SNA model.

physical layer convergence procedure See PLCP.

physical media See media.

physical medium See media.

physical medium dependent   See PMD.

physical sublayer   See PHY.

physical unit   See PU.

Physical Unit 2   See PU 2.

Physical Unit 4   See PU 4.

Physical Unit 5   See PU 5.

PIM   Protocol Independent Multicast - Multicast routing architecture that allows the addition of IP multicast routing on existing IP networks. PIM is unicast routing protocol independent and can be operated in two modes: dense mode and sparse mode.

PIM dense mode   One of the two PIM operational modes. PIM dense mode is data-driven and resembles typical multicast routing protocols. Packets are forwarded on all outgoing interfaces until pruning and truncation occurs. In dense mode, receivers are densely populated, and it is assumed that the downstream networks want to receive and will probably use the datagrams that are forwarded to them. The cost of using dense mode is its default flooding behavior. Contrast with PIM sparse mode. PIM dense mode is also known as dense mode PIM or PIM DM.

PIM DM   See PIM dense mode.

PIM SM   See PIM sparse mode.

PIM sparse mode   One of the two PIM operational modes. PIM sparse mode tries to constrain data distribution so that a minimal number of routers in the network receive it. Packets are sent only if they are explicitly requested at the RP. In sparse mode, receivers are widely distributed, and the assumption is that downstream networks will not necessarily use the datagrams that are sent to them. The cost of using sparse mode is its reliance on the periodic refreshing of explicit join messages and its need for RPs. Sometimes called sparse mode PIM or PIM SM. Contrast with PIM dense mode.

pin location   A color-coded slot on a patch panel. Cable wires are punched down using a punch tool to make an electrical connection that allows the network to function.

ping   packet Internet groper - Utility to determine whether a specific IP address is accessible. It works by sending a packet to the specified address and waiting for a reply. PING is used primarily to troubleshoot Internet connections. PING is also known as Packet Inter-network Groper

pixel   picture element - The smallest element of a display image, corresponding to a single displayed spot or color triad on a display, or to a single input spot from a camera.

plain old telephone service   See PSTN.

PLC   Packet Line Card - Card on the LightStream 2020 ATM switch that can be configured only as an edge card. A PLC, in conjunction with an access card, supports up to eight Ethernet or two FDDI edge ports.

PLCP   Physical Layer Convergence Procedure - Specification that maps ATM cells into physical media, such as T3 or E3, and defines certain management information.

plesiochronous transmission   Term describing digital signals that are sourced from different clocks of comparable accuracy and stability. Compare with asynchronous transmission, isochronous transmission, and synchronous transmission.

PLP   Packet Level Protocol - Network layer protocol in the X.25 protocol stack. Packet Level Protocol is also known as X.25 Level 3 or X.25 Protocol.

PLU   Primary Logical Unit - The LU that is initiating a session with another LU.

PMD   Physical Medium Dependent - Sublayer of the FDDI physical layer that interfaces directly with the physical medium and performs the most basic bit transmission functions of the network.

PNNI Private Network-Network Interface - ATM Forum specification that describes an ATM virtual circuit routing protocol, as well as a signaling protocol between ATM switches. Used to allow ATM switches within a private network to interconnect. Private Network-Network Interface is also known as Private Network Node Interface.

PoE Power over Ethernet - PoE is the powering of network devices over Ethernet cable. IEEE 802.3af and Cisco specify two different PoE methods. Cisco power sourcing equipment (PSE) and powered devices (PDs) support both PoE methods.

point of presence See POP.

point-to-multipoint connection One of two fundamental connection types. In ATM, a point-to-multipoint connection is a unidirectional connection in which a single source end-system (known as a root node) connects to multiple destination end-systems (known as leaves). Compare point-to-point connection.

point-to-point connection One of two fundamental connection types. In ATM, a point-topoint connection can be a unidirectional or bidirectional connection between two ATM end-systems. Compare point-to-multipoint connection.

Point-to-Point Protocol See PPP.

poison reverse updates Routing updates that explicitly indicate that a network or subnet is unreachable, rather than implying that a network is unreachable by not including it in updates. Poison reverse updates are sent to defeat large routing loops. The Cisco IGRP implementation uses poison reverse updates.

polarization Polarization is the physical orientation of the element on the antenna that actually emits the RF energy. All Cisco Aironet antennas are set for vertical polarization. A vertical dipole antenna is vertically polarized.

policy routing Routing scheme that forwards packets to specific interfaces based on user-configured policies. Such policies might specify that traffic sent from a particular network should be forwarded out one interface, while all other traffic should be forwarded out another interface.

policy-based routing See policy routing.

poll/final bit See P/F.

polling Access method in which a primary network device inquires, in an orderly fashion, whether secondaries have data to transmit. The inquiry occurs in the form of a message to each secondary that gives the secondary the right to transmit.

POP Point of Presence - Point of presence is the point of interconnection between the communication facilities provided by the telephone company and the building's main distribution facility.

port 1) Interface on an internetworking device (such as a router). 2) In IP terminology, an upper-layer process that is receiving information from lower layers. 3) To rewrite software or microcode so that it will run on a different hardware platform or in a different software environment than that for which it was originally designed. 4) A female plug on a patch panel which accepts the same size plug as an RJ45 jack. Patch cords are used in these ports to cross connect computers wired to the patch panel. It is this cross connection which allows the LAN to function.

POS Power-on Servicing - Feature on the LightStream 2020 ATM switch that allows faulty components to be diagnosed, removed, and replaced while the rest of the switch continues to operate normally. Power-on servicing is also known as hot swapping.

POST Power-on Self Test - Set of hardware diagnostics that runs on a hardware device when that device is powered up. On a LightStream 2020 ATM switch, for example, the NP, switch card, and line card all perform the POST.

Post, Telephone, and Telegraph See PTT.

POTS   Plain Old Telephone Service - See PSTN (Public Switched Telephone Network).

power tray   Power supply for a LightStream 2020 ATM switch. A LightStream 2020 switch can have one or two bulk power trays. In a redundant system, the two power trays load share, but each can power the entire system in the event that the other fails. The power tray can provide either AC or DC power to the switch.

power-on self test   See POST.

power-on servicing   See POS.

PPK   Per-Packet Keying - Method of overcoming the exploitation of encryption keys with key hashing.

PPP   Point-to-Point Protocol - A successor to SLIP, PPP provides router-to-router and host-to-network connections over synchronous and asynchronous circuits.

PQ   Priority Queuing - Routing feature in which frames in an interface output queue are prioritized based on various characteristics such as packet size and interface type.

presentation layer   Layer 6 of the OSI reference model. This layer ensures that information sent by the application layer of one system will be readable by the application layer of another. The presentation layer is also concerned with the data structures used by programs and therefore negotiates data transfer syntax for the application layer. Corresponds roughly with the presentation services layer of the SNA model.

presentation services layer   Layer 6 of the SNA architectural model. This layer provides network resource management, session presentation services, and some application management. Corresponds roughly with the presentation layer of the OSI model.

Pretty Good Privacy   See PGP.

PRI   Primary Rate Interface - ISDN interface to primary rate access. Primary rate access consists of a single 64-Kbps D channel plus 23 (T1) or 30 (E1) B channels for voice or data. Compare to BRI.

primary   See primary station.

Primary LU   See PLU.

Primary Rate Interface   See PRI.

primary station   In bit-synchronous data link layer protocols such as HDLC and SDLC, a station that controls the transmission activity of secondary stations and performs other management functions such as error control through polling or other means. Primary stations send commands to secondary stations and receive responses. A primary station is also known as a primary.

print server   Networked computer system that fields, manages, and executes (or sends for execution) print requests from other network devices.

priority queuing   See PQ.

private branch exchange   See PBX.

Private Network Node Interface   See PNNI.

Private Network-Network Interface   See PNNI.

process switching   Operation that provides full route evaluation and per-packet load balancing across parallel WAN links. Involves the transmission of entire frames to the router CPU where they are repackaged for delivery to or from a WAN interface, with the router making a route selection for each packet. Process switching is the most resource-intensive switching operation that the CPU can perform.

Production environment Software, equipment, documentation, and procedures used in support of business operations when a network is brought into service.

programmable read-only memory See PROM.

PROM Programmable Read-Only Memory - ROM that can be programmed using special equipment. PROMs can be programmed only once. Compare with EPROM.

propagation delay Time required for data to travel over a network, from its source to its ultimate destination.

protocol 1) Formal description of a set of rules and conventions that govern how devices on a network exchange information. 2) Field within an IP datagram that indicates the upper layer (Layer 4) protocol sending the datagram.

protocol address See network address.

protocol analyzer See network analyzer.

protocol control information See PCI.

protocol converter Enables equipment with different data formats to communicate by translating the data transmission code of one device to the data transmission code of another device.

protocol data unit See PDU.

Protocol Independent Multicast See PIM.

protocol stack Set of related communications protocols that operate together and, as a group, address communication at some or all of the seven layers of the OSI reference model. Not every protocol stack covers each layer of the model, and often a single protocol in the stack will address a number of layers at once. TCP/IP is a typical protocol stack.

protocol translator Network device or software that converts one protocol into another, similar, protocol.

proxy Entity that, in the interest of efficiency, essentially stands in for another entity.

proxy Address Resolution Protocol See proxy ARP.

proxy ARP Proxy Address Resolution Protocol - Variation of the ARP protocol in which an intermediate device (for example, a router) sends an ARP response on behalf of an end node to the requesting host. Proxy ARP can lessen bandwidth use on slow-speed WAN links.

proxy polling Technique that alleviates the load across an SDLC network by allowing routers to act as proxies for primary and secondary nodes, thus keeping polling traffic off of the shared links. Proxy polling has been replaced by SDLC Transport.

PSDN Packet-Switched Data Network - See PSN (packet-switched network).

PSE Packet Switch Exchange - Essentially, a switch. The term PSE is generally used in reference to a switch in an X.25 PSN.

PSN 1) Packet-Switched Network - Network that utilizes packet-switching technology for data transfer. Packet-switched network is also known as packet-switched data network (PSDN). 2) Packet-Switching Node - Network node capable of performing packet switching functions.

PSNP Partial Sequence Number Protocol - PSNPs are used to request one or more LSPs and acknowledge receipt of one or more LSPs.

PSTN Public Switched Telephone Network - General term referring to the variety of telephone networks and services in place worldwide. PSTN is also known as plain old telephone service (POTS).

PTT Post, Telephone, and Telegraph - Government agency that provides telephone services. PTTs exist in most areas outside North America and provide both local and long-distance telephone services.

PU Physical Unit - SNA component that manages and monitors the resources of a node, as requested by an SSCP. There is one PU per node.

PU 2 Physical Unit 2 - SNA peripheral node that can support only DLUs that require services from a VTAM host and that are only capable of performing the secondary LU role in SNA sessions.

PU 4 Physical Unit 4 - Component of an IBM FEP capable of full-duplex data transfer. Each such SNA device employs a separate data and control path into the transmit and receive buffers of the control program.

PU 5 Physical Unit 5 - Component of an IBM mainframe or host computer that manages an SNA network. PU 5 nodes are involved in routing within the SNA path control layer.

public data network See PDN.

Public Switched Telephone Network See PSTN.

pull string Strong, heavy string used to pull cable in multiple runs.

pulse amplitude modulation See PAM.

pulse code modulation See PCM.

pulse density See ones density.

punch tool Spring-loaded tool used for cutting and connecting wire in a jack or on a patch panel.

PUP PARC Universal Protocol - Protocol similar to IP developed at PARC.

PVC Permanent Virtual Circuit - Virtual circuit that is permanently established. PVCs save bandwidth associated with circuit establishment and tear down in situations where certain virtual circuits must exist all the time. Compare with SVC. Permanent virtual circuit is known as permanent virtual connection in ATM terminology.

PVP Permanent Virtual Path - Virtual path that consists of PVCs. See also PVC and virtual path.

Q.920/Q.921 ITU-T specifications for the ISDN UNI data link layer.

Q.922A ITU-T specification for Frame Relay encapsulation.

Q.931 ITU-T specification for signaling to establish, maintain, and clear ISDN network connections.

Q.93B ITU-T specification signaling to establish, maintain, and clear BISDN network connections. An evolution of ITU-T recommendation Q.931.

QLLC Qualified Logical Link Control - Data link layer protocol defined by IBM that allows SNA data to be transported across X.25 networks.

QoS Quality of Service - Measure of performance for a transmission system that reflects its transmission quality and service availability.

QoS parameters Quality of Service parameter - Parameters that control the amount of traffic the source router in an ATM network sends over an SVC. If any switch along the path cannot accommodate the requested QoS parameters, the request is rejected, and a rejection message is forwarded back to the originator of the request.

Quadruple Phase Shift Keying A modulation technique used by IEEE 802.11b-compliant wireless LANs for transmission at 2 Mbps.

Qualified Logical Link Control   See QLLC.

quality of service   See QoS.

quartet signaling   Signaling technique used in 100VG-AnyLAN networks that allow data transmission at 100 Mbps over four pairs of UTP cabling at the same frequencies used in 10BASE-T networks.

query   Message used to inquire about the value of some variable or set of variables.

queue   1) Generally, an ordered list of elements waiting to be processed. 2) In routing, a backlog of packets waiting to be forwarded over a router interface.

queuing delay   Amount of time that data must wait before it can be transmitted onto a statistically multiplexed physical circuit.

queuing theory   Scientific principles governing the formation or lack of formation of congestion on a network or at an interface.

RACE   Research on Advanced Communications in Europe - Project sponsored by the European Community (EC) for the development of broadband networking capabilities.

raceway   Wall-mounted channel with a removable cover used to support horizontal cabling.

radio frequency   See RF.

radio frequency interference   See RFI.

RAM   Random-Access Memory - Volatile memory that can be read and written by a microprocessor.

random-access memory   See RAM.

range   A linear measure of the distance that a wireless transmitter can send a signal.

RARP   Reverse Address Resolution Protocol - Protocol in the TCP/IP stack that provides a method for finding IP addresses based on MAC addresses. Compare with ARP.

rate enforcement   See traffic policing.

rate queue   Value that is associated with one or more virtual circuits, and that defines the speed at which an individual virtual circuit will transmit data to the remote end. Each rate queue represents a portion of the overall bandwidth available on an ATM link. The combined bandwidth of all configured rate queues should not exceed the total bandwidth available.

RBHC   Regional Bell Holding Company - One of seven telephone companies created by the AT and T divestiture in 1984.

RBOC   Regional Bell Operating Company - Local or regional telephone company that owns and operates telephone lines and switches in one of seven U.S. regions. The RBOCs were created by the divestiture of AT and T. Regional Bell Operating Company is also known as Bell Operating Company (BOC).

rcp   Remote Copy Protocol - Protocol that allows users to copy files to and from a file system residing on a remote host or server on the network. The rcp protocol uses TCP to ensure the reliable delivery of data.

rcp server   Router or other device that acts as a server for rcp.

read-only memory   See ROM.

Ready To Send   See RTS.

reassembly   The putting back together of an IP datagram at the destination after it has been fragmented either at the source or at an intermediate node.

receiver sensitivity   A measurement of the weakest wireless signal a receiver can receive and still correctly translate it into data.

redirect   Part of the ICMP and ES-IS protocols that allows a router to tell a host that using another router would be more effective.

redirector   Software that intercepts requests for resources within a computer and analyzes them for remote access requirements. If remote access is required to satisfy the request, the redirector forms an RPC and sends the RPC to lower-layer protocol software for transmission through the network to the node that can satisfy the request.

redistribution   Allowing routing information discovered through one routing protocol to be distributed in the update messages of another routing protocol. Redistribution is also known as route redistribution.

redundancy   1) In internetworking, the duplication of devices, services, or connections so that, in the event of a failure, the redundant devices, services, or connections can perform the work of those that failed. See also redundant system. 2) In telephony, the portion of the total information contained in a message that can be eliminated without loss of essential information or meaning.

redundant system   Computer, router, switch, or other computer system that contains two or more of each of the most important subsystems, such as two disk drives, two CPUs, or two power supplies. For example, on a fully redundant LightStream 2020 ATM switch, there are two NP cards with disks, two switch cards, and two power trays. A partially redundant LightStream 2020 switch might have two NPs, one switch card, and one power tray.

reflection   Physical phenomenon which occurs when radio frequency waves bounce off objects (for example, metal or glass surfaces).

Refraction   The measure of how much a given material bends light.

Regional Bell Holding Company   See RBHC.

Regional Bell Operating Company   See RBOC.

registered jack connector   See RJ connector.

relay   OSI terminology for a device that connects two or more networks or network systems. A data link layer (Layer 2) relay is a bridge; a network layer (Layer 3) relay is a router.

reliability   Ratio of expected to received keepalives from a link. If the ratio is high, the line is reliable. Used as a routing metric.

Remote access solution   Provides the ability for users to get access to a computer or a network from a remote distance. In corporations, people at branch offices, telecommuters, and people who are travelling may need access to the corporation's network. Home users get access to the Internet through remote access to an ISP.

remote bridge   Bridge that connects physically disparate network segments via WAN links.

remote copy protocol   See rcp.

remote login   See rlogin.

Remote Monitoring   See RMON.

Remote Operations Service Element   See ROSE.

remote shell protocol   See rsh.

remote source-route bridging   See RSRB.

remote-procedure call   See RPC.

rendezvous point   See RP.

repeater Device that regenerates and propagates electrical signals between two network segments.

Request For Comments See RFC.

request/response unit See RU.

Research on Advanced Communications in Europe See RACE.

reserved Set to zero.

Reverse Address Resolution Protocol See RARP.

Reverse Path Multicasting See RPM.

RF Radio Frequency - Generic term referring to frequencies that correspond to radio transmissions. Cable TV and broadband networks use RF technology.

RFC Request For Comments - Document series used as the primary means for communicating information about the Internet. Some RFCs are designated by the IAB as Internet standards. Most RFCs document protocol specifications such as Telnet and FTP, but some are humorous or historical. RFCs are available online from numerous sources.

RFI Radio Frequency Interference - Radio frequencies that create noise that interferes with information being transmitted across unshielded copper cabling.

RIF Routing Information Field - Field in the IEEE 802.5 header that is used by a source-route bridge to determine through which Token Ring network segments a packet must transit. A RIF is made up of ring and bridge numbers as well as other information.

RII Routing Information Identifie - Bit used by SRT bridges to distinguish between frames that should be transparently bridged and frames that should be passed to the SRB module for handling.

ring Connection of two or more stations in a logically circular topology. Information is passed sequentially between active stations. Token Ring, FDDI, and CDDI are based on this topology.

ring topology Network topology that consists of a series of repeaters connected to one another by unidirectional transmission links to form a single closed loop. Each station on the network connects to the network at a repeater. While logically a ring, ring topologies are most often organized in a closed-loop star. Compare with bus topology, star topology, and tree topology.

RIP Routing Information Protoco - IGP supplied with UNIX BSD systems. The most common IGP in the Internet. RIP uses hop count as a routing metric.

RIPng Routing Information Protocol next generation - Distance vector routing protocol with a limit of 15 hops that uses split-horizon and poison reverse to prevent routing loops. It is based on IPv4 RIP v2 and similar to RIPv2, but uses IPv6 for transport. The multicast group address FF02::9 identifies all RIPng enabled routers.(RIPng, RFC 2080)

RIPv2 Routing Information Protocol version 2 - Defined in RFC 1723 and is supported in IOS versions 11.1 and later. RIPv2 is not a new protocol, just RIPv1 with some extensions to bring it up-to-date with modern routing environments. RIPv2 has be updated to supports VLSM, authentication, and multicast updates.

RJ connector Registered Jack connector - Standard connectors originally used to connect telephone lines. RJ connectors are now used for telephone connections and for 10BASE-T and other types of network connections. RJ-11, RJ-12, and RJ-45 are popular types of RJ connectors.

rlogin remote login - Terminal emulation program, similar to Telnet, offered in most UNIX implementations.

RMON Remote Monitoring - MIB agent specification described in RFC 1271 that defines functions for the remote monitoring of networked devices. The RMON specification provides numerous monitoring, problem detection, and reporting capabilities.

ROM   Read-Only Memory - Nonvolatile memory that can be read, but not written, by the microprocessor.

root account   1) Privileged account on UNIX systems used exclusively by network or system administrators. 2) One of the four default user accounts that are created in the factory on each LightStream 2020 ATM switch. The root account is for use by the system or network administrator only. Its default interface is the bash shell. See also bash.

root bridge   Exchanges topology information with designated bridges in a spanning-tree implementation in order to notify all other bridges in the network when topology changes are required. This prevents loops and provides a measure of defense against link failure.

ROSE   Remote Operations Service Element - OSI RPC mechanism used by various OSI network application protocols.

round-trip time   See RTT.

route   Path through an internetwork.

route extension   In SNA, a path from the destination subarea node through peripheral equipment to a NAU.

route map   Method of controlling the redistribution of routes between routing domains.

Route Processor   See RP.

route redistribution   See redistribution.

route summarization   Consolidation of advertised addresses in OSPF and IS-IS. In OSPF, this causes a single summary route to be advertised to other areas by an area border router.

Route/Switch Processor   See RSP.

routed protocol   Protocol that can be routed by a router. A router must be able to interpret the logical internetwork as specified by that routed protocol. Examples of routed protocols include AppleTalk, DECnet, and IP.

Router   A network device that forwards packets from one network to another.

router   Network layer device that uses one or more metrics to determine the optimal path along which network traffic should be forwarded. Routers forward packets from one network to another based on network layer information. Occasionally called a gateway (although this definition of gateway is becoming increasingly outdated). Compare with gateway.

Routers   A networking device whose software and hardware is tailored to the tasks of forwarding information.

routing   Process of finding a path to a destination host. Routing is very complex in large networks because of the many potential intermediate destinations a packet might traverse before reaching its destination host.

routing domain   Group of end systems and intermediate systems operating under the same set of administrative rules. Within each routing domain is one or more areas, each uniquely identified by an area address.

Routing Information Field   See RIF.

Routing Information Identifier   See RII.

Routing Information Protocol   See RIP.

routing metric   Method by which a routing algorithm determines that one route is better than another. This information is stored in routing tables. Metrics include bandwidth, communication cost, delay, hop count, load, MTU, path cost, and reliability. Routing metric is also known as metric.

routing protocol   Protocol that accomplishes routing through the implementation of a specific routing algorithm. Examples of routing protocols include IGRP, OSPF, and RIP.

Routing Sheets   Contains a list of departments, individuals or roles that need to review and/or take action on the attached document(s).

routing table   Table stored in a router or some other internetworking device that keeps track of routes to particular network destinations and, in some cases, metrics associated with those routes.

Routing Table Protocol   See RTP.

routing update   Message sent from a router to indicate network reachability and associated cost information. Routing updates are typically sent at regular intervals and after a change in network topology. Compare with flash update.

RP   1) Route Processor - Processor module on the Cisco 7000 series routers that contains the CPU, system software, and most of the memory components that are used in the router. Route processor is also known as supervisory processor. 2) Rendezvous Point - Router specified in PIM sparse mode implementations to track membership in multicast groups and to forward messages to known multicast group addresses. See also PIM sparse mode.

RPC   Remote-Procedure Call - Technological foundation of client-server computing. RPCs are procedure calls that are built or specified by clients and executed on servers, with the results returned over the network to the clients.

RPM   Reverse Path Multicasting - Multicasting technique in which a multicast datagram is forwarded out of all but the receiving interface if the receiving interface is one used to forward unicast datagrams to the source of the multicast datagram.

RP-TNC   A connector type unique to Cisco Aironet radios and antennas. Part 15.203 of the FCC rules covering spread spectrum devices limits the types of antennas that may be used with transmission equipment. In compliance with this rule, Cisco Aironet, like all other wireless LAN providers, equips its radios and antennas with a unique connector to prevent attachment of non-approved antennas to radios.

RS-232   Popular physical layer interface. RS-232 is known as EIA/TIA-232.

RS-422   Balanced electrical implementation of EIA/TIA-449 for high-speed data transmission. RS-422 is referred to collectively with RS-423 as EIA-530.

RS-423   Unbalanced electrical implementation of EIA/TIA-449 for EIA/TIA-232 compatibility. RS-423 is referred to collectively with RS-422 as EIA-530.

RS-449   Popular physical layer interface. RS-449 is known as EIA/TIA-449.

rsh   remote shell protocol - Protocol that allows a user to execute commands on a remote system without having to log in to the system. For example, rsh can be used to remotely examine the status of a number of access servers without connecting to each communication server, executing the command, and then disconnecting from the communication server.

RSP   Route/Switch Processor - Processor module used in the Cisco 7500 series routers that integrates the functions of the RP and the SP.

RSRB   Remote Source-Route Bridging - SRB over WAN links.

RSVP   Resource Reservation Protocol - Protocol that supports the reservation of resources across an IP network. Applications running on IP end systems can use RSVP to indicate to other nodes the nature (bandwidth, jitter, maximum burst, and so forth) of the packet streams they want to receive. Resource Reservation Protocol is also known as Resource Reservation Setup Protocol.

RTP   1) Routing Table Protocol - VINES routing protocol based on RIP. Distributes network topology information and aids VINES servers in finding neighboring clients, servers, and routers. Uses delay as a routing metric. See also SRTP. 2) Real-Time Transport Protocol. Commonly used with IP networks. RTP is designed to provide end-to-end network transport functions for applications transmitting real-time data, such as audio, video, or simulation data, over multicast or unicast network services. RTP provides such services as payload type identification, sequence numbering, timestamping, and delivery monitoring to real-time applications.

RTS   Ready To Send - EIA/TIA-232 control signal that requests a data transmission on a communications line.

RTT   Round-Trip Time - Time required for a network communication to travel from the source to the destination and back. RTT includes the time required for the destination to process the message from the source and generate a reply. RTT is used by some routing algorithms to aid in calculating optimal routes.

RU   Request/Response Unit - Request and response messages exchanged between NAUs in an SNA network.

run-time memory   Memory accessed while a program runs. On a LightStream 2020 ATM switch, this memory contains configuration data that is accessed while the switch operates.

safety ground wire   Circuit wire that connects to a local earth ground and the chassis of an electrical appliance or device via an electrical outlet and plug. It is used to ensure that no voltage potential exists between the chassis of the electrical device and the earth ground.

sag   Any decrease of below 80% in the normal voltage carried by a power line. A sag is sometimes referred to as a brownout.

sampling rate   Rate at which samples of a particular waveform amplitude are taken.

SAP   1) Service Access Point - Field defined by the IEEE 802.2 specification that is part of an address specification. Thus, the destination plus the DSAP define the recipient of a packet. The same applies to the SSAP. See also DSAP and SSAP. 2) Service Advertisement Protocol - IPX protocol that provides a means of informing network clients, via routers and servers, of available network resources and services. See also IPX.

satellite communication   Use of orbiting satellites to relay data between multiple earth-based stations. Satellite communications offer high bandwidth and a cost that is not related to distance between earth stations, long propagation delays, or broadcast capability.

Sbus   Bus technology used in Sun SPARC-based workstations and servers. The SBus specification has been adopted by the IEEE as a new bus standard.

Scalability   Feature of a network design to include new user groups and remote sites over time. A scalable network design should support new applications without impacting the level of service delivered to existing users.

scattering   Scattering is the physical phenomenon that occurs when radio frequency waves strike an uneven surface (for example, a rough surface) and are reflected in many directions.

SCR   Sustainable Cell Rate - Parameter defined by the ATM Forum for ATM traffic management. For VBR connections, SCR determines the long-term average cell rate that can be transmitted.

SCTE   Serial Clock Transmit External - Timing signal that DTE echoes to DCE to maintain clocking. SCTE is designed to compensate for clock phase shift on long cables. When the DCE device uses SCTE instead of its internal clock to sample data from the DTE, it is better able to sample the data without error even if there is a phase shift in the cable.

SDH   Synchronous Digital Hierarchy - European standard that defines a set of rate and format standards that are transmitted using optical signals over fiber. SDH is similar to SONET, with a basic SDH rate of 155.52 Mbps, designated at STM-1.

SDLC Synchronous Data Link Control - SNA data link layer communications protocol. SDLC is a bit-oriented, full-duplex serial protocol that has spawned numerous similar protocols, including HDLC and LAPB.

SDLC Transport Cisco router feature with which disparate environments can be integrated into a single, high-speed, enterprise-wide network. Native SDLC traffic can be passed through point-to-point serial links with other protocol traffic multiplexed over the same links. Cisco routers can also encapsulate SDLC frames inside IP datagrams for transport over arbitrary (non-SDLC) networks. Replaces proxy polling.

SDLLC Feature that performs translation between SDLC and IEEE 802.2 type 2.

SDSU Switched Multimegabit Data Service DSU - DSU for access to SMDS via HSSIs and other serial interfaces.

secondary See secondary station.

secondary station In bit-synchronous data link layer protocols such as HDLC, a station that responds to commands from a primary station. A secondary station is also known as a secondary.

security management One of five categories of network management defined by ISO for management of OSI networks. Security management subsystems are responsible for controlling access to network resources.

segment 1) Section of a network that is bounded by bridges, routers, or switches. 2) In a LAN using a bus topology, a segment is a continuous electrical circuit that is often connected to other such segments with repeaters. 3) Term used in the TCP specification to describe a single transport layer unit of information. The terms datagram, frame, message, and packet are also used to describe logical information groupings at various layers of the OSI reference model and in various technology circles.

sequence number Number used to ensure correct sequencing of the arriving data.

Sequenced Routing Update Protocol See SRTP.

serial clock transmit external See SCTE.

Serial Interface Processor See SIP.

Serial Line Internet Protocol See SLIP.

serial transmission Method of data transmission in which the bits of a data character are transmitted sequentially over a single channel. Compare with parallel transmission.

serial tunnel See STUN.

server Node or software program that provides services to clients.

Server Message Block See SMB.

Servers A centralized computer that runs the EHR application for a medical practice.

service access point See SAP.

Service Advertisement Protocol See SAP.

service point Interface between non-SNA devices and NetView that sends alerts from equipment unknown to the SNA environment.

Service Profile Identifier See SPID.

Service-Oriented Network Architecture See SONA.

session 1) Related set of communications transactions between two or more network devices. 2) In SNA, a logical connection enabling two NAUs to communicate.

session layer   Layer 5 of the OSI reference model. This layer establishes, manages, and terminates sessions between applications and manages data exchange between presentation layer entities. Corresponds to the data flow control layer of the SNA model.

SF   Super Frame - Common framing type used on T1 circuits. SF consists of 12 frames of 192 bits each, with the 193rd bit providing error checking and other functions. SF has been superseded by ESF, but is still widely used. Super Frame is also known as D4 framing.

SGMP   Simple Gateway Monitoring Protocol - Network management protocol that was considered for Internet standardization and later evolved into SNMP. Documented in RFC 1028.

shaping   See traffic shaping.

shielded cable   Cable that has a layer of shielded insulation to reduce EMI.

shielded twisted-pair   See STP.

Shipworm   See Teredo.

shortest path first algorithm   See SPF.

shortest-path routing   Routing that minimizes distance or path cost through application of an algorithm.

signal injector   Device used to measure attenuation of a signal on a network.

signal reference ground   Reference point used by computing devices to measure and compare incoming digital signals.

signaling   Process of sending a transmission signal over a physical medium for purposes of communication.

signaling packet   Generated by an ATM-connected device that wants to establish a connection with another such device. The signaling packet contains the ATM NSAP address of the desired ATM endpoint, as well as any QOS parameters required for the connection. If the endpoint can support the desired QOS, it responds with an accept message, and the connection is opened.

Signaling System number 7   See SS7.

SIIT   Stateless IP/ICMP Translation - Algorithm used in NAT-PT that translates the IP header fields. Compare with NAT-PT and DNS ALG.

Silicon Switch Processor   See SSP.

silicon switching   Switching based on the SSE, which allows the processing of packets independent of the Silicon Switch Processor (SSP) system processor. Silicon switching provides high-speed, dedicated packet switching.

silicon switching engine   See SSE.

Simple Gateway Monitoring Protocol   See SGMP.

Simple Mail Transfer Protocol   See SMTP.

Simple Multicast Routing Protocol   See SMRP.

Simple Network Management Protocol   See SNMP.

simplex   Capability for data transmission in only one direction between a sending station and a receiving station. Compare with full duplex and half duplex.

single-mode fiber   Fiber-optic cabling with a narrow core that allows light to enter only at a single angle. Such cabling has higher bandwidth than multimode fiber, but requires a light source with a narrow spectral width (for example, a laser). Single-mode fiber is also known as monomode fiber.

SIP 1) SMDS Interface Protocol - Used in communications between CPE and SMDS network equipment. Allows the CPE to use SMDS service for high-speed WAN internetworking. Based on the IEEE 802.6 DQDB standard. See also DQDB. 2) Serial Interface Processor - Obsolete interface processor for Cisco 7000 series routers that provided either two or four channel-independent ports for synchronous serial connections at speeds from 2.4 Kbps to 4 Mbps. The SIP has been replaced by the FSIP. Sometimes called SX-SIP or Pre-FSIP. See also FSIP.

site-local unicast address An IPv6 address which is very similar in function to the IPv4 private address space that includes ranges. These addresses are meant for internal communications and are not routable on the public Internet. Site-local addresses start with the prefix FEC0::/10. Compare with link-local unicast address.

sliding window Refers to the fact that the window size is negotiated dynamically during the TCP session.

sliding window flow control Method of flow control in which a receiver gives transmitter permission to transmit data until a window is full. When the window is full, the transmitter must stop transmitting until the receiver advertises a larger window. TCP, other transport protocols, and several data link layer protocols use this method of flow control.

SLIP Serial Line Internet Protocol - Standard protocol for point-to-point serial connections using a variation of TCP/IP. Predecessor of PPP.

slotted ring LAN architecture based on a ring topology in which the ring is divided into slots that circulate continuously. Slots can be either empty or full, and transmissions must start at the beginning of a slot.

slow switching Packet processing performed at process level speeds, without the use of a route cache. Contrast with fast switching.

SMAC Source MAC - MAC address specified in the Source Address field of a packet. Compare with DMAC.

SMB Server Message Block - File-system protocol used in LAN Manager and similar NOSs to package data and exchange information with other systems.

SMDS Switched Multimegabit Data Service - High-speed, packet-switched, datagram-based WAN networking technology offered by the telephone companies.

SMDS Interface Protocol See SIP.

SMI Structure of Management Information - Document (RFC 1155) specifying rules used to define managed objects in the MIB.

smoothing See traffic shaping.

SMRP Simple Multicast Routing Protocol - Specialized multicast network protocol for routing multimedia data streams on enterprise networks. SMRP works in conjunction with multicast extensions to the AppleTalk protocol.

SMT Station Management - ANSI FDDI specification that defines how ring stations are managed.

SMTP Simple Mail Transfer Protocol - Internet protocol providing electronic mail services.

SNA Systems Network Architecture - Large, complex, feature-rich network architecture developed in the 1970s by IBM. Similar in some respects to the OSI reference model, but with a number of differences. SNA is essentially composed of seven layers.

SNA Distribution Services See SNADS.

SNA Network Interconnection See SNI.

SNADS   SNA Distribution Services - Consists of a set of SNA transaction programs that interconnect and cooperate to provide asynchronous distribution of information between end users. One of three SNA transaction services.

SNAP   Subnetwork Access Protocol - Internet protocol that operates between a network entity in the subnetwork and a network entity in the end system. SNAP specifies a standard method of encapsulating IP datagrams and ARP messages on IEEE networks. The SNAP entity in the end system makes use of the services of the subnetwork and performs three key functions: data transfer, connection management, and QOS selection.

Snapshot routing   Method of gathering routing information during an active time, taking a snapshot of the information and using that routing information for a configured length of time (referred to as the quiet time).

SNI   1) Subscriber Network Interface - Interface for SMDS-based networks that connects CPE and an SMDS switch. See also UNI. 2) SNA Network Interconnection - IBM gateway connecting multiple SNA networks.

SNMP   Simple Network Management Protocol - Network management protocol used almost exclusively in TCP/IP networks. SNMP provides a means to monitor and control network devices, and to manage configurations, statistics collection, performance, and security.

SNMP communities   Authentication scheme that enables an intelligent network device to validate SNMP requests from sources such as the NMS. A LightStream 2020 ATM switch, for example, responds only to SNMP requests that come from members of known communities and that have the access privileges required for that request.

SNMP2   Simple Network Management Protocol version 2 - Version 2 of the popular network management protocol. SNMP2 supports centralized as well as distributed network management strategies, and includes improvements in the SMI, protocol operations, management architecture, and security.

SNPA   Subnetwork Point of Attachment Address - SNPA address is the point at which subnetwork services are provided. This is the equivalent of the Layer 2 address corresponding to the Layer 3, NET or NSAP, address and is therefore usually a MAC address on a LAN or Virtual Circuit ID in X.25, Frame-Relay, or ATM.

socket   Software structure operating as a communications end point within a network device.

SONA   Service-Oriented Network Architecture - Architectural framework that guides the evolution of the network to an Intelligent Information Network (IIN). It enables enterprises to optimize applications, processes, and resources to deliver greater business benefits.

SONET   Synchronous Optical Network - High-speed (up to 2.5 Gbps) synchronous network specification developed by Bellcore and designed to run on optical fiber. STS-1 is the basic building block of SONET. Approved as an international standard in 1988.

source address   Address of a network device that is sending data.

source and destination IP addresses   Field within an IP datagram that indicates the 32-bit source and destination IP addresses.

source MAC   See SMAC.

source port   Number of the calling port.

source service access point   See SSAP.

source-route bridging   See SRB.

source-route translational bridging   See SR/TLB.

source-route transparent bridging   See SRT.

Southeastern Universities Research Association Net   See SURAnet.

SP   Switch Processor - Cisco 7000-series processor module that acts as the administrator for all CxBus activities. Switch processor is also known as ciscoBus controller.

SPAN   1) Switched Port Analyzer - Feature of the Catalyst 5000 switch that extends the monitoring abilities of existing network analyzers into a switched Ethernet environment. SPAN mirrors the traffic at one switched segment onto a predefined SPAN port. A network analyzer attached to the SPAN port can monitor traffic from any of the other Catalyst switched ports. 2) Full-duplex digital transmission line between two digital facilities.

spanning tree   Loop-free subset of a network topology.

Spanning Tree Protocol   See STP.

spanning-tree algorithm   See STA.

spanning-tree protocol   See STP.

sparse mode PIM   See PIM sparse mode.

speed matching   Feature that provides sufficient buffering capability in a destination device to allow a high-speed source to transmit data at its maximum rate, even if the destination device is a lower-speed device.

SPF   Shortest Path First algorithm - Routing algorithm that iterates on length of path to determine a shortest-path spanning tree. Commonly used in link-state routing algorithms. SPF is also known as Dijkstra's algorithm.

SPID   Service Profile Identifie - Number that some service providers use to define the services to which an ISDN device subscribes. The ISDN device uses the SPID when accessing the switch that initializes the connection to a service provider.

spike   Any power impulse lasting between .5 and 100 microseconds and possessing an amplitude over 100% of peak power line voltage.

split-horizon updates   Routing technique in which information about routes is prevented from exiting the router interface through which that information was received. Split-horizon updates are useful in preventing routing loops.

spoofing   1) Scheme used by Cisco routers to cause a host to treat an interface as if it were up and supporting a session. The router spoofs replies to keepalive messages from the host in order to convince that host that the session still exists. Spoofing is useful in routing environments such as DDR, in which a circuit-switched link is taken down when there is no traffic to be sent across it in order to save toll charges. See also DDR. 2) The act of a packet illegally claiming to be from an address from which it was not actually sent. Spoofing is designed to foil network security mechanisms such as filters and access lists.

spread spectrum   A radio transmission technology that spreads the user information over a much wider bandwidth than otherwise required in order to gain benefits such as improved interference tolerance and unlicensed operation.

SR/TLB   Source Route/Translational Bridging - Method of bridging where source-route stations can communicate with transparent bridge stations with the help of an intermediate bridge that translates between the two bridge protocols. Compare with SRT.

SRAM   Type of RAM that retains its contents for as long as power is supplied. SRAM does not require constant refreshing, like DRAM. Compare with DRAM.

SRB   Source-Route Bridging - Method of bridging originated by IBM and popular in Token Ring networks. In a SRB network, the entire route to a destination is predetermined, in real time, prior to the sending of data to the destination. Contrast with transparent bridging.

SRT   Source-Route Transparent Bridging - IBM bridging scheme that merges the two most prevalent bridging strategies, SRB and transparent bridging. SRT employs both technologies in one device to satisfy the needs of all Ens. No translation between bridging protocols is necessary. Compare with SR/TLB.

SRTP   Sequenced Routing Update Protocol - Protocol that assists VINES servers in finding neighboring clients, servers, and routers.

SS7   Signaling System number 7 - Standard CCS system used with BISDN and ISDN. Developed by Bellcore.

SSAP   Source Service Access Point - The SAP of the network node designated in the Source field of a packet. Compare to DSAP.

SSCP   System Services Control Points - Focal points within an SNA network for managing network configuration, coordinating network operator and problem determination requests, and providing directory services and other session services for network end users.

SSCP-PU session   System Services Control Points - Physical Unit session - Session used by SNA to allow an SSCP to manage the resources of a node through the PU. SSCPs can send requests to, and receive replies from, individual nodes in order to control the network configuration.

SSE   Silicon Switching Engine - Routing and switching mechanism that compares the data link or network layer header of an incoming packet to a silicon-switching cache, determines the appropriate action (routing or bridging), and forwards the packet to the proper interface. The SSE is directly encoded in the hardware of the Silicon Switch Processor (SSP) of a Cisco 7000 series router. It can therefore perform switching independently of the system processor, making the execution of routing decisions much quicker than if they were encoded in software.

SSID   Service Set Identifier - The SSID is a code attached to all packets on a wireless network to identify each packet as part of that network. The code is a case sensitive text string which consists of a maximum of 32 alphanumeric characters. All wireless devices attempting to communicate with each other must share the same SSID. Apart from identifying each packet, SSID also serves to uniquely identify a group of wireless network devices used in a given service set.

SSP   1) Silicon Switch Processor - High-performance silicon switch for Cisco 7000 series routers that provides distributed processing and control for interface processors. The SSP leverages the high-speed switching and routing capabilities of the SSE to dramatically increase aggregate router performance, minimizing performance bottlenecks at the interface points between the router and a high-speed backbone. 2) Switch-to-Switc Protocol - Protocol specified in the DLSw standard that routers use to establish DLSw connections, locate resources, forward data, and handle flow control and error recovery.

STA   Spanning Tree Algorithm - Algorithm used by the Spanning Tree Protocol to create a spanning tree.

stack   See protocol stack.

standard   Set of rules or procedures that are either widely used or officially specified.

star topology   LAN topology in which end points on a network are connected to a common central switch by point-to-point links. A ring topology that is organized as a star implements a unidirectional closed-loop star, instead of point-to-point links. Compare with bus topology, ring topology, and tree topology.

StarLAN   CSMA/CD LAN, based on IEEE 802.3, developed by AT and T.

start-stop transmission   See asynchronous transmission.

stat mux   See statistical multiplexing.

stateless autoconfiguration   Plug-and-play IPv6 feature that enables devices to connect themselves to the network without any configuration and without any servers (like DHCP servers). This key feature enables deployment of new devices on the Internet, such as cellular phones, wireless devices, home appliances, and home networks.

Stateless IP/Internet Control Message Protocol (IC   See SIIT.

static electricity   Unpredictable electrical charges in the atmosphere that interfere with radio reception, computer networking, and the like.

static route   Route that is explicitly configured and entered into the routing table. Static routes take precedence over routes chosen by dynamic routing protocols.

Station Management   See SMT.

statistical multiplexing   Technique whereby information from multiple logical channels can be transmitted across a single physical channel. Statistical multiplexing dynamically allocates bandwidth only to active input channels, making better use of available bandwidth and allowing more devices to be connected than with other multiplexing techniques. Also referred to as statistical time-division multiplexing or stat mux. Compare with ATDM, FDM, and TDM.

statistical time-division multiplexing   See STDM.

STDM   StatisticalTime-Division Multiplexing - Technique whereby information from multiple logical channels can be transmitted across a single physical channel. Statistical multiplexing dynamically allocates bandwidth only to active input channels, making better use of available bandwidth and allowing more devices to be connected than with other multiplexing techniques. Also referred to as statistical time-division multiplexing or stat mux. Compare with ATDM, FDM, and TDM.

STM-1   Synchronous Transport Module level 1 - One of a number of SDH formats that specifies the frame structure for the 155.52-Mbps lines used to carry ATM cells.

store and forward packet switching   Packet-switching technique in which frames are completely processed before being forwarded out the appropriate port. This processing includes calculating the CRC and checking the destination address. In addition, frames must be temporarily stored until network resources (such as an unused link) are available to forward the message. Contrast with cut-through packet switching.

STP   1) Shielded Twisted-Pair - Two-pair wiring medium used in a variety of network implementations. STP cabling has a layer of shielded insulation to reduce EMI. Compare with UTP. 2) Spanning Tree Protocol - Bridge protocol that utilizes the spanning-tree algorithm, enabling a learning bridge to dynamically work around loops in a network topology by creating a spanning tree. Bridges exchange BPDU messages with other bridges to detect loops, and then remove the loops by shutting down selected bridge interfaces. Refers to both the IEEE 802.1 Spanning-Tree Protocol standard and the earlier Digital Equipment Corporation Spanning-Tree Protocol upon which it is based. The IEEE version supports bridge domains and allows the bridge to construct a loop-free topology across an extended LAN. The IEEE version is generally preferred over the Digital version.

StreamView network management   Cisco suite of SNMP-based network management tools used in conjunction with the LightStream 2020 ATM switch. The StreamView suite includes three GUI-driven applications: a configuration program (the configurator), a network topology map (the topology map), and a node monitoring program (the monitor); and a command-line interface (CLI).

Structure of Management Information   See SMI.

STS-1   Synchronous Transport Signal level 1 - Basic building block signal of SONET, operating at 51.84 Mbps. Faster SONET rates are defined as STS-n, where n is a multiple of 51.84 Mbps.

STS-3c   Synchronous Transport Signal level 3, concatenated - SONET format that specifies the frame structure for the 155.52-Mbps lines used to carry ATM cells.

stub area   OSPF area that carries a default route, intra-area routes, and interarea routes, but does not carry external routes. Virtual links cannot be configured across a stub area, and they cannot contain an ASBR. Compare to non-stub area.

stub network   Network that has only a single connection to a router.

STUN   Serial Tunnel - Router feature allowing two SDLC- or HDLC-compliant devices to connect to one another through an arbitrary multiprotocol topology (using Cisco routers) rather than through a direct serial link.

subarea   Portion of an SNA network that consists of a subarea node and any attached links and peripheral nodes.

subarea node   SNA communication controller or host that handles complete network addresses.

subchannel   In broadband terminology, a frequency-based subdivision creating a separate communications channel.

subinterface   One of a number of virtual interfaces on a single physical interface.

subnet   See subnetwork.

subnet address   Portion of an IP address that is specified as the subnetwork by the subnet mask.

subnet mask   32-bit address mask used in IP to indicate the bits of an IP address that are being used for the subnet address. Subnet mask is also known as mask.

subnet mask field   The subnet mask field contains a 32-bit mask that identifies the network and subnet portion of the IP address. The addition of this field is the single most important change made to the RIP v2 message structure.

subnetwork   1) In IP networks, a network sharing a particular subnet address. Subnetworks are networks arbitrarily segmented by a network administrator in order to provide a multilevel, hierarchical routing structure while shielding the subnetwork from the addressing complexity of attached networks. Subnetwork is also known as subnet. See also IP address, subnet address, and subnet mask. 2) In OSI networks, a collection of ESs and ISs under the control of a single administrative domain and using a single network access protocol.

Subnetwork Access Protocol   See SNAP.

subnetwork point of attachment   See SNPA.

Subscriber Network Interface   See SNI.

subvector   A data segment of a vector in an SNA message. A subvector consists of a length field, a key that describes the subvector type, and subvector specific data.

Super Frame   See SF.

supernetting   Aggregating IP network addresses advertised as a single classless network address. For example, given four Class C IP networks-192.0.8.0, 192.0.9.0, 192.0.10.0 and 192.0.11.0-each having the intrinsic network mask of 255.255.255.0, one can advertise the address 192.0.8.0 with a subnet mask of 255.255.252.0.

supervisory processor   See RP (route processor).

SURAnet   Southeastern Universities Research Association Network - Network connecting universities and other organizations in the Southeastern United States. SURAnet, originally funded by the NSF and a part of the NSFNET, is now part of BBN Planet.

surge   Any voltage increase above 110% of the normal voltage carried by a power line.

sustainable cell rate   See SCR.

SVC   Switched Virtual Circuit - Virtual circuit that is dynamically established on demand and is torn down when transmission is complete. SVCs are used in situations where data transmission is sporadic. Switched virtual circuit is also known as switched virtual connection in ATM terminology.

Switch   A device that channels incoming data from any of multiple input ports to the specific output port that will take the data toward its intended destination.

switch   1) Network device that filters, forwards, and floods frames based on the destination address of each frame. The switch operates at the data link layer of the OSI model. 2) General term applied to an electronic or mechanical device that allows a connection to be established as necessary and terminated when there is no longer a session to support.

switch card   Card on the LightStream 2020 ATM switch that handles communication between the other cards on the switch. Each LightStream 2020 switch has one or two switch cards. The second card, if present, serves as a backup for the first.

Switch Processor   See SP.

switched LAN   LAN implemented with LAN switches.

Switched Multimegabit Data Service   See SMDS.

Switched Port Analyzer   See SPAN.

switched virtual circuit   See SVC.

switched virtual connection   See SVC.

Switch-to-Switch Protocol   See SSP.

SwitchVision   Cisco SNMP-based network management software, running on Microsoft Windows, that offers a powerful set of tools to manage an entire network, including switches, hubs, routers, and bridges. SwitchVision can automatically discover and map any SNMP device on the network and show the status of network devices. SwitchVision allows network administrators to set event thresholds, activate actions when error conditions occur, and set up custom tables and graphs to view critical network variables.

synchronization   Establishment of common timing between sender and receiver.

Synchronous Data Link Control   See SDLC.

Synchronous Digital Hierarchy   See SDH.

Synchronous Optical Network   See SONET.

synchronous transmission   Term describing digital signals that are transmitted with precise clocking. Such signals have the same frequency, with individual characters encapsulated in control bits (called start bits and stop bits) that designate the beginning and end of each character. Compare with asynchronous transmission, isochronous transmission, and plesiochronous transmission.

Synchronous Transport Module level 1   See STM-1.

Synchronous Transport Signal level 1   See STS-1.

Synchronous Transport Signal level 3, concatenated   See STS-3c.

sysgen   System Generation - Process of defining network resources in a network.

system generation   See sysgen.

System ID   System ID is a NSAP address field that identifies an individual OSI device. In OSI, a device has an address, just as it does in DECnet, while in IP an interface has an address.

system services control points   See SSCP.

Systems Network Architecture   See SNA.

T1   Digital WAN carrier facility. T1 transmits DS-1-formatted data at 1.544 Mbps through the telephone-switching network, using AMI or B8ZS coding. Compare with E1.

T3   Digital WAN carrier facility. T3 transmits DS-3-formatted data at 44.736 Mbps through the telephone switching network. Compare with E3.

TAC   1) Terminal Access Controller - Internet host that accepts terminal connections from dial-up lines. 2) Technical Assistance Center - Cisco TACs provide technical assistance to partners and end users, and form the hub of Cisco global support.

TACACS   Terminal Access Controller Access Control System - Authentication protocol, developed by the DDN community, that provides remote access authentication and related services, such as event logging. User passwords are administered in a central database rather than in individual routers, providing an easily scalable network security solution.

TACACS+   Terminal Access Controller Access Control System Plus - Proprietary Cisco enhancement to TACACS. Provides additional support for authentication, authorization, and accounting.

tagged traffic   ATM cells that have their CLP bit set to 1. If the network is congested, tagged traffic can be dropped to ensure delivery of higher-priority traffic. Tagged traffic is also known as discard eligible (DE).

TAXI 4B/5B   Transparent Asynchronous Transmitter/Receiver Interface 4-byte/5-byte - Encoding scheme used for FDDI LANs as well as for ATM. Supports speeds of up to 100 Mbps over multimode fiber. TAXI is the chipset that generates 4B/5B encoding on multimode fiber.

T-carrier   TDM transmission method usually referring to a line or cable carrying a DS-1 signal.

TCP   Transmission Control Protocol - Connection-oriented transport layer protocol that provides reliable full-duplex data transmission. TCP is part of the TCP/IP protocol stack.

TCP/IP   Transmission Control Protocol/Internet Protocol - Common name for the suite of protocols developed by the U.S. DoD in the 1970s to support the construction of worldwide internetworks. TCP and IP are the two best-known protocols in the suite.

TCS   Test and Control System - Independently-powered subsystem used to initialize, monitor, and troubleshoot the hardware on a LightStream 2020 ATM switch. The TCS consists of a hub residing on the switch card and slaves on NPs and line cards.

TCU   Trunk Coupling Unit - In Token Ring networks, a physical device that enables a station to connect to the trunk cable.

TDM   Time-Division Multiplexing - Technique in which information from multiple channels can be allocated bandwidth on a single wire based on preassigned time slots. Bandwidth is allocated to each channel regardless of whether the station has data to transmit. Compare with ATDM, FDM, and statistical multiplexing.

TDR   Time Domain Reflectometer - Device capable of sending signals through a network medium to check cable continuity, length, and other attributes. TDRs are used to find physical layer network problems.

Technical Assistance Center   See TAC.

Technical Office Protocol   See TOP.

telco   Abbreviation for telephone company.

telecommunications   Term referring to communications (usually involving computer systems) over the telephone network.

Telecommunications Industry Association   See TIA.

telephony   Science of converting sound to electrical signals and transmitting it between widely removed points.

telepole   Telescoping pole with a hook at one end. It is used to get cable across a ceiling or attic quickly.

teleworker   Work arrangement in which employees enjoy limited flexibility in working location and hours. The daily commute to a central place of work is replaced by telecommunication links. Teleworking is also known as a Branch of One, telecommuting, e-commuting, telework, or working from home (WFH).

telex   Teletypewriter service allowing subscribers to send messages over the PSTN.

Telnet   Command used to verify the application layer software between source and destination stations. This is the most complete test mechanism available.

Tempest   U.S. military standard. Electronic products adhering to the Tempest specification are designed to withstand EMP.

Teredo   Teredo is a mechanism which tunnels IPv6 datagrams within IPv4 UDP. This method provides for private IPv4 address use and IPv4 NAT traversal. Teredo was formerly known as Shipworm.

termid   SNA cluster controller identification. Termid is meaningful only for switched lines. Termid is also known as Xid.

terminal   Simple device at which data can be entered or retrieved from a network. Generally, terminals have a monitor and a keyboard, but no processor or local disk drive.

Terminal Access Controller   See TAC.

Terminal Access Controller Access System   See TACACS.

terminal adapter   Device used to connect ISDN BRI connections to existing interfaces such as EIA/TIA-232. Essentially, an ISDN modem.

terminal emulation   Network application in which a computer runs software that makes it appear to a remote host as a directly attached terminal.

terminal server   Communications processor that connects asynchronous devices such as terminals, printers, hosts, and modems to any LAN or WAN that uses TCP/IP, X.25, or LAT protocols. Terminal servers provide the internetwork intelligence that is not available in the connected devices.

terminator   Device that provides electrical resistance at the end of a transmission line to absorb signals on the line, thereby keeping them from bouncing back and being received again by network stations.

test and control system   See TCS.

Texas Higher Education Network   See THEnet.

TFTP   Trivial File Transfer Protocol - Simplified version of FTP that allows files to be transferred from one computer to another over a network.

TH   Transmission Header - SNA header that is appended to the SNA basic information unit (BIU). The TH uses one of a number of available SNA header formats.

THC over X.25   Feature providing TCP/IP header compression over X.25 links, for purposes of link efficiency.

THEnet   Texas Higher Education Network - Regional network comprising over 60 academic and research institutions in the Texas (United States) area.

Thinnet   Term used to define a thinner, less expensive version of the cable specified in the IEEE 802.3 10BASE2 standard. Compare with Cheapernet.

throughput   Rate of information arriving at, and possibly passing through, a particular point in a network system.

TIA   Telecommunications Industry Association - Organization that develops standards relating to telecommunications technologies. Together, the TIA and the EIA have formalized standards, such as EIA/TIA-232, for the electrical characteristics of data transmission.

tie-wraps   Plastic ties used for holding cables together or for holding cables in place.

time domain reflectometer   See TDR.

time domain reflectometry   Technique of sending an electrical signal down a cable and then timing the signal's reflection back from the end of the cable.

Time Notify   See TNotify.

Time To Live   See TTL.

time-division multiplexing   See TDM.

time-out   Event that occurs when one network device expects to hear from another network device within a specified period of time, but does not. The resulting time-out usually results in a retransmission of information or the dissolving of the session between the two devices.

TKIP   Temporal Key Integrity Protocol - TKIP is a WPA feature used to ensure integrity in wireless data transmission.

TLV   Type, Length, Value - TLV is in the IS-IS and ES-IS PDUs that contain variable-length fields, depending on the function of the PDU. Each field contains a type code and length, followed by the appropriate values. These fields are identified by one octet of type (T), one octet of length (L) and "L" octets of value (V). The Type field indicates the type of items in the Value field. The Length field indicates the length of the Value field. The Value field is the data portion of the packet. Not all router imp

TN3270   Terminal emulation software that allows a terminal to appear to an IBM host as a 3278 Model 2 terminal. The Cisco TN3270 implementation allows users to access an IBM host without using a special IBM server or a UNIX host acting as a server.

TNotify   Time Notify - Specifies how often SMT initiates neighbor notification broadcasts.

to switch unit   See TSU.

token   Frame that contains control information. Possession of the token allows a network device to transmit data onto the network.

token bus   LAN architecture using token passing access over a bus topology. This LAN architecture is the basis for the IEEE 802.4 LAN specification.

token passing   Access method by which network devices access the physical medium in an orderly fashion based on possession of a small frame called a token. Contrast with circuit switching and contention.

Token Ring   Token-passing LAN developed and supported by IBM. Token Ring runs at 4 or 16 Mbps over a ring topology. Similar to IEEE 802.5.

TOP   Technical Office Protocol - OSI-based architecture developed for office communications.

topology   Physical arrangement of network nodes and media within an enterprise networking structure.

topology map   Tool for managing a LightStream 2020 ATM switch that examines a network and displays the status of its nodes and trunks. The topology map is an HP OpenView-based application that runs on an NMS.

ToS   Type of Service - Field within an IP datagram that indicates how the datagram should be handled.

total length   Field within an IP datagram that indicates total length of the header plus the data.

Totally stub area   An area that does not accept external autonomous system (AS) routes and summary routes from other areas internal to the autonomous system. Instead, if the router needs to send a packet to a network external to the area, it sends it using a default route.

TPC   Transmit Power Control - TPC is an IEEE 802.11h specification which has been used in the cellular telephone industry for years. TPC sets the transmit power of the access point and the client adapter to allow for different coverage area sizes and to conserve battery life.

trace route   Program available on many systems that traces the path a packet takes to a destination. It is mostly used to debug routing problems between hosts. There is also a traceroute protocol defined in RFC 1393.

traffic management   See ControlStream traffic management.

traffic policing   Process used to measure the actual traffic flow across a given connection and compare it to the total admissable traffic flow for that connection. Traffic outside of the agreed upon flow can be tagged (where the CLP bit is set to 1) and can be discarded en route if congestion develops. Traffic policing is used in ATM, Frame Relay, and other types of networks. Also know as admission control, permit processing, rate enforcement, and usage parameter control (UPC).

traffic profile   Set of COS attribute values assigned to a given port on a LightStream 2020 ATM switch. The profile affects numerous parameters for data transmitted from the port including rate, cell drop eligibility, transmit priority, and inactivity timer.

traffic shaping   Use of queues to limit surges that can congest a network. Data is buffered and then sent into the network in regulated amounts to ensure that the traffic will fit within the promised traffic envelope for the particular connection. Traffic shaping is used in ATM, Frame Relay, and other types of networks. Traffic shaping is also known as metering, shaping, or smoothing.

trailer   Control information appended to data when encapsulating the data for network transmission. Compare with header.

transaction   Result-oriented unit of communication processing.

transaction services layer   Layer 7 in the SNA architectural model. Represents user application functions, such as spreadsheets, word-processing, or electronic mail, by which users interact with the network. Corresponds roughly with the application layer of the OSI reference model.

transceiver   See MAU.

transceiver cable   See AUI.

transfer priority   See transmit priority.

transit bridging   Bridging that uses encapsulation to send a frame between two similar networks over a dissimilar network.

translational bridging   Bridging between networks with dissimilar MAC sublayer protocols. MAC information is translated into the format of the destination network at the bridge. Contrast with encapsulation bridging.

transmission control layer   Layer 4 in the SNA architectural model. This layer is responsible for establishing, maintaining, and terminating SNA sessions, sequencing data messages, and controlling session level flow. Corresponds to the transport layer of the OSI model.

Transmission Control Protocol   See TCP.

Transmission Control Protocol/Internet Protocol   See TCP/IP.

transmission group   In SNA routing, one or more parallel communications links treated as one communications facility.

transmission header   See TH.

transmission link   See link.

transmit power   A radio transmission technology that spreads the user information over a much wider bandwidth than otherwise required in order to gain benefits such as improved interference tolerance and unlicensed operation.

transmit priority   Queuing scheme in which each internal TOS of a LightStream 2020 ATM switch correlates to a relative priority in queues in the ATM network. This priority determines which traffic is serviced first in the case of contention for a network resource. Transmit priority is also known as forwarding priority or transfer priority.

TRANSPAC   Major packet data network run by France Telecom.

Transparent Asynchronous Transmitter/Receiver Inte   See TAXI 4B/5B.

transparent bridging   Bridging scheme often used in Ethernet and IEEE 802.3 networks in which bridges pass frames along one hop at a time based on tables associating end nodes with bridge ports. Transparent bridging is so named because the presence of bridges is transparent to network end nodes. Contrast with SRB.

transport layer   Layer 4 of the OSI reference model. This layer is responsible for reliable network communication between end nodes. The transport layer provides mechanisms for the establishment, maintenance, and termination of virtual circuits, transport fault detection and recovery, and information flow control. Corresponds to the transmission control layer of the SNA model.

trap   Message sent by an SNMP agent to an NMS, console, or terminal to indicate the occurrence of a significant event, such as a specifically defined condition or a threshold that has been reached.

tree topology   LAN topology similar to a bus topology, except that tree networks can contain branches with multiple nodes. Transmissions from a station propagate the length of the medium and are received by all other stations. Compare with bus topology, ring topology, and star topology.

Trivial File Transfer Protocol   See TFTP.

trunk   Physical and logical connection between two ATM switches across which traffic in an ATM network travels. An ATM backbone is composed of a number of trunks.

trunk card   Line card on a LightStream 2020 ATM switch that is configured to communicate with other ATM switches. LightStream 2020 trunk cards offer a variety of interface types. CLCs, LSCs, and MSCs can operate as trunk cards.

trunk coupling unit   See TCU.

Trunk Up-Down   See TUD.

TSU   To Switch Unit - Subsystem on each LightStream 2020 ATM switch line card that appends ATM routing information to outgoing cells and sends the cells to the switch card.

TTL   Time to Live - Field in an IP header that indicates how long a packet is considered valid.

TUD   Trunk Up-Down - Protocol used in ATM networks that monitors trunks and detects when one goes down or comes up. ATM switches send regular test messages from each trunk port to test trunk line quality. If a trunk misses a given number of these messages, TUD declares the trunk down. When a trunk comes back up, TUD recognizes that the trunk is up, declares the trunk up, and returns it to service.

tunneling   Architecture that is designed to provide the services necessary to implement any standard point-to-point encapsulation scheme.

TUV   German test agency that certifies products to European safety standards.

twisted pair   Relatively low-speed transmission medium consisting of two insulated wires arranged in a regular spiral pattern. The wires can be shielded or unshielded. Twisted pair is common in telephony applications and is increasingly common in data networks.

two-way simultaneous   See TWS.

TWS   Two-Way Simultaneous - Mode that allows a router configured as a primary SDLC station to achieve better utilization of a full-duplex serial line. When TWS is enabled in a multidrop environment, the router can poll a secondary station and receive data from that station while it sends data to or receives data from a different secondary station on the same serial line.

Type 1 operation   IEEE 802.2 (LLC) connectionless operation.

Type 2 operation   IEEE 802.2 (LLC) connection-oriented operation.

type of service   See ToS.

Type, Length, Value   See TLV.

UART   Universal Asynchronous Receiver/Transmitter - Integrated circuit, attached to the parallel bus of a computer, used for serial communications. The UART translates between serial and parallel signals, provides transmission clocking, and buffers data sent to or from the computer.

UBR   Unspecified Bit Rate - QOS class defined by the ATM Forum for ATM networks. UBR allows any amount of data up to a specified maximum to be sent across the network, but there are no guarantees in terms of cell loss rate and delay. Compare with available bit rate (ABR), CBR, and VBR.

UDP   User Datagram Protocol - Connectionless transport layer protocol in the TCP/IP protocol stack. UDP is a simple protocol that exchanges datagrams without acknowledgments or guaranteed delivery, requiring that error processing and retransmission be handled by other protocols. UDP is defined in RFC 768.

ULP   Upper-Layer Protocol - Protocol that operates at a higher layer in the OSI reference model, relative to other layers. ULP is sometimes used to refer to the next-highest protocol (relative to a particular protocol) in a protocol stack.

unbalanced configuration   HDLC configuration with one primary station and multiple secondary stations.

UNI   User-Network Interface - ATM Forum specification that defines an interoperability standard for the interface between ATM-based products (a router or an ATM switch) located in a private network and the ATM switches located within the public carrier networks. Also used to describe similar connections in Frame Relay networks.

unicast   Message sent to a single network destination. Compare with broadcast and multicast.

unicast address   Address specifying a single network device. Compare with broadcast address and multicast address.

uninsured traffic   Traffic within the excess rate (the difference between the insured rate and maximum rate) for a VCC. This traffic can be dropped by the network if congestion occurs.

Universal Asynchronous Receiver/Transmitter   See UART.

Universal Resource Locator   See URL.

UNIX   Operating system developed in 1969 at Bell Laboratories. UNIX has gone through several iterations since its inception. These include UNIX 4.3 BSD (Berkeley Standard Distribution), developed at the University of California at Berkeley, and UNIX System V, Release 4.0, developed by AT and T.

unnumbered frames   HDLC frames used for various control and management purposes, including link startup and shutdown, and mode specification.

unshielded twisted-pair   See UTP.

unspecified bit rate   See UBR.

UPC   Usage Parameter Control - See traffic policing.

upper-layer protocol   See ULP.

UPS   Uninterruptable Power Supply - Backup device designed to provide an uninterrupted power source in the event of a power failure. They are commonly installed on all file servers and wiring hubs.

Urgent Pointer   Indicates the end of the urgent data.

URL   Universal Resource Locator - Standardized addressing scheme for accessing hypertext documents and other services using a WWW browser.

usage parameter control   See UPC.

USENET   Initiated in 1979, one of the oldest and largest cooperative networks, with over 10,000 hosts and a quarter of a million users. Its primary service is a distributed conferencing service called news.

User Datagram Protocol   See UDP.

User-Network Interface   See UNI.

UTP   Unshielded Twisted-Pair - Four-pair wire medium used in a variety of networks. UTP does not require the fixed spacing between connections that is necessary with coaxial-type connections. There are five types of UTP cabling commonly used: Category 1 cabling, Category 2 cabling, Category 3 cabling, Category 4 cabling, and Category 5 cabling. Compare with STP.

V.24   ITU-T standard for a physical layer interface between DTE and DCE. V.24 is essentially the same as the EIA/TIA-232 standard.

V.35   ITU-T standard describing a synchronous, physical layer protocol used for communications between a network access device and a packet network. V.35 is most commonly used in the United States and in Europe, and is recommended for speeds up to 48 Kbps.

V.42   ITU-T standard protocol for error correction using LAPM.

variable bit rate   See VBR.

Variable Length Subnet Masking   See VLSM.

VBR   Variable Bit Rate - QOS class defined by the ATM Forum for ATM networks. VBR is subdivided into a real time (RT) class and non-real time (NRT) class. VBR (RT) is used for connections in which there is a fixed timing relationship between samples. VBR (NRT) is used for connections in which there is no fixed timing relationship between samples, but that still need a guaranteed QOS. Compare with ABR, CBR, and UBR.

VC   Virtual Circuit - Logical circuit created to ensure reliable communication between two network devices. A virtual circuit is defined by a VPI/VCI pair, and can be either permanent (PVC) or switched (SVC). Virtual circuits are used in Frame Relay and X.25. In ATM, a virtual circuit is called a virtual channel.

VCC Virtual Channel Connection - Logical circuit, made up of VCLs, that carries data between two end points in an ATM network. Virtual channel connection is also known as virtual circuit connection.

VCI Virtual Channel Identifier - 16-bit field in the header of an ATM cell. The VCI, together with the VPI, is used to identify the next destination of a cell as it passes through a series of ATM switches on its way to its destination. ATM switches use the VPI/VCI fields to identify the next network VCL that a cell needs to transit on its way to its final destination. The function of the VCI is similar to that of the DLCI in Frame Relay. Compare to DLCI.

VCN Virtual Circuit Number - 12-bit field in an X.25 PLP header that identifies an X.25 virtual circuit. Allows DCE to determine how to route a packet through the X.25 network. Virtual circuit number is also known as logical channel identifier (LCI) or logical channel number (LCN).

VINES Virtual Integrated Network Service - NOS developed and marketed by Banyan Systems.

VLSM Variable Length Subnet Mask - Ability to specify a different subnet mask for the same network number on different subnets. VLSM can help optimize available address space.

WAN Wide Area Network - Data communications network that serves users across a broad geographic area and often uses transmission devices provided by common carriers. Frame Relay, SMDS, and X.25 are examples of WANs.

Weighted fair queuing See WFQ.

WEP Wired Equivalent Privacy - An optional security mechanism defined within the 802.11 standard designed to make the link integrity of wireless devices equal to that of a cable.

WFQ Weighted Fair Queuing - Queuing method that prioritizes interactive traffic over file transfers in order to ensure satisfactory response time for common user applications.

Wi-Fi Alliance The Wi-Fi Alliance offers certification for interoperability between vendors of 802.11 products. It helps to market a WLAN technology by promoting interoperability between vendors. Certification includes all three 802.11 RF technologies and WPA.

Wi-Fi Protected Access See WPA.

wireless controller A wireless controller is a device used in a centralized WLAN topology which handles authentication, association, mobility, and frame translation and bridging.

Wireless LAN Two or more computers or devices equipped to use spread-spectrum technology based on radio waves for communication within a limited area.

WLAN Wireless LAN - A WLAN a wireless local area network, which permits a network connection between two or more computers without using wires. It uses radio communication to accomplish the same functionality that a wired LAN has.

WLSE Wireless LAN Solution Engine - WLSE is a CiscoWorks option which allows centralized configuration and monitoring of the Cisco Aironet autonomous access points and provides RF management, rogue access point detection, and interference detection. WLSE is used with autonomous access points in the distributive WLAN model.

WPA Wi-Fi Protected Access - WPA is a security model for WLANs released in 2003, based on the IEEE 802.11i standard. It is a standards-based, interoperable security enhancement that strongly increases the level of data protection and access control for existing and future wireless LAN systems. It is derived from and will be forward-compatible with the upcoming IEEE 802.11i standard. WPA leverages Temporal Key Integrity Protocol (TKIP) for data protection and 802.1X for authenticated key management.

WWW browser World Wide Web browser - GUI-based hypertext client application, such as Mosaic, used to access hypertext documents and other services located on innumerable remote servers throughout the WWW and Internet.

zero code suppression Line coding scheme used for transmission clocking. Zero line suppression substitutes a one in the seventh bit of a string of eight consecutive zeros.

X.121 ITU-T standard describing an addressing scheme used in X.25 networks. X.121 addresses are sometimes called IDNs (International Data Numbers).

X.25 ITU-T standard that defines how connections between DTE and DCE are maintained for remote terminal access and computer communications in PDNs. X.25 specifies LAPB, a data link layer protocol, and PLP, a network layer protocol. Frame Relay has to some degree superseded X.25.

X.25 Level 3 See PLP.

X.25 Protocol See PLP.

X.400 ITU-T recommendation specifying a standard for electronic mail transfer.

X.500 ITU-T recommendation specifying a standard for distributed maintenance of files and directories.

XID 1) exchange identification. Request and response packets exchanged prior to a session between a router and a Token Ring host. If the parameters of the serial device contained in the XID packet do not match the configuration of the host, the session is dropped. 2) See termid.

Understanding the
Properties of Matter

Second Edition

Understanding the Properties of Matter

Second Edition

Michael de Podesta
National Physics Laboratory
UK

London and New York

First edition published 1996 by UCL Press

This edition published 2002 by Taylor & Francis
11 New Fetter Lane, London EC4P 4EE

Simultaneously published in the USA and Canada
by Taylor & Francis Inc,
29 West 35th Street, New York, NY 10001

Taylor & Francis is an imprint of the Taylor & Francis Group

© 2002 Taylor & Francis

Printed and bound in Great Britain
by St Edmundsbury Press, Bury St Edmunds, Suffolk

Every effort has been made to ensure that the advice and information in this
book is true and accurate at the time of going to press. However neither the
publisher nor the authors can accept any legal responsibility or liability for
any errors or omissions that may be made. In the case of drug
administration, any medical procedure or the use of technical equipment
mentioned within this book, you are strongly advised to consult the
manufacturer's guidelines.

Publisher's Note
This book has been prepared from camera-ready copy provided
by the author.

British Library Cataloguing in Publication Data
A catalogue record for this book is available from the British Library

Library of Congress Cataloging in Publication Data
De Podesta, Michael
    Understanding the properties of matter / Michael de Podesta. – 2nd ed.
        p. cm.
    Includes bibliographical references and index.
1. Matter – Properties. 2. Matter – Properties – Problems, exercises, etc.

QC173.3 .D42 2001 *2002*   2001052292
530.4 – dc21

ISBN 0-415-25787-5 (hbk)
ISBN 0-415-25788-3 (pbk)

For...

Maxwell and Christian
John and Maíre
You and me

Contents

Chapter 9: Liquids: Comparison with experiment

Chapter 10: Changes of phase: Background theory

Chapter 11: Changes of phase: Comparison with experiment

Chapter 12: Questions

Appendices

Index

Foreword to first edition

Professor Sir Brian Pippard, FRS

One of the greatest transformations of physics began about 70 years ago, when quantum mechanics was formulated. Many of the outstanding puzzles of atomic structure suddenly became clear, and it was not long before a start was made on understanding the chemical bond. Before 1930 the new ideas were applied to solids; one of the first successes was to explain how electrons can move so easily between the closely-packed atoms of a metal, and soon after this came the explanation of why some solids conduct electricity well, but others are insulators. Since then there has been no slackening of effort; many more phenomena have been revealed and explained, and new technologies have grown up out of the successes, to transform our lives. One example will suffice. The transistor was invented in 1947 by solid-state physicists, and without it modern communication and information systems would never have been developed.

There are more people engaged in research into condensed matter, and its applications, than on any other branch of physics. One consequence of this activity is that the assimilation of new facts and theories is an almost overwhelming task, and we are forced to rely on the efforts of those who can put together a readable account of the main themes. It is not surprising that most of the recent text books meet the challenge by concentrating on general principles and the theoretical treatment of rather simple examples, to such a degree that a casual reader might consider that the whole subject is dominated by theory. One cannot deny that without theory we should be left with a miscellaneous ragbag of facts, lacking the means to find any underlying structure. On the other hand, without the challenge of the facts, the deep general theories like quantum mechanics would never have been looked for.

Nowadays most physicists specialise in either experiment or theory, and there are few to rival those of earlier days who, like Maxwell, Rayleigh, Helmholtz and Fermi, were superlatively good at both. Nevertheless, all modern specialists acknowledge their dependence on the different skills of others. A theoretician ignorant of facts is no more to be trusted than an engineer who takes a textbook diagram of a bridge as the basis for a design, never having seen the real thing or tested a model. Unfortunately the prevalence of software packages for almost every conceivable task encourages the mistaken belief that they incorporate all the experience needed for success in their application. If you read Michael de Podesta's book seriously you are unlikely to fall into such a grievous error. Once its lesson has been learnt, it will remain a source of information and, more important still, an incentive to continue with the process of self-education, which is the key to achievement.

Of all the messages that this book conveys there is especially one with which I feel the strongest sympathy. It is not that facts are things you have to assimilate before you settle down to interesting theories – rather, it is that the facts themselves, if well presented, are interesting in their own right and raise a host of questions that make you want to find out how everything ties together. All too rarely do most of us stop to think about apparently trivial everyday observations. How often, for example, do we wonder why there are such things as liquids? You will not find a complete answer here because the complete answer is not known (and perhaps least understood about water, that most extraordinary of liquids) but you will discover the beginning of an answer, and you will find that the beautiful simplicities of thermodynamics help you to see what happens when a solid melts, and give hints of the difficulties that one may yet hope to

eventually overcome. And this is only one of the tantalising problems discussed here in the hope that you will discover (if you have not done so already) both the lovely certainties and the stimulating mysteries that together make physicists enjoy their work, and continue to enjoy it as long as they can carry on with physics.

Acknowledgements

Despite the fact that only one name appears on the cover, and despite the essentially solitary nature of writing, no book of this kind can ever truly be written by a single person. Every author is indebted in all kinds of ways, to all kinds of people, and I am no exception. What follows is a list of the major debts I have incurred while writing this book. I would like to thank my benefactors and ask simply for some time to be able to repay them.

My first, and largest, debt is to Stephanie Bell, my wife, and to Maxwell and Christian, my children. They have tolerated, supported and encouraged me, through months of late nights and working weekends.

My second debt is to the many academic colleagues with whom I have worked over the years. From the Physics Department at Birkbeck College; the Condensed Matter group at University College London; and at the Open University.

My third debt is to those who were kind enough to comment on the First Edition, particularly Bertil Dynefors, Gabe Spalding and Paulo Manuel de Araújo Sá, who produced detailed (and embarrassingly long) lists of errata. Every one of *these* mistakes has been eliminated!

My fourth debt is to the staff at *Taylor and Francis*. In particular, Grant Soanes for allowing me the opportunity to work on this revised edition, and Peter Willis for his help, kind words, and attention to detail.

I now work for the UK's National Physical Laboratory and I would like to thank my many colleagues there who have (often unknowingly) contributed to this book. I would also like to thank David Robinson for permission to take a months leave during which I was able to complete my first revision of the text.

And, as with the first edition, I would like to acknowledge the work of those scientists, living and dead, who have faithfully recorded their observations of the physical world. Without their care and attention to detail, it would not have been possible to write this book.

Finally, if you have any comments, good or bad, I would be happy to receive them. Any helpful comments on the text will be posted on the web site for the book (www.physicsofmatter.com).

Michael de Podesta

michael@physicsofmatter.com

February 2002

Constants

The fundamental physical constants are known to much greater precision than is shown in this table, but the precision shown is sufficient for all the work in this text, and almost all work related to the physics of matter. For more precise values and uncertainty estimates the reader should consult *Tables of physical and chemical constants* by *Kaye and Laby*, referred to in §1.4.1

Constant and symbol	Value	Unit
Speed of light in vacuum, c	2.998×10^{8}	m s^{-1}
Electric charge on proton, e	1.602×10^{-19}	C
Planck constant, h	6.626×10^{-34}	J s
Planck constant, $(h/2\pi)$	1.054×10^{-34}	J s
Mass of proton, m_p	1.673×10^{-27}	kg
Mass of electron, m_e	9.109×10^{-31}	kg
Atomic mass unit, u	1.661×10^{-27}	kg
Electron volt, eV	1.602×10^{-19}	J
Bohr magneton, μ_B	9.274×10^{-24}	J T^{-1}
Boltzmann constant, k_B	1.381×10^{-23}	J K^{-1}
Avogadro number, N_A	6.022×10^{23}	mol^{-1}
Molar gas constant, R	8.314	$\text{J K}^{-1}\text{mol}^{-1}$
Permeability of free space, μ_o	$4\pi \times 10^{-7}$	H m^{-1}
Permittivity of free space, ε_o	8.854×10^{-12}	F m^{-1}
Stephan–Boltzmann constant, σ	5.671×10^{-8}	$\text{W m}^{-2}\text{ K}^{-4}$

CHAPTER 1

The quest for an understanding of matter

1.1 Welcome

People have wondered about the properties of matter for many centuries and have written many excellent books on the subject. Even books that were printed half a century ago are relevant today. The properties of matter, and our theories about matter, have changed relatively little in this time. This is not to say that new phenomena have not been discovered and explained: for example superfluidity and superconductivity have been exciting areas of advance in understanding. However, the laws of thermodynamics have not changed and the speed of sound in copper is the same as it was 100 years ago. The scientists who have worked during this century have left you, students of physics in the new century, a truly vast legacy of experimental results and theoretical analysis. Your mission, should you choose to accept it, is to acquaint yourselves with this legacy.

The study of the properties of matter is like an ancient party. Over millennia, it has at times been quiet, at times riotous. Famous figures have attended, but most of the people here are just like you and me. As I write today, the party is bustling after a century or so of explosive chitter chatter. What will happen next? I have no idea, but I expect it will be interesting. I hope you will stay to find out.

1.2 Personal experience

More than half a lifetime ago I was a student of physics. From the manner in which I was I taught the various elements that comprise the study of matter, I learned several lessons that it has taken me a long time to unlearn. Firstly, I learned that it was not necessary to actually know what the properties of matter were in order to debate them earnestly. This is, of course, rubbish. However, fear of my own ignorance prevented me from realising this earlier. Secondly, I learned to avoid thinking about awkward subjects. I imagined that cleverer people than myself had sorted these things out. This is rubbish too, but fear of my own ignorance still haunts me here.

In hoping that your experience will differ from my own, I would urge you develop your study of the properties of matter along the following lines. Firstly, 'make friends' with matter: become familiar with what the properties of matter actually are. These properties have been determined and tabulated for thousands of substances so it is not difficult. I believe that unless you are familiar with the properties of matter it is impossible ever to say that you understand them. Secondly, and also secondarily, try to think about why things are the way they are. Often the data seem perplexing, but they usually make sense eventually.

1.3 A historical perspective

1.3.1 Discovery and rediscovery

Before embarking on this contemporary study of the properties of matter, it is instructive to spend some time reviewing the historical context in which this study takes place.

In all aspects of my own work as a scientist, I am constantly reminded that 'others have been here before'. That although I am discovering particular facts for the first time, these facts are leading me to re-discover the insights of previous generations of scientists. These scientists lacked the technical resources available today, but in their place used resourcefulness, dedication and imagination in a truly inspiring combination.

After overcoming my depression at the dimly retreating prospect of scientific stardom, I have realised that this process of rediscovery is not failure. Indeed it was – and is – the essential process through which the health of the scientific body is maintained. Further, I realise the process is not the work of a degree course, but of a lifetime. If you wish to learn about physics, the only way is to rediscover it for itself.

Unfortunately, rediscovery is as hard as discovery, but without the glory. In writing this book I have tried to ease your work of rediscovery of the properties of matter. I have written this book by collating data on the properties of matter, writing down a list of questions that occurred to me as I examined the data, and then trying to answer these questions on your behalf.

1.3.2 Familiarity and over-familiarity

The initial section of each topic in this book is a discussion of the data on that topic. Before discussing the theories about what happens, I wish you to become familiar with what actually happens. In this way I hope to allow you to rediscover some of the more striking properties of matter for yourself.

However in encouraging this familiarisation I encounter a severe problem. The problem of an im-

proper over-familiarity with rather sophisticated theories about matter. For example, many of you reading this will have seen images of atoms: you will have heard or even taken part in discussions of their detailed structure. I would go so far as to say that many of you believe in atoms. However I would also venture that many of you believe in atoms not because of insights you have made yourself, but because you have been told that they exist and you have been told that they possess certain properties. I am sure your teachers have taught you well, but being told something is different from convincing yourself it must be so. This is the sense in which I would like you to embark upon the study of matter. Do not believe it until you have seen the data! I would like you to be sceptical about the data in this book, about the theories presented here, and most of all about your own credulity.

1.3.3 Consciousness lowering

In order to help get in the mood to rediscover the properties of matter, you may care to take part in an exercise in 'consciousness lowering'.

Picture yourself in the late seventeenth century, look around you. The 'stuff' of the world – the matter – is diverse in its properties. You can probably see wood, metal, stone, paper and – most amazingly – animated flesh. Your task is to categorise these substances and their experimental properties. What do they have in common? How do they differ?

In other words, you must decide on a set of organisational principles which will allow you to found an understanding of matter. Notice that you cannot include references to concepts which we now accept such as atoms, or electric charge. These are concepts which you must develop by studying matter – categorising results, preparing hypotheses, worrying about exceptions – and trying to convince a sceptical group of colleagues that your insights are valid. I think you will find it extraordinarily difficult to know where to begin,

and if you wish to see the task through, I should set aside a lifetime or so for the purpose. The bewildering variety of the properties of matter will provide exceptional cases for just about any scheme of categorisation you adopt.

And if you find this process of categorisation difficult, pity then people from earlier times who reflected on the nature of matter. They suffered both from a lack of reliable data, a lack of validated concepts for understanding the data, and the experimental equipment of the same type as a 13-year old might use in a modern teaching laboratory. I wonder how long it would have taken you to 'discover' atoms and determine their properties; to 'discover' that there are two types of electric charge; to 'discover' that heat is not a substantive fluid.

All your present clarity of vision, such as your wise belief in the existence of atoms, has been constructed on a foundation of centuries of sceptical enquiry.

1.3.4 Organisational principles

What the above exercise is intended to show is that it is not obvious what organisational principles we should use in attempting to categorise matter. And without the appropriate organisational principles, the properties of matter are bewilderingly diverse and explanations appear arbitrary and unconvincing. So, how should we choose to categorise matter?

Animate/inanimate

The first categorisation that suggests itself to me is that between animate and inanimate matter. Historically, division of the study of matter in this way allowed the emerging science of physics to

appear successful at explaining and parameterising the simpler properties of inanimate matter. By contrast, the study of animate matter is still barely beyond the stage of naming and categorising.

Solids, liquids and gases

Considering the inanimate world, the next most apparent organisational scheme is the classification of matter into one of three categories: solid, liquid or gas. This rather natural categorisation is now seen as by no means exhaustive. (Indeed it never was: our own bodies are made from matter which is half-liquid and half-solid.) Liquid crystals for example disclose by their very name that the solid-liquid-gas categorisation is inadequate. Further, substances normally considered to be in one category (such as 'solid' rock) when viewed over geological time scales shows properties associated with the liquid state (such as flow and convection). However the solid–liquid–gas division is still a useful one, and forms the basis for the structure of this book.

The conceptual division of matter into distinct categories of solid, liquid and gas was historically extremely important. Once made, real progress became possible in understanding the properties of the simplest of the category of matter: the gaseous state. In studies of gases over the two hundred years from 1700 to 1900 an enormous number of ideas emerged and were tested. In particular the nature of four key concepts were distilled into a form somewhat similar to the one we hold today. The key concepts were descriptions of the properties of matter in terms of atoms, the nature of heat, electricity, and light As we examine the properties of gases in Chapter 5, bear in mind that with the exception of our reference to quantum mechanics, the study would not have been out of place a century ago!

1.4 The structure of this book

The structure of this book is shown in Figure 1.1. Chapters 1 to 3 provide respectively, the context of the book, a mini revision course on some relevant background theory, and a discussion of some

aspects of the process of measurement. Chapters 4 to 11 comprise the main text of the book. Gases are discussed in Chapters 4 and 5, solids in Chapters 6 and 7, liquids in Chapters 8 and 9. The tran-

sitions between these states of matter are considered in Chapters 10 and 11. The first of each pair of chapters outlines relevant background theory, while the second considers the experimental data, and the extent to which they can be understood using the background theory. Where relevant, the theory is extended to understand the data.

Chapter 12 contains a set of 30 questions which are considerably more involved than the end of chapter exercises. They are arranged under the headings of gases, liquids, solids and phase changes.

The appendices contain detailed points of theory which are important, but which would tend to distract attention from the flow of the text if placed within the chapters.

At www.physicsofmatter.com
In any book there is a conflict between the desire to include more material, and the desire to prevent the book becoming unreadably large. In this second edition, I have attempted to improve on the compromise I chose for the first edition by placing additional material on the internet. This has allowed me to present additional material on several important topics that were briefly covered in the first edition, while simultaneously keeping the core text at the same size. All the extension topics are available for free download from the web site:

```
http://www.physicsofmatter.com/
```

At this site, you will find copies of all the figures and tables used in the text. You will also find copies of several of the data tables in a format which may be used with the spreadsheet programs available on most personal computers.

1.4.1 Data sources and bibliography
The data in this book has been compiled from a variety of sources. All the sources are secondary: that is they have already been compiled by somebody else from primary data in research literature. These secondary sources are enormously useful in all areas of physics and I would urge anyone contemplating a career in physics to buy them and treasure them. The main sources of data used in

Figure 1.1 The structure of this book.

In the text:

2	**Background theory**	
3	**Measurement**	
4	**Gases**	Background theory
5		Comparison with experiment
6	**Solids**	Background theory
7		Comparison with experiment
8	**Liquids**	Background theory
9		Comparison with experiment
10	**Changes of Phase**	Background theory
11		Comparison with experiment
12	**Questions**	
	Appendices	

At www.physicsofmatter.com:

W1	**Band theory of solids**
W2	**Magnetic properties of solids**

the compilation of this book are:

- G. W. C. Kaye and T. H. Laby, *Tables of Physical and Chemical Constants*: 14th, 15th and 16th Editions, published by Longman (Harlow) in the UK and Wiley (New York) in the USA. This is referred to as *Kaye & Laby* in the text.

- Weast *CRC Handbook of Chemistry and Physics: 65th Edition* [also known as the 'Rubber Bible'], published by Chemical Rubber Publishing Company (Chicago, Ill)

- John Emsley, *The Elements*, published by Clarendon Press / Oxford University Press (Oxford).

References to electromagnetic theory are to the excellent

- B.I. Bleaney and B. Bleaney, *Electricity and Magnetism* [two volumes] published by Oxford University Press (Oxford).

Other sources are given in the text. Where no reference is given in the text, the data have been compiled and cross-checked from several sources. I have tried, by several techniques, to eliminate erroneous data from my compilations. However, I

cannot guarantee this, and you are referred to the original compilations and the references therein.

The web site for the book also contains an up-to-date list of errata.

1.5 Exercise

Exercises marked with a P prefix are 'normal' exercises. Those marked with a C prefix are best solved numerically by using a computer program or spreadsheet. Exercises marked with an E prefix are in general rather more challenging that the P and C exercises. Answers to all the exercises can be found on the web at www.physicsofmatter.com

P1. Isaac Newton was (obviously!) unaware of developments in electromagnetism, quantum mechanics, genetics and evolutionary theory. However, in my opinion, his view of the world was undoubtedly 'modern'. Obtain a copy of Newton's work *Opticks* (New York: Dover) and read the final section marked 'Queries' (page 339 in the Dover edition). This consists of a number of questions over which Newton had puzzled, and to which he had arrived at tentative answers. After reading his 'Queries', carry out the following exercise.

Imagine that Newton were to return to life in our time, and it fell to you to explain to him the key developments in modern science since his death. Write the script of a half-hour conversation between the two of you. Remember, you haven't got long so (a) don't waste time telling him about what he already knows and (b) be sure to script Newton's part as well as your own. I imagine he would be rather ill-tempered and aggressive, but compulsively curious. So he would be sure to interrupt if he didn't understand the language you were using and would be sure to say things like 'Yes, yes, I suspected that all along'.

Background theory

2.1 Introduction

My general aim in writing this book is to help you, and incidentally myself, to understand the properties of matter. In general, the properties that we seek to understand are the large scale (or macroscopic) properties of matter. These properties are familiar to us: for example density, colour or viscosity. In our explanations of why these properties have the values that they do, reference will often be made to the microscopic components of matter. So from the outset we need to be clear about what the components of matter are, and what general principles we may use to analyse their behaviour.

In this context, the principles are analogous to 'tools' for understanding 'components', which we may think of as the 'nuts and bolts' of matter. Historically, the principles evolved to allow analysis of particular problems, in rather the same way that mechanical tools have evolved. For example, screwdrivers have evolved to be good at turning screws. However, for the uninitiated, it is often difficult to distinguish between the 'tools' used to analyse a problem and the 'nuts and bolts' of the problem itself: it all looks like 'just so much metal'.

In the context of this book we consider the following 'components' of the world: *electrons*, *neutrons*, and *protons*; and the *electromagnetic field*. The 'tools' which we shall use are: *classical mechanics* and *quantum mechanics*; *thermodynamics* and *statistical mechanics*.

In what follows I assume that readers will have had some introduction to the topics outlined above. However, my experience tells me that, for many students, their understanding of some of these subjects remains scanty. For this reason, the presentation here assumes as little as possible in the way of background knowledge and confines itself to a few words of explanation together with the key results that students will need in the later chapters.

This chapter is divided into four sections:

§2.2   **Matter:** Here we outline our assumptions about what constitutes the matter of the world.

§2.3   **The electromagnetic field:** Here we look at the general properties of all the known fields, and focus on some detailed properties of the electromagnetic field, which is by far the most important from our point of view.

§2.4   **Classical and quantum mechanics:** Having looked at the components of the world, we will look at some of the tools we use to understand how the components interact.

§2.5   **Thermodynamics and statistical mechanics:** Finally we look at techniques for calculating the properties of large numbers of particles.

At www.physicsofmatter.com

In addition to copies of the figures and tables, you will also find animations of some of the key equations in this chapter, and some colour pictures of atomic wave functions.

2.2 Matter

2.2.1 Electrons, neutrons and protons

In what follows we assume that electrons, protons and neutrons are fundamental particles from which all matter is made. Some of their properties, as deduced from numerous experiments, are listed in Table 2.1. The mass and electric charge of the electron, proton and neutron do not require much further comment, except to note that they are all exceedingly small. Their smallness is significant because we are apt to bring to our study of these particles understandings gained with more familiar particles, which are usually substantially larger. As we shall see later in this chapter, because of their size, these particles must be described using the language of quantum mechanics. Although this allows a technical description of small particles and their properties, the description can be very difficult to understand.

But are protons electrons and neutrons *really* fundamental?

Electrons are currently considered fundamental particles at the deepest level at which scientists can study them. In other words, the properties of electrons are not explained in terms of 'component' particles. However, the properties of neutrons and protons *are* explained in terms of a yet deeper layer of structure. They are considered to consist of particles called *quarks*: when certain types of quarks are bound together, they create what we call a proton: when other types of quark are bound together, they create a neutron. This is imagined to be broadly analogous to the way that electrons, neutrons and protons are bound into atoms, and cause atoms to have different properties depending on the precise numbers and arrangement of electrons, neutrons and protons within them.

In the current cosmological view, all the electrons, protons and neutrons in the universe were created shortly after the start of the universe as the temperature of a primordial 'gas' fell. Initially the gas contained free quarks, but as the gas cooled the quarks 'condensed', i.e. bound together to form the particles we now know.

2.2.2 Nuclei

The total number of protons and neutrons in the universe is not thought to have changed very much since shortly after the start of the universe. This total number of protons and neutrons, estimated to be $\approx 10^{87}$, constitutes the raw material from which the physical universe is made. The protons and neutrons interact strongly in the regions of high temperature and pressure within the cores of stars to bind together into particles of varying sizes that

Table 2.1 The properties of particles that are treated as fundamental in this book. The most important properties of the particles for understanding the properties of matter are the first two rows of the table: mass and electric charge. The internal angular momentum (spin) and magnetic moment of the particles are discussed in the text below.

Property	Units	Electron	Neutron	Proton
Mass	Atomic mass units $u = 1.661 \times 10^{-27}$ kg	5.485×10^{-4} $\approx 1/1836$	1.0085	1.0071
Electric charge	Proton charge $e = 1.602 \times 10^{-19}$ C	-1	0	$+1$
Magnetic moment	Bohr magneton $\mu_B = 9.274 \times 10^{-24}$ J T^{-1}	1.001	1.0419×10^{-3}	1.521×10^{-3}
Magnetic moment	Nuclear magneton $\mu_N = 5.051 \times 10^{-27}$ J T^{-1}	1837.8	1.913	2.793
Intrinsic (spin) angular momentum	Planck constant divided by 2π $\hbar = 1.054 \times 10^{-34}$ J s	$\frac{1}{2}$	$\frac{1}{2}$	$\frac{1}{2}$
Electric dipole moment	Cm	0	0	0
Lifetime		Stable	Stable within nuclei half life ≈ 15 minutes in free space.	Stable

we refer to as *nuclei*. The number of protons in a nucleus is called its *atomic number*, Z. Most nuclei that are formed are unstable and rapidly disintegrate. Thus most nuclei that we find around us now are the relatively stable nuclei that have not yet disintegrated. The stable nuclei have roughly equal numbers of protons and neutrons, usually with a slight excess of neutrons. Nuclei with the same number of protons but different numbers of neutrons are called *isotopes*.

Nuclei are held together by attractive forces that act between the quarks that make up the protons and neutrons. These attractive forces act roughly equally between protons and protons, protons and neutrons, and neutrons and neutrons. Thus it is common to use the collective term *nucleon* which does not distinguish between protons and neutrons. The mass of a nucleon is approximately one atomic mass unit (u). The attractive forces are extremely short range ($\approx 10^{-15}$ m), and essentially amount to a contact force between nucleons, as if

their 'surfaces' were 'sticky'. The *mass number* of a nucleus, A, is the total number of nucleons in a nucleus.

No stable nuclei are observed to exist with more than 83 protons; a fact which is ascribed to the strong electric repulsion between protons. The repulsive force on a proton within the nucleus is roughly proportional to $Z(Z-1)$. Thus, for example, the repulsive force on a proton in a nucleus for which $Z = 82$ is 74 times bigger than for $Z = 10$. Above $Z = 82$ the repulsive force between the protons overcomes the attractive forces between the quarks in the nucleons, and so the nucleus becomes unstable.

Nuclei are extremely small, with typical diameters of the order 10^{-14} m. At temperatures below about 10,000 K, electrons bind to nuclei until they become electrically neutral, i.e. until the number of electrons equals the number of protons. It is thought that the universe as a whole is electrically

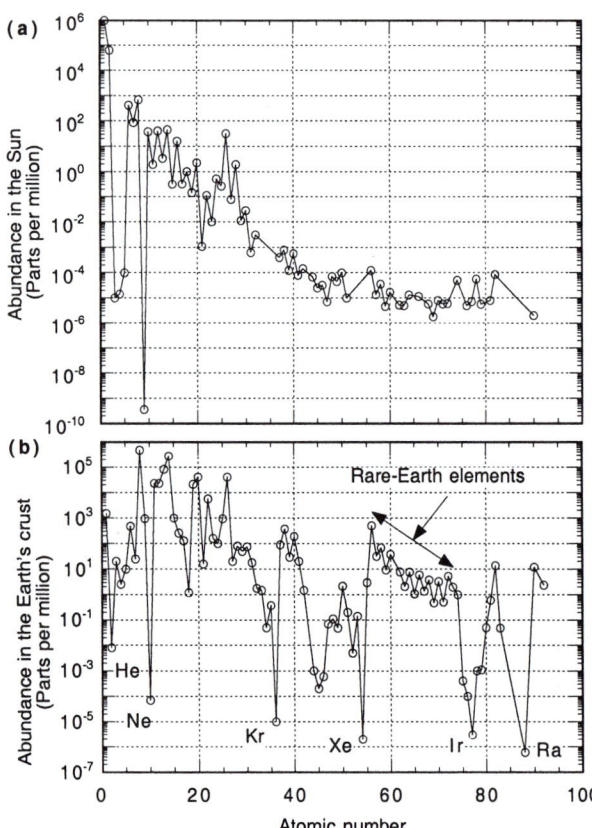

Figure 2.1 The relative abundance of the elements (a) in the outer part of the sun, and (b) in the solid, outer part of the Earth, its 'crust'. Notice that the vertical axis is logarithmic, so that points which are noticeably lower on the graph represent elements that are several orders of magnitude rarer than their neighbours.

The Sun is composed primarily of hydrogen, with all the other elements together accounting for only 6% of the total number of atoms. Further, with one or two exceptions, there is a relatively smooth variation with heavier nuclei becoming successively less common that lighter nuclei.

The distribution of elements in the Earth's crust is quite different from that in the Sun. Understanding the distribution of elements on Earth is considerably more difficult than for the Sun. For example, some of the rare elements in the Earth's crust are rare because they are chemically unreactive gases, which are relatively abundant in the Earth's atmosphere. This shows that the abundance of an element in the Earth's crust is not only related to the primordial composition of the Earth. Other factors are important, such as whether the element is a gas, liquid or solid at the Earth's mean temperature, or whether it will bind chemically with other elements. It is interesting to note that 'rare earth' elements are not particularly rare. Data from *Emsley* (§1.4.1)

9

neutral and that there are equal numbers of electrons and protons in existence. In this book, we restrict our study of matter to the temperature range below a few thousand kelvin. This excludes an explicit study of the state of matter known as a plasma because although it is by far the most common state of matter in the universe, it is relatively rare on our planet. The combination of a nucleus with sufficient electrons to achieve electrical neutrality is known as an *atom*.

2.2.3 Atoms

In later chapters, the arrangement of atoms in the different states of matter will be the main focus of our attention. Only occasionally will we refer separately to the existence of nuclei and their protons or neutrons. The structure of all atoms is broadly similar, consisting of two main features.

- A dense nucleus of A nucleons: Z protons and $(A - Z)$ neutrons. The nucleus therefore has an electric charge of $+Ze$, where e is the elementary charge on the proton, and an approximate mass of Au, where u is the atomic mass unit (see Table 2.1).

- A diffuse outer structure of Z electrons of total electric charge $-Ze$, held around the nucleus by electrical attraction to the oppositely-charged nucleus. The overall diameter of the electron structure is similar for most atoms and is $\approx 3 \times 10^{-10}$ m. The diameter of the electron structure around an atom is typically more than 10,000 times larger than the diameter of the nucleus.

A substance composed of only one type of atom only is called an *element*. Historically, it was through the realisation that some substances were elemental, and subsequent analysis of their properties that the basic properties of atoms were deduced. Table 2.2 lists the names and symbols of all the elements with atomic numbers up to 105.

Valence electrons

At separations greater than a few atomic diameters, atoms barely interact with one another. The interactions between atoms occur when they are brought close together and are caused *only by the electrical interactions between the atoms*. This single fact is worth repeating: the interactions between atoms are caused only by electrical interactions. The magnitude of the interaction is dominated by the outer part of the electronic structure around the atom. The electrons in the outer part of the structure are called *valence* electrons. The number and distribution of the valence electrons strongly affects the physical and chemical properties of atoms, and of the substances of which the atoms are a part.

Electrons tend to cluster around the nucleus in a sequence of spherically symmetric *shells*. This gives rise to a periodicity in the properties of atoms as function of Z, the number of electrons. For example, atoms with 2, 10, 18, 36, 54 and 86 electrons are able to pack electrons into successive shells with no electrons left over. Their physical and chemical properties are all strikingly similar, being the properties of atoms with no electrons outside a closed shell. Atoms with one electron outside a closed shell, i.e. those with 3, 11, 19, 37, 55 and 87 electrons also behave with striking similarity. For this reason, Mendeleyev and others grouped the elements into a so-called *Periodic Table* (Figure 2.2). In such a table, elements with similar properties, such as density, melting temperature, or chemical reactivity, were placed in columns. An example of the striking periodicity found in the properties of the elements can be seen in Figure 7.1, showing the densities of the solid elements as a function of atomic number.

Molecules and compounds

It is unusual on our planet to find matter in elemental form. Normally we encounter matter in which there are many types of atoms. The atoms are held together by electrical interactions between the outer electrons on each atom, known as *chemical bonds*. A set of atoms that are bonded together chemically is known as a molecule. Molecules range in size from two atoms to thousands of atoms. For example N_2, O_2 are two–atom molecules composed (as the subscript indicates) of two atoms of nitrogen and oxygen respectively. Examples of three atom molecules are H_2O (two atoms of hydrogen and one of oxygen) and CO_2 (one atom of carbon and two of oxygen). Molecules with thousands of atoms have chemical formulae which are too complicated to list here.

Figure 2.2. The periodic table of the elements. The shaded elements have only radioactive isotopes.

																1	2
																H	He

3	4												5	6	7	8	9	10
Li	Be												B	C	N	O	F	Ne
11	12												13	14	15	16	17	18
Na	Mg												Al	Si	P	S	Cl	Ar
19	20	21	22	23	24	25	26	27	28	29	30		31	32	33	34	35	36
K	Ca	Sc	Ti	V	Cr	Mn	Fe	Co	Ni	Cu	Zn		Ga	Ge	As	Se	Br	Kr
37	38	39	40	41	42	43	44	45	46	47	48		49	50	51	52	53	54
Rb	Sr	Y	Zr	Nb	Mo	Tc	Ru	Rh	Pd	Ag	Cd		In	Sn	Sb	Te	I	Xe
55	56		71	72	73	74	75	76	77	78	79	80	81	82	83	84	85	86
Cs	Ba		Lu	Hf	Ta	W	Re	Os	Ir	Pt	Au	Hg	Tl	Pb	Bi	Po	At	Rn
87	88		103	104	105	106	107	108	109									
Fr	Ra		Lr	Rf	Db	Sg	Bh	Hs	Mt									

57	58	59	60	61	62	63	64	65	66	67	68	69	70
La	Ce	Pr	Nd	Pm	Sm	Eu	Gd	Tb	Dy	Ho	Er	Tm	Yb
89	90	91	92	93	94	95	96	97	98	99	100	101	102
Ac	Th	Pa	U	Np	Pu	Am	Cm	Bk	Cf	Es	Fm	Md	No

Table 2.2. The elements with atomic numbers up to 105 together with their date of discovery. The term 'Old' as a date of discovery indicates that the element was known in antiquity. The names of the elements tell many fascinating stories about their discovery.

Z	Element, symbol, date of discovery	Origin of name
1	Hydrogen, H, (1766)	Greek: *Hydros Genes*: meaning Water Forming
2	Helium, He, (1895)	Greek: *Helios* meaning Sun
3	Lithium, Li, (1817)	Greek: *Lithos* meaning Stone
4	Beryllium, Be, (1797)	Greek: *Beryllos* meaning Beryl
5	Boron, B, (1808)	Arabic: *Buraq*
6	Carbon, C, (Old)	Latin: *Carbo* meaning Charcoal
7	Nitrogen, N, (1772)	Greek: *Nitron Genes* meaning Nitre Forming
8	Oxygen, O, (1774)	Greek: *Oxy Genes* meaning Acid Forming
9	Fluorine, F, (1886)	Latin: *Fluere* meaning To Flow
10	Neon, Ne, (1898)	Greek: *Neos* meaning New
11	Sodium, Na, (1807)	English: Soda: The symbol comes from the Latin *Natrium*
12	Magnesium, Mg, (1755)	Greek: Magnesia, a district in Thessaly
13	Aluminium, Al, (1825)	Latin: *alumen* meaning alum
14	Silicon, Si, , (1824)	Latin: *Silicis* meaning Flint
15	Phosphorus, P, (1669)	Greek: Phosphorus meaning Bringer of Light
16	Sulphur, S, (Old)	Sanskrit: *Sulvere* meaning Sulphur
17	Chlorine, Cl, (1774)	Greek: *Chloros* meaning Pale Green

Z	Element, symbol, date of discovery	Origin of name
18	Argon, Ar, (1894)	Greek: *Argos* meaning Inactive
19	Potassium, K, (1807)	English: Potash: The symbol comes from the Latin *Kalium*
20	Calcium, Ca, (1808)	Latin: *Calix* meaning Lime
21	Scandium, Sc, (1879)	Latin: *Scandia* meaning Scandinavia
22	Titanium, Ti, (1791)	*Titans*, Sons of the Earth Goddess.
23	Vanadium, V, (1801)	*Vanadis*, Scandinavian goddess
24	Chromium, Cr, (1780)	Greek: *Chroma* meaning Colour
25	Manganese, Mn, (1774)	Latin: *Magnes* meaning Magnet
26	Iron, Fe, (Old)	Saxon: Iron: The symbol comes from the Latin *Ferrum*
27	Cobalt, Co, (1735)	German: *kobald* meaning Goblin
28	Nickel, Ni, (1751)	German: *Kupfernickel* meaning either Devil's Copper or St Nicholas' Copper
29	Copper, Cu, (Old)	Latin: *Cuprum* meaning Cyprus
30	Zinc, Zn, (1400)	German: *Zink*
31	Gallium, Ga, (1875)	Latin: *Gallia* meaning France
32	Germanium, Ge, (1886)	Latin: *Germania* meaning German

11

Z	Element, symbol, date of discovery	Origin of name
33	Arsenic, As, (1280)	Greek: *Arsenikon* meaning Yellow Orpiment
34	Selenium, Se, (1817)	Greek: *Selene* meaning Moon
35	Bromine, Br, (1826)	Greek: *Bromos* meaning Stench
36	Krypton, Kr, (1898)	Greek: *Kryptos* meaning Hidden
37	Rubidium, Rb, (1861)	Latin: *Rubidius* meaning Deepest Red
38	Strontium, Sr, (1790)	English: *Strontian* in Scotland
39	Yttrium, Y, (1794)	The town of Ytterby in Sweden
40	Zirconium, Zr, (1789)	Arabic: *Zargun* meaning Gold Colour
41	Niobium, Nb, (1801)	Greek: *Niobe*, a daughter of Tantalus: Also called Columbium in USA
42	Molybdenum, Mo, (1781)	Greek: *Molybdos* meaning Lead
43	Technetium, Tc, (1937)	Greek: *Technikos* meaning Artificial
44	Ruthenium, Ru, (1808)	Latin: *Ruthenia* meaning Russia
45	Rhodium, Rh, (1803)	Greek: *Rhodon* meaning Rose
46	Palladium, Pd, (1803)	The asteroid *Pallas*
47	Silver, Ag, (Old)	Saxon: *Siolfur* meaning Silver: The symbol comes from the Latin *Argentum*
48	Cadmium, Cd, (1817)	Latin: *Cadmia* meaning *Calomine*
49	Indium, In, (1863)	Indigo
50	Tin, Sn, (Old)	Saxon: Tin: The symbol comes from the Latin *Stannum*
51	Antimony, Sb, (Old)	Greek: *Anti+Monos* meaning not alone. The symbol is from Latin *Stibium*
52	Tellurium, Te, (1783)	Latin: *Tellus* meaning Earth
53	Iodine, I, (1811)	Greek: *Iodes* meaning Violet
54	Xenon, Xe, (1898)	Greek: *Xenos* meaning Stranger
55	Caesium, Cs, (1860)	Latin: *Caesius* meaning Sky Blue
56	Barium, Ba, (1808)	Greek: *Barys* meaning Heavy
57	Lanthanum, La, (1839)	Greek: *Lanthanein* meaning To Lie Hidden
58	Cerium, Ce, (1803)	*Ceres*, an asteroid discovered in 1801
59	Praseodymium, Pr, (1885)	Greek: *Prasios Didymos* meaning Green Twin
60	Neodymium, Nd, (1885)	Greek: *Neos Didymos* meaning New Twin
61	Promethium, Pm, (1945)	Greek: *Prometheus*
62	Samarium, Sm, (1879)	The mineral Samarskite
63	Europium, Eu, (1901)	Europe
64	Gadolinium, Gd, (1880)	J. Gadolin, a Finnish chemist
65	Terbium, Tb, (1843)	The town of Ytterby in Sweden
66	Dysprosium, Dy, (1886)	Greek: *Dysprositos* meaning Hard To Obtain

Z	Element, symbol, date of discovery	Origin of name
67	Holmium, Ho, (1878)	Latin: *Holmia* meaning Stockholm
68	Erbium, Er, (1842)	The town of Ytterby in Sweden
69	Thulium, Tm, (1879)	*Thule*, meaning Ancient Scandinavia: The Uttermost North
70	Ytterbium, Yb, (1878)	The town of Ytterby in Sweden
71	Lutetium, Lu, (1907)	Latin: *Lutetia* meaning Paris
72	Hafnium, Hf, (1923)	Latin: *Hafnia* meaning Copenhagen
73	Tantalum, Ta, (1802)	Greek: *Tantalos*, the father of *Niobe*
74	Tungsten, W, (1783)	Swedish: *Tung Sten* meaning Heavy Stone: The symbol comes from the alternative name Wolfram
75	Rhenium, Re, (1925)	Latin: *Rhenus* meaning Rhine
76	Osmium, Os, (1803)	Greek: *Osme* meaning Smell
77	Iridium, Ir, (1803)	Latin: Iris meaning Rainbow
78	Platinum, Pt, (Old)	Spanish: *Platina* meaning Silver
79	Gold, Au, (Old)	Saxon: Gold
80	Mercury, Hg, (Old)	Latin: The planet Mercury: The symbol comes from the Latin *Hydragyrum* meaning Liquid Silver
81	Thallium, Tl, (1861)	Greek: *Thallos* meaning Green Twig
82	Lead, Pb, (Old)	Saxon: Lead: The symbol comes from the Latin *Plumbum*
83	Bismuth, Bi, (1450)	German: *Bisemutem*
84	Polonium, Po, (1898)	Poland
85	Astatine, At, (1940)	Greek: *Astatos* meaning unstable
86	Radon, Rn, (1900)	Radium
87	Francium, Fr, (1939)	France
88	Radium, Ra, (1898)	Latin: Radius meaning Ray
89	Actinium, Ac, (1899)	Greek: *aktinos* meaning Ray
90	Thorium, Th, (1815)	*Thor* The Scandinavian god of war
91	Protractinium, Pa, (1917)	Greek: *Protos* meaning First
92	Uranium, U, (1789)	The planet Uranus
93	Neptunium, Np, (1940)	The planet Neptune
94	Plutonium, Pu, (1940)	The planet Pluto
95	Americium, Am, (1944)	English: America
96	Curium, Cm, (1944)	Pierre and Marie Curie
97	Berkelium, Bk, (1949)	English: Berkeley
98	Californium, Cf, (1950)	English: California
99	Einsteinium, Es, (1952)	Albert Einstein
100	Fermium, Fm, (1952)	Enrico Fermi
101	Mendelevium, Md, (1955)	Dmitri Mendeleyev
102	Nobelium, No, (1958)	Alfred Nobel
103	Lawrencium, Lr, (1961)	Ernest O. Lawrence
104	Rutherfordium, Rf, (1964)	Ernest Rutherford
105	Dubnium, Db, (1967)	The town of Dubna, home to a centre for nuclear research

The phrase *chemical compound* generally refers to solids consisting of more than one type of atom, but for which there is no small group of atoms that may be considered independently. For example, carbon dioxide, CO_2, in its solid state would not be described as a compound. This is because even in its solid state the molecules are still clearly identifiable and interact only weakly with one other: it is thus referred to as a molecular solid. On the other hand, sodium chloride, NaCl, in its solid state is a chemical compound. This is because although its formula refers to only two atoms, each Na atom is bonded to six Cl atoms, and each Cl atom is bonded to six Na atoms. The bonding forms a network that extends throughout the solid.

Complex molecules

I have excluded from systematic inclusion in this book consideration of materials made from large complex molecules, i.e. those consisting of more than a small number of atoms. This is not because materials made from such molecules are not interesting; indeed the opposite is true. They are excluded because the study of their physical properties is still in its infancy and the variety of their properties is simply overwhelming. They are referred to in Chapters 8 and 9 on the properties of liquids (and liquid crystals) composed of organic molecules, and in passing at several other points.

2.3 The electromagnetic field

The matter of the world as we encounter it may be considered to be normally composed of atoms and molecules as described in §2.2.3. The primary method by which these atoms and molecules interact with one another is through the electromagnetic field, and in particular the electric aspect of the field

2.3.1 The concept of a field

It may be that you are not familiar with the concept of a field as a physical entity so let me start from the beginning. *Fields* are not composed of matter (electrons, protons and neutrons etc.), but they do still exist. Fields can be considered as a complementary component of the world to the particles of matter discussed in the previous section. Particles are localised with a relatively well-defined position whereas fields extend throughout all of space

Fields are found to affect matter, and matter to affect fields, and it is through their mutual effects that we determine the properties of both matter and fields. For example, consider two particles X and Y. We can imagine the interaction between X and Y as a three-stage process:
- Particle X affects the field around it,
- The disturbance of the field around X spreads away from X,
- A little later, particle Y is affected by the disturbance of the field created by X.

Notice that the field itself is not an observable 'object'. We infer its properties from systematic studies of the way one particle affects other particles around it. Currently we can explain all observable phenomena in the universe in terms of three different types of fields: the *gravitational*, *electroweak* and *colour* (or strong) fields. It is hoped that eventually all these fields will be understood as separate aspects of a single 'unified' field.

For our purposes, we need to examine the properties of only one of the above fields, the electroweak field. Before leaving the other two fields we note that:
- The colour field, while existing everywhere, acts only between particles that possess a property called *colour charge* and it is through this field that quarks interact with one another. As mentioned previously, the forces between quarks are extremely short range $\approx 10^{-15}$ m, and they thus act only within nuclei. In attempting to understand the properties of matter we ignore any processes that take place within nuclei and treat nuclei as if they were point masses with an electric charge $+Ze$.

- The gravitational field acts between all particles that possess mass, but its effects are generally negligible unless the masses involved are large, which will not happen over the length scales that we are interested in. We do however use the fact that particles possess mass, but only to discuss the way in which their motion is affected under the action of electrical forces. In other words we use mass in the sense of *inertial* mass, but not *gravitational* mass.

We note that we will be unable to understand some quite common phenomena, such as radioactivity or convection, without recourse to explanations that involve these two fields. However, to understand most properties of the matter which we find around us we need concern ourselves only with the electroweak field. In fact, in the regions in which we shall be discussing it, the 'weak' part of this field represents only a tiny correction to the 'electro' part of the field. The 'weak' part of the field causes a small difference between the interactions of:

- electrons which move with their internal spin axis oriented in the same direction as their direction of motion

and

- electrons which move with their internal spin axis oriented in the opposite direction as their direction of motion.

We will neglect these small effects caused by the 'weak' aspect of the field entirely and concentrate on the 'electro' part of the field, conventionally called the *electromagnetic field*.

2.3.2 Electric fields and forces

In what follows we consider the electric part of the electromagnetic field, and look at results for the properties of isolated electric charges, electric dipoles and their interaction with electric fields. I have followed the phraseology of electromagnetism textbooks in using phrases such as "a charge of 0.01 coulomb is placed at…". In this context I would like to remind you that there is no such thing as 'a charge': when the phrase is used it is shorthand for 'a particle of matter with a charge of…'. Electric charge is property of matter, and cannot be isolated from it.

Electric charges

Force on an electric charge q in an electric field

The electric field $\mathbf{E}$ in the region of a point charge of magnitude q is given by:

$$\mathbf{E} = \frac{q}{4\pi\varepsilon_0 r^2}\hat{\mathbf{r}} \qquad (2.1)$$

where r is the distance from the point charge, and $\hat{\mathbf{r}}$ is a unit vector from q to the point under consideration. The constant ε_0 (pronounced 'epsilon zero') is a universal constant known as *the permittivity of free space* and has the value $\varepsilon_0 = 8.854 \times 10^{-12}$ F m^{-1}. (The units F m^{-1} are Farads per metre.) The force $\mathbf{F}$ on a charge q_1 in an electric field $\mathbf{E}$ is given by:

$$\mathbf{F} = q_1\mathbf{E} \qquad (2.2)$$

and so the force on a point charge q_1 a distance r from q is given by combining 2.1 and 2.2 to give:

$$\mathbf{F} = \frac{q_1 q}{4\pi\varepsilon_0 r^2}\hat{\mathbf{r}} \qquad (2.3)$$

The electrical force $\mathbf{F}$ described in Equation 2.3 is sometimes referred to as the *Coulomb force*. The potential energy of the two charges is:

$$u = \frac{q_1 q}{4\pi\varepsilon_0 r} \qquad (2.4)$$

The potential energy per unit charge, the *electric*

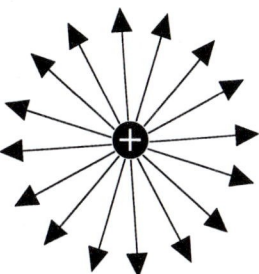

Figure 2.3 Conventional illustration of the electric field in the region of a positive point charge. The arrowed lines indicate the direction of the electric field, and their closeness indicates the intensity (strength) of the electric field.

Example 2.1

What is the electric field a distance 10^{-10} m from a proton?

The field is given by Equation 2.1 with:
$q = +1.6 \times 10^{-19}$ C
$r = 1 \times 10^{-10}$ m
We thus have:

$$E = \frac{1.6 \times 10^{-19}}{4\pi \times 8.85 \times 10^{-12} \times \left(10^{-10}\right)^2}$$

$$= +1.44 \times 10^{11} \text{ V m}^{-1}$$

This field is *enormous* in comparison to the electric fields commonly experienced in laboratories.

---

potential, around charge q is u/q_1, i.e.

$$V = \frac{q}{4\pi\varepsilon_o r} \tag{2.5}$$

Electric dipoles

In the study of matter, we frequently need to consider electrical charges that are grouped together so as to remain electrically neutral overall. However, for a variety of reasons, the positive and negative electrical charges may not be distributed such that they have the same centre of symmetry. For example, in the absences of an applied electric field, atoms and molecules are generally electrically neutral. However, in an applied electric field, the electrons and nuclei of all atoms move in opposite directions and the atom or molecule then acquires a so-called *electric dipole moment*. Sometimes the distribution of electric charge within some molecules is such that the molecules possess intrinsic electric dipole moments even in the absence of an applied electric field.

A simple electric dipole moment is illustrated in Figure 2.4 (a). The electric dipole moment considered as vector is given by:

$$\mathbf{p} = q\mathbf{d} \tag{2.6}$$

where **d** is a vector from the negative charge centre to the positive charge centre. The electric dipole moment has magnitude:

Example 2.2

Calculate the force, acceleration, and potential energy of an electron a distance 10^{-10} m from a proton. This distance is typical of separations between charges found in atoms. From Table 2.1 we see that protons possess an electric charge $+e$ and electrons possess an electric charge $-e$ where e has the value 1.6×10^{-19} C.

The force is given by Equation 2.3 with $q_1 = -1.6 \times 10^{-19}$ C, $q = +1.6 \times 10^{-19}$ C and $r = 10^{-10}$ m . We thus have:

$$F = \frac{-1.6 \times 10^{-19} \times 1.6 \times 10^{-19}}{4\pi \times 8.85 \times 10^{-12} \times (10^{-10})^2}$$

$$= -2.31 \times 10^{-8} \text{N}$$

where the negative sign indicates that the force is attractive. The force acts attractively along the line joining the two particles.

The acceleration of an electron is given by Newton's third law $a = F/m$ and so since $m_e = 9.1 \times 10^{-31}$ kg. We thus have:

$$a = \frac{F}{m} = \frac{-2.31 \times 10^{-8}}{9.1 \times 10^{-31}}$$

$$= -2.53 \times 10^{22} \text{ ms}^{-2}$$

Notice the colossal magnitude of this acceleration in comparison with the accelerations we experience daily $\approx g \approx 10 \text{ ms}^{-2}$.

The potential energy of the electron–proton pair is given by Equation 2.4 so we have:

$$u = \frac{-1.6 \times 10^{-19} \times 1.6 \times 10^{-19}}{4\pi \times 8.85 \times 10^{-12} \times 10^{-10}}$$

$$= -2.31 \times 10^{-18} \text{J}$$

where the negative sign indicates attraction. In other words the particles have a lower energy than if they were separated by a large distance. The small energies involved in Coulomb interactions between electrons and protons are often expressed in units of electron volts where:

$$1 \text{ eV} = 1.6 \times 10^{-19} \text{ J}$$

In these units the energy of interaction of a proton and electron separated by 10^{-10} m is:

$$u = \frac{-2.31 \times 10^{-18}}{1.6 \times 10^{-19}} = -14.4 \text{ eV}$$

$$p = qd \qquad (2.7)$$

Force on an electric dipole p in an electric field

As illustrated in Figure 2.4 (b) the net force on an electric dipole in a uniform electric field is zero, because the force on each component of the dipole cancels.

$$\mathbf{F} = 0 \qquad (2.8)$$

Torque on an electric dipole p in an electric field

As illustrated in Figure 2.4 (b), although a uniform electric field exerts no force on an electric dipole, it does exert a torque. The torque Γ is perpendicular to both $\mathbf{E}$ and $\mathbf{p}$ and is given by the vector product:

$$\Gamma = \mathbf{p} \times \mathbf{E} \qquad (2.9)$$

which has magnitude:

$$\Gamma = pE\sin\theta \qquad (2.10)$$

where θ is the angle between $\mathbf{p}$ and $\mathbf{E}$.

Electric field due an electric dipole

As well as being subject to forces and torques in electric fields, electric dipoles also act as sources of electric fields. At distances r greater than d (the separation of the charges in the dipole) the electric potential due the dipole may be written approximately as:

Example 2.3

In a carbon monoxide (CO) molecule, slightly more electric charge clusters around the oxygen atom than the carbon due to details of structure of electronic orbits around C and O atoms. The molecule thus has a 'built-in' electric dipole moment of approximately 0.1×10^{-30} Cm. (The unit of 1×10^{-30} Cm is typical of the electric dipole moments found in molecules and is sometimes called a *debye* unit. CO has an electric dipole moment of 0.1 debye.) Estimate the torque on a CO molecule in an electric of 1000 Vm^{-1}.

Assuming the moment is oriented perpendicular to the field, then Γ is given by:

$$\Gamma \approx pE = 0.1 \times 10^{-30} \times 10^3$$

$$= 10^{-28} \text{ Nm}$$

Notice that 1000 V m^{-1} is not a particularly strong electric field. It corresponds to the electric field between two plates 1 mm apart with a potential difference of 1 volt. As we saw in Example 2.1, the field near a proton is $\approx 10^{11}$ V m^{-1}.

$$V = \frac{\mathbf{p} \cdot \hat{\mathbf{r}}}{4\pi\varepsilon_o r^2} \qquad (2.11)$$

where $\mathbf{p}$ is defined in Equation 2.6 and $\hat{\mathbf{r}}$ is a unit vector from the dipole centre to the position at which the potential is evaluated. The electric field of a dipole (Figure 2.4(d)) is related to the gradient of the potential function and varies roughly as $1/r^3$.

(a)

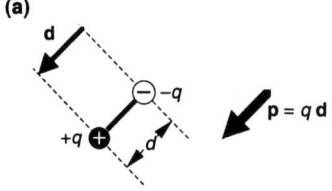

Figure 2.4 (a) An electric dipole consists of two equal and opposite charges and its magnitude p, the *electric dipole moment*, has magnitude $p = qd$. As a vector, it is considered to point from the negative to the positive charge. (b) In a uniform applied electric field, an electric dipole experiences no net force, but (c) is subject to a torque $\Gamma = pE\sin\theta$. (d) Electric field lines in the region of an electric dipole.

(b)

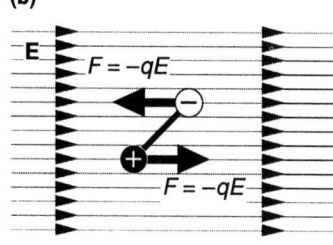

(c)

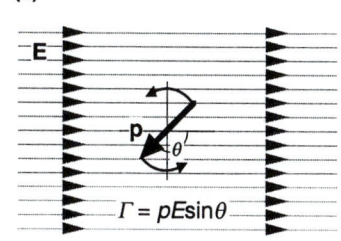

(d)

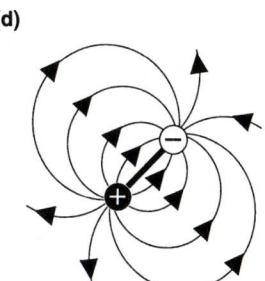

16

Electric dipole induced by an electric field

In the absence of an electric field, all atoms and many molecules have no electric dipole moment. However, in the presence of an applied electric field $\mathbf{E}$, a dipole moment $\mathbf{p}_i$ is *induced* on *all* atoms and molecules. The electric dipole moment induced on a molecule is related to the applied field $\mathbf{E}$ by:

$$\mathbf{p}_i = \alpha\mathbf{E} \tag{2.12}$$

where α is the *molecular polarisability*, which has a characteristic value for each type of atom or molecule.

Electric fields and matter

Only very occasionally do we observe the effect of an electric field in a vacuum. Generally, we observe electric fields through their effect on matter. In the presence of matter, the electric field is modified compared to how it would have been if the matter had not been there. In general, the field is reduced in value. This change is characterised by the *dielectric constant* ε of the substance in question. For a vacuum, $\varepsilon = 1$, and as long as the charges on question are not oscillating, we find that in general $\varepsilon > 1$. For substances such as air, ε has a value of around 1.001; for solid insulating substances such as glass, ε has a wide range of values, usually in the range 1.1 to 10. For metals, ε is effectively infinite since charges can move within metals to almost perfectly screen the effect of a charge.

To modify the formulae in Equations 2.1 to 2.5 for use within matter, the general rule is as follows: find ε_0 in the formula and replace it with $\varepsilon\varepsilon_0$.

Magnetic dipoles and forces

A summary of the properties of magnetic dipoles, and of forces on electric charges in a magnetic field, can be found on the Web in Chapter W2 on the magnetic properties of solids.

2.3.3 Changes in electromagnetic fields

The speed of light in a vacuum

The speed of electromagnetic disturbances in a region of the electric field in which there is no matter (a vacuum) is a universal constant c. In the *SI* system of units, this is defined to be exactly $2997922458.0 \text{ ms}^{-1}$ or roughly $2.998 \times 10^8 \text{ m s}^{-1}$. The theory of electromagnetic wave propagation predicts that c is related to other constants that characterise the electric field in a vacuum by:

$$c = \frac{1}{\sqrt{\varepsilon_0\mu_0}} \tag{2.13}$$

where μ_0 is a constant known as the *permeability of free space* and ε_0 is the permittivity of free space. Since $\varepsilon_0 = 8.854 \times 10^{-12} \text{ F m}^{-1}$, μ_0 (pronounced 'mew zero') has the value:

$$\mu_0 = \frac{1}{c^2\varepsilon_0}$$
$$= 1.257 \times 10^{-6} \text{ H m}^{-1} \tag{2.14}$$

Interestingly, from a historical point of view, this value of μ_0 is exactly equal to $4\pi \times 10^{-7} \text{ H m}^{-1}$. (The units H m^{-1} are Henrys per metre).

The constants ε_0 and μ_0

ε_0 is a constant of proportionality that characterises the strength of the electric field produced by a given charge. For example, in a hypothetical universe in which ε_0 was little smaller than it is in our universe, electric charges would induce slightly more intense electric fields than they do in our universe. Similarly, if μ_0 was a little smaller than it is in our universe, electric currents would create slightly larger magnetic fields than they do in our universe. Bearing these rough definitions in mind we can see that Equation 2.13 states that the speed of an electromagnetic disturbance in free space is inversely proportional to the square root of the 'spring constants' for the electromagnetic field.

The speed of light in a material substance

The speed v of electromagnetic disturbances through a region containing matter varies with the frequency of the disturbance and with properties of the matter through which the disturbance passes. The theory of electromagnetic wave propagation predicts that v is given by:

$$v = \frac{1}{\sqrt{\varepsilon \varepsilon_o \mu \mu_o}} \qquad (2.15)$$

where μ is the *relative magnetic permeability* and ε is the *relative dielectric permittivity* (sometimes called the *dielectric constant*) of the substance. Commonly μ has a value very close to unity in which case Equation 2.15 may be written approximately as:

$$v = \frac{c}{\sqrt{\varepsilon}} \qquad (2.16)$$

The ratio of the speed of light in free space, to the speed of light in a material, is known as the refractive index of a material, n_{light}. We can thus note that the refractive index of a non-magnetic substance is given by:

$$n_{\text{light}} = \frac{c}{v} \qquad (2.17)$$
$$\approx \sqrt{\varepsilon}$$

As we shall see when we examine data on the subject in section §5.8.2, §7.9.5 and §9.13.2, Equation 2.17 does not always hold. In general, we will be able to understand this by realising that ε can change with frequency.

The electromagnetic spectrum

When charged particles are accelerated or decelerated, an electromagnetic disturbance spreads outward from the particle at the speed of light. Commonly the acceleration is periodic, resulting from a simple harmonic motion of the charge. In such a case, the electromagnetic disturbance has a well-defined frequency f and wavelength λ. Table 2.3 illustrates the different names given to disturbances in different frequency ranges.

Table 2.3 Photon energies, frequencies, and wavelengths.

Frequency (Hz)	Wavelength (m)	Energy (eV)	Comment
10^6	3×10^2	4.14×10^{-9}	Radio broadcasts
10^7	3×10^1	4.14×10^{-8}	
10^8	3	4.14×10^{-7}	Television broadcasts
10^9	3×10^{-1}	4.14×10^{-6}	A gigahertz: microwave ovens and mobile phones
10^{10}	3×10^{-2}	4.14×10^{-5}	Infra-red
10^{11}	3×10^{-3}	4.14×10^{-4}	Infra-red
10^{12}	3×10^{-4}	4.14×10^{-3}	A terahertz: Infra-red: Typical frequency of atomic vibration
6.6×10^{12}	4.55×10^{-4}	2.5×10^{-2}	Infra-red: corresponds to processes occurring at around room temperature (290K)
10^{13}	3×10^{-5}	4.14×10^{-2}	Infra-red
4×10^{14}	7.5×10^{-7}	1.654	Red light: Corresponds to processes involving electrons in the outer (valence) shells of atoms
10^{15}	3×10^{-7}	4.14	Blue light: corresponds to processes involving electrons in the outer (valence) shells of atoms
10^{16}	3×10^{-8}	4.14×10^1	Ultra-violet light
10^{17}	3×10^{-9}	4.14×10^2	Ultra-violet light
10^{18}	3×10^{-10}	4.14×10^3	Ultra-violet light
10^{19}	3×10^{-11}	4.14×10^4	X-rays
10^{20}	3×10^{-12}	4.14×10^5	X-rays: corresponds to processes involving electrons in the inner shells of atoms
10^{21}	3×10^{-13}	4.14×10^6	X-rays
10^{22}	3×10^{-14}	4.14×10^7	X-rays
10^{23}	3×10^{-15}	4.14×10^8	Gamma rays: Corresponds to processes that occur within nuclei

Photons

The electromagnetic field can gain or lose energy only in small packets called photons. The energy E required to create a photon with a frequency f is given by:

$$E = hf \qquad (2.18)$$

where h is a universal constant known as the *Planck constant*, with the value 1.054×10^{-34} J s. The magnitude of the energy required to excite photons of different frequencies and wavelengths is summarised in Table 2.3.

2.4 Classical and quantum mechanics

2.4.1 Classical mechanics *or* quantum mechanics?

Classical mechanics concerns itself with the motion of 'relatively large' particles of matter. *Quantum mechanics* is concerned with the motion of particles of matter of all sizes, but is used mainly when the particles involved are 'relatively small'. Where to draw the distinction between 'relatively small' and 'relatively large' is a subject of both physical and philosophical controversy. Broadly speaking, particles larger than a few atomic diameters in size ($\approx 10^{-9}$ m to 10^{-8} m) may be treated classically, whereas particles smaller than this must be treated using quantum mechanics. However, this is not a hard and fast rule. Even for atomic sized particles, classical mechanics can give 'a feel' for a problem, and is often useful for obtaining order-of-magnitude estimates. Similarly, there are occasions where quantum mechanics is necessary to understand macroscopic phenomena.

2.4.2 Classical mechanics

'Laws of motion'

Classically, particles are assumed to obey the three 'laws of motion' first enunciated clearly by Isaac Newton. The first and second laws may be summarised as:

$$\mathbf{F} = m\mathbf{a} \qquad (2.19)$$

where $\mathbf{F}$ is the force acting on a body of mass m and $\mathbf{a}$ is the resulting acceleration. Equation 2.19 may be restated in terms of momentum $\mathbf{p}$, velocity $\mathbf{v}$, or position $\mathbf{r}$:

$$\mathbf{F} = \frac{d\mathbf{p}}{dt}$$
$$= m\frac{d\mathbf{v}}{dt} \qquad (2.20)$$
$$= m\frac{d^2\mathbf{r}}{dt^2}$$

If we rewrite the first equality in Equation 2.20 for short times, we find an expression which allows us to estimate $\mathbf{F}$ when a particle changes momentum by $\Delta\mathbf{p}$ in a short time Δt:

$$\mathbf{F} \approx \frac{\Delta\mathbf{p}}{\Delta t} \qquad (2.21)$$

This formula is useful when considering the impacts between colliding particles.

Simple harmonic oscillator

The motion of many objects may be described (to some extent at least) as being similar to that of an idealised *simple harmonic oscillator*. In a simple harmonic oscillator, a particle is attracted to a central position x_0 by a force which increases linearly with increasing displacement from x_0, i.e.

$$F = -K(x - x_0) \qquad (2.22)$$

The proportionality constant K in Equation 2.22 is generally known as the 'spring constant' of the oscillator. The larger the value of K, the greater the force attempting to restore the particle to position x_0. The potential energy of the particle in a simple harmonic oscillator is given by:

$$V = \tfrac{1}{2}K(x - x_0)^2 + V_0 \qquad (2.23)$$

where V_0 is energy of the particle when it is at rest at $x = x_0$.

Natural oscillations

A particle in a simple harmonic oscillator potential has a natural frequency of oscillation f_0. This natural frequency arises from the combination of the mass m of the oscillating particle and the spring constant K with which it is attracted to x_0. When a particle has a large mass, a given spring will return the particle to x_0 more slowly than it would a particle of low mass. Similarly, for a given particle mass, a 'stiff' spring with a large spring constant will return a particle to the origin more quickly than a 'floppy' spring with a small spring constant. The natural frequency of oscillation is given by the surprisingly simple expression:

$$f_0 = \frac{1}{2\pi}\sqrt{\frac{K}{m}} \qquad (2.24)$$

The natural frequency may also be expressed in terms of angular frequency ω (pronounced 'omega') as:

$$\omega_o = \sqrt{\frac{K}{m}} \qquad (2.25)$$

Forced oscillations: resonance

If the particle is subject to an externally applied force oscillating with angular frequency ω_o then the amplitude of the resulting oscillations shows a pronounced maximum when $\omega = \omega_o$, a phenomenon known as *resonance*. In order to calculate the oscillation amplitude at resonance, we must take account of the loss of energy from the oscillator system. The process of energy loss from the oscillations may often be fairly represented by a damping (or frictional) force proportional to the particle velocity v:

$$F = -\alpha v \qquad (2.26)$$

Notice the minus sign in Equation 2.26, which indicates that the damping force always acts in the opposite direction to the direction of motion. The term α (pronounced 'alpha') is large when the oscillations are heavily damped. If the applied (driving) force has the form:

$$F = F_o \cos(\omega t) \qquad (2.27)$$

then the particle position varies as:

$$x = A\cos(\omega t + \phi) \qquad (2.28)$$

The amplitude of oscillation A is given by:

$$A = \frac{F_o / m}{\sqrt{\left(\omega_o^2 - \omega^2\right)^2 + 4\left(\frac{\alpha}{2m}\right)^2 \omega^2}} \qquad (2.29)$$

and the phase difference ϕ (pronounced 'phi') between the particle motion and the applied force satisfies:

$$\tan\phi = \frac{\alpha\omega}{m\left(\omega_o^2 - \omega^2\right)}$$
$$= \frac{\alpha f}{2\pi m\left(f_o^2 - f^2\right)} \qquad (2.30)$$

Examples of the application of equations 2.29 and 2.30 are illustrated in Figure 2.6. There are two key features of these results that are worthy of notice. The first feature (Figure 2.6a) is the resonantly large amplitude of the vibrations of the particle when the forcing frequency f is close to its natural frequency of oscillation f_o. The second feature (Figure 2.6b) concerns the phase difference between the particle motion and the driving force, F. Notice that if the frequency of the driving force is well below f_o, the particles oscillate essentially

Figure 2.5 Simple harmonic oscillator. (a) A particle trapped by springs in a physical situation that would result in simple harmonic motion. (b) The force on a particle as a function of its displacement. The three lines correspond to three different values of K, the 'spring constant', with the steepest lines representing the stiffest spring. (c) The potential energy of a particle as a function of its displacement. The three curves correspond to different values of K, the 'spring constant', with the narrowest, most strongly curving parabola representing the stiffest spring.

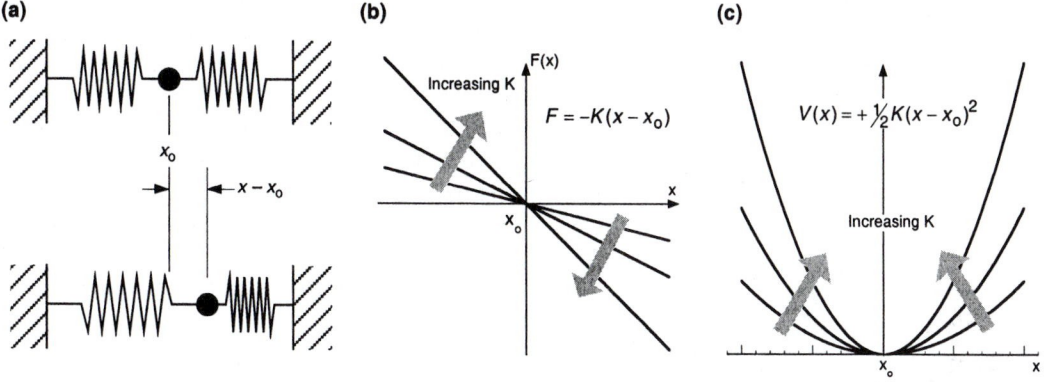

in phase with the driving force. However, if the frequency of the driving force is well above f_0, the particles oscillate essentially 180° *out of phase* with the driving force.

Small simple harmonic oscillators: electrons and atoms

The resonant frequency of a particle of mass m in a simple harmonic oscillator of spring constant K is given by:

$$\omega_0 = \sqrt{\frac{K}{m}} \qquad (2.25^*)$$

Because ω_0 is inversely proportional to m, the resonant frequencies of particles of atomic mass may be very large. The 'spring constants' that keep electrons and atoms in place in a solid are rather difficult to calculate accurately, but are generally of a similar order to those found in common household and industrial springs. Typical values lie in the range from 100 N m^{-1} to 1000 N m^{-1} (Example 2.5).

The forces acting on electrons and ions originate solely from their Coulomb interaction, and since electrons and ions have charges of a similar magnitude ($\pm e$) they have 'spring constants' of a similar magnitude. The 'spring constants' binding electrons to ions, and the low mass of the electron, yield resonant frequencies in the range 10^{15} Hz to 10^{16} Hz. Electromagnetic waves with these frequencies lie in the optical and ultra-violet regions of the electromagnetic spectrum. However, atoms or ions are typically 10^4 times heavier than electrons, and so their resonant frequencies are of the order of $\sqrt{10^4} = 10^2$ times lower than the resonant frequencies of electrons. Consequently, ions and atoms have resonant frequencies in the range 10^{13} to 10^{14} Hz. Electromagnetic waves with these frequencies lie in the infra-red region of the electromagnetic spectrum.

However, in order to describe small simple harmonic oscillators *accurately*, we must use the quantum mechanical description outlined in the following section.

Figure 2.6 The response of a simple harmonic oscillator to an applied oscillating force. The oscillator has a low damping coefficient $\alpha = 0.02$, a spring constant $K = 1$, and the response is depicted for particles of three different masses, $m = 0.5$, $m = 1.0$, $m = 2.0$.

(a) The amplitude of the oscillations as a function of frequency. Notice the increase in the resonant frequency as the mass of the particle decreases. Notice also the increase in the low frequency amplitude as the mass decreases. (b) The phase ϕ of the oscillations as a function of frequency. At frequencies much less than the resonant frequency, the particle oscillates essentially in phase with the applied force. The graphs in (a) and (b) were calculated using a spreadsheet program to evaluate Equations 2.36 and 2.37 at a set of closely spaced frequencies.

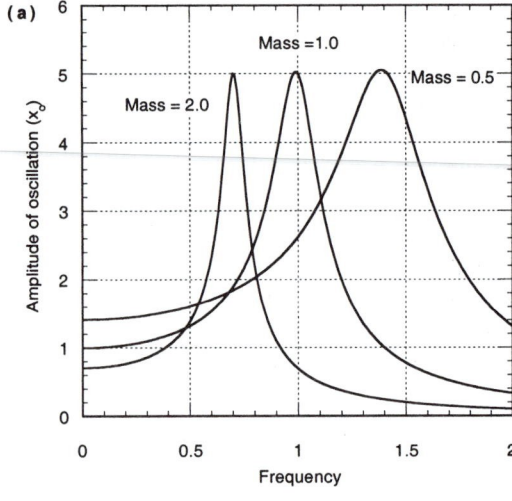

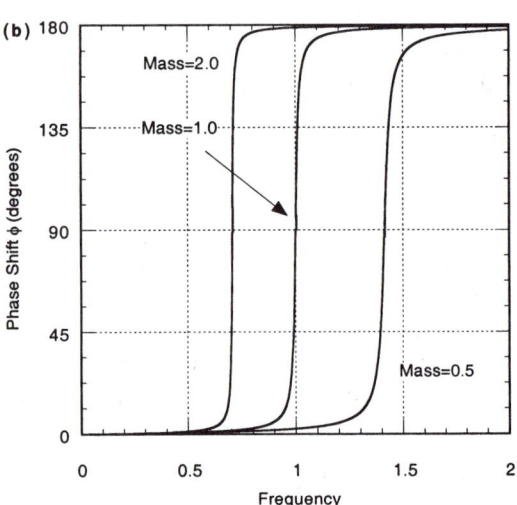

2.4.3 Quantum mechanics

Quantum states

Classically a particle may be described by listing the values of its physical properties, for example its mass, position, momentum, energy, electric dipole moment and so on. Taken together, these properties constitute a specification of the *state* of a particle. The laws of classical mechanics describe the way in which the state of a particle changes with time.

In quantum mechanics, we use the concept of a *quantum state* to describe the possible states of a particle. The laws of quantum mechanics describe which states are physically realistic, and specify the ways in which a particle moves from one quantum state to another. Each quantum state is characterised by a *unique* set of *quantum numbers* that 'index' the quantum state. Sometimes quantum numbers have continuously variable values, but commonly quantum numbers are restricted to a set of discrete values, i.e. values outside this set do not describe physically realistic quantum states. For example, for a particle of mass m confined to a cubic box of side L, the physically realistic quantum states have energies described by:

$$E(n_x, n_y, n_z) = \frac{h^2}{8mL^2}\left[n_x^2 + n_y^2 + n_z^2\right] \qquad (2.31)$$

where h is the *Planck constant* and n_x, n_y, n_z are the quantum numbers that uniquely label each particular quantum state.

Importantly, we frequently discuss the properties of a quantum state even if no particle is actually occupying the state. (Figure 2.7 (a) and (b)). Although this seems strange at first, it is merely analogous to (say) discussing the potential merits of theatre seats even when no one is sitting in them. Thus, in addition to specifying the properties of quantum states, we then describe a physical situation by specifying which quantum states are occupied.

It is also important to note that a quantum state can describe a *state of motion*. Thus a particle in a quantum state (and remaining in that state) may

---

Example 2.4

A diatomic molecule of nitrogen consists of two atoms of nitrogen of mass $m = 14 \times 1.66 \times 10^{-27}$kg. The distribution of electric charge throughout the molecule which has the minimum Coulomb energy is illustrated right. Vibrations of such molecules are observed to take place with resonant frequencies of the order of 10^{13} Hz.

IN EQUILIBRIUM

During these vibrations, the charge distribution changes and Coulomb forces act to restore the atoms to their minimum energy position. These vibrations may be modelled as a simple harmonic oscillator with spring constant K.

VIBRATIONS OF THE MOLECULE

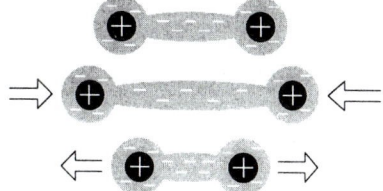

What is the approximate value of K?

Our model of the molecule is illustrated above, and we can use Equation 2.24 to estimate the resonant frequency f_o.

$$f_o = \frac{1}{2\pi}\sqrt{\frac{K}{m}} .$$

We can re-arrange this to yield an expression for K:

$$K = 2\pi m f_o^2 .$$

Substitution into this expression yields

$$K = 2\pi \times 14 \times 1.66 \times 10^{-27} \times \left[10^{13}\right]^2$$

$$= 91.7 \ \text{Nm}^{-1}$$

Note The correct mass to use in the calculation is actually the so-called *reduced mass* of the particle:

$$m_R = (1/m + 1/m)^{-1}$$

$$= m/2$$

However this does not affect the order of magnitude of the answer and so we conclude that for resonant frequencies in the region of 10^{13} Hz, K is of the order of 100 Nm^{-1}. It is interesting, and not entirely coincidental, to note that values of this order of magnitude are similar to those found in ordinary springs.

---

have a velocity. This is particularly significant in discussing the quantum states of electrons near atoms. Classically we describe the electrons as 'orbiting' the atom and indeed the quantum states are often called *orbitals*. This implies that the classical state of the particle is changing as it moves around the nucleus. However, quantum mechanically this 'state of motion' is simply described by specifying the quantum state which corresponds to that 'state of motion'.

Quantum states and energy levels

In any particular physical situation, there are in general many possible quantum states that a particle may occupy (Figure 2.7c). It is possible to have several quantum states that all have the same energy, although other properties of the quantum states will be different. Quantum states with the same energy are said to belong to the same *energy level*. An energy level with more than one quantum state is, curiously, said to be *degenerate*.

The wave function

Each quantum state has associated with it a wave function $\Psi(\mathbf{r},t)$ (Ψ is pronounced 'psi'). The wave function is a complex function, i.e. it has two components, a real part Ψ_r and an imaginary part Ψ_i. Please note that the technical mathematical terms 'real' and 'imaginary' can be used to describe many two-component quantities: the terms do not refer to the 'existence' (ontology) of

the components of the wave function. The probability of finding a particle in a region of space of volume $\mathbf{dr}$ around a position $\mathbf{r}$ is given by:

$$P(\mathbf{r})d\mathbf{r} = |\Psi(\mathbf{r})|^2 d\mathbf{r}$$
$$= \Psi^*(\mathbf{r})\Psi(\mathbf{r})d\mathbf{r} \qquad (2.32)$$
$$= \left[\Psi_r^2 + \Psi_i^2\right]d\mathbf{r}$$

where $\Psi^*(\mathbf{r})$ is the complex conjugate of $\Psi(\mathbf{r})$. Since the particle must be somewhere, the integral of $P(\mathbf{r})$ over all space must equal unity, i.e.

$$\int_{\text{all space}} P(\mathbf{r})d\mathbf{r} = \int_{\text{all space}} |\Psi(\mathbf{r})|^2 d\mathbf{r} = 1 \qquad (2.33)$$

This property is a key feature of the quantum mechanical description of matter: the probability of finding a particle near a particular position is related to the value of $|\Psi(\mathbf{r})|^2$ near that position.

The Schrödinger equation

Erwin Schrödinger has given his name to two equations relevant to our discussion of wave functions. These are the *time-independent Schrödinger equation* and the *time-dependent Schrödinger equation*. The first equation determines the form of the wave functions which correspond to particular allowed quantum states, and the second governs how a wave function evolves in time. In this book we will be mainly concerned with the

Figure 2.7 A simple representation of a collection of quantum states. Each line represents a particular quantum state, and its vertical position represents its energy. A filled circle indicates that the quantum state is occupied. (a) A set of quantum states with different energies. (b) The same set of states with just one state occupied. (c) A different set of quantum states, again with only one state occupied. Notice that at some energies there are several distinct quantum states, i.e. some of the *energy levels* are degenerate.

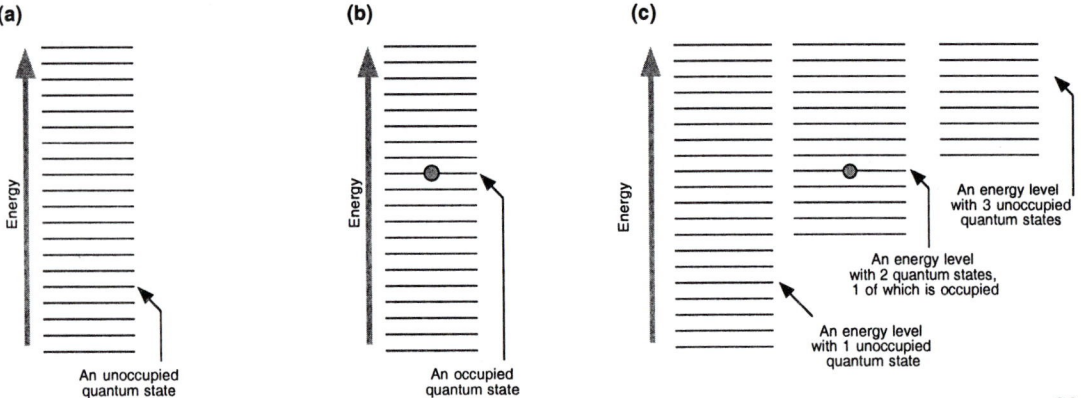

time-independent Schrödinger Equation, which is:

$$\frac{-\hbar^2}{2m}\nabla^2\Psi(\mathbf{r})+V(\mathbf{r})\Psi(\mathbf{r})=E\Psi(\mathbf{r}) \qquad (2.34)$$

or in one dimension:

$$\frac{-\hbar^2}{2m}\frac{\partial^2}{\partial x^2}\Psi(x)+V(x)\Psi(x)=E\Psi(x) \qquad (2.35)$$

In equations 2.34 and 2.35

- $V(\mathbf{r})$ is the function describing how the potential energy of the particle varies with position, e.g. for a one-dimensional harmonic oscillator $V(x)=\frac{1}{2}K(x-x_{\mathrm{o}})^2$.
- m is the mass of the particle under discussion.
- $\partial^2\Psi(x)/\partial x^2$ is the second derivative of the wave function. Colloquially the second derivative of a function is known as its *curvature*.
- E is the total energy of the particle under discussion.

At each point in space, the Schrödinger equation determines the relative values of the curvature of the wave function and its magnitude in terms of the energy E of the wave function. Suppose a given wave function (E fixed) has amplitude Ψ_{a} at position x_{a}, in a region of low potential energy. Suppose now that at position b the potential energy V is larger than at a. The Schrödinger equation (Figure 2.9) tells us that at b either the amplitude of the wave function must be reduced, or the curvature must be lessened. Finding solutions to the Schrödinger equation is in general quite tricky. Below we list a few solutions appropriate to some of the situations we shall encounter in later chapters.

Examples of quantum mechanics

A free particle

For a particle in free space the potential energy is a constant V_{o} independent of position. If this is the case then the Schrödinger equation:

$$\frac{-\hbar^2}{2m}\frac{\partial^2}{\partial x^2}\Psi(x)+V(x)\Psi(x)=E\Psi(x) \qquad (*2.35)$$

becomes:

Figure 2.8 Illustration of the way the modulus of the wave function squared $|\Psi(x)|^2$ is interpreted. The figures show a possible variation of $|\Psi(x)|^2$.

(a) If a particle occupies the quantum state that the wave function represents, it is more likely to found near x_1 than x_2 because $|\Psi(x_1)|^2 dx > |\Psi(x_2)|^2 dx$ (b) If a particle occupies the quantum state that the wave function represents, then it must be found somewhere between $x = -\infty$ and $x = +\infty$. Therefore the equation shown must hold true.

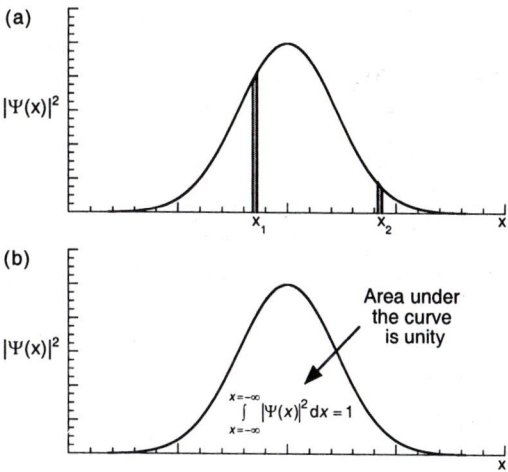

Figure 2.9 Illustration of the significance of each term in the Schrödinger equation. At each value of position x, the Schrödinger equation relates the curvature of the wave function at x, the value of the wave function itself at x, the potential energy at x and the value of the energy of the quantum state.

$$\underbrace{\frac{-\hbar^2}{2m}}_{\text{constants}}\times\underbrace{\frac{\partial}{\partial x^2}\Psi(x)}_{\substack{\text{curvature}\\ \text{of }\Psi(x)}}+\underbrace{V(x)}_{\substack{\text{potential}\\ \text{energy}\\ \text{at }x}}\times\underbrace{\Psi(x)}_{\substack{\text{value}\\ \text{of }\Psi\\ \text{at }x}}=\underbrace{E}_{\text{energy}}\times\underbrace{\Psi(x)}_{\substack{\text{value}\\ \text{of }\Psi\\ \text{at }x}}$$

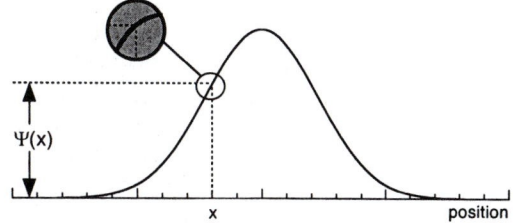

$$\frac{-\hbar^2}{2m}\frac{\partial^2}{\partial x^2}\Psi(x)+V_0\Psi(x)=E\Psi(x) \qquad (2.36)$$

Taking the V_0 term over to the right-hand side of the equation, and re-arranging the constants gives:

$$\frac{-\hbar^2}{2m}\frac{\partial^2}{\partial x^2}\Psi(x)=\left(E-V_0\right)\Psi(x)$$

$$\frac{\partial^2}{\partial x^2}\Psi(x)=-\left[\frac{2m}{\hbar^2}\left(E-V_0\right)\right]\Psi(x) \qquad (2.37)$$

Since all the quantities in square brackets are constants, this may be rewritten as:

$$\frac{\partial^2}{\partial x^2}\Psi(x)=-A^2\Psi(x) \qquad (2.38)$$

where A is a constant given by:

$$A=\sqrt{\frac{2m}{\hbar^2}\left(E-V_0\right)} \qquad (2.39)$$

Equation 2.38 is a differential equation that has solutions of the form:

$$\Psi(x)\approx\sin(Ax)\ or\ \Psi(x)\approx\cos(Ax) \qquad (2.40)$$

If $(E-V_0)$ is positive, then $2m/\hbar^2(E-V_0)$ will be a positive number, and its square root will be a real number (positive or negative). The solutions to the equation are sketched for several different positive values of $(E-V_0)$ in Figure 2.10.

The wavelength, λ, of the wave function (Equation 2.40) for the particle is given by:

$$A=\frac{2\pi}{\lambda} \qquad (2.41)$$

The *de Broglie hypothesis* is that the momentum, p, of the particle is given by:

$$p=\frac{h}{\lambda} \qquad (2.42)$$

Substituting Equation 2.41 into Equation 2.42 :

$$p=\frac{hA}{2\pi}=\hbar A \qquad (2.43)$$

Figure 2.10 Portions of wave functions $\psi(x)$ satisfying Equation 2.47 for three different values of $E-V_0$. From (a) to (c) the value of $E-V_0$ is increasing. Notice that for a given V_0, the higher values of E result in wave functions with shorter wavelengths.

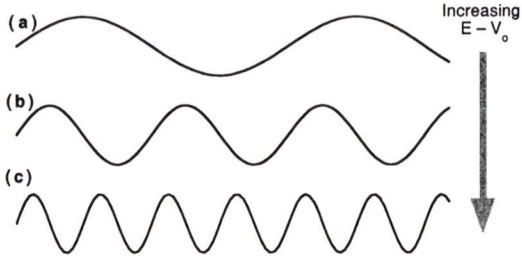

$$p=\hbar\sqrt{\frac{2m}{\hbar^2}\left(E-V_0\right)}$$

$$=\sqrt{2m\left(E-V_0\right)} \qquad (2.44)$$

The energy in the case of Figure 2.10 is entirely kinetic energy, and is related to the momentum by the usual relationship:

$$KE=E-V_0$$

$$=\frac{1}{2}mv^2=\frac{p^2}{2m} \qquad (2.45)$$

The square-well potential or the one-dimensional box

Figure 2.11 shows the variation of potential energy in a one-dimensional square potential well, the walls of which are extremely high. The concept of this type of potential energy well is of great use in physics. This is because, although the situation never actually occurs in nature, it is one of the few problems that it is possible to solve exactly. Furthermore, it often makes a good first approximation to many real problems, such as the problem of electrons trapped in a metal, or on an atom. It is considered further in §6.5, §7.7.3 and Chapter W1.

There are several features to note about the wave functions of the two lowest quantum states sketched in Figure 2.11:

- The wave functions satisfy the time-independent Schrödinger equation (Eq. 2.35).
- At the edges of the potential well, the wave function is zero where the potential energy is very large.
- In the central region of the potential well, the potential energy term $V(x)$ is zero. This is equivalent to a 'small part of free space'. The solution in this region will therefore be similar to that described in Figure 2.10.
- Unlike the case of the particle in free space (Figure 2.10), the wavelength is restricted to just a few special values that cause the wave function to be zero at the edges of the potential well. The wave functions which satisfy this condition are known as *eigenfunctions*.
- By virtue of the de Broglie hypothesis (Equation 2.42), the wavelength is restricted to special values. Consequently, the momentum and energy of the particles trapped in the potential well are also restricted to a few special values known as *eigenvalues*.

The wavelengths are restricted to the set of values,

$$\lambda = 2L, \ L, \ \frac{2}{3}L, \ \frac{1}{2}L, \ \frac{2}{5}L, \ ..., \ \frac{2L}{n}$$
$$= \frac{2L}{1}, \ \frac{2L}{2}, \ \frac{2L}{3}, \ \frac{2L}{4}, \ \frac{2L}{5}, \ ..., \ \frac{2L}{n} \qquad (2.46)$$

where n is an integer. I have written the series in two ways because the second way emphasises the structure of the sequence of allowed wavelengths. The energy of a particle trapped in this well is therefore restricted by Equation 2.46 to be:

$$E(n) = \frac{p^2}{2m}$$
$$= \frac{h^2}{2m[2L/n]^2} \qquad (2.47)$$

or more simply:

$$E(n) = \frac{h^2 n^2}{8mL^2}. \qquad (2.48)$$

where $n = 1, 2, 3, ...$ but not zero.

The two-dimensional box

Figure 2.12 (a) shows the variation of potential energy in a two-dimensional square potential well, the walls of which are extremely high. The two-dimensional square-well is an interesting intermediary between the one-dimensional and three-dimensional square well potentials. The primary purpose of discussing the two-dimensional example is that its wave functions can be visualised relatively easily, whereas the three-dimensional wave-functions are rather more difficult to depict. The wave functions in Figure 2.12 have energies

Figure 2.11 The variation of potential energy in a one-dimensional square potential well. The figure shows the wave functions $\psi(x)$ and probability densities $|\psi(x)|^2$ of the two lowest energy quantum states ($n = 1$ and $n = 2$).

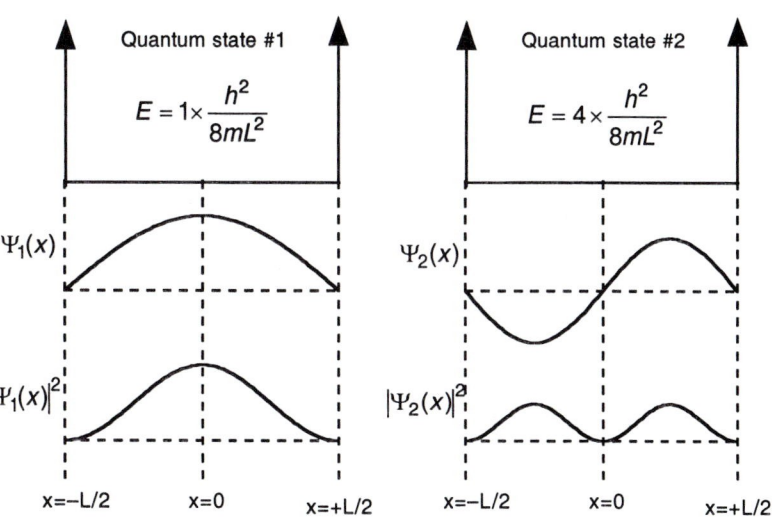

given by:

$$E(n_x, n_y) = \frac{h^2}{8mL^2}\left[n_x^2 + n_y^2\right] \qquad (2.49)$$

where n_x and n_y have values 1, 2, 3, ...etc., but not zero. In addition to the points noted in the one-dimensional example, notice that the wave functions and energies of each quantum state are determined by *more than one quantum number*. This raises the possibility that two or more distinct quantum states might possess the same energy, a phenomenon known as *degeneracy*. For example, referring to the state with $n_x = 1$, $n_y = 2$ as the (1,2) state, Figure 2.13 shows that the (1,2) and (2,1) states have quite distinct wave functions and probability densities, but the same energy. The significance of this degeneracy is discussed more fully in the section below on the three-dimensional box.

The three-dimensional box

A particle confined to a cubic 'box' of side L has wave functions described by *three* quantum numbers, n_x, n_y and n_z, and the wave functions have energies given by an expression similar to Equation 2.49:

$$E(n_x, n_y, n_z) = \frac{h^2}{8mL^2}\left[n_x^2 + n_y^2 + n_z^2\right] \qquad (2.50)$$

where n_x, n_y and n_z may take integer values 1, 2, 3, ...etc., but not zero. As with the two-dimensional box, degeneracy also occurs. Labelling the quantum state with $n_x = 3$, $n_y = 4$ and $n_z = 1$ by (3,4,1), we see that quantum states such as (1,2,2), (2,2,1) and (2,1,2) all have the same energy. Using the terminology mentioned above, we may refer to this *energy level* as being three-fold degenerate. The degeneracy of other energy levels is indicated in Figure 2.14.

Figure 2.12 (a) Illustration of a two-dimensional square well potential .

$V(x)$

Particle is trapped in here

(b) The wave functions and probability densities of the four lowest-energy quantum states for the two-dimensional square well

	Wave Function $\Psi(x,y)$	Probability Density $|\Psi(x,y)|^2$
$n_x = 1 : n_y = 1$ $E(1,1) = \frac{h^2}{8mL^2}[2]$		
$n_x = 2 : n_y = 1$ $E(2,1) = \frac{h^2}{8mL^2}[5]$		
$n_x = 1 : n_y = 2$ $E(1,2) = \frac{h^2}{8mL^2}[5]$		
$n_x = 2 : n_y = 2$ $E(2,2) = \frac{h^2}{8mL^2}[8]$		

Figure 2.13 The three-dimensional particle in a box problem. The figure shows a histogram of the number of quantum states with a given energy. The energy is indicated in units of $h^2/8mL^2$ and is calculated according to Equation 2.59.

For the first few energy levels, the quantum numbers of the states that comprise those energy levels are also shown.

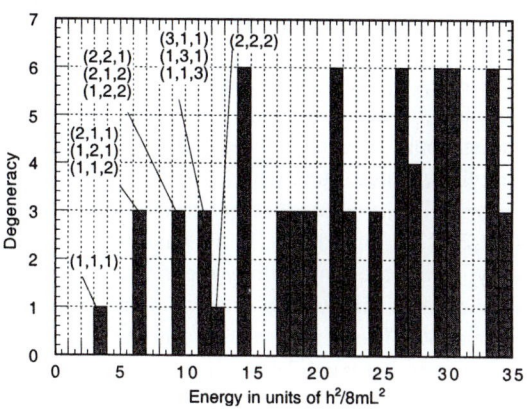

Figure 2.14 The variation of potential energy in a one-dimensional simple harmonic potential well. The wave functions $\psi(x)$ and probability densities $|\psi(x)|^2$ of the two lowest energy quantum states are also shown.

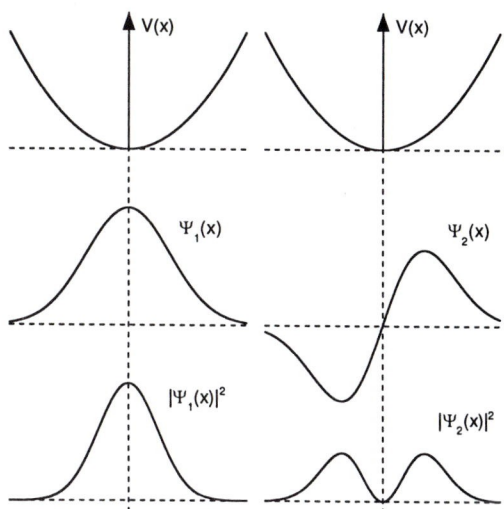

The simple harmonic oscillator

The potential energy of a particle in a one-dimensional simple harmonic oscillator

$$V(x) = \tfrac{1}{2}K(x - x_0)^2 \qquad (2.51)$$

is shown in Figure 2.15. As in the classical treatment of such an oscillator (§2.4.2), the frequency

$$f_0 = \frac{1}{2\pi}\sqrt{\frac{K}{m}} \quad \text{or} \quad \omega_0 = \sqrt{\frac{K}{m}} \qquad (2.52)$$

is significant because the energy of a quantum state with quantum number n is given by:

$$\begin{aligned} E(n) &= (n + \tfrac{1}{2})hf_0 \\ &= (n + \tfrac{1}{2})\hbar\omega_0 \end{aligned} \qquad (2.53)$$

The allowed energies of a particle trapped in a three-dimensional harmonic oscillator potential:

$$V(x) = \tfrac{1}{2}K\left[(x - x_0)^2 + (y - y_0)^2 + (z - z_0)^2\right] \qquad (2.54)$$

are given by:

$$E(n_x, n_y, n_z) = (n_x + n_y + n_z + \tfrac{3}{2})hf_0 \qquad (2.55)$$

Notice that the energy levels are equally spaced, unlike those of a particle in three-dimensional box where the energy gap between quantum states becomes smaller for higher energy states.

Atomic wave functions

The nature of the wave functions of electrons bound to atoms is of great interest. The characteristics of these functions determine many physical and chemical properties of the substances of which they form a part. Nowadays, the nature of the wave functions around most atoms is known rather well. Unfortunately, however, for most atoms the wave functions do not have any simple functional form, and the energy levels within the atom have a complex structure. Happily there is one simple case which is extremely informative: the hydrogen atom.

The hydrogen atom is the simplest atom, consisting of just one electron and one proton. The electrostatic potential energy around the proton varies roughly as $1/r$ (Eq. 2.5), binding the electron to the proton. Figure 2.16 illustrates the nature of the potential and some of the wave functions. The web site for this book has some attractive colour im-

Figure 2.15 The variation of potential energy in a one-dimensional $1/r$ potential well. The wave functions $\psi(r)$ and probability densities $|\psi(r)|^2$ of the two lowest energy quantum states are also shown. Representations of the three-dimensional $1/r$ potential are available on the web site for this book

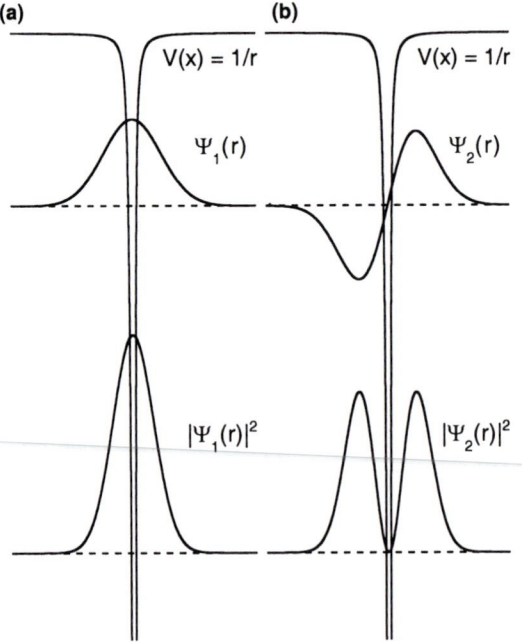

(a) **(b)**

$V(x) = 1/r$ $V(x) = 1/r$

$\Psi_1(r)$ $\Psi_2(r)$

$|\Psi_1(r)|^2$ $|\Psi_2(r)|^2$

ages of the wave functions of hydrogen-like atoms.

When many particles interact: the exclusion principle

The three fundamental particles (electrons, protons and neutrons) that we considered as our basic set of particles belong to a class of particles called *fermions* (Table 2.1). They can be identified as fermions by the fact that their intrinsic spin (in units of the Planck constant, $\hbar$) is half an odd integer, in this case $\frac{1}{2}$. It is worth noting that it is not known what the property referred to as *spin* actually corresponds to. However, we do know that (confusingly) it does *not* correspond to any kind of spinning motion. We know that it corresponds to an *intrinsic property* of a particle, and that it gives the particle an internal 'axis' or special direction.

Particles with spins of magnitude $\frac{1}{2}\hbar$, $\frac{3}{2}\hbar$, ... etc. obey the *Pauli exclusion principle*. This states that:

> At any one time, no more than one fermion may occupy an individual quantum state.

Notice however that it *is* possible for many fermions to have the same *energy*, as long as the energy level has many individual quantum states.

The application of this principle is critical to understanding the properties of matter and is discussed further in §2.5 on statistical mechanics. For example, it is a consequence of this principle that only one electron is allowed to occupy the lowest energy quantum state within an atom, and other electrons are forced to occupy higher energy states. Also, when atoms collide in a gas, it is the combination of the exclusion principle with the Coulomb repulsion between valence electrons that causes the atoms to 'bounce' off one another.

2.5 Thermodynamics and statistical mechanics

2.5.1 Introduction

Historically, the approach to understanding the large-scale properties of matter has developed along two rather separate lines.

In the *thermodynamic* approach, we assume as little as possible about the microscopic nature of matter. For example, we do not have to posit the existence of atoms. We then derive relationships between measurable large-scale properties of materials. In the *statistical mechanical* approach, we first make assumptions about the properties of the basic microscopic entities involved in a problem, usually atoms or molecules. We then try to deduce the properties of large numbers of these basic entities. This approach takes account of the fact that atoms are very small and the large-scale properties of a substance are the *average properties* of a very large number of atoms. Statistical mechanics makes calculations of these average values.

In this book, I have used some ideas from thermo-

dynamics and some from statistical mechanics. My aim has been to choose the explanation which seems to make most sense in the context of the book. Let us look at some ideas important to both approaches.

Temperature

In the statistical-mechanical approach, the key property of temperature is related to the *average kinetic energy* per basic entity of the substance, usually per molecule or per atom. Thus, if the temperature of a substance is high, its atoms possess relatively large amounts of kinetic energy. The relationship between temperature and average kinetic energy implies that there must exist an *absolute zero* of temperature, when the average kinetic energy per basic entity is reduced to zero. A more carefully worded definition of temperature is given at the end of this section, after we have described some specialised terminology.

Thermal equilibrium

Thermal equilibrium is the state reached by a material after it has been in contact with a large object at a constant temperature for a long time. The large object is known technically as a constant temperature *heat bath*. If a substance is in a state of thermal equilibrium, then its temperature (i.e. the average kinetic energy of its particles) is uniform throughout its volume, and does not change with time.

2.5.2 First law of thermodynamics

The first law of thermodynamics is essentially a restatement of the principle of conservation of energy. It defines a property called the *internal energy* of a sample of material in terms of heat supplied to a sample and work done on the sample. The first law takes account of the conversion of energy between *work* and *heat*.

Thermodynamics does not try to explain the properties of matter by reference to any microscopic structure. However, we understand from a statistical mechanical perspective that *work* is an example of a *mechanical* form of energy: energy is tied up in the *coherent motion* of molecules. In contrast, *heat* is energy which is tied up in the *random motion* of molecules. The first law states:

The change in internal energy	=	The heat supplied **to** the object	+	The work done **on** the object

$$\Delta U = \Delta Q + \Delta W \qquad (2.57)$$

First law of thermodynamics

This law relates changes between one state of thermal equilibrium and another, in terms of the work done on, and the heat supplied to, an object. In its simplest form, the work done on the object includes only mechanical work, but may be extended to include electrical or magnetic work.

2.5.3 Counting quantum states

Matter as we encounter it generally contains vast numbers of atoms or molecules. A mole (typically a few tens of grams of most substances) contains roughly 10^{23} atoms. Numbers of this magnitude are almost inconceivably large. For the purposes of comparison, it is hard to find meaningful numbers that even approach this size. For example, the universe is currently believed to have begun around 15 billion years ago: a long time by any reckoning. However, the number of seconds which have elapsed since then is *only* of the order 10^{17}. Other examples of stunningly large numbers are considered in Exercises C19 and C20. The large numbers of atoms involved in even tiny pieces of

---

Example 2.5

2 joules of heat is dissipated in an object which then expands and does 0.1 joules of work. By how much is its internal energy U increased?

We use Equation 2.55 with

$$\Delta Q = 2 \text{ J}$$
$$\Delta W = -0.1 \text{ J}$$

Notice the negative sign of ΔW arises because the object does work on its environment. Substituting into Equation 2.55

$$\Delta U = \Delta Q + \Delta W$$
$$= 2.0 - 0.1$$
$$= 1.9 \text{ J}$$

matter makes the task of determining the macroscopic (i.e. large-scale) properties of matter in some ways easier, and in some ways more difficult.

Big numbers make life easy

The large numbers of atoms means that average properties may be extremely well-defined. For example, in §4.4 we will see that at around room temperature, gas molecules move with speeds ranging from zero to several thousand metres per second. Despite this variability, the *average* speed of a gas molecule may be defined with high precision, and shows only tiny fluctuations. If just a few tens of molecules were involved in the gas, the fluctuations would be considerably larger, and the average value of their speed would be less significant.

Big numbers make life difficult

However, large numbers of molecules mean that in order to calculate the average properties, we need a coherent and consistent framework for counting the particles, their speeds and energies. This framework can be rather intimidating at first, but has an elegance which can be inspiring. In the next section we discuss the systematic approach to particles and the quantum states that they occupy

2.5.4 Statistical mechanics

In the context of this book, we consider statistical mechanics to be a scheme or plan for calculating average quantities. The plan has three stages:

Stage 1: Make a list of all the quantum states of a system and hence define a *density of quantum states* function.

Stage 2: Consider whether the particles which will occupy these states are fermions or bosons, and hence choose an *occupation function* that describes how the quantum states will be occupied.

Stage 3: Combine the *density of quantum states* function from stage 1, and the occupation function from stage 2 to yield a *distribution function*. The distribution function describes the way the particles are distributed among quantum states.

Stage 1a: A list of quantum states

Our first step is to produce a list of the possible quantum states that the individual particles which comprise a substance may occupy. This is usually in the form of a general formula saying how the energy E of a quantum state depends on its other quantum numbers. For example, the possible energies of particles in a three-dimensional particle in a box are:

$$E(n_x, n_y, n_z) = \frac{h^2}{8mL^2}\left[n_x^2 + n_y^2 + n_z^2\right] \quad (2.50^*)$$

Table 2.4 lists the energies of a few low-energy quantum states, and the number of electrons that can be accommodated in these states.

Stage 1b: The density of states function

From the list derived in stage 1a, we can calculate the form of a function which answers the question 'How many quantum states are there with energy between E and $E + dE$?'. This function is known as the *density of states function* and in this book has a symbol $g(E)$. In §6.5 and web Chapter W1 we show that the density of quantum states for a particle in a box increases with energy as:

$$g(E) = A\sqrt{E} \quad (2.58)$$

However, in order to observe the square-root dependence of $g(E)$ on energy, we must generally consider a few thousand quantum states at least. Even for large numbers of quantum states, if we consider $g(E)$ on a very fine energy scale, then we will discover 'graininess' and fluctuations around the average square root behaviour. This graininess is illustrated qualitatively in Figure 2.16. The detailed behaviour is also illustrated in Figure 2.13.

Stage 2: Fermions or bosons? The occupation function

In the second stage of our plan to calculate average quantities, we consider whether the particles which will occupy the quantum states are bosons or fermions. It is a fundamental assumption of statistical mechanics that in equilibrium, the average number of particles in an individual quantum state depends on *only* three factors:

Table 2.4 The first few energy levels for particles trapped in a box. The columns show in order (i) the quantum numbers of the states, (ii) the energy of the states with these quantum numbers, (iii) the number of quantum states with the same energy level (the degeneracy of the level), and (iv) the running total of the number of quantum states.

Quantum numbers (n_x, n_y, n_z)	Energy $\times \dfrac{h^2}{8mL^2}$	Number of quantum states with this energy	Cumulative total of quantum states
(1,1,1)	3	1	1
(1,1,2) (1,2,1) (2,1,1)	6	3	1 + 3 = 4
(1,2,2) (2,1,2) (2,2,1)	9	3	1 + 3 + 3 = 7
(1,1,3) (1,3,1) (3,1,1)	11	3	1 + 3 + 3 + 3 = 10
(2,2,2)	12	1	1 + 3 + 3 + 3 + 1 = 11

- the type of particle, which may be either a fermion or a boson
- the temperature
- the energy of the state.

Thus for a given type of particle, states of equal energy are equally likely to be occupied. This is very important. It means that even if the motions associated with these two states are completely different, the probability that the quantum states will be occupied is identical. For example, if a vibrational state of a molecule has the same energy as a rotational state, then both states will be occupied with equal probability.

- Fermions have a spin of half an odd integer ($\frac{1}{2}\hbar$, $\frac{3}{2}\hbar$, ...) and only a single particle may occupy the same quantum state at the same time. All the particles of matter that we commonly encounter are fermions.

- Bosons have a spin of zero or half an even integer ($0, \hbar, 2\hbar, ...$) and may multiply occupy the same quantum state. The most common bosons that we encounter are *photons* and *phonons*. These are 'particles', but they have with no rest mass. Photons describe the state of excitation of the electromagnetic field, and phonons describe the waves of displacement of atoms in a solid. Bosons can also be used to describe particles of matter, such as atoms of the isotope of helium, ^{4}He.

Figure 2.16 The three-dimensional particle-in-a-box problem. (a) The figure shows a histogram of the number of quantum states with a given energy and (b) shows the limiting behaviour of the histogram. In (a) the energy is indicated in units of $h^2/8mL^2$ and is calculated according to Equation 2.50. The histogram shows the number of quantum states in an energy range ($10 \times h^2/8mL^2$). If L is ≈ 1 metre, and m corresponds to a nitrogen molecule (=28 × 1.66 × 10^{-27} kg) then the $10 \times h^2/8mL^2$ evaluates to $\approx 10^{-43}$ joules. From (a) we can see, for example, that there are roughly 60 quantum states in an energy range $10\ h^2/8mL^2$ around an energy of 100 $h^2/8mL^2$. So the average spacing between quantum states in this range is roughly $(10\ h^2/8mL^2)/60 \approx 10^{-44}$ J. The detailed behaviour at the low-energy end of the graph is shown in Figure 2.13 and the inset to (b).

(a)

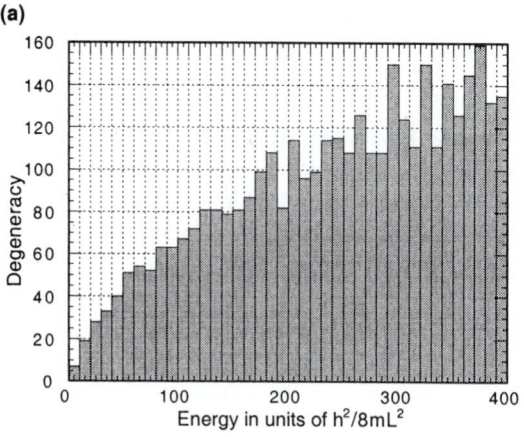

(b)

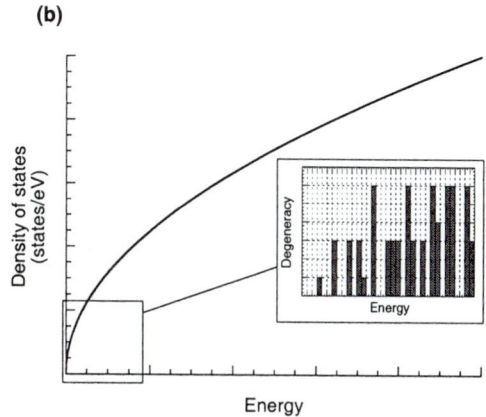

Example 2.6

For a box of volume V, the density of quantum states that may be occupied by electrons is $g(E) = \sqrt{E}$ states/eV. Sketch this function and evaluate how many quantum states there are with energies (a) between 9.0 and 9.1 eV, and (b) between 0 and 9 eV.

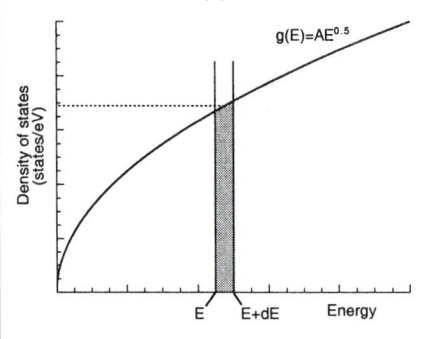

(a) Since the energy range $\Delta E = 0.1$ eV is small in comparison with the total energy, we may use the definition of the density of states function: '$g(E)\Delta E$ is the number of quantum states ΔN with energies in the range E to $E + \Delta E$'.

(b) In this case, energy range $\Delta E = 9$ eV is significant in comparison with the total energy, and so we must integrate the density of states function:

In this case this is given by:

$$\Delta N = g(E)\Delta E$$
$$= A\sqrt{E} \times \Delta E$$
$$= A\sqrt{9} \times 0.1$$
$$= 0.3A$$

$$N = \int_{E=0}^{E=9\mathrm{eV}} g(E)\mathrm{d}E = \int_{E=0}^{E=9\mathrm{eV}} AE^{\frac{1}{2}}\mathrm{d}E$$
$$= A\left[\frac{2}{3}E^{\frac{3}{2}}\right]_{E=0}^{E=9\mathrm{eV}}$$
$$= A \times \frac{2}{3} \times 9^{\frac{3}{2}}$$
$$= 18A$$

At low densities of particles, both of these sets of statistics reduce to a simpler form known as classical or *Maxwell Boltzmann* statistics (§2.5.5).

Based on the type of particle populating the quantum states under discussion, we can deduce an occupation function $f(E,T)$:

> $f(E,T)$ yields the average occupancy of an individual quantum state
> (2.59)

Fermions

For fermions the appropriate occupation function is called the *Fermi–Dirac function*

$$f_{FD}(E,T) = \frac{1}{\exp\left[(E-\mu)/k_BT\right]+1} \qquad (2.60)$$

where μ is a characteristic energy for the system of particles. Technically μ is known as the *chemical potential*, but for electrons to which we shall apply Equation 2.60, the chemical potential is generally referred to the *Fermi energy* E_F, i.e.

$$f_{FD}(E,T) = \frac{1}{\exp\left[(E-E_F)/k_BT\right]+1} \qquad (2.61)$$

For quantum states with energy equal to the Fermi energy ($E = E_F$), the probability a quantum state is occupied is exactly $\frac{1}{2}$.

Bosons

For bosons the appropriate occupation function is called the *Bose–Einstein function*

$$f_{BE}(E,T) = \frac{1}{\exp\left[(E-\mu)/k_BT\right]-1} \qquad (2.62)$$

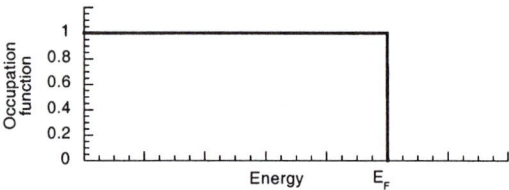

Figure 2.17 The Fermi–Dirac (FD) occupation function shows the average occupancy of an *individual quantum state*. (a) The FD function appropriate to absolute zero.

(b) How the function changes with increasing temperature. Notice that as the temperature changes, the maximum value of the function never exceeds unity. This is because the function is the 'embodiment' of the exclusion principle, which forbids multiple occupancy of quantum states. Notice also that at E_F, the average occupancy always has the value 0.5.

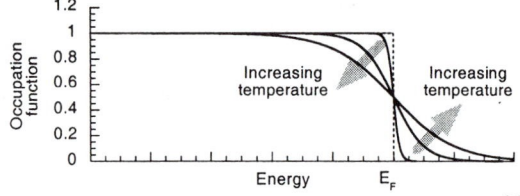

33

Unlike atoms and molecules, photons and phonons are not conserved. Photons and phonons may be absorbed or created, and for such particles the chemical potential may be set equal to zero.

$$f_{BE}(E,T) = \frac{1}{\exp[E/k_B T] - 1} \qquad (2.63)$$

This function is sketched in Figure 2.19

Stage 3: The distribution function

In the first stage of our plan to calculate average quantities, we worked out how many quantum states have energies between E and $E + dE$. In the second stage, we stated that the occupation factor $f(E,T)$ yields the average occupancy of each individual quantum state of energy E at temperature T. In the final stage of the plan, we will see that we can calculate the average number of particles actually *occupying* quantum states with energies between E and $E + dE$. To do this we take the product of the density of states function $g(E)$, and the occupation function $f(E,T)$ to yield the average occupancy of an individual quantum state.

$$\begin{array}{c} \text{Distribution} \\ \text{function} \end{array} = \begin{array}{c} \text{Density of} \\ \text{states} \end{array} \times \begin{array}{c} \text{Occupation} \\ \text{function} \end{array}$$

$$D(E,T)dE = g(E) \times f(E,T)dE \qquad (2.64)$$

Figure 2.18 The Bose–Einstein occupation function shows the average occupancy of an *individual quantum state*. Notice that the maximum value of the function may exceed unity, and indeed becomes infinite at zero energy.

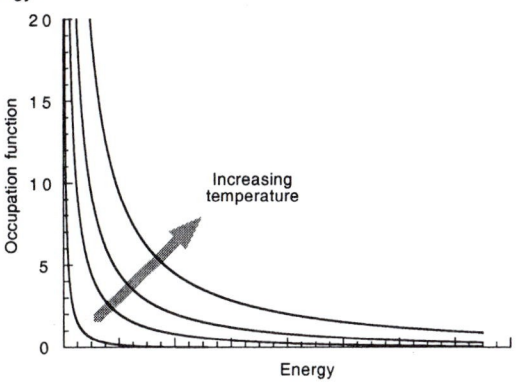

Calculating average quantities

Using the expressions derived in the three stages above, we can define several useful expressions. In particular, the number of particles occupying quantum states with energies in some energy range is given by:

$$N = \int_{\substack{\text{minimum} \\ \text{energy}}}^{\substack{\text{maximum} \\ \text{energy}}} D(E,T)dE \qquad (2.65)$$

or, using Equation 2.64, by:

$$N = \int_{\substack{\text{minimum} \\ \text{energy}}}^{\substack{\text{maximum} \\ \text{energy}}} g(E)f(E,T)dE \qquad (2.66)$$

Similarly the total energy of those particles may be written as:

$$E_{\text{total}} = \int_{\substack{\text{minimum} \\ \text{energy}}}^{\substack{\text{maximum} \\ \text{energy}}} g(E)f(E,T) \times E dE \qquad (2.67)$$

Figure 2.19 An illustration of the relationship between the density of states function, the occupation function, and the distribution function (Equation 2.64).

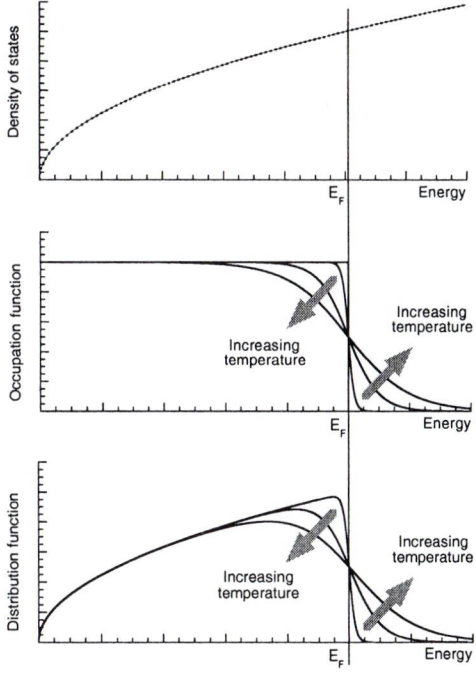

So if we divide Equation 2.67 by Equation 2.65, we obtain the *average energy* of a particle in that energy range:

$$\overline{E} = \frac{E_{\text{total}}}{N} = \frac{\int\limits_{\substack{\text{minimum} \\ \text{energy}}}^{\substack{\text{maximum} \\ \text{energy}}} g(E)f(E,T)E\mathrm{d}E}{\int\limits_{\substack{\text{minimum} \\ \text{energy}}}^{\substack{\text{maximum} \\ \text{energy}}} g(E)f(E,T)\mathrm{d}E} \quad (2.68)$$

To evaluate equation 2.68 in any particular situation is, in general, not particularly straightforward. However, what it represents is a systematic prescription for how to calculate these important quantities.

Some technical terms

Degrees of freedom

A strict definition of the *degrees of freedom* of a system might be something like that given below:

> The number of degrees of freedom of a physical system is the number of independent squared terms which enter into the expression for the energy of the system
>
> (2.69)

However, this gives little clue as to the usefulness of the concept. For example, the energy of an isolated atom of mass m is:

$$E = \tfrac{1}{2}mv_x^2 + \tfrac{1}{2}mv_y^2 + \tfrac{1}{2}mv_z^2 \quad (2.70)$$

which has three independent squared terms. We would thus describe such a molecule as having three degrees of freedom. Other degrees of freedom may be associated with vibrational or rotational motions. In a sense, the idea of stating the number of degrees of freedom that a molecule possesses adds nothing to what we know about the molecule. Nonetheless, it does give a shorthand and easily intelligible description of molecular motion. The usefulness of the idea arises because, in many circumstances, the average amount of energy associated with each degree of freedom is directly related to the temperature. Importantly this does not depend on the nature of the motion

Example 2.7

Work out the average energy of an electron gas at $T = 0$ K. (We will use this result in §6.5.)

According to Equation 2.75 we can define the number of electrons in our system as:

$$N = \int\limits_0^{E=\infty} g(E)f_{\text{FD}}(E,T)\mathrm{d}E$$

At absolute zero, $f_{\text{FD}}(E,0)$ has the value 1 for all energies below E_F, and 0 for all energies above. We may therefore write the integral for N as:

$$N = \int\limits_0^{E_F} g(E)\mathrm{d}E$$

Substituting for $g(E)$ from Example 2.7 and integrating we find:

$$N = \int\limits_0^{E_F} AE^{\frac{1}{2}}\mathrm{d}E$$

$$= \left[\tfrac{2}{3}AE^{\frac{3}{2}}\right]_0^{E_F}$$

$$= \tfrac{2}{3}AE_F^{\frac{3}{2}}$$

We may follow a similar procedure to arrive at an expression for the total energy:

$$E_{\text{Total}} = \int\limits_0^{E_F} AE^{\frac{1}{2}}E\mathrm{d}E = \int\limits_0^{E_F} AE^{\frac{3}{2}}\mathrm{d}E$$

$$= \left[\tfrac{2}{5}AE^{\frac{5}{2}}\right]_0^{E_F}$$

$$= \tfrac{2}{5}AE_F^{\frac{5}{2}}$$

Using Equation 2.77, we can evaluate the average energy of an electron as:

$$E_{\text{average}} = \frac{\text{total energy}}{\text{number of electrons}}$$

$$= \frac{\tfrac{2}{5}AE_F^{\frac{5}{2}}}{\tfrac{2}{3}AE_F^{\frac{3}{2}}}$$

$$= \frac{3}{5}E_F$$

If you look at Figure 2.19, which illustrates the distribution function, you will see that a figure of around 60% of the Fermi energy makes sense as an estimate of the average value of the energy.

associated with each degree of freedom. This will prove to be very important when we try to understand data on the heat capacity of gases in §5.3.

Temperature

In thermal equilibrium, the *average* energy associated with each accessible degree of freedom of the system is:

$$\overline{E} = \tfrac{1}{2} k_\mathrm{B} T \qquad (2.71)$$

where k_B ($= 1.38 \times 10^{-23}$ J K^{-1}) is the *Boltzmann constant* and T is a constant of proportionality familiar to us as the *absolute temperature*. The term 'accessible' is discussed below.

Accessibility

The occupation function $f(E,T)$ determines the average occupancy of a quantum state. As I mentioned above, in a sense there is nothing more to be said about the matter of occupying quantum states than is contained in the occupation function. However, the terminology of *accessibility* is commonly used to describe the occupancy of quantum states. When a quantum state has a low

average occupancy, it may in certain circumstances be described as *inaccessible*. As illustrated in Table 2.5, the term applies when the separation ΔE between quantum states is much greater than $k_\mathrm{B} T$.

2.5.5 Classical statistics: Boltzmann factor

Both the Bose–Einstein and the Fermi–Dirac occupation functions can be greatly simplified when there is a great excess of quantum states over particles. In such cases, bosons and fermions occupy quantum states in a similar way. We can see how this happens if we consider the situation of Figure 2.20. If there is just one particle occupying this system of quantum states, then clearly there are no restrictions placed by its fermion/boson nature on the quantum states it may occupy. Now consider the case where there are two particles in the same system of quantum states. If the two particles are

Table 2.5 Illustration of the use of the term *accessibility* of quantum states. Notice that increasing the temperature always increases the number of 'accessible' quantum states.

Inaccessible	Marginal accessibility	Fully accessible
$k_\mathrm{B}T \ll \Delta E$	$k_\mathrm{B}T \approx \Delta E$	$k_\mathrm{B}T \gg \Delta E$
e.g. $k_\mathrm{B}T < 0.1\Delta E$	e.g. $0.1\,\Delta E < k_\mathrm{B}T < 1.5\Delta E$	e.g. $k_\mathrm{B}T > 1.5\Delta E$
In this case, only occasionally do molecules make transitions to higher quantum states. We can consider the degrees of freedom associated with these transitions to be inaccessible.	In this case, molecules make transitions to the higher quantum states. Detailed calculations are required to assess the extent to which the quantum state can be considered accessible.	In this case, molecules frequently make transitions to higher quantum states. We can consider the degrees of freedom associated with these transitions to be fully accessible.
In colloquial terms, the processes associated with transitions between quantum states occur so rarely that they may generally be ignored.		In colloquial terms, the processes associated with transitions between quantum states occur so frequently that the quantum nature of the states may generally be ignored.

Figure 2.20 Classical and Fermi–Dirac statistics for fermions. In cases (a) and (b) the fermion nature of a particle does not become apparent and classical statistics may be used. In case (c) we must use Fermi–Dirac statistics. In (a) there is only a single particle and so the exclusion principle places no restrictions on which state it may occupy. In (b) there are two particles, but in most configurations, the particles do not attempt to occupy the same state. In (c) the density of particles is so high that the distribution of the particles amongst the available quantum states is dominated by the fermion nature of the particles.

Figure 2.21 Qualitative illustration of the energy ranges in which (a) the Fermi–Dirac and (b) the Bose–Einstein occupation factors may be approximated by a Boltzmann factor.

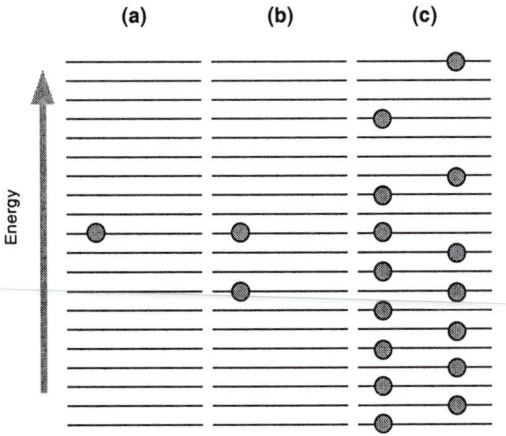

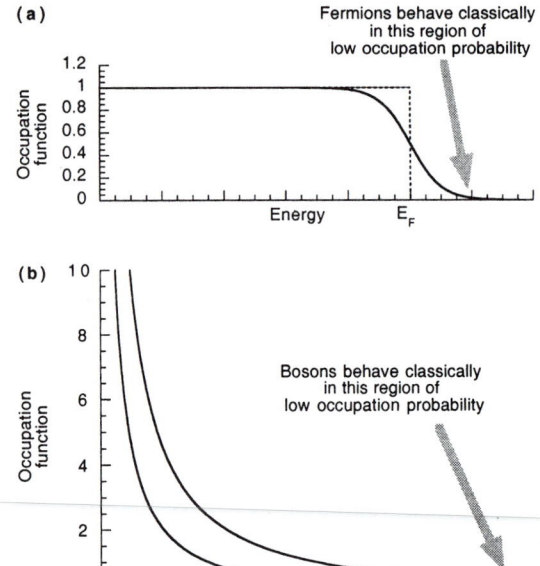

fermions, there will be a restriction that a single quantum state may be not be doubly occupied. However, if the chance of double occupation is low, the actual distribution of particles among available quantum states will not be much affected.

Under the conditions of low occupancy (say, with average occupancy less than ≈ 0.1) described above and in Figures 2.20 and 2.21, both Fermi–Dirac and Bose–Einstein occupation factors reduce to a simpler form known as a Boltzmann factor:

$$f(E,T) = A\exp(-E/k_{\mathrm{B}}T) \qquad (2.72)$$

where A is a constant determined by the requirement of Equation 2.64 that the total number of particles is:

$$N = \int_{\substack{\text{minimum} \\ \text{energy}}}^{\substack{\text{maximum} \\ \text{energy}}} g(E)f(E,T)\mathrm{d}E \qquad (2.73)$$

The deduction of Equation 2.72 from Equation 2.61 or 2.63 is discussed in Appendix A1

So, under conditions where the average occupancy of a quantum state is low, both quantum occupation functions reduce to a simpler Boltzmann factor. In this regime – the *classical regime* – the probability of occupying a state of particular energy varies exponentially with temperature. The Boltzmann factor manifests itself in many physical properties of substances, such as:

- the distribution of the energies of molecules of a gas (Appendix A1)
- the excitation of electron carriers in an insulator or semiconductor (§7.7.7)
- the evaporation of molecules from the surface of a liquid (§9.5).

In fact, we will meet the Boltzmann factor wherever we encounter systems whose physical properties display an exponential dependence on temperature.

Example 2.8

In the classical regime, what is the relative probability that two particular quantum states with energies E_1 and E_2 will be occupied at temperature T?

The average occupancy of a quantum state with energy E_1 is equal to:

$$f(E_1, T) = A \exp\left[\frac{-E_1}{k_B T}\right]$$

where A is a constant for system under consideration and in general depends on the number density of particles in the system. Similarly, the average occupancy of a quantum state with energy E_2 is equal to:

$$f(E_2, T) = A \exp\left[\frac{-E_2}{k_B T}\right]$$

Supposing that $E_2 - E_1 = \Delta E$, we can write the ratio of the probability of occupation of states with E_1 and E_2 as:

$$ratio = \frac{A \exp\left[\dfrac{-E_2}{k_B T}\right]}{A \exp\left[\dfrac{-E_1}{k_B T}\right]} = \exp\left[\frac{-E_2 - (-E_1)}{k_B T}\right]$$

$$= \exp\left[\frac{-(E_2 - E_1)}{k_B T}\right]$$

$$= \exp\left[\frac{-\Delta E}{k_B T}\right]$$

2.6 Exercises

Exercises marked with a P prefix are 'normal' exercises. Those marked with a C prefix are best solved numerically by using a computer program or spreadsheet. Exercises marked with an E prefix are in general rather more challenging that the P and C exercises. Answers to all the exercises may be found at www.physicsofmatter.com

The elements

P1. Which element is the most common in the outer part of the Sun? Approximately how many parts per million of gold are there in the outer part of the Sun? (Figure 2.1)

P2. Is gold really rare on Earth? What are the relative abundances of copper and gold? Gold tends to cost ≈ 60 times more than silver: is this factor related to their relative abundance on Earth? (Figure 2.1)

C3. A histogram of the number of elements discovered in a given decade shows that discoveries of elements were clumped in certain decades over the last 300 years. Download the data from Table 2.2 and plot the histogram. Can you suggest why this grouping occurred?

P4. A mnemonic for remembering the first row of the transition elements is: 'Katie Can't S(c)kate Till Very Cold Morning F(e)ollows Cold Night Copper Zinc'. Compose a mnemonic for the second row of the transition metals (Figure 2.2) beginning with rubidium.

Electromagnetism

P5. Example 2.2 shows that the force between an electron and a proton separated by a distance of 0.1 nm is 2.31×10^{-8} N. Work out the attractive force between an electron and a proton if they are separated by (a) 0.105 nm and (b) 0.095 nm. Assuming that the force varies roughly linearly with separation over this small range, show that the 'spring constant' K that describes the variation of electric force with distance is approximately $K = 460$ Nm^{-1}. Estimate the resonant frequency of the electron on the atom based on Equation 2.24. What is the wavelength of light with this frequency?

Compare this with the result of Example 7.24 and Figure 7.54 based on the analysis of the optical properties of glasses.

P6. The speed of light through a transparent substance is $c/2$. Estimate its refractive index and dielectric constant (Equation 2.17).

P7. A photon of X-radiation with a wavelength 3×10^{-11} m is completely absorbed by an atom within a complex biological molecule. How many photons of light with wavelength 3×10^{-7} m would have to be absorbed to impart a similar total energy to the molecule? (Equation 2.18)

Classical mechanics

P8. Two atoms are bonded together in a molecule. They vibrate in a stretching vibration with a frequency

1.13×10^{13} Hz. If their atomic mass is 14 u, what is the 'spring' constant that characterises the stiffness of their atomic bond? (Example 2.4)

(Note. In this case the mass you should use in Equation 2.24 is the *reduced mass* μ given by $1/\mu = (1/m + 1/m)$ i.e. $\mu = m/2$. See a classical mechanics text on relative motion.)

P9. Two particles have the same mass and resonant frequency ω_0, but are subjected to different damping mechanisms. The particles are subjected to the same sinusoidally oscillating force at frequency ω_0, but one particle has an amplitude of motion twice that of the other. Use Equation 2.29 to evaluate the relative magnitudes of the damping constant α in Equation 2.26.

P10. Based on the answer to Question P9, outline how an apparatus could be constructed and operated to determine the relative viscosities of two liquids.

C11. Program a computer or use a spreadsheet to plot the Equations 2.29 and 2.30 and so reproduce Figures 2.6 (a) and (b). Change the constant α in these equations to see the effect of damping on the dynamics of the particle.

Quantum mechanics

P12. According to Equation 2.31, what is the minimum kinetic energy of (i) an electron and (ii) a proton confined inside a cubic region of (a) side $L = 0.1$ nm and (b) side $L = 1$ nm.

P13. According to Equation 2.64, what is the minimum energy of (a) an electron and (b) a proton confined by a simple harmonic potential of spring constant 430 Nm^{-1}. What is the 'resonant frequency' f_0 in each case?

Statistical mechanics

P14. Following Table 2.4 for a particle trapped in a three-dimensional cubic box, how many quantum states have energy $14 \times h^2/8mL^2$? You may check your answer against Figure 2.13.

C15. Following Figure 2.17, write a computer program to calculate the degeneracy of all quantum states of a three-dimensional particle in a box with energies less than $40 \times h^2/8mL^2$.

P16. For a box of volume, V the density of quantum states that may be occupied by electrons is $g(E)=A\sqrt{E}$ states/eV. Derive an expression for the number of quantum states (a) with energies between 4 eV and 4.01 eV and (b) with energies between 0 eV and 4.5 eV. (Example 2.6)

C17. Use a calculator or a spreadsheet program to make an accurate sketch of the Fermi–Dirac function for μ (i.e. E_F) = 3 eV and temperatures of T = 10 K, 100 K and 1000 K.

C18. Use a calculator or a spreadsheet program to make an accurate sketch of the Bose–Einstein function for $\mu = 0$ and temperatures of T = 10 K, 100 K and 1000 K.

Large numbers

Numbers used in statistical mechanics can be very large. Try the following exercises to get used to making guesstimates with these large numbers.

C19. There are thought to be around 10^{87} protons in the universe. If they were all assembled into iron atoms with an appropriate number of neutrons and electrons: (a) What would be the mass and volume of the universe? (For the purposes of this calculation, take iron to have a density of $\approx 10^4$ kg m^{-3}.) (b) What would be the ratio of the volume of this 'condensed universe' to volume of the Earth (radius ≈ 6400 km). Is this bigger or smaller than you would have anticipated?

C20. The clock speed of the computer on which I am writing this text is 400 MHz? How long must I leave it running before it has executed the Avogadro number ($N_A = 6.02 \times 10^{23}$ mol^{-1}) of clock cycles? Will the warranty have expired? Estimate very roughly the number of clock cycles executed by *every* computer that that has *ever* existed.

CHAPTER 3
Measurement

3.1 Introduction

The importance of measurement

No matter what the context, the basic idea of measurement is to enable *quantitative comparison* of one property or thing with another. The ability to numerically compare quantities may be considered one of the defining characteristics of a science: without measurement, there is only speculation.

This book contains a chapter on measurement because in the teaching of physics, the insights achieved as a result of studying measurements are often taught as secondary to insights derived from theoretical approaches to a subject. Indeed, I have attended entire lecture courses where no reference was made to a single measurement in the outside world. However, in practice it is exceedingly rare for physicists to proceed in such a fashion. The beliefs that physicists hold about the world are, in a sense, *forced upon them* by measurements. The results of measurements act as guides, and constraints, for developing explanatory ideas about the world. So familiarity with measurements and the way they are made is as important an aspect of physics as familiarity with (say) mathematics. Although a student might be forgiven for thinking otherwise, it is not mathematics but measurement, that makes physics a science rather than a philosophy.

This chapter is divided into four sections:

§3.2 **Units:** Measurement units are in some ways a most mundane subject. Units are the standard quantities which enable the quantitative comparison, of which I spoke above, to be realised. However in other ways things are not so simple.

§3.3 **Key measurement techniques:** Given the importance of measurement, the techniques used to carry out this process are of considerable interest. Here we look at some of the more common techniques. Throughout the twentieth century there has been astonishing progress in techniques driven by the availability of specific technological tools. Three trends stand out above all others: the exploitation of the phenomenal accuracy with which *time* may be measured; the use of digital voltmeters and the concept of a sensor; and most recently the use of lasers and opto-electronic techniques.

§3.4 **Environments:** In considering measurements of the properties of matter we are interested in how matter behaves in differing environments, for example high and low temperatures. In this section we see in rough terms how these environments are created.

§3.5 **Uncertainty:** All measurements have an associated uncertainty. In this section we mention the uncertainty associated with the extensive tabulations and graphs in this book.

At www.physicsofmatter.com

You will find copies of the figures and tables used in this chapter, along with links to several of the world's leading National Measurement Institutes mentioned in the chapter.

3.2 Units

Recalling the fundamental idea of a measurement as a comparison, *units* act as *standard comparison quantities*. This notion of a unit is apparent in the names given to historical units of length such as the *foot*. These units referred to the length of a standard object against which all else in the 'kingdom' would be compared. Unfortunately, neighbouring kingdoms frequently had different definitions for quantities which made *quantitative comparison* exceedingly difficult. For example, in 1686, Newton was attempting to show *quantitatively* that his theory of gravity could explain both phenomena on the Earth as well as the motion of the Moon and other astronomical bodies. In searching for observations in support of his theory (Book III of *Principia Mathematica*) he describes the diameter of the Earth and the motion of the Moon in terms of *Paris* feet, as distinct from *English* feet used elsewhere in his work. Clearly the units of measurement are getting in the way of comparison rather than making it easier.

Historically, there have been two trends that have taken the science of measurement away from the use of units like the foot. These trends are:

- towards the use of a system of units that are agreed internationally
- towards defining standard quantities in terms of *phenomena* that can be *realised* by anyone. This is a move away from the use of defining objects or *artefacts*.

3.2.1 National standards and international agreements

Each country employs a system of *legal metrology*, the main aim of which is to facilitate trade rather than science, but which serves for both purposes. The UK has currently nearly completed adoption of the SI system of measurement units detailed below. The aim of having a coherent system of measurement units is a major scientific and management challenge.

The scientific part of the challenge is the tackled by National Measurement Institutes (NMIs): in the UK, the National Physical Laboratory (NPL); in the USA, the National Institute of Science and Technology (NIST); and in Germany the Physikalisch Technische Bundesanstalt (PTB). These laboratories manufacture and maintain apparatus that allow the *realisation* of accurate representations of the units (Tables 3.1 to 3.3). For example, each of the above NMIs has an apparatus which produces a known voltage against which a voltmeter belonging to a customer may be calibrated. You might now ask the question 'How do the NMIs know the value of the "known voltage" that they produce?' The answer is that they base the value on fundamental physical laws and principles. For the case of voltage, the known voltages are produced by so-called Josephson devices. They also work with each other and NMIs worldwide to ensure that their *realisations* of measurement units are internationally consistent.

The management part of the challenge is tackled by a quality assurance organisation: in the UK, the United Kingdom Accreditation Service (UKAS). This organisation ensures that laboratories bearing its seal of approval carry out valid calibrations and do not claim measurement uncertainties lower than they can actually achieve. Part of this validation is to ensure that relevant measuring instruments used in these laboratories are regularly recalibrated at the NPL. This system maintains a hierarchy of measurement accuracy and ensures that the lower orders of the hierarchy maintain as much as is practicable of the accuracy achieved at the apex of the hierarchy, NPL. However, at each tier of the hierarchy, extra measurement uncertainties are inevitably introduced. This makes it particularly important that the realisations of the base quantities at the NMIs have the smallest measurement uncertainties possible.

In 1999, the trend towards the international harmonisation of measurement units was cemented by the signing of the *Mutual Recognition Arrangement*. The 19 signatories agreed to recognise each other's realisations of measurement units through a programme of key inter-comparisons.

3.2.2 Artefacts and realisations

There are two ways in which we can agree on a measurement standard. Countries can agree on either:

- a standard *object* of which there is only one, and against which all others are compared. This object is referred to in measurement circles as an *artefact*

or

- a standard *physical phenomenon* or situation which it is practical for all countries to create. This situation is referred to in measurement circles as a *realisation* of a measurement unit.

The reason for the trend away from defining units by artefacts to definitions in terms of realisations may be seen by considering the one measurement unit that is still defined by an artefact: the kilogram.

The kilogram

There is only one kilogram. It is a unique piece of platinum–iridium alloy kept at the International Bureau of Weights and Measures (BIPM), Paris. It has its own special symbol, a gothic letter 'K' $\mathcal{K}$, which refers the object itself and not its mass. There are 41 copies of the kilogram in existence: the United Kingdom holds copy number 18. After it was last cleaned, the UK copy of the kilogram weighed 59 ± 3 μg more than the prototype kilogram, and then gained mass at a rate of 1 μg per month for a year and now gains mass at a rate of approximately 1 μg per year. However, the UK kilogram is so valuable that it spends it days in carefully controlled conditions inside three bell jars. Every time it is removed from its protective surrounding its mass changes a little as it reacts slowly with the air and adsorbs (or desorbs) a little moisture. Periodically the UK's copy of the kilogram is returned to Paris to make sure that its mass has not changed too much. But what if the international prototype kilogram, $\mathcal{K}$ itself, changed its mass? In fact recent inter-comparisons have shown that $\mathcal{K}$ definitely *has* changed mass, and a small coterie of scientists keep track of its changes by inter-comparing the copies of it.

Thus defining a standard quantity in terms of an object makes life very difficult for everyone concerned, and allows for the possibility of long term drift in the magnitude of measurement units. Definitions of standard quantities in terms of *artefacts* of any kind have died out leaving 'standard metres' as museum pieces. The reason for the anomalous longevity of the kilogram arises for the simple reason that despite the unsatisfactory nature of the arrangement, the resulting measurement uncertainties are lower than can be achieved by any competitive technique.

Other units are defined in terms of physical phenomena which may, in principle at least, be *realised* by anyone. The phenomena chosen are believed to be well understood, so that the definitions are unlikely to require revision, and hence the system of units will not change with time.

For example, the phenomena of the coexistence in equilibrium of water vapour, liquid water and ice defines the *triple point* of water (see Chapter 10 for more details). The temperature at which the triple point of pure water occurs is *defined* to be 273.16 kelvin. All one needs to do in order to realise this temperature is to obtain some pure water, manufacture a simple vessel, and stick it into ice at close to 0 °C. After equilibration, the temperature inside is *defined* to be 273.16 kelvin. This is a physical phenomenon which may be realised with relative ease and which will not change from one year to the next, or from one place to another.

3.2.3 The international system of units

All rational physicists use the system of units known as the *International System of Units*, or *Le Système International d'Unités*, or more normally *SI units*. At least they use SI units when discussing subjects other than their own. For discussing their own field of expertise, they frequently use sets of *colloquial units,* which for historical reasons, and reasons of genuine convenience, have not died out. In this book, I have chosen always to use the SI units, adding colloquial units where appropriate.

The SI units consist of seven base or fundamental quantities in terms of which all other quantities are derived. The SI base units and definitions are given Table 3.1.

Table 3.1 The SI base units. Notice that, with the exception of the kilogram, the definitions are in terms of physical phenomena and not defining artefacts. Although the definitions seem obscure, the language is carefully chosen in order to make accurate realisations of the standards feasible.

Quantity: Unit (abbreviation)	Definition
Time: second (s)	The second is the duration of 9,192,631,770 periods of the radiation corresponding to the transition between two hyperfine levels of the ground state of the caesium-133 atom.
Length: metre (m)	The metre is the length of the path travelled by light in vacuum during a time interval 1/299,792,458 of a second. Note: This defines 299,792,458 ms^{-1} as the *exact* speed of light in a vacuum.
Mass: kilogram (kg)	The kilogram is the unit of mass; it is equal to the mass of the international prototype of the kilogram
Electric Current: ampere (A)	The ampere is that constant current which, if maintained in two straight parallel conductors of infinite length, of negligible circular cross-section, and placed 1 metre apart in vacuum, would produce between these conductors a force equal to 2×10^{-7} newton, per metre of length.
Thermodynamic temperature: kelvin (K)	The kelvin, unit of thermodynamic temperature, is the fraction 1/273.16 of the thermodynamic temperature of the triple point of pure water.
Amount of substance: mole (mol)	The mole is the amount of substance of a system which contains as many elementary entities as there are atoms in 0.012 kilogram of carbon 12.
Luminous Intensity: candela (cd)	The candela is the luminous intensity, in a given direction, of a source that emits monochromatic radiation 540×10^{12} hertz and that has a radiant intensity of 1/683 watt per steradian

There are two other units (Table 3.2), called supplementary units, which are used to distinguish between quantities that are of a different nature, but which would otherwise have the same SI units. For example *angular velocity* is specified in units of rad s^{-1} even though the radian is dimensionless. This distinguishes the units of *angular velocity* from those of *frequency*.

Other units are derived from these base units, and have names given in terms of the base units involved. For example *mass density* is expressed in a unit called the *kilogram per cubic metre* and has the symbol kg m^{-3}. Other units derived from these base units are specially named in honour of various scientists. These are listed in Table 3.3.

I think it is important to realise that although SI is the culmination of a century of work in devising a rational system of units, alternative systems are still in use.

3.2.4 An example of the realisation of units: the mole

As an example of the way that SI defines the magnitude of a unit, let us consider what SI has to say about *the mole*: the unit of the *amount of substance*. First recall the definition from Table 3.1:

The mole is the amount of substance of a system which contains as many elementary entities as there are atoms in 0.012 kilogram of carbon 12.

A supplementary note to the agreement of this definition mentions that it is important to specify which elementary entities are being referred to.

Table 3.2 SI supplementary units.

Quantity	Name	Symbol	Expression in terms of SI base units
plane angle	radian	rad	m m^{-1} =1
solid angle	steradian	sr	m^2 m^{-2} =1

Table 3.3 SI derived units with special names. The name of the units are all written with lower case letters (with the exception of degree Celsius), but that the symbols for the units have upper case letters: be careful to distinguish between seimens (S) and seconds (s). The symbol for the ohm, Ω, is the greek letter 'W', called omega.

Quantity	Name	Symbol	Expression in terms of other units	Expression in terms of SI base units
frequency	hertz	Hz		s^{-1}
force	newton	N		$m\ kg\ s^{-2}$
pressure	pascal	Pa	$N\ m^{-2}$	$m^{-1}\ kg\ s^{-2}$
stress				
energy	joule	J	$N\ m$	$m^2\ kg\ s^{-2}$
work				
quantity of heat				
power	watt	W	$J\ s^{-1}$	$m^2\ kg\ s^{-3}$
radiant flux				
electric charge	coulomb	C		$s\ A$
quantity of electricity				
electrical potential	volt	V	$W\ A^{-1}$	$m^2\ kg\ s^{-3}\ A^{-1}$
potential difference				
electromotive force				
capacitance	farad	F	$C\ V^{-1}$	$m^2\ kg^{-1}\ s^4\ A^{-1}$
electric resistance	ohm	Ω	$V\ A^{-1}$	$m^2\ kg\ s^{-3}\ A^2$
electric conductance	siemens	S	$A\ V^{-1}$	$m^2\ kg^{-1}\ s^3\ A^{-1}$
magnetic flux	weber	Wb	$V\ s$	$m^2\ kg\ s^{-2}\ A^{-1}$
magnetic flux density	tesla	T	$Wb\ m^{-2}$	$kg\ s^{-2}\ A^{-1}$
inductance	henry	H	$Wb\ A^{-1}$	$m^2\ kg\ s^{-2}\ A^{-2}$
Celsius temperature	degree celsius	°C		K
luminous flux	lumen	lm		$cd\ sr$
illuminance	lux	lx	$lm\ m^{-2}$	$m^{-2}\ cd\ sr$

They may be ions, electrons, atoms, molecules, other particles or groups of particles.

Notice that this definition leaves it up to the scientific community to invent practical realisations of the definition. Let us look at a couple of ways in which, starting from first principles, we might determine the *amount of substance* in a sample of material.

Realisation #1

If the substance is a gas then we can use the fact that, as we show in Table 5.3, the volume of 1 mole of any gaseous substance held at standard temperature and pressure (STP), is close to $22.413 \times 10^{-3}\ m^3$. In §5.2.2 we see that we can understand *why* this is so based on an analysis of a microscopic theory of the behaviour of a gas. This analysis produces the perfect gas equation $PV = zRT$ (Eq. 4.1), while more sophisticated analyses (§4.4.2) arrive at slightly different equations that enable us to understand the small deviations of the volume at STP from the ideal value. We thus have a piece of physics which contains no 'fudge factors'. Thus, we can use the perfect gas equation to realise any of the quantities in the perfect gas equation (P, V, z, T) in terms of other quantities.

Thus by measuring the pressure of the gas at 0 °C in a container of known volume V we can infer the number of moles z of gaseous substance in the container. In fact, $PV = zRT$ is more commonly used to realise the definition of temperature T in terms of the pressure P of z moles of gaseous material in a container of fixed volume V.

Realisation #2

If the material is a solid or liquid and its chemical composition is known, then the number of moles

can be determined by weighing. If we consider a material A of chemical composition $X_p Y_q$ then we note that the molar mass of A is given by:

$$M(A) = \frac{m[A]}{m\left[^{12}C\right]} \times 0.012 \ \text{kg mol}^{-1} \qquad (3.1)$$

Here $m(A)$ indicates the mass of a single entity of the substance A. In this case 'a single entity' refers to a collection of p atoms of type X and q atoms of type Y. Similarly $m(^{12}C)$ indicates the mass of a single atom of ^{12}C. Note that although neither of these masses is known with great accuracy, the *ratio* expressed in Equation 3.1 can be measured with high accuracy by, for example, a *mass spectrometer*. Similarly the ratios:

$$\frac{m[X]}{m\left[^{12}C\right]} \ \text{and} \ \frac{m[Y]}{m\left[^{12}C\right]} \qquad (3.2)$$

can also be determined accurately. We can thus state that the mass of 1 mole of A is:

$$M(A) = \left[\left(p \left(\frac{m[X]}{m\left[^{12}C\right]} \right) + q \left(\frac{m[Y]}{m\left[^{12}C\right]} \right) \right) \right] \times 0.012 \ \text{kg mol}^{-1}$$

$$(3.3)$$

This enables the quantity of elementary entities in a sample of substance A to be determined as shown in Example 3.1

Example 3.1

How many moles of calcium fluoride (CaF_2) are there in 4.3209 kg of the substance ?

For CaF_2 we write X = Ca, Y = F, p = 1 and q = 2. The ratios of Equation 3.3 are noted in *Kaye and Laby* to be:

$$\frac{m(Ca)}{m(^{12}C)} = \frac{40.08}{12} = 3.34$$

and

$$\frac{m(F)}{m(^{12}C)} = \frac{18.9984}{12} = 1.5832$$

So the mass of a mole specified by Equation 3.3 is:

$$M(CaF_2) = [1 \times 3.34 + 2 \times 1.5832] \times 0.012$$

$$= 0.07808 \ \text{kg mol}^{-1}$$

If we have 4.3209 kg of CaF_2 we can determine the amount of CaF_2 by dividing the sample mass by the molar mass:

$$\text{Amount of } CaF_2 = \frac{4.3209}{0.07808} \ \text{mol}$$

$$= 55.34 \ \text{mol}.$$

Notice that the definition of a mole does not specify which realisation should be used: this is a matter for scientists and engineers to choose. As improvements in our understanding develop, or new techniques become available, the definition need not change. But the realisations of the definition may change, and hopefully become more accurate or easy to use.

3.3 Key measurement techniques

Certain techniques of measurement occur commonly in a wide variety of situations. The commonness, and hence the importance, of these techniques make them worth mentioning separately.

3.3.1 Time

Time, or its inverse, *frequency*, can be measured with stupendous accuracy. The UK National Physical Laboratory can realise a second with an accuracy of 1 part in 10^{13}. In part this is the result of hard work, but it is also due to the fact that time

lends itself to being measured accurately. For example, through what is known as the *piezo-electric effect*, a quartz (SiO_2) crystal mechanically oscillates at a frequency dependent on its size, shape, temperature, and applied electric field. If all these quantities are stabilised, it is possible for such a crystal (costing perhaps 10 pence) to oscillate at a frequency of about 10^8 Hz stable to a few parts in 10^9 over a few hours. These oscillations can be detected and converted into a stream of electrical pulses. Because we have the technology to count

pulses extremely reliably, we can determine how many pulses occur in a given interval of time. Indeed, in measurement circles *counting* is not generally considered a measurement because it has no uncertainty associated with it! The uncertainty in our count will then be two pulses at most, one at the beginning and one at the end of the timing interval. So, by counting these pulses, we can determine elapsed times of the order of one second with a resolution of 2 parts in 10^8. All that remains is to determine the actual frequency of the crystal by comparison with an instrument calibrated at a National Measurement Institute.

Voltage to frequency conversion

The ease with which high resolution is achieved for time and frequency measurements has caused people to seek ways to convert the quantity they wish to measure into a time measurement. The most important example of this is the development of techniques for measuring voltage, i.e. electrical potential difference. A simplified example of the conversion of a voltage measurement to a time measurement is the *integrating analogue to digital converter* (ADC). An integrating ADC (Figure 3.1) consists of three parts: an *integrator*, a *comparator* and a source of clock pulses as described above. There are three stages to the measurement:

- First, a circuit generates a current accurately proportional to an input voltage. This is arranged to charge a capacitor for a fixed period

Figure 3.1 An integrating analogue to digital converter.

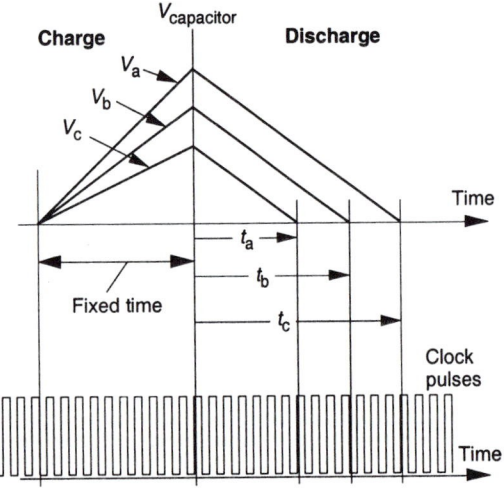

of time, i.e. for a fixed number of clock pulses.

- Second, with the input disconnected, the capacitor is discharged by a constant current circuit until the voltage reaches zero, as determined by a comparator circuit. The time taken for this discharge is measured by counting the number of clock pulses that occur during the discharge. The count of clock pulses required for the capacitor to discharge has been designed to be accurately proportional to the magnitude of the input voltage. So the larger the input voltage, the longer the discharge time and hence the more pulses that are counted.

- Third, digital circuitry converts this count to the correct units. Thus a measurement of time performed by counting clock pulses has been converted into a measurement of voltage.

Many variations of this technique exist under the general heading of *charge balancing* or *voltage to frequency* conversion techniques. Example 3.2 shows the high precision which may be achieved using such techniques. In all cases the result of the measurement is now held in the state of digital circuitry and may be easily 'read' by a computer for subsequent analysis.

3.3.2 Voltage measurement and transducer technology

The accuracy and ease with which voltage can be measured has caused a trend towards the creation

---

Example 3.2

If the clock of an integrating ADC runs at 10 MHz, how accurately could a voltage be measured if the integrating period was 1 second?

If the counting is accurate to ± 1 pulse then the discharge period can be timed with an uncertainty of roughly $0.1\,\mu s$. If the discharge period is roughly 0.1 s then the fractional uncertainty due to the integration is only of the order $0.1 \times 10^{-6}/0.1 \approx 1$ part in 10^6. If the voltage was of the order of 0.1 V this would correspond to an uncertainty of only a fraction of a microvolt. In practice, other factors make it difficult to achieve uncertainties at this low level.

of devices, known as *transducers* or *sensors*, which convert changes in physical quantities into changes in a voltage. Once a voltage that is related to the physical quantity to be measured has been generated, electrical circuits can act on the voltage to actuate a display or an alarm. Alternatively, once a voltage which corresponds to the quantity to be measured has been created, analogue-to-digital converters (Figure 3.1) can convert the voltage, and hence the quantity being measured, into a *digital code*. The data can then be conveniently analysed and stored using ever more powerful computers. Below we will look at just a few of the more important sensors.

Temperature sensors

In general, temperature sensors operate by passing an electric current through a piece of material and measuring changes in the flow of electric current as the temperature changes.

Platinum resistance thermometer

A *platinum resistance thermometer* (PRT) consists of a length of thin platinum wire. The electrical resistivity of platinum has been investigated extensively over many years and is now well documented (Figures 3.2 and 7.35). Ideally the wire should be strain-free and held delicately, but more commonly the requirement that the PRT be robust and easy to use is valued more highly than the absolute accuracy of the results. Practical PRTs are commonly formed by using a *thin film* of platinum on a substrate which conducts heat well, but is electrically insulating,. Alternatively, they may be wound on a frame and then held in place by a thermally-conducting, but electrically-insulating, cement.

Platinum is chosen in preference to other metals with similar electrical properties because of its exceptional resistance to chemical corrosion. This means that the diameter of wires made of platinum does not decrease as the wire slowly corrodes. The insensitivity to corrosion allows PRTs to be used up to temperatures as high as 1000 °C.

The length and diameter of the platinum wire are commonly chosen to give the PRT a resistance of 100 Ω at 0 °C.

Thermistor

Thermistors are pieces of semiconducting materials operated in a similar fashion to PRTs, but with a dramatically different dependence on temperature (Figure 3.2). Thermistors are particularly useful because their sensitivity to temperature changes is much higher than a PRT, but only over a limited range of temperatures.

Semiconducting diodes

Semiconducting diodes are used as temperature sensors in almost exactly the same way as resistance thermometers. A constant current of typically $10 \mu A$ is passed through the diode, and the voltage across the diode is measured (Figure 3.3) Diodes are considered separately from thermistors and PRTs because at constant temperature the voltage–current characteristic is highly non-linear, or non-ohmic i.e. V is not proportional to I However, at constant current, the voltage across the diode varies linearly over a wide temperature range.

Thermocouples

A thermocouple is one of the oldest, cheapest, and most difficult to explain methods of measuring temperature. A thermocouple is an arrangement of

Figure 3.2 Schematic variation of the electrical resistance of a platinum resistance thermometer (PRT) and a thermistor. Figure 7.36 shows a more accurate representation of the electrical resistance of platinum. Notice that the resistance of a PRT increases gradually with increasing temperature. In contrast, the resistance of a thermistor falls dramatically as the temperature is increased.

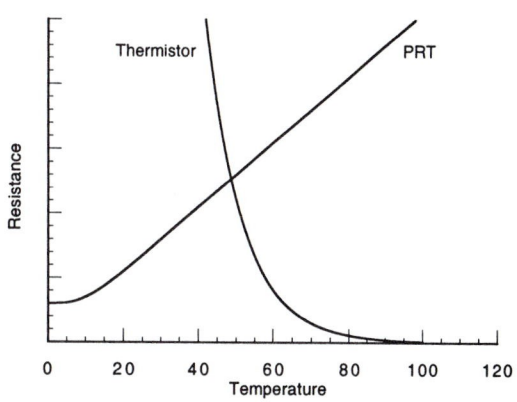

Figure 3.3. Illustration of the operation of a semiconductor diode thermometer. The variation of the voltage across the diode (a) is a non-linear, i.e. a non-ohmic function of the current through the diode. However if the current through the diode is fixed, the variation of the voltage with absolute temperature (b) is surprisingly linear over a wide temperature range.

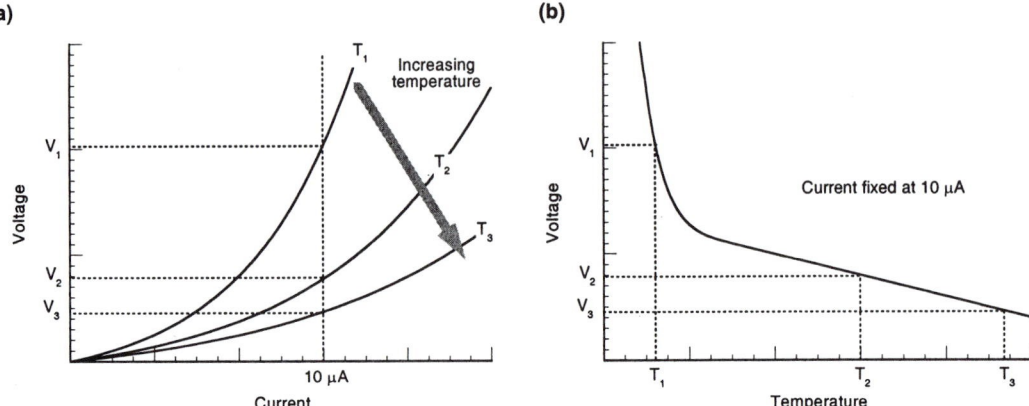

two metals, generally in wire form, and commonly configured as shown in Figure 3.4. In the arrangement shown, a potential difference (voltage) is generated across the terminals of the thermocouple, which is related to the temperature *difference* between the two junctions. For commonly

chosen materials, this voltage is nearly linearly proportional to the temperature difference. If one junction is held at a reference temperature (commonly 0 °C), then the temperature in Celsius of the second junction can be determined.

In practice thermocouples represent a cheap and relatively easy way to determine temperature. The metals in a thermocouple can be chosen to enable temperature measurement from a few kelvin to over 2000 °C (but not with the same thermocouple). However, because of difficulties with calibration, thermocouples are rarely used where the minimum uncertainty in temperature is required. Their main advantages are their low cost and the low mass of the sensing junction

Figure 3.4 Illustration of a common configuration for the use of a thermocouple. The thermocouple junction is placed where the temperature needs to be measured, and the other ends of the wires are joined to copper wires in a reference bath held at a known, stable temperature (typically that of melting ice). The thermocouple voltage (typically 40 μV for each degree celsius difference between the junction temperature and the reference temperature) is measured by a high-resolution voltmeter or analogue to digital converter.

Physically, it is a curious fact that the measured thermovoltage is *not* generated at the measurement junction. Instead, the measured voltage results from any region of the *entire length* of the wires in the circuit in which there is a *temperature gradient*. The magnitude of the thermovoltage generated in each length of wire depends on (a) the composition of the wire and (b) the integral of the temperature gradients along the wire. It is really rather surprising that such complex physics results in a simple and easy to use device. The theory of thermocouples is outlined further at the end of this chapter (§3.6 Exercise P6).

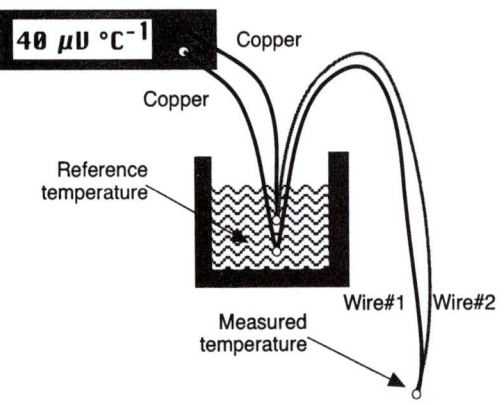

49

3.3.3 Lasers and optical techniques

What is special about lasers?

The word *laser* has now joined the mainstream of the English language. Until relatively recently however, it was merely an acronym, LASER, standing for *Light Amplification by the Stimulated Emission of Radiation*. The basic idea of laser operation is summarised in Figure 3.5. The discovery of the phenomenon of laser action in 1960 marked the start of a revolution. Since then, techniques have been developed to exploit the interaction of laser light with matter to determine all kinds of properties of matter. Lasers have many properties as light sources that are unmatched by any other source. For example:

- Lasers are very bright: this makes the beams easy to detect
- Laser light beams have (or can have) a very low divergence. This makes it possible to control the region of interaction between a laser beam and a substance being probed
- Laser light is (or can be) monochromatic
- Laser light is (or can be) coherent
- Lasers can produce very short pulses of light
- Lasers are very intense
- Laser light in the infra-red region of the spectrum can be transmitted through optical fibres with extremely low losses.

In different applications, different properties of lasers are exploited. However, the combination of properties available makes laser techniques extremely powerful. Importantly, such techniques can permit measurements in which there is no physical contact with the substance being investigated.

Light intensity transducers

The importance of optical techniques, not least for fibre-optic communication systems, has led to many developments in the field of transducers that convert variations in light intensity into electrical signals.

Photoresistors

The earliest of these detectors consisted of a resistor made from the element selenium. When illuminated the electrical resistance of the selenium falls dramatically. So if a constant current is passed through a selenium resistor, the voltage across the resistor will fall at high light levels and

---

Figure 3.5 The principle of laser action. (a) Consider a gas of atoms each of which has two quantum states which we can refer to as A and B.

(b) The relative proportions of atoms in the quantum states depends on their energies (E_A, E_B) and is given by a Boltzmann factor $\exp[-(E_B - E_A)/k_B T]$. This ensures that *in equilibrium* there are always more atoms in quantum state A (with lower energy) than quantum state B (with higher energy). When light of just the correct frequency $f = (E_B - E_A)/h$ is shone through the gas, transitions between quantum states are stimulated *with equal probability in either direction*. However, because there are many more atoms in quantum state A with lower energy, there are many more upward transitions ($A \Rightarrow B$) than downward transitions ($B \Rightarrow A$) so on average light is absorbed by the gas.

(c) In a laser, a non-equilibrium situation is arranged by one of many techniques in which there is a *population inversion* where many more atoms are in quantum state B with higher energy. Now the passage of light of just the correct frequency stimulates more *downward* than *upward* transitions and *on average* the medium emits more light at frequency f than initially entered the gas: Hence the name *Light Amplification by the Stimulated Emission of Radiation*

To create a population inversion it is in fact necessary that there be at least one other quantum state with energy greater than E_B, but I have not shown that state on these figures.

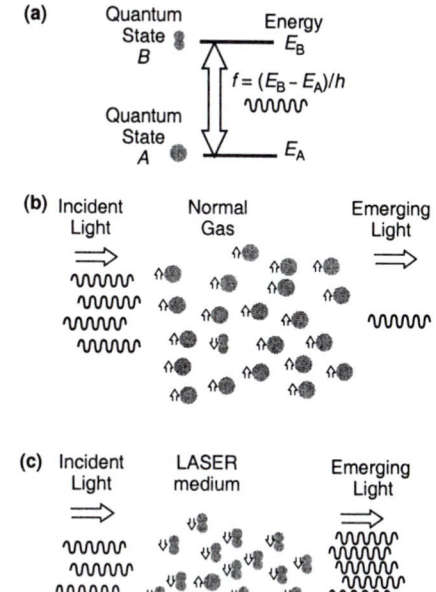

rise at low light levels. The microscopic processes that cause the change in resistance are discussed in Chapter 7, along with the optical behaviour of the better-known semiconducting elements silicon and germanium. The photo-resistive response is generally rather slow, and except in the cheapest applications, photoresistors have now been superseded by silicon photodiodes. The exception to this is the detection of far infrared light, with wavelengths greater than around 2 microns where photoresistors have a superior performance.

Photodiodes

Currently, *photodiodes* provide the most common elements in light detecting electrical circuits. The operation of the devices is complex, but may be summarised as follows. A *photodiode* is manufactured out of a semiconductor in which there is a junction between regions with different impurities. The impurities are chosen so that at the interface between the different regions, there arises a thin region of intense electric field known as the *depletion layer*. In a photodiode, this region is arranged to occupy as large a volume as possible.

When light interacts with valence electrons in a semiconductor, the electrons may become detached from a particular atom and made available to travel through the semiconductor. Normally, the electron is drawn back to the atom it has come from by the residual positive electric charge that it leaves behind it. However if the valence electron that absorbs the energy is located in a strong electric field, such as that which exists within the *depletion layer*, then it can be drawn away from its parent atom. It then contributes to an electric current that has been induced by the interaction of light with the semiconductor.

If photodiodes could operate perfectly they would generate one electron for each *photon* that was absorbed. By measuring the current generated between the two terminals of the diode we can determine the number of photons arriving at the *depletion layer* between the two impurity regions of the semiconductor. Importantly, photodiodes are most commonly made of silicon, which can be interfaced directly with silicon integrated circuits.

Figure 3.6 Light Transducers. Devices that generate a voltage or current when illuminated are technologically and experimentally important.

Photoresistors (a) are generally semiconducting substances in which extra carriers are created when illuminated with light whose photon energy exceeds its band gap. The extra carriers lower the electrical resistance of the substance. Although photoresistors are cheap, their change in resistance is not directly proportional to light intensity.

Photodiodes (b) are devices consisting of a junction of two semiconducting substances, most commonly *p* and *n* type silicon. When light is absorbed in the *depletion layer* between the *p* and *n* type silicon, a hole and an electron carrier are created and are drawn apart by the intense electric field in the depletion layer. Silicon photodiodes can measure light with wavelength s in the range 400 nm to 1050 nm. Although not equally sensitive to all wavelengths in this range, for any particular wavelength, the current is directly proportional to the light intensity. This is also the basic process used in silicon solar cells used to generate electricity from sunlight. See also Figure 7.56.

Photomultipliers (c) consist of a series of specially-coated electrodes inside a vacuum container. As explained in the text, a photon of light first liberates a few electrons at the first cathode. These electrons are then accelerated towards a second electrode where they release secondary electrons. These are then accelerated and after 7 or 8 electrodes, a detectable current pulse is produced in response to even a single photon.

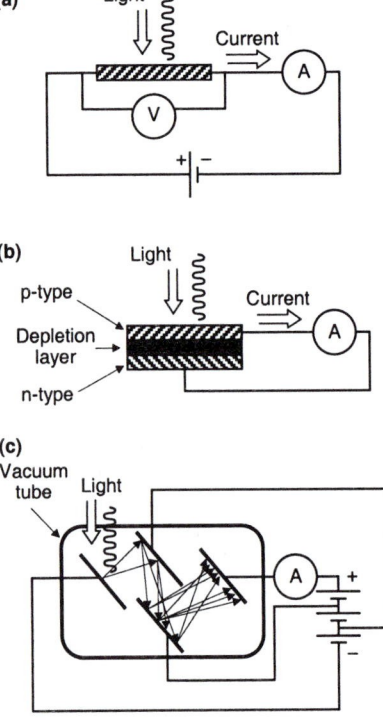

Photomultipliers

The most sensitive of all light-detecting devices are *photomultipliers*. These are evacuated glass tubes with a series of metal plates, *cathodes*, held at different voltages. Light illuminates the first plate, called the *photocathode*. By means of the photoelectric effect, a photon incident upon the photocathode can cause the emission of an electron. The electric field around the *photocathode* is such as to accelerate the emitted electron towards the second cathode. As the electron strikes the second cathode, it causes the emission of typically 6 or 7 *secondary electrons*, which are then drawn towards the third cathode. Here each of these secondary electrons causes a further 6 or 7 electrons to be emitted. Thus between $6^2 = 36$ and $7^2 = 49$ electrons are drawn towards a fourth cathode, and so on. A photomultiplier might contain as many as ten cathodes, after which the number of electrons has increased to between $6^{10} \approx 6.0 \times 10^7$ and $7^{10} \approx 2.8 \times 10^8$.

Thus, each photon produces a current pulse of typically 10^8 electrons. Although this amplification is impressive, it still presents a measurement challenge. In terms of voltages, it represents a voltage pulse of perhaps 1 mV lasting for a fraction of a microsecond, on top of the total voltage across the photomultiplier tube of around 1000V.

Interferometry

Measurement of distances or of motion can be achieved by using the techniques of optical interferometry with a resolution of less than a wavelength of light $\approx 7 \times 10^{-7}$ m, almost independent of the distance in question. The use of these techniques is made enormously more straightforward by the existence of cheap and robust sources of coherent light: lasers.

The basic principle of interferometry is illustrated in Figure 3.7. Light from a source S travels along two (or more) paths, say A and B, to a detector D.

First of all recall that light is the name we give to oscillations of the electric field when the oscillations occur with frequencies in the range 400×10^{12} Hz (blue) and 1000×10^{12} Hz (red). The electric field at D is the sum of the electric fields due to light arriving via path A and path B. If light from a source S follows a route which passes a point D via point A then the electric field at D oscillates rapidly with amplitude E_A volts per metre. If light from S travels to D by a second route, say via B, then the electric field at D is the sum of two oscillating electric fields, one with amplitude E_A and the other with amplitude E_B.

If the light from S is derived from several random sources of light within S (such as the atoms within a light bulb) then the electric field at D due to the waves arriving via A and B will sometimes add up, and sometimes subtract. On average this results in a value of electric field amplitude greater than the either E_A or E_B independently, but not equal to the sum $E_A + E_B$. Importantly, the average resultant amplitude of the electric field oscillation, given by:

$$\sqrt{\left[E_A^2 + E_B^2\right]})$$

does not depend on the precise lengths of paths A and B, or on the *details* of the conditions experienced along those paths.

Figure 3.7 Illustration of the use of an optical interferometer. Experiments placed in either of the experimental regions can affect the interference of light from source S at detector D. To detect small movements an experiment could be arranged to move a mirror in the optical path. To detect changes in optical properties of a material, the material could be placed directly in the optical path

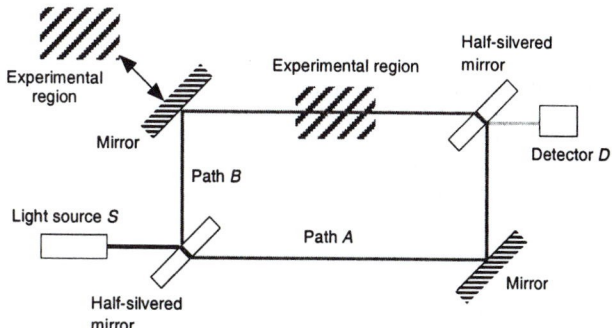

However, things are different if the light from S is derived from a *coherent* source of light, i.e. one in which all the atoms in S emit light *in phase* with each other. In this case, the waves arriving at D will add up *on every oscillation*, subtract *on every oscillation*, or do something in between *on every oscillation*. Exactly which situation occurs depends on the details of the conditions experienced along the paths A *or* B (for example, the presence or absence of a gas) and on the precise length of the paths. For a given set of conditions along the paths, the amplitude of the electric field oscillations varies between 0 and $(E_A + E_B)$. Let us say, for example, that under a given set of conditions along paths A and B the electric field oscillations have zero amplitude: then either:

- a shift in the position of the mirror by approximately one half a wavelength of light ($\approx 10^{-7}$m) or
- a delay of the light wave by $\approx 10^{-15}$ s caused by a change in some property of the medium through which the light travels,

is sufficient to change the amplitude of the electric field oscillations at D from zero amplitude to maximum amplitude $(E_A + E_B)$.

There are a many examples of the use of laser interferometry but space permits the inclusion of only two. The first example (Figure 3.8) is the detection of changes in the height of a liquid surface, and the second (Figure 3.9) is the direct measurement of the optical properties of a gas.

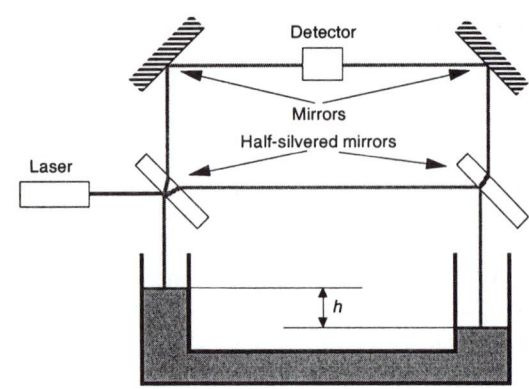

Figure 3.8 An optical interferometer used for the determination of change in height of a column of mercury.

In measurements of *pressure* it is common to use a U-tube filled with liquid as a simple manometer. This translates pressure differences into changes in the heights of liquid in the arms of the manometer. Using an optical interferometer the change in the liquid height can be detected with a resolution of the order 10^{-7} m.

The speed of light travelling through a gas differs slightly from the speed of light in a vacuum. As is discussed more fully in §5.8.2, the speed difference is related to the polarisability of the molecules of the gas. The device shown in Figure 3.9 is designed to measure small changes in the speed of light as the pressure of the gas in an experimental cell is changed (§5.8).

Figure 3.9 An optical interferometer used for the determination of the electrical polarisability of a gas. The apparatus is first set to a reference state by evacuating both the reference cell and the experimental cell. The reference cell is then kept under vacuum while the gas under investigation is introduced into the experimental cell. The light travelling through the experimental cell is then slowed down slightly by the interaction of its oscillating electric field with the electric charge on each atom. This results in a change in the intensity of light at the detector because the interference condition now depends on the transit time through the experimental cell.

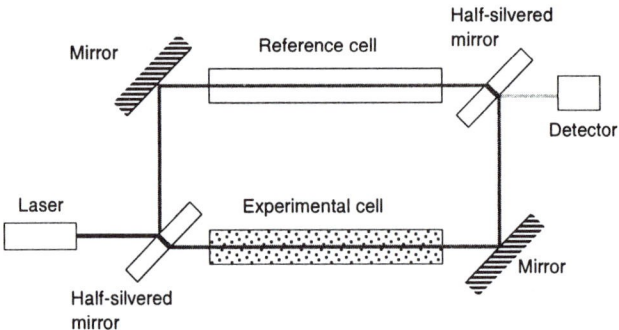

3.3.4 Bridges and balances

In studying the properties of matter, it is an unfortunate fact that many substances show only relatively small changes in their properties in response to changes in their environment. Consider the examples *A* and *B* below.

Example A

The volume of solids and liquids changes by typically 1 part in 10^5 when the temperature changes by 1 °C. The thermal expansion of most solids is of a similar order of magnitude, and so in order to compare the thermal expansion of different materials, we need to detect a length change of 1 part in 10^5 with a resolution of, say, 1 % or better. In other words, we need an apparatus that will detect a length change of 1 part in 10^7. In an experimental sample that might be $\approx$ 1cm $\times$ 1cm $\times$ 1cm, a change of 1 part in 10^7 corresponds to detecting a length change of $\approx 10^{-9}$ m, or about 3 atomic diameters.

Example B

In order to determine the heat capacity of a substance we need to change the temperature by a small amount ΔT at an absolute temperature of T. Ideally ΔT will be a small fraction T, typically perhaps 1%. But ΔT must be measured with a resolution of $\approx$ 1 part in 10^3 in order to determine the heat capacity with an accuracy of 0.1%. Thus it seems that the temperature must be measured to 1 part in 10^5.

Situations such as these, and a variety of others, call for the application of *comparison* or *bridge techniques*. What these techniques have in common is that they are sensitive not to the static background quantity (e.g. length or temperature in our examples), but to *small changes* in it.

Wheatstone bridge

The simplest example of this is the case of the *Wheatstone Bridge* electrical circuit shown in Figure 3.10.

The circuit, consisting of four resistors, a voltmeter and a voltage source, has two key features of its response.

- The circuit is said to be *balanced* when $R_a = R_b$ and $R_c = R_d$. At this point there will be no potential difference across the detector **V**. Thus the voltmeter is not sensitive to the magnitude of any of the resistances in the circuit, but it is sensitive to whether the resistances are *balanced*.

- Suppose that the circuit is initially balanced, and then R_d changes slightly from its balance condition by an amount ΔR. The voltmeter may be used on its most sensitive range to detect the out-of-balance voltage, which is given by:

$$\Delta V = i_{bridge}\left[\frac{\Delta R(R_a + R_b)}{R_a + R_b + R_c + R_d}\right] \qquad (3.4)$$

where we have assumed $\Delta R \ll R_a + R_b + R_c + R_d$. Suppose the voltmeter can resolve a change of

Figure 3.10 The Wheatstone Bridge circuit. A voltage source drives a current i_{bridge} through the resistance network illustrated. The detector **V** need not have, but most commonly will have, an impedance much greater than any of the other resistances in the circuit. The bridge is balanced when $R_a = R_b$ and $R_c = R_d$.

Figure 3.11. The alternative to a Wheatstone Bridge circuit. A voltage source drives a current i_{bridge} through the resistance R_d. The detector **V** must have an impedance much greater than R_d. If R_d changes by ΔR then the voltage across R_d changes by $\Delta V = i_{bridge}\Delta R$.

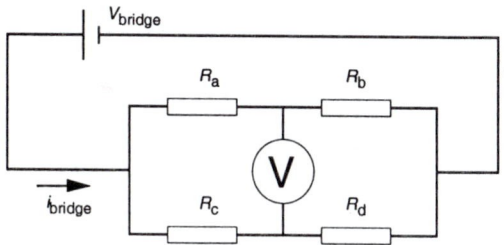

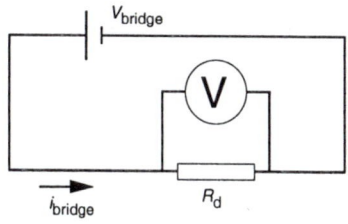

1 μV in 100 mV, a common specification. If R_a, R_b, R_c, and R_d were all 1000 Ω, $\Delta R_d = 1$ Ω and $i_{bridge} = 10$ mA, then ΔV would be 5mV. The voltmeter would then be able to detect a change of 1 Ω in a total resistance of 1000 Ω with a resolution of 1 part in 5000. The bridge circuit would thus just be able to detect resistance changes of the order of one thousandth of an ohm, i.e. 1 part in 10^6 of the total resistance.

Notice that the voltage change at the detector in a bridge circuit (5mV in the above example) is less than the voltage change which would occur if we passed the entire current i_{bridge} through the resistor R_d (Figure 3.11). If we did this we would get a change in voltage $\Delta V = i_{bridge}\Delta R$. This would be equal to 10 mV in the above example. So why bother with the complication of a bridge circuit? When using the bridge, the signal is 5 mV, increased from nothing, i.e. 0 mV $\Rightarrow$ 5mV. However, in the direct measurement configuration, the 10 mV is on top of a 1 V background, i.e. 1.000 V $\Rightarrow$ 1.010 V. Although the bridge has halved the voltage due to the resistance change, the 5mV signal is easier to measure with high resolution

because the background signal has been subtracted.

This is exactly the technique used for example *B* above. The element R_d of the circuit is arranged to be a resistance thermometer. The temperature step ΔT is applied by a resistive heater and results in a small change ΔR in the value of the resistance thermometer. The magnitude of the change ΔR is inferred from measurement of ΔV, and then converted to an equivalent temperature change ΔT.

Similarly, for example *B* above changes in the sample length can be converted into changes in the separation of two metal plates forming a capacitor (Figure 3.13). The changes in capacitance can be detected with high resolution by a circuit called a *capacitance bridge*, which is analogous to the Wheatstone bridge but which operates with alternating current.

The examples above represent ways of detecting *small changes* in quantities in a way that is insensitive to the magnitude of the quantities themselves.

The use of bridges has one more advantage. Consider again Equation 3.4 and the circuit it refers to in Figure 3.10 . Suppose that instead of measuring the out-of-balance voltage ΔV, we adjusted R_C so as to restore the balance condition $\Delta V = 0$. This would allow us to determine ΔR in terms of the four resistances R_a, R_b, R_c, R_d and the only requirement placed on the detector is that it should show a true zero. It does not need to be linear or even calibrated! There are occasions where this relatively simple approach produces results with the lowest measurement uncertainty.

Figure 3.12 The Wheatstone bridge may be used to detect small changes in a resistance thermometer due to a temperature change ΔT.

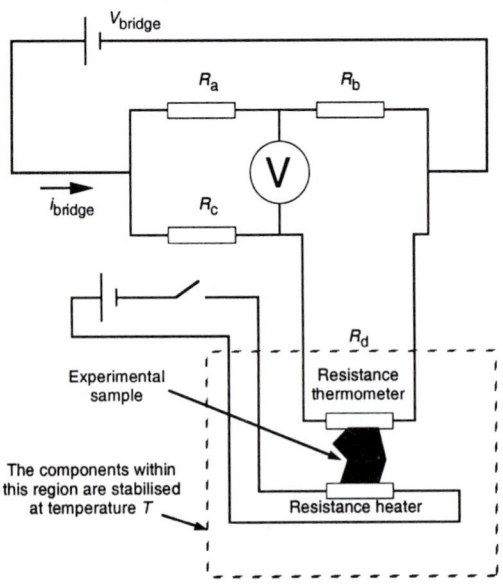

Figure 3.13 A schematic view of a capacitance cell. Small changes in the length of a sample cause changes in the separation between the two plates of a capacitor.

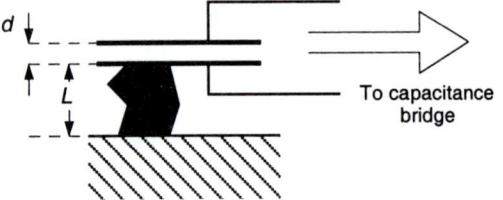

3.4 Environments

As well as being able to measure different physical quantities, we also need to be able to create and maintain environments in which we can perform experiments on samples of matter.

3.4.1 Temperature

High temperatures

Temperatures above room temperature are usually created by ovens or furnaces that are heated electrically. It is not difficult or particularly expensive to create an environment of a volume of 10 cm^3 or so with temperatures up to 900 °C. For temperatures above this, special materials (e.g. platinum or silicon carbide) must be used to resist the high rates of oxidation which would otherwise reduce the material of the heating filament to a powder. An alternative way to avoid oxidation is to operate a furnace either in vacuum or with an inert atmosphere. For example, graphite is commonly used as both as a heater and as a constructional material in furnaces operating up to 2000 °C in vacuum. However, it would burn rapidly if any oxygen were present.

Low temperatures

Low temperature environments are usually created by placing experiment samples in contact with a cold fluid. For temperatures only slightly below room temperature, we can use liquid refrigerants that are similar to those found in a domestic refrigerator. For lower temperatures it is common to use liquid nitrogen, which boils at atmospheric pressure at a temperature of around 77 K (–197 °C). For still lower temperatures, the refrigerant used is liquid helium, which boils at atmospheric pressure at a temperature of around 4.2 K (–269°C). By lowering the vapour pressure above the liquid, we can reduce the boiling temperature to ≈ 1.2 K, which suffices for most purposes.

3.4.2 Pressure

The pressure under which an experiment is performed may be altered from below atmospheric pressure $\approx 10^5$ Pa, to values as large as 10^{10} Pa (10 GPa). The devices used to change the pressure are all based on, or adapted from, the *piston* (Figure 3.14).

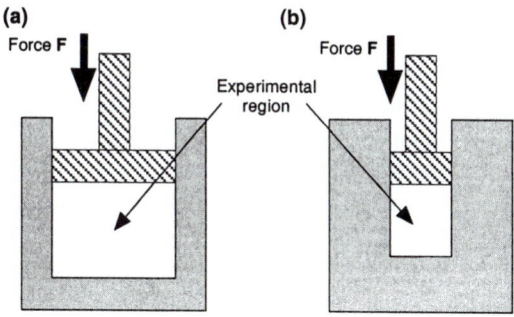

Figure 3.14 Example of the use of piston to create pressure environments. In (a) a force F acts over area A to produce a pressure $P_1 = F/A$. In (b) the force acts over a smaller area $A/4$ to produce a pressure $4P_1$, even though the force used is the same in both cases.

Figure 3.15 Illustration of techniques for applying high pressures to solid samples. The technique (a) uses a fluid around the sample to ensure that the pressure is transmitted hydrostatically. For application of the very highest pressures (b) the hardest material known, diamond, is used as a pressure anvil. The transparency of diamond allows relatively easy optical access. However the expense of large unflawed diamonds limits the size of the apparatus illustrated in (b), and all such experiments represent a considerable challenge to the experimenter.

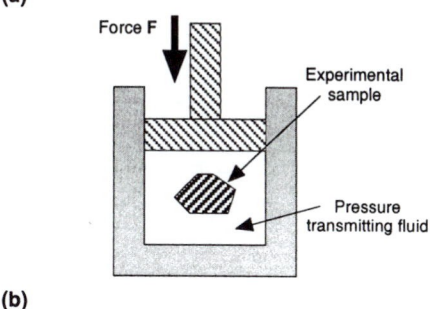

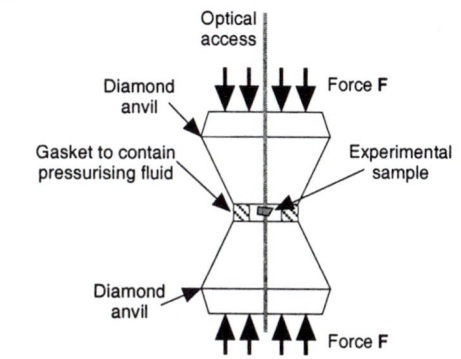

Figure 3.16 Illustration of the principle of operation of a mechanical vacuum pump. In (a) a piston/chamber is enlarged and 'sucks in' gas through A from the region in which the pressure is to be lowered. In (b) the connection A to the area in which the pressure is to be lowered is closed, and the piston lowered to compress the gas until the pressure exceeds atmospheric pressure (c), when a valve B opens to permit the compressed gas to be expelled. This process (d) can be used to lower the pressure in an experimental enclosure. Note: Modern vacuum pumps usually operate on a rotational rather than a reciprocating cycle as shown in (a) to (d) and they rarely look anything like this diagram might intimate.

(a)   **(b)**   **(c)**   **(d)**

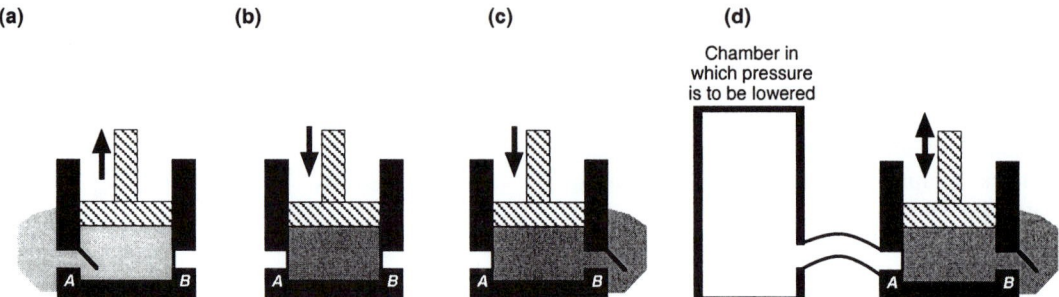

For gases and liquids it is a straightforward extension of Figure 3.14 to see how pistons can be used to apply pressure. The experimental sample is placed in a suitable container, and a force applied to the piston. The force is often amplified by means of a lever or a hydraulic arrangement. At high pressures it is often a matter of considerable ingenuity to extract measurements from within the high pressure environment, but that need not concern us here.

For solids, it is important to ensure that pressure is applied uniformly in all directions, otherwise samples are easily damaged. To ensure that pressure is *hydrostatic* a pressure-transmitting fluid which does not itself solidify under pressure is used (Figure 3.15).

Achieving low pressures is no less a matter for ingenuity. Figure 3.16 shows schematically how the pressure may be lowered within a chamber by a simple mechanical *vacuum pump*, generally called a *rotary* or *roughing* pump. Devices operating on this principle can fairly easily reduce the pressure in a chamber to around 10 Pa. This is one ten thousandth part of atmospheric pressure, and corresponds to the removal of 99.99% of all the molecules in the chamber. However there would still typically be 10^{21} molecules left per cubic metre (see Example 4.2). A number of devices are available which can achieve so-called high vacuum of 10^{-4} Pa, and with great care and expense, *ultra high vacuum* pressures of around 10^{-10} Pa may be achieved.

3.5 Uncertainty

In most of the tables in the following chapters, there is no mention of uncertainty. Of course, all measurements are accompanied by uncertainty, and strictly speaking the uncertainty of all the measurements in the book should be stated. The reason that statements of measurement uncertainty are lacking is that most of the sources from which I have obtained the data do not quote uncertainties. As a guide, all the figures I give in measured quantities are usually significant figures. For example, the density of the element Hafnium is given in Table 7.1 as 13276 kg m^{-3}. A realistic uncertainty for this is likely to ± 2 or 3 in the last figure given.

The bibliography in Chapter 1 contains the sources of the data used in the tables and figures in this book. You should consult these sources, and go beyond them to the original research papers if you wish to establish the uncertainties of the measurements with greater... certainty!

3.6 Exercises

Exercises marked with a P prefix are 'normal' exercises. Those marked with a C prefix are best solved numerically by using a computer program or spreadsheet. Exercises marked with an E prefix are in general rather more challenging that the P and C exercises. Answers to all the exercises may be downloaded from www.physicsofmatter.com

Some more demanding exercises relating to material in this Chapter and others may be found in Chapter 12.

Units

P1. What are the SI units (Tables 3.1 and 3.3) for the specification of:

(a) Magnetic flux density

(b) Temperature

(c) Electrical conductance

(d) Electrical resistance

(e) Electrical capacitance

(f) Amount of substance

(g) Mass

P2. What is the mass of (a) 1 mole of carbon atoms, (b) 1 mole of nitrogen atoms, and (c) 1 mole of nitrogen molecules (N_2).

P3. Given that the density of platinum/iridium is approximately 22×10^3 kg m^{-3}. Roughly how big is *the* kilogram $\mathcal{K}$? Assuming that $\mathcal{K}$ is a cube (which it is not) how thick is a 1 microgram layer of H_2O? You should find a result which is surprisingly thin. How many layers of H_2O molecules would be needed to make such a layer?

Measurement techniques

P4. If the frequency standard of NPL (§3.3.1) were used as the basis of a clock, how many years would it take before the time as determined by the clock was uncertain by 1 second? If the clock lasted for 100 years before it had to be replaced, how uncertain would the time be when the clock was replaced?

P5. I have read in *Scientific American* magazine that the United States of America and the Europe are moving apart from one another at a rate around one centimetre per year. How many metres per second does this correspond to? How many extra rows of atoms per second appear between the USA and Europe? How does this compare with the speed at which your hair grows? Suggest how, given a sufficient research budget, you would attempt to confirm this result. How long would your measurement take?

P6. We mentioned in §3.3 that the voltage generated by a thermocouple did not arise at the junction between the two dissimilar metals. Instead it arose all along the wires and depended on the product of the so-called *Seebeck* coefficient $S(x)$ for a material and the temperature *gradient* dT/dx at each point on the wire.

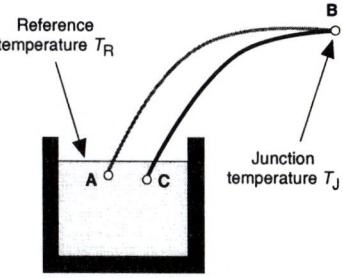

In the figure above, points A and C are at the same reference temperature T_R and point B is the measurement junction with temperature T_J. A is connected to B by wire with Seebeck coefficient S_1 and C is connected to B by wire with Seebeck coefficient S_2. The voltage V_{AC} is given by:

$$V_{AC} = \int_A^C S(x) \frac{dT}{dx} dx$$

Show that if the Seebeck coefficients are constant along each type of wire, that V_{AC} is indeed proportional to the temperature difference between T_R and T_J and given by:

$$V_{AC} = \left[T_R - T_J \right] \times \left[S_2 - S_1 \right]$$

P7. Suggest a practical measurement application for (a) a slow-reacting photo-resistor costing 10 pence and (b) a fast-reacting (within a microsecond) photodiode costing £1.

P8. In the experiment on which I am presently working at the NPL, I have to measure quite precisely the amount of light which is Rayleigh–scattered by a gas. Rough 0.1 nW of green light with a wavelength of 532 nm falls onto my detector. The detector (known as a *trap detector*) is a combination of three silicon photodiodes carefully arranged to capture essentially all incoming radiation. Assuming that one photoelectron is generated for each photon that falls on the detector, how much current should I expect to flow from my detector. If I had used a photomultiplier instead of a photodiode how much current might I reasonably have expected? So why have I used a photodiode?!

P9. On a bright moonlit night it is quite possible to see one's way home from a friend's house. How many optical photons per second are striking each square metre of the Earth in order to make this possible? I suggest you assume that 1 kW m^2 of entirely optical energy (average frequency 7×10^{14} Hz) strikes both the Earth and the Moon from the Sun. Assume that the light striking the Moon is reflected with 100% efficiency. The Moon–Earth separation is approximately 384×10^6 m and Sun–Earth (or Sun–Moon) separation is 150×10^9 m. The Moon's diameter is approximately 3.5×10^6 m.

P10. There is a link which I have not brought out in this book between the measurement of temperature (§3.3.2) and the detection of optical radiation (§3.3.3). This arises because all surfaces emit radiation which is characteristic of (a) their temperature and (b) an intrinsic surface property known as the *emissivity*. If the emissivity of a surface is known (which in practice it rarely is!), then its temperature can be inferred simply by exposing a detector to radiation coming from the surface. Such devices are the basis of many *non-contact thermometers*. The emission into a hemisphere around a surface of area A of a body with emissivity ε is given by $P = A\varepsilon\sigma T^4$ where σ is the *Stephan–Boltzmann* constant with the value 5.67×10^{-8} W m^{-2} K^{-4}. The Sun has a radius of 7×10^8 m and the Sun–Earth separation is 150×10^9 m. roughly 1 kW m^{-2} of radiant energy arrives at the Earth from the Sun. Estimate the temperature of the surface of the sun assuming it emits like a so-called *black body* with emissivity $\varepsilon = 1$

Assuming your body has a surface temperature of 22 °C, how much energy is radiated from your skin every second?

P11. An apparatus similar to Figure 3.9 is constructed. Show that the number of wavelengths of light in the reference cell of length L may be expressed as Ln_{light}/λ_0 where n_{light} is the refractive index of the gas and λ_0 the wavelength of the light in free space. Using:

- $n = P/k_B T$ from Example 4.2 where n is the number density of molecules

- Equation 2.17

- Equation 5.109 and Table 5.17

show that the refractive index of a gas is given approximately by $1 + P\alpha/2\varepsilon_0 k_B T$ where P and T are the temperature and pressure of the gas. Hence, describe how α, the molecular polarisability of an individual gas molecule, may be determined. If you think about it I hope you will find even the possibility of this kind of measurement very impressive.

P12. Verify Equation 3.4 for a Wheatstone bridge near to the balance condition. What assumption has been made about the internal resistance of the voltmeter? Compare the magnitude of the voltage change ΔV with the voltage change $i_d \Delta R_d$ across R_d and state what advantages a bridge circuit offers.

P13. A capacitance bridge (Figure 3.13) can detect a change of capacitance of 1 part in 10^8. If used in conjunction with a parallel-plate capacitor ($C = \varepsilon_0 A/d$) of area $A = 1$ cm^2 and separation $d = 0.1$ mm, estimate the smallest length change that can be detected. Roughly what fraction of the diameter of an atom does that correspond? Could this sensitivity really be achieved in practice?

P14. A mass of 10 kg is dropped through 1 metre onto the blunt end of a tapered piece of steel. The blunt end of the steel has a diameter of 30 mm and the sharp end of the steel has a diameter of 0.2 mm. Estimate the maximum pressure under the tip of the taper. Could such a device be constructed on similar principles for achieving high pressures in a laboratory environment?

P15. A mechanical vacuum pump such as that described in §3.4 removes a fixed *volume* of gas from a chamber each second. This volume (known technically as the *speed S* of the pump) is just the volume of the chamber times the number of cycles per second that the pump piston executes. As the pressure of the gas in the chamber is lowered, a fixed volume of gas contains fewer and fewer molecules at the rate of reduction of pressure slows down. It can be shown that the pressure P in the chamber is described by:

$$P = P_0 \exp\left(-\frac{St}{V}\right)$$

where P_0 is the initial pressure, V is the volume of the chamber being evacuated, S is the pump speed and t is the time.

A modest mechanical vacuum pump might have a speed of 8 m^3 hour^{-1}. Estimate the time to lower the pressure in a chamber of volume 100 litres from 1 atmosphere (10^5 Pa) to 1 Pa. This is about the low pressure limit for such a pump. At this pressure, the vapour pressure of the oil used to cool the moving piston is equal to the pressure in the chamber and net flow of molecules from the chamber is zero.

Although it requires further research outside the scope of this book, you might be interested to find out how such a chamber be evacuated to a pressure of 10^{-3} Pa or lower? The lowest pressure achievable is around 10^{-8} Pa which takes exceptional effort to achieve.

CHAPTER 4

Gases: background theory

4.1 Introduction

In this chapter, we will develop one of the earliest and most successful theories of matter: the so-called ideal gas theory. This theory envisages a gas as being a collection of molecules whose average *kinetic energy* is so large that the *potential energy* of interaction between the molecules is unable to hold them together. This model will probably be familiar, but just in case it is not, Figure 4.1 shows how one imagines the motion of the molecules in a gas.

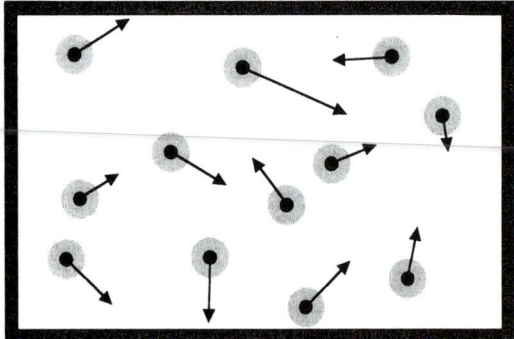

Figure 4.1. A schematic illustration of the motion of molecules in a gas. The molecules are shown as a central darkly-shaded region, where the electron charge density is high, and a peripheral lightly-shaded region. Although there is no electronic charge in this peripheral region, the electric field there will significantly affect the motion of any other molecules that enter that region. Notice that on average, the distance between the molecules is large compared with the extent of their region of influence. The arrows indicate the velocities of the molecules. Notice that the velocities are randomly oriented and that the length of the velocity vectors is varied, indicating that the molecules have a wide range of speeds.

Ideal gas theory tells us some amazing things are happening in the air around us. It predicts that the average speed of the molecules is around 500 m s^{-1} and that molecules collide with every square centimetre of the skin on your body roughly 10^{23} times every second. It also predicts that separation between the molecules is around 3.5 nm compared with the typical separation between molecules in their solid state of around 0.3 nm. As we shall see in Chapter 5, we have every reason to believe these predictions because quantitative explanations of the properties of gases based on the ideal gas model are extraordinarily successful.

§4.2   **The ideal gas model:** Here we outline the basic assumptions of the ideal gas theory. Importantly these assumptions are approximately true for almost every real gas that we will encounter! Then we derive from first principles an equation that relates the density of an ideal gas to its temperature and pressure

§4.3   **Calculating microscopic quantities:** In this section we look at some results which allow us to calculate some microscopic properties of gas.

§4.4   **Beyond the ideal gas equation:** Finally we look at how we can extend the ideal gas theory in order to take account of a more realistic set of assumptions than those we made in §4.2.

At www.physicsofmatter.com

In addition to copies of the figures and tables, you will find animations of several of the important equations in this chapter and a computer program which realistically simulates the dynamics of simple molecules in gases, liquids and solids.

4.2 The ideal gas model

4.2.1 Assumptions

The simplest model of a real gas is known as the ideal or perfect model of a gas. It consists of a list of real properties of molecules that are systematically ignored! The justification for this is that the model is relatively simple and yet has wide range of applicability. It predicts an astoundingly simple expression for the macroscopic properties of any gas, independent of the type of molecules that make up the gas. This universal relationship is summarised in the so-called *ideal gas equation*:

$$PV = zRT \qquad (4.1)$$

where:

P is the pressure of the gas (Pa)
V is the volume of the gas (m^3)
z is the number of moles of the gas under consideration (mol).
T is the absolute temperature (K)
R is the molar gas constant ($J\ K^{-1}\ mol^{-1}$)

What we assume :	What we neglect :
The molecules behave as perfect point masses, i.e. they have zero volume.	The molecules have a small, but finite, volume.
The molecules do not interact with each other except instantaneously as they collide.	The molecules of gases do interact with each other.
The collisions between molecules are elastic.	Not much: this is a very good assumption. The only time it is not appropriate is when we discuss electrical conduction through a gas.

These will be our initial assumptions. As we proceed through Chapters 4 and 5 we will see that these assumptions are sufficient to understand many properties of gases. However, we will on occasion need to go beyond some of these basic assumptions.

4.2.2 Derivation of the ideal gas equation

To derive this equation we need to make two connections between microscopic properties of the molecules and the macroscopic properties of the gas.

- First, we will identify the pressure (force per unit area) of a gas against the walls of its container with the average effect of the very large number of collisions of the molecules of the gas with the wall.

- Second, we will identify the temperature of the gas as being proportional to the average energy of molecules in the gas. (We will define this relationship more precisely in the following sections.)

In order to do this, we will first establish a relationship between the *average momentum* and the *average energy* of a gas molecule. Then, because of the identifications above, we will be able to establish a relationship between the pressure of the gas and its temperature.

Step 1: An average molecule, S

We consider z moles of a substance, i.e. zN_A molecules of just one type, each with mass m. We assume that in the gaseous state molecular collisions are relatively infrequent, and that most of a molecule's time is spent 'cruising' between collisions.

Consider a particular molecule, S, representative of all the molecules in the box. S has mass m and velocity $\mathbf{v}$, and thus has momentum $\mathbf{p} = m\mathbf{v}$. S's kinetic energy is given by $KE_S = \frac{1}{2}m\mathbf{v}^2$, and if we express this in terms of the individual components of its velocity v_x, v_y and v_z we find:

$$KE_S = \tfrac{1}{2}m\mathbf{v}\cdot\mathbf{v}$$
$$KE_S = \tfrac{1}{2}m(v_x, v_y, v_z)\cdot(v_x, v_y, v_z) \qquad (4.2)$$

$$KE_S = \tfrac{1}{2}m(v_x^2 + v_y^2 + v_z^2) \qquad (4.3)$$

Step 2: Hitting the wall of the box

We first of all imagine a limiting case of a low density gas with just one molecule, S, bouncing

Figure 4.2 The molecule S is alone in a box travelling with a kinetic energy which is the same as the *average* kinetic energy of all the molecules that will eventually inhabit the box.

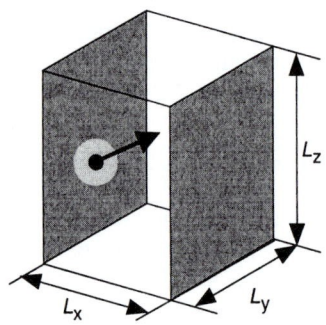

around inside a box of sides L_x, L_y and L_z and volume V (Figure 4.2). The speed of S is chosen such that its kinetic energy KE_S is the same as the average kinetic energy of the molecules with which we will eventually populate the box.

An elastic collision with the wall imparts momentum to the wall. Figure 4.3 (a) and (b) show a molecule before and after such a collision. The x-component of the velocity of S causes it to bounce backwards and forwards between the two walls that have been shaded. The y- and z- components cause it to bounce between the other walls. When it hits a wall it imparts some momentum to the wall. When it leaves the wall and re-enters the interior of the box the wall imparts momentum to it, and so it is subject to a reaction force. Although these forces are tiny, we will eventually populate the box with sufficiently large numbers of molecules so as to make the sum of these forces appre-

ciable. We will add up the forces that S produces as she bounces around.

Imagine that S's collisions with the walls are simple elastic collisions. If they are, then we are considering an event similar to the one depicted in Figure 4.3. More realistic assumptions concerning the interactions between the gas molecules and the molecules of the walls of the box are considered under *Complication 1* below.

If momentum is conserved, we can analyse the situation by equating momentum before and after the collision. We must consider the momentum both of the wall and the molecule.

Momentum before collision:

$$m\mathbf{v} + \mathbf{p}_{\text{wall}} \tag{4.4}$$

Momentum after collision:

$$m\mathbf{v}' + \mathbf{p}'_{\text{wall}} \tag{4.5}$$

Equating momentum before and after the collision, we have:

$$m\mathbf{v} + \mathbf{p}_{\text{wall}} = m\mathbf{v}' + \mathbf{p}'_{\text{wall}} \tag{4.6}$$

Noting that the initial momentum of the wall is zero ($\mathbf{p}_{\text{wall}} = 0$), we have

$$\mathbf{p}'_{\text{wall}} = m\mathbf{v} - m\mathbf{v}' \tag{4.7}$$

This means that the momentum imparted to the wall is just the difference between S's initial and final momentum. Imagining this to be an ideal collision, we assume v_y is unchanged by the collision and so there is no change in its y-component of momentum, and no force on the wall in the y-direction. However its x-component of velocity is exactly reversed. The momentum acquired by the wall is thus:

$$\mathbf{p}'_{\text{wall}} = mv_x\hat{\mathbf{x}} - mv'_x\hat{\mathbf{x}} \tag{4.8}$$

$$\mathbf{p}'_{\text{wall}} = mv_x\hat{\mathbf{x}} - m(-v_x)\hat{\mathbf{x}}$$
$$= 2mv_x\hat{\mathbf{x}} \tag{4.9}$$
$$= \Delta p_x\hat{\mathbf{x}}$$

So the momentum imparted to the wall is twice

Figure 4.3 An elastic collision with the wall imparts momentum to the wall. (a) and (b) show a molecule before and after such a collision.

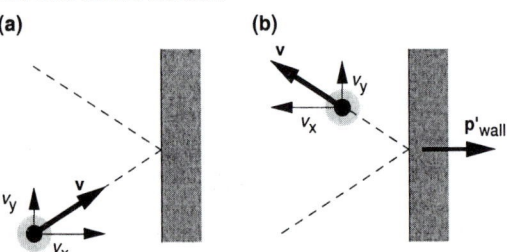

63

S's initial momentum. Not surprisingly this momentum transfer will be maximised if S is travelling quickly and has a large mass.

Step 3: Bouncing around in the box

After a collision, S will head off into the box, bounce off the other wall, and eventually return to the same wall for another collision. Notice that in the analysis above, if S collides with the other walls of the box then the x-component of its velocity will be unaffected. Thus we may confine our attention to the one wall we considered in Step 1. How long does it take for S to return to the same wall? If it travels with velocity v_x then it will take L_x / v_x seconds to reach the opposite wall, and a further L_x / v_x seconds to return. It thus makes collisions such as that described in Step 1 every $\Delta t = 2L_x / v_x$ seconds. Thus the average rate at which S imparts momentum to the wall is approximated by:

$$\frac{\Delta p_x}{\Delta t} = \frac{2mv_x}{2L_x / v_x} = \frac{mv_x^2}{L_x} \qquad (4.10)$$

The rate at which momentum is transferred to the wall is nothing more than the force on the wall (Newton's second law of motion):

$$F = \frac{\Delta p_x}{\Delta t} = \frac{mv_x^2}{L_x} \qquad (4.11)$$

Thus the force per unit area on the wall, i.e. the *pressure* due to S alone, is:

$$P = \frac{F}{Area} = \frac{mv_x^2 / L_x}{L_y L_z} \qquad (4.12)$$
$$= \frac{mv_x^2}{L_x L_y L_z} = \frac{mv_x^2}{V}$$

Comparing this with the formula for S's kinetic energy (Equation 4.3), this is just twice the kinetic energy associated with the x-component of its motion, divided by the volume.

Step 4: Pressure and kinetic energy

Now S is not just any molecule: its speed is chosen such that its kinetic energy is the same as the *average* kinetic energy of the real molecules with

64

which we will fill the box in Step 5. Neglecting the small gravitational energy term, there is no difference between the three directions in the box, and so we expect that S's average speed will be the same in each direction. Hence, the kinetic energy associated with motion in each of the three directions will be equal, i.e.

$$\tfrac{1}{2}mv_x^2 = \tfrac{1}{2}mv_y^2 = \tfrac{1}{2}mv_z^2 \qquad (4.13)$$

Notice that because S does not interact with the other molecules it only has kinetic energy; it has no potential energy. So in terms of its total kinetic energy KE_S we expect that the kinetic energy associated with S's motion in the x-direction will be just one third of its total kinetic energy, i.e.

$$\tfrac{1}{2}mv_x^2 = \tfrac{1}{3}KE_S \qquad (4.14)$$

Similar expressions will hold for the energy terms associated with motion in the y- and z-directions. Remembering S's role as an average molecule, we expect the average kinetic energy associated with a molecule moving in the x-direction will be just one third of the average of its total kinetic energy

Now returning to the expression (Equation 4.12) for the pressure that S exerts on the wall perpendicular to the x-direction:

$$P = \frac{mv_x^2}{V} \qquad (4.15)$$

We can rewrite this as:

$$P = 2\frac{\tfrac{1}{2}mv_x^2}{V} = 2\frac{\tfrac{1}{3}KE_S}{V} \qquad (4.16)$$

i.e.

$$P = \frac{2}{3}\frac{KE_S}{V} \qquad (4.17)$$

Or, in words: *the pressure due to a single molecule travelling with a velocity representative of the average kinetic energy of a large number of molecules is just two-thirds of the kinetic energy per unit volume, i.e. two-thirds of the kinetic energy density.*

Step 5: Filling the box

Suppose now the box contains not just one representative molecule, but z moles of ideal gas, i.e. zN_A molecules, where N_A is Avogadro's number. Now if there were two molecules, the pressure would be twice as great. So a first guess would be that if there were zN_A molecules, the pressure on the wall would simply be zN_A times larger:

$$P = zN_A \times \frac{2}{3}\frac{KE_S}{V} \tag{4.18}$$

In *Complication 2* below, we consider to what extent it is really true that the pressure on the wall will simply be zN_A times larger. In Equation 4.18 we can already see the skeleton of the ideal gas equation emerging. To see this we can rearrange it and compare it with our 'target' equation:

$$PV = zN_A \times \frac{2}{3}KE_S \tag{4.19}$$

$$PV = zRT$$

Comparing these two equations, we see we need to establish a relationship between the temperature and the average kinetic of a molecule in the gas.

Step 6: Temperature

We now come to a microscopic definition of that familiar macroscopic property, temperature. Temperature is defined as being a quantity proportional to the average energy per degree of freedom (see *Complication 3* for more details).

$$T \propto \frac{\text{Average energy per}}{\text{degree of freedom}} \tag{4.20}$$

For historical reasons, this relationship is usually written the other way around, and a slightly confusing factor of $\frac{1}{2}$ introduced:

$$\frac{\text{Average energy per}}{\text{degree of freedom}} = \tfrac{1}{2}k_B T \tag{4.21}$$

The constant of proportionality is called the *Boltzmann constant* $k_B = 1.38 \times 10^{-23}$ J K^{-1}. Now S has 3 degrees of freedom and so we can now relate the temperature of a gas to the average kinetic energy of its molecules:

$$\tfrac{1}{3}KE_S = \tfrac{1}{2}k_B T \tag{4.22}$$

In other words, the temperature of the gas is defined in terms of the average kinetic energy per degree of freedom of a gas molecule. If scientific understanding of matter had developed along different lines, it is quite possible that we might not today have a separate unit for temperature, but would measure it directly in joules!

Step 7: The ideal gas equation

Inserting the definition of temperature (Equation 4.22) into the expression for pressure (Equation 4.18), we can eliminate reference to KE_S. We begin with:

$$P = zN_A \times \frac{2}{3}\frac{KE_S}{V} \tag{4.23}$$

and substitute:

$$KE_S = \tfrac{3}{2}k_B T \tag{4.24}$$

and hence arrive at:

$$P = zN_A \times \frac{2}{3}\frac{\left[\tfrac{3}{2}k_B T\right]}{V} \tag{4.25}$$

After cancelling terms and rearranging the equation we find:

$$PV = z\left[N_A k_B\right]T \tag{4.26}$$

The product of the Boltzmann constant and the Avogadro number is known as the *molar gas constant*, R, which has the value:

$$R = \left[6.023\times10^{23} \text{ mol}^{-1}\right]\left[1.38\times10^{-23} \text{ J K}^{-1}\right] \tag{4.27}$$

$$= 8.314 \text{ J K}^{-1}\text{mol}^{-1}$$

We have thus arrived at:

$$PV = zRT \tag{4.28}$$

This is a predicted relationship between the pressure P, temperature T, and volume V, of z moles of ideal gas material. It is an example of what is called an *equation of state* for a substance: it links the properties that define the state of the substance. We will see that many real gases agree closely with the predictions for an ideal gas.

Example 4.1

Let's make a rough check of $PV = zRT$ on the nearest gas we have to hand: air. Air is a mixture of $\approx$ 78.1% N2, 20.1% O_2, 0.9% Ar, 0.03% CO_2 and a variable fraction of typically 0.5% H_2O. *Kaye and Laby* give the measured value of the density of air at 20 °C and 101.3 kPa (typical values) as 1.199 kg m^{-3}. What value does the perfect gas equation (Eq. 4.29) predict?

Rearranging $PV = zRT$, we write the number of moles per unit volume, the molar density z/V, as:

$$\frac{z}{V} = \frac{P}{RT}$$

If the *molar density* of air is z/V, then the *mass density* is Mz/V, where M is molar mass in kilograms. Thus according to perfect gas theory the density of air should be close to:

$$\rho = \frac{Mz}{V} = \frac{MP}{RT}$$

Let us evaluate this formula. If we ignore the minor constituents of air and treat it as a gas with an effective molecular weight given by the average of nitrogen (28), oxygen (16), and argon (40), we have the average molecular weight of air is:

$$M = (78.1\% \text{ of } 28) + (20.1\% \text{ of } 16) + (0.9\% \text{ of } 40)$$

$$= (0.781 \times 28) + (0.201 \times 16) + (0.009 \times 40)$$

$$= 28.66$$

and so the molar mass is $M = 28.66 \times 10^{-3}$ kg. Substituting $T = 293.15$ K, $P = 101.3$ kPa, and $R = 8.314$ JK^{-1} mol^{-1}, we find:

$$\rho = 1.191 \text{ kg m}^{-3}$$

Comparing the theoretical value with the experimental value of 1.199 kg m^{-3}, we can see that the perfect gas equation has predicted the density of air – a complex gas – with an accuracy of around 0.7%. If we had taken account of water vapour, our answer would be even closer to the experimental value. Impressive.

Example 4.2

Use the ideal gas equation to derive an expression for the number density of molecules in a gas and estimate the number density of molecules in a gas at *STP*.

There are a number ways to rearrange the ideal gas equation $PV = zRT$ to make it even more useful. First of all, we start by rearranging this equation for the molar density:

$$\frac{z}{V} = \frac{P}{RT} \text{ mol}^{-1} \text{ m}^{-3}$$

This tells us the number of moles of gas per cubic metre in terms of the pressure and temperature of the gas. Each mole of gas contains the Avogadro number of molecules, so we can write the number density as:

$$n = N_A \frac{z}{V}$$

$$= N_A \frac{P}{RT}$$

As we saw just before Equation 4.29, the molar gas constant is the product $R = N_A k_B$ where k_B is the Boltzmann constant. So we can divide through by N_A to give:

$$n = N_A \frac{P}{[N_A k_B]T}$$

$$= \frac{P}{k_B T}$$

At STP this evaluates to:

$$n = \frac{P}{k_B T} = \frac{1.013 \times 10^5}{1.38 \times 10^{-23} \times 273.15}$$

$$= 2.69 \times 10^{25} \text{ molecules m}^{-3}$$

In some older texts, this number is sometimes referred to as the *Loschmidt number*, being named for the scientist who first estimated this quantity in 1865.

If you skip to Chapter 5, in which the theory is compared with experimental data, you will see that the model can account for many properties of gases with a typical accuracy of around 1%. However, in order to understand some of the experimental results discussed in Chapter 5 it will be necessary to read through §4.3 on *Calculating microscopic quantities*. Alternatively you can read through the *Complications and reservations* section below to find out about the limits of the sim-

plifications and assumptions we have made in our seven-step derivation of $PV = zRT$.

Complications and reservations

Complication 1: Hitting the wall – what really happens?

The collision of a molecule with a wall is really quite a complex process. However, we will see that in terms of the exchange of momentum with the wall, the results of a more sophisticated analysis are identical with those arrived at in Step 1.

The real story is illustrated in Figure 4.4 and goes something like this. Molecules hit the wall, interact electrically with the atoms of the wall and then, in general, stick to wall. While they are on the wall, they can either stay vibrating about some attractive point on the wall, or move around on the surface. Then, typically after a nanosecond or so, they leave the wall and return to the gas. A nanosecond may seem rather short time to you, but in a nanosecond, a typical atom will vibrate around 10,000 times and so a great deal can happen. How can this complex process be approximated by the simple 'bouncing' model outlined in Step 1? The reasoning is as follows:

- Since molecules hit the wall from random directions and leave in random directions then on average there is no net momentum transfer parallel to the plane of the wall. This validates our assumption that on average the y-component of S's momentum is unaffected by the collision process.
- If we look at the initial and final situations, without asking about the details of the reflection process, then we find that the two processes are rather similar. In each case the molecule is first approaching the wall, and

Example 4.3

Suppose we have 1.3 moles of helium gas in a container of volume 1 litre at a temperature of 20 °C. (a) What is the pressure of the gas? (b) If the temperature is changed to 100 °C, but the gas is contained in the same volume, what is the pressure?

(a) Use $PV = zRT$ and substitute:

$V = 1$ litre

$\quad = 10^{-3} \text{ m}^{-3}$

$z = 1.3$ mol

$R = 8.31 \text{ J}^{-1}\text{K}^{-1}\text{mol}$

$T = 20$ °C

$\quad = 273.15 + 20 = 293.15$ K

To find:

$$P = \frac{zRT}{V} = \frac{1.3 \times 8.314 \times 293.15}{10^{-3}}$$

$$= 3.168 \times 10^6 \text{ Pa}$$

or approximately 31 times atmospheric pressure.

(b) Use $PV = zRT$ and substitute:

$V = 1$ litre

$\quad = 10^{-3} \text{ m}^{-3}$

$z = 1.3$ mol

$R = 8.31 \text{ J}^{-1}\text{K}^{-1}\text{mol}$

$T = 100$ °C

$\quad = 273.15 + 100 = 373.15$ K

To find:

$$P = \frac{zRT}{V} = \frac{1.3 \times 8.314 \times 373.15}{10^{-3}}$$

$$= 4.033 \times 10^6 \text{ Pa}$$

or approximately 40 times atmospheric pressure.

(a)　(b)　(c)

Atoms in the wall　Atoms in the wall　Atoms in the wall

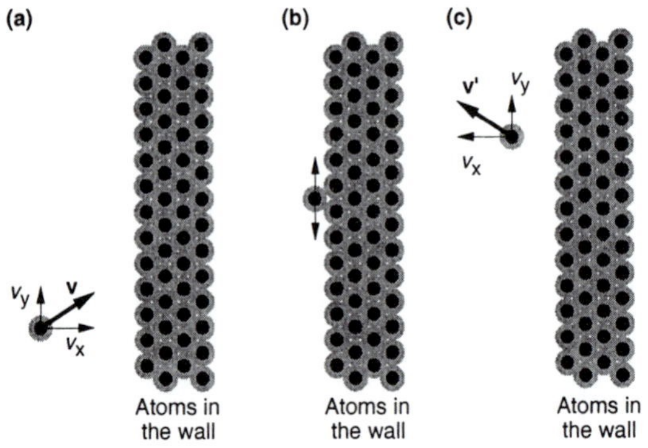

Figure 4.4. When a molecule hits a wall, what really happens is that it sticks to the wall for a short while (typically 10^{-12} s), and eventually leaves the wall and rejoins the gas with no 'memory' of the trajectory with which it hit the wall. It sticks to the wall because the wall is made of molecules with which it will have some kind of interaction. The figure shows (a) the approach to the wall, (b) the adsorption on the wall and (c) the escape from the wall. On each molecule, the area shaded grey indicates the region in which the molecule interacts strongly with neighbouring molecules.

then leaving the wall, with a velocity component v_x characteristic of the temperature of the gas and wall. Thus the average momentum transfer is the same in both cases. Thus the x-component of momentum imparted to the wall is unaffected by the detailed nature of the collision process.

The fact that S has spent some time on the wall instead of travelling through the box means the average time between its collisions with the wall will be slightly greater than we assumed in Equation 4.10. This will tend to reduce the pressure of a real gas as compared to an ideal gas.

Note that the argument above is only valid when both the walls and the gas are at the same temperature. If this is not so, then S will return to the gas with kinetic energy appropriate to the temperature of the wall and not the temperature of the gas. This is the mechanism by which a gas can be cooled or warmed by contact with a hotter or colder solid surface.

Complication 2: Collisions with other molecules.

While S may be able to bounce around happily from side to side of the container when it is in the box alone, it will not be free to do so when the box is filled with other molecules. Does the analysis break down if S cannot bounce back and hit the wall again after $2L_x / v_x$ seconds? No. However the reason it doesn't is quite subtle.

What happens is that although S does not travel from side to side in the box, the *momentum* that it

carries does (Figure 4.5). In each collision with another molecule the momentum is conserved, and so the momentum does bounce from side to side of the container. In addition to this there are many other molecules whose momentum is being 'bounced' across the box. In practice this makes calculations rather complicated, but in the end it amounts to exactly the same thing as our simple assumption in Step 1.

Complication 3: Degrees of freedom.

The idea of a degree of freedom is important in statistical mechanics and has already been mentioned in this chapter and in Chapter 2. There are three questions we need to ask in this context:

- What is a degree of freedom?
- What is an *accessible* degree of freedom?
- How is the energy distributed amongst accessible degrees of freedom?

1. What is a degree of freedom?

Colloquially, a *degree of freedom* of a molecule is a 'thing it can do' or a 'way it can possess energy'. Technically this corresponds to an independent 'squared term' in the expression for the energy of a molecule.

- For example, an atom in a gas can move in three dimensions and has kinetic energy associated with each of those possibilities. So it has at least three degrees of freedom:

$$KE = \tfrac{1}{2}mv_x^2 + \tfrac{1}{2}mv_y^2 + \tfrac{1}{2}mv_z^2 \qquad (4.29)$$

- The same atom in a solid has more possibilities open to it. As it jiggles around it can possess kinetic energy in the same way as a molecule in a gas can, but it also has potential energy. This is stored in the deformation of its 'bonds' with its neighbours as it vibrates. For small displacements from its equilibrium position x_0, y_0, z_0, the potential energy can be written as:

$$PE = \tfrac{1}{2}K_x(x - x_0)^2 + \tfrac{1}{2}K_y(y - y_0)^2$$
$$+ \tfrac{1}{2}K_z(z - z_0)^2 \qquad (4.30)$$

where K_x, K_y, K_z are the spring constants describing the variation of potential energy with position.

Figure 4.5 When there is more than one molecule in the box, a 'representative' molecule can no longer travel freely across the box and bounce from side to side in a time $2L_x/v_x$

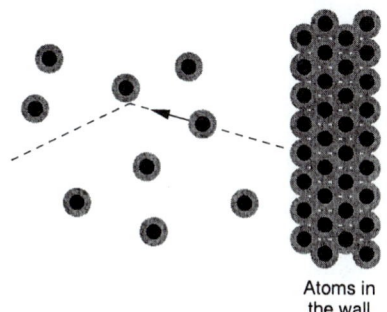

Atoms in
the wall

These are the three independent squared terms in Equation 4.28, which correspond to an additional three degrees of freedom.

- A diatomic molecule in a gas has three degrees of freedom associated with its kinetic energy, but may also have kinetic energy of vibration and rotation, and potential energy of vibration, and so has more degrees of freedom than an atom by itself. As a rule of thumb, the more atoms making up a molecule in a gas, then the greater will be the number of degrees of freedom.

2. What is an accessible degree of freedom?

The term *degrees of freedom* refers to things that a molecule *can* do, not to whether it is doing them. Due to the importance of the quantum nature of matter on small scales, some processes cannot take place because an energy gap ΔE separates quantum states in which the process does not occur, from quantum states in which it does occur. If the average energy available to a particular molecule is much less than the energy gap ΔE, then the process will only take place occasionally when (rare) local fluctuations cause the particular molecule's energy to exceed the energy gap.

The average energy per degree of freedom available to a molecule in an environment at temperature T is by definition of Equation 4.22, $\frac{1}{2}k_B T$. If this energy is much less than the energy gap then the process will not take place and the degree of freedom associated with that process is said to be inaccessible. If the temperature increases so that $\frac{1}{2}k_B T$ is much greater than the energy gap, then the process becomes accessible.

The idea of accessibility will be extremely important when we try to understand the heat capacity of gases in §5.3. Indeed, historically the inability of classical theories to explain something as apparently simple as the heat capacity of gases was (according to Lord Kelvin) one of the two outstanding problems remaining for physicists at the end of the nineteenth century.

3. How is the energy distributed amongst accessible degrees of freedom?

It is a fundamental assumption of statistical mechanics that, on average, energy is stored equally in all accessible degrees of freedom. This is a sound assumption, but one which is extremely important.

Consider the example of a molecule which has just the three degrees of freedom of translational motion. It is perhaps not surprising that on average, the kinetic energy associated with each degree of freedom will be equal. The *principle of equipartition of energy* allows us to go one step further by stating that *on average*, the kinetic energy associated with each degree of freedom will *definitely* be equal.

Consider now a molecule with extra accessible degrees of freedom associated, for example, with internal vibration. It is not at all obvious that on average, the energy associated with each translational degree of freedom will be equal to the energy associated with each vibrational degree of freedom. The principle of equipartition of energy allows us to state that *on average*, the energy associated with each accessible degree of freedom will be equal, independent of the type of motion each accessible degree of freedom corresponds to.

What the principle implicitly assumes is that there exists some mechanism for coupling one degree of freedom with another. A molecule travelling through space which never collided or interacted with another molecule would not exchange energy between its degrees of freedom: if it was not vibrating initially it would not spontaneously slow down and start vibrating. However, if it interacts with other molecules then it can exchange energy between its own degrees of freedom and other degrees of freedom on other molecules. We rely on the randomising effect of these interactions to ensure that energy is on average equally distributed amongst all the accessible degrees of freedom. Thus during a collision a molecule which was not vibrating could start vibrating at the expense of energy in another accessible degree of freedom.

Finally we consider degrees of freedom associated with different molecules. Again, collisions or interactions of some kind are an essential assumption of the principle of equipartition of energy. Molecular collisions act to share out energy

69

equally between different accessible degrees of freedom. If one degree of freedom of a molecule has much more than the average energy associated with a degree of freedom ($\frac{1}{2}k_{B}T$), then in interactions with other molecules, the energy associated with that degree of freedom will tend to be lost to other degrees of freedom which have less than the average energy per degree of freedom.

4.3 Calculating microscopic quantities

To understand some properties of gases we need go no further than the ideal gas theory outlined above. However, in order to understand, for example, the thermal conductivity of gases, we need to develop the theory still further. This development is generally referred to as the *kinetic theory* of an ideal gas. However, we need to go beyond some of the assumptions of the ideal gas model. In particular we need to find out about:

- the size of a gas molecule
- the root mean square speed of a gas molecule
- the mean speed of a gas molecule
- the mean free path of a gas molecule,

These quantities are important for understanding the behaviour of gases. However, unlike P, V and T, the quantities are not directly measurable in a straightforward way.

4.3.1 The size of a gas molecule

In the discussion of the complications of our derivation of the ideal gas equation we mentioned the idea of molecular collisions as being important in establishing the averaging of energy amongst degrees of freedom of the gas molecules. It is clear that molecules must have a finite size in order to collide. However, it is not clear what we mean by 'size' exactly, and how do we represent the 'size' of a molecule which may have a complex shape?

There are many definitions of the 'size' of atoms, slightly differing from one another. In general they refer to a radius within which (say) 90% of the electric charge distribution is found. For molecules which are non-spherical, we could specify complex shapes to describe the same criteria. In this chapter however we shall use the idea of an 'effective' cross-sectional area of a molecule. We will specify an 'effective diameter' a such that the chance of collision with a spherical molecule of diameter a is the same as that of colliding with the

molecule in question. We note that it is possible for a to change with temperature. For example, rotational degrees of freedom may be made accessible at high temperatures, which might tend to increase its effective cross-sectional area. Alternatively, the average speed of molecules may become so high that the region of electrical interaction around a molecule no longer affects the trajectory of nearby molecules. This would have the effect of reducing the effective cross-sectional area.

4.3.2 The distribution of molecular speeds

Clearly not all molecules in a gas move at the same speed. Even if by some clever contrivance we arranged that all the molecules did have the same speed at some time, things would not stay that way for long. Collisions between the molecules would cause one molecule to speed up and another to slow down. It might seem that it would be impossible to say anything about the range of molecular speeds present in a gas. Surprisingly, we can in fact say rather a lot, but only if the gas is in equilibrium at a temperature T. If this is the case, then using an analysis outlined in Appendix A1, we can show that the probability that a molecule has a speed between v and $v + dv$ is given by the Maxwell speed distribution $P_{M}(v)$:

$$P_{M}(v)dv = \frac{4}{\sqrt{\pi}}\left[\frac{m}{2k_{B}T}\right]^{\frac{3}{2}} v^2 \exp\left[\frac{-\frac{1}{2}mv^2}{k_{B}T}\right]dv$$

(4.31)

The general form of the Maxwell speed distribution curve is illustrated in Figure 4.6, and specific examples are shown in Figures 4.7 and 4.8. Given the Maxwell speed distribution function, one can define three distinct speeds, all similar in order of

magnitude and all characterising the speed distribution curve in slightly different ways. These speeds are:

The average speed	The root mean square speed	The most probable speed
$\bar{v}$	$v_{RMS} = \left(\overline{v^2}\right)^{1/2}$	v_{prob}

In general, either the average speed $\bar{v}$ or the root mean square speed v_{RMS} are the relevant averages. These two speeds differ by about 8%, $\bar{v} = 0.921 v_{RMS}$, and you should take care to the use right one. Special care needs to be taken in expressions in which the speed enters as a 'squared' term. We must distinguish between $\bar{v}^2$ and $\overline{v^2}$: the two are not the same! The most probable speed v_{prob} is the speed marking the peak of the speed distribution curve, but is of no special physical significance: you may now happily forget about it.

4.3.3 The number of molecules hitting unit area per second

There will be several occasions below, for example in considering the thermal conductivity of a gas, when it will prove useful to know how many molecules are crossing a unit area within the gas per second. We can get an estimate of this if we return to situation depicted in Figure 4.2 in our derivation of the ideal gas equation.

The molecule S is alone in a box travelling with a kinetic energy which is the same as the *average* kinetic energy of all the molecules that will eventually inhabit the box. We consider its collisions with the wall of area $A = L_x L_y$. S collides with this wall, bounces off into the box, bounces off the opposite face of the box, and eventually returns to the same wall for another collision. It takes S a time L_x / v_x seconds to reach the opposite wall, and a further L_x / v_x seconds to return: it thus makes collisions with the wall in question every $\Delta t = 2 L_x / v_x$ seconds. Thus the number of collisions with the wall per unit area per second is given by:

$$\text{Number of collisions per unit area per second} = \frac{1}{A\Delta t} \qquad (4.32)$$

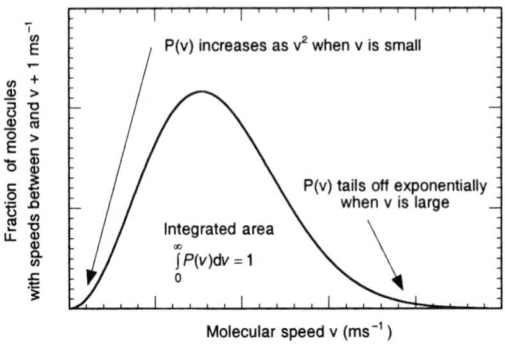

Figure 4.6 The general form of the Maxwell speed distribution curve for a gas (Equation 4.31)

Figure 4.7 Three curves showing the Maxwell distribution of molecular speeds in nitrogen gas and hydrogen. The vertical axis is the probability $P(v)$ that a molecule has a speed between v and $v + 1$ ms^{-1}. Two of the curves show the distribution for nitrogen at temperatures of 100 K and 1000 K. Notice that the peak of the curves shifts to higher speeds at higher temperatures. The third curve is for hydrogen at 100 K. Notice that because of the low mass of hydrogen compared with nitrogen, the curve is similar to the curve for nitrogen at 1000 K.

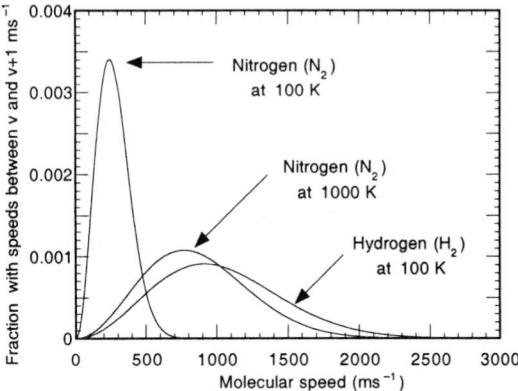

Figure 4.8 Illustration of the special speeds relevant to the Maxwell speed distribution curve. The curve shown refers to nitrogen molecules at a temperature of 1000 K (approximately 730 °C). Notice the three speeds shown are all near the peak of the curve, but differ significantly from each other.

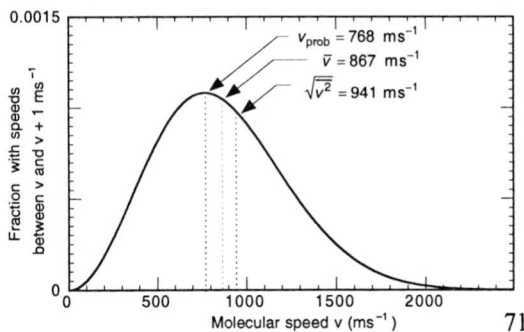

This can be simplified in several steps as follows:

$$\frac{1}{A\Delta t} = \frac{1}{A\left[2L_x / v_x\right]} = \frac{1}{L_y L_z \left[2L_x / v_x\right]}$$

$$= \frac{v_x}{2L_x L_y L_z} \qquad (4.33)$$

$$= \frac{v_x}{2V}$$

where I have used the fact that:

$$L_x L_y L_z = V \qquad (4.34)$$

If there are N molecules in the box with an x-velocity similar to that of S, then the number of collisions with the wall per unit area per second is given by:

$$\begin{array}{l} \text{Number of collisions} \\ \text{per unit area} \\ \text{per second} \end{array} \quad \begin{array}{l} = \dfrac{1}{2}\dfrac{Nv_x}{V} \\ \\ = \dfrac{1}{2}nv_x \end{array} \qquad (4.35)$$

where n is the number density of molecules. Next we notice that in this argument v_x was chosen such that the kinetic energy of S represented the average kinetic energy of the molecules in the box. Thus, in terms of the discussion of the distribution of molecular speeds in the previous section, we can write that:

$$KE_S = \frac{1}{2}m\overline{v^2} \qquad (4.36)$$

Now since:

$$\overline{v^2} = v_x^2 + v_y^2 + v_z^2 \qquad (4.37)$$

we see that $v_x^2 = \frac{1}{3}\overline{v^2}$ and so v_x in equation 4.35 is given by $v_x = \left(\frac{1}{3}\overline{v^2}\right)^{\frac{1}{2}}$. Substituting this value into Equation 4.35 yields our final expression for the number of collisions with the wall per unit area per second:

$$= \frac{1}{2}n\left(\frac{1}{3}\overline{v^2}\right)^{\frac{1}{2}} = \frac{1}{2\sqrt{3}}nv_{RMS} \qquad (4.38)$$

This remarkably simple expression is nearly, but

72

Example 4.4

What is the probability that a molecule of nitrogen in nitrogen gas at 1000 K has a speed between 750 ms^{-1} and 751 ms^{-1}?

We need to evaluate Equation 4.32 to find $P_M(v)dv$ with $v = 750$ ms^{-1} and $dv = 1$ ms^{-1}.

$$P_M(v)dv = \frac{4}{\sqrt{\pi}}\left[\frac{m}{2k_BT}\right]^{\frac{3}{2}}v^2\exp\left[\frac{-\frac{1}{2}mv^2}{k_BT}\right]dv$$

From Table 7.2 we find that the mass m of an individual molecule of N_2, is $2 \times 14u = 28u$ where $u = 1.661 \times 10^{-27}$ kg. Substituting this into Equation 4.32 along with $T = 1000$ K and remembering that the Boltzmann constant $k_B = 1.38 \times 10^{-23}$ J K^{-1} we arrive at:

$$P_M(750) = \frac{4}{\sqrt{\pi}}\left[\frac{28\times1.661\times10^{-27}}{2\times1.38\times10^{-23}\times1000}\right]^{\frac{3}{2}}(750)^2$$

$$\times\exp\left[\frac{-\frac{1}{2}\times28\times1.661\times10^{-27}(750)^2}{1.38\times10^{-23}\times1000}\right]$$

$$= \frac{4}{\sqrt{\pi}}\left[1.685\times10^{-6}\right]^{\frac{3}{2}}\times5.63500\times\exp[-0.948$$

$$= \frac{4}{\sqrt{\pi}}2.187\times10^{-9}\times562500\times\exp[-0.948]$$

And so:

$$P_M(750) = 1.076\times10^{-3}$$

This point is near the peak of the 1000 K curve for nitrogen in Figure 4.8.

---

not quite, correct. It is an underestimate of the correct value because of our simplified assumption that all molecules move with the same speed. Using a considerably more complicated analysis it can be shown that:

$$\begin{array}{l} \text{Number of collisions} \\ \text{per unit area} \\ \text{per second} \end{array} \quad = \frac{1}{4}n\overline{v} \qquad (4.39)$$

an answer which exceeds our simple estimate by about 25%. Example 4.6 shows that the number of collisions with the wall per second is *extremely* large. This is important because it allows us to understand how the tiny forces of molecular collisions can add up to the substantial force exerted by a gas on the walls of its container.

Example 4.5

In nitrogen gas at 1000 K, what fraction of molecules have speeds greater than 867 ms^{-1}. You will definitely need to use the following result:

$$\int_{x=867}^{x=\infty} x^{\frac{1}{2}} \exp[-x]dx = 0.4164$$

The required fraction is the integral of $P(v)dv$ (Equation 4.32) over the required speed range, which in this case is from $v = 867$ ms^{-1} to $v = \infty$. This is the area under the high-speed end of the Maxwellian speed distribution curve:

$$fraction = \int_{v=867}^{v=\infty} P(v)dv$$

$$= \int_{v=867}^{v=\infty} \frac{4}{\sqrt{\pi}} \left[\frac{m}{2k_BT}\right]^{\frac{3}{2}} v^2 \exp\left[\frac{-\frac{1}{2}mv^2}{k_BT}\right]dv$$

Now to solve this kind of integral we need to transform into a standard form. To do this we substitute:

$$x = mv^2/2k_BT$$

We also need to find expressions for all the other terms involving v:

$$\frac{dx}{dv} = \frac{2mv}{2k_BT} \quad \Rightarrow \quad dv = dx\left[\frac{k_BT}{mv}\right]$$

Substituting we find:

$$fraction = \int_{v=867}^{v=\infty} \frac{4}{\sqrt{\pi}} \left[\frac{m}{2k_BT}\right]^{\frac{3}{2}} \underbrace{v^2 \exp\left[\frac{-\frac{1}{2}mv^2}{k_BT}\right]}_{x} \underbrace{dv}_{dx\left[\frac{k_BT}{mv}\right]}$$

$$= \int_{v=867}^{v=\infty} \frac{4}{\sqrt{\pi}} \left[\frac{m}{2k_BT}\right]^{\frac{3}{2}} \left[\frac{k_BT}{mv}\right] v^2 \exp[x]dx$$

$$fraction = \int_{v=867}^{v=\infty} \frac{4}{\sqrt{\pi}} \left[\frac{m}{2k_BT}\right]^{\frac{3}{2}} \left[\frac{k_BT}{m}\right] \underbrace{v}_{\sqrt{\frac{2k_BT}{m}}x^{\frac{1}{2}}} \exp[x]dx$$

The integral then becomes:

$$= \frac{4}{\sqrt{\pi}} \underbrace{\left[\frac{m}{2k_BT}\right]^{\frac{3}{2}} \left[\frac{k_BT}{m}\right]\sqrt{\frac{2k_BT}{m}}}_{=1} \int_{v=11200}^{v=\infty} x^{\frac{1}{2}} \exp[x]dx$$

$$= \frac{4}{\sqrt{\pi}} \int_{v=867}^{v=\infty} x^{\frac{1}{2}} \exp[x]dx$$

where the upper limit x_2 is infinity, and we will work out the value x_1 using $x = mv^2/2k_BT$. We have:

$$x_1 = \frac{28 \times 1.66 \times 10^{-27} \times (867)^2}{2 \times 1.38 \times 10^{-23} \times 1000}$$

$$= 1.266$$

where we have used the fact that a nitrogen molecule has two atoms of nitrogen each of mass $14u$. Substituting for the lower limit of the integral:

$$fraction = 2\sqrt{\frac{1}{\pi}} \int_{x=1.266}^{x=\infty} x^{\frac{1}{2}} \exp[-x]dx$$

We can now substitute for the standard integral given at the start of the question. Hence:

$$fraction = 2\sqrt{\frac{1}{\pi}} \times 0.4164 = 0.4695$$

Thus around 47% of molecules have speeds greater than 867 ms^{-1}. We can use this kind of analysis to solve problems, such as working out how many molecules of a given type have a speed greater than the escape velocity of the Earth. (Chapter 12: Exercises 4 and 5)

4.3.4 The mean free path of a gas molecule

Collisions between molecules play an important part in the transport of both heat and electricity through a gas. The distance molecules travel before colliding with other molecules is particularly important. On average, a slowly moving molecule travels a considerably shorter distance before colliding than a fast moving molecule. For this reason we define the *mean free path* of a gas molecule, λ_{mfp}, as the average distance a gas molecule travels before colliding with another molecule.

We can fairly easily estimate the average free path for molecules that either move much slower than, or much faster than, the mean speed of a gas molecule. To do this we will treat molecules as hard spheres, and ignore the region of electrical interaction sketched in grey around the molecules in Figures 4.4 and 4.5. We will consider the effect of these interactions briefly at the end of this chapter. Recall that if molecules are not spherical, then the diameter, a, represents an average dimension related to the average cross-sectional area that the molecule presents to other molecules.

Example 4.6

Some nitrogen gas is held at a temperature of 1000 K inside a cubical container of dimensions 10 cm $\times$ 10 cm $\times$ 10 cm at a pressure of one atmosphere. What is the number of collisions per second with each wall of the container?

We use the fact that the number of collisions per unit area per second is $\frac{1}{4}n\bar{v}$.

- The molecular density n can be estimated using the ideal gas equation from the *molar density z/V*.

$$\frac{z}{V} = \frac{P}{RT}$$

Multiplying both side by the Avogadro constant yields an expression for the molecular density.

$$n = \frac{zN_A}{V} = \frac{PN_A}{RT} = \frac{P}{k_B T}$$

where k_B is the Boltzmann constant.

- The mean speed $\bar{v}$ can be evaluated using the Maxwell speed distribution Equation 4.31. However, in this case we can cheat by taking the answer directly from Figure 4.8.

The area of each wall is $0.1 \times 0.1 = 10^{-2}$ m^2, so the number of collisions with each wall is given by:

$$= \frac{1}{4} \times n \times \bar{v} \times A$$

$$= \frac{1}{4}\left[\frac{1.0135 \times 10^5}{1.38 \times 10^{-23} \times 1000}\right] \times 867 \times 10^{-2}$$

$$= 1.6 \times 10^{25}$$

We find the answer is given by 1.6×10^{25} collisions per second. This is an immense number. For comparison, as this book is being prepared for publication in the year 2001, it exceeds by several orders of magnitude the number of clock cycles completed by *every* computer that has *ever* existed!

Average free path of molecules moving much faster than $\bar{v}$

Imagine taking a snapshot of the molecules of gas at some particular time t and concentrating our attention on a particularly fast-moving molecule, M. The situation might look like the one depicted in Figure 4.9.

On average, M travels a distance λ before colliding with another molecule. In the limit of M moving extremely quickly it will be as if the other

Figure 4.9 A method for making an approximation for the mean free path for fast-moving molecules. A molecule travels on average a distance λ before colliding with another molecule. If the other molecules are effectively stationary while M travels through the gas then there must on average be no other molecules whose centres lie within a volume $\pi a^2 \lambda$.

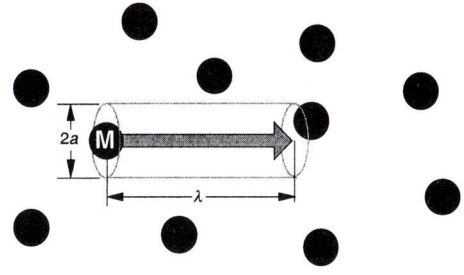

Figure 4.10 A method for making an approximation for the mean free path for slow moving molecules. A stationary molecule C presents a cross-sectional area

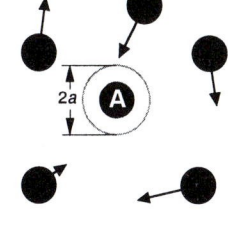

$$\pi(a/2)^2$$

to other moving molecules. If the centre of other molecules pass within an area

$$\pi a^2$$

around the centre of C there will a collision.

molecules did not move at all. In this case, there must on average be no other molecules whose centres lie within a cylinder of volume $\pi a^2 \lambda$ where a is the effective diameter of an atom. Since there is just one molecule (M) in a volume $\pi a^2 \lambda$, the number density of molecules n must be given by:

$$n = \frac{1}{\pi a^2 \lambda} \tag{4.40}$$

Rearranging this gives an expression for λ:

$$\lambda = \frac{1}{n\pi a^2} \tag{4.41}$$

This equation is an estimate for the average free path appropriate to fast-moving molecules. The effect of the motion of the other molecules (which

we have neglected entirely above) is difficult to account for quantitatively. However, it can be seen that in general other molecules will be likely to encroach on M's 'free space'. Thus Equation 4.41 represents an overestimate of the average free path appropriate to more typical molecules.

Average free path of molecules moving much slower than $\bar{v}$

Imagine taking a snapshot of the molecules of gas at some particular time t, and concentrate attention on a particularly slow-moving molecule, C. The situation might look like the one depicted in Figure 4.10.

If C were essentially stationary in comparison to the speeds of the other molecules then, as outlined in Figure 4.10, other molecules passing within an area πa^2 around the centre of C would collide. Considering a surface through C's centre we recall from §4.3.3 that the average number of molecules crossing unit area per second is $\frac{1}{4}n\bar{v}$. Thus the average number of molecules per second colliding with C from each of the two sides of the surface is given by:

$$= 2 \times \frac{1}{4}n\bar{v} \times \pi a^2 \qquad (4.42)$$

and so the average time between collisions is:

$$\Delta t = \frac{1}{2 \times \frac{1}{4}n\bar{v} \times \pi a^2} = \frac{2}{\bar{v}n\pi a^2} \qquad (4.43)$$

Now if C is not quite stationary, but moves with a speed v much less than the mean speed $\bar{v}$, then the average distance travelled by C before a collision, (the average free path) will be given by:

$$\lambda = v\Delta t$$
$$= \frac{2}{n\pi a^2}\left(\frac{v}{\bar{v}}\right) \qquad (4.44)$$

The mean free path of all molecules

We have calculated that for slow-moving molecules the average free path is given by Equation 4.44 which corresponds to a molecule being struck by other molecules at a constant average rate. Thus the faster it moves, the further it travels on

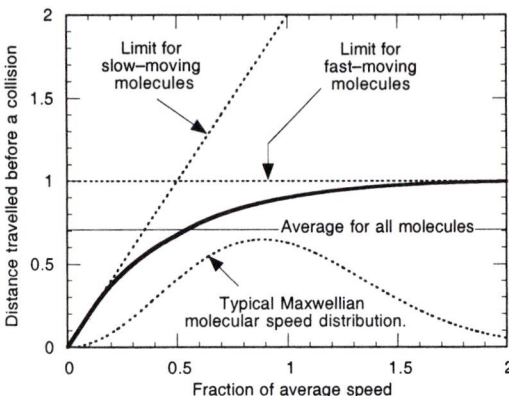

Figure 4.11 The variation of the mean free path λ of molecules as a function of the speed of the molecules expressed as fraction of the mean speed in units of $1/n\pi a^2$. The figure indicates the limiting behaviour of λ for low-speed molecules, high-speed molecules, and the average value for all molecules, λ_{mfp}. Also shown is a qualitative indication of the distribution of molecular speeds (Figures 4.6 , 4.7 & 4.8)

average between collisions. This increase of free path with speed cannot continue indefinitely: a molecule moving so fast that other molecules appear stationary cannot travel an indefinite distance before colliding. As shown above, the limiting average free path is:

$$\lambda = \frac{1}{n\pi a^2} \qquad (4.41)^*$$

Establishing these low and high speed limits has not been too difficult. However, finding the correct expression for the mean free path of all molecules, λ_{mfp}, is rather complex. We will however not be surprised to find (in common with Equations 4.41 and 4.45) that λ_{mfp} is proportional to $1/n\pi a^2$. It is perhaps rather surprising to find that the result of the complex calculation is simply that this factor is multiplied by $1/\sqrt{2} \approx 0.71$, to give:

$$\lambda_{mfp} = \frac{1}{\sqrt{2}n\pi a^2} \qquad (4.45)$$

The slow molecule, fast molecule, and average behaviours are summarised in Figure 4.11.

Example 4.7

It would be interesting to estimate λ_{mfp} for some typical situations. But how can we estimate the number density of molecules n and the diameter of a molecule a?

First of all we use Example 4.2 to rewrite the perfect gas equation for z moles of gas, Eq. 4.28 $PV = zRT$, as:

$$n = \frac{P}{k_B T} = \frac{10^5}{1.38 \times 10^{-23} \times 293}$$

$$= 2.5 \times 10^{25} \text{ molecules m}^{-3}$$

Using a typical value of the spacing between atoms in a solid as an estimate for the molecular diameter $a \approx 0.3$nm, we have:

$$\lambda_{mfp} = \frac{1}{\sqrt{2} n \pi a^2}$$

$$= \frac{1}{\sqrt{2} \times 2.5 \times 10^{25} \times 3.1415 \times \left(0.3 \times 10^{-9}\right)^2}$$

$$\approx 10^{-7} \text{m} \quad \text{i.e. about 100 nm}$$

In the air around us there are approximately 2.5×10^{25} molecules per cubic metre. Thus, the average separation between molecules can be estimated:

$$average \ spacing \approx \frac{1}{\sqrt[3]{2.5 \times 10^{25}}}$$

$$\approx 3.4 \times 10^{-9} \text{ m}$$

$$\approx 3 \text{ nm}$$

So we find that:

- The average spacing between molecules (3 nm) is approximately 10 times the diameter of a molecule (0.3 nm).
- The molecules travel on average, about 100 nm before colliding with another molecule. This is about 300 times the diameter of a molecule, or 30 times the average separation between molecules.

Thus our initial assumptions (§4.2.1) about our model of a gas are at least consistent with the predictions of the ideal gas theory.

4.4 Beyond the ideal gas model

In this chapter, we have developed a simple model of a gas. The extent to which this has been worthwhile depends on how well the model actually describes the properties of real gas. In Chapter 5 we will consider a variety of experimental data on gases and see to what extent we can understand the real behaviour of gases in terms of the theory developed above. We will find that the answer is, broadly, that the ideal gas model describes real gases well under a wide range of experimental circumstances.

Before moving on to compare the predictions of the ideal gas model with experiment, it is worth considering in what way a more general theory would differ from ideal gas theory. More advanced theories must take account of two key features of molecules that have been ignored (§4.1). These are first, the finite size of the molecules, and second, the interactions between the molecules, which, though weak do have measurable effects.

4.4.1 The Van der Waals equation

The Van der Waals equation of state is an interesting modification of the ideal gas equation. It is derived by considering a gas composed of hard spheres, each with volume v and a binding energy per pair of atoms of Δu. Since the molecules now have a finite volume, we can plausibly argue that the actual volume available for molecules to move in is reduced. This reduction is roughly equivalent to the volume which would be occupied by the hard spheres themselves. Thus we can write for a gas with molar volume V_m:

$$P\left(V_m - b\right) = RT \qquad (4.46)$$

where b is the approximate volume of N_A hard-sphere molecules, i.e. $b \approx N_A v$. A more sophisticated analysis indicates that the volume is in fact reduced by more than just the volume of the molecules and normally we estimate b as:

$$b = 4N_A v \qquad (4.47)$$

However, Equation 4.46 has taken no account of the attraction between the molecules. This effect is not modelled quite so realistically in the Van der Waals model of a gas, but some account may be taken by introducing a term of the form:

$$\left(P + \frac{a}{V_m^2}\right)(V_m - b) = RT \qquad (4.48)$$

Van der Waals equation

where the coefficient a is given by:

$$a = \frac{2}{3}N_A b\Delta u \qquad (4.49)$$

The additional a/V_m^2 term in Equation 4.48 is small when the molar volume of the gas is large, but becomes significant as the molar volume is reduced. Commonly Equation 4.48 is used to model real gases with the parameters a and b determined experimentally from the small deviations of gases from $PV = RT$. Surprisingly, the Van der Waals Equation not only predicts deviations from ideal gas behaviour, but at small molar volumes and low temperatures, it predicts a region of solid-like behaviour.

4.4.2 The virial equation

Modern theories of gases represent the equation of state of a gas using a so-called *virial expansion*:

$$Z = \frac{PV_m}{RT}$$
$$= 1 + \frac{B(T)}{V_m} + \frac{C(T)}{V_m^2} + \dots \qquad (4.50)$$

The virial expansion

Z is known as the *compression factor* of a gas, and the coefficients $B(T)$, $C(T)$ etc. are known as the *second virial coefficient*, the *third virial coefficient* etc., and are functions of temperature only. The second virial coefficients of many gases are tabulated in *Kaye and Laby*. Notice that if the virial coefficients are taken as zero, then Equation 4.50 is the ideal gas equation. Thus the virial coefficients model deviations from perfect gas behaviour. In general the virial coefficients are determined experimentally, and their values tabulated in reference books such *Kaye and Laby*. However in certain theories of gases, the coefficient $B(T)$ can be understood as arising from interactions between pairs of molecules, and $C(T)$ as arising from interactions between clusters of three molecules. In general knowledge of the second virial coefficient is sufficient to understand the properties of gases at a level of a few parts per million.

Figure 4.12 Molecular interactions are sometimes poorly modelled by the hard sphere approach used in determining the mean free path of a molecule λ_{mfp}. Each of the following cases shows a molecule A colliding with a stationary molecule B.

(a) In the hard sphere approach, A would completely 'miss' B.

(b) This shows the effect of long-range attractive interactions between molecules (grey region). If A is moving slowly, interactions such as this produce quite different results from those envisioned in (a).

(c) This shows how the same collision as in (b) might be affected if molecule A were moving more quickly. Notice the deviation of A's trajectory is less than in (b).

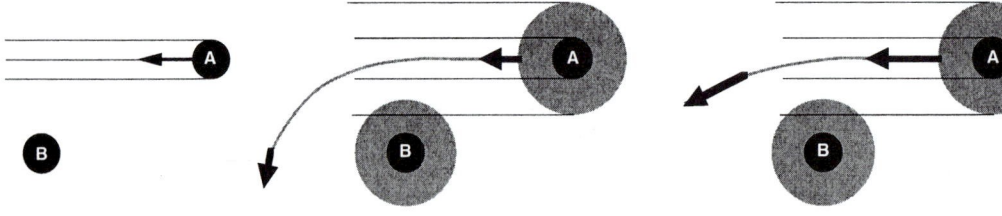

4.4.3 Molecular collisions

Finally, we consider the effect of molecular interactions on molecular collisions. The interactions between molecules are generally weakly attractive at long range (modelled by a grey area around the molecules in Figure 4.12), but repulsive at short range (modelled by the central black area of the molecules in Figure 4.12). Notice that assuming hard-sphere instantaneous-contact collisions will model the collision process correctly in most cases. However, some types of collision, such as those illustrated in Figure 4.12 (b) and (c), are not modelled at all well. The importance of this is that the 'effectiveness' of such collisions is reduced when the average kinetic energy of molecules is much larger than the attractive potential energy between molecules. This leads to a temperature dependence of the apparent average cross-sectional area used to evaluate the mean free path of a molecule.

4.5 Exercises

Exercises marked with a P prefix are 'normal' exercises. Those marked with a C prefix are best solved numerically by using a computer program or spreadsheet. Exercises marked with an E prefix are in general rather more challenging that the P and C exercises. Answers to all the exercises may be downloaded from www.physicsofmatter.com

Some more demanding exercises relating to material in this chapter and others may be found in Chapter 12.

P1. If 4 moles of gas are contained in a chamber of volume 1 litre at around room temperature, what is the pressure inside the container (Equation 4.29)? Is this above or below atmospheric pressure? To what temperature would you have to heat/cool the chamber in order to increase/decrease the pressure to atmospheric pressure?

P2. What is the number density of molecules in (a) air and (b) helium, at room temperature and atmospheric pressure (Example 4.2)?

C3. The probability that a molecule of mass m in a gas at temperature T has a speed between v and $v + dv$ is given by the Maxwell speed distribution curve. Program the formula for Equation 4.32 into a spreadsheet and so reproduce Figure 4.7.

P4. The average number of molecules colliding with unit area of wall per second is $\frac{1}{4} n\bar{v}$ (Equation 4.39). Produce an order of magnitude estimate for this quantity in air at atmospheric pressure and room temperature.

If an atom in the wall of a chamber has an 'area' of approximately 0.3 nm × 0.3 nm exposed to the chamber, estimate the frequency with which this atom is struck by atoms of the gas. To what pressure must the gas be lowered in order to reduce this frequency to 1 collision in 1000 seconds? (See also question P15 at the end of Chapter 3)

P5. By equating the average thermal energy per molecule $1.5k_BT$ with the kinetic energy of a molecule, (Equation 4.26) estimate the average speed of a molecule of argon at atmospheric pressure and room temperature. Assuming that argon molecules have a typical 'effective diameter' of around 0.3 nm, estimate the mean free path of an argon molecule in argon at atmospheric pressure and room temperature (Equation 4.45). Estimate the mean time between collisions and the average number of collisions per second.

P6. Appendix A1 outlines how the Maxwell speed distribution curve may be derived. Write an essay summarising the key stages of the calculation and suggest an experimental method by which the speed distribution curve might be determined.

P7. Academics! (a) You are a professor at Oxford University and a colleague claims that the ideal gas law does not agree well with experiment. Think of an experiment to demonstrate that the gas law is in fact obeyed rather well by most gases. (Hint: Try looking at the next chapter!) (b) Another colleague claims that the ideal gas law agrees well with experiment. Think of an experiment to demonstrate that under some circumstances the gas law breaks down completely.

P8. Measurements are made of the speed of 20 molecules sampled from some argon gas with the following results (in m s^{-1}) :

101.3	308.5	451.7	500.8
126.3	357.5	468.6	503.2
152.0	379.2	478.1	527.9
174.3	379.9	482.1	574.4
304.5	417.0	492.1	867.0

(a) Estimate $\bar{v}$ and v_{RMS} and their ratio. How closely does this result agree with what you might have expected from Figure 4.8

(b) Estimate the temperature and hence the pressure and number density of the gas.

C9. From www.physicsofmatter.com you can download a small program illustrating the dynamics of molecules in 2-dimensions. In the help section of the demo are some suggestions for phenomena you might like to observe. In particular you should set the program going with the option to plot molecular trajectories ON. After a while, switch the MOLECULAR INTERACTIONS off and notice the change in the character of the molecular motions. Write a paragraph summarising your observations.

P10. In Example 4.1 we compared the theoretical density of an air-like mixture of oxygen, nitrogen and argon with experimental values for the density of air. We said that the two estimates would agree more closely if we took account of the presence of water vapour. Let us see if that is right.

The vapour pressure of water (H_2O) at 20 °C is around 2000 Pa (Figure 9.22b). This would be pressure of water vapour if there were liquid water present in the container. However, more typically the vapour pressure would be about half of this value (i.e. 50% relative humidity). Estimate how much this would contribute to the density of air. Does this explain the small discrepancy of Example 4.1?

P11. In the derivation of the ideal gas equation we specifically neglected the effect of gravity. As we shall see in several questions in Chapter 12, this is sometimes not a good approximation. In fact, the pressure of a gas falls with increasing height, z, according to:

$$P = P_0 \exp\left[-mgz/k_B T\right]$$

where m is the mass of an individual molecule. Estimate the difference in the pressure between the top and bottom of the room you are in.

Gases: comparison with experiment

5.1 Introduction

In Chapter 4 we described the theory of a hypothetical *ideal gas*. The extent to which this endeavour has been worthwhile will become apparent as we compare the actual behaviour of real gases with the predictions of the theory. In the sections which follow we will familiarise ourselves with the experimental behaviour of real gases, and then develop ideal gas theory to compare its predictions with the experimental results. By juxtaposing predictions and experimental results we will see both the successes and the failures of ideal gas theory, and see how the theory can be developed to model the properties of real gases more closely.

§5.2   **Density:** As we saw in Example 4.1, ideal gas theory makes astonishingly accurate predictions.

§5.3   **Heat capacity:** If you had been studying physics at the start of the twentieth century rather than at the start of the twenty-first, you would have regarded the data on the heat capacity of gases as utterly mystifying. The explanation requires an understanding of the detailed structure and dynamics of the individual molecules that constitute the gas.

§5.4   **Expansions:** Gases can be compressed much more easily than liquids or solids which leads to interesting connections between their mechanical and thermal properties.

§5.5   **Thermal conductivity:** The key process in the transport of thermal energy through gases is collisions between gas molecules. In this section we will see that the 'hard sphere' model of molecular collisions we introduced in §4.3.4 needs to be significantly modified to explain the experimental data.

§5.6   **Speed of sound:** When we examine the data we will find that to explain the results we will again need to consider the detailed structure of the molecules of the gas. In particular we will find a connection with the heat capacity of gases that I still find surprising.

§5.7   **Electrical properties:** The insulating properties of gases are well known, but when subject to high electric fields gases break down and conduct electricity. At low electric fields, we will find that the properties of the gas again depend on the detailed distribution of electric charge within the molecules of the gas.

§5.8   **Optical properties:** The main optical property of gases is that they are almost completely transparent. It turns out that this property arises from an interesting relationship between the electronic properties of molecules and the process of evolutionary biology! When examining the data we will find interesting links to the electrical properties of gases, and to the detailed structure of the gas molecules.

At www.physicsofmatter.com

In addition to copies of the figures and tables, you will find animations of several of the important equations in this chapter and a computer program which realistically simulates the dynamics of simple molecules in gases, liquids and solids.

5.2 Density

5.2.1. Data on the density of gases

The most striking property of gases is their ability to expand to fill any container. In other words, a fixed number of gas molecules has no fixed volume and hence no fixed density. However, we can reasonably discuss the density of gases so long as we specify the conditions under which the density is determined. Table 5.1 contains data on the density of gases at a temperature of 0 °C (273.15 K) and a pressure 101325 Pa, conditions referred to as *standard temperature and pressure* (STP). Notice that this pressure is usually fairly close (but rarely equal to) the average atmospheric pressure close to sea level on Earth.

Notice that the densities in Table 5.1 are generally of the order of 1 kg m^{-3}. This is much lower than the densities of any solid or liquid substance, which generally have densities of the order of 1000 kg m^{-3} or higher.

Air

Air is a mixture of several gases whose relative abundances vary slightly from place to place. The main relatively constant components of the mixture are given in Table 5.2. The variability of both the composition and the density of air derives mainly from variations in water content. The density of *dry air* (i.e. with zero water content) and containing no carbon dioxide is 1.293 kg m^{-3} at STP. The density of 'normal' air is very sensitive to temperature and pressure. At 20 °C the value is typically 1.200 kg m^{-3}, and falls by roughly 0.004 kg °C^{-1} and increases by $\approx$ 0.012 kg kPa^{-1}. At 20 °C, the density fluctuations due to water content only exceptionally exceed $\pm$ 0.003 kg m^{-3}.

The density data show no apparent structure until we consider not the *mass density* (measured in kg m^{-3}), but the *molar density* (measured in mol m^{-3}). Table 5.3 shows the molar density and its inverse, the molar volume for each of the gases from Table 5.1 (see Example 5.1). The results in Table 5.3 indicate strongly that at STP, *every gas* has the same density of approximately 44.61 mol m^{-3}. We can also restate this in terms of

Table 5.1 The density of various gases at STP in units of kg m^{-3}. The lines in the table separate gases of monatomic, diatomic and polyatomic molecules.

Gas	A (u)	Density (kg m^{-3})
Helium, He	4.0030	0.1786
Neon, Ne	20.180	0.9003
Argon, Ar	39.948	1.782
Krypton, Kr	83.800	3.739
Xenon, Xe	131.29	5.858
Hydrogen, H$_2$	2.0160	0.08995
Nitrogen, N$_2$	28.014	1.250
Oxygen, O$_2$	31.998	1.428
Chlorine, Cl$_2$	70.906	3.164
Methane, CH$_4$	16.043	0.7158
Ethane, C$_2$H$_6$	30.070	1.342
Propane, C$_3$H$_8$	44.097	1.968

Table 5.2 The major components of *dry* atmospheric air. Typically water vapour is also present at a level of roughly 0.5%.

Gas	Molecular mass	% by volume
Nitrogen, N$_2$	28.01	78.09
Oxygen, O$_2$	32.00	20.95
Argon, Ar	39.95	0.93
Carbon dioxide, CO$_2$	44.00	0.03

Table 5.3 The molar volume of various gases at STP in units of 10^{-3} m^3. The lines in the table separate gases of monatomic, diatomic and polyatomic molecules.

Gas	Molar density (m^{-3})	Mass of 1 mol ($\times$ 10^{-3} kg)	Molar volume ($\times$ 10^{-3} m^3)
Helium, He	44.6158	4.0030	22.4136
Neon, Ne	44.6152	20.180	22.4139
Argon, Ar	44.6162	39.948	22.4134
Krypton, Kr	44.6168	83.800	22.4131
Xenon, Xe	44.6174	131.29	22.4128
Hydrogen, H$_2$	44.6160	2.0160	22.4135
Nitrogen, N$_2$	44.6168	28.014	22.4131
Oxygen, O$_2$	44.6162	31.998	22.4134
Chlorine, Cl$_2$	44.6172	70.906	22.4129
Methane, CH$_4$	44.6170	16.043	22.4130
Ethane, C$_2$H$_6$	44.6178	30.070	22.4126
Propane, C$_3$H$_8$	44.6182	44.097	22.4124

Example 5.1

One mole of helium gas (i.e. the Avogadro number 6.022×10^{23} of helium atoms), is held in a container at standard temperature and pressure. As illustrated below, the container is free to expand or contract, allowing the gas to assume its equilibrium volume for STP.

What is the equilibrium molar volume V_m?
First we note that 1 mole of helium gas has a mass of number 4.003×10^{-3} kg. From Table 5.1 the density of helium gas at STP is 0.1786 kg m^{-3}. From the expression *density = mass/volume* we can find the equilibrium volume:

$$V_m = \frac{mass}{density} = \frac{4.003 \times 10^{-3}}{0.1786}$$

$$= 22.413 \times 10^{-3} \ m^3$$

i.e. approximately 22.4 litres.

the molar volume i.e. the Avogadro number of molecules of any gas occupies a volume of roughly 22.41×10^{-3} m^3 at STP. Let me stress again that this result appears to be completely independent of the mass or complexity of the molecules of the gas.

So the questions raised by our preliminary examination of the experimental data on the density of real gases are:

- Why is the molar density of any of the gases in Table 5.3 approximately 44.61 mol m^{-3}, independent of the substance of which the gas is composed?
- Why are the densities of all gases at STP low when compared with those of solids (Tables 7.1 and 7.2) and liquids (Tables 9.1 and 9.2)?

5.2.2 Understanding the density data

We can answer the first question raised in §5.2.1. by rearranging the perfect gas equation:

$$PV = zRT \qquad \text{(4.29 and 5.1)}$$

into an expression for the molar density. We write this as:

$$\frac{z}{V} = \frac{P}{RT} \qquad (5.2)$$

Putting $P = 101325$ Pa and $T = 273.15$ K we have:

$$\text{molar density} = \frac{101325}{8.314 \times 273.15} \qquad (5.3)$$

$$= 44.6175 \text{ mol m}^{-3}$$

Consulting Table 5.3 reveals that the prediction of Equation 5.3 is strikingly accurate. It is clear that the perfect gas equation realistically describes at least some properties of real gases.

Consider now the second question raised in §5.2.1, the relatively low value of the densities as compared with those of solids and liquids. We can see that this is a natural feature of the model illustrated in Figure 4.1. In this model, we see that compared with the size of the molecules, a gas has large spaces between the molecules. Comparing this picture with the simple pictures of solids (Figure 6.1) and liquids (Figure 8.1) shows that a given number of molecules occupies a much larger volume in the gaseous state than in either of the 'condensed' states of matter.

5.2.3 Data on the thermal expansivity of gases

Gases, like most things, expand when heated. At least, they expand if they are free to do so. If they are constrained to stay at a constant volume, then the pressure they exert on their container increases. So, as with our discussion of density, we need to specify clearly the conditions under which the heating takes place.

Heating at constant pressure
The change in volume ΔV of a gas held at constant pressure in an initial volume V_o due to a temperature change ΔT can be expressed as:

$$\Delta V = V_o \beta_V \Delta T \qquad (5.4)$$

i.e. the volume change is proportional to the initial volume and the magnitude of the temperature

Figure 5.1: Heating a gas at constant pressure. Notice the increase in volume and reduction in density.

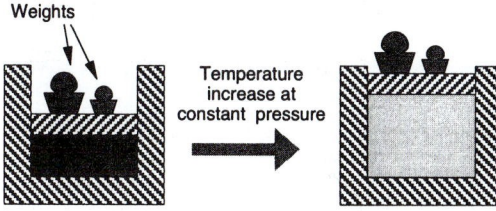

Figure 5.2: Heating a gas at constant volume. Notice the pressure (indicated by the weights) has increased.

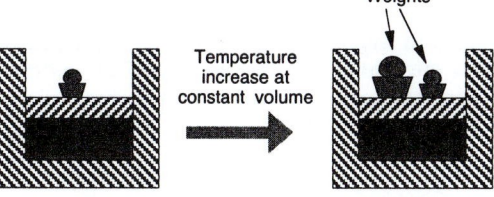

change, with constant of proportionally β_V. So the volume of the gas is given by:

$$V = V_0 + \Delta V$$
$$= V_0 + V_0 \beta_V \Delta T \qquad (5.5)$$
$$= V_0 (1 + \beta_V \Delta T)$$

The constant β_V is a called the *volume coefficient of thermal expansivity*. If β_V is small then the change in the volume of a gas due to a given temperature change will be small; if β_V is large then the change in the volume will be large.

Heating at constant volume

Similarly, when the temperature changes the increase in pressure of a gas held at *constant volume* (Figure 5.2) at initial pressure P_0 is:

$$\Delta P = P_0 \beta_P \Delta T \qquad (5.6)$$

and so the pressure P of the gas is given by:

$$P = P_0 + \Delta P$$
$$= P_0 + P_0 \beta_P \Delta T \qquad (5.7)$$
$$= P_0 (1 + \beta_P \Delta T)$$

where ΔT is the change in temperature.

The constant β_P is called the *pressure coefficient of thermal* expansivity. If β_P is small then the change in the pressure of a gas due to a temperature change will be small; if β_P is large then the change in the pressure of a gas due to a temperature change will be large.

Table 5.4 shows experimental values for β_P and β_V valid at around room temperature and pressure. We see that both the volume and the pressure coefficients of expansivity of all the gases shown

is close to $3.66 \times 10^{-3}\,°C^{-1}$, independent of the type of molecules of which the gas is composed. Looking ahead to Tables 7.7 and 9.5 shows that the figure for β_V is between 10 and 100 times larger than the thermal expansivity of many liquids, and around 100 to 1000 times larger than the expansivity of most solids.

So the main questions raised by our preliminary examination of the experimental data on the expansivity of gases are:

- Why are the expansivities of the five gases in Table 5.4 so similar, independent of the substance of which the gas is composed?
- Why are the expansivities of gases much greater than those shown by solids (Table 7.7) and liquids (Table 9.5)?

5.2.4 Understanding the data on the thermal expansivity of gases

We can answer the questions raised by our examination of the experimental data by rearranging the ideal gas equation $PV = zRT$. Equation 5.5 expressed the expansivity of a gas, β_V in a form

Table 5.4 Values of the expansivity coefficients β_V and β_P for gases whose initial pressure is 0.1333 MPa at 0 °C, valid in the temperature range 0 °C to 100 °C. The pressure 0.1333 MPa is a little greater than normal atmospheric pressure.

Gas	β_V (°C^{-1})	β_P (°C^{-1})
Helium, He	3.6580×10^{-3}	3.6605×10^{-3}
Hydrogen, H_2	3.6588×10^{-3}	3.6620×10^{-3}
Nitrogen, N_2	3.6735×10^{-3}	3.6744×10^{-3}
Air	3.6728×10^{-3}	3.6744×10^{-3}
Neon, Ne	3.6600×10^{-3}	3.6617×10^{-3}

which predicts the volume of a given amount of gas in terms of its volume V_o at some initial temperature T_o:

$$V = V_o(1 + \beta_v \Delta T) \qquad (5.8 \ \& \ 5.5^*)$$

where $\Delta T = T - T_o$. In order to compare the ideal gas theory with experiment, we need to rearrange $PV = zRT$ into a form similar to Equation 5.8. At temperatures T and T_o the volumes of z moles of gas are V and V_o respectively, i.e.

$$V = \frac{zR}{P_o}T \qquad V_o = \frac{zR}{P_o}T_o \qquad (5.9)$$

Notice that both measurements are made at the same pressure P_o. Taking the ratio of the two volumes and simplifying,

$$\frac{V}{V_o} = \frac{(zR/P_o)}{(zR/P_o)}\frac{T}{T_o}$$
$$= \frac{T}{T_o} \qquad (5.10)$$

we predict that:

$$V = \left[\frac{V_o}{T_o}\right]T \qquad (5.11)$$

i.e. the volume is directly proportional to the absolute temperature T, with a constant of proportionality V_o/T_o. Equating the right-hand sides of Equations 5.5 and 5.11, we have:

$$V_o(1 + \beta_v \Delta T) = \left[\frac{V_o}{T_o}\right]T \qquad (5.12)$$

Rearranging this to find β_v:

$$1 + \beta_v(T - T_o) = T/T_o$$
$$\beta_v = \frac{T/T_o - 1}{T - T_o}$$
$$= \frac{(T - T_o)/T_o}{T - T_o} \qquad (5.13)$$
$$= \frac{1}{T_o}$$

Table 5.5 Comparison of experimental and theoretical expansivities of gases. See also Table 5.4.

Gas	β_v (°C^{-1})	% difference between theory and experiment
Helium, He	3.6580×10^{-3}	− 0.082
Hydrogen, H$_2$	3.6588×10^{-3}	− 0.060
Nitrogen, N$_2$	3.6735×10^{-3}	+ 0.342
Air	3.6728×10^{-3}	+ 0.323
Neon, Ne	3.6600×10^{-3}	− 0.027

So the ideal gas theory predicts that all gases should have the same value of β_v. In Table 5.4 $T_o = 0 \ ^\circ C = 273.15$ K so we expect that:

$$\beta_v = \frac{1}{273.15} = 3.6610 \times 10^{-3} \ ^\circ C^{-1} \qquad (5.14)$$

which compares well with the experimental values of Table 5.4 in Table 5.5.

As Table 5.5 shows, the prediction of Equation 5.14 is accurate at the level better than 0.1% for some gases, and better than 1% even for complex mixed gases such as air: impressively close for such a simple theory.

An alternative interpretation of this data is to see it as way of defining the reference temperature T_o in Equation 5.13. Given the 'size' of a degree of temperature, the expansivity of gases provides a way of determining the absolute value of any chosen reference temperature.

Whichever interpretation of the results is chosen, the consistency of the results between different gases is striking. This indicates the general validity of the assumptions of the ideal gas theory outlined in the statements below Equation 4.1:

- The molecules behave as perfect point masses, i.e. they have zero volume
- The molecules do not interact with each other except momentarily as they collide
- The collisions between molecules are elastic

Now we need to consider the second question raised by examining the data: why the expansivities of gases are considerably greater than those of solids and liquids. To understand this, notice the significance of the second assumption above, that the molecules interact with each other only instantaneously as they collide. This amounts to

Example 5.2

Some helium gas is held in a fixed volume of 1 litre at a pressure of 0.1333 MPa and a temperature $T_0 = 0\,°C$. The pressure at another temperature T_1 is measured to be 0.1821 Mpa. What is T_1?

We can solve this problem using Equation 5.9, with the following values:

$$V_0 = 1 \text{ litre} = 1\times10^{-3} \text{ m}^{-3}$$

$$T_0 = 0\,°C$$

$$P_0 = 0.1333 \text{ MPa} = 0.1333\times10^6 \text{ Pa}$$

$$P_1 = 0.1821 \text{ MPa} = 0.1821\times10^6 \text{ Pa}$$

$$\beta = 3.6605\times10^{-3}\ °C^{-1} \text{ or } K^{-1}$$

$$\Delta T = ?$$

We rearrange Equation 5.9:

$$P = P_0(1+\beta\Delta T)$$

to solve for T_1:

$$\Delta T = T_1 - T_0 = \frac{1}{\beta}\left[\frac{P}{P_0}-1\right]$$

$$T_1 = T_0 + \frac{1}{3.6605\times10^{-3}}\left[\frac{0.1821}{0.1333}-1\right]$$

$$= 0\,°C + 273.186[0.3661]$$

$$= 0\,°C + 100.01\,°C$$

$$= 100.01\,°C$$

This calculation illustrates the mode of operation of *constant volume gas thermometers*. These devices allow the determination of temperature from first principles.

Example 5.3

Some nitrogen gas is held at a fixed pressure of 0.1333 MPa and an initial volume of 1 litre at a temperature of 0 °C. At what temperature (according to Equation 5.7) would the volume reach zero?

We use Equation 5.7 with the following values:

$$V_0 = 1 \text{ litre} = 1\times10^{-3} \text{ m}^{-3}$$

$$V_1 = 0$$

$$P_0 = 0.1333 \text{ MPa}$$

$$\alpha = 3.6735\times10^{-3}\ °C^{-1} \text{ or } K^{-1}$$

$$\Delta T = ?$$

We rearrange $V = V_0(1+\alpha\Delta T)$ to solve for T_1:

$$V = V_0(1+\alpha\Delta T) = 0$$

$$\Delta T = \frac{-1}{\alpha}$$

$$T_1 = T_0 + \frac{-1}{3.6735\times10^{-3}}$$

$$= 0\,°C - 272.2\,°C$$

$$= 0.93 \text{ K}$$

According to this analysis, the volume should reach zero at a temperature of $-272.2\,°C$ (≈ 0.95 K). If this experiment were performed it would be found that before this temperature was reached the nitrogen would first have liquefied at about $-196°C$ (77K) and later solidified at about ≈ 63K. In these states its expansion and contraction would be much smaller than in the gas phase.

---

assuming that the internal energy of a gas is held entirely by the kinetic energy of its molecules, neglecting the effect of the potential energy of interaction between molecules. The extent of the agreement between ideal gas theory and experiment arises because this neglect of the potential energy is valid.

However, the average kinetic energy of a molecule is proportional to the temperature. Remember that $KE_{average} = 1.5k_BT$ (Eq. 4.23) so as the temperature is reduced, the average kinetic energy becomes smaller and smaller. At lower temperatures the average kinetic energy will become comparable with the potential energy of interaction between the molecules. As the temperature is lowered, the molecules will tend to appear 'sticky' and form short-lived clusters. Eventually, at low enough

temperatures, they coalesce into a liquid or solid. What constitutes a 'low enough' temperature depends on the strength of interactions between gas molecules.

From the fact that solids and liquids form at low temperatures we can see that the interactions between molecules generally act to reduce the separation between molecules, and hence reduce the volume of the gas. The high expansivity of gases as compared with solids and liquids can be now be understood: it is the high temperature limit of the expansivity of all materials. When the temperature of the gas is high enough to allow us to neglect the molecular interactions that tend to restrict the volume of the gas, the expansivity of real gases approaches that predicted for an ideal gas.

5.3 Heat capacity

The heat capacity of a gas is defined as the limiting value of the ratio of the heat energy input ΔQ to the resulting temperature rise ΔT:

$$C = \frac{\Delta Q}{\Delta T}\bigg|_{\lim \Delta T \to 0} = \frac{dQ}{dT} \; JK^{-1} \qquad (5.15)$$

The value obtained for this ratio depends on the conditions under which the heat input is made. The two principal measurement conditions are those of:

- *constant pressure*, in which the heat input can cause an expansion of the gas, and
- *constant volume*, in which the heat input can cause a rise in pressure of the gas.

The heat capacity associated with measurements at constant pressure is referred to as C_P and that associated with measurements at constant volume is referred to as C_V. The heat capacity of a substance is usually quoted either for a given *mass* of material, the *specific heat capacity* (e.g. $J K^{-1} kg^{-1}$), or per mole, the *molar heat capacity* ($J K^{-1} mol^{-1}$).

Instead of examining data on C_P and C_V independently, we will look first at data for C_P in §5.3.1 and then at data for γ, the ratio of C_P to C_V, in §5.3.2.

5.3.1 Data on the heat capacity of gases at constant pressure

Tables 5.6 and 5.7 show the molar heat capacity C_P at several temperatures for a variety of monatomic and diatomic gases respectively. Figures 5.3 and 5.4 show graphs of the data from Tables 5.6 and 5.7.

The most striking feature of the data is the constancy of the value 20.8 $J K^{-1} mol^{-1}$ for all the monatomic gases shown, independent of temperature. In contrast, the diatomic gases have a rather larger heat capacity at low temperatures, which then increases still further as the temperature is increased, tending to a maximum of around 37 $J K^{-1} mol^{-1}$.

Thus for either monatomic or diatomic gases, we can make a 'ball park' estimate of the molar heat

Table 5.6 The molar heat capacities at constant pressure C_P($J K^{-1} mol^{-1}$) for the monatomic noble gases. These data are graphed in Figure 5.3.

- The shaded figures correspond to data taken in the liquid or solid phase. For each gas the boiling temperature and melting temperature are separated by less than 5 K.
- The data between the two double lines is from a separate source from the rest of the table. Notice that the extra measurement resolution still shows agreement between the heat capacities of the different gases.

T(K)	He	Ne	Ar	Kr	Xe
50	—	—	24.8	25.1	25.1
100	—	—	20.8	31.6	28.2
150	—	—	20.8	20.8	33.6
200	—	—	20.8	20.8	20.8
298.15	20.786	20.786	20.786	20.786	20.786
400	20.8	20.8	20.8	20.8	20.8
600	20.8	20.8	20.8	20.8	20.8
800	20.8	20.8	20.8	20.8	20.8
1000	20.8	20.8	20.8	20.8	20.8
1500	20.8	20.8	20.8	20.8	20.8
2000	20.8	20.8	20.8	20.8	20.8
2500	20.8	20.8	20.8	20.8	20.8

Table 5.7 The molar heat capacities at constant pressure C_P($J K^{-1} mol^{-1}$) for some diatomic gases. These data are graphed in Figure 5.4.

- The shaded figures correspond to data taken in the liquid or solid phase.

T(K)	H_2	O_2	N_2	F_2	Cl_2	Br_2	I_2
50	—	46.1	41.5	—	29.2	33.3	35.8
100	—	29.1	29.1	—	42.3	43.6	45.6
150	—	29.1	29.1	—	51.0	49.2	49.6
200	—	29.1	29.1	—	54.2	53.8	51.5
400	29.2	30.1	29.2	33.0	35.3	36.7	80.3
600	29.3	32.1	30.1	35.2	36.6	37.3	37.6
800	29.6	33.7	31.4	36.3	37.2	37.5	37.8
1000	30.2	34.9	32.7	37.0	37.5	37.7	37.9
1500	32.3	36.6	34.9	37.9	38.0	38.0	38.2
2000	34.3	37.8	36.0	38.4	38.3	38.2	38.5
2500	36.0	38.9	36.0	38.8	38.6	38.5	38.8

capacity as 30 ± 10 J K^{-1} mol^{-1} at all temperatures.

The main questions raised by our preliminary examination of the experimental data on C_P are:

- Why are the constant pressure heat capacities of monatomic or diatomic gases usually in the range 30 ± 10 J K^{-1} mol^{-1}?
- Why does $C_P = 20.8$ J K^{-1} mol^{-1} for monatomic gases, with almost no dependence on temperature, or on the type of molecule from which the gas is formed?
- Why do some diatomic gases have a low temperature value of C_P rather greater than the value for monatomic gases, but which increases with increasing temperature?

We will consider these questions in §5.3.3, after we have considered data on the ratio of heat capacities $\gamma = C_P/C_V$.

5.3.2 Data on heat capacity ratio ($\gamma = C_P/C_V$)

The data given in Tables 5.6 and 5.7 refer to the heat capacity at constant pressure C_P, i.e. the gas is allowed to expand as the heat input is made. C_P differs significantly from the heat capacity at constant volume C_V. Experimentally it is found that the ratio of C_P to C_V (known as γ, pronounced 'gamma') varies with the number of atoms in a molecule of the gas. Table 5.8 records values of γ classified by the number of atoms in a molecule of the gas.

Figure 5.5 shows a histogram of all the data from Table 5.8, and indicates which values correspond to which type of molecule. It is clear from the histogram that the data cluster according to the number of atoms in a molecule of the gas. Monatomic and diatomic gases have γ values of around 1.66 and 1.4 respectively, and tri- and poly-atomic gases have widely scattered smaller values, but always greater than one.

Interestingly, it seems that for air at high pressures the values for γ are strongly increased, even beyond the values for a monatomic gas.

Figure 5.3: The heat capacity of monatomic gases C_P versus absolute temperature (Table 5.6). Data for temperatures less than the boiling point are not plotted. Notice that at the resolution of the measurement, the gases have the same heat capacity across a temperature variation of over an order of magnitude.

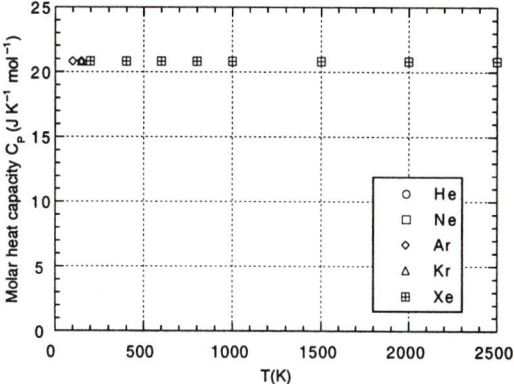

Figure 5.4: The heat capacity of diatomic gases versus absolute temperature (Table 5.7). Data for temperatures below the boiling point are not plotted. Notice that the heat capacities increase with temperature. The lines through the data points are drawn to guide the eye

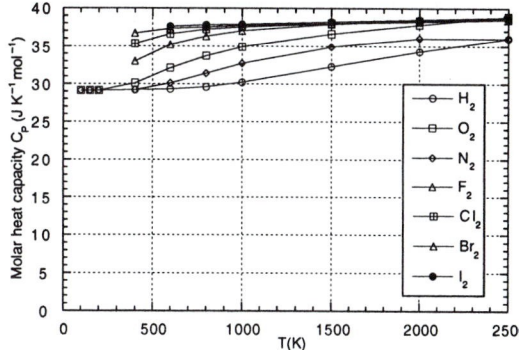

Figure 5.5 Histogram of values of γ in Table 5.8. The column height indicates how common it is to find γ within ± 0.01 of the value specified on the x-axis. Notice how the data are clustered in groups that are identifiable as monatomic, diatomic, polyatomic or high pressure.

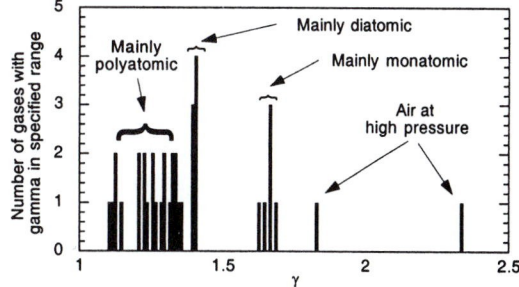

Example 5.4

Samples of four gases are heated from room temperature (20 °C or 293K) to 100 °C (373K) in a piston device at a constant pressure of $\approx 0.1MPa$:

A consists of 1 kg of helium

B consists of 1 kg of xenon

C consists of 1 kg of nitrogen

D consists of 1 kg of unknown *monatomic* gas.

(a) Work out how much heat energy is required to raise samples A, B and C to the required temperature.

(b) Sample D requires 41.65×10^3 joules to raise it to 100 °C. Considering only those gases tabulated in Table 5.6, work out which gas is being heated.

(a) The heating takes place at constant pressure so we use C_P to relate the heat input to the temperature rise.

Sample A: Helium

The heat required to raise one mole of gas from T_1 to T_2 is given by:

$$Q = \int_{T_1}^{T_2} C_P dT$$

Consulting Table 5.6 and Figure 5.3 we see that for helium C_P is constant over the range of heating, so the energy required to heat one mole of gas from T_1 to T_2 is given by:

$$Q = C_P \int_{T_1}^{T_2} dT$$
$$= C_P [T_2 - T_1]$$

and similarly for z moles of gas we have:

$$Q = z C_P [T_2 - T_1]$$

1 kg of helium, molecular mass 4, is $1/(4 \times 10^{-3}) = 250$ moles of helium. Substituting for z, C_P, T_2, and T_1 we have:

$$Q = 250 \times 20.8[373 - 293]$$
$$= 4.16 \times 10^5 \text{ J}$$

Sample B: Xenon

Similarly to sample A we find $Q = zC_P[T_2 - T_1]$. Now however we have 1 kg of Xe, which has a molecular mass of 131.3 and hence contains only:

$$z = \frac{1}{0.1313} = 7.62 \text{ moles}$$

Hence it takes only

$$Q = 7.62 \times 20.8[373 - 293]$$
$$= 12.68 \times 10^3 \text{ J}$$

to heat the same *mass* of gas through the same temperature rise! The reason for this somewhat counterintuitive result is related to the fact that we have many fewer molecules in sample B than in sample A.

Sample C: Nitrogen

We proceed exactly as with samples A and B except now there is a possibility that C_P will change over the range of heating because nitrogen gas consists of *diatomic* N_2 molecules. Detailed consultation of Table 5.7 shows that the variation from 200 K to 400 K is less than 1% and so may be assumed constant over our more restricted range.

Now however we have 1 kg of N_2 which has a molecular mass of $2 \times 14 = 28$. Notice that it is the mass of the *molecule* that is important. Hence we have :

$$z = \frac{1}{0.028} = 35.71 \text{ moles}$$

So it takes:

$$Q = 35.71 \times 29.1[373 - 293]$$
$$= 83.132 \times 10^3 \text{ J}$$

(b)

Sample D: Unknown monatomic gas

Sample D requires 41.65×10^3 J to raise it to 100 °C. We can use the formula we derived for helium (sample A) to work out z, the number of moles of gas present:

$$Q = z C_P [T_2 - T_1]$$

We know C_P because for all monatomic gases $C_P = 20.8$ J K^{-1} mol^{-1} and so we can find out how many moles z are contained in 1 kg of the unknown gas. Thus we can work out its relative molecular mass, and identify the gas by its molecular mass. We find that:

$$z = \frac{Q}{C_P[T_2 - T_1]} = \frac{41.65 \times 10^3}{20.8[373 - 293]}$$
$$= 25.03 \text{ moles}$$

Thus the relative molecular mass is given by:

$$M = \frac{1}{25.03 \times 10^{-3}} = 39.95$$

This identifies the monatomic gas unambiguously as argon.

So the main questions raised by our preliminary examination of the experimental data for γ are:

- Why is the heat capacity at constant pressure always greater than the heat capacity at constant volume, i.e. $\gamma > 1$?
- Why does the value of γ depend on whether the gas is monatomic, diatomic or polyatomic? In particular we would like to understand why:
  - Monatomic gases have values for γ close to 1.66 ($\pm$ 0.02)
  - Diatomic gases in the table have values for γ close to 1.4 ($\pm$ 0.1), except at high pressure
  - Polyatomic gases have lower values of γ than either monatomic or diatomic gases.
- Why is γ for air at extremely high pressures increased to values above those for monatomic gases?

Example 5.5

What is the *specific* heat capacity of helium gas?

One mole of helium gas has a mass of 4×10^{-3} kg and the value of its molar heat capacity at constant pressure C_P is 20.8 J K^{-1} mol^{-1} (Table 5.6). So it takes 20.8 J to raise the temperature of 4×10^{-3} kg of helium by 1 °C. The number of moles in 1 kg of helium is:

$$\frac{1}{4 \times 10^{-3}} = 250 \text{ moles of helium}$$

The *specific* heat capacity at constant pressure is therefore $250 \times 20.8 = 5200$ J K^{-1} kg^{-1}.

Example 5.6

For helium gas, Table 5.8 gives $\gamma = 1.63$ and Table 5.6 gives $C_P = 20.8$ J K^{-1} mol^{-1} over a wide temperature range. What is C_V for helium?

Since $\gamma = C_P / C_V$ we can work out C_V as:

$$C_V = \frac{C_P}{\gamma} = \frac{20.8}{1.63} = 12.8 \text{ J K}^{-1} \text{ mol}^{-1}$$

Table 5.8 The ratio of the principal heat capacities ($\gamma = C_P / C_V$) of some gases. The shaded results correspond to a pressure of 200 atmospheres (20 MPa). The notes below each section of the table summarise the results for that class of gases. There appears to be a trend towards a reduction in γ as the temperature is increased. Where no temperature shown, the temperature of the measurement is not known but is probably either 0 °C or close to 20 °C.

Gas	T(°C)	T(K)	γ	Gas	T(°C)	T(K)	γ
Monatomic gases				**Triatomic gases**			
He	0.0	273.20	1.630	O_3	—	—	1.290
Ar	0.0	273.20	1.667	H_2O	100.0	373.20	1.334
Ne	19.0	292.20	1.642	CO_2	10.0	283.20	1.300
Kr	19.0	292.20	1.689	CO_2	300.0	573.20	1.220
Xe	19.0	292.20	1.666	CO_2	500.0	773.20	1.200
Hg	310.0	583.20	1.666	NH_3	—	—	1.336
All the above results are close to 1.66				N_2O	—	—	1.324
Diatomic gases				H_2S	—	—	1.340
H_2	10.0	283.20	1.407	CS_2	—	—	1.239
N_2	20.0	293.20	1.401	SO_2	20.0	293.20	1.260
O_2	10.0	283.20	1.400	SO_2	500.0	773.20	1.200
CO	1800.0	2073.2	1.297	*All the above results are close to 1.3*			
NO	—	—	1.394	**Polyatomic gases**			
Most of the above results are close to 1.4				CH_4	—	—	1.313
C: Air				C_2H_6	—	—	1.220
Air	-79.3	193.90	1.405	C_3H_8	—	—	1.130
Air	10.0	283.20	1.401	C_2H_2	—	—	1.260
Air	500.0	773.20	1.357	C_2H_4	—	—	1.264
Air	900.0	1173.2	1.320	C_6H_6	20.0	293.20	1.400
Air	0.0	273.20	1.828	C_6H_6	99.7	372.90	1.105
Air	-79.3	193.90	2.333	$CHCl_3$	30.0	303.20	1.110
Most of the above results are close to 1.4 except for those shaded.				$CHCl_3$	99.8	373.00	1.150
				CCl_4	—	—	1.130
				The above results are between 1.1 and 1.4			

Example 5.7

What is the *difference* between the values of C_P and C_V for (a) helium and (b) nitrogen, i.e. how much extra energy is needed to raise 1 mole of gas through 1 kelvin if the process takes place at *constant pressure*, as compared with the same process at *constant volume*?

From Example 5.6 we find C_V as $C_V = C_P / \gamma$. So the difference between C_P and C_V is given by:

$$C_P - C_V = C_P - \frac{C_P}{\gamma} = C_P \left[1 - \frac{1}{\gamma} \right]$$

(a) For helium, using Tables 5.6 and 5.8,

$$C_P = 20.8 \text{ J K}^{-1} \text{ mol}^{-1}$$
$$\gamma = 1.63$$

so $\quad C_P - C_V = 20.8 \left[1 - \frac{1}{1.63} \right] = 8.04 \text{ J K}^{-1} \text{ mol}^{-1}$

(b) For nitrogen, using Tables 5.7 and 5.8,
$C_P = 20.8 \text{ J K}^{-1} \text{ mol}^{-1}$ at around room temperature
$\gamma = 1.63$:

so $\quad C_P - C_V = 29.2 \left[1 - \frac{1}{1.401} \right] = 8.36 \text{ J K}^{-1} \text{ mol}^{-1}$

5.3.3 Understanding the data on the heat capacity of gases

In this section we will attempt to understand the questions raised in §5.3.1 and §5.3.2 on C_P and γ respectively. In order to do this we will develop the theory of an ideal gas further than we did in Chapter 4. Our plan will be to derive expressions first for C_V, then for C_P and finally for their ratio γ.

Heat capacity: background theory

As we saw in §2.5.2, the first law of thermodynamics can be stated as:

$$\Delta U = \Delta Q + \Delta W \qquad (2.57^*)$$

where:
ΔQ is the heat supplied *to* a substance
ΔW is the work done *on* a substance
ΔU is the change in the internal energy of the substance.

For our purposes, we will rearrange this equation as an expression for ΔQ:

$$\Delta Q = \Delta U - \Delta W \qquad (5.16)$$

Arranged in this way first law tells us that when heat ΔQ is supplied to a substance, it may either:
(a) increase the internal energy of the substance ΔQ, or
(b) cause the substance to do ΔW of work on its environment.

This is a statement of the principle of conservation of energy. Notice that ΔW is defined in Equations 2.57 and 5.16 as *the work done on the gas by its* *environment*. Thus if the gas does net work on its environment (for example by expanding and pushing a piston) ΔW will be negative. We will develop our theory of the heat capacity of a gas in the following four stages:

Stage 1: We derive an expression the work done by a gas when it changes its volume.

Stage 2: We derive an expression for the heat capacity of a gas when no work is done by the gas during the heating process. This will be our result for C_V.

Stage 3: We combine the first two steps to derive an expression for the heat capacity of a gas when it does work on its environment during the heating process. This will be our result for C_P.

Stage 4: Finally, we combine the previous two results for C_V and C_P to yield an expression for their ratio γ.

Stage 1: Work done by an expanding gas

First of all recall that in general work is done when *a force moves its point of action*. Thus in order to do work, a gas must change its volume. Figure 5.6 illustrates a hypothetical experiment that will allow us to calculate the work done during a volume change.

If the piston apparatus of Figure 5.6 has an area A and the pressure of the gas is P, then the total force on the piston is $F = PA$. Now suppose the piston moves outward an infinitesimal amount dx. In this case the gas volume has increased by a small amount dV. Notice two things: first, the

Figure 5.6 The input of heat into a gas under conditions of constant pressure. The figure shows gas trapped in a thermally insulated piston device with cross-sectional area A. The piston is free to move so that it will finally stop when the net force on the piston is zero.

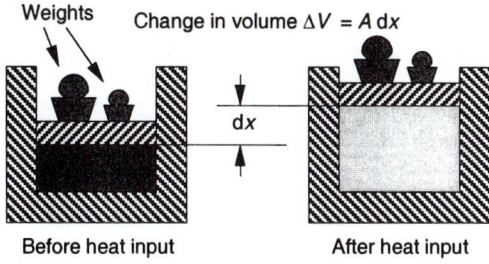

Before heat input   After heat input

work done *by the environment* on the gas is a negative quantity: this expresses the fact that in an expansion, the gas is doing work on its environment. Second, notice that we can write dW as follows:

$$dW = -F dx$$
$$= -PA dx \qquad (5.17)$$
$$= -P dV$$

where we noticed that $A dx$ is an infinitesimal element of volume dV. So the work done *by the environment* on the gas is given by:

$$dW = -P dV \qquad (5.18)$$

To obtain the work done *by the environment* on the gas in a finite expansion we must integrate this expression:

$$\Delta W = \int_{V}^{V+\Delta V} -P dV \qquad (5.19)$$

In general, P will change as the gas expands. However, if we consider the case when heat is added in order to maintain constant pressure during the expansion, then P can slip outside the integral to yield:

$$\Delta W = -P \int_{V}^{V+\Delta V} dV$$
$$= -P[V]_{V}^{V+\Delta V} \qquad (5.20)$$
$$\Delta W = -P\Delta V$$

Using the ideal gas equation $PV = zRT$ we may eliminate $P\Delta V$ in favour of $zR\Delta T$, where ΔT is the temperature change required to keep the pressure constant during the expansion. Hence, if z moles of ideal gas expands at constant pressure, the work done *by the environment* on the gas is:

$$\Delta W = -P\Delta V$$
$$= -zR\Delta T \qquad (5.21)$$

Before we move on to stage 2, I would like to remind you that when attempting to solve problems relating to this kind of process, it is important to take care with regard to the sign of ΔW.

Stage 2: Heat capacity at constant volume

If the heat is supplied to a gas at constant volume, then by Equation 5.21 no work is done either by or on the gas. Thus the first law of thermodynamics tells us that:

$$\Delta Q = \Delta U - 0$$
$$\Delta Q = \Delta U \qquad (5.22)$$

Under these conditions the heat energy input goes entirely into increasing the average energy of the molecules, and hence by Equation 4.19, the internal energy, U, of the gas. Recall that for an ideal gas, the internal energy of an ideal gas is just the sum of the kinetic energies of the individual molecules. A molecule of an ideal gas has just three degrees of freedom (§4.2: Complication 3). However we can generalise our calculation to a gas containing real molecules which have other degrees of freedom. If we consider a gas molecule to have p degrees of freedom, each with $0.5k_BT$ of energy, the internal energy of z moles of gas, i.e. zN_A molecules will be:

$$U = zN_A \times p \times \tfrac{1}{2}k_BT$$
$$= \tfrac{1}{2}zpN_Ak_BT \qquad (5.23)$$

Using $N_Ak_B = R$, this simplifies to:

$$U(T) = \tfrac{1}{2}zpRT \qquad (5.24)$$

The internal energy of the gas at $T + \Delta T$ will be given by:

$$U(T + \Delta T) = \tfrac{1}{2}zpR[T + \Delta T] \qquad (5.25)$$

So the change in internal energy ΔU on heating from T to $T + \Delta T$ is:

$$\Delta U = U(T + \Delta T) - U(T)$$
$$= \tfrac{1}{2} zpR[T + \Delta T] - \tfrac{1}{2} zpR[T] \qquad (5.26)$$
$$= \tfrac{1}{2} zpR\Delta T$$

By Equation 5.22 this change in internal energy must be supplied by the heat ΔQ, and so we may write:

$$\Delta Q = \tfrac{1}{2} zpR\Delta T \qquad (5.27)$$

So the heat capacity at constant volume of z moles of gas is given by:

$$C_V = \frac{\Delta Q}{\Delta T}$$
$$= \frac{\tfrac{1}{2} zpR\Delta T}{\Delta T} \qquad (5.28)$$
$$= \tfrac{1}{2} zpR$$

We thus predict that the molar (i.e. $z = 1$) constant-volume heat capacity of a gas will be:

$$C_V = 4.157p \quad \text{J K}^{-1} \text{mol}^{-1} \qquad (5.29)$$

in general, and:

$$C_V = 12.471 \quad \text{J K}^{-1} \text{mol}^{-1} \qquad (5.30)$$
$$\text{for } p = 3$$

These are simple results. Importantly they indicate that a measurement of C_V for a gas allows us to immediately infer the number of internal degrees of freedom of the molecules of the gas.

Stage 3: Heat capacity at constant pressure

In the previous two stages we developed an expression for the change in internal energy of a gas when it is heated at constant volume:

$$\Delta U = \tfrac{1}{2} pR\Delta T \qquad (5.31 \text{ and } 5.26^*)$$

and an expression for the work done *by the environment* on the gas in expanding at constant pressure:

$$\Delta W = -P\Delta V \qquad (5.32 \text{ and } 5.21^*)$$
$$= -R\Delta T$$

We can now combine these to arrive at an expression for C_P. Taking note of the sign of ΔW as discussed following Equation 5.16, we may substitute these expressions into the first law of thermodynamics:

$$\Delta Q = \Delta U - \Delta W$$
$$= \tfrac{1}{2} pR\Delta T - [-R\Delta T] \qquad (5.33)$$
$$= \left[\tfrac{1}{2} p + 1\right] R\Delta T$$

Remembering that $C_P = \Delta Q / \Delta T$ we find:

$$C_P = \frac{\Delta Q}{\Delta T} = \frac{R\Delta T\left[\tfrac{1}{2} p + 1\right]}{\Delta T} \qquad (5.34)$$
$$= R\left[\tfrac{1}{2} p + 1\right]$$

We thus predict that the molar (i.e. $z = 1$) constant-pressure heat capacity of a gas will be:

$$C_P = 8.314 \times \left[\tfrac{1}{2} p + 1\right] \quad \text{J K}^{-1} \text{mol}^{-1} \qquad (5.35)$$

in general, and:

$$C_P = 20.785 \quad \text{J K}^{-1} \text{mol}^{-1} \qquad (5.36)$$
$$\text{for } p = 3.$$

Stage 4: Gamma (γ)

Finally, we can combine Equation 5.28 for C_V:

$$C_V = \tfrac{1}{2} zpR \qquad (5.28^* \text{ and } 5.37)$$

and Equation 5.34 for C_P:

$$C_P = R\left[\tfrac{1}{2} p + 1\right] \qquad (5.34^* \text{ and } 5.38)$$

to obtain an expression for γ:

$$\gamma = \frac{C_P}{C_V} = \frac{zR\left[\tfrac{1}{2} p + 1\right]}{\tfrac{1}{2} zpR} = \frac{\left[\tfrac{1}{2} p + 1\right]}{\tfrac{1}{2} p} \qquad (5.39)$$

which simplifies to:

$$\gamma = 1 + \frac{2}{p} \qquad (5.40)$$

5.3.4 Comparison with experiment

We now have expressions for the heat capacities of a gas at either constant pressure or constant volume, and for their ratio gamma. So we are now in a good position to consider the extent to which they enable us to answer the questions raised at the end of §5.2.2 and §5.2.3 .

Why are the constant-pressure heat capacities of monatomic or diatomic gases usually in the range 30 ± 10 J K^{-1} mol^{-1}?

From Equation 5.38 for C_P, we expect the heat capacity at constant pressure to vary with p, the number of degrees of freedom of the molecules of the gas. We can rearrange Equation 5.38 as an expression for p:

$$p = 2\left[\frac{C_P}{R} - 1\right] \qquad (5.41)$$

in terms of C_P. Now we can interpret the range of values of C_P as being due to the different numbers of internal degrees of freedom of the molecules of the gas. Substituting $C_P = 30 \pm 10$ J K^{-1} mol^{-1} implies values for p in the range 5.2 ± 2.4, or $3 < p < 8$. As we shall see, this is a very plausible range of results.

Why, for monatomic gases, does $C_P = 20.8$ J K^{-1} mol^{-1}, with almost no dependence on temperature or the type of molecule from which the gas is formed?

For monatomic gases, we expect molecules to have no internal degrees of freedom. Therefore, there should be just three degrees of freedom per molecule, corresponding to the kinetic energy of molecule in each of the x-, y- and z- directions. Using $p = 3$ in Equation 5.38 gives a prediction of $C_P = 20.786$ J K^{-1} mol^{-1}. As we can see from Figure 5.7, this value agrees closely with the data for monatomic gases given in Table 5.6 and Figure 5.3. We may take this as an indication that that the internal energy of a monatomic gas really is held in the kinetic energy of its constituent atoms, and in no other way.

Why do diatomic gases have a low temperature value of C_P rather greater than the value for monatomic gases, and which increases with increasing temperature?

Using Equation 5.41

$$p = 2\left[\frac{C_P}{R} - 1\right] \qquad (5.41^*)$$

we can understand these results by supposing that diatomic molecules possess extra degrees of freedom. These would be in addition to the three degrees of freedom associated with the kinetic energy of a molecule as a whole. Furthermore, it appears that not only are there more degrees of freedom, but the number of degrees of freedom required to explain the data gets larger as the temperature increases. In the following section on the heat capacity ratio γ we will see that we can associate these extra degrees of freedom with certain types of *internal* molecular motion. Here we note that the diatomic gases in our sample appear to have a heat capacity corresponding to around 5 degrees of freedom at low temperatures, increasing to around 7 or 8 at higher temperatures.

Gamma, γ

Why is the heat capacity at constant pressure always greater than the heat capacity at constant volume, i.e. $\gamma > 1$?

We can see immediately why this must so. The first law of thermodynamics tells us that :

$$\Delta Q = \Delta U - \Delta W \qquad (5.16^* \text{ and } 5.42)$$

In order to achieve a given change in temperature ΔT, Equation 5.26 tells us that we need to increase the internal energy U of the gas by $\Delta U = \frac{1}{2} zpR\Delta T$. So in order to raise the temperature of the gas by ΔT the *minimum* energy required is $\Delta Q = \Delta U$ which occurs when $\Delta W = 0$, i.e. when the gas is held at fixed volume. If the gas is allowed to expand during heating then additional energy must be supplied to do the work ΔW involved in the expansion. Thus C_P must always be greater than C_V and hence γ must always be greater than one.

Why does the value of γ depend on whether the gas is monatomic, diatomic or polyatomic? In particular we would like to understand why:

- **monatomic gases have values for γ close to 1.66**
- **diatomic gases have values for γ close to 1.4 except at high pressure**
- **polyatomic gases have lower values of γ than either monatomic or diatomic gases.**

From Equation 5.40, we see that we expect γ to depend directly on the number of degrees of freedom per molecule p:

$$\gamma = 1 + \frac{2}{p} \qquad \text{(5.40* and 5.43)}$$

Figure 5.7 Comparison of the prediction of theory with experimental results for monatomic gases. The right-hand axis shows C_P in units of the gas constant R.

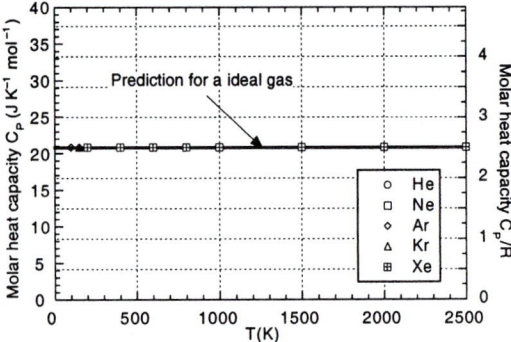

Figure 5.8 The experimental results for diatomic gases compared with the prediction for monatomic gases. The right-hand axis shows C_P in units of the gas constant R. The data exceed the prediction for monatomic gases by at least R at low temperatures, increasing to around 2 to 2.5R at high temperatures.

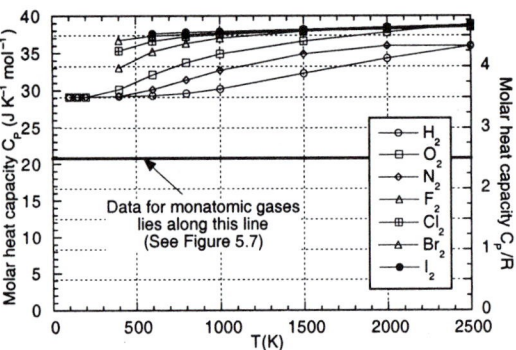

Rearranging this, we can obtain an expression for the number of degrees of freedom per molecule in terms of γ:

$$p = \frac{2}{\gamma - 1} \qquad (5.44)$$

Experimentally, Table 5.8 shows that monatomic gases have values of γ = 1.66 ± 0.02. Interpreting this using Equation 5.44 implies $p \approx 3$ (within ± 0.1). Recall that three degrees of freedom are exactly what we expected when we derived the ideal gas equation. Using Equation 5.44 to interpret the values of γ for all the gases in Table 5.8, yields the results in Table 5.9.

We see that we can plausibly explain the data for γ in terms of quite reasonable numbers of degrees of freedom per molecule. By this I mean that the values of p are all greater than three, but are not too much greater. We now need to understand the way in which the values of p vary across Table 5.9. In particular we need to understand why p varies with:

- the different molecules constituting the gas
- the temperature
- the pressure.

Given the answers to the previous questions we are now reasonably sure that all molecules in a gas possess three degrees of freedom associated with their kinetic energy in each of the x-, y- and z-directions. However, there are other possibilities.

Figure 5.9 Three degrees of freedom of a gas molecule are associated with kinetic energy of motion in each of the x-, y-, and z- directions.

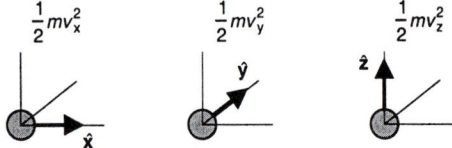

Rotational degrees of freedom

More complicated molecules also possess degrees of freedom associated with *rotation* about each of the x-, y- and z- axes. We can imagine this as a kind of 'tumbling motion', with the molecule spinning round randomly as it moves from one collision to another. The energy associated with

Figure 5.10 The three degrees of freedom of a diatomic molecule associated with rotation about the x-, y- and z-axes.

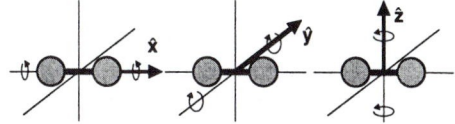

rotations differs depending on the axis of rotation. Figure 5.10 illustrates the rotation of a diatomic molecule. Just by symmetry, we can see that rotation about the y- and z-axes needs to be considered separately from rotation about the x-axis, the one through the centres of the two atoms. A quantum mechanical analysis of this problem shows that rotation about the x-axis is much less likely. This is because, as discussed in Table 2.5, the energy separation ΔE between the non-rotating quantum state of the molecule and the rotating quantum state is much greater for rotations about the x-axis

than for rotations the y- or z-axes. The idea that the energy ΔE separating non-rotating states from rotating states is anything other than zero can only be understood through consideration of the quantum mechanics of molecular motion. Classically, we could put as little energy as we chose into the rotation of molecule: there was no lower limit on the rotational speed of a molecule. Quantum mechanically, there is a lower limit to the energy tied up in rotation given by $\Delta E = \hbar\omega$ where ω is the minimum angular frequency of rotation.

It might surprise you that the data on heat capacity of diatomic gases can only be understood with recourse to a quantum mechanical explanation. If so, you would not be alone. At the start of the twentieth century, the fact that classical physics could not explain the heat capacity of gases led Lord Kelvin to call this a 'cloud over the dynamical theory of heat'. At that time, it represented (along with the Michelson–Morley experiment), the greatest challenge to physicists of that era.

Table 5.9 The number of degrees of freedom p for the molecules of a variety of gases predicted from the measured value of γ according to Equation 5.48. Values are plotted only for those gases included in Table 5.8.

Gas	γ	T(K)	p	Gas	γ	T(K)	p
A: Some monatomic gases				**D: Some triatomic gases**			
He	1.630	273.20	3.17	O_3	1.290	—	6.90
Ar	1.667	273.20	3.00	H_2O	1.334	373.20	5.99
Ne	1.642	292.20	3.12	CO_2	1.300	283.20	6.67
Kr	1.689	292.20	2.90	CO_2	1.220	573.20	9.09
Xe	1.666	292.20	3.00	CO_2	1.200	773.20	10.00
Hg	1.666	583.20	3.00	NH_3	1.336	—	5.95
				N_2O	1.324	—	6.17
B: Some diatomic gases				H_2S	1.340	—	5.88
H_2	1.407	283.20	4.91	CS_2	1.239	—	8.37
N_2	1.401	293.20	4.99	SO_2	1.260	293.20	7.69
O_2	1.400	283.20	5.00	SO_2	1.200	773.20	10.00
CO	1.297	2073.2	6.73				
NO	1.394	—	5.08	**E: Some polyatomic gases**			
				CH_4	1.313	—	6.39
C: Air				C_2H_6	1.220	—	9.09
Air	1.405	193.90	4.94	C_3H_8	1.130	—	15.4
Air	1.401	283.20	4.99	C_2H_2	1.260	—	7.69
Air	1.357	773.20	5.60	C_2H_4	1.264	—	7.58
Air	1.320	1173.2	6.25	C_6H_6	1.400	293.20	5.00
Air	1.828	273.20	2.42	C_6H_6	1.105	372.90	19.0
Air	2.333	193.90	1.50	$CHCl_3$	1.110	303.20	18.2
				$CHCl_3$	1.150	373.00	13.3
				CCl_4	1.130	—	15.4

Vibrational degrees of freedom

The rotational degrees of freedom we discussed previously refer to rigid rotation of the molecule, i.e. to motion in which there is no relative motion of the component atoms of the molecule. In general however, the atoms within molecules have several modes of vibration. For example, the relative separation of the two atoms in a diatomic molecule can vary, and the atoms will then oscillate about their average positions. The atoms then possess both kinetic energy of vibration and potential energy of vibration corresponding to a further two degrees of freedom.

Figure 5.11 The degree of freedom of a diatomic molecule associated with internal vibration.

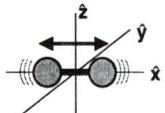

Diatomic molecules

For diatomic molecules we can understand how a molecule can have:

- three translational degrees of freedom
- three rotational degrees of freedom
- two vibrational degrees of freedom

making a total of eight degrees of freedom in all. Using Equation 5.38 $C_P = nR[p/2 + 1]$ with $p = 8$ predicts a maximum value of $C_P = 5R$ or $41.6 \text{ J K}^{-1}\text{mol}^{-1}$. This is just greater than the largest value in Figure 5.4. However C_P takes this value only at high temperatures. We can understand this as being due to the fact that some types of motion do not take place at low temperatures. Or in the language of statistical mechanics, some degrees of freedom are inaccessible at low temperatures (§2.5.3).

Table 5.10 (and Table 2.5) Illustration of the use of the term *accessibility* of quantum states. Notice that increasing the temperature always increases the number of 'accessible' quantum states.

Inaccessible	Marginal accessibility	Fully accessible
$k_B T \ll \Delta E$	$k_B T \approx \Delta E$	$k_B T \gg \Delta E$
e.g. $k_B T < 0.1\Delta E$	e.g. $0.1\,\Delta E < k_B T < 1.5\Delta E$	e.g. $k_B T > 1.5\Delta E$
In this case, only occasionally do molecules make transitions to the higher quantum state. We can consider the degrees of freedom associated with these transitions to be inaccessible.	In this case, molecules make transitions to the higher quantum state. Detailed calculations are required to assess the extent to which the quantum state can be considered accessible	In this case, molecules frequently make transitions to the higher quantum state. We can consider the degrees of freedom associated with these transitions to be fully accessible.
In colloquial terms, the process associated with transitions between quantum states occurs so infrequently that it may generally be ignored.		In colloquial terms, the process associated with transitions between quantum states occurs so frequently that the quantum nature of the states may generally be ignored.

Figure 5.12 The experimental C_P results for helium and oxygen plotted as a function of temperature, extracted from Figures 5.3 and 5.4 respectively. The left-hand axis gives C_P in units of $J\,K^{-1}\,mol^{-1}$ while the right-hand axis shows the number of accessible degrees of freedom inferred using Equation 5.48.

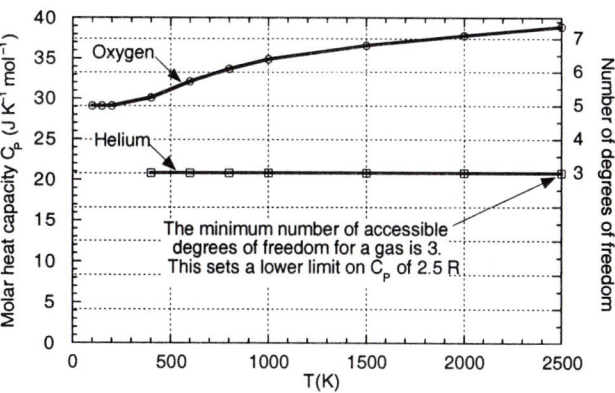

Tri- and polyatomic molecules

In general, we expect the number of degrees of freedom to increase as the number of atoms in a molecule increases, since more types of motion will become available. This tendency is clearly borne out by the data of Table 5.9. Diatomic molecules have more degrees of freedom than monatomic molecules, and polyatomic molecules have more degrees of freedom than diatomic molecules. As discussed below, the actual number observed depends on the way in which the atoms within the molecule are bonded together, and the temperature.

Variation of γ with temperature

As the temperature of the gas is increased, by definition the average energy per degree of freedom of the molecules is increased. In order to assess whether a particular degree of freedom is accessible or not, we compare $k_B T$ with ΔE, the energy difference between the quantum states of the molecule. There are three general situations, which are summarised in Tables 2.5 and 5.10.

The data for oxygen (O_2) (Figures 5.4 and 5.12) clearly indicate the gradual transition in which quantum states are inaccessible at low temperature, but become accessible at higher temperature.

If we compare the data at around 2000 K with that at 100 K, we see that oxygen molecules have acquired two extra degrees of freedom. Based on the discussion above we can tentatively assign these degrees of freedom to either the two easier modes

of rotation, or the potential and kinetic energies of internal molecular vibration. Detailed calculations indicate that (for diatomic molecules) the two extra degrees of freedom already accessible at low temperatures are due to molecular rotation. We thus infer that the two or three extra degrees of freedom becoming available over the temperature range up to 1000 K are associated with internal vibration of the molecule. From this we infer that the separation of the energy levels involved in these vibrational degrees of freedom is:

$$\Delta E \approx k_B T \approx 1.38 \times 10^{-23} \times 2000 \ \text{J}$$
$$\approx 2.76 \times 10^{-20} \ \text{J} \qquad (5.45)$$
$$\approx 0.173 \ \text{eV}$$

In §2.4 we noted that the frequency of vibration f_o of a simple harmonic oscillator is related to the energy separation between quantum states by $\Delta E = h f_o$. Since h is the Planck constant $(6.62 \times 10^{-34} \ \text{J s})$, this implies a vibrational frequency of $\approx 4.2 \times 10^{-13}$ Hz, a frequency in the infra-red part of the electromagnetic spectrum.

So as more degrees of freedom become available, we expect that γ (given by Equation 5.40 as $\gamma = 1 + 2/p$) should fall at higher temperatures, in broad agreement with the data.

Variation of γ with pressure

The data for air in Table 5.8 indicate that γ increases with increasing pressure. Comparing the datum for air at around atmospheric pressure $(\approx 0.1 \ \text{MPa})$ and $T = 283.2 \ \text{K}$ with the datum at

98

around 200 atmospheres (≈ 20 MPa) and $T = 273.2$ K, we see that increasing the pressure has reduced the number of accessible degrees of freedom. The extent of the reduction is quite dramatic, from a plausible 4.99 (i.e. 5), to a value of 2.42. This latter value is less than the three degrees of freedom that must be possessed by a gas whose molecules are free to move in three dimensions. How can we understand this?

Increasing the pressure of a gas at a fixed temperature implies an increase in the number density of molecules and hence a reduction in the average separation between molecules. This increases the frequency of molecular collisions and interactions, and these interactions restrict the motion of molecules. And so the associated degrees of freedom become inaccessible.

Consider the degrees of freedom associated with rotation. Because of its inertia, an O_2 molecule requires a certain time to rotate, typically 10^{-10} seconds, and if the molecules on average collide before this rotation can be completed then the degree of freedom is restricted. Calculations of the extent of this restriction are complicated, and we will not go through them here. However, we note that if the pressure is increased sufficiently the gas

will condense into a liquid. (Or it will enter a state where the molecules are so close together that it is not clear whether it should be called a liquid or a gas.) Gases compressed to this extent begin to show significant deviations from ideal gas behaviour, and the simple interpretation of γ according to Equation 5.40 is no longer realistic. Gases compressed so much that they cannot be distinguished from a liquid are discussed in §10.7.2, on the critical point.

Summary of heat capacity

Broadly speaking, we have been able to plausibly explain the behaviour of the heat capacity of gases on the basis of a relatively simple extension of the ideal gas theory. The key feature of the theory was the assumption that the internal energy of the gas is 'held' in the individual degrees of freedom of the gas molecules. Importantly we introduced the idea that molecules possessed *internal* degrees of freedom associated with vibrations and rotations of gas molecules. In order to understand the temperature dependence, it was necessary to develop the idea of the *accessibility* of degrees of freedom. This required acknowledgement of the quantum mechanical nature of the vibrations and rotations of gas molecules.

5.4 Compressibility: a discussion

5.4.1 Introduction

I would have liked at this point to present you with data on the compressibility of gases. However, there are two reasons why I cannot do this. The first is that the data are not tabulated in the reference books that I have consulted. And the second is *the reason* that the data are not tabulated: we need additional information about the constraints on the gas before we can say what its compressibility will be.

When we considered the heat capacity of a gas in §5.3, we calculated two special values C_P and C_V. These corresponded to *mechanical constraints* where, respectively, the pressure or the volume was kept constant during the heating or cooling

process. Similarly, when we consider the compressibility of a gas, we will have to specify the *thermal constraints* on the gas. In particular we will consider two specific types of volume changes: *adiabatic* and *isothermal*.

In an *adiabatic* volume change, no heat flows into or out of the gas. Thus if the gas expands and does some work, then the first law of thermodynamics tells us that the work must be done at the expense of the internal energy of the gas, and so the gas will cool.

In an *isothermal* volume change, the temperature of the gas is kept constant, and so heat must flow into or out of the gas. Thus if the gas expands and

Figure 5.13 (a) The variation of pressure with volume during an isothermal and adiabatic expansion. (b) An apparatus for realising an isothermal expansion requires some means of adding heat to the gas. (c) In an adiabatic expansion no heat flows into or out of the gas. Notice in (b) and (c) that the pressure in both cases is the same at the end of the expansion, but the volume is larger in the isothermal case, as indicated in (a).

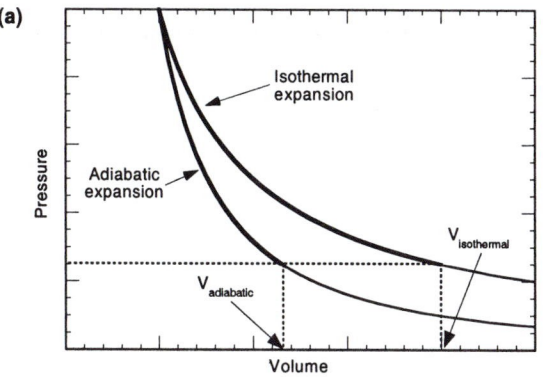

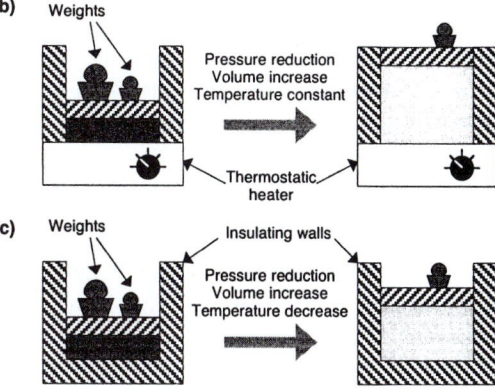

does some work, then work that is done is at the expense of the heat energy supplied to the gas during the expansion.

These effects are illustrated in Figure 5.13. We will look in some detail at both adiabatic and isothermal expansions below.

Compressibility and bulk modulus

The compressibility K, of a substance is defined as:

$$K = -\frac{1}{V}\frac{\partial V}{\partial P} \qquad (5.46)$$

Figure 5.14 *PV* diagram showing the gradient of the pressure volume curve and the relationship to the bulk modulus and compressibility.

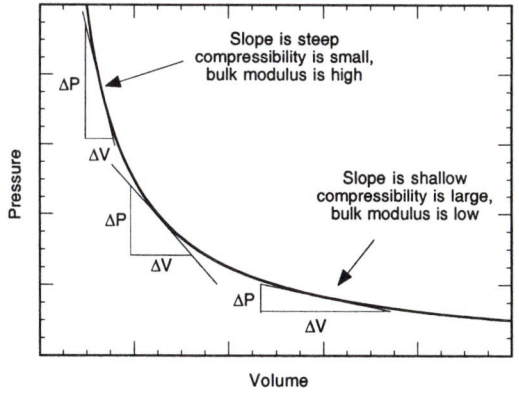

The bulk modulus, B, of a substance is the inverse of the compressibility, i.e.

$$B = \frac{1}{K} = -V\frac{\partial P}{\partial V} \qquad (5.47)$$

There are three points you should note about these expressions. The first is that they are both related to the slope of the pressure versus volume graph. (Figure 5.13). If material is incompressible, then the volume changes slowly with applied pressure (i.e. $\partial V/\partial P$ is small). This means that a small compressibility implies a large bulk modulus. The second point to note is the minus sign: this is because the slope $\partial V/\partial P$ is always negative, and it is conventional for physical properties of materials to be defined as positive quantities. Finally we note the factor V: this just normalises the data. You can see the effect of the factor V by considering that when pressurised, a large volume will have a bigger rate of change of volume than a small volume. However this is just to do with the size of the sample, and is not an intrinsic property of the gas.

5.4.2 Isothermal volume changes

In both isothermal and adiabatic expansions we assume that at all times the gas is in equilibrium. This allows us to make use of the fact that whatever the gas is doing, its pressure, volume and temperature are related by $PV = zRT$. In other

words, the pressure is related to the volume by:

$$P = \frac{zRT}{V} \qquad (5.48)$$

and so differentiating we find:

$$\frac{\partial P}{\partial V} = \frac{\partial}{\partial V}\left[\frac{zRT}{V}\right] \qquad (5.49)$$

In an isothermal expansion, the temperature is by definition constant, and so the pressure and volume are related by:

$$\frac{\partial P}{\partial V} = zRT\frac{\partial}{\partial V}\left[\frac{1}{V}\right] \qquad (5.50)$$

i.e.

$$\frac{\partial P}{\partial V} = zRT\left[\frac{-1}{V^2}\right] \qquad (5.51)$$

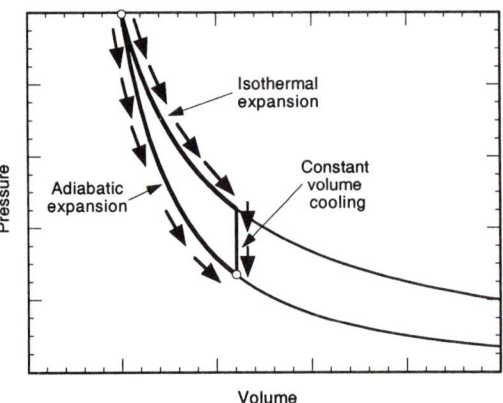

Figure 5.15 Two-step analysis of an adiabatic expansion. An adiabatic expansion can be considered as the sum of two steps which are simpler to analyse: an isothermal expansion, and then an isochoric (constant volume) cooling. This analysis allows us to determine the relationship between the initial pressure and volume and the final pressure and volume.

Substituting for V using $PV = zRT$ and then cancelling we arrive at:

$$\begin{aligned}\frac{\partial P}{\partial V} &= zRT\left[\frac{-1}{V^2}\right] \\ &= \frac{-zRT}{V}\left[\frac{1}{V}\right] \qquad (5.52) \\ &= \frac{-P}{V}\end{aligned}$$

This gives us a surprisingly simple result for the isothermal bulk modulus B_{iso}:

$$\begin{aligned}B_{iso} &= -V\frac{\partial P}{\partial V} \\ &= -V\left[\frac{-P}{V}\right] \qquad (5.53) \\ B_{iso} &= P\end{aligned}$$

5.4.3 Adiabatic volume changes

To derive the adiabatic bulk modulus we start with Equation 5.49

$$\frac{\partial P}{\partial V} = \frac{\partial}{\partial V}\left[\frac{zRT}{V}\right] \qquad (5.49*)$$

Unlike an isothermal expansion where the temperature does not change, the temperature does

change during an adiabatic expansion. This makes analysis of the expansion curve rather more complicated. However, we can analyse the adiabatic curve in two steps (Figure 5.15). We can consider a small adiabatic expansion as the sum of:

- an isothermal expansion in which heat ΔQ flows *into* the gas
- a constant volume temperature change in which heat ΔQ flows *out* of the gas.

We can then write:

$$\Delta P = \left.\frac{\partial P}{\partial V}\right|_{iso}\Delta V + \left.\frac{\partial P}{\partial T}\right|_V\Delta T \qquad (5.54)$$

Now we can evaluate the two parts of the differential of $P = zRT/V$ relatively easily. The first part is our previous result (Equation 5.52) and the second is a straightforward differentiation:

$$\Delta P = \frac{-P}{V}\Delta V + \frac{zR}{V}\Delta T \qquad (5.55)$$

However, we still do not know ΔT, the temperature change during the expansion. We can derive an expression for ΔT by considering the first law of thermodynamics:

$$\Delta U = \Delta Q + \Delta W \qquad (2.57* \,\&\, 5.56)$$

Analysing the adiabatic expansion as the sum of two steps, we notice that in the first step, the internal energy of the gas does not change (since its temperature remains constant). So in this first step heat ΔQ_1 flows *into* the gas during the isothermal expansion:

$$\Delta Q_1 = -\Delta W \qquad (5.57)$$

where ΔW is equal to the work done *on* (not by) the gas. As we saw in the steps leading to Equation 5.21, the work done *on* the gas during an expansion is:

$$\Delta W = -P\Delta V \qquad (5.58)$$

So at the end of the first step in our analysis we can state that the heat which has flowed into the gas is:

$$\Delta Q_1 = +P\Delta V \qquad (5.59)$$

In the second step in our analysis, the gas is cooled at constant volume until all the heat supplied in the first step has been removed. In terms of the constant volume heat capacity of the gas we can write:

$$\Delta Q_2 = zC_V\Delta T \qquad (5.60)$$

In order to make our two steps add up to an adiabatic change, the sum of Equations 5.58 and 5.59 must amount to zero, i.e. $\Delta Q_1 + \Delta Q_2 = 0$. Substituting we can derive an expression for the temperature change during an adiabatic expansion:

$$\Delta T = -\frac{P\Delta V}{zC_V} \qquad (5.61)$$

We can now substitute for ΔT into Equation 5.55:

$$\Delta P = -\frac{P}{V}\Delta V - \frac{zR}{V} \times \frac{P\Delta V}{zC_V} \qquad (5.62)$$

We can now separate terms and take the limiting value for small changes as follows:

$$\frac{\Delta P}{\Delta V} = -\frac{P}{V} - \frac{P}{V} \times \frac{R}{C_V}$$

$$\left.\frac{\partial P}{\partial V}\right|_{ad} = -\frac{P}{V}\left[1 + \frac{R}{C_V}\right] \qquad (5.63)$$

Remembering that $C_P = C_V + R$ (Equations 5.40 and 5.41) and that we can express the ratio of the principle heat capacities as γ, we can simplify this expression:

$$\left.\frac{\partial P}{\partial V}\right|_{ad} = -\frac{P}{V}\left[1 + \frac{R}{C_V}\right]$$

$$= -\frac{P}{V}\left[\frac{C_V + R}{C_V}\right]$$

$$= -\frac{P}{V}\left[\frac{C_P}{C_V}\right] \qquad (5.64)$$

$$\left.\frac{\partial P}{\partial V}\right|_{ad} = -\frac{\gamma P}{V}$$

We can then evaluate the adiabatic bulk modulus and arrive at another surprisingly simple result:

$$B_{ad} = -V\left.\frac{\partial P}{\partial V}\right|_{ad} = -V\left[\frac{-\gamma P}{V}\right] \qquad (5.65)$$

$$B_{ad} = \gamma P$$

5.2.6 Summary

Results

The previous sections have been quite mathematically involved, so it worthwhile pausing here to review the results of our calculations. We have calculated $\partial P/\partial V$ for both adiabatic and isothermal expansions. This is just the slope of the graph of pressure versus volume. For an isothermal expansion, we found $\partial P/\partial V = -P/V$. For adiabatic expansions, we found that the curve was always steeper than for isothermal expansions by a factor γ, i.e. $\partial P/\partial V = -\gamma P/V$.

From these results we derived expressions for the bulk modulus for both adiabatic and isothermal expansions:

$$B_{iso} = P \qquad (5.53*)$$

$$B_{ad} = \gamma P \qquad (5.65*)$$

We can also state values for the compressibility of the gas:

$$K_{ad} = \frac{1}{\gamma P} \qquad K_{iso} = \frac{1}{P} \qquad (5.66)$$

Example 5.8

A mixture of air and fuel in the cylinder of a motor car engine is ignited and increases temperature essentially instantaneously from ambient temperature to around to 1000 °C. The combustion products then rapidly expand from an initial volume of 100×10^{-6} m^3 to 400×10^{-6} m^3. If there is 0.005 mol of N$_2$ in the cylinder, estimate the work done in the expansion. If there were 4 such cylinders executing 40 such expansions each second, estimate the power that could be delivered by the engine.

The work done is given by the integral PdV (Eq. 5.60):

$$W = \int_i^f PdV$$

We can substitute for P using Equation 5.69 to find:

$$W = \int_i^f PdV = \int_i^f CV^{-\gamma}dV = C\int_i^f V^{-\gamma}dV$$

This can be integrated to yield:

$$W = C\left[\frac{V^{-\gamma+1}}{-\gamma+1}\right]_i^f = \frac{C}{-\gamma+1}\left[V^{-\gamma+1}\right]_i^f$$

Before we can evaluate this we need to work out the constant C. To do this we use the ideal gas law to work out the initial pressure:

$$P = \frac{zRT}{V} = \frac{0.005 \times 8.31 \times [273.15+30]}{100 \times 10^{-6}} = 1.26 \times 10^5 \ \text{Pa}$$

which allows us to evaluate C. We use $\gamma = 1.4$ for nitrogen from Table 5.8:

$$C = PV^\gamma = 1.26 \times 10^5 \left[100 \times 10^{-6}\right]^{1.4} = 0.316$$

We can now calculate the work done in the expansion:

$$= \frac{0.316}{0.4}\left[\left[100 \times 10^{-6}\right]^{-0.4} - \left[400 \times 10^{-6}\right]^{-0.4}\right]$$

$$= 0.791[39.81 - 22.87] = 13.4 \ \text{J}$$

If there are 4 cylinders executing 40 similar expansions per second then the power delivered by the engine is:

$$\text{Power} = 13.4 \times 4 \times 40 = 2144 \ \text{W} = 2.144 \ \text{kW}$$

PV$^\gamma$ constant

The result that $\partial P / \partial V = -\gamma P / V$ for an adiabatic expansion is often stated in more succinct and easily memorable manner:

$$PV^\gamma = \text{constant} \tag{5.67}$$

for an adiabatic expansion. To see how we arrive at this result we start with Equation 5.64:

$$\frac{\partial P}{\partial V} = -\frac{\gamma P}{V} \tag{5.64*}$$

We then rearrange this equation and integrate the results to find a relationship between P and V that holds during all adiabatic processes.

$$\frac{dP}{P} = -\frac{\gamma dV}{V}$$

$$\int \frac{dP}{P} = \int -\frac{\gamma dV}{V} = -\gamma \int \frac{dV}{V} \tag{5.68}$$

We now use the result that $\int dx / x = \ln x + C$, where C is a constant. We find:

$$\ln P = -\gamma \ln V + C$$

$$\ln P + \gamma \ln V = C \tag{5.69}$$

which simplifies to:

$$\ln P + \ln V^\gamma = C$$

$$\ln PV^\gamma = C \tag{5.70}$$

If the last equation above is valid, i.e. the natural logarithm of PV^γ is a constant, then it must also be true that PV^γ itself is constant during an adiabatic process.

Adiabatic or isothermal compressions?

Having taken all this trouble to compare results for isothermal and adiabatic volume changes, you might think that both results were equally useful. In fact, in a great many circumstances, changes to a gas are effectively adiabatic. This occurs because (as we shall see in the next section) the thermal conductivity of gases is generally very low. This means that when a change in a gas takes place, unless the change takes place very slowly, heat does not have time to flow into the gas to maintain the temperature. For example, when large volumes of air move around in the Earth's atmosphere (what we call 'weather'), the volume changes are effectively adiabatic because the changes take place too quickly. Similarly, the expansions and contractions of a gas in a sound wave are also adiabatic. We shall say more about this in §5.6.

5.5 Thermal conductivity

Heat flow through fluids can be *extremely* complex. This is because in addition to the normal flow of heat that takes place through any material, it is also possible for the fluid itself to move from one place to another. This process, known as *convection*, allows fluid to 'carry' heat with it in the form of its heat capacity. Thus, for example, a fluid flow of z moles per second from a part of a container which is ΔT hotter than a cold part will result in a delivery of heat energy to the colder part of the container of $zC_P\Delta T$ joules per second. This effect is illustrated in Figure 5.16.

Convection arises from the interaction of two effects:

- The density of a gas changes significantly on heating (see §5.1.2 on the expansivity of gases.)
- Most experiments we perform on gases take place in a gravitational field. If this were not so there would be no tendency for the hotter, less-dense, gas to 'rise' or 'fall'.

Both factors are necessary for convection. When heat flow by convection occurs in a fluid it can easily overwhelm any other thermal conduction processes through the 'still' fluid. Furthermore, heat flow by convection varies dramatically from one measurement apparatus to another and so is difficult to quantify. For this reason, even though convection is important in many practical situations, more fundamental information can be extracted from experiments on fluids where the fluid itself does not flow. The measurements presented below are made in the absence of convection on 'still gas'.

The thermal conductivity κ of a gas may defined by the equation

$$\frac{dQ}{dT} = -\kappa A \frac{dT}{dx} \qquad (5.71)$$

where:

$\dfrac{dQ}{dT}$ is the rate of heat flow (W)

κ is the thermal conductivity (W m^{-1} K^{-1})

A is the cross sectional area across which heat is flowing (m^2)

$\dfrac{dT}{dx}$ is the temperature gradient (K m^{-1}).

The minus sign in Equation 5.71 indicates that heat flows *down* a temperature gradient, i.e. from regions of high temperature to regions of low temperature.

5.5.1 Data on the thermal conductivity of gases

The data in Table 5.11 show the still-gas values of the thermal conductivity of a selection of monatomic, diatomic and tri-atomic gases at several temperatures. All the data refer to gases at pressures around one atmosphere. A typical value of κ for gases is ≈ 0.1 W m^{-1} K^{-1}. This is much less than for a metal such as copper (≈ 400 W m^{-1} K^{-1}: Table 7.16) or an electrical insulator such as quartz (≈ 1 to 10 W m^{-1} K^{-1} Table 7.17).

Figure 5.14 graphs data from Table 5.11 and shows there is clear qualitative similarity in the thermal conductivity of all the gases. The thermal conductivity increases as temperature rises, but the increase is not linear: the *rate* of increase becomes less at higher temperatures.

Figure 5.16 Convection occurs when heating produces a region of low-density gas (hot) which is beneath a region of high-density gas (cold). This arrangement is unstable and the low-density (hot) gas rises and moves to the colder part of the chamber. When it reaches the colder part of the chamber, it cools. It then gives up thermal energy $zC_P\Delta T$. When convection occurs, the heat flow does not depend on the intrinsic thermal conductivity of gas, but on its heat capacity and the rate of flow of gas.

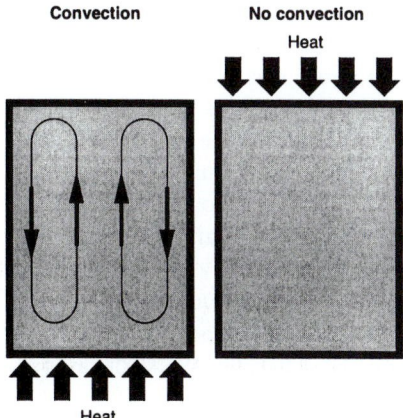

More surprisingly, Figure 5.18 shows that the thermal conductivity of a gas is independent of pressure across a wide range of pressures around atmospheric pressure: notice the logarithmic pressure range on the x-axis. Thus removing 99% of the molecules from a gas at atmospheric pressure, i.e. reducing the pressure by a factor 100, produces no change in the thermal conductivity of the gas!

The main questions raised by our preliminary examination of the experimental data on the thermal conductivity of gases are:

- Why does the thermal conductivity of gases increase at high temperatures?
- Why is the thermal conductivity of gases independent of pressure across a wide range of pressures around atmospheric pressure?
- Why are the thermal conductivities of gases as low as they are?

5.5.2 Understanding the data on the thermal conductivity of gases

Before considering the theory of the thermal conductivity, we note that the thermal conductivity of a gas is a different type of property from the heat capacity of a gas. The heat capacity relates the temperature at the beginning and end of a heating

Table 5.11 Measured values of the thermal conductivities of some gases. The units are 10^{-2} W m^{-1} K^{-1}. For example, the thermal conductivity of argon at 273.2 K is 1.63×10^{-2} W m^{-1} K^{-1}.

	Temperature (K)				
Gas	73.2	173.2	273.2	373.2	1273
Monatomic gases					
Helium, He	5.95	10.45	14.22	17.77	41.90
Neon, Ne	1.74	3.37	4.65	5.66	12.80
Argon, Ar	—	1.09	1.63	2.12	5.00
Krypton, Kr	—	0.57	0.87	1.15	2.90
Xenon, Xe	—	0.34	0.52	0.70	1.90
Radon, Ra	—	—	0.33	0.45	—
Diatomic gases					
Hydrogen, H_2	5.09	11.24	16.82	21.18	—
Fluorine, Fl_2	—	1.56	2.54	3.47	—
Chlorine, Cl_2	—	—	0.79	1.15	—
Bromine, Br_2	—	—	0.40	0.60	—
Nitrogen, N_2	—	1.59	2.40	3.09	7.40
Oxygen, O_2	—	1.59	2.45	3.23	8.60
Carbon monoxide, CO	—	1.51	2.32	3.04	—
Air, N_2/O_2	—	1.58	2.41	3.17	7.60
Polyatomic gases					
Ammonia, NH_4	—	—	2.18	3.38	—
Carbon dioxide, CO_2	—	—	1.45	2.23	7.90
Ethane, C_2H_6	—	1.80	—	—	—
Ethene, C_2H_4	—	1.40	—	—	—
Methane, CH_4	—	1.88	3.02	—	—
Sulpur dioxide, SO_2	—	—	0.77	—	—
Water/Steam, H_2O	—	—	1.58	2.35	—

Figure 5.17 Variation of the thermal conductivity of the gases from Table 5.11 with absolute temperature. All the curves, monatomic, diatomic and polyatomic behave broadly similarly, but the absolute magnitude of conductivity varies significantly from one gas to another. The lines joining the data points are a guide to the eye only.

Figure 5.18 Variation of the thermal conductivity of argon with pressure. The lines join the data points and are a guide to the eye only. Notice that the pressure scale is logarithmic and represents a pressure range of 5 orders of magnitude.

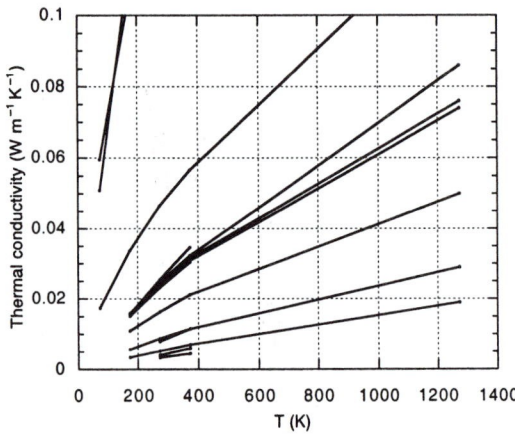

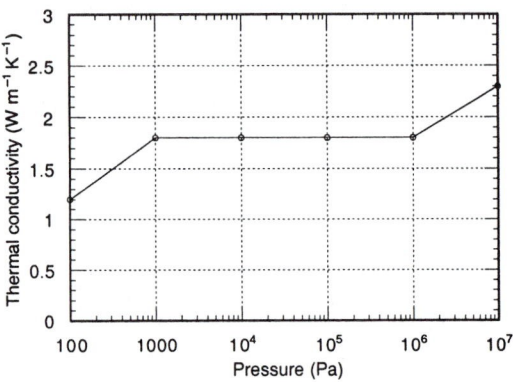

process to the heat added to the gas. In each state (before and after heating) the gas is in thermal equilibrium. In contrast, the thermal conductivity relates to the process of heat flow, which necessarily implies that the gas is not in equilibrium. It is a general feature of physics that equilibrium properties are easier to understand than transport processes.

Background theory

In order to understand the thermal conductivity of gases, we will need to use some of the ideas that we developed in §4.3. In particular we will use the following results:

- The mean free path, λ_{mfp}, of a gas molecule, is given by:

$$\lambda_{mfp} = \frac{1}{\sqrt{2}\pi n a^2} \qquad (4.45^* \ \& \ 5.72)$$

where n is number density of molecules and a is the effective diameter of a gas molecule.

- The average energy of a molecule with p degrees of freedom is given by:

$$\bar{u} = \tfrac{1}{2} p k_B T \qquad (5.73)$$

- The number of molecular collisions with an area A per second is given by:

$$\tfrac{1}{4} n \bar{v} A \qquad (4.39^* \ \& \ 5.74)$$

where n is number density of molecules and $\bar{v}$ is the mean speed of a gas molecule.

Figure 5.19 illustrates a gas in which there is a temperature gradient, and highlights an area A perpendicular to the temperature gradient. Molecules strike area A from both the hotter side and the colder side. On average, molecules striking A have travelled a distance λ_{mfp}, and so have come from within a sphere of radius λ_{mfp}. In order to work out the net energy transported across A per second we will make a simplifying assumption. We will assume that the molecules have come not from a sphere, but from two planes a distance λ_{mfp} from A in either direction along the temperature gradient. The energy transported from these planes will be in the form of the kinetic energy of the molecules, plus the energy associated with any internal degrees of freedom.

Example 5.9

A container of cross-sectional area 25 cm^2 and length 30 cm is heated from the top such that air at the bottom is at approximately 100 °C and that air at the top is approximately 10 °C warmer. What is the rate at which energy is transported down the tube?

We first note the situation is stable against convection, and so we may use the intrinsic values of the thermal conductivity listed in Table 5.11. We then note that the pressure is not mentioned in the question so we assume it is within an order of magnitude of atmospheric pressure and will thus be same as the figures listed in Table 5.11. We are now in a position to use Equation 5.72 in a fairly straightforward manner. We have:

110 °C

100 °C

$$\frac{dQ}{dt} = -\kappa A \frac{dT}{dx}$$

with:

$$\kappa = 3.17 \times 10^{-2} \ \text{W m}^{-1} \text{K}^{-1}$$

$$A = 25 \times 10^{-4} \ \text{m}^2$$

The temperature difference across the length of tube is 10 °C and the length of tube is 30×10^{-2} m, so we can estimate the temperature gradient within the tube as:

$$\frac{dT}{dx} \approx \frac{\Delta T}{\Delta x} = \frac{10}{0.3} \approx 33 \ \text{°C m}^{-1}$$

Thus the rate of heat flow down the tube is given by:

$$\frac{dQ}{dt} = -3.17 \times 10^{-2} \times 25 \times 10^{-4} \times 33$$

$$= 2.62 \times 10^{-3} \ \text{W}$$

Thus the maintenance of a 10 °C temperature difference across the length of the tube requires a heat input of only around 2.6 mW.

The number of molecules crossing unit area per second from each direction is given by Equation 5.74 as $\tfrac{1}{4} n \bar{v}$ and each molecule brings with it on average $\tfrac{1}{2} k_B T$ of energy per accessible degree of freedom. Thus if each molecule has p accessible degrees of freedom, on average the energy crossing area A per second from each side is:

$$\tfrac{1}{4} n \bar{v} \times A \times p \times \tfrac{1}{2} k_B T \qquad (5.75)$$

Now at $x + \lambda_{mfp}$, the temperature is approximately:

Figure 5.19 Illustration of the basic process by which we imagine heat flow to take place. Notice that the *average* speed of molecules (represented by the length of the arrows) in the hotter region is greater than the *average* speed in the colder region.

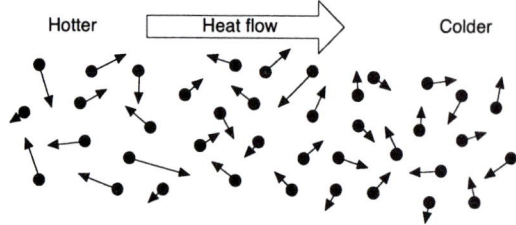

Hotter   Heat flow   Colder

$$T + \frac{\partial T}{\partial x}\lambda_{mfp} \qquad (5.76)$$

and at $x - \lambda_{mfp}$, the temperature is approximately:

$$T - \frac{\partial T}{\partial x}\lambda_{mfp} \qquad (5.77)$$

The small difference in temperature between Equations 5.76 and 5.77 means that molecules striking area A from $x + \lambda_{mfp}$ carry on average slightly more energy than molecules striking area A from $x - \lambda_{mfp}$. The difference between the two energy fluxes gives the net energy transported across A per second. Notice that in Figure 5.20 the temperature increases in the positive x-direction and so heat flow will be in negative x-direction.

So the energy flow per second across area A in the positive x-direction is:

$$\tfrac{1}{8}n\bar{v}Apk_B\left[T - \frac{\partial T}{\partial x}\lambda_{mfp}\right] \qquad (5.78)$$

and the energy flow per second across area A in the negative x-direction is:

$$\tfrac{1}{8}n\bar{v}Apk_B\left[T + \frac{\partial T}{\partial x}\lambda_{mfp}\right] \qquad (5.79)$$

Subtracting Equation 5.79 from Equation 5.78 yields the net energy per second in the positive x-direction:

$$\frac{dQ}{dt} = \frac{1}{8}n\bar{v}Apk_B\left[T - \frac{\partial T}{\partial x}\lambda_{mfp} - T - \frac{\partial T}{\partial x}\lambda_{mfp}\right]$$

$$= \frac{1}{8}n\bar{v}Apk_B\left[-2\frac{\partial T}{\partial x}\lambda_{mfp}\right]$$

$$= -\underbrace{\left[\tfrac{1}{4}n\bar{v}pk_B\lambda_{mfp}\right]}_{\kappa}A\frac{\partial T}{\partial x}$$

$$(5.80)$$

Comparing Equation 5.80 with the standard form of the heat flow Equation 5.71 we see that the expression within the square brackets is just κ:

$$\kappa = \tfrac{1}{4}n\bar{v}pk_B\lambda_{mfp} \qquad (5.81)$$

This expression requires only refinement and rearrangement before we can compare it with experimental results. If we had been more careful in our averaging of the heat flows across area A, we would have found an expression identical to Equation 5.81 but with the '4' in the denominator replaced by a '6'. This modified expression is the one we will now work with, namely:

$$\kappa = \tfrac{1}{6}n\bar{v}pk_B\lambda_{mfp} \qquad (5.82)$$

Figure 5.20 Simplified illustration of the calculation of thermal conductivity of a gas. The figure shows three planes in the gas perpendicular to a temperature gradient. The separation of the planes is λ_{mfp}. the mean free path of the molecules. Thus molecules that are travelling in the appropriate direction in either the top or the bottom plane will (probably) cross the central plane before colliding. Energy is carried across A in both directions, but *on average* more energy flows across A from the plane in the hotter region of the gas. The analysis of the thermal conductivity centres on the problem of evaluating the net energy flow across an area A.

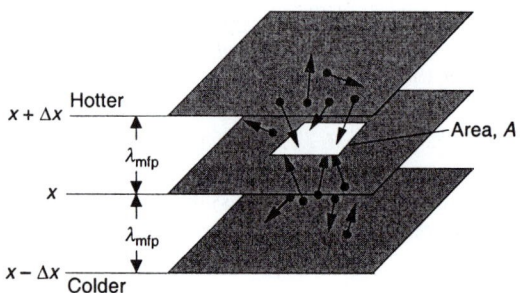

$x + \Delta x$ Hotter

λ_{mfp}

x

λ_{mfp}

$x - \Delta x$ Colder

Area, A

Example 5.10

Evaluate Equation 5.84 for argon gas at temperature *T*.

$$\kappa = \frac{\bar{v}pk_B}{6\sqrt{2}\pi a^2}$$

There are three quantities in Equation 5.84 that we need to estimate:
- the number of accessible degrees of freedom p
- the average molecular speed $\bar{v}$
- the effective molecular diameter a.

Let us look at each of these in turn.
- From the analysis of heat capacity measurements (§5.3.3) we can be sure that for a monatomic gas there are exactly three degrees of freedom, $p=3$.
- We can make an estimate of $\bar{v}$ in terms of the *root mean square velocity* $\sqrt{v^2}$. Remember that for any molecule there are three degrees of freedom associated with kinetic energy. Because of the equipartition of energy between degrees of freedom, we can write the *average* kinetic energy:

$$\frac{1}{2}mv^2 = 3 \times \frac{1}{2}k_B T$$

where m is the mass of a molecule. As mentioned in §4.32,

$$\sqrt{v^2} = 1.085\bar{v}$$

so we can estimate $\bar{v}$ as:

$$\bar{v} = \frac{1}{1.085}\sqrt{v^2}$$

$$= \frac{1}{1.085}\sqrt{\frac{3k_B T}{m}}$$

- Finally we estimate a from a typical value for the separation between atoms in the solid state, which is $a \approx 0.3 \times 10^{-10}$ m. This is not a very accurate estimate, and it does not allow us to quantitatively compare results for different gases. However, it should be a constant for each type of gas and be of the correct order of magnitude.

Putting these estimates together and substituting them into the equation for the thermal conductivity:

$$\kappa = \frac{\bar{v}pk_B}{6\sqrt{2}\pi a^2}$$

$$= \frac{1}{1.085}\sqrt{\frac{3k_B T}{m}} \times \frac{3k_B}{6\sqrt{2}\pi a^2}$$

$$= \left[\frac{3}{1.085 \times 6 \times \sqrt{2}}\sqrt{\frac{3k_B}{m}} \times \frac{k_B}{\pi a^2}\right]\sqrt{T}$$

$$= \left[0.326\sqrt{\frac{3k_B}{m}} \times \frac{k_B}{\pi a^2}\right]\sqrt{T}$$

Substituting for argon (relative atomic mass 39.95):

$$k_B = 1.38 \times 10^{-23} \ \text{J K}^{-1}$$

$$a = 0.3 \times 10^{-9} \ \text{m}$$

$$m = 39.95u = 39.95 \times 1.66 \times 10^{-27} \ \text{kg}$$

we find:

$$\kappa = \left[0.326\sqrt{\frac{3 \times 1.38 \times 10^{-23}}{39.95 \times 1.66 \times 10^{-27}}} \times \frac{1.38 \times 10^{-23}}{\pi\left(0.3 \times 10^{-9}\right)^2}\right]\sqrt{T}$$

$$= 3.98 \times 10^{-4}\sqrt{T} \ \text{W m}^{-1}\text{ K}^{-1}$$

If we substitute for λ_{mfp} using Equation 5.72, we arrive at an expression which has no reference to n, the number density of molecules

$$\kappa = \frac{1}{6}n\bar{v}pk_B \times \frac{1}{\sqrt{2}\pi na^2} \tag{5.83}$$

$$\kappa = \frac{\bar{v}pk_B}{6\sqrt{2}\pi a^2} \tag{5.84}$$

We are now in a position to compare our theoretical prediction with the experimental results of §5.5.1.

Comparison with experiment

Let us consider the questions raised at the end of §5.5.1 in turn

Why does the thermal conductivity of gases increase at high temperatures?

Example 5.10 below shows how we may use Equation 5.84 to estimate the thermal conductivity of a gas. The example shows that we expect a $T^{0.5}$ dependence for κ. Broadly speaking, this describes the behaviour of all the gases in Figure 5.17. However, we shall see that the theory as we have developed it is not able to fully explain the experimental in more than this qualitative manner.

We can make some more progress if we concentrate on results for argon, and examine the extent of detailed agreement between the calculation of κ in Example 5.10 and the experimental data. Table 5.12 shows this calculation repeated for each of the temperatures for which we have data. The predictions are clearly of the correct order of magnitude, but differ by a factor of roughly 2 to 3 from the data. Noting that our estimate of the diameter of an argon atom in Example 5.10 was just a ball-park guess, we could improve the overall level of agreement between theory and experiment if we revised our estimate for the diameter of an argon atom. The diameter required to match experimental data is shown on the rightmost column of Table 5.12. The magnitude of the diameters are entirely plausible; however in order to explain the data we have to suppose that the molecules become effectively smaller at higher temperatures.

A more quantitative approach

We can quantitatively examine the deviations of the data from the dependence if we re-plot some of the data from Figure 5.17 in a different form. Example 5.10 predicts that $\kappa = AT^{0.5}$ and so a plot of $\log\kappa$ versus $\log T$ should have a slope of 0.5 and an intercept of $\log A$ where:

$$A = \frac{k_{\mathrm{B}}}{2.17\pi a^2}\sqrt{\frac{3k_{\mathrm{B}}}{2m}} \qquad (5.85)$$

Figure 5.21 plots the data for the monatomic gases in this way. The slopes and intercepts of the best-fit lines of the form AT^x are recorded in Table 5.13. The intercepts A behave qualitatively as expected, becoming smaller for the gases with the larger molecules. In the bottom line of Table 5.13 we have used the experimental values for A to extract a value for the low-temperature limit of the effective diameter a of the noble gas atoms from Equation 5.85. The data indicate a low-temperature effective diameter of an argon atom of 0.391 nm which can be compared with a value of 0.21 nm at 173.2 K. We see that the effective diameter at low temperatures is considerably greater than the effective diameter at high temperature.

The origin of this effect lies in the effect discussed in §4.4.3 (Figure 4.13) concerning the detailed

Table 5.12 Calculated and experimental values for κ for argon at various temperatures. Also shown is the inferred value(a) for the molecular diameter.

	Data	Prediction		a
T (K)	(W m⁻¹ K⁻¹)	(W m⁻¹ K⁻¹)	Ratio	(nm)
173.2	1.09×10^{-2}	5.23×10^{-3}	2.08	0.21
273.2	1.63×10^{-2}	6.57×10^{-3}	2.48	0.19
373.2	2.12×10^{-2}	7.68×10^{-3}	2.76	0.18
1273	5.00×10^{-2}	14.19×10^{-3}	3.52	0.16

Figure 5.21 A log–log plot of thermal conductivity κ of the monatomic gases versus temperature. Thick lines connect data points. Thin dotted lines are the best-fit lines of the form AT^x. The thin solid line illustrates what a line of slope 0.5 looks like. The parameters of the lines fitted to the data are shown in Table 5.13.

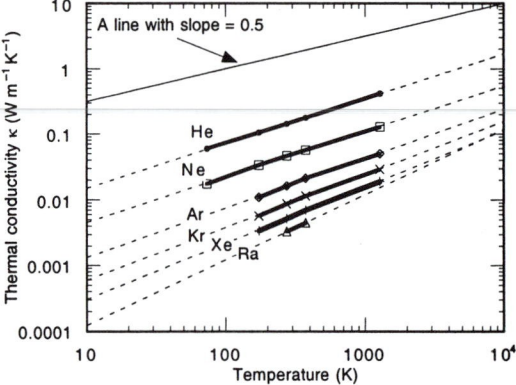

Table 5.13 Results from an analysis of the thermal conductivity data assuming the data has the form $\kappa = AT^x$. The significance of a is discussed in the text.

Gas	A	x	a (nm)
Helium, He	30.91×10^{-4}	0.685	0.108
Neon, Ne	9.14×10^{-4}	0.695	0.198
Argon, Ar	2.34×10^{-4}	0.754	0.391
Krypton, Kr	0.93×10^{-4}	0.806	0.620
Xenon, Xe	0.42×10^{-4}	0.857	0.923
Radon, Ra	0.12×10^{-4}	0.994	1.73

nature of molecular collisions. At low temperatures, the average speed of molecules is relatively slow, and molecules may be strongly affected by the weak attraction between molecules. At higher temperatures, the higher average speed of molecules causes their trajectories to be only slightly affected by the weak inter-molecular interactions.

109

We can find further evidence for the idea that molecular interactions are the source of the deviations of the thermal conductivity theory from the data. If we examine the slopes x from Figure 5.21 (Table 5.13) we note that the experimental values are all higher than the predicted 0.5, and that the difference from 0.5 becomes larger for the gases with heavier atoms.

We have not yet discussed the detailed nature of the interactions between molecules, but we will do so in §6.2. Perhaps surprisingly, §6.2 is concerned with the properties of noble gas molecules *in their solid state*. This does in fact make sense since in the properties of these molecular solids are dominated by interactions between molecules. This can be compared with the properties of the gas phase, in which we have had to search quite hard even to detect the properties of molecular interactions. In §6.2 we will see that the strength of the interaction between molecules is related to the *electrical polarisability* of a molecule (§5.7). This property is related to the ease with which the electron distribution around an atom may be distorted. The heavy noble gas atoms (such as xenon) have relatively large, easily distorted (i.e. highly polarisable) electron distributions. Hence they also have relatively strong interatomic interactions. In contrast the light noble gas atoms (such as helium) have small, very rigid (i.e. weakly polarisable) electron distribution, and hence relatively weak interatomic interactions. This picture corresponds well with the data of Table 5.13

Before moving on we note that we have come to an explanation of the deviations from a $T^{0.5}$ dependence of the thermal conductivity of gases. However in order to achieve this we have had to consider details of the interatomic interactions in the gas. In contrast we could understand the heat capacity data on monatomic gases without any consideration of the details of interatomic interactions. This is typical of the difference between an equilibrium property of a substance and a non-equilibrium transport property. It is generally a more straightforward matter to interpret equilibrium properties than it is to interpret transport properties. However, by studying the deviations from a $T^{0.5}$ dependence, we were able (in princi-

ple) to compare particular models of molecular interactions with experiment.

Why is the thermal conductivity of gases independent of pressure across a wide range of pressures around atmospheric pressure?

Figure 5.18 shows that, for argon at least, the thermal conductivity is independent of pressure over a range of at least three orders of magnitude. We can understand this immediately from the form of Equation 5.84:

$$\kappa = \frac{\bar{v} p k_B}{6\sqrt{2}\pi a^2} \qquad (5.84^*)$$

This equation does not mention pressure, and so the theory predicts correctly that κ is independent of pressure. But how does this come about? If we examine the precursor equations to 5.84, such as Equation 5.81, we can see that the formula includes the product of n and λ_{mfp}. This makes sense since the thermal conductivity will maximised if:

- there are more molecules to carry the thermal energy (i.e. n is large)
- each molecule can travel unimpeded through the gas (i.e. λ_{mfp} is large).

However λ_{mfp} is inversely proportional to n and so increasing n reduces λ_{mfp} by an exactly compensating factor.

Figure 5.18 shows that κ is independent of pressure only over a certain (large) range. At lower pressures κ gets smaller, and at higher pressures κ gets larger. We can understand the low-pressure behaviour quite simply. As the pressure is reduced, the number density of molecules n falls, and so λ_{mfp} gets larger. However a point will be reached where λ_{mfp} is so large that the molecules are simply bouncing from side to side in their container and only rarely colliding with each other. Lowering the pressure beyond this point will not cause any further increases in λ_{mfp} and κ will simply be proportional to n. We can estimate the pressure at which this occurs: if we fix $\lambda_{\mathrm{mfp}} \approx L$, the dimension of the gas container which might be, say, 1 cm (10^{-2} m). From Equation 5.72 λ_{mfp} will reach this value when:

$$n = \frac{1}{\sqrt{2}\pi L a^2} \qquad (5.86)$$

Using our usual estimate of a molecular diameter of $a = 0.3$ nm we find $n = 2.5 \times 10^{20}$ m^{-3}. We can estimate the pressure and temperature at which this occurs using the formula from Example 4.2:

$$n = \frac{P}{k_B T} \qquad (5.87)$$

Assuming a temperature of 300 K, we have

$$
\begin{aligned}
P &= n k_B T \\
&= 2.5 \times 10^{20} \times 1.38 \times 10^{-23} \times 300 \\
&\approx 1.04 \ \text{Pa} \\
&\approx 1.04 \times 10^{-2} \ \text{mBar}
\end{aligned}
\qquad (5.88)
$$

Atmospheric pressure is approximately 10^5 Pa (1000 mbar) so this phenomenon does not occur until relatively low pressure, a regime known as the high-vacuum regime. For example, the pressure inside the wall of a 'vacuum flask' is typically 10^{-5} mbar (approximately 10^{-8} Pa) and so the thermal conductivity of the gas in the flask is well into the high-vacuum regime. Notice that lowering the pressure through five orders of magnitude from atmospheric pressure would have had no effect on the thermal conductivity! Only when the pressure is reduced below the critical pressure indicated by Equation 5.88 is the thermal conductivity affected.

The rise in thermal conductivity at higher pressures occurs because the molecules are becoming so densely packed that the assumptions about molecular trajectories become invalid. Again, the mean free path is becoming fixed, but now at a distance of approximately one atomic diameter.

Why are the thermal conductivities of gases as low as they are?

The rise in thermal conductivity at very high pressures (Fig 5.18) gives a clue to the origin of the small absolute magnitude of the thermal conductivity in gases as compared with solids or liquids. The smallness of κ arises because the number density of molecules, n, is so small for a gas. If we consider a highly compressed gas in which λ_{mfp} is estimated as a small fraction of a molecular diameter a, and n as approximately $1/a^3$, then estimates of the order of magnitude of κ from Equation 5.84 produce answers similar to those found for liquids. We will consider this regime further when analysing the thermal conductivity of liquids in §9.11.

5.6 Speed of sound

5.6.1 Data on the speed of sound in gases

Sound is a displacement wave, or pressure wave, which propagates through a gas. At any particular moment, the wave consists of layers of compressed gas at a pressure slightly higher than ambient pressure, and rarefied gas at a pressure slightly lower than ambient pressure. Figure 5.20 illustrates the variation of the pressure/density within the wave.

Notice that only one type of sound wave, a longitudinal pressure wave, is able to propagate in gas. This is in contrast with solids, which can support three types of sound wave: one longitudinal and two transverse. This is because in order for a wave to propagate, there must be a restoring force which acts to reverse any strain in the material. For gases, there is no restoring force for so-called shear strains, and so transverse waves cannot be sustained.

Some illustrations and a more rigorous discussion of wave propagation are given in Appendix A2.

Sound travels considerably slower through gases than through solids or liquids. As shown in Table 5.14, the maximum speed at 0°C is approximately 1000 ms^{-1} for the gases with the lightest molecules, helium and hydrogen. This may be

compared with the values for solids (Table 7.6) and liquids (Table 9.5) which are typically of the order of 3000 ms^{-1}.

One important datum not included in Table 5.14 is for the speed of sound in air. At 1.0 kHz, in dry air with 0.03 % CO_2, at a temperature of 273.15 K and a pressure of 101325 Pa, the speed of sound is 331.45 ± 0.05 ms^{-1}.

Figure 5.19 shows a graph of c_{sound} versus M, the relative molecular mass of the molecules of the gas. It is fairly clear that the mass of the molecules of the gas plays a significant role in determining the speed of sound. Table 5.14 does not contain enough data to allow a systematic study of the effects of temperature and other factors on the speed of sound. However, we can obtain some clues about which other factors affect the speed of sound by looking in detail at the shaded entries in the table. These have at least one other 'partner entry' referring either to a gas with the same molecular mass, or to the same gas but at a different temperature. We will examine each of the shaded entries in turn.

Extract from Table 5.14

Gas		M	T(K)	c_{sound} (ms^{-1})
Helium	He	4.0	273.2	971.9
Deuterium	D_2	4.0	273.2	890

The data for helium and deuterium are taken at the same temperature, but the sound velocities differ by $\approx$ 9%. So there must be a factor other than temperature and molecular weight affecting c_{sound}.

Extract from Table 5.14

Gas		M	T(K)	c_{sound} (ms^{-1})
Water (steam)	H_2O	18.0	373.2	473
Water (steam)	H_2O	18.0	407.2	494

The data for steam show an increase in the speed of sound with increasing temperature.

Extract from Table 5.14

Gas		M	T(K)	c_{sound} (ms^{-1})
Nitrogen, N_2		28.0	273.2	337
Carbon monoxide, CO		28.0	273.2	337
Ethylene, C_2H_4		28.0	273.2	318

Table 5.14 The speed of sound in a selection of gases listed in order of increasing molecular mass M in atomic mass units u. The shaded entries in the table are gases that have a 'partner' gas in the table with the same molecular mass. See the text for more details.

Gas	M	T(K)	c_{sound} (ms^{-1})
Hydrogen, H_2	2.0	273.2	1286
Helium, He	4.0	273.2	971.9
Deuterium, D_2	4.0	273.2	890
Methane, CH_4	16.0	273.2	430
Ammonia, NH_3	18.0	273.2	415
Water (steam), H_2O	18.0	373.2	473
Water (steam), H_2O	18.0	407.2	494
Fluorine, F_2	19.0	373.2	332
Heavy Water (steam), D_2O	20.0	373.2	451
Neon, Ne	20.2	273.2	434
Acetylene, C_2H_2	26.0	273.2	329
Nitrogen, N_2	28.0	273.2	337
Carbon monoxide, CO	28.0	273.2	337
Ethylene, C_2H_4	28.0	273.2	318
Ethane, C_2H_8	30.0	283.2	308
Ethane, C_2H_6	30.0	304.2	316
Nitric oxide, NO	30.0	283.2	324
Nitric oxide, NO	30.0	289.2	334
Oxygen, O_2	32.0	303.2	332
Methanol, CH_3OH	32.0	370.2	335
Hydrogen sulphide, H_2S	33.1	273.2	310
Hydrogen chloride, HCl	36.5	273.2	296
Argon, Ar	40.0	273.2	307.8
Nitrous oxide, N_2O	44.0	298.2	268
Propane, C_3H_8	44.0	273.2	238
Carbon dioxide, CO_2	44.0	273.2	259
Ethanol, C_2H_5OH	46.0	326.2	258
Sulphur dioxide, SO_2	64.0	273.2	211
Chlorine, Cl_2	70.9	293.2	219
Carbon disulphide, CS_2	76.0	273.2	192
Benzene, C_6H_6	78.0	273.2	177
Bromine, Br_2	79.9	331.2	149
Hydrogen bromide, HBr	80.9	273.2	200
Krypton, Kr	83.8	273.2	213
Cyclohexane, C_6H_{12}	84.0	303.2	181
Hydrogen iodide, HI	127.9	273.2	157
Xenon, Xe	131.3	273.2	170
Sulphur hexafluoride, SF_6	146.0	284.2	133
Carbon tetrachloride, CCl_4	153.8	370.2	145
Iodine, I_2	263.8	453.2	138

The data for nitrogen and carbon monoxide are taken at the same temperature, and have the same speed of sound: the level of agreement is striking. However ethylene with the same molecular mass and at the same temperature has a sound velocity about 6% lower. Let us hypothesise that the number of atoms in the gas molecule is also a factor affecting c_{sound} .

Reviewing the data so far we have some evidence that:

- c_{sound} is increased at higher temperatures
- c_{sound} is decreased if a molecule of the gas has many atoms.

These hypotheses are consistent with all the data so far. Let us examine the rest of the data:

Extract from Table 5.14

Gas	M	$T(K)$	c_{sound} (ms^{-1})
Ethane, C_2H_6	30.0	283.2	308
Ethane, C_2H_6	30.0	304.2	316
Nitric oxide, NO	30.0	283.2	324
Nitric oxide, NO	30.0	289.2	334

We now have data that allow comparison of the effects of both temperature (over a limited range) and molecular complexity. We see that these data

Figure 5.22. A graph of c_{sound} (ms^{-1}) versus M, the relative molecular mass (u). The graph seems to show that the molecular weight of the molecules of the gas plays a significant role in determining the velocity of sound through the gas.

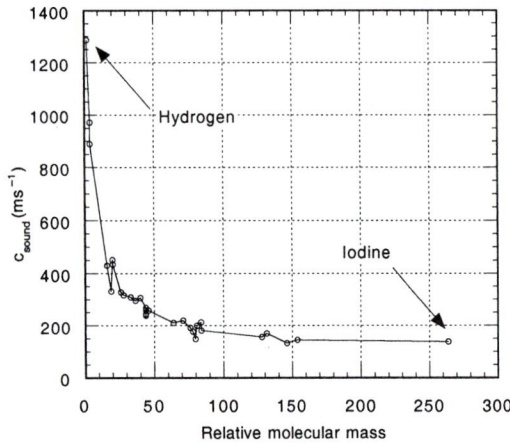

are again consistent with the hypotheses above: the more complex molecule has the lower c_{sound}; the higher temperature data have higher values of c_{sound}.

Extract from Table 5.14

Gas	M	$T(K)$	c_{sound} (ms^{-1})
Oxygen, O_2	32.0	303.2	332
Methanol, CH_3OH	32.0	370.2	335

These data correspond both to different numbers of atoms per molecule, and to different temperatures. The data are not inconsistent with the hypotheses because the effects of temperature and molecular complexity could be compensating one another.

Extract from Table 5.14

Gas	M	$T(K)$	c_{sound} (ms^{-1})
Nitrous oxide, N_2O	44.0	298.2	268
Propane, C_3H_8	44.0	273.2	238
Carbon dioxide, CO_2	44.0	273.2	259

Again the hypotheses are confirmed. Comparing propane and carbon dioxide we see that the molecule with more atoms has the lower c_{sound}. Comparing nitrous oxide and carbon dioxide, both triatomic molecules, we see that the substance at the higher temperature has the greater c_{sound}. Thus, our hypotheses set out above seem to be confirmed by all the data in Table 5.14. There is little data available on the dependence of the speed of sound on pressure, because, surprisingly, the speed of sound is broadly independent of the pressure.

So the questions raised by our preliminary examination of the experimental data on the velocity of sound in gases are:

- Why is the speed of sound greater at higher temperatures, but roughly independent of pressure?
- Why is the speed of sound reduced by molecular complexity, i.e. for different gases of the same molecular mass, sound travels faster in the gas with the least complex molecules?
- Why is the speed of sound higher in gases with low molecular mass?
- Why is the speed of sound in gases at about atmospheric pressure around a few hundred metres per second?

113

5.5.2 Understanding the data on the speed of sound

Appendix A2 contains a derivation of an expression for the speed of sound in any medium: solid, liquid or gas. There we predict that the speed of sound, c_{sound} in a gas is given in terms of its mass density ρ, and either the compressibility K or the bulk modulus B:

$$c_{sound} = \sqrt{\frac{1}{K\rho}}$$
$$= \sqrt{\frac{B}{\rho}} \quad (5.89)$$

We can see that this prediction makes physical sense by considering a region of compressed gas. The ease with which the gas will 'spring back' to try to restore ambient pressure depends on the quantities in Equation 5.89.

- It depends on the compressibility of the gas K because if the gas is easily compressed, then the restoring force will be small, i.e. the gas is not very 'springy'. Thus, highly compressible gases will tend to have a low speed of sound.
- It depends on the density of the gas ρ because if the density of the gas is high then the mass per unit volume will be high. This means that a given restoring force will produce less acceleration of the gas. Thus dense gases will 'spring back' slower and hence tend to have lower speed of sound.

The compressibility and its inverse $(1/K)$, the bulk modulus, were discussed at some length in §5.4. They are defined as:

$$K = -\frac{1}{V}\frac{\partial V}{\partial P} \quad \text{and} \quad B = -V\frac{\partial P}{\partial V} \quad (5.90)$$

There we saw that compressibility has different values depending on whether the gas is compressed at constant temperature, or whether the gas is isolated during the compression, in which case the temperature may rise on compression. In the former case the compressions are said to be *isothermal*; in the latter, the compressions are said to be *adiabatic*. The value of K corresponding to each of these types of compression is discussed below.

Adiabatic or isothermal compressions?

It is not obvious at first sight which type of compression takes place in a sound wave. We are not aware of temperature oscillations when a sound wave passes by, but this doesn't mean they don't exist: if they are small and oscillating at several hundred times per second, we may not notice them. In order to decide which type of compression takes place in a sound wave we will work out the predicted speed of sound in air (Equation 5.89) for each of the two cases in turn. Then by comparing the predictions with experiment we will see that it is possible to deduce which type of compression actually occurs. We saw in §5.4 that the

Figure 5.23 Two illustrations of the variation of pressure within a sound wave at a given time. (a) A perspective drawing of planes of constant pressure: shaded planes represent compressed regions of the gas, un-shaded planes represent rarefied regions of gas. (b) The pressure as a function of position in a sound wave. The pressure amplitude of a sound wave rarely exceeds 1% of the ambient pressure.

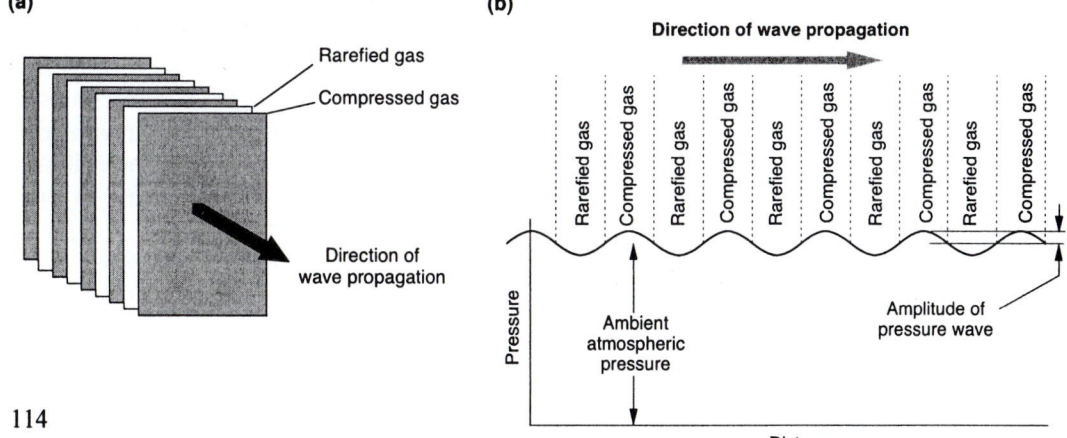

isothermal compressibility of an ideal gas is:

$$K_{\text{iso}} = \frac{1}{P} \qquad (5.66^*)$$

where P is the pressure of the gas and the subscript 'iso' indicates that compression is isothermal. Similarly, we saw that the adiabatic compressibility of a ideal gas is given by:

$$K_{\text{ad}} = \frac{1}{\gamma P} \qquad (5.66^*)$$

where γ is the ratio of the principal heat capacities C_P/C_V and the subscript 'ad' indicates that compression is adiabatic.

Taking the Equations 5.66 for K_{iso} and K_{ad} we can compare predictions for the speed of sound with experimental values. For air under the standard conditions of 0 °C (273.15 K) and pressure 1.013×10^5 Pa we find (§5.2) that the density of air is 1.293 kg m^{-3}. Taking a value of $\gamma = 1.4$ (Table 5.8) we can predict values for the speed of sound assuming either isothermal or adiabatic compressions in the sound wave.

$$c_{\text{sound}} = \sqrt{\frac{1}{K\rho}} \qquad (5.91)$$

Isothermal prediction

$$c_{\text{sound}} = \sqrt{\frac{1}{K_{\text{iso}}\rho}}$$

$$= \sqrt{\frac{P}{\rho}}$$

$$= \sqrt{\frac{1.013 \times 10^5}{1.293}}$$

$$c_{\text{sound}} = 279.9 \ \text{m s}^{-1}$$

Adiabatic prediction

$$c_{\text{sound}} = \sqrt{\frac{1}{K_{\text{ad}}\rho}}$$

$$= \sqrt{\frac{\gamma P}{\rho}}$$

$$= \sqrt{\frac{1.4 \times 1.013 \times 10^5}{1.293}}$$

$$c_{\text{sound}} = 331.2 \ \text{m s}^{-1}$$

Comparing these predictions with the experimental value of 331.45 ± 0.05 ms^{-1} clearly favours the theory in which the compressions of the gas are adiabatic. In retrospect, we can understand this fairly easily. The wavelength of a sound wave is typically of the order of one metre at a frequency of 1 kHz. If the compressions and rarefactions of the wave are adiabatic, then there will be small temperature differences created in the wave. In order for the compressions and rarefactions of the wave to be isothermal, heat would have to flow between compressed and rarefied regions of the wave in about half a cycle of the sound wave. The small temperature differences in the wave would have to equalise over a distance of half a wavelength (roughly 0.5 metre) in around 0.5 ms. For a poor thermal conductor such as a gas this is unrealistic. Thus for all sound waves in gases over all practical frequencies, the compressions and rarefactions are adiabatic, and the speed of sound is given by:

$$c_{\text{sound}} = \sqrt{\frac{\gamma P}{\rho}} \qquad (5.92)$$

The temperature oscillations associated with sound waves are considered in Exercise P34 at the end of this Chapter and Exercise 6 in Chapter 12.

Comparison with experiment

The pressure and temperature dependence of the speed of sound

Equation 5.92 allows us to understand immediately why the speed of sound is not significantly dependent on pressure: the density of a gas is proportional to its pressure. Thus changing the pressure of a gas affects the compressibility of a gas, but changes its density by an exactly compensating amount. This lack of pressure dependence becomes clearer if we rearrange Equation 5.92 by substituting for P and ρ: this allows direct comparison with the results of Table 5.14. We use the perfect gas equation to substitute for both $P = zRT/V$, and for $\rho = zM/V$ (where z/V is the number of moles per unit volume, and M is the mass in kg of one mole of gas). We find the speed of sound may thus be expressed as:

$$c_{\text{sound}} = \sqrt{\frac{\gamma z RT}{V} \times \frac{V}{zM}}$$

$$= \sqrt{\frac{\gamma RT}{M}} \qquad (5.93)$$

Equation 5.93 shows that if the temperature of the

115

Example 5.11

What is the predicted speed of sound in helium at 0 °C?

Equation 5.93 tells us that:

$$c_{sound} = \sqrt{\frac{\gamma R T}{M}}$$

The data for helium is:

$\gamma = 1.63$ (from Table 5.8)

$R = 8.31\ \text{J K}^{-1}\ \text{mol}^{-1}$

$T = 273.1\ \text{K}$

$M = 4.0 \times 10^{-3}\ \text{kg}$

So we find:

$$c_{sound} = \sqrt{\frac{1.63 \times 8.31 \times 273.1}{4.0 \times 10^{-3}}}$$

$$= 961.3\ \text{m s}^{-1}$$

This compares with the experimental value (Table 5.14) of 971.9 ms^{-1} an error of around 1 %.

gas is kept constant, then we expect to find no variation with pressure.

It is actually rather hard to compare the predictions of Equation 5.93 with experiment. It might seem to be a fairly straightforward task to look up the values of γ and M for the gas, and then note the temperature T at which c_{sound} was measured. However the tables of c_{sound} are commonly compiled by assuming that Equation 5.93 holds true and then deducing γ from measurements of c_{sound} and T. Hence we cannot then use the γ values to check the values of c_{sound}! However, we can look

at questions raised by examination of the data, with the aim of checking the overall consistency of Equation 5.93 in describing gases of different types of molecules.

The effect of molecular complexity

We saw in §5.3.2 that the number of degrees of freedom of a molecules could be determined from measurements of γ using Equation 5.44:

$$p = \frac{2}{\gamma - 1} \qquad (5.44^*)$$

This predicts that more complex molecules have more degrees of freedom (p) and hence lower values of c_{sound}. Thus through Equation 5.93:

$$c_{sound} = \sqrt{\frac{\gamma R T}{M}} \qquad (5.93^*)$$

we expect gases of more complex molecules to have a lower speed of sound. We can examine the dependence on p and γ by looking for gases which have the same molecular mass M but different numbers of molecules, and hence different values of γ. Searching through Table 5.14 we see that we have several examples of which I have chosen just the two whose details are set out in Table 5.15 below.

For the monatomic or diatomic molecules, the agreement is excellent if we assume that at around room temperature there are two accessible rotational degrees of freedom, but no vibrational degrees of freedom. However, for more complex molecules such as ethylene (CH_2CH_2), it is difficult to arrive at an estimate for γ which is any-

Table 5.15 Details of gases whose molecules have relative molecular mass of 4 and 28. The table enables a detailed comparison of theoretical expectations and experimental results for the dependence of the speed of sound upon molecular complexity.

Gas	M	Number of atoms per molecule	Expected γ	T(K)	c_{sound} (theoretical) $\sqrt{(\gamma R T/M)}$	c_{sound} (experimental) Table 5.14
He	4.0	1	1.667 (p=3)	273.2	972.8	971.9
D_2	4.0	2	1.400 (p=5)	273.2	891.5	890.0
N_2	28	2	1.400 (p=5)	273.2	336.9	337.0
CO	28	2	1.400 (p=5)	273.2	336.9	337.0
CH_2CH_2	28	6	1.2 (p=10?)	273.2	≈312	318.0

thing more than a guess. In order to improve on guess work we would need to carefully calculate the molecular dynamics of an ethylene molecule, a task well beyond the scope of this book.

Why gamma?

It is interesting to ask why γ, the ratio of the heat capacities C_P / C_V, is involved in an expression for the speed of sound. The answer lies in the effect that extra degrees of freedom have on the magnitude of the temperature oscillations in the sound wave. We can see how this happens by considering the compression/expansion of the gas that occurs in the wave. Since the compression/expansion is adiabatic, the gas is successively heated/cooled. By the equipartition theorem (§2.5), the increased/decreased internal energy of the gas caused by the compression/expansion is shared equally amongst the p accessible degrees of freedom of the molecules. So if the average energy of each molecule is increased/decreased by Δu, the temperature rise/fall ΔT will be such that $\Delta u = 0.5 p k_B \Delta T$. So ΔT is given by:

$$\Delta T = \frac{\Delta u}{0.5 p k_B} \tag{5.94}$$

Equation 5.94 implies that ΔT is inversely proportional to p. So, for example, if $p = 3$ then the temperature rise/fall ΔT will be larger than if $p = 5$

Figure 5.24. Graph of the speed of sound (m s^{-1}) versus $1/\sqrt{A}$ where A is the molecular mass in atomic mass units u. The data show a clear linear relationship as indicated by the least-squares fit shown as a line on the graph.

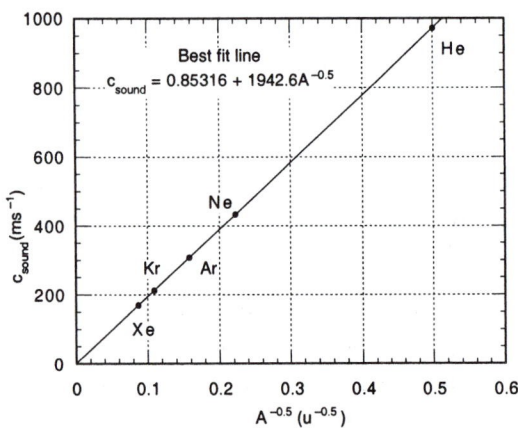

because the energy of compression/expansion is shared amongst fewer degrees of freedom. This temperature rise/fall causes the gas pressure to increase/decrease more quickly as its volume is reduced/enlarged. In other words, having fewer degrees of freedom increases the magnitude of the temperature oscillations that accompany the pressure oscillations in the sound wave. The temperature oscillations act to oppose the pressure oscillations that cause them, and so make the gas less compressible. And the larger the temperature rise, the greater the reduction in compressibility. Thus if two types of gas have molecules of the same mass, the gas whose molecules have fewer internal degrees of freedom will be 'springier'.

Dependence of c_{sound} on M

The strong dependence of c_{sound} on the molecular mass M was clearly shown in Figure 5.22. With hindsight we can now see how this dependence arises, and by plotting c_{sound} versus $M^{-\frac{1}{2}}$ we should find that the data lie close to a straight line through the origin. Further, if we draw this plot using a set of gases for which γ is the same we should be able to reduce the apparently random scatter on Figure 5.22. Figure 5.24 shows such a plot for the monatomic gases for which we are confident from analysis of heat capacity data that there are exactly three degrees of freedom, i.e. $p = 3$.

If we substitute the expression for γ (Equation 5.40) into Equation 5.93, and then separate out the dependence on molecular mass, we find:

$$c_{sound} = \sqrt{\left[1 + \tfrac{2}{3}\right] RT} \times M^{-\frac{1}{2}} \tag{5.95}$$

Now M is the mass of one mole of gas i.e. N_A times the mass of a molecule, Au. Evaluating this yields:

$$slope = \sqrt{\left[1 + \tfrac{2}{3}\right] RT}$$

$$= \sqrt{\left[1 + \tfrac{2}{3}\right] \frac{8.314 \times 273.1}{6.022 \times 10^{23} \times 1.661 \times 10^{-27}}} \tag{5.96}$$

$$= 1945.1 \text{ m s}^{-1} \text{ kg}^{-1/2}$$

which differs from the experimental slope (1942.6 m s^{-1} kg$^{-1/2}$) by $\approx 0.13\%$ i.e. less than two

117

parts in 1000. Clearly we understand all the factors at play in determining the speed of sound, in monatomic gases at least.

Order of magnitude of c_{sound}

Why does c_{sound} have the value it has for a gas? One answer is to refer to Equation 5.93 and its derivation and say 'it just does'. Another answer is to consider whether we could have said anything about the speed of sound in a gas before considering the derivation of Equation 5.93. In fact we can establish a rough upper limit for the maximum possible speed of sound in a gas. It is reasonable to suppose that *a sound wave cannot travel through a gas more quickly than the molecules of the gas are moving*. We can see this by noting that if we have a compressed region of gas, the pressure changes that constitute the sound wave clearly cannot move faster than the fastest molecules, and will probably move at a speed related to the average speed of molecules. Since the average speed of molecules in air at room temperature is ≈ 500 m s^{-1}, and the speed of sound is ≈ 340 m s^{-1}, we can see that there is some experimental support for this idea. We can in fact do better than this and convert Equation 5.93 for c_{sound} into a relationship between c_{sound} and $\overline{v^2}$.

First, we recall that T is defined by the fact that the average energy per accessible degree of freedom is

$0.5 k_B T$. So for the three degrees of freedom of the kinetic energy of the gas we have:

$$\tfrac{1}{2} m \overline{v^2} = \tfrac{3}{2} k_B T \qquad \text{(4.23 and 5.97)}$$

Substituting for T in Equation 5.93 yields:

$$c_{sound} = \sqrt{\frac{\gamma R T}{M}}$$
$$= \sqrt{\frac{\gamma R m \overline{v^2}}{3 k_B M}} \qquad (5.98)$$

Now M is the mass in kilograms of one mole of the gas, i.e. $M = N_A m$ where m is the mass of one molecule. Remembering that by definition $R = k_B N_A$ we have:

$$c_{sound} = \sqrt{\frac{\gamma R m \overline{v^2}}{3 k_B M}}$$
$$= \sqrt{\frac{\gamma R m \overline{v^2}}{3 k_B N_A m}} = \sqrt{\frac{\gamma \overline{v^2}}{3}} \qquad (5.99)$$
$$= \left[\sqrt{\frac{\gamma}{3}}\right] \sqrt{\overline{v^2}} = \left[\sqrt{\frac{\gamma}{3}}\right] v_{RMS}$$

Since γ ranges from roughly 1.7 to 1, c_{sound} should vary between 58% and 75% of the root mean square speed of the molecules.

5.7 Electrical properties

The electrical properties of gases are complex, and difficult to describe succinctly. However we can simplify our discussion by dividing the properties of the gas into behaviour observed in weak electric fields and strong electric fields.

In this section we will look mainly at the properties of gases under weak, static electric fields. The term 'static' in this context refers to electric fields varying at frequencies much lower than the frequencies of molecular vibration and rotation, i.e. less than approximately 10^9 Hz. The response to

electric fields varying at infrared frequencies or higher is discussed in the §5.8 on the optical properties of gases.

We will look briefly at the phenomenon of electrical breakdown that occurs in strong electric fields in §5.7.3.

5.7.1 Data on the electrical properties of gases in weak electric fields

The application of a weak electric field to a gas does not produce any dramatic effects. A 'weak'

electric field may be defined as one which is less than the *dielectric strength* of the gas. The dielectric strength varies with temperature and pressure, but at around room temperature and normal atmospheric pressure, it is of the order of 10^6 volts per metre ($V\,m^{-1}$).

For electric fields less than the dielectric strength of the gas it is not a trivial matter to detect *any* effect of the electric field on the gas! To a first approximation we may ignore the presence of a gas in a region of weak electric field and treat the situation as if there were no matter present, i.e. as a vacuum. However, careful experiments show that there is a small effect which may be described in terms of the *dielectric constant*, ε (§2.3.2). The dielectric constant has the value unity for a vacuum and is often tabulated as $(\varepsilon - 1)$. Tabulations in this form emphasise the difference between the presence and absence of molecules of the substance. For gases, ε usually differs only slightly from unity with typical values (Table 5.16) in the range 1.0001 to 1.001.

A gas weakens the interaction between electric charges by reducing the electric field around a charge, and so we find $\varepsilon \ge 1$. The quantity $(\varepsilon - 1)$ is tabulated for various gases around room temperature and atmospheric pressure in Table 5.16.

Table 5.16 and Figure 5.25(a) both show a good deal of apparently random variability. However despite this, it is possible to discern some systematic trends in the data. From Figure 5.22 it appears that, with striking exceptions, there is a weak trend towards larger dielectric constants in gases with large molecules. Further, in the two cases where Table 5.16 has data for a gas at several temperatures (carbon dioxide and ammonia), the data show a systematic decrease of $(\varepsilon - 1)$ with increasing temperature.

Figure 5.25(b) shows the variation of $(\varepsilon - 1)$ for carbon dioxide as a function of pressure at a temperature of 100 °C. We see that $(\varepsilon - 1)$ depends linearly on the pressure, with a slight sign of curvature at the highest pressures.

The main questions raised by our preliminary examination of experimental data on the dielectric

Table 5.16 The relative dielectric permittivity ε of various gases at atmospheric pressure (1.013×10^5 Pa). For pressures below atmospheric pressure ε varies linearly with pressure. The relative permittivity of vacuum is exactly 1, and all the gases in the table have values of ε within 1% of unity. The table shows the value of $10^4\,(\varepsilon - 1)$, which clearly shows the variation between gases. The table also shows the relative molecular mass of the molecules of the gas.

Different experimenters find different values of ε and the data for $10^4\,(\varepsilon - 1)$ should all be treated as accurate to only about 10%. The entry for ethanol has two alternative values to indicate two particularly divergent values for $10^4\,(\varepsilon - 1)$. For other entries I have taken averages of tabulated results, or ignored entries in tables that were clearly in error.

The data refer to values obtained with electric fields oscillating at radio frequencies, $\approx 10^6$ Hz. The shaded entries in the table, i.e. helium, hydrogen, argon, oxygen, nitrogen, and air, are typical results for ε valid from DC up to optical frequencies $\approx 10^{15}$ Hz. The variation over that range is within ± 2 of the least significant figure in the table.

Gas	M	T (°C)	$10^4(\varepsilon - 1)$
Monatomic gases			
Helium, He	4.0	20	0.65
Neon, Ne	20.2	0	1.3
Argon, Ar	40.0	20	5.16
Mercury, Hg	200.6	180	7.4
Mercury, Hg	200.6	180	7.4
Diatomic gases			
Hydrogen, H_2	2.0	0	2.72
Hydrogen, H_2	2.0	20	2.54
Nitrogen, N_2	28.0	20	5.47
Oxygen, O_2	32.0	20	4.94
Air (dry, no CO_2)	28.8	20	5.36
Carbon monoxide, CO	28.0	23	6.92
Triatomic gases			
Carbon dioxide, CO_2	44.0	0	9.88
Carbon dioxide, CO_2	44.0	20	9.22
Carbon dioxide, CO_2	44.0	100	7.23
Nitrous oxide, N_2O	44.0	25	11
Water (steam) H_2O	18.0	100	60
Polyatomic gases			
Ethane, C_2H_6	30.0	0	15
Benzene, C_6H_6	65.0	100	32.7
Methanol, CH_3OH	32.0	100	57
Ethanol, C_2H_5OH	44.0	100	61 or 78
Ammonia, NH_3	18.0	0	8.34
Ammonia, NH_3	18.0	100	4.87

permittivity of gases are:

- Why does the value of $(\varepsilon - 1)$ depends linearly on pressure?
- Why does the value of $(\varepsilon - 1)$ decreases with increasing temperature?
- Why does the value of $(\varepsilon - 1)$ depend on the type of molecule of the gas? There is some indication that $(\varepsilon - 1)$ may be larger for larger molecules. However, some molecules display particularly large dielectric constants.
- Why, under the action of weak electric fields, is the relative dielectric permittivity $(\varepsilon - 1)$ so close to unity?

5.7.2 Understanding the electrical properties of gases in weak electric fields

In order to understand the phenomena described above, we must first develop a theory of the dielectric constant of a gas. We do this in the following sections and then later proceed to compare the predictions of the theory with experiment.

Background theory

The theory we develop below models a gas as a collection of molecules which do not interact with one another. Thus the properties of the gas will depend directly on just two factors: the response of individual molecules to an applied electric field, and the number density of the molecules. Our previous discussion of ideal gas theory gives us the tools we need to understand how to calculate the number density of molecules. From Example 4.2 we can write that:

$$n = \frac{P}{k_B T} \qquad (5.100)$$

So let us now turn our attention to the response of individual molecules to an applied electric field. It is found that the responses fall into two distinct classes:

- Atoms or molecules which, in the absence of an applied electric field, possess no *electric dipole moment*. Such atoms and molecules are called *non-polar*. All atoms are non-polar, but only a few molecules (those with a high degree of symmetry such as N_2 or O_2) fall into this category.

Figure 5.25 (a) The data of Table 5.16 showing $10^4(\varepsilon - 1)$ as a function of the mass of the molecules of the gas. Uncertainty indications represent ±10% of the values in the Table 5.16. The value for Mercury (Hg) has not been plotted because its large molecular mass distorts the scale of the graph. (b) The variation of the dielectric constant plotted as $10^4(\varepsilon - 1)$ for carbon dioxide as a function of pressure at a temperature of 100 °C. We see that $(\varepsilon - 1)$ is depends linearly on the pressure, with a slight sign of curvature at the highest pressures.

(a)

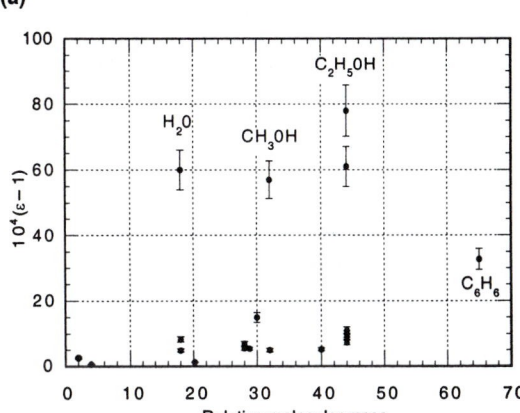

(b)

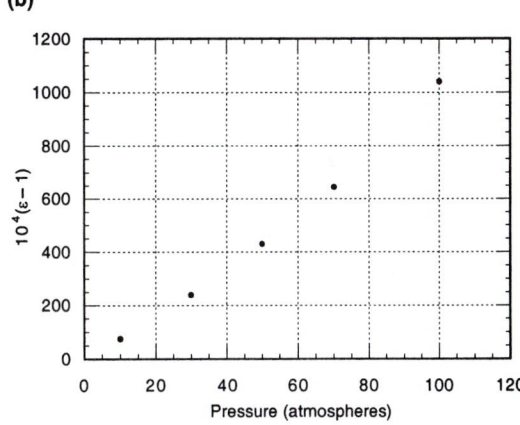

- Molecules which, in the absence of an applied electric field, possess a finite *electric dipole moment*. Such atoms and molecules are called *polar*. Most molecules fall into this category, though the magnitude of their dipole moment varies considerably from one type of molecule to another.

Let us examine the cases of non-polar and polar molecules in turn.

120

Non-polar molecules

The situation when a weak applied field is applied to an atom (or molecule) with no intrinsic electric dipole moment is illustrated in Figure 5.26. The electric field perturbs the electronic charge distribution around the nucleus of each atom, drawing the electrons slightly to one side of the nucleus. Thus an electric dipole moment is induced on each atom and the atoms are said to be *polarised*. However the atoms are still electrically neutral and so there is no net force on them in the applied electric field. The magnitude of the induced dipole moment p_i is given by the product of the total charge on the nucleus Ze multiplied by Δx, the distance between the centres of symmetry of the electronic and nuclear charge distributions. In general Δx is extremely small, typically a small fraction of an atomic diameter. Atomic dipole moments are sometimes tabulated in units of 10^{-30} C m, called *debye* units.

Physically we can see that the extent of the disturbance of the charge distribution depends on the ratio of the *applied* electric field to the *internal* field. Usually this ratio is extremely small (Example 2.1)

Polar molecules

The situation when a weak external field is applied to a molecule which has a permanent electric dipole moment p_p is illustrated in Figure 5.27.

Commonly, the permanent electric dipole moment p_p is much larger than the induced electric dipole moment p_i. In this case the main effect of the electric field is to rotate the molecule. Recall (§2.2.3) that the energy of an electric dipole $\mathbf{p}$ in a field $\mathbf{p}$ is $-\mathbf{p} \cdot \mathbf{E}$ and that the torque on an electric dipole $\mathbf{p}$ in a field $\mathbf{E}$ is $\Gamma = \mathbf{p} \times \mathbf{E}$.

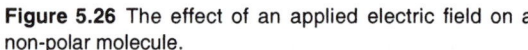

Figure 5.26 The effect of an applied electric field on a non-polar molecule.

Diagrams (a) and (c) refer to the situation when there is no electric field applied. In (a) the charge distribution of the electrons is symmetrically arranged around the nucleus. This is because the coulomb potential energy of an electron, which varies approximately as $1/r$ as shown in (c), is symmetric.

Diagrams (b) and (d) refer to the situation when there is an external electric field applied. In (b) the charge distribution of the electrons is now asymmetrically arranged around the nucleus. This is because the coulomb potential energy of an electron (d) is now asymmetric.

The extent of the disturbance of the charge distribution depends on the ratio of the applied electric field to the internal field. Usually this ratio is extremely small (Example 2.1).

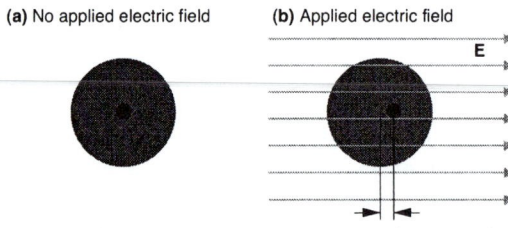

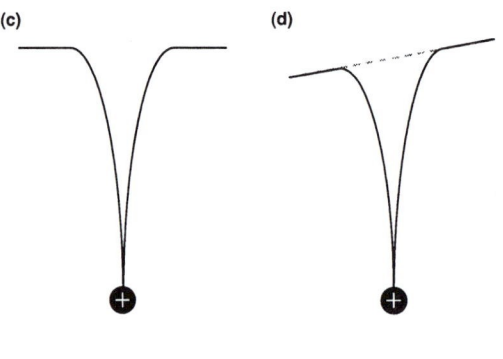

Figure 5.27 (a) Schematic illustration of a charge distribution which possesses a dipole moment. (b) For many purposes, a real molecule may be modelled as a permanent dipole moment. (c) The forces acting on a dipole moment form a torque that twists the molecule until $\mathbf{p}$ lies parallel to $\mathbf{E}$.

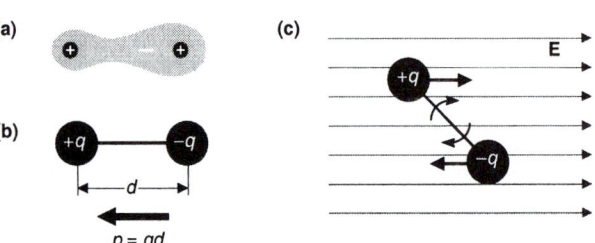

Dielectric constant of a non-polar gas

We start off by assuming that the electric field $\mathbf{E}$ around each molecule induces a electric dipole moment $\mathbf{p}_i$ on the molecule, given by:

$$\mathbf{p}_i = \alpha \mathbf{E} \qquad (2.12^* \ \& \ 5.101)$$

where α is called the *molecular polarisability*. If there are n such molecules per unit volume then the total polarisation per unit volume $\mathbf{P}$ is:

$$\begin{aligned} \mathbf{P} &= n\mathbf{p}_i \\ &= n\alpha\mathbf{E} \end{aligned} \qquad (5.102)$$

Now the average electric field $\mathbf{E}$ around each molecule is slightly reduced from the applied electric field $\mathbf{E}_{app}$ according to two relations. The first is:

$$\mathbf{E} = \frac{\mathbf{E}_{app}}{\varepsilon} \qquad (5.103)$$

which defines the dielectric constant ε. The second expression defines the polarisation (*Bleaney and Bleaney*: see §1.4.1 for a detailed reference):

$$\mathbf{E} = \mathbf{E}_{app} - \frac{\mathbf{P}}{\varepsilon_o} \qquad (5.104)$$

The minus sign arises because the induced electric field $\mathbf{P}/\varepsilon_o$ at a molecule due to all the other molecules opposes the applied field. Combining Equation 5.103 with Equation 5.104 we have:

$$\frac{\mathbf{E}_{app}}{\varepsilon} = \mathbf{E}_{app} - \frac{\mathbf{P}}{\varepsilon_o} \qquad (5.105)$$

Substituting for $\mathbf{P}$ using Equation 5.102 we find:

$$\frac{\mathbf{E}_{app}}{\varepsilon} = \mathbf{E}_{app} - \frac{n\alpha\mathbf{E}}{\varepsilon_o} \qquad (5.106)$$

Neglecting the small difference between the applied field $\mathbf{E}_{app}$ and average field around each molecule $\mathbf{E}$ we arrive at:

$$\frac{1}{\varepsilon} = 1 - \frac{n\alpha}{\varepsilon_o} \qquad (5.107)$$

which simplifies to:

$$\begin{aligned} \varepsilon &= \left[1 - \frac{n\alpha}{\varepsilon_o} \right]^{-1} \\ &\approx \left[1 + \frac{n\alpha}{\varepsilon_o} + ... \right] \end{aligned} \qquad (5.108)$$

where we have used the fact that $n\alpha/\varepsilon_o$ is very much less unity. We finally arrive at:

$$\varepsilon - 1 = \frac{n\alpha}{\varepsilon_o} \qquad (5.109)$$

This final expression may be compared with the exact expression for $\varepsilon - 1$ obtained after considerably more trouble (*Bleaney and Bleaney*) by *Clausius and Mossotti*:

Example 5.12

In an applied electric field, the centre of electronic symmetry of an argon atom moves a distance of around 10^{-13} m away from the nucleus. What is the magnitude of the electric dipole moment induced on the atom?

An argon nucleus has a charge $+18e$ and the electrons have a total charge $-18e$. If we assume that the entire charge distribution moves rigidly by a distance 10^{-13} m then the induced electric dipole moment is (§ 2.2.3):

$$\begin{aligned} p &= qd \\ &= 18 \times 1.6 \times 10^{-19} \times 10^{-13} \\ &= 2.88 \times 10^{-31} \ \text{C m} \\ &= 0.288 \ \text{Debye units} \end{aligned}$$

In fact, it is unlikely that the entire charge distribution would shift rigidly in the applied field. The electric field of the nucleus falls of as $\sim 1/r^2$ and so is much weaker in the outer regions of the atom than near the nucleus. (Figure 5.26) The electrons respond to the *total electric field* due to both the nucleus and the applied electric field. Near the nucleus, the applied electric field is a small fraction of the total electric field, but for electrons in the outer regions of the atom, the applied electric field may be a significant fraction of the total field. Thus, the outer (valence) electrons tend to move more than the inner electrons in an applied field. These considerations would reduce the actual dipole moment below that predicted above.

$$\varepsilon - 1 = \frac{n\alpha}{\varepsilon_{o}}\left[\frac{\varepsilon + 2}{3}\right] \qquad (5.110)$$

Expressions 5.109 and 5.110 yield a prediction for $\varepsilon - 1$ expressed in terms of the number density of molecules n, the permittivity of free space ε_{o}, and the molecular polarisability α. The molecular polarisability may (with some difficulty) be calculated from first principles for each type of molecule. Its magnitude depends on the ease with which the electronic charge around a molecule may be deformed by an applied electric field.

Dielectric constant of a polar gas

For a gas of polar molecules we have to take account of two different effects of the applied electric field.

- First the molecules will have an electric dipole moment $\mathbf{p}_i$ *induced* on them as described in the preceding section.
- Second, the orientation of molecules will be affected by the torque on their permanent electric dipole moment $\mathbf{p}_p$.

The first of these effects has been discussed in the previous section, so we will consider here only the second effect. In the absence of an applied electric field, the permanent electric dipole moments are randomly oriented, resulting in zero net polarisation of the gas. In the presence of an applied field, there will be a tendency for more molecules to orient their permanent dipole moments $\mathbf{p}_p$ parallel to the applied field, resulting in a net polarisation $\mathbf{P}$. We thus expect that the polarisation to be:

$$P \propto n \times fraction \times \mathbf{p}_p \qquad (5.111)$$

where n is the number density of molecules, and *fraction* (the fractional excess of molecules oriented parallel to $\mathbf{E}$) varies between 0 and 1. The *fraction* depends on the ratio of two energies: the random kinetic energy of the molecules which is of the order of $k_B T$; and the orientational energy of the molecule in the applied field, which is $\mathbf{p}_p \cdot \mathbf{E} \approx p_p E$. We thus expect the *fraction* in Equation 5.111 to be of the form:

$$fraction \propto \frac{p_p E}{k_B T} \qquad (5.112)$$

at least for small electric fields. Hence, we expect the polarisation of the gas to be given by an expression of the form:

$$\mathbf{P} \propto n \times fraction \times \mathbf{p}_p$$

$$\mathbf{P} \propto n \times \frac{p_p E}{k_B T} \times \mathbf{p}_p \qquad (5.113)$$

or dropping the vector notation:

$$P \propto \frac{n p_p^2 E}{k_B T} \qquad (5.114)$$

An exact calculation (*Bleaney and Bleaney*) shows the constant of proportionality in Equation 5.114 to be $\frac{1}{3}$ and so the polarisation is then:

$$P = \frac{n p_p^2 E}{3 k_B T} \qquad (5.115)$$

This expression has exactly the same form as the expression known as the *Curie Law* for the magnetisation of a substance containing freely-rotating permanent magnetic dipole moments (See Web Chapter W2). Following the argument of Equations 5.105 to 5.110 in the preceding section, we can convert this expression for the polarisation into an expression for the dielectric constant due to the re-orientation of the permanent dipole moments:

$$\varepsilon - 1 = \frac{n p_p^2}{3 \varepsilon_o k_B T}. \qquad (5.116)$$

Comparison with experiment

We are now in a position to compare the data on the dielectric constants of gases with the predictions of the preceding sections. We expect that for gases of non-polar molecules $\varepsilon - 1$ should be given by:

$$\varepsilon - 1 = \frac{n\alpha}{\varepsilon_o} \qquad (5.109^*)$$

where the molecular polarisability α is an intrinsic property of a molecule. For gases of polar molecules we expect that in addition to any induced

dipole moment there should be an additional term given by:

$$\varepsilon - 1 = \frac{np_p^2}{3\varepsilon_o k_B T} \qquad (5.116^*)$$

where p_p is an intrinsic property of a molecule.

Let us now turn to the questions raised by the data.

Pressure dependence

We notice that both expressions for $\varepsilon - 1$ (Equations 5.109 and 5.116) depend linearly on n, the number density of molecules. Hence at fixed temperature, we expect $\varepsilon - 1$ to vary linearly with pressure in accord with the experimental behaviour of CO_2 in Figure 5.25 (b).

Temperature dependence of non-polar molecules

The temperature dependence of $\varepsilon - 1$ is slightly harder to understand than the pressure dependence. From a wider understanding of the structure of molecules, we expect that the CO_2 molecule should have no permanent dipole moment and so it should obey Equation 5.109 for non-polar molecules. If this is so then we would expect $\varepsilon - 1$ to show no temperature dependence. However the data below (extracted from Table 5.16) show a clear dependence on temperature.

From Table 5.16

Gas	$T\,(°C)$	$T\,(K)$	$10^4\,(\varepsilon - 1)$
Carbon dioxide, CO_2	0	273	9.88
Carbon dioxide, CO_2	20	293	9.22
Carbon dioxide, CO_2	100	373	7.23

In fact, the temperature dependence is 'hidden' in the expression for the number density n. The data in Table 5.16 are taken at constant pressure, and increasing the temperature at constant pressure implies a reduction in the number density n according to:

$$n = \frac{P}{k_B T} \qquad (5.100^*)$$

This shows that, at constant pressure, n is proportional to $1/T$. Substitution into Equation 5.109 predicts that:

$$\varepsilon - 1 = \frac{P\alpha}{\varepsilon_o k_B T} \qquad (5.117)$$

If this is the origin of the temperature dependence, then we should expect the value of $\varepsilon - 1$ at 373 K to be a factor $273/373 = 0.732$ less than its value at 273 K. Comparing this with the data from Table 5.16 predicts that the value at 100 °C should be $0.732 \times 9.88 \times 10^{-4} = 7.23 \times 10^{-4}$, in agreement with the experimental value.

Temperature dependence of polar molecules

Using this knowledge of the of the 'hidden' temperature dependence of n we now expect the value of $\varepsilon - 1$ for polar molecules to vary as:

$$\varepsilon - 1 = \frac{p_p^2}{3\varepsilon_o k_B T}$$
$$= \frac{Pp_p^2}{3\varepsilon_o k_B^2 T^2} \qquad (5.118)$$

i.e. with a $1/T^2$ temperature dependence. Examining the data for the polar molecule ammonia in Table 5.16, we expect the value of $\varepsilon - 1$ at 373 K to be a factor $(273/373)^2 = 0.536$ less than its value at 273 K. Comparing this with the data from Table 5.16 predicts that the value at 100 °C should be $0.536 \times 8.34 \times 10^{-4} = 4.46 \times 10^{-4}$, in rough agreement with the experimental value of 4.87×10^{-4}.

From Table 5.16

Gas	$T\,(°C)$	$T\,(K)$	$10^4(\varepsilon - 1)$
Ammonia, NH_3	0	273	8.34
Ammonia, NH_3	100	373	4.87

The discrepancy between experiment and theory can be understood as arising from the fact that polar molecules have contributions to $\varepsilon - 1$ from both the re-orientation of their permanent electric dipole moments, and from their induced dipole moment. Thus we can plausibly assign the difference between the observed and predicted value to the induced electric dipole moment.

Dependence of $(\varepsilon - 1)$ on the type of molecule

The final points we need to understand concern the general magnitude of $\varepsilon - 1$ and the occasional occurrence of some extremely large values (Figure

5.25). We can understand this by considering as examples the distribution of electric charge within two simple diatomic molecules: O_2 and CO.

Even without knowing the details of the charge distribution within an oxygen molecule, we can say that we would expect the charge to be distributed symmetrically between the two atoms. We say this because each oxygen atom is identical and hence has an equal attraction (or *affinity*) for electrons. If we think now about carbon monoxide CO, we would expect the charge to be distributed asymmetrically between the two atoms. We say this because each atom is different and so has a different characteristic electron affinity. In this case, the electrons are more attracted to the oxygen atom than the carbon atom and so the oxygen atom becomes negatively charged with respect to the carbon atom. In other words, a CO molecule has permanent electric dipole moment.

We can estimate the magnitude of the permanent dipole moment p_p by considering the CO datum from Table 5.16: $10^4(\varepsilon - 1) = 6.92$ at 23 °C (296 K). Rearranging Equation 5.118, into an expression for p_p we obtain:

$$p_p = \sqrt{\frac{3k_B^2 T^2 (\varepsilon - 1)\varepsilon_0}{P}} \qquad (5.119)$$

Evaluating this at atmospheric pressure we find:

$$p_p = \sqrt{\frac{3\left(1.38\times10^{-23}\times296\right)^2 \times 6.92\times10^{-4} \times 8.85\times10^{-12}}{1.013\times10^5}}$$

$$= 1.74\times10^{-30} \text{ Cm} \qquad (5.120)$$

$$= 1.74 \text{ debye}$$

Does this make sense? Imagine that some fraction f of an entire electronic charge e is transferred from CO. The separation r_0 of the atoms in a CO molecule is given in *Kaye and Laby* as 0.1131 nm. We thus expect that the permanent dipole moment will be given by:

$$p_p = 1.74\times10^{-30}$$

$$= r_0 f e \qquad (5.121)$$

$$= 0.113\times10^{-9} \times f \times 1.6\times10^{-19}$$

which predicts $f = 0.096 \approx 0.1$, which seems reasonable. Notice that the magnitude of p_p yields the product of fe and r_0 and so we may interpret the magnitude of p_p as being:

- the transfer of a fractional charge fe across the entire length of the molecule, or
- the transfer of an entire electronic charge e across a fraction f of the entire length of the molecule, or
- any combination of the above two effects.

The discussion above allows us to understand why larger molecules tend to possess larger dipole moments. In larger molecules it is possible for an amount of charge of the order of e to be transferred across relatively large distances, and hence give rise to relatively large dipole moments. This charge transfer arises as part of the processes of chemical interaction between the atoms within a molecule. The larger physical extent of larger molecules allows charge to be spread across larger distances and hence give rise to larger permanent electric dipole moments.

Considering the non-polar gases in Table 5.16, we see that $\varepsilon - 1$, and hence the *induced* dipole moments, tends to increase with increasing atomic number, i.e. the molecular polarisability α is larger for larger atoms. We can understand this by considering the electric field which acts on the valence electrons in an atom (Figure 5.26 (c) and (d)). For an atom such as helium, the two electrons are extremely close to the electric charge on the nucleus $+2e$. In an atom such as xenon, however, the outer electrons are further away from the nucleus and experience a much weaker electric field. As a consequence the electric field around the valence electrons in xenon is much less than that around the valence electrons in helium. Thus an applied electric field of a given strength affects the valence electrons around a xenon atom more strongly than the electrons around a helium atom. This amounts to making a xenon atom more deformable (i.e. more polarisable) than a helium atom.

Finally we note that in Figure 5.25(a), all three of the substances with anomalously large dipole moments contain an OH group of atoms. A wide range of chemical experiments indicate that the

OH group, known as a hydroxyl group, has a particularly strong affinity for electrons, thus causing a large amount of charge to be transported away from the centre of the molecule.

5.7.3 Data on the electrical properties of gases in strong electric field

In weak electric fields, gases form effective electrical insulators with low values of electrical conductivity. In strong electric fields however, electric charge can move through a gas producing a variety of interesting phenomena. The value of electric field at which this change in behaviour takes place is known as the *breakdown electric field* or *dielectric strength* of the gas.

Taking air as a typical gas, the dielectric strength of air at 25 °C and normal atmospheric pressure (0.1013 MPa) is 3.13×10^6 V m^{-1}. The variation of dielectric strength of air with temperature and pressure is shown in Figure 5.28.

The value of electric field at which breakdown occurs varies between gases, and also depends critically on several 'minor' properties of the gas. In particular, the presence of ions, i.e. atoms which are not electrically neutral, significantly lowers the dielectric strength of a gas. In practice, we must also consider the humidity of the gas: humid air can deposit a microscopic layer of water on solid surfaces with which it is in contact. Although this extremely thin layer is only a weak conductor of electricity, it can 'short circuit' the even more highly resistive air. In different experiments this can lead to anomalous apparent increases or decreases in the dielectric strength of humid air.

In the nineteenth century great efforts were put into understanding the nature of the flow of electric current through a gas, and a considerable understanding of the phenomena associated with 'cathode rays' was achieved. These experiments advanced our understanding of the nature of gases and of the internal structure of atoms enormously. A selection of the phenomena we have to understand are succinctly described by one of the fore-

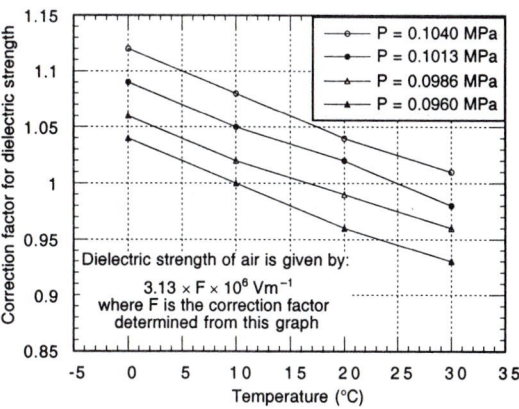

Figure 5.28 The variation of dielectric strength of air with temperature and pressure in the region of ambient temperature and pressure. The dielectric strength is increased at low temperatures and high pressures.

Example 5.13

An air-cored parallel-plate capacitor has a plate separation of $d = 1$ mm. If the air pressure is 0.1 MPa and the temperature is 5 °C, what is the maximum voltage that can be applied between the plates before sparking occurs?

From the text, the dielectric strength of air at 25 °C and normal atmospheric pressure (0.1013 MPa) is 3.13×10^6 Vm^{-1}. We use the graph (Figure 5.28) to find a corrected value for our temperature and pressure. Looking up the 5 °C line on the graph reveals that the correction factor will be between 1.04 (which would be appropriate at a pressure of 0.0986 MPa) and 1.07 (which would be appropriate at a pressure of 0.1013 MPa). Our pressure lies roughly midway between these values and so we estimate a value of 1.055. The dielectric strength of air at 5 °C and 0.100 MPa is therefore:

$$= 1.055 \times 3.13 \times 10^6 \text{ V m}^{-1} = 3.30 \times 10^6 \text{ V m}^{-1}$$

The electric field between the plates of a capacitor is given approximately by $E = V/d$. If we work out the voltage which will yield the maximum sustainable field we have:

$$V = Ed = \left[3.30 \times 10^6\right] \times \left[10^{-3}\right] = 3.30 \times 10^3 \text{ V}$$

Thus the capacitor can, in principle, be used up to 3.3 kV. However, the electric field around the edge of a capacitor plate can be significantly greater the field between the plates, and breakdown would occur there before it would between the plates. A more likely value of maximum working voltage is ≈ 1 kV. Notice that for very small gaps of the order of a micron (10^{-6} m) this breakdown voltage can be only a few volts.

most scientists of that age, J.J. Thomson, in his book *Conduction of Electricity Through Gases*. In the following extract he describes the general nature of the phenomena which occur when an electric current is passed through a glass tube containing gas at low pressure.

> When the electric discharge passes through a gas at low pressure, differences in the appearance of the gas at various points in its path become very clearly marked. The discharge, as illustrated [in Figure 5.29], presents the following features: starting from the cathode (negative terminal) there is a thin layer of luminosity (1) spread over its surface; next to this there is a comparatively dark space called 'Crookes dark space' (2), the width of which depends on the pressure of the gas, increasing as the pressure diminishes – it also depends, under some conditions on the intensity of the current. The boundary of the dark space is approximately the surface traced out by normals of constant length drawn to the surface of the cathode. Beyond the dark space there is a luminous region (3) called the 'negative glow'. Beyond this again is another comparatively dark region (4) called by some writers the 'second negative dark space' and by others the 'Faraday dark space'. Its length is very variable, even when the pressure is constant. Beyond this again there is a luminous column (5) reaching right up to the anode and called the positive column. When the current and pressure are within certain limits this column exhibits remarkable alternations of dark and bright spaces: these are called striations. In long tubes the positive column constitutes by far the greater part of the discharge, for the Crookes space, negative glow and Faraday dark space do not depend markedly on the length of the tube. So that when the length of the discharge is increased, the increase is practically only in the length of the positive column. Thus for example in a tube about 15 metres used by one of us, the positive column occupied the whole of the tube with the exception of two or three centimetres close to the cathode.

J. J. Thomson
Conduction of Electricity Through Gases,
published by Cambridge University Press in 1933

The colour of the 'luminosity', particularly within the positive column (feature 5 in Figure 5.29) depends on the type of gas. Hydrogen for instance has a red glow, as does neon, but argon has a bluish tint. If one examines the spectrum of the light then one finds that the spectrum is characteristic of the type of gas in the tube. More details of these

Figure 5.29 An illustration of the pattern of light emitted when an electric current flows through a gas, called a *discharge*. The details of the pattern (1 to 5) are discussed in the text. The shaded areas in the figure represent luminous regions of the gas and the unshaded regions represent regions from which no light is emitted.

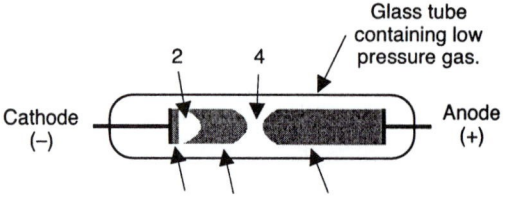

emission spectra are given in §5.7.5 on the optical properties of gases.

The main questions raised by our preliminary examination of the experimental data for on the properties of gases under strong electric fields are:

- Why is the dielectric strength largest at low temperatures and high pressures, i.e. when the gas is most dense?

- Why, below a critical electric field, the dielectric strength, do gases behave as electrical insulators, while above that they behave as electrical conductors, displaying a variety of optical effects?

5.7.4 Understanding the data on the electrical properties of gases in strong electric fields

When the electric field exceeds the dielectric strength, the gas changes from behaving like an insulator to become an electrical conductor. In this section, we will propose a formula for the dielectric strength of a gas, and then using the ideas developed for this formula we will qualitatively discuss the phenomena observed in a discharge tube by J.J. Thompson.

Background theory

In order to understand how the breakdown of the insulating properties of the gas occurs we need to consider the situation where a single charged particle, an ion, is present in the gas when an electric field $\mathbf{E}$ is applied. The ion might be the result of an interaction between an atom and a fast-moving particle from a cosmic ray shower. In the absence

of an electric field, the electron and ion created by the ionisation will quickly recombine (Figure 5.30).

In the presence of an electric field, the electron and ion created by the ionisation may be prevented from recombining and can be accelerated through the gas by the applied electric field (Figure 5.30).

Given that a free ion, separated from 'its' electron, has been created, it will experience force qE which will accelerate it. Hence its speed will increase and it will acquire more kinetic energy the further it travels in the field. If the *mean free path* λ_{mfp} of the ion in the gas is long enough, or the electric field strength is great enough, then it may acquire enough kinetic energy to ionise the atom with which it next collides. The consequences of this can be enormous.

There will now be two ions, instead of just one. What happened to the first ion may also happen to the second one, and if it does, the two ions will cause further ions to be created. Hence starting with just a single ion, the number of ions in a gas can increase in an effect called an *avalanche*. Also under the influence of the applied electric field, the second ion will move along in the same direction as the first, whereas the electron released from the second ion will travel in the opposite direction (Figure 5.30). After many collisions an electric current flows through the gas, with electrons travelling in one direction and ions travelling in the other.

Thus the presence of a single ion has caused the gas to become an electrical conductor instead of an electrical insulator. The electric field which must be applied to a gas to cause it to become a conductor is called the *breakdown electric field*, or the *dielectric strength* of the gas.

Pressure and temperature dependence of the dielectric strength

We can consider the ionisation process which initiates and maintains the density of ions responsible for conduction in gas, as a two-step process. In the first stage, an electron or ion (charge q) accelerates for a distance λ under the action of the electric field and gains energy u, given by:

Figure 5.30 Ionisation of an atom in the absence and the presence of a strong electric field.
(a) Initially (1) we have a neutral atom, then (2) one of the causes described in the text causes an ionisation event. In the absence of an applied field the negatively-charged electron and the positively-charged ion quickly recombine (3). Finally we return to the situation (1) we started with. Thus the gas is stable against the formation of ions.

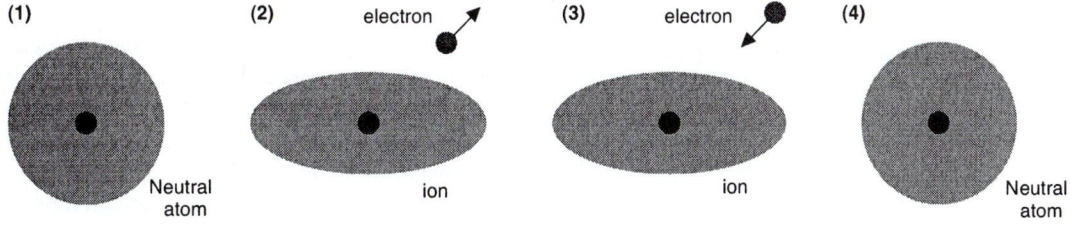

(b) Initially (1) we have a neutral atom, then (2) one of the causes described in the text causes an ionisation event. In contrast with (a), an applied electric field (3) acts to draw apart the negatively-charged electron and the positively-charged ion, and recombination is prevented.

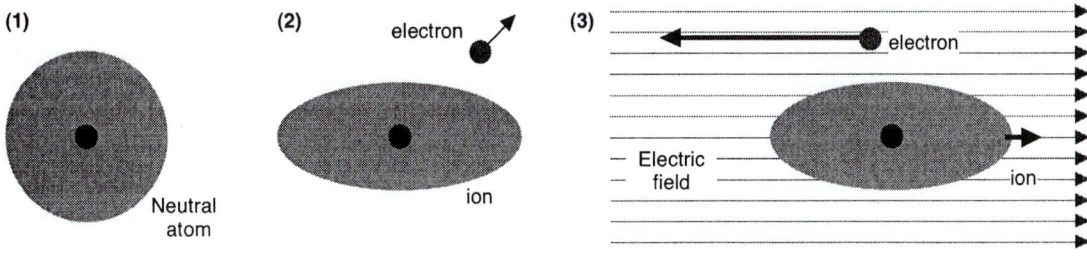

$$u = \int_0^\lambda q\mathbf{E} \cdot \mathrm{d}s \qquad (5.122)$$
$$= qE\lambda$$

In the second stage, some of this energy (typically of the order of few hundredths of an eV) is given up in collisions with molecules. These collisions lead, on average, to a further ionisation process.

However, although this two-stage process is easy to describe at this level, working out λ, the average path length of an ion or an electron between collisions, is rather difficult. Notice that because the ions and electrons are electrically charged, ion–molecule and electron–molecule interactions are considerably stronger than molecule–molecule interactions. Calculating the effective diameters or cross-sectional areas of molecules for ionic collisions is not an easy problem. However, we can say one thing for sure: whatever λ is, it will be inversely proportional to n, the number density of molecules in the gas.

So from Equation 5.122 we expect that the break down field E_B will be defined when the work done in accelerating an ion or electron is sufficient to ionise a molecule, i.e. when:

$$u_o = qE_B\lambda \qquad (5.123)$$

where u_o is the ionisation energy. Since u_o is characteristic of the molecules of the gas we therefore expect to find that E_B is proportional to $1/\lambda$. Hence based on the arguments in the preceding paragraph we expect quite generally to find:

$$E_B \propto \frac{1}{\lambda} \propto n \qquad (5.124)$$

Recalling that $n = P/k_B T$ we therefore expect that:

$$E_B \propto A\frac{P}{T} \qquad (5.125)$$

where A is an expression involving λ and u_o. Thus we expect the dielectric strength to be proportional to pressure and inversely proportional to absolute temperature.

Examining Figure 5.28, we see that at 0 °C, the correction factor increases from 1.04 at a pressure of 0.096 MPa to 1.12 at 0.104 MPa. Thus the dielectric strength increases by a factor $(1.12/1.04) = 1.08$ as a result of a pressure increase of $(0.104/0.0960) = 1.08$. At limited resolution, this is fairly good agreement.

Similarly, at a pressure of 0.1013 MPa, the correction factor of 1.09 at $T = 273.2$ K falls to a correction factor of 0.98 at a $T = 273.2 + 30$ K. Thus the dielectric strength decreases by a factor $(0.98/1.09) = 0.90$ as a result of a temperature increase by a factor $(303.2/273.2) = 1.11$. Since $1/1.11 = 0.90$ this is fairly good agreement, albeit at limited resolution.

At first sight, this result may appear counterintuitive. It might be thought that the best way to stop a gas from conducting would be to use a low gas pressure i.e. an approximation to a vacuum, which is an excellent insulator. It is not too difficult to reduce the pressure of a gas by a factor of about 10^9 from atmospheric pressure (10^{-6} mbar $\approx 10^{-4}$ Pa). However even here there are still $\approx 10^{16}$ molecules m^{-3}. In these circumstances, if a single ion is created it will travel straight across the vacuum chamber with virtually no chance of collision with another molecule. Thus the mean free path becomes fixed at the dimension of the container and does not get any longer as the pressure is lowered. This situation is similar to the behaviour of the pressure dependence of the thermal conductivity of a gas (§5.5). The relevant ionisation energy is then that of the atoms in the walls in the container. If an ion hits the walls and creates more ions, then ions will simply bounce between the walls of the container. Lowering the gas pressure will make no difference until there are no atoms at all, something which is not technically achievable.

The phenomena within a discharge tube

In the light of our discussions above, Table 5.17 explains the phenomena described by J.J. Thomson, in the passage from his book *Conduction of Electricity Through Gases* that was reproduced in §5.7.3. The spectra of the 'luminosity' is discussed below in §5.8 on the optical properties of gases. The state in which a substantial fraction of gas

molecules are ionised is generally referred to as a *plasma*. By far the majority of the matter in the universe exists in this state, but on Earth it is relatively rare, and we pass it by without further mention.

Figure 5.29 (Reproduced here for your convenience) The details of the pattern (1 to 5) are discussed in Table 5.17. The shaded areas in the figure represent luminous regions of the gas and the unshaded regions represent regions from which no light is emitted.

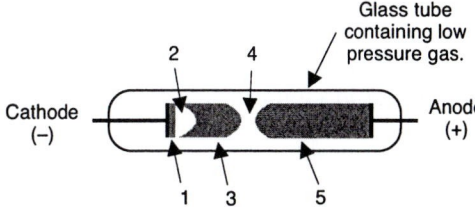

Table 5.17

Thompson's description	What is happening
Starting from the cathode (negative terminal) there is a thin layer of luminosity (1) spread over its surface.	The luminosity is caused by positive ions striking the surface of the cathode.
Next to this there is a comparatively dark space called 'Crookes dark space' (2), the width of which depends on the pressure of the gas, increasing as the pressure diminishes — it also depends, ·under some conditions on the intensity of the current. The boundary of the dark space is approximately the surface traced out by normals of constant length drawn to the surface of the cathode.	In this region electrons liberated from the cathode (by the impact of positive ions) are being accelerated by the electric field in the tube. They are colliding with atoms and ions in this region but give off no light because they do not have sufficient energy to excite the atoms. The boundary of the region has this form because electrons have travelled in straight lines for a distance of around one ionic mean free path from the cathode.
Beyond the dark space there is a luminous region (3) called the 'negative glow'.	Now electrons *do* have sufficient energy to excite the atoms.
Beyond this again is another comparatively dark region (4) called by some writers the 'second negative dark space' and by others the 'Faraday dark space'. Its length is very variable, even when the pressure is constant.	Having collided inelastically with atoms of the gas in region (3), the electrons lost kinetic energy and are now being accelerated again.
Beyond this again there is a luminous column (5) reaching right up to the anode and called the positive column. When the current and pressure are within certain limits this column exhibits remarkable alternations of dark and bright spaces: these are called striations. In long tubes the positive column constitues by far the greater part of the discharge, for the Crookes space, negative glow and Faraday dark space do not depend markedly on the length of the tube. So that when the length of the discharge is increased, the increase is practically only in the length of the positive column. Thus for example in a tube about 15 metres used by one of us, the positive column occupied the whole of the tube with the exception of two or three centimetres close to the cathode.	The striations are caused by alternating regions of the gas in which: • electrons and ions are accelerated and do not yet have sufficient energy to ionise/excite the atoms of the gas: these are the non-luminous dark regions • electrons and ions accelerated in the above 'dark' regions now have sufficient energy to ionise/excite the atoms of the gas; these are the luminous regions. In some circumstances where the geometry of the acceleration is not very well defined, or where the cathode is heated to created a spread of initial electron velocities, the dark and light striations become blurred and overlap one another.

5.8 Optical properties

'Light' is the name given to oscillations of the electromagnetic field which take place with frequencies in the range 400 THz (Red) to 1000 THz (Blue). Remember that 1 THz = 10^{12} Hz. Below we concentrate entirely on the effect of the oscillations of the *electric* component of the electromagnetic field.

5.8.1 Data on the speed of light in gases: refractive index

Light travels at a slightly slower speed, c_g, through a gas than its speed through vacuum c. You may be forgiven for not having noticed this difference because it is generally rather small; typically a small fraction of a per cent. An apparatus illustrating how such changes may be measured is illustrated in Figure 3.9. The ratio c/c_g is known as the *refractive index* of the gas (§2.3.3), and normally has the symbol n. In order to avoid confusion with n used to signify number density, the refractive index in this text has the symbol n_{light}. The refractive indices of various gases are shown in Table 5.18 and plotted as a function of

relative molecular mass in Figure 5.31. Because n_{light} for gases is close to unity, the table records data in the form $10^6(n_{light} - 1)$. Thus the refractive index of air recorded as 293 is actually 1.000293 and so the speed of light in air is $c/1.000293$, 99.97% of the speed of light in vacuum.

Figure 5.31 shows that there is a general trend towards large molecular mass molecules display-

Table 5.18 The refractive index of various gases as $10^6(n_{light}-1)$ together with the molecular weight of the molecules of the gas. The data refer to gases at STP (P = 0.1013 MPa: T = 0 °C). The refractive index is that appropriate to the bright yellow 'D' lines in the emission spectrum of sodium vapour and varies slightly with frequency.

Gas	M	$(n_{light}-1) \times 10^6$
Hydrogen, H_2	2	132
Helium, He	4	36
Methane, CH_4	18	444
Water vapour, H_2O	18	254
Ammonia, NH_4	18	376
Neon, Ne	20	67
Nitrogen, N_2	28	297
Carbon monoxide, CO	28	338
Air	29	293
Nitric oxide, NO	30	297
Oxygen, O_2	32	271
Methanol, CH_3OH	32	586
Hydrogen sulphide, H_2S	34	633
Hydrogen chloride, HCl	36	447
Fluorine, F_2	38	195
Argon, Ar	40	281
Nitrous oxide, N_2O	44	516
Carbon dioxide, CO_2	44	451
Ethanol, C_2H_5OH	46	878
Sulphur dioxide, SO_2	64	686
Chlorine, Cl_2	71	773
Carbon disulphide, CS_2	76	481
Benzene, C_6H_6	78	1762
Hydrogen bromide, HBr	81	570
Krypton, Kr	84	427
Hydrogen iodide, HI	128	906
Xenon, Xe	131	702
Bromine, Br_2	160	1132

Figure 5.31 The refractive index n of gases from Table 5.17 plotted as a function of the relative molecular weight of the gas molecules. The refractive indices of the gases are all within 0.2 % of unity and so the quantity $10^6(n-1)$ has been plotted so as to make visible differences in the data. The crosses (×) mark the data points for the noble gases helium, neon, argon, krypton, and xenon.

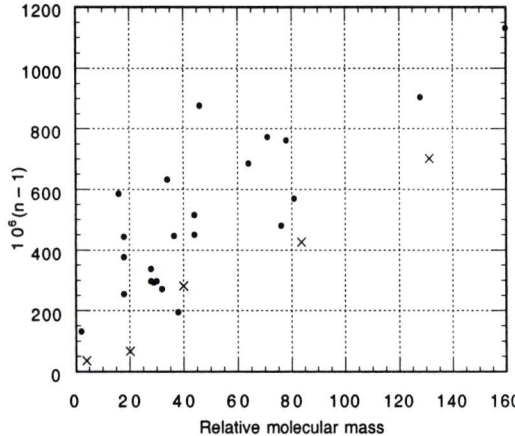

ing a higher refractive index, but the wide variation in n_{light} shows that there are significant factors other than molecular mass. Figure 5.31 shows the data for monatomic noble gases helium, neon, argon, krypton, and xenon as crosses ($\times$), indicating that amongst similar molecules, the link between n_{light} and M is relatively direct.

The main questions raised by our preliminary examination of the experimental data on the refractive indices of gases are:

- Why do the refractive indices of a wide variety of gases at STP all lie between 1.000 and 1.002?
- Why, within this range, is there a significant dependence of n_{light} upon the molecular mass?

5.8.2 Understanding data on the refractive index of gases

Introduction

Our explanation of the interaction of light with gases follows on from the discussion of the dielectric constant data (§5.7.2). We assume that each molecule responds independently to the oscillating electric field of the light wave, and that in response to this field the molecule either:

- acquires an induced dipole moment p_i, or
- orients its own permanent dipole moment p_p (if it has one) parallel to the instantaneous value of the electric field.

As we shall see, in general the second process is not as important as the first because the time taken for a molecule to rotate is typically of the order 10^{-10} seconds (Example 5.15). Although this may seem like a short time, it is much longer than the period of the electric field oscillation in a light wave, which is of the order 10^{-15} seconds.

So the main effect of a light wave is to induce an oscillating electric dipole moment on the molecules of the gas (Figure 5.33). In general, the magnitude of the induced dipole moment varies with frequency, and generally grows resonantly large at a frequency in the ultraviolet region of the spectrum. The frequency dependence of the dipole moments induced on atoms and molecules is considered more fully in the analysis of the optical

132

Example 5.14

It is required to split a laser beam in two, and to delay one beam with respect the other travelling through vacuum by 4.7 ps (4.7×10^{-12} s). To achieve this delay one part of the split beam light is passed through a length L of gas. For reasons of its inertness and cost, argon is thought suitable to fill the tube. What length of tube is required if the gas within is at STP? Is this method really practical?

We require a tube which will take a light signal 4.7 ps longer to traverse than an equivalent tube filled with vacuum. If the tube were evacuated the transit time would be:

$$t_0 = \frac{L}{c}$$

but when filled with gas will be:

$$t_g = \frac{L}{c_g}$$

We need a device in which $t_g - t = 4.7$ ps, i.e.

$$t_g - t = \frac{L}{c_g} - \frac{L}{c} = 4.7 \times 10^{-12}$$

We now note that Table 4.10 tells us that for argon at STP the refractive index is given by:

$$n - 1 = 281 \times 10^{-6}$$
$$n = 1.000281$$

From the definition of the refractive index this implies

$$\frac{c}{c_g} = 1.000281$$

Rearranging our equation we have:

$$4.7 \times 10^{-12} = L\left[\frac{1}{c_g} - \frac{1}{c}\right] = L\left[\frac{1}{c/1.000281} - \frac{1}{c}\right]$$

This simplifies to:

$$4.7 \times 10^{-12} = \frac{L}{c}[1.000281 - 1]$$

which can be solved for L:

$$L = \frac{4.7 \times 10^{-12} \times 2.998 \times 10^8}{0.000281} = 5.01 \text{ m}$$

This is rather an inconveniently long tube for practical use, given that the tube needs to be kept temperature stabilised. However, the technique can be (and is) used by reflecting the light backwards and forwards (say) ten times between an array of mirrors 0.5 m apart.

Figure 5.32 Comparison of the wavelength of blue light with the size of an atom. Notice that in order to be clearly printed the atom has been shown at approximately 10 times its correct scale size.

Figure 5.33 Illustration of the origin of the oscillating dipole moment on a non-polar molecule subject to an oscillating electric field. Notice that in the very short time between successive periods of the light field, only the low-mass electrons can move a significant distance. The heavy nucleus moves relatively little.

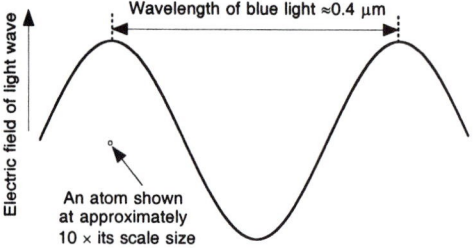

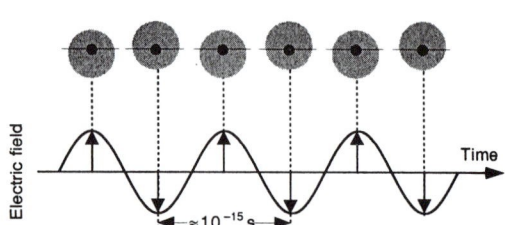

properties of solids (§7.5). Here we concentrate on the effect of these induced dipole moments on the speed of light through the gas.

As outlined in §2.3.3, for most substances the refractive index is given by:

$$n_{light} = \sqrt{\varepsilon} \qquad (2.17^*)$$

We can check Equation 2.17 by using values of $\varepsilon - 1$ from Table 5.16 to predict values for $n_{light} - 1$ (Table 5.19).

The non-polar gases (helium, neon, argon) show excellent agreement. Recalling that $\varepsilon - 1$ is determined at low frequencies (i.e. $<10^9$ Hz), this indi-

cates that the molecular polarisability of these atoms is relatively constant from radio frequencies (MHz) up to optical frequencies (1000 THz).

When we consider the polar molecules in Table 5.19 we find that this agreement is not as good: knowing the value of $\varepsilon - 1$ does not enable us to predict the value of $n_{light} - 1$. This disagreement is slight in the case of ammonia, but for water vapour the difference is dramatic. The reason is that the value of $\varepsilon - 1$ for polar molecules (determined at low frequency) is generally dominated by the effect of molecular rotation. However, as we mentioned above, the oscillations of electric field at optical frequencies are too rapid to allow molecules to rotate. So the refractive index is sensitive

Table 5.19 Comparison of the experimental values of the refractive index of gases with the prediction of their refractive index based on Equation 2.17. Before comparing the data, the dielectric constant data have been corrected to STP using factors discussed in §5.6.2. The first three entries in the table are for non-polar gases and the last two are for polar gases. Notice the good agreement between theory and experiment for the non-polar gases, and the massive disagreement for water vapour.

Gas	$10^4(\varepsilon - 1)$	T	Correction factor	$10^4(\varepsilon - 1)$ (STP)	Prediction $10^6(\sqrt{\varepsilon} - 1)$	Experiment $10^6(n_{light} - 1)$
Non-polar gases						
He	0.65	20	293/273	0.70	35	36
Ne	1.3	0	1	1.3	65	67
Ar	5.16	20	293/273	5.54	277	281
Polar gases						
NH_3	8.34	0	1	8.34	416	376
H_2O	60	100	$(293/273)^2$	69.1	3449	254

only to the induced component of the electric dipole moment of a molecule.

Turning to the questions raised at the end of §5.8.1, we can understand both these phenomena in terms of the connection outlined in Equation 2.17 between n_{light} and ε. The small magnitude of $n_{light} - 1$ results from the small magnitude of $\varepsilon - 1$ (Equation 5.109)

$$\varepsilon - 1 = \frac{n\alpha}{\varepsilon_o} \qquad (5.109^*)$$

which in turn is small because of the intrinsic magnitude of molecular polarisability α and the low number density of molecules in the gas. The dependence of $n_{light} - 1$ upon molecular mass arises because larger molecules tend to have larger values of molecular polarisability.

Example 5.15

Consider a diatomic polar molecule (i.e. one with a 'built-in' electric dipole moment) which has a permanent electric dipole moment of approximately 0.1×10^{-30} Cm.
(a) Estimate the torque on the molecule in an electric field of 1000 Vm^{-1}.
(b) Calculate the time for it to rotate through 90 °.

(a) Assuming the moment is oriented perpendicular to the field, then Γ is given by:

$$\Gamma \approx pE \doteq 0.1 \times 10^{-30} \times 10^3 = 10^{-28} \text{ N m}$$

(b) This is tricky if you are unfamiliar with dealing with rotational calculations. We recall that we use the rotational analogues to the equations of linear motion analogous to $F = ma$ we have:

$$\Gamma = I \frac{d^2\theta}{dt^2}$$

where Γ is the torque described above, I is the *moment of inertia* defined below, and $d^2\theta/dt^2$ is the *angular acceleration*. Similarly, one familiar equation states that $s = ut + \frac{1}{2}at^2$, or with $u = 0$ this becomes $s = \frac{1}{2}at^2$. The rotational analogue of that equation is:

$$\theta = \frac{1}{2}\left[\frac{d^2\theta}{dt^2}\right]t^2$$

These two equations allow us to calculate the time taken for a rotation due to a particular torque. The final formula we need is for the moment of inertia of the molecule and this is given by:

$$I = m_1 \times d_1^2 + m_2 \times d_2^2$$

where d_1 and d_2 are the distances to the two atoms from the centre of mass of the molecule. Approximately this amounts to:

$$I \approx [average \ mass \ of \ the \ two \ atoms] \times \left[\frac{1}{2}r\right]^2$$

where r is the distance between the two atoms, typically $\approx 1.3 \times 10^{-10}$ m (*CRC Handbook*)

Assuming average masses of the two atoms of $\approx 14u$ (i.e. like CO), the moment of inertia is approximately:

$$I \approx [14u] \times \left[\frac{1}{2} \times 1.3 \times 10^{-10}\right]^2$$

$$\approx [14 \times 1.66 \times 10^{-27}] \times \left[0.65 \times 10^{-10}\right]^2$$

$$= 9.8 \times 10^{-47} \approx 10^{-46} \text{ kg m}^2$$

Substituting this into the analogue of $F = ma$, we find an angular acceleration of:

$$\frac{d^2\theta}{dt^2} = \frac{\Gamma}{I} \approx \frac{10^{-28}}{10^{-46}} \approx 10^{18} \text{ rad s}^{-2}$$

So, we can now find out how long it takes the molecule to rotate. Starting with:

$$\theta = \frac{1}{2}\frac{d^2\theta}{dt^2}t^2$$

we can rearranging this to solve for t:

$$t = \sqrt{\frac{2\theta}{d^2\theta/dt^2}}$$

Substituting $\theta = \pi/2$ (i.e. 90°) we find:

$$t = \sqrt{\frac{2 \times \pi/2}{10^{18}}} \approx \sqrt{\pi \times 10^{-18}} \approx 1.8 \times 10^{-9} \text{ s}.$$

So we find that it takes a molecule a couple of nanoseconds to rotate in a weak electric field. This has been a very approximate calculation, but the result is still valid. Molecules take a time of the order of nanoseconds to rotate in an applied electric field.

This may seem like a short time, but in fact when compared to some other processes it is rather slow. For example, the electric field of a light wave oscillates at around 10^{15} times per second. In a field oscillating this fast the molecule will have no time to rotate, whereas in a DC field the molecule will have plenty of time to rotate. This causes a difference between the electrical properties of gases at DC and optical frequencies.

5.8.3 The scattering of light by gases

At optical frequencies, most gases are extremely transparent. However they are not 100% transparent. This can be easily seen by looking through a few kilometres of our most readily available gas, air: objects viewed at a distance can appear 'hazy' or 'coloured'. Also, looking upwards into the air, we see mainly blue light coming apparently from nowhere (we say 'the sky is blue'). If the atmosphere were truly transparent, we would instead see the blackness of space and the stars. Furthermore, the Sun, which appears to be yellow during the day, appears red as it rises or sets. All these effects are due to the scattering of light by the molecules of the gases in the atmosphere. The main questions raised by our qualitative observations of the scattering of light are:

- Why are gases highly, but not completely, transparent?
- Why are some colours scattered more strongly than others?

Let us begin our attempt to answer these questions by first considering the nature of the scattering process.

What is scattering?

The scattering of light caused by atoms in a gas is known as *Rayleigh scattering* (Figure 5.34). The process may be considered in two stages:

- An incoming electromagnetic wave polarises molecules of the gas, and induces an oscillating electric dipole moment.
- The induced oscillating electric dipole moment re-radiates energy in a complicated pattern. The re-radiated (or scattered) wave is at the same frequency as the incoming wave, but travels radially away from the centre of the scattering.

The 'scattering power' of an individual molecule depends on the magnitude of the dipole moment induced on it by the electric field of the light wave. Clearly, if no dipole moment is induced, then there will be no scattering. Recall that as we saw in examining the data on the refractive indices of gases (§5.8.2), at optical frequencies, only the *induced* dipole moment needs to be considered. This is because polar molecules have no time to rotate in a single cycle of the oscillating electric

Figure 5.34 Rayleigh scattering. An incoming plane wave causes an oscillating electric dipole moment (Figure 5.33). The oscillating dipole moment then re-radiates some of the incoming wave as a spherical wave emanating from the molecule. The figure shows a two-dimensional analogue to the scattering such as might occur with water waves on the surface of a pond.

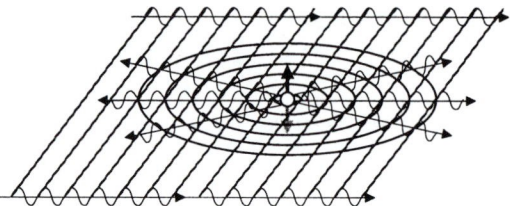

field of the light wave. The theory of an oscillating dipole radiator (*Bleaney and Bleaney*: see §1.4.1 for a detailed reference) indicates that the power radiated by a dipole whose magnitude varies as $p = p_o \cos(2\pi ft)$ is given by:

$$\text{Power} = \left[\frac{4\mu_o \pi^3 p_o^2}{3c}\right] \times f^4 \qquad (5.126)$$

Equation 5.126 shows that the scattered power depends on the fourth power of the frequency i.e. f^4. Blue light has a frequency of $f \approx 10^{15}$ Hz and red light has a frequency of $f \approx 4 \times 10^{14}$ Hz, so according to Equation 5.126, blue light should be scattered at least $(10/4)^4 \approx 2.5^4 \approx 39$ times more strongly than red light.

Blue skies, sunsets, and the difficulty of seeing stars in the daytime

We all know that we cannot see the stars in the daytime. But why not? And we all know that the sky is blue. But what exactly is it that is blue? Let us look at how our understanding of Rayleigh scattering helps us to answer these questions

First of all let us consider a person standing on Earth looking out into space, attempting to gaze at the stars during the daytime (Figure 5.35). They are looking out into space through a column of gas (air) which is about 20 km long. Intense light from the Sun is passing through this column, though it is not travelling directly towards the stargazer. The reason he or she cannot see the stars is because the small amount of light which has been Rayleigh

Figure 5.35 At Kelvin's position on Earth it is sunset and the Sun appears red because the blue light has been scattered out of the sunlight to make the 'sky' appear blue for people like Maxwell. This blue light is much brighter than starlight.

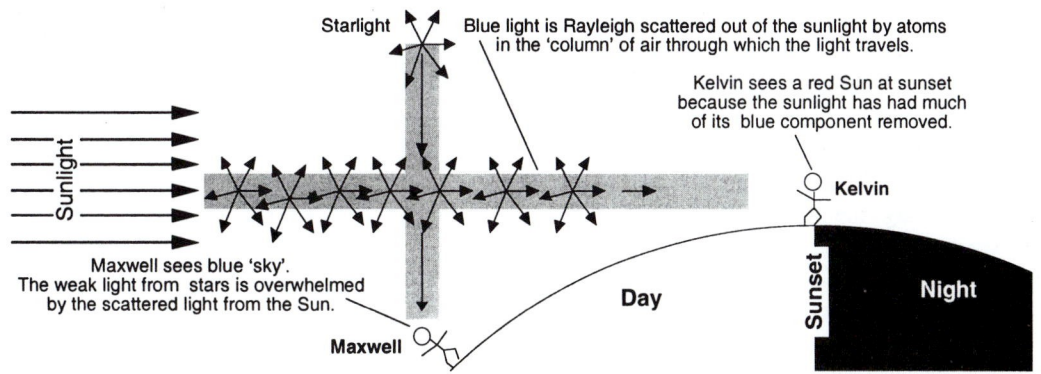

scattered from the sunlight, is *much* brighter than the feeble light from the stars.

The scattered light is primarily blue, because as we noted above, blue light is more strongly scattered than red light. So what we see when we look at blue 'sky' is a kind of glow from the atmosphere caused by its illumination with sunlight.

Furthermore, if our stargazer waited for a more conventional time to observe the stars, he or she might spend a few moments observing the light from the Sun at sunset. They would notice that the Sun appears considerable dimmer as it nears the horizon, and that its colour is distinctly redder than during the daytime. We can understand both these phenomena by noting that in order for sunlight to reach our stargazer at sunset, the sunlight must pass through a considerably greater thickness of the atmosphere than it would have had to during the day. As Figure 5.35 shows, this is a very large effect because the atmosphere is so thin (roughly 20 km) in comparison with the diameter of the Earth (roughly 12800 km).

This immediately allows us to understand why the Sun is less bright at sunset than at midday: more light has been scattered out of sunlight. Furthermore, because the blue light has been scattered more strongly than the red (in order to make blue skies for other observers) the light reaching our sunset stargazer has a stronger yellow/red component than the original spectrum of sunlight.

Another way of looking at it

There is another way of arriving at Equation 5.126 for the Rayleigh scattered power, which starts from quite different assumptions about the scattering process.

We start by noting that the theory of the propagation of electromagnetic waves through substances predicts that a *homogeneous substance* does not scatter light at all. A homogeneous substance is one in which there is no change in refractive index from one region of the substance to another. This is in fact correct. It is perhaps most dramatically demonstrated by the ability of light to travel through the glass of optical fibres with attenuation as low as 1 % per kilometre! What happens in a homogeneous substance is that the light which is re-radiated from the oscillations of the atomic dipoles interferes constructively only in the forward direction. The homogeneity of the medium ensures that destructive interference in the sideways direction is complete.

We might then ask why gases produce Rayleigh scattered light when solids do not. Surely, gases are homogeneous? The answer is that optically they are not. Example 4.2 tells us that the number density of molecules in a gas, $n = P / k_B T$, is of the order of 10^{25} molecules per cubic metre. Since the molecules move independently of each other, statistically, we would then expect that this number should show fluctuations of the order of $\sqrt{n}$. This means that if we counted the molecules in one cubic metre, and compared the result with a

count of the molecules in a neighbouring cubic metre, we would expect both results to be close to 10^{25}, with differences of the order $\sqrt{10^{25}} \approx 3 \times 10^{12}$. Thus the fluctuations represent changes of around 3 parts in 10^{12} of the overall number density. We thus expect the refractive index (Equation 2.17) of each cubic metre to be the same to roughly 3 parts in 10^{12}. However, if we consider how the refractive index might vary from one wavelength of light to the next we arrive at quite a different conclusion.

If we consider a cube of side equal to a wavelength of light λ then the average number of molecules in such a cube is $n\lambda^3$ and the fluctuations from one wavelength to the next are of the order $\sqrt{n\lambda^3}$. The refractive index of each small cube will vary by roughly $\sqrt{n\lambda^3}/n\lambda^3 = 1/\sqrt{n\lambda^3}$. Substituting $n \approx 10^{25}$ molecules per cubic metre and $\lambda = 4 \times 10^{-7}$ m (blue light) we note that there are only around 6.4×10^5 molecules in each small volume. So the fluctuations in this number are around one part in a thousand. These fluctuations in density from one wavelength to the next mean that the amplitude of radiation scattered from each small volume is not quite the same. This in turn leads to the result that the destructive interference between neighbouring sources of scattered radiation is not quite total. In this view of Rayleigh scattering, it is not the molecules themselves which we consider to do the scattering, but the fluctuations in their density on the scale of a wavelength of light.

5.8.4 Data on the emission spectra of gases

As outlined in §5.7.3 on the electrical properties of gases, when an electric current is passed through a gas, the gas gives off light from its *positive column*. The colour of the light is indicative of the type of gas through which the current is passed. However 'colour' is a subjective description of the light which can be made quantitative by examination of the *spectrum* of the light.

A spectrometer is a device which separates out the different frequencies of electromagnetic wave present in light by means of a prism or, more usu-

Figure 5.36 A prism spectrometer. Light is collimated by passing it through slits and then reaches a prism. The different speeds (refractive indices) of different frequencies of light through the glass of the prism (Table 7.49) causes the different colours to take different paths through the prism. The light is then projected onto a screen (or other detector). If the light is from an incandescent lamp, then the intensity varies across the screen in a way similar to that illustrated as *A*. This would look like our familiar 'rainbow' spectrum. However light from the positive column of a discharge tube (*B*) produces a line spectrum, and the precise positions and relative intensities of the lines are uniquely characteristic of the type of gas within the discharge tube.

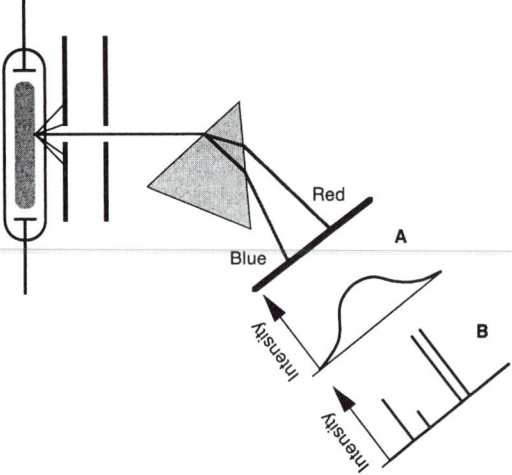

ally, a diffraction grating (Figure 5.36). If we examine the spectrum of a narrow slit illuminated by light from the gas, then we observe striking differences between white light from a heated filament lamp or the Sun, and light from the gas.

The emission spectrum of a gas is discrete: only certain frequencies (colours) characteristic of the molecules of the gas are present. For example, the presence of two very bright 'lines' close together with an average frequency of 509×10^{12} Hz (i.e. a wavelength of 589 nm in vacuum indicates the presence of sodium atoms in the gas. These lines appear 'yellow' to our eyes. Details of the spectra of sodium (vapour) and neon are shown in Figure 5.37.

By spectroscopic investigations, the composition of an unknown gas can be assessed by comparing its spectrum with reference spectra for known sub-

stances. This technique is used to determine the composition of the outer layers of stars, and in the examination of unknown materials as an alternative to 'wet' chemical analysis. This is the technique used to obtain the data on the composition of the outer part of the Sun detailed in Figure 2.1.

Historically, it was from studying the emission spectra of gases that our understanding of atomic structure was derived and checked. Thus the emission spectra of gases have played a key role in the development of the theory of quantum mechanics used to describe the electronic structure of atoms.

So the main question raised by this preliminary discussion of the experimental data on the emission spectra gases fields is:

- Why are the emission spectra of gases in the positive column of a discharge tube discrete, and characteristic of the atoms of the gas?

5.8.5 Understanding the data on the emission spectra of gases

The emission spectra of gases is more properly the subject of a book on atomic physics, but we can see roughly why the emission spectra are characteristic, without trying to calculate why the spectra have the particular form they have.

First we notice that within the positive column of a discharge tube we have molecules in several different states: electrically-neutral molecules, singly-ionised molecules, doubly-ionised molecules, and possibly higher ionisation states of the molecule. The internal electronic structure of each

Figure 5.37 The intensity of the light emitted as function of wavelength for sodium vapour and neon gas. On each spectrum the dotted curve represents the average sensitivity of the human eye. Note that:

- The vertical axis is logarithmic and is plotted in arbitrary units.
- Only about half the lines (those with intensities greater than 300) have been plotted.
- The positive column of a sodium vapour discharge lamp appears bright yellow because of the two closely spaced intense lines (the 'D' lines) at around 589nm, close to the peak of the spectral sensitivity of the eye.
- The positive column of a neon discharge lamp appears red because of the relative scarcity of *any* intense lines near the peak of the eye's sensitivity. The intense cluster of peaks at the red of the spectrum thus dominates the appearance of the spectrum even though the eye is very insensitive in this region of the spectrum.

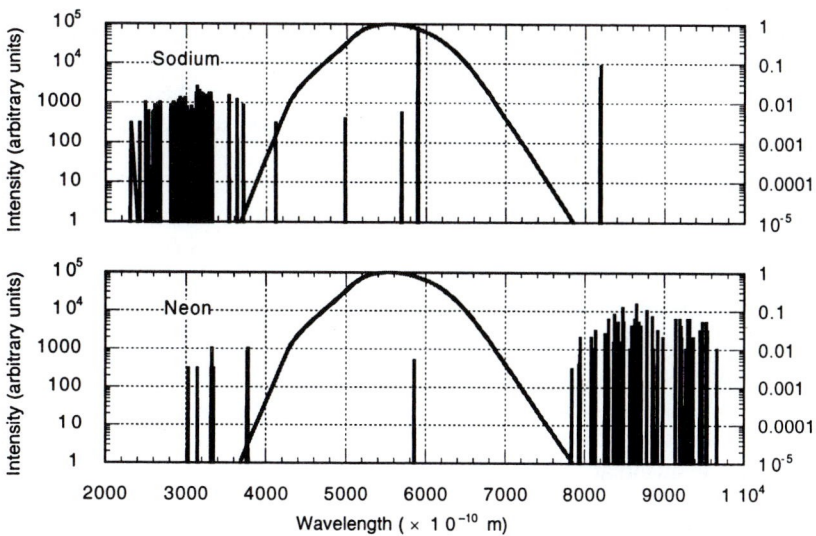

of these states of the molecule is similar, but slightly different. Let us assume for the moment that the molecules within the positive column are predominantly electrically neutral. These molecules are being continually bombarded by (a) other molecules as in a non-conducting gas, and (b) by ions and electrons with energies ranging up to the ionisation energy of the molecules.

Taking the analogy of a mechanical object, this high-energy bombardment sets a molecule 'ringing' at its natural resonant frequencies. In the same way, striking a bell sets it oscillating in characteristic patterns. Importantly, the resonant frequencies of a bell and the sound it produces are more characteristic of the size, shape and mass of the bell than they are of the way it was struck. Similarly, the molecules in a discharge tube oscillate in a characteristic manner, with characteristic frequencies depending on their internal electronic structure. These frequencies and their relative amplitudes depend more on the structure of the molecules than on the nature of what is exciting them. The oscillation of charge density within the molecules causes radiation of energy according to Equation 5.126. The radiated power is proportional to the magnitude of the oscillating dipole moment p. If the resonant vibration of the charge within the atom is large, then the oscillating dipole moment p also becomes resonantly large, and the radiated power at that frequency is intense.

As mentioned in §2.4, quantum mechanically the phenomenon of resonance is described as a transition between quantum states. Thus in the correct quantum mechanical description, a resonance of frequency f_o is described in terms of the emission or absorption of quanta of radiation with energy $E = hf_o$. Thus the frequencies of light (the colours) emitted from the positive column of a discharge tube are the characteristic frequencies of the oscillation of electric charge within the molecules of the gas.

5.9 Magnetic Properties.

Gases in general have subtle magnetic properties, which may for many purposes be ignored, i.e. the magnetic permeability of the gas is very close to unity. However in detailed studies of the emission spectra (see above) of gases in magnetic fields it was observed that under the action of a strong applied magnetic field, some of the lines in the spectrum of light from a gas could either change their position, or split into several lines. The observation and explanation of this *Zeeman effect* historically proved important in attempts to understand atomic structure.

5.10 Exercises

Exercises marked with a P prefix are 'normal' exercises. Those marked with a C prefix are best solved numerically by using a computer program or spreadsheet. Exercises marked with an E prefix are in general rather more challenging that the P and C exercises. Answers to all the exercises are downloadable from www.physicsofmatter.com

P1. Of the properties of gases listed below, which properties do not depend strongly on the microscopic properties of gas molecules other than their mass?

(a) Thermal conductivity (§ 5.4)

(b) Heat capacity at constant volume (§ 5.3)

(c) Heat capacity at constant pressure (§ 5.3)

(d) Density (§ 5.2)

(e) Thermal Expansivity (§ 5.2)

(f) Speed of Sound (§ 5.5)

(g) Dielectric Constant (§ 5.6)

(h) Refractive Index (§ 5.7)

(i) Emission Spectrum (§ 5.7)

Density and expansivity

P2. What is the approximate volume of 1 mole of any gas (a) at STP and (b) at room temperature and pressure? Work out the volume of the room you are in *now*:

Considering air to be made of 80% nitrogen and 20% oxygen (Table 5.2) approximately how many moles of oxygen and nitrogen are in the room? What is the mass of the air? If all the air were condensed into a solid, what volume would it occupy (Table 5.2 and Table 7.2)?

P3. Air held in a fixed volume of 1 litre has a pressure of 0.1333 MPa and a temperature of 0 °C. What is the mass of air in the container and what is the expected pressure at 100 °C (§ 5.2.2)?

P4. Compare the experimental results on the pressure coefficient β_P (Table 5.4) with those of a theory of your own devising. What is the relationship between the deviations from theory of the pressure and volume coefficients (Table 5.5)?

E5. The cylinder of a petrol engine initially contains approximately 10^{-3} mole of gas in a volume of 60 cm³ at a temperature of around 200 °C. During the subsequent explosion, the gas pressure peaks at approximately 3×10^5 Pa before the cylinder expands adiabatically to a volume of 240 cm³.

(a) What is the initial pressure of the gas (§ 5.2.3)?

(b) What is the peak force on the piston if its diameter is 5 cm?

(c) What is the peak temperature of the gas (§ 5.2.3)?

(d) Assuming the gas obeys:

$$PV^\gamma = \text{constant}$$

throughout the expansion, with $\gamma = 1.3$, estimate the pressure and temperature at the end of the expansion.

P6. Objects float if their *average* density is less than the density of the fluid in which they are immersed. A balloon of mass 10 g is made of a material with negligible wall thickness which does not stretch under pressure (a fair approximation for the plastic *Mylar*). It is filled with helium gas at 0°C and 1.1×10^5 Pa until it just floats in air at STP. (a) What is the volume of the balloon? (You should find that the volume of the balloon (expressed in m³) is very roughly the same as the total load on the balloon (expressed in kg). (b) What volume must the balloon have if it is to lift the weight of an adult human being, say 70 kg? (c) If the balloon just floats at STP, will it float or sink if the temperature is increased to room temperature? (Assume the volume of the balloon stays constant.)

P7. A solid object of density 2000 kg m⁻³ is weighed on a simple balance against weights of density 8000 kg m⁻³. (a) Derive an expression for the buoyancy (uplift) force on both the object and the weights if the measurement is carried out in air at room temperature and normal atmospheric pressure. (§5.2 and Tables 5.1 & 5.2). (b) Use the answer to (a) to show that no balance can be read with an accuracy greater than around 1 part in 10^4 unless the relative densities of the weights

and the object being weighed are considered.

P8. Approximately how many moles of gas are there in the Earth's atmosphere? What is the mass of this gas? Assume that: (i) the atmosphere exists at a uniform pressure of around half the normal atmospheric pressure at sea level; (ii) the average temperature is around 0 °C; (iii) that the atmosphere exists only up to a height of 10 km and (iv) that the atmosphere has the same composition as given in Table 5.2. The radius of the Earth is approximately 6400 km.

Assuming that the atmosphere has the same composition as given in Table 5.2, estimate the mass of CO_2 in the atmosphere. If the concentration of CO_2 increases by 1% each year, what mass of carbon joins the atmosphere each year? (§5.2.3). **Note:** The concentration of CO_2 in the atmosphere reflects the balance between processes which produce CO_2 (e.g. animals breathing, fuel-burning) and processes which remove CO_2 (e.g. rain, plant-growth). Understanding the actual concentrations is rather complex.

Heat capacity

P9. What is the molar heat capacity at constant pressure of (a) argon at 2000 K, (b) oxygen at –73.15 °C, (c) oxygen at 1000 K? (Tables 5.6 & 5.7)

P10. What is the molar heat capacity at constant pressure of the three major components of air (Table 5.2) at around room temperature? (Tables 5.6 & 5.7)

P11. At around room temperature and pressure, what is the value of γ (the ratio of the heat capacity at constant pressure to the heat capacity at constant volume), for (a) oxygen, (b) nitrogen (c) argon (d) carbon dioxide and (e) air. (Table 5.8). For each gas work out the number of degrees of freedom per molecule according to Equation 5.44 and compare your calculated values with mine in Table 5.9. To what extent is it fair to assume that, with regard to thermal properties, air behaves similarly to nitrogen?

P12. What is the ratio of the principal heat capacities γ for (a) helium at 0 °C, (b) mercury vapour at 0 °C, (c) krypton at 20 °C, (d) air at 500 °C, (e) steam at 100 °C, (f) methane and (g) ethane (Table 5.8)?

For each gas estimate the number of degrees of freedom of molecules of the gas according to Equation 5.44 and write a paragraph suggesting the molecular motions to which these degrees of freedom might correspond.(Tables 5.8 & 5.9)

P13. (a) What is the *heat capacity per kilogram* (at constant pressure) of argon gas at STP? Is it greater than or less than the *heat capacity per kilogram* of helium? (b) What is the heat capacity per cubic metre (at constant pressure) of argon gas at STP? Is it greater than or less than the heat capacity per cubic metre of helium?

P14. The room in which I am writing this question is approximately 3m × 4m × 5m in size. Assuming that no heat is lost through the walls or my newly double-glazed windows, estimate how long I will have to run a 1 kW fan heater if I am to raise the air temperature in the room from 8 °C to 25 °C? (Tables 5.2, 5.8 & Question P2 above)

Do this experiment in your own room and compare the results of your experiment with your calculation. Based on the results of your experiment, state to what extent the heat in a room is stored in the air, and to what extent it is stored in a thin layer of plaster on the inside of the walls.

P15. From analysis of the variation with temperature of the heat capacity of oxygen, the text estimates that oxygen molecules vibrate with a frequency of around $f_o = 4.2 \times 10^{13}$ Hz. Following a similar method, estimate the vibrational frequencies of (a) hydrogen (H_2) and (b) chlorine (Cl_2) (Table 5.7, Figure 5.4). By considering the relative mass of hydrogen, oxygen and chlorine atoms, estimate the effective 'spring constant' K for each type of molecular bond (Equation 2.24 and Example 2.4).

Note: as discussed following Example 2.4 and Question P9 of Chapter 2, the correct mass to use in Equation 2.24 is actually the so-called *reduced mass*. However, since this calculation is 'order of magnitude' only, this does not affect our general conclusions.

P16. Following on from Question P8, estimate the heat capacity at constant pressure of the Earth's atmosphere.

Expansions and contractions

P17. Following on from the statement in §5.4.4 that:

$$PV^\gamma = \text{constant}$$

during an adiabatic volume change, show that it is also true that:

$$TV^{\gamma-1} = \text{another constant}$$

during an adiabatic volume change.

C18. To appreciate the distinctions between isothermal and adiabatic expansions try the following computer exercise. (a) For a given amount of gas, use a spreadsheet to evaluate P as a function of V for a range of different values of γ for both adiabatic and isothermal expansions. (b) Plot a graph of both (i) P as a function of V and (ii) T as a function of V for both adiabatic and isothermal expansions.

P19. If the 10 cc of air at atmospheric pressure in a bicycle pump are adiabatically compressed to 2.5 cc, work out the expected pressure and temperature of the gas. If you have a bicycle pump, see if the compression ratio of four that I have suggested above is about right and check whether the air really does get this hot.

Thermal conductivity

C20. Plot the thermal conductivity at 100 °C of the noble gases (Table 5.11) as a function of molecular mass, m. By re-plotting the data as a function of $m^{-1/2}$, discuss to what extent the data agree with the theory summarised in Example 5.9. Now repeat the analysis for diatomic gases in Table 5.11 at both 0 °C and 100 °C: do the same general conclusions apply?

C21. From www.physicsofmatter.com you can download a small program illustrating the dynamics of molecules in 2-dimensions. In the 'help' section of the demo are some suggestions for phenomena you might like to observe. In particular you should set the program going with the option to plot molecular trajectories ON and MOLECULAR INTERACTIONS switched ON. You should look carefully to see if you can observe the 'orbiting collisions' referred to at the end of Chapter 4.

P22. Estimate the mean free path λ_{mfp} of helium molecules at a pressure of 1 Pa based on the molecular size data of Table 5.13. If the gas is contained in a region where the walls are separated by a distance of 1 mm, will the gas still be in the plateau region of thermal conductivity, or will the thermal conductivity have begun to decrease? (Figure 5.18).

P23. A *Pirani gauge* is a device to measure the pressure of a gas at low pressures. The device consists of a heated filament which is cooled by the gas. In the pressure range where the thermal conductivity of the gas changes with pressure, the temperature of the filament varies with gas pressure. Thus, after calibration, measurement of the temperature of the filament by a thermocouple or resistance thermometer (Chapter 2) allows determination of the pressure. By considering Figure 5.18 and Equation 5.85, estimate the size of the container in which the element should be suspended if the device works only at pressures below 100 Pa.

P24. A cubic container of volume 1 m³ is heated from the bottom such that air at the bottom is approximately 10 °C hotter than air at the top (Figure 5.13). (a) If the box is at a temperature around room temperature and at normal atmospheric pressure, approximately how many moles of gas are in the box? (b) Convection lifts 0.1 mole per second of air from the bottom to the top. Estimate the heat flow across the container due to convection? Is it greater or less than would be expected due to the 'still air' thermal conductivity listed in Table 5.11 alone?

C25. Table 5.12 shows the reduction of the effective diameter a of monatomic gas molecules as the temperature is increased. Plot a graph of a^2 versus $1/T$. You should see straight-line behaviour, a phenomenon noted by Sutherland. From the $1/T = 0$ intercept (i.e. corresponding to $T = \infty$), estimate the high-temperature 'hard core' diameter of an argon atom.

Analyse the data for the thermal conductivity of a diatomic gas (e.g. N_2) in same way as the text analyses the thermal conductivity of the monatomic gases. Does this analysis support or contradict the conclusions that the text draws from the analysis of the monatomic gas data?

Speed of sound

P26. What is the speed of sound in (a) helium and (b) deuterium at STP? What conclusion can be drawn from the difference between these results? (Table 5.14)

P27. What is the speed of sound in dry air at STP? (§5.6.1) What value would you expect for the speed of sound in air at normal room temperature (approximately 20 °C)? (Equation 5.93 and Example 5.11).

P28. During a thunderstorm, you observe that a lightning flash and the start of a peel of thunder are separated by t seconds. By considering the likely speed of sound in the atmosphere (§5.6.1 and Equation 5.93), derive a rule of thumb for estimating the distance of a lightning strike (in kilometres), based on a measurement of t.

E29. A siren in a flat region of England emits sound waves upwards and outwards in a hemispherical pattern. If the speed of sound were constant, the wave-fronts would form concentric hemispheres centred on the siren. However the speed of sound falls with decreasing temperature, and since the atmosphere becomes progressively colder with increasing altitude, the wave-fronts become distorted. Sketch the wave-fronts for (a) the normal situation and (b) the rare occasion (known as a *temperature inversion*) when warm air is trapped above colder air. In (b) show graphically how sound can be 'focussed' back onto the ground at large distances from the siren.

[**Aside**: Its interesting that the fall in pressure with height in the atmosphere does not affect this problem to first order, but look at Chapter 12: Q6 to discover the link between the decline in pressure with altitude and the decline in temperature.]

P30. You may have learned in your school years that 'sound cannot travel in a vacuum'. This is certainly true, but interestingly Equation 5.93 for the speed of sound has no explicit dependence on pressure. So consider a chamber into which a loud speaker is emitting a continuous tone. Write a short discussion of what will happen to the sound wave as the air is removed.

P31. If a volcano explosion near Australia were loud enough to be heard in England, roughly how long after the explosion would it be heard? (§5.6.1) If, instead, seismometers were used to detect the sound waves that travelled directly through the earth, estimate very roughly (Table 7.9) when the explosion would be detected. The radius of the Earth is 6,400 km

P32. Could a device be built which would measure the temperature of the air by measuring the speed of sound through it (§5.6)? If you did build such a device, what problems would you expect to have? What frequency of sound would you choose if the device were to be portable?

E33. A *flame* is a region of very hot gas (typically in the range 1500 °C to 2000 °C) that occurs close to exothermic chemical reactions. Determining the temperature of flames is important for optimising the combustion process, i.e. reducing unwanted combustion products and maximising energy output. However determining the temperature accurately is very difficult by conventional means. One way is to measure the speed of sound through a small region of the flame. An intense laser heats a small region of the gas rapidly. A pressure pulse (sound wave) moves away from the heated region and the change in refractive index a short distance away is measured by the effect on a second pulse beam. By measuring the time delay between the laser pulse and the effect on the probe beam the speed of sound can be determined. By considering Equation 5.93, estimate the uncertainty with which the temperature can be determined given a plausible level of uncertainty in (a) knowledge of the molecules present in the flame and (b) the change of γ with temperature.

P34. In Chapter 12 Question 7 you are asked to show that the magnitude of the temperature oscillations, ΔT, in a sound wave in a gas at temperature T and pressure P is given by:

$$\frac{\Delta T}{T} = \left(1 - \frac{1}{\gamma}\right)\frac{\Delta P}{P}$$

where ΔP is the magnitude of the pressure oscillations in the sound wave. For a sound wave in air with a pressure amplitude of 0.2 Pa estimate the magnitude of the temperature oscillations. How could you imagine measuring such oscillations? [Aside: if a sound wave has this amplitude is said to have a sound pressure level in decibels of 80 db. At a frequency of around 1 kHz, sound waves of this amplitude would be subjectively experienced as very loud — equivalent to standing near a road as a lorry passes by]

P35. Based on the speed of sound in air at STP (§5.6.1) estimate the root mean square (RMS) speed of molecules in air at STP according to Equation 5.99. How does this estimate compare with the one derived from the Maxwell speed distribution for nitrogen at 0 °C. (Table 5.8, Question C3 in §4.5).

P36. Describe, with the aid of labelled sketches, an apparatus that could be used to determine γ for gases at a range of temperatures by measuring the speed of sound in the gas. In analysis of your results, how would you separate out the $T^{1/2}$ dependence of the speed of

sound from the variations of γ with temperature? (Equation 5.93)

P37. We saw in §5.6.2 that the compressions and expansions in sound waves are always adiabatic. This is because the thermal conductivity of gases is so poor that the hotter (high-pressure) and colder (low-pressure) regions cannot communicate over a distance of half a wavelength, in the half-period before the wave reverses phase. If we wanted to observe a hypothetical isothermal sound wave, should we try moving to very low frequencies, or very high frequencies?

Electrical properties

P38. A parallel-plate capacitor of plate area $A = 1$ cm^2 and plate separation $d = 1$ mm has a capacitance of $C = \varepsilon\varepsilon_0 A/d$. Work out the capacitance if there is a vacuum between the two plates. What would be the percentage change in the capacitance if the space between the two plates was filled with (a) air at STP (b) CO_2 at STP (c) CO_2 at 1 atmosphere and 100 °C and (d) CO_2 at 100 atmospheres and 100 °C. (Table 5.16, Figure 5.25)

P39. What is the dielectric constant of (a) helium, (b) neon (c) argon and (d) nitrogen at STP? (Table 5.16) Use Equation 5.109 to estimate the polarisability of a single molecule of the each of the gases (a) to (d). State which molecule is the least polarisable, and which the most, and briefly suggest the features of each kind of atom which determine its polarisability (Figure 5.24).

P40. What is the dielectric constant of water (steam) at 100 °C (Table 5.16) Use Equation 5.116 to estimate the size of the permanent dipole moment on a water molecule in Debye units.

P41. What is the approximate breakdown field of air around room temperature and atmospheric pressure (Figure 5.28)?

P42. Around high voltage apparatus such as *Van der Graaf* generators, electrical breakdown may be prevented by enclosing the entire apparatus in an atmosphere of sulphur hexafluoride gas (SF_6). Given that the device must operate at around room temperature, should the gas be at high or low pressure (Figure 5.28)? What is the maximum conceivable breakdown field for the gas?

Optical properties

P43. What are (i) the refractive index and (ii) the speed of light, in (a) a vacuum (b) air at STP (c) helium at STP and (d) xenon at STP.(Table 5.18)?

P44. What is the ratio of the wavelength of light to the approximate diameter of an argon atom (Table 5.13 and Figure 5.32)?

P45. Equations 5.117 and 5.118 predict that at constant temperature, the difference of the dielectric constant of a gas from unity ($\varepsilon - 1$) is proportional to pressure. By considering Equation 2.17, show that as long as $(\varepsilon - 1) \ll 1$, the difference between the refractive index of a gas and unity is also proportional to pressure.

P46. What is the wavelength of (yellow) light with a frequency of 5.09×10^{14} Hz (a) in a vacuum and (b) in air at STP (0 °C and 1.013×10^5 Pa). As you may have shown in the previous question, the difference of the refractive index of a gas from unity is proportional to pressure. (c) Use the answers to part (a) and (b) to estimate the wavelength of the light in air at 0 °C and 1.023×10^5 Pa. (Table 5.18)

Why is the above calculation relevant? Before it reaches us, light from stars passes through the atmosphere, which is not quite uniform. The pressure of the air fluctuates slightly over a time scale of a few seconds, and differs slightly above neighbouring points on the ground. Show with the aid of a sketch how this effect can lead to distortions of the initially parallel wavefronts from a distant star. Explain how this leads to the 'twinkling' of stars when observed from the ground.

P47. A star is observed through a ground-based telescope to be at an angle of 45° above the horizon. Taking account of the refraction by the Earth's atmosphere, estimate the actual angle above the horizon.

P48. Figure 3.8 shows the use of an optical interferometer to determine the refractive index of light in a gas. Initially the sample arm of the apparatus is at vacuum. For a path length in the gas of 50 cm and yellow light with a frequency of 5.09×10^{14} Hz, calculate the pressure of helium gas required to produce a single wavelength phase shift between the two beams. (See also problem P11 in Chapter 3)

P49. The intensity, I, of a light beam is reduced (due to scattering) as it travels a distance x through the atmosphere according to $I = I_0 \exp(-x/\lambda)$. Derive an order of magnitude estimate of λ for air under typical conditions based on your own observations of the atmosphere.

P50. Figure 5.37 shows the emission spectra of sodium and neon. Both spectra have emission peaks in the range 580 nm to 590 nm, close to the peak sensitivity of the human eye. Taking note of the logarithmic scale, explain why an electrical discharge through sodium vapour appears yellow and through neon appears red.

P51. Estimate the refractive index of water vapour at STP by extrapolation from the refractive index of liquid water. How accurate is your estimate? (Table 5.18, §9.13 and Table 9.21)

Solids: background theory

6.1 Introduction

We envisage a solid as a collection of atoms whose *average* positions are fixed with respect to one another. When we studied the properties of gases we essentially ignored the potential energy of interaction of the atoms, but in solids we cannot do this: solids exist *because* of the potential energy of interaction between atoms. The atoms of a solid can vibrate about their average position, but can only exceptionally change their position with respect to their neighbours. This picture will probably be familiar to you, but just in case it is not, Figure 6.1 illustrates how we imagine the motion of the atoms in a solid.

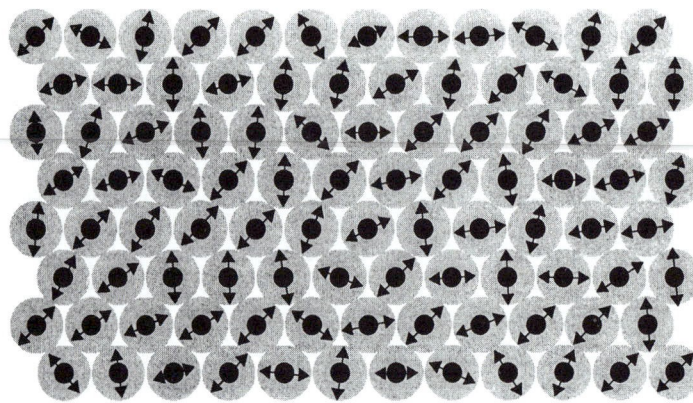

Figure 6.1 An illustration of the motion of atoms in a solid. The arrows indicate the direction of atomic motion. Notice the small separation between the atoms and the random orientation of their vibrations. The atoms themselves are shown as a central darkly-shaded region, where the electron charge density is high, and a peripheral lightly-shaded region. The electric field in this peripheral region significantly affects the motion of neighbouring atoms, and disturbs the electronic charge density of neighbouring atoms.

When we discussed the properties of gases we were able to arrive at the theory of a 'ideal gas', which for many purposes was a good approximation to the properties of real gases. Solids, however have many fewer properties that can be explained in terms of a theory of an 'ideal solid'. The diversity of properties exhibited by solids calls for us to make *several* simple models to serve as starting points for attempts to understand the behaviour of real solids. Despite the diversity in the properties of solids, it is important to realise that in all the materials, the only force acting between atoms is the electrostatic coulomb force. The coulomb force, coupled with the different configurations of electrons in the outer parts of the 100 or so different types of atoms, is sufficient to produce solids with the diversity that you find around you. In this chapter, we will discuss four simplified models solids which represent idealised categories. However, most real solids do not fall neatly into one category or another. Our hope is that by looking at a few (rather rare) 'simple solids' which do fit this categorisation scheme, we will be able to shed light on what is happening in more common, but more complex, solids.

At www.physicsofmatter.com

In addition to copies of the figures and tables you will find: animations of some of the important equations in this chapter; a computer program which realistically simulates the dynamics of simple molecules in solids, liquids and gases; and Chapter W1 on the *band theory of solids*, which extends some of the topics dealt with in this chapter.

The four simple models of solids which we discuss in §6.2 to §6.5 are illustrated in Figure 6.2. As this figure indicates, it is the arrangement of the outer (valence) electrons on atoms in a solid that is the basis of our categorisation. The interaction of valence electrons with neighbouring atoms is responsible for *bonding* atoms together into a solid, and the four models correspond to four, relatively distinct, bonding mechanisms between atoms.

6.2 Molecular solids

6.2.1 General description

In molecular solids, the electronic structure of the atoms or molecules that make up the solid is the same (or similar to) the electronic structure of the atoms or molecules which move around independently in the gas. The solid is held together by the weak interactions that take place between all molecules, exactly the same interactions which we ignored when we considered such molecules in the gaseous state. This kind of solid is formed when the molecules that make up the gas are chemically stable enough that the outer electrons of each molecule stay with their 'parent' molecule when they form a solid.

The types of substance in which molecular bonding plays a key role are:
- the noble 'gases', i.e. the same gases which are such fine exemplars of the ideal gas law also make fine molecular solids
- the halogen molecules, i.e. F_2, Cl_2, Br_2 and I_2
- many long chain polymer molecules, such as polyethylene or polyvinyl chloride.

Two important factors affect the properties of solids made from these molecules: the *shape* of the molecules, and the *strength* of the interaction between the molecules. In this section, we will look quantitatively at the effect of the strength of the interaction on the properties of simply shaped molecules. The effects of molecular shape are discussed further in §6.6.1 on organic solids, §7.2 on the thermal expansivity of plastics and §8.4.4 on the properties of organic liquids.

6.2.2 Attractive and repulsive forces between neutral molecules

The attractive force between neutral molecules

The origin of the attraction

The distribution of electric charge around molecules in a molecular solid is broadly unchanged from the distribution when the molecules are in the gaseous state. In particular each molecule is

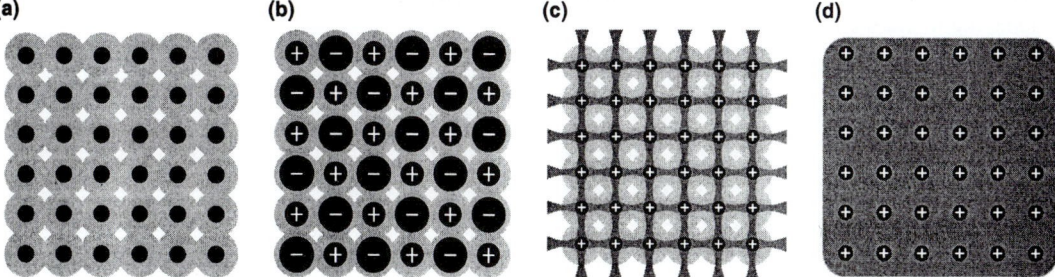

Figure 6.2 The four types of simple solid discussed in this chapter. (a) Molecular solids in which the entities which make up the solid (atoms or molecules) are essentially the same as the entities which made up the gas. (b) Ionic solids in which the entities that make up the solid are ions rather than atoms or molecules. Electrons from the outer part of one atom have moved *wholly* to another atom. (c) Covalent solids in which the entities that make up the solid (atoms or molecules) are greatly altered from their state in the gas. Electrons from the outer part of one atom have changed their 'orbits' so that they now move round more than one atom. This leads to a high electronic charge density in regions *in between* the mean positions of the atoms. (d) Metallic solids in which the electrons from the outer parts of the atoms can move anywhere within the solid and are not attached to any individual atom.

(a) **(b)** **(c)** **(d)**

electrically neutral. So what holds the molecules together? The force which holds the molecules together is the Coulomb force, but the action of the force is subtle. The attraction between molecules arises not because each molecule has a net charge, but because the distribution of electrons around each molecule *fluctuates*. Consider a series of imagined snapshots of the electronic distribution around a single atom. (Figure 6.3)

Figure 6.3 A representation of the fluctuations of charge density around a neutral atom. The figure shows the charge distribution at three times separated by $\approx 10^{-16}$ second.

(a) $t = 0$ **(b)** $t = 1 \times 10^{-16}$ s **(c)** $t = 2 \times 10^{-16}$ s

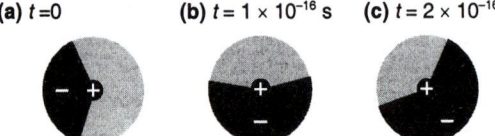

(d) Time-averaged charge distribution

Averaged over a time greater than a *few* $\times 10^{-16}$ s, the charge distribution is symmetrical (Figure 6.3(d)). However, on a shorter time scale, the charge distribution fluctuates and is in general slightly 'imbalanced'. This means that the atom behaves as a tiny *electric dipole*, the direction of which is constantly changing. An electric dipole has a weak electric field around it that can affect other atoms nearby (§2.3.2), and it is through the action of this field that bonding, sometimes known as *Van der Waals bonding*, takes place.

Rough calculation

Suppose that at a particular instant the charge distribution is asymmetrical such that an atom has an electric dipole p. As we mentioned in §2.3.2, the electric field due to p is given approximately by:

$$E(r) \approx \frac{p}{4\pi\varepsilon_0 r^3} \qquad (6.1)$$

A second atom placed in this field becomes electrically polarised by an amount that is proportional to the magnitude of the electric field. (See §5.7.2 on gases.) The electric dipole moment *induced* on the second atom, p_2, will be given by:

Figure 6.4 Fluctuations of the charge-density distribution on atom 1 lead to a temporary electric dipole moment. The electric field from the electric dipole moment *induces* a dipole moment on neighbouring atoms, causing the two atoms to be attracted to one another.

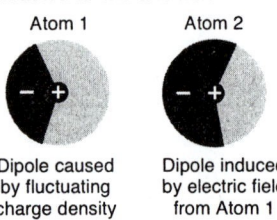

Atom 1   Atom 2

Dipole caused by fluctuating charge density   Dipole induced by electric field from Atom 1

$$p_2 = \alpha E(r) \qquad (6.2)$$

where α is the *molecular polarisability* of atom 2 (Figure 6.4). The second atom will have an energy of interaction u with the first atom given by:

$$u = -p_2 E(r) \qquad (6.3)$$

We now substitute for p_2 using Equation 6.2 and $E(r)$ using Equation 6.1 to yield:

$$
\begin{aligned}
u &\approx -\alpha E(r) E(r) \\
&\approx -\left[\alpha \frac{1}{r^3}\right]\frac{1}{r^3} \qquad (6.4)\\
&\approx -\frac{\alpha}{r^6}
\end{aligned}
$$

which predicts that the energy of interaction between the two atoms therefore varies as $1/r^6$, and is proportional to the molecular polarisability α of the atoms involved. The attractive energy varies with distance more rapidly than the $1/r$ variation that occurs between uncompensated charges, which means that the interactions of this type are relatively short-range. As we saw in §5.7.2, the polarisability of atoms and molecules is generally rather small, and so the energy of interactions is also rather low.

The repulsive force between neutral molecules

The attractive force described above cannot be the only term involved in the interaction between two neutral atoms. If this were so the energy would become more negative without limit as the atoms came closer. There must be another term in the

147

energy which increases as the separation between the atoms gets smaller.

The origin of the repulsion

The repulsion arises because as the atoms get closer, the outer electrons on each atom come close together. The processes that take place as atoms approach each other closely are complex, but we can identify two separate ways in which bringing atoms closer together costs energy.

- First, the outer electrons of one atom have to attempt to occupy orbitals around the other atom. The lowest-energy orbitals are all occupied and so the Pauli exclusion principle forces electrons to occupy higher-energy orbitals.
- Second, when the electrons on the outer part of each atom get very close they begin to repel each other directly through their coulomb interaction.

There is no simple direct way to derive the variation of the repulsion with distance, but two approximate forms are commonly used that capture some of the behaviour of real solids. It is sometimes assumed that the repulsive energy varies as either:

$$u \approx +\frac{\text{constant}}{r^{12}}$$

or as:

$$u \approx +\text{constant} \times e^{-r/\rho} \qquad (6.5)$$

where ρ is a 'range parameter'. We will choose the first of these alternative forms because it is mathematically easier to manipulate.

6.2.3 Pair potential: the Lennard-Jones potential

We can combine the attractive and repulsive terms (Equations 6.4 and 6.5) into an expression for the potential energy of a pair of interacting neutral atoms:

$$u_{\text{pair}}(r) = -\frac{A}{r^6} + \frac{B}{r^{12}} \qquad (6.6)$$

where A and B are constants that determine the relative size of the attractive and repulsive terms. Because it describes the interaction of just two

Figure 6.5 The potential energy versus separation of two atoms interacting via a Lennard-Jones potential. The energy scale is drawn in units of ε and the separation scale is drawn in units of σ where ε and σ are defined according to Equation 6.8.

(a) The relationship between σ and the representation of a molecule shown in Figure 6.1. The steeply rising potential makes the atom behave as if it has a hard core. The shallow minimum gives rise to a region which is weakly attractive to other atoms.

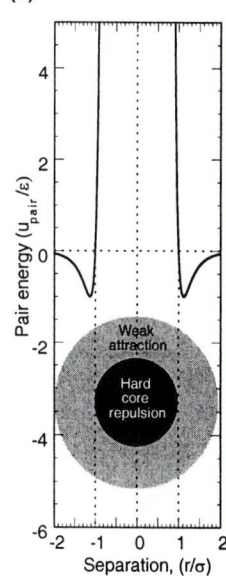

(b) The Lennard-Jones pair potential. Notice the shallowness of minimum in the potential energy,

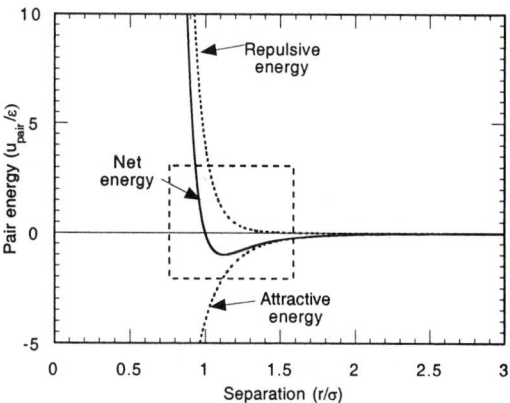

(c) Detail from the rectangle in (b) showing that the minimum occurs at $r = 1.12\sigma$ and $U = -\varepsilon$

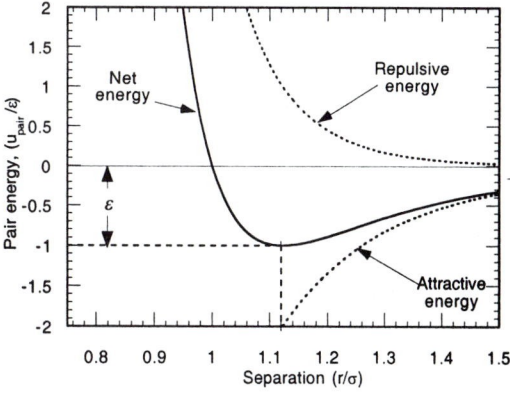

atoms, expressions such as Equation 6.6 are known as *pair potentials*. This particular form of pair potential (with powers of '12' and '6') was discovered by Professor Lennard-Jones to be particularly appropriate to molecular solids and so is called a *Lennard-Jones* pair potential.

The Lennard-Jones potential is often rearranged into the form:

$$u_{pair}(r) = -4\varepsilon \left\{ \left[\frac{\sigma}{r} \right]^6 - \left[\frac{\sigma}{r} \right]^{12} \right\} \qquad (6.7)$$

where:

$$\sigma = \left[\frac{B}{A} \right]^{1/6} \quad \text{and} \quad \varepsilon = \left[\frac{A^2}{4B} \right] \qquad (6.8)$$

Although Equation 6.7 looks more complicated than Equation 6.6, it has the advantage that the parameters σ and ε have a clear physical interpretation in terms of the form of the $u_{pair}(r)$ (see Figure 6.5)

- σ is a *range* parameter and indicates the approximate 'size' of an atom. At $r = \sigma$ the value of u_{pair} is zero.
- ε is an *energy* parameter and indicates the *strength* of the interaction between atoms. At the minimum of the $u_{pair}(r)$ curve u_{pair} has the value $-\varepsilon$.

It is important to note that the interactions between molecules described above take place in the solid state *and in the gaseous state*. In the gaseous state, the most important feature is the strong repulsion that makes atoms which collide with one another behave as if they are hard spheres with radius of around 0.8σ (Figure 6.5). After extensive analysis we were just able to detect the effect of the attractive part of intermolecular interactions in §5.5.2 on the thermal conductivity of gases. In the solid state, the key feature of the pair potential is the shallow minimum. Molecules try to achieve positions relative to other molecules that allow them to sit as close to this minimum as possible.

6.2.4 Calculation of cohesive energy

In this section we will calculate the electrostatic energy of one mole of molecules which interact with each other through the Lennard-Jones pair potential. This quantity is known as the *cohesive energy U* of a substance and is generally measured of kJ mol^{-1} or eV per molecule.

We will assume that the molecules are arranged in a regular crystal structure, and in §6.1.4 we shall work out which crystal structure the molecules would choose if they were to maximise their cohesive energy.

Calculation: Stage 1

To begin, we consider a particular molecule i surrounded by all the other molecules j in the crystal. We write its energy u_i as:

$$u_i = u_{pair}(r_{i1}) + u_{pair}(r_{i2}) + \dots [\text{not } u_{pair}(r_{ii})]$$
$$\dots + u_{pair}(r_{ij}) + \dots + u_{pair}(r_{iN_A})$$

$$u_i = \sum_{j \neq i}^{N_A} u_{pair}(r_{ij})$$

$$(6.9)$$

where r_{ij} is the distance between the ith molecule and each other molecule j in the crystal. The energy for N_A molecules in one mole of the solid is then given by:

$$U = \frac{N_A u_i}{2} \qquad (6.10)$$

Notice the factor $\frac{1}{2}$ which arises because the energy u_i is the sum of the electrostatic energy of *pairs* of molecules, and we wish to calculate the energy per *individual* molecule. Remembering the form of the Lennard-Jones potential, (Equation 6.7) we can then write:

$$U = -\frac{N_A}{2} \sum_{j \neq i} 4\varepsilon \left[\left(\frac{\sigma}{r_{ij}} \right)^6 - \left(\frac{\sigma}{r_{ij}} \right)^{12} \right] \qquad (6.11)$$

Calculation: Stage 2: A trick

Now we use a mathematical trick. We write the distance between the ith and j^{th} atoms as a multiple of the nearest neighbour distance r_o (as yet unknown):

$$r_{ij} = \alpha_{ij} r_o \qquad (6.12)$$

Note α_{ij} is a just a number, not a distance. So, for example, for one pair of atoms, say $i = 1$ and $j = 4$, α_{ij} might take the value 2.314. This means that the distance from atom 1 to atom 4 is 2.314 times the distance r_0. We can now rewrite our expression for U using this substitution:

$$U = -2\varepsilon N_A \sum_{j \neq i} \left[\left(\frac{1}{\alpha_{ij}} \right)^6 \left(\frac{\sigma}{r_0} \right)^6 - \left(\frac{1}{\alpha_{ij}} \right)^{12} \left(\frac{\sigma}{r_0} \right)^{12} \right]$$

(6.13)

We can then separate the summation into two terms:

$$U = -2\varepsilon N_A \sum_{j \neq i} \left[\left(\frac{1}{\alpha_{ij}} \right)^6 \left(\frac{\sigma}{r_0} \right)^6 \right]$$
$$+ 2\varepsilon N_A \sum_{j \neq i} \left[\left(\frac{1}{\alpha_{ij}} \right)^{12} \left(\frac{\sigma}{r_0} \right)^{12} \right]$$

(6.14)

Notice that the fraction σ / r_0 does not depend on the index j in either summation. Hence, it may be brought outside the summation sign since it is a common factor to each term in the sum:

$$U = -2\varepsilon N_A \left(\frac{\sigma}{r_0} \right)^6 \sum_{j \neq i} \left[\left(\frac{1}{\alpha_{ij}} \right)^6 \right]$$
$$+ 2\varepsilon N_A \left(\frac{\sigma}{r_0} \right)^{12} \sum_{j \neq i} \left[\left(\frac{1}{\alpha_{ij}} \right)^{12} \right]$$

(6.15)

Each of the two terms in Equation 6.15 now has two parts, a term in σ / r_0 and a quantity in square brackets known as a *lattice sum*. The lattice sums are referred to as A_6 and A_{12} respectively.

$$A_6 = \sum_{j \neq i} \left[\left(\frac{1}{\alpha_{ij}} \right)^6 \right] \qquad A_{12} = \sum_{j \neq i} \left[\left(\frac{1}{\alpha_{ij}} \right)^{12} \right] \quad (6.16)$$

On substituting for A_6 and A_{12}, the expression for the cohesive energy begins to look a little more tractable:

Example 6.1

Calculate the lattice sum A_{12} for the face-centred cubic lattice.

The lattice sum A_{12} is defined according to Equation 6.16 as:

$$A_{12} = \sum_{j \neq i} \frac{1}{\alpha_{ij}^{12}}$$

where α is the 'multiplier' of the nearest-neighbour distance required to reach a particular atom j from a chosen atom i. The figure shows a central atom i and the distance to several neighbouring atoms.

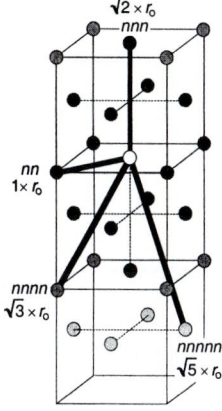

- Each nearest neighbour has a multiplier distance of 1 ($\times r_0$) and there are 12 such atoms (labelled *nn* in the figure).
- Each next-nearest neighbour has a multiplier distance of $\sqrt{2}$ ($\times r_0$) and there are 6 such atoms (labelled *nnn* in the figure).
- Each next next-nearest neighbour has a multiplier distance of $\sqrt{3}$ ($\times r_0$) and there are 24 such atoms (labelled *nnnn* in the figure).

Proceeding to successively more distant atoms we see that the expression for the lattice sum is given by:

$$A_{12} = 12 \times \frac{1}{1^{12}} + 6 \times \frac{1}{\left(\sqrt{2}\right)^{12}} + 24 \times \frac{1}{\left(\sqrt{3}\right)^{12}} + 24 \times \frac{1}{\left(\sqrt{5}\right)^{12}} + \ldots$$

Evaluating the terms we find:

$$A_{12} = \frac{12}{1} + \frac{6}{64} + \frac{24}{729} + \frac{24}{15625} + \ldots$$
$$= 12 + 0.09375 + 0.03292 + 0.00154 + \ldots$$
$$= 12.128\ldots$$

This sum converges rapidly and only a few terms are required to estimate A_{12} with good precision. The A_6 summation converges more slowly and to attain equivalent precision to A_{12} one must consider more distant neighbours than those in the figure above.

$$U = -2\varepsilon N_A \left(\frac{\sigma}{r_0}\right)^6 A_6 + 2\varepsilon N_A \left(\frac{\sigma}{r_0}\right)^{12} A_{12} \quad (6.17)$$

Calculation: Stage 3: Lattice sums

Evaluating lattice sums is a straightforward mathematical exercise (Example 6.1). The lattice sums A_6 and A_{12} depend only on the *form* of the lattice, i.e. on the *type* of crystal structure (e.g. face-centred cubic, body-centred cubic, etc.) and not on the particular separation between the molecules in the crystal of σ or r_0. In other words A_6 and A_{12} are just numbers and each different crystal structure has uniquely characteristic values of A_6 and A_{12}.

The cohesive energy of an assembly of N_A atoms is now conveniently expressed in terms of the lattice sums as:

$$U = -2\varepsilon N_A \left[\left(\frac{\sigma}{r_0}\right)^6 A_6 - \left(\frac{\sigma}{r_0}\right)^{12} A_{12} \right] \quad (6.18)$$

Calculation: Stage 4: Minimising the cohesive energy

Equation 6.18 tells us the cohesive energy of a solid with particular values of σ/r_0, ε, A_6 and A_{12}. What we need to do now is to find the particular set of values that yields the minimum value of the cohesive energy. We will do this in two steps. First we will find the value of σ/r_0 that minimises U. In the section we will consider the effect of the lattice sums.

To find the optimum value of σ/r_0 we differentiate Equation 6.18 for U with respect to σ/r_0 and set the result equal to zero. Differentiating we find:

$$\frac{dU}{d(\sigma/r_0)} = -2\varepsilon N_A \left[6\left(\frac{\sigma}{r_0}\right)^5 A_6 - 12\left(\frac{\sigma}{r_0}\right)^{11} A_{12} \right] (6.19)$$

Setting this equal to zero requires that:

$$12\left(\frac{\sigma}{r_0}\right)^{11} A_{12} = 6\left(\frac{\sigma}{r_0}\right)^5 A_6 \quad (6.20)$$

Simplifying and rearranging we find:

Example 6.2

Calculate the cohesive energy per mole for a substance whose atoms interact via a Lennard-Jones potential.

According to Equation 6.18 the cohesive energy per mole is given by:

$$U = 2N_A \varepsilon \left[A_{12}\left(\frac{\sigma}{r_0}\right)^{12} - A_6\left(\frac{\sigma}{r_0}\right)^6 \right]$$

and in equilibrium r_0 is given by Equation 6.23 as

$$r_0 = \sigma \left[\frac{2A_{12}}{A_6} \right]^{1/6}$$

Substituting the equilibrium value of r_0 into the expression for U should therefore yield the equilibrium value of cohesive energy per mole. The expression for U has two brackets in it: $(\sigma/r_0)^{12}$ and $(\sigma/r_0)^6$. These brackets simplify to:

$$\left[\frac{\sigma}{r_0}\right]^{12} = \left[\frac{\sigma}{\sigma(2A_{12}/A_6)^{1/6}} \right]^{12} = \left[\frac{A_6}{2A_{12}}\right]^2$$

and

$$\left[\frac{\sigma}{r_0}\right]^6 = \left[\frac{\sigma}{\sigma(2A_{12}/A_6)^{1/6}} \right]^6 = \left[\frac{A_6}{2A_{12}}\right]$$

Substituting into the expression for U we find:

$$U = 2N_A \varepsilon \left[A_{12}\left(\frac{A_6}{2A_{12}}\right)^2 - A_6\left(\frac{A_6}{2A_{12}}\right) \right]$$

$$= 2N_A \varepsilon \left[\frac{A_6^2}{4A_{12}} - \frac{A_6^2}{2A_{12}} \right]$$

$$= -N_A \varepsilon \left[\frac{A_6^2}{2A_{12}} \right]$$

$$\left(\frac{\sigma}{r_0}\right)^6 = \frac{A_6}{2A_{12}} \quad (6.21)$$

$$\frac{\sigma}{r_0} = \left(\frac{A_6}{2A_{12}}\right)^{1/6} \quad (6.22)$$

$$r_0 = \sigma \left(\frac{2A_{12}}{A_6}\right)^{1/6} \quad (6.23)$$

This is the value of the nearest-neighbour distance that minimises the potential energy of the lattice. Notice that r_o is a multiple of σ, the 'range' parameter in the Lennard-Jones potential. In order to evaluate the cohesive energy of the lattice, we can substitute the value for σ/r_o from Equation 6.23 into Equation 6.18. This calculation is performed in Example 6.2.

According to Example 6.2 the cohesive energy per mole is given by:

$$U = -\left(\frac{A_6^2}{2A_{12}}\right)N_A\varepsilon \qquad (6.24)$$

and so the cohesive energy per molecule $u = U/N_A$ is:

$$u = -\left(\frac{A_6^2}{2A_{12}}\right)\varepsilon \qquad (6.25)$$

Summary of cohesive energy calculation
The calculation culminating in expressions 6.24 and 6.25 has involved the use of technical tricks such as the use of lattice sums. Because of this it is worth recalling that these tricks have been used in order to perform the (simple in principle) task of adding up the electrostatic interactions of a large number of molecules. The final question we need to answer is what values of A_6 and A_{12} minimise the cohesive energy. We will find the answer to this question in the next section.

6.2.5 Equilibrium crystal structure

Equation 6.25 succinctly expresses the cohesive energy of a crystal in terms of the lattice sums A_6 and A_{12}. But notice that A_6 and A_{12} could refer to *any crystal structure*. When a crystal forms from a melt, the crystal structure adopted is generally the one with the lowest (i.e. most negative) cohesive energy. (This matter is discussed further in Chapter 10.)

In order to predict which crystal structure actually forms, we need to calculate u according to Equation 6.25 for all likely crystal structures. We then work out which crystal structure has the largest

152

Figure 6.6 When a crystal forms it could conceivably form any one of several different structures. The actual structure formed depends strongly on the cohesive energy U of the structure. For atoms that interact via the Lennard-Jones potential Equation 6.7, the cohesive energy can be expressed in terms of the lattice sums A_6 and A_{12} described in the text. The figures illustrate two crystal structures showing (i) that the *number* of nearest-neighbour atoms differs from crystal structure to crystal structure and (ii) that the relative distances to next-nearest neighbours also differs from one structure to another. The calculation of the lattice sums for fcc is considered in Example 6.1.

(a) Body-centred cubic

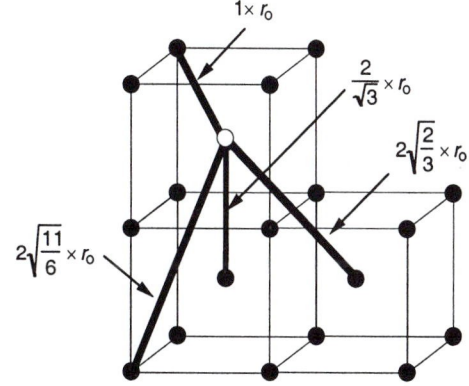

(b) Simple cubic

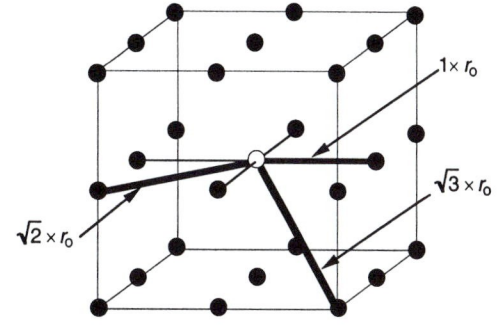

value of $A_6^2/2A_{12}$. Table 6.1 shows the lattice sums and calculated cohesive energy for three different crystal structures in which a molecular solid might conceivably crystallise. The face-centred cubic structure is illustrated in Example 6.1 and the body-centred cubic and simple cubic structures are illustrated in Figure 6.6

Table 6.1 Values of the lattice sums A_6 and A_{12} for three crystal structures. The bottom line of the table shows the cohesive energy U for each crystal structure calculated in terms of A_6 and A_{12} according to Equation 6.25.

	Simple cubic	Body-centred cubic	Face-centred cubic
A_6	8.4	12.25	14.45
A_{12}	6.2	9.11	12.13
Cohesive energy, U	-5.69ε	-8.24ε	-8.61ε

All the crystal structures in Table 6.1 have a negative cohesive energy, i.e. they all represent arrangements of molecules which are energetically favourable compared to molecules being separated from one another by large distances. The crystal structure naturally chosen however will be the one with the *largest* cohesive energy (i.e. the most negative value) which in this case is the face-centred cubic (*fcc*) structure. This expectation is indeed borne out and all the noble gases neon, argon, krypton and xenon form solids with an *fcc* structure at low temperature.

Comparison with experiment for noble gases

Once the crystal structure is known to be *fcc*, the appropriate values of A_6 and A_{12} can be substituted into Equation 6.23 for r_o. For *fcc*, the predicted values of r_o and u are $r_o = 1.09\ \sigma$ and $u = -8.6\varepsilon$. Values of σ and r_o can be deduced from analysis of the deviations of gases from perfect gas behav-

iour (e.g. §5.5 on the thermal conductivity of gases), i.e. σ and ε are estimated from the behaviour of the substance *in the gaseous phase*! Using values of σ and ε derived from these experiments, allows us to predict values of r_o and u which may be compared with experimental values deduced from analysis of data on X-ray scattering, and latent heat of vaporisation of the substances. Table 6.2 compares predicted and experimental values of the cohesive energy per molecule and the lattice spacing in the *fcc* crystal structure. We see that there is fair agreement between theory and experiment.

Table 6.2 Values of the lattice constant r_o and the cohesive energy per atom u calculated according to Equations 6.23 and 6.25 are compared with experimental values for neon, argon, krypton, and xenon. The values of σ and ε for each substance have been deduced from measurements in the *gaseous* phase of each substance by observing the deviations from perfect gas behaviour.

	Substance			
	Ne	Ar	Kr	Xe
$\sigma \times 10^{-10}$ m	2.74	3.44	3.65	3.98
$r_o(=1.09\sigma) \times 10^{-10}$ m	2.99	3.71	3.98	4.34
r_o(expt) $\times 10^{-10}$ m	3.13	3.75	3.99	4.33
Ratio(theory/expt)	0.955	0.989	0.997	1.002
$\varepsilon \times 10^{-3}$ eV	3.1	10.3	14.0	20.0
$u = -8.6\varepsilon \times 10^{-3}$ eV	-27	-89	-120	-172
u(expt) $\times 10^{-3}$ eV	-20	-80	-110	-170
Ratio(theory/expt)	1.35	1.11	1.09	1.01

6.3 Ionic solids

6.3.1 General description

In ionic solids, the 'entities' that make up the solid are essentially *ions*, atoms stripped of one or more of their electrons, or with one or two more added.

As with molecular solids, it is the Coulomb force which holds the substance together, but in ionic solids not all the forces are attractive. There are equal numbers of positively and negatively charged ions, and although the positively and negatively charged ions attract one another, the negative ions repel the other negative ions and the positive ions repel the other positive ions. The fact that ionic solids actually exist tells us that the at-

tractive forces will eventually outweigh the repulsive forces, but we need to make a detailed calculation in order to see why.

6.3.2 Calculation of the cohesive energy

The calculation of the cohesive energy of an ionic solid is similar to the calculation in §6.2 for the cohesive energy of a molecular solid. We have to add up all the pair-interactions between ions in the solid. Before we do the calculation for a real three-dimensional crystal, we can get the flavour for what the calculation involves by looking at a two-dimensional problem.

A two-dimensional problem

What is the potential energy of a single ion in a large 'net' of charges, of which a section is illustrated in Figure 6.7?

In order to answer this question, consider one particular ion, a positive ion say, and add up the energy of interaction of all the other ions with the chosen ion. We must be careful to consider the ions systematically in order to make sure that all of them are counted (but only once!). We start by adding up the Coulomb terms as follows:

$$Energy = \frac{-e^2}{4\pi\varepsilon_o r_o} + \frac{-e^2}{4\pi\varepsilon_o r_o} + \frac{-e^2}{4\pi\varepsilon_o r_o} +$$

$$\frac{-e^2}{4\pi\varepsilon_o r_o} + \frac{-e^2}{4\pi\varepsilon_o (\sqrt{2}r_o)} + \dots \quad (6.26)$$

Notice that *energy* in Equation 6.26 is the sum of energies of ion *pairs*. The energy associated with the central ion is just ½ this quantity. We therefore write the coulomb energy per ion, u as:

$$u = \frac{1}{2}\left[\frac{-e^2}{4\pi\varepsilon_o r_o} + \frac{-e^2}{4\pi\varepsilon_o r_o} + \frac{-e^2}{4\pi\varepsilon_o r_o} +\right.$$

$$\left.\frac{-e^2}{4\pi\varepsilon_o r_o} + \frac{-e^2}{4\pi\varepsilon_o (\sqrt{2}r_o)} + \dots\right] \quad (6.27)$$

If we collect together the terms that correspond to ions at the same distance from the origin, and take out a common factor, we find a series, the first four terms of which are:

$$u = \frac{e^2}{8\pi\varepsilon_o r_o}\left[4\times\frac{-1}{1} + 4\times\frac{+1}{\sqrt{1^2+1^2}} +\right.$$

$$\left.4\times\frac{+1}{2} + 8\times\frac{-1}{\sqrt{1^2+2^2}} + \dots\right] \quad (6.28)$$

This series is similar to the lattice sums considered in the previous section on molecular bonding (Example 6.1), except that in this case the sign of each term oscillates. In each term within the brackets in Equation 6.28:

- the first number (4 or 8 for the terms shown) is the number of ions at that distance,
- the sign in the numerator of the fraction is

154

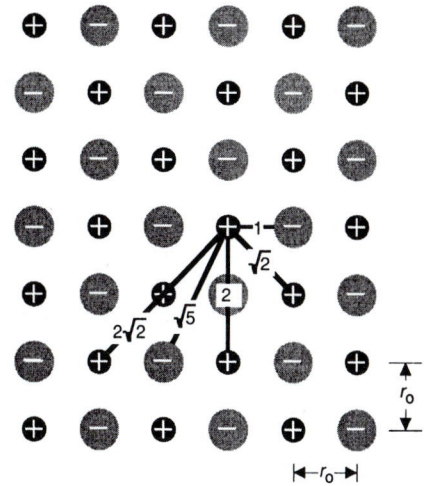

Figure 6.7 A section from an infinite two-dimensional 'net' of charges. The charge on each ion is either $+e$ or $-e$. The numbers on the lines indicate the number of times r_o must be multiplied to reach between the lattice sites indicated.

determined by whether the charges are of the same or opposite sign, and

- the denominator of the fraction is the distance from the origin in units of r_o.

Evaluating the terms we find the first eight terms are:

$$u = \frac{e^2}{8\pi\varepsilon_o r_o}\left[-4 + \frac{4}{\sqrt{2}} + 2 - \frac{8}{\sqrt{5}} + \frac{4}{2\sqrt{2}} - \frac{4}{3}\right.$$

$$\left. + \frac{8}{\sqrt{10}} - \frac{8}{\sqrt{13}} + \dots\right] \quad (6.29)$$

Term	Value	Running total
1	-4.0000000	-4.0000000
2	+2.8284271	-1.1715729
3	+2.0000000	+0.8284271
4	-3.5777088	-2.7492817
5	+1.4142136	-1.3350681
6	-1.3333333	-2.6684014
7	+2.5298221	-0.1385793
8	-2.2188008	-2.3573801

The problem with this summation may be becoming apparent to you. The terms are getting smaller, but only very slowly. Using a 'brute force' computer program to whip through the first few thousand terms in the sum yields an approximate answer of −1.57. This is likely to be close,

but not quite right. However this problem of adding up a long series of slowly converging terms will come to haunt us with a vengeance when we come to the three-dimensional problem in just a moment.

The significance of the calculation we have just done is that an ion in a net such as the one described will be bound into the net with an energy equal to approximately 1.57 times the energy of interaction of the ion with just one other ion of the opposite charge.

The three-dimensional problem

Now we proceed to the three-dimensional problem (Figure 6.8) actually encountered in ionic crystals. We approach the calculation in a similar way to the two-dimensional calculation, but the geometry is now a little more taxing. The summation for the energy of an ion now looks like:

$$u = \frac{e^2}{4\pi\varepsilon_o r_o} \times \frac{1}{2}\left[6\times\frac{-1}{1} + 12\times\frac{+1}{\sqrt{1^2+1^2}} + \right.$$

$$\left. 8\times\frac{-1}{\sqrt{1^2+1^2+1^2}} + 6\times\frac{+1}{2} + ...\right]$$

$$(6.30)$$

$$u = \frac{e^2}{4\pi\varepsilon_o r_o} \times \frac{1}{2}\left[-6 + \frac{+12}{\sqrt{2}} - \frac{8}{\sqrt{3}} + \frac{6}{2} + ...\right] \quad (6.31)$$

Term	Value	Running total
1	-6.0000000	-6.0000000
2	+8.4852813	+2.4852813
3	-4.6188022	-2.1335208
4	+3.0000000	+0.8664792
5	-10.7331263	-9.8666471
6	+9.7979589	-0.0685121
7	-6.0000000	-6.0685121
8	+7.5894666	+1.5209545

Again we have taken care to calculate the energy per ion and not per ion pair. Using a 'brute force' computer program to evaluate the sum (Eq. 6.31) yields a sum which does not clearly converge, but instead oscillates at a value of around −1.5. Series of this type are called *Madelung Sums* after the person who solved the three-dimensional problem. The sum evaluates to −1.748 for the NaCl type

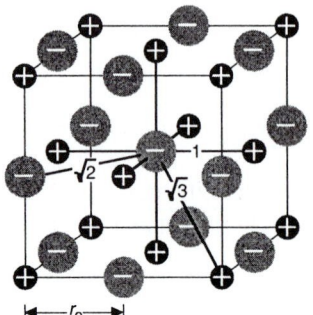

Figure 6.8 The arrangement of ions in a crystal with the same structure as NaCl. The numbers on the lines are the distance between the ions in units of r_o. This diagram should be compared with its two-dimensional equivalent in Figure 6.7.

crystal structure and to similar values for other common ionic crystal structures, i.e. the energy of an ion in an ionic crystal of the NaCl type is:

$$u = \frac{e^2}{8\pi\varepsilon_o r_o}[-1.748] \quad (6.32)$$

However, this seems to indicate that if r_o is reduced the energy of the ion will become very large and negative. Of course there must be some repulsive term between atoms which stops the crystal 'collapsing'. This repulsive term is due to the Pauli exclusion principle effect discussed in §6.2.2. It may be modelled once again as:

$$u = +\frac{c}{r_o^{12}} \quad (6.33)$$

Adding the repulsive effect between the ion and its six nearest neighbours we find its energy is:

$$u = \frac{-1.748e^2}{8\pi\varepsilon_o r_o} + \frac{6c}{r_o^{12}} \quad (6.34)$$

It is clear that reducing r_o makes the attractive term more negative, but it also rapidly increases the Pauli repulsion between the outer orbitals of each ion.

Finding the equilibrium separation

If we differentiate Equation 6.34 for u with respect to r_o we can find the value of r_o which minimises the cohesive energy per ion:

$$\frac{du}{dr_o} = \frac{+1.748e^2}{8\pi\varepsilon_o r_o^2} - \frac{12 \times 6c}{r_o^{13}} \qquad (6.35)$$

Equating this to zero yields:

$$\frac{+1.748e^2}{8\pi\varepsilon_o r_o^2} = \frac{72c}{r_o^{13}} \qquad (6.36)$$

Solving for r_o yields:

$$r_o^{11} = \frac{576c\pi\varepsilon_o}{+1.748e^2} \qquad (6.37)$$

$$r_o = \left[\frac{576c\pi\varepsilon_o}{+1.748e^2}\right]^{1/11} \qquad (6.38)$$

This formula predicts the nearest-neighbour ionic separation in terms of the Madelung sum (-1.748) and the constant c that determines the magnitude of the repulsive forces between atoms.

6.3.3 Crystal structure

Determining the crystal structure of an ionically-bonded substance from first principles is considerably more difficult then the equivalent task for molecularly-bonded substance(§ 6.2.3). This is because in the molecularly-bonded solid that we considered there, all the molecules were identical. For ionically-bonded substances there are always at least two different types of ions. This introduces a new consideration: the relative sizes of the ions.

We are however able to say some general things about the types of crystal structure we may expect ionically-bonded substances to form. The presence of both positive and negative ions rules out densely-packed crystal structures with large numbers of nearest neighbours. To see why, consider the two-dimensional situation illustrated in Figure 6.9. Suppose a single ion A surrounded itself with six nearest neighbours of opposite charge to itself (Figure 6.9(a)). This would lower A's electrostatic energy considerably, however the six neighbours would all have the same sign of charge and thus *their* energy would be *increased* considerably. Further, the structure could not be extended throughout the crystal while keeping the crystal

electrically neutral overall. Similar arguments apply to the equivalent three-dimensional close-packed structures.

Figure 6.9 Two possible local arrangements of ions; see text for details.

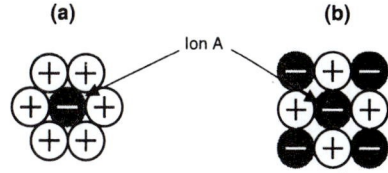

For this reason ionically-bonded substances form crystal structures that are more 'open'. Notice that in Figure 6.9(b) nearest neighbours always have opposite charges: only next-nearest neighbours have the same charge.

6.3.4 Cohesive energy

We have already gone a substantial way to calculating the cohesive energy of an ionic solid by calculating the separation between ions in equilibrium (Equation 6.38). In this section we will complete the calculation by substituting the expression for the equilibrium separation back into the expression for the cohesive energy.

The expression for the cohesive energy per ion (Equation 6.34) is:

$$u = \frac{-1.748e^2}{8\pi\varepsilon_o r_o} + \frac{6c}{r_o^{12}} \qquad (6.34*)$$

We can make the substitution for r_o much simpler if we first take out a factor $1/r_o$ from each term, to yield:

$$u = \frac{1}{r_o}\left[\frac{-1.748e^2}{8\pi\varepsilon_o} + \frac{6c}{r_o^{11}}\right] \qquad (6.39)$$

Substituting for r_o inside the bracket only yields:

$$u = \frac{1}{r_o}\left[\frac{-1.748e^2}{8\pi\varepsilon_o} + \frac{6c}{\left[\frac{576c\pi\varepsilon_o}{+1.748e^2}\right]^{11/11}}\right] \qquad (6.40)$$

Simplifying, and cancelling terms we arrive at:

$$u = \frac{1}{r_o}\left[\frac{-1.748e^2}{8\pi\varepsilon_o} + \frac{1.748e^2}{96\pi\varepsilon_o}\right] \qquad (6.41)$$

$$u = \frac{-1.748e^2}{8\pi\varepsilon_o r_o}\left[1 - \frac{1}{12}\right] \qquad (6.42)$$

This evaluates to:

$$u = \frac{-1.602e^2}{8\pi\varepsilon_o r_o} \qquad (6.43)$$

Notice that the repulsive component in Equation 6.42 is one twelfth of the attractive component. The expression yields the cohesive energy per ion in a simple-cubic ionic solid. In order to convert this into a cohesive energy per mole, we must multiply this figure by the number of formula units in a mole. Note that in the simple two-component ionic solids we have been considering, each chemical formula unit contains two ions (e.g. Na^+ and Cl^-). We therefore expect to find that the cohesive energy per mole for such a substance is:

$$U = 2N_A u \quad \text{mol}^{-1} \qquad (6.44)$$

Following Example 6.3 we conclude that the molar cohesive energy of NaCl is given by:

$$U = 2 \times 6.02 \times 10^{23} \times 6.55 \times 10^{-19} = 789 \text{ kJ mol}^{-1}$$

This is the energy required to separate a mole of NaCl into one mole of Na^+ ions and one mole of Cl^- ions. The value of U inferred from experiments is given in C. Kittel: *Introduction to Solid State Physics (seventh edition)*: Table 7 as 774 kJ mol^{-1}. We may take this agreement at the level of a few per cent as validation of the theory we have developed so far.

Cohesive energy per atom

The cohesive energy determined in Equation 6.44 is the energy required to separate an ionic solid into its constituent *ions*. It is interesting to consider what would be the energy required to separate an ionic solid into its constituent *atoms*. In order to calculate this we need to know:

- the energy u_1 (known as the *ionisation energy*) required to remove an electron from a

Example 6.3

Evaluate the cohesive energy per ion (Equation 6.41) for NaCl (common salt).

We can evaluate r_o from the density (Table 7.2); the atomic masses of Na and Cl (Table 7.2); and the crystal structure which is known from X-ray diffraction patterns to be of the simple type described in Figure 6.8. We have:

- 1 mole of Na has a mass of 22.99×10^{-3} kg
- 1 mole of Cl has a mass of 35.45×10^{-3} kg

So 1 mole of NaCl has a mass of 58.44×10^{-3} kg and one chemical formula unit of NaCl has a mass of:

$$m = \frac{58.44 \times 10^{-3}}{N_A} = 9.708 \times 10^{-26} \text{ kg}$$

Consideration of Figure 6.8 indicates that one chemical formula unit of NaCl occupies a volume of $2r_o^3$ and hence a density of $\rho = m/2r_o^3$.

The experimental determined density of NaCl is $\rho = 2165$ kg m^{-3} and so we deduce that:

$$r_o = \left[\frac{m}{2\rho}\right]^{\frac{1}{3}} = \left[\frac{9.708 \times 10^{-26}}{2 \times 2165}\right]^{\frac{1}{3}}$$

$$= 2.82 \times 10^{-10} \text{ m}$$

Using this value in Equation 6.46 for the cohesive energy per ion we have:

$$u = -\frac{-1.602 \times \left(1.6 \times 10^{-19}\right)^2}{8\pi \times 8.85 \times 10^{-12} \times 2.82 \times 10^{-10}}$$

$$= -6.55 \times 10^{-19} \text{ J/ion}$$

This can also be expressed as 4.09 eV per ion.

sodium atom

$$Na \xrightarrow{+u_1} Na^+ + e^-$$

- The energy u_2 (known as the *electron affinity*) required to add an electron to a chlorine atom

$$Cl + e^- \xrightarrow{+u_2} Cl^-$$

For NaCl, u_1 = +5.139 eV per Na ion and u_2 = −3.617 eV per Cl ion (*Emsley*). Thus to take two neutral atoms of Na and Cl and form an Na^+ and a Cl^- ion requires $u_1 + u_2$ = + 5.139 − 3.617 = 1.522 eV per NaCl formula unit. Equivalently this can be stated as 146.9 kJ mol^{-1} of NaCl. Notice that it actually costs energy to transfer an electron from the sodium atom to the chlorine atom. However if

we take account of the cohesive electrostatic energy of the ions when they are arranged in a crystal, there is an additional energy gain u given by Equation 6.44 and which we evaluated as -789 kJ mol^{-1}. Thus the cohesive energy of NaCl relative to neutral atoms is $+146.9 - 789 \approx -642$ kJ mol^{-1} (or -6.65 eV per NaCl formula unit).

Summary
We have seen in this section that we can understand the magnitude of the cohesive energy of ionic solids in terms of the coulomb interaction of ions distributed on a crystal lattice.

6.4 Covalent solids

6.4.1 General description
In covalent solids, electrons, which in isolated atoms occupied quantum states localised around a single atom, occupy orbitals that are distributed around at least one other atom in addition to their 'parent' atom: literally 'co-valence'. The materials which tend to form covalent solids are:

- elements from the centre of the periodic table e.g. C, Si and Ge
- compounds of elements from the centre of the periodic table
- many compounds of oxygen (oxides), sulphur (sulphides) and nitrogen (nitrides)

Covalency often occurs when the outer valence electrons have orbitals that are not spherical, but have 'lobes' that point in different directions. This gives rise to some directionality in the attraction between atoms. In other words, atoms will be attracted to one another if their orbitals point in a certain direction (perhaps towards each other), but if the orbitals point in a slightly different direction the atoms may well repel one another.

Notice that because of the directionality of the attraction/repulsion, we cannot simply write down

a law of attraction that depends only on the separation between atoms, such as the Lennard-Jones equation (Equation 6.7). Thus calculating the properties of covalent solids is considerably more complex than calculating the properties of molecular solids. However, we will attempt a simple calculation for one of the simplest (but rarest!) covalent solids: carbon in the form of diamond.

6.4.2 Calculation of covalent bond length or strength

A 'point charge' model of a covalent bond
We can make a simple model of a covalent bond as follows. We consider a 'solid' consisting of just carbon atoms, and imagine the charge in the region between the atoms to be distributed as shown below:

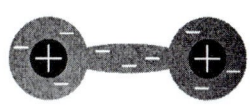

Figure 6.11 A simple model of the charge distribution in a C–C bond

The C–C bond of Figure 6.11 is electrically neutral overall, but electrons 'originally' from each atom spend some time 'orbiting' both atoms, and some time in the bond region. We will assume that each electron spends some fraction f of its time orbiting the atoms at each end of the bond. It therefore spends a fraction $(1 - 2f)$ of its time in the region between the atoms. We see that if $f = 0.5$ then the electrons spend essentially no time in the bond region and if $f = 0$ the electron spends all its time in the bond region. If we recall that one electron from each atom will take part in the bond, then *on average* we can make a 'point charge' model of the charge distribution in the bond like that illustrated in Figure 6.12.

Figure 6.10 A simple model of a covalent bond between atoms illustrating the directional nature of the bond. In (a) two similar atoms are shown with overlapping electron orbits. The increased charge density in between the atoms pulls the atoms together, as shown by the black arrows. In (b) a misalignment of the atoms causes a repulsion (indicated by the arrows) between the atoms.

(a)   **(b)**

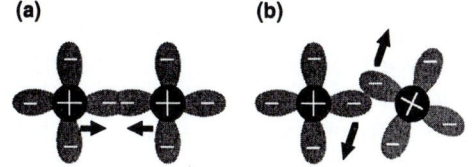

Figure 6.12 A point-charge model of a covalent bond. The term 'core charges' refers to the electrical charges in the core electrons and the nucleus.

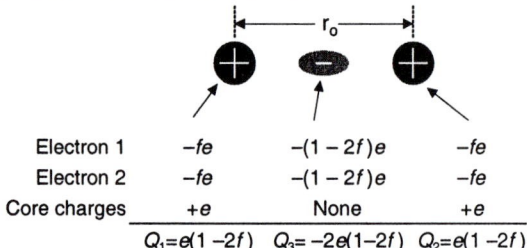

Electron 1	$-fe$	$-(1-2f)e$	$-fe$
Electron 2	$-fe$	$-(1-2f)e$	$-fe$
Core charges	$+e$	None	$+e$

$$Q_1 = e(1-2f) \quad Q_3 = -2e(1-2f) \quad Q_2 = e(1-2f)$$

Notice that when an electron leaves an atom, the atom is left positively charged due to the balance of nuclear and core electrons. If we imagine the charges Q_1, Q_2 and Q_3 to be point charges, we can work out the approximate energy of this charge distribution using Coulomb's Law. We have:

$$u = \frac{Q_1 Q_2}{4\pi\varepsilon_0 r_0} + \frac{Q_1 Q_3}{4\pi\varepsilon_0 (r_0/2)} + \frac{Q_2 Q_3}{4\pi\varepsilon_0 (r_0/2)} \quad (6.45)$$

Substituting for Q_1, Q_2 and Q_3 from Figure 6.12

$$u = \frac{e^2(1-2f)^2}{4\pi\varepsilon_0 r_0} + \frac{-2e^2(1-2f)^2}{4\pi\varepsilon_0 (r_0/2)} + \frac{-2e^2(1-2f)^2}{4\pi\varepsilon_0 (r_0/2)} \quad (6.46)$$

and taking out a common factor we have:

$$u = \frac{e^2(1-2f)^2}{4\pi\varepsilon_0 r_0}\left[\frac{1}{1} + \frac{-2}{\frac{1}{2}} + \frac{-2}{\frac{1}{2}}\right] \quad (6.47)$$

which simplifies to:

$$u = \frac{e^2(1-2f)^2}{4\pi\varepsilon_0 r_0}[-7] \quad (6.48)$$

Equation 6.48 indicates that if an electron spends no time in the bond region ($f = 0.5$) then the binding energy $u = 0$. This corresponds to two neutral atoms which do indeed have zero electrostatic attraction. The maximum binding energy occurs for $f = 0$ which corresponds to an electron spending all its time in the bond region. We find:

$$u_{\max} = [-7]\frac{e^2}{4\pi\varepsilon_0 r_0} \quad (6.49)$$

Comparison with experiment: a plausibility test

In *Kaye and Laby*, we can find tabulated values of the C–C bond length and binding energy in different compounds and molecules. Taking the C–C bond length in a typical diatomic molecule, we have $r_0 = 0.1312$ nm and a cohesive energy per bond (actually tabulated as a *dissociation energy D*) of $D = 603$ kJ mol^{-1}. Converting this into a cohesive energy per bond $u = D/N_A$ evaluates to $603 \times 10^3/6.02 \times 10^{23} = 1.00 \times 10^{-18}$ J $= 6.25$ eV.

We can use these *experimental* values to deduce an estimate for f. Rearranging Equation 6.48 and solving for f we have:

$$(1-2f)^2 = -\frac{4\pi\varepsilon_0 r_0 u}{7e^2} \quad (6.50)$$

$$f = 0.5\left[1 - \sqrt{-\frac{4\pi\varepsilon_0 r_0 U}{7e^2}}\right] \quad (6.51)$$

Substituting the values discussed above:

$$f = 0.5\left[1 - \sqrt{-\frac{4\pi\times8.85\times10^{-12}\times0.1312\times10^{-9}\times-1.00\times10^{-18}}{7(1.6\times10^{-19})^2}}\right]$$

$$f = 0.5[1 - \sqrt{0.08146}] = 0.357 \quad (6.52)$$

Equation 6.52 indicates that an electron in a C–C covalent bond spends roughly 35% of its time orbiting the atoms at either end of the bond, and around 30% of its time in the central bond region. This estimate for f is unlikely to be accurate. However, it does show at least that our assumptions are self-consistent.

The above calculation is extremely crude: we have ignored, for example, the quantum mechanical rules that govern the distribution of charge around the atom and in the bond region. However, the purpose of the calculation has *not* been to calculate a realistic answer for the charge distribution in a covalent bond. If we wanted to do this we would have to quantum mechanically calculate (or experimentally determine) the charge density around, and in between, each atom. The purpose of this calculation is to show that, given the exis-

tence of the bond structure (i.e. its length and strength) we can understand the connection between the two using only Coulomb's Law.

We have also ignored the fact that in a solid, each carbon atom takes part in other covalent bonds with other atoms. There will therefore be other contributions to the binding energy of a solid because the neighbouring electrically-negative bond regions will repel one another. The consequences of this are discussed in the next section on crystal structure and illustrated in Figures 6.13, 6.14 and 6.15.

6.4.3 Crystal structure

The directionality of the covalent bond means that solids with covalent bonds tend to form crystals with quite different structures from those formed by molecular solids. In molecular solids, the maximum cohesive energy was achieved by atoms packing themselves in a way which achieved the largest possible number of nearest neighbours. In covalent solids, the structures are dictated by the geometry of the electron orbitals around atoms: adding extra nearest neighbours in general results in no extra bonding. For this reason, covalent solids often form rather 'open' structures with relatively low numbers of nearest neighbours.

For example, a carbon atom has four valence electrons and so can take part in, at most, four covalent bonds. It will therefore be of no benefit to form a crystal structure with more than four nearest neighbours. Each lobed orbital on the atom points in a different direction, and since each orbital has an excess of negative charge in it, it will repel the other orbitals in the same atom. The lobes therefore point away from one another, in the directions towards the corners of the regular tetrahedron (Figure 6.13)

In order to benefit from a covalent bond, other atoms must orient their orbitals with respect to the first atom so they can create overlapping orbital regions (Figure 6.13 (b)). The crystal structure formed is rather difficult to describe in words but is sketched in Figures 6.14 and 6.15.

Figure 6.13 (a) An illustration of the arrangement electric charge around a carbon atom. The four valence electrons orient their orbitals towards the points of a regular tetrahedron in order to minimise their repulsive Coulomb interaction. (b) An illustration of the arrangement of orbitals in two C atoms covalently bonded together.

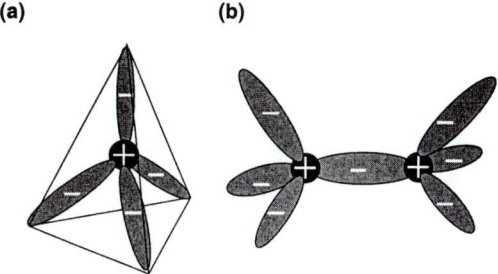

(a)   **(b)**

Figure 6.14 The crystal structure of diamond as deduced from X-ray scattering. The separation between atoms is 0.154 nm. The lines indicate the bonding regions and the spheres indicate the location of the atoms. The different shading is to aid the clarity of the picture, and allow identification of the four atoms entirely contained within the outer cube.

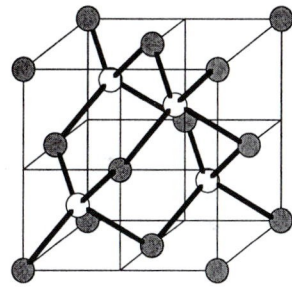

Figure 6.15 A simplified model of a small region of a diamond lattice. The model uses point charges to represent the continuous charge distribution that exists in the real lattice. It is a three-dimensional extension of the two-atom point charge model discussed in the text.

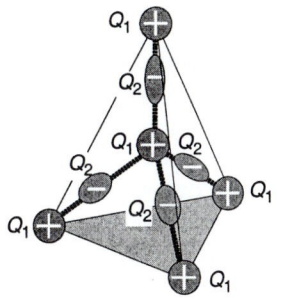

6.4.4 Cohesive energy calculations

The cohesive energy of a covalently-bonded solid is rather difficult to calculate, and we will not proceed to a full calculation here. However, we can indicate how such a calculation would be made. Consider the case of diamond which has the crystal structure illustrated in Figure 6.14 and 6.15. The complex three-dimensional nature of the charge distribution throughout the lattice makes a systematic evaluation of the electrostatic energy of the structure more complicated than it was for ionic substances (§ 6.3). In particular the situation of the positively-charged ions and the negatively-charged bond regions are not equivalent. However, we may reasonably imagine how we could determine the cohesive energy of such a lattice in a way broadly similar to that discussed in §6.3.1.

6.5 Metals

6.5.1 General description

In metals, the entities that make up the solid are essentially positive ions (i.e. atoms stripped of one or more of their electrons) and electrons free to move in between the ions. One can think of this as a kind of delocalised covalent bond. However in order to understand even the simplest properties of metals we need to look at one factor which has been ignored in the previous three models of solids: *quantum mechanics*.

The 'particle in a box' problem

In this section, we will develop a strikingly simple model of a metal. We envisage that the electrons are unable to leave the metal, but that they are free to move around within it. This is a description of a metal as a 'box' and the determination of the quantum states of electrons in a metal is then reduced to the 'particle in a box' problem (§2.3). The way in which the Coulomb potentials around single ions can add up to form a box-like potential is illustrated in Figure 6.16.

The approximation that the potential energy experienced by an electron is box-like is known as the *free electron approximation*, and amounts to neglecting the corrugated details on the bottom of the expected potential in Figure 6.16 (c). The main justification of this approximation is that (as we shall see) the electrical properties of metals are generally rather similar to each other and very different from non-metals. This being so, their properties might be expected to arise from some general feature of their situation, and not on details particular to certain types of atoms.

Figure 6.16 The variation of the potential energy of a single electron in the vicinity of (a) a single ion, (b) two ions close together, and (c) a collection of ions close together. In (a) the potential will vary approximately like the Coulomb law $\approx 1/r$. In (b) the two potentials add together to make the region in between the ions a particularly attractive place to be for an electron. In (c) the ions have formed a box-like region capable of containing an electron with its walls, but allowing it to move within the box if its energy is not so low as to get trapped into the 'corrugations' at the bottom of the box. The dotted line shows the essence of the free electron approximation discussed in the text.

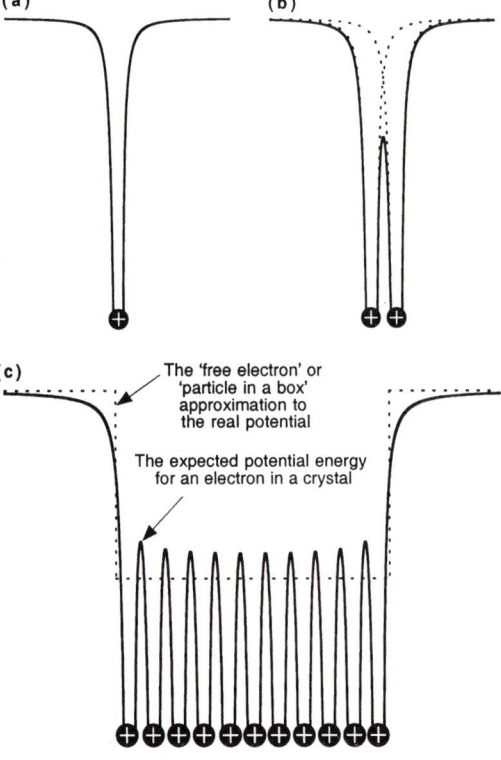

(a)

(b)

(c)

The 'free electron' or 'particle in a box' approximation to the real potential

The expected potential energy for an electron in a crystal

Quantum mechanics tells us (§2.3) that the energy of an electron in a cubic box of side L is given by:

$$E\left(n_x, n_y, n_z\right) = \frac{h^2}{8mL^2}\left[n_x^2 + n_y^2 + n_z^2\right] \qquad (6.53)$$

where n_x, n_y, n_z are quantum numbers allowed to take only integer values 1, 2, 3,.... The quantum state with lowest energy is the state with $n_x = n_y = n_z = 1$, which we denote as $E(1,1,1)$. The quantum state with the next lowest energy is $E(1,1,2)$. There are three states with this same energy since from Equation 6.53, $E(1,1,2) = E(1,2,1) = E(2,1,1)$. The properties of a few of the low energy states are listed in Table 6.3.

The Pauli exclusion principle (§2.4) allows only one electron in each quantum state. In order to apply the exclusion principle correctly we need to recall that because an electron in a state (n_x, n_y, n_z) can have two possible spin states, there are *two* electron quantum states associated with each unique (n_x, n_y, n_z) combination. Importantly, because of the exclusion principle, if we place several electrons in the same box, then not all electrons will be able to occupy the lowest energy state. Some electrons are forced to occupy higher energy states.

An example: an eight-atom metal

In order to see how these quantum mechanical results affect our understanding of metals, we will consider a specific example of a cluster of eight atoms. We consider that each atom has one valence electron which could be relatively easily detached from its parent atom. We thus have eight electrons to be accommodated in one of two ways. Let us call them options A and B.

- In Option A we model each atom as a box of side a, with each box containing a single electron. The solid is then just a collection of these eight separate boxes
- In Option B we model the solid as a single large box of side $2a$ which contains all eight electrons.

Notice that both options refer to electrons with the same overall electron density, $n = 1/a^3$. The energy of option B is dramatically lower than the energy of option A. This means that electrons prefer to be in 'one big box' rather than eight small boxes. Although this calculation is specific, the result is quite general: electrons 'like to spread out if they can'. Of course, what we are really interested in is not the properties of an eight-atom piece of metal, but the limit of this problem for large numbers of atoms. In other words, we need to compare the

Table 6.3 The first few energy levels for particles trapped in a box. The columns show (i) the quantum numbers of the states, (ii) the energy of the states in units of $h^2/8mL^2$, for example $E(1,1,3) = A[1^2 + 1^2 + 3^2] = 11A$ where $A = h^2/8mL^2$, (iii) the number of quantum states with the same energy, (iv) the number of electrons that can be accommodated at that energy, and (v) the running total of the number of electrons able to be accommodated with energy equal to or less than the current energy, i.e. the running total of column (iv).

Quantum numbers n_x, n_y, n_z	Energy in units of $h^2/8mL^2$	Number of states	Number of electrons able to be accommodated with this energy (including spin)	Number of electrons able to be accommodated with energy less than or equal to the current energy
(1,1,1)	3	1	2	2
(1,1,2) (1,2,1) (2,1,1)	6	3	6	2 + 6 = 8
(1,2,2) (2,1,2) (2,2,1)	9	3	6	2 + 6 + 6 = 14
(1,1,3) (1,3,1) (3,1,1)	11	3	6	2 + 6 + 6 + 6 = 20
(2,2,2)	12	1	2	2 + 6 + 6 + 6 + 2 = 22
(1,2,3) (1,3,2) (2,1,3) (2,3,1) (3,2,1) (3,1,2)	14	6	12	2 + 6 + 6 + 6 + 2 + 12 = 34

Figure 6.17 Options *A* and *B* for accommodating eight electrons within a solid.

| Option *A* | Option *B* |

Option *A*

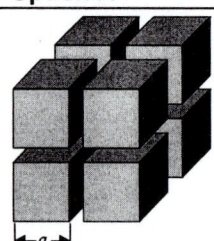

Each electron is confined to its own separate box (atom) with side $\approx a$. Each electron enters the ground state in its own box, and so the total energy will be:

$$E = 8 \times \frac{h^2}{8ma^2} \times [3]$$

And so the total energy of Option *A* is:

$$E_{\text{option A}} = 24 \times \frac{h^2}{8ma^2}$$

Option *B*

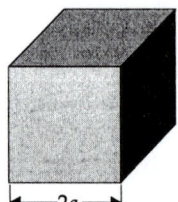

Each electron is contained in the same box with side $\approx 2a$. The electrons enter the lowest quantum states available. Two electrons can occupy the ground state and so the total energy of these two electrons will be:

$$2 \times \frac{1}{4} \times \frac{h^2}{8ma^2} \times [3]$$

The factor 1/4 arises from Equation 6.59 because the box has side $L = 2a$ as opposed to $L = a$ in Option *A* The next six electrons can occupy the states (1,1,2), (1,2,1), (2,1,1) so their total energy will be:

$$6 \times \frac{1}{4} \times \frac{h^2}{8ma^2} \times [6]$$

Adding up these terms we find that the total energy of Option *B* is:

$$E_{\text{option B}} = \left[\frac{2 \times 3}{4} + \frac{6 \times 6}{4} \right] \frac{h^2}{8ma^2}$$

$$= 10.5 \times \frac{h^2}{8ma^2}$$

---

energy of *N* electrons trapped in boxes of side *a* with energy of *N* electrons trapped in a single box of side $\sqrt[3]{N}a$. We consider this problem in §6.5.4, but surprisingly, the result does not change much.

The importance of quantum mechanics

Considering again the 8-atom metal of the previous section, we see that is not difficult to imagine how changes in electron density could result in different total energies. However in both options *A* and *B*, *the electron density was the same*, $n = 1/a^3$, so the change in energy has not arisen from a change in electron density. The lowered energy is a result of the change in the nature of the electron wave functions. Thus an arrangement of atoms can lower their energy by allowing their electrons to become *delocalised* i.e. to move freely through the crystal, while still being trapped within the crystal and not allowed to leave. This is nothing more than a gigantic version of option *B*, the big box. In other words, the cohesive energy of metals derives from this delocalisation energy.

The importance of Coulomb interactions

Notice that no mention has been made of the Coulomb interaction either: between *electrons and ions* or; between *electrons and the other electrons* with whom they share a 'box'. Since we have seen the importance of Coulomb interactions in the other three types of bonding, we can assume that Coulomb interactions are important and that a full theory must consider them. The theory we have outlined is known as the theory of a *free electron gas*. The neglect of Coulomb interactions is dignified by giving it two special names:

- The *Free Electron Approximation* assumes we can neglect the interactions between electrons and ions,

  except that occasionally electrons are scattered by vibrations of the lattice.

- The *Independent Electron Approximation* assumes we can neglect the interactions between electrons and other electrons,

  except that electrons somehow(!) know about each other sufficiently to obey the exclusion principle.

We take the first few steps in going beyond the free electron approximation in Web Chapter W1. Going beyond the independent electron approximation is beyond the scope of this book.

6.5.2 Counting quantum states

In a real metal, we have to deal with more than 'just a few' electrons in a box, and counting the occupied quantum states individually becomes impossible. If you think this is not so, please try Exercise 7 at the end of this chapter! In order to cope with the large number of electrons, several statistical mechanical techniques have been developed to allow calculations to be made about metals. They correspond to rather sophisticated ways of counting quantum states whose energies lie in particular energy ranges, as opposed to the rather laborious method of 'just counting' adopted for Table 6.3. The methods are discussed in some detail in Web Chapter W1, and here we just note the general approach.

The counting methods are based on the following rather simple idea. We plot points representing allowed states on a three-dimensional graph. The graph is generally called a k-space graph, or sometimes just 'k-space'. Importantly, the points, which represent the allowed states, are distributed in a fine *uniform* mesh on the graph. So by measuring 'volumes' on this three-dimensional k-space graph, we can also count states.

k-space

So far we have used the quantum numbers (n_x, n_y, n_z) to represent each allowed quantum state. In order to make the most of the k-space idea, we need to change our description of the quantum states and use three different quantum numbers (k_x, k_y, k_z). The rationale for this is that (n_x, n_y, n_z) represent *standing wave* solutions of the Schrödinger equation, while (k_x, k_y, k_z) represent *travelling wave* solutions. As you may know, a standing wave can be considered as the sum of two travelling waves moving in opposite directions. The key advantage of this change from a physicist's point of view is that it allows us to visualise electrons as *moving* within a metal.

The mathematical complexities of this change are discussed in Web Chapter W1, but here I would like you to note three important points.

- First, not all values of (k_x, k_y, k_z) are valid solutions of the Schrödinger equation. This should not really surprise you since it just reflects the fact that only integer values (n_x, n_y, n_z) were allowed.

- The second point concerns the significance of (k_x, k_y, k_z). In fact, (k_x, k_y, k_z) are no longer just numbers: they are directly related to the wavelength of the wave function, and hence to the energy and momentum of the quantum state that they represent.

- The final point is that the k-space scheme can seem very abstract, so it is important to remember why we have needed to introduce the concept. It allows us to count large numbers of quantum states, and in particular it allows us to calculate the *density of states* function that we discussed in §2.5.3.

Let us look at each of these three points in turn.

1. Allowed values of k_x, k_y and k_z

Whereas the quantum numbers n_i in Equation 6.59 had allowed values $n_i = 1, 2, 3\ldots$ where $i = x, y, z$, the quantum numbers k_i can have negative or positive values corresponding to mo-

Figure 6.18 k-space is a concept which enables for counting quantum states of the particle in a box problem when lots of particles are present. Each quantum state is represented by a point on a k_x, k_y, k_z graph. The energy of the state is proportional to the square of its distance from the origin on this graph. So in order to minimise their energy the occupied quantum states cluster in sphere around the origin.

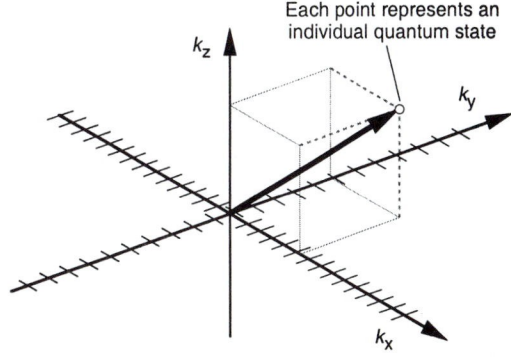

tion in either direction. The k_i's are related to the wavelength of each quantum state as follows. If our waves were just one-dimensional, then we would simply write:

$$\lambda = \frac{2\pi}{k} \qquad (6.54)$$

In three dimensions, things are a little more complicated. We imagine the k_i's are components of a vector $\mathbf{k}$ that points from the origin to the point $\mathbf{k} = (k_x, k_y, k_z)$. Now the wavelength of the wave represented by $\mathbf{k} = (k_x, k_y, k_z)$ is given by:

$$\lambda = \frac{2\pi}{|\mathbf{k}|} = \frac{2\pi}{\sqrt{k_x^2 + k_y^2 + k_z^2}} \qquad (6.55)$$

In our particle in a box problem, we found that the allowed wavelengths of the wave functions formed the following series:

$$\lambda = 2L, L, L/3, L/4 \ldots \qquad (6.56)$$

There is a pattern here, but it might not be clear to you. You may be able to see the pattern more clearly if I write it out again in a different format:

$$\lambda = \frac{2L}{1}, \frac{2L}{2}, \frac{2L}{3}, \frac{2L}{4} \ldots$$
$$= \frac{2L}{m} \qquad (6.57)$$

where $m = 1, 2, 3\ldots$ etc. We can express this series in λ as a series in k:

$$k = \frac{2\pi}{\lambda} = \frac{2\pi}{2L/m}$$
$$k = \frac{\pi m}{L} \qquad (6.58)$$

In fact, because we separated each standing wave into *two* travelling waves, this expression needs to be altered. The analysis in Web Chapter W1 shows that the allowed values of (k_x, k_y, k_z) are in fact given by:

$$k_x = \frac{2m_x \pi}{L_x}, k_y = \frac{2m_y \pi}{L_y}, k_z = \frac{2m_z \pi}{L_z} \qquad (6.59)$$

where $m_x = \pm1, \pm2, \pm3 \ldots$ and L_x is length of the piece of metal in the x-direction. There are similar

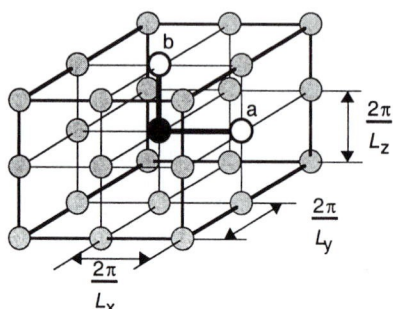

Figure 6.19 Close up view of 'k-space'. The circles represent allowed values of $\mathbf{k}$. If the central point represents a solution of the Schrödinger equation with a particular value of k_x, k_y, k_z, then point a represents a solution with k_x component increased by $2\pi/L_x$. Similarly point b represents a solution with k_z component increased by $2\pi/L_z$.

relationships for y and z. Thus the allowed states form a mesh in k-space (Figure 6.18) and the distance from one allowed value of k_x to the next is:

$$\Delta k_x = \frac{2(m_x + 1)\pi}{L_x} - \frac{2(m_x)\pi}{L_x}$$
$$= \frac{2\pi}{L_x} \qquad (6.60)$$

So, as illustrated in Figure 6.19, each allowed $\mathbf{k}$-state occupies a small cuboid of 'volume':

$$\Delta k_x \Delta k_y \Delta k_z = \frac{2\pi}{L_x} \times \frac{2\pi}{L_y} \times \frac{2\pi}{L_z}$$
$$= \frac{8\pi^3}{V} \qquad (6.61)$$

where V is the total volume of the crystal. I have used the word 'volume' in quotation marks above Equation 6.61 because I am referring to 'volume' on a k-space graph. As you can see from Equation 6.61, the 'volume' on the k-space graph actually has the dimensions of inverse volume, i.e. m^{-3} rather than m^3. The final point we need to make is that we need to take account of the internal spin of electrons. This allows two electrons with opposite spin to occupy each k-state. Thus, the 'volume' of k-space required for each electron is given by half the value in Equation 6.61:

$$\Delta \mathbf{k} = \frac{4\pi^3}{V} \qquad (6.62)$$

2. Energy and momentum

Equation 6.55 allows us to use the de Broglie relation (Equation 2.42) to infer the momentum and energy of the wave represented by (k_x, k_y, k_z)

The momentum may be written as:

$$p = \frac{h}{\lambda} = \frac{h}{\frac{2\pi}{|\mathbf{k}|}}$$

$$= \hbar|\mathbf{k}| \tag{6.63}$$

$$p = \hbar\sqrt{k_x^2 + k_y^2 + k_z^2}$$

Notice that the quantum states with small amounts of momentum have small values of $|\mathbf{k}|$. Thus in k-space they will be represented by points near the origin. The energy, which is just the kinetic energy of a free particle, may be written as:

$$E = \frac{1}{2}m_e v^2 = \frac{p^2}{2m_e}$$

$$E = \frac{\hbar^2|\mathbf{k}|^2}{2m_e} \tag{6.64}$$

$$E = \frac{\hbar^2}{2m_e}\left[k_x^2 + k_y^2 + k_z^2\right]$$

Notice again that the low-energy quantum states have small values of $|\mathbf{k}|$. Thus in k-space they will be represented by points near the origin. Importantly, Equation 6.64 is the equation of a sphere. Thus, all quantum states with energy E will be represented by points in k-space which lie on the surface of a sphere with radius:

$$|\mathbf{k}| = \sqrt{\frac{2m_e E}{\hbar^2}} \tag{6.65}$$

3. The density of states function

Using the concept of k-space allows to work out the *density of states* function $g(E)$ that we met §2.5.3. The density of states function answers the question: how many quantum states are there with energy between E and $E + dE$? The answer is $g(E)dE$. To find $g(E)$ in terms of our k-space graph, we can ask a related question: how many quantum states are there with k-vector of length

---

Example 6.4

An electron occupies a quantum state with:

$$k_x = 10^{-10}\ \text{m}^{-1} \qquad k_y = 10^{-10}\ \text{m}^{-1} \qquad k_z = 0\ \text{m}^{-1}$$

Work out the wavelength, energy, and speed of an electron occupying this state.

Wavelength
The total magnitude of the electrons k-vector is:

$$|\mathbf{k}| = \sqrt{k_x^2 + k_y^2 + k_z^2} = 10^{10}\sqrt{1^2 + 1^2 + 0^2}$$

$$= 1.41 \times 10^{10}\ \text{m}^{-1}$$

So the wavelength is given by Equation 6.55:

$$\lambda = \frac{2\pi}{|\mathbf{k}|} = \frac{2\pi}{1.41 \times 10^{10}} = 4.44 \times 10^{-10}\ \text{m}$$

Energy
The energy is given by Equation 6.64:

$$E = \frac{\hbar^2|\mathbf{k}|^2}{2m_e} = \frac{\left(1.054 \times 10^{-34}\right)^2\left(1.41 \times 10^{10}\right)^2}{2 \times 9.1 \times 10^{-31}}$$

$$= 1.21 \times 10^{-18}\ \text{J}$$

$$= 7.58\ \text{eV}$$

Speed
The speed can be calculated from the momentum $p = mv$ and $p = \hbar k$:

$$v = \frac{\hbar|\mathbf{k}|}{m_e} = \frac{1.054 \times 10^{-34} \times 1.41 \times 10^{10}}{9.1 \times 10^{-31}}$$

$$= 1.633 \times 10^6\ \text{m s}^{-1}$$

---

between k and $k + dk$? We can work out the answer to this question by working out the 'volume' of a spherical shell with inner radius k and thickness dk. The answer is:

$$\text{'volume'} = 4\pi k^2 dk \tag{6.66}$$

The number of states in this 'volume' is:

$$dN = \frac{4\pi k^2 dk}{4\pi^3 / V}$$

$$= \frac{V k^2 dk}{\pi^2} \tag{6.67}$$

We can convert this to an expression for $g(E)$ by changing references to k to references to E. We note that $k^2 = 2m_e E / \hbar^2$ and that dk is given by:

$$k = \left(2m_e / \hbar^2\right)^{\frac{1}{2}} E^{\frac{1}{2}}$$

$$\frac{dk}{dE} = \left(2m_e / \hbar^2\right)^{\frac{1}{2}} \frac{1}{2} E^{-\frac{1}{2}} \qquad (6.68)$$

$$dk = \frac{1}{2}\left(2m_e / \hbar^2\right)^{\frac{1}{2}} E^{-\frac{1}{2}} dE$$

Substituting for k^2 and dk in Equation 6.67 we find:

$$dN = \frac{V}{\pi^2} k^2 dk$$

$$= \frac{V}{\pi^2} \times \frac{2m_e E}{\hbar^2} \times \frac{1}{2}\left(\frac{2m_e}{\hbar^2}\right)^{\frac{1}{2}} E^{-\frac{1}{2}} dE \qquad (6.69)$$

$$= \underbrace{\left[\frac{V}{\pi^2} \frac{\sqrt{2m_e^3}}{\hbar^3} E^{\frac{1}{2}}\right]}_{g(E)} dE$$

This is the sought-after density of states function:

$$g(E) = \frac{V\sqrt{2m_e^3 E}}{\pi^2 \hbar^3}$$

$$= \left[\frac{V\sqrt{2m_e^3}}{\pi^2 \hbar^3}\right]\sqrt{E} \qquad (6.70)$$

Notice that $g(E)$ depends only a group of fundamental constants, and increases as the square root of the energy. It is illustrated in Figure 2.16 and is used in Examples 2.6 and 2.7 to calculate the average energy of an electron in a metal.

Occupying k-states

In the previous few paragraphs we have seen how the idea of k-space can be used to help develop a theoretical model of a metal. We have seen that the k-vectors of the allowed quantum states are distributed on a uniform mesh throughout k-space. Now we need to consider which of these quantum states are occupied by electrons.

We could answer this question by following the formal approach described in §2.5.3. To do that we would combine the density of states function (Eq. 6.70) with the Fermi–Dirac occupation function (Eq. 2.61) to calculate the distribution function (Eq. 2.64), which we could use to calculate

the properties of metals. We used that approach in Example 2.7 where we calculated the average energy of an electron in a metal. However, here we will approach the question of the occupancy of quantum states in a slightly simpler way, by considering the case of a metal at absolute zero. At $T = 0$ the Fermi–Dirac function (Figure 2.17) tells us that the N electrons in the metal occupy the N lowest energy quantum states.

Consider the following analogy: k-space is like an 'auditorium' into which we allow an 'audience' (electrons) to enter. The first electrons to enter occupy the 'cheapest seats' (low-energy k-states), and those who enter later have to occupy 'more expensive seats' (higher-energy k-states). The density of states function tells us exactly how many seats (k-states) there are in each 'price range' (energy range). The Fermi–Dirac function tells us that at $T = 0$ the N electrons in the metal occupy the N 'cheapest seats' (lowest energy quantum states).

The low-energy quantum states are those clustered around the origin on a k-space graph. The mesh of allowed states is actually very fine indeed, so by the time the first few thousand electrons have been accommodated, the region of occupied states looks rather like a sphere centred on the origin (Figure 6.20). By the time a number of the order of 10^{23} electrons have been accommodated, the region of occupied states forms an essentially perfect sphere, known as the *Fermi sphere*, with Fermi radius k_F. Since each electron requires a 'volume' of k-space $4\pi^3 / V$ we can write:

$$\frac{\frac{4}{3}\pi k_F^3}{4\pi^3 / V} = N \qquad (6.71)$$

where we have remembered that a sphere of radius r has a volume $\frac{4}{3}\pi r^3$. If we cancel some terms, and solve for k_F we find:

$$k_F^3 = 3\left[\frac{N}{V}\right]\pi^2$$

$$k_F = \left(3n\pi^2\right)^{\frac{1}{3}} \qquad (6.72)$$

where $n = N/V$ is the electron density. We can

also work out an expression for the energy (called the *Fermi energy*) of electrons on the 'surface' of the Fermi sphere:

$$E_F = \frac{\hbar^2 k_F^2}{2m_e} \tag{6.73}$$

6.5.4 A real metal

The previous section has been rather theoretical and so in this section we will evaluate some of the key results from the last section for a real metal: copper.

A numerical example

To estimate the number density n of 'free electrons' in a metal we can proceed as follows. We first work out the number density n of atoms in a metal. Then we imagine that (say) 1, 2, or 3 electrons, the *valence electrons* from each atom, can leave the 'parent' atom to form the electron gas. Which integer value we choose will depend upon our prior knowledge of the metal under consideration. There are several ways to estimate n, but perhaps the simplest is to divide the *density* by the mass of an atom to get the *number density* of atoms. If we then multiply by the valence we arrive at n. From Table 7.2 we see that the density of copper is 8.933×10^3 kg m^{-3}, and the mass of an atom is $63.55 \times 1.66 \times 10^{-27}$ kg. Assuming copper has a valence of one, then our estimate for n is:

$$n = \frac{1 \times 8.933 \times 10^3}{63.55 \times 1.66 \times 10^{-27}} \tag{6.74}$$

$$= 8.47 \times 10^{28} \text{ electrons m}^{-3}$$

If we use this estimate for n in Equation 6.72 for the Fermi wave vector k_F we find:

$$k_F = (3 \times 8.47 \times 10^{28} \times \pi^2)^{\frac{1}{3}} \tag{6.75}$$

$$= 1.36 \times 10^{10} \quad \text{m}^{-1}$$

Substituting this in Equation 6.73 for the Fermi energy E_F we find:

$$E_F = \frac{(1.054 \times 10^{-34})^2 (1.36 \times 10^{10})^2}{2 \times 9.1 \times 10^{-31}}$$

$$= 1.13 \times 10^{-18} \text{ J} \tag{6.76}$$

$$= 7.06 \text{ eV}$$

Figure 6.20 (a) In three-dimensions the occupied states form a sphere in k-space known as the *Fermi sphere* which is shown shaded in the figure. If we imagine slicing through the Fermi sphere in plane where $k_z = 0$ we would find a situation represented in (b). Each small circle represents an allowed travelling wave solution to the Schrödinger Equation. The filled circles represent occupied quantum states and the unfilled circles represent empty quantum states. At absolute zero, only the lowest energy states (low k = long wavelength = low energy) are occupied. For any macroscopic piece of metal the quantum states would be much more densely packed than in the figure.

(a)

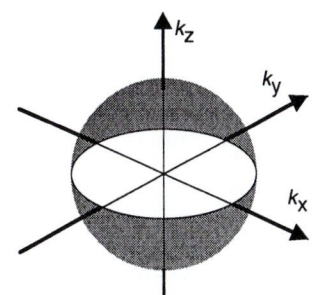

(b)

We can evaluate $g(E)$ per unit volume from Equation 6.70:

$$\frac{g(E)}{V} = \left[\frac{\sqrt{2 \times (9.1 \times 10^{-31})^3}}{\pi^2 (1.054 \times 10^{-34})^3} \right] \sqrt{E} \tag{6.77}$$

$$= 1.062 \times 10^{56} \sqrt{E} \text{ states J}^{-1}\text{m}^{-3}$$

And we can evaluate this at the Fermi energy:

$$\frac{g(E_F)}{V} = \left[1.062 \times 10^{56}\right]\sqrt{1.13 \times 10^{-18}} \qquad (6.78)$$

$$= 1.13 \times 10^{47} \quad \text{states} \quad J^{-1}m^{-3}$$

Let us look at the significance of k_F, E_F and $g(E)$ in turn.

The significance of k_F

The significance of k_F can be seen more easily if we look at the wavelength of electrons with wave vector k_F. Since k_F is the *maximum* k-vector, then electrons with this k-vector will have the *minimum wavelength* since $k = 2\pi/\lambda$. Substituting from Equation 6.75:

$$\lambda_{min} = \frac{2\pi}{1.36 \times 10^{10}} \qquad (6.79)$$

$$= 4.63 \times 10^{-10} \quad m$$

We find a wavelength comparable to the spacing a between atoms. We can see the significance of this if we consider again Figure 6.16, which was the basis of the free-electron approximation. We have been able to ignore the 'corrugations' on the bottom of the potential well because the wavelengths of electron wave functions are not related to the spacing between ions a. Thus the peaks in the probability density $|\Psi|^2$ sometimes fall exactly on an ion, and sometimes in between ions. On average, each electron experiences a smoothly-averaged potential.

However, if the periodicity of the electron probability density has a periodicity which *exactly* matches the lattice periodicity, then the peaks in the probability density will either always fall on an ion, or always fall between ions. In either case, the electron–ion interaction becomes much significantly larger, and can no longer be ignored. This phenomenon is critical to understanding the detailed electronic properties of solids, and we consider it further in Chapter W1 on the band theory of solids.

The significance of E_F

The significance of E_F can be seen if we compare it with the typical amount of thermal energy an electron might expect to receive as interacts with the ions in a metal crystal ($\approx \tfrac{3}{2}k_BT$). Evaluating this at room temperature $\approx 290K$:

$$\tfrac{3}{2}k_BT = 6.0 \times 10^{-21} \quad J \qquad (6.80)$$

$$= 0.038 \quad eV$$

This energy is smaller than E_F by a factor ≈ 200.

The electrons with energies near E_F also travel very fast. Since E_F is the kinetic energy of the electron, $\tfrac{1}{2}mv_F^2$, we can work out the Fermi speed v_F as:

$$v_F = \sqrt{\frac{2E_F}{m}} = \sqrt{\frac{2 \times 1.122 \times 10^{-18}}{9.1 \times 10^{-31}}} \qquad (6.81)$$

$$= 1.6 \times 10^6 \quad m\,s^{-1}$$

which is $\approx 1\%$ of the speed of light. Also, notice that the electrons with energies near E_F travel with this speed independent of the temperature. This may be contrasted with the situation of molecules in a *molecular* gas whose distribution of speeds depends strongly on temperature (Figure 4.7).

The significance of $g(E_F)$

As we heat a metal above absolute zero, some quantum states above the Fermi energy will become occupied, and some states below the Fermi energy will become empty. However, the exclusion principle restricts this process very strongly. Only electrons occupying quantum states with energies within about k_BT of the Fermi energy are able to change state. This is because only those electrons have access to the empty quantum states above the Fermi energy. As we saw above, $k_BT << E_F$, and so the number of electrons able to accept thermal energy is rather small, of the order of $\Delta N = g(E_F)k_BT$. Hence the *fraction* of electrons able to accept thermal energy is:

$$\frac{\Delta N}{N} = \frac{g(E_F)k_BT}{N}$$

$$= \frac{1.13 \times 10^{47} \times 1.38 \times 10^{-23}}{8.47 \times 10^{28}}T \qquad (6.82)$$

$$= 1.84 \times 10^{-5}T$$

It is important to note how small this fraction is.

Even at a temperature of 2000 K, which is above the melting temperature of most metals, only around $1.84 \times 10^{-5} \times 2000 \approx 4\%$ of the 'free'

electrons in the metal have changed their quantum state. We shall see the effect of this when we consider the heat capacity of metals in §7.6

6.5.4 Cohesive energy

The cohesive energy of a metal is rather difficult to calculate accurately. However, even at the level of this book, we can show that the cohesive energy is quite large, potentially of the order of several electron volts per atom (several hundred kJ mol^{-1}).

Cohesive energy of the eight-electron metal

Consider again the calculations illustrated in Figure 6.17. These showed the energy of eight electrons on eight isolated atoms of volume a^3 (Option A) was significantly greater than the energy of eight electrons able to move around a single box of volume $8a^3$ (Option B). Table 6.4 summarises the total energy of the eight electrons, the average energy per electron, and the difference between the average energy per electron in the two options.

Now for a metal, a has a typical value of ≈ 0.3 nm and so a typical energy benefit per electron in Table 6.4 is given by:

$$u = -1.69 \times \frac{h^2}{8ma^2}$$

$$= -1.69 \times \frac{(6.626 \times 10^{-34})^2}{8 \times 9.1 \times 10^{-31}(0.3 \times 10^{-9})^2}$$

$$= -3.4 \times 10^{-18} \quad \text{J per electron} \qquad (6.83)$$

$$= -21.2 \qquad eV \text{ per electron}$$

$$= -2043 \qquad \text{kJ per mole}$$

The cohesive energy of a 'real' metal

In order to calculate the cohesive energy of real metal consisting of more than eight electrons, we need to calculate the average energy per electron. This is done in Example 2.8, where it is shown that the average energy per electron in the free electron approximation is $\frac{3}{5}E_F$

Table 6.5 summarises the calculation we need to make. Let us try to evaluate this energy difference. First of all we can express E_F in terms of k_F (see Equation 6.73)

Table 6.4 Evaluating the energy difference between options A and B in Figure 6.17 for eight electrons.

	Option A (separate atoms)	Option B (metallic state)
Energy of 8 electrons	$24 \times h^2/8ma^2$	$10.5 \times h^2/8ma^2$
Average energy per electron	$3 \times h^2/8ma^2$	$1.31 \times h^2/8ma^2$
Energy *difference* per electron		$-1.69 \times h^2/8ma^2$

$$u = \frac{3}{5}E_F - \frac{3h^2}{8ma^2}$$
$$= \frac{3}{5} \times \frac{\hbar^2 k_F^2}{2m} - \frac{3h^2}{8ma^2} \qquad (6.84)$$

Now we write k_F in terms of n (Equation 6.72):

$$u = \frac{3}{5} \times \frac{\hbar^2 (3n\pi^2)^{2/3}}{2m} - \frac{3h^2}{8ma^2} \qquad (6.85)$$

Finally, we recall that $\hbar = h/2\pi$ and that the number density of electrons is just $n = 1/a^3$:

$$u = \frac{3}{5} \times \frac{h^2(3\pi^2)^{2/3}}{4\pi^2 \times 2ma^2} - \frac{3h^2}{8ma^2} \qquad (6.86)$$

Taking out common factors we arrive at:

$$u = \left[\frac{(3\pi^2)^{2/3}}{5\pi^2} - 1\right] \times \frac{3h^2}{8ma^2}$$
$$= -0.806 \times \frac{3h^2}{8ma^2} \qquad (6.87)$$

Table 6.5 Evaluating the energy difference between options A and B in Figure 6.17 for a free electron gas.

	Option A (separate atoms)	Option B (metallic state)
Energy of N electrons	$3N \times h^2/8ma^2$	$N \times 3E_F/5$
Average energy per electron	$3 \times h^2/8ma^2$	$3E_F/5$
Energy *difference* per electron		$3E_F/5 - 3h^2/8ma^2$

which amounts to roughly 50% of the cohesive energy per electron of the eight electron metal we considered earlier. We therefore find for the cohesive energy of a typical metal a figure of:

$$u \approx -1.6 \times 10^{-18} \quad \text{J per electron}$$
$$\approx -10.11 \qquad \text{eV per electron} \qquad (6.88)$$
$$\approx -974 \qquad \text{kJ per mole}$$

Clearly, this is a potentially strong form of bonding. Astonishingly, we arrived at this figure without any consideration of the Coulomb interaction between electrons! When we consider the Coulomb interactions between electrons and other electrons, and between electrons and ions, then the problem becomes considerably more complex. These matters are discussed in Chapter W1 on the band theory of solids.

6.6 Real solids

The four types of bonding we discussed in §6.2 to §6.5 represent ideal situations: only rarely can solids be understood by considering just one type of bonding. The solids which can be understood this way are sometimes called *simple* (although they are not!) and have been studied extensively in the first 70 years or so of modern solid-state physics. However most solids are not simple, in the sense of having only type of bonding: most materials have two or more types of bonding. Indeed, in general it is not always possible to clearly separate the types of bonding present: there are just interacting electrons following the Coulomb law and the rules of quantum mechanics. However, despite this reservation, we consider below some combinations of types of bonding found in real solids.

6.6.1 Organic solids

Many of the most common solids that we encounters in normal life are classed as organic in nature. Originally the term *organic* meant that the substance was derived from a living organism. In modern terms however it denotes a substance composed primarily of carbon and hydrogen atoms. If we consider plastics, just one class of organic substance, one can begin to appreciate the astonishingly diverse properties of organic solids. Clearly we cannot specify everything about bonding in organic substances, but we can make one or two generalisations.

Bonding between molecules

Organic substances are composed of molecules which are bound to each other by Van der Waals bonding similar to that discussed in §6.1. The relatively weak Van der Waals force acts between all molecules, and is non-directional in nature.

However, some molecules have other types of bonds between them. In particular, hydrogen bonds are especially important for molecules which contain the OH chemical group. We discuss them further in Chapter 8.

Bonding within molecules

Organic molecules can consist of anything from just a few to many thousands of atoms. Within each organic molecule, the atoms are held together by relatively strong covalent bonding similar to that discussed in §6.3. Since the covalent bonding is directional in nature, this leads to organic molecules having relatively well-defined shapes. The broad picture is shown in Figure 6.21.

When we consider complex organic molecules we have to consider yet another effect we have glided over in this chapter, but which we will return to in Chapter 10: *entropy*. Consider, for example, a collection of organic molecules which are each, say, 100 carbon atoms long and studded with various hydrogen and other atoms. By considering the shape of the molecules and the interactions between them, we can predict the crystal structure for the substance with the lowest energy. However, in practice this crystal structure will never be attained because the molecules will become tangled in a way which is essentially irreversible.

171

For such materials, their equilibrium properties are dominated by this disorder and their minimum energy state is nearly irrelevant. This highlights an important feature that we discuss again in Chapter 10. The equilibrium structure for *any substance* is *not* the lowest energy structure, but the one which minimises a combination of entropy and internal energy known as the *Gibbs free energy*.

6.6.2 Hydrogen bonding

Hydrogen bonding is a specific combination of ionic and covalent bonding that occurs in substances which contain oxygen and hydrogen atoms bonded together, e.g. H_2O. It is given a specially category to itself because of its importance in organic substances where it acts between molecules and is much stronger than the Van der Waals force. The nature of the hydrogen bond is discussed in detail in §9.1 where we consider its effect on the density of liquid water.

6.6.3 The ionic–covalent continuum

In 'pure' ionic bonding, an electron is transferred completely from one atom to another. Of course, once this transfer is complete, the electric forces will act to try to pull this electron back to its parent ion. If these forces partially succeed then there will be some electron density in the region in be-

tween the ions, which is the situation in a covalent bond. Thus 'pure' ionic and 'pure' covalent bonds can be seen as two extremes of a continuum. Symmetry considerations dictate that a 'pure' covalent bond can only exist between two identical atoms. Any difference in the electron affinity of the atoms at either end of the bond will result in an asymmetric charge distribution which has both ionic and covalent character (Figure 6.22).

The figure illustrates four possible electronic charge distributions in between two atoms. In the lower picture, the atoms have identical electron affinity. The other three cases refer to situations where the right-most atom has increasing electron affinity compared to the left-most atom.

The differing electron affinities of atoms are caused by the different distributions of charge around the nucleus of the atoms. Atoms with complete shells of electrons have essentially zero electron affinity. Atoms with one electron missing from a shell have particularly high electron affinity the 'gap' in the shell allows other electrons to 'see' the nuclear charge and hence be attracted to the atom.

6.6.4 Transition metals

Most elements are metallic. However most ele-

Figure 6.21 Within an organic substances there are in general at least two types of bonding:

- **Within** an organic molecule the atoms are held together by relatively strong, directional covalent bonds

- **Between** organic molecules the bonding is due to relatively weak, non-directional, Van der Waals bonds.

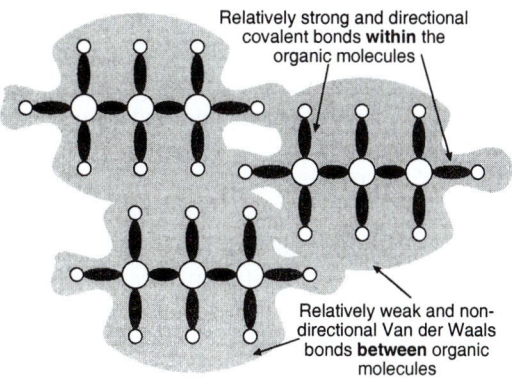

Relatively strong and directional covalent bonds **within** the organic molecules

Relatively weak and non-directional Van der Waals bonds **between** organic molecules

Figure 6.22 An illustration of the ionic-covalent continuum. In the text ionic and covalent bonding were presented as distinct categories. In practice, many substances have bonding which is intermediate between the two cases. The figure illustrates four possible electronic charge distributions in between two atoms. In the lower picture, the atoms have identical *electron affinity*. The other three cases refer to situations where the rightmost atom has increasing electron affinity compared to the leftmost atom.

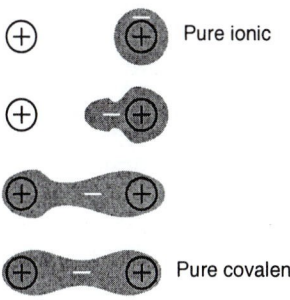

Pure ionic

Pure covalent

ments are bonded in a way which is a mixture of metallic and covalent bonding. In the transition metals for example, electrons in *d*-orbitals form bonds which are partly covalent and partly metallic, while electrons occupying *s*-orbitals form almost purely metallic bonds. The situation is too complex for detailed consideration here.

6.6.5 What have we neglected?

In considering molecular, ionic and covalent bonding in §6.2 to §6.4 we concentrated entirely on the effect of Coulomb interactions, and neglected to take account of quantum mechanics.

Clearly this cannot be quite right, since we saw when considering metals in §6.5, that quantum mechanics played a critical role in determining, for example, the cohesive energy of metals. Also, in metallic bonding, when we did consider the effect the of quantum mechanics, we then neglected to take account of the Coulomb interaction between electrons.

In reality, both Coulomb interactions and quantum mechanics are important considerations in all types of bonding. Table 6.6 summarises some of the effects we neglected in §6.2 to §6.5.

Table 6.6 Summary of what has been considered and neglected in Chapter 6.

Bonding type	What we considered	What we neglected
Molecular	We calculated the cohesive energy of an array of neutral molecules interacting through fluctuations of their electric charge distribution.	We neglected to consider the origin of the charge distributions, and the origin of their fluctuations. These can only be properly calculated using quantum mechanics.
Ionic	We calculated the cohesive energy of an array of positive and negative ions interacting through the coulomb interaction.	We neglected to consider why electrons transfer themselves completely from one ion to another. This can only be understood by quantum mechanical calculations of the charge distribution around atoms and ions.
Covalent	We calculated the cohesive energy of a covalent bond in terms of a simple model of the charge distribution within the bond.	We neglected to consider *why* that particular charge distribution occurs. This can only be understood by quantum mechanical calculations of the electron wave functions near both atoms. Notice that in addition to the Coulomb energy which we calculated, there will be an additional 'delocalisation' term analogous to that which occurs on a larger scale in metals
Metallic	We calculated the cohesive energy of a metal by considering the change in energy of the wave functions as they were allowed to expand into a large volume.	We neglected to include the effects of the strong Coulomb interactions between electrons and other electrons, and between electrons and ions.

6.7 Exercises

Exercises marked with a P prefix are 'normal' exercises. Those marked with a C prefix are best solved numerically by using a computer program or spreadsheet. Exercises marked with an E prefix are in general rather more challenging that the P and C exercises. Answers to all the exercises are downloadable from www.physicsofmatter.com

C1. Download the molecular dynamics simulation from the web site www.physicsofmatter.com and observe the

dynamics of molecules in a solid. Notice how the initial 'square' structure spontaneously 'collapses' into a 'hexagonal' structure. Can you explain why this happens?

C2. Use a spreadsheet program to draw the functional form of Equation 6.6 for a range of values of *A* and *B*.

P3. Given the entries in Table 6.2 for σ and ε for krypton, estimate (a) the molar cohesive energy and (b) the density. Check your answers in Table 11.5 and Table 7.2 respectively.

C4. Write a computer program to evaluate the Madelung

sum for an ion at the centre of a small ionic crystal with $12 \times 12 \times 12$ ions. Re-evaluate the Madelung sum for an ion displaced from its equilibrium position by an amount Δ and plot a graph of the Madelung sums versus Δ. You should find a roughly quadratic variation with Δ indicating that the ion will vibrate in a roughly simple harmonic potential.

P5. In §6.3 we considered calculations of the potential energy of electrons in a covalent bond, but did not consider their kinetic energy. The kinetic energy is difficult to calculate accurately, but one can estimate it roughly be considering the electrons in the bond region of length L to be confined to a three dimensional box of side L. The kinetic energy of an electron in such a box may be estimated using Equation 2.39 (or Equation 6.59). Calculate this energy.

The calculated kinetic energy for the C–C bond is large, but a more realistic calculation would compare the kinetic and potential energies of electrons on isolated atoms, with the kinetic and potential energies of electrons when bonded. Unfortunately, this is a much more difficult calculation than the simple estimates we have made.

P6. Work out the separation between neighbouring atoms in (a) silicon and (b) germanium given that their crystal structure is illustrated in Figure 6.14. The densities of silicon and germanium may be found from Table 7.1. (See also Example 7.3)

P7. Repeat the Option A/Option B (Figure 6.17) exercise for metals with $3^3 = 27$ and $4^3 = 64$ electrons. Compare the energy per electron with the value calculated for the 8-electron metal and the value for 'real' metal. (Tables 6.4 and 6.5)

C8. Download the molecular dynamics simulation from the web site www.physicsofmatter.com and run the simulation for the solid state. When the simulations is running turn off the radio button for molecular interactions and observe the destruction of the solid. Would the solid state be possible without molecular interactions?

CHAPTER 7

Solids: comparison with experiment

7.1 Introduction

I do not know where you are reading this, but I expect that you are close to some solids with extraordinary properties. This is true for me as I write this on my computer. Beneath my fingers is a keyboard made of plastics, some transparent and some opaque. In front of me is a screen made of glass, the reverse of which is coated with solids that glow under bombardment by electrons. Nearby are paper, cloth and wood. I can see metals, some at temperatures in excess of 2000 °C. And 50 centimetres away is a chip of patterned silicon which enables my computer to function. There is also the semi-solid matter I call my body, which possesses the capacity for abstract thought. This diversity of properties makes comparison with the simple models outlined in Chapter 6 particularly difficult. There are so many 'special cases' and 'exceptions' that it is unusual to find strict numerical agreement between theory and experimental data. However, we will find that often we can understand *the order of magnitude* of results, and the *trends* of the results from one material to another. With these limitations on our ambition in mind, let us see what Chapter 7 holds.

§7.2, §7.3, and §7.4 Density, Compressibility, Thermal expansivity: We will find that the density of solids reflects the *type of bonding* present; the compressibility tells us about the *pair-potential* between atoms; and thermal expansivity tells us about the *asymmetry* of the pair-potential .

§7.5 **Speed of sound:** Sound waves in solids are considerably more complex than in gases. However we relegate much of this complexity to Appendix A2 and focus on the trends in the data, allowing us to get a good feel for the factors involved.

§7.6 **Heat capacity:** The heat capacity of most solid elements at around room temperature can be understood using an exceptionally simple model of a solid. However, the temperature-dependence of the data, and the data which *cannot* be explained by this model, will lead us to a more realistic model, and a surprising connection to §7.5 on the speed of sound.

§7.7 **Electrical properties:** The difference in conductivity between *metals* and *insulators* is an amazing 20 orders of magnitude. Not surprisingly, we will use quite different models to understand the two categories of solids. More surprising is the simplicity of each of the models that we will use. For *metals* we will use the free electron model of a solid we discussed in §6.5, and for insulators we will ignore the bonding between the atoms almost entirely!

§7.8 **Thermal conductivity:** Although simple in principle, the data and the theory are surprisingly complex, and we attempt to understand only the temperature-dependence of the data.

§7.9 **Optical properties:** In Chapter 2 we said that the refractive index of a material is related to its dielectric constant. Using this result and Newton's laws of motion we will be able to explain the values, and the variation with wavelength, of the refractive index of transparent solids. Amazing.

At www.physicsofmatter.com

In addition to copies of the figures and tables you will find: animations of some of the important equations in this chapter; a computer program which realistically simulates the dynamics of simple molecules in solids, liquids and gases; Chapter W1 on the *Band theory of solids* which extends some of the topics dealt with in this chapter; and Chapter W2 on the *Magnetic properties of solids*.

7.2 Density

In contrast with gases, the most striking property of solids is that they have both a well-defined *volume and shape*. Further, unlike gases, neither the volume nor the shape are particularly sensitive to changes in temperature or pressure.

7.2.1 Data on the density of solids

The densities of most solids lie in the range between 0.5 and 20 times that of water. Historically, the *gram* was defined as the mass of one cubic centimetre of water at 4 °C. Thus the density of water lies close to 1 gram per cubic centimetre, or in the rather incongruous *SI* units, 1000 kg m^{-3}. So solid densities lie in the range from around 500 kg m^{-3} to around 20000 kg m^{-3}. Table 7.1 gives the density of an arbitrary selection of substances. The density of the elements is recorded in Table 7.2 and graphed as a function of atomic number in Figure 7.1.

The first point we note is that solid densities are of a similar order of magnitude to liquid densities (Tables 9.1 and 9.2), but around a thousand times greater than the densities of gases at around STP (Table 5.1).

From the data in Table 7.2 we can work out many quantities that are useful for understanding the properties of solids, for example:

- the number densities of atoms in the elements
- the volume per atom taken up by atoms in the elements
- the typical separations between atoms in the elements in the solid state and
- the molar volume of the elements.

These calculations are carried in out Example 7.1. The densities of the elements as recorded in Table 7.2 appear to vary almost randomly, but when plotted as a function of atomic number (Figure 7.1) it becomes apparent that there is a significant amount of structure in the data. The most striking features are the periodic increases and decreases in density, and the curious linear portion between elements 57 to 71. There are also more subtle

Table 7.1 The approximate values of the density of some solids.

Solid	ρ(kg m^{-3})
Metals	
Aluminium/Dural	2700–2800
Phosphor–bronze	8900
Brass	8400–8500
Gold (22 carat)	17500
Gold (9 carat)	11300
Mild steel	7900
Stainless steel	7700–7800
Wrought iron	7800
Invar	8000
Platinum/Iridium	21500
Wood	
Balsa	200
Pine	500
Oak	700
Beech	750
Teak	850
Ebony	1200
Natural materials	
Amber	1100
Beeswax	950
Granite	2700
Ice	920
Coal	1.4–1.6
Mica	2800

features. Notice for instance the 'shoulders' on the high atomic number side of each peak *e*, *f* and *g*, or the periodicities at small atomic. We also note that there is a general trend towards elements with high atomic number having higher densities.

So, the main questions raised by our preliminary examination of the experimental data on the density of solids are:
- Why are the densities of solids much greater than those of gases?
- Why is there a general trend to increasing density for elements with increasing atomic number?
- Why are there periodic increases and decreases in density?
- Why is there a linear density increase between elements with atomic numbers from 57 to 71?

Table 7.2 The density of the elements (kg m^{-3}). Also shown is the atomic number Z and the atomic weight A in units of the atomic mass unit u = 1.66 × 10^{-27} kg. For example, the density of *magnesium*, whose atoms each contain 12 protons, is 1.738 × 10^3 kg m^{-3}. The mass of an atom of magnesium is 24.31 × 1.66 × 10^{-27} kg. The densities of elements that are normally gaseous at room temperature are evaluated at a temperature just below their freezing point at atmospheric pressure. For helium, which does not solidify at atmospheric pressure at any temperature, the density is evaluated at 4.2 K and 25 atmospheres (25 ×10^5 Pa) pressure which is sufficient to cause solidification.

Z	Element and symbol	A	Density	Z	Element and symbol	A	Density
1	Hydrogen, H	1.008	89				
2	Helium, He	4.003	120	51	Antimony, Sb	121.7	6692
3	Lithium , Li	6.941	533	52	Tellurium, Te	127.6	6247
4	Beryllium, Be	9.012	1846	53	Iodine, I	126.9	4953
5	Boron, B	10.81	2466	54	Xenon, Xe	131.3	3560
6	Carbon (graphite), C	12.01	2266	55	Caesium, Cs	132.9	1900
6	Carbon (diamond), C	12.01	3513	56	Barium, Ba	137.3	3594
7	Nitrogen, N	14.01	1035	57	Lanthanum, La	138.9	6174
8	Oxygen, O	16.00	1460	58	Cerium, Ce	140.1	6711
9	Fluorine, F	19.00	1140	59	Praseodymium, Pr	140.9	6779
10	Neon, Ne	20.18	1442	60	Neodymium, Ne	144.2	7000
11	Sodium, Na	22.99	966	61	Promethium, Pm	145.0	7220
12	Magnesium, Mg	24.31	1738	62	Samarium, Sm	150.4	7536
13	Aluminium, Al	26.98	2698	63	Europium, Eu	152.0	5248
14	Silicon, Si	28.09	2329	64	Gadolinium, Gd	157.2	7870
15	Phosphorus, P	30.97	1820	65	Terbium, Tb	158.9	8267
16	Sulphur, S	32.06	2086	66	Dysprosium, Dy	162.5	8531
17	Chlorine, Cl	35.45	2030	67	Holmium, Ho	164.9	8797
18	Argon, Ar	39.95	1656	68	Erbium, Er	167.3	9044
19	Potassium, K	39.10	862	69	Thulium, Th	168.9	9325
20	Calcium, Ca	40.08	1530	70	Ytterbium, Yb	173.0	6966
21	Scandium, Sc	44.96	2992	71	Lutetium, Lu	175.0	9842
22	Titanium, Ti	47.90	4508	72	Hafnium, Hf	178.5	13276
23	Vanadium, V	50.94	6090	73	Tantalum, Ta	180.9	16670
24	Chromium, Cr	52.00	7194	74	Tungsten, W	183.9	19254
25	Manganese, Mn	54.94	7473	75	Rhenium, Re	186.2	21023
26	Iron, Fe	55.85	7873	76	Osmium, Os	190.2	22580
27	Cobalt, Co	58.93	8800	77	Iridium, Ir	192.2	22550
28	Nickel, Ni	58.70	8907	78	Platinum, Pt	195.1	21450
29	Copper, Cu	63.55	8933	79	Gold, Au	197.0	19281
30	Zinc, Zn	65.38	7135	80	Mercury, Hg	200.6	13546
31	Gallium, Ga	69.72	5905	81	Thallium, Th	204.4	11871
32	Germanium, Ge	72.59	5323	82	Lead, Pb	207.2	11343
33	Arsenic, As	74.92	5776	83	Bismuth, Bi	209.0	9803
34	Selenium, Se	78.96	4808	84	Polonium, Po	209.0	9400
35	Bromine, Br	79.90	3120	85	Astatine, At	210.0	—
36	Krypton, Kr	83.80	3000	86	Radon, Rn	222.0	4400
37	Rubidium, Rb	85.47	1533	87	Francium, Fr	223.0	—
38	Strontium, Sr	87.62	2583	88	Radium, Ra	226.0	5000
39	Yttrium, Y	88.91	4475	89	Actinium, Ac	227.0	10060
40	Zirconium, Zr	91.22	6507	90	Thorium, Th	232.0	11725
41	Niobium, Nb	92.91	8578	91	Protractinium, Pa	231.0	15370
42	Molybdenum, Mo	95.94	10222	92	Uranium, U	238.0	19050
43	Technetium, Tc	97.00	11496	93	Neptunium, Np	237.0	20250
44	Ruthenium, Ru	101.1	12360	94	Plutonium, Pu	244.0	19840
45	Rhodium, Rh	102.9	12420	95	Americium, Am	243.0	13670
46	Palladium, Pd	106.4	11995	96	Curium, Cm	247.0	13300
47	Silver, Ag	107.9	10500	97	Berkelium, Bk	247.0	14790
48	Cadmium, Cd	112.4	8647	98	Californium, Cf	251.0	15100
49	Indium, In	114.8	7290	99	Einsteinium, Es	254.0	—
50	Tin, Sn	118.7	7285	100	Fermium, Fm	257.0	—

7.2.2 Understanding the data on the density of solids

Of the questions raised at the end of the previous section, we can understand the first one immediately: why the density of solids is much greater than the density of gases. All the models of solids we discussed in Chapter 6 consist of atoms arranged close to one another, whereas a gas consists of molecules with large spaces between them. It is not really surprising therefore that the amount of mass per unit volume in a solid is greater than for a gas.

However understanding the other questions is rather more complicated because it is difficult to make predictive calculations of the expected density of a particular solid. The reason for this is that the atoms of a solid can arrange themselves in any of several different ways. So even if we could calculate the equilibrium separation between atoms, each different arrangement of atoms would have a different density. Thus in order to predict the density of a material one needs to be able to predict the atomic separation *and* the crystal structure that

Figure 7.1 The densities of the elements plotted against atomic number, i.e. the number of electrons on each atom. A great deal of structure is evident. The troughs *a, b, c, d* occur just after the completion of the main electron shells of the atoms; *a* = K (Potassium); *b* = Rb (Rubidium); *c* = Cs (Caesium); *d* = Fr (Francium). The peaks *e, f,* and *g* are between the middle and end of the filling of the *d* - electron states in the three rows of *transition metals*; *e* = Zn (Zinc); *f* = Rh (Rhodium); *g* = Os (Osmium); the regular slope *h* represents the *Lanthanides*.

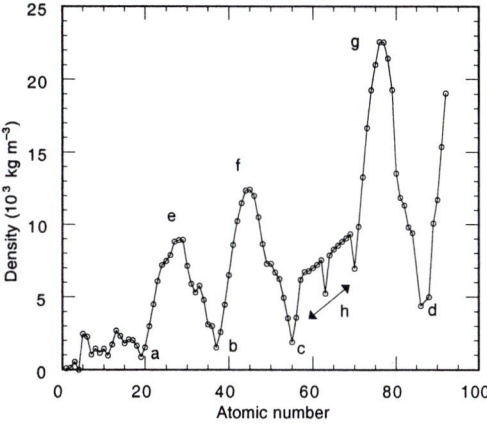

the material will adopt. To achieve this one needs to evaluate the energy of several different 'competing' crystal structures with high accuracy and then compare the results to find out which crystal structure the atoms will naturally choose. Although we managed to do this for the noble gas solids (§6.2.3) for most solids this task is still a challenge for even the most modern and sophisti-

---

Example 7.1

Estimate:

- **the number density of iron atoms in solid iron**
- **the volume per iron atom in solid iron**
- **the typical separation between iron atoms in solid iron**
- **the molar volume of the iron.**

We can answer these questions as follows:

- From Table 7.2 we see that iron (atomic number Z =26) has a density of 7.873×10^3 kg m^{-3} and that the average mass of an iron atom is $55.85u = 55.85 \times 1.66 \times 10^{-27}$ kg. Thus dividing the mass density by the mass per atom yields the number density of atoms:

$$n = \frac{7.783 \times 10^3}{55.85 \times 1.66 \times 10^{-27}} = 8.39 \times 10^{28} \text{ m}^{-3}$$

- If there are n atoms per cubic metre, then the volume per atom $v = 1/n$, which for iron is

$$v = \frac{1}{8.39 \times 10^{28}} = 1.19 \times 10^{-29} \text{ m}^3 \text{ atom}^{-1}$$

- It is not possible to evaluate the exact separation between atoms without knowledge of the crystal structure of the iron. However we can make an estimate of the separation if we imagine an atom to be confined in a tiny cube of side a. We can then estimate a by using

$$a = \sqrt[3]{v}$$
$$= \sqrt[3]{1.19 \times 10^{-29}}$$
$$= 2.28 \times 10^{-10} \text{ m}$$

Finally, we can work out the volume of 1 mole, i.e. N_A atoms of iron. This is just $N_A v$, which is:

$$V_m = N_A v = 6.022 \times 10^{23} \times 1.19 \times 10^{-29}$$
$$= 7.18 \times 10^{-6} \text{ m}^{-3}$$

This corresponds to a cube of iron a little less than 2 cm on each side.

---

cated theories of solids. Bearing these reservations in mind, let us look at the questions raised about this data in turn.

General trend to increasing density

The general trend towards increasing density arises because the atoms that make up solids get heavier as their atomic number increases. The heavier atoms in Figure 7.2 have masses over 200 times greater than the lighter atoms on the graph, and so it would be surprising if materials made from heavier atoms were not denser.

However, we need also to consider the way the spacing between atoms changes. The simplest model of a solid we can envisage assumes that (a) the spacing between atoms remains roughly constant, and that (b) the crystal structures of the elements are all the same. Example 7.2 is a calculation of the density of the elements assuming that they all have a simple-cubic crystal structure (which in fact none of them do) with an atomic spacing is 0.3 nm. The results of this calculation are plotted on Figure 7.2. It seems that these simple assumptions produce density estimates that are of the correct order of magnitude and which reproduce the trend towards increasing density.

This broad agreement implies that, as a general trend, the separation between atoms must be staying roughly constant as the atoms get heavier. However this approach clearly cannot explain the periodic variations the density.

Periodic increases and decreases in density

To understand the periodic increases and decreases in density, we need to examine the data in more detail and to consider the type of bonding present in different elements. Let us look at the low-density and high-density elements in turn.

Low-density elements

The lowest-density elements (near a, b, c, d on Figure 7.2) occur for elements made from atoms which have either:

- filled electron shells, i.e. the molecularly bonded noble gases Ne, Ar, Kr, Xe, or
- one electron outside a filled electron shell, i.e. the alkali metals, Na, K, Rb, Cs.

Example 7.2

If all the elements had a simple cubic crystal structure with nearest neighbour separation $a = 0.3$ nm, what would be the density of all the elements?

On these assumptions the *number density* of all elements would be $1/a^3$. Since the mass of each atom is Au where A is the relative atomic mass and u is an atomic mass unit, we conclude that the *mass density* ρ of the elements would be:

$$\rho = \frac{Au}{a^3}$$

Substituting $a = 0.3 \times 10^{-9}$ m and $u = 1.66 \times 10^{-27}$ kg yields:

$$\rho = \frac{A \times 1.66 \times 10^{-27}}{\left(0.3 \times 10^{-9}\right)^3} = 61.5A$$

This line is plotted on Figure 7.2.

In the first case we have seen that the bonding mechanism between the atoms is the weak Van der Waals attraction (§6.1) and so we are not surprised if the atoms do not pull each other together tightly. In the second case the addition of one proton and one electron changes Ne to Na, Ar to K, Kr to Rb and Xe to Cs, and the dominant bonding changes from molecular to metallic, but the density changes rather little. We can understand this by recalling that molecularly-bonded

Figure 7.2 The densities of the elements plotted against atomic number. The solid line represents the expected density of the solid elements if they all had a simple cubic crystal structure with a nearest neighbour separation of 0.3 nm. (See Example 7.2)

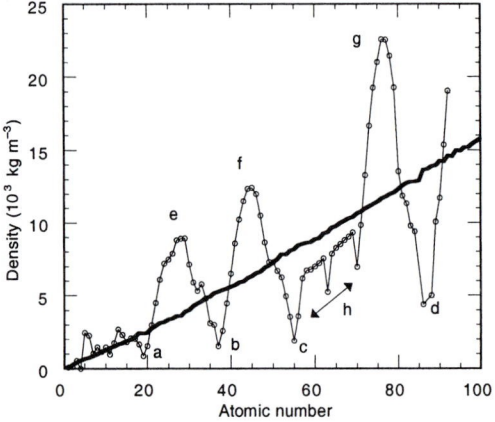

179

Table 7.3 The atomic number Z, atomic mass A and the density ρ of the lanthanide elements extracted from Table 7.2. The row marked %A is the % density increase (compared with La) expected if the separation between atoms is unchanged and only the atomic mass changes. The row marked %ρ is the % density increase (compared with La) actually found. It shows that the 59% density increase is much greater than can be explained by the 26% increase in atomic mass alone.

	La	Ce	Pr	Nd	Pm	Sm	Eu	Gd	Tb	Dy	Ho	Er	Tm	Yb	Lu
Z	57	58	59	60	61	62	63	64	65	66	67	68	69	70	71
A	138.9	140.1	140.9	144.2	145	150.4	152.0	157.3	158.9	162.5	164.9	167.3	168.9	173.0	175.0
%A	0	0.87	1.44	3.84	4.39	8.28	9.40	13.21	14.41	16.99	18.74	20.41	21.62	24.57	25.96
ρ	6174	6711	6779	7000	7220	7536	5248	7870	8267	8531	8797	9044	9325	6966	9842
%ρ	0	8.7	9.8	13.4	16.9	22.1	-15.0	27.4	33.9	38.2	42.5	46.5	51.4	12.8	59.4

solids choose close-packed crystal structures (face-centred cubic) to allow as many atoms as possible to get as close together as their pair potential allows. However metals achieve their lowest energy state by allowing their conduction electrons 'extra room' to move around in. The alkali metals thus choose a crystal structure (body-centred cubic) that allows for this 'extra room'. Thus although the metallic bonding is stronger, as indicated by the higher melting and boiling temperatures of the alkali metals (Table 11.2) the density does not increase much compared with their molecularly-bonded neighbours.

High-density elements

The high-density elements occur in the middle of rows of the periodic table. For these materials, in addition to metallic bonding there is also strong covalent bonding between atoms, and the *number* of covalent bonds that an atom can make reaches a maximum in the middle of a row of the periodic table. Elements from near the centre of a row in the periodic table can form more covalent bonds than elements from near the ends of rows. This is because elements in the middle have both electrons which are able to form covalent bonds *and* unoccupied quantum states which can accommodate bond-forming electrons from neighbouring electrons. Each covalent bond pulls atoms more tightly together and thus lead to higher densities.

The discussion above seems to indicate that there might be a correlation between the density of substances and their cohesive energy. This is in fact so and the relationship is discussed in §11.5.2.

Elements 57 to 71

Finally we need to understand the striking linear density increase of elements 57 to 71. These elements are known as the *Lanthanide series* or the *Rare Earth elements*, although as Figure 2.1 shows they are not particularly rare. Remember that as we move across Figure 7.2, each step corresponds to

- the addition of one electron to the atom
- one proton to the nucleus
- and one or two more neutrons to the nucleus.

Normally the extra electron occupies a quantum state which places it in an orbit which results in most of its charge density being around the outer part of the atom, i.e. in the valence electron states. In the lanthanides a new orbital is available (called the $4f$ orbital) which can hold 14 electrons. Recall that s orbitals hold 2 electrons, p orbitals 6 electrons, and d orbitals 10 electrons.

Figure 7.3 An entirely schematic diagram showing the location of the peak of the charge density associated with the $4f$ orbitals, and contrasting their position with that of the valence orbitals and the core orbitals.

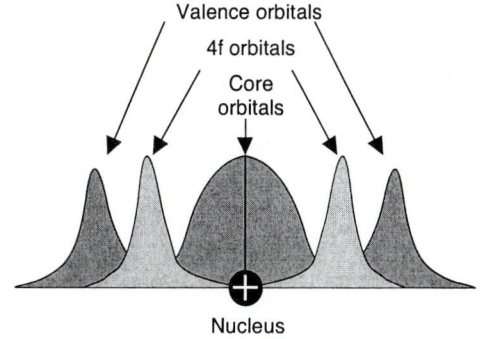

Valence orbitals

4f orbitals

Core orbitals

Nucleus

This orbital results in the additional electronic charge residing *inside the atom* rather than near the outside of the atom. This has two consequences for the density of the lanthanides. First, as the charge density in the outer part of the atom is not changed, the bonding to neighbouring atoms (which is both metallic and covalent) is broadly unaffected. If this was the only effect then the density of elements would increase as the mass of atoms increased, while the separation between atoms would remain roughly constant. Second, the effect of the each extra nuclear charge pulls all the

---

Example 7.3

Work out the density of diamond

To calculate this we need to know (a) the length of a C–C bond in diamond, and (b) the crystal structure of diamond. As we saw in the discussion of the covalent bond in §6.4 we could not predict the length of the bond until we knew the precise distribution of charge within the bond. In this example we take the length of the bond as being determined experimentally, and work out the density by looking at a representative sample of the material. The bond length and crystal structure of diamond are both deduced from X-ray scattering. The crystal structure is shown on the right and the separation between nearest-neighbour atoms is 0.154 nm. The thick lines indicate the bonding regions and the spheres indicate the location of the atoms. The different shading is to aid the clarity of the picture, and allow identification of the four atoms *entirely* contained within the outer cube.

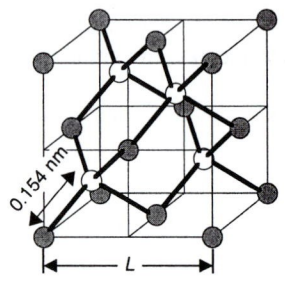

The sample of material shown in the figure is a representative section of an entire crystal known as a *unit cell*. If we work out the density of the unit cell we will find the same density as the entire crystal. If the cube shown has a side L then the density will be:

$$\rho = \frac{number\ of\ atoms \times mass\ of\ atom}{a^3}$$

The mass of a carbon atom is $12u$, i.e. $12 \times 1.67 \times 10^{-27}$ kg. The number of atoms is easy to work out in principle, but can be rather confusing in practice. We just count the number of atoms in the figure right, but we must take account of the fact that some atoms at the edge of the unit cell will also be counted in neighbouring unit cells. For cubic unit cells the rules for dealing with this are listed below and illustrated on the figure right:

- atoms shared between *faces* of neighbouring cells count as only 1/2 an atom
- atoms shared between *edges* of neighbouring cells count as only 1/4 an atom
- atoms shared between *corners* of neighbouring cells count as only 1/8 an atom.

Counting carefully on the diamond structure we find:

$$\left[8 \times \frac{1}{8} corner\ atoms\right] + \left[6 \times \frac{1}{2} face\ atoms\right] + [4 \times 1 whole\ atoms] = 8\ atoms$$

Finally we need to work out the side of this unit cell in terms of the separation between two atoms. If you examine the *body diagonal AD* shown you will see that using Pythagoras' theorem it can be shown to be equal to:

$$AD = \sqrt{L^2 + L^2 + L^2} = L\sqrt{3}$$

The spacing between nearest-neighbour atoms is just 1/4 of this distance i.e. $r_o = \sqrt{3}L/4$ so that $L = 4r_o/\sqrt{3}$. We can now put the numbers into our calculation. *Emsley* give the C–C distance as $r_o = 1.54 \times 10^{-10}$m and so we find:

$$\rho = \frac{8 \times 12 \times 1.67 \times 10^{-27}}{\left[4 \times 1.54 \times 10^{-10} \Big/ \sqrt{3}\right]^3} = 3564\ kg\ m^{-3}$$

This can be compared with the experimental value of 3513 kg m^{-3}, a disagreement of 1.5%. Since the temperatures of the various measurements are not given we conclude that, to the extent that we understand why the C–C separation is approximately 1.54×10^{-10}m, we can also understand the observed density of diamond.

orbitals a little closer to the nucleus. This makes the orbitals, and hence the atom itself, become systematically smaller as one proceeds across the series, an effect known as the *lanthanide contraction*.

Table 7.3 shows a calculation of how the density of the lanthanides would be expected to vary if the separation between atoms stayed constant. It is clear the 59% density increase which actually occurs is much greater than can be explained by the 26% increase in atomic mass alone.

The dips in the density of Eu (europium) and Yb (ytterbium) occur for reasons that are connected with the detailed arrangement of electrons within the 4f shell.

Summary

So we conclude that we can understand the density of elemental solids rather well, even though there are few materials for which we can *a priori* predict the density. Broadly speaking the variation of the density of the elements arises from the combination of two trends: a periodic variation connected with the type of bonding present; and a linear trend to higher densities for elements with high mass atoms.

7.3 Compressibility and bulk modulus

7.3.1 Background

In the previous. section (§7.2), we examined data on the density of solids. Unless noted otherwise, this data was appropriate at around room temperature and atmospheric pressure. In this section (§7.3), we shall examine data on the density of solids changes when the pressure is increased, i.e. the compressibility of solids. In the following section (§7.4), we shall examine the effect of temperature on the density.

In fact, we rarely discuss changes in density *per se*. We normally examine changes in the volume or length as a function of pressure or temperature. The changes in volume as a function of pressure are generally characterised by either the bulk modulus B, or the compressibility K. These are merely the inverse of each other, and are defined by:

$$B = -V \frac{\partial P}{\partial V}$$
$$K = \frac{1}{B} = -\frac{1}{V} \frac{\partial V}{\partial P}$$

(7.1)

In our discussion of the compressibility of gases, we needed to take care to distinguish between *adiabatic* and *isothermal* moduli. For solids, the two moduli differ by much less than for gases, and often the data tables do not state which value is

plotted. If the data are derived at high pressure, then generally it is only possible to determine the isothermal modulus. If the data are determined by using speed of sound measurements then, as for gases, the appropriate modulus to use is the adiabatic modulus, except at the highest frequencies.

For many materials, the bulk modulus can be related to the other common elastic moduli: Young's modulus, and the rigidity modulus, as discussed in Appendix A2. If the material is easily compressed then it will have a small bulk modulus, and large compressibility.

7.3.2 Data on the compressibility of solids

Table 7.4 shows the bulk modulus for the elements and Figure 7.4 shows a graph of this data as function of atomic number.

The first and most obvious observation is that the graph is reminiscent of Figure 7.2 showing the density of the elements. This indicates that denser elements tend to be less compressible. We can probe a little deeper to see if the data for the simple solids we described in the last chapter actually agree with our expectations. The data for the molecularly bonded noble gases (§6.2) and the alkali metals (§6.5) are shaded in Table 7.4.

Table 7.4 The bulk modulus of the elements in their solid state. The temperature of the measurements varies considerably and there are discrepancies of the up to 50% in figures from different sources.

Z	Element	B (GPa)	Z	Element	B (GPa)	Z	Element	B (GPa)
1	Hydrogen	0.2	29	Copper	137.8	59	Praseodymium	30.6
2	Helium	0.1	30	Zinc	72.0	60	Neodymium	32.7
3	Lithium	11.1	31	Gallium	56.9	61	Promethium	35.0
4	Beryllium	100.3	32	Germanium	7.7	62	Samarium	39.4
5	Boron	178.0	33	Arsenic	22.0	63	Europium	14.7
6	Carbon (diamond)	542.0	34	Selenium	8.3	64	Gadolinium	38.3
6	Carbon (graphite)	33.0	35	Bromine	1.9	65	Terbium	39.9
7	Nitrogen	1.2	36	Krypton	3.5	66	Dysprosium	38.4
8	Oxygen		37	Rubidium	1.9	67	Holmium	39.7
9	Fluorine		38	Strontium	1.2	68	Erbium	41.1
10	Neon	1.1	39	Yttrium	36.6	69	Thulium	39.7
11	Sodium	6.4	40	Zirconium	83.3	70	Ytterbium	13.3
12	Magnesium	44.7	41	Niobium	170.2	71	Lutetium	41.1
13	Aluminum	75.5	42	Molybdenum	231.0	72	Hafnium	109.0
14	Silicon	98.8	43	Technetium	297.0	73	Tantalum	200.0
15	Phosphorous (Red)	10.9	44	Ruthenium	320.8	74	Tungsten	323.2
15	Phosphorous(White)	4.9	45	Rhodium	270.4	75	Rhenium	372.0
16	Sulphur	17.8	46	Palladium	182.0	76	Osmium	418.0
17	Chlorine		47	Silver	100.7	77	Iridium	355.0
18	Argon	2.7	48	Cadmium	41.6	78	Platinum	228.0
19	Potassium	3.1	49	Indium	41.1	79	Gold	217.0
20	Calcium	17.2	50	Tin	58.2	80	Mercury	25.0
21	Scandium	43.5	51	Antimony	42.0	81	Thallium	35.9
22	Titanium	105.1	52	Tellurium	23.0	82	Lead	45.8
23	Vanadium	161.9	53	Iodine	7.7	83	Bismuth	31.3
24	Chromium	160.1	54	Xenon	3.6	84	Polonium	26.0
25	Manganese	118.0	55	Caesium	1.6	29	Copper	137.8
26	Iron	169.8	56	Barium	10.3	30	Zinc	72.0
27	Cobalt	191.4	57	Lanthanum	24.3			
28	Nickel	186.0	58	Cerium	23.9			

So the main questions we would like to address are:

- What is the origin of the periodic increases and decreases in the bulk modulus in Figure 7.4?
- Do the data on noble gas solids match our theoretical expectations?
- Do the data on alkali metals match our theoretical expectations?

7.3.3 Understanding the data on the compressibility of solids

Background

We can get some idea of the kind of information that the bulk modulus data gives us if we consider a very simple case: two atoms interacting via a

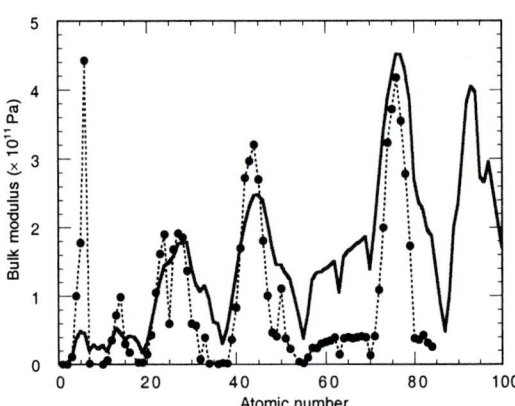

Figure 7.4 The bulk modulus of the elements plotted as function of atomic number. Also shown as a grey continuous line (and on an arbitrary scale) is the density of the elements shown in Figure 7.1.

pair potential. We know that if the molecule is stable, then the interaction between the molecules $u_{pair}(r)$ must be of the general form shown in Figure 7.5 (a). i.e. the atoms must repel at small separations and be attracted at large separations. The equilibrium separation r_0 of the atoms will be determined by the condition that:

$$\frac{du_{pair}(r)}{dr} = 0 \qquad (7.2)$$

A graph of $du_{pair}(r)/dr$ as a junction of r is shown in Figure 7.5 (b). When we compress this molecule, then the energy required to reduce r_0 by a certain amount is related to the *slope* of this curve. The steeper this curve, then harder it is to compress the molecule. Thus the 'bulk modulus' of this one-dimensional molecule to be related to the first derivative (the gradient) of $du_{pair}(r)/dr$, or to the second derivative, (the curvature) of $u_{pair}(r)$, evaluated at $r = r_0$ i.e.

$$B \propto \frac{d}{dr}\left(\frac{du_{pair}(r)}{dr}\right)$$
$$\propto \left.\frac{d^2 u_{pair}(r)}{dr^2}\right|_{r=r_0} \qquad (7.3)$$

Many solids can be described as the sum of pair potentials between its constituent atoms. For such materials, it will not surprise you to find that the general formula for the bulk modulus of a substance at absolute zero is:

$$B = V\left.\frac{\partial^2 U}{\partial V^2}\right|_{V=V_0} \qquad (7.4)$$

where U is the cohesive energy of the solid. However, Equation 7.4 is in fact applicable even to solids such as metals which cannot (in general) be analysed as a sum of pair interactions.

Let us consider the questions raised by the data.

Elements

The periodic changes in bulk modulus are reminiscent of the changes we saw when we examined the data on the density of the elements (Figure 7.1). However, if we examine the data for B in

184

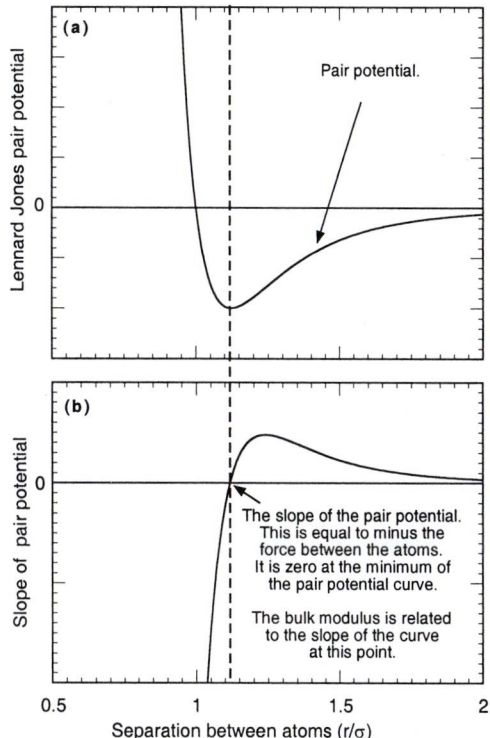

Figure 7.5 (a) A pair potential curve and (b) its derivative. The bulk modulus us related to the slope of the first derivative at the point where the slope is zero.

Table 7.4, we can see that the difference between the smallest and largest values of B is a factor of the order of 1000. This is strikingly larger than the factor of around 30 that spans the density of the elements. The fact that the patterns for density and bulk modulus are correlated tells us that the origin of both patterns is the same: the types of bonding present in the different regions of the periodic table. In the next two sub-sections we will calculate the bulk modulus for two of the especially 'simple' solids that we considered in Chapter 6. Here we will focus on the general trend of the data.

We see that the most compressible elements are those near the ends of the periods on the periodic table. The noble gases and alkali metals are shaded in Table 7.4 to give an indication of where the periods end. The elements in this region are held together either by molecular bonding (§6.2), or by metallic bonding (§6.5). The data tells us that these two types of bonding give rise to relatively

compressible solids. In the next two sub-sections we will describe the detailed calculation of the bulk modulus each of these types of bonding.

In the middle of rows, the high values of bulk modulus are due to extensive covalent bonding (§6.4). As we discussed in §7.2.2, elements near the *centre* of a row in the periodic table can form more covalent bonds than elements near the *ends* of rows. This is because elements in the middle have both electrons which are able to form covalent bonds *and* unoccupied quantum states which can accommodate bond-forming electrons from neighbouring atoms. It is pretty clear that the covalent bonds which are formed are extremely rigid. In other words, the bonds have an optimal length. When pressure is applied to the substance, it takes a great deal of energy to shorten the bonds to any significant extent.

The lanthanide series elements ($Z = 57$ to $Z = 71$) stand out on Figure 7.4 as they did on Figure 7.1. We note that their compressibility is relatively constant as we proceed across series. As explained in §7.2.2, this is because the valence electrons of the lanthanide atoms are in the same orbitals for *all the lanthanides*. The additional electrons added as Z increases across the series are accommodated in $4f$ orbitals. These are located inside the valence orbitals and do not take part in bonding. The small increase in bulk modulus as one proceeds across the series is *probably* due to the additional nuclear charge added as Z increases across the series. This effect gives rise to lanthanide contraction described in §7.2.2. However, the lanthanide elements also show extremely strong magnetic effects. Interestingly the lanthanide elements which show a drop in bulk modulus, (Ce, Eu and Yb), are elements in which there is a sometimes rearrangement of electrons between the f-orbitals and the valence orbitals.

Noble gas solids

For the noble gas solids, He, Ne, Ar, Kr and Xe, we developed in §6.2 a theory which predicts U in terms of atomic parameters σ and ε. So we can predict a value of B for these elements in terms of σ and ε by directly evaluating:

$$B = V \frac{\partial^2 U}{\partial V^2}\bigg|_{V=V_0} \qquad (7.4^*)$$

where the molar cohesive energy U is given by:

$$U = -2\varepsilon N_A \left[\left(\frac{\sigma}{r_0}\right)^6 A_6 - \left(\frac{\sigma}{r_0}\right)^{12} A_{12} \right] \qquad (6.18^*)$$

The differentiation of U is straightforward, but takes many steps. For this reason, I have put these detailed steps in Appendix 5. The result of all the work is pleasingly simple: We find a prediction that:

$$B = \left[\frac{4A_6^2}{A_{12}} \sqrt{\frac{A_6}{A_{12}}} \right] \frac{\varepsilon}{\sigma^3} \qquad (7.5)$$

Evaluating this using the values of A_6 and A_{12} appropriate to the face-centred cubic structure (Table 6.1) we find:

$$B = 75.13 \frac{\varepsilon}{\sigma^3} \qquad (7.6)$$

Table 7.5 shows the results of evaluating Equation 7.6 for noble gases.

Table 7.5 Values of the bulk modulus of the noble gas solids calculated according to Equation 7.6, compared with experimental data from Table 7.4.

	Substance			
	Ne	**Ar**	**Kr**	**Xe**
σ ($\times 10^{-10}$ m)	2.74	3.44	3.65	3.98
ε ($\times 10^{-3}$ eV)	3.1	10.3	14.0	20.0
$75.13\varepsilon/\sigma^3 (\times 10^9$ Pa)	1.81	3.18	3.46	3.81
Data	1.1	2.7	3.5	3.6
Ratio (theory/expt)	**1.65**	**1.18**	**0.99**	**1.06**

The agreement between theory and experiment shown in Table 7.5 is not great. However, there are several reasons why we might not expect particularly good agreement. The first is that the temperature at which the data is taken is above absolute zero. The crystals 'soften' significantly on warming. The second reason is that the curvature of the Lennard-Jones potential is a rather subtle feature of the pair potential. It is a relatively easy to invent a pair potential which has a minimum in

185

the correct place. However, it is much harder to invent a curve which has the minimum in the right place *and* has the correct curvature around that minimum. The third reason for discrepancies is the effect of the zero point energy. This effect is strongest in He where it prevents solidification at any temperature (unless pressure is applied). It is also quite strong in Ne. The ground state energy of a Ne atom in a box of side $\approx r_0$ is sufficiently large to cause the lattice to swell above what would be expected based on the Lennard-Jones theory (Table 6.2). This makes the lattice slightly easier to compress because the atoms do not sit at the bottom of the pair potentials.

Simple metals

In §6.5 we developed the free-electron model of a metal. There were no pair potentials, or indeed electrostatic interactions of any kind, included in this model. The cohesive energy derived entirely from the *delocalisation* of electrons as they entered quantum states in a large volume rather than being confined to atomic sized 'boxes'. We predicted that the molar cohesive energy was:

$$U = \frac{3}{5}N_A\varepsilon_F - N_A E_{atomic} \qquad (6.84^* \text{ \& } 7.7)$$

where ε_F is the Fermi energy and E_{atomic} is the energy of the localised atomic state from which our electrons came. We assume that E_{atomic} does not depend on volume. Let us now evaluate the bulk modulus:

$$B = V\frac{\partial^2 U}{\partial V^2}\bigg|_{V=V_0} \qquad (7.4^*)$$

for a free electron gas and see how it compares with the experimental data for the elements. At first sight, it might appear that U does not depend on V at all. However, if we write out the expression for ε_F we see that it depends on k_F, which in urn depends on n, the electron number density. Thus, compressing the free-electron gas will increase, the number density, and hence k_F and hence in turn ε_F.

$$\varepsilon_F = \frac{\hbar^2 k_F^2}{2m_e}$$

$$= \frac{\hbar^2}{2m_e}\left[\left(3n\pi^2\right)^{\frac{1}{3}}\right]^2 \qquad (6.79^* \text{ \& } 7.8)$$

$$= \frac{\hbar^2}{2m_e}\left[\left(\frac{3N_A\pi^2}{V}\right)^{\frac{1}{3}}\right]^2$$

Separating out the term in V we can write:

$$\varepsilon_F = \underbrace{\frac{\hbar^2}{2m_e}\left(3N_A\pi^2\right)^{\frac{2}{3}}}_{constant = A}V^{-\frac{2}{3}} \qquad (7.9)$$

$$= AV^{-\frac{2}{3}}$$

And so:

$$\frac{\partial^2\varepsilon_F}{\partial V^2} = A\left[-\frac{2}{3}\right]\left[-\frac{5}{3}\right]V^{-\frac{8}{3}} - 0$$

$$= \left[\frac{10}{9}\right]AV^{-\frac{8}{3}} \qquad (7.10)$$

$$= \left[\frac{10}{9}\right]\frac{\varepsilon_F}{V^2}$$

Substituting into the expression for B we find the pleasingly simple result:

$$B = V\left(\frac{3}{5}N_A\left[\frac{10}{9}\frac{\varepsilon_F}{V^2}\right]\right)$$

$$= \frac{2}{3}\frac{N_A}{V}\varepsilon_F \qquad (7.11)$$

$$= \frac{2}{3}n\varepsilon_F$$

This is evaluated for the alkali metals, (Li, Na, K, Rb and Cs) in Table 7.6. We see that agreement is not great, but our predictions are of the correct order of magnitude and in some cases within 10% of the experimental result. This is a truly remarkable result. We have predicted the compressibility of some real pieces of metal, by considering an entirely abstract model: that of the free-electron gas (i.e. the particle in a box). This gives us confidence that in the alkali metals, a good deal of the cohesive energy really does derive from electron

delocalisation, with very little in the way covalent bonding.

Summary

We conclude that we can understand the bulk modulus of elemental solids rather well. Broadly speaking, the periodic variation of the bulk modulus of the elements arises from the periodic variation in the amount of covalent bonding present. For some simple molecular solids and metals, we developed a theory which made modestly successful predictions for the bulk modulus.

Table 7.6 Values of the bulk modulus of the alkali metals calculated according to Equation 7.11, compared with experimental data from Table 7.4.

	Substance				
	Li	Na	K	Rb	Cs
$n\ (\times 10^{28}\ m^{-3})$	4.63	2.53	1.33	1.08	0.86
$\varepsilon_F\ (\times\ eV)$	4.7	3.14	2.05	1.78	1.53
$2n\varepsilon_F/3(\times 10^9\ Pa)$	23.2	8.5	2.9	2.06	1.41
Data	11.1	6.4	3.1	1.9	1.6
Ratio (theory/expt)	**2.10**	**1.33**	**0.94**	**1.08**	**0.88**

7.4 Thermal expansivity

7.4.1 Background

In general, solids expand when heated. If a solid has initial volume V_0, the increase in volume ΔV on raising the temperature by ΔT at constant pressure may be expressed as:

$$\Delta V = V_0 \beta \Delta T \qquad (7.12)$$

where β is the *coefficient of volume expansion* or sometimes the *coefficient of cubical expansion*. Hence the volume may be written as:

$$V = V_0 + \Delta V$$
$$= V_0 (1 + \beta \Delta T) \qquad (7.13)$$

For solids it is also possible to define α, the *coefficient of linear expansion*, which describes the way the *length* of a sample of solid will change with temperature. It does not make much sense to describe a coefficient of linear expansion for a gas or a liquid, which does not have the constancy of shape possessed by solids.

If a solid has initial length L_0, the increase in length ΔL on raising the temperature by ΔT at constant pressure may be expressed as:

$$\Delta L = L_0 \alpha \Delta T \qquad (7.14)$$

where α is the *coefficient of linear expansion*. Hence the length may be written as:

$$L = L_0 + \Delta L$$
$$= L_0 (1 + \alpha \Delta T) \qquad (7.15)$$

As illustrated in Figure 7.4, the coefficients of linear and volume expansivity are linked by the simple relationship:

$$\beta = 3\alpha \qquad (7.16)$$

Example 7.4

What is the relationship between the coefficient of linear expansivity and the coefficient of volume expansivity?

Consider a sphere of initial volume $4\pi r_0^3/3$. Each dimension increases in length by a factor $(1 + \alpha\Delta T)$ and so the volume increases by a factor:

$$(1 + \alpha\Delta T)^3 = 1 + 3\alpha\Delta T + 3(\alpha\Delta T)^2 + (\alpha\Delta T)^3$$

Since $\alpha\Delta T$ is usually $\ll 1$, this is given to an excellent approximation by:

$$(1 + \alpha\Delta T)^3 \approx 1 + \underbrace{3\alpha\Delta T}_{\beta}$$

Thus the volume expansivity β (Equation 7.2) is given by:

$$\beta \approx 3\alpha$$

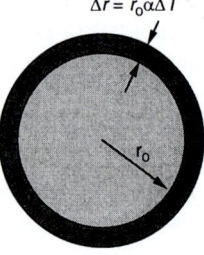

$\Delta r = r_0 \alpha \Delta T$

r_0

Table 7.7 The coefficient of linear expansivity α for various solids at temperatures around room temperature. (*Kaye & Laby*). The volume expansivity of the elements is given by $\beta = 3\alpha$ as shown in Example 7.4.

Elemental metals	α (°C^{-1})	Miscellaneous	α (°C^{-1})	Alloys	α (°C^{-1})
Aluminium (Al)	23	Brick	3–10	Brass (68% Cu/32% Zn)	18–19
Antimony (Sb)	≈ 11	Cement and concrete	10–14	Bronze (80% Cu/20% Sn)	17–18
Bismuth (Bi)	≈ 13	Marble	3–15	Constantan (60% Cu/40% Ni)	15–17
Cadmium (Cd)	≈ 30	Lead glass (46% pbo)	≈ 8	Duralumin (95% Al/4% Cu)	23
Chromium (Cr)	≈ 7	Typical glass	≈ 8–10	Magnalium (90% Al/10% Mg)	≈ 23
Cobalt (Co)	≈ 12	Porcelain	2–6	Nickel steel(10% Ni/90%Fe)	13
Copper (Cu)	16.7	Silica	0.4	Nickel steel(36% Ni/64%Fe)	0–1.5
Gold (Au)	13	Typical wood (along grain)	3–5	Nickel steel(43% Ni/57%Fe)	7.9
Iridium (Ir)	6.5	Typical wood (across grain)	35–60	Nickel steel(58% Ni/42%Fe)	11.4
Iron (Fe)	11.7			Carbon steel	≈ 11
Lead (Pb)	29	**Plastics**		Stainless steel (74%Fe/18%Cr/8%Ni)	29
Magnesium (Mg)	25	Epoxy resins	45–65	Phosphor-bronze	17
Nickel (Ni)	12.8	Epoxy resins	45–65	Platinum–Iridium (90% Pt/10% Ir)	8.7
Palladium (Pd)	≈ 11	Polycarbonates	66		
Platinum (Pt)	8.9	Low-density polyethylene	40–150	**Carbon**	
Rhodium (Rh)	8.4	Medium-density polyethylene	80–220	Diamond	1.0
Silver (Ag)	19	High density polyethylene	200–360	Graphite (polycrystalline)	7.1
Tantalum (Ta)	6.5	Natural rubber	220		
Thallium (Tl)	≈ 28	Hard rubber	60		
Tin (Sn)	≈ 21	Perspex	50–90		
Titanium (Ti)	≈ 9	Nylon	80–280		
Tungsten (W)	4.5	Polystyrene	34–210		
Vanadium (V)	≈ 8	Polyvinyl chloride (pvc)	70–80		
Zinc (Zn)	≈ 30				

7.4.2 Data on the thermal expansivity of solids

The coefficients of linear expansivity for a variety of solids are shown in Table 7.7 A, B, and C, and plotted by category as a histogram in Figure 7.6. In general these results indicate that for metals, either elements or alloys, a typical expansivity is of the order 10^{-5} °C^{-1}, but with significant variability about this figure. This is considerably less than the expansivities of gases $\approx 3 \times 10^{-3}$ °C^{-1} at around STP (Table 5.4). Notice in particular the results for nickel-iron alloys in Table 7.7: for a composition of 36% Ni and 64% Fe (i.e. just under 2:1 ratio of iron atoms to nickel atoms) the expansivity falls by a factor 10 to $\approx 10^{-6}$ °C^{-1}. Alloys with this composition, known as *Invar* alloys (short for *invariable*), are technologically important. They are used in the construction of devices in which mechanical stability must be maintained over a range of temperatures, for example in sci-entific instruments, or the 'shadow mask' of a colour television tube.

Figure 7.6 Histogram of the data from Table 7.4 Where a range of values indicated in Table 7.4 the midpoint of the range has been used for plotting purposes.

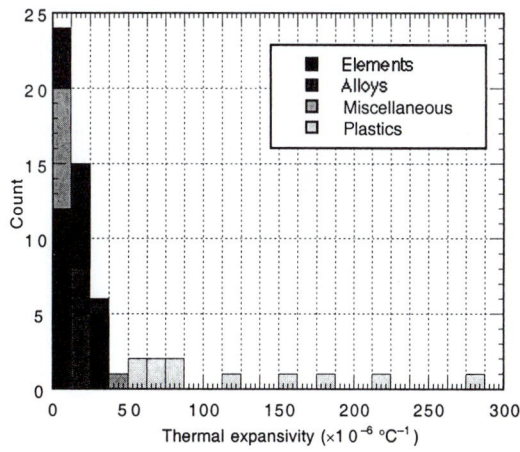

The typical figure of $\alpha \approx 10^{-5}\,°\text{C}^{-1}$ is also a reasonable guide to the materials in the first column of the 'miscellaneous' section of Table 7.7. However the plastics and rubbers in the second column have expansivities that are typically 10 times larger than this. In fact all the substances in Figure 7.6 with expansivities greater than $50 \times 10^{-6}\,°\text{C}^{-1}$ belong to this category.

So the main questions raised by our preliminary examination of the experimental data on the expansivity of solids are:

- Why is the expansivity of solids much smaller than that shown by gases?
- Why does the expansivity of alloys appear not to be the average of the expansivity of its components?
- Why is the expansivity of plastics much larger than that of metals?

7.4.3 Understanding the expansivity of solids

Background

First of all let us see how we can understand the expansion of solids in general terms and then turn to the questions raised above. Consider two neighbouring atoms or ions in a crystalline solid such as any of those we considered in §6.2 to §6.5. We can understand the thermal expansion of the crystal only if the average separation between the two atoms or ions increases with temperature. In general, heating the crystal increases the amplitude of vibration of atoms, so the separation between the two atoms oscillates, typically at around 10^{13} Hz.

The harmonic approximation

If the potential energy of interaction of the two atoms is symmetric about r_o, then the *average* separation of the atoms neither increases nor decreases with increased vibrational amplitude (Figure 7.7 (a). It is as if the atoms are connected together by a perfect spring whose potential energy may be written as:

$$u(r) = u_o + \tfrac{1}{2} K(r - r_o)^2 \qquad (7.17)$$

where K is the 'spring constant' of the bond. Assuming a pair potential such as Equation 7.17 is

---

Example 7.5

Three samples of copper, perspex, and invar, each of length 2 metres at 20 °C are warmed to 30 °C. Calculate the *change* in length of each sample.

The data for our calculations are as follows:
$L_0 = 2$ m
$\alpha = 16.7 \times 10^{-6}\,°\text{C}^{-1}$ for copper
$\alpha = 50\text{-}90 \times 10^{-6}\,°\text{C}^{-1}$ for perspex
$\alpha = 0\text{-}1.5 \times 10^{-5}\,°\text{C}^{-1}$ for invar i.e. nickel/steel (36/64)
$\Delta T = 30°\text{C} - 20°\text{C} = 10$ K

We start with Equation 7.4:

$$L = L_0(1 + \alpha \Delta T)$$

Remembering that $L = L_o + \Delta L$ we write this as:

$$L = L_o + \underbrace{L_0 \alpha \Delta T}_{\Delta L}$$

$$\Delta L = L_0 \alpha \Delta T$$

For our examples this becomes $\Delta L = 2 \times 10 \times \alpha = 20\alpha$
Thus the changes in length are:

Copper: $\Delta L = 20 \times 16.7 \times 10^{-6}\,°\text{C}^{-1} = 0.33$ mm
Perspex: $\Delta L = 20 \times 50 \rightarrow 90 \times 10^{-6}\,°\text{C}^{-1} = 1 \rightarrow 1.8$ mm
Invar: $\Delta L = 20 \times 0 \rightarrow 1.5 \times 10^{-6}\,°\text{C}^{-1} = 0 \rightarrow 0.03$ mm

This example is intended to illustrate that while the thermal expansion of solids is indeed small, it is still appreciable and must be taken into account in many real measurements.

Example 7.6

In Example 7.1 we estimated the typical separation between atoms in a piece of iron at 20 °C to be 2.29×10^{-10} m. How much does this average separation change if the iron is heated to 100 °C?

Table 7.7A gives the coefficient of linear expansion of iron as $\alpha = 11.7 \times 10^{-6}\,°\text{C}^{-1}$. Thus each length of a piece of iron changes by a factor $(1 + \alpha \Delta T)$ when the temperature changes by ΔT. In this case

$$\Delta T = 100\ °\text{C} - 20\ °\text{C}$$
$$= 80\ °\text{C}$$

We thus have:

$$L = L_0(1 + \alpha \Delta T) = L_0\left(1 + 11.7 \times 10^{-6} \times 80\right)$$
$$= L_0(1.000936)$$

So the average separation between iron atoms changes from $L_o = 2.29 \times 10^{-10}$ m to $L_o = 2.292 \times 10^{-10}$ m, i.e. it increases by roughly 1 part in 1000.

189

known as the *harmonic approximation*, and is quite sufficient for many purposes. However it is not possible to understand thermal expansion using the harmonic approximation.

Anharmonic vibrations

In general the potential energy of interacting atoms or ions is not quite symmetrical. As the amplitude of atomic oscillations increases, so does the average separation between the atoms (Figure 7.7 (b)). We can describe the potential energy of the two atoms by an equation such as:

$$u(r) = u_0 + \tfrac{1}{2} K (r - r_0)^2 + \tfrac{1}{6} K' (r - r_0)^3 \quad (7.18)$$

where K' determines the magnitude of the asymmetric or so-called *anharmonic* contribution. Notice that if $(r - r_0)$ is small enough we may always neglect the anharmonic part of the potential energy, because the $(r - r_0)^3$ term goes to zero faster than the $(r - r_0)^2$ term. Thus at low temperatures, where the vibrational amplitudes are small, the anharmonic term is generally negligible. At higher temperatures, the anharmonic term begins to contribute to the potential energy of the atoms. When the anharmonic term contributes to u, we see that $u(r - r_0) \neq u(r_0 - r)$ and the vibrations of the atoms in the potential become asymmetric, with atoms on average spending more time at separations greater than r_0, giving rise to an increase in the average separation of the atoms, i.e. thermal expansion.

Unfortunately, estimating the magnitude of the anharmonic coefficient K' and determining its effect on the average separation between atoms are both rather difficult. Thus in general we shall attempt to understand the data on thermal expansion in terms of the *shape* of a graph of potential energy of interaction between two atoms versus their separation. If this explanation of the thermal expansion of solids is correct, we should find ourselves able to naturally understand the questions raised by the experimental data of §7.4.2.

Why the thermal expansivity of solids is less than that of gases

We can understand fairly directly why the thermal expansivity of solids is less than that of gases. A

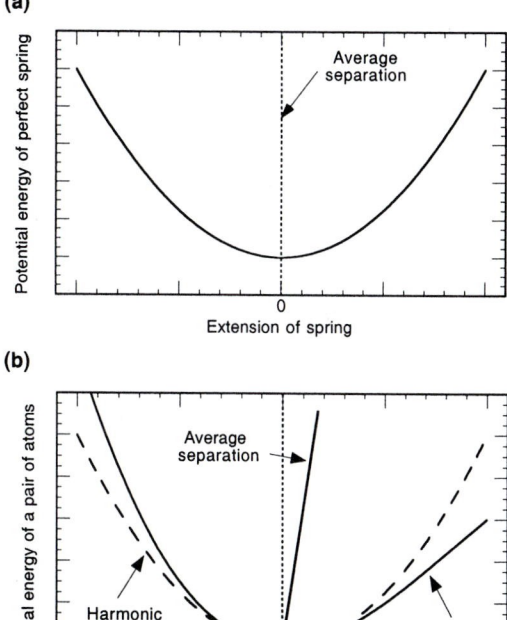

Figure 7.7 The potential energy of interaction between atoms in a solid. (a) The *harmonic approximation*: How the energy would vary if the atoms were connected by 'perfect springs'. (b) The typical deviation from the harmonic approximation of a real interatomic potential. The sloping line indicates the increasing average separation as the average energy of oscillation (i.e. the temperature) is increased.

gas represents the high-temperature limit of the thermal expansivity of a substance. When the temperature of a gas is raised, one may usually ignore the potential energy of interaction between the molecules which would act to constrain the volume of the gas. However, in a solid atoms are restrained from 'flying away' by their potential energy of interaction with their neighbours. Thus the thermal expansivity of solids is 'restricted' by the potential energy of interaction between atoms.

It is a surprising fact that the oscillation amplitudes of atoms in solids are never very large. In §11.3.2 we show that solids melt when the oscillation amplitude reaches around 5% of the atomic separation. So well below the melting temperature,

the amplitude of atomic oscillations are rather small, and the anharmonic contributions to the potential energy that give rise to thermal expansion are generally smaller then the harmonic contributions.

The thermal expansivity of alloys: invar

Given our basic thesis of the underlying origin of thermal expansion, let us now look at why the expansivity of alloys appears sometimes not to be the average of the expansivity of its components.

A one-dimensional alloy

For simplicity let us imagine a row of atoms in a sort of one-dimensional alloy of two elements A and B. Figure 7.8 shows rows of atoms representing both the pure elements and the 'alloy'. From the point of view of the expansivity of the alloy we need to concentrate not on the distribution of atoms themselves, but on the distribution of *bonds between atoms*. In pure A material, there are just A–A bonds and in pure B material, there are just B–B bonds. However in the alloy there is a third type of bond, an A–B bond, which in general will have different characteristics to either A–A or B–B bonds.

Figure 7.8 An illustration of the arrangement of bonds in one-dimensional models of pure A, pure B, and an alloy of A and B. Notice that the alloy contains an type of interatomic bond which is present in neither of the pure substances.

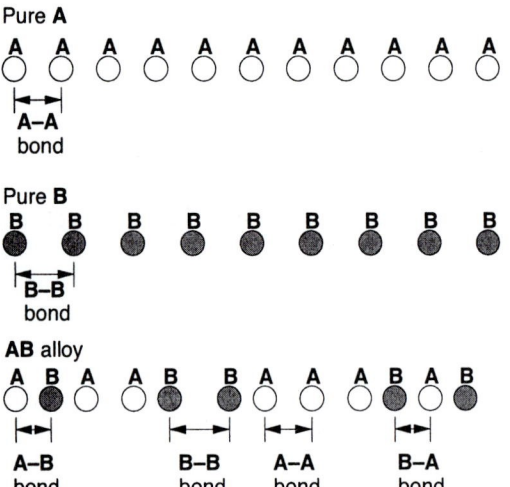

A three-dimensional alloy

If we envisage a real random alloy as collection of one-dimensional alloys held parallel to one another, then we can understand the thermal expansivity of alloys as being due to the average number of A–A, A–B, and B–B bonds in the alloy. Since we can measure the properties of A–A and B–B bonds by studying the pure material, alloys give us a chance to study the behaviour of A–B bonds.

The composition of a random alloy may be specified as $A_X B_{1-X}$ where X varies between 0 (pure B) and 1 (pure A), and in general X will be some arbitrary number e.g. for $X = 0.47$ we have $A_{0.47}B_{0.53}$. The probability that the atom at a particular site in the alloy will be type A is X, and so the probability that a particular bond will be an A–A bond is X^2. Similarly, the probability that a particular atom will be type B is 1–X, and so the probability of a B–B bond is $(1-X)^2$. Finally, the probability that a particular bond will either A–B or B–A is $2X(1-X)$. The expansivity of the alloy will be given by the average of the three types of bond within the material:

$$Expansivity \ of \ alloy =$$
$$(Expansivity \ of \ A-A \ bond)X^2$$
$$(Expansivity \ of \ B-B \ bond)(1-X)^2$$
$$(Expansivity \ of \ A-B \ bond)2X(1-X)$$
$$(7.19)$$

With the ideas summarised in Equation 7.19 in mind, let us examine the data from Table 7.7. Each table has an 'expected' column, which is the average expansivity of the elements, weighted by the percentage of the two elements present. This column represents an estimate of the thermal expansivity which neglects the final term in Equation 7.19. Thus if the 'expected' value in Table 7.8 is close to the 'Experimental' value then the 'A–B' bonds between the alloy components are similar to the average of an A–A and B–B bond.

For the aluminium, copper and platinum alloys, the 'expected' value of expansivity is close to the 'experimental' value. However, the data for iron-nickel alloys shows that an Fe–Ni bond behaves dramatically differently from either an Fe–Fe or

Ni–Ni bonds. In particular $Fe_{0.64}Ni_{0.36}$ shows essentially zero expansivity: this seems to imply that under certain circumstances an Fe–Ni bond must have a *negative* expansivity in order to compensate for the fact that Fe–Fe and Ni–Ni bonds have a positive expansivity. This corresponds to an interatomic potential between an iron and a nickel atom that is asymmetric in the opposite way to the normal potential (Figure 7.9)

The origin of this unusual behaviour is connected with the ferromagnetism shown by these elements. In addition to normal contributions to the energy of an Fe–Ni bond there is an additional term in the potential energy associated with the magnetic interaction between neighbouring atoms. The dependence of this energy on the separation between iron and nickel atoms is critical, and increases strongly with only a small increase in separation r (Figure 7.9). Over a certain temperature range this effect can give rise to a *contraction* in the average length of an Fe–Ni bond, which can compensate for the expansion of the Fe–Fe and Ni–Ni bonds. Outside this temperature range, the expansivity of the invar alloy assumes values closer to those in the 'expected' column of Table 7.8

The thermal expansivity of plastics

The thermal expansivity of plastics is typically one order of magnitude or more greater than that of crystalline solids (Table 7.7 and Figure 7.6). Since all the plastics in Table 7.7 share high thermal expansivity values, we would expect the explanation to be general for the class of materials, rather than specific to particular features of each individual substance. So what general features of plastics cause them to have a high thermal expansivity?

All the plastics in Table 7.7 are made from organic *polymer* molecules. These molecules are extremely long, varying from a few hundred to many thousands of atomic bonds in length. The molecules are made of repeating units of a simple *monomer* such as ethylene, linked together in a chain whose length varies with the conditions under which the *polymerisation* is carried out. The bonding in polymers is similar to that present in other organic substances (§6.6.1). The bonding

Table 7.8 Expected and experimentally determined values the coefficient of linear expansivity thermal expansivity α for some alloys and their component metals.

Alloy composition	Expected (see text)	Experimental α ($°C^{-1}$)
Aluminium alloys		
Duralumin (95% Al/4% Cu)	22.5×10^{-6}	23×10^{-6}
Magnalium (90% Al/10% Mg)	23.2×10^{-6}	$\approx 23 \times 10^{-6}$
Aluminium	—	23×10^{-6}
Copper	—	16.7×10^{-6}
Magnesium	—	$\approx 25 \times 10^{-6}$
Copper alloys		
Brass (68% Cu/32% Zn)	21×10^{-6}	$18\text{-}19 \times 10^{-6}$
Bronze (80% Cu/20% Sn)	17.6×10^{-6}	$17\text{-}18 \times 10^{-6}$
Constantan (60% Cu/40% Ni)	15.1×10^{-6}	$15\text{-}17 \times 10^{-6}$
Copper	—	16.7×10^{-6}
Zinc	—	$\approx 30 \times 10^{-6}$
Tin	—	$\approx 21 \times 10^{-6}$
Ni	—	12.8×10^{-6}
Platinum alloys		
Platinum-Iridium (90% Pt/10% Ir)	8.66×10^{-6}	8.7×10^{-6}
Platinum	—	8.9×10^{-6}
Iridium	—	6.5×10^{-6}
Iron alloys		
Nickel steel (10% Ni/90%Fe)	11.8×10^{-6}	13×10^{-6}
Nickel steel (36% Ni/64%Fe)	12.1×10^{-6}	$0\text{-}1.5 \times 10^{-6}$
Nickel steel (43% Ni/57%Fe)	12.2×10^{-6}	7.9×10^{-6}
Nickel steel (58% Ni/42%Fe)	12.3×10^{-6}	11.4×10^{-6}
Stainless steel (74%Fe/18% Cr/8%Ni)	10.9×10^{-6}	29×10^{-6}
Iron	—	11.7×10^{-6}
Nickel	—	12.8×10^{-6}
Chromium	—	7×10^{-6}

Figure 7.9 Schematic illustration of the potential energy of an Fe–Ni bond in an invar alloy (Table 7.8). The asymmetry of the potential (over a certain range) is opposite to that which occurs in normal bonds (Figure 7.7).

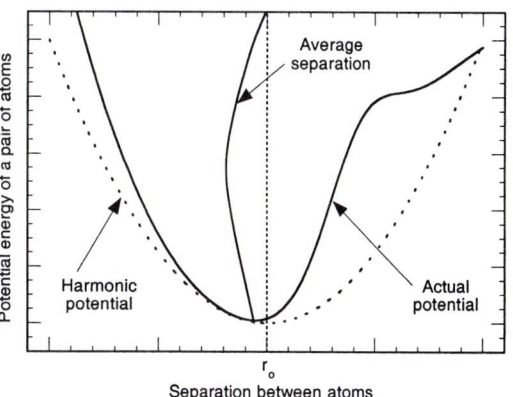

within the molecules is covalent and thus relatively strong. However, the bonding *between* the molecules is the relatively weak Van der Waals interaction and this allows molecules to move relatively easily with respect to one another.

For polymers we must also consider the extreme length of the molecules which causes them to become *entangled* in one another. In other words, although the molecules are not strongly bonded to each other, their physical entanglement holds them together in the solid state. In §8.4 and §9.9 on the cell model of liquids, we will see that the complex shapes of organic molecules lead to their having a relatively large viscosity, i.e. it is relatively diffi-cult for organic molecules to move relative to one another. The entanglement of polymer molecules in a solid is an extreme limit of this 'viscosity' effect.

The thermal expansivity of plastics is therefore not dominated by the variation in average separation of bonded molecules, but by rearrangements of the *shapes* of the molecules that become possible as the level of thermal excitation is increased. The processes of molecular rearrangement are too complex to consider here but we can imagine that this rearrangement, in combination with weak intermolecular forces, could lead to large values of thermal expansivity.

7.5 Speed of sound

7.5.1 Introduction

The passage of sound through a solid is more complicated to describe than the passage of sound through a gas. This is because in addition to the longitudinal (compressive) waves supported by gases, solids can support waves of transverse (shear) stress. Recall that in a longitudinal sound wave, the material is alternately compressed and rarefied as one travels along the direction of wave propagation (Figure 5.20 and in Figure 7.9 (a)). In a transverse sound wave, the material is transversely stressed or *sheared* in alternating directions as one travels along the direction of wave propagation (Figure 7.9 (b) and (c)).

7.5.2 Data on the speed of sound in solids

The speed of longitudinal and transverse sound waves in various bulk media are shown Table 7.6. The data for the elements are graphed as a function of relative atomic mass in Figure 7.10, which also shows the speed of sound in gases at STP for comparison (Figure 5.20). It is apparent that sound travels considerably faster through solids than gases at STP: typically by a factor of ten. The data for solids also show considerably more variability than was seen in the equivalent data for gases. It is

also clear that the speed of longitudinal and transverse sound waves differ considerably. The ratio of the two speeds is graphed for the elements as a function of relative atomic mass in Figure 7.11. It is apparent that longitudinal sound waves travel typically twice as fast as transverse sound waves, but that there are one or two striking exceptions to this rule.

So, the main questions raised by our preliminary examination of the experimental data on the velocity of sound in solids are:

- Why is the speed of sound in solids is typically a few thousand metres per second, about 10 times faster than in gases at STP?
- Why do longitudinal sound waves travel about twice as fast as transverse waves?
- Why does the speed of sound tend to be less in elements with large atomic mass?

7.5.3 Understanding the speed of sound in solids

All these questions can be answered fairly well with reference to the formulae for the velocities of sound in a solid. These are derived in Appendix A2 and discussed below.

Figure 7.10 The variation of the speed of longitudinal and transverse sound waves (Table 7.9) with relative atomic mass. For comparison, a section of the data for gases from Table 5.14 is also plotted. There appears to be a tendency towards lower speeds at larger atomic masses, similar to the tendency shown by gases in Figure 5.19. Data points are joined by straight lines to highlight trends in each data set.

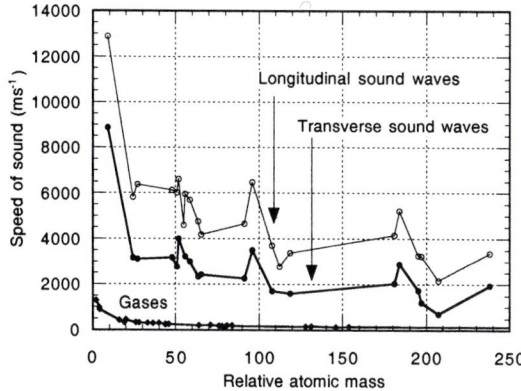

Figure 7.11 The variation of the ratio of the longitudinal to transverse sound velocities with relative atomic mass for the elements in Table 7.9. Typically $c_L \approx 2c_T$, but in some cases the results differ significantly from this value.

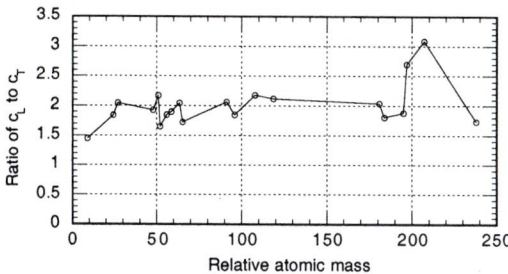

Table 7.9 The speed of sound in solids at 20 °C showing c_L, the speed of longitudinal waves, and c_T, the speed of transverse (shear waves).

Elemental metals	Speed of sound	
	$c_L(\mathrm{ms^{-1}})$	$c_T(\mathrm{ms^{-1}})$
Aluminium, Al	6374	3111
Beryllium, Be	12890	8880
Cadmium, Cd	2780	–
Chromium, Cr	6608	4005
Copper, Cu	4759	2325
Gold, Au	3240	1200
Iron, Fe	5957	3224
Lead, Pb	2160	700
Magnesium, Mg	5823	3163
Manganese, Mn	4600	—
Molybdenum, Mo	6475	3505
Nickel, Ni	5700	3000
Niobium, Nb	5068	2092
Platinum, Pt	3260	1730
Silver, Ag	3704	1698
Tantalum, Ta	4159	2036
Tin, Sn	3380	1594
Titanium, Ti	6130	3182
Tungsten, W	5221	2887
Uranium, U	3370	1940
Vanadium, V	6023	2774
Zinc, Zn	4187	2421
Zirconium, Zr	4650	2250

Insulators	$c_L(\mathrm{ms^{-1}})$	$c_T(\mathrm{ms^{-1}})$
Carbon (diamond)	18350	9200
Glass (crown)	5660	3420
Glass (heavy flint)	5260	2960
Glass (pyrex)	5640	3280
Quartz crystal X-cut	5720	—
Quartz fused	5970	3765
Concrete	4250–5250	—
Ice (-20°C)	≈3840	—

Plastics	$c_L(\mathrm{ms^{-1}})$	$c_T(\mathrm{ms^{-1}})$
Polyethylene	2000	3111
Polystyrene	2350	1120
PVC	2300	–
Rubber	1600	4005

Compressive and shear strain

Sound is a *strain wave* which propagates through a solid. The nature of a sound wave in a solid is more complex than in a gas, because as well as *compressive* strains (such as those in gases), a solid can sustain *shear* strain. Shear strain is more complicated than compressive strain, but mathematically it can be described in similar terms.

The basic idea is that if there is any distortion of the solid from its equilibrium shape (Figure 7.12), the average separation of the atoms within the solid is no longer optimal. Some atoms will be too close to their neighbours, and some too far apart. In either case there will be a restoring force which

will act to return the atoms to their equilibrium separations. The dynamics of the sound wave will be affected by the way the solid responds to the restoring force. The two factors most critical in determining this response are the restoring force per unit displacement (the natural 'springiness' of the substance), and the density of the substance. Let us look at each of these factors in turn.

194

The restoring force per unit strain.

The restoring force on a small region of a solid depends on the type of distortion (strain) that has taken place. The parameters that describe the restoring force per unit strain are known as the *elastic moduli* of a substance. There are three such moduli, each defined by an equation of the form:

Restoring force = Elastic modulus × strain

Young's modulus, E

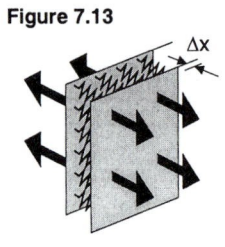

Figure 7.13

This characterises the restoring forces appropriate to longitudinal extensions of a substance. Figure 7.13 opposite shows two rigid planes of area A separated in equilibrium by a distance a and held together by 'springs' (analogous to planes within a solid held together by atomic bonds). Young's modulus is defined by:

$$\frac{F}{A} = E\frac{\Delta x}{a} \qquad (7.20)$$

where F is the force exerted on each plane. Notice that if a rod of material is stretched in this way, it will tend to 'neck' i.e. its cross-sectional area will be reduced (Figure 7.15). This tendency is characterised by the *Poisson ratio*, σ, of a substance. If we apply a stress S_x (force per unit area) in the x-direction, we induce stress S_y in the y-direction. The Poisson ratio is defined as:

$$\sigma = \frac{S_y}{S_x} \qquad (7.21)$$

This is discussed more fully in Appendix 2.

Figure 7.12 Sound waves in solids: (a) longitudinal (b) and (c) transverse waves. The figure shows planes of material perpendicular to the direction of propagation of a sound wave. In the longitudinal wave (a) the strength of shading indicates the degree of compression or rarefaction. In (b) and (c) a transverse wave displaces layers of material perpendicular to the direction of propagation. In (b) the layers are displaced from side to side and in (c) they are displaced up and down.

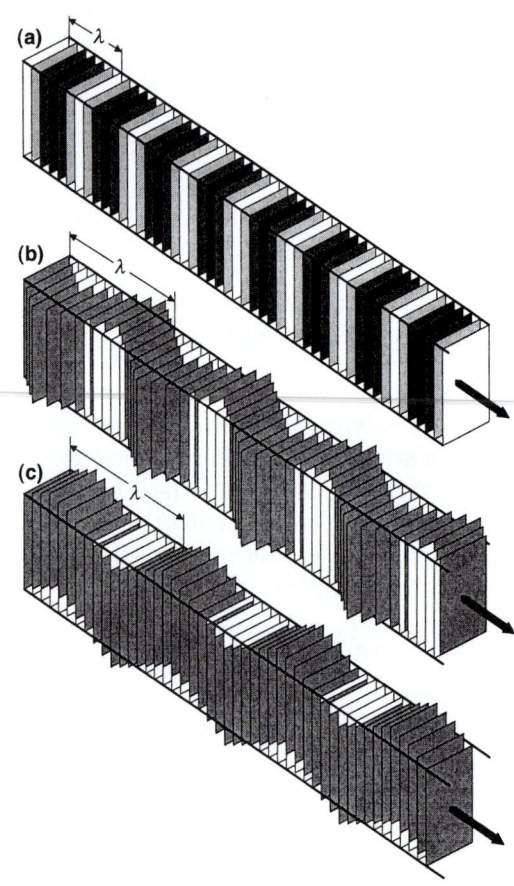

Figure 7.14 (a) Two planes in a solid in their equilibrium position. In (b) and (c) the same planes are subject to two types of shear strain and in (d) to compressive strain.

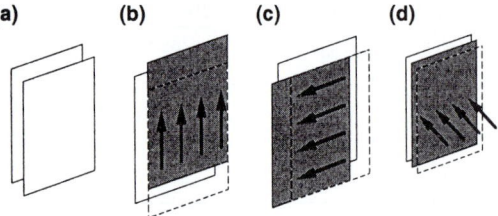

Figure 7.15 Illustration of the way in which a rod of material necks and bulges as a compressive sound wave travels along a long thin rod.

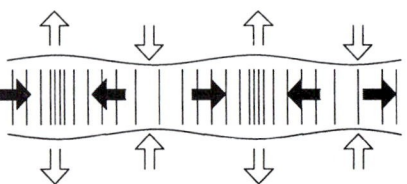

Shear or rigidity modulus, G

This characterises the restoring forces appropriate to shear or transverse deformations of the substance. Figure 7.16 opposite shows two rigid planes of area A held together by 'springs' (analogous to planes within a solid held together by atomic bonds). The rigidity modulus is defined by:

Figure 7.16

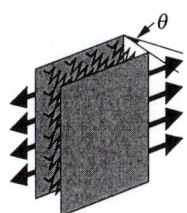

$$\frac{F}{A} = G\theta \qquad (7.22)$$

where F is the force on each plane. But see Appendix A2 for a qualification of this definition.

Bulk modulus, B

We have already discussed the bulk modulus of solids extensively in §7.3. Here we just remind ourselves that the bulk modulus (and its inverse, the compressibility K) describes the restoring forces appropriate to volume compressions of the substance. It is defined by:

$$B = -V\frac{\partial P}{\partial V} \qquad (7.23)$$

where P is the pressure and V is the volume of the substance.

If the material is easily compressed or easily sheared, then for a given strain, the restoring force will be small. In other words, a high modulus (E, G, or B) indicates that the corresponding deformation of the solid is difficult and the solid has a strong tendency to 'spring' back to its equilibrium position.

The density of the solid, ρ

If the density of a solid is high, i.e. if the *mass per unit volume* is high, then by Newton's second law ($F = ma$) the acceleration due to a given restoring force will be low. If the acceleration of a piece of solid is low then it will return to its equilibrium position only slowly, and the wave disturbance will propagate only slowly.

196

Example 7.7

A pulse of sound of frequency 100 MHz and lasting for 1 µs long is fired into one face of an experimental copper sample of dimensions $10 \times 10 \times 10$mm. If all modes of sound propagation are excited:

- **What is the wavelength of the sound wave?**
- **How far has the front of the pulse travelled by the time the pulse transmission is stopped?**
- **What will be the duration (width) of the pulse by the time it has returned to its point of origin after being reflected from the far side of the cube?**

Transmitter

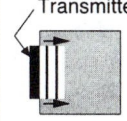  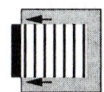

To work out the wavelength of the sound wave we rearrange $c_{sound} = f\lambda$ i.e. $\lambda = c_{sound}/f$ and so for the longitudinal waves we have for longitudinal and transverse waves respectively:

$$\lambda_L = \frac{4759}{100\times10^6} = 47.6\times10^{-6} \text{ m} \approx \tfrac{1}{20} \text{ mm}$$

$$\lambda_T = \frac{2325}{100\times10^6} = 23.3\times10^{-6} \text{ m} \approx \tfrac{1}{40} \text{ mm}$$

How far has the front of the pulse travelled by the time the pulse excitation is stopped? In 1 µs the longitudinal waves in the pulse have travelled a distance of:

$$c_{sound}^L \times t = 4759\times10^{-6} = 4.76 \text{ mm}$$

$$c_{sound}^T \times t = 2325\times10^{-6} = 2.33 \text{ mm}$$

What will be the duration (width) of the pulse by the time it has returned to its point of origin after being reflected from the far side of the cube? The waves in the pulse will return to their original face after a travelling once each way across the cube, a distance of 20 mm.

The longitudinal (*fast*) waves at the *start* of the pulse will return to the original face after a time:

$$t = \frac{20\times10^{-3}}{c_{sound}^L} = \frac{20\times10^{-3}}{4759} = 4.20 \text{ µs}$$

The transverse (slow) waves at the *end* of the pulse will return to the original face after a time:

$$t = 10^{-6} + \frac{20\times10^{-3}}{c_{sound}^T} = 10^{-6} + \frac{20\times10^{-3}}{2325} = 9.60 \text{ µs}$$

where we have remembered that the pulse was originally 1µs long. The pulse width has therefore grown from 1µs to $9.60 - 4.20 = 5.4$ µs.

Formulae for the speed of sound in solids

In experimental situations, we commonly encounter three similar expressions for the speed of sound. Given the discussion above, the general form of these expressions should not be at all surprising. What is surprising is how simple the expressions are! However, the derivation of these simple equations is rather complex and so has been confined to Appendix A2.

The speed of a longitudinal sound wave in a long thin rod

The speed of a longitudinal sound wave along a narrow rod is given by:

$$c_{\text{rod}} = \sqrt{\frac{E}{\rho}} \qquad (7.24)$$

where E is the Young's modulus. The types of compressive and extensive strains that take place within the rod are illustrated by shaded arrows in Figure 7.15. Notice that in the regions where the substance is compressed, the rod tends to bulge slightly, while in the regions where the substance is extended, the rod tends to 'neck' slightly. It is important to realise that this is *not* the situation of a bulk longitudinal sound wave.

The speed of a transverse sound wave in a bulk solid

Similarly, the speed of a transverse sound wave, c_{T}, in a bulk solid is given by:

$$c_{\text{T}} = \sqrt{\frac{G}{\rho}} \qquad (7.25)$$

where G is the rigidity modulus.

The speed of a longitudinal sound wave in a bulk solid

The speed of a longitudinal sound wave in a bulk solid is given by an expression similar to Equation 7.10. However, it includes an extra factor γ to take account of the fact that the *lateral accommodation* (the 'necking' and 'bulging' shown in Figure 7.15) does not take place for longitudinal waves in a bulk solid. The speed of sound is given by:

$$c_{\text{L}} = \sqrt{\frac{\gamma E}{\rho}} \qquad (7.26)$$

Example 7.8

Evaluate the Poisson ratio for the situation depicted below in which the *volume* of the bar is conserved in the extension.

Consider a rectangular bar of material of cross-sectional area $A = x^2$ and length L subject to a stretching force **F**.

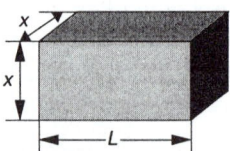

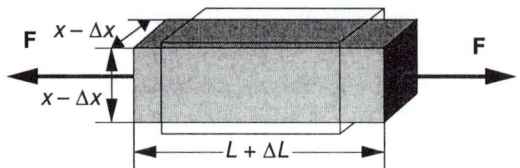

- The bar will in increase its length by an amount ΔL and the extent of its stretching is determined by Young's modulus E according to:

$$E = \frac{\text{tensile stress}}{\text{tensile strain}} = \frac{F/A}{\Delta L/L}$$

- However, it is perhaps not so obvious that the lateral dimensions of the bar will, in general, contract to some extent. If the lateral contraction is Δx then the ratio of the lateral strain $\Delta x/x$ to the tensile strain $\Delta L/L$ is known as the *Poisson* ratio, σ. To evaluate this for a volume-conserving strain we equate the unstrained and strained volumes

unstrained volume = strained volume

$$x^2 L = (x - \Delta x)^2 (L + \Delta L)$$
$$x^2 L = \left(x^2 - 2x\Delta x + \Delta x^2\right)(L + \Delta L)$$
$$x^2 L = \left(x^2 - 2x\Delta x + \Delta x^2\right)(L + \Delta L)$$

Multiplying out the terms and neglecting small quantities we find:

$$x^2 L = x^2 L - 2xL\Delta x + x^2 \Delta L + \text{small quantities}$$

Neglecting these small quantities, cancelling the term $x^2 L$ and rearranging yields:

$$\frac{\Delta x}{x} = \frac{1}{2}\frac{\Delta L}{L}$$

The fraction of the left is the lateral strain and the fraction on the right is the tensile strain. By definition therefore the Poisson ratio in this example is just 0.5. If, as one would expect, the volume of the material expands under the tensile strain, then the lateral strain would be less than that predicted in this example and the Poisson ratio would be less than 0.5. Commonly the Poisson ratio is roughly 1/3.

where γ is factor :

$$\gamma = \frac{(1-\sigma)}{(1-2\sigma)(1+\sigma)} \qquad (7.27)$$

and σ is the *Poisson ratio* for the substance. Note however the factor γ in Equation 7.26 is not related at all to the factor γ in the formula for the speed of sound in gases.

The physical significance of the Poisson ratio is illustrated in Example 7.8. It quantitatively expresses the tendency of a substance to 'neck' or 'bulge' when strained longitudinally. Technically it is the ratio of the *lateral* strain to the *direct* strain and has typical values between 0.2 and 0.4. A substance that does not 'neck' or 'bulge' at all has $\sigma = 0$ and one that changes shape so its volume is unchanged has $\sigma = 0.5$. The Poisson ratio can be used to find relationships between the different elastic moduli, and these are discussed further in §A2.4 at the end of Appendix A2.

Comparison of theory and experiment

Having examined the theoretical predictions for the speed of sound in solids, we are now in a position to look at the questions that arose from our examination of the data on the speed of sound in solids.

Comparison of the speed of sound in gases and solids

Equations 5.29 and 7.24 to 7.26 indicate that the speed of sound in both gases and solids is determined by the ratio of the 'springiness' of a substance to its density. So if we combine the fact that:

- the speed of sound in solids is typically one order of magnitude greater than the speed of sound in gases at around STP

with the fact that:

- the density of solids (§7.2) is typically 10^3 to 10^4 times greater than the density of gases at STP,

then together these facts imply that the 'springiness' of solid is around 10^5 to 10^6 times greater than gases. Thus it requires around a million times more energy to reduce the volume of a solid by a given factor than it does for a gas. It is easy to understand why this is so. Reducing the volume of a

---

Example 7.9

The experimentally determined values of Young's modulus and Poisson ratio for copper are $E = 129.8$ GPa and $\sigma = 0.343$ (*Kaye and Laby*). What is the expected value for the speed of longitudinal and transverse sound waves in copper?

Equations 7.25 and 7.26 give us the formulae we require. Evaluating the expected value of γ we write:

$$\gamma = \frac{(1-\sigma)}{(1-2\sigma)(1+\sigma)} = \frac{(1-0.343)}{(1-0.686)(1+0.343)}$$
$$= 1.558$$

From Table 7.2 we find the density of copper is 8933 kg m^{-3} and substituting into the expression for the speed of sound we find:

$$c_L = \sqrt{\frac{\gamma E}{\rho}} = \sqrt{\frac{1.558 \times 129 \times 10^9}{8933}}$$
$$= 4758 \ \mathrm{m\,s^{-1}}$$

We can estimate the speed of transverse sound waves in solids by using Equation 7.24 to determine the rigidity modulus G in terms of the Young's modulus E. Using the values of E and σ given we find:

$$G = \frac{E}{2(1+\sigma)} = \frac{129.8 \times 10^9}{2(1+0.343)}$$
$$= 48.32 \times 10^9 \ \mathrm{Pa}$$

Substituting this value for G into Equation 7.11 we find:

$$c_T = \sqrt{\frac{G}{\rho}} = \sqrt{\frac{48.32 \times 10^9}{8933}}$$
$$= 2326 \ \mathrm{m\,s^{-1}}$$

These values can be compared with the experimental values from Table 7.9 of $c_L = 4759$ m s^{-1} and $c_T = 2325$ m s^{-1}, a suspiciously good agreement!

---

gas mainly increases the number density of molecules and so increases the frequency with which they hit the walls. However, in order to reduce the volume of a solid we need to rearrange the valence electrons of strongly interacting atoms. The bulk modulus of many solids are discussed in §7.3 and listed in Table 7.4. Typical values of B for elements, or for engineering solids, are of the order 10^{10} Pa to 10^{11} Pa. We use these values in Example 7.9 to show that Equations 7.25 and 7.26 predict the speed of sound with good accuracy.

The relative speed of longitudinal and transverse sound waves

Equations 7.25 and 7.26 yield the speeds of longitudinal and transverse sound waves through bulk solid. If we take their ratio, we predict that:

$$\frac{c_L}{c_T} = \frac{\sqrt{\gamma E / \rho}}{\sqrt{G / \rho}} = \sqrt{\frac{\gamma E}{G}} \tag{7.28}$$

Substituting the expression for γ (Equation 7.27) and the relationship between E and G (Equation 7.14) we find:

$$\frac{c_L}{c_T} = \sqrt{\frac{\frac{(1-\sigma)}{(1-2\sigma)(1+\sigma)}E}{\frac{1}{2(1+\sigma)}E}}$$

Cancelling and simplifying we arrive at:

$$\frac{c_L}{c_T} = \sqrt{\frac{2(1+\sigma)(1-\sigma)}{(1-2\sigma)(1+\sigma)}} = \sqrt{\frac{2(1-\sigma)}{(1-2\sigma)}} \tag{7.29}$$

Thus the experimental fact that c_L is typically $\approx 2c_T$ (Figure 7.11) may be reinterpreted as a statement that:

$$\frac{2(1-\sigma)}{(1-2\sigma)} \approx 4 \tag{7.30}$$

Rearranging and solving for σ we find:

$$4 - 8\sigma \approx 2 - 2\sigma$$
$$\sigma \approx \tfrac{1}{3} \tag{7.31}$$

If you consult *Kaye and Laby* you will find that $\sigma = \tfrac{1}{3}$ is indeed a typical value of the Poisson ratio.

The dependence of the speed of sound in solids on atomic mass

Equations 7.24 to 7.26 indicate that one should expect the speed of any kind of sound wave to vary inversely as the square root of the density $c \propto 1/\sqrt{\rho}$. In §7.2 (Figure 7.2) we saw that there is a general trend amongst the elements for high atomic number elements to be relatively more dense. However, in addition to the trend to high density, there are also periodic increases and decreases in density associated with the different

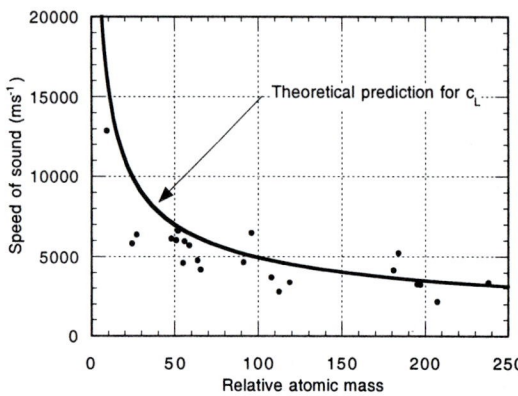

Figure 7.17 A simple prediction for the speed of longitudinal sound waves in the elements assuming that:
- All elements have the same value of Young's modulus E of ≈ 100 GPa
- All elements have Poisson ratio $\approx 1/3$
- The density of the elements is given by the formula (Example 7.2) $\rho = 61.5A$.

The final formula evaluated is $c_L = \sqrt{1.5 \times 10^{11}/61.5A}$

types, and strengths, of bonding amongst the elements. Based on the density data we would therefore expect to find a general trend towards a lower speed of sound for high atomic number elements, and fluctuations in the speed of sound associated with the density variations. This is, broadly speaking, just what is depicted in Figure 7.10.

A simple calculation

We can construct a simple model that allows us to understand the variation of the speed of sound amongst the elements. We assume that:

- All elements have the same value of Young's modulus E of ≈ 100 GPa. This is a typical value of E (see §7.3 for details) but there are considerable variations around this figure.
- All elements have Poisson ratio $\sigma = \tfrac{1}{3}$.
- The density of the elements is given by $\rho = 61.5A$ (Example 7.2). This line is indicated on Figure 7.2 and follows the trend of the data, but not the periodic increases and decreases in density.

Figure 7.17 shows the speed of longitudinal sound waves calculated according to Equation 7.26 and based on these assumptions. It is clear that the line captures the trend of the data rather well.

7.6 Heat capacity

7.6.1 Introduction

The *heat capacity* of an object is a measure of the temperature rise of that object for a given input of heat energy. It is defined in terms of the temperature rise ΔT resulting from an input of heat energy ΔQ, by the ratio:

$$C = \frac{\Delta Q}{\Delta T} \text{ joule kelvin}^{-1} \text{ (J K}^{-1}) \qquad (7.32)$$

If the temperature of an object rises by only a small amount due a given heat input, then the object has a large heat capacity. Equation 7.32 is the formula used to determine the heat capacity from experimental measurements of ΔQ and ΔT. It approximates the theoretical definition, which is the limit of Equation 7.32 as ΔT tends to zero:

$$C = \frac{\mathrm{d}Q}{\mathrm{d}T} \text{ joule kelvin}^{-1}(\text{J K}^{-1}) \qquad (7.33)$$

When we discuss the heat capacity of a *substance*, rather than an object, we need also to state the amounts of the substance to which we are referring. This is usually quoted either for a given mass of material, the *specific heat capacity* (e.g. $\text{J K}^{-1} \text{ kg}^{-1}$) or per mole, the *molar heat capacity* ($\text{J K}^{-1} \text{ mol}^{-1}$). For practical calculations the specific heat capacity is usually more convenient, but from a fundamental point of view, the molar heat capacity is far more interesting. Remember the molar heat capacity is the heat capacity of the Avogadro number ($N_A = 6.023 \times 10^{23}$) of atoms or molecules .

The heat capacities at constant pressure and constant volume are designated by C_P and C_V respectively. For solids we normally assume that measurements are made at constant pressure unless told otherwise. The difference between C_P and C_V is usually smaller than for gases because the expansivity of solids is so much smaller. C_P is usually a few per cent greater than C_V at around room temperature, with the difference becoming smaller at lower temperatures and increasing at higher temperatures.

7.6.2 Data on the heat capacity of the elements

The molar heat capacities at constant pressure C_P for the elements at 20 °C (293.1K) are recorded in Table 7.10 and a histogram showing the distribution of values of C_P for the solid elements is shown in Figure 7.18. The histogram indicates a striking phenomenon: more than 50% of the solid elements have a heat capacity within about 10% of 25 J K^{-1} mol^{-1}, and nearly all elements have C_P between 22 and 32 J K^{-1} mol^{-1}. Let me stress that this is a remarkable fact. It means that if we collect one mole of almost any element (i.e. the Avogadro number of atoms) then it takes roughly 25 J to raise their temperature by 1 K. Amazingly, this is independent of the type of atom, the crystal structure or the nature of the bonding!

There are some exceptions. On the low side, the three light elements beryllium, boron and carbon have molar heat capacities of 16.4, 11.1 and 8.5 J K^{-1} mol^{-1} respectively. On the high side, the three alkali metals rubidium, caesium and francium have molar heat capacities of 31.1, 32.2 and 31.7 J K^{-1} mol^{-1} respectively, while the value for the ferromagnetic element gadolinium has C_P of 37.0 J K^{-1} mol^{-1}.

Figure 7.18 Histogram of C_P for the solid elements in J K^{-1} mol^{-1} at around room temperature (25 °C = 298.15 K). More than 50% of the elements have a heat capacity close to 25 J K^{-1} mol^{-1}, and nearly all elements have C_P between 22 and 32 J K^{-1} mol^{-1}.

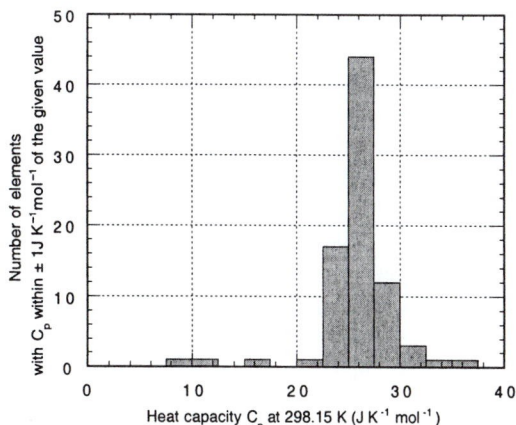

Table 7.10 The molar heat capacity at constant pressure C_P of the elements at room temperature 25 °C (298.15K). The shaded data are elements that are either liquids or gases at this temperature.

Z	Element	A	ρ (kg m⁻³)	C_P (J K mol⁻¹)	Z	Element	A	ρ (kg m⁻³)	C_P (J K mol⁻¹)
1	Hydrogen, H	1.008	89	28.824	49	Indium, In	114.8	7290	26.74
2	Helium, He	4.003	120	20.786	50	Tin, Sn	118.7	7285	26.99
3	Lithium , Li	6.941	533	24.770	51	Antimony, Sb	121.7	6692	25.23
4	Beryllium, Be	9.012	1846	16.44	52	Tellurium, Te	127.6	6247	25.73
5	Boron, B	10.81	2466	11.09	53	Iodine, I	126.9	4953	54.438
6	Carbon (graphite), C	12.01	2266	8.53	54	Xenon, Xe	131.3	3560	20.786
6	Carbon (diamond), C	12.01	3513	6.11	55	Caesium, Cs	132.9	1900	32.17
7	Nitrogen, N	14.01	1035	29.125	56	Barium, Ba	137.3	3594	28.07
8	Oxygen, O	16.00	1460	29.355	57	Lanthanum, La	138.9	6174	27.11
9	Fluorine, F	19.00	1140	31.300	58	Cerium, Ce	140.1	6711	26.94
10	Neon, Ne	20.18	1442	20.786	59	Praseodymium, Pr	140.9	6779	27.20
11	Sodium, Na	22.99	966	28.24	60	Neodymium, Ne	144.2	7000	27.45
12	Magnesium, Mg	24.31	1738	24.89	61	Promethium, Pm	145.0	7220	26.81
13	Aluminium, Al	26.98	2698	24.35	62	Samarium, Sm	150.4	7536	29.54
14	Silicon, Si	28.09	2329	20.0	63	Europium, Eu	152.0	5248	27.66
15	Phosphorus, P	30.97	1820	23.84	64	Gadolinium, Gd	157.2	7870	37.03
16	Sulphur, S	32.06	2086	22.64	65	Terbium, Tb	158.9	8267	28.91
17	Chlorine, Cl	35.45	2030	33.907	66	Dysprosium, Dy	162.5	8531	28.16
18	Argon, Ar	39.95	1656	20.786	67	Holmium, Ho	164.9	8797	27.15
19	Potassium, K	39.10	862	29.58	68	Erbium, Er	167.3	9044	28.12
20	Calcium, Ca	40.08	1530	25.31	69	Thulium, Th	168.9	9325	27.03
21	Scandium, Sc	44.96	2992	25.52	70	Ytterbium, Yb	173.0	6966	26.74
22	Titanium, Ti	47.90	4508	25.02	71	Lutetium, Lu	175.0	9842	26.86
23	Vanadium, V	50.94	6090	24.89	72	Hafnium, Hf	178.5	13276	25.73
24	Chromium, Cr	52.00	7194	23.35	73	Tantalum, Ta	180.9	16670	25.36
25	Manganese, Mn	54.94	7473	26.32	74	Tungsten, W	183.9	19254	24.27
26	Iron, Fe	55.85	7873	25.10	75	Rhenium, Re	186.2	21023	25.48
27	Cobalt, Co	58.93	8800	24.81	76	Osmium, Os	190.2	22580	24.70
28	Nickel, Ni	58.70	8907	26.07	77	Iridium, Ir	192.2	22550	25.10
29	Copper, Cu	63.55	8933	24.44	78	Platinum, Pt	195.1	21450	25.86
30	Zinc, Zn	65.38	7135	25.40	79	Gold, Au	197.0	19281	25.42
31	Gallium, Ga	69.72	5905	25.86	80	Mercury, Hg	200.6	13546	27.98
32	Germanium, Ge	72.59	5323	23.35	81	Thallium, Th	204.4	11871	26.32
33	Arsenic, As	74.92	5776	24.64	82	Lead, Pb	207.2	11343	26.44
34	Selenium, Se	78.96	4808	25.36	83	Bismuth, Bi	209.0	9803	25.52
35	Bromine, Br	79.90	3120	75.69	84	Polonium, Po	209	9400	25.75
36	Krypton, Kr	83.80	3000	20.79	85	Astatine, At	210		
37	Rubidium, Rb	85.47	1533	31.06	86	Radon, Rn	222	4400	20.786
38	Strontium, Sr	87.62	2583	26.40	87	Francium, Fr	223	2410	31.70
39	Yttrium, Y	88.91	4475	26.53	88	Radium, Ra	226	5000	25.76
40	Zirconium, Zr	91.22	6507	25.36	89	Actinium, Ac	227	10060	27.20
41	Niobium, Nb	92.91	8578	24.60	90	Thorium, Th	232	11725	27.32
42	Molybdenum, Mo	95.94	10222	24.06	91	Protractinium, Pa	231	15370	27.20
43	Technetium, Tc	97	11496	25.88	92	Uranium, U	238	19050	27.66
44	Ruthenium, Ru	101.1	12360	24.06	93	Neptunium, Np	237	20250	29.62
45	Rhodium, Rh	102.9	12420	24.98	94	Plutonium, Pu	244	19840	32.80
46	Palladium, Pd	106.4	11995	25.98	95	Americium, Am	243	13670	25.86
47	Silver, Ag	107.9	10500	25.35	96	Curium, Cm	247	1330	27.70
48	Cadmium, Cd	112.4	8647	25.98					

Figure 7.19 The variation with temperature of the molar heat capacity of copper, silver and gold. All three curves tend to a value ≈ 25J K^{-1} mol^{-1} at high temperatures in accord with the results of Table 7.10 and Figure 7.18. At low temperatures all three curves tend to zero.

Figure 7.20 The variation with temperature of the heat capacity of sapphire (Al$_2$O$_3$). The data tends to a value ≈ 130 J K^{-1} mol^{-1} at high temperatures, much higher than the elemental values of Table 7.10 and Figure 7.18. At low temperatures the data tend to zero in a similar manner to the data for copper, silver and gold (Figure 7.19)

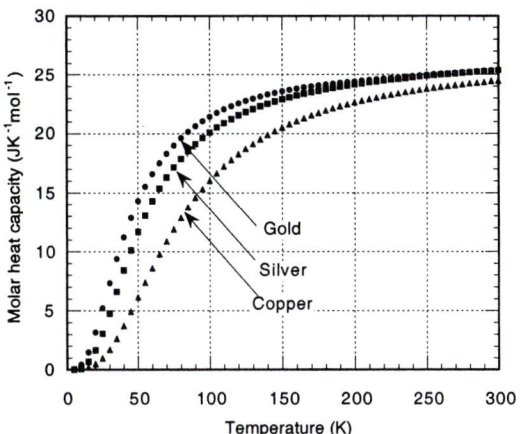

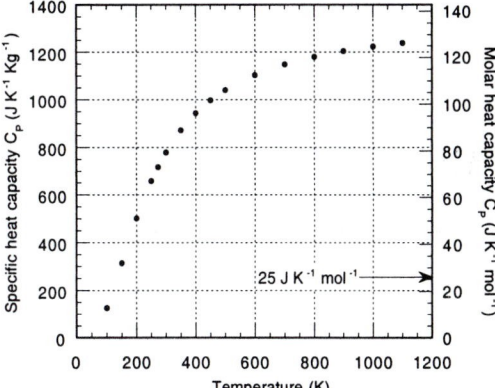

The variation of heat capacity with temperature in solids

The heat capacities of three metallic elements are depicted as a function of temperature in Figure 7.19. The data chosen are typical of the behaviour of many crystalline materials.

Figure 7.19 shows that the molar heat capacities of copper, silver and gold tend to roughly the same value at high temperatures. The behaviour below room temperature is qualitatively similar, apparently tending to zero at absolute zero. Figure 7.19 shows the heat capacities of crystalline aluminium oxide (Al$_2$O$_3$). In powdered form, this substance is known as *alumina*, and in crystalline form it is referred to as *sapphire*. The behaviour below about 1000 K is qualitatively similar to the behaviour of the metallic elements below room temperature, apparently tending to zero at absolute zero.

The main questions raised by our preliminary examination of the experimental data on C_P are:

- Why, at room temperature, is C_P for the elements often close to 25 J K^{-1} mol^{-1}?
- Why does C_P for the solid elements become smaller below room temperature, tending to zero at low temperatures?

7.6.3 Understanding the heat capacity of solids

To answer the questions raised in the previous section, we will construct a model of solids that is simpler even than any of those discussed in Chapter 6! We can justify this level of simplicity because, as we noted above, the universality of the value of 25 J K^{-1} mol^{-1} means that the value cannot be related to the details of the bonding type. We will then develop the model further to try to understand the reduction of heat capacity at low temperatures.

A simple model of a solid

Our model takes into account the fact that atoms in all solids have an equilibrium position about which they vibrate. This is their minimum energy position, and any displacement from this position takes them into a region where their potential energy of interaction with neighbouring atoms is higher. The atom will therefore experience a restoring force trying to return it towards its minimum energy position. This is exactly as if the atom were held in position with microscopic springs (Figure 7.21). This is a fanciful idea, but it can be helpful as long as one remembers that in reality the forces involved are mainly electrostatic.

Figure 7.21 Analogy to the situation of atoms in a crystal. An atom behaves *as if* it were held at its minimum energy position by springs. First (a) shows the atom in its equilibrium position and (b) shows the atom displaced from its equilibrium position. Notice that the springs in (b) are all either compressed or extended compared with their equilibrium length of r_0.

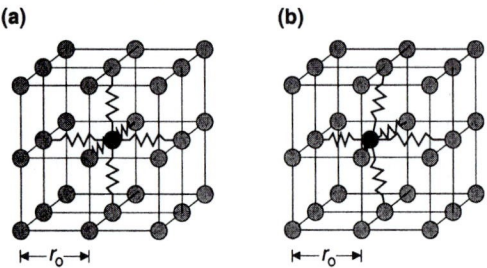

(a)   **(b)**

If we consider all the 'springs' in Figure 7.21 to have the same spring constant K, then we can write the potential energy of a single spring to be:

$$v = \frac{1}{2}K(x - x_0)^2 \qquad (7.34)$$

where $(x - x_0)$ is the displacement in the x-direction of the atom from its equilibrium x-coordinate. Similar equations apply for displacements in the y- and z- directions. (Displacing the atom in the x-direction will slightly stretch the y- and z- springs too, but we neglect this small effect in this analysis). Taking account of the kinetic energy of motion in each of the x-, y- and z-directions we can write down the total energy u associated with vibration of an atom:

$$u = \frac{1}{2}K(x - x_0)^2 + \frac{1}{2}mv_x^2$$
$$+ \frac{1}{2}K(y - y_0)^2 + \frac{1}{2}mv_y^2 \qquad (7.35)$$
$$+ \frac{1}{2}K(z - z_0)^2 + \frac{1}{2}mv_z^2$$

At any instant of time some of these terms will be large, and others small, but over time we would expect the average value of the energy associated with each of these six energy terms to be equal. Why? There are three reasons:

- The first relates to the symmetry of the situation. There is no difference in the crystal between the x-, y- and z-directions and so there is no reason why one vibration *on average* should have a higher energy of vibration than the other directions. If this were so at one

---

Example 7.10

Use Figure 7.19 to work out how much heat energy is required to raise the temperature of a cube of copper of side 2.42 cm from (a) 273 K to 283 K (b) 173 K to 183 K (c) 73 K to 83 K (d) 3 K to 13 K.

First we need to work out how many moles of copper are contained in our sample. If it has side L then its volume is L^3 and its mass is ρL^3, where its ρ is the density of copper (Table 7.2). The number of moles z in the cube is then:

$$z = \frac{\rho L^3}{molar\ mass}$$

For the sample in question this becomes:

$$z = \frac{8933 \times (0.0242)^3}{63.55 \times 10^{-3}} = 2.00\ mol$$

From Figure 7.19, we see that in the ranges indicated the heat capacity is approximately:
(a) 273 K to 283 K— $C_P \approx 24$ J K^{-1} mol^{-1}
(b) 173 K to 183 K — $C_P \approx 21.5$ J K^{-1} mol^{-1}
(c) 73 K to 83 K — $C_P \approx 11.8$ J K^{-1} mol^{-1}
(d) 3 K to 13 K — too small to infer directly from the graph but definitely $C_P < 0.1$ J K^{-1} mol^{-1}.

Thus the amount of heat energy required to heat the sample through 10 K in each range is:

$$\Delta Q = zC_P\Delta T = 2.00 \times C_P \times 10$$

(a) 273 K to 283 K — $\Delta Q = 2.00 \times 24.0 \times 10 = 480$ J
(b) 173 K to 183 K — $\Delta Q = 2.00 \times 21.5 \times 10 = 430$ J
(c) 73 K to 83 K — $\Delta Q = 2.00 \times 11.8 \times 10 = 236$ J
(d) 3 K to 13 K — $\Delta Q < 2.00 \times 0.1 \times 10 < 2$ J

Notice just how small the heat capacity becomes at low temperatures!

---

particular time, then that direction of vibration would tend to lose energy to the other directions of vibration.

- The second concerns the exchange of energy between potential and kinetic energy. It is a standard exercise in analysing simple harmonic motion to show that the *average* values of kinetic and potential energy are exactly equal.

- Finally, we remind ourselves that this is merely a special case of the equipartition of energy between degrees of freedom discussed in §2.5.

We might imagine that if the spring constant was

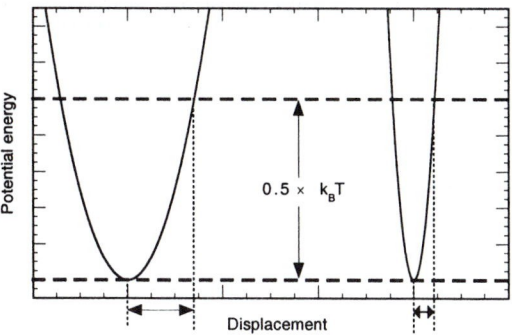

Figure 7.22 An illustration of two simple harmonic potentials with different spring constants. A given amount of energy (for example 0.5 $k_B T$) results in smaller oscillations of the stiffer-springed potential.

different in one direction then the average energy associated with vibration in that direction would be different from the other terms. However this conjecture would be mistaken! For example (Figure 7.22), suppose the x-spring was stiffer than the others, i.e. $K_x > K_y$ or K_z. Then the amplitude of x-vibration would be less than in the y- and z-directions, but this smaller amplitude x-vibration would 'cost' the same energy as the larger amplitude y- and z-vibrations because the spring constant K_x is larger.

Thus, using the standard notation of representing the average of a quantity by a 'bar' over the top of it, we expect the average of each term in 7.35 to be equal:

$$\overline{\tfrac{1}{2}K(x-x_0)^2} = \overline{\tfrac{1}{2}mv_x^2}$$
$$= \overline{\tfrac{1}{2}K(y-y_0)^2} = \overline{\tfrac{1}{2}mv_y^2} \qquad (7.36)$$
$$= \overline{\tfrac{1}{2}K(z-z_0)^2} = \overline{\tfrac{1}{2}mv_z^2}$$

Each of the terms in Equation 7.36 constitutes a degree of freedom for the atom in the sense discussed in §2.4, §4.2, and §5.3.3. As you may recall from those discussions, temperature is defined so that the average energy per degree of freedom is $\tfrac{1}{2}k_B T$, where k_B is the Boltzmann constant. Thus molecules in a gas each have three degrees of freedom associated with kinetic energy of motion in the x-, y-, and z-directions. From Equation

7.36 we can see that atoms in a solid each have six degrees of freedom associated with kinetic and potential energy of motion in the x-, y-, and z-directions. Thus, according to our simple model, if we have one mole of an element, i.e. the Avogadro number N_A of atoms, we expect the internal energy of that substance at temperature T to be:

$$U = U_0 + N_A \times 6 \times \tfrac{1}{2} k_B T \qquad (7.37)$$

where U_0 is the cohesive energy at $T = 0$ K. This equation will only apply for substances with one atom per chemical formula unit. For example, it would not refer to sodium chloride, NaCl. One mole of NaCl contains $2N_A$ atoms: N_A each of Na and Cl. Generalising Equation 7.37 to take account of solids with p atoms per chemical formula unit, we obtain a prediction for the internal energy of a solid:

$$U = U_0 + pN_A \times 6 \times \tfrac{1}{2} k_B T \qquad (7.38)$$

By remembering that $N_A k_B = R$, the molar gas constant, we can rewrite this as:

$$U = U_0 + 3pRT \qquad (7.39)$$

By the first law of thermodynamics (Equation 2.57), changes in internal energy are related to the heat supplied to a substance and the work on that substance by:

$$\Delta U = \Delta Q + \Delta W \qquad (7.40)$$

If we consider first the effect of a temperature change at constant volume, then $\Delta W = P\Delta V$ is zero. In this case we may differentiate Equation 7.39 to find the heat capacity at constant volume C_V:

$$C_V = \frac{dQ}{dT} = \frac{dU}{dT}$$
$$= \frac{d}{dT}(U_0 + 3pRT) \qquad (7.41)$$
$$C_V = 3pR$$

where we have used the fact that U_0 does not depend on temperature. If the heat is supplied at constant pressure, then we need to take account of the thermal expansivity and the volume dependence of

Example 7.11

How does the experimental value of the heat capacity of NaCl $(0.88 \text{ J K}^{-1}\text{g}^{-1}$ @ 10 °C; *Kaye and Laby*) compare with the value predicted by the law of Dulong and Petit?

We can work out the theoretically expected value using Equation 7.41:

$$C_V = 3pR$$

For NaCl, there are two atoms per chemical formula unit, i.e. $p = 2$ and so we predict a heat capacity of:

$$C_V = 3 \times 2 \times 8.31$$

$$= 49.86 \text{ J K}^{-1}\text{mol}^{-1}$$

Since one mole of NaCl has a mass of 22.99 + 35.45 = 58.44 g (Table 7.2), we see that 1 g is 1/58.44 = 17.1×10^{-3} mole and so the experimental value of the molar heat capacity is $58.44 \times 0.88 = 51.4 \text{ J K}^{-1}\text{mol}^{-1}$, within 3% of the predicted value of $49.86 \text{ J K}^{-1}\text{mol}^{-1}$.

Example 7.12

How does the high-temperature limiting value of the heat capacity of sapphire Al_2O_3 depicted in Figure 7.19 compare with the value predicted by the law of Dulong and Petit?

We can work out the theoretically expected value using Equation 7.41:

$$C_V = 3pR$$

For Al_2O_3, there are five atoms per chemical formula unit, i.e. $p = 5$ and so we predict a heat capacity of:

$$C_V = 3 \times 5 \times 8.31$$

$$= 124.7 \text{ J K}^{-1}\text{mol}^{-1}$$

There is some uncertainty in predicting the high-temperature limiting value of the heat capacity of sapphire depicted in Figure 7.19 but by my estimation the value is $\approx 127 \pm 3 \text{ J K}^{-1}\text{mol}^{-1}$, within 2% of the value predicted by the law of Dulong and Petit.

---

the internal energy. However, although the latter effect is large, the thermal expansivity is generally small (Table 7.7). At or below room temperature, C_P and C_V generally differ by only a few per cent at most. In what follows we assume $C_V \approx C_P$.

If we evaluate Equation 7.41 for elements ($p=1$) we have a startlingly simple prediction that $C_V = 3R$, independent of the mass of atoms, type of bonding, or crystal structure! Evaluating this prediction we find:

$$C_V = 3 \times 8.31 = 24.93 \text{ J K}^{-1}\text{mol}^{-1} \qquad (7.42)$$

Comparison with Table 7.10 shows that this estimate is accurate for C_P to within 10 % for most elements at room temperature (Figure 7.23). When we consider the diverse properties of the solids involved, this is indeed a remarkable result. This result was noted as early as the nineteenth century and is called the *law of Dulong and Petit*.

The analysis leading to Equation 7.41 allows us to understand the heat capacity of elements and compounds at around room temperature. We can even understand some of the exceptions in Figure 7.18. Three of the elements with particularly high values of C_P are the alkali metals rubidium, caesium and francium with molar heat capacities of 31.1, 32.2

and $31.7 \text{ J K}^{-1}\text{mol}^{-1}$ respectively. These elements melt at unusually low temperatures (39.1 °C, 28.4 °C, and 27 °C respectively) and so at 20 °C they are close to their melting temperature. In this region their thermal expansivity is particularly large and the difference between the experimental

Figure 7.23 Histogram of the heat capacities at constant pressure C_P of the solid elements in J K^{-1} mol^{-1} at room temperature 25 °C = 298.15 K (also shown as Figure 7.18). The bold line shows the prediction of Equation (7.42) for the heat capacity of all elements.

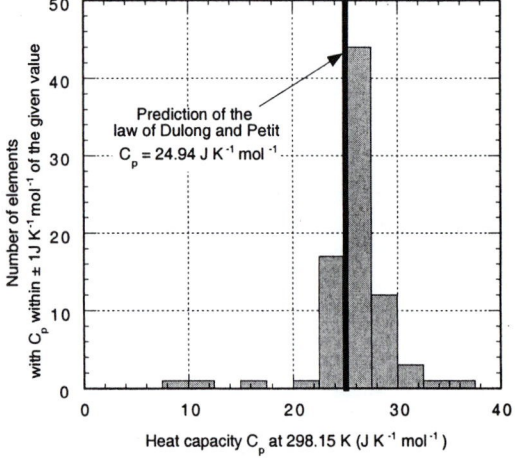

205

value of C_P and the predicted value of $3R$ is just the difference between C_P and C_V that we neglected for the other elements. The unusual datum for the ferromagnetic element gadolinium has C_P of $37.0 \text{ J K}^{-1} \text{ mol}^{-1}$ is connected with the transition to the ferromagnetic state.

The heat capacity of solids at low temperatures

The approach developed so far can plausibly explain the unusually high values of C_P at around room temperature, but it cannot explain the unusually low values. Neither can it explain the reduction of the heat capacity observed at low temperatures (Figures 7.19 and 7.20).

Degrees of freedom

Based on the analysis of the heat capacity of gases in §5.3, we might surmise that the reduction in heat capacity at low temperatures arises because some of the six degrees of freedom available to each atom (Equation 7.25) have become constrained, i.e. they are not fully accessible. It is at first difficult to see where this restriction on the accessible degrees of freedom of vibration comes from. It might appear that at low temperatures, the amplitude of the vibration of the atoms of solid would be reduced, but would otherwise be similar to the situation at high temperatures. However, this is plainly not so since if it were, the heat capacity would not be reduced at low temperatures!

The origin of the restriction on the vibration of each atom lies in the quantum mechanical nature of the vibration. If the potential energy of the atom of mass m varies with position approximately like a simple harmonic oscillator (the theory of which is summarised in §2.4.3) then we write:

$$v = \tfrac{1}{2}K(x-x_0)^2 \qquad (2.51^* \text{ and } 7.43)$$

where $(x-x_0)$ is the displacement in the x-direction of the atom from its equilibrium x-coordinate. The frequency of vibration is given by:

$$f_0 = \frac{1}{2\pi}\sqrt{\frac{K}{m}} \qquad (2.52^* \text{ and } 7.44)$$

and the amplitude of vibration is quantised such that the total energy of vibration is limited to one of the values:

$$u = (n_x + \tfrac{1}{2})hf_0 \qquad (2.53^* \text{ and } 7.45)$$

where h is the Planck constant, and n_x is any positive integer starting from 0.

Figure 7.24 An illustration of the relationship between energy levels, particle mass and spring constant for a simple harmonic potential. If (a) represents the energy levels of a particle of mass M bonded in a particular way, then (b) would represent the energy levels of a heavier particle in the same potential, and (c) would represent the energy levels of a particle of a similar mass, but more stiffly constrained.

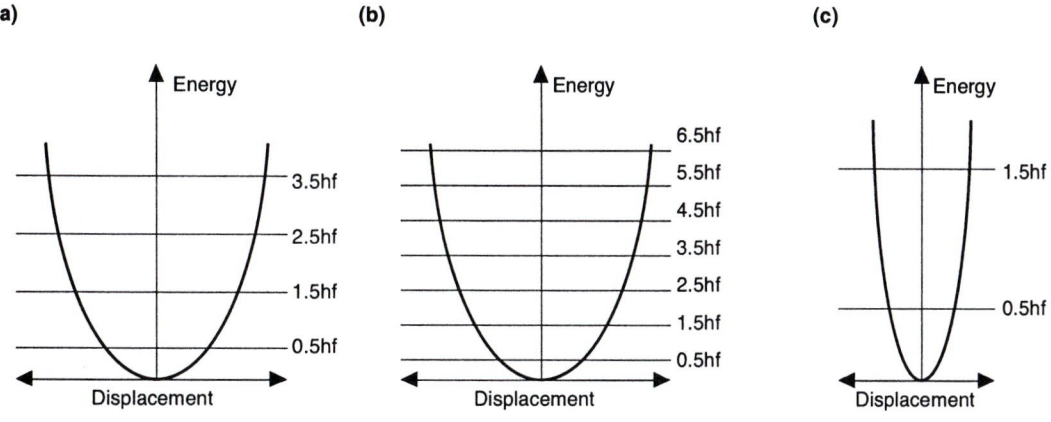

The transition to inaccessibility

In §5.3.3 we noted that a quantum state becomes inaccessible when the thermal energy $\tfrac{1}{2}k_BT$ is significantly less than the energy gap ΔE between quantum states. In this case ΔE is the difference in energy between successive quantum states. So considering the gap between successive values of Equation 7.45, we would expect to observe the reduction in the accessibility of quantum states when $k_BT < hf_o$:

$$k_BT < \frac{h}{2\pi}\sqrt{\frac{K}{m}}$$

$$T < \frac{\hbar}{k_B}\sqrt{\frac{K}{m}} \tag{7.46}$$

This idea, due to Einstein, captures some of the essential physics of the reduction of the heat capacity of solids at low temperatures. Equation 7.46 defines a temperature below which excited vibrational quantum states begin to become inaccessible. The *Einstein theory* correctly predicts that the heat capacity of solids becomes smaller below a characteristic temperature known as the *Einstein temperature* Θ_E defined by:

$$\Theta_E = \frac{hf_o}{k_B} = \frac{\hbar}{k_B}\sqrt{\frac{K}{m}} \tag{7.47}$$

Θ_E varies from one solid to another depending on the stiffness constant K of the bonds and the mass m of the atoms.

The Einstein theory of the heat capacity of solids

The Einstein theory of the heat capacity is developed fully in Appendix 4. In many ways it is similar to the classical theory developed earlier in this section. The key difference is that the average energy associated with each (x, y or z) harmonic oscillator is no longer given by the simple expression:

$$\bar{u} = 2 \times \tfrac{1}{2}k_BT \tag{7.48}$$

but by a more complex expression:

$$\bar{u} = \tfrac{1}{2}hf_o + \frac{hf_o}{\exp(hf_o/k_BT) - 1} \tag{7.49}$$

Example 7.13

Assuming an Einstein temperature of 230 K, use Equation 7.47 to predict the frequency f_o at which all the copper atoms are supposed to vibrate. Also estimate a value for K, the spring constant of a copper–copper 'bond'.

Using Equation 7.47:

$$f_o = \frac{k_B\theta_E}{h} = \frac{1.38\times10^{-23}\times230}{6.63\times10^{-34}}$$

$$= 4.79\times10^{12} \text{ Hz}$$

Recall that f_o is defined by (Equation 7.44) as:

$$f_o = \frac{1}{2\pi}\sqrt{K/m}$$

Rearranging to solve for K we find: $K = 4m\pi^2 f_o^2$

From Table 7.2 we find that the mass of copper atom is $63.55 \times 1.66 \times 10^{-27}$ kg and so we predict that:

$$K = 4\times63.55\times1.66\times10^{-27}\times\pi^2\times(4.79\times10^{12})^2$$

$$= 95.6 \text{ J m}^{-2}$$

This value may be compared with the value worked out from the speed of sound (§7.11: Exercise 7P32).

Notice however that at high temperatures, i.e. when $k_BT \gg hf_o$, the exponential in the denominator of Equation 7.49 can be expanded:

$$\bar{u} \approx \tfrac{1}{2}hf_o + \frac{hf_o}{[1+(hf_o/k_BT)+...]-1}$$

$$\approx \tfrac{1}{2}hf_o + \frac{hf_o}{hf_o/k_BT} \tag{7.50}$$

$$\approx \tfrac{1}{2}hf_o + k_BT$$

This agrees with the classical result except for the so-called zero-point energy term $\tfrac{1}{2}hf_o$. Since this correction is not temperature-dependent, it is usually considered as a correction to the cohesive energy U_o rather than the thermal energy. Proceeding as we did in the classical case (Equation 7.37) we write the molar internal energy as:

$$U = U_o + 3pN_A\bar{u} \tag{7.51}$$

where p is the number of atoms per chemical formula unit. Recalling that for temperature changes at constant volume $dU/dT = dQ/dT$ we write:

207

$$C_V = \frac{dU}{dT} = \frac{d}{dT}\left(3pN_A \bar{u}\right)$$

$$= 3pN_A \frac{d}{dT}(\bar{u}) \qquad (7.52)$$

Substituting for $\bar{u}$:

$$C_V = 3pN_A \frac{d}{dT}\left(\tfrac{1}{2}hf_o + \frac{hf_o}{\exp(hf_o/k_BT)-1}\right)$$

$$(7.53)$$

and differentiating we find:

$$C_V = \frac{hf_o \exp(hf_o/k_BT)}{k_BT^2} \times \frac{3pN_A hf_o}{\left[\exp(hf_o/k_BT)-1\right]^2}$$

$$(7.54)$$

Recalling that $R = N_A k_B$, this may be written as:

$$C_V = 3pR\left(\frac{hf_o}{k_BT}\right)^2 \frac{\exp(hf_o/k_BT)}{\left[\exp(hf_o/k_BT)-1\right]^2} \qquad (7.55)$$

Finally, recalling the definition of $\Theta_E = hf_o/k_B$ (Equation 7.47) this may also be written as:

$$C_V = 3pR\left(\frac{\Theta_E}{T}\right)^2 \frac{\exp(\Theta_E/T)}{\left[\exp(\Theta_E/T)-1\right]^2} \qquad (7.56)$$

Figure 7.25 shows the heat capacity of copper from Figure 7.18 plotted together with the Einstein prediction for the heat capacity based on $\Theta_E = 230$ K. This value has been chosen by trial and error to give good agreement across most of the temperature range. It is clear that the theory does indeed capture the trend of the data. However, careful examination of Figure 7.25 shows that the agreement between the theory and experiment becomes rather poor at low temperatures.

The discrepancy at low temperatures in Figure 7.25 looks small and it would be nice if we could neglect it and move on. However, it turns out to be important because it is a clue that there is something wrong with the way the Einstein theory models the vibrations within solids. In the next section, we will develop our simple model of a solid further in order to reflect correctly the types of vibrations that actually take place in solids.

208

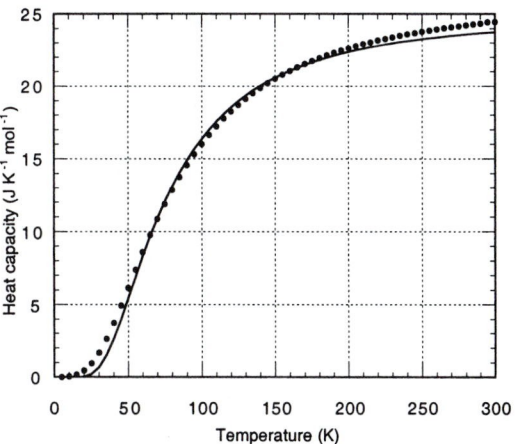

Figure 7.25 The heat capacity of copper from Figure 7.19 plotted together with the Einstein prediction for the heat capacity based on $\Theta_E = 230$ K. The predicted Einstein temperature corresponds to a spring constant of $K = 2.423$ J m^{-2}, and a frequency of vibration of $f_0 = 4.79 \times 10^{12}$ Hz It is clear that the theory captures the trend of the data. However, careful examination shows that the agreement between the theory and experiment becomes poor at low temperatures. **Note:** The Einstein theory prediction is for C_V, but the data with which it is compared is based on C_P.

Lattice waves, sound waves and phonons

The key problem with the Einstein theory as applied to ordinary solids is that it assumes that each atom is in the situation of Figure 7.26 (a). This supposes that each atom is surrounded by neighbours which do not themselves vibrate. Clearly this cannot be the case. In the Einstein theory, it is assumed that all the atoms vibrate at the same frequency. However a little thought shows that the model illustrated in Figure 7.26 (b) is likely to be more realistic. The difficulty with this new model is that the atoms no longer vibrate independently.

Consider the following thought experiment. Imagine displacing the central atom in Figure 7.26 (b) and then letting it go. The atom would not vibrate at frequency f_o leaving its neighbours unaffected. What would happen is that a wave-like disturbance would spread out from the central atom. This is what is wrong with the Einstein model at low temperatures. It assumes that the vibrational energy of the lattice is held as individual and independent vibrations of atoms, whereas

Figure 7.26 Analogy to the situation of atoms in a crystal. The forces on an atom are such that the atom behaves *as if* it were held at its minimum energy position by springs. First (a) shows the simple model used in our initial analysis, then (b) shows a more realistic representation of the situation within the solid. Motion of the central atom in (b) causes all the atoms around it to move as well, creating a tremendously difficult situation to analyse.

(a)   **(b)**

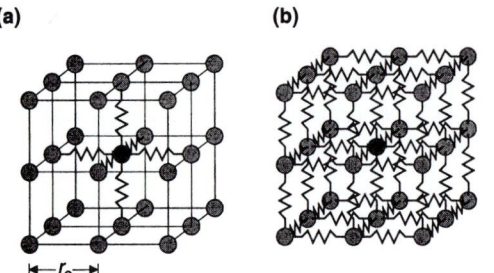

in fact the energy is held in waves of displacements running through the lattice.

Now we have already considered waves of displacement in a solid: they are nothing more than sound waves (§7.5). However, the frequencies of the naturally occurring displacement waves in solids are typically of the order of 10 THz i.e. $\approx 10^{13}$ Hz (Example 7.13). This is considerably greater than the frequencies considered in §7.5.

In seeking to describe the vibrations of the lattice at an atomic level, we need to develop a language which (a) correctly describes the wave-like nature of the excitations in the lattice, and (b) incorporates the quantum mechanical nature of the vibrations of the atoms. These requirements are resolved with the introduction of the concept of a *phonon*.

What is a phonon?

The concept of a phonon is analogous to the concept of a photon (§2.3.3): a phonon describes the wave-like excitations of the displacements in a lattice; a *photon* describes the wave-like excitations of the electromagnetic field. The phonon concept allows us to describe realistically the wave-like nature of the vibrations in a lattice and yet incorporates the quantum mechanical nature of the vibrating atoms.

Figure 7.27 Illustration of the concept of a phonon in 1-dimensional crystal. The filled circles represent the instantaneous positions of atoms and the empty circles represent their equilibrium positions. Case (a) shows the crystal when there are no phonons present. Case (b) would be described by saying there is one transverse phonon present in the lattice with relatively long wavelength λ_1 and relatively low frequency f_1. In case (c) the amplitude of the wave is larger than in (b) which would be described by saying there are two transverse phonons with the same wavelength λ_1 and relatively low frequency f_1 as in (b). Case (d) would be described by saying there is one transverse phonon present in the lattice with relatively short wavelength λ_2 and relatively high frequency f_2. Case (e) would be described by saying there are two transverse phonons in the lattice: one with long wavelength and low frequency and other with short wavelength and high frequency.

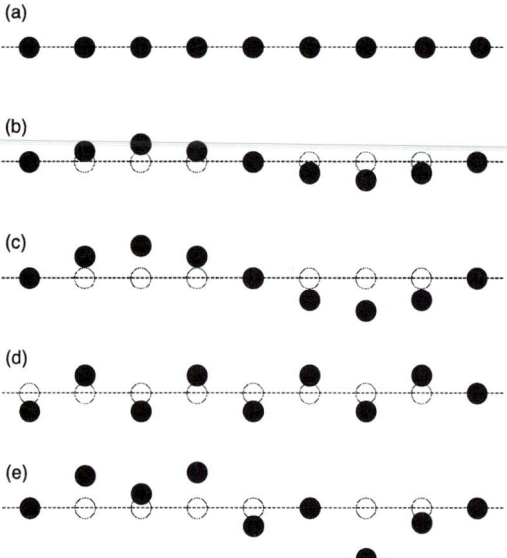

Figure 7.28 The relationship between frequency and wavelength assuming a speed of sound of 4000 ms^{-1}. For wavelengths less than an atomic spacing (typically 3×10^{-10} m), the idea of a compression wave becomes meaningless, because there is nothing to be compressed! This estimates that the maximum frequency of atomic vibrations is $\approx 10^{13}$ Hz.

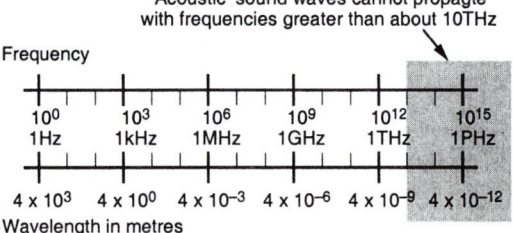

Four important features of the phonon description of lattice vibrations are outlined below and illustrated in Figure 7.27.

Quantised vibration amplitude

A displacement wave of frequency f in a lattice cannot have arbitrary amplitude. Its amplitude may only increase in such a way that the energy associated with the wave is limited to one of a set of values:

$$u = \left(n + \tfrac{1}{2}\right)hf \qquad (7.57)$$

where n may have the value $0, 1, 2 \dots$. If $n = 0$ then we say 'there are no phonons in that mode of vibration'. Otherwise we say 'there are n phonons in that mode of vibration'. Notice the similarity of Equation 7.44 with Equation 7.33

Boson nature

The terminology above allows us to treat phonons as particles with a boson nature. The 'mode of vibration' represents a quantum state which is 'occupied' by phonons. Importantly this allows us to use the Bose–Einstein occupation function (Equation 2.62) to predict the average occupancy of an individual mode of vibration:

$$f_{BE}(u, T) = \bar{n}(u, T)$$
$$= \frac{1}{\exp(u / k_B T) - 1} \qquad (7.58)$$

where u is given by Equation 7.44. The chemical potential μ has been set equal to zero because phonons are not 'conserved' particles like electrons or protons. Phonons are destroyed and created by putting energy into or out of the lattice.

No minimum phonon energy

There is no minimum phonon energy. Long wavelength waves have low frequencies, and hence hf in Equation 7.57 can take arbitrarily small values. This means there is no 'energy gap' in the spectrum of possible vibrational energies of the atoms in a lattice. This is in distinct contrast with the Einstein model, in which atoms were assumed to either vibrate at f_o, or not at all.

Maximum phonon energy

There is a maximum phonon energy. It makes no sense to imagine waves with a wavelength shorter than a lattice spacing, i.e. ≈ 0.3 nm. Since there is a short-wavelength limit to λ, there must be a consequent high-frequency limit hf_{max} and hence there is a maximum phonon energy, hf_{max}. Assuming that the speed of these very high frequency sound waves is the same as the more familiar sound waves (i.e. ≈ 4000 ms^{-1}) then we can use $c_{sound} = f\lambda$ to estimate the maximum phonon frequency:

$$f_{max} \approx \frac{4000}{3 \times 10^{-10}} \approx 1.3 \times 10^{13} \text{ Hz} \qquad (7.59)$$

The Debye theory of the heat capacity of solids

The theory of the heat capacity of solids in which the internal energy of the lattice is held as phonons (quantised sound waves) is known as the *Debye theory* of the heat capacity. The theory is more fully developed in Appendix 4. In a similar manner to the Einstein model, the heat capacity is predicted in terms of a characteristic temperature, known in this case as the *Debye temperature*, Θ_D. Just as the Einstein temperature is related to the frequency of the vibration of the atoms f_o by Equation 7.35, so the Debye temperature is related to the maximum phonon frequency f_D by:

$$\Theta_D = \frac{hf_D}{k_B} \qquad (7.60)$$

However, unlike the Einstein theory, the predictions cannot be expressed by a closed-form formula such Equation 7.43. Table 7.11 shows the predicted values for the heat capacity of solids tabulated at $0.1\Theta_D$, $0.2\Theta_D$, etc.

Figure 7.29 shows the heat capacity of copper from Figure 7.19, plotted together with both the Debye and Einstein predictions for the heat capacity. The Debye curve is based on $\Theta_D = 310$ K (c.f. $\Theta_E = 230$ K) chosen by trial and error to give good agreement across most of the temperature range. Both curves capture the trend of the data, but at low temperatures the Debye prediction falls off

more slowly than the Einstein prediction. This is because in the Debye model (and in reality) there is a continuum of low-energy vibrational modes which can be excited at low temperatures.

Key features of the Debye theory

The Debye theory predicts that at temperatures less than $\approx 0.1\Theta_D$ (i.e. less than around 30 K for copper) C_V should vary as T^3 according to:

$$C_V = \left[\frac{1944p}{\Theta_D^3}\right]T^3 \quad \text{J K}^{-1}\text{ mol}^{-1} \qquad (7.61)$$

where p is the number of atoms per chemical formula unit, and has the value $p = 1$ for elements. Equation 7.61 allows us to estimate Θ_D from the low temperature heat capacity (Figure 7.32).

At $T = \Theta_D$ the heat capacity is predicted to be around 95% of its classical value ($C_V = 3pR$) as predicted by the law of Dulong and Petit.

Table 7.12 contains a selection of Debye temperatures for elements determined from their low temperature heat capacity according to Equation 7.61. Figure 7.30 shows the predicted variation of the heat capacity for substances with Debye temperatures of 100 K, 300 K and 1000 K. We see that at room temperature, the heat capacity values will be close to $C_V = 3R$ if Θ_D is of the order of room temperature or less. However if Θ_D is much greater than room temperature, then the heat capacity at room temperature will appear to anomalously low. This is the origin of the anomalously low values in the histogram 7.18.

Relationship between speed of sound and Θ_D

The Debye theory assumes that the thermal energy of the lattice is held in the form of high frequency sound waves. If this is so then we might expect to find a relationship between the Debye temperature of a substance and the speed of sound in that substance. Recalling the definition of Θ_D (Equation 7.60) as the temperature corresponding to maximum phonon frequency, and thus the minimum phonon wavelength, we can write:

$$\Theta_D = \frac{h}{k_B}\times f_D \approx \frac{h}{k_B}\times\frac{c_{\text{sound}}}{\lambda_{\text{min}}} \qquad (7.62)$$

Table 7.11 The predicted value of the heat capacity of monatomic solids according to the Debye theory. Also tabulated is the fraction of the high temperature limiting value ($3R$) expected at the temperature indicated.

T/Θ_D	$C(T)$ J K^{-1} mol^{-1}	$C(T)/R$
0	0	0
0.01	1.944×10^{-3}	7.7927×10^{-5}
0.02	1.555×10^{-2}	6.2342×10^{-4}
0.03	5.248×10^{-2}	2.1040×10^{-3}
0.04	0.1244	4.9873×10^{-3}
0.05	0.2430	9.7408×10^{-3}
0.06	0.4198	1.6829×10^{-2}
0.07	0.6658	2.6693×10^{-2}
0.08	0.9903	3.9702×10^{-2}
0.09	1.399	5.6074×10^{-2}
0.1	1.891	7.5821×10^{-2}
0.2	9.195	0.36863
0.3	15.158	0.60770
0.4	18.604	0.74585
0.5	20.588	0.82541
0.6	21.795	0.87380
0.7	22.572	0.90495
0.8	23.098	0.92603
0.9	23.469	0.94089
1.0	23.739	0.95173
1.1	23.942	0.95987
1.2	24.098	0.96612
1.3	24.221	0.97103
1.4	24.318	0.97495
1.5	24.398	0.97813
1.6	24.463	0.98074
1.7	24.517	0.98291
1.8	24.562	0.98474
1.9	24.601	0.98629
2.0	24.634	0.98761

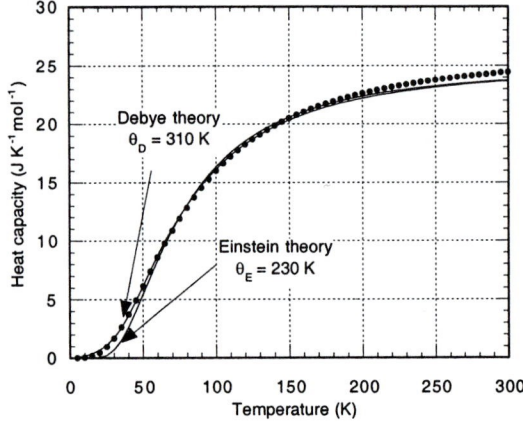

Figure 7.29 The Debye prediction for the heat capacity of copper compared with the Einstein prediction shown in Figure 7.25.

211

Since λ_{min} is of the order of a typical lattice spacing ($a \approx 3 \times 10^{-10}$ m) which is roughly the same for many elements, Equation 7.62 suggests that the Debye temperature ought to be roughly proportional to the speed of sound. Figure 7.31 shows a graph of the speed of transverse sound waves (Table 7.9) as a function of the Debye Temperature (Table 7.12) and it is evident that there is a roughly linear relationship between the two. I personally find Figure 7.31 fascinating. It indicates a relationship between a characteristic temperature determined from heat capacity measurements, and the speed of sound determined from acoustic measurements. The fact there is any relationship at all between the two quantities gives us confidence that our explanation of the heat capacity in terms of lattice waves (phonons) really is correct.

Metals

In the Debye theory of the heat capacity of solids, the thermal energy of a solid is considered to be

Table 7.12 The Debye temperatures θ_D of several elements as determined by analysis of the T^3 behaviour of their low-temperature heat capacity (Equation 7.61).

Element	Z	θ_D (K)	Element	Z	θ_D (K)
Beryllium	4	1440	Zirconium	40	291
C(Diamond)	6	2230	Molybdenum	42	450
Magnesium	12	400	Silver	47	225
Aluminium	13	428	Cadmium	48	209
Titanium	22	420	Tin	50	200
Vanadium	23	380	Tantalum	73	240
Chromium	24	630	Tungsten	74	400
Manganese	25	410	Platinum	78	240
Iron	26	470	Gold	79	165
Nickel	28	450	Lead	82	105
Copper	29	343	Uranium	92	207

tied up in vibrations of the atoms of the substance. We saw that these vibrations could be analysed as 'sound' waves in the lattice. However, as discussed in §6.5, within metals there is a high density of 'free' electrons, which we analysed as a 'gas' of electrons. However, this gas does not appear to have a heat capacity of $3R/2$ per mole that

Figure 7.30 The Debye prediction for the heat capacity of solids with Debye temperatures of 100 K, 300 K and 1000 K. At room temperature, the heat capacity values will be close to $C_V = 3R$ if θ_D is less than room temperature. However if θ_D is much greater than room temperature, then the heat capacity at room temperature appears to anomalously low. This is the origin of the anomalously low values of C_P for beryllium, boron and carbon in Figure 7.18.

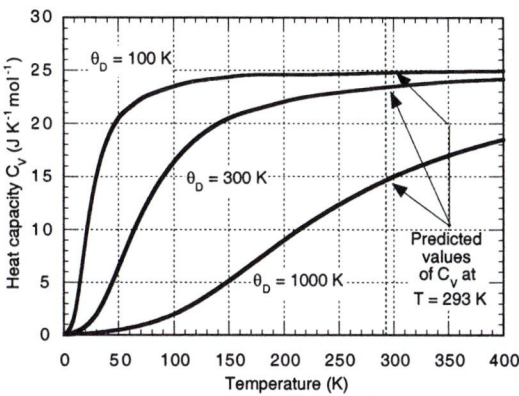

Figure 7.31 The speed of transverse sound waves in some elements (Table 7.9) plotted as a function of their Debye temperature (Table 7.12). It is clear that there is a roughly linear relationship between the two quantities.

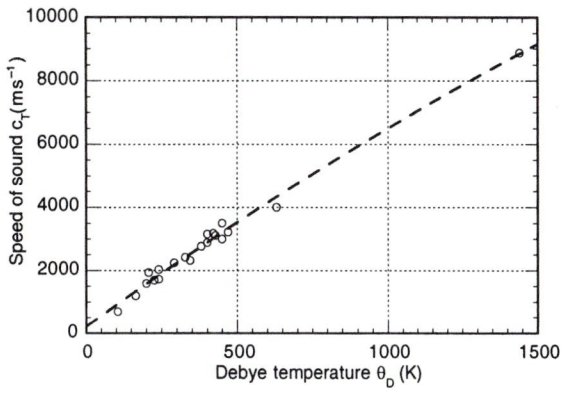

one would expect monatomic gas (§5.3). In fact, if we look only at high temperature data, the 'electron gas' appears to have a negligibly small heat capacity. For example, the C_P for copper at its Debye temperature of 343 K ($\approx 70\,°C$) is $\approx 25\ J\ K^{-1}\ mol^{-1}$ which can all be plausibly understood (within the uncertainties of our study) by the effect of atomic vibrations. This result is typical of metals and raises the question: What has happened to the heat capacity of the free 'electron gas' that we suppose to exist within metals?

By now the answer may be becoming familiar to you: whenever the full heat capacity expected is not observed then we should look to see if some of the degrees of freedom of the system are not accessible. We saw this with diatomic, triatomic, and polyatomic molecules (§5.3.3), with atoms in solids at low temperature (§7.6), and now with electrons. For electrons we anticipate three degrees of freedom corresponding to kinetic energy of motion in each of the x-, y-, and z- directions. The question of what has happened to the heat capacity of the free electron 'gas' may now be interpreted as the question. What has happened to these degrees of freedom?

The answer lies in our consideration (§6.5) of the effect that quantum mechanics has on the cohesive energy of metals. We described the quantum states with the aid of a 'k-space graph', with the electrons occupying quantum states nearest the origin,

and forming a 'sphere' of occupied states (Figure 7.32). This correctly describes the occupancy of quantum states at absolute zero. However, when the temperature is raised, this picture is slightly altered because some electrons can accept energy and move into higher quantum states. However, because of the Pauli exclusion principle, (see §2.4) most electrons are unable to accept thermal energy because there are no vacant quantum states into which they can move. Only electrons in quantum states with energies close to the Fermi energy E_F can accept energy, and as we saw in §6.5.3, at room temperature $k_B T \ll E_F$.

With this model we can now understand the behaviour of the electron gas in a metal. If the gas had been a classical molecular gas then the three degrees of freedom would have resulted in an internal energy U of:

$$U = U_o + N_A \times \tfrac{3}{2} k_B T$$
$$= U_o + \tfrac{3}{2} RT \quad mol^{-1} \qquad (7.63)$$

and hence a molar heat capacity $C_V = 3R/2$. However, the internal energy due to thermal excitations of electrons is only a small fraction of the classically expected value (Equation. 7.63). So we write:

$$U = U_o + \left[\begin{smallmatrix}\text{number of electrons}\\\text{able to accept energy}\end{smallmatrix}\right] \times \tfrac{3}{2} k_B T \quad mol^{-1} \quad (7.64)$$

Figure 7.32. A close-up view of the occupation of quantum states in the region near the occupied quantum states with the maximum energy of E_F. A filled circle represents an occupied quantum state, and an empty circle represents an empty quantum state. As the temperature increases, electrons in quantum states within a range $\approx \pm k_B T$ of E_F can change states. The exclusion principle prevents electrons in states with energy much more than $\approx k_B T$ below the maximum energy from accepting energy. This is because there are no vacant states for these electrons to move into.

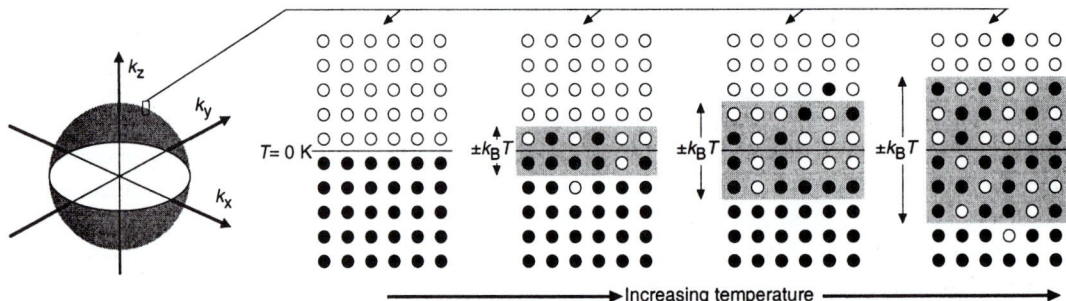

Although we do not know the precisely the *number of electrons* in Equation 7.64, we can say that it should be:

- related to the number of available quantum states with energies in a small range close to E_F. This is directly proportional to the density of quantum states at the Fermi energy $g_m(E_F)$ (Equation 6.70). The subscript 'm' indicates that the density of states is evaluated for a volume equal to the molar volume.
- proportional to $k_B T$. As shown in Figure 7.32, electrons occupying quantum states within a range $\approx k_B T$ are able to accept thermal energy.

We can thus write Equation 7.64 as:

$$U = U_o + \left[g_m(E_F) \times k_B T\right] \times \tfrac{3}{2} k_B T \quad \text{mol}^{-1} \quad (7.65)$$

where the factor $\left[g_m(E_F) \times k_B T\right]$ is the number of quantum states (in one mole of substance) in a range $k_B T$ around the Fermi energy. Hence the molar heat capacity is given by:

$$C_V^{el} = \frac{dU}{dT}$$

$$= \frac{d}{dT}\left(U_o + \left[g_m(E_F) \times k_B T\right] \times \tfrac{3}{2} k_B T\right) \quad (7.66)$$

$$= \underbrace{\left[3g_m(E_F) \times k_B^2\right]}_{\gamma} T$$

This is generally written as:

$$C_V^{el} = \gamma T \quad (7.67)$$

where γ is the *coefficient of electronic heat capacity*:

$$\gamma = 3g_m(E_F) k_B^2 \quad \text{mol}^{-1} \quad (7.68)$$

The rough theory outlined above predicts the electronic heat capacity of a metal is much less than would be expected of a classical gas, and is proportional to absolute temperature. We can test this theory by looking at the heat capacity of metals at low temperatures. When $T \ll \Theta_D$, the heat capacity due to phonons is much smaller than at room temperature, and we can more easily observe the electronic contribution to the heat capacity.

214

Example 7.14

At 300 K, what is the expected value of the electronic contribution to the molar heat capacity of copper?

We can estimate the electronic contribution to C by using Equation 7.67 and substituting for $g(E_F)$ from Equation 6.70:

$$g(E) = \frac{V\sqrt{2m^3 E}}{\pi^2 \hbar^3}$$

Equation 6.77 expresses the density of quantum states around energy E in a volume V of metal. We need first to substitute V for the molar volume V_m. Using the density data for copper (Table 7.2) (molar mass 63.55×10^{-3} kg) we find $V_m = 63.55 \times 10^{-3}/8933 = 7.11 \times 10^{-6}$ m^3. In Equation 6.76 we worked out that (according the theory of a free-electron gas) the Fermi energy in copper is 1.13×10^{-18} J (7.0 eV). Substituting these values into the $g(E_F)$ yields:

$$g(E_F) = \frac{7.11 \times 10^{-6}\sqrt{2 \times (9.1 \times 10^{-31})^3 \times 1.13 \times 10^{-18}}}{\pi^2 (1.054 \times 10^{-34})^3}$$

$$= \frac{7.11 \times 10^{-6}\sqrt{1.703 \times 10^{-108}}}{11.56 \times 10^{-102}}$$

$$= 8.026 \times 10^{41} \quad \text{states J}^{-1} \text{ mol}^{-1}$$

which predicts an electronic heat capacity of:

$$C_V^{el} = \frac{\pi^2 k_B^2 g(E_F) T}{3}$$

$$= \frac{\pi^2}{3}(1.38 \times 10^{-23})^2 \times 8.026 \times 10^{41} \times 300$$

$$= 0.151 \quad \text{J K}^{-1} \text{ mol}^{-1}$$

This is to be compared with the contribution due to the lattice of around 25 J K^{-1} mol^{-1}. In other words, the electronic contribution to the heat capacity is only around 0.6% of the total heat capacity.

We note that γ varies from one metal to another and depends on the number of (mainly occupied) quantum states just below the Fermi energy and the number of (mainly empty) quantum states just above the Fermi energy. Thus, determination of the quantity γ by heat capacity measurements tells us how many quantum states there are with energies close to the Fermi energy. This quantity is just the density of electronic quantum states evaluated at the Fermi energy, i.e. $g_m(E_F)$. A more detailed theory of the heat capacity of metals predicts that γ is given by:

$$\gamma = \frac{\pi^2}{3} g_m(E_F) k_B^2 \quad \text{mol}^{-1} \qquad (7.69)$$

which differs from Equation 7.68 by just a few per cent.

Low-temperature heat capacity

Measurements of the heat capacity of materials at low temperatures provide a way of testing both the Debye theory of the heat capacity of solids and the theory of metallic heat capacity. In a metal at high temperatures the electronic heat capacity is much smaller than the lattice heat capacity, which makes it difficult to identify experimentally the small electronic component on top of the large lattice heat capacity. At low temperatures, i.e. less than about a tenth of the Debye temperature, the lattice term is much smaller, and we have clear predictions for the behaviour of both lattice and electronic terms.

At $T \ll \Theta_D$ we expect from Equation 7.64 that the lattice heat capacity $C^L = \alpha T^3$ and at all temperatures we expect that the electronic heat capacity $C^{el} = \gamma T$. Thus, we predict the total heat capacity to be given by:

$$\begin{aligned} C_{total} &= C^{el} + C^L \\ &= \gamma T + \alpha T^3 \end{aligned} \qquad (7.70)$$

We can see clearly whether or not this is valid if we plot some data in the following form C_{total}/T versus T^2. If the data conform to Equation 7.70 than they will form a straight line with slope α and intercept γ:

$$\frac{C_{total}}{T} = \gamma + \alpha T^2. \qquad (7.71)$$

The fact that Figure 7.33 shows straight-line behaviour indicates that the heat capacity of copper does indeed conform to the theoretical expectation that $C_{total} = \gamma T + \alpha T^3$.

7.6.4 Summary

We began our investigation of the heat capacity of solids by first noting the remarkable fact that the heat capacity of nearly all the elements is close to

Figure 7.33 My own measurements of the low-temperature heat capacity of copper plotted as C/T versus T^2. Since the graph has T *squared* as its x-axis, the data shown correspond to the temperatures between 2 K and 10 K. Note that as predicted by Equation 7.71, the data conform to a straight line. From the slope of the line, α and hence the Debye temperature can be found, and from the intercept we may determine γ and hence $g(E_F)$.

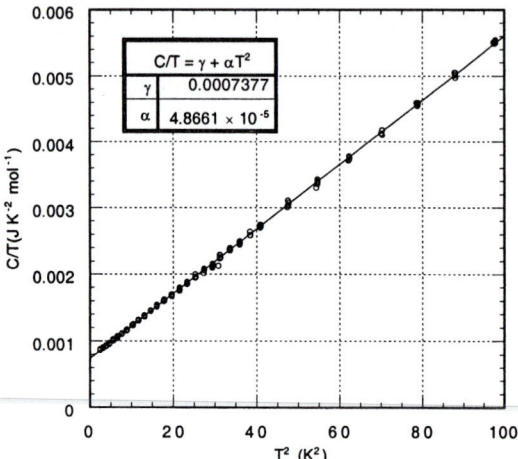

25 J K^{-1} mol^{-1}. We came to understand that this is due to the equal distribution of energy among the six degrees of freedom of the atoms vibrating in the lattice.

We then noted that the heat capacity of all substances falls as the temperature approaches absolute zero. We understood this as being due to the restriction of some of the vibrational degrees of freedom of the atoms. The relatively simple Einstein model allowed us to understand the general form of the temperature dependence. However, in order to understand the details of the low-temperature behaviour, we needed to develop Debye model, and the concept of the phonon.

Finally, we considered 'the dog which did not bark': the apparent absence of a contribution to C_P of the 'free electron' gas we had hypothesised to exist within metals. We understood this as being due to the fermion nature of the electrons. The exclusion principle restricted their ability to accept thermal energy, except for a few electrons occupying quantum states close to the Fermi energy.

7.7 Electrical properties

7.7.1 Introduction

There is a sense in which *every* property of a solid can be considered an electrical property. This is because the particles that make up solids are fundamentally electrical in nature. However, in this section we use the term *electrical property* to refer to the response of solids to externally applied electric fields.

Conductors and insulators

When *any substance* is subject to an applied electric field E, a current of electronic charge flows through the substance. The magnitude of the resultant current density, j, is characterised by the *electrical resistivity* ρ or the electrical conductivity σ of the substance. The two measures are the inverse of each other, $\rho = 1/\sigma$, and so for most purposes there is no advantage to using one measure or the other. The electrical resistivity and conductivity are defined by:

$$j = \sigma E \qquad (7.72a)$$

and

$$E = \rho j \qquad (7.72b)$$

If the current density is measured in amperes per square metre ($A\,m^{-2}$) and the electric field in volts per metre ($V\,m^{-1}$) then the units of σ are $\Omega^{-1}\,m^{-1}$ or $S\,m^{-1}$. The SI symbol S stands for *seimens* not to be confused with 's' for second. The units of resistivity are ohm metres ($\Omega\,m$). For a sample of cross-sectional area A and length L, the resistivity is related to the *electrical resistance R* by:

$$\rho = \frac{RA}{L} \quad \Omega\,m \qquad (7.73)$$

The electrical conductivity and resistivity of the elements is listed in Table 7.13 and plotted as a function of atomic number in Figure 7.33. Looking at Table 7.13, the data appear to vary almost randomly. However, in Figure 7.33 we can see that the resistivities of the elements fall into two rather distinct categories:

- Most elements are metals and have resistivities in the range $10^{-6}\,\Omega\,m$ to $10^{-8}\,\Omega\,m$

Example 7.15

A piece of platinum wire is 1 m long and 1 mm in diameter. What is its electrical resistance at round room temperature?

We rearrange Equation 7.73: $R = \dfrac{\rho L}{A}$ where ρ is resistivity, L is the length of the wire, and A is the cross-sectional area. We use the following values:

$$\rho = 1.06 \times 10^{-7} \ \Omega\,m$$
$$L = 1 \ m$$

$$A = \pi\left[\frac{d}{2}\right]^2 = 3.142\left[\frac{0.5 \times 10^{-3}}{2}\right]^2 = 7.854 \times 10^{-7} \ m^2$$

to work out that:

$$R = \frac{1.06 \times 10^{-7} \times 1}{7.855 \times 10^{-7}} = 0.135 \ \Omega$$

- The rest of the elements are much poorer electrical conductors. Note again the logarithmic scale of Figure 7.33.

A few elements have resistivities much greater than $1\,\Omega\,m$ ($\log R = 0$ on Figure 7.34) and are effectively *electrical insulators*. The elements silicon (Si), (Ge), (Se) and (Te) have resistivities intermediate between metals and insulators and are known as *semiconductors*. There are two interesting points to note. First, the conductivities of the solid elements span 23 orders of magnitude at room temperature. On cooling to temperatures close to absolute zero, some substances become superconducting, at which point the range of conductivities spans at least 40 orders of magnitude. This is easily the greatest range exhibited by *any* physical property of solids. Second, the term *electrical insulator* can be misleading. It can imply that no current flows in response to an applied electric field. In fact, a current *always* flows in response to an applied electric field. In substances called electric insulators this current is generally extremely small, but is definitely not zero. This point is discussed further in §7.7.6.

Table 7.13 The electrical resistivity of the elements which are solid at around room temperature. Take care with the exponents of values in this table which vary from entry to entry and column to column by 46 orders of magnitude.

Z	Element	$\rho(\Omega\,m)$	$\sigma(S\,m^{-1})$	Z	Element	$\rho(\Omega\,m)$	$\sigma(S\,m^{-1})$
1	Hydrogen, H	—	—	49	Indium, In	8.37×10^{-8}	1.19×10^{7}
2	Helium, He	—	—	50	Tin, Sn	1.1×10^{-7}	9.1×10^{6}
3	Lithium , Li	8.55×10^{-8}	1.17×10^{7}	51	Antimony, Sb	3.9×10^{-7}	2.56×10^{6}
4	Beryllium, Be	4×10^{-8}	2.5×10^{7}	52	Tellurium, Te	0.00436	229
5	Boron, B	18000	5.56×10^{5}	53	Iodine, I	1.37×10^{-7}	7.30×10^{8}
6	Carbon (diamond), C	10^{11}	10^{-11}	54	Xenon, Xe	—	—
7	Nitrogen, N	—	—	55	Caesium, Cs	2×10^{-7}	5×10^{6}
8	Oxygen, O	—	—	56	Barium, Ba	5×10^{-7}	2×10^{6}
9	Fluorine, F	—	—	57	Lanthanum, La	5.7×10^{-7}	1.75×10^{6}
10	Neon, Ne	—	—	58	Cerium, Ce	7.3×10^{-7}	1.37×10^{6}
11	Sodium, Na	4.2×10^{-8}	2.38×10^{7}	59	Praseodymium, Pr	6.8×10^{-7}	1.47×10^{6}
12	Magnesium, Mg	4.38×10^{-8}	2.28×10^{7}	60	Neodymium, Ne	6.4×10^{-7}	1.56×10^{6}
13	Aluminium, Al	2.66×10^{-8}	3.77×10^{7}	61	Promethium, Pm	5×10^{-7}	2×10^{6}
14	Silicon, Si	0.001	1000	62	Samarium, Sm	9.4×10^{-7}	1.06×10^{6}
15	Phosphorus, P	1×10^{-9}	1×10^{9}	63	Europium, Eu	9×10^{-7}	1.11×10^{6}
16	Sulphur, S	2×10^{15}	5×10^{-16}	64	Gadolinium, Gd	1.34×10^{-6}	7.46×10^{5}
17	Chlorine, Cl	—	—	65	Terbium, Tb	1.14×10^{-6}	8.77×10^{5}
18	Argon, Ar	—	—	66	Dysprosium, Dy	5.7×10^{-7}	1.75×10^{6}
19	Potassium, K	6.15×10^{-8}	1.63×10^{7}	67	Holmium, Ho	8.7×10^{-7}	1.15×10^{6}
20	Calcium, Ca	3.43×10^{-8}	2.92×10^{7}	68	Erbium, Er	8.7×10^{-7}	1.15×10^{6}
21	Scandium, Sc	6.1×10^{-7}	1.64×10^{6}	69	Thulium, Th	7.9×10^{-7}	1.27×10^{6}
22	Titanium, Ti	4.2×10^{-7}	2.38×10^{6}	70	Ytterbium, Yb	2.9×10^{-7}	3.45×10^{6}
23	Vanadium, V	2.48×10^{-7}	4.03×10^{6}	71	Lutetium, Lu	7.9×10^{-7}	1.27×10^{6}
24	Chromium, Cr	1.27×10^{-7}	7.87×10^{6}	72	Hafnium, Hf	3.51×10^{-7}	2.85×10^{6}
25	Manganese, Mn	1.85×10^{-6}	5.41×10^{5}	73	Tantalum, Ta	1.25×10^{-7}	8.03×10^{6}
26	Iron, Fe	9.71×10^{-8}	1.03×10^{7}	74	Tungsten, W	5.65×10^{-8}	1.77×10^{7}
27	Cobalt, Co	6.24×10^{-8}	1.60×10^{7}	75	Rhenium, Re	1.93×10^{-7}	5.18×10^{6}
28	Nickel, Ni	6.84×10^{-8}	1.46×10^{7}	76	Osmium, Os	8.12×10^{-8}	1.23×10^{7}
29	Copper, Cu	1.67×10^{-8}	5.98×10^{7}	77	Iridium, Ir	5.3×10^{-8}	1.89×10^{7}
30	Zinc, Zn	5.92×10^{-8}	1.69×10^{7}	78	Platinum, Pt	1.06×10^{-7}	9.43×10^{6}
31	Gallium, Ga	2.7×10^{-7}	3.70×10^{6}	79	Gold, Au	2.35×10^{-8}	4.26×10^{7}
32	Germanium, Ge	0.46	2.1739	80	Mercury, Hg	9.41×10^{-7}	1.06×10^{6}
33	Arsenic, As	2.6×10^{-7}	3.85×10^{6}	81	Thallium, Th	1.8×10^{-7}	5.56×10^{6}
34	Selenium, Se	0.01	100	82	Lead, Pb	2.07×10^{-7}	4.84×10^{6}
35	Bromine, Br	—	—	83	Bismuth, Bi	1.068×10^{-6}	9.36×10^{5}
36	Krypton, Kr	—	—	84	Polonium, Po	1.4×10^{-6}	7.14×10^{5}
37	Rubidium, Rb	1.25×10^{-7}	8×10^{6}	85	Astatine, At	—	—
38	Strontium, Sr	2.3×10^{-7}	4.35×10^{6}	86	Radon, Rn	—	—
39	Yttrium, Y	5.7×10^{-7}	1.75×10^{6}	87	Francium, Fr	—	—
40	Zirconium, Zr	4.21×10^{-7}	2.37×10^{6}	88	Radium, Ra	1×10^{-6}	1×10^{6}
41	Niobium, Nb	1.25×10^{-7}	8×10^{6}	89	Actinium, Ac	—	—
42	Molybdenum, Mo	5.2×10^{-8}	1.92×10^{7}	90	Thorium, Th	1.3×10^{-7}	7.69×10^{6}
43	Technetium, Tc	2.26×10^{-7}	4.42×10^{6}	91	Protractinium, Pa	1.77×10^{-7}	5.65×10^{6}
44	Ruthenium, Ru	7.6×10^{-8}	1.32×10^{7}	92	Uranium, U	3.08×10^{-7}	3.25×10^{6}
45	Rhodium, Rh	4.51×10^{-8}	2.22×10^{7}	93	Neptunium, Np	1.22×10^{-6}	8.20×10^{5}
46	Palladium, Pd	1.08×10^{-7}	9.26×10^{6}	94	Plutonium, Pu	1.46×10^{-6}	6.85×10^{5}
47	Silver, Ag	1.59×10^{-8}	6.29×10^{7}	95	Americium, Am	6.8×10^{-7}	1.4706×10^{6}
48	Cadmium, Cd	6.83×10^{-8}	1.46×10^{7}				

In the following sections we will examine in turn the electrical behaviour of metals and insulators, and then briefly discuss the properties of semiconductors.

7.7.2 Data on the electrical properties of metals

The most striking property of metallic conductors is their ability to conduct electricity in an arbitrarily small electric field. In other words there is no equivalent of the 'breakdown' effect observed in electrical insulators (§7.7.6).

Data on the resistivity of the elements

From Table 7.13, it is clear that most elements are metals, with resistivity at around room temperature between $10^{-6}\,\Omega$ m to $10^{-8}\,\Omega$ m. Figure 7.35 shows detail from the lower part of Figure 7.34 on a linear scale. The data show significant non-random variations, but there are too many details to attempt a direct explanation of the conductivity of each element. The structure in the data is reminiscent of the density data for the elements shown in Figure 7.1, but the peaks and troughs in the data are not so regular.

If we take the best conductors from Table 7.13, we find that they are silver, copper and gold (the noble metals), closely followed by aluminium. These four elements are marked on Figure 7.35, and the temperature dependence of their resistivity is shown in Figure 7.36 along with that of platinum. The variation is broadly linear with the resistivity tending towards small values at low temperatures.

Data on the resistivity of alloys

Alloys are mixtures of elemental metals, but as illustrated in Figure 7.37, the mixtures are at the atomic level.

Alloys are usually made by melting metallic elements together and mixing them while they are molten. The electrical resistivity of three alloys is compared with the electrical resistivity of their constituent elements in Table 7.13. There is one surprising feature of this table. In all cases the resistivity of the alloy is considerably greater than the resistivity of either component element. This is particularly striking for the Pt(10% Ir) and

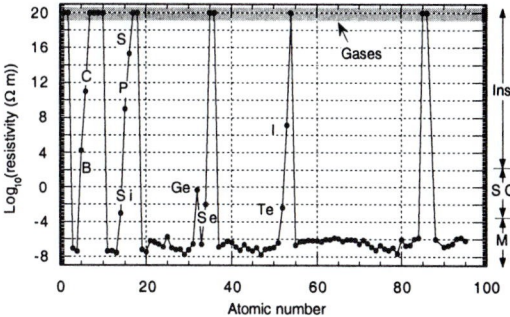

Figure 7.34 The logarithm of the resistivity of the elemental metals (M), semiconductors (SC) and insulators (Ins) plotted as a function of atomic number. The elemental gases are plotted as having a resistivity of $10^{20}\,\Omega$m to show how they fit the pattern of conducting and insulating behaviour.

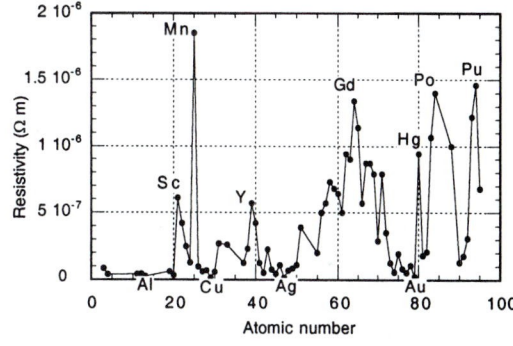

Figure 7.35 The resistivities of the metallic elements plotted on a linear scale as a function of atomic number. Elements with date off the graph have not been plotted.

Figure 7.36 The resistivities of five metallic elements plotted on a linear scale as a function of temperature. The data for platinum is the result of many closely-spaced measurements and is plotted as a continuous curve. The data for Al, Cu, Ag and Au consists of just a few points with lines drawn to connect the data points.

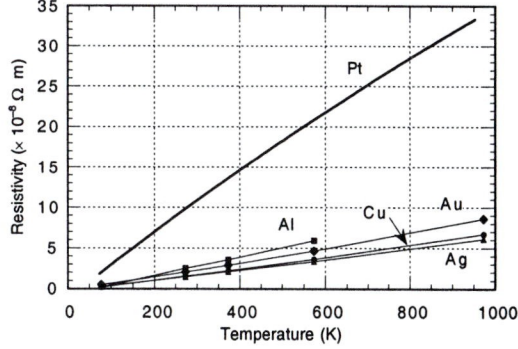

Pt(10% Rh) alloys. For example, replacing 1 in 10 platinum atoms with an iridium atom causes the resistivity to more than double. This is despite the fact that iridium has a lower resistivity than platinum!

Superconductivity

Many metals and alloys when cooled to temperatures within a few degrees of absolute zero display an extraordinary set of properties, including the ability to conduct electricity with no detectable resistivity. This phenomenon is known as *superconductivity* and occurs only below a certain critical temperature T_C. The critical temperatures of a variety of elemental superconductors and alloys are shown in Table 7.15.

Interestingly, the three elements that are the best conductors at room temperature (copper, silver and gold) do not become superconductors. (Or if they do their transition temperatures are below a few microkelvin). Further, it is interesting to note that the conductivity of a substance in the superconducting state, while not known to be strictly infinite is better than that of pure copper at 4K by

Figure 7.37 illustration of the difference between (a) a random binary alloy, and (b) a mixture of two elements.

(a)   **(b)**

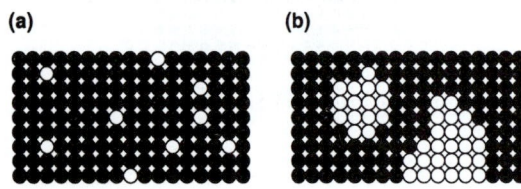

Table 7.14 The resistivities (Ω m) of three alloys at around room temperature is shown in centre of the three tables below. On either side of the data for the alloy, are the resistivities of the component elements.

Component 1	Alloy	Component 2
Cu	Cu(Zn)	Zn
1.55×10^{-8}	6.3×10^{-8}	5.5×10^{-8}
Pt	Pt(10% Ir)	Ir
9.81×10^{-8}	24.8×10^{-8}	4.7×10^{-8}
Pt	Pt(10% Rh)	Rh
9.81×10^{-8}	18.7×10^{-8}	4.3×10^{-8}

Example 7.16

Consider two wires of equal length and circular cross-section, one made from aluminium and one from copper. What will be the ratio of diameters of the wires if the resistance of the wires is equal?

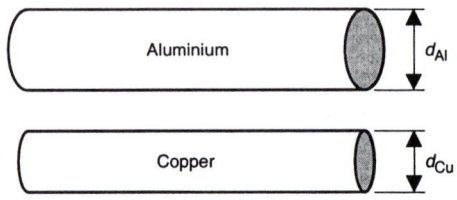

For a wire of length L and cross-sectional area $A = \pi d^2/4$ the electrical resistance is given by:

$$R = \frac{\rho L}{\pi d^2 / 4}$$

If the two wires have equal resistance ($R_{Cu} = R_{Al}$) and equal length then:

$$\frac{4\rho_{Cu}L}{\pi d_{Cu}^2} = \frac{4\rho_{Al}L}{\pi d_{Al}^2}$$

which simplifies to:

$$\left[\frac{d_{Al}}{d_{Cu}}\right]^2 = \frac{\rho_{Al}}{\rho_{Cu}} \quad \Rightarrow \quad \frac{d_{Al}}{d_{Cu}} = \sqrt{\frac{\rho_{Al}}{\rho_{Cu}}}$$

Substituting from Table 7.13:

$$\rho_{Al} = 2.655 \times 10^{-8} \ \Omega \, m \qquad \rho_{Cu} = 1.673 \times 10^{-8} \ \Omega \, m$$

we find:

$$\frac{d_{Al}}{d_{Cu}} = \sqrt{\frac{2.655 \times 10^{-8}}{1.673 \times 10^{-8}}} = 1.26$$

and so the diameter of aluminium wire would have to be about 26% greater than the copper wire.

The volume of aluminium used would thus be greater in the ratio of the square of the diameters (1.59). Interestingly, the densities of the aluminium (2698 kg m^{-3}) and copper (8933 kg m^{-3}) are such that the aluminium cable would be lighter in the ratio:

$$\frac{\text{density of aluminium}}{\text{density of copper}} \times \left[\frac{d_{Al}}{d_{Cu}}\right]^2 = \frac{2698}{8933} \times 1.59 = 0.49$$

In other words, an aluminium cable of similar electrical resistance to a copper cable would be slightly larger, but would weigh only around half as much. In some circumstances, this proves to be an important engineering advantage.

Table 7.15 Examples of substances which display superconducting behaviour below the temperature shown.

Substance	Alloy
Low-temperature superconductors: elements	
Aluminium	1.75
Lead	7.2
Niobium	9.25
Tin	3.72
Vanadium	5.4
Low-temperature superconductors: alloys	
V_3Si	17.1
Nb_3Sn	18.3
MgB_2	39
High-temperature superconductors	
$YBa_2Cu_3O_{7-\delta}$	93
$Hg_1Ba_2Ca_2Cu_3O_{10}$	133

a factor in excess of 10^{15}. In other words, the conductivity in the superconducting state is better than the conductivity in the metallic state by a factor similar to that by which the conductivity in the metallic state is better than the conductivity of some insulators (Table 7.17 below).

Summary

The main questions raised by our preliminary examination of the experimental data on the electrical resistivities of metals are:

- Why is there no 'breakdown field' for metals?
- Why are most elements metals?
- Why do the resistivities of metals vary roughly linearly with temperature?
- Why are the resistivities of alloys larger than the resistivities of their component metals?
- Why do some metals become superconducting at low temperatures?

7.7.3 Understanding the electrical properties of metals

To answer these questions we need to develop further the quantum mechanical description of an electron gas that we began in §6.5.

Quantum theory of conduction in metals

The basis of the quantum mechanical approach to the problem is illustrated in Figure 7.38. This approach strictly applies only at $T = 0$ K. However, the exclusion principle strongly restricts the ability

Figure 7.38 Illustration of the effect of an electric field on the occupation of quantum states in a simple model of a metal. First, (a) shows the case when no electric field is applied, then (b) shows the case when an electric field is applied in the negative-x direction. Notice that in (b) the distribution is not symmetric but is shifted by an amount Δk and so has a net excess of electrons with positive k-vectors. In the figures each small circle represents an allowed travelling wave solution to the Schrödinger equation. The shaded circle represents the Fermi sphere of occupied states which is shifted by Δk as discussed in the text.

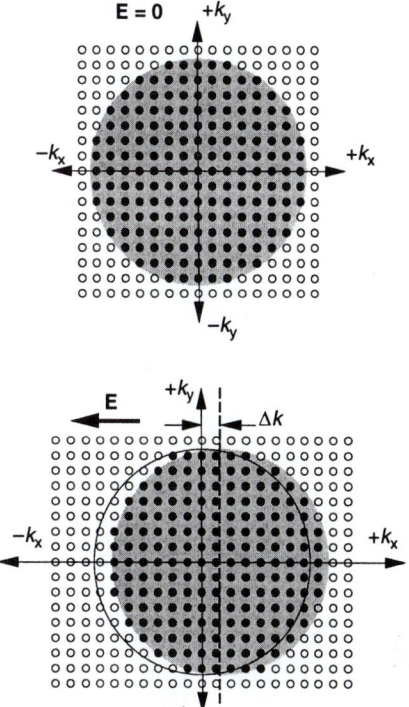

of electrons to change quantum states, and we will find that the theory is actually applicable at finite temperatures.

When no electric field is applied, electrons occupy travelling-wave quantum states inside the *Fermi sphere* on a k-space graph. The travelling-wave states outside the sphere are unoccupied. Notice that because of the symmetry of the situation in which electrons find themselves, *on average* as many electrons will be travelling in one direction as in opposite direction. So the *average* electron velocity must be zero.

When an electric field is applied, electrons occupying quantum states with energies near the Fermi energy are able to make transitions into unoccupied quantum states just above the Fermi energy. The net effect of this is to change the balance of occupied and unoccupied states as shown in Figure 7.38 (b).

In the theory we will develop below, we will suppose that the primary effect of the electric field is to alter the balance of occupancy between travelling wave states with velocities parallel to the applied electric field E, and those with velocities anti-parallel, to the applied electric field E.

Scattering

Inside a metal, electrons undergo several processes that are grouped together under the term *scattering*. Scattering in this context is a process whereby an electron in one quantum state (with, say, wave vector k_1) makes a transition to a second quantum state (with, say, wave vector k_2). For electrons in metals, the factors which determine the relationship between k_1 and k_2 have a large random element. In other words, knowing which quantum state an electron is in does not tell you much about which quantum state it is going to be scattered into. Scattering occurs when the quantum state occupied by an electron is no longer the 'appropriate' quantum state to occupy. Consider the following examples.

Electron–phonon scattering

Suppose an electron is in a quantum state k_1 appropriate to a region of the crystal with electron density n. In a nearby region of the crystal, a lattice distortion (a phonon) may have temporarily increased (or decreased) the lattice spacing. This region would therefore also have an increased (or decreased) equilibrium number density of electrons. Such a situation might enhance the probability for an electron to make a transition from k_1 and k_2 where k_2 would be a state 'more appropriate' to the new situation. However, since the lattice vibrations are highly random, the new quantum state will in general be only distantly related to k_1. This process is described as *electron-phonon scattering*.

Electron–impurity scattering

Suppose an electron is in a quantum state k_1 appropriate to a region of the crystal with electron density n. Now suppose that it encounters a region of the crystal with an impurity. In general the impurity will have a complicated distribution of electric charge around it which may cause an electron to make a transition from k_1 to another quantum state k_2 which is 'more appropriate' to the new situation. This process is described as *electron–impurity scattering*.

It is important to note that in the absence of scattering processes such as those described above, electrons would stay in their quantum state indefinitely. Thus in a perfect crystal, with no phonons (i.e. at $T = 0$ K), and no impurities (and no surfaces!: in this context surfaces count as an electron scatterer), the conductivity would be infinite.

Working out the conductivity

According to the de Broglie hypothesis, an electron in a travelling-wave quantum state with wave vector k has momentum:

$$\begin{aligned} |\mathbf{p}| &= \hbar k \\ &= \frac{h}{2\pi} \times \frac{2\pi}{\lambda} \\ &= \frac{h}{\lambda} \end{aligned} \qquad (7.74)$$

The effect of the applied electric field is to change this momentum in accord with Newton's second law:

$$\begin{aligned} \mathbf{F} &= \frac{d\mathbf{p}}{dt} \\ &\approx \frac{\Delta \mathbf{p}}{\Delta t} \end{aligned} \qquad (7.75)$$

We consider that each electron can be accelerated under the action of the applied electric field for some time Δt, after which it is 'scattered'. We consider that each scattering event completely destroys the momentum that the electron gained in the time Δt. (Aside: This assumption is in fact not quite correct. Often the electron is scattered only through a small angle, and much of its momentum is preserved. However, any other assumption

leads to theory that is considerably more complex. We note therefore that the value of Δt that we deduce from our theory may be longer than the actual time between scattering events. This is because for some scattering processes, the 'before' and 'after' wave vectors k_1 and k_2 may in fact be weakly related. Thus, it may take several actual scattering events to completely destroy the momentum acquired by an electron). In between the scattering events, the electron changes its momentum by:

$$\Delta \mathbf{p} = \mathbf{F}\Delta t \qquad (7.76)$$

and since the force on each electron is $\mathbf{F} = q\mathbf{E}$, where q is the charge on the electron, we have:

$$\Delta \mathbf{p} = q\mathbf{E}\Delta t \qquad (7.77)$$

Now a change in momentum $\Delta \mathbf{p}$ corresponds to a change in wave vector $\Delta \mathbf{p} = \hbar \Delta \mathbf{k}$, so every electron in the metal will on average shift its wave vector by an amount $\Delta \mathbf{k}$ (Figure 7.38) given by:

$$\Delta \mathbf{k} = \frac{q\mathbf{E}\Delta t}{\hbar} \qquad (7.78)$$

Notice that $\Delta \mathbf{k}$ is in the opposite direction to $\mathbf{E}$ because the electron charge, q, is negative. The momentum shift $\Delta \mathbf{p}$ corresponds to a velocity shift $\Delta \mathbf{v}$ given by $\Delta \mathbf{v} = \Delta \mathbf{p}/m$, i.e.

$$\Delta \mathbf{v} = \frac{q\mathbf{E}\Delta t}{m} \qquad (7.79)$$

Notice that $\Delta \mathbf{v}$ is *on average* the same for every electron and is known as the *drift velocity*.

The drift velocity

In the absence of an applied electric field, we expect that the average velocity of electrons is zero, i.e.

$$(\mathbf{E} = 0)$$

$$\bar{\mathbf{v}} = \frac{\sum\limits_{i=1}^{N} \mathbf{v}_i}{N} = 0 \qquad (7.80)$$

because in the absence of an applied electric field on average as many electrons are travelling in one direction as another. Now when an electric field

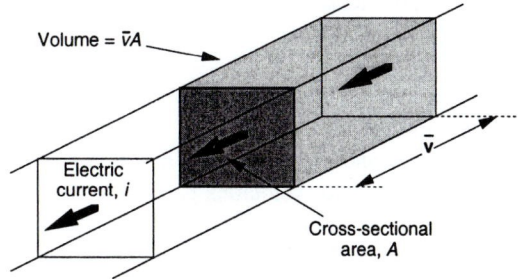

Figure 7.39 Electrons flowing through a piece of metal. In one second all the charge within a distance $\bar{v}$ 'upstream' of a cross-section perpendicular to the current flow will pass the cross-section. In this case the volume of charge that will flow past the cross sectional area is $\bar{v} A$. The amount of charge in this volume is $qnA\bar{v}$

has been applied the average velocity is no longer zero, but just $\Delta \mathbf{v}$ given by Equation 7.79, i.e.

$$(\mathbf{E} \neq 0)$$

$$\bar{\mathbf{v}} = \frac{\sum\limits_{i=1}^{N} (\mathbf{v}_i + \Delta \mathbf{v})}{N}$$

$$= \frac{\sum\limits_{i=1}^{N} (\mathbf{v}_i)}{N} + \frac{\sum\limits_{i=1}^{N} (\Delta \mathbf{v})}{N} \qquad (7.81)$$

$$= 0 + \frac{\sum\limits_{i=1}^{N} (\Delta \mathbf{v})}{N} = \frac{N\Delta \mathbf{v}}{N}$$

$$= \Delta \mathbf{v}$$

Current flow

Consider a metal sample through which a current i is flowing. Let us calculate the relationship between the current density and the average speed of the charged particles carrying the current. If we consider a particular cross-section of area A then the total current which flows past the cross-section per second is, by the definition of current, just i coulombs. However, we can also see that *on average*, all the charge within a volume $A\bar{v}$ will flow past the cross-section per second. If the number density of current carriers is n and each carrier has charge q, then the total charge in volume $A\bar{v}$ is just $nqA\bar{v}$.

We thus find $\mathbf{i} = nqA\bar{\mathbf{v}}$, and after substituting for

222

$\bar{\mathbf{v}} = \Delta\mathbf{v}$ from 7.79 we have:

$$i = nqA \times \frac{qE\Delta t}{m} \qquad (7.82)$$

Rearranging this to give an expression for the current density $\mathbf{j}$ we find:

$$j = \frac{i}{A} = nq \times \frac{qE\Delta t}{m}$$

$$j = \underbrace{\left[\frac{nq^2\Delta t}{m}\right]}_{\sigma}E \qquad (7.83)$$

Comparing this with Equation 7.72(a) we see that the quantity in brackets is the conductivity σ shown in Table 7.13. Hence:

$$\sigma = \frac{nq^2\Delta t}{m} \qquad (7.84)$$

The scattering time Δt

Let us now compare the expression 7.84 for σ with experiment. The quantities n, q and m are either well-known or can be fairly easily estimated. However the quantity Δt, the average time to 'scatter', is not easy to estimate. What we can do is to use measured values of conductivity to predict values for Δt and then see whether we can understand the predicted values.

According to this theory, at around room temperature electrons remain in their travelling wave quantum states for approximately 10^{-14} s to 10^{-13} s

---

Example 7.17

Estimate the scattering time Δt for mobile electrons in copper at room temperature.

From Table 7.2 we estimate a number density of electrons of $n = 8.417 \times 10^{28}$ m^{-3}. Using Equation 7.84 we estimate Δt according to:

$$\Delta t = \frac{m\sigma}{nq^2} = \frac{9.1\times10^{-31}\times5.98\times10^7}{8.417\times10^{28}\times\left(1.60\times10^{-19}\right)^2}$$

$$\approx 2.5\times10^{-14} \text{ s}$$

In this calculation we have taken the value $\sigma = 5.98 \times 10^7$ seimens for copper at 20 °C from Table 7.13.

---

seconds before being scattered. This might seem like a very short time, but in fact is quite reasonable if we consider how we expect the electron to be scattered. In §7.6.3 we saw that the naturally occurring displacement waves in a lattice had frequencies of the order 10^{13} Hz. Thus 10^{-13} seconds is a typical time over which a region of a solid may first be compressed and then dilate. If it is indeed these atomic vibrations that scatter electrons then we would expect scattering to take place after the positions of the atoms have changed substantially, i.e. after some fraction of an oscillation time.

The questions raised by the data

Absence of a 'breakdown field' for metals

Within this model we can understand the first question raised by the data: why there is no 'breakdown field' for metals. This arises from the extreme closeness in energy of the quantum states in Figure 7.38. No matter in what direction an electric field is applied, electrons in occupied states are easily able to access vacant states and so change their momentum.

In an insulator, things are rather different. The quantum states with energy closest to the Fermi energy are at the top of a so-called *band* of electronic states. If an electron is to move through the crystal, it must find an unoccupied quantum state into which it can move. In general, this requires quite a lot of energy, of the order of an electron volt or more. Since the available thermal energy $(\approx k_B T)$ is of the order $\frac{1}{40}$ electron volt, this kind of process is very rare. The conduction process in insulators is discussed further in §7.7.7, and the distinction between insulators and metals is discussed again in the context of band theory in Web Chapter W1.

The temperature-dependence of the resistivity

When an electron scatters from a lattice distortion as described above, the lattice gives up momentum $\Delta\mathbf{p}$ and energy ΔE to the electron. However as we saw in §7.6.3, the lattice can lose energy only in quantised amounts. In order to scatter an electron,

the amplitude of vibration of a displacement wave with frequency f must be reduced such that the energy tied up in the wave falls from $(n_{ph} + \frac{1}{2})hf$ to $(n_{ph} + \frac{1}{2} - 1)hf$. Here n_{ph} refers to the number of *phonons* in the vibrational mode with frequency f. Clearly this process cannot take place if $n_{ph} < 1$. Further it seems plausible that the process becomes more likely as the number of phonons associated with that mode of vibration increases. Thus at high temperatures, where there are many phonons associated with each mode of vibration of the lattice, electrons are more likely to be scattered, and the 'scattering time' Δt in Equation 7.84 is reduced.

The average number of phonons associated with a displacement wave of frequency f is given by the Bose–Einstein occupation factor (Equation 7.58) as:

$$n_{ph} = \frac{1}{\exp(hf / k_B T) - 1} \quad (7.85)$$

If the temperature is high enough that $k_B T >> hf$ then we may expand the denominator of Equation 7.85 to yield:

$$n_{ph} = \frac{1}{\left[1 + (hf / k_B T) + \ldots\right] - 1} \approx \frac{k_B T}{hf} \quad (7.86)$$

This indicates that at high temperatures, the number of phonons in any particular mode of vibration is proportional to absolute temperature. Following on from this argument, we would therefore expect the 'scattering time' Δt to be proportional to $1/T$ and hence the resistivity to be proportional T. This is indeed broadly what happens (Figure 7.36).

The argument above is certainly correct at temperatures such that $k_B T$ is greater than the maximum phonon energy, i.e. when $T > \Theta_D$. However, Figure 7.36 indicates that the linear behaviour actually continues well below Θ_D. This indicates that the approximation in Equation 7.56 remains valid even below Θ_D. At first this might not seem possible, but in fact we can understand it by appreciating that the phonons which are actually giving rise to most of the resistivity in metals have frequencies well below the maximum possible phonon frequency.

Commonness of metallic behaviour among elements

Let us now turn to the question of why most elements are metals. This is what is known as 'a good question': it is very difficult to answer in simple terms.

As discussed in §6.5, the origin of metallic behaviour lies in the tendency for the outer (valence) electrons on an atom to lower their energy by spreading their wave function, allowing motion from one atom to another. This tendency is quite general and will occur unless electrons can lower their energy more effectively in some alternative way. As you may be aware, it is actually rather rare to come across pure elements naturally, and those one does find are rarely metallic. Normally elements form chemical compounds in which the outer electron of one element finds a low energy quantum state to occupy on another atom. The outer electrons are then bound to either one atom or the other, or alternatively, are tied up in covalent/ionic bonds.

In elements however, there is only one type of atom. Hence electron transfer does not occur because the electron will merely find itself in an identical situation on the neighbouring atom. Thus in elements, the formation of delocalised states is one of a limited number of strategies for reducing the electron energies. If we chemically combine metallic elements with the common insulating elements, e.g. oxygen or nitrogen, then in general the metallic properties are destroyed as the valence electrons find low-energy, *localised* quantum states.

Superconductors

The phenomenon of superconductivity is too complex for us to attempt even a simple analysis of the data in Table 7.15. However, the phenomenon is so fascinating that I feel I must write a few words on the subject. The key feature of all theories of superconductivity is the appreciation that the electron 'gas' described in §6.5 undergoes a kind of 'condensation' at low temperatures. The electron 'fluid' which 'condenses out' from the electron 'gas' has the unusual properties that are characteristic of the superconducting state.

In the transition of a normal molecular gas to a

molecular liquid, the cause of the condensation is a weak attractive interaction between molecules. Similarly, a weak attraction between electrons is the origin of the condensation into the superconducting state. However, for electrons in a metal it is not at all obvious what the origin of this weak attractive interaction between electrons might be. In fact, so elusive was the source of this interaction, that it took scientists around 40 years to work out what it was!

In low-temperature superconductors, some electrons within a metal can interact with other electrons by distorting the lattice of ions. We say the lattice *mediates* an attractive interaction between electrons. In technical terms the *electron–electron* attraction is actually an electron–*phonon*–electron interaction. Thus metals with a strong electron-phonon interaction, and hence a high resistivity, are more likely to become superconductors. This is why the best elemental conductors (Cu, Ag, and Au), in which the electrons are weakly scattered by phonons, do not become superconducting.

In high temperature superconductors the origin of the attractive interaction between electrons is (at the time of writing) still unknown, but is thought to be of the form electron–*something*–electron. Whoever discovers precisely what the *something* is, will undoubtedly be destined for a Nobel Prize.

The resistivity of alloys

The resistivity of an alloy is larger than the resistivity of either its component elements. For example, data for an alloy of platinum (Pt) and its neighbour in the periodic table iridium (Ir) extracted from Table 7.14 is shown below.

Pt	Pt(10% Ir)	Ir
9.81×10^{-8}	24.8×10^{-8}	4.7×10^{-8}

This data is at first hard to understand. Surely adding 10 % of 'low-resistivity iridium' to 'higher-resistivity platinum' will lower the overall resistivity? The answer to this question is 'No', but in order to understand why, we have to think again about the processes by which electron waves are scattered.

On page 221 we discussed two ways in which electrons could be scattered. We noted that in a perfect lattice at absolute zero, electrons would remain in their quantum states indefinitely. We noted that it was deviations from the perfect periodicity of the lattice which scattered electrons, and considered two ways in which a perfect lattice might be disrupted: by lattice waves, or by impurities of any kind. Importantly, *any* disruption will cause an increase in resistivity. The appearance of a plane of atoms in an alloy of two elements A (e.g. Pt) and B (e.g. Ir) is illustrated in Figure 7.40.

Figure 7.40: Arrangements of atoms in a binary alloy.

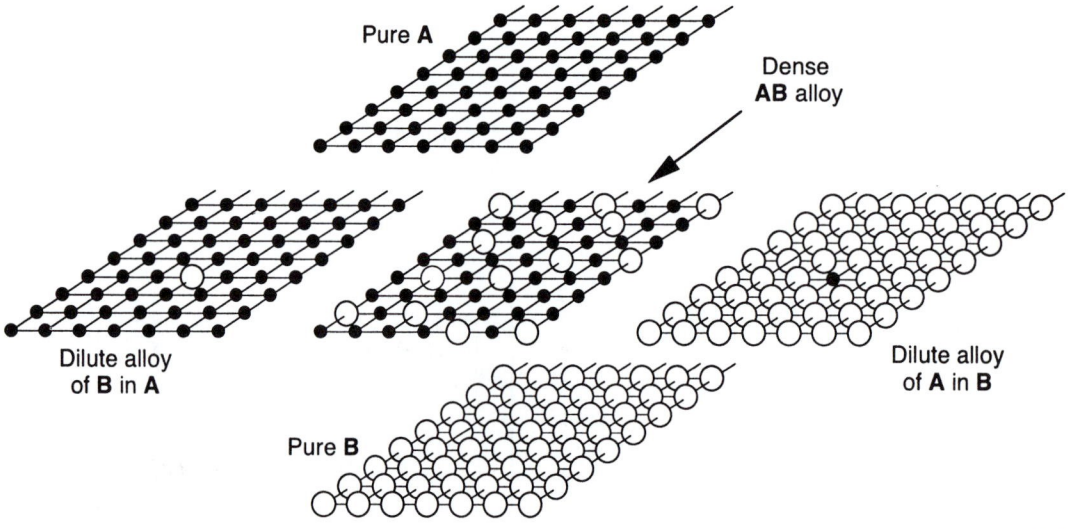

Pure **A**

Dense **AB** alloy

Dilute alloy of **B** in **A**

Dilute alloy of **A** in **B**

Pure **B**

The resistivity of pure A or pure B arises entirely from lattice waves (phonons) within the material as discussed previously. In addition to this, the resistivity of alloys has scattering contributions from each of the impurities. For dilute impurities (i.e. just a few per cent of A atoms substituted by B atoms) it is fairly easy to identify which is the 'pure' substance and which is the 'impurity'. However for non-dilute alloys, estimates of the resistivity are extremely difficult. It is worth noting that the resistivity data for Pt(Ir) is evaluated at 20°C and thus consists of both contributions from impurities and from lattice vibrations.

7.7.4 Data on insulators in weak electric fields

Conduction and polarisation

The simplest electrical property of electrical insulators (or *dielectrics*, as they also known) is that for small electric fields they are poor electrical conductors! Neglecting the tiny electric current that flows in response to the applied electric field, the main effect of the electric field is to *polarise* the material. This weakens applied electric fields within the material to an extent measured by the *relative dielectric permittivity* (or *dielectric constant*) ε of the material (§2.2). From Table 7.16 it seems that typical values of ε are in the range 2 to 10 for a variety of common solids. This is around a factor 1000 greater than typical values for gases (§5.6.1), but of a similar order to that found for liquids (§9.7.3). However materials such as strontium titanate and strontium zirconate show dramatically enhanced dielectric constants. This implies that in these substances, an applied electric field has an enormous effect on the distribution of electric charge within the material.

So the main questions raised by our preliminary examination of the experimental data on the electrical properties of insulators are:

- Why is the difference of the dielectric constant from unity $\varepsilon - 1$ in solids typically 1000 times greater than for gases?
- Why is the dielectric constant of some solids anomalously large?

7.7.5 Understanding the behaviour of insulators in weak electric fields

In this section we consider the data on the properties of insulators under weak static electric fields. The response to rapidly varying electric fields is covered in §7.9 on the optical properties of insulators.

Table 7.16 The relative dielectric permittivity ε of various insulators (and semiconductors) The relative permittivity of vacuum is exactly 1. All measurements refer to 20°C, but are insensitive to small changes $\approx \pm 10°C$ around this temperature.

Substance		ε
Elements		
Silicon	Si	11.9
Germanium	Ge	16.0
Ceramics		
Alumina	Al_2O_3	8.5
Strontium titanate	$SrTiO_3$	200
Strontium zirconate	$SrZrO_3$	38
Glass		
Quartz	SiO_2	4.5
Borosilicate glass	SiO_2 with BO	4 – 5
Lead glass	SiO_2 with PbO	7
Plastics		
Polyethylene		2.3
Polystyrene		2.6
Polytetrafluoroethylene	PTFE	2.1
Polyamide	Nylon	3 – 4

Example 7.18

A capacitor is made from two plates of metal of area 1 cm^2 separated by 0.1 mm? Calculate the capacitance if the intervening material is (a) air, (b) PTFE, or (c) strontium titanate.

The capacitance of a parallel plate capacitor is given by $C = \varepsilon\varepsilon_0 A/L$ which for the capacitor in question is:

$$C = \varepsilon \times \frac{8.854 \times 10^{-12} \times 10^{-4}}{10^{-4}} = 8.854\varepsilon \times 10^{-12} \text{ F}$$

$$= 8.854\varepsilon \text{ pF}$$

From Table 5.16 we find ε (air) ≈ 1.000 and from Table 7.16 we find ε (PTFE) ≈ 2.1 and ε ($SrTiO_3$) ≈ 200. Substituting for ε yields:

$C = 8.86$ pF	air
$C = 18.6$ pF	PTFE
$C = 1771$ pF	strontium titanate

Comparison with gases

In the discussion of the electric properties of gases (§5.7) we saw that in order to understand the dielectric constants of gases we had to divide gas molecules into two classes:

- Those with a permanent 'built-in' electric dipole moment, called *polar molecules*; and
- those without any 'built-in' electric dipole moment, called *non-polar molecules*.

In an applied electric field both types of molecules acquired *induced* electric dipole moments. In addition to this, polar molecules also experience a torque that allows them to rotate in order line up with the applied electric field. This additional mechanism usually gives polar molecules a significantly stronger response to applied fields than non-polar molecules.

In a solid, the mechanism of molecular rotation is, in general, not possible: atoms and molecules within a solid are usually unable to rotate because of the constraints of the bonds to neighbouring atoms. Bearing this in mind we will make our first attempt to understand the behaviour of the dielectric constant of solids by considering a solid to be the limit of a very dense gas, in which the molecules cannot rotate. Clearly, this is not a sophisticated model of a solid. However, as we shall see, it is able to explain the first question raised by the data: why the difference of the dielectric constant from unity $(\varepsilon - 1)$ in solids is typically 1000 times greater than for gases.

Equation 5.109 predicts that for a non-polar gas:

$$\varepsilon - 1 = \frac{n\alpha}{\varepsilon_0} \qquad (7.87)$$

where n is the number density of molecules and α is the polarisability of a single molecule. For gases we found values of $10^4(\varepsilon - 1)$ between 1 and 10 for non-polar molecules (Table 5.16) at STP. The number density of gas molecules at STP is given by:

$$n = \frac{P}{k_B T} \qquad (5.87*)$$

which evaluates to:

$$n = \frac{1.013 \times 10^5}{1.38 \times 10^{-23} \times 273.15} \qquad (7.88)$$
$$= 2.68 \times 10^{25} \text{ molecules m}^{-3}$$

For solids, number densities are closer to 10^{29} m^{-3} and so considering a solid as a dense gas we expect to find the dielectric constants enhanced by a factor of approximately $10^{29}/2.68 \times 10^{25} \approx 3700$. Since values for $10^4(\varepsilon - 1)$ for gases were between 1 and 10, our predicted range of values of ε is from 0.37 to 3.7. Comparison with Table 7.16 shows that this is indeed the correct order of magnitude for the dielectric constants of most insulators.

We have understood the order of magnitude of ε as being due to the change in molecular number density between a solid and a gas. We can now interpret differences in ε between different solids as being due to differences in either the number density of the atoms in the solid, or α the 'molecular polarisability' of a solid. Notice that for solids other than molecular solids, we can no longer identify individual molecules within the solid and so the molecular polarisability refers to the polarisability of a chemical formula unit of the solid. However, the molecular polarisability of a solid still depends on the same factors that determined the polarisability of molecules.

Anomalously large values of ε

The remaining question to be answered from §7.7.4 is why the dielectric constant of some solids is anomalously large. For example, strontium titanate $SrTiO_3$ has a value of ≈ 200. Following Equation 7.87 we see that since n cannot increase by a factor of the order 20 from one material to another, the origin of the enhanced value of must lie in an enhanced 'molecular' polarisability α.

The enhancement of the polarisability is but one of the extraordinary properties of strontium titanate. The structure of $SrTiO_3$ is complex, with both covalent and ionic bonds. Importantly, the atoms can arrange themselves in two different crystal structures, which have nearly the same cohesive energy. One arrangement is favoured at high temperatures and another at low temperatures, with the crossover between the two structures at around

125 K. In the presence of an applied electric field, all the positive ions are pulled in one direction, and all the negative ions move in the opposite direction. Because of the delicate balance between the two crystal structures, an applied electric field causes the ions within the crystal structure to move anomalously large distances. and hence develop an anomalously large electric dipole moment.

7.7.6 Data on insulators in strong electric fields

Resistivity

As mentioned in the previous section, insulators are poor conductors of electricity, but their conductivity, though small, is still finite (Table 7.17)

The measured resistivity of an insulator depends strongly on its purity and the temperature at which the measurement is made. In general, increasing the temperature dramatically lowers the resistivity. The measured resistivity also depends on several factors we might not at first have considered relevant, such as the length of time we wait after the applying the electric field before making the measurement. The result also depends on whether the surface of the experimental sample is rough or smooth. Given these qualifications, the data of Table 7.17 should be considered as only an indication of the order of magnitude of the result to be expected. However, one things is clear: the resistivity of insulators can be as much as 10^{20} greater than the resistivity of metals.

Dielectric strength

If the strength of the electric field used to determine the resistivity of an insulator is increased, then eventually the current rises dramatically, often catastrophically destroying the substance being measured. This phenomenon is known as *electrical breakdown*, and the value of electric field at which breakdown occurs (known as the *dielectric strength*) is of the order $10\ \mathrm{MV\,m^{-1}}$. This sounds like an enormous electric field, but is not perhaps quite so impressively large as it first appears. In practical terms its corresponds to a voltage of roughly 10 kV across a piece of material 1mm

thick, or a voltage of only 10 V across a piece of material 1 μm thick. It is also of interest to put the magnitude of the breakdown field in solids into some sort of context. First, in Example 2.1(b) we worked out a typical figure for the electric field strength in the region of an atom of around 10^{11} V m^{-1}. So when electrical breakdown occurs, the field, the *applied* electric field $\approx 10^7$ V m^{-1} is still a tiny fraction of the *intrinsic* fields experienced by electrons within the material. Second, we can compare the dielectric strength with that of air at 25 °C and normal atmospheric pressure. In §5.7.3 we saw that this figure was 3.1×10^6 V m^{-1}, so solid insulators have dielectric strengths which are of a similar order, though actually slightly greater than, those found for gases at around room temperature and pressure.

The main questions raised by our preliminary examination of the experimental data on the electrical properties of insulators are:

- Why is the conductivity of insulators so much worse than that of metals?
- Why does the dielectric strength of solid insulators exceed those of gases at around room temperature and pressure by a factor as great as 10?

Table 7.17 Typical orders of magnitude of the resistivity of some insulating substances at around room temperature. The data correspond to values of ρ determined one minute after the electric field is applied.

Insulator	ρ (Ω m)	Insulator	ρ (Ω m)
Alumina Al$_2$O$_3$	$10^9 - 10^{12}$	Paper	$\approx 10^{10}$
QuartzSiO$_2$	$\approx 10^{16}$	PTFE	$10^{15} - 10^{19}$
Diamond C	$10^{10} - 10^{11}$	Polystyrene	$10^{15} - 10^{19}$
Boron B	$10^{10} - 10^{11}$	Varnish	10^7
Iodine I$_2$	10^{13}	Soil	$10^2 - 10^4$
Glass	$10^9 - 10^{12}$	Distilled water	$10^2 - 10^5$

Table 7.18 Typical values (and ranges of values) of the dielectric strength of some insulating substances.

Insulator	Vm^{-1}
Alumina, Al$_2$O$_3$	$10 - 35 \times 10^6$
Sapphire, Al$_2$O$_3$	17×10^6
Quartz, SiO$_2$	$25 - 40 \times 10^6$
Beryllia	$10 - 14 \times 10^6$

7.7.7 Understanding the data on insulators in strong electric fields

The conduction process in insulators

When we discussed the absence of a breakdown field in a metal, we noted that conduction in an insulator was by a quite different process from that in a metal. The quantum states with the energy closest to the Fermi energy are at the top of a so-called *band* of electronic states. If an electron is to move through the crystal, it must find an unoccupied quantum state into which it can move. The quantum states occupied by the most energetic electrons can, for many purposes, be visualised as being essentially *localised* at or near a particular atom. When an electric field is applied, the electrons in these states are unable to change quantum state and remain bound to their 'parent' atoms.

In order to cause them to move through the crystal, we must supply some energy ΔE to move an electron from its quantum state around one atom into a vacant quantum state around a neighbouring atom. In metals ΔE is infinitesimally small, but in an insulator it is usually a relatively large energy, typically several electron volts. At room temperature the typical vibrational energy of an atom is around $k_B T$, which is around $\frac{1}{40}$ of an electron volt. The probability of an electron spontaneously moving from to an unoccupied quantum state on a neighbouring atom therefore contains a Boltzmann factor term (§2.5) like:

$$\text{probability} \approx \text{factor} \times \exp\left[\frac{-\Delta E}{k_B T}\right] \quad (7.89)$$

For a typical value of $\Delta E = 3$ eV, the exponential Boltzmann factor evaluates to $\exp(-120) \approx 10^{-52}$. This makes the process of excitation to a quantum state in which electrical conduction is possible extremely unlikely. However, unlikely as it is, it still occurs. There is a low, but finite, rate at which electrons are 'freed' into quantum states in which they can conduct electricity.

However a 'free electron' electron in an insulator will leave an uncompensated positive charge behind, and will return to a localised quantum state similar to that from which it derived relatively

---

Example 7.19

1 kV is applied across the two faces of a sheet of glass 1 mm thick and with an area 1 cm × 1 cm.
(a) Estimate the current which flows across the sheet 1 minute after the electric field is applied?
(b) How many electrons per second does this current correspond to?
(c) Estimate the number density of electrons able to conduct electricity.

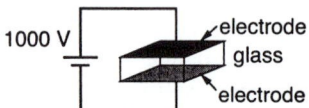

(a) From Table 7.17 the expected resistivity is in the range 10^9 Ω m to 10^{12} Ω m. To estimate the resistance of the glass we use: $R = \rho L/A$ with $L = 10^{-3}$ m and $A = 10^{-4}$ m². Substituting $\rho = 10^9$ Ω m we find:

$$R = \frac{10^9 \times 10^{-3}}{10^{-4}} = 10^{10} \ \Omega$$

And so we expect a resistance of between 10^{10} Ω and 10^{13} Ω. For a voltage of 1 kV Ohm's Law tells us:

$$I = \frac{V}{R} = \frac{10^3}{10^{10}} = 10^{-7} \ A$$

and so we expect a current of between 0.1 nA and 0.1 μA.

(b) A current of I ampere corresponds to:

$$n = \frac{I}{1.6 \times 10^{-19}} \approx \frac{10^{-7} \rightarrow 10^{-10}}{1.6 \times 10^{-19}}$$

which evaluates to between 10^9 and 10^{12} electrons per second.

(c) We use the general formula (Equation 7.84):

$$\sigma = \frac{ne^2 \Delta t}{m_e}$$

to evaluate n the charge carrier density . In this formula m_e and e are the mass and charge of the electron, and Δt is the time over which a carrier is free to be accelerated by the electric field. Estimating Δt to have a similar value to that found in metals, and substituting in orders of magnitude only with $\sigma = 1/\rho \approx 10^{-9}$ S we have:

$$n = \frac{\sigma m_e}{e^2 \Delta t} \approx \frac{10^{-9} \times 10^{-30}}{10^{-19} \times 10^{-19} \times 10^{-14}} \approx 10^{13} \ m^3$$

This may be compared with the number density of atoms of $\approx 10^{29}$ m³.

quickly. This process is termed *recombination*. In other words, carriers are not only created relatively rarely, they are also destroyed relatively quickly after their creation. As Example 7.19 shows, for a substance with a resistivity of 10^9 Ω m, on average there are only of the order of 10^{13} free electrons per cubic metre. This may be compared with a typical value of roughly 10^{29} atoms per cubic metre. Thus typically there is *on average* only one carrier per 10^{16} atoms. The chance that an electron on a particular atom will be in an excited state in such a substance is about a billion times less than the chance of winning the UK national lottery.

This description of the conduction process allows us to understand directly why insulators are poor conductors. Further, the mechanism described above also allows us to understand why the conductivity depends strongly on temperature. Assuming $\Delta E = 3$ eV we may evaluate the Boltzmann factor:

$$\exp\left[\frac{-\Delta E}{k_{\mathrm{B}}T}\right] \qquad (7.90)$$

for $T = 293$ K (20 °C) and $T = 303$ K (30 °C). At 20 °C the factor evaluates to 2.5×10^{-52} and at 30 °C it evaluates to 1.25×10^{-50}. Thus heating the substance by 10 °C increases the rate of carrier formation by a factor ≈ 100. We will see in the next section that this sensitivity to temperature is at the heart of understanding breakdown in solids.

Dielectric strength

The detailed mechanism of dielectric breakdown in solids differs considerably from that in gases (§5.6.4). However, the two processes do have some features in common. In both processes there is a low density of charge carriers in equilibrium and breakdown occurs when each carrier can *on average* create at least one more carrier before it is removed from the conduction process. In other words, both processes are *avalanche* effects. In gases, electrons and ions create new carriers by ionisation of neutral molecules. In solids, electrons create a region which is hotter than the equilibrium temperature, making it considerably more likely that a new carrier will be formed locally.

230

> ### Example 7.20
>
> **In a transistor, which forms part of many microcircuits, a potential difference is applied between two regions of the circuit. The so-called *gate electrode* is separated from the conducting channel of the transistor by a thin layer of silicon dioxide, SiO_2, which is a good electrical insulator. In order to make circuits smaller this layer must be made thinner and thinner. If the breakdown field for SiO_2 is 40×10^6 V m^{-1}, what is thinnest layer that can be made if the applied voltage is 5 V?**
>
> Simply, the electric field in the SiO_2 layer is given by:
>
> $$E = \frac{V}{d}$$
>
> so the minimum thickness of the layer is given by:
>
> $$d \geq \frac{V}{E_{\max}} \geq \frac{5}{4 \times 10^7}$$
>
> $$\geq 1.2 \times 10^{-7} \text{ m} \approx 120 \text{ nm}$$

Let us again consider the case of the insulator we considered above with an excitation energy of $\Delta E = 3$ eV between states on neighbouring atoms. Suppose that a carrier is created and travels one lattice spacing a before being lost to the conduction process. In an electric field E Vm^{-1} it will have acquired an extra Ea electron volts of energy from the electric field. For $E \approx 10^7$ Vm^{-1} (typical of the values in Table 7.18) and $a \approx 0.3$ nm this amounts to 3×10^{-3} eV of energy. If this energy is given up to vibrations of the atom on which it now resides, this is equivalent to local heating. So what temperature rise does this correspond to? Although the actual calculation is quite tricky, we can get a sense of the orders of magnitude involved by considering the following. At $T \approx 293$ K:

$$k_{\mathrm{B}}T \approx \tfrac{1}{40} \text{ eV} = 25 \times 10^{-3} \text{ eV}.$$

Thus locally the effective temperature is increased such that:

$$k_{\mathrm{B}}T \approx 25 \times 10^{-3} + 3 \times 10^{-3} \text{ eV}$$

$$\approx 28 \times 10^{-3} \text{ eV}$$

which corresponds to $T \approx 325$ K. The Boltzmann factor governing the rate of carrier formation is

thus increased to 3×10^{-47}. So it is now around 10^5 times more likely than previously that an electron carrier will be created in this region.

This amplification of probability is exactly the kind of process which gives rise to avalanche, and will eventually create a hot, high carrier density region (a plasma) within the solid. Typically this region will grow rapidly and breakdown will take place, potentially vaporising the insulator in the process.

The physics of conduction and breakdown in insulators is considerably more complex than I have indicated above. However, even in this simple analysis we have been able to understand the fundamental processes underlying electrical conduction and breakdown. We will consider these conduction processes again when we discuss conduction in semiconductors (§7.7.9).

7.7.8 Data on semiconductors

Semiconductors are indicated on Figure 7.34 as having a resistivity at room temperature of around $1\ \Omega\,m$. This is around a million times higher than metals, but more than a million times lower than the insulators discussed in §7.7.6. As with insulators, the resistivity of semiconductors depends strongly on the purity and temperature of the semiconductor.

Figure 7.41 shows the sensitivity of the resistivity of silicon to phosphorus impurities. The main feature to note is that low levels of impurity, even at the level of a few parts per million, significantly *reduce* the resistivity. This is in direct contrast to metals, where we saw that resistivity is *increased* by the addition of impurities. The highest concentration shown in Figure 7.41 corresponds to a replacement of around 1% of silicon atoms with phosphorus atoms, and the resistivity is about 100 times higher than the resistivity of typical metals.

Figure 7.42 illustrates the sensitivity of the resistivity of silicon to temperature. The main feature to note is that resistivity *decreases* dramatically as the temperature is increased. This is in direct contrast to metals, where we saw that resistivity *increases* as the temperature increases.

Figure 7.41 The resistivity at 300 K of silicon alloyed with small amounts phosphorus, both plotted on logarithmic axes. Alloying at this low level – the highest impurity concentration shown is just over one P atom for every 100 Si atoms – is generally referred to as *doping*. Notice that doping phosphorus dramatically reduces the resistivity of the silicon even at low levels. Notice also that even at its lowest value the resistivity is 100 times worse than that of typical metallic elements (Figure 7.34).

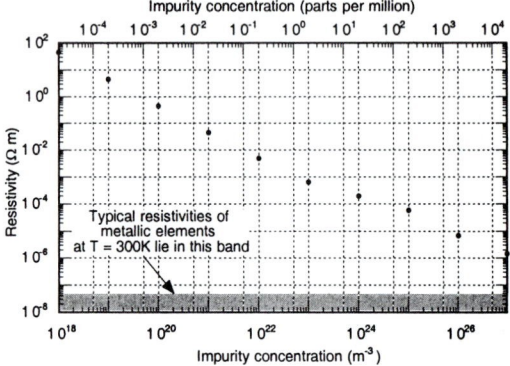

Figure 7.42 Calculation of the resistivity of relatively pure silicon plotted on a logarithmic scale versus temperature. Also shown for contrast is the resistivity of platinum also plotted on Figure 7.35. Note: The silicon data has been calculated from data tabulated in various sources. It should be taken as indicative of the trend of data only.

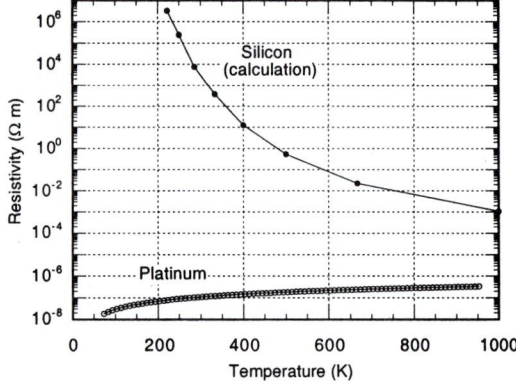

So the questions raised by our preliminary examination of the experimental data on the electrical resistivities of semiconductors are:

- Why does the resistivity of semiconductors increase strongly with decreasing temperature?

- Why does the resistivity of silicon decrease when small amounts of other elements are added as impurities?

7.7.9 Understanding the electrical properties of semiconductors

We approach the behaviour of semiconductors by considering them to be essentially insulators. As discussed in §7.7.7, the conduction process in insulators is dramatically different from that in metals. When considering insulators we saw that the main effect of an applied electric field was to polarise the electronic structure around the atoms of the substance. Only occasionally did local fluctuations conspire to excite an electron from a bound quantum state to a state in which conduction was possible. The difference between the term *insulator* and *semiconductor* lies only in the magnitude of ΔE, the energy required to excite an electron into a quantum state in which electrical conduction is possible.

Background theory

The creation of charge carriers

The arrangement of quantum states on an atom of semiconducting substance is shown in Figure 7.43. A low-energy quantum state, generally corresponding to an electron taking part in a covalent bond, is occupied by an electron. There is also a higher-energy quantum state, which is in general empty. The relative probability of occupancy of the two quantum states is proportional to a Boltzmann factor (§2.5). Thus, the relative probability that the higher energy of the two quantum states is occupied is proportional to:

Figure 7.43 An illustration of the situation on an atom of semiconducting substance at $T = 0$ K. A low-energy quantum state is occupied, and a higher-energy quantum is empty. The energy difference ΔE between the two states is very much greater than $k_B T$. The figure is drawn approximately to scale so that if ΔE is 1 eV, then $k_B T$ is $\approx$ 1/40 eV, the value of $k_B T$ at around room temperature.

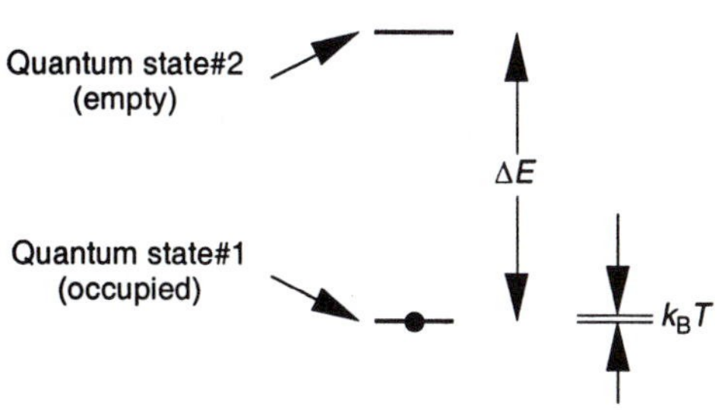

$$P \propto \exp\left[\frac{-\Delta E}{k_B T}\right] \qquad (7.91)$$

For semiconductors, the energy gap ΔE is rather less than for insulators, typically of the order of 1 eV. However the Boltzmann factor in Equation 7.79 is still extremely small: at room temperature it is typically $\exp(-40) \approx 4 \times 10^{-18}$. This is much greater than for the insulators, but still leads to a slow rate of excitation of electrons into the upper quantum state.

Notice that when an electron is in the upper quantum state it is able to conduct electricity. In an applied electric field, the electron may move into a neighbouring quantum state, which is almost certainly empty, and so move through the crystal. This contrasts with the situation when there are no excited electrons. In this case electrons cannot move easily onto neighbouring atoms because there is no low-energy quantum state available for them. In order to move into an upper quantum state an electron would require ΔE of energy, which it would have to acquire at the expense of the electric field. If the spacing between atoms is a, then the electric field would have to exceed $\Delta E/a$ V m^{-1}, which amounts to roughly 10^9 V m^{-1}: well in excess of the breakdown field.

So thermal excitation of electrons into the upper quantum state makes them available for an electric field to draw them into a conduction process. Notice also that the atom the electron has left now has an vacant lower-energy quantum state. This allows neighbouring electrons to move into this quantum state as shown in Figure 7.44 (c) and (d). In this process, the vacant lower quantum state is effectively transferred in the same direction as the applied electric field. Since this vacant state has an uncompensated positive electric charge, we see that the excitation of single electron allows conduction in the lower quantum states. This conduction process is quite distinct from the conduction associated with the motion of electrons.

Carrier recombination

Notice that if no external electric field acts on the semiconductor, then the excited electron will still be attracted to its 'original' atom by the uncom-

Figure 7.44 The situation of electrons within a semiconducting substance. (a) At $T = 0$ K the electrons occupy the lowest energy states, but (b) above $T = 0$ K a few higher energy states are populated. In (c) and (d) $T > 0$ K and an applied electric field causes electrons to move to neighbouring quantum states. Notice that field makes the electron in the upper state move one way, and the uncompensated positive charge in the lower quantum state move in the opposite direction.

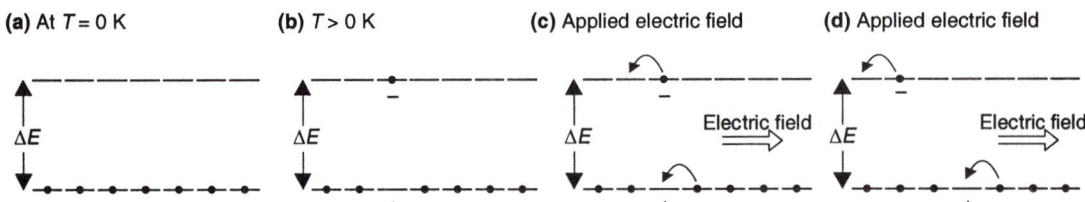

(a) At $T = 0$ K   **(b)** $T > 0$ K   **(c)** Applied electric field   **(d)** Applied electric field

pensated positive charge. After a short time, the electron will in general return to its low-energy quantum state, giving up its excess energy in the form of a photon and/or a phonon. This process is called *carrier recombination* and 'annihilates' two charge carriers.

Terminology

The lower-energy quantum states are generally referred to as *valence* states, and the upper quantum states as *conduction* states. Electrons in the conduction states are called *electron carriers* and the vacant valence states left behind by a excited electron carrier are called *hole carriers*.

In equilibrium

At a temperature T in a semiconductor, electron and hole carriers are created at a characteristic rate which is proportional to $\exp(-\Delta E / k_B T)$. After a short while these carriers annihilate. Thus at any instant there is an equilibrium concentration of electron carriers and hole carriers able to conduct electricity. These carriers form two dilute interpenetrating charged 'gases' within the semicon-

ductor as shown in Figure 7.45. Notice that because of the way they are created, the number densities of hole and electron carriers are equal. Also, because of the exponential dependence of the creation rate, the number density of both types of carriers increases rapidly with increasing temperature.

Conductivity

Consider a single charge carrier with charge q within the semiconductor. Under the action of an applied electric field, carriers make transitions from quantum state to quantum state, and so move through the crystal (Figure 7.44 (c) and (d)). The rate at which these transitions are made depends on details of the quantum states involved and, in general, is not equal for the hole and electron carriers. Since the rate at which the electron is accelerated by an electric field would normally be determined by its mass, we characterise the rate at which these transitions are made by means of an *effective mass m^**. In a manner similar to the case for electrons in metals (Equation 7.84) we derive an expression for the drift velocity Δv of the

Figure 7.45. A region of a semiconductor with the lattice of atoms represented by a grey box. The number densities of hole and electron carriers are equal, and increase strongly with temperature. In fact the change in density with temperature is much more dramatic than figure indicates.

(a) Low temperature

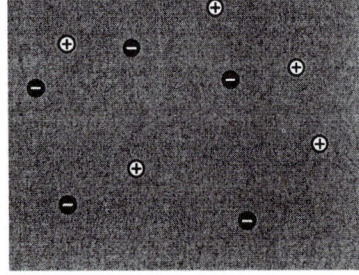

(b) High temperature

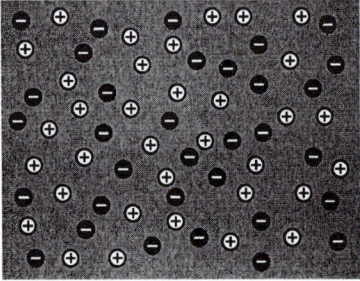

charge carriers. We start with Newton's law:

$$F = m^* \frac{\Delta v}{\Delta t} \qquad (7.92)$$

where Δt is average time between scattering events, and F is the extra force on the electrons due to the *external* electric field (qE). Rearranging this as an expression for the drift velocity we find:

$$\Delta v = \frac{qE}{m^*} \Delta t \qquad (7.93)$$

Using a similar argument to that following Figure 7.83 we may write the current density due to a carrier density n of such carriers as:

$$j = nq\left(\frac{q\Delta t}{m^*}\right) E \qquad (7.94)$$

If we have two such 'gases' of carriers, one of which is composed of hole carriers and the other of which is composed of electron carriers, then the current density will be given by:

$$j = n_h q \underbrace{\left[\frac{q\Delta t_h}{m_h^*}\right]}_{\mu_h} E + n_e q \underbrace{\left[\frac{q\Delta t_e}{m_e^*}\right]}_{\mu_e} E \qquad (7.95)$$

I have used the subscripts 'h' and 'e' to refer to hole and electron carriers respectively. The quantity $q\Delta t / m^*$ that I have drawn in brackets in the above equations is known as the *carrier mobility*, μ. In terms of μ we may write an expression for the conductivity as:

$$j = \underbrace{\left[n_h q\mu_h + n_e q\mu_e\right]}_{\sigma} E \qquad (7.96)$$

$$\sigma = n_h q\mu_h + n_e q\mu_e$$

Comparison with experiment

We can understand the temperature-dependence of the resistivity of semiconductors in terms of a temperature-dependence of the terms in Equation 7.96. Since the charge q on either type of carrier is unlikely to change with temperature, we concentrate our attention on the temperature-dependence of the mobility, μ, and the carrier density, n.

234

The temperature dependence of the mobility

The mobility of a carrier is defined by:

$$\mu = \frac{q\Delta t}{m^*} \qquad (7.97)$$

From our study of metals, we would expect the carrier lifetime Δt to change with temperature. However, we would expect in general that the carrier lifetime would get *shorter* at high temperatures, which would cause an *increase* in resistivity at higher temperatures: this is exactly the opposite of what is observed. The details of the quantum states that determine m^* do not change strongly with temperature and we cannot explain

---

Example 7.21

Estimate number density of electron and hole carriers in pure silicon at 300 K.

Let us first estimate the *mobility* of the carriers according to Equation 7.97: $\mu = q\Delta t/m^*$. Since we have no direct information on the quantities in this equation we must make some plausible guesses. We estimate the effective masses of both types of carrier are of the order of the mass of a free electron m_e and that the scattering lifetime of carriers is similar to that which we worked out for copper in Example 7.16 $\approx 2.5 \times 10^{-14}$ s. We thus write the mobility of either hole or electron carriers as:

$$\mu_e \approx \mu_h \approx \mu$$

$$\mu \approx \frac{1.6\times10^{-19}\times2.5\times10^{-14}}{9.1\times10^{-31}}$$

$$= 4.4\times10^{-3} \ \text{C s kg}^{-1}$$

(Note: This is in fact a significant underestimate of the mobility). Recalling that we expect $n_h = n_e$ we therefore write Equation 7.96 as:

$$\sigma = 2nq\mu$$

where n is the number density of either holes or electrons. Rearranging to solve for n we find:

$$n \approx \frac{\sigma}{2q\mu} \approx \frac{1}{2\rho q\mu}$$

$$= \frac{1}{2\times3\times10^3\times1.6\times10^{-19}\times4.4\times10^{-3}}$$

$$\approx 2.4\times10^{17} \ \text{m}^{-3}$$

where we have used $\rho \approx 3 \times 10^3$ at around 300 K read from Figure 7.42.

the changes in resistivity as being due to changes in m^*. So we expect the mobility of either electrons or holes to fall slightly, but not dramatically, as the temperature is increased.

The temperature-dependence of the carrier density

The source of the temperature-dependence of the resistivity lies in the temperature-dependence of the number density of charge carriers. As we saw above, the rate at which electrons make transitions to conduction states (and hence the creation rate of hole and an electron carriers) is proportional to $\exp(-\Delta E / k_B T)$. However the recombination rate does not increase so dramatically. It will still increase because there is now an enhanced probability of an encounter between a hole and an electron carrier. Overall, this leads to an exponential temperature dependence of the equilibrium number density of charge carriers.

The estimate of Example 7.21 is extremely instructive. There are roughly 10^{29} atoms per cubic metre in silicon, and so a carrier density of 2.4×10^{17} per cubic metre corresponds to around one carrier for 10^{12} atoms. Even given the uncertainties and assumptions involved in this calculation, the key result remains. The density of the gases of electron and hole carriers that occur spontaneously within silicon is *extremely* low.

The effect of impurities on the resistivity of silicon

Example 7.21 indicates that the number density of either hole or electron carriers in silicon at room temperature is extremely small, around 1 carrier for every 10^{12} silicon atoms. This is the number of carriers which exist due to processes *intrinsic* to the silicon lattice itself. When an impurity is added to silicon in such a way that it replaces the silicon atom within the lattice, then quantum states in the region of the impurity are altered. For some impurities, this alteration is such as to make it much easier to create either a hole (a so-called *p*-type impurity) or an electron carrier (a so-called *n*-type impurity). If each impurity atom creates one carrier, impurities present in silicon at a level of 1 impurity atom per 10^9 silicon atoms will create around 1000 times more carriers than occur intrin-

sically within the silicon. This is the origin of the extreme sensitivity of the resistivity of semiconductors to impurities. The excess carriers which are created as a result of impurities, are known as *extrinsic* carriers. Please notice the staggering purities involved. For almost all substances, purity at a level of around 1 part per million is considered 'extremely pure'. However, for silicon at room temperature, we would not observe the intrinsic electronic behaviour until we made the substance around a million times purer than this!

The effect of n-type (donor) impurities

Let us consider the way in which the quantum states within a lattice are affected when an atom of phosphorus is substituted for an atom of silicon (Figure 7.46).

Phosphorus has five valence electrons, one more than silicon, and one extra nuclear charge. The extra electron will occupy the next available quantum state, which will be at roughly the same energy as the empty conduction states in silicon. However, in general, the quantum state is at a slightly lower energy than the conduction states in silicon. This is because of the electrical attraction of the extra nuclear charge.

Notice that the energy required to remove this extra electron and place it in a conduction state on the silicon atom, ΔE_d, is much less than the ΔE required to remove an electron from a valence state and place it into a conduction state. The reduction is in fact quite dramatic. For example, for silicon the energy gap ΔE is around 1.1 eV, but the ΔE_d is only 0.044 eV. At room temperature, where $k_B T$ is around 0.025 eV, it becomes highly likely that the electron derived from the phosphorus impurity will be able to move easily into the conduction states. Thus each phosphorus impurity effectively donates one electron to the number density of electron carriers. But notice that in this process, no equivalent hole carriers have been created.

So we see that phosphorus impurities in silicon at a level of 1 part per billion can easily create sufficient electron carriers to completely dominate the conduction process.

235

The effect of p-type (acceptor) impurities

Let us consider the way in which the quantum states within a lattice are affected when an atom of aluminium is substituted for an atom of silicon (Figure 7.47).

Aluminium has three valence electrons, one less than silicon, and one less nuclear charge. Thus the valence quantum state which is occupied in silicon is empty at the aluminium impurity. The empty aluminium valence state will be at roughly the same energy as the occupied valence states in silicon. However, in general, the quantum state is at a slightly higher energy than the valence states in silicon. This is because of the attraction effect of the nuclear charge in aluminium is less than in

silicon. Notice now that the energy required to remove an electron from a valence state in silicon and place it into the empty state on the aluminium atom ΔE_a is much less than the ΔE required to remove an electron from a valence state and place it into a conduction state. Just as for donor impurities, the reduction is dramatic. For example, for silicon the energy gap ΔE is around 1.1 eV, but ΔE_a is only 0.057 eV. At room temperature, where $k_B T$ is around 0.025 eV, it is highly likely that the electrons will be able to move easily into this acceptor state. Notice that each aluminium impurity effectively accepts an electron and hence creates a hole carrier in the valence states of silicon, but no equivalent electron carrier is created.

Figure 7.46 The mechanism by which a donor impurity causes an increase in the number of carriers available for conduction. (a) At $T = 0$ K, the extra electron on the phosphorus impurity is in a quantum state with an energy just below the conduction quantum states on neighbouring ions. The energy ΔE_d required to 'ionise' the impurity and place the donated electron into the conduction states is much less than the band gap ΔE. Thus at relatively low temperatures the electron leaves its localised quantum state and an electron carrier is created in the conduction band. (b) Notice that unlike the case of a carrier arising from processes intrinsic to the silicon, the electron carrier in the conduction states does not have a partner hole carrier in the valence states. There is however an immobile net positive charge left on the phosphorus impurity.

Figure 7.47 The mechanism by which an acceptor impurity causes an increase in the number of carriers available for conduction. (a) At $T = 0$ K, the quantum state on an aluminium equivalent to the valence state in silicon is unoccupied. The energy of this state is just above the valence quantum states on neighbouring ions. The energy ΔE_a required by an electron to occupy this quantum state is much less than the band gap ΔE. At relatively low temperatures, this capture can occur with high probability resulting in the creation of a hole carrier in the valence states of the silicon. (b) Notice that unlike the case of a carrier arising from processes intrinsic to the silicon, the hole carrier in the valence states does not have a partner electron carrier in the conduction states. There is however an immobile net negative charge left on the aluminium impurity.

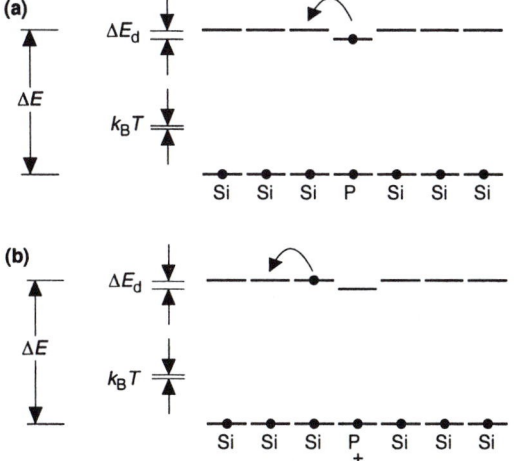

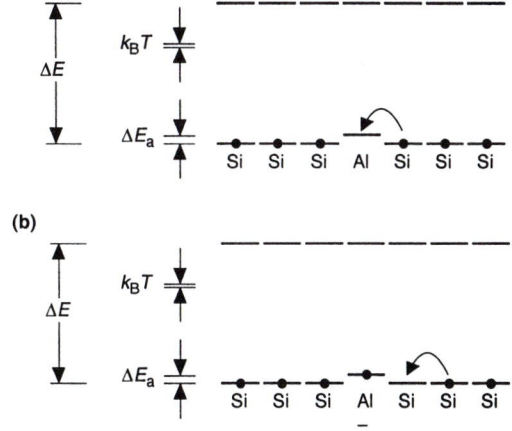

7.8 Thermal conductivity

7.8.1 Introduction

The thermal conductivity of a substance is a measure of the ease or difficulty with which heat flows through the substance. Good thermal conductors, such as many metals, have high values of thermal conductivity. Poor thermal conductors, such as many electrical insulators or fibrous materials, have low values of thermal conductivity.

The thermal conductivity of a substance is defined by the equation:

$$\frac{dQ}{dt} = -\kappa A \frac{dT}{dx} \qquad (7.98)$$

In this equation:

$\dfrac{dQ}{dt}$ is the rate of heat flow (W)

κ is the thermal conductivity, $(W\ m^{-1}\ K^{-1})$

A is the cross-sectional area across which heat is flowing (m^2)

$\dfrac{dT}{dx}$ is the temperature gradient $(K\ m^{-1})$

The minus sign in Equation 7.98 indicates that heat flows against the temperature gradient, from high temperatures to low temperatures.

7.8.2 Data on the thermal conductivity of solids

The thermal conductivity data of some solid elements is given in Table 7.19, and summarised in Figure 7.48.

The most striking feature of the data is the astonishing thermal conductivity of diamond, between two and five times greater than copper at room temperature.

Perhaps surprisingly, the metallic elements do not show up as being dramatically better conductors of heat than the electrically insulating elements. However, there is a distinct difference between the temperature-dependence of the thermal conductivity. In particular, the thermal conductivity of

Figure 7.48 Selected data from Table 7.19 The upper graph shows the data for all the insulators and semiconductors in Table 7.16 with the exception of diamond. The thermal conductivity of diamond is so much greater than any other material that it distorts the scaling of the graph. The two unlabelled curves close to the temperature axis belong to tellurium and sulphur. The lower graph shows the data for a selection of metals. The vertical scale is the same as the upper graph showing that a typical value of the metallic conductivity is slightly greater for insulators. More striking is the different temperature dependence shown by metals and insulators. The metals show a less pronounced temperature dependence. In general the thermal conductivity appears to increase with decreasing temperature. However, two of the insulators show peaks in thermal conductivity as the temperature is lowered.

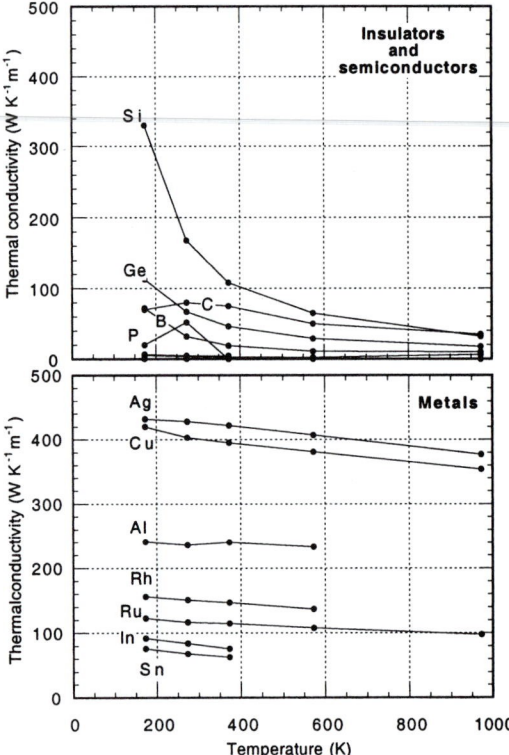

insulators falls more rapidly than that of metals as the temperature is increased. We should note however that the elemental insulators in Table 7.19 refer to rather specialised materials which are quite different from the day-to-day substances we refer to as 'insulators'. The thermal conductivities of a variety of materials (including those we

would more commonly refer to as thermal insulators, such as wool) are given in Table 7.20. Notice that in the alloy section of Table 7.20, the thermal conductivity of bronze (made from 90% copper and 10% tin) is closer to that of tin than copper.

So the main questions raised by our preliminary examination of the experimental data on the thermal conductivity of solids are:

- Why does the thermal conductivity of elements fall into two classes, electrical conductors and electrical insulators, distinguished by the temperature-dependence of their thermal conductivity?
- Why, in general, does the thermal conductivity of most solids increase on cooling, with some materials showing a peak in the thermal conductivity as the temperature is lowered?
- Why are the thermal conductivities of the elemental solids large compared with those of gases (Table 5.4)? However, many common materials such as wool or paper have values that are similar to those of gases?

Table 7.19 Thermal conductivity κ of solid elements (W K^{-1} m^{-1}) as a function of absolute temperature. The shaded entries refer to data above the melting temperature of the element. The labels M, I and SC stand for metal, insulator and semiconductor respectively. The two results for phosphorus at 173.2 K correspond to different crystal structures known as 'black' and 'yellow' phosphorus respectively.

Element and type of material		Temperature (K)				
		73.2 K	173.2 K	273.2 K	373.2 K	1273 K
Lithium, Li	M	94	86	82	47	59
Beryllium, Be	M	367	218	168	129	93
Boron, B	I	72	32	19	11	10
Carbon (Graphite), C	I	70–220	80–230	75–195	50–130	35–70
Carbon (Diamond), C	I	1700–4900	1000–2600	700–1700	—	—
Sodium, Na	M	141	142	88	78	60
Magnesium, Mg	M	160	157	154	150	—
Aluminium, Al	M	241	236	240	233	92
Silicon, Si	SC	330	168	108	65	32
Phosphorous, P	I	20	13/0.25	0.18	0.16	—
Sulphur, S	I	0.39	0.29	0.15	0.17	—
Potassium, K	M	105	104	53	45	32
Scandium, Sc	M	15	16			
Titanium, Ti	M	26	22	21	19	21
Vanadium, V	M	32	31	31	33	38
Chromium, Cr	M	120	96.5	92	82	66
Manganese, Mn	M	7	8	—	—	—
Iron, Fe	M	99	83.5	72	56	34
Cobalt, Co	M	130	105	89	69	53
Nickel, Ni	M	113	94	83	67	71
Copper, Cu	M	420	403	395	381	354
Zinc, Zn	M	117	117	112	104	66
Gallium, Ga	M	43	41	33	45	—
Germanium, Ge	SC	113	67	46.5	29	17.5
Selenium (c-axis), Se	I	6.8	4.8	4.8	—	—
Rubidium, Rb	M	59	58	32	29	22
Yttrium, Y	M	16.5	17	—	—	—
Zirconium, Zr	M	26	23	22	21	23
Niobium, Nb	M	53	53	55	58	64
Molybdenum, Mo	M	145	139	135	127	113
Technetium, Tc	M	—	51	50	50	—
Ruthenium, Ru	M	123	117	115	108	98
Rhodium, Rh	M	156	151	147	137	—
Palladium, Pd	M	72	72	73	79	93
Silver, Ag	M	432	428	422	407	377
Cadmium, Cd	M	100	97	95	89	445
Indium, In	M	92	84	76	42	—
Tin, Sn	M	76	68	63	32	40
Antimony, Sb	M	33	25.5	22	19	27
Tellurium(c-axis), Te	I	5.1	3.6	2.9	2.4	6.3

7.8.3 Understanding the thermal conductivity of solids

Background theory

Thermal energy can be transferred through a solid in two quite distinct processes.

In the first process, heating a region of the solid causes an increase in the amplitude of atomic vibrations in that region. The mechanism of heat transfer is quite simple. Consider an atom A with a large vibrational amplitude, interacting with a neighbouring atom B with a smaller vibrational amplitude. A will tend to lose energy until the *average* energies per degree of freedom of A and B are equal. Since the *average* energy per degree of freedom is directly related to the temperature, the exchange of energy takes place until the local temperatures at A and B are equal. In terms of phonons (§7.2), the increased amplitude of atomic vibration is described as the creation of phonons, technically an increased number density of phonons $n_{ph}(T)$. These phonons then travel at the speed of sound to the colder regions of the lattice taking with them the excess energy of vibration from the hotter regions.

In the second process, which takes place only in metals, 'free' electrons can accept a small amount of thermal energy and then carry it to colder regions of the metal. Notice that in metals this second process takes place *in addition* to the first process and so, other things being equal, we would expect metals to have a higher thermal conductivity than insulators.

Both processes may be analysed in a manner analogous to that used to examine the thermal conductivity of gases (§5.4: Figure 7.48). In these analogies, the first process described above is analysed as a *gas of phonons* and the second process as a *gas of electrons*.

Detailed analysis

In what follows, we consider a 'gas' in which there is a temperature gradient, and consider 'particles' striking an area A perpendicular to the temperature gradient. This analysis could be applied to any gas. However, as we use the terms 'gas' and 'particle', you should bear in mind that at the end of this section, we will apply the formulae we develop first to a phonon gas, and then second to an electron gas.

Table 7.20 Thermal conductivity of a variety materials (WK^{-1} m^{-1}). The tables refer to metallic alloys, refractory materials, i.e. those suitable for use in high temperatures without degradation, and a selection of everyday materials.

	173.2K	273.2K	373.2K	573.2K	873.2K	973.2K	1473.2K
Brass (Cu70%,Zn30%)	89	106	128	146	—	—	—
Bronze (Cu90%,Sn10%)	—	53	60	80	—	—	—
Carbon steel	48	50	48.5	54.5	—	30.5	—
Silicon steel	—	25	28.5	31	—	28	—
Stainless steel	—	24.5	25	25.5	—	24.8	—
Alumina (Al$_2$O$_3$)	—	40	28	—	9.2	—	5.7
Beryllia (BeO)	—	300	213	—	61	—	22
Fire brick	—	—	—	—	1.1	—	1.3
Silica (SiO$_2$) fused quartz	—	1.33	1.48	—	2.4	—	—
Zirconia (ZrO$_2$)	—	—	1.8	—	2.0	—	2.2

Substance	κ (WK^{-1} m^{-1})	Substance	κ (WK^{-1} m^{-1})	Substance	κ (WK^{-1} m^{-1})
Brick wall	≈1	Porcelain	1.5	Glass wool	0.037
Plaster	≈0.13	Rubber	≈0.2	Cotton wool	0.03
Timber	≈ 0.15	Polystyrene	≈0.1	Sheep's wool	0.05
Balsa wood	≈0.06	Glass (crown)	1.1	Nylon	0.25
Paper	0.06	Glass (flint)	0.85	Epoxy resins	≈0.2
Cardboard	0.21	Glass (pyrex)	1.1	Cellular polystyrene	≈0.04

As we did for molecular gases in §5.5.2, we consider an area A within the gas perpendicular to a temperature gradient. On average, particles striking A have a travelled a mean free path λ_{mfp} without any 'collisions'. So they bring with them thermal energy characteristic of the region about λ_{mfp} distant. Now particles strike A from both the hotter side and the colder side, but there may be more particles striking A from one side or the other. Alternatively, the average energy they bring with them may be greater for particles arriving from one side or the other. In either case, there would be a net heat flux across A. In this analysis we make the following assumptions.

- The average speed of the particles, $\bar{v}$, is relatively weakly affected by temperature. This is true in both for the electron and the phonon gas we will consider, but would not be true a molecular gas.

- The number of particles crossing unit area per second is given by Equation 4.39 as $\frac{1}{4}n\bar{v}$, where n is the number density of the particles. We will consider that in general the number density of particles may change with temperature, i.e. $n = n(T)$.

- Each particle brings with it *on average* a small amount of energy, which may be passed on to other particles in a collision.

Combining these three assumptions, we estimate that the rate of energy flow due to particles crossing area A from the hotter side at $x + \mathrm{d}x$ is:

$$\left.\frac{\mathrm{d}Q}{\mathrm{d}t}\right|_{+} = \frac{1}{4}n(T+\Delta T)\bar{v} \times A \times \bar{E}_{\mathrm{th}}(T+\Delta T) \quad (7.99)$$

Similarly, the rate of energy flow due to particles crossing area A from the colder side at $x - \mathrm{d}x$ is:

$$\left.\frac{\mathrm{d}Q}{\mathrm{d}t}\right|_{-} = \frac{1}{4}n(T-\Delta T)\bar{v} \times A \times \bar{E}_{\mathrm{th}}(T-\Delta T) \quad (7.100)$$

The net rate of energy flow is therefore just the difference between Equations 7.100 and 7.99:

$$\left.\frac{\mathrm{d}Q}{\mathrm{d}t}\right|_{+} - \left.\frac{\mathrm{d}Q}{\mathrm{d}t}\right|_{-} = \frac{1}{4}n(T+\Delta T)\bar{v} \times A \times \bar{E}_{\mathrm{th}}(T+\Delta T)$$

$$- \frac{1}{4}n(T-\Delta T)\bar{v} \times A \times \bar{E}_{\mathrm{th}}(T-\Delta T)$$

$$(7.101)$$

Figure 7.49 Simplified illustration of the calculation of thermal conductivity of 'a gas'. This is the same as figure 5.20, but now we are applying it more generally to phonon and electron gases instead of just molecular gases.

The Figure shows three planes in 'a gas' perpendicular to a temperature gradient. The separation of the planes is λ_{mfp}, the mean free path of the particles. Thus particles that are travelling in the appropriate direction in either the top or the bottom plane will (probably) cross the central plane before colliding. Energy is carried across A in both directions, but *on average* more energy flows across A from the plane in the hotter region of the gas. The analysis of the thermal conductivity centres on the problem of evaluating the net energy flow across an area A.

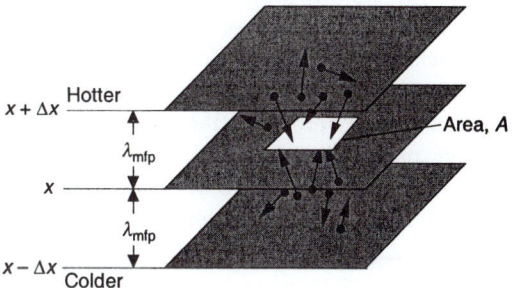

which simplifies to:

$$\frac{\mathrm{d}Q}{\mathrm{d}t} = \frac{1}{4}\bar{v}A\big[n(T+\Delta T)\bar{E}_{\mathrm{th}}(T+\Delta T)$$

$$- n(T-\Delta T)\bar{E}_{\mathrm{th}}(T-\Delta T)\big] \quad (7.102)$$

From the above equation, you may be able to see that heat is transferred because the temperature gradient causes a gradient in either:

- the number density of particles, or

- in their average energy, or

- both these terms.

Since gradients in either or both terms can give rise to heat flow, and since they occur as product, let's just consider gradients of *the product* of the two terms. Writing the product $n(T)\bar{E}_{\mathrm{th}}(T)$ as a single quantity, $\overline{nE}_{\mathrm{th}}(T)$ we have:

$$\frac{\mathrm{d}Q}{\mathrm{d}t} = \frac{1}{4}\bar{v}A\big[\overline{nE}_{\mathrm{th}}(T+\Delta T)$$

$$- \overline{nE}_{\mathrm{th}}(T-\Delta T)\big] \quad (7.103)$$

If we expand $\overline{nE}_{\mathrm{th}}(T)$ to first order we find:

$$\frac{dQ}{dt} = \frac{1}{4}\bar{v}A\left[\overline{nE}_{\text{th}}(T) + \Delta T\frac{d}{dT}(\overline{nE}_{\text{th}})\right.$$
$$\left. - \left(\overline{nE}_{\text{th}}(T) - \Delta T\frac{d}{dT}(\overline{nE}_{\text{th}})\right)\right] \quad (7.104)$$

Subtracting the two terms in Equation 7.104 yields:

$$\frac{dQ}{dt} = \frac{1}{4}\bar{v}A\left[2\Delta T\frac{d}{dT}(\overline{nE}_{\text{th}})\right] \quad (7.105)$$

Finally, we may substitute for ΔT using:

$$\Delta T = \frac{dT}{dx}\lambda_{\text{mfp}} \quad (7.106)$$

Rewriting Equation 7.105 using this substitution, we arrive at an expression for the heat flow in terms of the temperature gradient:

$$\frac{dQ}{dt} = \frac{1}{2}\bar{v}A\left[\frac{dT}{dx}\lambda_{\text{mfp}} \times \frac{d}{dT}(\overline{nE}_{\text{th}})\right] \quad (7.107)$$

If we rearrange this equation so that we can easily compare it with the standard form of Equation 7.98, we can derive an estimate for the thermal conductivity:

$$\frac{dQ}{dt} = \frac{1}{2}\bar{v}\underbrace{\left[\lambda_{\text{mfp}} \times \frac{d}{dT}(\overline{nE}_{\text{th}})\right]}_{\kappa}A\frac{dT}{dx}$$

$$\kappa = -\frac{1}{2}\bar{v}\lambda_{\text{mfp}}\frac{d}{dT}(\overline{nE}_{\text{th}}) \quad (7.108)$$

So our efforts above have arrived at an expression for the thermal conductivity of a gas that depends upon:

- the mean speed $\bar{v}$ of the particles of the gas
- the mean free path λ_{mfp} of the particles of the gas
- the *rate* at which the product $\overline{nE}_{\text{th}}$ changes with temperature.

Each factor in Equation 7.108 is difficult to estimate. However, the value of the last term $d(\overline{nE}_{\text{th}})/dT$ is the most problematic. For this reason, we restrict ourselves to trying to understand only the *temperature-dependence* of the thermal conductivity, rather than its absolute magnitude.

Let us now move on to see how Equation 7.108 can help us understand the temperature-dependence of the thermal conductivities, first in insulators and then in metals.

Electrical insulators: a phonon gas

For electrical insulators, there are no 'free' electrons to carry excess thermal energy. So we assume that it is the vibrations of the lattice alone that are responsible for heat transfer. We will estimate the temperature dependence of the thermal conductivity of a *phonon gas* by considering how Equation 7.108 applies in detail to such a gas.

The data given in Table 7.16 refer mainly to temperatures which are greater than (or at least of the order of) Θ_{D}, the Debye temperature (Table 7.12) and so we treat the three factors in Equation 7.108 as follows:

- We approximate the speed of all phonons to be c_{sound}, an average of the speeds of sound for different modes. The speed of sound in a solid is roughly temperature independent.
- We consider that at these high temperatures, the main source of scattering of phonons is other phonons. This is in fact correct, but it is rather a difficult matter to establish that it should be so. At low temperatures, when the amplitude of atomic vibrations is small, the main sources of phonon scattering are impurities, crystalline defects and surface irregularities. Considering the phonon gas in the same light as a molecular gas (§4.3.4), we expect that the mean free path for phonons will be inversely proportional to the number density of phonons, i.e.

$$\lambda_{\text{mfp}}^{\text{ph}} \propto \frac{1}{n_{\text{ph}}(T)} \quad (7.109)$$

- The number of phonons in each mode of vibration with energy E_{ph} is given by the Bose–Einstein factor :

$$n_{\text{ph}}(E_{\text{ph}},T) = \frac{1}{\exp(E_{\text{ph}}/k_{\text{B}}T) - 1}$$

$$(2.63^* \text{ and } 7.110)$$

When T is high enough, so that $k_{\text{B}}T$ is greater than the maximum phonon energy (which is

241

of the order of $k_B \Theta_D$), then we can expand the exponential to first order to give:

$$n_{ph}(E_{ph},T) = \frac{1}{\left[1 + E_{ph}/k_B T + ...\right] - 1}$$
$$\approx \frac{k_B T}{E_{ph}} \qquad (7.111)$$

So for all phonon modes, the product $\overline{nE}_{th}$ we introduced previously is given by:

$$\overline{nE}_{th} = n_{ph}(E_{ph},T)E_{ph} \approx k_B T \qquad (7.112)$$

which is linearly proportional to temperature. Since this happens for each individual phonon mode, the product $\overline{nE}_{th}$ involving the total phonon density must also increase linearly as the absolute temperature.

Let us combine the three factors above to work out just the temperature-dependence (rather than the absolute magnitude) of the thermal conductivity κ. Combining only the temperature-dependencies of these factors in Equation 7.108 we find:

$$\kappa = -\frac{1}{2} \times \underbrace{c_{sound}}_{constant} \times \underbrace{\lambda_{mfp}^{ph}}_{\frac{1}{constant \times T}} \times \underbrace{\frac{d}{dT}\left(\overline{nE}_{th}\right)}_{\frac{d}{dT}(constant \times T)}$$

$$\kappa(T) \propto constant \times \frac{1}{constant \times T} \times constant$$
$$(7.113)$$

which simplifies to:

$$\kappa(T) \propto \frac{1}{T} \qquad (7.114)$$

for insulators at $T > \Theta_D$.

So at high temperatures we expect to find that $\kappa(T) \propto T^{-1}$ i.e. that electrical insulators become poorer conductors as they are heated. This comes about because the increased density of phonons at higher temperatures shortens the phonon mean free path. This agrees (at least qualitatively) with the high-temperature data on insulators in Figure 7.48.

Insulators at low temperatures

At temperatures below the Debye temperature Θ_D, this trend does not continue. The thermal conductivity reaches a peak and then begins to get worse. This comes about because in this regime, the phonon density is reduced to such an extent that the dominant source of scattering is from impurities and defects. Since their density does not change with temperature, we find that λ_{mfp}^{ph} does not depend on temperature. The temperature dependence of the product $\overline{nE}_{th}$ also changes in this regime. It may be shown that well below Θ_D, $n_{ph} \propto T^3$ and $E_{ph} \propto T$. Equation 7.108 therefore becomes:

$$\kappa = -\frac{1}{2} \times \underbrace{c_{sound}}_{constant} \times \underbrace{\lambda_{mfp}^{ph}}_{constant} \times \underbrace{\frac{d}{dT}\left(\overline{nE}_{th}\right)}_{\frac{d}{dT}(constant \times T^4)}$$
$$(7.115)$$

$$\kappa(T) \propto constant \times constant \times constant \times T^3$$

So we expect the thermal conductivity of insulators to falls quite dramatically ($\propto T^3$) at temperatures well below the Debye temperature.

Metals: an electron gas

For metals, in addition to thermal conduction by phonons, the electron gas (§6.5) is able to conduct heat. Once again we note that the data of Table 7.16 refer mainly to temperatures which are greater than (or at least of the order of) Θ_D. Bearing this in mind, we treat the three factors in Equation 7.108 as follows:

- We approximate the speed of all electrons to the Fermi speed v_F. As in our discussion of electrical conductivity in a metal, only those electrons in quantum states with energies close to the Fermi energy E_F are able to accept thermal energy.

- We consider that at high temperatures the main source of scattering of electrons is phonons. (Notice that in the last section on insulators, the main source of phonon scattering was also phonons.) From the discussion of electrical conductivity, we concluded that the scattering time for electrons Δt varied inversely with absolute temperature (Equation 7.86). Since the speed of the electrons (v_F) is temperature-independent, we conclude that the mean free path of electrons will also vary

242

inversely as temperature, i.e.

$$\lambda^e_{mfp} = v_F \Delta t$$

$$\propto constant \times \frac{1}{T} \tag{7.116}$$

As we discussed in §7.6 on the electronic heat capacity of solids, only a small fraction of electrons are able to accept thermal energy from the lattice. This fraction is proportional to $k_B T$ and the typical energy of an electron in this fraction is $E_F + k_B T$. Notice that only the latter component of this energy may be given up in thermal interactions, and so the *thermal* energy $\overline{E}_{th}$ of electrons in the fraction is $k_B T$. Hence the product $n\overline{E}_{th}$ we introduced previously has the form:

$$n\overline{E}_{th} \propto \underbrace{n}_{\substack{constant \\ \times k_B T}} \times \underbrace{\overline{E}_{th}}_{k_B T} \tag{7.117}$$

In the above equation the first factor $k_B T$ arises from the *number* of electrons able to contribute to the thermal current and the second $k_B T$ factor arises because of the *thermal energy* of those which do contribute to the thermal current.

Combining only the temperature dependencies of these factors in the Equation 7.108 for κ:

$$\kappa = -\frac{1}{2} \times \underbrace{v_F}_{constant} \times \underbrace{\lambda^e_{mfp}}_{\substack{constant \\ \frac{1}{T}}} \times \underbrace{\frac{d}{dT}(n\overline{E}_{th})}_{\frac{d}{dT}(constant \times T^2)} \tag{7.118}$$

we arrive at:

$$\kappa(T) \propto constant \times \frac{1}{T} \times \frac{d}{dT}(constant \times T^2) \tag{7.119}$$

which simplifies to:

$$\kappa(T) \propto constant \tag{7.120}$$

for metals at $T > \Theta_D$.

Hence we conclude that at high temperatures we should expect to find κ is temperature-independent. This agrees (at least qualitatively)

with the high-temperature data on metals in Figure 7.48. We see however that the metallic data does show a small decrease with increasing temperature. We can understand this as being due to the fact that in metals, thermal conduction also occurs through the phonon gas described in the previous section. The thermal conductivity of the phonon gas is proportional to $1/T$, which explains the slight fall of κ with T. A rough estimate from Figure 7.48 indicates that at around room temperature, around 95% or so of the thermal conductivity of elemental metals is due to conduction by electrons.

Metals at low temperatures

As the temperature is lowered below the Debye temperature Θ_D, the thermal conductivity of metals does not stay roughly constant. There are two reasons for this. The first reason is that the thermal conductivity of the lattice gets better as the temperature is lowered. Now the total thermal conductivity that we measure is the 'parallel' sum of the electron and phonon contributions. Since phonon thermal conductivity increases as the temperature is lowered, so will the total thermal conductivity. The second reason is that the thermal conductivity of the electron gas itself changes. As the phonon density declines, a regime is reached where phonons are no longer the dominant source of scattering for electrons.

Instead, the main source of scattering arises from impurities and defects. Since their density does not change with temperature, we find that λ^e_{mfp} does not depend on temperature. The temperature dependence of the product $n\overline{E}_{th}$ does not change as the temperature is lowered because, as we have seen, temperatures around the Debye temperature barely disturb the free-electron gas from its configuration at absolute zero. We can thus rewrite Equation 7.118 as:

$$\kappa = -\frac{1}{2} \times \underbrace{v_F}_{constant} \times \underbrace{\lambda^e_{mfp}}_{constant} \times \underbrace{\frac{d}{dT}(n\overline{E}_{th})}_{\frac{d}{dT}(constant \times T^2)} \tag{7.121}$$

so we arrive at:

$$\kappa(T) \propto \text{constant} \times \text{constant} \times \frac{\text{d}}{\text{d}T}(\text{constant} \times T^2)$$

$$(7.122)$$

which simplifies to:

$$\kappa(T) \propto \text{constant} \times T \qquad (7.123)$$

So the thermal conductivity of the electron gas also falls at temperatures well below the Debye temperature.

Summary of temperature-dependency

Table 7.21 draws together the results from this section of our analysis.

Table 7.21 Summary of our predictions for the temperature dependence of the thermal conductivity of phonon and electron gases at high and low temperatures.

	Low temperature	High temperature
Phonon gas	KT^3	$1/T$
Electron gas	T	constant

The results of Table 7.21 do not permit a simple application to the data. This is because, for example, metals contain both phonon and electron gases, and we have not calculated the relative magnitudes of the conductivity due to each mechanism. However, we can make three general comments.

The first is that for both conduction mechanisms, it is phonon scattering that is the dominant cause of scattering at high temperatures, and impurity or defect scattering that is the dominant scattering term at very low temperatures. In this regime the lattice vibrates so violently that neither lattice waves or electrons can travel uninterrupted.

The second is that, except at the lowest temperatures, the thermal conductivities of both types of gases (as they exist in solids) are linked. Again, this is because phonons are the dominant source of scattering for both electron and phonon gases.

The final comment is that the change from low-temperature to high-temperature behaviour leads in general to a peak in the thermal conductivity of all materials. The temperature at which the peak occurs is very variable between materials. It is even variable amongst different samples of the same material dependent on the defect and impurity concentration in each particular sample. However typically the peak will occur at a few tens of kelvin.

Inhomogeneous materials

The final questions raised by the data concern the order of magnitude of the data in Table 7.19 and 7.20 when compared with those of gases in Table 5.11. Given that we have analysed solids as merely containers for electron and phonon gases, there was considerable similarity in the approach taken here and in §5.5. This similarity of approach allows us to identify immediately the simple reason why typical solid thermal conductivities (≈ 10 W K^{-1} m^{-1}) are so much greater than those of gases ($\approx 10^{-2}$ W K^{-1} m^{-1}). It is simply that the density of atoms present in a solid is roughly 1000 times greater than a molecular gas.

However in *inhomogeneous* materials such as paper or wool, gases (usually air) may be trapped within a solid. Such materials may have a thermal conductivity which differs only slightly from that of a gas. This low thermal conductivity arises even when the conductivity of the solid itself (the individual wool or paper fibres) may be relatively good. It arises because the material is constituted so that heat must take an extremely long path through the substance, often with an extremely small effective cross-sectional area. For example, in wool, heating one end of an individual wool fibre will quickly transfer heat along the whole length of the fibre. However, each fibre only touches its neighbouring fibres at a few points. This dramatically reduces the effective cross-sectional area across which heat is transported. If the reduction in thermal conduction is sufficiently large, then we may actually neglect the heat flowing through the fibres of the inhomogeneous substance. In this case the weak thermal conduction through the trapped gas in the material may prove the limiting thermal conduction process.

7.9 Optical properties

7.9.1 Introduction

The optical properties of solids are extremely varied: from strongly absorbent to transparent to strongly reflecting. This indicates considerable variety in the way solids respond to oscillating electric fields with frequencies between 400×10^{12} Hz (red light) and 1000×10^{12} Hz (blue light). The optical properties of solids are rather difficult to characterise succinctly, since typically this requires a specification of their absorbtion and reflection across the optical frequency range. However for many purposes, substances may be characterised by two parameters: the *refractive index* and the *absorption coefficient*. In general, these two parameters are related to one another, but in our analysis we will not emphasise this links, instead looking at each parameter independently.

7.9.2 Data on the optical properties of metals

Metal samples thicker than roughly 10 nm are essentially opaque to visible light and are strongly reflective. With the exceptions of copper and gold, all the metallic elements have the same 'silvery' colour, i.e. they are strongly reflective at all optical wavelengths.

Table 7.22 The reflectivity of polished surfaces of several metals. The figures represent averages across the optical spectrum.

	Reflectivity (%)
Steel	58
Aluminium	92
Silver	98
Copper	67
Gold	81

7.9.3 Data on the optical properties of insulators

The refractive index of a transparent substance is related to the speed of light v in the substance by:

$$n_{light} = \frac{c}{v}. \tag{7.124}$$

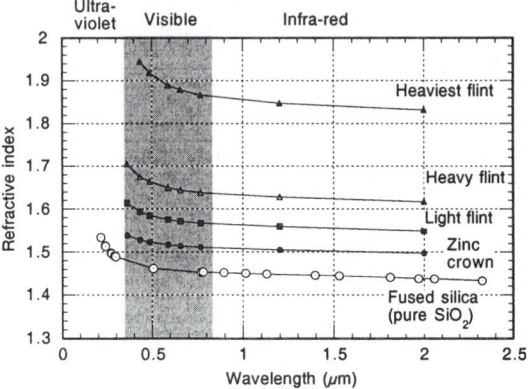

Figure 7.50 The refractive index of some optical glasses as a function of wavelength. The shaded region corresponds to the visible region of the spectrum. Longer wavelengths are described as infra-red, and shorter wavelengths as ultra-violet.

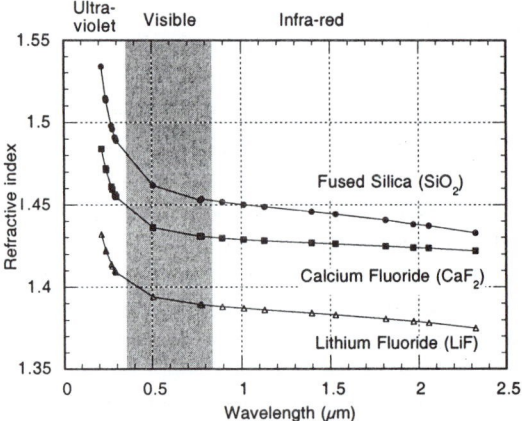

Figure 7.51 The refractive index of a three transparent insulators as a function of wavelength. The SiO_2 curve is also plotted on Figure 7.49 for comparison. The shaded region corresponds to the visible region of the spectrum. The longer wavelengths are therefore in the infra-red region of the spectrum, and the shorter wavelengths in the ultra-violet region.

where c is the speed of light in a vacuum. The symbol n_{light} is used instead of the more usual n to prevent confusion with the use of n to represent the number density of atoms. The measured refractive index n_{light} of various transparent substances is plotted as a function of wavelength in Figures 7.50 and 7.51. The figures show that n_{light}

245

increases (i.e. the light travels slower) at shorter (bluer) wavelengths. The glasses in Figure 7.49 are composed of mainly SiO_2 with a variety of oxides, typically barium oxide (BaO) or lead oxide (PbO), added at various concentrations. The glasses shown represent the range of refractive indices available for optical designers. The high refractive index glasses tend to tarnish (oxidise) quickly, which means they are not used unless they are essential to an optical design. They also tend to absorb in the blue, which makes them look slightly 'yellowish'. The exception to this rule is carbon (in the form of diamond) which (as you may know) is completely transparent and yet has a refractive index of 2.4. Figures 7.50 and 7.51 show that in general the refractive index is greater for shorter wavelengths than longer wavelengths. Interestingly, the *rate* at which the refractive index increases with wavelength also increases as the wavelength is reduced.

The questions raised by our preliminary examination of the experimental data on the optical properties of solids are:

- Why are some insulators transparent to visible light? However, light travels through these materials with a speed between 50% and 70% of its speed in free space.
- Why does the speed of light in these materials depends on the wavelength of light and become slower as the wavelength decreases?
- Why are metals highly reflective?

7.9.4 Understanding the data on the optical properties of solids

We have considered previously what happens to metals and insulators when they are subject to *static* electric fields (§7.7). We saw that:

- In metals, a static electric field causes a flow of electrons, which are essentially free to move through the metal. The current was limited by scattering, which occurred after roughly 10^{-14} seconds.
- In insulators, (aside from a tiny fraction of mobile electrons) most electrons remain attached to their 'parent' atoms or molecules. However the charge within each atom or molecule becomes displaced or *polarised*.

Example 7.22

A 10 W laser beam is focussed to a spot with a radius of 10 μm at the surface of a silver-coated glass mirror. Will the mirror surface be damaged?

It is interesting to note the intensity of *optical* radiation intensity at the beam spot is:

$$I_{\text{optical}} = \frac{10}{\pi\left(10\times10^{-6}\right)^2} = 3.18\times10^{10} \ \text{W m}^{-2}$$

so this is certainly an intense beam. The reflectivity of the mirror is 98% and so the power dissipated in the mirror is:

$$P_{\text{thermal}} = \left(1-0.98\right)P_{\text{optical}} = 0.02\times10 \ \text{W} = 0.2 \ \text{W}$$

This is not a great deal of power, but the beam is highly concentrated, and so the temperature might rise significantly at the mirror surface. The geometry makes the exact problem difficult to solve, but if we imagine the situation shown below, where the beam delivers its power to the end of a rod-shaped sample, then we can calculate the temperature gradient along this rod fairly easily using Equation 7.98 $dQ/dt = -\kappa A dT/dx$. The two calculations will probably differ only by a factor of the order unity.

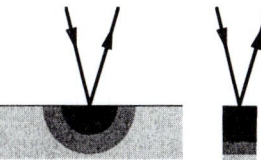

For the rod we write:

$$A = \pi r^2 = \pi\left(10^{-5}\right)^2 = 3.142\times10^{-10} \ \text{m}^2$$

We then note that κ for glass from Table 7.17 is roughly $1 \ \text{W K}^{-1} \ \text{m}^{-1}$. Substituting $dQ/dt = 0.2$ W we find

$$\frac{dT}{dx} = -\frac{1}{\kappa A}\frac{dQ}{dt} = \frac{1}{1\times3.142\times10^{-10}}\times0.2$$

$$= 637\times10^6 \ \text{K m}^{-1}$$

If we assume that 1 mm or so below the surface the temperature is around room temperature, then the temperature at the mirror surface would be approximately:

$$\frac{T-T_0}{\Delta x} \approx \frac{dT}{dx} = 637\times10^6 \ \text{K m}^{-1}$$

$$T \approx T_0 + \Delta x\left[\frac{dT}{dx}\right] \approx 20 \ °C + 10^{-3}\times637\times10^6$$

$$\approx 630000 \ °C$$

Even allowing for changes to any of the parameters in this calculation, it is clear that such a beam could not be bounced of any solid surface at this spot size without vapourising it.

At optical frequencies the distinction between metallic and insulating response remains, but now the currents and polarisations which are caused by the electric field of a light wave are *oscillating* currents and *oscillating* polarisations. In the analyses which follow we assume (correctly) that the electric component of the electromagnetic field affects atoms much more strongly than the magnetic component of the field.

7.9.5 Insulators

In considering the optical properties of insulators, we will neglect the tiny fraction of mobile electrons within the insulator. We consider that the main effect of light is to cause oscillations of the electrons trapped in the valence states around each atom or ion. And amazingly, that is just about all we need to assume to understand a great deal about the optical properties of insulators.

Example 7.23

Snell's law relates the deviation of a light ray at an interface to the refractive indices of the material of either side of the interface.

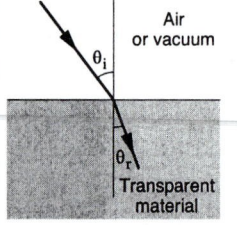 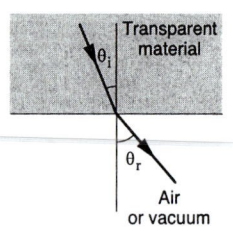

If the refractive indices of the materials on the incident and refracted sides of the interface are n_i and n_r respectively, then Snell's law predicts that the incident angle θ_i and the refracted angle θ_r are related by:

$$\frac{\sin \theta_r}{\sin \theta_i} = \frac{n_i}{n_r}$$

For blue light ($\lambda \approx 0.4$ µm) incident on a glass surface at 45°, work out both the angle of refraction and angle of deviation $(\theta_i - \theta_r)$ of the light if the glass surface is made from (a) crown glass, (b) heavy flint glass and (c) heaviest flint glass. Repeat the exercise for red light ($\lambda \approx 0.7$µm).

Reading from Figure 7.49 we can assemble the following table of approximate refractive indices:

	Crown glass	Heavy flint glass	Heaviest flint glass
Red light	1.51	1.63	1.88
Blue light	1.53	1.68	1.94

So for crown glass if we substitute into Snell's law we get:

$$\frac{\sin \theta_r}{\sin(45°)} = \frac{1}{1.51} = 0.6623$$

where we have assumed that the refractive index of air is ≈ 1 (Table 5.17). Solving for θ_r we find:

$$\sin \theta_r = 0.6623 \times \sin(45°) = 0.4683$$

$$\theta_r = \sin^{-1}(0.4683)$$

$$= 27.93°$$

This situation is illustrated below, where it is clear that the angle of deviation is $45° - 27.93° = 17.07°$.

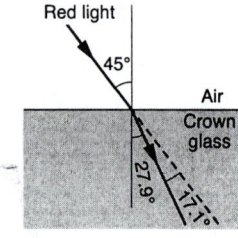

Repeating this calculation for the other glasses yields the table of angles of deviation:

	Crown glass	Heavy flint glass	Heaviest flint glass
Red light	17.07°	19.29°	22.91°
Blue light	17.47°	20.11°	23.62°
Difference	0.40°	0.82°	0.71°

The *difference* between the angles through which red and blue light are refracted is calculated in the last row of the table. Notice that the glass with the greatest angle of deviation (the heaviest flint glass) does not produces the greatest *dispersion* between the red and blue light (the heavy flint glass).

We consider the electrons to occupy a 'shell' with mass M and electric charge Q distributed around the atom. We assume that the electric field of light wave causes this 'shell' to move rigidly with respect to the rest of the atom. This amounts to assuming that the electric fields *within* the shell (which give rise to its structure and shape) are much stronger than the external field of the light wave. This is true for all but the most intense laser light sources, which can give rise to so-called *nonlinear* optical behaviour. We note also that the 'shell' will have a much smaller mass than an atom as a whole.

At the position of an atom, the electric field due to the light is given by $E = E_o \cos(\omega t)$. So the shell experiences a periodic force $F = QE_o \cos(\omega t)$. In addition to this force, there is a restoring force due to the internal electric fields within the atom. We do not know the precise form of this force, but we do know that the force acts to restore the charge shell to its initial position around the atom. We assume that the force has the form $-Kx$, where K is the 'spring constant' acting to restore the shell of charge to its optimum position, and x is the displacement of the charge shell from its optimum position. Newton's second law of motion states that:

$$F = ma \qquad (2.19^*)$$

which in our case amounts to:

$$\overbrace{-Kx + QE_o \cos(\omega t)}^{F} = M\overbrace{\frac{d^2x}{dt^2}}^{a} \qquad (7.125)$$

Since this is a differential equation we must assume a solution and then show that our solution is appropriate. So assuming that the displacement of the charge x is given by:

$$x = x_o \cos(\omega t + \phi) \qquad (7.126)$$

where x_o is the amplitude of the charge displacement, and ϕ is the phase difference between the charge oscillations and the oscillations of the light field. From Equation 7.126 we can work out that:

$$\frac{dx}{dt} = -\omega x_o \sin(\omega t + \phi) \qquad (7.127)$$

Figure 7.52 A simple model of the polarisation of an atom in an applied electric field. (a) The electron shells around an atom are much lower in mass than the nucleus. (b) & (c): When the direction of the applied electric field is reversed, the heavy nucleus moves much less than the charged electron shells.

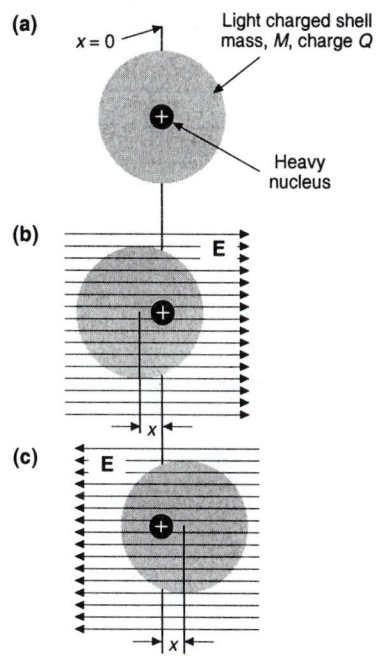

and so:

$$\frac{d^2x}{dt^2} = -\omega^2 x_o \cos(\omega t + \phi) \qquad (7.128)$$
$$= -\omega^2 x$$

Substituting 7.126 and 7.128 into 7.125 we arrive at:

$$-Kx_o \cos(\omega t + \phi) + QE_o \cos(\omega t) = -M\omega^2 x_o \cos(\omega t + \phi) \qquad (7.129)$$

We can now rearrange this to obtain an expression for x_o. First we write:

$$QE_o \cos(\omega t) = Kx_o \cos(\omega t + \phi) - M\omega^2 x_o \cos(\omega t + \phi) \qquad (7.130)$$

$$QE_o \cos(\omega t) = x_o \cos(\omega t + \phi)\left[K - M\omega^2\right] \qquad (7.131)$$

and finally we arrive at an expression for x_0:

$$x_0 = \frac{QE_0}{K - M\omega^2}\left[\frac{\cos(\omega t)}{\cos(\omega t + \phi)}\right] \qquad (7.132)$$

This equation describes a situation in which the amplitude of the charge displacement grows resonantly large when the frequency (colour) of the light is such that $K = M\omega^2$. The theory as we have developed it predicts (incorrectly) that the charge displacement will be infinite when $K = M\omega^2$. This is because we have neglected the *damping term* in our differential equation (Equation 7.125) (for further details see §2.3.2 on the simple harmonic oscillator). Because of this difficulty we must only apply Equation 7.132 at frequencies that are much less than the resonant frequency. We note however that the amplitude of oscillation will still grow large when $K = M\omega^2$, but that the actual amplitude of the oscillations will depend on the extent of damping of the charge oscillations.

Low frequency approximation

As long as we work well below the resonant frequency, the phase difference ϕ between the forcing field and the charge displacement stays small (Figure 2.6), and the time-dependent factor in brackets in Equation 7.132 stays close to unity. With this proviso, we write the amplitude of the charge oscillations as:

$$x_0 \approx \frac{QE_0}{K - M\omega^2} \qquad (7.133)$$

The resonant frequency is reached when ω satisfies the condition $K = M\omega^2$, i.e. when $\omega = \omega_0$ given by:

$$\omega_0 = \sqrt{\frac{K}{M}} \qquad (7.134)$$

Substituting 7.121 into 7.120 we arrive at:

$$x_0 \approx \frac{QE_0}{M(\omega_0^2 - \omega^2)} \qquad (7.135)$$

If this is the amplitude of the oscillations of charge displacement, then the amplitude of the electric dipole moment caused by this displacement is:

$$p_0 = Qx_0 \approx \frac{Q^2 E_0}{M(\omega_0^2 - \omega^2)} \qquad (7.136)$$

If we recall the definition of the polarisability, α, of an atom (Equations 2.12 and 5.101):

$$p_0 = \alpha E_0 \qquad (7.137)$$

then by comparing 7.136 and 7.137 we can derive an expression for the polarisability:

$$\alpha \approx \frac{Q^2}{M(\omega_0^2 - \omega^2)} \qquad (7.138)$$

Recalling that the approximations we have made restrict the theory to frequencies such that $\omega^2 \ll \omega_0^2$, we can write the molecular polarisability at such low frequencies as:

$$\alpha \approx \frac{Q^2}{M\omega_0^2} \text{ when } \omega \ll \omega_0 \qquad (7.139)$$

Notice that even at low frequencies, the molecular polarisability α still depends on the value of the resonant frequency ω_0.

The dielectric constant and the refractive index

Recalling from §5.6.2 Equation 5.104 that the dielectric constant of a substance consisting of n non-interacting molecules per unit volume may be expressed as:

$$\varepsilon - 1 = \frac{n\alpha}{\varepsilon_0}. \qquad (7.140)$$

Substituting from Equation 7.139 for α this becomes:

$$\varepsilon - 1 = \frac{nQ^2}{\varepsilon_0 M\omega_0^2}. \qquad (7.141)$$

As mentioned in §2.3.3, the refractive index of a medium may be expressed as:

$$n_{\text{light}} = \frac{c}{v} \approx \sqrt{\varepsilon}$$

$$n_{\text{light}}^2 \approx \varepsilon \qquad (7.142)$$

where ε is the dielectric constant. Substituting for ε from Equation 7.141 we find:

$$n_{\text{light}}^2 = 1 + \frac{nQ^2}{\varepsilon_o M \omega_o^2} \qquad (7.143)$$

This expression predicts the 'low frequency' value of the refractive index in terms of some simple quantities and ω_o the frequency of the resonant vibration of the electron shell within the atom.

Finding the resonant frequency

We can now solve for ω_o in terms of the experimental values of the 'low frequency' value of the refractive index. Rearranging Equation 7.143 as an expression first for ω_o:

$$\omega_o = \sqrt{\frac{nQ^2}{\varepsilon_o M(n_{\text{light}}^2 - 1)}} \qquad (7.144)$$

and then for f_o, the frequency rather than the angular frequency:

$$f_o = \frac{1}{2\pi} \sqrt{\frac{Q^2}{\varepsilon_o M}} \sqrt{\frac{n}{(n_{\text{light}}^2 - 1)}} \qquad (7.145)$$

Finally we can derive an expression for the wavelength of light which would resonantly excite the atom $\lambda_o = c / f_o$:

$$\lambda_o = \frac{c}{f_o}$$
$$= \frac{2\pi c \sqrt{\varepsilon_o M}}{Q} \sqrt{\frac{n_{\text{light}}^2 - 1}{n}} \qquad (7.146)$$

Evaluating the pre-factor numerically for an electron shell with a single electron this evaluates to:

$$\frac{2\pi c \sqrt{\varepsilon_o M}}{Q} = \frac{2\pi \times 3.0 \times 10^8 \sqrt{8.85 \times 10^{-12} \times 9.1 \times 10^{-31}}}{1.6 \times 10^{-19}} \qquad (7.147)$$
$$= 3.34 \times 10^7$$

$$\lambda_o = 3.34 \times 10^7 \sqrt{\frac{n_{\text{light}}^2 - 1}{n}} \quad \text{metre} \qquad (7.148)$$

where n_{light} is the refractive index and n is the number density of atoms. According to our simple theory, Equation 7.148 should apply to all solids, liquids or gases which have just a single electron which can be polarised.

250

Example 7.24 shows that we can understand the range of experimental values of refractive index by assuming that atoms contain charged 'shells' which have resonances in the ultra-violet region of the spectrum (λ_o from 0.1 μm to 0.3 μm). Recall that visible light has a wavelength range from roughly 0.35 μm (violet) to roughly 0.77 μm (red).

The questions raised by the data

In the light of theory outlined above, let us look at the questions raised by our examination of the data in turn:

The value of the refractive index

The reason that insulators are transparent to visible light is that there are no mechanisms for absorbing the light within the insulator. This is because the resonant frequencies of electron shells typically lie in the ultra-violet region of the spectrum. Thus the amplitude of the charge oscillations induced by the (relatively) low-frequency oscillations of the electric field of the light wave are relatively small.

In a 'pure' glass (mainly SiO_2) the resonant frequencies of electron shells lie in the far ultra-violet. However, impurities with many electron shells (such as lead) have lower resonant frequencies, closer to the visible region of the spectrum. As Equation 7.143 suggests, lowering ω_o has the effect of increasing the refractive index and so adding such impurities to a glass increases the

---

Example 7.24

A typical number density of atoms in a solid is $n_o \approx 5 \times 10^{28}$ m^{-3}. For solids with refractive indices $n_{\text{light}} = 1.2$, 1.5 or 2, evaluate the expected value of the wavelength of radiation corresponding to the resonant frequency of the charges within the solid.

Using Equation 7.148 for $n \approx 5 \times 10^{28}$ m^{-3} and $n_{\text{light}} = 1.2$ we write:

$$\lambda_o = 3.34 \times 10^7 \sqrt{\frac{(1.2)^2 - 1}{5 \times 10^{28}}}$$

which evaluates to $\lambda_o = 0.099 \times 10^{-6}$ m. Similarly we find for $n_{\text{light}} = 1.5$, $\lambda_o = 0.167 \times 10^{-6}$ m and for $n_{\text{light}} = 2$, we find $\lambda_o = 0.259 \times 10^{-6}$ m.

overall refractive index of the mixture. However the refractive index cannot be increased indefinitely.

If the resonant frequency is lowered too much, then the substance will start to absorb light at frequencies around ω_0. The theory outlined above has ignored the role of absorption, but we can see fairly directly how this absorption occurs. If the oscillations of a charge shell grow large, then nearby atoms will be set in motion by their electrical interactions with the oscillating charge shell. This dissipates the energy of oscillation in the form of lattice waves (phonons). In addition, an oscillating charge radiates electromagnetic energy at the frequency at which it is oscillating in a process known as *Rayleigh scattering* (§5.8.3). Both processes limit the useable refractive index of a transparent substance to $n < \approx 2$. The exception to this limit is diamond.

The origin of diamond's exceptional optical properties lie in the very rigid covalent bonds between carbon atoms and the relatively light mass of the carbon atoms themselves. In itself the refractive index of diamond ($n_{\text{light}} \approx 2.4$) is not uniquely high. *Kaye and Laby* list several materials with a refractive index in this range. For example, strontium titanate has a refractive index of 2.42 at a wavelength of 0.56 μm. What *is* unique is the combination of this high refractive index with low absorbtion. Optically, diamond is clear whereas strontium titanate, though transparent, is slightly yellowish. The reason for the low absorbtion is complex, but roughly speaking it is because of the exceptionally high energy required to create a *phonon* in diamond. This high energy is reflected in the exceptionally high Debye temperature of diamond (≈ 2000 K) and the amazingly fast speed of sound waves ($\approx 18,350$ m s^{-1}). These in turn derive from the light mass of the atoms and the exceptionally rigid nature of the C–C covalent bonding network.

Quantum mechanics

In discussing the dynamics of a 'charged shell' inside an atom under the action of an electromagnetic field, we need to be aware that the laws of quantum mechanics limit the realm in which the classical approach we have taken is applicable. In particular it is important to understand that the process that we have called *resonance*, using our classical vocabulary, describes a process which is described in a quantum mechanical vocabulary as a *transition between quantum states* (Figure 7.53). Thus the 'resonances' which occur in the ultra-violet are properly described as transitions between quantum states by electrons in the outer parts of the atom.

Infra-red response

The shells of charge *within* each atom of a substance are not the only charged objects that can move in response to the oscillating electric field in a light wave: the ions themselves can move as whole. However, the process in which whole ions move in response to an oscillating electric field occurs at much lower frequencies. Equation 7.148 gives the wavelength of the radiation which will cause resonance in a bound particle of mass M and charge Q. Example 7.24 shows that λ_0 for an electron lies in the ultra-violet region of the spectrum. However although an ion has a similar magnitude of charge to an electron, an ionic mass may be 10^4 times greater than an electron mass. Substituting $M \approx 10^4 m_e$ in Equation 7.148 we find:

$$\lambda_0 \approx 3.34 \times 10^9 \sqrt{\frac{n_{\text{light}}^2 - 1}{n}} \qquad (7.149)$$

Figure 7.53 Classical and quantum mechanical description of resonance in a simple harmonic oscillator. (a) Classically, the amplitude of an oscillation grows dramatically when the oscillator is subject to a force at frequency $\omega - \omega_0 = \sqrt{(K/M)}$ (b) Quantum mechanically, when $\omega = \omega_0$ photons with energy $\hbar\omega$ are absorbed and the oscillator makes transitions between its quantum states.

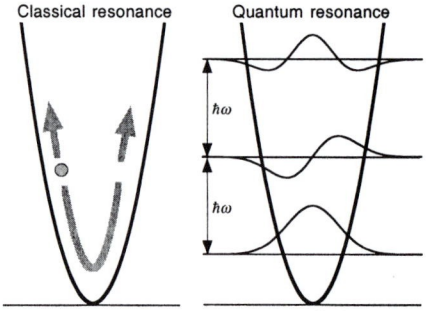

Classical resonance   Quantum resonance

Assuming that the refractive index and the number density of ions are similar to those in Example 7.24, then the resonant wavelength is 100 times longer i.e. of the order of 10 μm. Such wavelengths lie far into the infra-red part of the electromagnetic spectrum. Thus at optical frequencies (of the order 10 to 100 times greater than the resonant frequencies corresponding to ionic vibration) the electric field oscillates so quickly that the relatively heavy ions have no time to respond before the field reverses and a new oscillation begins. Thus at optical frequencies only the electrons are light enough to oscillate in response to field and so we may ignore the polarisability of the lattice in our considerations.

Aside: the visible range of the spectrum

The visible range of the electromagnetic spectrum lies in between the region in which ionic vibrations absorb radiation (infra-red), and that in which electronic vibrations within atoms absorb radiation (ultra-violet). This is not a coincidence. The considerations above apply equally to electrons and ions in molecules in the gaseous, liquid or solid phases. Our eyes have evolved so as to be useful to us. They would be of precious little use if the gas in which we lived, and the fluid in which we evolved, were opaque. We have evolved sensitivity in the range of the electromagnetic spectrum in which many substances are transparent.

Variation of n_{light} with wavelength

The dependence of the refractive index on wavelength arises quite naturally from the equation for $\alpha(\omega)$. Rearranging Equation 7.138:

$$\alpha(\omega) \approx \frac{Q^2}{M\omega_o^2\left[1-\left(\omega/\omega_o\right)^2\right]} \quad (7.150)$$

and expanding the bracket to first order in ω/ω_o we obtain:

$$\alpha(\omega) \approx \underbrace{\frac{Q^2}{M\omega_o^2}}_{\alpha(\omega=0)}\left[1+\left(\omega/\omega_o\right)^2+...\right] \quad (7.151)$$

This should be valid as long as $\omega \ll \omega_o$. Comparing this with Equation 7.126 for the zero-

frequency polarisability, we can write:

$$\alpha(\omega) \approx \alpha(\omega=0)\left[1+\left(\omega/\omega_o\right)^2+...\right] \quad (7.152)$$

Finally, we can rearrange this as an expression for λ to yield:

$$\alpha(\lambda) \approx \alpha(\lambda=\infty)\left[1+\left(\lambda_o/\lambda\right)^2+...\right] \quad (7.153)$$

This revised wavelength-dependent polarisability $\alpha(\lambda)$ feeds through to an expression for the refractive index in the same way that the infinite wavelength polarisability $\alpha(\lambda=\infty)$ fed through to the infinite-wavelength refractive index (Equations 7.137 to 7.143). We thus find the wavelength-dependent refractive index is given by:

$$n_{light}(\lambda) \approx n_{light}(\lambda=\infty)\left[1+\left(\lambda_o/\lambda\right)^2\right]$$
$$\approx n_{light}(\lambda=\infty) + n_{light}(\lambda=\infty)\lambda_o^2 \times \frac{1}{\lambda^2}$$
$$(7.154)$$

This predicts that if we plot $n_{light}(\lambda)$ as function of $1/\lambda^2$ then we should expect a straight-line variation with intercept $n_{light}(\lambda=\infty)$ and slope $\lambda_o^2 n_{light}(\lambda=\infty)$. Figure 7.54 shows the refractive index data from Figure 7.50 plotted versus $1/\lambda^2$. We see that the data conform rather well to straight lines and that analysis of the slopes predicts similar values of λ_o to those inferred from an analysis of the $n_{light}(\lambda=\infty)$ theory. Of the two predictions for λ_o the slope analysis is to be preferred. This is because in order to evaluate Equation 7.148 we needed to assume a certain number of electrons per shell, a number which cannot be accurately estimated without some detailed knowledge of the charge distribution of the substance under examination.

Before proceeding, it is worth reflecting on the astonishing results predicted here. Based on little more than the theory of a harmonic oscillator and Coulomb's law we have plausibly explained the optical properties of glasses! The tiny masses in-

Figure 7.54 The data of Figure 7.50 re-plotted to show the refractive index of various glasses plotted as a function $1/\lambda^2$. The straight lines are least-squares fits to the data. The equations of the lines and the value of λ_0 inferred from the slope of the lines is given in the inset. In Example 7.24 we found that for $n_{light}(\infty) \approx 1.5$ implied $\lambda_0 \approx 0.167$ μm whereas from this data we deduce $0.059\mu m$. This factor 3 difference arises because in Example 7.24 we assumed just one electron per atom and used only an approximation for the electron density. However both analyses are simplified and *neither* should be trusted absolutely.

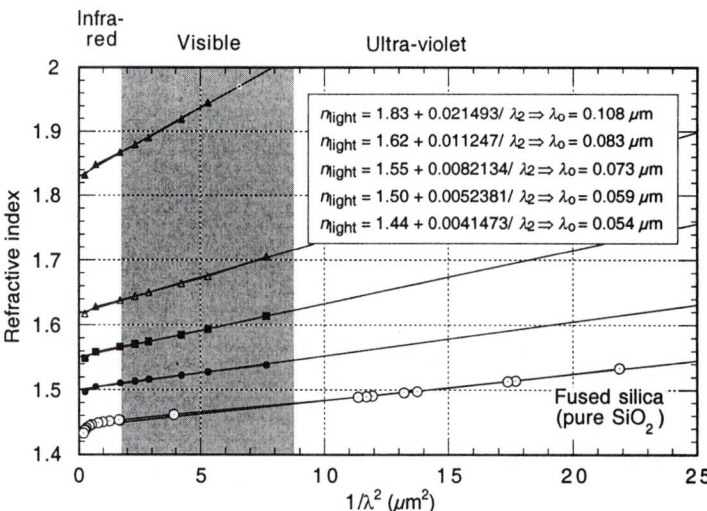

Inset equations:
$$n_{light} = 1.83 + 0.021493/\lambda_2 \Rightarrow \lambda_0 = 0.108\ \mu m$$
$$n_{light} = 1.62 + 0.011247/\lambda_2 \Rightarrow \lambda_0 = 0.083\ \mu m$$
$$n_{light} = 1.55 + 0.0082134/\lambda_2 \Rightarrow \lambda_0 = 0.073\ \mu m$$
$$n_{light} = 1.50 + 0.0052381/\lambda_2 \Rightarrow \lambda_0 = 0.059\ \mu m$$
$$n_{light} = 1.44 + 0.0041473/\lambda_2 \Rightarrow \lambda_0 = 0.054\ \mu m$$

Fused silica (pure SiO_2)

volved in atomic size oscillators have shifted the resonant frequencies to the optical regime, but the basic results still apply. As long as we consider regions of the spectrum where resonances (electronic transitions between quantum states) are absent, then the classical model will serve us well.

Another way of looking at things

Our simple analysis has allowed us to understand a great deal about the optical properties of insulators. As we saw in §5.8.3, there is another way of looking at these phenomena. There we considered the *Rayleigh scattering* from a gas. This scattering arose because each small region of a gas could be considered as an oscillating electrical dipole radiator. The radiation from each region was emitted as a spherical wave, and the resultant scattering from the gas was the sum of these spherical waves.

In a gas, the *amplitude* of each spherical wave differed slightly from one region of the gas to another. This was because the random nature of the positions of the gas molecules gave rise to small density fluctuations. The amplitude differences caused the radiation scattered at right angles to the wave to just fail to cancel.

In a solid, we can apply exactly the same model. The oscillating dipole moments induced by the wave have a much greater amplitude in a solid

than in a gas, because of the higher density. Thus, the amplitude of the scattered waves are also much larger. However, the regular arrangement of atoms in a solid, and the much higher density, lead to much smaller *fluctuations* in density from one region (of volume $\approx \lambda^3$) to the next. This homogeneity reduces the Rayleigh scattering in solids to a level low enough to permit light to travel through a kilometres of optical fibre with only a few per cent reduction in amplitude. However, in the direction *parallel* to the direction of the light wave, the scattered radiation always adds in phase. It may be shown that it is the addition of a slightly phase-shifted scattered wave to the original wave that leads to the reduction in the speed of light through the solid.

7.9.5 Metals

The main question raised by our examination of the optical properties of metals is why metals are highly optically reflective. We will consider this question in a largely qualitative manner.

Insulators can be optically transparent if the charges within the insulators are bound sufficiently tightly that their resonant frequencies lie well into the ultra-violet region of the spectrum. If the resonant frequency is too close to the optical region of the spectrum, then visible light will be

253

able to cause relatively large charge oscillations. These oscillations can dissipate the energy of the wave either as phonons or photons. In contrast, it is easy for the electric charges within metals to move in response to the electric field of the light wave. We envisage reflection as a three stage process.

Stage 1: The skin depth

In the first stage (Figure 7.55 (a)) the incoming electromagnetic wave is heavily damped as it enters the metal. This damping occurs as the electric field does work in accelerating the many free electrons in the surface of the metal. The more free electrons, the greater the damping of the wave. The electric field decays over a distance known as the *skin depth* δ, related to the conductivity σ of the metal by (*Bleaney and Bleaney*):

$$\delta = \sqrt{\frac{2}{\mu_0 \sigma \omega}}.$$ (7.155)

Substituting for μ_0 yields:

$$\delta \approx \sqrt{\frac{2}{4\pi \times 10^{-7} \times 2\pi}} \sqrt{\frac{1}{f\sigma}}$$

$$= 503 \sqrt{\frac{1}{f\sigma}} \quad \text{metre}$$ (7.156)

Notice that the damping of the wave is *not* due to dissipation of the electrons energy into heat. If that were so then the skin depth would get shorter in more resistive substances, but as Equation 7.156 shows, δ behaves in exactly the opposite manner.

For aluminium, $\sigma = 4 \times 10^7$ S at around room temperature (Table 7.13) and for (say) green light $f \approx 5 \times 10^{14}$ Hz, Equation 7.156 predicts a skin depth $\delta \approx 4$ nm. Since the wavelength of light with this frequency is of the order of 600 nm we see that light penetrates the metal for only a small fraction of its wavelength.

Stage 2: Current flow

In the second stage (Figure 7.55 (b)) we consider the oscillating currents which flow in the small region of depth δ in which the electric field is not zero. We noted in §7.7.3 that the mean time before

scattering in a metal was around 10^{-14} s. However, in this time a light wave makes ≈ 10 oscillations. So the currents induced at the surface of a metal are not strongly damped by electron scattering.

Figure 7.55 The processes underlying reflection of light from a metallic surface. (a) The incoming electromagnetic wave is strongly damped as it enters the metal. The length over which the field decays is known as the skin depth, δ, and is related to the conductivity, σ, of the metal as shown in Equation 7.155. (b) In the thin region, δ, in which the electric field is not zero, oscillating currents will flow. The currents are driven by the electric field of the light wave. (c) The oscillating currents re-radiate electromagnetic waves. Waves radiated into the solid are strongly absorbed, but waves radiated away from the surface can propagate easily.

(a) Incoming wave

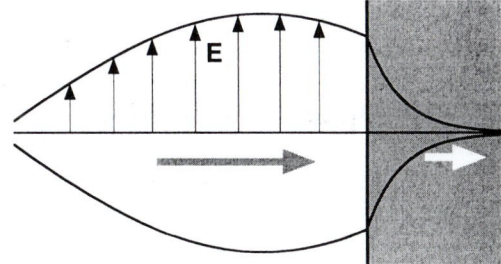

(b) Charge oscillations due to incoming wave (a)

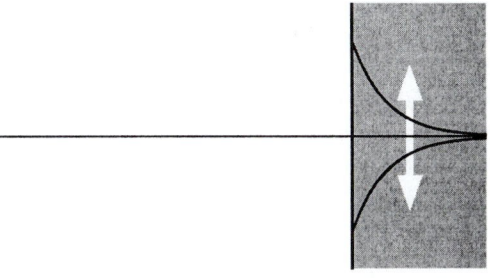

(c) Re-radiated (reflected) wave due to the charge oscillations (b)

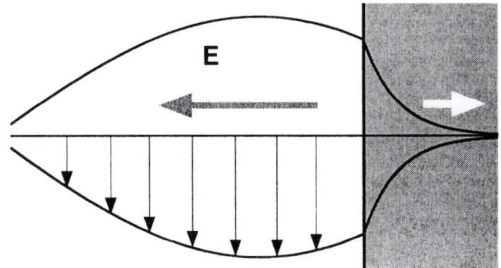

Stage 3: Re-radiation

In the third stage (Figure 7.55 (c)) we note that the oscillating currents will radiate electromagnetic waves. The wave radiated into the metal decays strongly and but the wave radiated back out of the metal can propagate. Because currents in Stage 2 are not strongly dissipated, most of the energy is re-radiated.

The colour of copper

Figure 7.55 allows us to understand where the burnished red colour of copper arises. In a thin layer at the metal surface, the copper ions will be subjected to an oscillating electric field. As we saw previously, §7.9.5, electron shells within ions typically have resonances in the ultra-violet region of the spectrum. However, in copper, a resonance occurs in the blue region of the visible spectrum. At this resonance there is strong absorbtion, and the charge oscillations are converted into phonons (heat) within the solid. So when white light illuminates the surface of copper, the blue end of the spectrum is absorbed, and the red and orange part of the spectrum is reflected.

Quantum mechanically, the resonance in the blue region of the spectrum corresponds to an electronic transition within the copper ions in which an electron moves from a quantum state which is part of a covalent bond, to a state on the surface on the 'Fermi sphere'. This transition occurs for light with wavelength $\lambda < 6.2 \times 10^{-7}$ m (blue) which corresponds to frequencies $f < 4.8 \times 10^{14}$ Hz. Photons with these frequencies have energy $E = hf$ given by:

$$
\begin{aligned}
E &= hf \\
&= 6.6 \times 10^{-34} \times 4.8 \times 10^{14} \\
&= 3.2 \times 10^{-19} \text{ J} \\
&= 2.0 \text{ eV}
\end{aligned}
\tag{7.157}
$$

By examining the frequencies at which light (ultra-violet, visible and infra-red) is transmitted through (or reflected from) solids, one can experimentally determine key features of the energy differences between quantum states in solids. This topic is also discussed briefly in Web Chapter W1 on the *band theory of solids*.

7.9.6 Semiconductors

In discussing electrical conduction (§7.7.9) I categorised semiconductors as electrical insulators in which electrical carriers could be created relatively easily, either thermally or by the addition of impurities. However, even in the most highly-doped semiconductors, the carrier density was only $\approx 1\%$ of that in typical metals. So, in discussing the optical properties of semiconductors, we expect to find properties characteristic of insulators, with additional characteristics appropriate to a metal with a low carrier density.

Both these expectations are borne out, but there are additional processes that take place in semiconductors that make them especially complicated to describe, but potentially especially useful. These extra complications arise because the 'resonances' which occurred in the ultra-violet region of the spectrum in transparent insulators, occur in the optical or infra-red regions of the spectrum in semiconductors. Indeed, they are the reason that semiconductors are not transparent! We recall from §7.9.5 that these 'resonances' corresponded to processes in which electrons make transitions between quantum states within the solid. In semiconductors, the transitions are made by electrons in quantum states in covalent bonds (valence states), to other states in which they can move through the semiconductor (conduction states). The energy above which such electronic transitions become possible is called the *energy gap* of a semiconductor and has a typical value of the order of an electron volt (1 eV).

Optical absorbtion

Since the conductivity of semiconductors is much less than that of metals, the skin depth (Equation 7.156) is much greater than for metals. So the electric field of a light wave can penetrate a semiconductor for a distance of typically a few wavelengths (i.e. a few μm). In this distance, it is able to interact with atoms and excite electrons from valence states into conduction states. This creates an electron carrier and a hole carrier which in the presence of an electric field will be drawn apart and contribute to the current flow through the semiconductor. Thus, the current flow through a semiconductor may be made light-dependent.

Light-emitting diodes and photodiodes

Consider a situation within a semiconductor in which conduction states are populated with electron carriers to a level above their equilibrium density. After a short while, the electron carriers will find hole carriers and annihilate. The excess energy of the electron carrier may be emitted in the form of phonons and photons. The photon energy will correspond to the energy gap of the semiconductor, typically ≈ 1 eV. This corresponds to emission of infra-red light with a wavelength of around 1 μm.

An excess of carriers may be created at the junction between two pieces of semiconductor, one of which has mainly n-type impurities, and the other with mainly p-type impurities. Such a device is called a pn junction or a *diode* (a general name for any two-terminal electrical device). There are many technologically significant applications for pn junctions, including the ability to allow current to flow in only one direction. But here we concentrate on their ability to emit and absorb light.

The situation at the junction between p-type and n-type material is complicated, but the key features are summarised in Figure 7.56 (a) and (b). Close to the junction electron carriers from the n-type region diffuse across the physical boundary and annihilate with holes in the p-type region. Similarly holes from the p-type region diffuse across the physical boundary and annihilate with electrons in the n-type region. The result is a region near the boundary with very low carrier density

Figure 7.56 Illustration of the use of a semiconductor pn junction as a photodiode and light emitting diode (LED). (a) How we imagine the arrangement of carriers at the moment a pn junction is formed. (b) The arrangement a short while later. The carriers have diffused a short distance across the junction and annihilated the 'native' carriers. This leaves uncompensated donor and acceptor charges in the so-called *depletion layer*. (c) When used as an LED, an electric current across junction injects holes and electrons into the depletion layer where they annihilate. (d) When used as a photodiode light with photon energy greater than the energy gap can create hole–electron pairs. If these are created in the depletion layer they are pulled apart by the built in electric field and give rise to a current.

(a) pn junction at the moment of formation

(b) Depletion layer

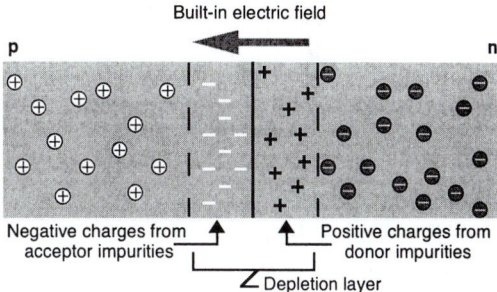

(c) Light-emitting diode

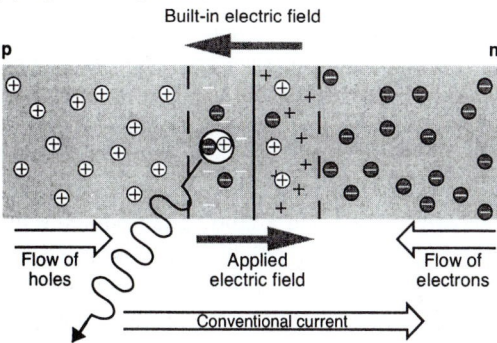

(d) Photodiode

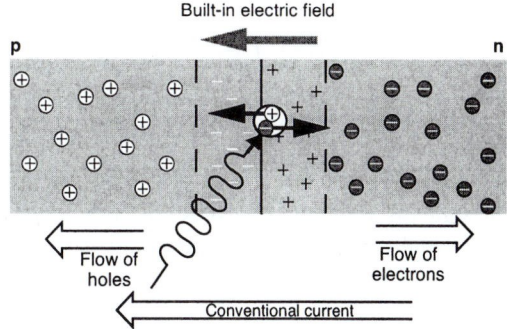

known as a *depletion layer*. In this layer there are charged impurities with no compensating carriers. This results in an intense electric field in this region (Figure 7.56(b)).

If current is driven across a *pn* junction as shown in Figure 7.56 (c), then in the junction region, the current must change from being carried mainly by hole-carriers in the *p*-type material, to being carried mainly by electron-carriers in the *n*-type material. In order to do this electron-carriers and hole-carriers annihilate intensely in the depletion layer. As well as emitting phonons, which heat the material, photons with energy equal to the band gap are emitted. When a *pn* junction has been op-

timised for this purpose, it is known as a *light-emitting diode*.

Now consider a *pn* junction, in which no current is flowing as shown Figure 7.56 (d). If light is absorbed in this region, then an electron–hole pair will be created. However, they will not recombine because the intense electric field draws them in opposite directions. In fact they give rise to a current known as a *photo-current*. When a *pn* junction has been optimised for this purpose, it is known as a *photodiode*. Such devices can be used either as sensitive detectors of optical radiation, or for the generation of useful electrical currents from sunlight.

7.10 Magnetic properties

The magnetic properties of solids are discussed in Web Chapter W2.

7.11 Exercises

Exercises marked with a P prefix are 'normal' exercises. Those marked with a C prefix are best solved numerically by using a computer program or spreadsheet. Exercises marked with an E prefix are in general rather more challenging that the P and C exercises. Answers to all the exercises may be downloaded from www.physicsofmatter.com

Density

P1. Figure 7.1 shows a graph of the density of the elements versus atomic number. The peaks *e, f* and *g* have 'shoulders' on the high atomic number side. To what features on the periodic table (Figure 2.2) do these 'shoulders' correspond?

C2. Re-plot the graph of density versus atomic number (Figure 7.1) up to element 20 to see the detail in Table 7.1. Is there still evidence of periodic behaviour?

P3. What are the densest and second densest elements? Are these also the elements with the greatest *number density* of atoms? Would you expect to find that a compound or alloy of the densest element was denser than the element itself? (Table 7.2)

C4. Which element has the greatest *number* density of atoms? (Table 7.2 and Example 7.1)

P5. Work out approximately (a) the number density, (b) the molar density, (c) the molar volume, (d) the atomic volume and (e) the typical separation between atoms in (i) tungsten and (ii) aluminium. (Table 7.2 and Example 7.1)

P6. What types of wood will sink in water (Table 7.1)? What types of wood would sink in ethanol (Tables 7.1 and 9.2)?

P7. The density of the element with atomic number 50 is the same as that predicted by the simple theory of Example 7.2. Does this imply that element 50 has a simple cubic crystal structure with a lattice spacing of 0.3 nm? If not, what does it imply? (Figure 7.2 and Example 7.1)

Compressibility

P8. By considering the correlation between compressibility and density data, estimate the compressibility of Uranium (Z = 92) (Figure 7.4).

P9. Which two elements listed in Table 7.4 have the highest bulk modulus. For these elements, estimate roughly the pressure required to reduce the average distance between atoms by 1%. Compare the pressure change required with the temperature change required to *increase* the average distance between atoms by 1% ?

Thermal expansivity

P10. Of the elements listed in Table 7.7, which has (a) the largest and (b) the second largest thermal expansivity?

P11. Estimate a typical figure for the linear thermal expansivity of brick and cement. (Table 7.7). A house has walls made from brick and cement and the mean temperature of the walls can change by around 10 °C between summer and winter. Estimate (a) the change in mean height of a house 10 metres high and (b) the change in height of a door frame 2.2 metres high. (Example 7.5)

P12. Show that the area expansivity of a substance is given by 2α. (Example 7.4)

P13. Example 7.4 shows that the volume expansivity may be given by $\beta = 3\alpha$. Show that this same relationship holds for a cuboid of initial dimension $x \times y \times z$. Show that if the linear expansivity in each direction is different, the volume expansivity is given by the sum of the linear expansivities in each of the three directions.

P14. Use order of magnitude estimates from Table 11.1 and Table 7.7 to estimate how much an elemental solid expands before it melts.

P15. A sphere of copper just fails to fit through a circular carbon-steel hole. The is machined to be exactly 10.000 mm diameter at 20 °C. On cooling to –50 °C, the copper sphere *just* falls through the hole. What is the diameter of the copper sphere at room temperature?

P16. Estimate the percentage change in the *average* separation of two neighbouring atoms in a piece of copper when the temperature is changed from (a) 20 °C to 100 °C, (b) 20 °C to 1000 °C, and (c) 20 °C to 10 K. (Table 7.7, Examples 7.5 and 7.6)

P17. Write an explanation (about half a page) for a non-scientific friend outlining what an *alloy* is, and explaining why the thermal expansion of alloys is not always given by the average of its component metal. (Table 7.7)

P18. Write a briefing paper for a fellow student explaining what *invar* is (Tables 7.7 and 7.8) and how its thermal expansivity is related to that of iron and nickel. By considering the brief outline of the origin of ferromagnetic interactions at the end of Web ChapterW2, speculate as to how the anomalous pair potential of Figure 7.9 may be produced.

P19. Write an explanation ($\approx$ half a page) for a non-scientific friend explaining why plastics expand more than crystalline solids. Show the explanation to the friend and ask them to ask the first question which comes into their mind. Answer the question. (§7.4)

Speed of sound

P20. What is the speed of the longitudinal sound waves in (a) domestic glassware, (b) ice, (c) polyethylene, (d) aluminium, (e) copper, and (f) lead. (Table 7.9)

P21. Typically what is the *ratio* of the speed of longitudinal sound waves to the speed of transverse sound waves in elements (Figure 7.11). Name (a) one element in which the ratio lies close to this typical value, (b) one element in which the ratio lies well below this value, and (c) one element in which the ratio lies well above this value. Evaluate the Poisson ratio for each element (a) to (c) (Equation 7.29).

P22. The sounds from musical instruments, such as the xylophone, are made by striking blocks of metal that are free to 'ring'. If the fundamental resonance of a block of length L occurs when $L = \lambda/2$, estimate the length of a block that will resonate at 440 Hz (the note A above middle C). Take a look at a real xylophone and see if you can spot something unexpected about the relative lengths of the keys.

P23. Write an explanation for a colleague summarising the definitions of shear modulus G and Young's modulus E. Explain briefly why we might reasonably expect the shear modulus of a solid to be less than Young's modulus. (Figures 7.14 and 7.16)

P24. Based on Equations 7.25 to 7.27, estimate the shear modulus G, Young's modulus E and Poisson ratio σ of copper, silver, and gold (Tables 7.2 and 7.9). Use Equation A2.33 in Appendix 2 to estimate the bulk modulus B and compare it with the experimental values from Table 7.4.

P25. Describe an experiment to directly demonstrate to a non-scientific friend that sound travels faster through solids than through gases. (Tables 5.14 and 7.6).

Heat capacity

P26. What is the molar heat capacity of (a) gold and (b) neodymium at around room temperature? (Table 7.10)

P27. Which elements have the highest and lowest molar heat capacity ($J\,K^{-1}\,mol^{-1}$) at 298 K? (Table 7.10)

C28. Which elements have the highest and lowest *specific* heat capacity ($J\,K^{-1}\,kg^{-1}$) at 298 K? (Tables 7.2 and 7.10)

P29. Estimate C_P for copper, silver and gold at the boiling temperature of liquid nitrogen. (Figure 7.19 and Table 11.1)

E30. Liquid helium costs around £3.00 per litre and is used routinely to cool apparatus for use in low-temperature experiments. The latent heat of liquid helium is around 2000 joules per liquid litre. Estimate roughly how much it would cost to cool 1 kg of copper from room temperature to the boiling temperature of liquid helium (Figure 7.19 and Table 11.1). In fact, a simple calculation overestimates the amount of helium

required by a factor of roughly 50: can you suggest why?

P31. Following Example 7.13 and Figures 7.19 and 7.25, estimate an Einstein temperature for gold. Based on that estimate, calculate the Einstein frequency and the spring constant between gold atoms.

P32. By considering the spring constant K estimated in Example 7.13, and the model of a solid sketched in Figure 7.14, show that Young's modulus for a substance may be estimated as $E \approx K/a$, where a is the lattice spacing (≈ 0.3 nm). How well does the estimate for E for copper derived from analysis of the heat capacity data (Example 7.13) tie up with E estimated from the bulk modulus data (Tables 7.4 and Equation A2.33 in Appendix 2)?

P33. Figure 7.30 indicates a roughly linear relationship between the Debye temperature and the speed of sound wave in a substance. Estimate the constant of proportionality using Equation 7.48 and discuss how well it agrees with the experimental value of approximately 7. Use this correlation to estimate the Debye temperature for niobium and seek confirmation of your estimate in the scientific literature. (Tables 7.9 and 7.12)

C34. Compare the heat capacity predicted by Equation 7.61 with the tabulated values of the Debye function (Table 7.11). Up to what fraction of Θ_D is the Equation accurate within (a) 1%, and (b) 10%?

P35. Explain to a friend what is meant by the terms *phonon* and *photon* and outline the correct usage of each term.

P36. Evaluate the ratio $k_B T/E_F$ for a copper at 10 K, 100 K and 1000 K (Equations 6.72 and 6.76).

E37. Estimate the ratio of $C_{el}/C_{lattice}$ for silver at (a) room temperature and (b) 1K. (Example 7.14, Table 7.12, Equation 7.47)

P38. A single photon of energy 3×10^4 eV is absorbed in a block of silicon ($\Theta_D \approx 630$ K) of volume 1 cm^3. Estimate the temperature rise if the silicon is held at initial temperatures of (a) 1 mK, (b) 10 mK and (c) 100 mK (Equation 7.47 and Table 7.2). Could such a cryogenic device be used as a photon detector at any of these temperatures?

Electrical properties

P39. Which four elements are the best electrical conductors at room temperature (Table 7.13 and Figures 7.35 and 7.36)? Are these still the best conductors at a $T = 1$ K (Table 7.15)? Amongst the lanthanide elements (Figure 7.1) which is the worst and which the best electrical conductor around room temperature? (Table 7.13)

P40. What is the resistivity of (a) copper, (b) brass, and (c) zinc at around room temperature? (Table 7.14)

P41. A copper wire is 50 km in length, has a diameter of 10 cm, and a potential difference of 3×10^5 V across it. Estimate the current through the wire and the power dissipated per metre. (Table 7.13 and Example 7.15)

P42. The resistivity ρ_z of an element with atomic number Z is required in a calculation, but your tables record only the value of ρ_{z+1} for the element with atomic number $Z + 1$. How good a guide is this to the likely value of ρ_z (Figure 7.34 and 7.35)? If you had to choose a single figure as a ballpark estimate of the resistivity of *all* elemental metals, what value would you choose?

P43. The resistivity ρ of rhodium is 4.51×10^{-8} Ω m at room temperature. Estimate ρ at 77 K. (Hint: Look at Figure 7.36 and make some assumptions)

P44. Work out the scattering time for electrons in Au, Cu, Zn, Cu(Zn) and Nd (Example 7.17). Discuss briefly the origin of the differences in Δt.

P45. Ask your tutor why metallic behaviour is common amongst the elements. Write down their answer, think about it, and then send it to me.

P46. Element A has resistivity ρ_A and element B has resistivity ρ_B. Sketch how you would expect the resistivity of a random alloy $A_X B_{1-X}$ to vary for $0 < X < 1$. (Table 7.14)

P47. Work out the thickness of a parallel plate capacitor made with a quartz dielectric with an area 10 mm^2 and a capacitance of 1 nF (Example 7.18). If the capacitor has a voltage of 100 V across its plates, roughly what is the current (known as the *leakage current*) which flows through the capacitor? (Table 7.14 and Example 7.19)

If an AC voltage at a frequency of 1 kHz is now applied to the capacitor, the reactive current through the capacitor has a magnitude $VC/2\pi f$. Compare the magnitudes of the capacitative and leakage currents through the capacitor. A good dielectric substance for a capacitor has a low leakage current and a high dielectric constant. In these terms is quartz or polystyrene a better material with which to make a capacitor? (Table 7.14)

P48. A parallel-plate capacitor is made with a quartz dielectric, an area 10 mm^2, and has a capacitance of 1 nF (Example 7.18). What is the maximum voltage that may be applied to the capacitor (Table 7.18)? How would you expect this maximum voltage to change with temperature? (§7.5.7)

Semiconductors

P49. What is the resistivity of silicon with 1 part per million phosphorus impurity at around 300 K? How many phosphorus atoms per cubic metre does this correspond to? (Figure 7.40)

P50. What is a typical value of the energy gap for a semiconductor? (Figure 7.43 and Equation 7.79)

P51. Estimate the number density of electron and hole carriers in pure silicon at 1000 K (Example 7.21 and Figure 7.42). How does this compare with the number density of carriers in copper at 1000 K?

P52. Based on the discussion around Figures 7.45 and 7.46, suggest elements that would make good donor or acceptor dopants for (a) silicon and (b) germanium. Speculate which dopants would have the smallest activation energies, i.e. have quantum states with energy most similar to the host material.

Thermal conductivity

P53. A question about frying pans. Roughly 1 kW of heat flows through the base of a cast iron frying pan (diameter 30 cm, thickness 5 mm) and heats the oil beneath some sausages to around 200 °C. Estimate the temperature of the underneath of the frying pan. The handle is 15 cm long, 2 cm in diameter, and made from epoxy resin. Make some simple assumptions and estimate the temperature half way down the handle. (Tables 7.16 and 7.17).

P54. The room in which I am sitting has one outside wall, which has an area of approximately 3 m × 4 m. Roughly half of this area is taken up with glass 5 mm thick. Neglecting leaks around the window frame, and assuming that the wall has two layers of bricks (approximately 20 cm total thickness) but no cavity, estimate the rate at which energy must be dissipated inside the room in order to keep it at 23 °C when it is –2 °C outside. (Tables 7.16 and 7.17)

Based on this calculation, would you recommend that I invest in double-glazing? Describe with the aid of a sketch how even a thin cavity of trapped air would help improve the thermal insulation of both the brick wall and the window. (Table 5.11)

Optical Properties

P55. What is the average optical reflectivity of aluminium? (Table 7.22)

C56. The reflectivity of glass to light normally incident upon it is given by the formula:

$$R = \left[\frac{\left(n_{\text{light}} - 1\right)}{\left(n_{\text{light}} + 1\right)} \right]^2$$

so that, for example, when $n_{\text{light}} = 1.5$, $R = 0.04$ and so 4% of the incident light intensity is reflected. Using a spreadsheet or otherwise, plot R as function of n_{light} for n_{light} in the range 1 to 3. Since glass with $R > 0.1$ is not useful for many applications, what is the maximum useful refractive index.

P57. If the refractive index of glass were the same for all wavelengths across the spectrum, would a high refractive index prism split white light into different colours more strongly than a low refractive index prism? (Example 7.24)

P58. Diamonds are commonly used in jewellery. Suggest which optical properties of diamonds are responsible for this popularity? Justify your suggestion.

P59. What conclusions can be drawn from the level agreement between the theory of refractive index and experimental data in Figure 7.53?

P60. Estimate the wavelength of *UV* resonance (or *UV* electronic transition) for glass with a refractive index of 1.3 (Example 7.24). From your estimate of λ_o produce an estimate of f_o, the resonant frequency. By considering Equation 2.25, and supposing only a single electron to be excited, estimate the 'spring constant' K with which the electron is bound within the glass. Compare your answer with the result of Question P5 at the end of Chapter 2

P61. Estimate the skin depth of copper at a frequency of: (a) 50 Hz (mains frequency); (b) 50 MHz (the clock frequency of a computer when the first edition was published); (c) 1 GHz (the clock frequency of a computer when the second edition was published; (d) 10 THz (infra red); (e) 1000 THz (optical) (Equation 7.155). How thick should the aluminium screening around a computer be in order to reduce the strength of the radiated electric field by a factor of 100?

CHAPTER 8
Liquids: background theory

8.1 Introduction

If we raise the temperature of a solid it will, commonly, become liquid, and then on further heating it will evaporate to become a gas. In this sequence of states (solid $\Rightarrow$ liquid $\Rightarrow$ gas) the liquid state is intermediate between the solid and gaseous states. This intermediate position is a reflection of the fact that the arrangement of atoms or molecules in a liquid is, in general, intermediate between the crystalline order of the solid state and the random molecular motions of the gaseous state. In what follows we will discuss liquids as being *structurally* intermediate between solids and gases.

In general, we will find that most properties of liquids can be understood by explanations that begin in one of two ways. Either we will begin by saying that liquids are similar to solids, but more disordered and slightly less

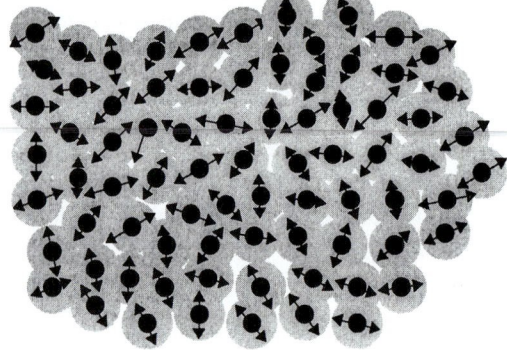

Figure 8.1 Illustration of the motion of atoms in a liquid. Notice the small separation between the atoms, and the random orientation of the vibrations of the molecules. The atoms themselves are shown as a central darkly-shaded region, where the electron charge density is high, and a peripheral lightly-shaded region. The electric field in this peripheral region significantly affects the motion, and disturbs the electronic charge density, of neighbouring atoms.

dense, *or* we will begin by saying that liquids are similar to gases, but more ordered and much more dense. Both approaches are useful for understanding the behaviour of liquids.

When we discussed the properties of gases we were able to arrive at the theory of an 'ideal gas' which was, for many purposes, a good approximation to the properties of real gases. However, there was no single model of an 'ideal solid' that could explain the diverse properties of solids. Liquids fall into an intermediate category and we will discuss their properties in terms of two simplified models. One model describes the *structure* of a liquid (§8.3): we will use this model to understand properties such as the density. The other model describes the *dynamics* of the liquid molecules (§8.4): we will use this model to understand properties such as the viscosity. We will find that we are able to understand many of the properties of real liquids in terms of these models. However, the models are so simplified that we will not really be able to 'believe' them in the way that we 'believe' the model of an ideal gas. The models capture just one or two key features of liquid behaviour and ignore many properties of the molecules that make up the liquid. The predictions of the models tend to be rather qualitative, allowing to us to examine trends among groups of substances, or variations with temperature, rather than predicting that the viscosity of, say, water at temperature T will be X.

At www.physicsofmatter.com

In addition to copies of the figures and tables, you will find a computer program which realistically simulates the dynamics of molecules in liquids, solids and gases.

8.2 Bonding in liquids

8.2.1 Bonding in liquids

Liquids consist of a 'condensed' collection of atoms or molecules with less average kinetic energy than a gas of the molecules, but too much kinetic energy to allow them to form a solid. We can divide the electrostatic bonding mechanisms into the same four categories as for solids (molecular, ionic, covalent and metallic) plus one exceptional category, *hydrogen bonding*, which is discussed below.

8.2.2 Hydrogen bonding

Hydrogen bonding is of special importance in discussing organic liquids, and also our most precious liquid, water. It occurs in substances composed of molecules which contain the chemical group OH: a combination of a hydrogen atom and an oxygen atom. This combination occurs in water (H_2O or HOH), in alcohols such as methanol (CH_3OH) or ethanol (C_2H_5OH), and numerous other organic molecules. Hydrogen bonding also occurs to a lesser extent in bonds between H and N, and H and a halogen F, Cl, or Br.

In liquids made from organic molecules, the *atoms within the molecules* are held together by primarily covalent bonding. However, the molecules are attracted to each other by the relatively weak *Van der Waals* force. The hydrogen bond is an attractive mechanism that acts between different molecules in addition to the Van der Waals force. It is much stronger and more directional than the Van der Waals force and is similar in effect to the covalent bonding that occurs within molecules.

The OH covalent bond within a water molecule is highly asymmetric, with the centre of charge symmetry being much closer to the oxygen rather than hydrogen atom. This leaves the hydrogen atom slightly positively charged, and the oxygen atom negatively charged. The extra electron charge density around the oxygen atom distributes itself so as to minimise its coulomb repulsion from the other electrons on the oxygen atom. The electron density in the region of an oxygen atom in a water molecule is shown in Figure 8.2 (a). Notice that the charge density forms two lobes on the

Figure 8.2 Types of bonding in liquids. (a) In molecular liquids the entities which make up the liquid (atoms or molecules) are essentially the same as the entities which made up the gas. Internally the atoms that comprise the molecules are bound within each molecule by primarily covalent bonding. Externally the molecules are bound together by the Van der Waals force discussed in §6.2. (b) In ionic liquids the entities which make up the liquid are ions rather than atoms or molecules. Locally most ions experience a situation similar to that experienced within a solid, but the regular periodicity of the solid lattice is absent. (c) In covalent liquids the entities which make up the liquid (atoms or molecules) are greatly altered from their state in the gas. In particular there is a high electronic charge density on some regions in between the mean positions of the atoms. Locally most ions experience a situation similar to that experienced within a solid, but the regular periodicity of the solid lattice is absent. (d) In metallic liquids the electrons from the outer parts of the atoms can move anywhere within the liquid and are not attached to any individual atom. Notice that the electrons are still free to move from ion to ion in any direction even though the regular periodicity of the lattice has been destroyed.

(a) **(b)** **(c)** **(d)**

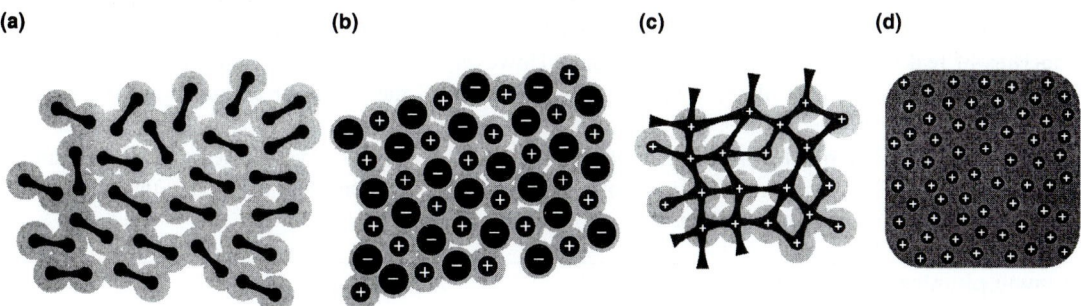

other side of the oxygen atom from the covalent bond regions.

A second water molecule may orient itself with respect to the first so that one of its hydrogen atoms is close to electron orbitals around the oxygen atom. This structure is known as a hydrogen bond and has many of the features of a covalent bond. For example, although it has only about one-tenth the strength of the OH covalent bond, it is rigid like a covalent bond. By 'rigid' I mean that the O–H–O link in Figure 8.3 (b) has a minimum energy when the three atoms are in line. Hydrogen bonding will be discussed further in §9.2.2.

8.2.3 Organic liquids

In this context, the term 'organic' historically referred to substances which originated from a once-living organism. In modern parlance the term has a technical sense in which it refers to substances the molecules of which contain *both* carbon and hydrogen atoms. Thus carbon tetrachloride CCl_4 and ammonia NH_3 are *inorganic* but methane CH_4 is organic. The distinction into organic and inorganic is important in this context, as data books frequently separate substances along these lines, and we shall follow suit in discussions of the experimental data in Chapter 9. Understanding the bonding in organic substances is particularly important, since much of the experimental data on liquids refers to organic liquids. The key features of this bonding may be fairly easily stated.

*Intra*molecular bonding

The atoms within each molecule are held together by primarily covalent bonds that are extremely strong and highly directional. This gives the molecules of organic substances characteristic *shapes*.

*Inter*molecular bonding

The molecules of the substance are (in general) attracted to each other by much weaker forces, primarily the non-directional Van der Waals force, and sometimes augmented by directional hydrogen bonds.

Figure 8.3 Qualitative indication of the structure of a hydrogen bond between water molecules. (a) The distribution of electric charge within an isolated water molecule. The hydrogen atoms are slightly positively charged and the oxygen atoms slightly negatively charged. The excess charge on the oxygen atom resides in two orbitals oriented so as to minimise their coulomb repulsion from the covalent bonds. (b) A second molecule may orient itself so as to place its hydrogen atoms close to the negatively charged electron orbitals around the oxygen atom. The two oxygen atoms shown are linked by a hydrogen atom and two bond regions: one bond is covalent and the other is known as a *hydrogen bond*.

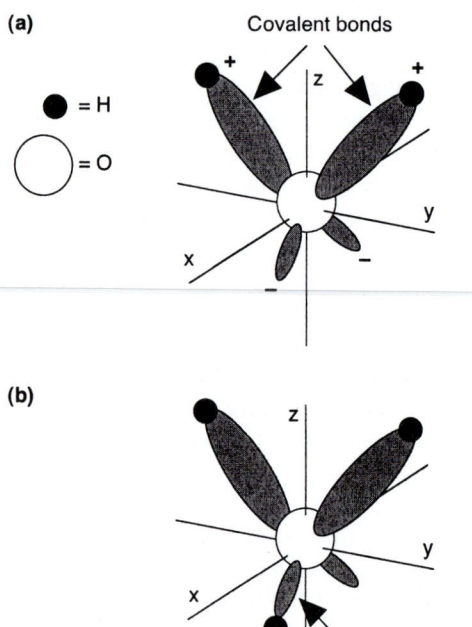

The combination of strong intramolecular bonding and relatively weak intermolecular bonding results, as we shall see, in a complex array of properties.

8.3 The structure of liquids

8.3.1 Structural description

Having reviewed what actually holds liquids together, we will now develop a general model of the structure of a liquid. The structural description concentrates on a single atom or molecule, and then describes the *average* positions of its neighbours within the liquid.

Figure 8.1 shows our imagined picture of the situation of atoms or molecules in the liquid state. It might represent the result of taking a 'snapshot' of a microscopic amount of liquid. The atoms are vibrating about their average positions rather like the equivalent picture for a solid, Figure 6.1. The atoms are highly constrained by the closeness of neighbouring atoms and so their vibrational frequencies are similar to those in solids: around 10^{13} Hz. The equivalent picture taken, say, one vibrational period (i.e. roughly 10^{-13} second) later would look in detail almost exactly the same. However the equivalent picture taken say 10^{-10} second later (i.e. after around a thousand or so atomic oscillations) would typically look qualitatively similar, but in detail the picture would be completely different. All the positions of the atoms would have changed. This changing structure is the origin of difficulties in adopting a universally appropriate model of liquids.

I have said previously that the structure of a liquid is similar to that of a disordered solid, but that the structure of a liquid changes on a time-scale of a fraction of a nanosecond. Given this, it might at first seem that it would be impossible to say anything *quantitative* about the structure of liquids. In fact we can make rather precise statements about liquid structure as long as we are content with descriptions of the *average* structure. Obviously this will not describe the many individual and unique situations in which each molecule is placed. However, we have seen in previous chapters that many properties of materials depend on average properties of a substance (e.g. average speed, average separation, and average energy). So if we can calculate these averages, we may well be able make progress in understanding the relation-ship of liquid structure to the properties of liquids. So with the aim of quantitatively describing the average arrangement of molecules in a liquid, we use two related mathematical functions, called the *radial distribution function $N(r)$* and the *radial density function $n(r)$*

8.3.2 The radial distribution function for spherical molecules

The radial distribution function is a mathematical function which describes the *average* distribution of molecules around a particular molecule. It specifies the average number of molecules that are found at a certain distance from a particular molecule. For spherical molecules the function answers the question:

On average, *how many molecules have centres which lie within a spherical shell of inner radius r and thickness dr centred on a particular molecule?*

The idea is complicated to depict in three dimensions, but is illustrated in Figure 8.4 for a two-dimensional liquid-like arrangement of molecules. In two dimensions we ask the question:

On average, *how many molecules have centres which lie within an annular area of inner radius r and thickness dr centred on a particular molecule?*

The number of molecules with centres in the annular area of inner radius r and thickness dr will increase as r increases. This is because annular areas of larger radius have a larger area and so tend to have the centres of more molecules within them. In two dimensions, an annulus has area $2\pi r dr$ and so its area increases linearly with its radius r. In three dimensions, a spherical shell has volume $4\pi r^2 dr$ and its volume increases quadratically with r. However, in addition to the smooth increase we can discern shorter-range variations in the functions in either two or three dimensions. It is these variations that reflect the structure present within a liquid.

The significance of the radial distribution may become clearer if we work out the radial distribution function for the two-dimensional liquid-like arrangement of circles pictured in Figure 8.4. Within the annular area shown, lie the centres of 15 circles. If we count the numbers within similar rings of different radii then we obtain results similar to those shown in Figure 8.5. The procedure for constructing a radial distribution function for a two-dimensional liquid similar to that in Figure 8.4 is outlined in Example 8.1.

8.3.3 The radial density function

Of more fundamental significance in the study of liquids is a function closely related to the radial distribution function known as the *radial density* function $n(r)$ This function charts local variations in the *average* density of the substance as a function of distance from the centre of a molecule. At large distances from a particular molecule this function tends to the value of the bulk density of the substance. However, on an atomic scale we see peaks and troughs corresponding to the average separations of nearest and next-nearest neighbour molecules. In Example 8.1 we work out both the radial density and radial distribution functions for a two-dimensional solid, liquid and gas.

Having worked out the radial density function $n(r)$, the question arises of how to interpret it. The first point apparent from Figure 8.6 is that $n(r)$ for a liquid is rather similar to $n(r)$ for a solid. This indicates that around each molecule there remains some degree of order that was typical of the solid state. However that observable periodicity is reduced as we move further from the molecule under consideration. This is quite unlike a crystalline solid where the positions of the molecules remain correlated over long distances. Positional order of this type is called *short-range order*.

The question remains of precisely over what range the $n(r)$ of a liquid loses its correlations? The rate at which this occurs depends on the temperature of the liquid. Just above the melting temperature, $n(r)$ for the liquid is similar to that for a solid. But as the temperature is increased $n(r)$ becomes increasingly smoothed out, with the correlations between the positions of the molecules becoming

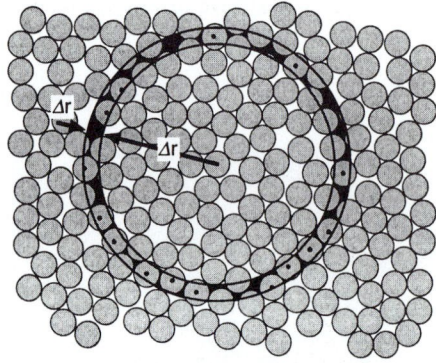

Figure 8.4 The radial distribution function describes the *average* distribution of molecules around any particular molecule. My count of the number of molecules reveals that there are 15 molecules in the ring shown.

Figure 8.5 Qualitative illustration of the radial distribution function for simple liquid-like structures in (a) two-dimensions, and (b) three-dimensions. Notice the linear trend of the two-dimensional function, and the quadratic trend of the three-dimensional function. Constructing a radial distribution function for a two-dimensional liquid-like structure is described in Example 8.1.

(a)

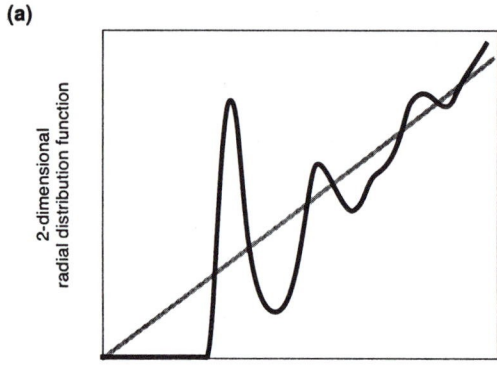

Distance from central molecule

(b)

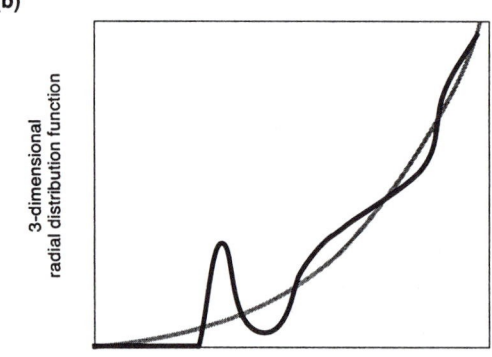

Distance from central molecule

Example 8.1

The *radial distribution function* for a two-dimensional solid, liquid and gas. The figures below represent two-dimensional solids, liquids and gases. Superimposed on these drawings is a ring structure that allows us to determine how many circles (atoms) have centres that lie within any particular annular area. The sums from each annular area are shown totalled in each figure and then transferred to Table 8.1.

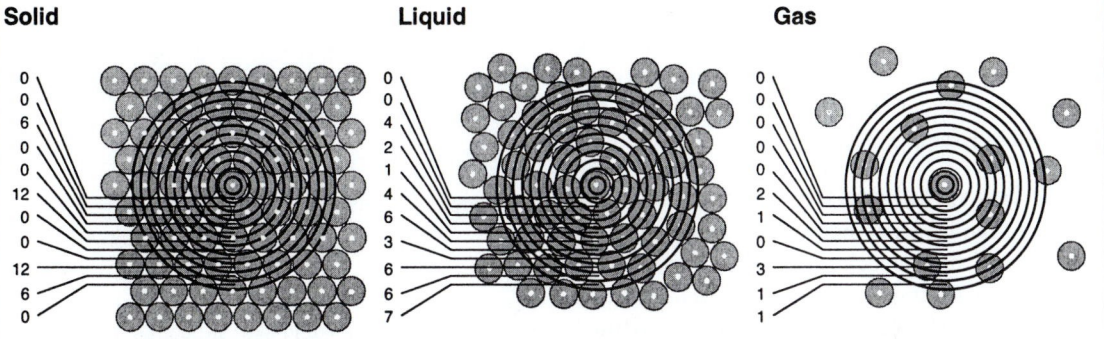

less pronounced. Just below the transition to the gaseous state the correlations may be considerably weakened. This is illustrated in Figure 9.22.

The exercise of constructing the two-dimensional radial density function $n(r)$ in Example 8.1 is clearly somewhat artificial, but the conclusion drawn is in fact rather general: liquids retain some degree of short-range order in the positioning of their molecules.

8.3.4 Non-spherical molecules

Many substances that form liquids around room temperature are organic in nature and have molecules that are not in the least spherical. Such molecules may have rings of atoms that make

them essentially planar in shape, or they may have chains of atoms that make them essentially linear in shape. There are also many complicated combinations of rings and chains that are not well described by the idea of a simple spherical molecule that we have used in the previous section.

Thus for organic molecules, $n(r)$ can describe the positional correlations of the centres of molecules, but does not include information about the relative *orientations* of neighbouring molecules. Consider a molecule such as that illustrated schematically in Figure 8.7. The picture is intended to illustrate a molecule which is not symmetric, and which has covalent bonds within the molecule that give it a relatively fixed shape. Figure 8.8 illustrates two

Table 8.1 Data from Example 8.1. The table shows the mean radius of each ring in Example 8.1, and summarises the data for the solid, liquid and gas examples. For each ring, it divides the number of circles (atoms) found in each ring by the approximate area of that ring, $2\pi r\Delta r$. The units are such that the width of each ring $\Delta r = 1$. This is an approximation to the radial density function for the substance. The results for the solid and liquid case are plotted in Figure 8.6.

Ring	Radius	Solid N	Solid $n = \dfrac{N}{2\pi r\Delta r}$	Liquid N	Liquid $n = \dfrac{N}{2\pi r\Delta r}$	Gas N	Gas $n = \dfrac{N}{2\pi r\Delta r}$
1	1.5	0	0	0	0	0	0
2	2.5	0	0	0	0	0	0
3	3.5	6	0.273	4	0.182	0	0
4	4.5	0	0	2	0.071	0	0
5	5.5	0	0	1	0.029	0	0
6	6.5	12	0.294	4	0.098	2	0.049
7	7.5	0	0	6	0.127	1	0.021
8	8.5	0	0	3	0.056	0	0
9	9.5	12	0.201	6	0.101	3	0.050
10	10.5	6	0.091	6	0.091	1	0.015
11	11.5	0	0	7	0.097	1	0.014

Figure 8.6 The radial density function of the two-dimensional 'liquid' and 'solid' shown in Example 8.1 and calculated in Table 8.1. The peaks in the solid data correspond to nearest neighbours, next-nearest neighbours, etc. Notice that these peaks are maintained in the liquid state, but that they are smoothed by the increased disorder of the liquid state. The figure also shows the limiting values of the macroscopic liquid and solid density.

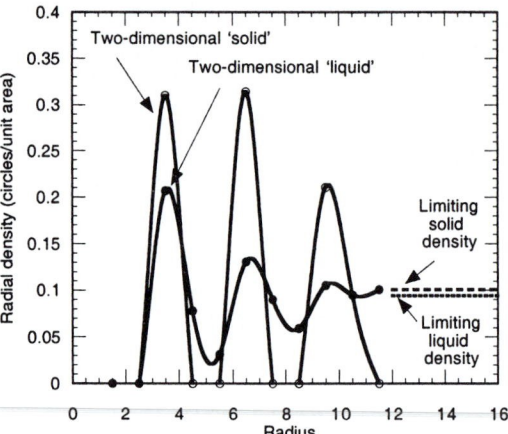

Figure 8.7 A representation of an asymmetric molecule with relatively fixed shape.

8.3.5 Liquid crystals

Many molecules which have some of the properties of the molecule in Figure 8.7 exhibit a strong tendency to align themselves with their neighbours. For example, they may prefer to orient themselves so that their long axis is parallel with that of their neighbours. If we consider the centres of the molecules, defined as the position of the centre of mass of each molecule, we find that the radial density function is highly anisotropic. In some directions it may show essentially crystalline order, while in other directions it indicates order more typical of a liquid. States with this mixed order are known as *liquid crystals* or *meso-phase* states. The prefix *meso* is from the Greek for *middle* or *intermediate* and indicates that such states are structurally mid-way between the solid and liquid state.

Solid and liquid structures

We can look at the generic types of structures that arise in liquid crystal mesophases by considering the interactions between the molecules such as those illustrated in Figure 8.7. The molecules will have some relative orientation in which they can minimise their energy of interaction. Five possible orientations are shown in Figure 8.8. In this example, let us suppose that they have a low energy when they are aligned parallel, as indicated in Figure 8.9

such molecules in several different relative orientations but separated by the same distance between centres. It is not difficult to imagine that the interaction energy of one molecule with another depends not only on the separation of the two molecules, but also on their relative orientation. This orientation dependence of the interaction energy would be particularly significant if the molecules were *polar* (§5.7.2), i.e. if they had some regions that were electrically positive and others that were electrically negative. The hydrogen bond in Figure 8.3 is a special example of interactions between polar molecules.

The importance of the molecular shape will be seen in §9.9 when we compare data on organic liquids with data derived from molten metals which are better described by the spherical molecules model we have considered in §8.2.2.

Figure 8.9 We suppose that the molecules illustrated in Figure 8.7 have their lowest energy when they are oriented as shown

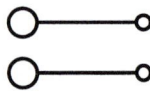

Figure 8.8 Five possible arrangements of pairs of the molecules from Figure 8.7.

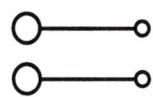 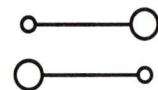 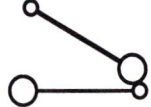 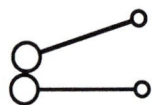 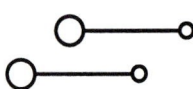

The *solid* formed from such molecules might look something like either of the options in Figure 8.10.

In the liquid state, the positions of the molecules are disordered in a similar way to a 'normal liquid' and the orientations of the molecules are also highly randomised.

Liquid crystal structures

There are a number of possible states, known as *mesostates*, or more commonly as *liquid crystal states*, that are intermediate between the order of the solid and the disorder of the liquid. Perhaps the simplest state to describe is the *nematic state*. The word drives from the Greek *nema*, meaning 'thread', and the state describes thread-like molecules which remain roughly parallel to one another, but the positions of their centres are disordered. The orientation of the molecules within the liquid is indicated by a vector **n** known as the *director*. In general the director will change from one region to another, producing the equivalent of crystalline defects in a solid that are known as *disinclinations*. Figure 8.12 illustrates a nematic liquid crystal state of molecules which have a minimum energy configuration like that illustrated in Figure 8.7.

One special type of variation of **n** has important applications in the use of liquid crystals in digital displays, and is known as a *cholesteric* liquid crystal. The term cholesteric derives from two words: *chole* which is the Greek prefix for the bile or gall duct from which these chemicals were originally derived; and *stereo* which in this context refers to the three-dimensional waxy nature of the substance. Within any layer of the structure, the substance looks like a nematic liquid crystal structure, but its key feature is that the director *rotates* from one region of the crystal to another. As illustrated in Figure 8.13, the rotation of the

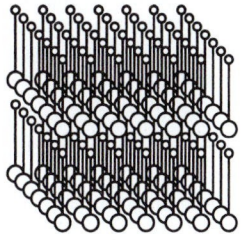 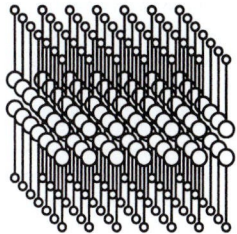

Figure 8.10 Two plausible solid structures that might be formed from molecules such as those illustrated in Figure 8.7 above.

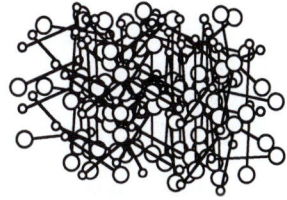

Figure 8.11 A plausible liquid structure that might be formed from molecules such as those illustrated in Figure 8.7 above.

director is perpendicular to the plane containing the nematic director. Molecules such as those illustrated in Figure 8.7 would be unlikely to form a cholesteric phase liquid crystal.

The final type of liquid crystal state is known as a *smectic* state, in which molecules form layers similar to the layers indicated in the solid state (Figure 8.10). The word *smectic* derives from the Greek *smektikos* meaning *to wash*, because of the soap-like consistency of substances in this state. Different varieties of smectic liquid crystal are distinguished by the different relative orientations of the director **n** with respect to the layers of the structure, and by the degree of order within each layer. Molecules such as those illustrated in Figure 8.7 could quite feasibly form smectic structures.

Table 8.2 The transition temperatures of some substances which form liquid crystal mesophases.

Ethyl-anisal-p-aminocinnamate:

Crystal $\xleftarrow{\text{83 °C}}$ Smectic B $\xleftarrow{\text{91 °C}}$ Smectic A $\xleftarrow{\text{118 °C}}$ Nematic $\xleftarrow{\text{139 °C}}$ Liquid

Cholesterol benzoate $C_{34}H_{50}O_2$: relative molecular mass 491

Crystal $\xleftarrow{\text{146 °C}}$ Cholesteric $\xleftarrow{\text{178.5 °C}}$ Liquid

Figure 8.12 Conceivable nematic liquid crystal structure of molecules which have a minimum energy configuration like that illustrated in Figure 8.9. In (a) the vector **n** is the *director* which describes the direction of the texture of the structure, while (b) illustrates a region in which two directors meet at a disinclination.

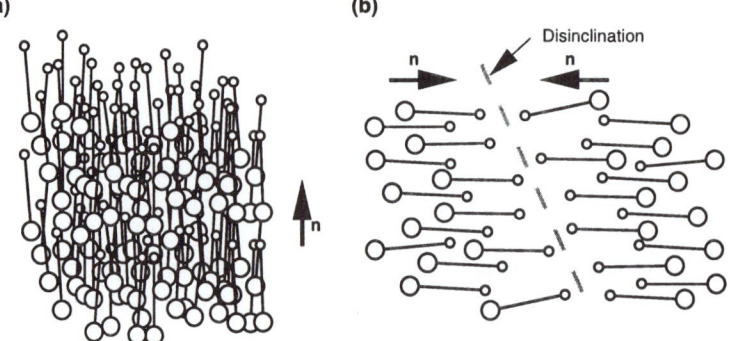

With a little imagination, you might be able to envisage other combinations of positional and orientational disorder that constitute what are known to be a multitude of different liquid crystal states. The liquid crystal phases discussed above generally exist over limited temperature ranges, commonly only a few degrees celsius, in between the solid and liquid states (Table 8.2).

Figure 8.13 Cholesteric liquid crystal. Within any layer of the structure, the substance appears to be nematic. To appreciate the structure, consider for example the top layer on the diagram, which has a director pointed to the right. If we consider a neighbouring layer its nematic director is rotated with respect to the top layer. Similarly, the layer below is rotated with respect to the second layer. In this way the substance has a director which rotates in a plane whose normal is perpendicular to all the directors.

Summary

At the level of this book it has been impossible to survey all the types of liquid crystal state. However it is important to notice that liquid crystal phases are a natural and common phenomenon in liquids whose molecules have anisotropic properties. Since many living organisms are constructed from large anisotropic molecules in a near-fluid state, liquid crystals have profound, but still poorly understood, effect on the functioning of biological systems, including our own bodies.

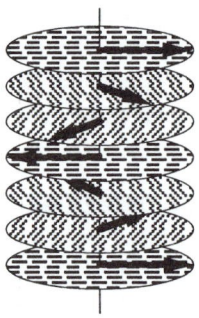

Figure 8.14 Some smectic liquid crystal structures. Smectic B is the most solid-like of the liquid crystal states, having positional order within each layer of the smectic structure. Smectic A is a structure in which this positional order *within* the layer is lost, but the orientational order within the layer is retained along with the layer structure itself. In Smectic C the layer structure remains, but the molecules orient themselves at an angle with respect to the layers.

(a) Smectic A

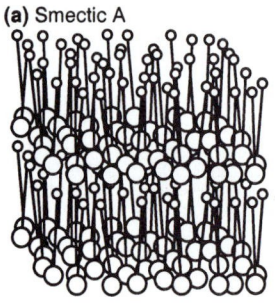

(b) Smectic B

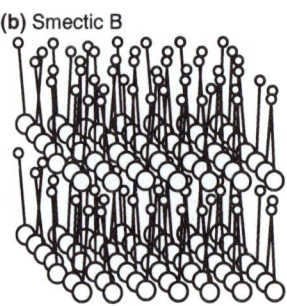

(c) Smectic C

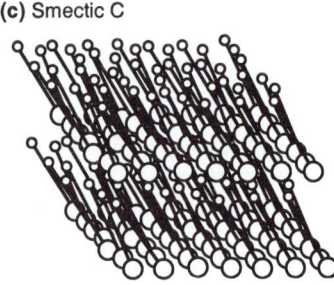

8.4 The dynamics of a liquid: the cell model

8.4.1 The need for a dynamical description

In the previous section we considered how we could describe the structure of the liquids. We introduced the radial density function $n(r)$ as a method of describing the structure of a liquid of spherical molecules. We then considered some of the factors relevant to non-spherical molecules, and saw that ultimately these factors could give rise to liquid crystal structures.

However, in order to understand many phenomena that are characteristic of the liquid state, we need to describe the way the structure *changes*. For example the *viscosity* of liquid, which describes the ease with which a liquid changes shape, is essentially a measure of the ease with which the structure of a liquid can *change*. We will try to understand the dynamics of a liquid by first considering how the structure of a liquid of spherical molecules might change. The we will see how our conclusions would be affected if the molecules of the liquid were non-spherical.

8.4.2 Spherical molecules: a cell model

The following model of liquids, known generally as the *cell model*, is an attempt to develop a near universal model of liquids. It assumes that each molecule is constrained by its neighbours into a 'cell' of roughly atomic dimensions: this is certainly the case in real liquids. Each molecule vibrates within a 'cage' created by its neighbours.

However, as consideration of Figure 8.15 (b) shows, molecules such as B take part in the formation of several cells. In the figure B is part of the 'cell wall' constraining molecules A and C amongst others. In addition B is itself constrained within another cell not shown in Figure 8.15, in which A and C form part of the 'cell wall'. In order to break through this kind of complex analysis we need to make a dramatic simplification.

The simplification of the cell model is that it considers only the properties of an *average molecule* in an *average cell*. The cell model has four parameters:

- The average size of the cell a illustrated in Figure 8.15 (b).
- The size of the energy barrier which must be overcome in order to move a molecule from one cell to another ΔE_h. The subscript 'h' on ΔE_h is intended to indicate the 'hopping' process by which molecules move through the liquid.
- The energy cost to entirely remove a molecule from the liquid ΔE_e. The subscript 'e' on ΔE_e is intended to indicate 'escape' or 'evaporation' processes through which molecules leave the liquid.
- The energy cost to move a molecule from the body of the liquid to the surface of the liquid ΔE_s. The subscript 's' on the ΔE_s stands for 'surface'.

As Figure 8.16 illustrates, it is important to realise that the actual process by which a molecule moves through a liquid is not a single-particle process. It will in general involve the chance motions of several molecules conspiring to allow a molecule to

Figure 8.15 The cell model of a liquid. (a) A simple representation of a molecule. (b) The way closely-packed molecules form a cell or cage around other molecules.

(a)

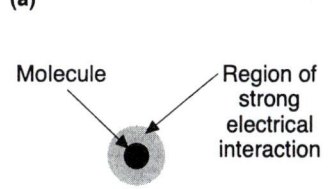

Molecule | Region of strong electrical interaction

(b)

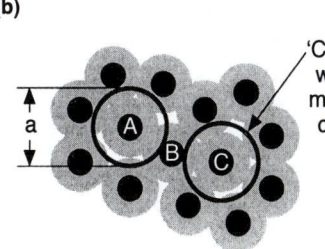

a

'Cage' or 'cell' within which molecule C is constrained

Figure 8.16 Illustration of the significance of the potential energy in the cell model of a liquid. In (a) a typical molecule *A* is shown trapped by its neighbours. This is represented on the potential energy diagram by a single *average* molecule vibrating inside a fixed *average* potential well. Occasionally, as illustrated in (b), the vibrations of neighbouring molecules conspire to allow a molecule to change its cell. Notice that, although this process of moving from cell to cell will normally involve two or more molecules, it is represented on the potential energy diagram as the motion of the single representative particle.

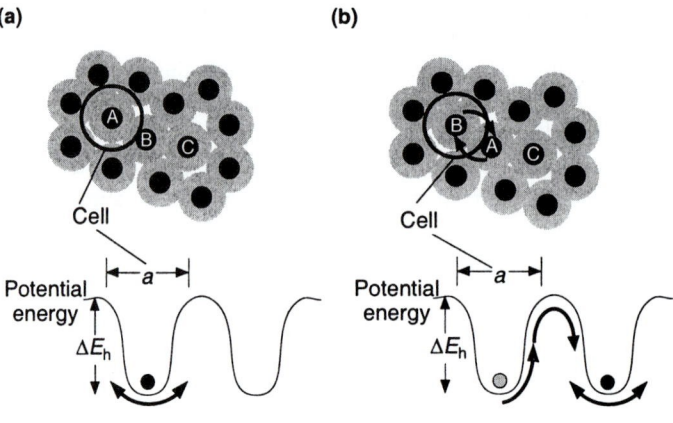

move. However, the simplification of the cell model is that it considers only the motion of a single *average* particle moving through an *average* potential which is empty of other molecules. The cell model thus represents a considerable simplification of the real situation. However it does capture the essence of the situation, in that molecules tend to vibrate about a position for a certain time but are still able move away from their neighbours, although with a relatively low probability. The chance of escape from a cell is determined by the strength of the interactions between molecules, by the shape of the molecules, and by temperature.

If the molecules were completely trapped in their cells then the model would describe a solid, i.e. a set of molecules vibrating about fixed positions. The solid would lack the crystalline order we normally assumed in Chapter 7 and would be known as an *amorphous* solid.

8.4.3 The potential energy in the liquid state

Let us consider how the (electrical) potential energy of an average molecule in the liquid state will vary with position throughout the liquid. As illustrated in Figure 8.17, we expect a potential which repeats through out the liquid, since the *average* experience of each molecule will be similar, independent of where it is the liquid.

Figure 8.17 indicates two different potentials, one

with a barrier to hopping from cell to cell, ΔE_h, much greater than the other. Since a substance in which atoms remain in their original potential cells is a solid, we expect the liquid with the larger ΔE_h will be more solid-like, i.e. able change its shape less easily than one with the smaller ΔE_h. The ease of changing shape is related to the *viscosity* of a substance (§9.6), so we expect that a small ΔE_h will give rise to a low viscosity.

As the temperature increases the probability per unit time that a molecule will escape from its cell also increases, since the average kinetic energy of the molecule is roughly $\approx k_B T$. We thus expect that the viscosity of a liquid will be reduced at higher temperatures, a prediction which is compared with experimental data in §9.6.

Figure 8.17 The variation of the potential energy of an average molecule with position according to the cell model of a liquid. The upper curve represents a liquid in which the 'hopping' process described in Figure 8.16 is more difficult than for the liquid represented by the lower curve.

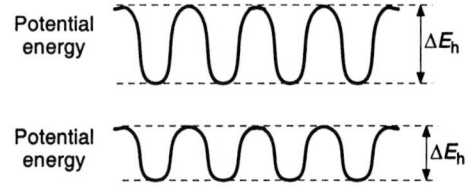

The energy required to activate 'hopping' from cell to cell within a liquid may be compared to the energy required to remove a molecule from the liquid altogether, ΔE_e. In general a molecule in the liquid will be interacting with a number of other adjacent molecules, typically between 8 and 11. The bonds with all these molecules must be broken if the molecule is to escape from the body of the liquid. The energy ΔE_e required to do this will thus in general be rather greater than ΔE_h.

The ease with which a molecule can leave the body of the liquid is related to the vapour pressure that a liquid creates above its surface. This matter is discussed more fully §9.8. However, we can say already that we expect that substances with a high ΔE_h will tend to have a high ΔE_e. Hence we can expect to find that the more viscous a substance, the lower its vapour pressure at a given temperature, i.e. the less volatile the substance will be.

Finally, we consider the situation of a molecule at the surface of a liquid. This molecule will only be bonded to perhaps 5 or 6 others, as opposed to between 8 and 11 others for a molecule in the body of the liquid. Its binding energy might therefore only be only around 50% of that a molecule in the body of the liquid. Thus we might expect that it will cost ΔE_s (roughly 50% of ΔE_e) to take a molecule from the body of the liquid and place it at the surface. This energy cost is the origin of the surface energy (or surface tension) of a liquid and is discussed more fully in the comparison with experimental surface energy data (§9.7)

Figure 8.19 encapsulates the essence of the cell model of liquid dynamics. The three activation energies will have very different values for say molten sodium and molten aluminium, but we might expect that for each substance, the *ratio* of the activation energies $\Delta E_h : \Delta E_s : \Delta E_e$ should be similar. Furthermore, we might hope to find some similarities between the behaviour of molten metals and very different liquids, such as water or organic liquids. The extent to which the cell model achieves this is reviewed in §9.9

8.4.4 Non-spherical molecules

The dynamics of liquids formed from non-spherical molecules is likely to be more complex than for the simple liquids discussed above. However, within the framework of the cell model, we expect to find just two significant differences between non-spherical and spherical molecules.

First we expect that the 'hopping' or 'swapping places' process discussed for spherical molecules will be considerably more difficult. Long molecules will become 'tangled' and 'hooked' in a way which has no analogy for the simple liquids. We thus expect that for a given binding energy ΔE_e, substances with non-spherical molecules will have relatively large values of ΔE_h.

Second, we expect that it will be considerably easier to place a molecule on the surface. We expect this because it will be possible to orient the

Figure 8.19 The variation of the potential energy of an average molecule with position according to the cell model of a liquid, showing the relative values of ΔE_h, ΔE_s, and ΔE_e. The curve is likely to be most appropriate to spherical molecules which can 'hop' past one another relatively easily. The curve should be contrasted with the one shown in Figure 8.20, which is likely to be appropriate for non-spherical molecules.

Figure 8.18 The variation of the potential energy of an average molecule with position according to the cell model of a liquid, showing the relative values of ΔE_h and ΔE_e.

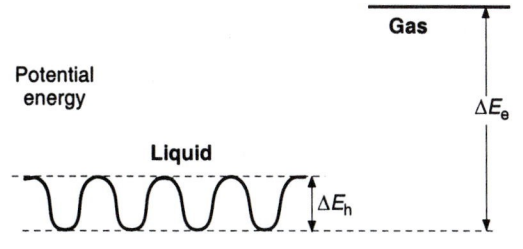

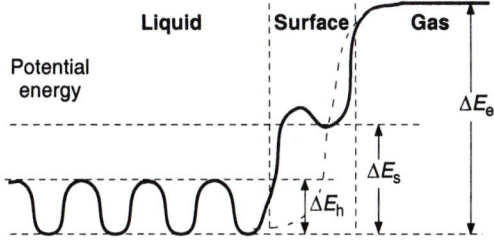

molecule so that most of it stays 'under' the surface, i.e. still within the body of the liquid. Since this *can* happen relatively easily, we can expect that it *will* happen. So we expect that for a given binding energy ΔE_e, substances with non-spherical molecules will have relatively small values of ΔE_s, and appropriately low values of surface tension.

Thus, a cell model picture for non-spherical molecules might now look something like Figure 8.20. Notice the changes in the relative magnitudes of ΔE_h and ΔE_s compared with those for spherical molecules in Figure 8.19. Figure 8.20 describes a liquid that forms surfaces relatively easily, but which is more viscous than we would expect on the basis of its binding energy. The extent to which this change in the relative magnitudes of ΔE_h and ΔE_s actually occurs in real liquids is discussed in §9.9.

Finally, before leaving this description of the cell model of liquids, we stress again that the parameters of the cell model are not single-particle parameters. They are merely parameters allowing complex many-molecule correlations to be described in rather simple terms.

8.4.5 Non-Newtonian liquids

The two options outlined in Figures 8.19 and 8.20 for spherical and non-spherical molecules shows some of the flexibility of cell model. It can describe liquids that result from a wide variety of different molecular constituents. However, it is common to find liquids that are not well described by *any* variant of the cell model. These liquids are frequently:

- formed from very long molecules, often polymers, that may be hundreds of times longer than they are wide. Clearly such a molecule will not 'hop' from cell to cell. Its motion is dominated by the nature of its entanglements with its neighbours

- dissolved in a solvent, a more 'normal' liquid made of smaller molecules.

It is not possible to discuss the dynamics of these complex liquids here, but I can point out some interesting properties of such liquids and invite the you to experiment with the following:

Soup: When stirring a smooth, thick soup in a bowl, if you stop stirring you find that the soup may 'spring back' and briefly rotate in the opposite direction. This is quite contrary to the expected behaviour for a simple fluid, which would continue to rotate. This phenomenon is known as *visco-elasticity*

Non-drip paint: Paints are composed of pigments in specially formulated 'carrier liquids'. Some carrier liquids are manufactured such that in the low-stress situation of a can, or on a paintbrush, they behave as a solid and retain their shape, i.e. they do not drip. Indeed, they may wobble like a jelly indicating elastic behaviour and some sense of a 'shape'. However under the stress of brush stroke they behave as a liquid and leave the brush. Substances behaving in this way are known as *thixotropic*.

Cornflour and water: Pour a small amount of cornflour (containing a natural medium-length polymer) onto a flat surface. Add water a drop at a time and stir thoroughly. Eventually a state is reached in which the substance may be 'torn' in two or 'broken' if pulled sharply, but which heals and flows like a liquid over the time scale of a few seconds.

Controlling the properties of substances with

Figure 8.20 The variation of the potential energy of an average molecule with position according to the cell model of a liquid, showing the relative values of ΔE_h, ΔE_s, and ΔE_e. This curve is likely to be appropriate for non-spherical molecules which cannot 'hop' past one another easily. The curve should be contrasted with the curve appropriate for spherical molecules shown in Figure 8.19.

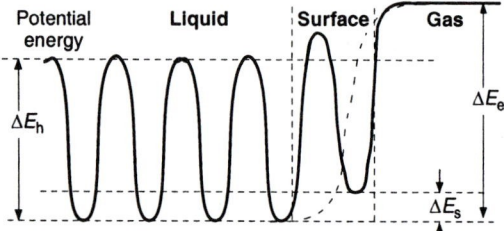

many molecules in solution is a problem of great complexity, one which still presents many challenges for scientists in both academic and industrial concerns.

8.5 Exercises

Exercises marked with a P prefix are 'normal' exercises. Those marked with a C prefix are best solved numerically by using a computer program or spreadsheet. Exercises marked with an E prefix are in general rather more challenging that the P and C exercises. Answers to all the exercises are downloadable from www.physicsofmatter.com

Molecular dynamics

To answer questions 1 to 3 you need to download the molecular dynamics simulation from the web site www.physicsofmatter.com

C1. Set the simulation 'phase' control to 'liquid' and make some notes about the key features of the dynamics of molecules in a simple two-dimensional liquid. Contrast these with the dynamics of molecules in (a) a simple two-dimensional solid and (b) a simple two-dimensional gas.

C2. Run the simulation for the liquid phase with at least 25 molecules and allow it to run until the molecules form 'a blob'. Stop the simulation and examine the instantaneous positions of the molecules. To what extent do the figures in Example 8.1 and Figure 8.4 reflect the patterns seen in the simulation?

C3. Run the simulation for the liquid phase with at least 25 molecules and allow it to run until the molecules form 'a blob'. Look for the occurrence of processes in which molecules swap places in a manner similar to that described in Figure 8.16. One of the molecules is coloured red to allow you to keep track of it more easily. Notice that it requires the motion of many molecules to allow an individual molecules to change 'cells'.

Radial density functions

P4. Construct (a) the radial density function and (b) the radial distribution function for the data of Table 8.1.

P5. Construct two-dimensional liquid and solid structures (like those in Example 8.1) by positioning coins on a surface. Draw evenly-spaced, concentric circles (like those in Example 8.1) onto tracing paper or an overhead transparency, and use this to count the number of molecules within a certain distance of a central molecule. From this data you can construct an analogue to Table 8.1 and hence determine the radial density function and the radial distribution function. This is a fairly standard (if time-consuming) exercise and as long as you average your results sufficiently and make realistic liquids your results should be similar to those shown in Figures 8.4 (a) and 8.6

If you have more time on your hands you may make a liquid with two components, e.g. from penny pieces (component P) and two-penny pieces (component Q). To describe this liquid you need four radial distribution functions. You need one to describe the distribution of P molecules around a P molecule; one to describe the distribution of P molecules around a Q molecule; one to describe the distribution of Q molecules around a Q molecule; and finally, one to describe the distribution of Q molecules around an P molecule. You should find relationships amongst the functions, but what you find will depend on the relative sizes of the coins you use. Amazingly, it is possible to actually measure such distribution functions for real three-dimensional liquids!

Liquids: comparison with experiment

9.1 Introduction

Most elements are in the solid state at room temperature and only enter the liquid state at elevated temperatures (Table 11.1). For this reason, data on elemental liquids is somewhat rarer than data on the properties of substances that are in their liquid state at around room temperature. Thus, we shall refer commonly to the so-called organic liquids mentioned in §8.2.3. Many properties of liquids are intermediate between those of gases and solids. Recall that the most striking property of matter in its solid state is that it displays both a well-defined volume *and* shape. This is in contrast with matter in its gaseous state, which expands to fill a container of any shape or volume. In line with its intermediate status, matter in its liquid state has a relatively well-defined volume, but no well-defined shape.

§9.2, §9.3, §9.4 **Density, Compressibility** and **Thermal expansivity:** In these three sections we will extend our discussion in §8.3 to allow us to understand the effects of liquid structure. We will attempt to understand the magnitude of the density change on melting, and (in more handwaving terms) the evolution of the density under changes in both pressure and temperature.

§9.5, §9.11 **Speed of sound** and **Thermal conductivity:** Here we deal with transport of energy through liquids, and in both sections we will develop simple 'hybrid' models of liquids. We will consider the transport as being the sum of transport through disordered solid-like regions and small gas-like regions. We will find that even though this approach allows us to model a wide range of behaviour, it is not really sophisticated enough to accurately describe the data.

§9.6, §9.7, §9.8 **Viscosity, Surface energy** and **Vapour pressure:** In these sections we discuss properties which are especially characteristic of the liquid state. We interpret them in terms of the dynamical *cell model* outlined in §8.4, and then in §9.9 we consider just how applicable the cell model is to liquids. Our conclusion is that with some reservations, the cell model does allows us to understand the temperature-dependence of viscosity and vapour pressure, and the way in which all these properties vary from one liquid to another.

§9.10 **Heat capacity:** We will find that the heat capacity in the liquid state is, in general, greater than in the solid or gaseous states. Exploiting our understanding of heat capacities of gases and solid, we will explain this as being due to the accessibility of extra degrees of freedom in the liquid state as compared with the other two states.

§9.12, §9.13 **Electrical** and **Optical properties:** For transparent liquids, our main approach will be to treat liquids as dense gases, and we will find that this approach is surprisingly successful. However, we will also find that its shortcomings highlight the importance of understanding the time-scale on which the liquid structure changes and the importance of molecular interactions. Similarly, for liquid metals, appreciating the time-scale of electron scattering will allow us to understand how it is that the metallic state survives the melting transition.

At www.physicsofmatter.com

In addition to copies of the figures and tables, you will find a computer program which realistically simulates the dynamics of molecules in liquids, solids and gases.

9.2 Density

9.2.1 Data on the density of liquids

Liquids have roughly similar densities to solids, with typical values between half and twenty times that of water. Historically, the *gram* was defined as the mass of one cubic centimetre of water at 4 degrees centigrade. So, we find that the density of water lies close to 1 gram per cubic centimetre, or in the rather incongruous SI units, 1000 kg m^{-3}. We thus find liquid densities in the range 500 kg m^{-3} to 20 000 kg m^{-3}.

Table 9.1 contains data on the density of about half the elements measured in the liquid state at their melting temperature. The table also shows the ratio of the stated liquid density, to the density in the solid state at 25 °C reported in Table 7.2. The thermal expansion of the solid between 25 °C and the melting temperature is generally less than 1% and does not alter the general conclusion drawn from Table 9.1 and illustrated in Figure 9.1: liquids are generally around 10% less dense than the corresponding solids. Notice however that four elements, silicon, germanium, gallium and bismuth are a few per cent more dense in the liquid state.

Figure 9.1 Histogram of the ratio of the density in the liquid phase at the melting temperature to the density in the solid phase of elements at 25 °C. The data is for 45 elements, of which 41 expand and 4 contract as they enter the liquid phase.

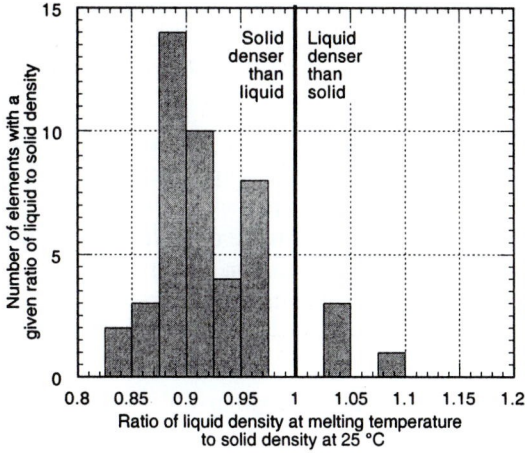

Ratio of liquid density at melting temperature to solid density at 25 °C

Table 9.1 The density of some elements at their melting temperatures in the liquid state. Also given is the ratio of the liquid density to the density of the solid at 25 °C (Table 7.2). The four elements which contract on melting: (silicon, gallium, germanium and bismuth) are shaded.

Z	Element	A	Liquid density (kg m^{-3})	Ratio of liquid/solid density
3	Lithium	6.941	516	0.968
5	Boron	10.81	2080	0.843
11	Sodium	22.99	930	0.962
12	Magnesium	24.31	1580	0.909
13	Aluminium	26.98	2400	0.889
14	Silicon	28.09	2525	1.080
16	Sulphur	32.06	1819	0.872
19	Potassium	39.10	824	0.955
20	Calcium	40.08	1365	0.892
22	Titanium	47.90	4130	0.916
23	Vanadium	50.94	5550	0.878
25	Manganese	54.94	6430	0.860
26	Iron	55.85	7100	0.901
28	Nickel	58.70	7800	0.875
29	Copper	63.55	8000	0.895
30	Zinc	65.38	6600	0.925
31	Gallium	69.72	6113.6	1.035
32	Germanium	72.59	5530	1.038
34	Selenium	78.96	4000	0.832
37	Rubidium	85.47	1470	0.959
40	Zirconium	91.22	5800	0.891
41	Niobium	92.91	7830	0.913
42	Molybdenum	95.94	9350	0.915
44	Ruthenium	101.1	10900	0.889
45	Rhodium	102.9	10850	0.874
46	Palladium	106.4	10700	0.892
47	Silver	107.9	9300	0.886
48	Cadmium	112.4	8020	0.927
50	Tin	118.7	6980	0.958
51	Antimony	121.7	6490	0.970
52	Tellurium	127.6	5770	0.924
55	Caesium	132.9	1845	0.971
56	Barium	137.3	3323	0.925
72	Hafnium	178.5	12000	0.904
73	Tantalum	180.9	15000	0.900
74	Tungsten	183.9	17600	0.914
75	Rhenium	186.2	18800	0.894
76	Osmium	190.2	20100	0.890
77	Iridium	192.2	20000	0.887
78	Platinum	195.1	19700	0.918
79	Gold	197.0	17320	0.898
81	Thallium	204.4	11290	0.951
82	Lead	207.2	10690	0.942
83	Bismuth	209.0	10050	1.025
92	Uranium	238.0	17907	0.940

Table 9.2 contains data on the measured density of substances, mainly organic, that are liquids at around room temperature. The densities are within a factor two of the density of water. Interestingly, Figure 9.2 illustrates the fact that the density of similarly constituted organic liquids does not increase with the mass of the molecules from which the liquid is composed. This is in contrast with the elemental solids (Figure 7.1), for which there is a strong dependence on atomic mass.

Water is a more complicated liquid than a simple entry in Table 9.2 might imply. Table 9.3 and Figure 9.3 show the density of ice and water as function of temperature from −10 °C to 100 °C. Notice

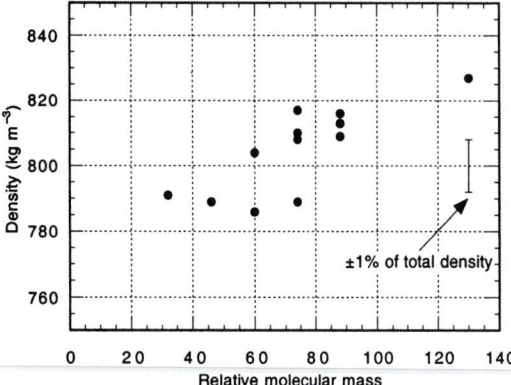

Figure 9.2 A graph of selected data from Table 9.2 showing the density of liquids with an OH group known as *alcohols* as a function of the relative molecular mass of the molecules.

Figure 9.3 The density of water (H_2O) and heavy water (D_2O) as a function of temperature at atmospheric pressure. Data points plotted below 0°C refer to the density of ice. The inset shows the density of water between 0 °C and 10 °C showing the weak maximum in density at 3.98 °C.

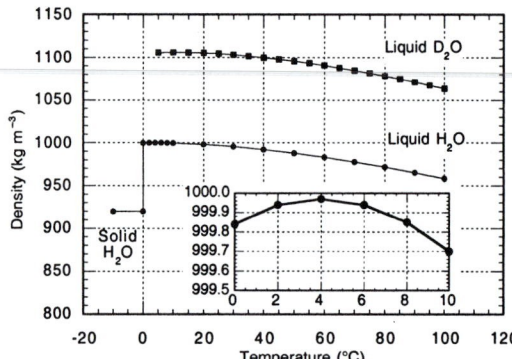

Table 9.2 The density of substances that are liquids at room temperature. The table gives the name of the substance, the chemical formula for its molecules, the relative molecular mass of each molecule, the density and the temperature of the density measurement. Only the last three entries in the table are *inorganic*.

Liquid and chemical formula		MW	Density (kg m⁻³)	
Organic liquids				
Methanol	CH_3OH	32	791	@20°C
Ethanol	C_2H_5OH	46	789	@20°C
Propan-1-ol	C_3H_7OH	60	804	@20°C
Propan-2-ol	C_3H_7OH	60	786	@20°C
2 Methyl-propan-1-ol	C_4H_9OH	74	817	@20°C
2 Methyl-propan-2-ol	C_4H_9OH	74	789	@20°C
Butan-1-ol	C_4H_9OH	74	810	@20°C
Butan-2-ol	C_4H_9OH	74	808	@20°C
2 Methyl-butan-1-ol	$C_5H_{11}OH$	88	816	@20°C
2 Methyl-butan-2-ol	$C_5H_{11}OH$	88	809	@20°C
Pentanol	$C_5H_{11}OH$	88	813	@20°C
Octanol	$C_8H_{17}OH$	130	827	@20°C
Aniline	C_6H_7N	86	1026	@15°C
Acetone	C_3H_6O	58	787	@25°C
Benzene	C_6H_6	78	879	@20°C
Inorganic liquids				
Carbon disulphide	CS_2	76	1293	@0 °C
Carbon tetrachloride	CCl_4	154	1632	@0 °C
Water (see Table 9.3)	H_2O	18	1000	@0 °C

Table 9.3 The density of water (H_2O) and heavy water (D_2O) as a function of temperature at atmospheric pressure.

T (°C)	H₂O	D₂O	T (°C)	H₂O	D₂O
0	999.84	—	40	992.22	1100.0
2	999.94	—	45	—	1097.9
4	999.97	—	50	988.04	1095.7
5	—	1105.6	55	—	1093.3
6	999.94	—	60	983.20	1090.6
8	999.85	—	65	—	1087.8
10	999.70	1106.0	70	977.77	1084.8
15	—	1105.9	75	—	1081.6
20	998.20	1105.3	80	971.79	1078.2
25	—	1104.4	85	—	1074.7
30	995.65	1103.2	90	965.31	1071.1
35	—	1101.7	95	—	1067.4
			100	958.36	1063.5

Figure 9.4 The density of mercury in its liquid state plotted as a function of temperature. Notice the linearity and large magnitude of the thermal expansion: the density changes by about 7%.

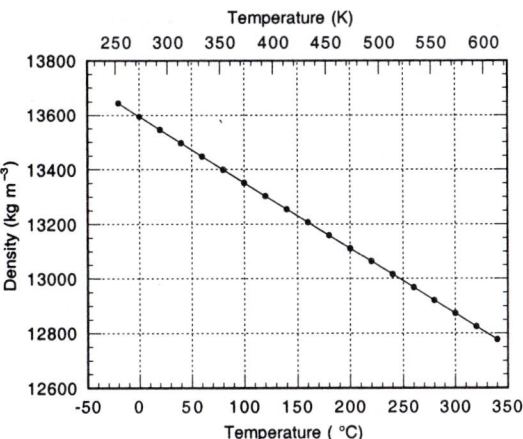

that water, like silicon, germanium, gallium and bismuth in Table 9.1, is more dense in its liquid phase than its solid phase. The density in the liquid phase is roughly constant, but shows a non-linear 4% fall in density as it is heated from 0 °C to 100 °C. There is a maximum in the density curve which occurs at 3.98 °C. The non-linear thermal expansion is in contrast with the strikingly linear behaviour of liquid mercury (Figure 9.4).

Using data from Tables 9.1 and 9.2, Example 9.1 shows how we can work out both the number of *molecules* per unit volume and the number of *atoms* per unit volume in the liquid state.

So the main questions raised by our preliminary examination of the experimental data on the density of liquids are:

- Why are the densities of most liquids of a similar order to that of solids?
- Why is the density of most liquid elements about 10% lower than their density in the solid state?
- Why is the density of a few liquids around 10% *higher* than in the solid state?
- Why, within a group of similar liquids such as the alcohols, is there only a weak dependence of density on molecular mass?

Example 9.1

Using the data from Table 9.2, work out:
- **the number the molecules per unit volume, and**
- **the number of atoms per unit volume**

in liquid ethanol and liquid pentanol.

Ethanol

The molecular mass of ethanol is 46, i.e. there are Avogadro's number of ethanol molecules in 46×10^{-3} kg of ethanol. The molar volume of of ethanol is:

$$V_{\mathrm{m}} = \frac{46 \times 10^{-3}}{789} = 5.83 \times 10^{-5} \ \mathrm{m}^3$$

which is around 58 cm^3. The number density of ethanol molecules is therefore:

$$n = \frac{N_{\mathrm{A}}}{V_{\mathrm{m}}} = \frac{6.02 \times 10^{23}}{5.83 \times 10^{-5}} = 1.033 \times 10^{28} \ \mathrm{molecules} \ \mathrm{m}^{-3}$$

Each ethanol molecule consists of 2 carbon atoms, 6 hydrogen atoms and 1 oxygen atom: 9 atoms in total. Thus the density of atoms is approximately: $9n = 9.29 \times 10^{28}$.

Pentanol

The molecular mass of pentanol is 88, i.e. there are Avogadro's number of pentanol molecules in 88×10^{-3} kg of pentanol. The molar volume of pentanol is:

$$V_{\mathrm{m}} = \frac{88 \times 10^{-3}}{813} = 1.082 \times 10^{-4} \ \mathrm{m}^3$$

which is around 108 cm^3. The number density of pentanol molecules is therefore:

$$n = \frac{N_{\mathrm{A}}}{V_{\mathrm{m}}} = \frac{6.02 \times 10^{23}}{1.082 \times 10^{-4}} = 5.56 \times 10^{27} \ \mathrm{molecules} \ \mathrm{m}^{-3}$$

Each pentanol molecule consists of 5 carbon atoms, 12 hydrogen atoms and 1 oxygen atom: 18 atoms in total. So we can estimate the density of atoms to be approximately: $18n = 1.00 \times 10^{29}$.

The atomic number density of both types of liquid is close to the typical atomic number density of a solid. The molecular number density for pentanol is around half the value for ethanol because the pentanol molecules are around twice as large and twice the mass, leading to a similar mass per unit volume for the two liquids.

This implies that the separation between atoms *within* molecules is not greatly different from the separation between atoms in neighbouring molecules.

9.2.2 Understanding the density data

Normal liquids

Our discussion of the density of liquids begins with our basic assumptions about the structure of liquids outlined in §8.2. This section describes a liquid as being like a disordered solid, but with a detailed structure which changes every few nanoseconds or so (Figure 8.1). Given this description, we can see immediately why liquids might in general be less dense than solids: the packing of molecules in liquids is less 'efficient' leaving 'holes' in the structure. We can take this supposition one stage further by following the lessons of §8.3 and directly evaluating the 'area' density of a two-dimensional liquids and solids. We can then extend the two-dimensional example to three dimensions.

Figures 9.5 and 9.6 represent a hypothetical two-dimensional substance in its solid and liquid states respectively. The area density of spheres in this substance may be evaluated by considering the number of spheres within a given area. The odd shaped area shown in Figures 9.5 and 9.6 is chosen in order to eliminate edge effects where whole rows of spheres fall just in, or just out of the counting area. The solid density evaluates to 136 spheres/area and the liquid density evaluates to 126 spheres/area. Taking the ratio indicates that the liquid density is around 126/136 ≈ 93% of the solid density — an area density decrease of 7%. This is for two dimensions: if we apply the considerations of Example 7.4 we would find the three-dimensional density decrease to about be $\frac{3}{2}$ times this amount, around 11%.

This is in good agreement with the general level of density changes observed as solids change into liquids. The simplicity of the explanation makes it rather convincing, but raises a more difficult question: how can we understand those few substances in which the density *increases* on melting?

Substances which contract on melting

The answer lies again in the efficiency with which molecules pack together. We have seen that substances which bond *covalently* form crystal structures of relatively low density (§6.4). This is because, energetically, it is better for neighbouring molecules to adopt the optimum orientation and separation rather than merely to get as close as

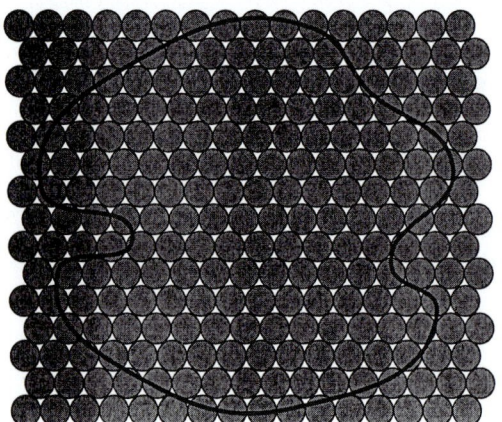

Figure 9.5 The figure may be used to calculate the 'area density' of close-packed two-dimensional circles that are analogous to a two-dimensional solid. The curved area is the same in this figure as in Figure 9.6 and contains the centres of 136 circles. The curved area is chosen to avoid counting bias near the edge of the area.

Figure 9.6 The figure may be used to calculate the 'area density' of close-packed two-dimensional circles that are analogous to a two-dimensional liquid. The curved area is the same in this figure as in Figure 9.5 and contains the centres of 126 circles.

possible (Figure 6.10). Similar considerations also apply to ionically bonded substances. This is in contrast to the situation of substances that are held together by Van der Waals or metallic bonding, which seek as many near neighbours as possible.

In the liquid phase of covalently-bonded substances, the random and constantly changing structure leads to difficulty in maintaining the correct orientation with respect to neighbouring molecules. As a consequence of this, the open structure of the solid *collapses* as the substance enters the liquid state. If this hypothesis is correct then we ought to find that the substances which contract on melting have primarily covalent bonding. Is this the case? Yes and No.

The first two examples, silicon and germanium, do fall clearly into this category. In §6.4 we mentioned that they are covalently-bonded solids and form an open crystal structure based around the tetrahedral symmetry of their electron orbitals. Water is a more complicated case, but the hydrogen bonding present in water is certainly highly directional: this is discussed below. The case of

gallium, our last example, is more puzzling. Gallium is a metal and so ought to have at least some component of non-directional bonding. However, the general run of the argument concerning the density of liquids suggests that the fact that gallium contracts as it enters the liquid state must indicate that it too must have a directional (i.e. covalent) bonding mechanism in addition to its metallic bonding.

Water

Finally we come to the case of water. In water, the directional bonds which make the solid state (ice) lower in density than the 'collapsed' liquid state are the *hydrogen bonds* between the molecules. In the 'collapsed' liquid state a great deal of the structure present in ice remains and advanced studies indicate that only a few per cent of the hydrogen bonds are bent (not broken) in the liquid state. The process that leads to the melting of ice is the progressive weakening of the ice structure (Figure 9.7) by thermal vibrations which cause the hydrogen-bonded part of the oxygen=oxygen linkages to bend. It is as if in the skeletal steel frame of a skyscraper, a few of the steel girders were

Figure 9.7 Qualitative indication of the structure of ice. (a) A central water molecule linked to two others. Concentrating on the oxygen atoms, we can see that each oxygen can link to four other oxygen atoms arranged roughly tetrahedrally around it. Two of these links are of the form **O=covalent bond=H=hydrogen bond=O** and two are of the form **O=hydrogen bond=H=covalent bond=O**. (Notice the change in order of the covalent and hydrogen bonds.) One example of each form of O=O linkage is shown as a straight line in (b). In (c) the structure of ice is indicated with the circles representing only the oxygen atoms and the lines representing either of the two types of O=O linkages discussed. Different bonds have been drawn either as thin, bold or shaded lines to emphasise the structure. In fact all the bonds are equivalent.

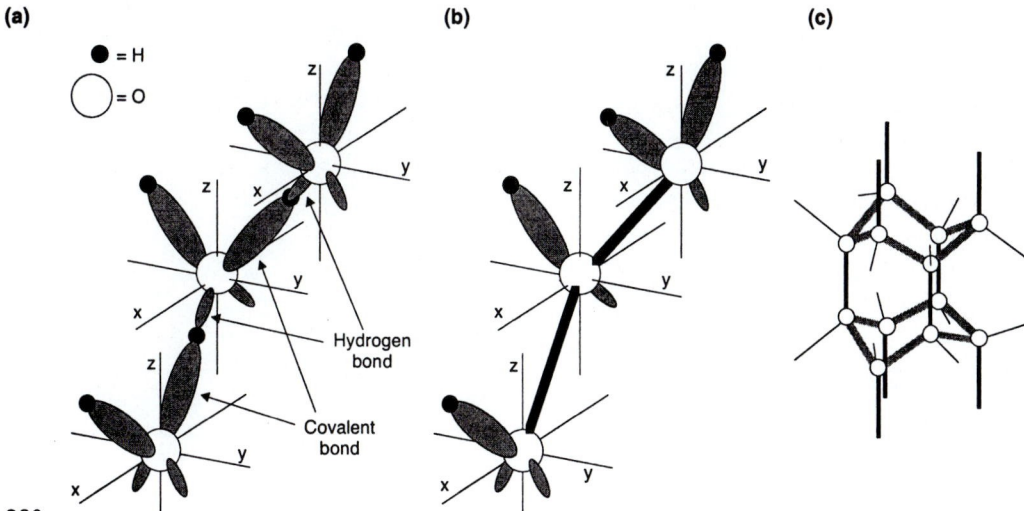

(a) **(b)** **(c)**

replaced with rubber ones: large parts of the structure would remain intact, but the structure as a whole would collapse. The melting of ice is a similar, though less spectacular, phenomenon.

The density of organic liquids

Finally, we come to the question of why, within a group of similar liquids such as the alcohols, there is only a weak dependence of density on molecular mass (Table 9.2 and Figure 9.2). Molecules which differ in mass by a factor 4, form liquids whose densities changes by less than 5%. The conclusion to be drawn from this striking fact is that the separation between atoms *in different molecules* is similar to the separation between atoms *within a molecule*. This is at first rather surprising.

As we mentioned in §8.2.4, the forces acting *between* organic molecules are relatively weak. The alcohols of Table 9.2 do not have a strong contribution from hydrogen bonding, and so a good deal of their bonding energy is the weak Van der Waals

force due to the fluctuations of electronic charge on the molecules. There is also a term which results from the slightly polar nature of the carbon-hydrogen C–H bonds that constitute most of the bonds in the molecule. The forces acting between atoms *within* a molecule are the strong covalent bonds due to either C–H or C–C bonds.

However the larger molecules have more 'surface area' and so the more molecules can be attracted through the non-directional Van der Waals mechanism. This factor will compensate somewhat for the weakness of the interaction. We should also realise that although the atomic separation between atoms within a molecule and atoms in neighbouring molecules is similar, the *strength* of their interactions differs dramatically. The *inter*molecular forces between the atoms are overcome at the boiling temperature (≈ 300 K), whereas the *intra*molecular forces are not overcome until the molecule decomposes ($\approx$ several thousand kelvin).

9.3 Compressibility and bulk modulus

9.3.1 Background

In the previous section (§9.2), we examined data on the density of liquids. In this section (§9.3), we shall examine data on how the density of liquids changes when the pressure is increased, i.e. their compressibility. In the following section (§9.4), we shall examine the effect of temperature on the density. In fact, we rarely discuss changes in density *per se*. We normally talk about changes in the volume or length as a function of pressure or temperature. The changes in volume as a function of pressure are generally characterised by either the bulk modulus B, or the compressibility K. These are merely the inverse of each other, and are defined by:

$$B = -V \frac{\partial P}{\partial V}$$

$$K = \frac{1}{B} = -\frac{1}{V} \frac{\partial V}{\partial P}$$

(7.1*)

In our discussion of the compressibility of gases, we needed to take care to distinguish between *adiabatic* and *isothermal* moduli. For liquids, the two moduli differ by much less than for gases, and often the data tables do not state which value is plotted. If the data are derived at high pressure, then generally it is only possible to determine the isothermal modulus. If the data are determined by using speed of sound measurements then, as for gases, the appropriate modulus to use is the adiabatic modulus, except at the highest frequencies. We shall also discuss the bulk modulus of liquids when we consider the speed of sound data in §9.5

9.3.2 Data

Table 9.4 shows the bulk modulus for a number of, mainly organic, liquids.

The most striking feature of the data in Table 9.4 is that there is not much of it! This reflects the fact that liquids are relatively under-studied in comparison with their solid relatives. On inspection there are, however, some quite striking results contained in the data. Firstly, the data for ether and water indicate that the bulk modulus increases with increasing pressure. This implies that it is easier to compress a liquid initially, but that it becomes harder and harder as the pressure increases. Secondly, the compressibility of nearly all the organic liquids is of the order of 1 GPa, about a factor 10 to 100 less than the bulk moduli of the elemental solids. Admittedly, the data here is essentially for organic liquids which we would expect to be considerably more compressible than (mostly metallic) elements. However the factor 10 difference is still quite large. This tells us that in general it is much easier to compress a liquid than it is a solid.

So the main questions we would like to address are:

- Why is the compressibility of nearly all the organic liquids of the order of 1 GPa, about a factor 10 to 100 less than the bulk moduli of the elemental solids?
- Why does the bulk modulus of liquids tend to increase with increasing pressure?

9.3.3 Understanding the data on the compressibility of liquids

Background

In attempting to analyse the rather scant data for the compressibility of liquids, we immediately encounter a problem: we have no simple theory with which to compare the data. The reason why there is no simple theory is that even the simplest analysis shows that this is not a simple problem! To see this we note that applying pressure to a liquid will have two distinct effects. The first is *structural* (§8.3), and the second *dynamical* (§8.4). Applying pressure in general causes the structure of the liquid (i.e. the radial density function) to evolve into a generally more solid-like structure. In addition, the change in structure reduces the volume for a molecule and hence alters the ease

Table 9.4 The bulk modulus of some liquids at the pressure and temperature shown. The pressure is shown in units of atmospheres, where one atmosphere is approximately 0.1 MPa.

Liquid and formula	P (Atm)	B (GPa)	T (°C)
Organic liquids			
Methanol, CH_3OH	37	0.97	14.7
Ethanol, C_2H_5OH	1	1.32	0
Propan-1-ol, C_3H_7OH	8	1.04	17.7
Propan-2-ol, C_3H_7OH	8	0.983	17.8
Butan-1-ol, C_4H_9OH	8	1.13	17.4
Butan-2-ol, C_4H_9OH	8	1.03	17.9
Ether	1	0.689	0
Ether	1000	1.56	0
Benzene, C_6H_6	8	1.10	17.9
Inorganic liquids			
Carbon disulphide, CS_2	8	1.16	15.6
Carbon tetrachloride, CCl_4	1	1.12	20
Water, H_2O	1	2.05	15
Water, H_2O	1000	2.75	15
Water, H_2O	2500	3.88.	14.2

with which molecules can move within the liquid. In terms of the cell model of liquid dynamics, applying pressure reduces the cell volume and increases the hopping barrier height ΔE_h. This effect on liquid dynamics is illustrated in Figure 11.12. To calculate the bulk modulus of liquids we need a theory which links the structural and dynamical models we developed in Chapter 8. Developing such a model in any serious sense is beyond the scope of this book. However, in §9.5.2 we will develop an extremely simple model of exactly this kind linking dynamical and structural properties. In this section, we restrict ourselves merely to trying to understand the order of magnitude of the data, and its qualitative dependence on pressure.

Order of magnitude of the bulk modulus

Our general model of liquid structure (§8.3) allows us to understand this is in a pretty straightforward manner. We consider that a liquid is similar to a solid, but that its molecules are packed together with around 10% of extra space. So it would not be surprising to find that it would be relatively easy to 'reclaim' this 10% when the liquid is compressed.

Increase in bulk modulus with pressure

We would then expect to find that on trying to compress a liquid beyond this point, the bulk modulus would become closer to that in the solid state. (We shall see in §10.7 that the application of large pressure can also serve to solidify a liquid.) In Example 9.2 we see that in order to compress any of the liquids in Table 9.4 by around 10 % we would need to apply a pressure of roughly 1000 atmospheres. We would expect that at this point the bulk modulus would have increased significantly. Looking at the data for ether and water from Table 9.4 we see that the changes are indeed significant, roughly 100 % for ether ($B = 0.689$ GPa $\Rightarrow B = 1.56$ GPa) and around 35% for water ($B = 2.05$ GPa $\Rightarrow B = 2.75$ GPa). It is important to remember that water has many anomalous properties, particularly with regard to its structure and so its properties are probably not very typical of liquids as a whole.

Summary

At a qualitative level, we can understand the bulk modulus of liquids quite well. Liquids are more compressible than solids because there is roughly 10 % of extra space in the liquid state which can be relatively easily recovered under the application of pressure. Under around 1000 atmospheres, the bulk modulus increases significantly for the two liquids for which we had data, though not by quite as much as the factor 10 that we might have expected. We consider the bulk modulus of liquids again in §9.5 when we try understand the data on the speed of sound in liquids.

Example 9.2

What pressure would be required to reduce the volume of a liquid from Table 9.4 by 10%?

We start out with the definition of the bulk modulus:

$$B = -V \frac{\partial P}{\partial V} \qquad (*7.1)$$

We rearrange this as an expression for dP and then integrate:

$$dP = -B \frac{dV}{V}$$

$$P = -B \int_{V_0}^{V_0 - \Delta V} \frac{dV}{V}$$

$$= -B \left[\ln(V)\right]_{V_0}^{V_0 - \Delta V}$$

$$= -B \left[\ln(V_0 - \Delta V) - \ln(V_0)\right]$$

$$= -B \ln\left[\frac{V_0 - \Delta V}{V_0}\right]$$

Substituting $\Delta V = 0.1 V_0$ into this:

$$P = -B \ln[0.9]$$

$$\approx -B \times -0.10$$

$$\approx 0.1B$$

This tells us that in order to reduce volume by 10% we need to apply a pressure equal to around $0.1B$. Given the general values for organic liquids, this implies a pressure of around 0.1 GPa. Since atmospheric pressure is roughly 10^5 Pa, this corresponds to a pressure of roughly 1000 atmospheres.

9.4 Thermal expansivity

9.4.1 Data on the thermal expansivity of liquids

The increase in volume on heating a liquid held at constant pressure P_0 with initial volume V_0 can be expressed as:

$$V = V_0(1 + \beta \Delta T) \qquad (9.1)$$

where ΔT is the change in temperature from the initial temperature, and β is the *coefficient of volume expansion*.

The data of Table 9.5 show that the volume thermal expansivity of liquids is in general rather greater than that of solids (Table 7.4), but still considerably less than for gases (Table 5.4). This is true for organic, inorganic and elemental liquids. Notice that some liquids display anomalous thermal expansivities close to their melting temperature. For example, water (Figure 9.3) displays a *negative* thermal expansion: it contracts as it is heated from 0 °C and 4 °C. Other liquids, such as mercury (Figure 9.4), display extremely linear

behaviour from their melting temperature up to their boiling temperature.

In summary, these results indicate that for elements and organic liquids, a typical volume expansivity varies between $10^{-3} \, °C^{-1}$ and $10^{-4} \, °C^{-1}$. Notice, however, that the volume expansivity of molecular liquids, with the exception of water, is considerably greater than for the molten metals.

So the main questions raised by our preliminary examination of the experimental data on the expansivity of solids are:

- Why is the expansivity of liquids (in general) larger than for solids, but smaller than that shown by gases?
- What determines the particular values of α for each material?
- What is the origin of the thermal expansivity anomaly in water?

9.4.2 Understanding the thermal expansivity of liquids

In §7.4 we explained the expansivity of solids as being due to the asymmetry of the potential energy variation between atoms. At low temperatures, the atoms vibrate with low amplitude around the minimum of the interatomic potential. These low amplitude vibrations are essentially symmetric about the position of mean separation. As the temperature increases, the atomic vibrations become systematically larger in amplitude and increasingly asymmetric in nature. This asymmetry increases the mean separation of the atoms of the substances and leads to the phenomenon of thermal expansion.

Thus the key element in understanding the thermal expansivity of solids lay in understanding the detailed manner in which the potential energy of each pair of atoms varied as a function of their average separation.

Table 9.5 The coefficient of volume expansivity β for various liquids at temperatures around room temperature. The shaded column shows the value of the volume expansivity of the corresponding solid substance. N/A indicates that data is not available.

Substance		MW	$T\,(°C)$	$\beta\,(°C^{-1})$ Liquid	$\beta\,(°C^{-1})$ Solid
Organic liquids					
Acetic acid	CH_3COOH	60	20	107×10^{-5}	N/A
Acetone	CH_3COCH_3	58	20	143×10^{-5}	N/A
Methanol	CH_3OH	46	20	119×10^{-5}	N/A
Ethanol	C_2H_5OH	32	20	108×10^{-5}	N/A
Aniline	C_6H_7N	86	20	85×10^{-5}	N/A
Benzene	C_6H_6	78	20	121×10^{-5}	N/A
Toluene	$C_6H_5CH_3$	92	20	107×10^{-5}	N/A
Inorganic liquids					
Carbon Disulphide	CS_2	76	20	119×10^{-5}	N/A
Carbon Tetrachloride	CCl_4	154	20	122×10^{-5}	N/A
Water	H_2O	18	20	21×10^{-5}	N/A
Metals					
Lithium	Li	23	400-1125	19×10^{-5}	16.8×10^{-5} @ 20 °C
Sodium	Na	39	96.5	25×10^{-5}	21.2×10^{-5} @ 20 °C
Potassium	K	85.5	64 - 1400	29×10^{-5}	24.9×10^{-5} @ 20 °C
Rubidium	Rb	133	39	30×10^{-5}	27.0×10^{-5} @ 20 °C
Copper	Cu	63.6	1084	10×10^{-5}	4.95×10^{-5} @ 20 °C
Copper	Cu	63.6	1084	10×10^{-5}	6.09×10^{-5} @ 527 °C
Mercury	Hg	200.6	0 - 100	18.1×10^{-5}	N/A

The atoms in a liquid are held together by exactly the same forces that hold the atoms of a solid together, and so we may reasonably expect the thermal expansivity of liquids to be similar to those of solids. Experimentally we find that the thermal expansivity of liquids is similar to that of the equivalent solids (Table 9.5) but with a tendency to be slightly larger. This may be understood as being due to the fact that the thermal expansivity of solids tends to increase with temperature, and the liquid data is necessarily obtained at a higher temperature than the equivalent solid data.

However, there is one further way in which a liquid can expand that is unavailable to a solid: it can change its structure. This happens in a slow undramatic manner, evolving from a solid-like structure near its melting temperature to a more gas-like structure near its boiling temperature. The evidence of Table 9.5 is that in elements for which data is available for both for liquids and solids, this method of expansion is a relatively small component of the total thermal expansivity.

However, the thermal expansivity of the organic liquids is nearly three times larger than elemental liquids which melt at a similar temperature. This arises because the molecules of organic liquids are attracted to one another by the weak Van der Waals forces that make it relatively easy for molecules to move apart and adopt structures that optimise their energy. Since the covalent bonds *within* the molecules are considerably stronger than the Van der Waals bonds *between* molecules, molecules tend to retain their optimal *shape* on heating but to change the relative orientation and separation as a function of temperature.

Figure 9.8 Detailed view of the thermal expansivity anomaly in water. Notice the tiny scale of the anomaly.

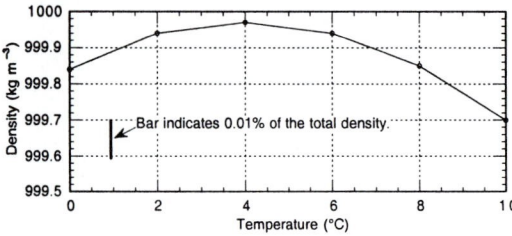

Example 9.3

Liquid-in-glass thermometers consist of a reservoir of liquid connected to a thin tube called a capillary tube. The volume of the liquid reservoir changes with temperature and this change in volume is reflected in a variation of the length of the liquid column in the capillary tube.

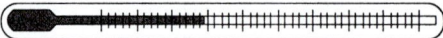

A given liquid-in-glass thermometer has a reservoir of volume 1 cm^3 and is connected to a capillary tube with an internal diameter of 0.1 mm. For mercury and ethanol, the two most commonly used working liquids, work out the sensitivity of such a thermometer, i.e. the number of millimetres per degree celsius that the liquid surface moves along the tube.

The basic equation is 9.1: $V = V_0(1 + \_\Delta T)$ and we need first to evaluate the volume change $V - V_0 = \Delta V$ of the liquid for a change in temperature of 1 °C. Rearranging Equation 9.1:

$$V - V_0 = \Delta V = V_0 \beta \Delta T$$

This volume change is accommodated by the expansion of the fluid up the capillary tube. The extra volume is therefore given by $\pi r^2 \Delta L$ where ΔL is the distance the fluid expands up the tube and r is the radius of the capillary tube. We thus have $\Delta V = V_0 \beta \Delta T = \pi r^2 \Delta L$ and so rearranging with $\Delta T = 1$ °C this gives:

$$\Delta L = \frac{V_0 \beta}{\pi r^2}$$

Substituting $r = 0.05 \times 10^{-3}$ m and $V_0 = 1 cm^3 = 10^{-6} m^3$:

$$\Delta L = \frac{10^{-6}\beta}{\pi\left(0.05 \times 10^{-3}\right)^2} = 127.3\beta$$

If we substitute the β values for mercury (18.1 × 10⁻⁵ °C⁻¹) and ethanol (108 × 10⁻⁵ °C⁻¹) we find:

$$\Delta L(\text{Mercury}) = 0.023\text{m} = 23 \text{ mm}$$
$$\Delta L(\text{Ethanol}) = 0.137\text{m} = 137 \text{ mm}$$

Both displacements are easily appreciable and both liquids are commonly used in liquid-in-glass thermometers. A fuller calculation would take into account the expansion of the tube and the container of the liquid reservoir which tends to slightly reduce the sensitivity of the thermometers. Notice that water could not be used as the working liquid in such a thermometer because its thermal expansivity (which corresponds to the *slope* of the data in Figure 9.3) varies considerably across the small temperature range in which it is a liquid. This is in contrast to the data for mercury shown in Figure 9.4. Furthermore cooling below 0°C would cause the liquid to freeze, and the expansion of water on freezing would almost certainly break the reservoir container.

The final question concerns the thermal expansivity anomaly in water which causes water to become slightly denser as it warms from 0 °C to 3.98 °C. The origin of this anomaly is already clear from Figure 9.3, which shows the anomaly on the same scale as the 10 % volume collapse that ice undergoes on melting. The process that leads to the melting of ice is the progressive weakening of the ice structure (Figure 9.8) by thermal vibrations which cause the hydrogen-bonded part of the oxygen=oxygen linkages to bend. This process of bending and collapse continues in the liquid state, but is in competition with the normal processes of thermal expansion discussed above. Thus the maximum in the density arises at around 4 °C because at that temperature the process of collapse of the liquid structure is exactly balanced by the tendency to thermally expand. We should also note the small magnitude of the thermal expansivity anomaly, amounting to only 2 parts in 10^4.

9.5 Speed of sound

9.5.1 Data on the speed of sound

Sound travels considerably faster through liquids than gases: the maximum speed in Table 9.6 below is around 3350ms^{-1} for molten copper, which may be compared with a maximum of around 1000 ms^{-1} for hydrogen gas (Table 5.14). Examination of the data of Table 9.6 shows that the speed of sound in a liquid is around 30% less than the speed of sound in the corresponding solid. The *type* of wave which propagates has more in common with the single type of longitudinal wave which propagates in a gas. The shear waves (Figure 7.12 (b) and (c)) are heavily damped in liquids and we do not consider such waves here.

The main question raised by our preliminary examination of the experimental data on the velocity of sound in liquids is:

- Why is the speed of sound in liquids around 30% slower than in the equivalent solid below its melting temperature?

9.5.2 Understanding the data on the speed of sound

Having examined the speed of sound in both gases (§5.6) and solids (§7.5) we are now fairly confi-

Table 9.6 The speed of sound in liquids showing c_L, the speed of longitudinal waves. For the elements, where possible, the data for the solid state (taken from Table 7.12) is also included, in the shaded column, for comparison. Data for ice is also included.

Substance	T (°C)	c_L (ms⁻¹)	Substance	T (°C)	c_L (ms⁻¹)	Substance	T (°C)	c_L (ms⁻¹)	c_L (ms⁻¹)
Organic Liquids			*Elements*			*Elements*			
Acetic acid	20	1173	Hydrogen, H_2	−258	1242	Cadmium, Cd	360	2150	2780
Acetone	20	1190	Helium, He	−269	211	Copper, Cu	1350	3350	4759
Methanol	20	1121	Nitrogen, N_2	−189	745	Gallium, Ga	50	2740	
Ethanol	20	1162	Oxygen, O_2	−186	950	Mercury, Hg	20	1454	
Propanol	20	1223	Sodium, Na	110	2520	Silver, Ag	1150	2630	3704
Butanol	20	1258	Potassium, K	80	1869	Tin, Sn	240	2470	3380
iso-Pentanol	20	1255	Rubidium, Rb	50	1427	Zinc, Zn	450	2700	4187
Hexanol	20	1331	Caesium, Cs	40	980				
Hexanol	20	1331							
Heptanol	20	1343							
Water	0	1402							
Ice	−20	3840							

dent that we understand the physics of sound propagation. The speed of sound in a medium depends on two quantities: the compressibility of the medium, and its density. Our success in understanding the data for gases and solids leads us to rephrase our original questions as follows:

- Is the lower speed of propagation in a liquid as compared with a solid due to a change in *compressibility* or a change in *density*?

However, in liquids a complicating factor arises concerning the character of the waves in the liquid. Are the waves like those in a gas, or like those in a solid? In this section we will first deal with this complication, and then address the effect of density and bulk modulus in turn

The effect of the character of the sound waves

In solids, the speed of a longitudinal compressive wave c_L, is given by Equation 7.26 and 7.27 as:

$$c_L = \sqrt{\frac{\gamma E}{\rho}} \qquad \text{(7.26* and 9.2)}$$

where ρ is the density of the substance, E its Young's modulus, and γ a factor related to the Poisson ratio σ of the substance given by:

$$\gamma = \frac{(1-\sigma)}{(1-2\sigma)(1+\sigma)} \qquad \text{(7.27* and 9.3)}$$

Remember that γ in this context has no connection with the ratio of the heat capacities of gases found in formulae for the speed of sound in gases.

Our first step is to write Young's modulus in terms of the bulk modulus B, using a standard equation (Appendix A2):

$$B = \frac{E}{3(1-2\sigma)} \qquad (9.4)$$

Substituting Equation 9.4 into Equation 9.2 yields and expression for the speed of longitudinal sound waves in bulk solid as:

$$c_L = \sqrt{\frac{3B(1-\sigma)}{\rho(1+\sigma)}} \qquad (9.5)$$

Now for solids, the Poisson ratio has typical value

of $\sigma \approx 1/3$ which implies:

$$c_L^{\text{solid}} \approx \sqrt{\frac{3B(\tfrac{2}{3})}{\rho(\tfrac{4}{3})}}$$

$$\approx \sqrt{\frac{3}{2}}\sqrt{\frac{B}{\rho}} \qquad (9.6)$$

$$\approx 1.22\sqrt{\frac{B}{\rho}}$$

However, for liquids we expect a Poisson ratio closer to 0.5. This is the value of Poisson ratio relevant to compressions and rarefactions that are *volume conserving*. We expect this because liquids have the ability to change shape relatively easily. (See Example 7.8.) Substituting $\sigma = \tfrac{1}{2}$ we arrive at:

$$c_L^{\text{liquid}} = \sqrt{\frac{3B(\tfrac{1}{2})}{\rho(\tfrac{3}{2})}}$$

$$= \sqrt{\frac{B}{\rho}} \qquad (9.7)$$

which is similar to the equivalent result for a gas (§5.5.2).

Let us first make the (incorrect) assumption that the density and bulk modulus of a substance in its solid and liquid states are equal. If this were so then the expected difference in the speed of sound would arise entirely from the changed character of the sound waves in the liquid. Taking the ratio of Equations 9.6 and 9.7 predicts that the ratio $c_L^{\text{liquid}}/c_L^{\text{solid}}$ would be $\approx 1/1.22 \approx 0.82$, i.e. we would expect the speed of sound in liquids to be about 18% lower than in the equivalent solid.

The effect of density

In §9.2 we saw that the densities of liquids were generally of the order of 10% less than those of solids due to the less efficient 'packing' of atoms in the liquid state. According to Equation 9.7 this predicts that the speed of sound in liquids should be *increased* as compared to the speed of sound in an otherwise equivalent solid by a factor $\sqrt{1.1}$ which is roughly 1.05. So, taking into account both the change in the character of sound waves in

287

the liquid and the change in density, we should expect the speed of sound in liquids to be (1.05 × 0.82 ≈ 0.86) ≈ 14% lower than in the equivalent solids.

The effect of the bulk modulus

Consideration of both the character of waves in a liquid and of the changes of density in the liquid, has not explained the experimental fact of a 30% reduction in the speed of sound in liquids. So we must assume that the extra lowering in the speed of sound of a liquid is due to a lowering of the bulk modulus of the liquid.

Taking the ratio of Equations 9.7 and 9.6 yields an expression for the ratio of the speed of sound in liquid and solid c_L^{liquid}/c_L^{solid} :

$$\frac{c_L^{liquid}}{c_L^{solid}} = \sqrt{\frac{B^{liquid}}{\rho_{liquid}}} \bigg/ \sqrt{\frac{3}{2}}\sqrt{\frac{B^{solid}}{\rho_{solid}}}$$

$$= \sqrt{\frac{2}{3}}\sqrt{\frac{B^{liquid}}{B^{solid}} \times \frac{\rho_{solid}}{\rho_{liquid}}} \quad (9.8)$$

Experimentally we have $c_L^{liquid}/c_L^{solid} \approx 0.7$ and $\rho_{solid}/\rho_{liquid} \approx 1.1$ so Equation 9.8 simplifies to:

$$0.7 = \sqrt{\frac{2}{3} \times 1.1}\sqrt{\frac{B^{liquid}}{B^{solid}}} \quad (9.9)$$

Solving for the B^{liquid}/B^{solid} yields:

$$\frac{B^{liquid}}{B^{solid}} \approx 0.7^2 \times \frac{3}{2.2} \approx 0.67 \quad (9.10)$$

Equation 9.10 implies that liquids are around one third more compressible (less springy) than the equivalent solids. In retrospect this does not seem implausible. The inefficient packing of atoms in the liquid leads to an extra 10% of empty space within a liquid. Thus under pressure we would expect the liquid to relinquish some of this 'empty space' relatively easily. Thus, the same factors which enabled us to understand the lower density of the liquid state also enable us to understand the higher compressibility.

288

A simple calculation

In the previous part of this section, we explained the difference in the speed of sound between liquids and solids as being due to differences in the character of the sound wave, the density, and the bulk modulus. This is undoubtedly true. However, it would be nice to try gain a little more insight into what might be happening at a molecular level.

We can do this using a *very* simple-minded approach to state of liquid, which combines some elements of the structural model of a liquid (§8.2) and the cell model (§8.3). We consider a molecule trapped within its cell in the liquid. Energy may be transmitted through the cell in two modes, one characteristic of a gas, and the other more typical of a solid.

- In the first mode the molecule may move across its cell from one side to the other. Energy gained on one side of the cell is thus transmitted as in a gas through molecular motion, albeit with an extremely short mean free path.
- In the second mode, vibrations of one molecule may be transmitted vibrations to its neighbours, as in a solid.

Consider the time it takes for energy to move across a cell of width $a + \Delta a$, where a is the typical atomic separation in the solid. We must add two times: the time for a short gas-like trajectory through a distance Δa plus the time for solid-like transmission across the rest of the cell with dimension of the order a.

The time Δt taken for transmission in the liquid across a cell of width $\approx a + \Delta a$ is thus:

$$\Delta t = \frac{distance}{speed}$$

$$= \frac{a}{c_{solid}} + \frac{\Delta a}{c_{gas}} \quad (9.11)$$

and thus the speed of sound in a liquid should be:

$$c_{liquid} = \frac{distance}{\Delta t} = \frac{a + \Delta a}{\left[\dfrac{a}{c_{solid}} + \dfrac{\Delta a}{c_{gas}}\right]} \quad (9.12)$$

This simplifies in two stages:

$$c_{liquid} = \frac{a\left[1+\dfrac{\Delta a}{a}\right]}{\dfrac{a}{c_{solid}}\left[1+\dfrac{\Delta a c_{solid}}{a c_{gas}}\right]} \qquad (9.13)$$

and:

$$c_{liquid} = c_{solid}\frac{\left[1+\dfrac{\Delta a}{a}\right]}{\left[1+\left[\dfrac{\Delta a}{a}\right]\times\left[\dfrac{c_{solid}}{c_{gas}}\right]\right]} \qquad (9.14)$$

Notice that the two factors in this equation correspond to the two factors in the expression for the speed of sound. The term $\Delta a/a$ accounts for the change in density, and the term c_{solid}/c_{gas} takes account of the change in bulk modulus.

In order to estimate c_{liquid} we need to estimate $\Delta a/a$ and c_{solid}/c_{gas}. We can estimate the first factor from the density change on entering the liquid state, typically 10% (§9.2). Thus we estimate that the volume of the 'cell' is of the order $(a+\Delta a)^3$, which is around 10% larger than a^3. Noting that:

$$\begin{aligned}(a+\Delta a)^3 &\approx a^3+3a^2\Delta a\\ &\approx a^3\left[1+3\frac{\Delta a}{a}\right]\end{aligned} \qquad (9.15)$$

we estimate $\Delta a/a \approx 0.\frac{1}{3}$, which is roughly 0.033.

The ratio of c_{solid}/c_{gas} is difficult to estimate directly here because there are no common entries in the tables for the velocity of sound in the gaseous and solid states. However the solid values are all about 3000 ms^{-1} whereas the gaseous values are more typically in the region of 300 ms^{-1}. We thus estimate that $c_{solid}/c_{gas} \approx 10$.

Using these estimates in Equation 9.14 we find:

$$\begin{aligned}c_{liquid} &\approx c_{solid}\frac{[1+0.033]}{[1+0.033\times 10]}\\ &\approx 0.78c_{solid}\end{aligned} \qquad (9.16)$$

which agrees reasonably well with our experimental finding that $c_{liquid}\approx 0.7c_{liquid}$. The calculation, though thoroughly hand-waving, has produced a reasonable prediction for the speed of sound in a liquid in terms of the speed of sound in gases and solids. This reflects the intermediate status of liquids, and the difficulty in approaching phenomena in liquids that have mixed solid-like and gas-like character. Hand-waving as it is, we will use this model again when we consider transport of heat energy through a liquid (§9.11.4).

Figure 9.9 A molecule has more space available to it the liquid state than the solid state. We imagine that the molecules move freely as in a gas across the extra space Δa within the liquid state.

Solid

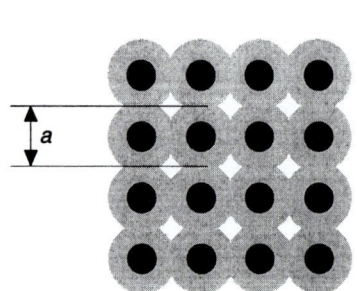

Liquid

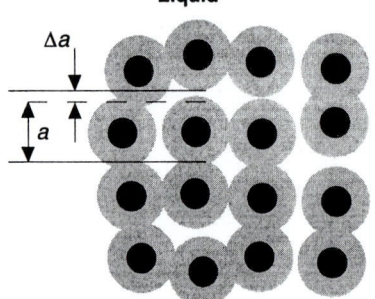

9.6 Viscosity

9.6.1 Introduction

I mentioned at the start of this chapter that liquids possess a relatively well-defined volume, but no well-defined shape. However, not all liquids can change their shape with similar ease, and the quantitative measure of the ease with which they can flow from one shape to another is the *viscosity* of the liquid.

We generally consider that solids do not flow at all. This is not quite strictly true: under the intense forces and at high temperatures, solids do flow, albeit extremely slowly. On Earth, the phenomenon of solid flow is responsible (among other things) for the drifting apart of the continents of Europe and America at an average speed of around 0.3 nanometres per second (10 millimetres per year).

The viscosity of liquids may be measured in a variety of ways. These methods depend on, for example, the rate of damping of oscillations of objects in the liquid, the speed with which objects fall through the liquid, or the rate of flow of the liquid through constrictions.

Formally, we define viscosity in terms of the *rate of transfer of momentum* (or *force*) exerted on a plane of liquid when a second plane of liquid is moved with velocity v. If the second plane is far away from the first, we expect the transfer of momentum to be smaller than if the plane is nearby. Also the quicker the first plane moves, the more momentum will be transferred to adjacent planes. For many liquids, the force between the planes is:

- proportional to the velocity v, and
- inversely proportional to the separation x of the two plates.

We thus write:

$$F = \eta \frac{v}{x} \qquad (9.17)$$

where the constant of proportionality is defined as the viscosity. Liquids for which this definition holds are known as *Newtonian liquids*. Figure 9.10 illustrates this definition.

Figure 9.10 (a) Cross-section through a liquid showing that when a plate is drawn through a liquid it drags with it layers of liquid. This corresponds to a transfer of z-momentum in the x-direction. The viscosity is a measure of the amount of z-momentum transferred. (b) Two plates, one fixed to a wall via a spring and one free to move. When the top plate is moved, the lower plate experiences a force which depends on the speed v of the first plate, and the distance x (Equation 9.17). (c) The viscosity of liquids can be more easily determined by measuring the damping of torsional oscillations of circular plates.

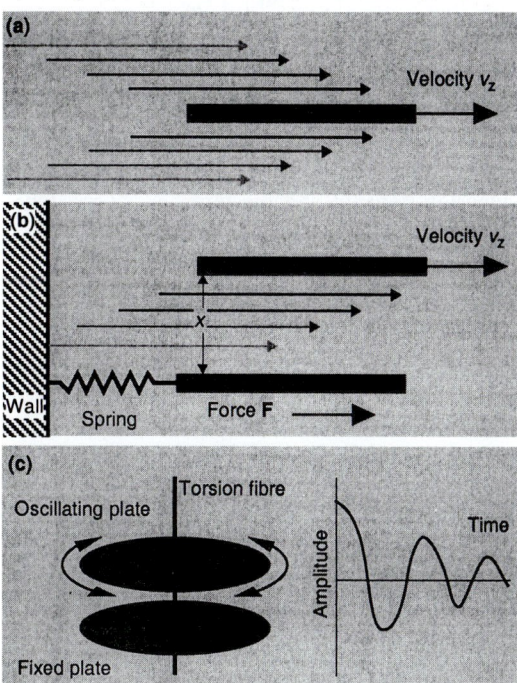

Figure 9.10 (a) is a schematic of the definition of viscosity. Moving a plate through a liquid will drag a few atomic layers adsorbed to its surface with it and thus create a moving liquid layer. A plate moving as indicated will tend to drag a second plate with it, creating a force F on the second plate, which could be measured by a spring balance apparatus. Figure 9.10 (b) illustrates an apparatus which might be used in practice. One plate oscillating above another would be damped by (i.e. lose momentum to) the liquid trapped between it and a fixed plate. Observations of the rate of damping allow a direct inference of the viscosity according to the definition Equation 9.17.

9.6.2 Data on the viscosity of liquids

The viscosity of various substances is recorded in Table 9.7 and selected data from the table is plotted in Figure 9.11. Figure 9.12 shows the detailed variation of the viscosity of water with temperature. It is clear from all these data that the viscosity of liquids depends strongly on temperature, becoming more viscous as a liquid is cooled.

Figure 9.11 shows viscosity of various liquids varying strongly with temperature. For example, the data for ethanol varies by at least two orders of magnitude as the temperature is increased from −100 °C to 100 °C. Similarly the data for water in Figure 9.12 shows a fall of around one order of magnitude between 0 °C and 100 °C. From Table 9.7 we note that substances with larger melting temperatures tend to have larger viscosities. So for example, sodium is more viscous than potassium, and ethanol is more viscous than methanol.

So the main question raised by our preliminary examination of the experimental data on the viscosity of liquids is:

• Why does the viscosity decrease strongly with increasing temperature?

9.6.3 Understanding the viscosity of liquids

Our approach here will be to use the cell model of a liquid to discuss the viscosity data. The fundamental process that takes place when a liquid changes shape is such that one layer of molecules

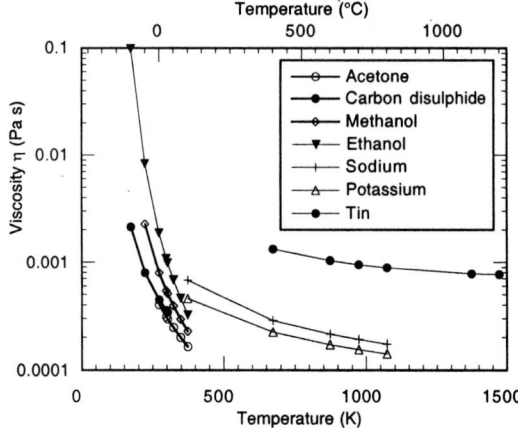

Figure 9.11 The viscosity η (Pa s) of various substances from Table 9.6 plotted as a function of the temperature. Note that the vertical scale is logarithmic covering three orders of magnitude.

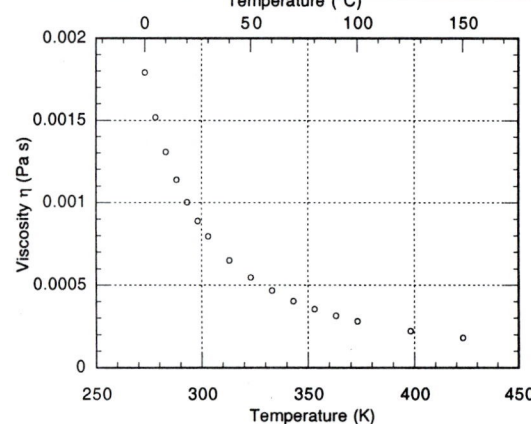

Figure 9.12 The viscosity η (Pa s) of water plotted as a function of the temperature. Note that the vertical scale is linear.

Table 9.7 The viscosity η of various substance in their liquid state in units of mPa s as a function of the temperature in °C. To obtain the viscosity in units of Pa s, multiply the entries in this table by 10^{-3}. For example, the viscosity of mercury at 25 °C is 1.528×10^{-3} Pa s.

Substance	Temperature (°C)												
	−100	−50	0	25	30	50	75	100	400	600	700	800	1100
Acetic acid	—	—	—	1.116	1.037	0.792	0.591	0.457	—	—	—	—	—
Acetone	—	—	0.402	0.310	0.295	0.247	0.200	0.165	—	—	—	—	—
Benzene	—	—	—	0.603	0.562	0.436	0.332	0.263	—	—	—	—	—
Carbon disulphide	2.132	0.796	0.445	0.357	0.343	—	—	—	—	—	—	—	—
Methanol	—	2.258	0.797	0.543	0.507	0.392	0.294	0.227	—	—	—	—	—
Ethanol	98.96	8.318	1.873	1.084	0.983	0.684	0.459	0.323	—	—	—	—	—
Sodium	—	—	—	—	—	—	—	0.680	0.286	0.215	0.192	0.174	—
Potassium	—	—	—	—	—	—	—	0.458	0.224	0.172	0.155	0.141	—
Mercury	—	—	1.616	1.528	1.497	1.401	1.322	1.255	—	—	—	—	—
Tin	—	—	—	—	—	—	—	—	1.33	1.04	0.950	0.890	0.780

has to 'slide past' another layer. In terms of the cell model this process requires molecules to 'hop' from one cell to another. Since the energy required to activate this hopping is ΔE_h, the probability P that any particular molecule will be able to hop into an appropriate cell is (§2.4):

$$P(\Delta E_h, T) = \text{constant} \times \exp\left(\frac{-\Delta E_h}{k_B T}\right) \quad (9.18)$$

In order to achieve a certain change of shape within the liquid, a certain (very large) number of individual molecular hops are necessary. So the more molecules that have energy greater than ΔE_h, the easier the change will be. If molecules have energy less than ΔE_h then they will be unable to move from their local cell, and the liquid will behave in a solid-like manner.

The ease of flow of the liquid (called its *fluidity*) is defined as $1/\eta$. From the considerations above we expect the fluidity to vary like:

$$\frac{1}{\eta} \propto \exp\left(\frac{-\Delta E_h}{k_B T}\right) \quad (9.19)$$

or that the viscosity will vary as:

$$\eta \propto \exp\left(\frac{+\Delta E_h}{k_B T}\right) \quad (9.20)$$

This is an easily testable proposition. If the viscosity varies as Equation 9.20 suggests, then a plot of $\ln(\eta)$ versus $1/T$ should yield a straight line. Figure 9.13 shows the data from Table 9.7 replotted in this form. The data in Figure 9.13 do seem to conform to Equation 9.20 and so represent good evidence for the exponential dependence of viscosity on inverse temperature, and hence indirectly for the cell model of a liquid.

We can evaluate the parameter ΔE_h from the slopes of the data in Figures 9.13 and 9.14. Since we have plotted $\ln(\eta)$ versus $1/T$ we should expect the slope to be $\Delta E_h / k_B$. We record the results in units of milli-electron volts (meV) in Table 9.8. The values in Table 9.8 are of the order 0.1 eV with values ranging from $\frac{1}{6}$ to $\frac{1}{20}$ of an

Figure 9.13 The viscosity η (Pa s) of various substances from Table 9.6 plotted on a logarithmic axis as a function of inverse temperature. Note that the vertical scale covers three orders of magnitude in viscosity. The lines are fits to the data points, with slopes indicated in Table 9.8.

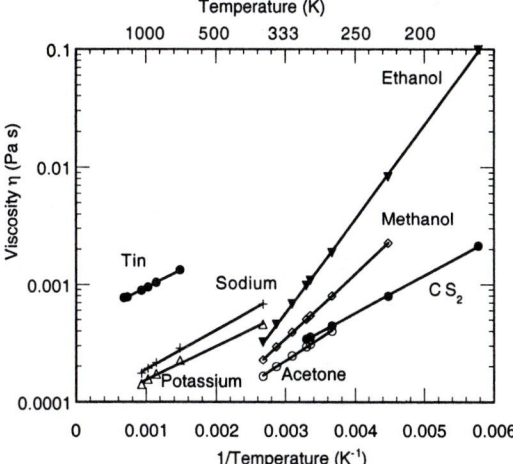

Figure 9.14 The viscosity η (Pa s) of water plotted on a logarithmic axis as a function of the inverse temperature. The two filled circle (•) data points are taken under pressure above 100 °C. The line is a fit to the data taken between 0 °C and 100 °C and has a slope of 1862 K. The data conform fairly closely to the line but clear signs of curvature are evident.

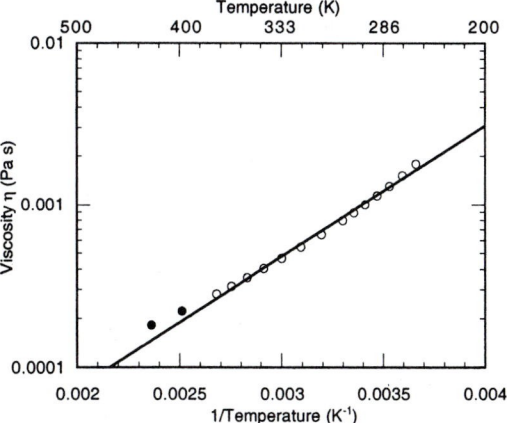

electron volt. Now if the cell model really does make sense then we should be able broadly to understand the magnitude of the predicted activation energies ΔE_h. The values of ΔE_h are considered in the light of estimates for ΔE_s and ΔE_e in §9.9.

Table 9.8 Analysis of the slopes found in Figures 9.13 and 9.14 in terms of Equation 9.20.

Substance	Slope (K)	ΔE_h (J)	ΔE_h (meV)
Acetone	907	12.52×10^{-21}	78.1
CS_2	736	10.16×10^{-21}	63.4
Methanol	1271	17.55×10^{-21}	109.5
Ethanol	1845	25.47×10^{-21}	159.0
Sodium	769	10.62×10^{-21}	66.3
Potassium	661	9.126×10^{-21}	57.0
Tin	688	9.50×10^{-21}	59.3
Water	1862	25.7×10^{-21}	160

Before discussing the values deduced in Table 9.8 it is important to keep in mind that ΔE_h is *not* the activation energy for a single molecule to 'hop' its way through the liquid. It is an energy which reflects the probability of complex multi-molecule correlations occurring which conspire to allow a molecule to 'jiggle' through the liquid.

Looking at the data in Table 9.8 by itself we see that broadly the values of ΔE_h seem reasonable. For example:

- ΔE_h for sodium is greater than ΔE_h for potassium in line with the fact that the interatomic bonding in sodium is slightly stronger than in potassium as evidenced by the boiling temperatures of the two (potassium 1047 K and sodium 1156 K).

- ΔE_h for methanol (CH_3OH) is less than for ethanol (CH_3CH_2OH) which is a larger, heavier and more awkwardly shaped molecule.

- ΔE_h for ethanol (CH_3CH_2OH) is similar to that of water. Here we see that the ease of motion of a molecule through the liquid arises both from bonding considerations, and from considerations of molecular shape. The water molecule is much smaller than the ethanol molecule, and so should find it easier move through its liquid. However water experiences strong hydrogen bonding which slows down its motion in comparison with the weaker bonding of the ethanol.

There are however data in Table 9.8 that seem at first sight surprising. For example, ΔE_h for ethanol (boiling temperature 345 K) is nearly three times greater than for tin (boiling temperature 2543 K). To understand this, we need once again to consider the relative ease with which a molecule moves is a product of :

- *geometrical considerations*: it is easier for the small essentially spherical tin atom to move through liquid tin than it is for the oddly-shaped ethanol molecule to move through liquid ethanol.

- *bonding strength considerations*: the bonding between ethanol molecules is considerably weaker than it is between tin atoms as evidenced by their differences in boiling temperature.

However, in order to understand the data of Table 9.8 in full we need to consider the data in the context of experimental values of the other cell model parameters ΔE_s and ΔE_e, a task undertaken in §9.9.

9.7 Surface energy

9.7.1 Introduction

The property of smooth surface formation is characterised by a *surface energy* or *surface tension*. This gives a numerical measure of the distinction between a liquid and a gas, which requires essentially no energy to form a new 'surface'. We are familiar with the fact, illustrated in Figure 9.15, that liquids on an impermeable surface frequently form droplets rather than spreading in a uniformly thin film.

This tendency arises because it takes energy to form a surface on a liquid. The energy per unit area required to form new surface on a liquid is known as the *surface energy* or more commonly, the *surface tension*, and is usually denoted by the symbol γ (pronounced 'gamma'). There is no connection between this use of the symbol gamma and that mentioned in the sections on heat capacity, bulk modulus and speed of sound.

Figure 9.15 (a) A (hypothetical) liquid with no surface tension and (b) a real liquid showing the effect of surface tension.

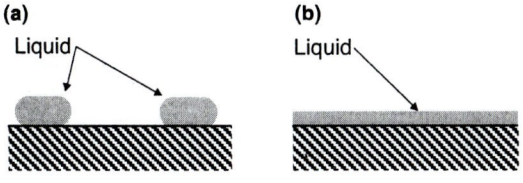

(a) Liquid

(b) Liquid

Figure 9.16 (a) A conceptually simple, but impractical, device for investigating the surface tension of liquids.

(b) Moving the arm by dx increases the area of a liquid film by 2Ldx. The factor of 2 arises because new surface area is created on both the upper and lower surfaces.

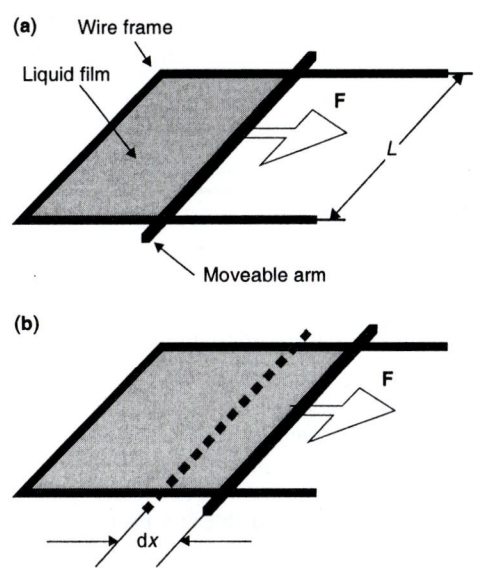

(a) Wire frame

Liquid film

F

L

Moveable arm

(b)

F

dx

If no energy were required to form a surface then liquids would seek to minimise other contributions to their energy, regardless of the amount of surface area created in this process. So for example, a liquid poured onto an impermeable surface would minimise its gravitational potential energy by forming a layer approximately one molecule thick. As pointed out in Figure 9.15, this does not happen, and small amounts of water form *droplets* with a restricted surface area.

An experiment (primarily a thought experiment) illustrating the concept of surface tension is depicted in Figure 9.16. The apparatus consists of a liquid film formed across a wire frame. Suppose that the arm is first balanced and then moved slowly to a new position. Moving the arm increases the area of the film by an amount $L\Delta x$, so extra liquid surface area has been created both on the top and the bottom of the film. The total extra area created is given by $\Delta A = 2L\Delta x$. By the definition of the surface energy, this requires energy $\gamma\Delta A$. This energy is supplied by the work ΔW done on the film, which is just $F\Delta x$. Thus the work ΔW done by the force in creating this surface is:

$$\Delta W = \gamma\Delta A$$
$$= 2\gamma L\Delta x \qquad (9.21)$$

When balanced, the force **F** applied to the moveable arm counteracts the tendency of the liquid film to contract and thus minimise its surface area. The magnitude of the force is given by $-dW/dx$, which in this case is approximately given by $-\Delta W/\Delta x$:

$$F = -\frac{\Delta W}{\Delta x} = -\frac{2\gamma L\Delta x}{\Delta x} \qquad (9.22)$$
$$= -2\gamma L$$

Comparing Equations 9.21 and 9.22 we see that the surface tension (the force per unit length of exposed surface) and the surface energy per unit area, are numerically equal. They have the units of [force]/[length] or [energy]/[area] = $N\,m^{-1}$.

9.7.2 Data on the surface tension and surface energy of liquids

Table 9.9 lists the surface tension of various substances and Figure 9.17 shows the variation of the surface tension with temperature for selected substances from Table 9.9. Figure 9.18 shows the variation of the surface tension of water with temperature on a more detailed scale.

It is clear from the data that there is a considerable range of values of surface tension. There appears to be some relationship between the melting temperature and the surface tension that the substance exhibits. This correlation causes high melting temperature substances to appear at the top of Figure 9.17. Mercury does not exactly fit in with this trend, but the other molten metals do fit quite well.

Table 9.9 The surface energy or surface tension of various substances in their liquid state (10^{-3} N m^{-1}) at a given temperature in °C. For example, the surface tension of benzene is 28.88×10^{-3} N m^{-1}.

Substance	Temperature (°C)	γ (mN m^{-1})
Acetic acid	20	27.59
Acetone	20	23.46
Benzene	20	28.88
Carbon disulphide	20	32.32
Methanol	20	22.50
Ethanol	20	22.39
Water	20	72.75
Sodium	100	209.9
Potassium	65	110.9
Mercury	25	485.5
Lead	350	444.5
Aluminium	700	900
Gold	1100	1120

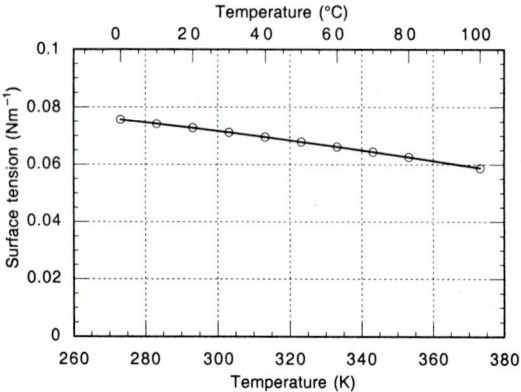

Figure 9.18 The surface energy or surface tension of water in units of N m^{-1} s as a function of temperature. Notice the large difference in scale between this figure and Figure 9.17.

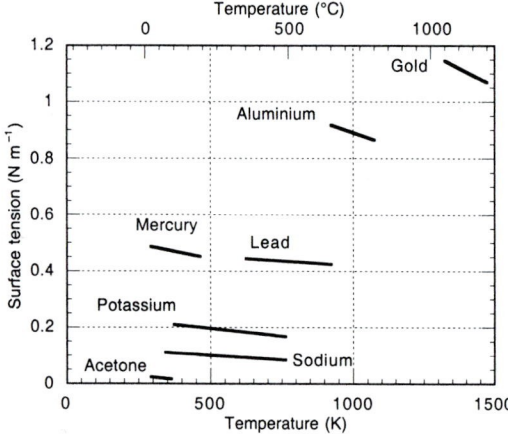

Figure 9.17 The surface energy or surface tension of various substances from Table 9.8 in units of mN m^{-1} s as a function of temperature. Notice the large difference in scale between this figure and Figure 9.18.

The second striking feature of Figure 9.17 and 9.18 is that all the data show a negative slope, indicating that the surface energy become less at higher temperatures. The slopes also appear to become steeper as the melting temperature of the substance increases. The variation with temperature appears to be approximately linear for the data shown, but the data for water show a slight curvature.

Thus the main questions raised by our preliminary examination of the experimental data on the surface energy of liquids are:

- Why do substances with high melting temperatures tend to have a high surface energy?
- Why does the surface tension of liquids decline approximately linearly with temperature?

9.7.3 Understanding the surface tension of liquids

Our approach here, as with the approach to understanding the viscosity data, will be to use the cell model of a liquid to discuss the data. In Figure 9.19 we consider the situation of molecule A near the surface of the liquid in comparison to molecule B deeper within the liquid. On average, molecules such as A have around half the number of nearest neighbours as molecules such as B. Thus molecules such as A may be considered as about 'halfway to being free of the liquid'. In the cell model of a liquid we assume that thus will take an energy ΔE_s of the order of 50% of ΔE_s.

So if it costs ΔE_s to have a single molecule at the surface of a liquid, then we can evaluate the surface energy of a liquid quite straightforwardly. We need only to count the number of molecules such as A per unit surface area. If we consider that each molecule is constrained within a cell of dimensions of the order a, then the number of molecules

Figure 9.19 A two-dimensional illustration of the situation of molecules near the surface of a liquid. In three-dimensions, molecules such as *A* still interact with roughly half as many molecules as a molecule within the liquid such as *B*.

Liquid surface

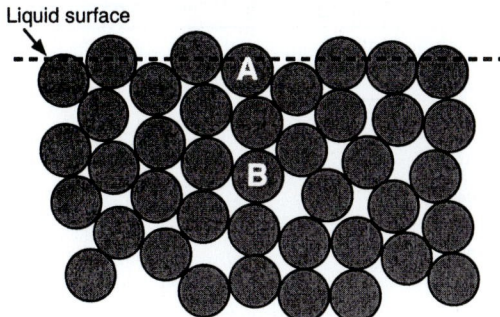

Figure 9.20 A view looking down on the surface of the liquid. In order to estimate the surface energy, we need to count how many molecules (such as A) there are per unit area. Roughly speaking the answer will be $\approx 1/a^2$.

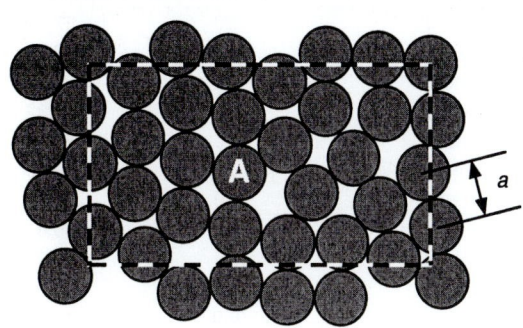

per unit surface area will be $\approx 1/a^2$. So we estimate that the surface energy γ is given simply by:

$$\gamma = \frac{\Delta E_s}{a^2} \qquad (9.23)$$

We can estimate a for a liquid by considering that a molecule of mass m has a 'volume' of the order a^3. Following this line of reasoning, we can estimate the density ρ of substance to be m/a^3. The mass of molecule is Mu, where M is its *relative molecular mass* and u an atomic mass unit. Substituting for a^2 in Equation 9.23 produces an estimate for γ:

$$\gamma = \Delta E_s \left[\frac{\rho}{Mu} \right]^{2/3} \qquad (9.24)$$

Equation 9.24 allows us to estimate the surface energy γ in terms of a few well-known properties of a substance, and a theoretical property ΔE_s which we have no independent method of estimating. In any case, due to the hand-waving nature of the arguments that preceded Equation 9.24 we would not be surprised if Equation 9.24 were out by a factor of 50% or so. However we can still make progress in assessing to what extent our theory of surface tension makes sense.

The relative value of ΔE_S

Although we cannot predict γ from experimental

values of ΔE_s, we can use experimental values of γ to predict ΔE_s by rearranging Equation 9.24:

$$\Delta E_S = \gamma \left[\frac{Mu}{\rho} \right]^{2/3} \qquad (9.25)$$

Based on the discussion of §8.3 we expect to find that for any particular liquid, ΔE_s should be:
- around 50% of ΔE_e as estimated from vapour pressure data (§ 9.8)
- a few times greater than ΔE_h as estimated from viscosity data (§9.6),

Values of ΔE_s deduced from surface tension experiments are collated for several liquids in Table 9.10.

The conclusions of Table 9.10 are broadly in line with our expectations: the surface energy of liquid metals is considerably higher than the surface energy of organic liquids. There are however one or two interesting comparisons to be made. For example, in §9.6 we saw that the activation energy for 'hopping' was broadly similar for water and ethanol. However, the data for surface energy indicate that it takes only two-thirds of the energy to place an ethanol molecule on the surface compared to that required to place a water molecule on the surface.

However, in order to appreciate the subtleties of

Table 9.10 The value of ΔE_s (evaluated according to Equation 9.25) deduced from surface tension data on various substances in their liquid state (Table 9.9).

Substance		MW	ρ (kg m^{-3})	T (°C)	γ (mN m^{-1})	ΔE_s (meV)
Acetic acid	CH_3COOH	60	1049	20	27.59	35.9
Acetone	CH_3COCH_3	58	790	20	23.46	36.0
Benzene	C_6H_6	78	877	20	28.88	50.4
Carbon disulphide	CS_2	76	1293	20	32.32	42.8
Methanol	CH_3OH	32	791	20	22.50	23.2
Ethanol	C_2H_5OH	46	789	20	22.39	29.5
Water	H_2O	18	1000	20	72.75	43.7
Sodium	Na	23	930	100	209.9	156
Potassium	K	39	824	65	110.9	127
Mercury	Hg	201	13600	25	485.5	256
Lead	Pb	207	10690	350	444.5	281
Aluminium	Al	27	2400	700	900	396
Gold	Au	197	17320	1100	1120	496

interpretations of these derived quantities, it is best to look at the relationships between all three parameters of the cell model ΔE_e, ΔE_s and ΔE_h for different liquids. These data are collated in Table 9.12 and discussed in §9.9 on the cell model.

The temperature variation of surface energy

The second point to note is that Equation 9.25 predicts that the surface energy is temperature-independent. This is in fact not quite true, but the temperature dependence is much weaker than the exponential temperature-dependence seen in the viscosity (§9.6) or the vapour pressure (§9.8). Is it possible to understand the roughly linear decline

in surface energy with temperature? If we consider the data for water (Figure 9.18) we see that γ falls by around 25% as the temperature increases from 273 K to 373 K. This is much too large to be explained in terms of the 4% density variation (Table 9.2). So we need to try to understand this reduction in the cost of forming a surface as being due to a reduction in ΔE_s itself. Understanding this reduction is rather complex, but essentially it results from the changing *structure* of the liquid. In §8.3 we described the average structure of a liquid in terms of the radial density function. Figure 9.21 illustrates the changes in the radial density function that take place as a liquid is warmed. The

Figure 9.21 Schematic diagram of the radial density function $n(r)$ at different temperatures in the liquid phase. For comparison, the figure also shows the $n(r)$ of the solid and of a (hypothetical) gas-like state with the same average density as the liquid. At higher temperatures the correlations between molecular positions that gives rise to the peaks and troughs in the $n(r)$, are weakened. It can be seen that, while still maintaining the same average density, the *average* separation of molecules increases. This results in a reduction of the overall binding energy. This occurs because there is an increase in the probability of molecules being at the troughs of the function, and a decrease in the probability of them being at the peaks.

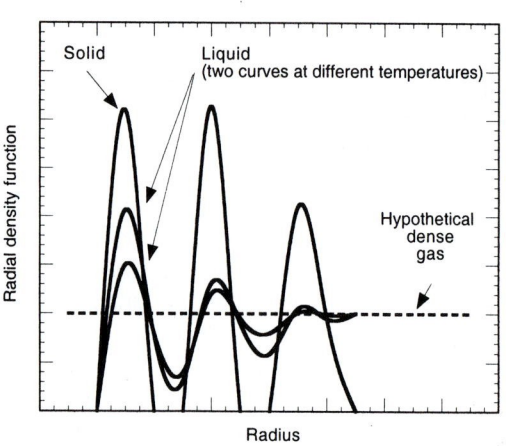

297

correlations between the average positions of molecules are weakened, leading to the lowering of the peaks and raising of the troughs of Figure 9.21. It can be seen that, while still maintaining the same average density, the *average* separation of molecules increases. This results in a reduction of the overall binding energy because there is a reduction in the *average* number of molecules at the optimum separation, and an increase in the number of molecules with slightly greater than the optimum separation.

These changes result in a reduction in all the activation energies in the cell model. Thus as the temperature rises it becomes easier for a molecule to:
- hop from cell to cell
- leave the liquid completely, or
- move to the surface.

However, the activation energies change only relatively slowly with temperature and so are difficult to discern in the temperature-dependence of the viscosity or the vapour pressure because they are overwhelmed by the exponential temperature-dependence. Thus it is only in the surface energy data that the slow decrease in activation is observed.

A second factor affecting ΔE_s is the effect of the vapour above the surface of the liquid. The density of the vapour rises approximately exponentially with temperature, but for water between 0 °C and 100 °C is still only of the order of one hundredth of the density of the liquid. Even so, the surface molecules do interact with the molecules in the gas phase, albeit more weakly than they do with

the molecules in the liquid phase. We thus expect the surface energy to be reduced according to:

$$\Delta E_s = \Delta E_s^o - [\text{gas factor}] \qquad (9.26)$$

where ΔE_s^o is the surface energy in the absence of any vapour above the liquid and the *gas factor* is related to:

- *the average distance from a surface molecule to gas molecule.* We might expect the interaction energy to vary as approximately $1/r^6$ if the interaction has a Van der Waals origin discussed in §6.2. This distance will be related to the density of molecules in the gas and we would expect that as the number density of gas molecules increased the *strength* of the interaction with surface molecules would increase
- *the number density of gas molecules.* In addition to the distance factor discussed above, the greater the number density of molecules in the gas, the greater the *number* of interactions that a surface molecule may have with molecules in the gas.

The interaction between surface molecules in the liquid and molecules in the vapour only becomes significant as we approach the temperature known as the *critical temperature*, at which the density of molecules in the gas becomes equal to the density of molecules in the liquid. At this temperature the surface energy of the liquid–gas interface falls to zero. The surface tension data are considered again in §11.4 where we discuss the data on the critical temperature and pressure of liquids.

9.8 Vapour pressure

9.8.1 Introduction

At any temperature, a liquid attempts to sustain above its surface a characteristic pressure of gas known as the *vapour pressure*. Graphs of the vapour pressure versus temperature are shown for water (Figure 9.22), the noble gas solids and liquids (Figure 9.23), and some molten metals (Figure 9.24). For all of these widely differing substances, the vapour pressure increases extremely

strongly with increasing temperature For example, the vapour pressure of silver in Figure 9.24 increases by three orders of magnitude as the temperature is increased by $\approx 50\%$ from 1650 K to 2450 K. Notice that the vapour pressure curves are nearly, but not quite, straight lines on the graphs. This indicates that on this logarithmic vertical scale, the vapour pressure is nearly, but not quite, an exponential function of temperature.

Figure 9.22 The vapour pressure of water as a function of temperature plotted on (a) a linear scale and (b) a logarithmic scale. The boiling temperature is defined as the temperature at which the vapour pressure equals atmospheric pressure (0.10135 MPa), which for water occurs at 99.975 °C.

(a)

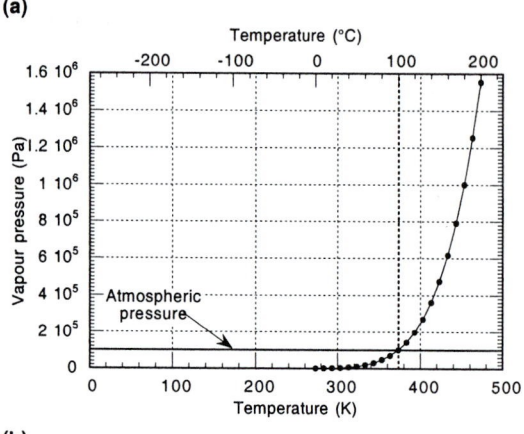

(b)

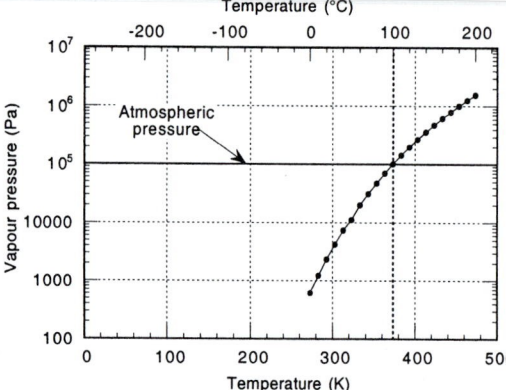

Figure 9.23 The vapour pressure of the rare gases as a function of temperature plotted on a logarithmic scale. The boiling temperature is defined as the temperature at which the vapour pressure equals atmospheric pressure (0.10135 MPa), which for these substances occurs at: He 4.22 K; Ne 27.1 K; Ar 87.3 K; Kr 119.8 K; Xe 165.1 K. Note: For much of the indicated range, most of these elements are solid, and the vapour co-exists with the solid rather than the liquid state. This is discussed further in Section 11.6 on the solid⇒gas transition.

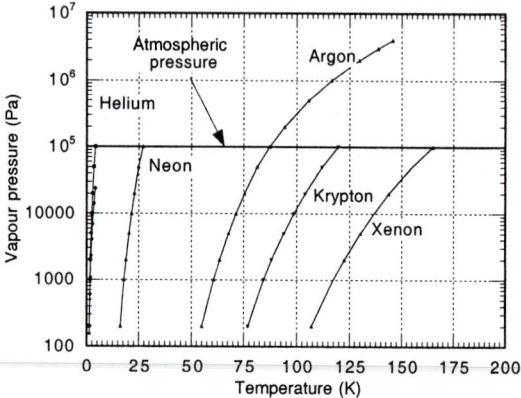

Figure 9.24 The vapour pressure of five metals as a function of temperature plotted on a logarithmic scale. The boiling temperature is defined as the temperature at which the vapour pressure equals atmospheric pressure (0.10135 MPa), which for these substances occurs at: Ag 2433 K; Al 2793 K; Cu 2833 K; Sn 2893 K; Au 3123 K.

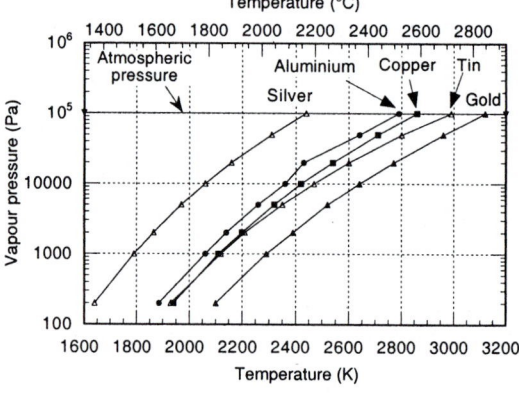

The main question raised by our preliminary examination of the experimental data on the liquid to gas transition is:

- Why does the vapour pressure of a substance increase strongly with temperature?

9.8.2 Understanding the vapour pressure data

We will try to understand the vapour pressure data by contructing a model for process of evaporation. To do this we need to model the substance in both the gas and liquid phases. When we discuss the substance in its gas phase, we will use the ideal gas model we developed in Chapter 4, and when we discuss the substance in its liquid phase we will use the cell model that we described in §8.4. In the cell model, the energy required to remove a molecule from the body of the liquid into the gaseous phase is ΔE_e. This activation energy leads to the rate at which molecules leave the

299

liquid being proportional to a Boltzmann factor (§2.5 Example 2.8) given by:

$$\exp\left[\frac{-\Delta E_e}{k_B T}\right] \tag{9.27}$$

This factor will prove to be the origin of the strong temperature dependence of vapour pressure. However, in order to calculate the vapour pressure above the liquid we need to derive expressions for both:

- the rate at which molecules *leave* the surface, and also
- the rate at which they *return* from the gas phase into the liquid.

We will derive expressions for the rates of each of these processes in the following two sections.

The rate at which molecules leave the surface

Consider a molecule just below the surface of a liquid vibrating within its 'cell' with frequency f. Remember that the frequency of molecular oscillations is typically 10^{13} Hz. So f times per second the molecule 'hits' the wall of its cell in an appropriate direction to leave the liquid. If the molecular energy exceeds ΔE_e it will succeed in leaving the liquid. Now, the probability that its energy is greater than ΔE_e is given approximately by $A \exp(-\Delta E_e / k_B T)$, where A is a temperature-independent constant. If the cell has dimensions roughly $a \times a \times a$ then the cross-section of the cell area perpendicular to the surface is given by a^2. We thus expect that the number of molecules leaving the surface per unit area per unit time is:

$$N_{leaving} = \frac{fA \exp(-\Delta E_e / k_B T)}{a^2} \tag{9.28}$$

The rate at which molecules return to the liquid

The number of molecules returning to the liquid from the gas per second is rather easier to estimate. In §4.3.3 we saw that the number of gas molecules crossing unit area per second is given by $\frac{1}{4} n_{gas} \bar{v}_{gas}$, where n_{gas} is the number density of molecules in the gas and $\bar{v}_{gas}$ is the average speed of a gas molecule. If we assume that every molecule which strikes the surface of the liquid returns to the liquid and does not rejoin the gas, then we

estimate the return rate (per unit area) of molecules rejoining the liquid is:

$$N_{returning} = \frac{1}{4} n_{gas} \bar{v}_{gas} \tag{9.29}$$

The equilibrium vapour pressure

In equilibrium, the rate at which molecules leave the liquid must be the same as that at which molecules return to it. Thus, in equilibrium, Equations 9.28 and 9.29 will be equal, and we expect:

$$\frac{1}{4} n_{gas} \bar{v}_{gas} = \frac{fA \exp(-\Delta E_e / k_B T)}{a^2} \tag{9.30}$$

or

$$n_{gas} = \frac{4 fA \exp(-\Delta E_e / k_B T)}{\bar{v}_{gas} a^2} \tag{9.31}$$

This equation can be simplified in two stages. First, we substitute for the number density of molecules in the liquid $n_{liq} \approx 1/a^3$ to give:

$$n_{gas} = \frac{4 n_{liq} faA \exp(-\Delta E_e / k_B T)}{\bar{v}_{gas}}$$
$$= 4 n_{liq} A \exp(-\Delta E_e / k_B T) \left[\frac{fa}{\bar{v}_{gas}}\right] \tag{9.32}$$

We now consider the fraction isolated on the right-hand side of Equation 9.32. The quantity fa is approximately equal to half the average speed of a molecule within a cell. Recall that f times a second, a molecule travels a distance $2a$ back and forth across the cell. Thus in each second they travel a distance $2fa$. Substituting $\bar{v}_{liq} = 2fa$ we find:

$$n_{gas} = 2 n_{liq} A \exp(-\Delta E_e / k_B T) \left[\frac{\bar{v}_{liq}}{\bar{v}_{gas}}\right] \tag{9.33}$$

We can estimate that the average molecular speeds within the liquid and gas at equal temperature are likely to be rather similar, if not exactly equal. If the fraction is close to unity we can proceed to estimate the vapour pressure in terms of n_{gas}. Using the ideal gas equation, (Example 4.2) we estimate the molecular number density in the gas as:

$$n_{\text{gas}} = \frac{P}{k_B T} \qquad (9.34)$$

and hence we estimate the vapour pressure above a liquid as:

$$P = k_B T n_{\text{gas}}$$
$$\approx 2 k_B T n_{\text{liq}} A \exp\left(-\Delta E_e / k_B T\right) \qquad (9.35)$$

If Equation 9.35 is a fair representation of the variation of the vapour pressure above a liquid in equilibrium, then a plot of $\ln(P/T)$ versus $1/T$ should yield a straight line with slope $-\Delta E_e / k_B$:

$$\ln\left[\frac{P}{T}\right] \approx \underbrace{\ln\left[2 k_B T n_{\text{liq}} A\right]}_{\text{Intercept}} - \underbrace{\left[\frac{\Delta E_e}{k_B}\right] \frac{1}{T}}_{\text{Slope}} \qquad (9.36)$$

The data from §9.8.1 when re-plotted in this manner (Figure 9.25) display a strikingly linear behaviour. If we take this linearity as evidence in favour of the cell model, then evaluating the slopes allows estimates of ΔE_e which are recorded in Table 9.11. The data of Table 9.11 give us two opportunities to test our assumptions about the process of evaporation.

First the values of ΔE_e evaluated from the slopes of Figures 9.25 (a) and (b) may be considered in relation to the other cell model parameters ΔE_h and ΔE_s. This comparison is performed in §9.9 where we evaluate the applicability of the cell model to real liquids. The conclusion there is that, with reservations, the cell model can help in understanding liquids.

Second we can use the value of ΔE_e calculated from the slope of Figures 9.25 (a) and (b) to predict a value for the latent heat of vaporisation. Remember that this is the amount of heat which must be supplied to convert one mole of substance from the liquid to the gaseous states at the boiling temperature. The expected value is just the number of molecules in one mole, N_A, times ΔE_e which is effectively the 'latent heat per molecule'. We compare this prediction with experimental results for the bulk latent heat L in §11.4 on the liquid ⇔ gas phase transition. There we will find that

Figure 9.25 The vapour pressure data from (a) Figure 9.23 and (b) Figure 9.24 re-plotted as P/T versus $1/T$ to test the prediction of Equation 11.36. The vertical axis of both graphs is logarithmic and so the linearity of the data indicates good agreement between theory and experiment. The lines on the graph represent least-squares fits to the data. The parameters of the fitted lines are listed in Table 9.11.

(a)

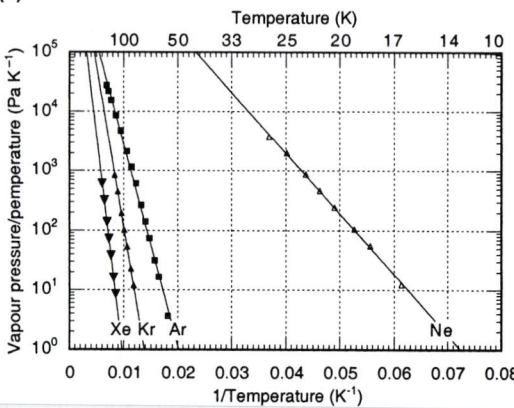

(b)

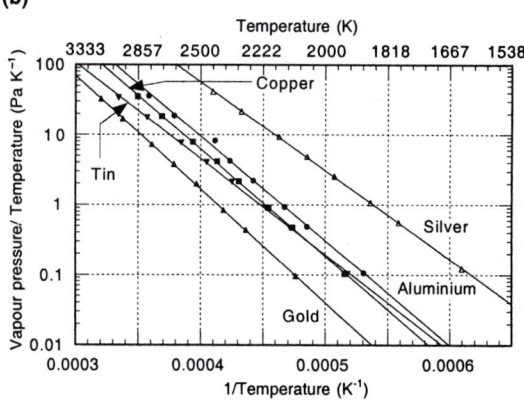

Table 9.11 Analysis of the slopes found in Figures 9.23 and 9.24 in terms of Equation 9.36.

Substance	Slope (K)	ΔE_e (J)	ΔE_e (eV)
Copper	−35209	486×10^{-21}	3.04
Silver	−29191	403×10^{-21}	2.52
Gold	−37355	516×10^{-21}	3.22
Aluminium	−34380	474×10^{-21}	2.96
Tin	−31616	436×10^{-21}	2.72
Helium	−9.51	0.13×10^{-21}	0.00082
Neon	−234	3.23×10^{-21}	0.020
Argon	−781	10.8×10^{-21}	0.067
Krypton	−1247	17.2×10^{-21}	0.107
Xenon	−1767	24.4×10^{-21}	0.152

$L \approx N_A \Delta E_e$ within about 10%, which gives us confidence in the model of evaporation that we have developed.

Finally we can answer the question raised by our preliminary examination of the data in §9.8.1: Why the vapour pressure of a substance increases strongly with temperature? We have seen that we can understand this in terms of the dynamics of molecules entering and leaving the surface of the liquid. But that is not all. In §10.8 we will find a very general relationship between any two phases of matter which co-exist is equilibrium. This relationship, known as the *Clausius–Clapeyron equation*, leads to prediction that the vapour pressure has a form very similar to Equation 9.36. However the Clausius–Clapeyron Equation makes almost no assumptions about the microscopic processes involved at the interface between the two phases.

9.9 The cell model: experimental results collated

Using the cell model of a liquid, we have made predictions for the temperature dependence of the viscosity (§9.6), surface tension (§9.7), and vapour pressure (§9.8). We have seen broad agreement between the model and the data. By analysing these experimental data, we can deduce estimates for all three activation energies in a simple cell model of the liquid: ΔE_e, ΔE_s and ΔE_h. To show the relationships between ΔE_e, ΔE_s and ΔE_h for the different liquids, the data from Tables 9.8, 9.10 and 9.11 are summarised in Table 9.12. The table also shows normalised values of the activation energies, i.e. $\Delta E_e = 1$, $\Delta E_s / \Delta E_e$ and $\Delta E_h / \Delta E_e$. After normalisation, the data show a surprising

Table 9.12 Collated value of ΔE_e, ΔE_s and ΔE_h (in units of milli electron volts) from Tables 9.8, 9.10 and 9.11. Also shown are the values of ΔE_s and ΔE_h normalised for each liquid. The small table at the foot of the main table presents a summary of the data from each category.

Substance		ΔE_e (meV)	ΔE_s (meV)	ΔE_h (meV)	$\Delta E_e/\Delta E_e$	$\Delta E_s/\Delta E_e$	$\Delta E_h/\Delta E_e$
Acetic acid	CH_3COOH	391	36	114	1	0.092	0.292
Acetone	CH_3COCH_3	319	36	78	1	0.113	0.245
Benzene	C_6H_6	373	50	106	1	0.134	0.284
Carbon disulphide	CS_2	—	43	63	1	—	—
Methanol	CH_3OH	379	23	110	1	0.061	0.290
Ethanol	C_2H_5OH	423	30	159	1	0.071	0.376
Water	H_2O	405	44	160	1	0.109	0.395
Sodium	Na	954	156	66	1	0.164	0.0692
Potassium	K	786	127	57	1	0.162	0.0725
Mercury	Hg	579	256	23	1	0.442	0.0397
Tin	Sn	2720	—	59	1	—	0.0217
Lead	Pb	1742	281	98	1	0.161	0.0563
Aluminium	Al	2790	396	96	1	0.142	0.0344
Gold	Au	3220	496	175	1	0.154	0.0543
Copper	Cu	3030	—	—	1	—	—
Silver	Ag	2520	—	—	1	—	—

Summary			
Substance	$\Delta E_e/\Delta E_e$	$\Delta E_s/\Delta E_e$	$\Delta E_h/\Delta E_e$
Organic	1	$\approx \frac{1}{10}$	$\approx \frac{1}{3}$
Metallic	1	$\approx \frac{1}{6}$	$\approx \frac{1}{20}$

Figure 9.26 Qualitative illustration of the formation of surfaces in (a) liquids made of atoms, such as liquid metals, and (b) liquids consisting of molecules, such as organic molecules. The shapes of the molecules in (b) are entirely illustrative and the gaps between the molecules are left to allow easy identification of the molecules. In (b) the cost of forming a surface may be relatively small if the molecules orient themselves appropriately. However, for organic liquids 'hopping' is considerably more difficult owing to the larger size of their molecules and their complex shapes.

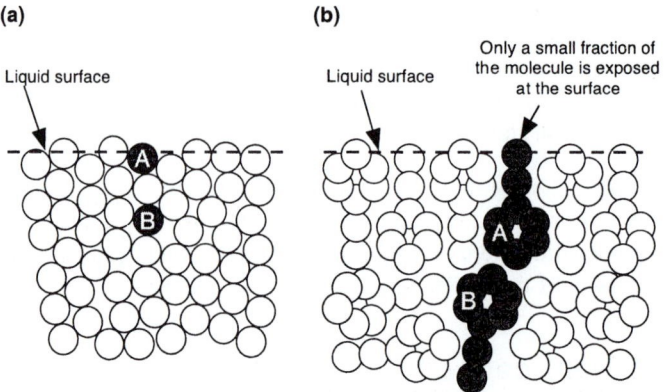

(a)

Liquid surface

(b)

Liquid surface

Only a small fraction of the molecule is exposed at the surface

degree of consistency concerning the *relative* values of ΔE_e, ΔE_s and ΔE_h. We notice immediately that, as might have been anticipated, the relative values are completely different for liquids composed of complex molecules (such as organic liquids) and liquids composed of atoms, (such as elemental metallic liquids).

The metallic data fit the picture envisaged in our simplest version of the cell model (Figure 8.19) rather well. We see that across metals with a wide range of melting temperatures there is a broad degree of consistency about the *relative* magnitudes of the activation parameters. The energy to place an atom on the surface of liquid is rather less than we had anticipated about $\frac{1}{6}$ rather than $\approx \frac{1}{2}$, but the activation energy for molecules to 'hop' or 'swap' cells ΔE_h, is always around three times smaller than ΔE_s.

The data for organic liquids also shows consistent relative magnitudes of the activation energies, but notably ΔE_h is considerably greater than ΔE_s. This implies that the situation for organic molecules is akin to that envisaged in our second version of the cell model (Figure 8.20). For liquids composed of these molecules, it is relatively easy to place molecules at the surface. However, it is relatively more difficult for molecules to move through the liquid than it is for metal atoms to move through a metallic liquid.

In discussing the viscosity data we have already mentioned that the shape of the molecules will

significantly affect their ability to move through the liquid. However, the shape of molecules will also have a significant effect on the ease with which surfaces are formed (Figure 9.26). For non-spherical molecules we may reasonably expect that at the surface the molecules will orient themselves so as to minimise their potential energy. So it is likely that most of the molecule will arrange to stay 'beneath the surface' of the liquid, 'exposing' only a small part of the molecule. By doing this, a liquid incurs only a fraction of the 'full cost' of placing a molecule completely at the surface.

The cell model: summary

The cell model provides a flexible framework for discussing *processes* in liquids. However its generality and applicability to a wide range of liquids makes the attempt to tune the parameters of the model to explain detailed features of the behaviour of particular liquids futile. In order to understand the details of the dynamics of molecules in liquids, and to predict quantitative values for the properties of liquids, we need to concern ourselves much more with the details of molecular shapes and interactions. This is something that extends well beyond the scope of this book, but is still an active area of research.

Perhaps the greatest 'danger' in applying the cell model to real liquids is that people (i.e. you) might believe the model to be 'realistic'. I feel obliged to stress yet again that the 'hopping' processes envisaged in the cell model are complicated many-

molecule correlated motions, and the parameters deduced characterise this complex motion. The simple one-molecule picture described in the cell model is merely analogous to (rather than descriptive of) the real situation.

In recent years the most direct way to understand dynamical processes in liquids has been by direct computer simulations of liquids. The forces between pairs of molecules are first estimated using quantum mechanical calculations of electron wave functions and charge densities. Then the motions of molecules are charted by using nothing more complicated than Newton's laws, albeit applied many millions of times to calculate the trajectories of the molecules. A computer program that uses this principle to simulate the motion of molecules in the liquid can be downloaded from www.physicsofmatter.com.

9.10 Heat capacity

9.10.1 Introduction

The *heat capacity* of an object is a measure of the increase in temperature of that object for a given input of heat energy. It is defined in terms of the temperature rise ΔT resulting from an input of heat energy ΔQ, by the ratio:

$$C = \frac{\Delta Q}{\Delta T} \quad \text{joule kelvin}^{-1}(\text{J K}^{-1}) \qquad (9.37)$$

If the temperature of an object rises by only a small amount due a given heat input, then the object has a large heat capacity. Equation 9.37 is the formula used to determine the heat capacity from experimental measurements of ΔQ and ΔT. It approximates the theoretical definition, which is the limit of Equation 9.28 as ΔT tends to zero:

$$C = \frac{\mathrm{d}Q}{\mathrm{d}T} \qquad (9.38)$$

When we discuss the heat capacity of a *substance*, rather than an object, we need also to state the amounts of the substance to which we are referring. This is usually quoted either for a given mass of material, the *specific heat capacity* (e.g. $\text{J K}^{-1}\text{kg}^{-1}$) or per mole, the *molar heat capacity* ($\text{J K}^{-1}\text{mol}^{-1}$). For practical calculations the specific heat capacity is usually more convenient, but from a fundamental point of view, the molar heat capacity is far more interesting. Remember the molar heat capacity is the heat capacity of the Avogadro number of atoms or molecules ($N_A = 6.023 \times 10^{23}$).

The heat capacities at constant pressure and constant volume are designated by C_P and C_V respectively. For liquids, we normally assume that measurements are made at constant pressure unless told otherwise. The difference between C_P and C_V is usually smaller than for gases, but larger than for solids.

9.10.2 Data on the heat capacity of liquids

The heat capacity of various liquids is shown in Table 9.13. If we plot the data as a function of the relative molecular mass of the molecules of the liquid we arrive at Figure 9.27. No particularly striking trends are evident, except perhaps a broad trend (with clear exceptions) towards increasing heat capacity for high-mass molecules.

Figure 9.27 The heat capacity of the liquids from Table 9.13 plotted as a function of the relative molecular mass of the molecules of the liquid.

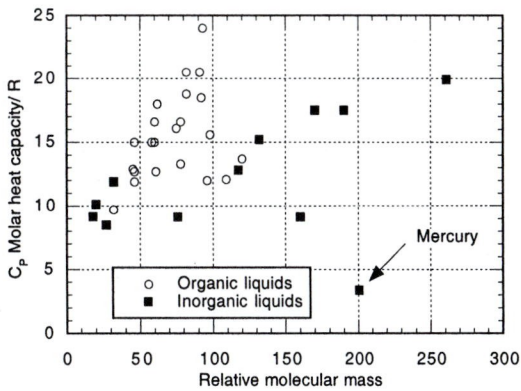

Table 9.13 The heat capacities at constant pressure C_p for a selection of substances that are liquids at around room temperature. The table records the substance name and chemical formula, the relative molecular mass of its constituent molecules, the number of atoms per molecule, and the temperature at which the measurement is made. The molar heat capacity is then recorded as in J K^{-1} and as a multiple of the gas constant R.

Substance		MW	N	T(°C)	C_p (J K^{-1} mol^{-1})	(R)
Organic liquids						
Methanol	CH_3OH	32	6	12	80.64	9.7
Ethanol	C_2H_5OH	46	9	0	105.3	12.7
Ethanol	C_2H_5OH	46	9	20	113.4	13.6
Ethanol	C_2H_5OH	46	9	40	124.7	15.0
Propanol	C_3H_7OH	60	12	18	138.0	16.6
Acetic acid	$C_2H_4O_2$	60	8	20	124.3	15.0
Acetone	C_3H_6O	58	10	20	124.7	15.0
Aniline	C_6H_7N	93	14	15	199.9	24.0
Benzene	C_6H_6	78	12	10	110.8	13.3
Benzene	C_6H_6	78	12	40	138.1	16.6
Bromoethane	C_2H_5Br	109	8	20	100.8	12.1
Chloroform	$CHCl_3$	120	5	20	113.8	13.7
Cyclohexane	C_6H_{10}	82	16	20	156.5	18.8
1,2 Dichloroethane	$C_2H_4Cl_2$	98	8	20	129.3	15.6
Dichloromethane	$C_2H_2Cl_2$	96	6	20	100.0	12.0
Ethanadiol	$C_2H_6O_2$	62	10	20	149.8	18.0
Ethyl acetate	$C_4H_8O_2$	82	8	20	170.1	20.5
Ethyl nitrate	$C_2H_5O_3N$	91	11	20	170.3	20.5
Formamide	CH_3ON	45	6	20	107.6	12.9
Formic acid	CH_2O_2	46	5	20	99.0	11.9
Nitromethane	CH_3O_2N	61	7	20	106.0	12.7
Nitroethane	$C_2H_5O_2N$	75	10	20	134.2	16.1
Toluene	C_7H_8	92	15	18	153.6	18.5
Inorganic liquids						
Arsenic trifluoride	AsF_3	132	4	20	126.6	15.2
Boron trichloride	BCl_3	118	4	20	106.7	12.8
Bromine	Br_2	160	2	20	75.7	9.11
Carbon disulphide	CS_2	76	3	20	75.7	9.11
Hydrogen cyanide	HCN	27	3	20	70.6	8.49
Water	H_2O	18	3	0	75.9	9.13
Heavy water	D_2O	20	3	0	84.3	10.1
Mercury	Hg	201	1	20	28.0	3.37
Hydrazine	N_2H_4	32	6	20	98.9	11.9
Silicon tetrachloride	$SiCl_4$	170	5	20	145.3	17.5
Tin tetrachloride	$SnCl_4$	261	5	20	165.3	19.9
Titanium tetrachloride	$TiCl_4$	190	5	20	145.2	17.5

But does this broad trend arise because the molecules are increasing in mass? Or is the trend related to the number of atoms in a molecule? This may seem like a stupid question, but it is not. When we analysed the heat capacity of gases (§5.3) and solids (§7.6), we saw that the molar heat capacity depended on the number of atoms per molecule, or the number of atoms per formula unit, respectively. Re-plotting the data as a function of the number of atoms per molecule (Figure 9.28) produces a slightly clearer trend. In particular, mercury, one of the two elemental liquids that

Figure 9.28 The heat capacity of the liquids from Table 9.13 plotted as a function of the number of atoms per molecule. The line has a slope $3R$ per atom as discussed in the text.

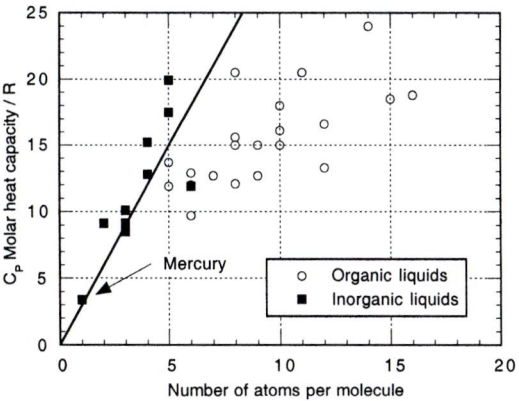

we have data for, now appears in a sensible position on the graph. In Figure 9.27 mercury is the isolated data point low down on the graph at a relative molecular mass of 201. But on Figure 9.28 mercury now forms part of the trend to increasing heat capacity with increasing molecular complexity. The line on Figure 9.28 is a line of slope $3R$ per atom. Recall that for solids, the heat capacity is roughly $3pR$ per mole where p is the number of atoms per formula unit (Equation 7.41). The line is drawn to see if there is any remnant of that behaviour in the liquid state. The line appears to in-

dicate roughly the trend of the data for small molecules, but for larger molecules (mainly organic molecules) the data fall below this trend line. However, we note again that there is good deal of variation in the data.

Variation of the heat capacity with temperature

There is unfortunately little data available in standard data books on the variation of the heat capacity of liquids with temperature. The exceptions to this are water and mercury: Figure 9.29 shows the heat capacity of these liquids and of the heat capacity of the benzene and ethanol taken from Table 9.13. Clearly the heat capacities of water and mercury are roughly constant over this temperature range, while the heat capacity of the organic liquids increases slightly with temperature. There is very little data for the organic liquids and so we draw (only tentatively) the conclusion that the heat capacity of organic liquids increases with temperature. In fact the data for water and mercury is available in reasonable detail and show variations with temperature as depicted in Figure 9.30.

Considering the scant information of Figures 9.27 to 9.29, the main questions raised by our preliminary examination of the experimental data on C_P are these:

- Why do the heat capacities of liquids tend to

Figure 9.29 The variation with temperature of the heat of various liquids around room temperature. The lines join the data points and are to guide the eye only.

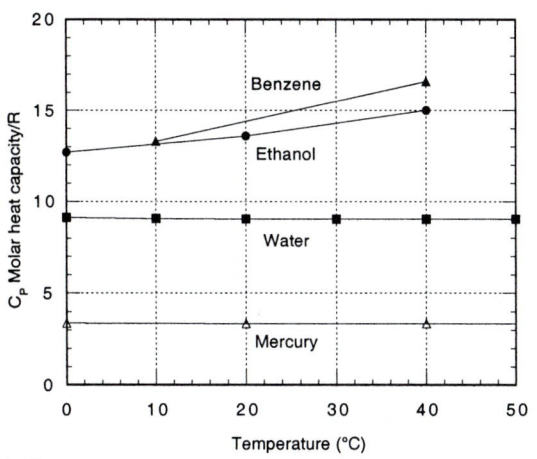

Figure 9.30 The constant pressure heat capacity of water and mercury showing data in all three phases. The melting and boiling temperatures are water; $T_M = 0°C$, $T_B = 100 °C$; and mercury $T_M = -38.9 °C$, $T_B = 356.6 °C$.

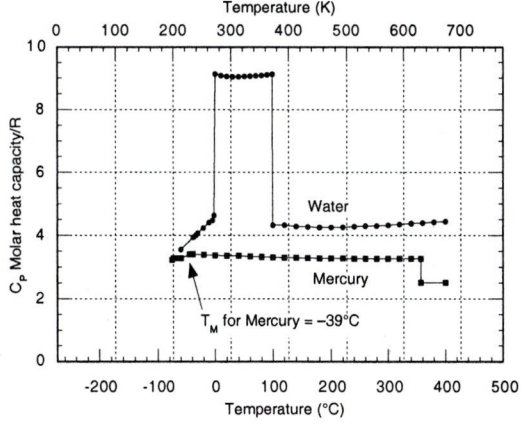

increase with increasing molecular complexity for small molecules, but not for larger (primarily organic) molecules?

- Why is the heat capacity of many substances in their liquid phase greater than the heat capacity of the gaseous or solid phases?
- Why do the heat capacities of liquids tend either to stay constant or to increase with temperature?

9.10.3 Understanding the heat capacity of liquids

We address these questions in the light of our experience in trying to understand the heat capacities of solids (§7.5) and gases (§5.3). Let us look at the questions raised by the data in turn:

- Why do the heat capacities of liquids tend to increase with increasing molecular complexity for small molecules, but not for larger (primarily organic) molecules?

Having previously considered the heat capacities of solids and gases, we are able to rephrase these questions in terms of the degrees of freedom of molecules of the liquid. What the data indicates is that the molar heat capacity tends to increase with the number of atoms in a molecule for small molecules. This is hardly surprising: in §7.5 we saw that the expression for the heat capacity of a solid:

$$C^{\text{solid}} = 3pR \tag{9.39}$$

was proportional to p, the number atoms per chemical formula unit of the substance. Thus the molar heat capacity of NaCl is close to twice the value of an elemental solid because there are twice as many atoms present. Thus the reason for the increase in molar heat capacity of substances as a function of molecular complexity is simply that there are more atoms present in a mole, and thus the possibility of more degrees of molecular vibration and rotation.

More interesting is the question of why the heat capacity of more complex liquids fails to continue to increase with molecular complexity. In our experience of solids and gases, whenever we failed to observe an expected heat capacity contribution, we concluded that some degrees of freedom of the

substance were inaccessible. In this case the degrees of freedom are those associated with molecular vibration and rotation. For small molecules, many of these degrees of freedom are available, but more complex molecules are often entangled with other molecules and so many of their degrees of freedom, particularly those associated with rotation, are restricted by the closeness of the other molecules. A more complex analysis might search for correlations between the reduction in the expected heat capacity and anomalous large values of the parameter ΔE_{h} in the cell model (§9.9). We shall not attempt this analysis

We now come to the second question raised in the previous section:

- Why is the heat capacity of many substances in their liquid phase greater than the heat capacity of the gaseous or solid phases?

Once again, we can reinterpret this datum as being a statement about the number of *accessible degrees of freedom* in the liquid state. It amounts to stating that there are more ways in which a molecule can possess energy in the liquid state. We can see how this comes about by comparing the situation of the molecules with their situation in the gaseous and solid states.

In the gaseous state the interactions between molecules are generally weak due to the large spaces between the molecules. Thus the degrees of freedom associated with the potential energy of interaction between molecules are not accessible. Thus on entering the liquid state, several more degrees of freedom become immediately available to the molecules. However some degrees of freedom associated with molecular rotation and internal vibration may become restricted in the liquid state due to the closeness of neighbours.

In the solid state the interactions between molecules are generally strong due to the closeness of other molecules, and the rigidity of the structure. This closeness and rigidity strongly restricts the ability of molecules to rotate and (at low temperatures) to vibrate. On entering the liquid state there is in general an extra 10% more space available to allow molecular rotation, or more precisely *rotational vibration*, which amounts to rotating

back and forth through some angle. We would therefore expect some increase in the possible motions of the molecules.

We can now consider to what extent these general ideas are borne out by the data of §9.10.1. We can make two fairly general predictions, the first concerning elemental liquids and the second concerning substances which are denser in the liquid state than the solid state.

For elemental liquids whose molecules consist of single atoms we would not expect a strong change in heat capacity on entering the solid state because there are no degrees of freedom associated with atomic vibration (or rotation) to be hindered in the solid state. However, on leaving the liquid state for the gaseous state we would expect a fall in the heat capacity due to the loss of degrees of freedom associated with the interactions between molecules. These predictions are broadly borne out by the data for mercury in Figure 9.30, which shows no jump on entering the solid state but does show a 25% fall on entering the gaseous state. This behaviour is typical of the behaviour of elements, and bears out the general ideas about the liquid state outlined above.

Some substances are denser in their liquid state than their solid state. From the previous argument, we might at first expect that on entering the solid state the molecules would have more 'room to manoeuvre' and so be *more* free to rotate and vibrate. If we consider the data for water (also shown in Figure 9.30) we see that this approach must be mistaken. We notice that on entering the gaseous state, there is a roughly 50% fall in heat capacity which we may interpret as being due to the loss of degrees of freedom associated with molecular interactions. However, the heat capacity also falls on entering the solid state, even though the molecules have around 10% more space in the solid. The reason lies in the nature of substances that contract on melting. As we saw in §9.2.2, they possess strongly directional bonding. Thus although the molecules have more room in the solid state, they are strongly constrained from any kind of rotation or rotational vibration by the *rigidity* of their bonds to their neighbouring molecules.

Thus the general idea that molecules have more degrees of freedom in the liquid state than either the solid or gaseous states seems to make sense.

We now turn to the third and final question raised by the data on heat capacities:

- Why do the heat capacities of liquids tend to either stay constant or to increase with temperature?

Referring to our previous studies of the heat capacities of gases and solids, we have ascribed any temperature-dependence of the heat capacity to a change in the accessibility of degrees of freedom of the substance. For both solid mercury and solid water (ice), the heat capacity increases with temperature in line with the discussion of §7.6 on the heat capacity of solids. This increase is due to the increasing average vibrational energy of the molecules in comparison with energy required to excite the highest energy vibrational modes within the solid.

On entering the liquid state the situation changes dramatically: for example, it is no longer possible to sustain transverse vibrational waves within the liquid. Thus the vibrational modes within the liquid are essentially vibrations of individual molecules. The constancy of the heat capacity in the liquid state then indicates that the local environment within which the vibration takes place, does not change strongly. Close examination of the data for water reveals detailed changes in the heat capacity that indicate that changes are taking place in the environment of the water molecule, but they are not significant in comparison to the massive change on entering the liquid state. These changes are related to the thermal expansivity anomaly in water, and the similarity between Figures 9.8 and 9.31 is striking.

Figure 9.31 Detail from Figure 9.29 showing the variation of the heat capacity of water in its liquid state.

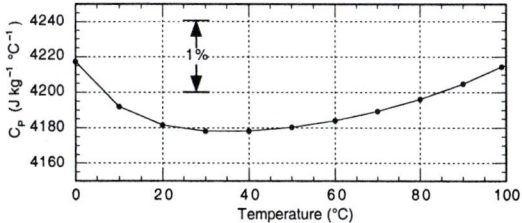

9.11 Thermal conductivity

9.11.1 Data on thermal conductivity of liquids

The thermal conductivity of a substance is a measure of the ease or difficulty with which heat flows through the substance. The thermal conductivity of a substance is defined by the equation:

$$\frac{dQ}{dt} = -\kappa A \frac{dT}{dx} \qquad (9.40)$$

In this equation:

$\dfrac{dQ}{dt}$ is the rate of heat flow (W)

κ is the thermal conductivity, $(\text{W m}^{-1}\,\text{K}^{-1})$

A is the cross-sectional area across which heat is flowing (m^2)

$\dfrac{dT}{dx}$ is the temperature gradient (K m^{-1}).

The minus sign in Equation 9.40 indicates that heat flows against the temperature gradient, from high temperatures to low temperatures. As with gases, note that when determining the thermal conductivity of liquids one must guard against the possibility of *convective* heat transfer as illustrated in Figure 5.16. This arises from the combination of the large thermal expansivities of liquids, their ability to flow, and the presence of a gravitational field in most experiments.

Table 9.14 Thermal conductivity of miscellaneous non-metallic liquids in units of $\text{WK}^{-1}\,\text{m}^{-1}$. The data is given at two temperatures T_1 and T_2, and varies roughly linearly between these two temperatures. (Figure 9.32 (a)).

Liquid	T_1	T_2	K_1	K_2
Acetone	193	333	0.198	0.146
Aniline	293		0.172	
Benzene	293	323	0.147	0.137
Methanol	233	333	0.223	0.186
Ethanol	233	353	0.189	0.150
N-butanol	213	353	0.167	0.106
N-propanol	233	353	0.168	0.148
Toluene	193	353	0.159	0.119
Carbon tetrachloride	253	333	0.115	0.102
Water	273	353	0.561	0.673
Xenon	173	223	0.07	0.05

Figure 9.32 (a) Data from Table 9.12 showing the thermal conductivity of miscellaneous non-metallic liquids in units of W m^{-1}K^{-1}. (b) Thermal conductivity of insulating liquids shown over a larger range. (c) The data from (b) re-plotted on a logarithmic scale.

(a)

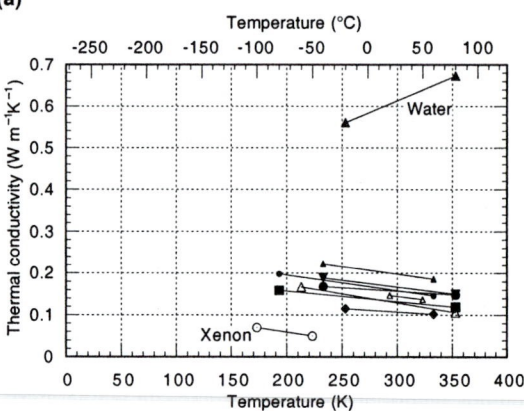

(b)

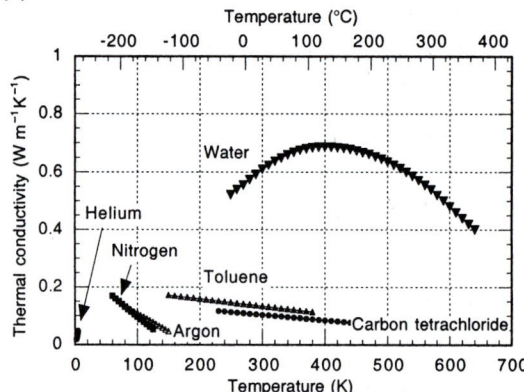

(c)

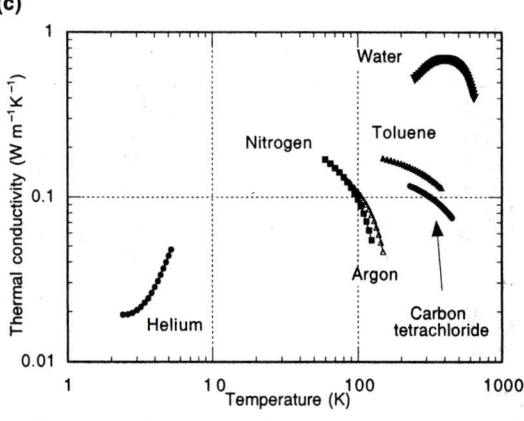

The thermal conductivity of several non-metallic liquids is given in Table 9.14 and illustrated in Figure 9.32 (a). There is little in the way of simple variation and the available data is rather limited. This makes it difficult to perceive any clear trends except that the thermal conductivity tends to get worse for most (but not all) liquids as the temperature increases. Figure 9.32 (b) and (c) shows thermal conductivity data over a wider range of temperatures.

The thermal conductivity of several elemental metals in their liquid state is given in Table 9.15 and illustrated in Figure 9.33. There are two striking features of this data. First, most of the elements shown show a decrease in their thermal conductivity as they enter the liquid state typically by around 50%. Second, the general magnitude of the thermal conductivities are a factor 100 greater than the thermal conductivities of the non-metallic liquids mentioned in Table 9.12. The temperature-dependence of the thermal conductivity is as varied as for the non-metallic liquids, with some liquids showing increases in thermal conductivity and others showing decreases.

The main questions raised by our preliminary examination of the experimental data on the thermal conductivity of liquids are:

- Why does the thermal conductivity of liquids sometimes increase and sometimes decrease with increasing temperature?
- Why is the thermal conductivity of liquid metals around a factor 100 greater than non-metallic liquids?

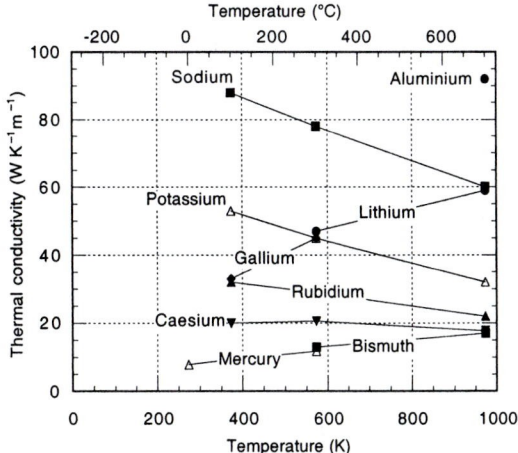

Figure 9.33 Data from Table 9.13 showing the thermal conductivity of elemental metals in their liquid state in units of W K^{-1} m^{-1}.

- Why is the thermal conductivity of elemental liquid metals generally less than in the corresponding solid?

9.10.2 Understanding the thermal conductivity of liquids

We will approach the data on the thermal conductivity of liquids by using the same simple model that we used when we considered the speed of sound data (§9.5.2). We consider heat to flow through a liquid in a combination of two strikingly different processes. One process is similar to that found in gases, and the other is similar to that found in solids:

Table 9.15 Thermal conductivity (W K^{-1} m^{-1}) of elemental metals in their liquid state. Shaded entries refer to the solid state. The data are graphed in Figure 9.33.

Liquid		173 K	273 K	373 K	573 K	973 K	K_L/K_S(%)
Lithium	Li	98	86	82	47	59	57
Sodium	Na	141	142	88	78	60	62
Potassium	K	105	104	53	45	32	51
Rubidium	Rb	59	58	32	29	22	55
Caesium	Cs	37	36	20	20.6	17.7	56
Mercury	Hg	29.5	7.8	9.4	11.7	—	26
Aluminium	Al	241	236	240	233	92	39
Bismuth	Bi	11	8.2	7.2	13	17	181
Gallium	Ga	43	41	33	45	—	80
Tin	Sn	76	68	63	32	40	51

310

- *In a gas*, a molecule moves bodily from one place to another, taking its kinetic energy with it.
- *In a solid*, molecules vibrate and the energy of vibration is passed on from one molecule to another. However, the molecules themselves do not change their average position.

The liquid state has elements in common with both solid and gaseous states. However, the distance that the molecules move before collisions is dramatically reduced in the liquid state as compared with the gaseous state. Further the liquid state lacks the rigidity exhibited by the solid state, which reduces the ease which vibrations are transmitted: recall that the speed of longitudinal sound waves is around 30% less in the liquid than the solid (§9.5). As in our discussion of the speed of sound, we will approach the liquid state by considering the extent to which energy transport within the liquid state is gas-like or solid-like.

Using the idea of thermal resistivity, we estimate the thermal resistance of the liquid as being the sum of the thermal resistivity of solid and gas fractions:

$$R_{\text{liquid}}^{\text{th}} = R_{\text{solid}}^{\text{th}} + R_{\text{gas}}^{\text{th}} \qquad (9.41)$$

Expressing this in terms of the thermal conductivity we have:

$$R_{\text{liquid}}^{\text{th}} = \frac{L}{A\kappa_{\text{solid}}} + \frac{\Delta L}{A\kappa_{\text{gas}}} \qquad (9.42)$$

where L is the length of the solid fraction in a liquid, ΔL is the length of the gas fraction, and A the cross-sectional area of the liquid. Multiplying by $A/(L + \Delta L)$ we find:

$$\frac{AR_{\text{liquid}}^{\text{th}}}{(L+\Delta L)} = \frac{L}{(L+\Delta L)\kappa_{\text{solid}}} + \frac{\Delta L}{(L+\Delta L)\kappa_{\text{gas}}} \qquad (9.43)$$

which simplifies to first order as:

$$\frac{1}{\kappa_{\text{liquid}}} = \left[1 - \frac{\Delta L}{L}\right]\frac{1}{\kappa_{\text{solid}}} + \frac{\Delta L}{L}\left[1 - \frac{\Delta L}{L}\right]\frac{1}{\kappa_{\text{gas}}} \qquad (9.44)$$

Recalling that the typical change in volume on entering the liquid state is 10% we estimate $\Delta L / L \approx (0.1)/3 = 0.033$ (§9.2.1 and Example 7.4). Substituting into Equation 9.35 produces:

$$\frac{1}{\kappa_{\text{liquid}}} = [0.967]\frac{1}{\kappa_{\text{solid}}} + 0.033 \times [0.967]\frac{1}{\kappa_{\text{gas}}} \qquad (9.45)$$

which simplifies to:

$$\kappa_{\text{liquid}} = \left[\frac{0.967}{\kappa_{\text{solid}}} + \frac{0.032}{\kappa_{\text{gas}}}\right]^{-1} \qquad (9.46)$$

In this simple model, the thermal conductivity of a substance in its liquid phase can be related to its thermal conductivity in the gas and solid phases. The idea is that heat travels a factor $\approx 0.967/0.032 \approx 30$ times further through the solid-like pat of a liquid than the gas-like part. So if the thermal conductivity of the solid-like fraction is 30 times greater than the conductivity of the gas-like fraction, then both terms in Equation 9.46 are equal. However, if the thermal conductivity of

Figure 9.34. From the point of view of thermal conductivity, a liquid may be considered as being a solid-like matrix with pockets of gas-like 'free space'. From the data on the density of liquids, we estimate that roughly 10% of a liquid is 'free space'. We can estimate the thermal conductivity of the liquid if we imagine separating out the free-space part of the liquid and considering heat to pass through a gas-like layer, and then a solid-like amount of substance. The arrow in each figure indicates the direction of heat transport.

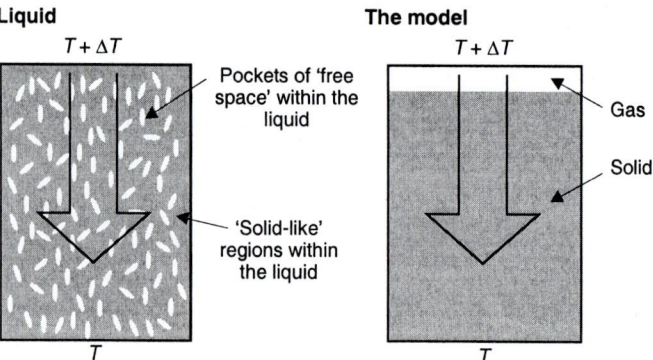

the solid is (say) $\approx$ 300 times that of the gas (quite typical), then the gas term is about 10 times larger than the solid term. We would then expect the thermal conductivity of the liquid to be dominated by the gas thermal conductivity. If this were so then the temperature-dependence of the liquid thermal conductivity should follow that of the gas thermal conductivity, and increase as $\approx T^{0.5}$ to T^1.

However, experimentally, over the temperature range shown, the thermal conductivity of most of the liquids *falls* with temperature. This can be understood in terms of this model as indicating that it is the solid-like fraction of the conductivity which is dominating the thermal conductivity of liquids, i.e. the data indicate that thermal conduction in liquids is dominated by processes analogous to those in solids. So we can interpret the decline in the conductivity as being due to an increase in the scattering of phonons with temperature.

Notice that the atomic vibrations that comprise most phonons have frequencies of roughly 10^{13} Hz and the phonons travel at the speed of sound $\approx$ 2000 m s^{-1}. We expect the structure of a liquid to change on a time-scale of the order of 10^{-10} seconds. Thus the phonons may travel considerable distances through the liquid without being aware of its fluid nature. As far as vibrations are concerned, the lattice looks like a highly disordered solid. It is this last point, the strong disorder, that is responsible for the relatively poor thermal conduction in liquids as compared with solids.

Notice that two liquids, helium and water, show an increase in thermal conductivity with temperature. In fact both liquids are highly anomalous and it is unwise to generalise on the basis of data either of these liquids. However the increase in helium is likely to be related to an essentially gaseous mechanism, but the increase in water is likely to be related to the low temperature case discussed at the end of §7.8.

Liquid metals

It is perhaps surprising, but as we shall see in (§9.12) when metals melt they retain their high electrical conductivity, albeit with a slightly increased value of resistivity. Thus for liquid metals, in addition to conduction by molecular vibrations transmitted in 'gas like' and 'solid-like' manner, thermal conduction may take place through the motion of the conduction electrons. Since the thermal conductivity of all the liquid metals is dramatically greater than all the non-metallic liquids, we conclude that (to a first approximation) we may ignore thermal conduction through molecular vibrations in liquid metals.

If electronic motion is the dominant conductor of heat *and* charge, then there should be a relationship between the electrical and thermal conductivity. When they move, electrons transport a fixed amount of charge, but an amount of heat ($\approx k_B T$) which depends on temperature. As shown in Table 9.16, the ratio $\kappa/\sigma T = \rho\kappa/T$ is indeed relatively constant both as a function of temperature and from one simple metal to another. We find $\rho\kappa/T$ consistently close to a value of 2.45×10^{-8} (W Ω K^{-2}), which confirms our suspicion that phonon conductivity is negligible in comparison with electrical conduction.

Table 9.16 Thermal conductivity (WK^{-1} m^{-1}) and electrical resistivity (Ω m) of elemental metals in their liquid state. Also evaluated is the quantity $\rho\kappa/T$ known as the *Lorentz number* and has theoretical value of 2.45×10^{-8} (W Ω K^{-2}).

Liquid	373 K			573 K			973 K		
	ρ	κ	$\rho\kappa/T$	ρ	κ	$\rho\kappa/T$	ρ	κ	$\rho\kappa/T$
Sodium	9.7×10^{-8}	88	2.3×10^{-8}	16.8×10^{-8}	78	2.3×10^{-8}	39.2×10^{-8}	60	2.4×10^{-8}
Potassium	17.5×10^{-8}	53	2.5×10^{-8}	28.2×10^{-8}	45	2.2×10^{-8}	66.4×10^{-8}	32	2.2×10^{-8}
Rubidium	27.5×10^{-8}	32	2.4×10^{-8}	48×10^{-8}	29	2.4×10^{-8}	99×10^{-8}	22	2.2×10^{-8}
Caesium	43.5×10^{-8}	20	2.3×10^{-8}	67×10^{-8}	20.6	2.4×10^{-8}	134×10^{-8}	17.7	2.4×10^{-8}
Mercury	103.5×10^{-8}	9.4	2.6×10^{-8}	128×10^{-8}	11.7	2.6×10^{-8}	214×10^{-8}	—	—

9.12 Electrical properties

9.12.1 Data on the electrical properties of liquid metals

When any substance is subject to an applied electric field E, a current of electronic charge flows through the substance. The magnitude of the resultant current density j is characterised by the *electrical resistivity* ρ or the *electrical conductivity* σ of the substance. The two measures are the inverse of each other, $\rho = 1/\sigma$ and so for most purposes there is no advantage to using one measure or the other. The electrical resistivity and conductivity are defined by:

$$j = \sigma E$$

and $$(9.47)$$

$$E = \rho j$$

If the current density is measured in Am^{-2} and the electric field in $V\,m^{-1}$ then the units of σ are $\Omega^{-1}\,m^{-1}$ or *seimens* (symbol 'S', not to confused with 's' for seconds). The units of resistivity are inverse seimens, S^{-1} or more commonly $\Omega\,m$. For a sample of cross-sectional area A and length L, the resistivity is related to the electrical *resistance* R by:

$$\rho = \frac{RA}{L} \quad \Omega\,m \quad \text{or} \quad S^{-1}\,m \qquad (9.48)$$

From Figure 7.34, it is clear that most elements are metals, with resistivity between $10^{-5}\,\Omega\,m$ and $10^{-8}\,\Omega\,m$ at around room temperature. Perhaps surprisingly, heating elements beyond their melting temperature does not destroy their metallic behaviour. Data on the temperature dependence of some low melting-point elemental metals is given in Table 9.17 and plotted in Figure 9.35. As is clear from Figure 9.35, and from the last row of Table 9.17, the resistivity in the liquid state, is significantly greater than the resistivity in the solid state, though still of a similar order of magnitude.

So the main questions raised by our preliminary examination of the experimental data on the electrical resistivity of liquid metals are:

- Why does the metallic state survive in liquids?

Table 9.17 The resistivity ($\times 10^{-8}\,\Omega\,m$) of elemental metals with low melting points. The shaded data above the line in the table refers to the metals in the solid state and data below line refer to data in the liquid state. The last row of the table shows the ratio of the resistivities in the solid and liquid states. The figure is derived from the ratio of the last datum in the solid region to the first datum in the liquid region.

$T(K)$	Na	K	Rb	Cs	Hg
0	0	0	0	0	0
78.2	0.76	1.30	2.59	4.1	5.8
273.2	4.33	6.49	11.5	18.8	94.1
373.2	9.51	15.8	27.3	44.5	103.5
573.2	17.4	27.7	45.1	67.3	128
973.2	38.9	64.7	93	128	214
1473.2	88	165	250	338	630
ρ_S/ρ_L (%)	46	41	42	42	6

Figure 9.35 The resistivity of elemental metals with low melting points. Notice that the data show a significant increase in resistivity from below the melting temperature to above it. Note: The lines which connect the data points are drawn only to guide the eye. In actuality data were available at closely spaced temperatures, it would show that at the transition from liquid to solid there would be a sharp increase in resistivity.

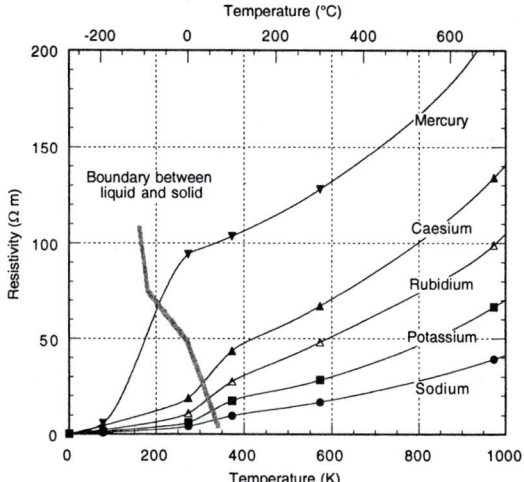

- Why is the electrical resistance worse in the liquid state than the solid state?

9.12.2 Understanding the electrical properties of liquid metals

Perhaps surprisingly, we can approach the results of our examination of the resistivity of liquid metals in exactly the same way that we approached the data for metallic solids. The reasons why this is so also shed light onto the question of why the resistivity in the liquid state is higher than the resistivity in the solid state.

As discussed in §7.7, our first picture of the electrons within a metal is as a free electron gas with a number density of around 10^{29} m^{-3}. The exclusion principle causes the many electrons in the gas to have extremely high energies which causes electrons move extremely quickly through a metal, at speeds of around the Fermi speed $v_F \approx 10^6$ m s^{-1}. In the introductory sections of this chapter we mentioned that atoms vibrate within their 'cells' in the liquid structure in a time of around 10^{-13} seconds. And typically we expected an atom to vibrate of the order of 1000 times before the detailed structure changed significantly.

During the time which it takes for an atom to vibrate once, an electron can travel around 10^6 m s^{-1} × 10^{-13} s = 10^{-7} m, which corresponds to around 300 'cell' diameters. Thus for the electrons the changes in liquid structure which take place on a time-scale of $\approx 10^{-10}$ seconds appear very slow indeed. Thus the change to the liquid state which is so apparent on a large time scale may not even be noticed by electrons! The liquid structure looks to a conduction electron like a strongly disordered solid, and it is this strong positional disorder which scatters the electrons in the same way that alloying increased the resistivity of a solid (§7.7). So the origin of the increase in resistivity on entering the liquid state is caused by increased scattering due to the loss of an ordered lattice.

As Example 9.3 makes clear, we are still not quite able to explain the resistivity values in the liquid state. The predicted resistivity is of the order 15 times larger than the experimental value. Reviewing the steps leading to the prediction reveals places where the calculation could be out by small factors, but only one place where a factor of the order 15 could be 'lost'. This is the assumption

314

Example 9.4

Let us use the theory of §7.7 for the free electron gas to estimate the resistivity of the liquid metal potassium. In its liquid state potassium (relative molecular mass 39.1) has a density of 824 kg m^{-3} and so the number density of atoms is:

$$n = \frac{\rho}{Mu} = \frac{824}{39.1 \times 1.66 \times 10^{-27}} = 1.27 \times 10^{28} \text{ atoms m}^{-3}$$

If we assume that one electron per atom joins the free electron gas, then this is also the number density of electrons. We can predict the wave-vector of the most energetic conduction electrons k_{max} according to Equation 6.72: $k_F = (3n\pi^2)^{1/3}$ and hence the maximum velocity of electrons is $v_F = \hbar k_F / m_e$.

Substituting we find:

$$v_F = \frac{\hbar(3n\pi^2)^{1/3}}{m_e} = \frac{1.054 \times 10^{-34}(3\pi^2 \times 1.27 \times 10^{28})^{1/3}}{9.1 \times 10^{-31}}$$

$$= 0.835 \times 10^6 \text{ ms}^{-1}$$

Let us assume that before being scattered an electron travels across roughly two 'cells' of diameter a in the liquid. This estimate seems reasonable given the strongly disordered 'lattice' present in the liquid state. From the liquid density we can estimate the density as Mu/a^3 and hence the cell diameter is of the order:

$$a \approx (Mu/\rho)^{1/3} \approx \left(\frac{39.1 \times 1.66 \times 10^{-27}}{824}\right)^{1/3}$$

$$= 4.3 \times 10^{-10} \text{ m}$$

The scattering time τ will be the time taken for an electron to travel a mean free path, roughly $2a$ which is $\tau \approx 2a/v_F$. Thus:

$$\tau \approx \frac{2a}{v_F} = \frac{2 \times 4.3 \times 10^{-10}}{0.835 \times 10^6} = 1.0 \times 10^{-15} \text{ s}$$

If we substitute this value in the expression for the resistivity of a free electron gas (Equation 7.71) we find:

$$\rho = \frac{m}{ne^2\tau}$$

$$\rho = \frac{9.1 \times 10^{-31}}{1.27 \times 10^{28} \times (1.6 \times 10^{-19})^2 \times 1.0 \times 10^{-15}}$$

$$= 280 \times 10^{-8} \text{ } \Omega\text{m}$$

This predicted value may be compared with the experimental value just above the melting temperature of 17.5 × 10^{-8} Ω m, i.e. a factor 15 lower than the prediction.

Figure 9.36 A schematic illustration of the way an electron wave can be scattered several times through small angles and eventually result in randomisation of the electrons initial momentum.

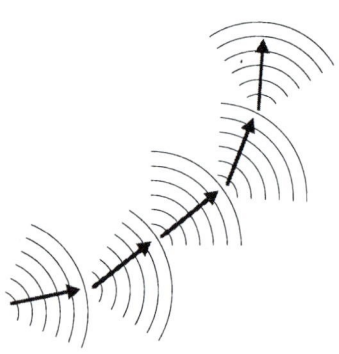

Table 9.18 The relative dielectric permittivity ε of various insulating liquids. The relative permittivity of vacuum is exactly 1.

Substance	MW	T	$\varepsilon - 1$	ε
Argon, Ar	40	82 K	0.53	1.53
Helium, He	4	4.19 K	0.048	1.048
Hydrogen, H_2	2	20.4 K	0.228	1.228
Nitrogen, N_2	28	70 K	0.45	1.45
Oxygen, O_2	32	80 K	0.507	1.507
Methanol, CH_3OH	32	25 °C	31.6	32.6
Ethanol, C_2H_5OH	46	25 °C	23.3	24.3
Propanol, C_3H_7OH	60	25 °C	19.1	20.1
Butanol, C_4H_9OH	74	20 °C	16.8	17.8
Pentanol, $C_5H_{11}OH$	88	25 °C	12.9	13.9
Hexanol, $C_6H_{13}OH$	102	25 °C	12.3	13.3
Aniline, C_6H_7N	86	20 °C	5.90	6.90
Acetone, C_3H_6O	58	25 °C	19.7	20.7
Carbon disulphide, CS_2	76	20 °C	1.64	2.64
Water, H_2O	18	20 °C	79.4	80.4

that because of the disorder in the 'lattice' in the liquid state, electrons travel only about two 'cells' before scattering must be wrong. In order to make our theory agree with the data, electrons must travel 15 times further i.e. of the order 30 'cells' before scattering. This does indeed seem a surprisingly large distance but we can understand it as follows.

First, we note that the scattering events assumed in the theory are *total* scattering events, after which the electron is likely to travel in any direction. If the electron is scattered every two 'cell' diameters or so (as seems inevitable given the level of disorder in the liquid state) then we can understand the resistivity value if we assume that these scattering events are *small-angle scattering events*. So every two cells or so, an electron is scattered by only a small angle. As illustrated in Figure 9.36, it would take several such scattering events before the electrons initial momentum would be randomised.

Figure 9.37 The difference of the relative dielectric permittivity from unity, $\varepsilon - 1$, plotted as function of the molecular mass of the molecules of various electrically insulating liquids. Lines have been drawn to attract attention to the trend in the alcohols, to which water appears be roughly related. All the elements in Table 9.16 appear as points close to the x-axis in this figure.

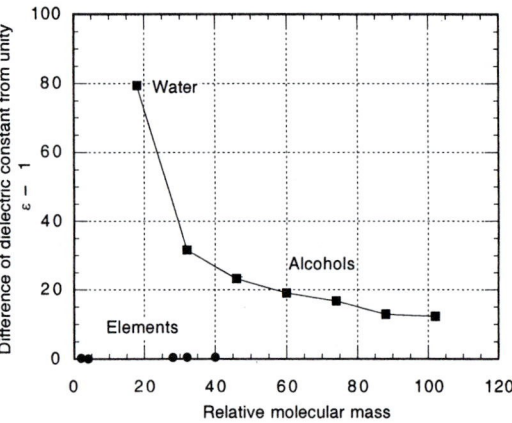

9.12.3 Data on the electrical properties of liquid insulators

Weak electric fields

The most basic electrical property of electrical insulators (or *dielectrics*) is that for small electric fields they are highly resistive! The primary effect of the electric field is to *polarise* the material,

causing electrical charges within the material to separate slightly. This weakens applied electric fields within the material to an extent measured by the relative dielectric permittivity ε of the material. The values of $\varepsilon - 1$ for the elements in Table 9.18 generally lie in the range 0 to 1. The organic alcohols have considerably higher values, which

315

become smaller for the larger molecules. The value for water, which may be considered as the limit of the small alcohol molecules, has an enormously large value, ≈ 80. This is of a similar order to the structurally-bistable compound, $SrTiO_3$.

The main questions raised by our preliminary examination of the experimental data on the electrical properties of insulators are:

- Why is the difference of the dielectric constant from unity $(\varepsilon - 1)$ in liquids typically 1000 times greater than for gases?
- Why does $(\varepsilon - 1)$ for some liquids exceed the values for elemental liquids by a factor of the order 10?

These questions will be addressed in §9.12.4 below.

Strong electric fields

As with solids and gases, liquids which are electrically insulating at low electrical fields eventually conduct at high electric fields. Unfortunately the data books I have been using have no references to the *dielectric strength* or *breakdown field* for liquid dielectrics.

9.12.4 Understanding the electrical properties of liquid insulators

We can consider the dielectric constant data from the point of view that a liquid is in essence a dense gas-like collection of molecules. In this approach we understand the dielectric properties of liquids as being essentially the dielectric properties of the constituent molecules of the liquid. The dielectric constant of the liquid is then increased above the gaseous value by the relatively high density of the liquid. In order to test this approach we need to estimate the number density of molecules in the gaseous and liquid states. This is done by means of Example 4.2:

$$n_{gas} = \frac{P}{k_B T} \qquad (5.100^* \text{ and } 9.49)$$

and Example 7.1:

$$n_{liq} = \frac{\rho}{Mu} \qquad (9.50)$$

where ρ is the density of the liquid, M the relative molecular mass of the molecules, and u an atomic mass unit. Further, we recall from §5.7 that the dielectric constant of a gas is given by two different expressions depending on whether the molecules are *polar* or *non-polar*.

Polar molecules have a permanent (intrinsic) electric dipole moment p_p due to the distribution of electric charge within each molecule. An applied electric field exerts a torque on the molecules, which tends to align them with the applied field. In addition, the electronic charge distribution within the molecule can itself be changed by the applied field, resulting in an *induced* electric dipole moment. The magnitude of the induced dipole moment is related to α, the polarisability of the molecule.

We expect that for gases, and hopefully liquids, composed of non-polar molecules ε should be given by:

$$\varepsilon - 1 = \frac{n\alpha}{\varepsilon_0} \qquad (5.109^* \text{ and } 9.51)$$

where the molecular polarisability α is an intrinsic property of a molecule. For collections of polar molecules we expect that in addition to any induced dipole moment there should be an additional term given by:

$$\varepsilon - 1 = \frac{np_p^2}{3\varepsilon_0 k_B T}. \qquad (5.116^* \text{ and } 9.52)$$

where p_p is the electric dipole moment built into a molecule, an intrinsic property of the molecule.

Non-polar molecules

Based on Equation 9.51, $\varepsilon - 1 = n\alpha / \varepsilon_0$ we can calculate the values of α per molecule in the liquid state and compare our results with the similar calculation for the substance in the gaseous state.

As Table 9.19 indicates, the molecular polarisability inferred from the dielectric constant data is roughly the same independent of whether ε is measured in the gaseous or the liquid states. In order to see the significance of this result, recall

Table 9.19 The results of calculations of the molecular polarisability of non-polar molecules based on dielectric constant data for both liquid and gaseous states. The value of on Equation 9.51 $\alpha/\varepsilon_o =(\varepsilon - 1)/n$ with n estimated by either Equation 9.49 or 9.50 as appropriate. The data for the densities of liquid hydrogen, nitrogen and oxygen are estimates based on a 10% decrease of the density of the solid. See Table 5.16 for gas data and Table 9.18 for liquid data. The gas data refer to atmospheric pressure (1.013×10^5 Pa). Notice that the inferred value of α is quite similar in liquid and gaseous states.

		Liquid				Gas			
Substance		ρ (kg m^{-3})	ε-1	n ($\times10^{28}$ m^3)	α/ε_o ($\times10^{-30}$)	ρ (kg m^{-3})	ε-1	n ($\times10^{28}$ m^3)	α/ε_o ($\times10^{-30}$)
Argon	40	1410	0.53	2.12	25	293	5.16	2.50	21
Helium	4	120	0.048	1.81	2.65	293	0.65	2.50	2.6
Hydrogen	2	≈80	0.228	2.41	9.5	293	2.54	2.50	10.2
Nitrogen	28	≈930	0.45	2.00	22.5	293	5.47	2.50	21.9
Oxygen	32	≈1300	0.507	2.45	20.5	293	4.94	2.50	19.8

again that α is an intrinsic property of a molecule related to the ease with which its electronic structure is deformed by applied fields. The fact that this property of the molecule is the same in the liquid and gaseous states implies that the electronic structure of the molecule is similar in both states.

Polar molecules

We can calculate the values of p_p per molecule in the liquid state and compare our results with the similar calculation for the substance in the gaseous state. We use:

$$p_p = \left[\frac{3\varepsilon_o k_B T(\varepsilon - 1)}{n} \right]^{1/2} \text{(5.119* and 9.53)}$$

with n estimated by either Equation 9.49 or 9.50 as appropriate. As Table 9.20 indicates, the value of intrinsic dipole moment p_p inferred from the dielectric constant data on liquids is roughly 2.4 times larger than the same quantity inferred from

the dielectric constant data on gases. The origin of this enhancement is at first puzzling but can in fact be understood fairly straightforwardly.

When we observe a molecule in a low-density gas, the molecules are separated by large distances and interact only weakly with each other. So their responses to the applied field are independent of one another. So when we measure the molecular polarisability α in a gas, we deduce its correct value. However, as the density of molecules is increased, this independence of response is lost. When the molecules are as close as they are in the liquid state, the interactions between molecules are significant and cannot be neglected. To see how this independence is lost, Example 9.5 considers a hypothetical molecule with an intrinsic electric dipole moment of the same order as those in Table 9.20. Example 9.5 shows that the electric field near a polar molecule may be exceedingly large. Electric fields of this magnitude will (a) strongly polarise the charge distributions on neighbouring molecules, and (b) affect the relative orientation of

Table 9.20 The results of the calculations of the permanent molecular dipole moment (in C m) of polar molecules according to Equation 9.53. The gas data refer to atmospheric pressure (1.013×10^5 Pa).

			Liquid					Gas		
Substance	M	T (K)	ρ (kg m^{-3})	ε-1	n ($\times10^{28}$ m^3)	p ($\times10^{-30}$)	T (K)	ε-1	n ($\times10^{28}$ m^3)	p ($\times10^{-30}$)
Methanol	32	298	791	31.6	1.49	15.2	373	57	1.97	6.29
Ethanol	46	298	789	23.3	1.03	15.7	373	61 or 78	1.97	6.5 or 7.4
Water	18	293	1000	79.4	3.35	16.0	373	60	1.97	6.45

neighbouring molecules. Thus when a molecule is turned to align with an external field, its electric field turns with it, and thus the polarisation also 'turns with' the molecule. Thus the electric dipole moment 'associated with' a particular molecule is equal to the original intrinsic dipole moment p_p, plus a second part related to the interaction with neighbouring molecules.

Conclusion

We are now in a position to understand the experimental data. The reason why the difference of the dielectric constant from unity $(\varepsilon - 1)$ in liquids is typically 1000 times greater than for gases is indeed as we supposed initially because of the density of molecules.

The reason why $(\varepsilon - 1)$ for some liquids exceeds values for elemental liquids by a large factor is because these high dielectric constant liquids are *polar* and the effect of an applied electric is to turn the molecules within the liquid. The applied field thus alters the distribution of electric charge within the liquid, which can correspond to a relatively large *structural* change in the liquid. This may be compared with the anomalously large values of dielectric constant observed in the structurally bistable solid, strontium titanate (Table 7.16)

The reason why $(\varepsilon - 1)$ for some liquids exceeds the predicted value based on density extrapolation by a factor of the order 2.5 is because these liquids are *polar* As each molecule rotates, it drags with it its polarisation of nearby molecules.

Example 9.5

Consider a molecule around 0.3 nm in length with a permanent electric dipole moment of $p_p = 6 \times 10^{-30}$ C m, similar to the experimental values in Table 9.18. This is equivalent to a situation in which charges of $+q$ and $-q$ are separated by a distance $d = 0.3$ nm such that § 2.2.3:

$$p_p = qd$$

We thus estimate that the charge at either end of the molecule q:

$$q = \frac{p_p}{d} = \frac{6 \times 10^{-30}}{0.3 \times 10^{-9}} = 2 \times 10^{-20} \text{ C}$$

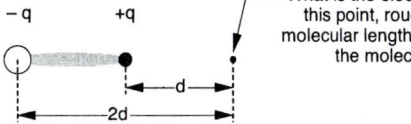

What is the electric field at this point, roughly one molecular length away from the molecule?

Let us now work out the electric field at a distance of roughly one molecular length away from the molecule along the axis of the molecule. The electric field may be calculated as the sum of the two contributions: one from the charge at either end of the molecule. Thus at a distance d from the positively-charged end of the molecule the electric field is:

$$E = \frac{+q}{4\pi\varepsilon_0 d^2} + \frac{-q}{4\pi\varepsilon_0 (2d)^2} = \frac{-q}{4\pi\varepsilon_0 d^2}\left[1 - \frac{1}{4}\right]$$

$$= \frac{2 \times 10^{-20}}{4\pi \times 8.85 \times 10^{-12} \times \left(0.3 \times 10^{-10}\right)^2}\left[\frac{3}{4}\right]$$

$$= 1.50 \times 10^9 \text{ V m}^{-1}$$

9.13 Optical properties

9.13.1 Dielectric materials: insulators

The optical properties of liquids may (for many purposes) be characterised by two parameters: the *refractive index* of the material and the *absorbtion coefficient*. In this section we consider only the refractive index of insulating liquids. The refractive index n_{light} of a transparent material is related to the speed of light v in the material by:

$$n_{light} = \frac{c}{v}, \qquad (2.17^*)$$

where c is the speed of light in a vacuum. The refractive index of various transparent liquids is recorded in Table 9.21. As with solids, the value of n_{light} varies with wavelength, and the data refer to the refractive index at the wavelength of the bright yellow D lines in the spectrum of sodium vapour. Figure 9.38 shows the variation of n_{light} with wavelength for water. The graph is strikingly similar to the data for the variation of the refractive index of glasses shown in Figures 7.50 and 7.51.

Figure 9.38 The refractive index of a water as a function of wavelength. The shaded region corresponds to the visible region of the spectrum.

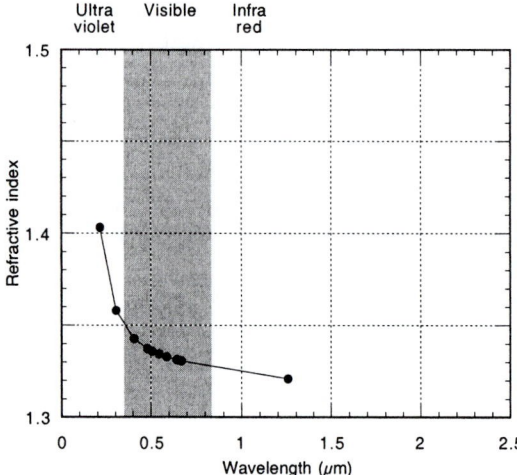

Table 9.21 The refractive index of various liquids for yellow light.

Substance and chemical formula	MW	n_{light}
Water, H_2O	18	1.33
Carbon tetrachloride, CCl_4	152	1.405
Toluene, C_7H_8	92	1.497
Methanol, CH_3OH	32	1.329
Ethanol, C_2H_5OH	44	1.3614
Propan-1-ol, C_3H_7OH	56	1.3852
Propan-2-ol, $C_2H_5OHCH_2$	56	1.3742
Acetic acid, CH_3COOH		1.3716
Benzene, C_6H_6	78	1.501
Aniline, C_6H_7N	86	1.586
Hydrogen disulphide, HS_2	65	1.885

The questions raised by our preliminary examination of the experimental data on the optical properties of liquids are:

- Why are the refractive indices of liquids similar to those of transparent solids, but different from unity by about 1000 times more than gases?
- Why is the variation with wavelength of the refractive index of liquids similar to that exhibited by transparent solids?

9.13.2 Understanding the optical properties of insulators

Our approach to the optical properties of liquids is similar to our approach to the dielectric properties of liquids. As a first step, we consider the optical properties of liquids as being essentially the optical properties of the constituent molecules of the liquid but enhanced above the gaseous properties by the relatively high density of the liquid.

From the discussion of the refractive index of gases, we recall that, in general, the refractive index is related to the dielectric constant of the substance by:

$$n_{light} = \sqrt{\varepsilon} \qquad (2.17^*)$$

From Equation 2.17 we see that if the dielectric constant is given by:

$$\varepsilon = 1 + \frac{n\alpha}{\varepsilon_0} \qquad (5.109^* \ \& \ 9.51^*)$$

then we expect the refractive index to be given by:

$$\begin{aligned} n_{light} &= \sqrt{\varepsilon} \\ &= \sqrt{1 + \frac{n\alpha}{\varepsilon_0}} \end{aligned} \qquad (9.54)$$

Now the low-frequency dielectric constant of a liquid with polar molecules has contributions both from the rotation of the polar molecules and from the polarisation of their charge distribution. However, at optical frequencies, the inertia of the molecules prevents them from rotating in response to the electric field of the light wave. Hence the refractive index is related only to the *induced* component of the dielectric constant.

In order to see whether we can explain the refractive index of a liquid in terms of only the change in the number density of molecules, we will proceed as follows. First we will estimate the molecular polarisability α using Equation 9.54 and the refractive index data on gases (Table 5.17). Then we will use the *same value* of α to estimate the refractive index we might expect in the liquid state assuming that the liquid is merely a dense gas. We will work through the calculation first for water.

Example calculation : water vapour

Rearranging Equation 9.54 as an expression for α we find:

$$\alpha = \frac{\varepsilon_o (n_{\text{light}}^2 - 1)}{n} \tag{9.55}$$

In order to evaluate Equation 9.55 we must first estimate the number density of molecules in the gaseous using Example 4.2:

$$n^{\text{gas}} = \frac{P}{k_B T} \tag{9.56}$$

where I have written the phase as a superscript to help to distinguish between the use of n as a symbol for both refractive index and number density. Since the water vapour data refers to STP this evaluates to:

$$n^{\text{gas}} = \frac{1.013 \times 10^5}{1.38 \times 10^{-23} \times 273} \tag{9.57}$$

$$= 2.689 \times 10^{25} \ \text{m}^{-3}$$

Substituting for n^{gas} and for the refractive index of water vapour (Table 5.17 $n_{\text{light}} = 1.000254$), Equation 9.55 evaluates to:

$$\alpha = \frac{8.854 \times 10^{12} ((1.000254)^2 - 1)}{2.689 \times 10^{25}} \tag{9.58}$$

$$= 1.647 \times 10^{-40} \ \text{F}^{-1} \ \text{m}^4$$

Example calculation: water liquid

We now need to estimate the number density of water molecules in liquid water at STP. To do this we use Equation 9.50 and substitute for the density of water $\rho = 1000 \ \text{kg m}^{-3}$ and the mass of a mole of water $M = 18 \times 10^{-3}$ kg to find:

$$n^{\text{liquid}} = \frac{N_A \rho}{M} \tag{9.59}$$

$$n^{\text{liquid}} = \frac{6.022 \times 10^{23} \times 1000}{18 \times 10^{-3}} \tag{9.60}$$

$$= 3.346 \times 10^{28} \ \text{m}^{-3}$$

Substituting this value for n^{liquid} and the value of molecular polarisability determined from the gas data (Equation 9.58) into Equation 9.54 for the refractive index yields:

$$n_{\text{light}} = \sqrt{1 + \frac{3.346 \times 10^{28} \times 1.647 \times 10^{-40}}{8.854 \times 10^{-12}}} \tag{9.61}$$

$$\approx 1.27$$

which is to be compared with the experimental value of 1.33. Tables 9.21 and 5.17 showing the refractive indices of liquids and gases have two entries in common aside from H_2O. Table 9.22 shows the results of the calculations similar to that outlined above for these two substances. Table 9.22 indicates that the predictions for $n_{\text{light}} - 1$ are 20 % to 25 % below the experimental values. This level of agreement is not bad if we consider the extent of the extrapolation of around a thousand fold in number density, and our neglect of any consideration of molecular interactions.

The effect of molecular interactions is difficult to predict accurately, but it is worth bearing in mind the results for the low-frequency dielectric constant values of polar liquids. We found that due to the molecular interactions, they were enhanced by a factor ≈ 2.4 over what would have been expected based on the gas data.

Table 9.22 Calculation of the refractive indices of liquid water, methanol and benzene from the data on the refractive index of their vapours (Table 5.18). The predictions for $n_{\text{light}} - 1$ are 20 to 25% below the experimental values. The method of calculation is described in Equations 9.55 to 9.61.

| | | Gas | | | | Liquid | | | |
| | | | Number | | Molecular polarisability | Density | Number density | Prediction | Actual |
Substance		MW	density (m^{-3})	n_{light}	α (F^{-1}m^4)	(kg m^{-3})	(m^{-3})	$n_{\text{light}} - 1$	$n_{\text{light}} - 1$
Water	H_2O	18	2.689×10^{25}	1.000254	1.647×10^{-40}	1000	3.346×10^{28}	0.27	0.33
Methanol	CH_3OH	32	2.689×10^{25}	1.000586	3.860×10^{-40}	791	1.489×10^{28}	0.284	0.329
Benzene	C_6H_6	78	2.689×10^{25}	1.001762	11.61×10^{-40}	879	6.786×10^{27}	0.375	0.501

Comparison of refractive index data and dielectric constant data

The refractive index measurements use light oscillating at a frequency of the order 10^{15} Hz. In one period of such a fast oscillation the molecules are unable to rotate to align their intrinsic dipole moments with the electric field. Thus the refractive index arises only from the molecular polarisability α because only the electrons within the molecule are able to move fast enough to respond on this time-scale. Recall for comparison that a molecule vibrates within its cell roughly once every 10^{-13} seconds, and that the structure of the liquid changes around every 10^{-10} seconds. In contrast the dielectric constant measurements are usually made at frequencies of only 10^6 Hz. In one period of such an oscillation there is plenty of time for molecules to optimally align their intrinsic dipole moment p_p with the electric field.

Bearing this in mind, it is interesting to compare the results of an analysis of dielectric constant data for the polar liquids water and methanol (§9.12.3), with the results of the analysis of the refractive index. For the dielectric constant data we found that the intrinsic dipole moment of a polar molecule in the liquid appeared to be enhanced by a factor of around 2.4. The reason for the enhancement was the low frequency ($\approx 10^6$ Hz) used for these measurements and the strong interaction between molecules.

However, the refractive index data is not sensitive to the permanent dipole moment on each molecule, but only to the *polarisability* of each molecule. The refractive index data could be interpreted as indicating that the molecular polarisability in the liquid is enhanced over its value in the gas by roughly 25%. (Using Equation 9.51 for liquid water predicts $\alpha = 2.035 \times 10^{-40}$ F^{-1} m^4 compared with $\alpha = 1.647 \times 10^{-40}$ F^{-1} m^4 for the gas (Equation 9.54).) This enhancement arises as follows. When a molecule is polarised by the electric field of the light wave, it acquires *an induced* electric dipole moment p_i. The electric field around this dipole moment can be intense (Example 9.4) and this polarises the neighbouring molecules. The extent of this additional polarisation depends on the density of the substance: if there are many molecules close to the 'source' molecules, then the effect is relatively large. Notice that the effect ($\approx 25\%$) is not as large as the static polarisation effect ($\approx 250\%$) because that effect involved the *rotation* of polar molecules. Such rotations require a nanosecond or so to complete, and so on the time scale of the oscillation of the light wave ($\approx 10^{-16}$ s) such processes can be neglected.

9.14 Exercises

Exercises marked with a P prefix are 'normal' exercises. Those marked with a C prefix are best solved numerically by using a computer program or spreadsheet.. Exercises marked with an E prefix are in general rather more challenging that the P and C exercises. Answers to all the exercises are downloadable from www.physicsofmatter.com

Density and expansivity

P1. Which element has (a) the largest, and (b) the smallest, ratio of solid density to liquid density at its melting temperature? (Table 9.1)

C2. Download the molecular dynamics simulation from the web site www.physicsofmatter.com. Run the simulation for the liquid phase with at least 25 molecules and allow it to run until the molecules form 'a blob'. Stop the simulation and examine the instantaneous positions of the molecules. To what extent do the figures in Example 8.1 and Figure 8.4 reflect the patterns seen in the simulation?

P3. By considering the densities in Table 9.2, estimate the density of *any* alcohol. Estimate the density of vodka, a mixture by volume of 60% water and 40% ethanol.

P4. To what extent are the relative densities of light water (H_2O) and heavy water (D_2O) related solely to their difference in atomic mass? (Table 9.3)

P5. Compare the change in the density of mercury over the temperature range 0 °C to 300 °C with the change in the density of gold over the same temperature range. (Figure 9.4, Table 7.4 and Example 7.4)

P6. Which liquid metal in Table 9.4 has the highest thermal expansivity?

P7. In many parts of the world it is common for a body of fresh water such as pond or a lake to freeze over in the winter and melt again in the spring. The cooling of the lake arises primarily from air cooling: the temperature of the Earth beneath the lake is relatively stable from one season to another. Write an explanation for a friend explaining how the two 'anomalous' properties of water (Figure 9.3: the density maximum at 4 °C and the low density of its solid phase) combine to create a situation in which the majority of the lake remains liquid even in extremely cold weather. (See also Question P22).

P8. Water substance increases its volume by roughly 10% when it freezes. The freezing of water trapped in cracks within a rock is a powerful tool for geological erosion. By considering a simply shaped crack, estimate roughly the pressure exerted on the rock by ice when it freezes. You will need to estimate the Young's modulus of the ice, which you may do using Equation 7.24 from information on its density (Figure 9.3), and the speed of sound in ice (Table 7.9).

Speed of sound

P9. What is the speed of longitudinal sound waves in (a) water and (b) ethanol?

P10. What is the ratio of the speed of longitudinal sound waves (a) in water and ice, and (b) in copper and molten copper?

P11. Based on the speed of longitudinal sound waves, estimate very roughly the Young's modulus E and bulk modulus B for ice, water, copper and molten copper. (Equations 9.2 to 9.10, Figure 9.3, Tables 9.1 and 9.6, Tables 7.2 and 7.9) . Where possible, compare your values with those in Tables 7.4 and 9.4.

Viscosity, surface tension, and vapour pressure

P12. Consider the descent of a solid sphere of radius r and density ρ_S through a liquid of density ρ_L and viscosity η. The viscous force (G. Stokes 1850) has been found to be $F = 6\pi r\eta v$ and so increases as the sphere accelerates until it exactly equals the net force due to gravity and buoyancy. Derive an expression for the viscosity of a liquid in terms of this terminal velocity of a sphere falling through it. Estimate the terminal velocity for both steel (Table 7.1) and nylon (density ≈ 1300 kg m^{-3}) spheres falling through water at (a) 0 °C and (b) 40 °C (Figure 9.12). Can you think of a *simple* experiment that you could carry out to see if your estimates are correct?

P13. What is the viscosity of water at (a) 0 °C and (b)

40 °C (Figure 9.15)? Using the Stokes formula from Question P12, estimate the time for an air bubble 1 mm in diameter to rise through a column of liquid water 15 cm high at each of these temperatures.

An air bubble would grow as it rose through the liquid (§5.2) because the pressure of the liquid around it would fall. Estimate the extent to which the bubble would grow on its journey, and state whether you would expect to be able to notice this.

P14. What is the surface energy (surface tension) γ for (a) water at 20 °C and (b) gold at 1100 °C ? (Table 9.9) What is the value of ΔE_s in milli electron volts for (a) water at 20 °C and (b) gold at 1100 °C ? (Table 9.10)

P15. Estimate the of vapour pressure at 2000 °C of (a) copper, (b) silver, (c) gold, and (d) aluminium? (Figure 9.24)

P16. Estimate the rate at which molecules leave the surface of liquid water at 20 °C according to Equation 9.28 and Table 9.11. What rate of mass loss does this correspond to? In other words how many grams evaporate per unit area per second. Compare this with your qualitative experience of water evaporating in a situation where little water vapour will re-enter the liquid e.g. spilling water outdoors onto a non-absorbent surface on a warm day with a slight breeze.

P17. Assuming the oceans of the world to be at an average surface temperature of 4 °C, and to have a surface area of 2/3 that of the Earth, estimate the rate at which the oceans are evaporating (Equation 11.8 and Table 9.10). If this mass loss were not replaced by rain, at what rate would the sea level decline? (Equation 11.8 and Table 9.10). The radius of the Earth is approximately 6400 km.

P18. Estimate the vapour pressure of water at the boiling temperature of ethanol. Based on the ratio of vapour pressures, estimate the minimum fraction of water (by molar concentration) that would be present in a distilled water/ethanol mix. By a similar technique estimate the minimum fraction of methanol present. (Equation 9.36 and Table 11.2)

P19. Write an essay summarising the cell model of a liquid dynamics. (§8.4 and §9.6 to §9.9).

Thermal properties

P20. What is the molar heat capacity of (a) water at 0 °C and (b) ethanol at 20 °C? (Table 9.13). Estimate roughly the heat capacity of vodka, a mixture by volume of 60% water and 40% ethanol.

P21. What is the thermal conductivity of (a) water at 20 °C (b) ethanol at 20 °C, (c) mercury at 20 °C and (d) molten sodium at 100 °C. (Table 9.14 and 9.15)

P22. As discussed in Question P7, lakes and ponds are cooled by contact with cold air above them. Consider a

frozen lake with a surface temperature of $-10°C$. Underneath a 1 cm thick ice layer at the ice–water interface, the temperature is 0 °C. (a) Using a value of 2.2 $W K m^{-1}$ for the thermal conductivity of ice, estimate the rate (in mm per second) at which ice forms on the underside of the frozen layer. You should find a surprisingly rapid value. (b) Alternatively, estimate the depth of water that can be cooled from 4 °C to 0 °C per second.

P23. Roughly how much energy does it take to heat (a) 1 mol and (b) 1 kg of liquid water from its melting temperature to its boiling temperature? Evaluate the same quantities for methanol, ethanol, and mercury. (Tables 9.13, 11.1 and 11.2)

P24. A cylinder of liquid water 5 cm deep with a base diameter of 10 cm is placed on a thermostatically controlled pad at a temperature of 4 °C. Work out the rate of heat flow through the liquid if the upper temperature is (a) 3 °C and (b) 5 °C. Consider carefully the effect of convection within the water. (Table 9.14, Figure 9.3 and Questions P22 and P7)

P25. A cubic container of volume $1 m^{-3}$ is heated from the bottom such that molten sodium metal at the bottom is approximately 100 °C hotter than sodium at the top. (a) Approximately how many moles of sodium are in the box? (b) Convection lifts 100 moles per second of sodium from the bottom to the top. Estimate the heat flow across the container due to convection? Is it greater or less than would be expected due to the thermal conductivity listed in Table 9.15 alone?

Electrical properties

P26. Estimate the electrical resistivity of (a) sodium and (b) potassium at 400 °C (Table 9.17 and Figure 9.35)

P27. Use the constancy of the Lorentz number (Table 9.14) to estimate the thermal conductivity of sodium and potassium at 400 °C (Question P26)

P28. Estimate the mean scattering time τ for electrons in molten potassium and sodium at 100 °C (Example 9.4).

P29. What is the dielectric constant of (a) water at 20 °C (b) ethanol at 20 °C and (c) liquid nitrogen at 70 K (Table 9.18 and Figure 9.37)

P30. One of your colleagues is unable to read §9.12.3 and §9.12.4 as a result of their research on the biological effects of 40% ethanol solutions. Write a report for them summarising the extent to which the dielectric constants of liquids of both polar and non-polar molecules can be understood by considering liquids to be dense gases. (Tables 9.19 and 9.20).

Optical properties

P31. What is the refractive index of (a) water at 20 °C and (b) ethanol at 20 °C. Estimate the refractive index of a mixture by volume of 40% ethanol with 60 % water.

P32. Estimate the refractive index of liquid methanol and liquid ethanol based on the analysis of the water given in the example calculation of Equations 9.59 to 9.61. Compare your results with my calculations in Table 9.22.

P33. Using data taken from Figure 9.38, estimate very roughly the frequency of the UV transition in water based on the analysis for glasses in §7.9.5.

P34. Would a prism made of water be more or less dispersive than one made of glass? (Figures 7.50, 7.51 and 9.38)

P35. The reflectivity of glass immersed in water to light normally incident upon it is given by the formula

$$R = \left[\frac{n_{light}^{water} - n_{light}^{glass}}{n_{light}^{water} + n_{light}^{glass}} \right]^2$$

Explain why it is difficult to see glass when it is underwater. (Table 9.21, Figure 7.50) Compare the calculated value of R with the value for light incident upon either water or glass from air. (Chapter 7 Question C56)

Changes of phase: background theory

10.1 Introduction

A collection of molecules of H_2O are capable of smashing the steel hull of an ocean liner if their temperature is 272 K. If their temperature is increased by less than 1 % to 274 K they pose no danger at all. When ice melts some of its properties change dramatically even though the temperature changes by only a tiny amount. The phenomenon of 'sudden change' of properties is the most general, and the most striking, characteristic of *phase changes*.

In the preceding chapters we have examined the properties of gases, solids and liquids, and seen how it is possible to understand their behaviour in terms of the atoms and molecules of which they are made. The division into just three phases is natural, since in our experience solids, liquids and gases behave strikingly differently. However, the division raises several questions that we will address in this chapter.

§10.2   **Free energy:** It is frankly impossible to understand phase transitions in anything more than a qualitative sense without understanding the role of *free energy*. In this section we will introduce the concept and use it to estimate the melting and boiling temperatures of potassium metal. The key result (which is demonstrated explicitly in Appendix 3) is that the equilibrium phase of a substance is the phase with the lowest Gibbs free energy.

§10.3, §10.4 **Phase transitions** and **Enthalpy change on transformation:** In these sections we look at the key result from §10.2 and extend our analysis to enable us to estimate not only the temperatures at which transitions take place, but also the amount of heat energy required to make them happen.

§10.5   **The 'order' of a phase transition:** The transition temperature of a phase transition can mark one of two things depending on its *order*. It can mark the temperature below which one phase has *completely changed* into another. This is the 'normal' or *first-order* type of phase change. For example, on cooling below its melting temperature, a substance becomes *completely* solid. Alternatively, for so called *non-first order* or *continuous* transitions, the transition temperature marks the temperature below which one phase *begins to change* into another.

§10.6   **Nucleation: supercooling and superheating:** In order to change from one phase (e.g. liquid) to another (e.g. solid) a substance has to somehow 'know' that a solid has a lower free energy than a liquid. But how can a liquid 'know' anything about a solid?

§10.7   **Phase diagrams:** The transition temperatures between phases change with pressure in an interesting and complicated manner. Sometimes we wish to summarise a great deal of information about the general form of these changes and this can be achieved with a phase diagram. Here we learn what phase diagrams are, how they are constructed, and the significance of some of their special features.

At www.physicsofmatter.com

You will find copies of the figures and tables from this chapter.

10.2 Free energy

10.2.1 Questions and answers

Consider the following questions:

- What factors determine that at a particular temperature a substance should be a liquid, but that at slightly higher temperature the substance should become a gas?
- What factors determine that at a particular pressure a substance should be a liquid, but that at slightly higher pressure the substance should become a solid?

These changes of *phase* are certainly complex in nature and in any particular case we could imagine considering many detailed microscopic features of a substance in search of understanding. However, there exists a general formalism for determining which phase of matter a substance adopts under specified circumstances. The formalism discusses the *equilibrium* phase of material in terms of five quantities listed below:

- **Temperature**: We are already aware that temperature is key factor in determining the equilibrium phase of substance.
- **Pressure**: We will see in §11.4 that the temperature at which the liquid⇔vapour transition occurs depends strongly on pressure. Similarly we shall see in §11.3 that the temperature at which the solid⇔liquid transition occurs depends weakly on pressure. So pressure is also a factor in determining the equilibrium phase of a substance.
- **Volume**: In most experiments the volume of a substance is allowed to vary, being determined by the experimenter's choice of temperature and pressure.
- **Internal energy**: As students of physics we are used to explaining phenomena by stating that objects try to 'minimise their energy'. So for example we noted in §6.1 that solids formed from noble gas atoms chose particular crystal structures in order to minimise their internal energy. It is not surprising therefore that internal energy is a factor in determining the equilibrium phase of a substance.
- **Entropy**: Entropy has not previously been discussed in this book for the reason that there is no simple way of explaining what entropy

is. Thus while we appreciate what heat, temperature, pressure and volume are, I have never met a scientist who had a 'sense of entropy'. This tends to make explanations of phenomena in terms of entropy confusing (at first). Now, however, we have no choice but to come to terms with entropy.

The five factors above that influence the equilibrium phase of a substance may be combined into a single mathematical function that reflects the balance between the various terms. The function is (to me at least) shockingly simple: as outlined in detail in Appendix 3, if a substance is in equilibrium at a temperature T and pressure P, the phase of the substance which minimises the function:

$$G = U - TS + PV \qquad (10.1)$$

is the equilibrium phase of the substance. The function G is called the *Gibbs free energy* of a substance and is an especially important quantity in understanding changes of phase. It is usually expressed in units of kJ mol^{-1} but may also be expressed in several other formats, commonly as electron volts per molecule (eV molecule^{-1})

Entropy: an aside

Microscopically, entropy is related to the amount of *order* in a substance. We can readily appreciate that heating a substance, i.e. adding heat energy ΔQ to a substance, will increase the amount of disordered motion of the constituent atoms of a substance. Macroscopically the quantitative measure of this disorder is the entropy S of the substance. If an amount of heat ΔQ is added to a substance at temperature T then the entropy S of the substance is increased by ΔS given by the surprisingly simple formula:

$$\Delta S = \frac{\Delta Q}{T} \text{ joule kelvin}^{-1} \left(J\,K^{-1} \right) \qquad (10.2)$$

The total entropy of a substance is conventionally assigned to be zero for a substance in equilibrium at absolute zero, and so the total entropy of a substance at temperature T is given by:

$$S = S_0 + \int_0^T \frac{\Delta Q}{T} dT \qquad (10.3)$$

as shown in Example 10.2.

Entropy is discussed a little further in Appendix A3, but at this point we note the similarity between the entropy and the internal energy U

$$U = U_0 + \int_0^T \Delta Q dT \qquad (10.4)$$

But what *is* entropy?

Nature has provided we humans with a sense of temperature, albeit with rather non-linear sensors. Also, we can fairly easily develop concepts of thermal energy (heat) and mechanical energy (work). Developing an appreciation of what entropy *is*, or refers to, is more difficult. Each of us has to make this journey towards understanding alone, and so I offer the following paragraphs as a gesture of friendship to those of you struggling with the concept.

Consider a solid made of long chain polymers. By considering the shape of each molecule, it is possible to calculate the equilibrium structure of such a solid. We did this kind of thing in §6.2 for simple molecules. However, in practice the solid is unlikely ever to be found in this structure. This is because long molecules are easily tangled up. You can observe this process if you fill a box with electrical leads with a plug on either end. If you place the leads in carefully (make a crystal), then shake the box (increase the temperature), then you can be pretty sure to find that the leads are tangled in ways which are extremely complicated. It requires careful untangling to restore the leads to their pristine structure. In particular, once tangled, no amount of shaking will *ever* return the leads to their untangled state. What you have observed is analogous to the tendency of atoms and molecules to try out different ways of arranging themselves. You have also seen that this tendency becomes stronger at higher temperatures.

Another analogy for the action of entropy can be found in the game of snooker (or 'pool'). Anyone who has ever played this game knows that the

---

Example 10.1

A quantity of heat $\Delta Q = 0.2$ J is added to a large amount of the substance at (a) 0.1 K, (b) 1 K, and (c) 10 K. Calculate the increase in entropy of the substance at each temperature.

We assume the amount of substance is large enough that the temperature rise in each case is small. The increase in entropy in each case is given by Equation 10.2:

$$\Delta S = \frac{\Delta Q}{T}$$

So in case (a) we have:

$$\Delta S_a = \frac{0.2}{0.1} = 2 \ \mathrm{J\,K^{-1}}$$

and in cases (b) and (c) we have $\Delta S_b = 0.2 \ \mathrm{J\,K^{-1}}$ and $\Delta S_c = 0.02 \ \mathrm{J\,K^{-1}}$ respectively. Notice that adding a given amount of heat at low temperatures causes a large increase in entropy (disorder), whereas the same quantity of heat added at higher temperature adds less entropy.

Colloquially we might consider that adding a certain amount of heat energy to a substance at low temperatures is the equivalent of placing an energetic bull into a calm shop selling porcelain: the result is a large increase in the disorder. Adding the same amount of energy to a substance at a higher temperature is the equivalent of placing another energetic bull into a shop already full of other energetic bulls: the amount of added disorder is less noticeable.

---

lowest energy state for the snooker balls is in the pockets. When they approach the pockets with just the right speed and from the correct angle, the balls are satisfyingly captured. However, this is irrelevant to the amateur snooker player for whom the balls just bounce around on the surface of the table without showing any tendency to be captured. The analogy with entropy is that molecules will only enter a low-energy state if they can find it. If there are many more high-energy ways of behaving, then molecules can essentially indefinitely resist the tendency to occupy low-energy states. This is the action and the effect of entropy.

10.2.2 The Gibbs free energy

The circumstances in which we imagine an experiment being performed on a substance are usually such as to maintain the temperature constant in a cryostat or a furnace, and the pressure is either

327

the ambient atmospheric pressure, or a controlled and stabilised pressure. Thus P and T are usually the controlled parameters of an experiment with the volume a 'free' parameter able to adjust itself appropriately to the temperature and pressure.

Let us look at each of the three terms on the right-hand side of Equation 10.4 and see how each contributes to G:

$$G = U - TS + PV \qquad (10.1*)$$

U The internal energy. Lowering U helps to minimise G.

TS The temperature times the entropy. In order to minimise G the substance should try to *maximise* this product. At a given temperature this means choosing a state with maximum S. The requirement to maximise S becomes less significant at low temperatures because T is a multiplying factor.

PV The pressure times the volume. In order to minimise G the substance should try to minimise this product. At a given pressure this means choosing a state with the *minimum* volume.

Consider a substance at a particular temperature T and pressure P, and imagine that the substance is able to 'try out' different phases in order to determine which phase minimises its *Gibbs free energy*. Let us consider the three terms in Equation 10.1 for each state: solid, liquid and gas. As we show in Appendix 3 the state which minimises G will form the equilibrium state of the system.

The factors which favour of one state or another are summarised in Tables 10.1. We see that at a given temperature and pressure, a substance may seek to minimise G in any of several ways. For example it may:

- minimise its internal energy: this is best achieved in the solid or liquid state
- maximise its entropy: this is best achieved in the liquid or gaseous state
- minimise its volume: this is best achieved in the solid or liquid state.

The state which minimises the *sum* of the three terms will depend on the balance of the terms.

Example 10.2

A substance is heated from T_1 to T_2. Neglecting thermal expansion, deduce an expression for the increase in entropy and internal energy of the substance.

Internal energy

Consider the temperature rise dT due to an infinitesimal input of heat dQ. If the substance expands only negligibly the work done by the substance on its environment dW is negligible. The first law of thermodynamics ($dU = dQ + dW$) then tells us that the heat input dQ goes entirely to increasing the internal energy of the substance dU. The heat input dQ is related to the temperature rise dT by the heat capacity $dQ = C\,dT$. So the change in internal energy dU due to dQ is given by $dU = C dT$. If C varies with temperature (as it generally does) then the total change in internal energy on heating from temperature T_1 to T_2 is given by:

$$\Delta U = \int_{T_1}^{T_2} C(T)\mathrm{d}T$$

Putting $T_1 = 0$ and $T = T_2$ we arrive at:

$$U(T) = U_0 + \int_0^T C(T)\mathrm{d}T$$

where U_0 is the cohesive energy of the substance in the solid state at $T = 0$.

Entropy

Consider the temperature rise dT due to an infinitesimal input of heat dQ. As above, we assume that dW is negligible so that $dU = dQ$ By the definition of entropy (Equation 10.2) the heat dQ carries with it entropy dS given by:

$$\mathrm{d}S = \frac{\mathrm{d}Q}{T}$$

By the definition of the heat capacity $dQ = C dT$ and so:

$$\mathrm{d}S = \frac{C\mathrm{d}T}{T}$$

Thus the total change in entropy on heating from temperature T_1 to T_2 is given by:

$$\Delta S = \int_{T_1}^{T_2} \frac{C(T)}{T}\mathrm{d}T$$

Putting $T_1 = 0$ and $T = T_2$ we arrive at:

$$\Delta S = S_0 + \int_{T_1}^{T_2} \frac{C(T)}{T}\mathrm{d}T$$

where S_0 is the entropy of the substance in the solid state at $T = 0$. Conventionally S_0 is take to be zero.

Table 10.1 Summary of the contributions to the Gibbs free energy in each of the possible states of matter.

	U	$-TS$	$+PV$
Solid	In a solid atoms are close together and interact strongly. This terms is therefore large and negative.	The entropy of a solid is very low. This is because solids are highly ordered, which is *a priori* a very unlikely state for matter to be in. However, the entropy is multiplied by temperature. If the temperature is low, TS will be small, but if the temperature is large this term will be very significant.	At a given pressure the volume of a solid is close to the minimum volume that a substance can occupy. This makes this term small.
Gas	The interaction between atoms is many orders of magnitude weaker in gases than in solids. In the Ideal Gas theory it is neglected entirely.	The entropy of a gas is very high. This is because gases are completely disordered collections of atoms.	At a given pressure the volume of a gas is as large as it is able to be.
Liquid	The interaction between atoms is of the same order as in the solid state, but the lack of organisation means that the internal energy is generally not quite as low as in a solid.	The entropy of a liquid is a little larger than a solid.	At a given pressure the volume of a liquid is similar to that of a solid.

At absolute zero

At absolute zero matters are relatively straightforward. The internal energy term is just U_o, the *cohesive energy* of the substance. The term TS containing the entropy is zero because $T = 0$. And the term PV is negligible in comparison with U_o. Considering all these factors we see that at $T = 0$, the equilibrium state of the substance (i.e. the state with minimum G) will be the state which minimises the internal energy of the substance. With the sole exception of helium, this state is always the solid state. This is the justification for our calculations in §6.2. There we tried to determine which crystal structure a substance would adopt by considering only the internal energy of the solid. If we wished to repeat that procedure at higher temperatures, we would need to consider the minimum value of G, which would be considerably more complicated to estimate.

If we consider a substance to have a cohesive energy per atom of u_o electron volts, then the internal energy of substance at $T = 0$ K will be just:

$$U_o = -u_o e N_A \ \mathrm{J\,mol^{-1}} \qquad (10.5)$$

where e is the charge on the proton, N_A is the Avogadro number, and the minus sign indicates that the energy is negative with respect to the state in which the atoms are widely separated from one another.

$$U_o = -u_o \times 1.6 \times 10^{-19} \times 6.02 \times 10^{23}$$
$$\approx -96 u_o \ \mathrm{kJ\,mol^{-1}} \qquad (10.6)$$

At finite temperature

Above absolute zero the other terms in the Gibbs free energy must be taken into account. As outlined in Example 10.2, we can estimate the internal energy $U(T)$ by:

$$U(T) = U_o + \int_0^T C(T)\mathrm{d}T \qquad (10.7)$$

where U_o is the cohesive energy of the substance in the solid state at $T = 0\,\mathrm{K}$. Similarly we can estimate the entropy $S(T)$:

$$S(T) = S_o + \int_0^T \frac{C(T)}{T}\mathrm{d}T \qquad (10.8)$$

However the calculations involved require two key pieces of information:

Example 10.3

Compare the terms U and PV in the Gibbs free energy for a solid at absolute zero.

Cohesive energies range from around 0.1 eV per atom for molecularly bonded substances to around 10 eV per atom for substances such as diamond. A typical figure of around 1 eV per atom yields a cohesive energy of $U_0 \approx -100 \text{ kJ mol}^{-1}$.

We can compare this with the PV term at atmospheric pressure. The volume of one mole of substance in the solid or liquid states is just the mass of one mole divided by the density of the substance. Using typical figures of $m \approx 100 \times 10^{-3}$ kg and $\rho \approx 10 \times 10^3 \text{ kg m}^{-3}$ indicates a molar volume of $\approx 10^{-5} \text{ m}^3 \text{ mol}^{-1}$ (i.e around 10 cm^3). At atmospheric pressure, the PV term evaluates to:

$$1.013 \times 10^5 \text{ Pa} \times 10^{-5} \text{ m}^3 \text{ mol}^{-1} \approx 1 \text{ J mol}^{-1}$$

Thus at zero temperature, the PV term in the Gibbs free energy amounts to only $\approx 10^{-5}$ of the cohesive energy.

- We must know the heat capacity as function of temperature $C(T)$ in order to calculate either $U(T)$ or $S(T)$
- We must know the cohesive energy U_0. In general, this involves rather complicated calculations, or complex inferences from experimental data.

So although straightforward in principle, accurately calculating G as a function of temperature is in practice rather difficult.

10.2.3 Gibbs free energy: an example

Let us examine the balance between contributions to the Gibbs free energy by means of an example. We will attempt to calculate the Gibbs free energy for potassium as a function of temperature. We do not have full data available for this element, but this will force us to rely on our general knowledge of the properties of matter. We shall have to make assumptions about what is typical for a substance, based on the data in Chapters 5, 7 and 9.

To determine the temperature at which a phase transition takes place, we need to estimate *all* of the terms in G for each of the phases under consideration. In Table 10.2 we summarise the contributions to $G = U - TS + PV$ in the solid and gaseous phases and suggests how we may estimate

these. The liquid state is considered later in Table 10.3.

In compiling Table 10.2 the following assumptions have been made. U_0 for the solid is taken from Table 11.5 and U_0 for the gas is taken as zero. S_0 for the solid is (in line with convention) taken as zero and S_0 for the gas is chosen so as to agree with the thermodynamic data from *Emsley*.

To compound the difficulty of estimating S for the gas phase, the behaviour of the heat capacity of the gas at low temperatures is not known either. This problem is overcome by considering the heat capacity of the gas to be that of an ideal gas, and then adding the S_0 constant so as to achieve agreement with the data from *Emsley*.

The results of calculations of these quantities have been evaluated using a spreadsheet computer program and are shown in Figure 10.1. We see that the balance of terms in G is such that at low temperatures, the $U + PV$ terms dominate and the substance seeks to have a low internal energy and a low volume. At higher temperatures however, the more disordered state minimises G.

We can consider the entropy S to be weighted by a factor T in the expression for G. So at low temperatures the TS term is weighted rather little, and substances choose phases which minimise $U + PV$, of which the internal energy term usually dominates. This is the situation which we met in §6.2, where we predicted the equilibrium crystal structure of argon from a consideration of its internal energy alone. At high temperatures the TS term is weighted more strongly and at high enough temperatures substances choose phases which maximise TS (or minimise $-TS$), i.e. phases which have a high degree of disorder.

In the case of potassium, the balance between terms is such that we predict that at atmospheric pressure, the solid state should transform into the gaseous state at around 824 K.

In fact, potassium transforms into the *liquid state* at around 336 K and then into the gaseous state at around 1033 K (Table 11.1): not a very good agreement.

Table 10.2 Summary of the contributions to the Gibbs free energy $G = U - TS + PV$ in the solid and gas phases. The results of the sum are plotted as a function of temperature in Figure 10.1.

	U (mol^{-1})	TS (mol^{-1})	PV (mol^{-1})
Solid	The cohesive binding energy is given by Table 11.5 as −90.1 kJ mol^{-1}. To estimate U we evaluate: $$-90.1 \times 10^3 + \int C_V(T)\, dT$$ where $C_V(T)$ is estimated from a Debye model of a solid with a Debye temperature of 100 K.	Estimated from: $$T\left[\int \frac{C_V(T)}{T} dT\right]$$ with $C_V(T)$ estimated from a Debye model of a solid with a Debye temperature of 100 K. The entropy at $T = 0$ K is taken as zero.	We neglect thermal expansion and estimate PV from the density and atomic mass (Table 7.2). At atmospheric pressure we find: $$PV = 1.013 \times 10^5 \times \frac{39 \times 10^{-3}}{830}$$ This term is very small.
Gas	Assuming perfect gas behaviour, we have no binding energy and so we estimate U as: $$0 + \int C_V(T)\, dT$$ where $C_V(T)$ is estimated from an assumption of perfect gas behaviour as $C_V = 1.5R$ independent of temperature.	Estimated from: $$T\left[\int \frac{C_V(T)}{T} dT\right]$$ with $C_V(T)$ estimated from an assumption of perfect gas behaviour as $C_V = 1.5R$ independent of temperature. The entropy at $T = 0$ K is chosen so as make the entropy of potassium vapour at 298 K agree with the data from *Emsley*.	We use the perfect gas equation for 1 mole of substance to evaluate : $$PV = RT$$

Let us see if matters are improved if we make a calculation of G for the liquid state. Unfortunately, this is a difficult thing to do realistically because we have no simple universal theory of the liquid state from which we can deduce the properties of liquids. However we do have sufficient information in Chapter 9 to make an informed guess at the behaviour of G_{liquid}.

- We know that $|U_{liquid}|$ is less than $|U_{solid}|$, because the atoms are not so efficiently packed in a liquid. We assume that if the potassium existed in its liquid phase at absolute zero its cohesive energy would be only around 90% of that found in crystalline potassium.

- Furthermore we know from §9.10.1 that at high temperatures the heat capacity of liquids is roughly temperature-independent and typically around 10% higher than that of solids.

- We do not know the residual entropy of the liquid state as compared with the solid state at $T = 0$ K. For the sake of simplicity we set this constant equal to zero, and merely acknowl-

edge that this detracts from the accuracy of the results.

- We know (§9.2) that the volume of liquids is typically 10 % higher than that of the equivalent solid. However the PV term is not large for either liquids or solids.

Our estimates for the three terms in G_{liquid} are shown in Table 10.3 and the results of this calculation performed on a spreadsheet are plotted along with those of Figure 10.1 in Figure 10.2

The calculated results shown in Figure 10.2 indicate that it is possible to understand how the liquid state can become more stable In a limited temperature range. This range can be thought of as a 'bridging region' linking the low entropy, high cohesive energy state at low temperatures with the high entropy, low cohesive energy state at high temperatures. Our only input to this calculation has been some plausible assumptions about the entropy, internal energy and heat capacity in the liquid state.

331

Table 10.3 Summary of the contributions to the Gibbs free energy $G = U - TS + PV$ in the liquid phase. The results are plotted as a function of temperature along with the results from Table 10.1 in Figure 10.2.

	U (mol^{-1})	TS (mol^{-1})	PV (mol^{-1})
Liquid	The cohesive binding energy of the solid is given by *Kittel* as -90.1 kJ mol^{-1}. Assuming a value of around 90% of this figure we estimate U as: $$-81 \times 10^3 + \int C_V(T)\mathrm{d}T$$ where $C_V(T)$ is estimated to be 10% greater than the equivalent solid and to have a lower Debye temperature.	Estimated from: $$T\left[\int \frac{C_P(T)}{T}\mathrm{d}T\right]$$ where $C_V(T)$ is estimated to be 10% greater than the equivalent solid and to have a lower Debye temperature. The entropy at $T = 0$ is set equal to zero as for a solid. This will underestimate the entropy of the liquid state.	We consider this term to be the same as the solid.

Sensitivity of transition temperatures to assumptions

Notice that at zero temperature G_{liquid} is just a little above G_{solid}. As we have seen, the heat capacities of liquids are only a little greater than solids and so the entropy rises at only a slightly greater rate than for solids. Because G_{solid} varies in a similar manner to G_{liquid}, the predicted transition temperature is sensitive to the assumptions made in the calculation.

Small changes in our assumptions lead to large changes in transition temperatures. For example, the calculation illustrated in Figure 10.2 predicts that potassium will melt at 498 K (experimental value 336 K) and that potassium will boil at 922 K (experimental value 1033 K). In Figure 10.3 we illustrate the result of a calculation assuming that the cohesive energy of the liquid state at $T = 0$ K would be 95 % of the solid value, instead of 90 % as assumed in Figure 10.2. This calculation pre-

Figure 10.1 The result of a calculation of the Gibbs free energy G for potassium in its solid and gaseous states. The simplest assumptions possible have been made about the behaviour of U, S and V in this temperature range. Notice that at zero temperature G_{gas} is zero but G_{solid} is large and negative. This arises because at low temperatures the internal energy U is the main contributor to G.

Figure 10.2 The result of a calculation of the Gibbs free energy G for potassium in its solid, liquid and gaseous phases. See also Figure 10.1. Notice that at zero temperature G_{liquid} is just a little above G_{solid}. As we have seen, the heat capacities of liquids are only a little greater than solids and so the entropy rises at only a slightly greater rate than for solids. The similar variation of G_{solid} and G_{liquid} means that the predicted transition temperature is sensitive to the assumptions made in the calculations.

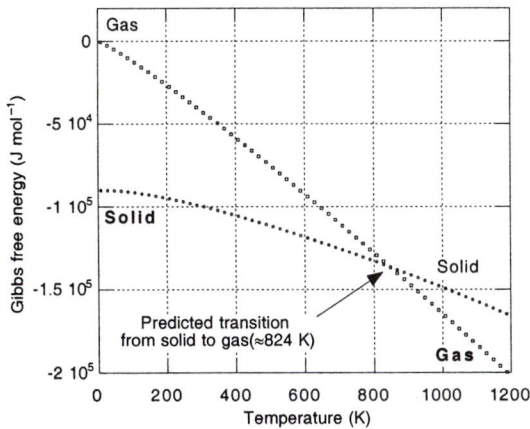

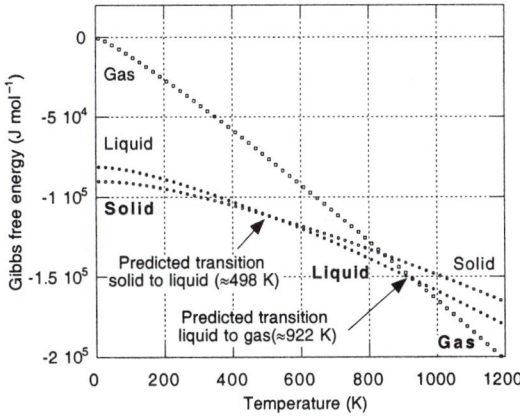

dicts that potassium will melt at 307 K and boil at 980 K, much closer to experimental values.

The better agreement between predicted and experimental values of T_M and T_B in Figure 10.3 should not be taken to indicate that the assumptions of the second calculation are any more realistic than the first. The two calculations are presented merely to indicate how sensitive the calculations are to assumptions made about the states involved. The success of both these calculations is that they predict a liquid state at all! Determining realistic values for T_M and T_B requires a good deal of attention to details that we have neglected to consider here.

Figure 10.3 The result of a calculation of the Gibbs free energy G for potassium in its solid, liquid and gaseous phases. See also Figure 10.2 above. In this figure we have assumed a cohesive energy in the liquid state of 95% of the solid value rather than 90% as assumed in Figure 10.2. The resulting predictions for T_M and T_B have changed significantly.

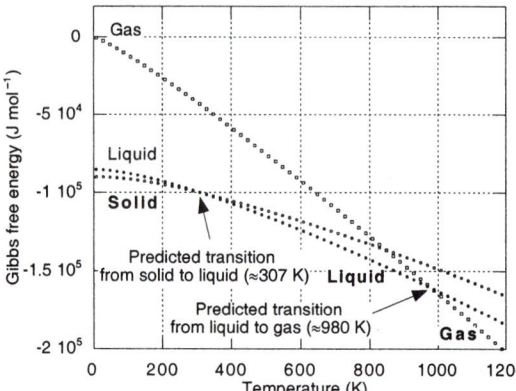

10.3 Phase transitions

We can now state in a general sense why phase transitions occur: they occur because the Gibbs free energy of one state of matter becomes less than that of another. It is important to realise that the free energy is a function which combines *both* the internal energy of the substance *and* the natural tendency of all states towards disorder. So the equilibrium state of substance is *not* (as students frequently maintain) the state which minimise the internal energy. If this were true, substances would remain solids at all temperatures.

Our general picture of solid ⇔ liquid ⇔ gas phase transitions is summarised in Figure 10.4. Notice that at each transition temperature the *slope* of the Gibbs free energy changes suddenly from one value to another. Let us perform some manipulations on the Gibbs free energy in order to look at its gradient with respect to temperature. In general we have:

$$G = U - TS + PV \qquad (10.1^*)$$

Changes in G result from changes in internal energy, temperature, entropy, pressure, and volume. Thus we may write a small (differential) change in G as:

$$dG = dU + PdV + VdP - TdS - SdT \qquad (10.9)$$

This is a complicated expression. However, the first law of thermodynamics asserts that:

$$\Delta U = \Delta Q + \Delta W \qquad (2.41^*)$$

From the definition of entropy we can substitute

Figure 10.4 A substance seeking to minimise its Gibbs free energy will jump from one curve to another at the temperature at which the Gibbs free energy of one phase becomes lower than another. In this case the substance jumps from the solid to the liquid curve at T_M and then to the gaseous curve at T_B.

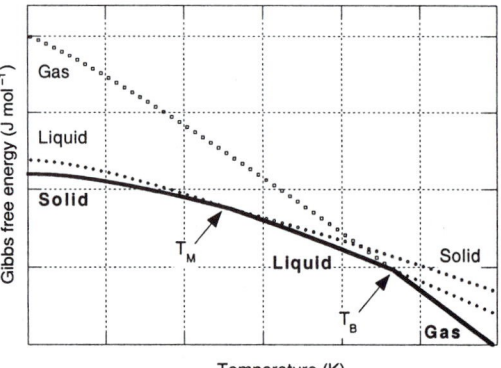

for ΔQ:

$$\Delta Q = T\Delta S \qquad (10.2^*)$$

If we are careful to account of the sign of the work done *on* the gas in expanding by ΔV we write the first law as:

$$\Delta U = T\Delta S - P\Delta V \qquad (10.10)$$

which in differential limit is:

$$dU = TdS - PdV \qquad (10.11)$$

We now re-arrange this so that all the terms are on the same side to find that:

$$dU + PdV - TdS = 0 \qquad (10.12)$$

We can now apply this result to Equation 10.5:

$$dG = \underbrace{dU + PdV - TdS}_{=\,0} + VdP - SdT \qquad (10.13)$$

which simplifies the equation considerably:

$$dG = VdP - SdT \qquad (10.14)$$

Now if the changes of phase in which we are interested take place at constant pressure (as they usually do) the alterations in G are not due to changes in pressure. So we put $dP = 0$. In this case we have:

$$dG = -SdT \qquad (10.15)$$

which amounts to:

$$\left.\frac{dG}{dT}\right|_{P} = -S \qquad (10.16)$$

This equation tells us that the slope of the Gibbs free energy with respect to temperature at constant pressure is just the negative of the entropy S. Thus all curves on graphs of G versus T (such as Figures 10.1 to 10.4) must have negative slopes. Also high entropy states have steeper slopes than low entropy states. This allows us to understand analytically what we already appreciate physically: the phase of matter with the highest entropy (colloquially the least amount or 'order' or 'structure') will eventually become the equilibrium phase of

334

the substance. The steepness of the curve will eventually overtake *any* amount of advantage given to a phase which has an large cohesive energy. Ultimately everything will enter the gaseous phase.

Around a phase transition point, we can apply Equation 10.10 to produce a particularly useful and interesting result. In what follows we use the subscripts '1' to indicate the lower temperature phase (which might be a solid or a liquid) and '2' to indicate the higher temperature phase (which might be a liquid or a gas).

At temperatures infinitesimally below and infinitesimally above a phase transition we have:

$$\left(\frac{dG}{dT}\right)_{1} = -S_1$$

and $\qquad (10.17)$

$$\left(\frac{dG}{dT}\right)_{2} = -S_2$$

Thus the difference in the slopes is given by

$$\left(\frac{dG}{dT}\right)_{2} - \left(\frac{dG}{dT}\right)_{1} = [-S_2] - [-S_1] \qquad (10.18)$$

$$\left(\frac{dG}{dT}\right)_{2} - \left(\frac{dG}{dT}\right)_{1} = S_1 - S_2 \qquad (10.19)$$

$$= -\Delta S$$

Since we are at a phase transition, we have $S_2 > S_1$ so ΔS in Equation 10.13 is a positive quantity. Thus in order to move from the lower temperature curve (1) to the higher temperature curve (2) and so accomplish the phase transition, a quantity of entropy must be supplied at the constant temperature of the transition temperature. In order to supply this entropy at the transition temperature T_T we must, from the definition of entropy (Equation 10.1), supply an amount of heat:

$$\Delta Q_T = T_T \Delta S \qquad (10.20)$$

This heat energy ΔQ_T transforms the substance at constant temperature from one phase to another, increasing the internal energy of the substance and (usually) its volume. The combination of terms

$U + PV$ is known as the *enthalpy* of a substance, and the heat ΔQ_T supplied at a transition is known as the *enthalpy change on vaporisation* or *fusion*. This is often shortened to *enthalpy of vaporisation* or *fusion*, or less commonly nowadays to *latent heat of vaporisation* or *fusion*. The terms are all equivalent. *Fusion* is an old-fashioned term for melting.

10.4 Enthalpy change on transformation

10.4.1 Introduction

Based on the theory outlined above we ought to be able to arrive at some general estimates about the typical magnitude of the enthalpies of fusion and vaporisation.

Let us pause to review our results so far. We saw in §10.3 that with some plausible assumptions, we could estimate U and S as a function of temperature and hence estimate the phase transition temperatures for potassium. In §10.3 we predicted that at a phase transition, we must supply an amount of entropy ΔS given by:

$$\left(\frac{\mathrm{d}G_2}{\mathrm{d}T}\right) - \left(\frac{\mathrm{d}G_1}{\mathrm{d}T}\right) = S_1 - S_2 \qquad (10.19^*)$$
$$= -\Delta S$$

which requires an amount of heat ΔQ_T:

$$\Delta Q_T = T_T \Delta S \qquad (10.20^*)$$

Further, at the transformation temperature, we know (by definition) that $G_2 = G_1$ and so:

$$U_1 - T_T S_1 + P_T V_1 = U_2 - T_T S_2 + P_T V_2 \qquad (10.21)$$

Re-arranging this yields:

$$\left(U_1 - U_2\right) + P_T\left(V_1 - V_2\right) = T_T\left(S_1 - S_2\right) \qquad (10.22)$$
$$= -T_T \Delta S$$

which may be compared to Equation 10.20 to give an expression for ΔQ_T:

$$\Delta Q_T = \left(U_2 - U\right)_1 + P_T\left(V_2 - V_1\right) \qquad (10.23)$$

In the next two sections we will move on from the calculations in §10.3 to try to estimate ΔQ_T, the enthalpy changes on phase transformation.

The relative values of ΔQ_M and ΔQ_B

One feature of calculations shown in Figure 10.2 and reproduced below in Figure 10.5 is already clear. The difference between the slope of the liquid and solid curves at the predicted melting temperature is rather small: the two curves run close to one another over a considerable range of temperature. In contrast, the difference between the slope of the gas and liquid curves at the predicted vaporisation temperature is rather large: the gas curve cuts the liquid curve rather steeply. Thus according to Equations 10.17 and 10.18 we should expect that the enthalpy change on vaporisation ΔQ_B should be considerably larger than the enthalpy change on fusion ΔQ_M. Here and in the following sections, I have used the subscript 'B' to stand for 'boiling' and the subscript 'M' to stand for 'melting'.

Figure 10.5 According to the considerations of sections 10.1 and 10.2, a general feature of the enthalpy changes on transformation is that the enthalpy change on fusion (melting) is less than the enthalpy change on vaporisation (boiling). On the $G(T)$ graph, the enthalpy changes are related to the differences in the *gradient* of the curves at their intersections.

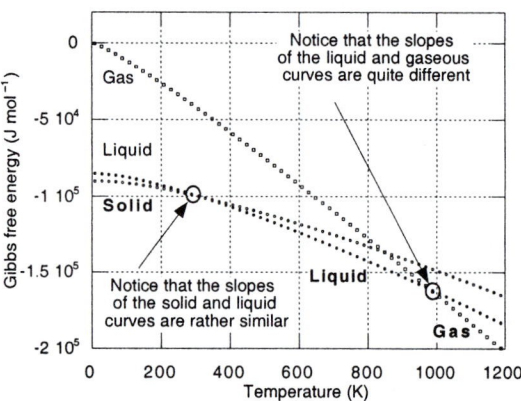

In the next two sections the enthalpy change at each of the melting and boiling transformations will be considered in turn.

10.4.2 Enthalpy change on fusion ΔQ_M

In order to estimate the enthalpy change on fusion (melting) ΔQ_M, we can make use of Equation 10.17 $\Delta Q_M = T_M \Delta S$ and estimate the melting temperature T_M, S_{liquid} for the liquid state at T_M and S_{solid} for the solid state at T_M. Alternatively, we can use Equation 10.23:

$$\Delta Q_M = \left(U_{liquid} - U_{solid}\right) + P_M \left(V_{liquid} - V_{solid}\right)$$

$$(10.24)$$

and estimate the internal energy and volume of the liquid state at T_M, and the internal energy and volume of solid state at T_M. Given the uncertainty in estimating the residual entropy of a liquid at $T = 0$ K, it is a more profitable to follow the second of these two options.

For the solid and liquid states, the PV term is negligible in comparison with the internal energy term and Equation 10.24 becomes:

$$\Delta Q_M \approx U_{liquid} - U_{solid} \qquad (10.25)$$

As in Example 10.2, we can estimate U by integrating the heat capacity:

$$\Delta Q_M = \left[U_0(\text{liquid}) + \int_{T=0}^{T} C_{liquid}(T)dT\right]$$

$$- \left[U_0(\text{solid}) + \int_{T=0}^{T} C_{solid}(T)dT\right] \qquad (10.26)$$

which becomes:

$$\Delta Q_M = \left[U_0(\text{liquid}) - U_0(\text{solid})\right]$$

$$+ \int_{T=0}^{T} [C_{liquid}(T) - C_{solid}(T)]dT \qquad (10.27)$$

Equation 10.27 is evaluated for potassium in Example 10.4. The result (5.22 kJ mol^{-1}) does not compare particularly well with the experimental value (Table 11.1) of 2.4 kJ mol^{-1}. However, we clearly have the correct order of magnitude, and

---

Example 10.4

Estimate Q_M for potassium.

Following on from the calculations of §10.2. We note that:

- The zero temperature cohesive energy of the liquid state amounts to only a fraction (typically 90%–95%) of the cohesive energy of the solid. The 95% yielded slightly better values for T_M so we use this estimate that $U_0(\text{liquid}) \approx 0.95\ U_0(\text{solid})$.
- The heat capacity in the liquid state is generally greater than in the solid state typically by around 10%.

We thus find:

$$Q_M = -0.05 U_0(solid) + 0.1 \times \int_0^T C_{solid}(T)dT$$

Now $U_0(\text{solid}) = 90.1$ kJ mol^{-1} (Table 11.5) and estimating the integral numerically as we did for the previous examples we find that at the experimentally determined melting temperature $T_M = 336$ K

$$Q_M \approx -0.05 \times \left(-90.1 \times 10^3\right) + 0.1 \times 7198$$

$$\approx 5.22\ \text{kJ mol}^{-1}$$

---

the poor detailed agreement is due mainly to the generality of the assumptions made in our estimates of the heat capacities of the liquid and solid state. We will consider the experimental data on the enthalpy change on melting in §11.3.

10.4.3 Enthalpy change on vaporisation ΔQ_B

Following a similar scheme to that outlined in the previous §10.4.2, we can estimate the enthalpy change on vaporisation by using Equation 10.23:

$$\Delta Q_B = \left(U_{gas} - U_{liquid}\right) + P_B \left(V_{gas} - V_{liquid}\right) \quad (10.28)$$

For the liquid state, the PV term is negligible, but for the gaseous state this is not so. Including the PV term only for the gaseous state, this equation becomes:

$$\Delta Q_B = \left(U_{gas} - U_{liquid}\right) + P_B V_{gas} \qquad (10.29)$$

As in Example 10.4, we can estimate U by integrating the heat capacity:

$$\Delta Q_B = \left[U_0(gas) + \int_{T=0}^{T} C_{gas}(T)dT \right]$$

$$- \left[U_0(liquid) + \int_{T=0}^{T} C_{liquid}(T)dT \right] \quad (10.30)$$

$$+ P_B V_{gas}$$

which becomes:

$$\Delta Q_B = \left[U_0(gas) - U_0(liquid) \right]$$

$$+ \left[\int_{T=0}^{T} C_{gas}(T)dT - \int_{T=0}^{T} C_{liquid}(T)dT \right]$$

$$+ RT_B$$

$$(10.31)$$

Equation 10.31 is evaluated for potassium in Example 10.5. The result (88.6 kJ mol^{-1}) does not compare particularly well with the experimental value (Table 11.1) of 77.5 kJ mol^{-1}. However we again have the correct order of magnitude, and attribute the poor detailed agreement to the generality of the assumptions made in our estimates of the heat capacities of the liquid and gaseous states. We will consider the experimental data on the enthalpy change on vaporisation for the elements in §11.3.

Example 10.5

Estimate Q_B for potassium.

Following on from the calculations of §10.1. If we make ideal gas assumptions for the gaseous phase we note that:

- The zero temperature cohesive energy of the gaseous state is zero
- The heat capacity in the liquid state is generally greater than in the solid state typically by around 10%
- The heat capacity in the gaseous state is $C_P = 2.5R$ (§5.3).

We thus find:

$$Q_B = \left[0 - 0.95 U_0(solid) \right] + 2.5RT_B$$

$$- 1.1 \times \int_0^T C_{solid}(T)dT + RT_B$$

Recalling $U_0(solid) = 90.1$ kJ mol^{-1} and estimating the liquid integral numerically as we did for the previous examples, we find that at the experimentally determined boiling temperature $T_M = 1047$ K

$$Q_B \approx \left[-0.95 \times \left(-90.1 \times 10^3 \right) \right] + 2.5 \times 8.31 \times 1047$$

$$- 1.1 \times 24914 + 8.31 \times 1047$$

$$\approx 85595 + 21751 - 27405 + 8700$$

$$\approx 88.6 \ \text{kJ mol}^{-1}$$

10.5 The 'order' of a phase transition

10.5.1 Introduction

At the transitions discussed in §10.3.1 and §10.3.2, a substance changes completely from one phase to another. For example at 0.01 K above T_M the substance is *completely* liquid; at 0.01 K below T_M the substance is *completely* solid. These transitions are characterised by a discontinuous change in the *gradient* of the Gibbs free energy. However, not all phase transitions take place in this way. Imagine cooling a substance slowly in its solid or liquid phases: it is conceivable that at a certain temperature some processes or behaviours *begin* to be possible. Below the transition temperature, the substance does not completely transform, but *begins* to show a new property, and the strength of this property grows as the substance is cooled further below the transition temperature.

At such a transition there is no discontinuity in the *gradient* of G, but there is a discontinuity in the *curvature* of G. This leads to a general technique of categorising phase transitions according to whether G has a discontinuity in its gradient or its curvature.

Figure 10.6 Schematic illustration of the changes in the Gibbs free energy G at (a) a first-order and (b) a second-order phase transition at temperature T_T. In a first-order transition, entropy (and hence heat energy) equal to the difference in gradients must be supplied. In a second-order transition there is no discontinuity in gradient, but there is a discontinuity in the *curvature* of G.

(a)

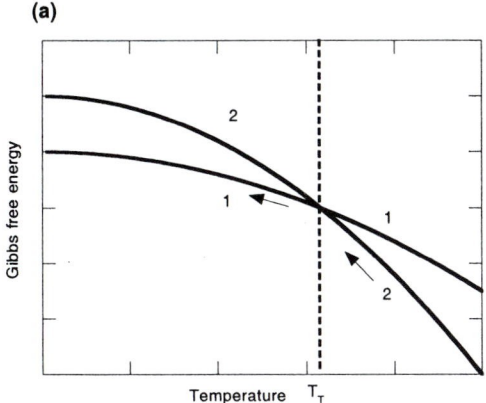

(b)

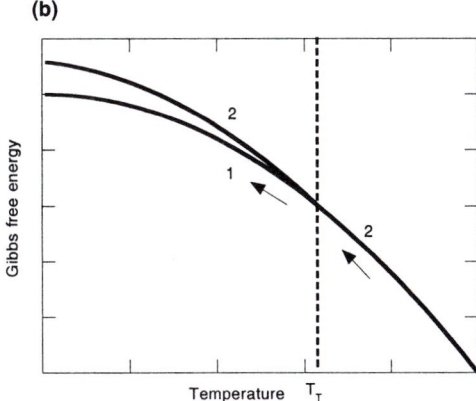

- Recalling that the gradient $\partial G/\partial T$ is the *first* derivative of G, transitions in which there is a discontinuity in gradient are called *first-order transitions*. These are characterised by the phenomena of an enthalpy of transformation, colloquially a *latent heat*.

- Recalling that the curvature $\partial^2 G/\partial T^2$ is the *second* derivative of G, transitions in which there is a discontinuity in curvature are called *second-order transitions*. These are characterised by the absence of any enthalpy of transformation, which means there is no latent heat associated with such a transition.

The characteristic behaviour of the Gibbs free energy close to first- and second-order transitions is illustrated schematically in Figure 10.6.

Now we might imagine that, having gone to the trouble of establishing this general framework for phase transitions, there must be a great many examples of both types of phase transition: not so. The vast majority of phase transitions are first-order, and only one or two examples of second-order phase transitions. It is possible to continue the sequence of categorising to ever more subtle degree. For example, for a third-order phase change, the transition temperatures would indicate the temperature at which the Gibbs free energy begins 'to begin' to change! In general, the catego-

risation of any phase transition as third-order is specious and is no longer made. So in general we simply categorise transitions as either first-order, or 'not first-order'. Transitions which are not first-order are called *continuous*.

In practice, it is often difficult to distinguish between first-order and continuous transitions. If a substance is not homogeneous, or there is a temperature gradient across it, then a transition may appear continuous, when it is in fact first-order. It usually requires careful experiments to distinguish the two cases. Notice that I have referred to phase transitions other than solid $\Leftrightarrow$ liquid $\Leftrightarrow$ gas transitions, something I shall justify in Chapter 11. However, structural phase transitions such as those between solids, liquids and gases are nearly always first-order.

Table 10.4 The orders of some phase transitions.

First-order	Continuous
Melting/freezing	Superconducting (in zero magnetic field)
Boiling/condensing	Ferromagnetic
Liquid crystals	
Superconducting (in a magnetic field)	

338

10.6 Nucleation: supercooling and superheating

10.6.1 The mechanism of a phase transition

So far in our discussion of phase changes we have assumed that a substance changes from one phase to another when the Gibbs free energy of one phase becomes lower than the Gibbs free energy of the other phase. However this raises the question of how the substance 'knows' what the Gibbs free energy of the other phase is going to be when it is not actually in that phase already! In other words how is a phase transition is initiated?

Microscopically, all phase transitions may be considered to occur in two stages: *nucleation* and *growth*.

Nucleation

In the *nucleation* stage, the random motions of the atoms or molecules conspire to create a local situation which is atypical of the *average* properties of the substance. These locally atypical regions (perhaps just a few atoms in size initially) are known variously as *nuclei, embryos* or *seeds*. The process of embryo formation occurs at all temperatures, although the rate of formation varies strongly with temperature. Alternatively some small irregularity within the substance, perhaps an impurity, or some feature of the container for the substance, provides a locally anomalous region capable of supporting a nucleus of a different phase.

Growth

In the *growth* stage, the nucleus of the second phase either (a) grows in size, (b) stays the same size, or (c) shrinks. In general, nuclei will not grow spontaneously even when the Gibbs free energy of the second phase becomes lower than the Gibbs free energy of the first phase. This is because for small nuclei the *surface energy* of the nuclei may be very high. Eventually the nucleus becomes able to grow in size and the macroscopic phase transition commences.

If there are no suitable nuclei available, a substance may pass its appropriate transition temperature and continue in the 'wrong' (or non-equilibrium) phase. This phenomenon is known as either *supercooling* or *superheating* depending on the direction of temperature change. Note that these phenomena are not caused by the experimental 'error' of heating or cooling 'too quickly' into a transient state. The supercooled or superheated substances may be quite stable until supplied with an appropriate 'seed' on which the second phase may grow.

Let us examine the process of nucleation and growth for each of the phase transitions we have considered so far.

10.6.1 Solid ⇒ liquid: melting

Superheating past the bulk melting temperature is extremely unusual in the solid ⇒ liquid transition. In terms of the nucleation and growth theory outlined above, this implies that suitable liquid nuclei exist in the solid phase near the melting temperature. There is considerable evidence that these nuclei exist at solid surfaces and cause solids to tend to melt from their surfaces inwards. Indeed it is possible that in equilibrium, even well below T_M there may be an atomic layer or two of essentially liquid substance present on the surface of a solid. The equilibrium thickness of this layer grows rapidly as the temperature approaches T_M and then grows without limit. In this theory we can understand the reluctance of solids to superheat, because liquid nuclei would always be available due to the so-called *pre-melting* of the surface. This theory predicts that, in general, solids should melt from their surfaces rather than from within the solid.

10.6.2 Liquid ⇒ solid: freezing

In contrast with the melting transition, the solid ⇒ liquid transition frequently shows significant supercooling. In line with the theory above, we can interpret this as being either due to a lack of nuclei, or to the presence of a strong barrier to the growth of nuclei.

Considering our simple conceptions of liquid and solid structures as envisaged in Figures 6.2 and 8.2, it seems unlikely that there will be any lack of nuclei. We expect that there will be many regions of liquid structure that are (transiently) similar to the solid structure. It seems that once such solid nuclei form they fail to grow either because the nuclei has a large surface energy or because the nuclei has broken apart before it had time to grow.

Suppose that a spherical nucleus of 'solid' of radius a exists in the liquid state. The nucleus will grow if increasing its size from a to $a + da$ lowers the free energy of the substance. There are two factors which determine whether this is so.

- The first is the free energy difference between the solid and liquid states $\Delta G_{LS}(T)$. At the melting temperature $\Delta G_{LS}(T_M)$ is zero by definition. If the temperature is lowered below T_M, then the solid state becomes increasingly favoured over the liquid state. However, as Figure 10.5 indicates, the *gradients* (dG/dT) of the free energies of liquid and solid states differ only slightly. So the free energy benefit of the solid state increases only slowly as the temperature is lowered below T_M. Notice that $\Delta G_{LS}(T)$ is proportional to the *volume* of the nucleus.

- The second factor is the energy cost of forming an interface between the solid and liquid states. Around the nucleus may be a region of strained material which is not optimally arranged for either the solid or the liquid states. If this surface layer has a cost $G_{surface}$ per unit area, then there will be a cost of allowing the nucleus to grow which will be proportional to the *surface area* of the nucleus.

We can write the total energy as:

$$G_{nucleus} = -[\text{volume}] \times \Delta G_{LS}(T) + [\text{surface area}] \times G_{surface} \tag{10.32}$$

$$G_{nucleus} = -\left[\frac{4}{3}\pi a^3\right] \times \Delta G_{LS}(T) + \left[4\pi a^2\right] \times G_{surface} \tag{10.33}$$

Note that in Equation 32 we have defined ΔG_{LS} as positive if the G_{solid} is less than G_{liquid}. Evaluating

$\partial G_{nucleus} / \partial a$ we find:

$$\frac{\partial G_{nucleus}}{\partial a} = -\left[4\pi a^2\right] \times \Delta G_{LS}(T) + \left[8\pi a\right] \times G_{surface} \tag{10.34}$$

Now the nucleus will grow if its total energy decreases as a increases, i.e. if $\partial G_{nucleus} / \partial a < 0$. This is true when:

$$-4\pi a^2 \times \Delta G_{LS}(T) + 8\pi a \times G_{surface} < 0 \tag{10.35}$$

i.e. when:

$$4\pi a^2 \times \Delta G_{LS}(T) > 8\pi a \times G_{surface} \tag{10.36}$$

which simplifies to:

$$a > \frac{2G_{surface}}{\Delta G_{LS}(T)} \tag{10.37}$$

This defines a critical size for a nucleus, $a_{critical}$, below which the surface energy cost of the nu-

Figure 10.7 The origin of the phenomena of supercooling. Nuclei of the solid state within the liquid state will not grow unless doing so lowers the free energy. This leads to the phenomenon of a critical size of nucleus. As the temperature falls below the melting temperature (at which the free energies of the bulk liquid and solid states are equal by definition), the free energy difference between liquid and solid states increases and causes a decrease in the critical nuclear size. Eventually, the critical size is reduced to the size of the nuclei that are spontaneously formed in the liquid state and the substance freezes.

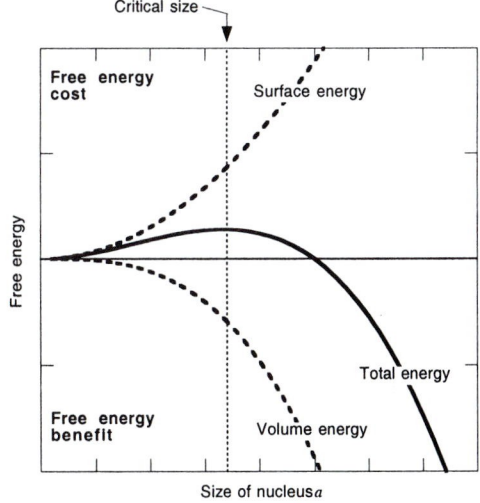

cleus impedes the transformation from liquid to solid. Notice that:

- At the melting temperature $a_{critical}$ is infinite since $\Delta G_{LS}(T_M)$ is zero by definition. Thus unless some external process initiates the transition, liquids will always supercool to some extent.
- As the temperature falls below T_M, $\Delta G_{LS}(T)$ increases, and thus decreases the critical size of a nucleus. When the temperature is sufficiently far below T_M that the critical size is less than the size of the nuclei actually formed in the liquid, then the nuclei will grow and the substance will freeze. Because $\partial G/\partial T$ for both solid and liquid are similar (Figure 10.5) it is possible for the temperature to fall considerably (several kelvin) below T_M before ΔG_{LS} becomes large enough to cause nuclear growth.

10.6.3 Liquid $\Rightarrow$ gas: boiling/vaporisation

Superheating at the liquid $\Rightarrow$ gas transition is also relatively common. Here a liquid may be heated to above its normal boiling temperature, but fails to boil because of the lack of suitable nuclei. Notice that at any free surface the vapour pressure will continue to increase exponentially with temperature (§9.8) above the normal boiling temperature. The process which is inhibited is the formation of bubbles of gas within the body of the liquid.

This is relatively easy to understand: to form a bubble it is necessary to form a new surface on the inside of the bubble and this requires a large surface energy. Since forming surfaces requires extra energy, this must be supplied in excess of the normal free energy difference between the liquid and gas phases. For this reason the presence of external nuclei (which minimise the initial surface energy required) is often critical to establishing boiling close to the equilibrium T_B.

10.6.4 Gas $\Rightarrow$ liquid: condensation

Supercooling at the gas $\Rightarrow$ liquid transition is considerably less common than superheating at the liquid $\Rightarrow$ gas transition. Once again this requires that we have a large number of nuclei, or a low barrier to growth.

Figure 10.8 Schematic illustration of the variation of temperature with time during the slow cooling of a pure substance through its equilibrium melting temperature. As discussed in the text, the liquid always supercools to some extent. This continues until the critical radius reduces to the same size as the typical nucleus size present in the liquid, at which point the nuclei begin to grow spontaneously. This causes the release of enthalpy of fusion, which (if the external cooling rate is slow enough) will reheat the solid/liquid melt back to the equilibrium melting temperature. The melt remains at this temperature until all the liquid is transformed to solid, after which cooling recommences.

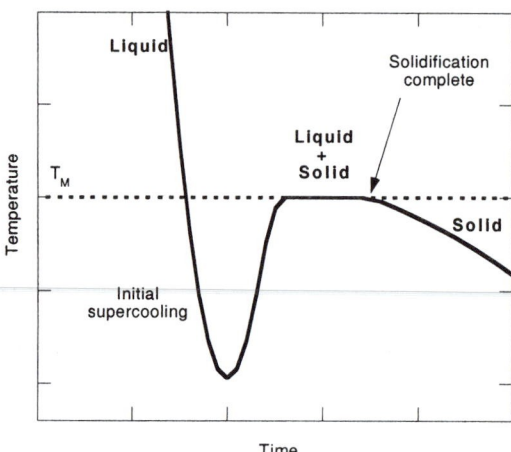

In a gas, large numbers of nuclei are constantly formed when molecules collide. Notice however, for simple molecules at least, it requires at least *three* molecules to interact in order to form a two-molecule 'droplet', technically called a *dimer*. The reason for this can be seen if we consider simple molecules such as argon, which consist of just a single atom. If two molecules collide, without any interactions with other molecules, then they will never stick together. This is because no matter how slowly they are moving when they collide, their interactions conserve energy and so they will always move apart again. In order to form a dimer, they must interact in the presence of a third molecule, which will take away some fraction of their total energy and leave the pair with less than they started with. For more complex molecules consisting of many atoms, it is possible for collisions between two molecules to result in dimer formation. This is because energy can be lost from their kinetic energy into other degrees of freedom of the molecules.

10.7 Phase diagrams

10.7.1 Introduction

It is often instructive to present information about the transitions between substances pictorially on what is known as a *phase diagram*. There are many different types of phase diagram but the aim of all such diagrams is to *summarise* the tremendous amount of information about the phases adopted by substance, in a way that can be readily appreciated. A schematic phase diagram is shown in Figure 10.9 below.

Consider a substance at atmospheric pressure: at absolute zero the substance will, with the sole exception of helium, be solid. As the temperature is increased at constant pressure, typically the substance will eventually melt at T_M and then boil at T_B. (Note that the volume of the substance will change significantly as it transforms from solid to gas, but this is not shown on this type of diagram.) This heating process, represented by the dotted

line on Figure 10.9, seems fairly straightforward to interpret. However other paths are not so straightforward to interpret. Consider for example that shown in Figure 10.10 which represents heating a solid in a vacuum.

The phase boundaries (lines) on Figures 10.9 and 10.10 represent sets of points at which a phase transition takes place. Thus traversing any of the solid lines in these figures takes us from one phase to another. We know, from our analysis of the changes in Gibbs free energy at transitions (§10.1.1), that at any point on the phase boundary, the Gibbs free energies of the two phases on either side of the boundary are equal. Let us consider two points A and B on a phase boundary at slightly different temperatures and pressures (Figure 10.11).

The Gibbs free energy at point A is G_A and the

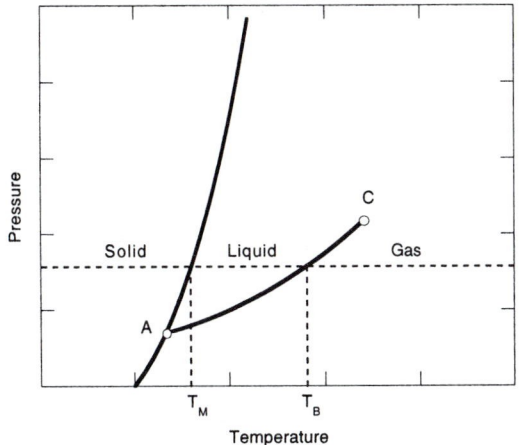

Figure 10.9 Schematic phase diagram of a typical substance on the *PT* plane. Note: The drawing is not to scale. This type of diagram refers to the state of a fixed amount of a substance, usually one mole. The volume of the substance is free to take any value and is not recorded on this type of diagram. The diagram must be interpreted subtly as discussed in the text. The solid lines connect temperatures and pressures at which more than one phase exists in equilibrium. The point A represents the so-called *triple point* (§10.7.3) of the substance and point C represents the so-called *critical point* (§10.7.2).

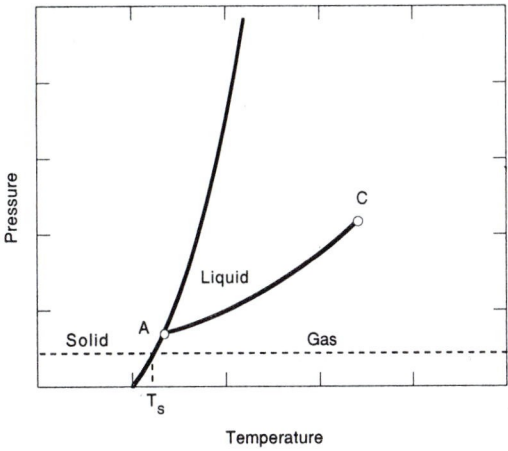

Figure 10.10 Schematic phase diagram of a typical substance on the *PT* plane. Note: The drawing is not to scale. If a solid is heated at low pressure, i.e. the pressure is not allowed to rise on heating, then at 'low enough pressure' the solid always transforms directly into the gas phase. This can be understood as being because the liquid phase always has a minimum vapour pressure above it, whereas a solid can sustain a much lower vapour pressure above its surface. The point A represents the so-called *triple point* (§10.7.3) of the substance and point C represents the so-called *critical point* (§10.7.2).

difference in free energy between A and B is ΔG. The free energy difference ΔG is due to differences in U, T, S, P and V and, as outlined in Equation 10.14, this may be simplified to:

$$\Delta G = V\Delta P - S\Delta T \qquad (10.38)$$

Now the change ΔG is the same for both phases, so using subscripts 1 and 2 for the two phases:

$$\Delta G_1 = \Delta G_2 \qquad (10.39)$$

or

$$V_1\Delta P - S_1\Delta T = V_2\Delta P - S_2\Delta T \qquad (10.40)$$

Rearranging this we have:

$$\Delta P(V_1 - V_2) = \Delta T(S_1 - S_2) \qquad (10.41)$$

$$\frac{\Delta P}{\Delta T} = \frac{(S_1 - S_2)}{(V_1 - V_2)} \qquad (10.42)$$

Or taking the differential limit we arrive at an equation known as the *Clausius–Clapeyron* equation:

$$\frac{dP}{dT} = \frac{(S_1 - S_2)}{(V_1 - V_2)} \qquad (10.43)$$

This is a very important equation!

Figure 10.11 A detailed view of the phase boundary between two phases 1 and 2 which might, for example, refer to a liquid⇔solid phase boundary. At each point along the phase boundary the Gibbs free energies of the phases on either side of the phase boundary are equal. At point A the Gibbs free energy of each phase is G_A and at point B (which is at a slightly different temperature and pressure) the Gibbs free energy of each phase is G_B.

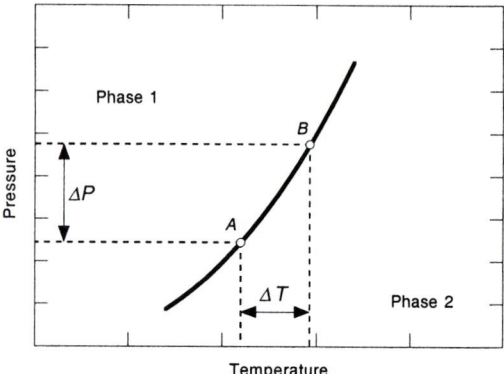

Example 10.6

Work out the rate of change of boiling temperature with pressure for water.

Consider 1 mole of water at around its normal boiling temperature of 100 °C. From Table 11.2 we find that the molar enthalpy change on vaporisation is around 40.6×10^3 J K^{-1} mol^{-1}. One mole of liquid has a mass of 18×10^{-3} kg and a volume of roughly $V_L = 18 \times 10^{-6}$ m^3 (Table 9.1). Assuming the gas to behave as a perfect gas, we can estimate the volume of one mole of gas as:

$$V_G = \frac{RT}{P} = \frac{8.3 \times 373}{10^5} = 0.031 \ \text{m}^3$$

or around 1700 times the liquid volume. Neglecting the liquid volume in comparison with the gas volume we can use Equation 10.47 to estimate dP/dT :

$$\frac{dP}{dT} = \frac{40.6 \times 10^3}{373 \times 0.031} = 3511 \ \text{Pa K}^{-1}$$

Thus if we increase the pressure above the liquid by 3511 Pa we increase the boiling temperature by 1 K.

Example 10.7

Work out the rate of change of boiling temperature with pressure for water.

Consider 1 mole of water at around its normal melting temperature of 0 °C. From Table 11.2 we find that the molar enthalpy change on fusion is around 5.99×10^3 J K^{-1} mol^{-1}. One mole of liquid has a mass of 18×10^{-3} kg and a volume of approximately $V_L = 18 \times 10^{-6}$ m^3 (Table 9.1). One mole of solid (ice) has a volume roughly 8% larger or around $V_s = 19.4 \times 10^{-6}$ m^3 (Figure 9.3). Using Equation 11.47 to estimate dP/dT :

$$\frac{dP}{dT} = \frac{5.99 \times 10^3}{273 \times \left[18 \times 10^{-6} - 19.4 \times 10^{-6}\right]}$$

$$= -15.6 \times 10^6 \ \text{Pa K}^{-1}$$

Thus if we increase the pressure above the solid by around 15.6×10^6 Pa which is around 150 times atmospheric pressure, i.e. we *decrease* the melting temperature by 1 K.

Notice (a) the relative insensitivity of the melting temperature to external pressure: this is typical of most solid⇔liquid transitions, and (b) the fact that increasing the pressure *decreases* the melting temperature: this is highly unusual. This depression of the melting temperature by pressure is a consequence of the unusual contraction of the substance as it enters the liquid phase. (Figure 9.3)

The Clausius–Clapeyron equation relates the slope of a phase boundary to the difference in entropy and volume of the phases on either side of the phase boundary. We have already seen that the difference in entropy between the two phases is the origin of the *enthalpy change on transformation (or latent heat)* Q_T and so we may write:

$$\frac{dP}{dT} = \frac{Q_T \big/ T_T}{(V_1 - V_2)}$$

$$= \frac{Q_T}{T_T(V_1 - V_2)}$$

(10.44)

The usefulness of the Clausius–Clapeyron equation is best illustrated by some examples, but we will return to Equations 10.43 and 10.44 several times in the following sections.

10.7.2 The critical point

The *critical point* is a special point on the liquid $\Leftrightarrow$ gas phase boundary. It marks the point at which the densities of the phases on the liquid side and the gas side of the phase boundary become equal. Let us calculate the general shape of the liquid $\Leftrightarrow$ gas phase boundary and then consider how the densities of the two terms vary as one moves along the boundary.

The liquid–gas phase boundary

In §9.8 we considered a microscopic model of evaporation and condensation, and came to the conclusion that we may reasonably expect the vapour pressure of a gas in equilibrium to vary like:

$$P \approx A \exp\left[\frac{-\alpha}{T}\right]$$

(10.45)

where α is a constant. A similar result also follows from the Clausius–Clapeyron equation with rather fewer assumptions about a particular liquid model. At the liquid $\Leftrightarrow$ gas phase boundary we have:

$$\frac{dP_B}{dT_B} = \frac{\Delta Q_B}{T_B(V_G - V_L)}$$

(10.46)

where the subscript 'B' indicates that P_B and T_B are the boiling pressure and temperature of the

liquid, and 'L' and 'G' indicate liquid and gas phases respectively. Let us first assume that:

- in the gas phase the substance behaves as an ideal gas
- has a volume very much greater than in the liquid phase, and
- the latent heat Q_B does not vary with temperature.

Under these assumptions, and remembering that the volume of one mole of ideal gas is:

$$V_G = \frac{RT}{P}$$

(10.47)

we find that Equation 10.46 becomes:

$$\frac{dP_B}{dT_B} = \frac{Q_B}{T_B\left[\frac{RT_B}{P_B}\right]}$$

$$= \frac{P_B Q_B}{RT_B^2}$$

(10.48)

Rearranging this yields:

$$\frac{dP_B}{P_B} = \left[\frac{Q_{LG}}{R}\right]\frac{dT_B}{T_B^2}$$

(10.49)

If we integrate this equation, we find:

$$\int\frac{dP_B}{P_B} = \left[\frac{Q_B}{R}\right]\int\frac{dT_B}{T_B^2}$$

(10.50)

which yields:

$$\ln\left[\frac{P_B}{P_o}\right] = \left[\frac{-Q_B}{RT_B}\right]$$

(10.51)

or:

$$P_B = P_o \exp\left[\frac{-Q_B}{RT_B}\right]$$

(10.52)

This equation has a form similar to that derived with the aid of a microscopic model of a liquid (Equation 9.35). Figure 10.12 shows a plot of Equation 10.56 for water using the value $Q_B = 40.6$ kJ mol^{-1} from Table 11.2 and a value of $P_o = 4.89 \times 10^{10}$ Pa chosen to give a vapour pressure of 1 atmosphere (1.013×10^5 Pa) at 373.15 K.

The volume of gas at the phase boundary

Figure 10.12 and Equation 10.52 indicate that the pressure at the liquid $\Leftrightarrow$ gas phase boundary rises exponentially with temperature. This rapid variation causes some of the assumptions on which this equation was based to relatively quickly become invalid. In particular we assumed that the gas behaved like a perfect gas and we neglected the volume of the liquid in comparison with the gas. While this assumption was valid at 373 K where the vapour pressure was 1 atmosphere, it is unlikely to be valid at around 800 K where the vapour pressure is around 1000 times higher. Using the perfect gas equation to derive a rough estimate of the volume of one mole of substance in the gas phase we find:

$$V_G = \frac{RT}{P}$$

$$= \frac{RT}{P_o \exp\left[-Q_B/RT_B\right]} \quad (10.53)$$

Figure 10.12 The equilibrium vapour pressure above liquid water predicted according to Equation 10.52. Consider point *A* on the graph which refers to water at a pressure of 5×10^7 Pa and a temperature of 400 K (127 °C). The graph tells us that the water would be in the liquid phase. At point *B*, which refers to water under a pressure of 5×10^7 Pa and a temperature of 800 K (527 °C) the graph tells us that the water would be in the gas phase. The line indicates temperatures and pressures in which water can co-exist as a liquid and as a gas, i.e. it defines the boiling temperature. Atmospheric pressure ($\approx 10^5$ Pa) is very close to the x-axis on this graph.

To see what this equation implies, consider a container with both liquid and gas present in equilibrium. Since both phases are present, we are by definition, at the phase boundary. As we increase the temperature, the pressure increases and we move along the phase boundary. Equation 10.53 tells us that for the material present in the gas phase, the volume of one mole of substance falls *exponentially*.

However, for the material present in the liquid phase, the molar volume does not vary so dramatically. In general the volume of liquid held on the co-existence curve increases slightly with temperature. The *critical point* refers to a point along the co-existence curve at which the volumes of the liquid and gas phases become equal. At this point it becomes impossible to distinguish between the two phases

Estimating the critical temperature and pressure

At what pressure the volume of one mole of gas will become equal to the volume of one mole of liquid? The ideal gas equation is obviously not going to produce a good estimate for this. Remember that the ideal gas equation ignores two key features of real molecules: the interactions between molecules, and the volume of the molecules themselves. We will first use the ideal gas

Figure 10.13 At the critical point the volume of a substance is the same in either the 'liquid' or the 'gas' phase.

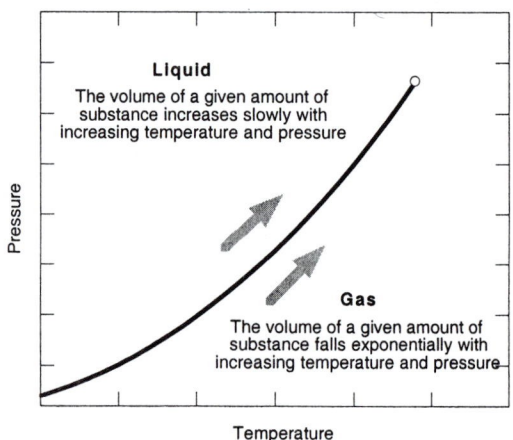

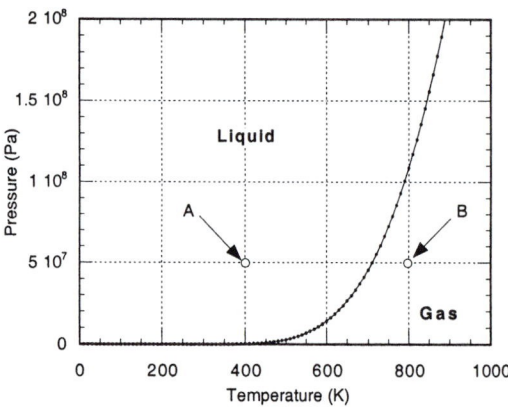

equation to make a rough estimate of the temperature and pressure at which the gas volume becomes equal to the liquid volume. We will then refine our estimates to take account of the factors that the ideal gas equation has neglected.

Ideal gas estimate

The molar volume of liquid water at around 373 K is 18.8×10^{-6} m^3 (Table 9.2). Ignoring any thermal expansion of the liquid, we use the ideal gas equation to predict a range of pressures and temperatures at which the volume *of the gas* is 18.8×10^{-6} m^3:

$$P = \frac{RT}{18.8 \times 10^{-6}} \qquad (10.54)$$

Equation 10.54 is satisfied for a range of temperatures and pressures. Plotting the points that satisfy this equation on the same graph as the vapour pressure, Equation 10.52, yields a rough estimate of the point at which the gas and liquid densities at the phase boundary are equal (Figure 10.14). This predicts that the critical temperature of water is greater than 1000 K and the critical pressure is around 4.5×10^8 Pa.

Including the effect of molecular volume

However, this estimate is certainly an overestimate of the critical temperature and pressure because of our neglect of the volume of the molecules (§4.4.1). If we re-evaluate the pressure required to contain a gas in a given volume, using the *experimentally determined* critical volume for water (Table 11.4) of 59.1×10^{-6} m^3 then we obtain an estimate of the critical temperature and pressure of 803 K and 1.13×10^8 Pa.

Including the effect of molecular interactions

However, even this is an overestimate of the critical temperature because we have assumed the latent heat Q_B would not vary with temperature. Clearly this cannot be quite right since at the critical point the liquid and gas phases are indistinguishable. So at that point there can be no latent heat associated with the transition. Thus somewhere between the boiling temperature and the critical temperature, the latent heat must fall to zero. This is due to changes in the structure of the liquid. In general, the way in which this happens is rather complicated, and much of the change is close to the critical point itself. However, we can see qualitatively what the effect of this is. Equation 10.52 predicts that the vapour pressure is:

$$P_B = P_o \exp\left[\frac{-Q_B}{RT_B}\right] \qquad (10.52^*)$$

If Q_B becomes smaller, the vapour pressure will increase, all other factors being equal. This will lower the point of intersection of the lines on Figure 10.14. Thus, through these relatively crude approximations, we can begin to approach an understanding of how, and under what conditions, the critical point of a substance is approached. Roughly speaking it occurs in the region of the intersection of:

- the vapour pressure curve of a gas above a liquid

- the pressure required to keep a gas constrained to a volume a little greater than that occupied by liquid at STP.

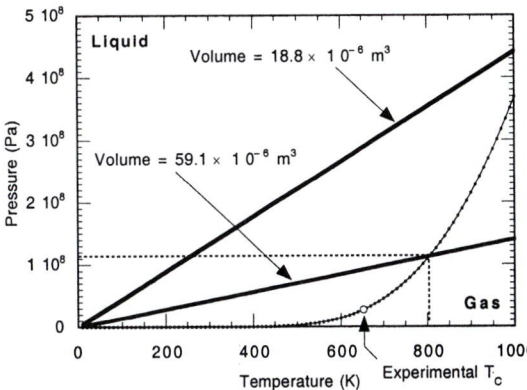

Figure 10.14 The curved line is the calculated coexistence curve for water shown in Figure 10.12. The upper straight line represents an estimate of the pressure required to keep water vapour confined to a volume equal to the volume of liquid water at around 373 K. The lower straight line represents an estimate of the pressure required to keep water vapour confined to a volume equal to experimentally determined critical volume of water: 59.1×10^{-6} m^3. The intersection of the curves represents a crude estimate of the critical temperature and pressure. The circle on the graph at ≈ 650 K represents the experimental value. Atmospheric pressure $\approx 10^5$ Pa is very close to the *x*-axis on this graph.

10.7.3 The triple point

The triple point, like the critical point discussed in §10.7.2, is another special point on a phase diagram. It marks the pressure and temperature at which the line representing the solid ⇔ liquid phase transition intersects with the line representing the liquid ⇔ gas transition. In order to determine where this intersection takes place, we will use the Clausius–Clapeyron equation (Equation 10.43). This will allow us to analyse the solid ⇔ liquid transition in the same way that we analysed the liquid ⇔ gas transition in §10.6.1 on the critical point.

The solid ⇔ liquid co-existence curve

We start once again with the Clausius–Clapeyron equation:

$$\frac{dP}{dT} = \frac{\Delta Q_T}{T_T(V_1 - V_2)} \quad (10.44^*)$$

where phase 1 is the liquid phase and phase 2 is the solid phase. In this case, ΔQ_T is the enthalpy change on fusion ΔQ_M, and T_T is the melting temperature T_M. So Equation 10.44 becomes:

$$\frac{dP_M}{dT_M} = \frac{\Delta Q_M}{T_M(V_L - V_S)} \quad (10.55)$$

We first of all notice the effect of the volume change ΔV_{LS} between the liquid and the solid.

For most substances ΔV_{LS} is positive – the liquid is less dense than the solid – and amounts to around 10 % of the volume of the solid (Figure 9.1). This volume change is dramatically smaller than the volume change between liquid and gas, perhaps by a factor 1000 or so. So the slope of the melting curve (where solid and liquid co-exist) is typically much steeper than the slope of the vaporisation curve (where liquid and gas co-exist).

For a few substances ΔV_{LS} is negative – the liquid is more dense than the solid – and again amounts to around 10% of the volume of the solid (Figure 9.1). For these substances, the slope of the melting curve will still be just as steep as it is for normal substances, but the slope will be negative (Figure 10.15).

Example 10.8

At atmospheric pressure ice melts at 273.15 K and undergoes a density change from around 920 kg m^{-3} (Table 7.1, Figure 9.1) to 999.84 kg m^{-3} (Table 8.1). The latent heat required to melt 1 mole of ice is 5994 Jmol^{-1}. What is the melting temperature at a pressure (a) twice atmospheric pressure, and (b) 1000 times atmospheric pressure?

We use the Clausius–Clapeyron Equation (10.43)

$$\frac{dP_M}{dT_M} = \frac{\Delta Q_F}{T_F(V_L - V_S)}$$

First we evaluate ΔV_{LS}, the volume change between liquid and solid. Considering one mole of water substance i.e. 18×10^{-3} kg, we have:

$$V_L = \frac{18 \times 10^{-3}}{999.84} = 18.00 \times 10^{-6} \text{ m}^3 \left(= 18.00 \text{ cm}^3\right)$$

and:

$$V_S = \frac{18 \times 10^{-3}}{920} = 19.57 \times 10^{-6} \text{ m}^3 \left(= 19.57 \text{ cm}^3\right)$$

so that :

$$V_{LS} = 18.00 \times 10^{-6} - 19.57 \times 10^{-6}$$

$$= -1.57 \times 10^{-6} \text{ m}^3$$

Substituting $\Delta Q_F = 5994$ J mol^{-1} and $T_M = 273.15$ K we find:

$$\frac{dP_M}{dT_M} = \frac{5994}{273.15 \times \left(-1.57 \times 10^{-6}\right)}$$

$$= -13.98 \times 10^6 \text{ Pa K}^{-1}$$

This indicates that to *lower* the melting temperature by 1K, we need to apply a pressure of around 10^7 Pa, which is roughly 100 times atmospheric pressure.

We can estimate the change in melting temperature ΔT_M due to a change in pressure ΔP_M using:

$$\frac{\Delta P_M}{\Delta T_M} \approx \frac{dP_M}{dT_M} = -13.98 \times 10^6 \text{ Pa K}^{-1}$$

and hence:

$$\Delta T_M \approx \frac{\Delta P_M}{-13.98 \times 10^6} = -7.15 \times 10^{-8} \text{ Pa}^{-1}$$

(a) For a pressure of twice atmospheric pressure $\Delta P_M = 1.013 \times 10^5$, ΔT_M evaluates to -7.25×10^{-3} K, i.e. a doubling of the pressure results in a *lowering* of melting temperature of only 7.25 mK.

(b) For a pressure of 1000 times atmospheric pressure $\Delta P_M = 1.013 \times 10^8$, ΔT_M evaluates evaluates to -7.25 K. Although much larger than the shift in (a) this large pressure only shifts the melting temperature by around 7 K in 273 K, i.e. a shift of only 3%.

Predicting the melting curve

If we plot the melting line on the same diagram on which we plotted the vapour pressure curve, then their intersection will provide an estimate of the location of the triple point. Starting with the Clausius–Clapeyron equation we equation we write:

$$\frac{dP_M}{dT_M} = \frac{\Delta Q_M}{T_M(V_L - V_S)} \qquad (10.56)$$

In order to estimate the order of magnitude of the quantities involved, we make two assumptions. First, we assume that the latent heat of fusion ΔQ_M does not vary with pressure or temperature. And second, we assume that the volume difference between the liquid and solid phase $V_L - V_S$ does not vary with pressure or temperature. In fact, both quantities do vary with pressure and temperature, but usually only rather slowly. This affects the detailed shape of the melting curve, but not its qualitative form. With these assumptions we write:

$$dP_M = \frac{\Delta Q_M}{\Delta V_{LS}} \frac{dT_M}{T_M} \qquad (10.57)$$

Integrating this from zero pressure yields:

$$\int_{P_M=0}^{P_M} dP_M = \frac{\Delta Q_M}{\Delta V_{LS}} \int_{T_M(P_M=0)}^{T_M(P_M)} \frac{dT_M}{T_M} \qquad (10.58)$$

Remembering that $\int dx/x = \ln(x)$ this becomes:

$$P_M = \frac{\Delta Q_M}{\Delta V_{LS}} \left[\ln(T_M(P_M=0)) - \ln(T_M(P_M)) \right] (10.59)$$

Re-writing this we find:

$$P_M = \frac{\Delta Q_M}{\Delta V_{LS}} \ln\left[\frac{T_M(P_M=0)}{T_M(P_M)} \right] \qquad (10.60)$$

This equation allows us to predict the pressure required to cause a liquid to solidify, in terms of the melting *temperature* of the substance at zero pressure $T_M(P_M=0)$. In fact at zero pressure a substance does not melt but sublimes; ignoring this for the moment, we choose a value for $T_M(P_M=0)$ to agree with the experimental melting temperature of 273.15 K for ice at $P_M = 1.013 \times 10^5$ Pa. The resulting curve is plotted

348

Example 10.9

Why is ice so slippery?

One theory commonly propounded is that when pressurised, ice melts because its melting temperature has been lowered. Does this make sense? Consider a car with a mass of around 1000 kg distributed equally across four wheels.

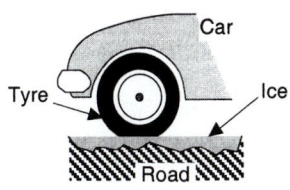

The weight of the car is supported on a relatively small area of contact on each tyre. Recalling that the tread of the tyre reduces the area of rubber in contact with the road by around 30%, we estimate this contact area as 70% of 15cm × 15 cm = 15.75×10^{-3} m^2 per tyre. The force supported over this area is the mass of the car times the acceleration due to gravity, which we take as 10 m s^{-2}. The force per tyre is therefore 1000 × 10/4 = 2500 N. The force per unit area under each tyre i.e. the pressure each tyre exerts is therefore approximately $2500/(15.75 \times 10^{-3}) = 1.6 \times 10^5$ Pa or an excess pressure of around 1.6 atmospheres. Taking into account the uncertainties in our estimates, and allowing for the excess pressure that may be generated if the car is motion, we might estimate that the maximum pressure under the tyres of a car is around 10^6 Pa.

Using Example 10.8 as a guide, 10^6 Pa will lower the melting temperature by around 0.1 K. Thus a car travelling over an iced surface will indeed increase the pressure on the ice such that the ice is taken to its melting temperature *if* the ice is already with approximately 0.1 K of its melting temperature. Do you think this is why ice is slippery?

Figure 10.15 Illustration of the difference between the melting curves of (a) normal substances and (b) substances whose liquid phase is more dense than their solid phase.

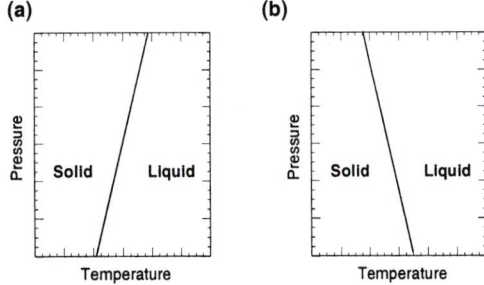

alongside the vaporisation curve (from Figure 10.12) in Figure 10.16 (a) and (b).

If we consider now what happens at low pressures, we see that the triple point marks the point below which the liquid phase disappears. As we shall see in §11.7, solids support a vapour pressure above their surface in much the same way as liquids do, and so the melting curve disappears. The vaporisation curve continues below the triple point in approximately the same way as it 'would have done' for the liquid ⇔ gas transition. Experimental data on the differences between the liquid ⇔ gas and solid ⇔ gas phase transitions is given in §11.7.

10.7.3 Constructing a phase diagram

Water
By combining the co-existence curves for liquid–gas, solid–gas and solid–vapour phases, we can construct a phase diagram for water substance. The result is shown in Figure 10.16 with the pressure plotted on both linear and logarithmic scales.

In fact, the phase diagram of water is not so simple as indicated in Figure 10.16(c). In different regimes of temperature and pressure there are at least ten known crystal structures of the solid phase of water (ice). The common crystal structure (known as ice Ih) collapses under the application of pressure ($\approx 2 \times 10^8$ Pa at -40 °C) to form ice II, which is denser than liquid water at that pressure. This changes the slope of solid–liquid coexistence curve from its initial negative slope to the more common positive slope. The experimental phase diagram is shown in Question 28 in Chapter 12.

Potassium
Let us look at a second example of a phase diagram, this time for the metal potassium discussed in §10.2. The procedure for constructing the phase diagram is exactly that discussed above for water.

We can predict the vaporisation curve using Equation 10.52:

Figure 10.16 The phase diagram for water (a) The curve of the melting pressure versus temperature. Also shown is the vaporisation curve for water from Figure 10.12. (b) The same graph as (a) but with the data plotted on a logarithmic scale. This shows the low-pressure behaviour more clearly and allows us to identify the triple point at the intersection of the vaporisation and melting curves. (c) The same as (b) but with the low-pressure end of the melting curve removed. This is the phase diagram for water substance.

(a)

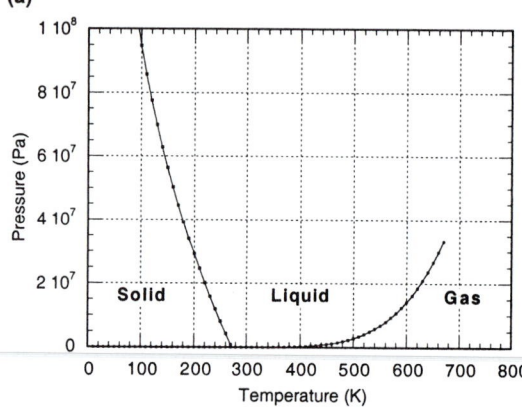

(b)

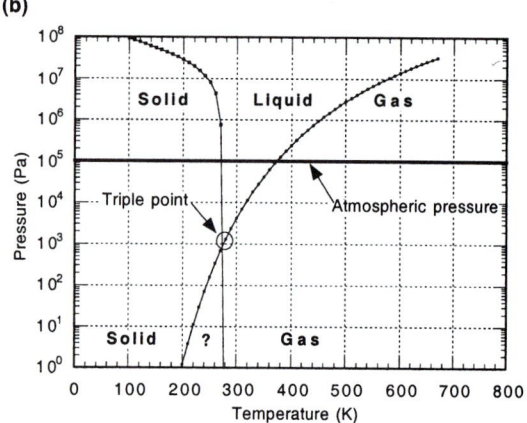

(c)

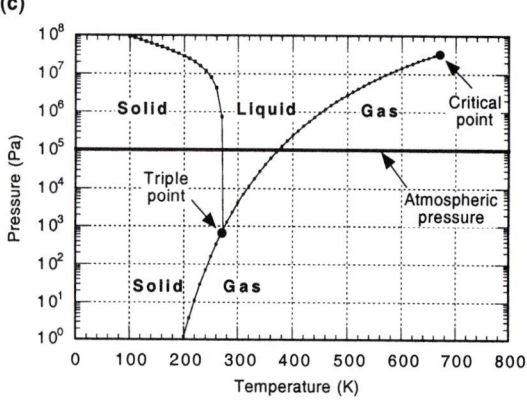

Figure 10.17 The phase diagram for potassium (a) with pressure shown on a linear scale and (b) with pressure shown on a logarithmic scale. The curves are predicted according to Equations 10.62 and 10.63 using data from Table 11.1 and Table 9.2: molar mass = 39.1 × 10^{-3} kg; solid density = 862 kg m^{-3}; liquid density = 824 kg m^{-3}; T_M = 336.8 K; T_B = 1047 K; Q_{LS} = 2.4 kJ mol^{-1}; Q_{LG} = 77.53 kJ mol^{-1}. Comparing this with Figure 10.16 (c), the vaporisation curve is much lower in pressure than that for water at the same temperature, and the slope of the melting curve is positive. The critical point has not been marked on the liquid ⇔ gas phase boundary.

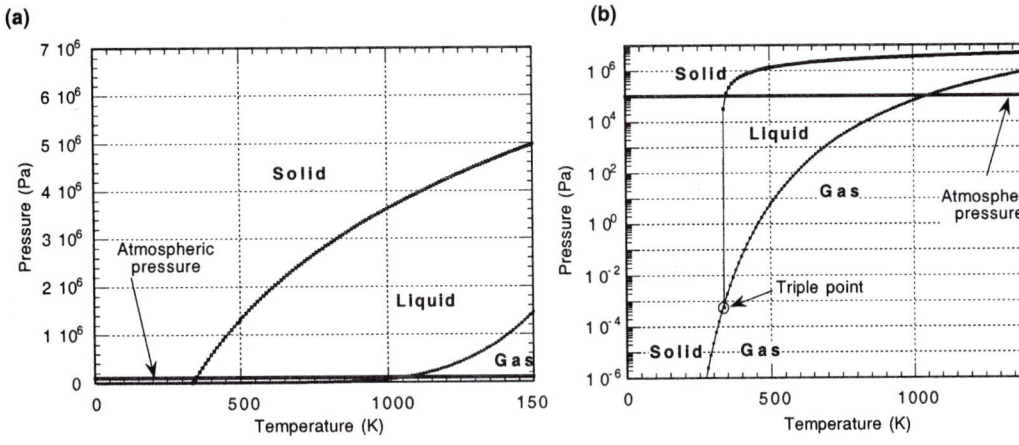

$$P_B = P_o \exp\left[\frac{-Q_B}{RT_B}\right] \quad (10.52^* \text{ and } 10.61)$$

with P_o adjusted to yield a vapour pressure of one atmosphere at 1047 K in agreement with the boiling temperature of potassium (Table 11.1).

The melting curve is predicted from Equation 10.60:

$$P_M = \frac{\Delta Q_M}{\Delta V_{LS}} \ln\left[\frac{T_M(P_M = 0)}{T_M(P_M)}\right] \quad (10.60^*)$$

with the melting temperature at zero pressure set to 336.8 K in rough agreement with the melting temperature at one atmosphere (Table 11.1).

The phase diagram constructed from these equations is shown in Figure 10.17.

Notice that because latent heat of vaporisation is considerably greater for potassium than for water, the vaporisation curve is much lower in pressure than that for water (Figure 10.16) at the same temperature. Notice also that because the volume of potassium increases as it melts, the slope of the melting curve is positive, i.e. the application of pressure suppresses the melting transition.

10.7.4 The *PVT* surface

Phase diagrams such as those shown in §10.7.3 are an enormously useful way to present a great deal of information about a substance in summary form. As we mentioned before, phase diagrams refer to a given amount of a substance – usually one mole – and give information about what phase (liquid, solid or gas) a substance will adopt at any pressure or temperature. However, there is an unplotted variable on these phase diagrams: the volume which the given amount of substance adopts in each of these three phases.

The volume varies by many orders of magnitude across the different experimental conditions outlined in the phase diagrams, and its variation with pressure and temperature is different in each of the different phases. There is a construction, known as the *PVT* surface, which indicates the volume of a given amount of substance at different points on the phase diagram. A schematic illustration of such a surface is shown in Figure 10.18. I think it is important for you to realise that the concept of a *PVT* surface is pedagogical rather than practical. It is generally used to indicate schematically the phases that substances adopt, rather than as an aid to any particular calculation.

Figure 10.18. (a) The *PVT* surface of a hypothetical 'typical' substance. The specification of this surface for a substance describes the equilibrium behaviour of a substance. In general each part of the surface may be described by an equation state. (b) The line *XY* represents a process in which the substance is heated at constant pressure. In the solid state (*A*) the volume changes only a little with temperature. The substance then melts (*C*) and expands at constant temperature until it is all transformed to the liquid state (*D*). There the thermal expansion is slightly larger than in the solid state. Eventually the substance reaches its boiling temperature and its volume increases dramatically as it vaporises (*E*). Eventually all the substance is transformed to the gas phase.

(a)   **(b)**

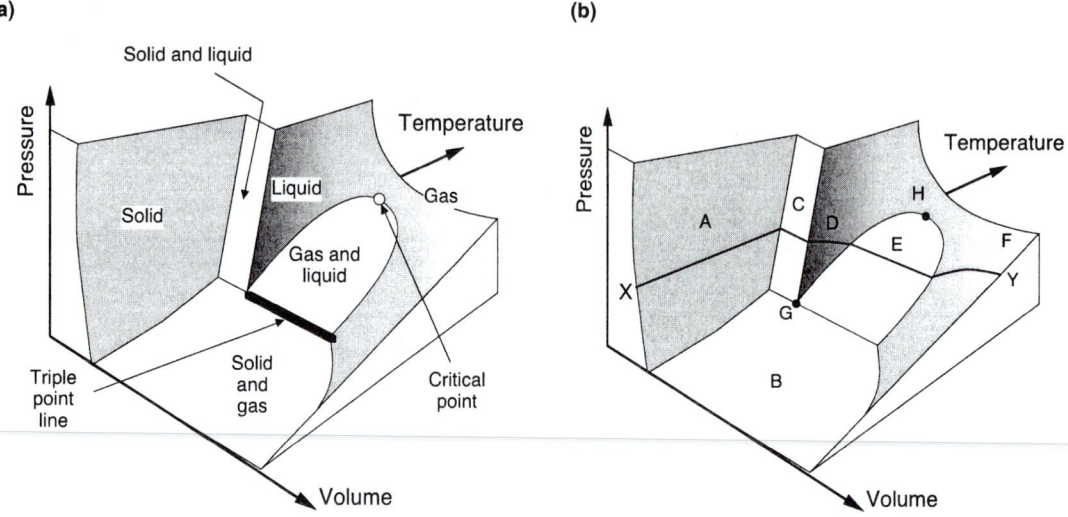

10.8 Exercises

Exercises marked with a P prefix are 'normal' exercises. Those marked with a C prefix are best solved numerically by using a computer program or spreadsheet.. Exercises marked with an E prefix are in general rather more challenging that the P and C exercises. Answers to all the exercises are downloadable from www.physicsofmatter.com

P1. At temperatures less than 30K, the heat capacity of metal varies like $C \approx \gamma T + \alpha T^3$ J K^{-1} mol^{-1} where $\gamma = 10^{-4}$ J K^{-2} mol^{-1} and $\alpha = 10^{-5}$ J K^{-4} mol^{-1}. Calculate the thermal contribution $U(T)$ to the internal energy of the solid at 1 K and 20 K. How does this compare with typical values of the internal energy due to electrostatic attraction U_o (Table 11.5).

P2. Assuming that the heat capacity of a substance follows the Debye law (Figures 7.28 and 7.29) sketch the approximate form of $U(T)$. Indicate clearly the value of $U(T)$ at $T = 0$ K and the limiting slope at temperatures greater than the Debye temperature.

P3. One mole of an elemental solid substance has a cohesive energy $U_o = 100$ kJ mol^{-1}. By considering this energy to arise from atoms arranged in a simple cubic structure ($a \approx 0.3$ nm) with nearest neighbour interactions only, show that each atomic bond contributes approximately 1/3 eV to the cohesive energy of the substance.

By considering the energy required to split a cube of the substance in two (or otherwise), show that the energy required to a form a new surface of the substance is approximately $\Delta G_S \approx 0.3$ J m^{-2}.

P4. The substance considered in P3 has a melting temperature $T_M = 700$ K. Close to the melting temperature, the Gibbs free energy of the liquid phase has a slope $\partial G_L/\partial T = -400$ J K^{-1} mol^{-1} and the Gibbs free energy of the solid phase has slope $\partial G_S/\partial T = -395$ J K^{-1} mol^{-1}. Use Equation 10.41 with a value of $\Delta G \approx 0.3$ J m^{-2} to estimate the size of a critical embryo if the substance supercools by 0.7 K before commencing solidification. Note that before you can substitute into Equation 10.41 you must convert the Gibbs free energy difference ΔG_{LS}

351

from $J\,mol^{-1}$ to $J\,m^{-3}$. Do you think your estimate for the critical embryo size is plausible?

P5. Following Example 10.7, work out the rate at which the freezing temperature of ethanol would increase with applied pressure. If the maximum achievable laboratory pressure is around 10^5 atmospheres, could a pressure be achieved at which the melting temperatures of ethanol and water were equal? (In fact the structure of ice changes at high pressure and slope of melting curve then becomes positive.)

P6. Following Examples 10.8 and 10.9, write a short report with calculations on whether the slipperiness of ice is evidence for the existence of a pre-melted surface (§10.5.1). As part of your report conduct informal ex-

periments with ice cubes that are cooled as far below $0\,°C$ as you can achieve (a three star domestic freezer will cool ice to $-18°C$). In particular, address the question of whether the slipperiness is connected with the temperature of the sliding object.

P7. Water substance is held in equilibrium at a series of temperatures and pressures (a) to (g). For each state (a) to (g) indicate the phase of the water substance according to Figure 10.16.

(a) 200 K, 10^5 Pa   (b) 200 K, 10^8 Pa

(c) 400 K, 10^8 Pa   (d) 400 K, 10^5 Pa

(e) 700 K, 10^5 Pa   (f) 700 K, 10^8 Pa

(g) 273.15 K, 611 Pa

CHAPTER 11
Changes of phase: comparison with experiment

11.1 Introduction

In the Chapter 10 we established that changes of phase can be described with the aid of a phase diagram. We spent some time establishing the general form of a phase diagram for a 'typical substance' and arrived at something like Figure 11.1. The three transitions between the phases that occur as a result of temperature changes at constant pressure are shown as double-ended arrows. In this chapter we would like to examine experimental data on all aspects of this diagram: the slopes of the phase boundaries and their points of intersection. In practice the amount of data involved is amazingly large so we restrict ourselves to data on the elements and a small range of relatively simple substances (§11.2).

Figure 11.1 A generic *PT* phase diagram

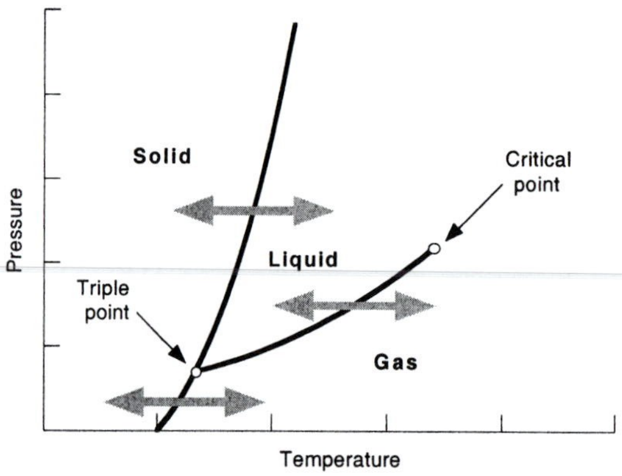

§11.3, §11.4 The solid ⇔ liquid and liquid ⇔ gas transitions: Although we refer to these transitions in the same manner, and they are both represented by the crossing of a single line in Figure 11.1, they are physically very different processes. We will find that we need to develop quite different microscopic models to understand each type of transition.

§11.5, §11.8 The critical point and triple point: Examining the data on these points reveals that they occur at similar relative positions on the phase diagrams of quite different substances.

§11.6 Scaling: laws of corresponding states: Throughout this book, we have discovered correlations between the physical properties of different substances. This raises the hope that we might be able to use *some* properties of a substance to predict an unknown property, either of that substance or another one. We will find that sometimes we can do this and sometimes we can not. But what is the origin of these partial correlations?

§11.7 The solid ⇔ gas transitions: Compared with the phase transitions considered in §11.3 and §11.4 the solid ⇔ gas transition is relatively understudied. We will find it is relatively easy to understand the process using a surprising extension of the cell model of a liquid.

§11.9 Other types of phase transitions: We mentioned in Chapter 10 that there is the concept of a phase transition could be applied more widely than to changes between solids in liquids and gas. In this section we look at what these transitions are and how they can be studied .

At www.physicsofmatter.com

You will find copies of the figures and tables from this chapter.

11.2 Data on the solid ⇔ liquid and liquid ⇔ gas transitions

This section consists of just two tables, which contain data that will be referred to in several of the following sections. Table 11.1 contains data relevant to the solid ⇔ liquid and liquid ⇔ gas transitions in the elements, and Table 11.2 contains the equivalent data for various substances.

Table 11.1 Thermal data for the elements: the melting and boiling temperatures in kelvin, and the enthalpies of fusion (melting) and vaporisation. The data refer to standard atmospheric pressure unless otherwise stated. Two elements – arsenic and carbon – which sublime when heated at atmospheric pressure. These are discussed in §11.7 on the solid ⇒ gas transition, and their the enthalpies of fusion and vaporisation are estimated from studies at high pressure.

Z	Name	Atomic weight	Density $(kg\,m^{-3})$	Melting point (K)	Boiling point (K)	Enthalpy of fusion $(kJ\,mol^{-1})$	Enthalpy of vaporisation $(kJ\,mol^{-1})$
1	Hydrogen	1.008	89	14.01	20.28	0.12	0.46
2	Helium	4.003	120	0.95	4.216	0.021	0.082
3	Lithium	6.941	533	453.7	1620	4.6	134.7
4	Beryllium	9.012	1846	1551	3243	9.8	308.8
5	Boron	10.81	2466	2365	3931	22.2	538.9
6	Carbon	12.01	2266	Sublimes at ≈ 3700		105	710.9
7	Nitrogen	14.01	1035	63.15	77.4	0.72	5.577
8	Oxygen	16	1460	54.36	90.188	0.444	6.82
9	Fluorine	19	1140	53.48	85.01	5.1	6.548
10	Neon	20.18	1442	24.56	27.1	0.324	1.1736
11	Sodium	22.99	966	371	1156.1	2.64	89.04
12	Magnesium	24.31	1738	922	1363	9.04	128.7
13	Aluminium	26.98	2698	933.5	2740	10.67	293.72
14	Silicon	28.09	2329	1683	2628	39.6	383.3
15	Phosphorous	30.97	1820	317.3	553	2.51	51.9
16	Sulphur	32.06	2086	386	717.82	1.23	9.62
17	Chlorine	35.45	2030	172	239.18	6.41	20.403
18	Argon	39.95	1656	83.8	87.29	1.21	6.53
19	Potassium	39.1	862	336.8	1047	2.4	77.53
20	Calcium	40.08	1530	1112	1757	9.33	149.95
21	Scandium	44.96	2992	1814	3104	15.9	304.8
22	Titanium	47.9	4508	1933	3560	20.9	428.9
23	Vanadium	50.94	6090	2160	3650	17.6	458.6
24	Chromium	52	7194	2130	2945	15.3	348.78
25	Manganese	54.94	7473	1517	2235	14.4	219.7
26	Iron	55.85	7873	1808	3023	14.9	351
27	Cobalt	58.93	8800	1768	3143	15.2	382.4
28	Nickel	58.7	8907	1726	3005	17.6	371.8
29	Copper	63.55	8933	1356.6	2840	13	304.6
30	Zinc	65.38	7135	692.73	1180	6.67	115.3
31	Gallium	69.72	5905	302.93	3676	5.59	256.1
32	Germanium	72.59	5323	1210.6	3103	34.7	334.3
33	Arsenic	74.92	5776	Sublimes at 886		27.7	31.9
34	Selenium	78.96	4808	490	958.1	5.1	26.32
35	Bromine	79.9	3120	265.9	331.93	10.8	30
36	Krypton	83.8	3000	116.6	120.85	1.64	9.05
37	Rubidium	85.47	1533	312.2	961	2.2	69.2
38	Strontium	87.62	2583	1042	1657	6.16	138.91
39	Yttrium	88.91	4475	1795	3611	17.2	393.3

Z	Name	Atomic weight	Density (kg m^{-3})	Melting point (K)	Boiling point (K)	Enthalpy of fusion (kJ mol^{-1})	Enthalpy of vaporisation (kJ mol^{-1})
40	Zirconium	91.22	6507	2125	4650	23	581.6
41	Niobium	92.91	8578	2741	5015	27.2	696.6
42	Molybdenum	95.94	10222	2890	4885	27.6	594.1
43	Technetium	97	11496	2445	5150	23.81	585.22
44	Ruthenium	101.1	12360	2583	4173	23.7	567.8
45	Rhodium	102.9	12420	2239	4000	21.55	495.4
46	Palladium	106.4	11995	1825	3413	17.2	393.3
47	Silver	107.9	10500	1235.1	2485	11.3	255.1
48	Cadmium	112.4	8647	594.1	1038	6.11	99.87
49	Indium	114.8	7290	429.32	2353	3.27	226.4
50	Tin	118.7	7285	505.12	2543	7.2	290.4
51	Antimony	121.7	6692	903.9	1908	20.9	67.91
52	Tellurium	127.6	6247	722.7	1263	13.5	50.63
53	Iodine	126.9	4953	386.7	457.5	15.27	41.67
54	Xenon	131.3	3560	161.3	166.1	3.1	12.65
55	Caesium	132.9	1900	301.6	951.6	2.09	65.9
56	Barium	137.3	3594	1002	1910	7.66	150.9
57	Lanthanum	138.9	6174	1194	3730	10.04	399.6
58	Cerium	140.1	6711	1072	3699	8.87	313.8
59	Praseodymium	140.9	6779	1204	3785	11.3	332.6
60	Neodymium	144.2	7000	1294	3341	7.113	283.7
61	Promethium	145	7220	1441	3000	12.6	—
62	Samarium	150.4	7536	1350	2064	10.9	191.6
63	Europium	152	5248	1095	1870	10.5	175.7
64	Gadolinium	157.2	7870	1586	3539	15.5	311.7
65	Terbium	158.9	8267	1629	3396	16.3	391
66	Dysprosium	162.5	8531	1685	2835	17.2	293
67	Holmium	164.9	8797	1747	2968	17.2	251
68	Erbium	167.3	9044	1802	3136	17.2	292.9
69	Thulium	168.9	9325	1818	2220	18.4	247
70	Ytterbium	173	6966	1097	1466	9.2	159
71	Lutetium	175	9842	1936	3668	19.2	428
72	Hafnium	178.5	13276	2503	5470	25.5	661.1
73	Tantalum	180.9	16670	3269	5698	31.4	753.1
74	Tungsten	183.9	19254	3680	5930	35.2	799.1
75	Rhenium	186.2	21023	3453	5900	33.1	707.1
76	Osmium	190.2	22580	3327	5300	29.3	627.6
77	Iridium	192.2	22550	2683	4403	26.4	563.6
78	Platinum	195.1	21450	2045	4100	19.7	510.5
79	Gold	197	19281	1337.6	3080	12.7	324.4
80	Mercury	200.6	13546	234.28	629.73	2.331	59.15
81	Thallium	204.4	11871	576.6	1730	4.31	162.1
82	Lead	207.2	11343	600.65	2013	5.121	179.4
83	Bismuth	209	9803	544.5	1833	10.48	179.1
84	Polonium	209	9400	527	1235	10	100.8
85	Astatine	210	—	575	610	23.8	—
86	Radon	222	4400	202	211.4	2.7	19.1
87	Francium	223	—	300	950	—	—
88	Radium	226	5000	973	1413	7.15	136.8
89	Actinium	227	10060	1320	3470	14.2	293

Z	Name	Atomic weight	Density (kg m^{-3})	Melting point (K)	Boiling point (K)	Enthalpy of fusion (kJ mol $^{-1}$)	Enthalpy of vaporisation (kJ mol $^{-1}$)
90	Thorium	232	11725	2023	5060	19.2	543.9
91	Protactinium	231	15370	2113	4300	16.7	481
92	Uranium	238	19050	1405	4018	15.5	422.6
93	Neptunium	237	20250	913	4175	9.46	336.6
94	Plutonium	244	19840	914	3505	2.8	343.5
95	Americium	243	13670	1267	2880	14.4	238.5

Table 11.2 Thermal data for the various substances: the melting and boiling temperatures in kelvin, and the enthalpies of fusion (melting) and vaporisation. The data refer to standard atmospheric pressure unless otherwise stated and (s) indicates that the substance sublimes rather than boils and the melting temperature is obtained under pressure. (*) indicates a large discrepancy of ± 20 K amongst data from different sources.

Substance		MW	Density (kg m^{-3})	Melting point (K)	Boiling point (K)	Enthalpy of fusion (kJ mol $^{-1}$)	Enthalpy of vaporisation (kJ mol $^{-1}$)
Acetic acid	CH_3COOH	60	1049	289.75	391.1	11.535	—
Acetone	CH_3COCH_3	58	787	177.8	329.3	5.691	—
Aniline	C_6H_7N	93	1026	266.85	457.6	10.555	—
Benzene	C_6H_6	78	877	278.65	353.2	9.951	—
Chloroform	$CHCl_3$	119	—	209.55	334.4	8.800	—
Cyclohexane	C_6H_{10}	82	779	279.65	353.8	2.630	—
Ethyl acetate	$C_4H_8O_2$	88	—	189.55	350.2	10.481	—
Methanol	CH_3OH	32	791	179.25	337.7	3.177	—
Ethanol	C_2H_5OH	46	789	155.85	351.5	5.021	—
Propan-1-ol	C_3H_7OH	60	804	146.65	370.3	5.195	—
Propan-2-ol	C_3H_7OH	60	786	—	—	—	—
Butan-1-ol	C_4H_9OH	74	810	183.65	390.35	9.282	—
Butan-2-ol	C_4H_9OH	74	808	298.55	372.65	6.786	—
Toluene	C_7H_8	92	867	178.15	383.8	6.851	—
Lithium fluoride	LiF	25.9	2635	1118	1949	—	—
Lithium chloride	LiCl	42.39	2068	878	1620(*)	—	—
Lithium bromide	LiBr	86.9	3464	823	1538	—	—
Sodium chloride	NaF	42.0	2558	1266	1968	—	—
Sodium fluoride	NaCl	58.4	2165	1074	1686	—	—
Sodium bromide	NaBr	102.9	3203	1020	1663	—	—
Potassium fluoride	KF	58.1	2480	1131	1778	—	—
Potassium chloride	KCl	74.6	1984	1043	1273(s)	—	—
Potassium bromide	KBr	119.0	2750	1007	1708	—	—
Carbon dioxide	CO_2	44	—	216.55	194.7	—	—
Carbontetrachloride	CCl_4	154	1632	—	—	—	—
Carbon disulphide	CS_2	76	1293	162.35	319.6	4.395	—
Carbon monoxide	CO	28	—	74.15	81.7	—	—
Water	H_2O	18	998	273.15	373.15	5.994	40.608

Example 11.1

Calculate the amount of energy required to complete the following processes:

(a) Melt 1 mole of ice at its melting temperature.
(b) Heat 1 mole of liquid (water) from 0°C to 100°C.
(c) Melt 1 mole of copper at its melting temperature.

The data required to answer these questions is given in Tables 11.2, 9.11 and 11.1 respectively.

(a) From Table 11.2 the enthalpy of fusion of water is 5.994×10^3 J mol^{-1}. Thus to melt 1 mole (0.018 kg) of ice requires $1 \times 5.994 \times 10^3 = 5994$ J.
(b) From Table 9.13 the heat capacity of water is given as 75.9 J K^{-1} mol^{-1}. Thus to raise 1 mole (0.018 kg) of water from 0°C to 100°C requires $1 \times 75.9 \times 100 = 7590$ J, i.e. about 25% more energy than that required to melt the same amount of water.
(c) From Table 11.2 the enthalpy of fusion of copper is 13×10^3 J mol^{-1}. Thus to melt 1 mole (0.0635 kg) of copper requires $1 \times 13 \times 10^3 = 13000$ J. This amounts to about twice that required to melt 1 mole of water.

Example 11.2

Calculate the amount of energy required to complete the following processes:

(a) Boil 1 mole of water at its boiling temperature.
(b) Heat 1 mole of liquid (water) from 0°C to 100°C.
(c) Boil 1 mole of copper at its melting temperature.

The data required to answer these questions is given in Tables 11.2, 9.11 and 11.1 respectively.

(a) From Table 11.2 the enthalpy of vaporisation of water is 40.608×10^3 J mol^{-1}. Thus to boil 1 mole (0.018 kg) of water requires $1 \times 40.608 \times 10^{-3} = 40608$ J, i.e. about 7 times as much energy as is required to melt the same amount of water.
(b) From Table 9.13 the heat capacity of water is given as 75.9 J K^{-1} mol^{-1}. Thus to raise 1 mole (0.018 kg) of water from 0°C to 100°C requires $1 \times 75.9 \times 100 = 7590$ J, i.e. about 80% *less* energy than that required to boil the same amount of water.
(c) From Table 11.2 the enthalpy of vaporisation of copper is 304.6×10^3 J mol^{-1}. Thus to boil 1 mole (0.0635 kg) of copper requires $1 \times 304.6 \times 10^3 = 304600$ J. This amounts to about 23 times as much energy as required to melt the same quantity of copper, and about 8 times as much energy as required to boil 1 mole of water.

11.3 The solid ⇔ liquid transition: melting and freezing

11.3.1 Introduction

For most substances, the transition from the solid to the liquid state occurs gradually, over a range of temperature. However for *pure substances*, melting takes place at a well-defined temperature known as the *melting temperature*, T_M, or *melting point*. Defining what we mean by a pure substance is not as easy as it might at first appear. A working definition is:

1. A pure substance is one composed of a single type of atom or molecule.

This definition requires occasional qualification, but it will serve for now.

At the melting temperature, a substance can be either a solid or a liquid. As illustrated in Figure 11.2, if a sample is 50% solid and 50% liquid it will stay that way until further heat is added to, or removed from, the substance. Heat input at the melting temperature does not raise the temperature of the solid/liquid mixture: it serves to transform more solid into liquid. The energy required to transform one mole of substance from solid to liquid at constant pressure is known by several equivalent terms: the molar *enthalpy change on fusion*; the molar *enthalpy of fusion*; the molar *latent heat of fusion*. The preferred form is the *enthalpy change on fusion*, the term *fusion* being an old term for melting.

11.3.2 Further data

The melting temperature T_M and molar enthalpy of fusion of the elements are recorded in Table 11.1 above, and plotted as a function of atomic number for the elements in Figures 11.3 and 11.4 respec-

Figure 11.2 The five pictures illustrate the effect of application of heat energy to a substance in the solid state at the melting temperature. The heat serves only to transform more solid into liquid, but does not raise the temperature of the mixture. Notice that the solid phase is usually more dense than the liquid and sinks in the mixture. This is not always the case: water, silicon, germanium gallium and bismuth are examples where the liquid phase is denser than the solid phase. (See Tables 9.1 and 9.2.)

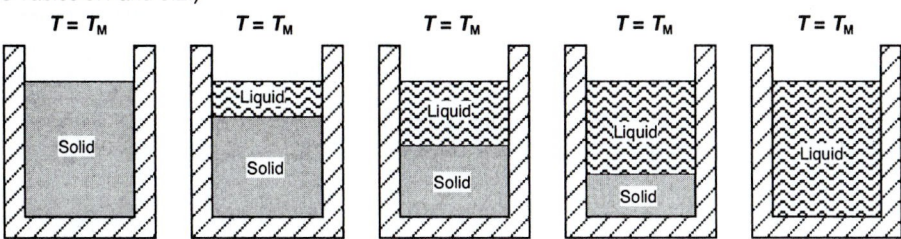

tively. The figures show a qualitative similarity to one another, indicating that elements with a high melting temperature tend to have a high enthalpy of fusion. Furthermore, the structure in the data shows similar patterns to those seen in Figure 7.1 showing the density of elements.

Note that the temperature of the transition from the solid to the liquid phase is dependent on the pressure to which the liquid/solid is subjected. In general, higher pressures tend to increase the temperature at which solid ⇔ liquid transitions take place. Interestingly, in substances which contract on melting, higher pressures tend to *lower* the temperature at which solid ⇔ liquid take place. Figure 11.4 shows data for the elements silver and gold, and the depression of the melting tempera-

ture for water is discussed in §11.3.4.

The main questions raised by our preliminary examination of the experimental data on the solid ⇔ liquid transition in the elements are:

- Why do elements with a high T_M tend to have a high enthalpy of fusion?

- Why does the variation of T_M of the elements with atomic number show a pattern similar to that seen in the density of elements?

- Why does T_M of most substances increase with pressure, but decrease for substances which contract on melting?

These questions will be considered in §11.3.4, after we have examined the Lindemann theory of melting.

Figure 11.3 The melting temperatures of the elements plotted as function of atomic number. Notice that the pattern has similarities to several other patterns such as those seen in Figures 7.1 and Figures 11.4.

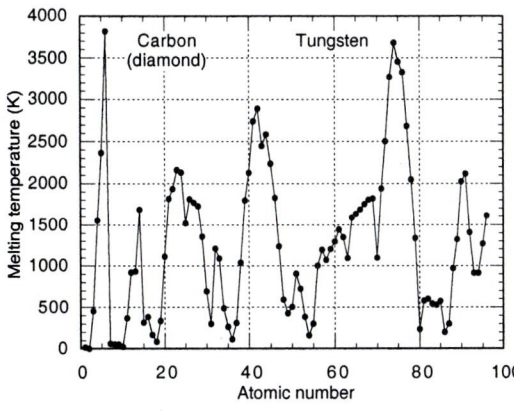

Figure 11.4 The molar enthalpy change of fusion of the elements plotted as function of atomic number. The datum for diamond has not been plotted so as to allow detail on the rest of the graph to be seen.

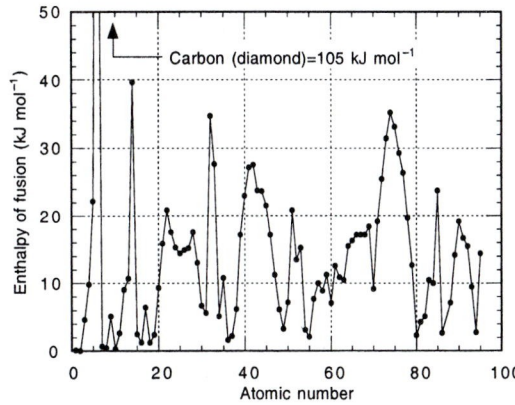

Figure 11.5 The elevation of the melting temperature of silver and gold as a function of applied pressure. Notice that the pressures are extremely large, 1 kBar is 1000 times atmospheric pressure and the pressure scale shown extends up to 200 kBar.

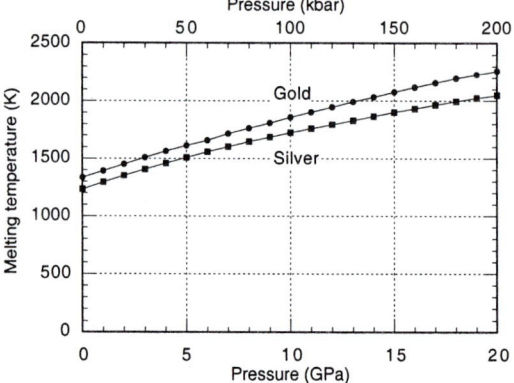

few per cent. Thus understanding what causes melting in anything more than a general sense is rather difficult. We can however still make a little headway into the problem.

First we can consider the process of melting in elemental substances only. Substances with more than one type of interatomic bond add an extra degree of complexity without adding more insight into the problem. Following the ideas of *Lindemann*, we hypothesise that melting is related to the amplitude of vibration of the atoms within the solid. Thus for small amplitude vibrations the solid state would be stable, but for larger amplitude vibrations the structure of the substance would lose rigidity and 'collapse' into the liquid state.

11.3.3 Lindemann theory of melting

The solid $\Rightarrow$ liquid transition – melting – is a considerably more complex process than the liquid $\Rightarrow$ gas transition – boiling. In the liquid $\Rightarrow$ gas transition, essentially all interactions between molecules are eliminated after the phase change. Thus we can understand the transition in terms of the dramatic change in the environment of each molecule. However, from our discussion of the nature of liquids in Chapters 8 and 9, we see that in the solid $\Rightarrow$ liquid transition the interactions and separations between molecules change by only a

Support for this idea may be gleaned by considering Figure 11.6, which shows the way in which melting temperature and Debye temperature vary amongst the elements. In §7.6, we saw that the Debye temperature of a substance, Θ_D, is (roughly) the temperature at which the atoms gain access to all their degrees of freedom. Above this temperature, they begin to vibrate essentially independently of their neighbours. The correlation seen in Figure 11.6 represents strong evidence that, not surprisingly, there is a relationship between the melting temperature and level of atomic vibration.

Figure 11.6 The melting and Debye temperatures of the elements plotted as function of atomic number. The temperatures are plotted on a logarithmic vertical axis. Notice the correlations between the two datasets. The data points are connected by straight lines in order to highlight trends in the data. Since data on the Debye temperature is not available for all the elements, some straight lines appear to indicate a Debye temperature higher than the melting temperature (e.g. elements 7 to 10): This is an artefact of the plotting procedure.

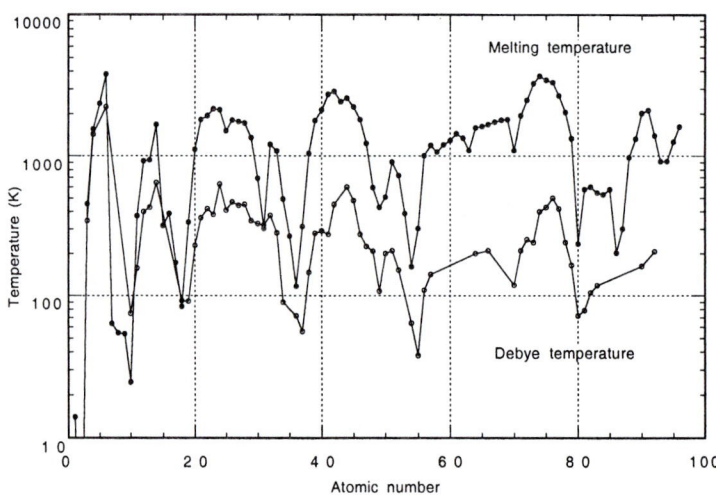

The Lindemann hypothesis

Lindemann hypothesised that melting occurred when the amplitude of vibration A reached a certain fraction f of the interatomic spacing a. This idea seems reasonable, and we can test it fairly straightforwardly.

We suppose that the atomic vibration is simple harmonic – so we neglect the asymmetry of the interatomic potential energy (Figure 7.7). The average energy of vibration of an atom in such a potential is $\overline{E_x} = k_B T$ for each direction of vibration: $\frac{1}{2} k_B T$ for the degree of freedom associated with *kinetic energy* of vibration in the x-direction and $\frac{1}{2} k_B T$ for the degree of freedom associated with *potential energy* of vibration in the x-direction (See §2.5). This average energy is also related to the potential energy of vibration at the extreme point of the oscillation, i.e. at $x = A$, the amplitude of vibration. We thus write:

$$\overline{E_x} = k_B T$$
$$= \tfrac{1}{2} K A^2 \qquad (11.1)$$

where K is the 'spring constant' of the harmonic potential. The Lindemann hypothesis is that melting occurs when the amplitude of vibration A is

Figure 11.7 To test the Lindemann hypothesis we assume that each atom vibrates in a simple harmonic potential with amplitude A, which is some fraction f of the interatomic spacing a. According to the equipartition theorem (§2.5) the mean energy of vibration $\overline{E_x}$ for vibration in one direction has the value $k_B T$. This is also equal to the potential energy of vibration at an extremum of vibration $\frac{1}{2} K A^2$.

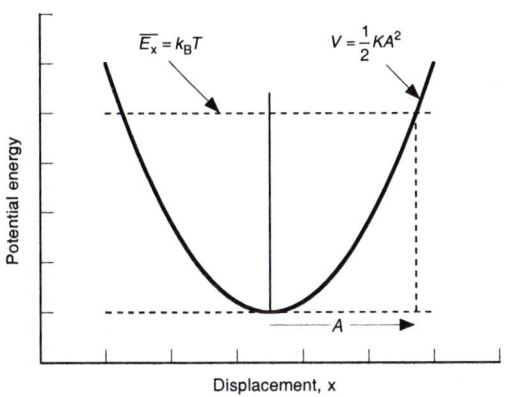

equal to a fraction f of the interatomic spacing a. Our task is to estimate this fraction f and see if it is similar for different elements. If it is, then we should find that:

$$k_B T_M = \tfrac{1}{2} K A^2 \qquad (11.2)$$

Substituting $A = fa$ and re-arranging we have:

$$f^2 = \frac{2 k_B T_M}{K a^2} \qquad (11.3)$$

Before we can estimate f we need to find expressions for K and a which we do as follows.

Estimating K

Firstly, we recall that the frequency of vibration ω of an atom in a simple harmonic oscillator potential is given by:

$$\omega = \sqrt{\frac{K}{m}} \qquad (11.4)$$

where m is the mass of an atom. Hence we can write $K = m\omega^2$. Further we note the Debye temperature Θ_D is the temperature at which the thermal energy of vibration $k_B \Theta_D$ is roughly equal to the energy separation between quantum states ($\hbar\omega$) of the simple harmonic oscillator potential. This is equivalent to using an Einstein approximation (§7.6) and then estimating the Einstein temperature Θ_E as Θ_D. This likely to be accurate at around the 50% level. So at this level of approximation we write:

$$K = m\omega^2$$
$$= m \left[\frac{k_B \Theta_D}{\hbar} \right]^2 \qquad (11.5)$$

Estimating a

Secondly we can make a rough estimate of a for the elements by imagining each atom of mass m to occupy a volume a^3, and thus to have a density $\rho = m/a^3$. We can thus use the density data of Table 7.1 to estimate a from:

$$a = \left[\frac{m}{\rho} \right]^{1/3} \qquad (11.6)$$

Estimating f

Substituting Equations 11.5 and 11.6 into Equation 11.3 we arrive at:

$$f^2 = \frac{2k_B T_M}{Ka^2}$$

$$= \frac{2k_B T_M}{m\left[\dfrac{k_B\Theta_D}{\hbar}\right]^2\left[\dfrac{m}{\rho}\right]^{2/3}} \qquad (11.7)$$

We can use Equation 11.7 to evaluate the fraction f for all the elements for which we have Debye Temperature data (Table 7.12). The results of this calculation are graphed in Figure 11.8.

The Lindemann fraction f has a value of around one twentieth of an interatomic spacing for a wide variety of different elements. The 25 % variability in the data ($f = 0.052 \pm 0.014$ to 1 standard deviation) is extremely small when we consider that it describes substances as different as argon and tungsten!

	T_M (K)	f
Argon	83.8	0.045
Tungsten	3680	0.044

Since we have completely ignored the crystal structure of the substances, small approximations such as $\Theta_E \approx \Theta_D$ in Equation 11.5 are relatively

Figure 11.8 The Lindemann Fraction f calculated according Equation 11.7 for the elements. Notice that the fraction is around one twentieth of a lattice spacing and the data in the graph have a mean value of 0.052 ± 0.014 at one standard deviation. By comparison with Figure 11.2 this variability is extremely small.

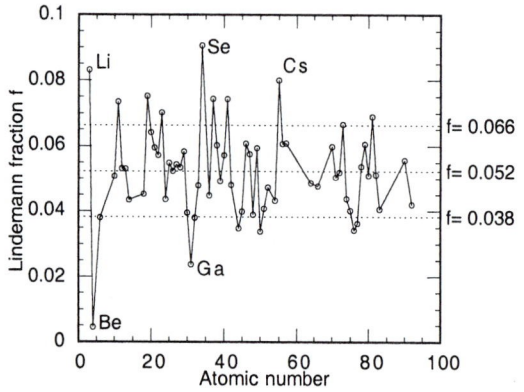

Example 11.3

Calculate the Lindemann fraction f for copper.

We have:
$k_B = 1.38 \times 10^{-23}$ J K^{-1}, $\hbar = 1.034 \times 10^{-34}$ J s,
$N_A = 6.02 \times 10^{23}$ mol^{-1}

and
$T_M = 1356.6$ K (Table 11.1)
$m = 63.55 \times 10^{-3}$ kg/N_A (Table 7.2)
$ = 1.056 \times 10^{-25}$ kg
$\rho = 8933$ kg m^{-3} (Table 7.2)
$\Theta_D = 343$ K (Table 7.12)

We thus estimate f as:

$$f^2 = \frac{2\times1.38\times10^{-23}\times1356.6}{1.056\times10^{-25}\left[\dfrac{1.38\times10^{-23}\times343}{1.054\times10^{-34}}\right]^2\left[\dfrac{1.056\times10^{-25}}{8933}\right]^{2/3}}$$

which evaluates to $f^2 = 3.388 \times 10^{-3}$ and $f = 0.0582$. This lies within the upper one standard deviation limit about the average value indicated in Figure 11.7

---

small contributors to the overall uncertainty in the estimate for f. From our perspective, it is the *constancy* of f which gives support to the Lindemann hypothesis. Thus melting occurs when the amplitude of atomic vibration reaches a fraction of roughly one twentieth of a lattice spacing. It is surprising – to me at least – that vibrations with this small amplitude are sufficient to destabilise a crystal structure to the extent that it melts.

11.3.4 Understanding the solid ⇔ liquid transition

Having established in general microscopic terms what happens when a substance melts, let us return to the questions raised by the data in §11.3.1 on the solid ⇔ liquid transition. These questions are considered in turn below.

Why do elements with a high melting temperature tend to have a high enthalpy of fusion?

This question is similar to the first question in the next section §11.4.1 on the liquid ⇔ gas transition: Why do elements with high boiling temperatures tend to have high enthalpies of fusion? We will proceed by first reviewing the data for the

Figure 11.9 The relationship amongst the elements between the enthalpy of transformation (fusion or vaporisation) and the temperature at which a transformation takes place. The figure shows:

- the ratio of the enthalpy of fusion to the melting temperature has a relatively constant value of around 0.01 in the units chosen
- the ratio of the enthalpy of transformation to the boiling temperature has a relatively constant value of around 0.1 in the units chosen.

The 0.01 and 0.1 figures have no absolute significance and are only the result of felicitous choice of units.

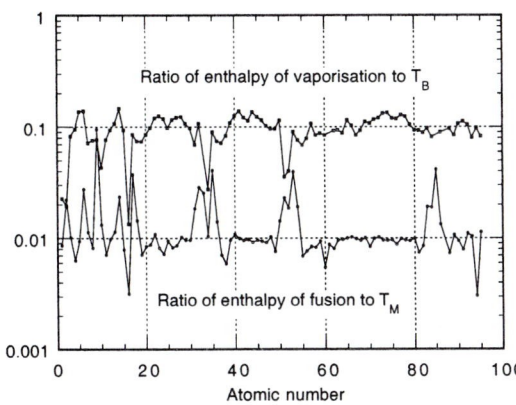

elements, and then consider both of these questions together, first in a simple way, and then using the more sophisticated Gibbs free energy analysis.

Simple analysis

Figure 11.9 combines data from different columns in Table 11.1 and shows that roughly speaking – and with some striking exceptions – that:

- the melting temperature in kelvin is around 1% of the enthalpy change on melting in kJ mol^{-1}
- the boiling temperature in kelvin is around 10% of the enthalpy change on vaporisation in kJ mol^{-1}.

First, we can then say that these correlations are exactly what we would expect. Using Lindemann theory (§11.3.3) we saw that melting occurs when the amplitude of vibration of atoms reaches around a twentieth of an interatomic spacing. If the bonds between atoms are very strong, then (a) it will (by definition) require a great deal of energy to break them, and (b) it will generally require a

great deal of energy to *stretch* or *bend* them. These two facts lead directly to correlations between enthalpy change on melting and – through the Lindemann criterion – the melting temperature.

Similarly with boiling: if the bonds between atoms are very strong, then (a) it will (by definition) require a great deal of energy to break them, and (b) the temperature at which atoms have sufficient energy ($\approx \frac{1}{2} k_B T$ per degree of freedom) to break the bonds will be very high. These two facts lead again to correlations between enthalpy change on vaporisation and the boiling temperature.

Gibbs free energy analysis

We can examine the matter further by considering the general form of the variation of the Gibbs free energy G of a substance with temperature T. There is no simple approximation to the form of the free energy curves, but as outlined in §10.2 and Figure 10.4, the solid and liquid free energy curves both have negative slopes and negative curvatures (i.e. they curve downwards).

The general effect of a large cohesive energy U_0 is to give rise to large *difference* between the cohesive energy of the liquid and solid states at $T = 0\,\text{K}$. Recall (Figure 11.10) this difference is typically a fraction ($\approx 5\%$) of the total cohesive energy of the solid. There are two important consequences of a large difference between the cohesive energies of the solid and liquid states:

- First, the point at which the liquid and solid free energies become equal – by definition, the melting temperature – is displaced to a higher temperature.
- Second, *at the transition temperature*, the difference in slopes of the free energy curves is the *entropy* change on transformation. If this entropy (Q_M / T_M) is supplied at higher temperatures, then the heat supplied Q_M – the enthalpy change on melting – must also be greater.

Thus, a high melting temperature and a large latent heat of melting are both correlated with a large cohesive energy. Similar arguments lead to correlations between the cohesive energy, the boiling temperature and the latent heat of vaporisation (Figure 11.11)

Figure 11.10 Analysis of the correlation between melting temperature and enthalpy change on transformation (ΔQ_{LS}). U_o represents the cohesive energy of either the solid or liquid states at 0 kelvin. The figures represent the variation of the Gibbs free energy of a substance with cohesive energy which is (a) small and (b) large. The general effect of the large U_O is to give rise to a large difference between U_0(liquid) and U_0(solid). So a high T_M and a large ΔQ_{LS} are correlated with each other, because they are both correlated with a large U_0.

(a) Small cohesive energy

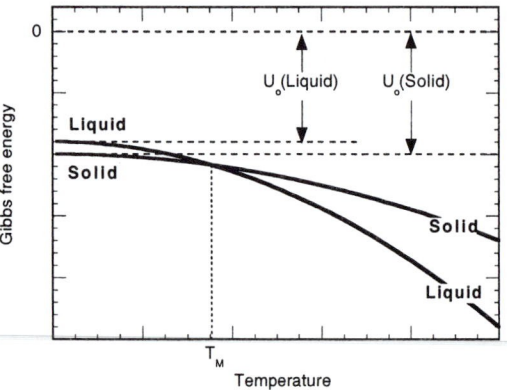

(b) Large cohesive energy

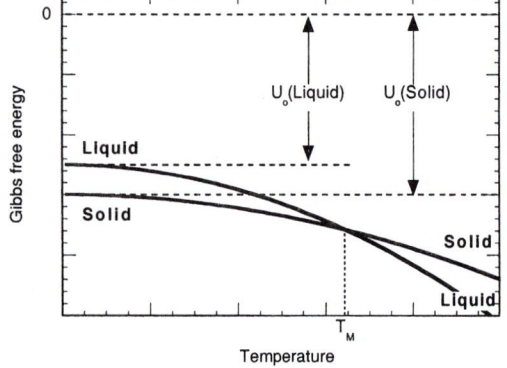

Figure 11.11 Analysis of the correlation between boiling temperature and enthalpy change on vaporisation (ΔQ_{LG}). U_o represents the cohesive energy of the liquid state at 0 kelvin. The figures represent the variation of the Gibbs free energy of a substance with cohesive energy which is (a) small and (b) large. The general effect of the large U_o is to give rise to a large difference between U_0(gas) and U_0 (liquid). So a high T_B and a large ΔQ_{LG} are correlated with each other, because they are both correlated with a large U_0.

(a) Small cohesive energy

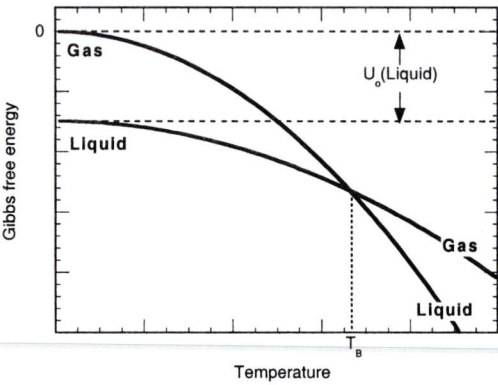

(b) Large cohesive energy

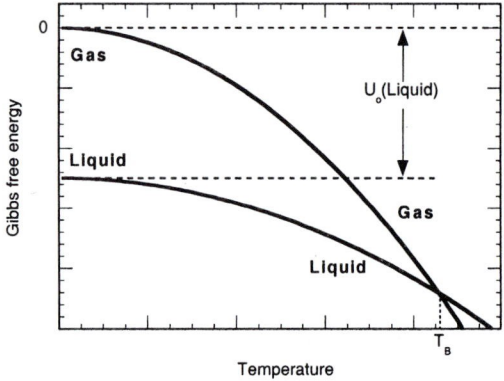

The variation of melting temperature with atomic number

The second question raised by our analysis of the solid ⇔ liquid transition is why the variation of the melting temperature of the elements with atomic number, shows patterns similar to that seen in the density of elements (Figure 7.1). The origin of this correlation, as with that between melting temperature and enthalpy of fusion, has its root in the cohesive energy of the substance. This implies, not wholly surprisingly, that substances with a high cohesive energy tend to be particularly dense.

This matter is considered further in §11.6.

Dependence of melting temperature on pressure

Finally, we come to the question of why the melting temperature of most substances increases with pressure, but decreases for substances which contract on melting. We will approach this question qualitatively, and then see how our considerations can be made more rigorous. In §9.2 we explained the origin of the expansion on melting, as being due to the inefficiency with which molecules are

packed together in the liquid state. The extra 'empty space' inside a liquid enabled us to understand why the liquid state was typically 33% easier to compress than the solid state (§9.4 on speed of sound in liquids). We assumed that the empty space within the liquid was relatively easy to 'reclaim' when pressure was applied.

If this idea is correct, then reclaiming the 'empty space' within a liquid must necessarily make the liquid more solid-like. In particular, it must reduce the ease with which a molecule may 'hop' from one 'cell' within the liquid to another. So we will attempt to understand the pressure dependence of the melting temperature by suggesting that (in general) the application of pressure at a fixed temperature makes a liquid more solid-like. If we imagine applying pressure at a temperature just above the melting temperature, then making the liquid more like a solid will tend to stabilise the solid phase. If the solid phase is stabilised at a temperature at which the liquid phase used to be stable, then we have (by definition) raised the melting temperature.

This is an idea we may test fairly straightforwardly: if it is more difficult for a molecule to 'hop' from 'cell' to 'cell', then a liquid should become more viscous as pressure is applied. Data on the change in viscosity of a liquid under pressure are shown in Figure 11.12. They indicate that for normal liquids, the viscosity increases under applied pressure as expected. However, for water – one of the few liquids which is more dense than its corresponding solid – the reverse process can happen. For water at a temperature just above its melting temperature, pressure first *decreases* the viscosity. Thus pressure makes a normal liquids more viscous (more solid-like), but makes water just above 0 °C less viscous (more liquid-like).

We understood the normal liquid by assuming that there is 'free space' in the liquid which is removed by pressure. For water – and other substances which contract on melting – it is the solid state which has the 'free space' due to the open hydrogen-bonded crystal structure. We can understand the pressure data by supposing that there is already too much 'free space' in the liquid state, and pres-

364

Figure 11.12 Change in viscosity of (a) various liquids and (b) water under applied pressure. Notice the very large pressures involved in these measurements: 100MPa is approximately 1000 times atmospheric pressure.

In (a) the data are taken at 30°C and show the change in viscosity of each substance relative to the viscosity of the same substance at zero pressure. In (b) the data are taken at various temperatures and show the change in viscosity of water relative to the viscosity at the same temperature and zero pressure. Notice that for temperatures below ≈ 30 °C the effect of pressure is first to cause a *decrease* in viscosity in contrast with the behaviours of 'normal' liquids shown in (a).

(a)

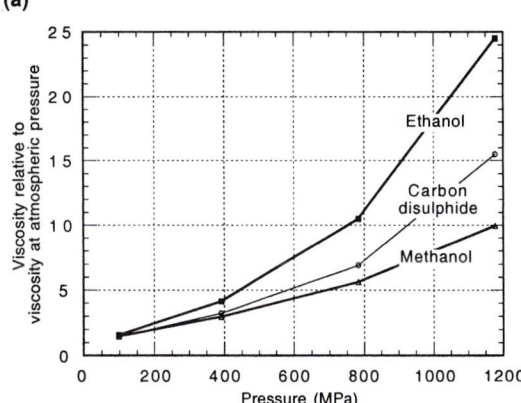

(b)

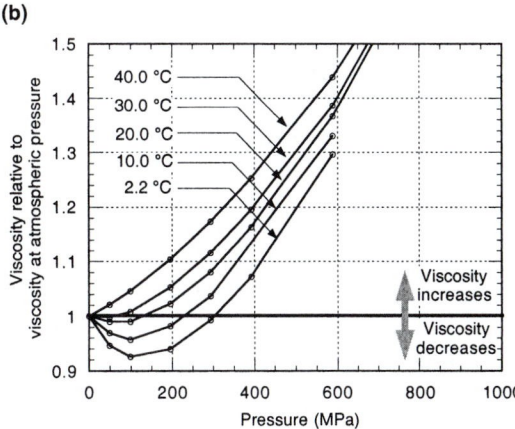

sure has the effect of increasing the forces which allow molecules to move past one another.

Thus pressure makes most liquids more the solid-like, but makes liquids which contract on melting more liquid-like. Thus it is not surprising that the effect of pressure is to raise the melting temperature, but for liquids which contract on melting the effect is to lower the melting temperature.

11.4 The liquid ⇔ gas transition: boiling and condensing

11.4.1 Introduction

Although the *boiling temperature* of a pure liquid substance is a well-defined temperature, *the process of transformation from liquid to gas occurs at all temperatures.* At any temperature, a liquid attempts to sustain above its surface a characteristic pressure of its vapour: the *vapour pressure*. We developed a theory for the equilibrium vapour pressure above a liquid based on the cell model of liquid in §9.8. We also developed a prediction based on more general grounds (the *Clausius-Clapeyron* equation) in §10.43. In both analyses, we predicted that (in agreement with experiment) the vapour pressure should increase exponentially with increasing temperature.

Since the liquid and gas phases of a substance co-exist at all temperatures at which the liquid is stable, a sensible choice is made as to the pressure of vapour which defines the transition to the gaseous phase. We define the transition temperature as the temperature at which the vapour pressure of liquid reaches standard atmospheric pressure $(1.0135 \times 10^5 \text{ Pa})$. This choice may be sensible, but it is important to realise that it is also arbitrary: another defining pressure could have been chosen. If for example we had evolved on a planet with a much lower atmospheric pressure, our table of the boiling temperatures of substances would all be considerably lower. (It is interesting to note that this is not the case for a solid⇔liquid phase change. This is because the melting curve is much steeper than the vaporisation curve (§10.7) and so the melting temperatures of substances do not depend strongly on atmospheric pressure.)

The phenomenon of 'boiling' in which bubbles form at the transition temperature from liquid to vapour is one with which we are familiar from observations of water. However, bubble formation (Figure 11.13) at the liquid⇒vapour transition is not really a fundamental feature of the transition. In liquid helium, normal boiling occurs at 4.2 K, but on cooling below 2.17 K, the bubbling associated with boiling ceases. However, despite this, evaporation of molecules from the liquid surface

Figure 11.13 What happens when a liquid boils? Temperature fluctuations within the liquid cause small bubbles to form. Initially these are only a few atomic diameters in size. Whether the bubble grows or shrinks depends on the balance between the pressure of the liquid around the bubble, and the vapour pressure within the bubble. If the temperature is such that the vapour pressure exceeds the external pressure then bubbles will form in the liquid and grow. Because of the density difference between the gas and the liquid, the bubbles rise within the liquid and 'burst' when they reach the surface. Changes in the external pressure therefore cause changes in the boiling temperature of the liquid.

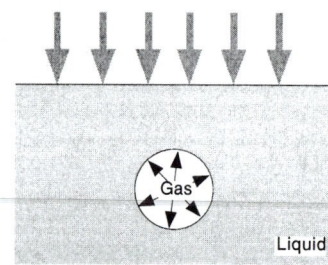

Figure 11.14 The boiling temperatures of the elements plotted as function of atomic number.

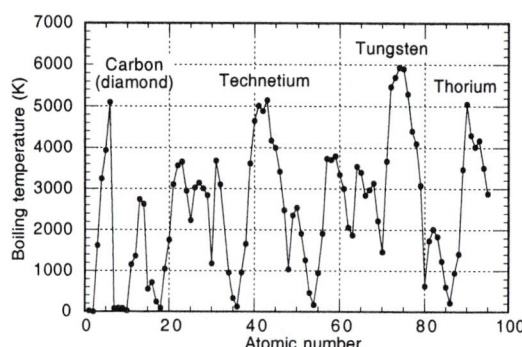

Figure 11.15 The enthalpy change on vaporisation of the elements plotted as function of atomic number.

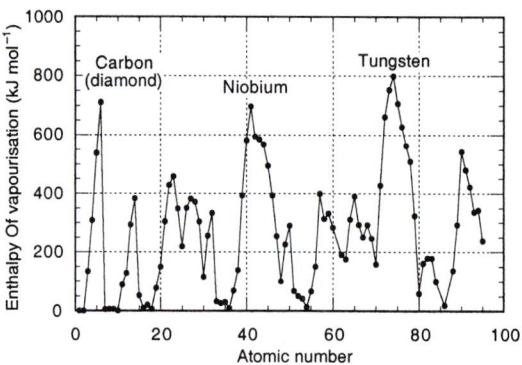

continues uninterrupted. What has happened is that at this temperature helium undergoes a transition to a new liquid structure with a thermal conductivity hundreds of times greater than in its 'normal' state. The excellent thermal conduction reduces the magnitude of thermal gradients and fluctuations within the liquid below the level sufficient to cause bubble formation. Helium is an unusual liquid (to be sure!), but it highlights an important insight about 'boiling'. The phenomenon is related to the magnitude of temperature gradients and fluctuations within the liquid, rather than being intrinsic to the liquid$\Rightarrow$vapour transition *per se*.

11.4.2 Data on the liquid$\Rightarrow$gas transition

The boiling temperatures of the elements and other substances are recorded in Tables 11.1 and 11.2 and graphed as a function of atomic number in Figures 11.14 and 11.15. These figures show that there are correlations between the boiling temperatures and enthalpy changes on vaporisation of the elements.

The main questions raised by our preliminary examination of the experimental data on the liquid to gas transition are:

- Why do elements with a high boiling temperature tend to have a high enthalpy of vaporisation?
- Why does the variation of the boiling temperature of the elements with atomic number show a pattern similar to that seen in the density of elements?
- Why does the vapour pressure of a substance increase strongly with temperature?

In fact we have already answered all three of these questions. The first two questions have already been addressed in §11.3.4 where they are considered along with similar questions from the solid $\Leftrightarrow$ liquid transition. The final question was addressed in §9.8, where we developed a theory of the vapour pressure of a liquid. However we are now in a position to extend the cell model theory so that one of its key parameters can be compared directly with experiment.

11.4.3 Understanding the value of the latent heat: the cell model re-visited

In §8.4 we saw that ΔE_e was the cell model parameter that characterised the energy required to remove an individual molecule from the liquid and move it into the vapour. In §9.10 we looked at values of ΔE_e deduced from the slopes of vapour pressure versus temperature graphs and compared them with other cell model parameters. We saw that, broadly speaking, we could understand the *relative* values of ΔE_e, ΔE_h, and ΔE_s. Now however we are in a position to relate the absolute value of ΔE_e to the latent heat of the liquid.

The theory is shockingly simple. If ΔE_e represents the energy required to remove a single molecule of a substance from the liquid, then $N_A \Delta E_e$ represents the energy required to remove N_A molecules of a substance from the liquid. This is nothing more than the latent heat of vaporisation of a mole of the liquid. In other words ΔE_e is effectively the 'latent heat per molecule'. We thus expect to find:

$$L = N_A \Delta E_e \qquad (11.8)$$

Based on Equation 11.8, we can predict a value for the latent heat of vaporisation for any liquid for which have a value of ΔE_e. The data for ΔE_e from Table 9.12 is reanalysed in Table 11.3 and compared with the experimental value of the latent heat from Table 11.1. We see to within about 10%, we can predict the latent heat of vaporisation

Table 11.3 Comparison of $N_A \Delta E_e$ with the experimental value of the latent heat of vaporisation L. The final column shows the ratio of these two quantities $N_A \Delta E_e/L$. The values of ΔE_e are drawn from Table 9.12.

Substance	ΔE_e(J) $\times 10^{-21}$	$N_A \Delta E_e$ (kJ mol^{-1})	L (kJ mol^{-1})	$N_A \Delta E_e/L$
Copper	486	292.7	300.5	0.97
Silver	403	242.7	255.06	0.95
Gold	516	310.7	324.43	0.96
Aluminium	447	269.2	290.8	0.92
Tin	436	262.6	290.37	0.90
Helium	0.13	0.078	0.08	0.98
Neon	3.23	1.95	1.77	1.10
Argon	10.8	6.50	6.52	0.99
Krypton	17.2	10.36	9.03	1.15
Xenon	24.4	14.69	12.64	1.16

of substances with greatly different boiling temperatures. This prediction is deduced from the temperature-dependence of the vapour pressure. This level of agreement gives us confidence that the cell model we developed in Chapter 9 is applicable to real liquids, and that ΔE_e has been realistically estimated.

11.5 The critical point

11.5.1 Introduction

The fact that the liquid and gaseous phases of a substance co-exist over a wide range of temperatures is a clue to the close relationship between the phases. Evidence for this is strengthened by the fact, above a certain temperature, known as the *critical temperature* T_C, there is no distinct transition from liquid to gas. Since there is no distinct transition, then we do not know whether to describe the state of the substance as a liquid or a gas. The correct designation is to describe a substance above its critical temperature as being a *supercritical fluid*. This is a state can be reached smoothly without a phase transition from *either* the liquid *or* the gas phase.

A *critical pressure* and *critical volume* can also be defined as the pressure and volume at which the densities of the *co-existing* gas and liquid phases are equal.

11.5.2 Further data

The critical parameters of various substances discussed are listed in Table 11.5.

Figure 11.17 represents an attempt to find structure in the critical parameter data from Table 11.5.

The data are plotted on a logarithmic scale and so a good deal of the variation amongst the data is not clearly shown. However, it is clear that, apart from the smallest molecular masses, the critical parameters are roughly independent of molecular mass. We can notice that there are, not surprisingly, significant correlations between the critical temperature pressure and volume for a particular substance.

Roughly speaking we find ballpark values of critical parameters in Table 11.5 are:

$$T_C \approx 500 \text{ K} \approx 200 \text{ °C}$$

$$P_C \approx 5 \text{ MPa} \approx 50 \text{ atmospheres}$$

$$V_C \approx 200 \times 10^{-6} \text{ m}^3 \text{ mol}^{-1} \approx \text{ a sphere about 7 cm in diameter per mole}$$

Table 11.5 also indicates that the density of most substances at the critical point is close to one-third their density at normal pressures and temperatures. Such figures indicate that in the critical condition there is little 'free space' around each molecule as compared to a gas. However, the density ratio indicates that at the critical point roughly two-thirds of the volume of the substance is free space (at least as compared with the liquid state).

Figure 11.16 The approach to the critical point. The five pictures illustrate the effect of application of heat energy to a substance in the liquid state in a closed container. As the temperature rises the density of the vapour increases exponentially with temperature. When the density of the vapour pressure approaches that of the liquid state, a reduction in volume may take the system to a situation where the density of the vapour and the liquid are equal – a situation known as the critical point.

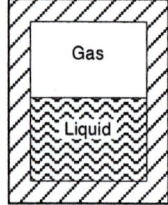 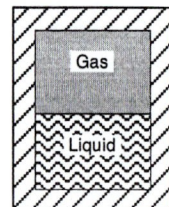 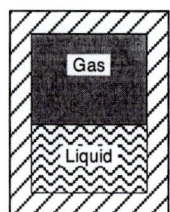 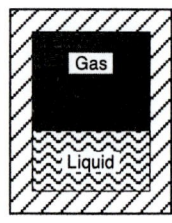 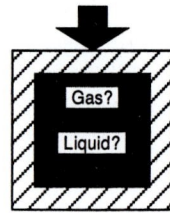

Table 11.4 The critical parameters of various substances discussed in Chapter 6 and Chapter 8. P_C, V_C and T_C are the critical pressure, molar volume and temperature. Z_C is the *compression factor* which is discussed in §11.5.3. The next column gives the density at the critical point, calculated from the molecular mass and V_C. This may be compared with the density of the substance in the liquid state well away from T_C. For the inorganic substances where the liquid density data is not available, the solid density has been used instead The final column gives the ratio of the density at the critical point to that at a temperature well below the critical point.

Substance	P_C (MPa)	V_C ($\times 10^{-6}$ m³ mol⁻¹)	T_C (K)	$Z_C=$ $P_C V_C/R T_C$	Critical Density (kg m⁻³)	Liquid Density (kgm⁻³)	Density Ratio
Methanol, CH_3OH	8.09	118	512.6	0.224	271	791	0.343
Ethanol, C_2H_5OH	6.14	167	513.9	0.240	275	789	0.349
Propan-1-ol , C_3H_7OH	5.17	219	536.8	0.254	274	804	0.340
Acetic acid, $C_2H_4O_2$	5.79	171	594.5	0.200	351	1049	0.334
Acetone, C_3H_6O	4.7	213	508.1	0.237	272	787	0.346
Aniline, C_6H_7N	5.3	274	698.9	0.250	339	1026	0.330
Benzene, C_6H_6	4.9	254	562.2	0.266	307	879	0.349
Bromoethane, C_2H_5Br	6.23	215	503.8	0.320	507	1456	0.348
Chloroform, $CHCl_3$	5.5	240	536.4	0.296	500	1498	0.333
Cyclohexane, C_6H_{10}	4.02	308	553.4	0.269	266	941.6	0.282
Ethyl acetate, $C_4H_8O_2$	3.83	286	523.2	0.252	287	900.6	0.319
Toluene, C_7H_8	4.11	320	591.8	0.267	288	868.8	0.331
Carbon monoxide, CO	3.50	93.1	133	0.295	300.75	—	—
Carbon dioxide, CO_2	7.38	94.0	304.2	0.274	468.09	—	—
Carbon disulphide, CS_2	7.9	173	552	0.298	439.31	1263	0.348
Carbon tetrachloride, CCl_4	4.56	276	556.4	0.272	550.72	1604	0.343
Hydrogen, H_2	1.294	65.5	32.99	0.309	30.534	89	0.343
Nitrogen, N_2	3.39	90.1	126.2	0.291	310.77	1035	0.300
Oxygen, O_2	5.08	78	154.8	0.308	410.26	1460	0.281
Chlorine, Cl_2	7.71	124	417	0.276	572.58	2030	0.282
Bromine, Br_2	10.3	135	584	0.287	1185.2	3120	0.380
Helium, He	0.229	58	5.2	0.307	68.966	120	0.575
Neon, Ne	2.73	41.7	44.4	0.309	479.62	1442	0.333
Argon, Ar	4.86	75.2	150.7	0.292	531.91	1656	0.321
Krypton, Kr	5.50	92.3	209.4	0.292	910.08	3000	0.303
Xenon, Xe	5.88	119	289.7	0.291	1100.8	3560	0.309
Radon, Rn	6.3	—	377		—	4400	
Water, H_2O	22.12	59.1	647.3	0.243	304.57	1000	0.305
Heavy water, D_2O	21.88	54.9	644.2	0.224	364.30	1100	0.331

Figure 11.17 The critical parameters (Table 11.5) of various substances discussed in Chapter 6 and Chapter 8 plotted as a function of their relative molecular mass. Note that the vertical axis is logarithmic, which compresses much of the actual variation amongst the data.

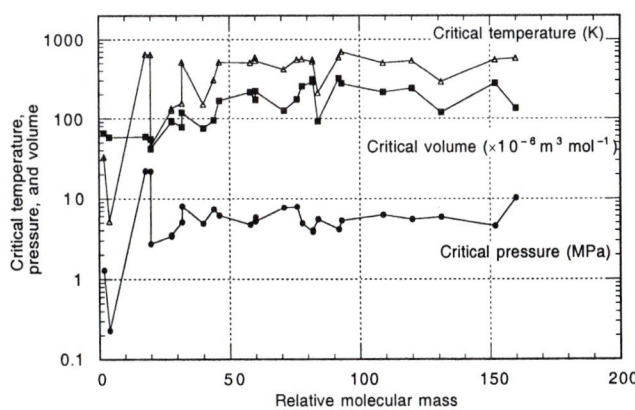

The main questions raised by our preliminary examination of the experimental data on the critical temperature of substances are:

- Why do the critical temperatures, volumes and pressures have broadly similar values for substances with a wide range of molecular masses?

- Why is the density at the critical point roughly one-third of the density at normal pressure and temperature?

11.5.3 Understanding the data on the critical temperature

To understand what is happening as a substance approaches its critical condition we may chart the development of the *radial density function* (§8.2.2). This is illustrated qualitatively in Figure 11.18, which is itself adapted from Figure 8.6. Figure 11.18 illustrates the continuous evolution of the liquid state:

- Just above the melting temperature, a great deal of the short-range order of the solid still remains.

- As the temperature is raised, the density of the liquid state falls continuously (Figures 9.3 and 9.4) the short-range order is systematically weakened.

- At the critical condition, the overall density of the liquid state is around 34% of its 'normal' value, and little of the short-range order remains.

We have already seen evidence of this evolution of the liquid state in Figure 9.21, where we looked at data on the surface tension of liquids. There we saw that the surface tension of all liquids declines roughly linearly with temperature. In Figure 11.19 we re-examine the data on water shown in Figure 9.18. We see clearly that the data, when extrapolated, indicate that water substance will have zero surface tension (i.e. be indistinguishable from a dense gas) at a temperature just above the critical temperature. Given the crude extrapolation, and the unusual properties of water, we see that even between 0 °C and 100 °C, the structure of water is already evolving in a way destined for 'completion' at T_C.

Returning to direct consideration of the questions

Example 11.4

Work out the volume occupied per molecule when ethanol is in its critical state.

Considering ethanol in Table 11.4 we see that it has a critical volume of $167 \times 10^{-6} \text{ m}^3 \text{ mol}^{-1}$. i.e. this volume contains the Avogadro number of molecules. Thus the volume per molecule in the critical state is:

$$\text{Volume per molecule} = \frac{167 \times 10^{-6}}{6.02 \times 10^{23}}$$
$$= 2.77 \times 10^{-28} \text{ m}^3$$

If we imagine each molecule confined to a cube of volume $a \times a \times a$ then the cube would have side:

$$a = \sqrt[3]{2.77 \times 10^{-28}}$$
$$= 6.5 \times 10^{-10} \text{ m}$$

This volume would contain one ethanol molecule C_2H_5OH, i.e. two carbon atoms, six hydrogen atoms and one oxygen atom. Considering that a typical atom has a diameter of a *few* $\times 10^{-10}$ m and that the bonds between atoms are separated by similar amount, this leaves little free space in between molecules.

---

raised in the previous section, we see that the key linking feature of the critical point data is that the density at the critical point is around one-third of the normal liquid density. Thus we can understand

Figure 11.18 Qualitative indication of the radial density function of a solid, a normal liquid and a liquid in the critical condition. In the solid state the peaks correspond to nearest neighbours, next-nearest neighbours etc. In the liquid state, the peaks are maintained but they are smoothed by the increased disorder of the liquid state. In the critical state the peaks are weaker still, and the overall density is much reduced in comparison with either liquid or solid states.

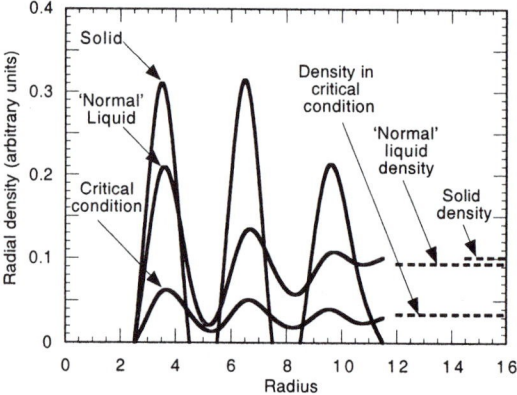

the relative uniformity of critical molar volumes merely by noting that the *normal* liquid densities of the substances in Table 11.4 only vary by a factor ≈ 3, which is considerably compressed on the logarithmic scale of Figure 11.17.

The virial approach to the critical condition

Let us consider approaching the critical temperature and pressure in two stages, as indicated on Figure 11.20. We start with a gas at around STP and then in stage 1 we heat the gas to the critical temperature, T_C. In stage 2 we then compress it until we arrive at the critical pressure P_C.

At around STP we know that the gas is 'well described' by the ideal gas equation, and in general, this will also be the case when the gas is heated to T_C. Let me say more precisely what I mean by 'well described'. In §4.4, we saw that the *compression factor Z* was defined by:

$$Z = \frac{PV_m}{RT} \qquad (4.50^* \text{ and } 11.9)$$

where V_m is the molar volume. We noted that the deviations from ideal gas behaviour could be described by a so-called *virial* expansion:

$$Z = 1 + \frac{B(T)}{V_m} + \frac{C(T)}{V_m^2} + ... (4.50^* \text{ and } 11.10)$$

Recall that in §4.4, I stated that the second virial coefficient $B(T)$ depended on strength of interactions between *pairs* of molecules, while the third virial coefficient $C(T)$ depended on strength of interactions between *clusters of three* molecules. Importantly, the virial coefficients depend *only* on temperature. The second and third virial terms amount to only a fraction of a per cent for gases at modest pressures and temperatures. So by 'well described', I mean that the compression factor for the substance is close to unity.

Now for a gas at around atmospheric pressure and the critical temperature, the terms $B(T)/V_m$ and $C(T)/V_m^2$ are small. In Stage 1 of our approach to the critical point, we increase the temperature and constant pressure. This can result in increases or decreases of the virial coefficients, but in general

370

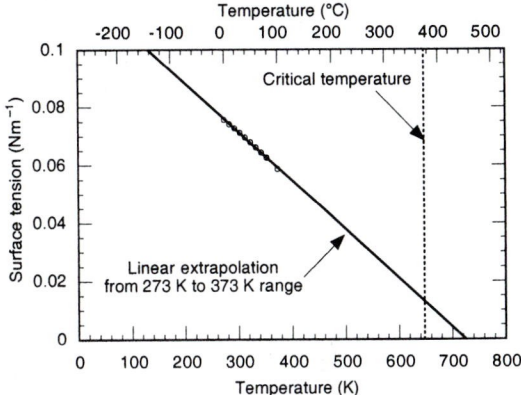

Figure 11.19 Data on the surface tension of water from Figure 9.21 re-plotted on a large scale. The linear extrapolation is based on a linear least squares fit to the data between 0 °C and 100 °C. The data imply that the surface tension will reach zero at a temperature just greater than the actual critical temperature. (T_C = 647 K)

the terms in the virial series remain small. However, as we increase the pressure in Stage 2, the terms in the virial expansion become larger. This is because, although the virial coefficients do not depend on pressure, the molar volume (which occurs in the denominator of all the terms) is decreased. Now the critical molar volume is typically of the order of $V_C \approx 200 \times 10^{-6}$ m^3 mol^{-1}

Figure 11.20 The virial approach to critical condition. Starting with a low-pressure gas we can approach the critical condition in two stages. In Stage 1, the gas is heated at constant pressure causing it to expand considerably. In Stage 2 the gas is compressed at constant temperature. In this stage the volume is reduced, increasing the importance of molecular interactions.

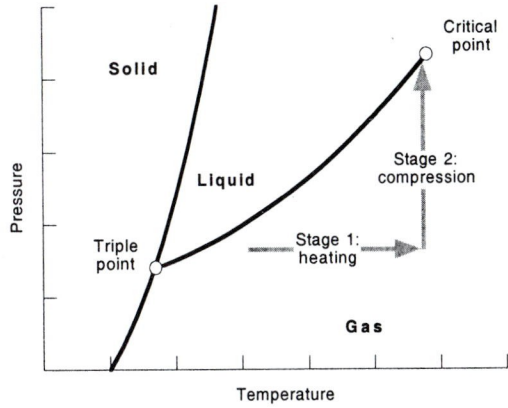

compared with 22.4 litres ($V_C \approx 22400 \times 10^{-6}$ $m^3\,mol^{-1}$) at STP. So, we see that at the critical point, the second term in the virial expansion is around 100 times larger than at STP, the third term is around $100^2 = 10^4$ larger, and subsequent terms larger still. Physically we can see the growth of the higher-order terms results from the increasing significance of ever larger clusters of molecules as the pressure approaches the critical value. As Table 11.5 makes clear, the compression factor *at* the critical point for many substances has a value of $Z_C = P_C V_C / RT_C$ in the range 0.2 to 0.3. This may be compared with a value very close to unity in the gas phase, well away from the critical point.

The question remains of *why* the density at the critical is point is roughly one-third the normal liquid density. The value of one-third is just what it turns out to be! We can see that the value does indeed correspond to an extremely dense gas as one would expect. The question of why the value – whatever might have turned out to be – is 'universal', is a question which is considered in the following section (§11.6) on laws of 'corresponding states'.

11.6 Scaling: laws of corresponding states

11.6.1 Introduction

Consider the following:

- In §11.3, we noted that substances with high boiling temperatures also tend to have high melting temperatures.

- In §11.3.3, Figure 11.9, we noted that the ratio of the enthalpy of fusion of an element to its melting temperature has a relatively constant value of around 0.01 J K^{-1} mol^{-1}. Also we saw that the ratio of the enthalpy of vaporisation of an element to its boiling temperature has a relatively constant value of around 0.1 J K^{-1} mol^{-1}.

- In §11.3.3.1 we noted that the Lindemann fraction for the elements had a common value of around $\frac{1}{20}$.

- In §11.5.2, Table 11.4 we noted that the densities of substances at their critical point were all roughly one-third of their value in the liquid phase.

- In §11.4.2 Equation 11.8 we noted that the value of $P_C V_C / RT_C$ has value of around 0.25 for a wide range of substances.

- In §9.9 we concluded that the *cell model* could plausibly describe the dynamic properties of a wide variety of liquids with just four 'free parameters'.

The observations above, and many others that you can find throughout the book, raise the hope that it

might be possible to find a model of an 'ideal substance' analogous to our model of an 'ideal gas'. In fact, the properties of substances, particularly solids are too diverse to make this a worthwhile endeavour.

However, many of the correlations between substances are particularly striking: Example 11.5 predicts the critical temperature of water based only on its boiling temperature, and the properties of liquid krypton! It is clear that there must be something physically significant underlying the observed universality. Such correlations offer the tantalising possibility that if we could understand them, then surely we must be on the verge of understanding at least 'something about everything'. In practice, what we arrive at are a great many 'rules of thumb', each applicable in most cases but with several exceptions. These rules tell us something approximately true about several substances, but nothing definite about any particular substance.

For instance, in Example 11.5 we also consider potassium and water. We notice that for these substances the melting temperature is poorly predicted from the boiling temperature. In the following sections we examine the data to see to what extent we may trust a simple scaling approach to all substances.

11.6.2 Further data on melting, boiling, and critical temperatures

In Figure 11.21 we compare the critical temperature T_C and melting temperature T_M with the boiling temperatures of various substances. As expected from Example 11.5, the figure shows that the critical temperature is strongly correlated with the boiling temperature of the liquid, and is typically a factor of roughly 1.6 higher. Recall from Example 11.5 that T_C for argon was a factor 1.73 higher than T_B.

So the main question raised by this preliminary examination of the experimental data on the melting, boiling, and critical temperatures of substances is simply:

- What is the origin of the common relationship between T_M, T_B and T_C observed in a variety of substances?

11.6.3 Understanding the origin of corresponding states

At high temperatures all substances enter the gaseous phase and, as we have seen, obey the perfect gas equation reasonably well, at least at low density. The reason for this is that the approximations underlying the derivation of $PV = zRT$ are well satisfied by real gases.

As a substance is cooled in the gas phase its density increase and eventually it reaches the point at which further cooling will cause it to enter one of the condensed states. The temperature and density at which this occurs depends on the strength of interaction between the molecules of the gas.

Recall that all molecules are naturally 'sticky': when molecules collide they stick together unless the kinetic energy of the molecules is high enough to prevent it. As we saw in §4.3, the average speed of the Maxwell distribution of molecular speeds falls as the temperature falls. Eventually, for any substance the average kinetic energy of the molecules is such that, on collision, the molecules stick together.

The temperature at which this happens will be related to the stickiness (binding energy) of the molecules. Thus the boiling temperature is related

Example 11.5

The table below shows the critical, boiling and melting temperatures for krypton.

T_C(K)	T_B(K)	T_M(K)
209.4	120.85	116.6

Does knowing these figures for krypton allow us to predict the equivalent quantities for the other solids knowing only their boiling temperature?

First let us normalise the data to the boiling temperature of the substance. The above table now looks like:

	T_C	T_B	T_M
Krypton	1.73	1.00	0.965

If the simplest form of scaling theory is correct then given the boiling temperature of other substances we should find that their melting temperature is around 96% of T_B and their critical temperature is around 73% higher than T_B. Let us see if it works:

	T_C(K)	T_B(K)	T_M(K)
Expectation for argon	151.0	87.3	84.2
Data for argon	150.7	87.3	83.8
Expectation for neon	46.9	27.1	26.1
Data for neon	44.4	27.1	24.6

The agreement for argon is rather good, while that for neon is not so good. But before we accept the scaling idea wholesale let us try it on a couple of other rather different substances.

	T_C(K)	T_B(K)	T_M(K)
Expectation for water	645.6	373.2	360.1
Data for water	647.3	373.2	273.2
Expectation for potassium	–	1047	1010
Data for potassium	–	1047	337

We see that the results are rather more mixed. The theory predicts the critical temperature of water astonishingly well, but predicts the melting temperature very poorly. Similarly, the melting temperature of potassium is very poorly predicted.

directly to the binding energy of molecules – and hence to the *cohesive energy* of the substance. It is this phenomenon which links the characteristic temperatures for a substance, to the binding energy per molecule. Ignoring factors of the order of 'a few', we write:

$$u_o \approx k_B T_B \qquad (11.11)$$

Figure 11.21 The critical temperature (Table 11.4) and melting temperature (Table 11.1) plotted as function of boiling temperature for various liquids. The boiling temperature line is a line of slope = 1. The vertical separation between the melting point datum and the boiling temperature line is an indication of the temperature range over which the substance exists as a liquid. The cluster of substances with boiling temperatures between 300 K and 400K are all organic substances.

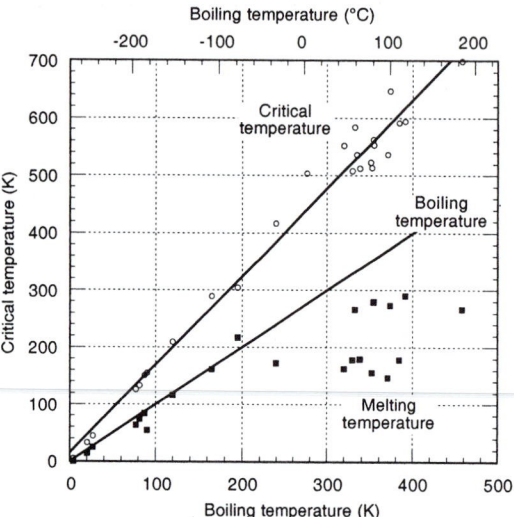

Figure 11.22 The melting temperature of the elemental metals plotted as a function of their boiling temperature. The vertical separation between the melting point datum and the boiling temperature line is an indication of the temperature range over which the substance exists as a liquid. Roughly, the melting temperatures are around two-thirds the boiling temperature, but there is a good deal of fluctuation around this figure. Some metals appear to have an anomalously large range of existence in the liquid phase. Gallium for example melts at only 302.9 K, but does not boil until 3676 K, a factor of 10 difference.

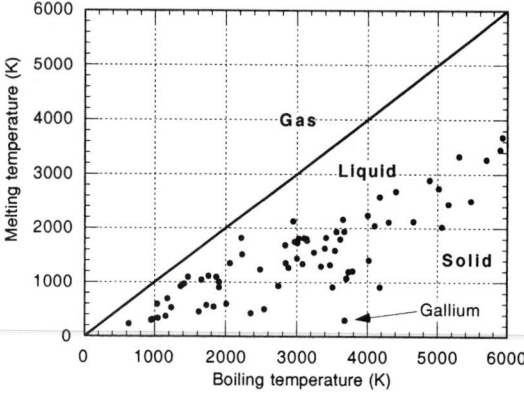

or using cohesive energies per mole:

$$U_o \approx xN_A k_B T_B$$
$$\approx xRT_B \tag{11.12}$$

where x is the number of bonds (roughly speaking, the number of nearest neighbours) with which a molecule interacts in the condensed state. Of course there are many other factors to be taken into account, for example, the shape of complex molecules. However for reasons of simplicity we stick with our Equation 11.12. Table 11.5 contains calculated data for the cohesive energies of the elements. These are the results both of complex calculations similar to those we embarked upon in Chapter 6, and analysis of experimental results. It is worthwhile recalling that this energy is *electrostatic in origin* (as mediated by the laws of quantum mechanics) and arises from the bonding mechanisms outlined in Chapter 6.

Cohesive energy and boiling temperature

Given the value of U_o, the boiling temperature

Figure 11.23 The boiling temperatures of the elements plotted as function of their cohesive energy (Table 11.5). It is clear that the data show a broad trend – with exceptions – indicating that substances with higher cohesive energies tend to have higher boiling temperatures. The solid line in the figure is the predicted melting temperature according to $T_B = (U_o/xR)$ with $x = 10$.

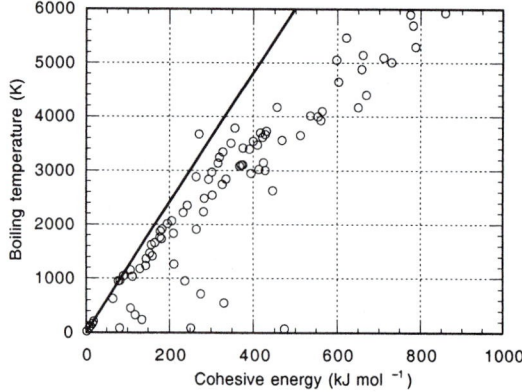

may be predicted according to Equation 11.20. The function $T_B \approx U_o / xR$ is graphed in Figure 11.27, along with the actual boiling temperature. We have assumed ten nearest neighbours as a

Table 11.5 The cohesive energies U_o of the elements in units of kJ mol^{-1}. U_o is the energy required to separate the atoms of a solid at $T = 0$ K into isolated neutral atoms.

Z	Element	U_o (kJ mol^{-1})	Z	Element	U_o (kJ mol^{-1})	Z	Element	U_o (kJ mol^{-1})
1	Hydrogen	—	32	Germanium	372	63	Europium	179
2	Helium	—	33	Arsenic	285.3	64	Gadolinium	400
3	Lithium	158	34	Selenium	237	65	Terbium	391
4	Beryllium	320	35	Bromine	118	66	Dysprosium	294
5	Boron	561	36	Krypton	11.2	67	Holmium	302
6	Carbon	711	37	Rubidium	82.2	68	Erbium	317
7	Nitrogen	474	38	Strontium	166	69	Thulium	233
8	Oxygen	251	39	Yttrium	422	70	Ytterbium	154
9	Fluorine	81	40	Zirconium	603	71	Lutetium	428
10	Neon	1.92	41	Niobium	730	72	Hafnium	621
11	Sodium	107	42	Molybdenum	658	73	Tantalum	782
12	Magnesium	145	43	Technetium	661	74	Tungsten	859
13	Aluminium	327	44	Ruthenium	650	75	Rhenium	775
14	Silicon	446	45	Rhodium	554	76	Osmium	788
15	Phosphorous	331	46	Palladium	376	77	Iridium	670
16	Sulphur	275	47	Silver	284	78	Platinum	564
17	Chlorine	135	48	Cadmium	112	79	Gold	368
18	Argon	7.74	49	Indium	243	80	Mercury	65
19	Potassium	90.1	50	Tin	303	81	Thallium	182
20	Calcium	178	51	Antimony	265	82	Lead	196
21	Scandium	376	52	Tellurium	211	83	Bismuth	210
22	Titanium	468	53	Iodine	107	84	Polonium	144
23	Vanadium	512	54	Xenon	15.9	85	Astatine	—
24	Chromium	395	55	Caesium	77.6	86	Radon	18.5
25	Manganese	282	56	Barium	183	87	Francium	—
26	Iron	413	57	Lanthanum	431	88	Radium	160
27	Cobalt	424	58	Cerium	417	89	Actinium	410
28	Nickel	428	59	Praseodymium	357	90	Thorium	598
29	Copper	336	60	Neodymium	328	91	Protactinium	—
30	Zinc	130	61	Promethium	—	92	Uranium	536
31	Gallium	271	62	Samarium	206			

rough estimate of the number of interacting pairs of molecules and we see that the prediction is of the correct order of magnitude and broadly captures the trend of the data

Having seen that condensation/boiling temperature is related to the cohesive energy, it is fairly straightforward to conceive how the melting temperature can be related to the boiling temperature using extensions of the arguments leading to the concept of the Lindemann fraction. Similarly the link with the Debye temperature follows plausibly. Further, as outlined in §11.3.4, the cohesive energy of a substance is linked directly to the enthalpy changes on fusion and vaporisation. If we

plot the calculated cohesive energy as a function of atomic number (Figure 11.24) we see the periodic variation with temperature that we have observed in many properties of the elements. It is the cohesive energy – modified differently in each case – which underlies all of the periodic variations of elemental properties that we have observed in:

- the density: Figure 7.1
- the Debye temperature: Figure 11.6
- the melting temperature: Figure 11.3
- the boiling temperature: Figure 11.14
- the enthalpy change on fusion: Figure 11.4
- the enthalpy change on vaporisation: Figure 11.15

374

Figure 11.24 The cohesive energy of the elements (Table 11.5) plotted as a function of atomic number. It is clear that the data show periodic increases and decreases which reflect the effect of the filling of electron shells and the type of bonding possible. It is this graph which is at the heart of the periodic variations observed amongst elemental density; melting, boiling and Debye temperatures; and the enthalpies of fusion and vaporisation.

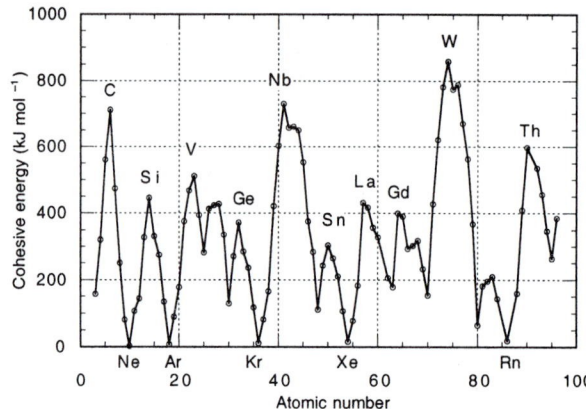

Thus, despite the bewildering variety of properties displayed by matter, on a course scale we can conceive as matter in a very simplistic way. We imagine each molecule to be just a 'blob' of mass m interacting with a cohesive energy somewhere in the range 0.1 eV per atom to 10 eV per atom. The universal behaviour arises because, roughly speaking, *all* matter can be described in this rather general way.

11.7 The solid ⇔ gas transition: sublimation

11.7.1 Introduction

The sections above have described a familiar story: solids melt into liquids, which evaporate to become gases. However, some substances transform straight from the solid state to the gaseous state in a process known as *sublimation*. The unfamiliarity of this transformation deserves some comment.

The vapour pressure above a solid

The transformation from solid to gas – like the transformation to liquid to gas – is a continuous process: solid and gas co-exist at all temperatures. However, the *vapour* pressure of many solids, such as iron, is exceedingly small at around room temperature. Figure 9.24 shows the vapour pressure of several metals and in Exercise 11.24 you can see just how small the vapour pressure is above a solid. However, even these substances are regularly evaporated, but they must first be heated to high temperatures often, but not always, melting in the process. This is the technique by which thin aluminium coatings are placed on, for example, compact discs.

However, for many solids the vapour pressure *is* appreciable even at around room temperature. The vapour pressure of water substance in both its liquid and solid phases is shown in Figures 11.25.

Notice that when water freezes, the vapour pressure does not suddenly fall to zero, but maintains a continuous curve. The figure shows the vapour pressure above the solid, and above supercooled liquid. It is clear from Table 11.6 and Figure 11.25, that the vapour pressure above the surface of liquid water is similar to (but slightly higher than) the vapour pressure above solid ice at the same temperature.

Similar behaviour is also seen in Figure 9.23 showing the vapour pressure above the solid noble 'gases': neon, argon, krypton, and xenon. Over most of the temperature range shown the substances (except helium) are solid – their liquid phase exists for only a few kelvin below their boiling temperature. However there is no striking discontinuity between the vapour pressure above their solid and liquid phases.

375

Sublimation

We may define a *sublimation temperature* for a solid – by analogy with the definition of the boiling temperature – as the temperature at which the vapour pressure above a solid reaches atmospheric pressure. By this definition, only two elements, carbon and arsenic, sublime.

We have noted previously that the application of pressure tends to increase the temperature of liquid $\Rightarrow$ gas transition and the same is true of the solid $\Rightarrow$ gas transition. Thus the temperature of the complete transition to the gaseous state can be moved to a higher temperature by the application of pressure. We also noted in §11.2 that the temperature of a solid $\Rightarrow$ liquid transition is also in general increased by application of pressure.

Consider a liquid at atmospheric pressure just above its melting temperature: application of pressure will raise the melting temperature and return the substance to the solid state. Similarly, application of pressure to a gas just above its boiling temperature may cause condensation of the substance into the liquid state. Thus in each case the application of pressure favours the more condensed of the phases available to the substance.

Similarly, application of pressure to a substance which sublimes may sometimes cause a stabilisation of the liquid phase, which allows the solid $\Leftrightarrow$ liquid and liquid $\Leftrightarrow$ gas transitions to be investigated. For example, arsenic is recorded in Table 11.2 as subliming at 886 K. However, under application of a pressure of 28 atmospheres (≈ 2.8 MPa) arsenic first melts at 1090 K, and then evaporates, allowing investigation of the enthalpies of fusion and vaporisation. Note that the boiling temperature conventionally refers to normal atmospheric pressure and so the boiling temperature 'under pressure' is not usually recorded.

The main questions raised by our preliminary examination of the experimental data on the solid to gas transition:

- Why does sublimation occur at all?
- Why is sublimation relatively so rare?

Table 11.6 The equilibrium vapour pressure (Pa) of water substance above the solid or liquid surface as a function of temperature. The shaded data on the liquid corresponds to data taken on supercooled water.

T(°C)	Solid	Liquid	T(°C)	Solid	Liquid
−90	0.009	—	−15	165.5	191.50
−80	0.053	—	−14	181.5	208.03
−70	0.258	—	−13	198.7	225.50
−60	1.077	—	−12	217.6	244.57
−50	3.940	—	−11	238.0	264.98
−40	12.88	—	−10	260.0	286.58
−30	38.12	—	−9	284.2	310.18
−29	42.27	—	−8	310.2	335.26
−28	46.80	—	−7	338.3	362.06
−27	51.87	—	−6	368.7	390.86
−26	57.34	—	−5	401.8	421.80
−25	63.47	—	−4	437.4	454.74
−24	70.14	—	−3	475.8	489.81
−23	77.34	—	−2	517.4	527.55
−22	85.34	—	−1	562.4	567.83
−21	94.01	—	0	610.6	610.6
−20	103.4	—	1	—	656.9
−19	113.8	—	2	—	706.0
−18	125.2	—	3	—	758.1
−17	137.5	—	4	—	813.6
−16	151.0	—	5	—	872.5
			6	—	935.2
			7	—	1002
			8	—	1073
			9	—	1148
			10	—	1228.1
			11	—	1312.7
			12	—	1402.6
			13	—	1497.7
			14	—	1598.5
			15	—	1705.3

11.7.2 The solid $\Leftrightarrow$ gas transition

From the data referred to §11.7.1, we first note that the vapour pressure above a solid is broadly similar to that above a liquid. From this we conclude that, broadly speaking, the process of sublimation is equivalent to 'boiling from the solid' in contrast with the more usual 'boiling from the liquid'. Normally when the temperature is high enough for a substance to have a significant vapour pressure the substance has already melted. However arsenic, for example, does not melt until a temperature which is higher than the temperature at which the vapour pressure is one atmosphere.

Figure 11.25 The vapour pressure of water and ice as function of temperature (Table 11.6) Plotted on (a) a logarithmic and (b) a linear vertical scale. Note the vapour pressure data is plotted logarithmic scale. The figure shows data for liquid water which has been supercooled below its freezing temperature, and for ice. Notice that at 0°C the vapour pressures of ice and water are extremely close, but that below this temperature the vapour pressure of the liquid is slightly greater than the vapour pressure of the solid.

(a)

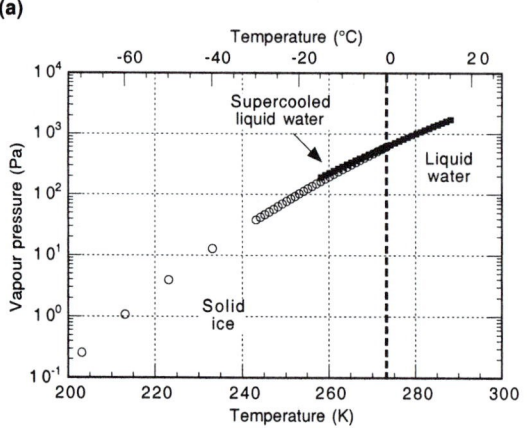

(b)

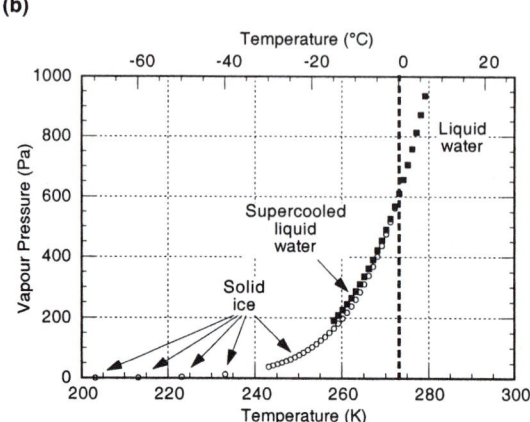

We will consider sublimation in two different ways: first microscopically, and then in terms of the Gibbs free energies of the phases.

Microscopic considerations

Let us use the cell model of liquid dynamics outlined in §8.4, to try to understand the situation of arsenic in its liquid state.

Figure 11.26, is intended as schematic illustration and is not to be considered quantitatively, but indicates plausibly the situation of arsenic. It shows a situation in which ΔE_h is greater than ΔE_e. In other words, the activation energy for the 'hopping' process is greater than the energy ΔE_e for escape from the substance altogether. Recall that ΔE_h is the activation energy involved when a liquid flows. Thus Figure 11.26 illustrates a substance which evaporates before it flows. We now need to understand how this could situation could arise.

Arsenic

For arsenic the situation is mainly due to anomalously weak and directional bonds between the atoms. Consider the data from Table 11.1 on the enthalpy of fusion of the elements around arsenic:

We see that the enthalpy of vaporisation for arse-

nic is anomalously low in comparison to its enthalpy of fusion. This indicates, as we supposed, that evaporation is relatively easy in comparison with melting. The high energy involved in forming the liquid state is likely to arise because of a high degree of directional covalent bonding between atoms. The weakness of the bonding is likely to arise because of the difficulty of fully bonding its

Figure 11.26 An illustration of the cell model with parameters appropriate to arsenic. Ignoring the situation at the surface of the liquid, we notice immediately that ΔE_h is greater than ΔE_e. In other words the activation energy for the 'hopping' process is less than the energy ΔE_e for escape from the substance altogether. Note: Be careful in interpreting ΔE_h. It is *not* a single-particle hopping process: see §8.4 for further details.

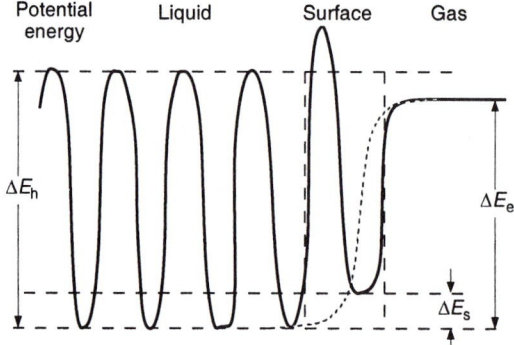

Extract from Table 11.1

Z	Name	Density (kg m^{-3})	Melting point (K)	Boiling point (K)	Enthalpy of fusion (kJ mol^{-1})	Enthalpy of vaporisation (kJ mol^{-1})
31	Gallium	5905	302.93	3676	5.59	256.1
32	Germanium	5323	1210.6	3103	34.7	334.3
33	Arsenic	5776	Sublimes at 886		27.7	31.9
34	Selenium	4808	490	958.1	5.1	26.32

five valence electrons. The crystal structure adopted by arsenic in trying to do this is complex and changes with temperature. In the structure adopted just below the sublimation temperature, the arsenic atoms first form strongly bonded tetrahedra, which are then relatively weakly bonded to each other.

Carbon

For carbon we can understand the reluctance to form a liquid state in terms of the exceptional strength and directionality of the C–C covalent bond. This makes the 'hopping' processes required for liquid behaviour extremely energetically costly.

Gibbs free energy considerations

In §10.2, we considered the transformation from solid to liquid by examining schematic Gibbs free energy diagrams. We noted that the *free energies* of the solid and liquid states were particularly sensitive to the difference in their *cohesive energy* at

$T = 0$ K. In Figures 10.2 and 10.3, we saw the effect on potassium of increasing the energy of the liquid state by 5 % of the cohesive energy of the solid. This caused the predicted melting temperature to increase by 62 %, from 307 K to 498 K. So if the cohesive energy of the liquid state $|U_{liquid}|$ is particularly small, then it seems quite plausible that this could shift the melting transition to considerably higher temperatures. In this case it appears that T_M is shifted even above T_B. The reason that the cohesive energy of the liquid state is high is due to the difficulty of optimally bonding to other atoms in the disordered liquid state,

In the case of arsenic matters are complicated by the complex crystal structure, and the structural transformation from one crystal structure to another at around 500 K. In order to represent this we would need to draw a fourth line on Figure 10.3 representing the Gibbs free energy of gas, liquid and the two solid phases. This situation is too complex for further consideration at this level.

11.8 The triple point

11.8.1 Data on the triple point

In the previous sections, we examined data on the transitions between the states of matter discussed earlier: solid ⇔ liquid, solid ⇔ gas and liquid ⇔ gas. These transitions take place over a range of temperatures depending on the pressure at which the substance is investigated. However, there is a temperature at which all three phases of matter can co-exist in equilibrium. This is called the *triple–point temperature* and is a characteristic temperature for each pure substance. Table 11.7 shows that the triple point occurs at a temperature just a little above the melting temperature.

So the main question raised by our preliminary examination of the experimental data on the triple points of substances is:

- Why is the triple-point temperature T_{Tr} so close to the melting temperature T_M of a substance at atmospheric pressure?

11.8.2 Understanding the triple-point data

As we saw in §10.7, the triple point lies at the intersection of the solid ⇔ liquid phase boundary (the melting curve) and liquid ⇔ gas phase boundary (the vaporisation curve). We have men-

Table 11.7 The melting, boiling and triple-point temperatures of various substances. The T_{tr} values are often known extremely accurately. The T_M and T_B values are typically known to within ≈ 10 mK.

Substance	T_M (K)	T_{Tr} (K)	T_B (K)
Oxygen	54.35	54.3584	90.188
Nitrogen	63.15	63.150	77.352
Argon	83.75	83.8058	87.29
Water	273.15	273.16	373.15

Figure 11.27 A schematic phase diagram illustrating the relative steepness of the solid $\Leftrightarrow$ liquid phase boundary in comparison with the liquid $\Leftrightarrow$ gas phase boundary. This means that points on the melting curve at different pressures – such as one atmosphere and the triple point pressure – occur at quite closely spaced temperatures.

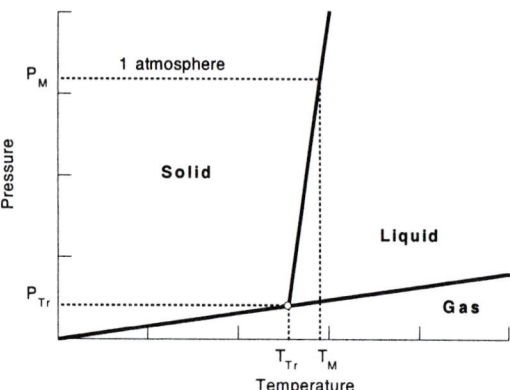

tioned previously (Examples 10.6 and 10.7) that the slope of the melting curve was very much steeper than the slope of the vaporisation curve. We shall make a calculation in moment, but before we calculate anything, it is worth just noting that it is the extreme steepness of the melting curve which causes the triple point to lie close to the melting temperature at atmospheric pressure. As illustrated in Figure 11.27, changing the pressure on a substance by several orders of magnitude has relatively little effect on the melting temperature.

The slope of each of these phase boundaries may be predicted using the Clausius–Clapeyron equation. At the solid $\Leftrightarrow$ liquid phase boundary:

$$\frac{dP_M}{dT_M} = \frac{(S_1 - S_2)}{(V_1 - V_2)}$$
$$= \frac{\Delta Q_M}{T_M(V_L - V_S)} \quad \text{(10.55* and 11.13)}$$

and at the liquid $\Leftrightarrow$ gas phase boundary:

$$\frac{dP_B}{dT_B} = \frac{(S_1 - S_2)}{(V_1 - V_2)}$$
$$= \frac{\Delta Q_B}{T_B(V_G - V_L)} \quad \text{(10.46* and 11.14)}$$

From Figure 11.9 we notice that the ratio $\Delta Q_B / T_B$ to $\Delta Q_M / T_M$ is around 10 for many elements, and so we write that roughly:

$$\frac{dP_M}{dT_M} \approx \left[10 \times \frac{(V_G - V_L)}{(V_L - V_S)} \right] \frac{dP_B}{dT_B} \quad \text{(11.15)}$$

Now the volume of a gas, though thoroughly variable, is around 1000 times the volume of the equivalent solid at around atmospheric pressure. The volume difference between a liquid and a solid (Figure 9.1) is typically $\approx 10\%$ of the solid volume. Using these approximations we find that:

$$\frac{dP_M}{dT_M} \approx \left[10 \times \frac{1000 V_S}{0.1 V_S} \right] \frac{dP_B}{dT_B}$$
$$\approx 10^5 \frac{dP_B}{dT_B} \quad \text{(11.16)}$$

Equation 11.16 indicates that the slope of the melting curve is typically 10^5 times steeper than the slope of the vaporisation curve. This is also clear graphically in either of the examples in Figures 10.16 and 10.17. The consequence of this is that, in comparison with the vaporisation curve, the melting curve on a phase diagram is nearly vertical. So the *pressure* at which the vaporisation curve intersects the melting curve hardly makes any difference to the *temperature* at which the intersection takes place. Recall that:

- the *melting temperature* is the intersection of the melting curve with a horizontal line at $P = 1$ atmosphere
- the *triple–point temperature* is the intersection of the melting curve with the vaporisation curve, and occurs at a different pressure.

However the extreme steepness of the melting curve means that the temperature difference between these two intersections is small, frequently less than a kelvin.

11.9 Other types of phase change

11.9.1 Introduction

The transitions between the three phases of matter are manifest to us all. However, other transitions take place *within* all three phases of matter that also merit the title 'phase change'. These phase changes are often not apparent by merely looking at a substance. Let us look at some examples of phase changes, and then look to see what they have in common with melting, freezing, condensation, evaporation, and sublimation. Perhaps the main criterion that we consider when classifying a physical change as being due to a phase transition is that it should occur *suddenly*.

The superconducting transition.

As discussed in §7.7, below a temperature T_C, known as the *critical temperature*, the electrical resistivity of some substances falls suddenly to values indistinguishable from zero. Thus electric currents can flow without energy loss in these materials.

As determined by the electrical resistivity, the transition is extremely sharp. In pure unstrained materials the width of the transition may be only a few micro kelvin. The heat capacity of a superconducting compound Nb_3Sn (niobium-three-tin) (Figure 11.28) shows a large jump at T_C. It is quite clear that something has suddenly happened, or at least suddenly *started* to happen, when Nb_3Sn is cooled below T_C.

Superfluid

Helium, which behaved as a closely ideal gas in its gaseous phase, behaves as an *extremely* anomalous liquid when it condenses. The list of unusual properties is too long to enumerate here, but one of the most striking is that at atmospheric pressure the liquid does not solidify on cooling. Helium can be cooled as close to absolute zero as is achievable and still does not solidify. The origin of this phenomenon is the large value of the zero-point energy of helium (due to its low mass) when compared with weakness of its interatomic forces (due to its rigid electronic structure). The normal boiling temperature of the liquid is 4.2 K, but if the

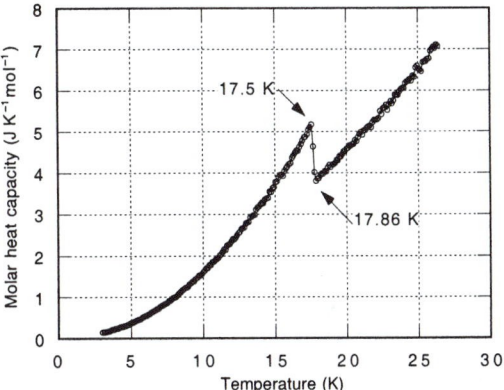

Figure 11.28 My own measurements of the heat capacity of Nb_3Sn. Notice the large jump in the heat capacity at the superconducting transition temperature T_C. The jump occurs on top of the heat capacity due to lattice vibrations discussed in §7.6.

temperature is lowered below 2.172 K (precisely) the liquid begins to display so-called *superfluid* properties. These include the ability to flow with absolutely zero viscosity. The heat capacity in this range displays a large, very sharp peak deemed by early researchers to be shaped like the Greek letter λ (lambda) and hence known as the λ-transition. It is again clear that something has suddenly happened, or suddenly *started* to happen, when liquid helium is cooled below its λ-point.

Liquid crystal states

As we saw in Chapter 8, many organic substances may exist in a form intermediate between the liquid and solid states known as a *mesophase* or *liquid crystal state*. In these states the substances display unusual optical properties. If these, normally transparent, liquids are viewed in an arrangement similar to that shown in Figure 11.34, they display striking properties. The key feature of the apparatus is the two polarising filters on either side of the liquid under examination. Normal liquids do not significantly affect the polarisation of light passing through them.

Thus if the polarising filters are crossed no light is transmitted. However, above a certain transition

Figure 11.29 Apparatus for observing liquid crystal phases.

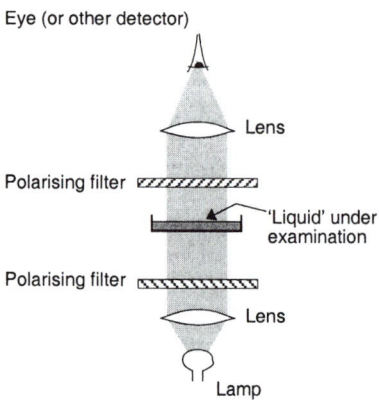

Eye (or other detector)

Lens

Polarising filter

'Liquid' under examination

Polarising filter

Lens

Lamp

temperature these liquids strongly affect the polarisation of light passing through them. When viewed through a microscope as shown, the liquids look like a window on a frosty morning: crystals appear to have grown in from the edges of the container. However, crystals have not grown: the liquid is still a liquid in the sense that it will still flow, but something has certainly changed within the liquid. The onset of the effect is sudden, and the destruction of the effect above a second critical temperature is also sudden.

Ferromagnetic materials

As discussed in Chapter W2, in the absence of an applied magnetic field, the magnetic moment of a piece of iron at 771 °C is exactly zero. However, at 769 °C the magnetic moment becomes finite even in the absence of an applied magnetic field. The magnetic moment then increases in magnitude as the temperature is lowered below the *Curie temperature* of 770 °C. Similar behaviour is observed in all ferromagnetic materials, although Curie temperatures vary significantly. Figure 11.30 shows the heat capacity of the alloy CePt which becomes ferromagnetic at around 6 K. The Curie temperatures of the ferromagnetic elements are: iron: 760 °C; nickel: 358 °C; cobalt: 1115 °C; gadolinium: 16 °C. All ferromagnetic substances show similar heat capacity anomalies close to their Curie temperature, and the anomaly in gadolinium is responsible for the unusually high value of its heat capacity at 20 °C noted earlier in Table 7.1.

11.9.2 Discussion

What these changes have in common is that at a particular temperature, 'something happens' or 'something starts to happen'. That is, 'some property' of the substance changes rapidly as the environment of the substance is changed by just a small amount. The differences between the different types of phase transition may be considered to be 'merely' to do with the physical property that changes suddenly. Many of these transitions are accompanied by heat capacity anomalies which often look somewhat similar, even though the processes taking place are dramatically different.

The main questions raised by our preliminary examination of the experimental data on different types of phase changes are:
- Why do phase changes occur suddenly at a well-defined temperature?
- Why do materials display similar anomalies in their heat capacity around these transitions?

That these questions are raised in the last section of the penultimate chapter of this book is perhaps something of a shame. Understanding and providing answers to these questions has been a triumph of twentieth-century mathematical physics. Indeed, as I write I have in front of me two books devoted entirely to answering these questions.

Perhaps the simplest way to consider these various transitions is to consider how they would look on a free energy diagram. In fact, for all the transi-

Figure 11.30 My own measurements of the heat capacity of CePt. This material becomes ferromagnetically ordered below ≈ 6 K.

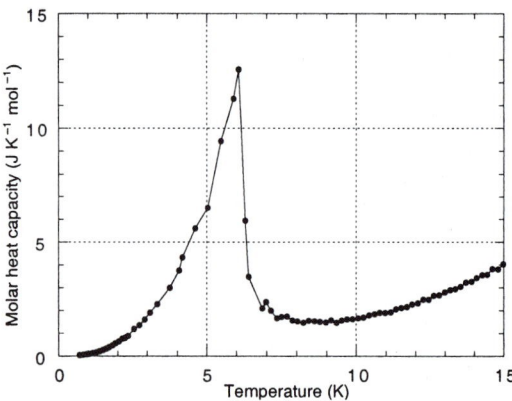

Molar heat capacity (J K^{-1} mol^{-1})

Temperature (K)

381

tions I have mentioned, the transitions are *continuous* rather *first-order*, in the sense used in Figure 10.6. What happens is that above the transition temperature, the substance fluctuates and 'discovers' that certain types of fluctuation have lower entropy, and lower energy. Recall the form of the Gibbs free energy:

$$G = U - TS + PV \qquad (10.1^*)$$

and that the equilibrium phase of a substance is the phase which minimises G. Lower *energy* states tend to minimise G, but lower *entropy* states in which there is extra order of some kind increase G. However as the temperature is lowered, the TS term becomes less significant and fluctuations into the ordered states become more likely. The fluctuations begin to grow, both in their time-scale, and their length-scale. Eventually, a point is reached at which the time-scale for the fluctuations has grown perhaps from picoseconds originally to microseconds and eventually to seconds. Similarly the length scale of the fluctuations grows from nanometres to metres. Below a certain temperature, the new type of behaviour exists throughout a sample.

In the previous paragraph, I have not discussed the type of order (i.e. what has happened) that has become established. In general, this is not at all obvious from the heat capacity curves. The heat capacity curves reflect the generic shape of he underlying free energy curves, and this is the reason for similar behaviour in $C(T)$ in widely differing substances.

To determine what has happened at a phase transition, we need to measure a property more directly related to type of order that the substance has 'discovered'. Measuring the magnetisation, resistivity or polarisability generally gives a good idea of the nature of the phase change involved.

Finally I should mention that not all phase changes within the liquid or solid are continuous in nature. Many such transitions, particularly structural transitions, are first-order.

11.10 Exercises

Exercises marked with a P prefix are 'normal' exercises. Those marked with a C prefix are best solved numerically by using a computer program or spreadsheet.. Exercises marked with an E prefix are in general rather more challenging that the P and C exercises. Answers to all the exercises are downloadable from www.physicsofmatter.com

C1. From Table 11.1 find out which element has:
(a) the highest melting temperature?
(b) the fourth highest melting temperature?
(c) the highest latent heat of melting (fusion) per mole?
(d) the highest latent heat of vaporisation per mole?
(e) the highest ratio of latent heat of vaporisation per mole to the latent heat of melting (fusion) per mole?
(You may need to use a spreadsheet for this last part.

P2. Which quantities in Table 11.1 are the best indicator of the cohesive energy of an element? Justify your answer. From Table 11.1, estimate which element has the highest cohesive energy per mole and compare your answer with the calculated results in Table 11.5.

P3. What is the boiling temperature of (a) methanol, (b) ethanol, and (c) acetone (Table 11.2)?

C4. The melting and boiling temperatures of the alkali halides are listed in Table 11.2. Do these temperatures show any systematic variation with the member of the halide family involved? Is the weak variation of melting temperature with components what you would have expected from the discussion of ionic and covalent bonding in §6.3?

P5. How much energy is required to melt 1 kg of (a) helium, (b) neon, (c) argon, (d) krypton? (Table 11.1)

P6. How much energy is required to melt 1 kg of (a) copper, (b) silver, (c) gold, (d) mercury? (Table 11.1)

P7. Based on Figures 11.3 and 11.4, indicate to what extent knowledge of the melting temperature and molar enthalpy of fusion of an element with atomic number Z are sufficient to predict the melting temperature and molar enthalpy of fusion of the element with atomic number $Z + 1$. Include a discussion of the relationship between the variation shown in Figures 11.3 and 11.4 and the periodic table (Figure 2.2)

P8. By how much does the melting temperature of gold (Table 11.1, Figure 11.5) change when atmospheric pressure changes from 1 to 1.1 atmospheres?

P9. Repeat the Lindemann melting theory calculation of Example 11.3 for gold. Does your answer lie within the one standard deviation limits drawn on Figure 11.8?

P10. How good are the rough estimates of the enthalpy of fusion and vaporisation of the elements indicated in Figure 11.9? Based on the rough figures in the legend to Figure 11.9, estimate the enthalpy of fusion and vaporisation for (a) an element with T_M = 1683 K and T_B = 2628 K, (b) an element with T_M = 1357 K and T_B = 2840 K, and (c) an element with T_M = 3680 K and T_B = 5930 K. Compare your results with the actual values in Table 11.1. Can you identify the elements?

P11. An unknown elemental metal has its melting temperature determined with an uncertainty of ±3 K. How well would this serve to uniquely identify the element? (Table 11.1 and Figure 11.3)

P12. How much energy is required to boil 1 kg of (a) helium, (b) neon, (c) argon, (d) krypton? (Table 11.1)

P13. How much energy is required to boil 1 kg of (a) copper, (b) silver, (c) gold, (d) mercury? (Table 11.1)

C14. The temperatures at which the vapour pressures of several organic substances reach 10^3, 10^4 and 1.013×10^5 Pa are listed below. Estimate their molar latent heat of vaporisation (kJ mol^{-1}) (Equations 9.16 & 11.8)

Substance	T (K) for $P=10^3$ Pa	T (K) for $P=10^3$ Pa	T_B (K)
Acetic acid, CH_3COOH	—	329	391.1
Acetone, CH_3COCH_3	237	349	329.3
Aniline, C_6H_7N	337	385	457.6
Benzene, C_6H_6	—	293	353.2
Chloroform, $CHCl_3$	240	278	334.4
Cyclohexane, C_6H_{10}	—	292	353.8
Ethyl acetate, $C_4H_8O_2$	255	294	350.2
Methanol, CH_3OH	253	288	337.7
Ethanol, C_2H_5OH	267	302	351.5
Propan-1-ol, C_3H_7OH	284	320	370.3
Propan-2-ol, C_3H_7OH	274	307	355.4
Butan-1-ol, C_4H_9OH	301	338	390.35
Butan-2-ol, C_4H_9OH	288	322	372.65
Toluene, C_7H_8	275	318	383.8

P15. What are the critical temperature, pressure and molar volume of (a) water (b) carbon dioxide and (c) ethanol? What is the density of each of these substances in the critical state, and roughly what fraction of the solid density does this correspond to? (Table 11.4)

P16. Calculate the volume per molecule of water in (a) its critical state and (b) its liquid state at 20 °C (Example 11.5, Figure 11.12)

C17. Based on the data in Table 11.1 estimate the average scaling law ratios between T_B, T_C and T_M for the elements. (Figures 11.22 and 11.23)

C18. Figure 11.6 indicates that there is a rough relationship between the Debye temperature of an element and its melting temperature. Use the data in Tables 7.12 and 11.1 to produce a rule of thumb relating θ_D and T_M

P19. Predict the Debye temperature of copper based on the melting temperatures of copper, silver and gold and the Debye temperatures of gold and silver (Tables 11.1 and 7.12). How good is your estimate?

P20. Identify the elements in Figure 11.23 which have anomalously low boiling points for their cohesive energy. Explain how these anomalies arise and why their existence does not invalidate the general correlation of boiling temperature and cohesive energy?

P21. What is the equilibrium vapour pressure above (a) ice and (b) water (if applicable) at a temperature of (i) 0 °C, (ii) –10 °C and (iii) –20 °C. (Table 11.6) Based on your answers to these questions discuss whether there are any conditions under which snow might evaporate directly without first melting.

P22. Suggest a reason why the equilibrium vapour pressure above ice is slightly less than that above water (Table 11.6 and Figure 11.25 (a) and (b)). How could you verify your suggestion?

P23. What is the triple point of (a) water and (b) argon (Table 11.7)

P24. In §9.8, the dependence of vapour pressure on temperature is discussed. Given the latent heat and the boiling temperature (Table 11.1) of the elements it is possible to estimate the vapour pressure at any temperature (Equation 9.35 and Table 11.3). Estimate the vapour pressure at 100 °C and 1000 °C of: (a) potassium, (b) copper, (c) iron and (d) tungsten

P25. A strong metal box containing water in its solid phase is heated from –20 °C to + 20 °C and the heat capacity of the combined object is measured continuously. If you had no *a priori* technique for separately accounting for heat supplied as latent heat and heat which raised the temperature of the box, then you would assume that there was 'anomaly' in the heat capacity of the box. Sketch the general form of the 'anomaly that you would observe. Discuss any similarities or difference between your graph and Figures 11.28 and 11.30.

Questions

12.1 Introduction

Questions, questions, questions. That is all you will find in this chapter. These questions are more challenging than those found at the end of the chapters, and some questions are completely open-ended! I hope you enjoy them. There are 30 questions: 1 to 10 are mainly about gases; 11 to 13 concern liquids; 14 to 27 are mainly about solids; and questions 27 to 30 concern changes between different phases.

12.2 Gases

1. Buoyancy and the Boltzmann factor

I have always found buoyancy fascinating. It is normally explained with reference to *Archimedes' principle*, and a loose statement that 'less dense objects float'. However, if we consider a helium balloon, or a football held under water, we are familiar with the fact that the object experiences an *upward* force. This can only come from the molecules that surround the object. Recall that gravity can only supply a downward force. This problem looks at the molecular origin of forces of buoyancy.

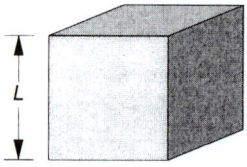

We will consider a cubic balloon(!) of side L in a medium, say air, of density ρ.

(a) What is the difference in potential energy of a molecule of mass m between the positions at the bottom of the balloon and the top?

(b) What is the relative probability that an individual quantum state will be occupied just above

the balloon as compared with just below the balloon? Hint: Look at Example 2.8

(c) What are the relative number densities of molecules just above the balloon as compared with just below the balloon?

(d) If the pressure below the balloon is P_0 then write an expression for the pressure above the balloon P in terms of P_0, m, g, L, k_B, and T.

(e) Express the formula in (d) as a linear function of L. To do this you will find it helpful to recall that an exponential function is approximated by $\exp(x) \approx 1 + x$ if $x \ll 1$.

(f) Using the formula derived in (e), determine the pressure difference between the top of the balloon and the bottom, and so derive a formula for the net upward force. You should find that this exactly reproduces the expression you would have derived if you had equated the upward force to the gravitational force on the mass of the air that the balloon displaced: $\rho L^3 g$.

2.Where is the sky?

When we look up we are familiar with the fact that the sky is blue. Having read §5.8 you will also be familiar with the fact that the colour blue comes from Rayleigh scattering by the molecules of the atmosphere. But where does most of the scattering come from? How high up would you have to go before the sky would look dark?

(a) For a molecule of mass m, what is the difference in the potential energy between being on the ground and being at height h?

(b) What is the relative probability that an individual quantum state will be occupied at the ground and at height h? Hint: Look at Example 2.8

(c) If the number density of molecules at the ground is n_0 show that the number density of molecules at height h is given by:

$$n = n_0 e^{-mgh/k_B T}$$

(d) The quantity $[k_B T / mg]$ is known as the *scale height*, λ, of the atmosphere. The scale height is the height at which the pressure would fall to $1/e$ of its value at the ground. Evaluate this quantity for the Earth.

(e) Recalling (!) that $\int e^{ax} = \dfrac{1}{a} e^{ax}$, show that 90% of the molecules in the atmosphere are below a height of approximately 2.3λ. So if we assume that the scattering power of the atmosphere is re-

lated to the number of molecules, show that, roughly, the blue of the sky originates at heights below ≈ 20 km.

(f) Do you think the approximation that the atmosphere is at a uniform temperature will seriously affect this result? A graph of mean atmospheric temperature as a function of height (at temperate latitudes) is shown in Question 6. Try comparing your predictions of the variation of number density (and hence pressure, if the temperature is constant) with the following data, which refer to the variation of pressure with height of a 'Standard Atmosphere' of the International Civil Aviation Organisation.

Height (km)	Pressure (kPa)
0	101.3
1	89.9
2	79.5
3	70.1
4	61.6
5	54.0
6	47.2
7	41.1
8	35.6
9	30.7
10	26.4

3. Relative concentrations of O_2 and N_2 at top of Mount Everest

Following on from your calculation of the scale height, λ, of the atmosphere in Question 2, it can be shown that the pressure of an isothermal atmosphere would vary as:

$$P = P_0 e^{-mgh/k_B T}$$

where m is the mass of a molecule in the atmosphere, and g is the acceleration due to gravity.

(a) What is the expected pressure of the air at the top of Mount Everest (height ≈ 8.9 km)?

(b) Work out the scale heights for oxygen and nitrogen molecules.

(c) Look up the relative concentrations of oxygen and nitrogen in the atmosphere at sea level (Table 5.2) and then work out the ratio of oxygen to nitrogen at top of Mount Everest.

(d) The Yetti are a mysterious and as yet undiscovered species which are believed to inhabit the upper slopes of the Himalayas. They can only live happily in an atmosphere where the air pressure is below 50 kPa. However, their delicate metabolism (which is still a mystery to medical science) also requires that the ratio of oxygen to nitrogen in the atmosphere exceeds 25%. Explain the difficulties that the Yetti face in their ecological niche.

4. Why is there no atmosphere on the Moon?

One can see why there is no atmosphere on the Moon if we compare the typical speeds of gas molecules with the speed necessary to escape the gravitational pull of the Moon, the so-called *escape velocity*. Interestingly, the escape velocity does not depend on the mass of the object trying to 'escape'. It applies equally to a rocket launching a satellite and molecule of a gas.

(a) The gravitational potential energy of an object of mass m at the surface of a planet of mass M and radius R is given by:

$$V = -\frac{GMm}{R}$$

where G is the Newtonian gravitational constant. By equating the magnitude of this energy to the kinetic energy of a particle at the Moon's surface, show that the escape velocity from the Moon is approximately 2380 ms^{-1}.

(b) Imagine that the Moon had an atmosphere of either (i) helium or (ii) nitrogen. For each case, follow Example 4.5 and calculate the fraction of

molecules that have speeds greater than the escape velocity. Assume a temperature of 273 K.

Your results for (a) should explain why the Moon has no helium in its atmosphere. Do they explain why the Moon cannot retain an atmosphere of nitrogen? How sensitive are your conclusions to the assumed temperature? What would happen if the average temperature was low, with occasional *very* hot days?

You will probably find the following integrals and values helpful

$$\int_{4.99}^{\infty} x^{\frac{1}{2}} e^{-x} dx \approx 0.017 \qquad \int_{34.9}^{\infty} x^{\frac{1}{2}} e^{-x} dx \approx 10^{-15}$$

$$G = 6.672 \times 10^{-11} \ \mathrm{m^3 \ kg^{-1} \ s^{-2}}$$

$$M_{\mathrm{Earth}} = 5.976 \times 10^{24} \ \mathrm{kg} \qquad R_{\mathrm{Earth}} = 6371 \ \mathrm{km}$$

$$M_{\mathrm{Moon}} = 0.0123 \times M_{\mathrm{Earth}} \qquad R_{\mathrm{Moon}} = 0.272 \times R_{\mathrm{Earth}}$$

5. Why is there so little helium in the Earth's atmosphere?

There is very little helium in the Earth's atmosphere. For example, at sea level, the concentration of helium is ≈ 5.2 PPM and neon ≈ 18 PPM (*Kaye and Laby*). This is even though helium is constantly being created on the Earth through the α-decay of radioactive elements. So why is there so little helium on Earth? It is tempting, but wrong, to ascribe this to the same reason that the Moon does not have an atmosphere, i.e. that the fast moving tail of the Maxwell–Boltzmann distribution 'leaks' molecules into outer space. That is what I thought until I came to set this and the previous question!

(a) Following the example of the previous question, calculate the fraction of helium molecules which, at 273 K, have speeds greater than the escape velocity of the Earth.

You should find an answer which is *extremely* small. So why is there so little helium in the atmosphere?

(b) Following on from Question 3, work out the scale height λ of an atmosphere composed of helium. This value is greater than for nitrogen by a factor ≈ 7 and indicates that the *relative* concen-

tration of helium increases with increasing height. Thus helium in the atmosphere tends to drift upwards. The temperature of the upper atmosphere increases rapidly above 100 km. This is due to the interactions between molecules and UV- and X-radiation from the Sun: notice the difference between day and night time temperatures. Recalculate your answer from (i) assuming a temperature of 1000 K. Can you understand the loss of helium now?

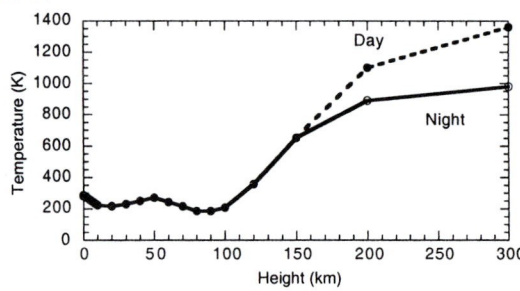

You may find the following values helpful.

$$\int_{110.5}^{\infty} x^{\frac{1}{2}} e^{-x} dx \approx 10^{-47} \qquad \int_{30}^{\infty} x^{\frac{1}{2}} e^{-x} dx \approx 10^{-12}$$

$$M_{\mathrm{Earth}} = 5.976 \times 10^{24} \ \mathrm{kg} \qquad R_{\mathrm{Earth}} = 6371 \ \mathrm{km}$$

387

6. Stability of the atmosphere against convection

The figure shows the how the mean temperature of the atmosphere changes with height at temperate latitudes. In this question you will attempt (and nobly fail!) to understand why the temperature of the atmosphere falls with height at *just* the rate that it does.

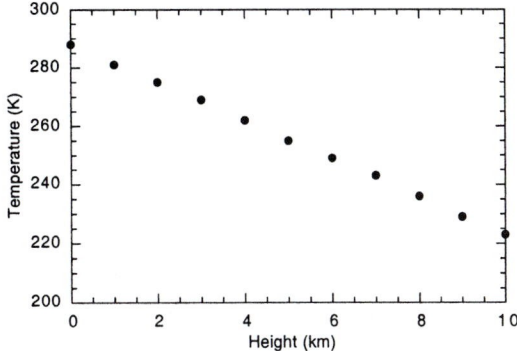

(a) What is the mean temperature gradient in the atmosphere in units of K km^{-1} ?

Consider a volume of gas near the ground. It will rise until its density matches that of the surrounding air. Its volume will adjust to match the surrounding air pressure, but its temperature may differ from that of the surrounding atmosphere. This is because the thermal conductivity of the gas is so poor that over relevant time-scales, the volume of gas is effectively isolated and so it undergoes changes adiabatically rather than isothermally.

(b) For a fixed amount of gas undergoing an isothermal change the quantity $PV = \text{constant}$. For a fixed amount of gas undergoing an adiabatic change the quantity $PV^\gamma = \text{constant}$, where $\gamma = C_P/C_V$ is the ratio of the principle specific heats of the gas (See §5.4). Show that for a fixed amount of gas undergoing an adiabatic change the quantity $P^{1-\gamma}T^{\gamma-1} = \text{constant}$, where *constant* has a different value from that in the previous expression.

(c) By first differentiating the expression $P^{1-\gamma}T^{\gamma-1} = \text{constant}$ with respect to height (remembering that both P and T change with height), show that the temperature and pressure gradients in the atmosphere are related by:

$$\frac{dT}{dh} = \frac{\gamma-1}{\gamma}\frac{T}{P}\frac{dP}{dh}$$

Assuming that atmospheric pressure varies as $P = P_0 e^{-mgh/k_B T}$ show that close to the ground the temperature gradient that would develop should be $\approx 9.4 \text{ K km}^{-1}$.

If the temperature gradient is greater than this, volumes of gas at ground level would spontaneously rise because the rapid fall in temperature would make the air above them more dense, 'overcompensating' for the reduction in density due to the falling pressure. (Recall that the density of a gas is given by $\rho = mP/k_B T$). Thus 9.4 K km^{-1} represents the maximum value of temperature gradient sustainable without convection in the Earth's atmosphere. The actual value is smaller than this due to the complicating effect of water vapour.

7. Adiabatic temperature oscillations in a sound wave

The amplitude of pressure oscillations in a sound wave is usually expressed as the ratio of the root mean square (r.m.s.) value of the pressure oscillations to a reference value of $P_0 = 2 \times 10^{-5}$ Pa. The ratio is usually expressed logarithmically in units of decibels (dB). Thus the amplitude of sound pressure waves is given by:

$$\text{pressure oscillation amplitude in Pa} = 20\ \log\frac{P_1}{P_0}$$

Thus, for example, if a sound wave had an amplitude of 0.2 Pa, then the pressure oscillation amplitude is 80 dB. This is known technically as the sound pressure level. If the oscillation were at a frequency of 1 kHz, such a sound would be experienced as very loud: equivalent to standing near a road as a large lorry passes.

(a) Starting from $PV^\gamma = \text{constant}$, show that $P^{1-\gamma}T^\gamma = \text{another constant}$.

(b) For a sound wave travelling through a gas with mean temperature T_0 and mean pressure P_0, show that the amplitudes of pressure and temperature oscillations (ΔP and ΔT) are related by:

$$\frac{T_0^\gamma}{\left(T_0 + \Delta T\right)^\gamma} = \frac{P_0^{\gamma-1}}{\left(P_0 + \Delta P\right)^{\gamma-1}}$$

(c) When ΔP and ΔT are small compared to P_0 and T_0, show that this reduces to:

$$\frac{\Delta T}{T_0} = \frac{(\gamma-1)}{\gamma}\frac{\Delta P}{P_0}$$

8. Diatomic molecules

The covalent bond between the hydrogen and the chlorine in a HCl molecule has a 'spring constant' of $K = 860\ \mathrm{Nm}^{-1}$.

(a) Assuming that the chlorine atom is heavy enough for it to scarcely vibrate at all, calculate the resonant frequency of oscillation of the hydrogen atom.

(b) How many degrees of freedom should you expect this gas to exhibit at around room temperature?

(c) Estimate the temperature above which you should expect this gas to show a heat capacity of $C_P = 37.4\ \mathrm{J\,K^{-1}\,mol^{-1}}$.

(d) Help! My poor graduate student has confused two flasks. One contains HCl and the other contains and equal number of moles of DCl. Remember deuterium is the name for the heavy isotope of

(d) Show that the magnitude of the temperature oscillations associated with an 80 dB sound wave are $\approx 0.16\ \mathrm{mK}$.

(e) How could you detect such tiny rapid temperature oscillations?

hydrogen D = ^{2}H. Its bonding to chlorine is identical to ordinary hydrogen, but of course it has twice the mass. I casually suggest that HCl and DCl can easily be distinguished at certain temperatures by the difference in their heat capacity. Can you suggest a good temperature range in which to try this experiment? Which gas would have the higher heat capacity in this range?

(e) I then remember that it would probably be easier to distinguish between the gases by measuring the speed of sound through the gases. Which would have the higher speed of sound? And how big would you expect the difference to be?

(f) Can you think of another (even simpler?) way to distinguish between the two gases?

9. My office.

The office in which I used to work was 5 m long by 4m wide and an amazing 5m high! It had a mean temperature of around 23 °C. Assume that the air is composed entirely of nitrogen and oxygen in the ratio 4:1.

(a) Calculate the total *translational* energy of the air molecules in my room.

(b) In order to stay cool, my colleague Dr. Zochowski and I used a fan. This device gives an excess velocity of $\approx 2\ \mathrm{ms}^{-1}$ to approximately 0.5 m³ of air per second. After the coherent directed velocity of the air has turned into random molecular motions, the temperature of the air in the room will rise slightly. Calculate the power input to the room from the fan.

(c) Calculate the rate of temperature rise in the room due to the fan. (Neglect convection and assume that the temperature of the room is uniform.)

(d) Write a paragraph explaining to one of your less scientific friends why a device which actually heats the room makes me feel cooler!

(e) The cooling effect of the fan is related to the so called 'wind chill' effect. But is it always a 'chill' effect? Explain how using a fan when defrosting a refrigerator would provide a 'wind heating' effect.

(f) In summer my office heats up to around 28 °C, but in winter the temperature falls to around 18 °C. How many molecules of oxygen are there in the room in winter? How many more (or is it how many fewer?) molecules of oxygen are there in summer?

(g) My lung capacity is around 2.5 litres, but when I relax, I generally inhale only around 0.5 litres of air in each breath. In each breath I use around 20% of the available oxygen in my lungs, expelling the rest. If my office were sealed so that no air could enter or leave, and I were alone (without even e-mail!), estimate how long I would survive. When the oxygen fraction in the room falls below around 15% I will become unconscious, and when it falls below 10% I will expire. 'Tell me the truth now… how long have I got?'

10. The virial equation

The ideal gas equation accurately describes the properties of nearly all gases in a wide variety of situations. However, if you want to be very careful indeed you can use the virial equation (Equation 4.50) to take account of deviations from ideal gas behaviour. This is written as:

$$\frac{PV_m}{RT} = 1 + \frac{B(T)}{V_m} + \frac{C(T)}{V_m^2} + \dots \tag{1}$$

where V_m is the molar volume. We can write the second virial coefficient $B(T)$ as:

$$B(T) = a - b\exp\left[\frac{c}{T}\right] \tag{2}$$

We can use Equations 1 and 2 to decide when deviations from ideal gas behaviour exceed 1%, i.e. when the second term on the right-hand side of Equation 1 exceeds 0.01.

(a) Explain why, if we are looking only for small deviations from ideal gas behaviour, we may write the right-hand side of the virial equation as:

$$1 + \frac{B(T)P}{RT}$$

(b) Using data in the table below, sketch the function $B(T)$ for nitrogen across the range in which the above formula is valid.

(c) Using data in the table below, estimate the *temperature* below which (at atmospheric pressure) the deviations from ideal gas behaviour are such that the second term in Equation 3 exceeds 0.01. (This needs to done numerically)

(d) Consider the temperatures calculated in (c) as a fraction of the boiling temperature of the appropriate liquid. Is there a pattern?

(e) For each of the gases in the table, estimate the mean separation between atoms when the deviations exceed 1%. Comment on your results.

Gas	a m³ mol⁻¹	b m³ mol⁻¹	c K	a, b and c valid From (K)	To (K)
Helium	114.1	98.7	3.245	7	150
Neon	81.0	63.6	30.7	44	973
Argon	154.2	119.3	105.1	80	1024
Krypton	189.6	148.0	145.3	110	700
Xenon	247.0	192.9	199.8	160	650
Water	33.0	15.2	1300.7	293	1248
Nitrogen	185.4	141.8	88.7	75	700
Oxygen	152.8	117.0	108.8	90	400

Liquids

11. Van der Waals equation of state

The Van der Waals (VdW) Equation of state for z moles is mentioned briefly in §4.5.2 as a development of the ideal gas equation. The equation for z moles of substance is given by (*c.f.* Equation 4.44):

$$\left[P + \frac{z^2 a}{V^2}\right][V - zb] = zRT \tag{1}$$

Equation 1 is in fact a good deal more interesting than just a modification to the ideal gas law. Amazingly – at least *I* find it amazing – this equation not only describes the small deviations from ideal gas behaviour, but also allows a fair description of the liquid state! However, working analytically with Equation 1 is considerably more complicated than the ideal gas equation.

(a) For nitrogen the parameters a and b are given by $a = 0.1408$ m³ Pa mol⁻¹ and $b = 3.913 \times 10^{-5}$ m³ mol⁻¹. Use a spreadsheet or graph-plotting program to plot the predicted graphs of P versus V for temperatures of 200 K, 130 K, 120 K and 100 K for $z = 1$ mol. Remember that b is (roughly speaking) the volume of 1 mole of the substance in the solid state. So plot V from say $1.1b$ to say $100b$ in suitably small steps. You will need to use a logarithmic scale on both axes to see clearly the behaviour of the $P(V)$ across this range. On the same graph plot the predicted behaviour using the ideal gas equation.

(b) The VdW graph at 200 K should look like an ideal gas at all volumes except that it is distorted so that the zero of volume corresponds to a volume of b. Explain briefly why this is so.

(c) The VdW graphs at 120 and 130 K should show a distinct kink. This is close to the critical temperature T_C of nitrogen. Recall that above T_C nitrogen can not be liquefied at any pressure. *At the critical temperature the graph should have a point of inflection but not a minimum.* Based on these graphs estimate the critical volume and pressure and compare your estimates with the data in Table 11.4.

(d) At 100 K, the graph shows a distinct kink with a maxima and minima. (This is unphysical: dP/dV is positive and if you think about it that cannot be right.) This region is discussed in many texts (e.g. *Flowers and Mendoza*) but the usual approach is to ignore it! The wiggle in this region corresponds roughly to the region in which liquid and gas co-exist. At volumes well below the kink region, the equation describes the properties of a liquid mod-

estly well. Estimate the compressibility of a liquid from the slope of your curve at around $V = 1.1b$. Following the discussion in §9.3, state briefly whether or not you consider this estimate to be reasonably accurate.

(e) If you still have not had enough, then compare the experimental and predicted critical temperatures for:

- Argon:
  $a = 0.1362$ m^3 Pa mol^{-1} and
  $b = 3.219\times10^{-5}$ m^3 mol^{-1},

- CO_2:
  $a = 0.3639$ m^3 Pa mol^{-1} and
  $b = 4.267\times10^{-5}$ m^3 mol^{-1}.

12. Radial density function of two-dimensional fluid

This question concerns a two-dimensional fluid, similar to that discussed at the start of Chapter 8 in Example 8.1. The 'molecules' of the fluid are, for the purposes of this calculation, impenetrable discs with radius $r_0 = 1.1 \times 10^{-9}$ m.

(a) If the molecules are in a low-density gas-like phase with a number density n per unit area, sketch the radial distribution function $g(r)$ and radial density function $\rho(r)$.

(b) The molecules interact via a pair potential with the form:

$$u_{pair}(r) = \frac{-5\times10^{-83}}{r^6} \ \text{J} \ \text{ if } r \geq 2r_0$$

and at 600 K the molecules are in a gas-like phase and occupy an area ten times greater than the total area of the discs themselves. Estimate (i) the molar internal potential energy using:

$$U = \frac{N_A}{2} \int_0^\infty g(r)u_{pair}(r)dr$$

and (ii) the molar internal kinetic energy assuming that the molecules exhibit two degrees of freedom. By comparing the results of (i) and (ii), comment on the validity of the assumption that the molecules are in a gas-like phase.

(c) At a lower temperature the radial distribution function has the form:

$$g(r) = 0 \ \text{ for } \ r < 2r_0$$
$$g(r) = 3Cr \ \text{ for } \ 2r_0 \leq r < 4r_0$$
$$g(r) = Cr \ \text{ for } \ 4r_0 \leq r < 5r_0$$
$$g(r) = 2Cr \ \text{ for } \ r \geq 5r_0$$

where C has the value 2×10^{18} m^{-2}. Sketch the radial distribution function $g(r)$ and radial density function $\rho(r)$.

(d) Evaluate the molar internal potential energy using formula given in (b).

13. Radial density function of three-dimensional liquid

The radial distribution function $N(r)$ in the liquid phase of the newly invented element *Hypotheticum* is shown below. The constant C has the value 1.5×10^{29} m^{-3}. The molecules of hypotheticum have a relative molecular mass of 70 and are per-

fectly spherical hard spheres, with a weak force of attraction between atoms.

(a) From the form of $N(r)$ estimate the diameter r_0 of an atom of Hypotheticum.

(b) Sketch a graph of the radial *density* function and so estimate the density of liquid hypotheticum at this temperature and pressure.

(c) The pair-potential function for these molecules is given by:

$$u_{\text{pair}}(r) = -1.6\times10^{-22} \text{ J if } 3r_0 \leq r < 6r_0$$

Sketch $u_{\text{pair}}(r)$ and then estimate the depth of the attractive potential expressed in kelvin.

$$u_{\text{pair}}(r) = -1.6\times10^{-22} \text{ J if } 3r_0 \leq r < 6r_0$$

Sketch $u_{\text{pair}}(r)$ and then estimate the depth of the attractive potential expressed in kelvin.

(d) Show that the contribution of the molecular interaction to the molar internal energy at this temperature and pressure is around −9.34 kJ mol^{-1}. It may help if you note that:

$$U = \frac{N_A}{2} \int_0^\infty N(r)u_{\text{pair}}(r)dr$$

(e) Sketch the form of the radial density function for the substance (i) at the same pressure but at

(d) Show that the contribution of the molecular interaction to the molar internal energy at this temperature and pressure is around −9.34 kJ mol^{-1}. It may help if you note that:

$$U = \frac{N_A}{2} \int_0^\infty N(r)u_{\text{pair}}(r)dr$$

(e) Sketch the form of the radial density function for the substance (i) at the same pressure but at higher temperatures, and (ii) at the critical point. higher temperatures, and (ii) at the critical point.

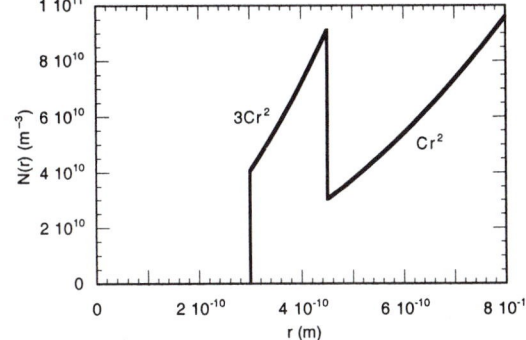

Solids

14. Young's modulus of simple solids

Many properties of solids can be understood on the basis of a simple model of a solid. The simplest version of the model assumes that each atom vibrates independently of its neighbours, like Figure 7.26(a) rather than Figure 7.26(b).

(a) The Einstein temperature of copper is 230 K and its density is 8933 kg m^{-3}. Based on the simple model above estimate values for (i) the Young's modulus, and (ii) the speed of longitudinal sound waves.

(b) Young's modulus E is defined by considering a long bar of unstressed length L under a tensile or compressive stress. In line with Equation 7.20:

$$\frac{\text{Force}}{\text{Area}} = E\frac{\Delta L}{L}$$

where [Force/Area] is known as the *tensile stress* and $\Delta L/L$ is the fractional extension of the bar and is know as the *tensile strain*. The 'trick' which allows us to do this is to think of the solid as being composed of essentially independent 'strings' of atoms. The key parameters you will need to esti-

mate are K the 'spring constant' for the bonds between atoms; and a the interatomic spacing.

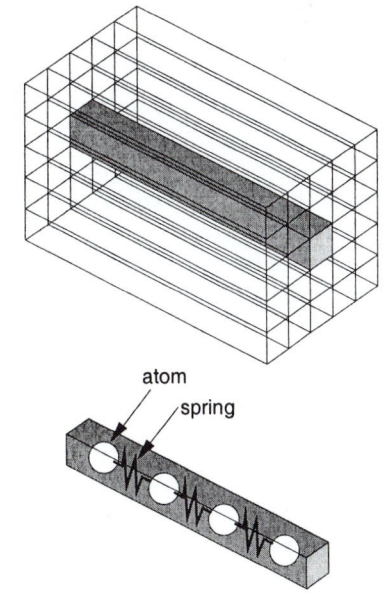

15. Schottky heat capacity anomaly

Consider a case where there are two quantum states on each atom in an elemental solid separated by $\Delta E = 2 \times 10^{-3}$ eV. This situation actually occurs at low temperature in some compounds where an ion is free to adopt two orientations. Normally there are more than two options, but the mathematics becomes even more complex and very little physics is added to the problem.

(a) Show that the probability of atom being in the upper and lower quantum states are given by:

$$P_{\text{lower}} = \frac{1}{1 + e^{-\Delta E/k_B T}}$$

$$P_{\text{upper}} = \frac{e^{-\Delta E/k_B T}}{1 + e^{-\Delta E/k_B T}}$$

Hint: The ion must be in one or other of these two orientations. So follow Example 2.8 and remember that $P_{\text{lower}} + P_{\text{upper}}$ must equal one.

(b) Show that the internal energy of 1 mole of the substance may be written as:

$$U(T) = U_o + N_A \left[\frac{\Delta E \, e^{-\Delta E/k_B T}}{1 + e^{-\Delta E/k_B T}} \right]$$

Make a graph of this function for temperatures from $T = 0$ K to $T = 3\Delta E/k_B$.

(c) Show that the constant volume heat capacity is:

$$C(T) = \frac{\Delta E^2 \times e^{\Delta E/k_B T}}{\left[e^{\Delta E/k_B T} + 1 \right]^2 k_B T^2}$$

Make a graph of this function for temperatures from $T = 0$ K to $T = 3\Delta E/k_B$. You should find that there is a large peak in the heat capacity (known as an *anomaly*).

(d) Numerically integrate $C(T)/T$ from $T = 0$ K to $T = 3\Delta E/k_B$ to show that the integrated entropy is close to $R\ln 2$.

The importance of this result is that from a measurement of the heat capacity of such a material, it is possible to identify the number of microscopic degrees of freedom available to the atoms. This relates to the entropy of the material (Example 10.2). The result holds in general and if the ions have p possible orientations the integral of $C(T)/T$ is $R\ln(p)$.

16. Asymmetry of pair potential: thermal expansion

In this question we will try to work out the coefficient of thermal expansion of a molecularly-bonded solid. Before starting I would just like to say that if you find this question straightforward you really should consider a career in physics. To do this we need to expand the Lennard-Jones 6-12 pair potential

$$u_{\text{pair}}(r) = -4\varepsilon \left[\left(\frac{\sigma}{r} \right)^6 - \left(\frac{\sigma}{r} \right)^{12} \right] \qquad (1)$$

about its minimum.

(a) For simplicity let us consider only a single 'bond' between a pair of molecules. Differentiating $u_{\text{pair}}(r)$ we can find the value of r_o at the minimum. Show that $r_o = \left[2^{1/6} \right] \sigma$.

(b) Differentiate $u_{\text{pair}}(r)$ twice and evaluate the double differential at r_o to estimate the *curvature* of the potential. This is just the 'spring constant'

of the bond, K. So if the curve were symmetric it would have the form:

$$u_{\text{pair}}(r) = u_{\text{pair}}(r_o) + K(r - r_o)^2 \qquad (2)$$

Now equations such as Equation 1 are not as simple as quadratic equations and to solve this problem we need to take advantage of the fact that we know that near the bottom of the potential well the potential is *nearly* quadratic. Deviations from quadratic (harmonic) behaviour are small in comparison with the quadratic term. So we can first estimate the amplitude of vibration assuming that the curve is harmonic (Equation 2). This would lead to an oscillation symmetric about the equilibrium separation with the atom vibrating across Range 1 in the figure [labelled (a)] over the page. However, in the actual potential we see that the atom vibrates across Range 2 in the figure. Notice that Range 2 is not centred on the equilibrium

393

separation but is shifted slightly to the right. The extent of this shift is what we wish to estimate.

(c) Estimate the amplitude of vibration A at temperature T assuming that the pair potential is quadratic.

(d) Figure (b) right shows how we can estimate Δx.

To do this we note that the slope of the actual potential close to the extrema of vibration at $(r_0 \pm A)$ is roughly:

$$\left.\frac{du_{pair}(r)}{dr}\right|_{(r_0 \pm A)} \approx \frac{\text{deviation from quadratic at } (r \pm A)}{\Delta x}$$

Use this equation to evaluate Δx. To do this you will need to evaluate the *slope* of the actual potential at around $r_0 \pm A$, and the difference between Equations 1 and 2 at these points. This yields the magnitude of the thermal expansion in a bond at temperature T. From this you can estimate the thermal expansion coefficient α, which is just the fractional bond expansion $(\Delta x/r_0)$ per degree.

(e) Estimate the thermal expansion coefficient α for argon using the data from Table 6.2. Make sure you evaluate your estimate well below (say 50%) the melting temperature. The answer for argon is rather larger than for most solids: can you suggest a reason?

If you got this far: well done!

17. Force as derivative of potential

Consider a hypothetical element, the solid phase of which is composed of atoms interacting via a pair potential of the form:

$$u_{pair}(r) = A\left(e^{-2r/a} - 0.01e^{-r/a}\right)$$

This element forms a simple cubic solid with equilibrium separation between nearest neighbour atoms r_0. We will consider the properties of this element only at $T = 0$ K and neglect all interactions other than those between nearest neighbours.

(a) Make a graph of the function $u_{pair}(r)$.

(b) Show that the total molar cohesive energy is

$$U(r_0) = 3AN_A\left(e^{-2r_0/a} - 0.01e^{-r_0/a}\right)$$

and show that the equilibrium separation is $r_0 = 5.3A$.

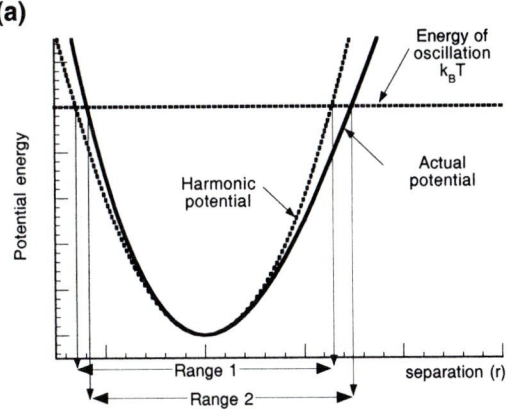

(a)

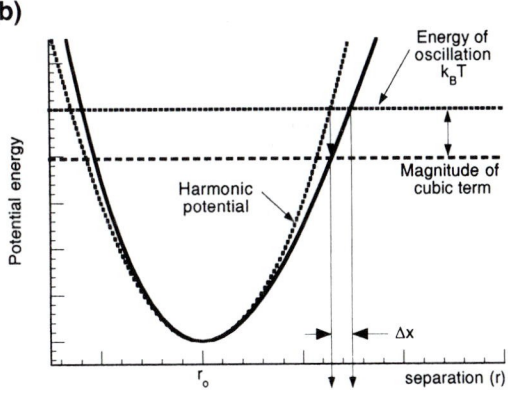

(b)

(c) What is the average cohesive energy per atom u_0 in the crystal in equilibrium.

(d) The force between two atoms can be written:

$$F(r) = -\left(\frac{du_{pair}(r)}{dr}\right)$$

Make a graph of $F(r)$ for a pair of atoms. On your graph of $F(r)$ identify: (a) the point at which $u_{pair}(r) = 0$; (b) the point at which $du_{pair}(r)/dr = 0$; (c) the point at which $u_{pair}(r)$ has a point of inflection.

(e) Assuming the simple solid model summarised in Figure 7.26 (a) and described in Question 14 is valid, estimate Young's modulus of this substance. Note: It may help you to remember that:

$$\frac{d}{dx}\left(e^{bx}\right) = be^{bx}$$

18. Heat capacity

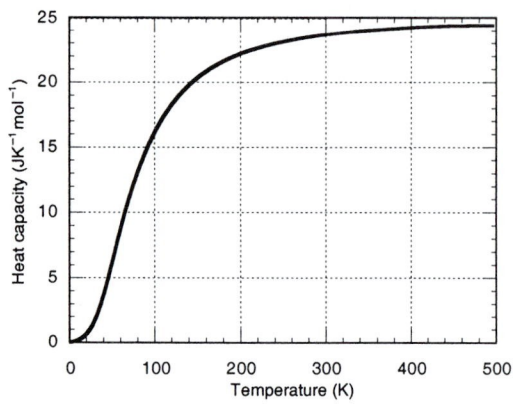

The graph shows the heat capacity of an elemental metal as a function of temperature. The density of the substance is 8.93×10^3 kg m^{-3} and the relative atomic mass is 64.

(a) Estimate the maximum energy of a phonon in this substance.

(b) Estimate roughly the speed of longitudinal and transverse sound waves in the substance.

(c) Estimate roughly the Young's modulus of the substance.

(d) Assuming the simple model of a solid summarised in Figure 7.26 and described in Question 14 is valid, estimate the 'spring constant' K for bonds between the atoms.

19. Hall effect

The Hall effect may be described as follows. When a magnetic field is applied perpendicular to a wafer of conducting material carrying a current along its length, then a potential difference appears across its width. This is illustrated schematically on the figure below.

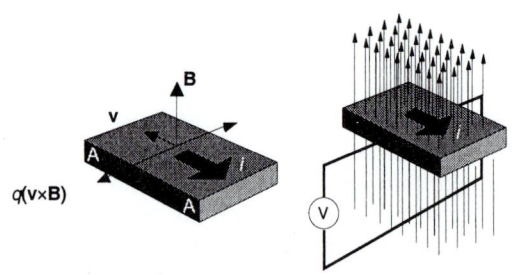

The magnetic field **B** gives rise to a *transverse* potential difference V_H which we can understand by considering the following four points.

First: Consider the directions in which electrons move in the absence of an applied magnetic field. On the figure above I have drawn two arrows, representing the drift velocity **v** of an electron in the metal and the direction of conventional current flow.

Second: In an applied magnetic field **B**, each electron experiences an additional magnetic force $\mathbf{F_m} = q\,(\mathbf{v} \times \mathbf{B})$. Notice that because of the negative charge of the electron, $\mathbf{F_m}$ points in the opposite direction to the vector $(\mathbf{v} \times \mathbf{B})$.

Third: The magnetic force acts to 'push' electrons to the side of the sample marked A in the figure. Since the electrons cannot leave the sample by the side, the side A becomes negatively charged. The charging process builds up until an electric field created is sufficient to prevent any more electrons being pushed to side A. In other words, in the steady state – which is established a few picoseconds after the current begins to flow – the magnetic and electric forces are balanced and are of equal magnitude but opposite sign. In other words the Lorentz force is zero, which implies that $\mathbf{F_e} = -\mathbf{F_m}$. In this geometry, both $\mathbf{F_e}$ and $\mathbf{F_m}$ act along the x-axis and so their y- and z- components are both zero. Considering only the x-component of the vectors we can then write:

$$qE_H = qvB \qquad (1)$$

where E_H is the Hall electric field. Finally, in order to work out the potential difference V_H measured across the sample we need to recall two results:

- first, the electric field is just V_H/d where d is the width of the sample,

- second, the current can be written as $i = nAqv$, where n is the number density of charge carriers, A the cross-sectional area of the wire, q the charge on an individual carrier and v the average speed of the carriers.

(a) Using the information above show that the Hall voltage may be written as:

$$V_H = \frac{i}{nqt} B \qquad (2)$$

where t is the thickness of the sample and q is the charge on an electron.

(b) Show that if the current were carried by positively charged carriers, the Hall voltage would have the opposite sign.

(c) For a gold film 1 μm thick a current of 1 mA produces a Hall voltage of 31.8 nanovolts in a perpendicular magnetic field of 0.3 T. Estimate the number density of electron carriers in gold.

(d) Semiconductors can have number densities of carriers n as low as (and sometimes much lower in fact!) than 10^{20} m^{-3}. For a sample 1 mm think estimate how many volts per tesla would be produced from the same measuring current if the semiconductor were used as a magnetic field detector. Would such a substance make a good magnetic field detector?

(e) Commonly the strength of the Hall effect for a substance is quantified in terms of a Hall constant R_H, which is the Hall electric field per unit *current density* per unit magnetic field:

$$R_H = \frac{E_H}{jB} \qquad (3)$$

where j is the current density through the sample, i.e. the current per unit cross sectional area $j = i/td$ if the thickness is t and the width is d. Starting from Equation 3, show that the predicted value of R_H is:

$$R_H = \frac{1}{nq} \qquad (4)$$

My own experiments (during my PhD) on potassium metal yielded a value of $R_H = -4.60 \times 10^{-10} \pm 0.14 \times 10^{-10}$ C^{-1} m^3. Is this the value that theory outlined in §6.5 would lead you to expect?

20. Intrinsic and extrinsic silicon

At absolute zero, a phosphorus impurity in silicon traps its 'extra' electron with a binding energy of $\Delta E_d \approx 0.044$ eV.

(a) Estimate the temperature T_1 above which essentially all the phosphorus impurities are ionised and their electrons donated to the conduction.

(b) If the phosphorus concentration is 1×10^{19} m^3 estimate the electron carrier density above T_1. What level of purity (in parts per million) does this correspond to? Would you describe such a material as 'pure'?

(c) The number density of electron carriers arising from the valence band n_e (as opposed to those arising from phosphorus impurities) is given *very roughly* by:

$$n_e = n_{Si} \exp\left[\frac{-\Delta E}{k_B T}\right] \qquad (1)$$

where n_{Si} is the number of silicon atoms per cubic metre and ΔE is the energy gap in silicon (≈ 1.1 eV). At what temperature T_2 will the number density of electron carriers arising from the

valence band equal the maximum number of donated electrons from the impurities. Above T_2 the silicon displays essentially the same properties as pure silicon and the impurities play only an insignificant part in conduction. Importantly, conduction is due to both electrons in the conduction band *and* an equal number of holes in the valence band. For silicon of this purity T_2 marks the temperature above which the sample behaves *intrinsically*. Below T_2 the conductivity of the silicon is dominated by the donated electrons from the phosphorus and this regime is known as the *extrinsic* regime. Between T_1 and T_2 the number of carriers is roughly constant.

(d) Estimate T_1 and T_2 for a sample with phosphorus impurities at a level of 10^{20} m^{-3}.

(e) Estimate the magnitude of the Hall constant (Question 19) from a sample of the above semiconductor (i) just above T_1 and (ii) just above T_2.

21. Mobility in metals and semiconductors

The resistivity of silver (the best conductor) at around room temperature is $\approx 1.59 \times 10^{-8}$ Ω m and the resistivity of silicon with a concentration of 10^{22} phosphorus atoms m^{-3} is $\approx 5\times 10^{-3}$ Ω m.

(a) Calculate the scattering time τ and the mobility μ for electron carriers in each element.

(b) Surprisingly you will find that the mobility of electrons in silicon is much greater than in silver. Suggest a reason why this should be so. (Hint; the Debye temperature of silicon is 635 K and for silver it is 225 K.)

(c) Calculate the mobility for electrons in copper, silver, and gold. Does phonon scattering explain the trend in the mobilities of copper, silver, and gold? (See Table 7.12 for Debye Temperature and Table 7.13 for resistivity.)

(d) Calculate the drift velocity for electrons in silver and in silicon with a concentration of 10^{22} phosphorus atoms m^{-3} when a current of 1 mA is passed down wires of cross sectional area 10^{-6} m^2. (Hint: Equation 7.72b will help you to estimate the electric field.)

(e) For silver, compare the result in (d) with a calculation of the Fermi velocity of electrons. For silicon, compare this result in (d) with the mean speed of electrons calculated as if they were a Maxwell–Boltzmann type classical gas. (See §4.3). Comment on your results.

22. Light bulb design

An incandescent light bulb is essentially a heater: a small section of wire – the filament – is heated until its temperature is sufficient to cause it to glow. You might be surprised at how hot the filament becomes: in most light bulbs the temperature is around 1700 °C! Such extreme temperatures are required because the hotter the filament, the 'whiter' the light. However this requirement severely restricts the materials that can be used for a filament. Most commonly, the element tungsten is used. Let us try to work out how to design a filament for a 60 watt light bulb to operate from a 220 V supply. This is the kind of light bulb you might be using in a desk lamp as you read this. It might not seem to be much of challenge to 'design a piece of wire' but as you will see, working out the length L and diameter d of the wire is more complicated than it seems.

The key to designing a light bulb is to realise that it is essentially an energy transducer, i.e. it changes electrical energy to radiant energy in the form of electromagnetic waves. Thus we want to put in 60 watts of electrical energy and get out 60 watts of radiant energy.

(a) Assuming that the electrical resistivity of tungsten at around 2000 K is $\approx 5 \times 10^{-7}\ \Omega$ m, work out the ratio of the length to the cross-sectional area of the wire L/d of a piece of wire that will dissipate $P = 60$ W.

The rate at which radiant energy leaves a surface of area S at absolute temperature T is given by Stefan's law: $P = \sigma S T^4$ where σ is the Stephan-Boltzmann constant $\sigma = 5.57 \times 10^{-8}$ W m^{-2} K^{-4}. In fact this Equation applies exactly only to the surface of a hypothetical material known as a 'black

body'. However, it can be used as a rough approximation for most real substances. (See part (d) for how to go beyond this approximation.)

(b) Show that the energy radiated from a wire in terms of its length and diameter d:

$$P = \left(\pi \sigma T^4\right) dL$$

(c) In order to make our light bulb work, we need to choose values for L and d which causes both 60 W energy electrical dissipation (part (a)) and 60 W of radiated energy to be radiated (part (b)). Hence derive separate expressions for d and L. Assuming that the light bulb will operate at around 2000 K, estimate the length and diameter of the filament.

(d) Break open a light bulb (carefully!) and check your calculation. You will probably find that you got the diameter of the wire about right, but overestimated the length of the wire. What factors do you think could account for this difference? One of the factors is the *emissivity* ε of tungsten, which describes the deviation of the emission of the surface from the black body condition. Thus the actual amount of energy radiated is given by $P = \varepsilon \sigma S T^4$. Can you estimate a value of ε for tungsten from your measurements?

(e) Finally, note that I have considered only conventional light bulbs. Tungsten halogen bulbs run much hotter than normal light bulbs, and this calculation will very severely overestimate the length of filament required for such bulbs. You can recognise such bulbs because they are (a) much smaller than normal bulbs and (b) much brighter, giving a whiter (or in fact bluer) light than normal light bulbs.

23. Low temperature heat capacity

T (K)	Molar heat capacity (mJ mol^{-1} K^{-1})
1.0	0.84
1.5	1.53
2.0	2.72
2.5	4.2
3.0	6.42
3.5	9.24
4.0	13.2

The table above shows data on the low temperature heat capacity C of a substance.

(a) Plot this data on a graph as C/T versus T^2. How can you tell this element is a metal?

(b) Estimate the density of states at the Fermi energy.

(c) Assuming that the density of states has the free electron form (See Equation 6.70 and Example 7.14) estimate the Fermi energy in electron volts.

(d) The Debye theory of the phonon heat capacity of a solid (Appendix A4) predicts that when $T \ll \Theta_D$:

$$C(T) = 9R\left(\frac{T}{\theta_D}\right)^3 \quad [25.976]$$

Use this equation and the data above to estimate the Debye temperature of the sample.

(e) Estimate the speed of sound in the sample.

(f) Estimate the heat capacity of the element at a temperature of 500 K.

24. Packing fractions

When thinking about crystal structures in solids it is often helpful to think of atoms as hard spheres. On this assumption, work out the fraction of space (known as the *packing fraction*) that is occupied by spheres when they are packed in

(a) simple cubic,

(b) body-centred cubic, and

(c) face-centred cubic structures.

Note that in the simple cubic structure, the spheres on adjacent corners just touch (or as it is known

technically: *kiss*). In a body-centred cubic structure, the eight spheres at the corners of the cube do not touch each other but they all kiss the central sphere. And in a face-centred cubic structure the sphere at the centre of each face kisses the four spheres at the corners of that face. You should find that face-centred cubic structure yields the most efficient packing, but you may be interested to know that it is currently not mathematically possible to *prove* that this is the case!

25. Solid helium

At low temperatures and atmospheric pressure, helium – uniquely – does not solidify. Under pressure, helium can be solidified, and as the pressure is increased, it goes through a succession of ever denser crystal structures. Under a pressure of 37 atmospheres at 1.7 K, helium has a body centred cubic (*bcc*) structure with a density of 200 kg m^{-3}. In this question we will try to understand why the crystal structure adopted is *bcc* (Figure 6.6 (a)) and not *fcc* (Figure in Example 6.1) as adopted by the other noble gases.

(a) Estimate the side of the *bcc* conventional unit cell and the nearest neighbour separation.

(b) The parameters of the Lennard–Jones pair potential estimated from the gas phase are $\sigma = 2.56 \times 10^{-10}$ m. and $\varepsilon = 1.406 \times 10^{-22}$ J. Using the values

of the lattice sums for *bcc* from Table 6.1, estimate the nearest neighbour separation you would expect to find and compare it with the answer in (a).

You should find that the answer to part (b) is considerably smaller than the experimental near neighbour separation determined in (a). So the phenomena we need to understand are (i) why helium first solidifies in a *bcc* structure and (ii) why the nearest-neighbour separation is greater than would be estimated on the basis of the Lennard–Jones potential.

The factor we have not considered is that the atoms are intrinsically quantum mechanical objects. When confined to a small volume there is a minimum energy – the so-called *zero point energy* – that the particle must have. Let us try to model this

by adding the energy of a particle in a box of side L (Equation 2.49) to Equation 6.18. We estimate that the energy per atom is:

$$\frac{U}{N_A} = 2\varepsilon A_{12}\left(\frac{\sigma}{r_o}\right)^{12} - 2\varepsilon A_6\left(\frac{\sigma}{r_o}\right)^6 + \frac{3h^2}{8m_{He}L^2} \quad (1)$$

where the last term is the lowest energy of a helium atom in a three-dimensional cubic box of side L. Of course, each helium atom is not confined to a cubic box of this (or any other) size, but is constrained by a complicated potential. In this question we will estimate roughly that $L \approx 0.7r_o$.

(a) Evaluate the coefficient of r_o or L in each term in Equation 1 and plot each term in Equation 1 as a function of r_o on the same graph.

(b) Plot (i) the sum of the first two terms and (ii) the sum of the first three terms in Equation 1 as a function of r_o (roughly from around σ to 1.2σ). You should see that the minimum of the curve has been moved to a larger value of r_o and reduced in its depth by a considerable amount. You will not be able to get the actual value of the new lattice constant right, but you should see that the new

curve has a minimum which is only just below the zero of energy, i.e. the binding is very weak.

(c) Evaluate the last term in Equation 1 – the quantum mechanical term – for neon, argon and krypton, and compare your results with the cohesive energy of these substances in Table 6.2. You should find that the quantum mechanical correction is small for substances other than helium and (to a much smaller extent) neon.

(d) The packing fraction for bcc is less than for fcc. Taking this into account, explain briefly why helium solidifies first in the bcc structure.

Optional. If you wish to understand solid helium more fully, consider Equation 1 evaluated with lattice sums appropriate to the fcc structure. Compare these results with the evaluation you made for the bcc structure. For fcc you will have to choose a value for L which will be a smaller fraction of r_o than the factor 0.7 chosen for bcc. This is because the more efficient packing of atoms in a fcc structure more tightly constrains the helium atoms.

26. Beyond Einstein!

The Einstein model of vibrations in solids assumes that all atoms are identical and all vibrate with a single frequency. The Debye model is more realistic, allowing for a spectrum of allowed vibrational frequencies. However, in between the two models there were historically a plethora of modifications of the Einstein model, which assumed 'a few' vibrational frequencies.

(a) Assuming that 50% of the atoms vibrate with frequency f_1 and 50% with frequency f_2, work through the equations in Appendix A4 (or Equations 7.48 to 7.56) and show in a similar fashion that the heat capacity predicted by such a model is given by:

$$C = \frac{3R}{2T^2}\left[\frac{\Theta_1^2 \exp(\Theta_1/T)}{\left(\exp(\Theta_1/T)-1\right)^2} + \frac{\Theta_2^2 \exp(\Theta_2/T)}{\left(\exp(\Theta_2/T)-1\right)^2}\right]$$

where $\Theta_1 = hf_1/k_B$ and $\Theta_2 = hf_2/k_B$.

(b) Show that this has the same high-temperature limiting value (law of Dulong and Petit) as the Einstein expression (Equation 7.56).

(c) Sketch - either qualitatively or by direct use of a spreadsheet - the general shape of this new curve when $f_1 = 10f_2$.

(d) Suggest (with some attempt at justification please) what kind of substances such a model might have been developed to describe.

27. Low-temperature resistivity of metals

The graph over the page shows the electrical resistivity of a sample of copper which contains small amounts of zinc impurity. The units of ρ on the vertical scale are 10^{-8} Ωm. At absolute zero, lattice vibrations are unable to scatter electrons. The scattering which gives rise to the so-called *residual resistivity* is due solely to impurities and defects in the crystal lattice.

A general rule, called *Mattheison's rule*, states that the resistivity arising from different sources may be simply added to give the total resistivity:

$$\rho_{total} = \rho_{impurity} + \rho_{phonons} \quad (1)$$

Assuming Mattheison's rule to hold:

(a) At 0 K, work out the resistivity due to impurities and that due to phonons.

(b) At 300 K, work out the resistivity due to impurities and that due to phonons.

(c) It is known that zinc impurities in copper add to the resistivity an amount:

$$\rho_{zinc/copper} = 4 \times 10^{-9} c_{zinc/copper} \ \Omega\,m$$

where $c_{zinc/copper}$ is the concentration of zinc in copper in atomic percent. (See discussion in §7.4 of an $A_x B_{1-x}$ alloy: the alloy has x atomic percent of element A.) Assuming no other significant amounts of impurity are present, what is the concentration of zinc in this particular sample?

(d) Make a sketch of the curve of $\rho(T)$ that you would expect if the concentration were twice as great as that found in (c).

(e) Estimate the time between scattering events at $T = 0$ K.

(f) Copper has a number density of electrons of around 8.65×10^{28} m^{-3}. Estimate the speed of electrons at the Fermi surface and hence estimate the mean free path between scattering events. Compare your answer with the expected distance between impurities inferred from your answer to (c). Do they agree?

(g) The measurements shown were deduced from measurements on a sample 3 cm long and 1 mm in diameter. If the measuring current was 50 mA, estimate the voltage measured experimentally. The resistivity of superconductors is known to be $<10^{-25}$ Ω m. Based on your answer to this question explain why data on the resistivity of superconductors has to be inferred from measurements other than direct measurements of resistivity.

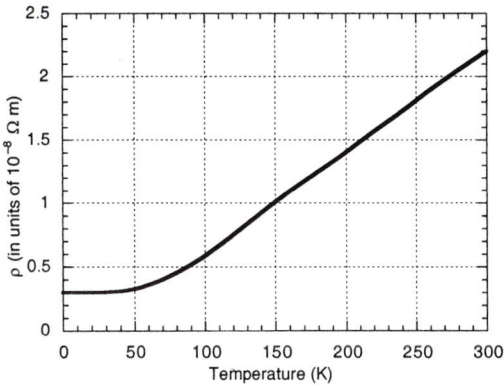

Changes of Phase

28. Water phase diagram

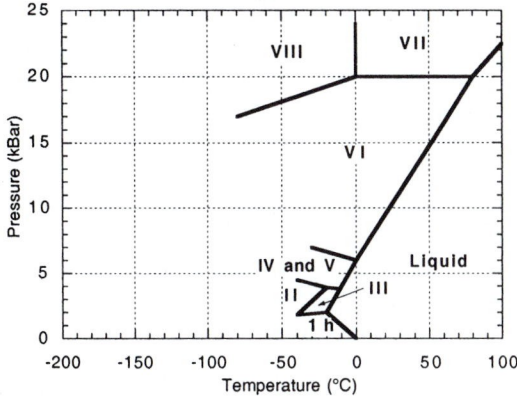

Figure 10.16 shows a phase diagram for water substance constructed on the basis of extrapolation of the theoretical expressions for the melting and vaporisation curves. These expressions do not remain accurate at very high pressures because the normal ice structure, called Ice I (or Ice Ih where the h stands for *hexagonal*), collapses into a series of ever-denser structures. The experimentally determined phase diagram of ice is shown above. The roman numerals indicate regimes of temperature and pressure in which ice adopts one its ten different crystal structures. The *full* phase diagram is even more complicated than the one shown and includes a large number of metastable crystal structures.

(a) The vertical scale on the pressure axis is in kilobar, where one bar is normal atmospheric pressure. On the diagram above sketch the area to which Figure 10.16 applies.

(b) What is the minimum melting temperature for ice, and at what pressure does it occur?

(c) Over roughly what temperature range would applying pressure to ice first cause the ice to melt, and then at higher pressures to solidify?

(d) What pressure would be required to solidify water at room temperature?

(e) At what pressure would water freeze at 100 °C? Is it feasible to ever measure this?

(f) Which solid structures have a volume less than that of the liquid at that pressure?

(g) Let us just suppose there is some water deep within the Earth near to the core–mantle boundary.

The pressure at this depth is around 10^{11} Pa. Extrapolating (wildly!) from the phase diagram, estimate the freezing temperature of water in this region. If the water were solidified, what structure would it adopt?

29. Corresponding states

The atoms of a hypothetical element *Podestium* have mass 10^{-25} kg and in their solid state adopt a simple cubic structure with nearest neighbours separated by 4×10^{-10} m. They undergo three-dimensional simple harmonic motion about fixed equilibrium positions with a period of 5×10^{-13} s.

(a) Estimate the melting temperature of the solid. What uncertainty would you ascribe to your estimate?

(b) Based on your answer to (a), estimate the boiling temperature of the liquid. What uncertainty would you ascribe to your estimate?

(c) Estimate the critical temperature of the substance.

(d) Estimate the critical volume of the substance.

30. *PVT* journey.

The figures on the right show two generic *PVT* surfaces. The drawings are poor, but in the upper figure, points *A* and *B* are intended to describe points at the same pressure, and in the lower figure, points *C* and *D* are intended to describe points at the same volume.

(a) A substance is taken on a 'journey' across the *PVT* surface shown from point *A* to point *B* and then back to point *A* by a different 'route'.

(b) A substance is taken on a 'journey' across the *PVT* surface shown from point *C* to point *D*.

Describe each journey (a) and (b) in as much detail as possible, including descriptions of:

- The phase (or phases) of the substance present at each stage on its journey. Where relevant discuss the relative amounts of the phases present.
- The rates of changes of *P*, *V* and *T*.
- The points along the paths where heat enters or leaves the substance;
- The points along the paths where work is done by or on the substance;
- Anything else relevant!

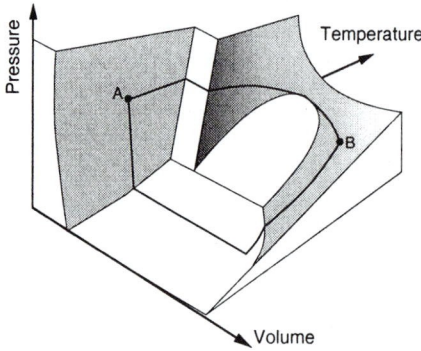

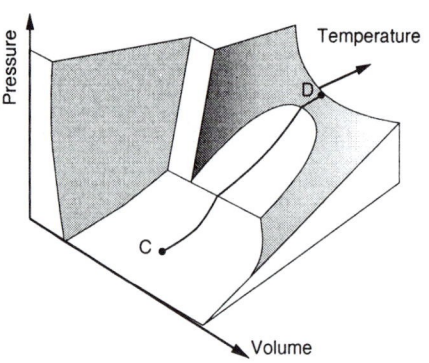

APPENDIX 1

Maxwellian speed distribution of a gas

A1.1 Introduction

In this appendix we will work out the distribution of molecular speeds in a gas by explicitly calculating three functions that describe the properties of dilute gases. These are:

- The *density of states function* $g(E)\mathrm{d}E$, which yields the number of quantum states with energies between E and $\mathrm{d}E$.
- The *occupation function* $f(E,T)$, which yields the average number of particles occupying a single quantum state with energy E and temperature T.
- The *distribution function* $D(E,T)$, which is the product $f(E,T)g(E)\mathrm{d}E$ and yields the average

number of particles occupying quantum states with energies between E and $\mathrm{d}E$ at temperature T.

Once we have worked out the distribution function, we will be able to state *on average* how many molecules in a gas have energies between E and $E + \mathrm{d}E$. Then, since we know that for simple molecules the energy of a molecule is entirely kinetic ($E = \frac{1}{2}mv^2$), we can deduce how many molecules have speeds between v and $v + \mathrm{d}v$. In what follows we consider only the properties of simple molecules of mass m and no internal degrees of freedom.

A1.2 The density of states function

Our determination of the density of states function is based on an analysis of the 'particle in a box' problem (§2.4.3 and §6.5.2). That is, we think of molecules of gas as occupying the quantum states of a 'particle in a box'. In §6.5 we considered this problem for the case of electrons packed densely together inside a metal, but now we consider the case of molecules packed at low density into an empty box. The first step is to develop a way of systematically counting the quantum states of a 'particle in a box' (Figure A1.1). We will consider two counting techniques: a simple way and a more complicated way. We will, of course, choose the more complicated way.

The quantum states: standing waves
The first method of counting is derived from Equation 2.49 for the energies of allowed quantum states:

$$E(n_x, n_y, n_z) = \frac{h^2}{8mL^2}\left[n_x^2 + n_y^2 + n_z^2\right] \quad (A1.1)$$

Figure A1.1 A scheme for counting quantum states in the 'particle in a box' problem when lots of particles are present. Each quantum state is represented by a point on an n_x, n_y, n_z graph. The energy of the state is proportional to the square of its distance from the origin on this graph. For this reason, the occupied quantum states cluster in a quadrant of a sphere around the origin

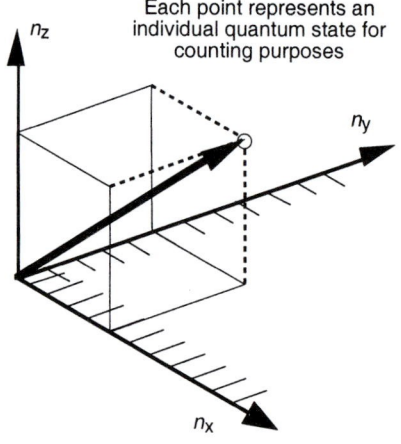

Each point represents an individual quantum state for counting purposes

403

We represent an allowed quantum state by a point on a three-dimensional graph whose axes are n_x, n_y, and n_z respectively. Thus each individual quantum state is represented by a single point on the graph, and the points representing the quantum states are distributed uniformly on a 'mesh' throughout the graph. Because of this, by measuring 'volumes' on this three-dimensional graph we can – with a fair degree of approximation – also count quantum states. Further, we can also simply state that the energy of a particular state is given by $h^2/8mL^2 \times$ [the square of the length of the vector from the origin to the point representing that quantum state](Figure A1.1).

However in order to develop the 'geometrical' method of counting quantum states further, we will change to a second view of the quantum states of a particle in a box.

The quantum states: travelling waves

The second method of counting arises from a reconsideration of the particle in a box problem. We will arrive at similar, but distinctly different, solutions to the Schrödinger equation: travelling wave solutions.

In §2.3.3 we required the wave functions to be zero at the edge of the box because we imagined the edge of the box to represent the walls of the box. We supposed that molecules were not allowed to penetrate the walls (otherwise they are not walls!) and so the wave functions of the particles must be zero there. Now, however, we consider a more complex situation. We imagine a volume of the gas which is *representative* of the gas as a whole and we imagine it to surrounded by *identical volumes* of gas. The differences between this situation and the standing wave situation are illustrated in Figure A1.2. You may consider this to be 'trickery', and it is. It is a mathematical trick, but it will allow us to see more clearly the physics of what is happening in the gas.

The key difference to the problem is that now instead of requiring that the wave functions be zero at the edges of the box, i.e. $\Psi(-x/2) = \Psi(+x/2) = 0$, we require that the wave functions be identical in neighbouring boxes, i.e.

$$\Psi(x) = \Psi(x + L_x) \tag{A1.2}$$

where L_x is the length of the box under consideration. If the solutions are $\sin(kx)$ or $\cos(kx)$ waves this is equivalent to requiring that:

$$\cos(k_x x) = \cos(k_x[x + L_x])$$

or $\hspace{6cm}$ (A1.3)

$$\sin(k_x x) = \sin(k_x[x + L_x])$$

The requirements A1.3 are known as *Born–von Karmen boundary conditions*, and lead to only discrete values of k being allowed solutions. Let us follow one of Equations A1.3 through explicitly to find these conditions for k_x. The boundary conditions require that:

$$\cos(k_x x) = \cos(k_x[x + L_x]) = \cos(k_x x + k_x L_x) \tag{A1.4}$$

Using the trigonometric identity:

$$\cos(A+B) = \cos A \cos B - \sin A \sin B \tag{A1.5}$$

Equation A1.4 can be rewritten as:

$$\cos(k_x x) = \cos(k_x x)\cos(k_x L_x) - \sin(k_x x)\sin(k_x L_x) \tag{A1.6}$$

Figure A1.2 Illustration of two approaches to the particle in a box problem. (a) The first approach uses the idea of an isolated box representing the entire crystal. The second approach (b) uses the idea of a box of representative material surrounded by identical copies of itself. The edges of the actual crystal are imagined to be far enough away that they do not significantly affect the particles deep inside the box.

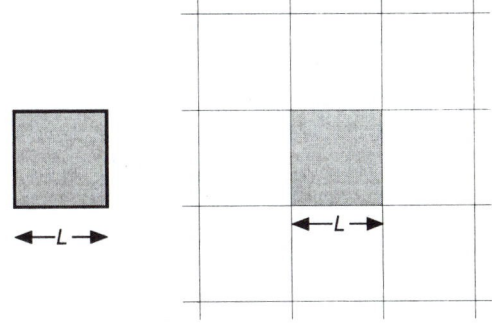

Clearly, in general this equation is not true! It is only true when $\cos(k_x L_x) = 1$ and when the second term is zero. Since x can vary, this will only be true when $\sin(k_x L_x) = 0$. Now $\cos(k_x L_x) = 1$ when $k_x L_x = 0, \pm 2\pi, \pm 4\pi,\ldots$etc, and these values of $k_x L_x$ also cause $\sin(k_x L_x)$ to be zero. So the Born-von Karmen boundary conditions are satisfied when:

$$k_x L_x = 0, \pm 2\pi, \pm 4\pi,\ldots \quad \text{(A1.7)}$$

i.e. when:

$$k_x = 0, \frac{\pm 2\pi}{L_x}, \frac{\pm 4\pi}{L_x},\ldots \quad \text{(A1.8)}$$

or in general when:

$$k_x = \frac{2m_x \pi}{L_x} \text{ where } m_x = 0, \pm 1, \pm 2\ldots \quad \text{(A1.9)}$$

I shall leave it to you to show that following the second of Equations A1.3 through in a similar way [using $\sin(A + B) = \sin A \cos B + \cos A \sin B$] results in exactly the same conclusion.

Figure A1.3 A cross-section through 'k-space'. Each small circle represents an allowed travelling wave solution to the Schrödinger equation. The filled (unfilled) circles represent occupied quantum states which are occupied (unoccupied). The configuration of occupied and unoccupied states shown is similar to that expected in a metal at absolute zero. Only the lowest energy states (low k = long wavelength = low energy) are occupied. In three dimensions the occupied states form a sphere in k-space known as the Fermi sphere.

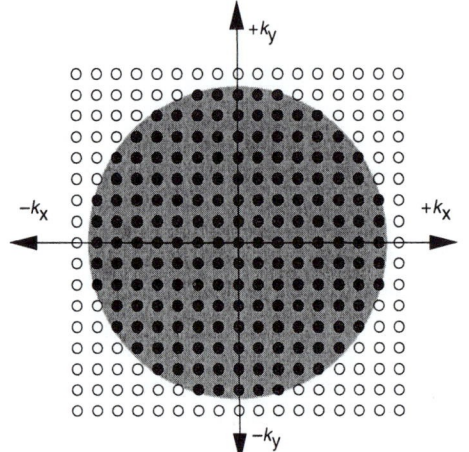

Figure A1.4 Close up view of 'k-space'. The circles represent allowed values of **k**. If the central point represents a solution of the Schrödinger equation with a particular value of k_x, k_y, k_z, then point a represents a solution with k_x component increased by $2\pi/L_x$. Similarly point b represents a solution with k_z component increased by $2\pi/L_z$.

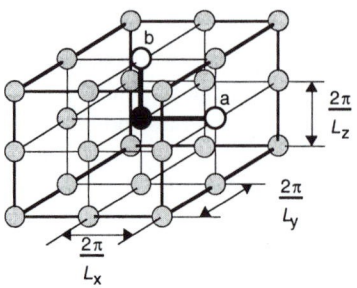

We can now make sketches analogous to Figure A1.1 for this new situation. In these sketches we plot points representing k_x, k_y and k_z, which serve to label individual quantum states. The main difference between this and the (n_x, n_y, n_z) representation discussed previously is that each allowed point in space now represents a travelling wave rather a standing wave. Hence we can have negative k values and so the quantum states are distributed all around the origin rather than being confined to the positive $|\mathbf{k}|$ octant (contrast Figures A1.1 and A1.3).

We know further that the allowed states are distributed uniformly through k-space so that if we consider a 'volume' of k-space we can work out how many allowed quantum states it contains. A close up view of our k-space graph is shown in Figure A1.4

It is clear from the Figure A1.4 that each state has around it a 'volume of k-space' $\Delta\Omega$ given by:

$$\Delta\Omega = \frac{2\pi}{L_x} \times \frac{2\pi}{L_y} \times \frac{2\pi}{L_z} \quad \text{(A1.10)}$$

and since $L_x L_y L_z = V$ this reduces to:

$$\Delta\Omega = \frac{8\pi^3}{V} \quad \text{(A1.11)}$$

This simple result embodied in Equation A1.11 is crucial. As we shall see, it enables us to count quantum states, and in particular, it enables us to

405

answer the following question: how many quantum states are there with wave vectors between k and $k + dk$?

How many quantum states are there with wave vectors between *k* and *k* + d*k* ?

All the quantum states with k vectors in this range correspond to points in a spherical shell of radius k and thickness dk. We can write down the 'volume' on the k-space graph that these points occupy as:

$$d\Omega = 4\pi k^2 dk \qquad (A1.12)$$

and since each point occupies a volume $\Delta\Omega = 8\pi^3 / V$ the number of quantum states dN in this shell is given by:

$$dN = \frac{4\pi k^2 dk}{8\pi^3/V} = \frac{Vk^2 dk}{2\pi^2} \qquad (A1.13)$$

How many quantum states are there with energy between *E* and *E* + d*E* ?

In order to answer this we need to rewrite Equation A1.13 replacing references to k – in this case k^2 and dk – with references to E. We start with:

$$E = \frac{1}{2}mv^2 = \frac{p^2}{2m} = \frac{\hbar^2 k^2}{2m} \qquad (A1.14)$$

We see that:

$$k^2 = \frac{2mE}{\hbar^2} \qquad (A1.15)$$

Differentiating Equation A1.14 we find:

$$dE = \frac{\hbar^2 k}{m} dk \qquad (A1.16)$$

and replacing the reference to k :

$$dE = \frac{\hbar^2 \sqrt{2mE/\hbar^2}}{m} dk \qquad (A1.17)$$

we arrive at:

$$dk = \frac{m}{\hbar^2 \sqrt{2mE/\hbar^2}} dE \qquad (A1.18)$$

We can now replace both the references to k in Equation A1.19 with references to E:

$$dN = \frac{V}{2\pi^2} \times \frac{2mE}{\hbar^2} \times \frac{m}{\hbar^2 \sqrt{2mE/\hbar^2}} dE \qquad (A1.19)$$

which simplifies to:

$$dN = \frac{Vm^{3/2}}{\sqrt{2}\pi^2\hbar^3} E^{1/2} dE \qquad (A1.20)$$

This expression is for the number of quantum states dN with energies between E and $E + dE$, which is exactly the definition of the density of states function $g(E)$. So we now have the expression we desire:

$$g(E) = \frac{dN}{dE} = \frac{Vm^{3/2}}{\sqrt{2}\pi^2\hbar^3} E^{1/2} \qquad (A1.21)$$

A1.3 The occupation function

We now have to consider whether the particles which will occupy the box will be bosons or fermions. Molecules are composed of many atoms and atoms are composed of protons, neutrons and electrons. Whether a molecule is a boson or a fermion depends on way in which the spins of the component particles add together. For example, helium atoms occur in two isotopes: the rare ^{3}He

and the more common ^{4}He. ^{3}He has 2 electrons, 2 protons, and 1 neutron, all with spin $\frac{1}{2}\hbar$. No matter which way these are added together, the net result is always half an odd integer times $\hbar$ and so ^{3}He atoms are fermions: they obey the exclusion principle and are described by Fermi–Dirac statistics. In contrast ^{4}He has 2 electrons, 2 protons and 2 neutrons which always add together to yield a

spin of zero or an integer multiple $\hbar$. Thus ^{4}He atoms are bosons: they do *not* obey the exclusion principle, and they are described by Bose–Einstein statistics.

However, at the low densities present in gases, both fermion and boson occupation functions are well approximated by the Boltzmann occupation function. Only when the density of the gas is such that the probability of multiple occupation of quantum states becomes significant can we distinguish between the two occupation functions. However this high density regime does not occur until we reach temperatures of a few kelvin, and densities similar to those in solids and liquids.

The Boltzmann occupation function

Independent of whether the molecules of the gas are fermions or bosons we may write the occupation function – the average occupancy of an individual quantum state – as:

$$f(E,T) = \frac{1}{\exp\left[\dfrac{E-\mu}{k_B T}\right] \pm 1} \qquad (A1.22)$$

where the upper sign corresponds to fermions and the lower sign corresponds to bosons (Equations 2.61 and 2.62). The energy μ is known as the *chemical potential*, but is sometimes referred to as the Fermi energy when dealing with fermions. Now we could proceed to evaluate the distribution function using Equation A1.22 directly. However, there is a useful approximation that may be made when the average occupancy of a quantum state is low. As mentioned in §2.5.5, when there is little chance of two particles occupying the same quantum state, the occupation functions of fermions and bosons must be similar since they have an essentially unrestricted choice of quantum states. Thus in the low-density (classical) limit of Equation A1.22 we always have:

$$f(E,T) \ll 1 \qquad (A1.23)$$

If this is true, then the denominator of Equation A1.22 must be much larger than unity, which implies that:

$$\exp\left[\frac{E-\mu}{k_B T}\right] \gg 1 \qquad (A1.24)$$

This being so, we may write:

$$f(E,T) \approx \exp\left[-\left(\frac{E-\mu}{k_B T}\right)\right] \qquad (A1.25)$$

which may be factorised as:

$$f(E,T) \approx \exp\left[\frac{+\mu}{k_B T}\right]\exp\left[\frac{-E}{k_B T}\right] \qquad (A1.26)$$

Now the chemical potential μ has not yet been determined, but we will be able to determine it if we notice that the average occupancy of a quantum state, when summed over all quantum states, must sum to N, the total number of particles, i.e.

$$N = \sum_{\substack{\text{All}\\\text{quantum}\\\text{states i}}} f(E_i,T) \approx \sum_{\substack{\text{All}\\\text{quantum}\\\text{states i}}} \exp\left[\frac{+\mu}{k_B T}\right]\exp\left[\frac{-E_i}{k_B T}\right]$$

$$(A1.27)$$

We can now factor out $\exp[+\mu/k_B T]$, which is common to all terms in the sum:

$$N = \exp\left[\frac{+\mu}{k_B T}\right] \sum_{\substack{\text{All}\\\text{quantum}\\\text{states i}}} \exp\left[\frac{-E_i}{k_B T}\right] \qquad (A1.28)$$

and rearrange to solve for $\exp[+\mu/k_B T]$:

$$\exp\left[\frac{+\mu}{k_B T}\right] = \frac{N}{\displaystyle\sum_{\substack{\text{All}\\\text{quantum}\\\text{states i}}} \exp\left[\frac{-E_i}{k_B T}\right]} \qquad (A1.29)$$

We can now substitute this expression for $\exp[+\mu/k_B T]$ back into Equation A1.26 to yield the desired expression for $f(E,T)$:

$$f(E,T) = \frac{N\exp\left[\dfrac{-E}{k_B T}\right]}{\displaystyle\sum_{\substack{\text{All}\\\text{quantum}\\\text{states i}}} \exp\left[\frac{-E_i}{k_B T}\right]} \qquad (A1.30)$$

Finally, we note that at a given temperature, both the denominator and N are constant so:

$$f(E,T) = A\exp\left[\frac{-E}{k_B T}\right] \qquad (A1.31)$$

which is the classical Boltzmann occupation function, Equation 2.72.

A1.4 The distribution function

Multiplying together Equations A1.21 for the number of quantum states between energies E and $E + dE$:

$$dN = \frac{Vm^{3/2}}{\sqrt{2}\pi^2\hbar^3} E^{1/2} dE \qquad (A1.21^*)$$

and Equation A1.31 for the average occupancy of a quantum state:

$$f(E,T) \approx A \exp\left[\frac{-E}{k_B T}\right] \qquad (A1.31^*)$$

we arrive at the arrive at the *distribution function*. This tells us the average number of *particles* which occupy quantum states with energies between E and $E + dE$:

$$dN = A \frac{Vm^{3/2}}{\sqrt{2}\pi^2\hbar^3} E^{1/2} \exp\left[\frac{-E}{k_B T}\right] dE \qquad (A1.32)$$

In order to evaluate this expression for dN we need to work out a way of eliminating the undefined constant A in Equation A1.32. We can do this by integrating Equation A1.32 to find an expression for N, the total number of particles:

$$\int_{E=0}^{E=\infty} dN = N = \int_{E=0}^{E=\infty} A \frac{Vm^{3/2}}{\sqrt{2}\pi^2\hbar^3} E^{1/2} \exp\left[\frac{-E}{k_B T}\right] dE$$
$$(A1.33)$$

Taking the constants outside of the integral we arrive at:

$$N = A \frac{Vm^{3/2}}{\sqrt{2}\pi^2\hbar^3} \int_{E=0}^{E=\infty} E^{1/2} \exp\left[\frac{-E}{k_B T}\right] dE \qquad (A1.34)$$

The integral is (fortunately) a standard integral which evaluates (using MathCAD or a Maths reference book) to:

$$\int_{x=0}^{x=\infty} x^{1/2} e^{-x/a} dx = \frac{\sqrt{\pi a^3}}{2} \qquad (A1.35)$$

where we have substituted $x = E$ and $a = k_B T$. With these substitutions Equation A1.34 becomes:

$$N = \frac{A Vm^{3/2}}{\sqrt{2}\pi^2\hbar^3} \times \frac{\sqrt{\pi k_B^3 T^3}}{2} \qquad (A1.36)$$

We can now eliminate A in Equation A1.32 by dividing through by Equation A1.36 for N, and hence calculating the *fraction* of the particles dN/N which occupy quantum states with energies in the range E to $E + dE$. We find :

$$\frac{dN}{N} = \frac{\dfrac{Vm^{3/2}}{\sqrt{2}\pi^2\hbar^3} E^{1/2} A \exp\left[\dfrac{-E}{k_B T}\right] dE}{\dfrac{A Vm^{3/2}}{\sqrt{2}\pi^2\hbar^3} \times \dfrac{\sqrt{\pi k_B^3 T^3}}{2}} \qquad (A1.37)$$

$$\frac{dN}{N} = 2 \sqrt{\frac{E}{\pi k_B^3 T^3}} \exp\left[\frac{-E}{k_B T}\right] dE \qquad (A1.38)$$

We may alternatively write this as the probability $P(E)dE$ that a molecule has energy between E and $E + dE$:

$$P(E)dE = 2 \sqrt{\frac{E}{\pi k_B^3 T^3}} \exp\left[\frac{-E}{k_B T}\right] dE \qquad (A1.39)$$

It is important to take note of the general form of Equation A1.39 which we may write more simply as:

$$P(E)dE = \text{constants} \times \sqrt{E} \times \exp\left[\frac{-E}{k_B T}\right] \qquad (A1.40)$$

We see that, at a given temperature, Equation A1.39 predicts *exactly the same* distribution of molecular energies for *all gases*. Example A1.1 shows how the curve may be used to make calculations about energy distribution in gases.

Figure A1.5 The distribution of energies of molecules in a gas at temperatures of 100 K and 300 K. Notice that the curves are universal, i.e. they apply to all simple molecules whatever their mass. Heavy molecules move more slowly than lighter molecules in such a way as to keep the energies their same.

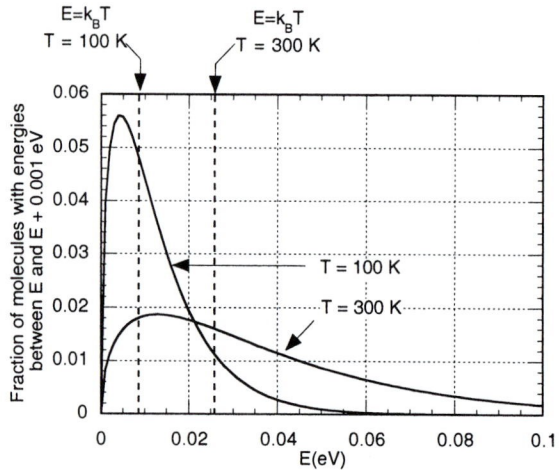

A1.5 The distribution of molecular speeds

We are now close to completing the task we set ourselves: to calculate the distribution of molecular speeds. To achieve this, we need to convert the references to energy E in Equation A1.38:

$$\frac{dN}{N} = 2\sqrt{\frac{E}{\pi k_B^3 T^3}} \exp\left[\frac{-E}{k_B T}\right] dE \quad (A1.38^*)$$

into references to molecular speed, using:

$$E = \tfrac{1}{2}mv^2 \quad (A1.42)$$

and:

$$dE = mv\,dv \quad (A1.43)$$

Notice that these substitutions assume the molecules have only the three degrees of freedom associated with molecular motion, and so we are implicitly neglecting the possibility of internal molecular vibrations and rotations. In fact, the presence or absence of these other degrees of freedom does not affect the conclusions that we draw here. On substituting Equations A1.42 and A1.43 into A1.38 we find:

$$\frac{dN}{N} = 2\sqrt{\frac{\tfrac{1}{2}mv^2}{\pi k_B^3 T^3}} \exp\left[\frac{-mv^2}{2k_B T}\right] mv\,dv \quad (A1.44)$$

which simplifies to:

$$\frac{dN}{N} = \sqrt{\frac{2}{\pi}}\left[\frac{m}{k_B T}\right]^{3/2} v^2 \exp\left[\frac{-mv^2}{2k_B T}\right] dv \quad (A1.45)$$

In terms of the probability that a molecule has a speed between v and $v + dv$, $P(v)dv$:

$$P(v)dv = \sqrt{\frac{2}{\pi}}\left[\frac{m}{k_B T}\right]^{3/2} v^2 \exp\left[\frac{-mv^2}{2k_B T}\right] dv \quad (A1.46)$$

This is the Maxwellian speed distribution curve. If you think its derivation from the 'particle in a box' problem has been magical, then consider this. Maxwell derived this curve 150 years ago, around 70 years before the discovery of quantum mechanics! The salient features of the curve are illustrated in Figures 4.6 to 4.8. An animation of the way in which the curve changes with temperature may be found on the web site for the book at www.physicsofmatter.com

Example A1.2 shows how the curve is used to make calculations about speed distributions in gases.

409

Example A1.1

In a gas at temperature T, what fraction of molecules have energies greater than k_BT, given that:

$$\int_{x=1}^{x=\infty} x^{\frac{1}{2}}e^{-x}dx = 0.507$$

The required fraction is the integral of dN/N (Equation A1.39) over the energy range specified, which in this case is from $E = k_BT$ to infinity. So:

$$fraction = \int_{E=k_BT}^{E=\infty} 2\sqrt{\frac{E}{\pi k_B^3 T^3}}e^{-E/k_BT}dE$$

If we substitute $x = E/k_BT$ we find $dx = dE/k_BT$ and the integral becomes:

$$fraction = \int_{x=1}^{x=\infty} 2\left[\sqrt{\frac{1}{\pi k_B^2 T^2}}\right]x^{\frac{1}{2}}e^{-x}k_BT\ dx$$

Taking the constants outside the integral sign, allows us to recognise the integral given in the question:

$$fraction = \left[2\sqrt{\frac{1}{\pi}}\right]\int_{x=1}^{x=\infty} x^{\frac{1}{2}}e^{-x}dx$$

and substituting for this integral we have:

$$fraction = \left[2\sqrt{\frac{1}{\pi}}\right]\times 0.507 = 0.572$$

Thus 57.2% of molecules have energy greater than k_BT. Notice that this is true at any temperature!

Example A1.2

In a nitrogen gas at 300 K, what fraction of molecules have speeds greater than 10^3 ms^{-1}, given that:

$$\int_{x=5.615}^{x=\infty} x^{\frac{1}{2}}e^{-x}dx = 9.345\times 10^{-3}$$

The required fraction is the integral of $P(v)dv$ (Equation A1.46) over the speed range specified, which in this case is from $v = 10^3$ ms^{-1} to infinity. So:

$$\int_{v=10^6}^{v=\infty} P(v)dv = \int_{v=10^6}^{v=\infty}\sqrt{\frac{2}{\pi}}\left[\frac{m}{k_BT}\right]^{\frac{3}{2}}v^2 e^{-mv^2/2k_BT}dv$$

If we substitute $x = mv^2/2k_BT$ then $dx = dv\sqrt{\frac{2m}{k_BT}}$ and the integral becomes:

$$fraction = \sqrt{\frac{2}{\pi}}\left[\frac{m}{k_BT}\right]^{\frac{3}{2}}\int_{x=x_1}^{x=\infty}\frac{2k_BTx}{m}e^{-x}\frac{dx}{\sqrt{x}}\sqrt{\frac{k_BT}{2m}}$$

where the upper limit is infinity, and we will work out the x-value corresponding to the lower limit presently. Taking the constants outside the integral sign:

$$fraction = \sqrt{\frac{2}{\pi}}\left[\frac{m}{k_BT}\right]^{\frac{3}{2}}\frac{2k_BT}{m}\sqrt{\frac{k_BT}{2m}}\int_{x=x_1}^{x=\infty}x^{\frac{1}{2}}e^{-x}dx$$

and re-arranging:

$$fraction = 2\sqrt{\frac{1}{\pi}}\left[\frac{m}{k_BT}\right]^{\frac{3}{2}}\left[\frac{k_BT}{m}\right]^{\frac{3}{2}}\int_{x=10^6}^{x=\infty}x^{\frac{1}{2}}e^{-x}dx$$

then cancelling we find:

$$fraction = 2\sqrt{\frac{1}{\pi}}\int_{x=x_1}^{x=\infty}x^{\frac{1}{2}}e^{-x}dx$$

Again we are able to recognise the numerical integral given in the question. We need to evaluate the lower limit of the integral using $x = mv^2/2k_BT$ we have:

$$x_1 = \frac{28\times 1.66\times 10^{-27}\times(10^3)^2}{2\times 1.38\times 10^{-23}\times 300} = 5.615$$

$$fraction = \left[2\sqrt{\frac{1}{\pi}}\right]\int_{x=5.6\times 10^6}^{x=\infty}x^{\frac{1}{2}}e^{-x}dx$$

and substituting for this integral we have:

$$fraction = \left[2\sqrt{\frac{1}{\pi}}\right]\times 9.345\times 10^{-3} = 0.0105$$

Thus just over 1% of molecules have speeds greater than 10^3 ms^{-1}.

Derivation of speed of sound formulae

A2.1 Introduction

Derivations of formulae for the speed of sound are similar for all types of sound waves in solids, liquids and gases. Here we consider the derivation of formula first for the speed of longitudinal sound waves in gases and solids, and then for shear sound waves in solids. Finally we consider relationships among the elastic moduli in solids.

All analyses of sound waves involve both small quantities (e.g. strain in a solid), and infinitesimal changes in these small quantities. This can make the analyses confusing at first so you will need to take particular care in the following sections.

A2.2 Longitudinal sound waves in a gas

The situation of planes of gas perpendicular to the direction of propagation (x-direction) of a plane sound wave is illustrated in Figure A2.1. Our analysis focuses on the changes in pressure and volume close to two planes (1 and 2) within the gas. In the absence of a sound wave, the equilibrium pressure is P_o and planes 1 and 2 are located at x and $x + \Delta x$ respectively. In the presence of a sound wave, the pressure at x oscillates about P_o and at any particular time the pressure at x is no longer in general the same as the pressure at $x + \Delta x$.

The effect of the sound wave is to compress (or rarefy) the gas which was originally between x and

$x + \Delta x$. The position of planes 1 and 2 changes from:
- x and $x + \Delta x$, to
- $x + u$ and $(x + \Delta x) + (u + \Delta u)$.

Table A2.1 below is a systematic analysis of the shifts in position of these planes and of the resulting volume and pressure changes within the gas. The aim of the analysis is to deduce the net unbalanced force on the gas that originally lay between x and $x + dx$. We can then use Newton's Law $F = ma$ to determine the dynamics of the gas, and hence deduce the speed of sound.

It is important to notice the direction of the forces acting on the gas in Figure A2.1(b). The net force

Figure A2.1 (a) A representation of the planes of constant pressure in a sound wave. The darkness of the shading indicates the amplitude of the pressure oscillations at a certain time. (b) Shows an analysis of the forces on a thin 'slab' of gas. It may help to refer to this figure when following the derivations in Table A2.1

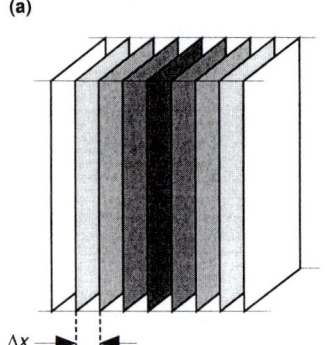
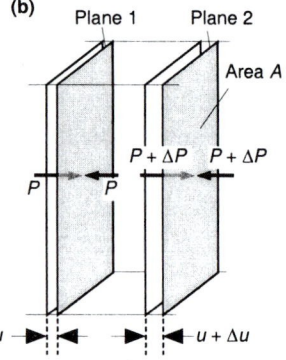

Table A2.1 Systematic derivation of the net force per unit area on the element of gas shown in Figure A2.1b.

	Value at x	Value at $x + dx$	Difference
Displacement from equilibrium position	u	$u + \Delta u$	Δu
Fractional volume change $\Delta V/V$	$\dfrac{A\Delta u}{A\Delta x} = \dfrac{\Delta u}{\Delta x} \approx \dfrac{\partial u}{\partial x}$	$\dfrac{A\Delta(u+\Delta u)}{A\Delta x} \approx \dfrac{\partial(u+\Delta u)}{\partial x}$ $= \dfrac{\partial u}{\partial x} + \dfrac{\partial}{\partial x}(\Delta u)$	$\left(\dfrac{\partial^2 u}{\partial x^2}\right)\Delta x$
Notice that if $\Delta u = 0$ then the gas is not compressed at all		Notice that we can also write Δu as: $\Delta u = \left(\dfrac{\partial u}{\partial x}\right)\Delta x$ and so substitution yields: $= \dfrac{\partial u}{\partial x} + \dfrac{\partial}{\partial x}\left(\dfrac{\partial u}{\partial x}\right)\Delta x$ $= \dfrac{\partial u}{\partial x} + \left(\dfrac{\partial^2 u}{\partial x^2}\right)\Delta x$	
Pressure change $\Delta P = -\dfrac{1}{K}\dfrac{\Delta V}{V}$	$-\dfrac{1}{K}\dfrac{\partial u}{\partial x}$	$-\dfrac{1}{K}\dfrac{\partial u}{\partial x} - \dfrac{1}{K}\left(\dfrac{\partial^2 u}{\partial x^2}\right)\Delta x$	$-\dfrac{1}{K}\left(\dfrac{\partial^2 u}{\partial x^2}\right)\Delta x$
(by definition)			
Force per unit area $\Delta F = -\Delta P$ to the right in Figure A2.1(b)	$+\dfrac{1}{K}\dfrac{\partial u}{\partial x}$	$+\dfrac{1}{K}\dfrac{\partial u}{\partial x} + \dfrac{1}{K}\left(\dfrac{\partial^2 u}{\partial x^2}\right)\Delta x$	$+\dfrac{1}{K}\left(\dfrac{\partial^2 u}{\partial x^2}\right)\Delta x$

on the slab results from the sum of P acting to the right and $P + \Delta P$ acting to the left. Notice that in the case indicated with Δu positive, ΔP would be *negative* and the force on the gas would be in the positive x direction.

The mass of the gas originally between x and $x + \Delta x$ is $\Delta m = \rho A\Delta x$ where ρ is the density of the gas. The difference ΔP between the pressure (force per unit area) at x and at $x + \Delta x$ gives rise to acceleration of this mass. Note that the 'background' pressure corresponds to the ambient pressure within the gas and does not change with time. Recalling that we may write the acceleration of the gas as $\partial^2 u/\partial t^2$ we write:

$$\Delta F = (\rho A\Delta x)\frac{\partial^2 u}{\partial t^2} \tag{A2.1}$$

Dividing through by A, substituting for $\Delta F/A = \Delta P$ from the rightmost column of Table A2.1 and cancelling yields:

$$\frac{1}{K}\frac{\partial^2 u}{\partial x^2}\Delta x = (\rho\Delta x)\frac{\partial^2 u}{\partial t^2} \tag{A2.2}$$

$$\frac{\partial^2 u}{\partial x^2} = (K\rho)\frac{\partial^2 u}{\partial t^2} \tag{A2.3}$$

Comparing Equation A2.3 with the standard form of the wave equation:

$$\left(\frac{\partial^2 f}{\partial x^2}\right) = \frac{1}{v^2}\left(\frac{\partial^2 f}{\partial t^2}\right) \tag{A2.4}$$

where $f(x)$ is the property that satisfies the wave equation. In this case we identify the displacement of the gas u as satisfying the wave equation with the speed of the displacement wave v given by:

$$v = \sqrt{\frac{1}{K\rho}} \tag{A2.5}$$

Equation A2.5 is also commonly written in terms of the bulk modulus B:

$$v = \sqrt{\frac{B}{\rho}} \tag{A2.6}$$

As outlined in §5.6.2, the bulk modulus and compressibility are those associated with *adiabatic* compression of the gas. Equation A2.6 also holds for liquids.

A2.3 Longitudinal sound waves in solid rods

A longitudinal wave in a solid rod is illustrated in Figure A2.2 and the forces on an 'elemental slab' are analysed in Figure A2.2(b) and in Table A2.2. The derivations are similar to those for longitudinal waves in a gas described in §A1.1.

The mass of the slab Δx per unit area is

$\Delta m = \rho A dx$ and the difference ΔF between the tensile force per unit area at x and at $x + \Delta x$ gives rise to acceleration of this mass. Note that the 'background' tensile force corresponds to a situation where $\Delta u = 0$, i.e. to a static background stress which does not change with time. Noticing that we may write the transverse acceleration of

Figure A2.2 (a) A representation of the planes of constant pressure in a sound wave. The darkness of the shading indicates the amplitude of the pressure oscillations at a certain time. (b) Shows an analysis of the forces on a thin 'slab' of solid. It may help to refer to this figure when following the derivations in Table A2.2

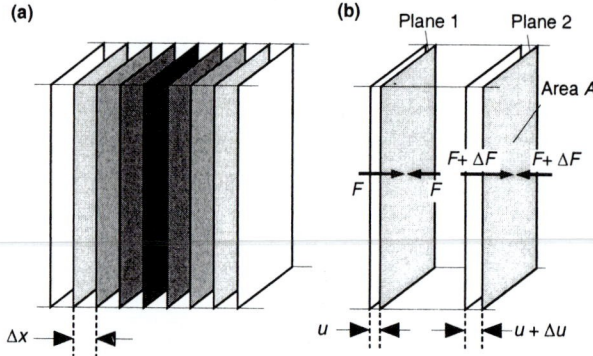

Table A2.2 Systematic derivation of the net tensile force per unit area on the element of solid shown in Figure A2.2b.

	Value at x	Value at $x + dx$	Difference
Longitudinal displacement	u	$u + \Delta u$	Δu
Tensile strain	$\varepsilon = \dfrac{\Delta u}{\Delta x} \approx \dfrac{\partial u}{\partial x}$	$\varepsilon + \Delta\varepsilon = \dfrac{\Delta(u + \Delta u)}{\Delta x}$	$\left(\dfrac{\partial^2 u}{\partial x^2}\right)\Delta x$
This is the *fractional* linear extension of the material originally between x and $x + \Delta x$.		$\approx \dfrac{\partial(u + \Delta u)}{\partial x}$	
		$\approx \dfrac{\partial u}{\partial x} + \dfrac{\partial(\Delta u)}{\partial x}$	
		Notice that we can also write Δu as:	
		$\Delta u = \left(\dfrac{\partial u}{\partial x}\right)\Delta x$	
		which substitutes to give:	
		$\dfrac{\partial u}{\partial x} + \dfrac{\partial}{\partial x}\left(\dfrac{\partial u}{\partial x}\right)\Delta x$	
		$\dfrac{\partial u}{\partial x} + \left(\dfrac{\partial^2 u}{\partial x^2}\right)\Delta x$	
Tensile stress	$S = E\varepsilon$	$S + \Delta S = E(\varepsilon + \Delta\varepsilon)$	$E\left(\dfrac{\partial^2 u}{\partial x^2}\right)\Delta x$
	$= E\dfrac{\partial u}{\partial x}$	$= E\dfrac{\partial u}{\partial x} + E\left(\dfrac{\partial^2 u}{\partial x^2}\right)\Delta x$	
Tensile force per unit area	$\dfrac{F}{A} = S = E\varepsilon = E\dfrac{\partial u}{\partial x}$	$\dfrac{F + \Delta F}{A} = E\dfrac{\partial u}{\partial x} + E\left(\dfrac{\partial^2 u}{\partial x^2}\right)\Delta x$	$\dfrac{\Delta F}{A} = E\left(\dfrac{\partial^2 u}{\partial x^2}\right)\Delta x$

the slab as $\partial^2 u / \partial t^2$ we write:

$$\Delta F = (\rho A \Delta x)\frac{\partial^2 u}{\partial t^2} \qquad (A2.7)$$

Dividing through by A, substituting for dF/A from the rightmost column of Table A2.2, we find:

$$E\frac{\partial^2 u}{\partial x^2}\Delta x = (\rho \Delta x)\frac{\partial^2 u}{\partial t^2} \qquad (A2.8)$$

$$\frac{\partial^2 u}{\partial x^2} = \left(\frac{\rho}{E}\right)\frac{\partial^2 u}{\partial t^2} \qquad (A2.9)$$

Comparing Equation A2.9 with the standard form of the wave Equation (A2.4) shows that the speed of a longitudinal sound wave in a solid is:

$$v = \sqrt{\frac{E}{\rho}} \qquad (A2.10)$$

In fact, this formula is only appropriate to longitudinal sound waves along long thin rods. The formula for the speed of longitudinal sound waves in bulk solid is discussed in §A2.4 on *stresses in solids*

A2.4 Transverse sound waves

A shear wave in a bulk solid is illustrated in Figure A2.3 and the forces on an elemental 'slab' are analysed in Figure A2.3(b) and in Table A2.3 below. The derivations are similar to those for longitudinal waves in a gas or a solid described previously.

The mass of the slab Δx is $\Delta m = \rho A \Delta x$ and the difference ΔF_s between the shear force per unit area at x and at $x + \Delta x$ gives rise to acceleration of this mass. Note that the 'background' shear force F_s corresponds to a situation where $\Delta u = 0$, i.e. to static background shear which does not change with time. Recalling that we may write the transverse acceleration of the slab as $\partial^2 u / \partial t^2$ we have:

$$\Delta F_s = (\rho A \Delta x)\frac{\partial^2 u}{\partial t^2} \qquad (A2.11)$$

Substituting for $\Delta F_s/A$ and cancelling:

$$G\frac{\partial^2 u}{\partial x^2}\Delta x = (\rho \Delta x)\frac{\partial^2 u}{\partial t^2} \qquad (A2.12)$$

$$\frac{\partial^2 u}{\partial x^2} = \left(\frac{\rho}{G}\right)\frac{\partial^2 u}{\partial t^2} \qquad (A2.13)$$

Comparing Equation A2.13 with the standard form of the wave Equation (A2.4) shows that the speed of a shear wave in a solid is:

$$v_S = \sqrt{\frac{G}{\rho}} \qquad (A2.14)$$

Figure A2.3 (a) A representation of the planes of constant shear in a sound wave. (b) Shows an analysis of the forces on a thin 'slab' of solid in a shear wave. It may help to refer to this figure when following the derivations in Table A2.3.

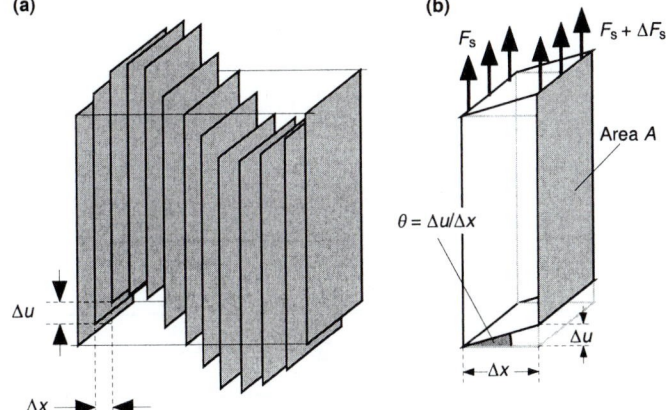

Table A2.3 Systematic derivation of the net shear force per unit area on the element of solid shown in Figure A2.3b.

	Value at x	Value at $x + dx$	Difference
Transverse displacement	u	$u + \Delta u$	Δu
Shear strain	$\theta = \dfrac{\Delta u}{\Delta x}$ $\approx \dfrac{\partial u}{\partial x}$	$\theta + \Delta\theta = \dfrac{\Delta(u + \Delta u)}{\Delta x}$ $\approx \dfrac{\partial(u + \Delta u)}{\partial x}$ $= \dfrac{\partial u}{\partial x} + \dfrac{\partial}{\partial x}(\Delta u)$ We now write Δu as: $\Delta u = \left(\dfrac{\partial u}{\partial x}\right)\Delta x$ which substitutes to give: $\theta + \Delta\theta = \dfrac{\partial u}{\partial x} + \dfrac{\partial^2 u}{\partial x^2}\Delta x$	$\Delta\theta = \left(\dfrac{\partial^2 u}{\partial x^2}\right)\Delta x$
Shear stress	$S_S = G\theta$ $= G\dfrac{\partial u}{\partial x}$	$S_S + \Delta S_S = G(\theta + \Delta\theta)$ $= G\dfrac{\partial u}{\partial x} + G\left(\dfrac{\partial^2 u}{\partial x^2}\right)\Delta x$	$\Delta S_S = G\left(\dfrac{\partial^2 u}{\partial x^2}\right)\Delta x$
Shear force per unit area	$\dfrac{F_S}{A} = S_S = G\theta = G\dfrac{\partial u}{\partial x}$	$\dfrac{F_S + \Delta F_S}{A} = G\dfrac{\partial u}{\partial x} + G\left(\dfrac{\partial^2 u}{\partial x^2}\right)\Delta x$	$\dfrac{\Delta F_S}{A} = G\left(\dfrac{\partial^2 u}{\partial x^2}\right)\Delta x$

A2.5 Stresses in solids

Under tensile stresses, solids behave in a more complicated way than has been described hitherto. In the derivation of the speed of longitudinal sound waves in solids, we assumed that the only effect of a tensile (or compressive) stress was to extend (or shorten) the solid in the direction of the applied stress. However in reality a tensile (compressive) stress applied to a solid in the x-direction, causes the some compressive (tensile) stress in the y- and z- directions. Colloquially we say that the solid tends to 'neck' ('bulge').

In this section we consider the state of strain of a solid under applied tensile stress S_x, S_y, S_z in the x-, y- and z-directions respectively (Figure A2.4). Notice that the net stress in the x- direction is not just the directly applied stress S_x but $+S_x - \sigma S_y - \sigma S_z$ where σ is the *Poisson ratio* (Example 7.8). Recall that σ describes the ratio of lateral to direct stress.

The minus signs arise because a tensile (+) stress in the y-direction results in a tendency to 'neck' in the x-direction i.e. in a compressive (−) strain. The net stress in the x-direction is related to the strain in the x-direction $\Delta x/x$ by Young's modulus E:

$$+S_x - \sigma S_y - \sigma S_z = E\frac{\Delta x}{x} \tag{A2.15}$$

Assuming the elastic properties of the material are isotropic, similar equations hold for the net stresses in the y- and z-directions:

$$-\sigma S_x + S_y - \sigma S_z = E\frac{\Delta y}{y} \tag{A2.16}$$

$$-\sigma S_x - \sigma S_y + S_z = E\frac{\Delta z}{z} \tag{A2.17}$$

A longitudinal sound wave running along the

Figure A2.4 A block of solid of dimensions $x \times y \times z$ subjected to tensile stresses in each of the x-, y- and z-directions. The stress in the y- and z-directions also gives rise to stresses in the x-direction because of the rigidity of solids. The magnitude of the stress in the x-direction due to a stress in the y-direction defines the *Poisson ratio* σ according to:

$$\sigma = \frac{S_x}{S_y}$$

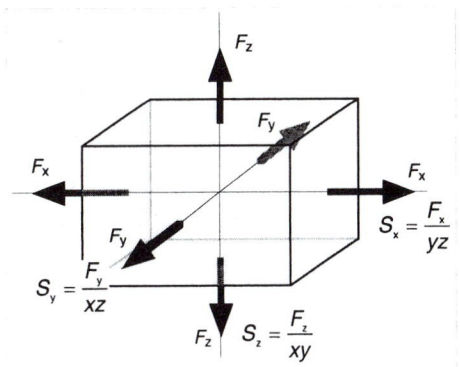

$$S_x = \frac{F_x}{yz}$$

$$S_y = \frac{F_y}{xz}$$

$$S_z = \frac{F_z}{xy}$$

length of a long thin rod causes necking and bulging of the rod, but results in no unrelieved transverse stress, i.e. for a wave travelling in the x-direction, S_x and S_y are zero and Equation A2.15 becomes:

$$S_x = E\frac{\Delta x}{x} \qquad (A2.18)$$

This is the relationship we assumed in Table A2.2 between stress and strain, and so Equation A2.18 correctly applies to longitudinal sound waves on a along a long thin rod.

However, for a longitudinal sound wave in bulk solid, the presence of constraining material means the tendency to neck or bulge is resisted, and there are now unrelieved stresses transverse to the direction of motion of the wave. Thus for a wave travelling in the x- direction, S_y and S_z are generally not zero, however the lateral strains, $\Delta y/y$ and $\Delta z/z$ are constrained to be zero. In this case we rewrite Equations A2.15 to A2.17 as:

$$+S_x - \sigma S_y - \sigma S_z = +E\frac{\Delta x}{x} \qquad (A2.19)$$

$$-\sigma S_x + S_y - \sigma S_z = 0 \qquad (A2.20)$$

$$-\sigma S_x - \sigma S_y + S_z = 0 \qquad (A2.21)$$

If we solve the last two equations simultaneously, we find:

$$S_y = S_x\frac{\sigma}{(1-\sigma)} \quad \text{and} \quad S_z = S_x\frac{\sigma}{(1-\sigma)} \qquad (A2.22)$$

which may substituted in Equation A2.19 to yield:

$$+S_x - \sigma\left[S_x\frac{\sigma}{(1-\sigma)}\right] - \sigma\left[S_x\frac{\sigma}{(1-\sigma)}\right] = E\frac{\Delta x}{x}$$

$$(A2.23)$$

Simplifying and rearranging yields:

$$S_x\left[1 - \frac{2\sigma^2}{(1-\sigma)}\right] = E\frac{\Delta x}{x} \qquad (A2.24)$$

$$S_x = \left[\frac{1-\sigma-2\sigma^2}{(1-\sigma)}\right]E\frac{\Delta x}{x} \qquad (A2.25)$$

which may be written as:

$$S_x = \gamma E\frac{\Delta x}{x} \qquad (A2.26)$$

where γ is given by:

$$\gamma = \frac{(1+\sigma)(1-2\sigma)}{(1-\sigma)} \qquad (A2.27)$$

Comparing A2.26 with A2.18, we see that for a longitudinal wave in a bulk solid, we should have used an extra factor γ in the analysis of Table A2.2. We would then have found that the speed of longitudinal sound waves in a bulk solid would be:

$$v = \sqrt{\frac{\gamma E}{\rho}} \qquad (A2.28)$$

Other useful expressions

The situation shown in Figure A2.4 and summarised in the trio of equations A2.15 to A2.17, or A2.19 to A2.21 may also be used to link the bulk modulus B to Young's modulus E. If we consider the block in figure A2.3 to be under uniform tensile stress, the strain in all three directions will be equal, as will the stresses S_x, S_y, and S_z be equal (to, say, S). In this case the first of the trio of equations becomes:

$$S - \sigma S - \sigma S = E \frac{\Delta x}{x} \qquad (A2.29)$$

$$S(1 - 2\sigma) = E \frac{\Delta x}{x} \qquad (A2.30)$$

Notice that in this case of uniform stress S is just the force per unit area over the surface of the block. Furthermore, the fractional volume change $\Delta V/V$ (Example 7.4) is given by $3\Delta x/x$. We can thus rewrite Equation A2.30 as:

$$P = \left(\frac{E}{(1 - 2\sigma)} \right) \frac{\Delta x}{x} = \left(\frac{E}{3(1 - 2\sigma)} \right) \frac{\Delta V}{V} \qquad (A2.31)$$

Comparing this with the definition of the bulk modulus:

$$P = B \frac{\Delta V}{V} \qquad (A2.32)$$

we see that:

$$B = \frac{E}{3(1 - 2\sigma)} \qquad (A2.33)$$

Using similar techniques it may also be shown that:

$$G = \frac{E}{2(1 + \sigma)} \qquad (A2.34)$$

The Gibbs free energy

A3.1 The Gibbs free energy in equilibrium

Consider a sample of a substance A in contact with a reservoir maintained at temperature T and pressure P. Such a situation broadly represents the most common experimental situation for experiments on liquids and solids. Samples are held at a particular temperature, in a cryostat or furnace, and are free to adjust their volume. The pressure of their environment (commonly atmospheric pressure) remains constant, independent of any volume changes of the sample.

This situation is represented schematically in Figure A3.1. Notice that initially we do not assume that the sample is at temperature T and pressure P. We merely assume that it is in contact with reservoirs in such a situation.

Let us consider the entropy S_{Total} of the combined system of the sample plus the reservoir, i.e. of $A_{\text{Total}} = A + A'$. Suppose there is a *spontaneous* exchange of heat between A and A'. Then since the total system is isolated, the entropy flow associated with such a heat flow must obey the second law of thermodynamics:

$$\Delta S_{\text{total}} = \Delta S + \Delta S' \geq 0 \qquad \text{(A3.1)}$$

Suppose that in this spontaneous process, some heat Q flows *from* the reservoir A' and is absorbed by the sample A. Then:

- Considering the definition of entropy and the heat flow *from* A' we conclude that the change in the entropy of the reservoir is:

$$\Delta S' = \frac{-Q}{T} \qquad \text{(A3.2)}$$

- Considering the first law of thermodynamics and the heat flow *into* A we conclude that:

$$Q = \Delta U + P\Delta V \qquad \text{(A3.3)}$$

Figure A3.1 The conceptual framework for discussion of the circumstances at equilibrium of system A which is placed in contact with a reservoir at temperature T and pressure P. The processes which occur spontaneously are those which tend to minimise the sum of quantities known as the Gibbs free energy (Equation A3.10) and equilibrium is characterised by a minimum value of the Gibbs free energy.

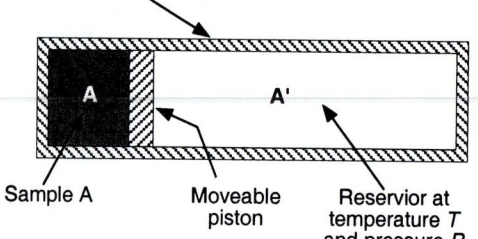

Adiabatic (insulating) wall

Sample A   Moveable piston   Reservior at temperature T and pressure P

Substituting A3.2 into A3.1 we have:

$$\Delta S_{\text{total}} = \Delta S - \frac{Q}{T} \qquad \text{(A3.4)}$$

Taking out a factor $1/T$ this becomes:

$$\Delta S_{\text{total}} = \frac{1}{T}\left[T\Delta S - Q\right] \qquad \text{(A3.5)}$$

and substituting Equation A3.3 into A3.5 we find:

$$\Delta S_{\text{total}} = \frac{1}{T}\left[T\Delta S - (\Delta U + PV)\right] \qquad \text{(A3.6)}$$

This may be rewritten as:

$$\Delta S_{\text{total}} = \frac{1}{T}\left[\Delta(TS - U - PV)\right] \qquad \text{(A3.7)}$$

In A3.7 we have used the fact that when ΔT and ΔP are zero, $\Delta(TS - U - PV)$ can be simplified. First we write the expression out in full and then simplify it as follows:

$$\Delta(TS - U - PV) = T\Delta S + \underbrace{S\Delta T}_{=0} - \Delta U - P\Delta V - \underbrace{V\Delta P}_{=0}$$

$$= T\Delta S - \Delta U - P\Delta V$$

$$\text{(A3.9)}$$

This is only true when ΔT and ΔP are zero, i.e. when P and T are held constant. If we now define the Gibbs free energy G of the system A as:

$$G = U - TS + PV \qquad \text{(A3.10)}$$

then Equation A3.7 becomes:

$$\Delta S_{\text{total}} = \frac{-\Delta G}{T} \qquad \text{(A3.11)}$$

Thus the total entropy change ΔS_{total} is now expressed in terms of quantities relating only to the system under study, A, and not to the reservoir. The second law of thermodynamics (Equation A3.1) tells us that in spontaneous processes, the total entropy ΔS_{total} can only either increase, or stay constant. Together with Equation A3.11 this implies:

$$\Delta G \leq 0. \qquad \text{(A3.12)}$$

In other words, if a sample A is placed in contact with a reservoir at temperature T and pressure P, the spontaneous processes which occur are such as to reduce the Gibbs free energy. So the equilibrium state is characterised by the Gibbs free energy attaining its minimum value.

You may also consult *Sears and Zemansky* (Published in 1996 by McGraw Hill College Division, ISBN: 0070170592) or *Reif* (Published in 1965 by McGraw-Hill Inc, ISBN: 007085615X) for further details.

The Einstein and Debye theories of heat capacity

A4.1 Introduction

Table A4.1 presents further details of the Einstein and Debye theories of the heat capacity of solids in such a way that their similarities become apparent. The main text has already stressed the key physical differences between the two theories (§7.6). The Einstein theory considers the thermal component of the internal energy U of a solid to be held by atoms vibrating *independently* in identical simple harmonic potentials. In contrast, the Debye theory considers the thermal component of the internal energy to be held by displacement (sound) waves.

- In the Einstein theory, the quantum states of the solid are the quantum states of each individual simple harmonic potential. All the quantum states have the same energy $(n + \frac{1}{2})\hbar\omega_E$. The thermal excitations of the solid are analogous to a set of fictitious particles which may multiply occupy a single quantum with energy $E_E = \hbar\omega_E$.

- In the Debye theory, the quantum states of the solid are considered to be wave-like states that are occupied by *phonons*. In order to work out the density of states one proceeds as in §6.5 or in Appendix A1. In §6.5 we showed that for electrons in a box the density of states varied like $g(E) = A\sqrt{E}$ (Equation 6.70). We derived the density of states functions for molecules in box in Appendix A1 and found it

to have the same form (Equation A1.21) However, for phonons there are two key differences in the analysis. First, there is only one quantum state for each value of $\mathbf{k} = (k_x, k_y, k_z)$. Second, for phonons the energy is directly proportional to $|\mathbf{k}|$ since the energy of a phonon is $E = \hbar\omega = \hbar v|\mathbf{k}|$. This expression has assumed that the speed of sound (v) that relates the frequency to the wavelength is independent of wavelength. This is not quite correct for wavelengths of the order of a lattice spacing or so, but this is neglected in the Debye theory. The reader is referred to any advanced text on solid state physics for more details.

The Einstein theory predicts:

$$C = 3R \frac{\Theta_E^2 \exp(\Theta_E / T)}{T^2 \left[\exp(\Theta_E / T) - 1\right]^2} \qquad (A4.1)$$

This function may be directly calculated once Θ_E is determined. The Debye theory predicts:

$$C = 9R \left[\frac{T^3}{\Theta_D^3}\right] \int_{x=0}^{x=\Theta_D / T} \frac{x^4 \exp(x)}{\left[\exp(x) - 1\right]^2} dx \qquad (A4.2)$$

This function is tabulated in Table 7.11.

Table A4.1

	Debye theory	Einstein theory
Density of quantum states This function is such that $g(E)\mathrm{d}E$ is the number of individual quantum states with energies between E and $E + \mathrm{d}E$.	There is a maximum phonon energy E_D. There are no quantum states with energies greater than E_D, and below E_D the density of states varies as: $$g(E) = AE^2$$ where A can be shown to have a value per mole of: $$A = \frac{9R}{k_B^4 \theta_D^3}$$ where Θ_D is the Debye temperature of the solid given theoretically by: $$\Theta_D^3 = \frac{18 N_A \pi^2 \hbar^3}{k_2^3 V_M \left[\frac{2}{c_T^3} + \frac{1}{c_L^3} \right]}$$ where c_T and c_L are the speeds of sound of transverse and longitudinal sound and V_M is the volume of one mole of the solid.	All quantum states have the same energy E_E and in 1 mole of elemental solid the density of states is: $$g(E) = 3N_A \delta(E - E_E)$$ where $\delta(E - E_E)$ is a delta function which is zero at all values of E except E_E where it is extremely large. Its integral over energy is defined to be 1.
Occupation function This function yields the average occupancy of an individual quantum state with energy E when a system of particles in equilibrium at temperature T.	The phonons are considered to be non-conserved bosons and so their occupation function is f_{BE} (§2.5.3 Equation 2.62). The value of the chemical potential μ is zero because these bosons are not conserved (phonons may be destroyed and created). $$f_{BE}(E,T) = \frac{1}{\exp\left(\frac{E}{k_B T}\right) - 1}$$	The excitations of atoms of the solid are considered as non-conserved bosons and so their occupation function is f_{BE} (§2.4.3 Equation 2.62). The value of the chemical potential μ is zero because these excitations may be destroyed or created. $$f_{BE}(E,T) = \frac{1}{\exp\left(\frac{E}{k_B T}\right) - 1}$$
Distribution function This function is such that the number of particles $(\mathrm{d}N)$ occupying quantum states with energies between E and $E + \mathrm{d}E$ is $D(E)\mathrm{d}E =$ $\quad f(E,T)\, g(E)\mathrm{d}E$	By definition: $$\mathrm{d}N = D(E,T)\mathrm{d}E$$ $$= f_{BE}(E,T)g(E)\mathrm{d}E$$ so the number of phonons in one mole of solid at temperature T is: $$N = \int_0^{E_D} \frac{AE^2}{\exp\left(\frac{E}{k_B T}\right) - 1}\, \mathrm{d}E$$	By definition: $$\mathrm{d}N = D(E,T)\mathrm{d}E$$ $$= f_{BE}(E,T)g(E)\mathrm{d}E$$ so the number of excitations in the solid at temperature T is: $$N = \int_0^\infty \frac{3N_A \delta(E - E_E)}{\exp\left(\frac{E}{k_B T}\right) - 1}\, \mathrm{d}E$$ $$= \frac{3N_A}{\exp\left(\frac{E_E}{k_B T}\right) - 1}$$
Total internal energy (Neglecting the cohesive energy U_o)	$$\mathrm{d}U = ED(E,T)$$ $$= Ef_{BE}(E,T)g(E)\mathrm{d}E$$ $$U = \int_0^{E_D} f_{BE}(E,T)Eg(E)\mathrm{d}E$$ $$U = \int_0^{E_D} \frac{AE^3}{\exp\left(\frac{E}{k_B T}\right) - 1}\, \mathrm{d}E$$	$$\mathrm{d}U = ED(E,T)$$ $$= Ef_{BE}(E,T)g(E)\mathrm{d}E$$ $$U = \int_0^{E_D} f_{BE}(E,T)Eg(E)\mathrm{d}E$$ $$= \frac{3E_E N_A}{\exp\left(\frac{E_E}{k_B T}\right) - 1}$$

	Debye theory	Einstein theory

Heat capacity

Since neither of these theories consider the an-harmonic inter-atomic potentials that give rise to thermal expansion, both these esti-mates for the heat capacity are esti-mates of C_V the molar heat capac-ity at constant vol-ume.

Debye theory

By definition:

$$C = \frac{dU}{dT}$$

$$= \frac{\partial}{\partial T}\left[\int_0^{E_D} \frac{AE^3}{\exp\left(\frac{E}{k_B T}\right) - 1} dE\right]$$

Noticing that the integral is with respect to en-ergy, we can take the differentiation inside the integral sign.

$$C = \int_0^{E_D} AE^3 \frac{\partial}{\partial T}\left[\frac{1}{\exp\left(\frac{E}{k_B T}\right) - 1}\right] dE$$

$$C = \int_0^{E_D} AE^3 \times \frac{-1 \times \left[\frac{-E}{k_B T^2}\right]}{\left[\exp\left(\frac{E}{k_B T}\right) - 1\right]^2} \times \exp\left(\frac{E}{k_B T}\right) dE$$

$$C = \int_0^{E_D} \frac{AE^4 \exp\left(\frac{E}{k_B T}\right)}{\left[\exp\left(\frac{E}{k_B T}\right) - 1\right]^2} \times \frac{1}{k_B T^2} dE$$

We can solve this integral by substituting:

$$x = \frac{E}{k_B T} \text{ i.e. } dE = k_B T dx$$

$$C = \int_0^{x_D} \left(\frac{A(k_B T)^4 x^4 e^x}{\left(e^x - 1\right)^2} \times \frac{1}{k_B T^2}\right) k_B T dx$$

Taking non x-dependent factors outside the integral we find:

$$C = A k_B^4 T^3 \int_0^{x_D} \frac{x^4 e^x}{\left(e^x - 1\right)^2} dx$$

The value of integral must (in general) be evaluated numerically. Noticing that the upper limit for the integral may be written as θ_D/T and substituting for A we find:

$$C = 9R\left[\frac{T^3}{\Theta^3}\right]\int_0^{\Theta_D/T} \frac{x^4 e^x}{\left(e^x - 1\right)^2} dx$$

Debye prediction

Einstein theory

By definition:

$$C = \frac{dU}{dT}$$

$$= \frac{\partial}{\partial T}\left[\frac{3E_E N_A}{\exp\left(\frac{E_E}{k_B T}\right) - 1}\right]$$

$$C = \frac{-3E_E N_A}{\left[\exp\left(\frac{E_E}{k_B T}\right) - 1\right]^2} \times \frac{-E_E}{k_B T^2} \times \exp\left(\frac{E_E}{k_B T}\right)$$

$$C = \frac{3E_E^2 N_A}{k_B T^2 \left[\exp\left(\frac{E_E}{k_B T}\right) - 1\right]^2} \times \exp\left(\frac{E_E}{k_B T}\right)$$

$$C = 3R \times \frac{E_E^2}{k_B^2 T^2 \left[\exp\left(\frac{E_E}{k_B T}\right) - 1\right]^2} \times \exp\left(\frac{E_E}{k_B T}\right)$$

This may be written in terms of the Einstein temperature as:

$$C = 3R \frac{\Theta_E^2}{T^2 \left[\exp\left(\frac{\Theta_E}{T}\right) - 1\right]^2} \times \exp\left(\frac{\Theta_E}{T}\right)$$

Einstein prediction

APPENDIX 5

Derivation of formula for bulk modulus

A5.1 Bulk modulus of noble gas solids

In this appendix we show the mathematical steps required to derive the formulae for the bulk modulus of noble gas solids. This was a topic we covered in §7.3 on the compressibility of solids, The task at hand is to evaluate the formula for the bulk modulus B:

$$B = V \frac{\partial^2 U}{\partial V^2}\bigg|_{V=V_0} \qquad (7.4^* \text{ \& A5.1})$$

where U is the molar internal energy. The subscript indicates that we are to evaluate $\partial^2 U / \partial V^2$ at the equilibrium volume: $V = V_0$. For molecular solids, we consider only the internal energy at $T = 0$ K. In this case:

$$U = -2\varepsilon N_A \left[A_6 \left(\frac{\sigma}{r_0}\right)^6 - A_{12} \left(\frac{\sigma}{r_0}\right)^{12} \right]$$

$$= 2\varepsilon N_A \left[A_{12} \left(\frac{\sigma}{r_0}\right)^{12} - A_6 \left(\frac{\sigma}{r_0}\right)^6 \right] \qquad (6.18^*)$$

This expresses U as a function of r_0, the equilibrium separation between atoms. In order to evaluate A5.1 we need to find the relationship between the volume of the solid and r_0. We know from §6.2.5 that the equilibrium crystal structure is face-centred cubic, so we can write the molar volume as a function of r_0:

$$V = \frac{N_A}{4}\left(\sqrt{2}r_0\right)^3 = \frac{N_A}{\sqrt{2}}r_0^3 \qquad (A5.2)$$

Differentiating we find:

$$\frac{\partial V}{\partial r_0} = 3\frac{N_A}{\sqrt{2}}r_0^2 \qquad (A5.3)$$

which we can rewrite as:

$$\frac{\partial r_0}{\partial V} = \frac{r_0}{3V} \qquad (A5.4)$$

We can use this expression as follows. Proceeding in two steps, we change the variable of differentiation from V to r_0:

$$B = V \frac{\partial^2 U}{\partial V^2}$$

$$= V \left[\frac{\partial r_0}{\partial V}\right]^2 \frac{\partial^2 U}{\partial V^2} \qquad (A5.5)$$

$$= V \left[\frac{r_0}{3V}\right]^2 \frac{\partial^2 U}{\partial V^2}$$

Now we substitute for U and differentiate twice:

$$B = V\left[\frac{r_0}{3V}\right]^2 \frac{\partial^2}{\partial r_0^2}\left(2N_A\varepsilon\left[A_{12}\left(\frac{\sigma}{r_0}\right)^{12} - A_6\left(\frac{\sigma}{r_0}\right)^6\right]\right)$$

$$= V\left[\frac{r_0}{3V}\right]^2 \frac{\partial}{\partial r_0}\left(2N_A\varepsilon\left[-\frac{12}{r_0}A_{12}\left(\frac{\sigma}{r_0}\right)^{12} + \frac{6}{r_0}A_6\left(\frac{\sigma}{r_0}\right)^6\right]\right)$$

$$= V\left[\frac{r_0^2}{9V^2}\right]\left(2N_A\varepsilon\left[\frac{12\times13}{r_0^2}A_{12}\left(\frac{\sigma}{r_0}\right)^{12} - \frac{6\times7}{r_0^2}A_6\left(\frac{\sigma}{r_0}\right)^6\right]\right)$$

$$(A5.6)$$

Now we simplify this expression and collect terms to find:

$$B = 2N_A\varepsilon\left[\frac{1}{9V}\right]\left(\left[\frac{12\times13}{1}A_{12}\left(\frac{\sigma}{r_0}\right)^{12} - \frac{6\times7}{1}A_6\left(\frac{\sigma}{r_0}\right)^6\right]\right)$$

$$= \left[\frac{2N_A\varepsilon}{9V}\right]\left[156A_{12}\left(\frac{\sigma}{r_0}\right)^{12} - 42A_6\left(\frac{\sigma}{r_0}\right)^6\right]$$

$$(A5.7)$$

425

We can now substitute the equilibrium value of σ/r_0 as determined by Equation 6.22

$$\left[\frac{\sigma}{r_0}\right]^6 = \left[\frac{A_6}{2A_{12}}\right] \qquad (*6.23)$$

And substitute this into Equation A5.7:

$$B = \frac{2N_A\varepsilon}{9V}\left[156A_{12}\left[\frac{A_6}{2A_{12}}\right]^2 - 42A_6\left[\frac{A_6}{2A_{12}}\right]\right] \qquad (A5.8)$$

We simplify the expression for B in several stages:

$$B = \frac{2N_A\varepsilon}{9V}\left[\frac{156}{4} - \frac{42}{2}\right]\left[\frac{A_6^2}{A_{12}}\right]$$

$$= \frac{2N_A\varepsilon}{9V}[39 - 21]\left[\frac{A_6^2}{A_{12}}\right]$$

$$= \frac{2N_A\varepsilon}{9V}[18]\left[\frac{A_6^2}{A_{12}}\right] \qquad (A5.9)$$

$$= \frac{4N_A\varepsilon}{V}\left[\frac{A_6^2}{A_{12}}\right]$$

Now we substitute for V in this expression using A5.2, which itself needs to be evaluated at the equilibrium separation A5.2. So we evaluate the molar volume as:

$$V = \frac{N_A}{\sqrt{2}}r_0^3$$

$$= \frac{N_A}{\sqrt{2}}\sigma^3\overbrace{\left[\frac{2A_{12}}{A_6}\right]^{1/2}}^{r_0^3} \qquad (A5.10)$$

We can substitute for V (Equation A5.10) into Equation A5.9:

$$B = \frac{4N_A\varepsilon}{\underbrace{\frac{N_A}{\sqrt{2}}\sigma^3\left[\frac{2A_{12}}{A_6}\right]^{1/2}}_{V}}\left[\frac{A_6^2}{A_{12}}\right] \qquad (A5.11)$$

and simplify this by cancelling terms:

$$B = \frac{4N_A\varepsilon}{\frac{N_A}{\sqrt{2}}\sigma^3\left[\frac{2A_{12}}{A_6}\right]^{1/2}}\left[\frac{A_6^2}{A_{12}}\right] \qquad (A5.12)$$

$$= \frac{4\varepsilon}{\sigma^3}\left[\frac{A_6^{5/2}}{A_{12}^{3/2}}\right]$$

Now we substitute $A_{12} = 12.13$ and $A_6 = 14.45$ for the *fcc* structure (Table 6.1) to find:

$$B = 75.12\frac{\varepsilon}{\sigma^3} \qquad (A5.13)$$

To evaluate this for a particular substance we use values from Table 6.2 for the range parameter σ and the energy parameter ε. For example for argon we find:

$$B = 75.12\frac{\varepsilon}{\sigma^3}$$

$$= 75.12 \times \frac{10.3 \times 1.6 \times 10^{-22}}{\left(0.344 \times 10^{-9}\right)^3}$$

$$= 75.12 \times 4.05 \times 10^7 \qquad (A5.14)$$

$$= 3.041 \times 10^9 \ \text{Pa}$$

$$= 3.041 \ \text{GPa}$$

This may be compared with the experimental value of 2.7×10^9 Pa (2.7 GPa). The calculated values for the other noble gas solids are tabulated in Table 7.6.

Index